ESSENTIALS OF BUSINESS LAW

ABOUT THE AUTHORS

Len Young Smith received an A.B., an M.A., and a J.D. from Northwestern University. He has been a member of the Illinois State Board of Law Examiners for thirty-eight years, and for the last thirty-five years he has served as President of the Board. He has served on the National Conference of Bar Examiners for over thirty years, and chaired the conference from 1955–56. He is also a former editor of *The Bar Examiner*. Len Smith is a member of the Illinois Bar and belongs to the Council of Legal Education ABA. Len Young Smith is a member of Who's Who in American Law, and Who's Who in the World. He is a co-author of *Smith and Roberson's Business Law, Sixth Edition*, as well as *Business Law and the Regulation of Business*.

Richard A. Mann received a B.S. in Mathematics from the University of North Carolina at Chapel Hill and a J.D. from Yale Law School. He is currently Professor of Business Law and Chairperson of Business Law at the University of North Carolina. Richard Mann is a past President of the Southeastern Regional Business Law Association. He is a member of Who's Who in American Law, Outstanding Young Men of America, and the North Carolina Bar.

Professor Mann has written extensively on a number of legal topics including bankruptcy, sales, secured transactions, real property, insurance law and business associations. He has received the *American Business Law Journal's* award for both the best article (1984) and the best comment (1979). He has served as a reviewer and staff editor for the *American Business Law Journal*. He teaches in several executive education programs and is a founder, managing director and instructor in the Carolina CPA Review. He is a co-author of *Smith and Roberson's Business Law, Sixth Edition*, as well as *Business Law and the Regulation of Business*.

Barry S. Roberts received a B.S. in Business Administration from Pennsylvania State University, a J.D. from the University of Pennsylvania and an LL.M. from Harvard Law School. He served as a judicial clerk for the Pennsylvania Supreme Court prior to practicing law in Pittsburgh. Barry Roberts is currently Professor of Business Law and Director of the Undergraduate Program at the School of Business Administration, University of North Carolina at Chapel Hill. He is a member of Who's Who in American Law, Outstanding Young Men of America, and the North Carolina Bar.

Professor Roberts has written numerous articles on such topics as antitrust, products liability, constitutional law, banking law, employment law, and business associations. He has been a reviewer and staff editor for the *American Business Law Journal*. Professor Roberts is a founder, managing director and instructor in the Carolina CPA Review. He is a co-author of *Smith and Roberson's Business Law, Sixth Edition*, as well as *Business Law and the Regulation of Business*.

ESSENTIALS OF BUSINESS LAW

Len Young Smith
Chairman of the Department of Business Law,
Northwestern University (Retired),
Member of the Illinois Bar

Richard A. Mann
Professor of Business Law,
The University of North Carolina at Chapel Hill,
Member of the North Carolina Bar

Barry S. Roberts
Professor of Business Law,
The University of North Carolina at Chapel Hill,
Member of the North Carolina and Pennsylvania Bars

WEST PUBLISHING COMPANY
St. Paul   New York   Los Angeles   San Francisco

Copy Editor: Carol Spencer
Cover Design: Delor Erickson
Artwork: Taly Design Group
Typesetter: Parkwood Composition

A STUDENT STUDY GUIDE

A study guide containing outlines and summaries of major topics plus review questions for additional practice is available with this text. If you cannot locate a copy of the study guide in your bookstore, please ask your bookstore manager to order a copy for you under the title *Study Guide to Accompany Essentials of Business Law.*

COPYRIGHT © 1984 By WEST PUBLISHING CO.
COPYRIGHT © 1986 By WEST PUBLISHING CO.
         50 West Kellogg Boulevard
         P.O. Box 64526
         St. Paul, Minnesota 55164-1003

Printed in the United States of America

Library of Congress Cataloging-in-Publication Data

Smith, Len Young, 1901–
    Essentials of business law.

    Rev. ed. of: Essentials of business law / Len Young
Smith . . . [et al.].
    Includes index.
    1. Commercial law—United States. I. Mann, Richard A.
II. Roberts, Barry S. III. Essentials of business
law. IV. Title.
KF889.S55   1986   346.73'07   85-22788
ISBN 0-314-93514-2   347.3067
1st Reprint—1986

G. Gale Roberson
1903–1985

This text is dedicated to G. Gale Roberson, a truly outstanding leader in the fields of law and business law. Gale is best known for his authorship of the sixth edition of *Smith and Roberson's Business Law*. In addition, he was also an author of the first edition of this text.

We all deeply feel the loss of this great scholar, educator, and attorney. We will attempt to carry on his tradition of excellence.

G. Gale Roberson received an A.B. from the University of Illinois and a J.D. from Harvard Law School. He spent eleven years as an attorney with the U.S. Securities and Exchange Commission and twenty-nine years in private practice in Chicago. In addition to practicing law, Gale Roberson taught at De Paul University Law School and served as a Professorial Lecturer at Northwestern University in Evanston. He was an Honorary President of the American Business Law Association. Professor Roberson was a member of Who's Who in American Law and the Illinois Bar.

CONTENTS IN BRIEF

CONTENTS

TABLE OF CASES

PREFACE

The second edition of *Essentials of Business Law* is in the tradition of accuracy, comprehensiveness, and authoritativeness long associated with *Smith and Roberson's Business Law*. This text covers all the material presented in the current edition of Smith and Roberson in a less technical, but nonetheless authoritative manner. It covers the material succinctly, yet in depth sufficient to be easily comprehended by today's students.

This text is designed for use in Business Law and Legal Environment courses generally offered in universities, colleges, and schools of business and commerce. By reason of the broad coverage and variety of the material this volume may be readily adapted to specially designed courses in Business Law by assigning and emphasizing different combinations of the subject matter. With the addition of material on Employment Law (chapter 27), Suretyship (chapter 37) and Accountants' Legal Liability (chapter 40), all topics included in the CPA exam are covered by the text.

Greater emphasis has been placed upon the regulatory environment of Business Law: The first six chapters are devoted to introductory coverage of the legal environment of business, including new chapters on Constitutional and Administrative Law and Criminal Law; Part Nine (Chapters 39 to 41) thoroughly addresses the area of government regulation of business; and each of the parts opens with an introductory discussion of the public policy, social issues and business ethics pertaining to that part.

We have deemed it desirable to place primary emphasis on the text and to present the cases in summary fashion. Cases are briefed and integrated into the chapters. The facts are summarized in clear and understandable narrative using the names of the parties. The legal issues and court decisions are carefully explained with a minimum of legal jargon. The opinions have been drastically shortened, the reductions affording more satisfactory material for purposes of instruction. Using the headings FACTS and DECISION, most cases are adequately covered in 25 lines or less.

From long classroom experience we are of the opinion that fundamental legal principles can be more effectively learned from text and case materials having at least a degree of human interest. To accomplish this objective a large number of recent cases have been included. Landmark cases, on the other hand, have not been neglected. Moreover, a new feature—Law in the News—has been added to provide the student with recent news articles that discuss the implications of the legal principles covered in the text.

To improve readability, all unnecessary "legalese" has been eliminated while necessary legal terms are printed in boldface and clearly defined, explained and illustrated. Definitions of essential terms also appear in the margins. The text has been enriched by the addition of numerous new, illustrative hypothetical and case examples which help students relate material to real life experiences.

Strong classroom tested problems appear at the end of the chapters to test the student's understanding of major concepts. We have used the problems and consider them excellent stimulants to classroom discussion. Students have found the problems helpful in enabling them to apply the basic rules of law to factual situations, many of which are taken from reported court decisions. The problems serve as a springboard for discussion and readily suggest other and related problems to the inquiring, analytical mind.

We have used over 100 classroom tested figures, charts, and diagrams. The diagrams help the student conceptualize the many abstract concepts in the law; the charts not only summarize prior discussions but also aid in pointing out relationships between different legal rules. In addition, each chapter ends with a chapter summary which graphically outlines and summarizes the topics to be covered. A list of key terms also appears at the end of each chapter to aid the student in checking his mastery of the subject matter.

We express our gratitude to the following Professors for their helpful comments:

Carroll Burrell
San Jacinto College

Joseph P. Davey
Hartnell College

Allan M. Gerson
Palm Beach Community College

Robert Inama
Ricks College

James Miles
Anoka Ramsey Community College

Sylvia Samuels
Skyline College

Susan Schoeffler
Central Piedmont Community College

John E. H. Sherry
Cornell University

Michael D. Sommerville
St. Mary's College

Stanley H. Stone
Valencia Community College-East Campus

We express our thanks and deep appreciation to Jean Riggsbee and Jean Watlington for typing the manuscript. For their support we extend our thanks to Helen T. Smith, Karlene Fogelin Knebel, and Joanne Erwick Roberts. And we are grateful to Richard Fenton, Bill Gabler and Tim Reedy of West Publishing Company for their invaluable assistance and cooperation in connection with the preparation of this text.

Len Young Smith
Richard A. Mann
Barry S. Roberts

PART ONE
THE LEGAL ENVIRONMENT OF BUSINESS

PART ONE

THE LEGAL ENVIRONMENT OF BUSINESS

PUBLIC POLICY, SOCIAL ISSUES AND BUSINESS ETHICS

Law concerns the relations of individuals with one another as they affect the social and economic order. It is both the product of civilization and the means by which civilization is maintained. As such, law reflects the social, economic, political, religious, and moral philosophy of society. Judge Learned Hand, in *The Spirit of Liberty,* captured the absolute importance of law when he stated: "Without it we cannot live; only with it can we insure the future which by right is ours. The best of man's hopes are enmeshed in its success; when it fails we must fail; the measure in which it can reconcile our passions, our wills, our conflicts, is the measure of our opportunity to find ourselves."

One of the essential roles that law performs is that of social control. As the legal philosopher Roscoe Pound observed in *An Introduction to the Philosophy of Law:*

For the purpose of understanding the law of today, . . . I am content to think of law as a social institution to satisfy social wants—the claims and demands and expectations involved in the existence of civilized society—by giving effect to as much as we may with the least sacrifice, so far as such wants may be satisfied or such claims given effect by an ordering of human conduct through politically organized society. For the present purposes, I am content to see in legal history the record of a continually wider recognizing and satisfying of human wants or claims or desires through social control; a more embracing and more effective securing of social interests; a continually more complete and effective elimination of waste and precluding of friction in human enjoyment of the goods of existence.

In this textbook we are primarily concerned with law as an agency of social control over economic activity. As we discuss in Chapter 1, law in this country arises in four different ways: constitutions, legislation, court decisions, and actions by administrative agencies. Together these sources of law form an intricate network that governs, regulates, and facilitates the conduct of business affairs. We refer to this network as the *legal environment of business.*

In Part One we deal with that portion of the legal environment of business that affects *all* economic activity. Chapters 1 and 2 provide an introduction to our legal system by briefly examining its nature, structure, origins, processes, and purposes. Chapter 3 covers constitutional law as it applies to business. Constitutional law involves the allocation of power to government and the preservation of individual liberty against governmental action. Consequently, you should understand constitutional law to appreciate the basic legal system of the United States. Moreover, a number of public policy issues affecting business have constitutional dimensions. For example, to what extent should commercial speech such as advertising be protected by the First Amendment? When do the activities of private corporations become "state action" and therefore subject to the constitutionally imposed requirements of due process?

Chapter 3 also addresses the law determining the powers and procedures of administrative agencies. This chapter provides the background for understanding the operation of these agencies (such as the Federal Trade Commission, the National Labor Relations Board, the Occupational Safety and Health Administration, and the Securities and Exchange Commission), which today play a dominant role in regulating business and protecting society.

Chapter 4 discusses the criminal law, which is of great importance in protecting the state and the individual. Many public policy issues involve the application of criminal law to the conduct of business. For example, should a corporation be held criminally liable for the conduct of its employees? Should punishment of criminal offenses by business be limited to fines or should management also be imprisoned?

Finally, Chapters 5 and 6 deal with the law of torts. The following passage is quoted in *Torts,* 5th ed. by Prosser and Keeton:

Arising out of the various and ever-increasing clashes of the activities of persons living in a common society, carrying on business in competition with fellow members of that society, owning property which may in any of a thousand ways affect the persons or property of others—in short, doing all the things that constitute modern living—there must of necessity be losses, or injuries of many kinds sustained as a result of the activities of others. The purpose of the law of torts is to adjust these losses, and to afford compensation for injuries sustained by one person as the result of the conduct of another. Wright, "Introduction to the Law of Torts," 1944, 8 *Camb.L.J.* 238.

In adjusting these losses the courts inevitably make decisions that affect public policy. For example, if the courts impose liability for injuries caused by defective products, then the manufacturer's cost of paying these claims will increase the price of the product to all customers.

We encourage you to think about these and other relevant policy, social, and ethical issues as you read the chapters in this text. As we stated earlier, the law reflects the social, economic, political, religious, and moral philosophy of society. Consequently, your understanding and appreciation of the law will be enhanced by considering the public policy behind the law as well as the social implications of the law.

1

INTRODUCTION TO LAW

The laws of the United States affect and influence the life of every American citizen, and the laws of each State affect and influence the life of each of its citizens as well as a large number of noncitizens. The rights and duties of every individual, as well as the safety and security of every individual and his property, depend on the law.

The law is pervasive. It interacts with and influences the political, economic, and social systems of every civilized society. It permits, forbids, and/ or regulates practically every known human activity and affects all persons either directly or indirectly.

It is also highly interrelated—or as lawyers often say—"the law is a seamless web." Accordingly, you will find it helpful in studying the different areas of business law first to consider law as a whole. This will enable you not only better to understand each specific area of law but also to understand its relationship to other areas of law.

Nature of Law

The law did not spring full blown from the mind of any person or the minds of any combination of persons at any one time. It evolved slowly, and it contains the seed of future change and development as new conditions and new needs arise in an era of technology and expanding population. The law has improved by change, and it will continue to change.

The law is not a pure science based on unchanging and universal truths. Rather, it is a continuous striving to attain a workable set of rules that adjust the individual and group rights of a society within the fixed framework of its political ideology and the constant progression of its sociology and technology. Nonetheless, the fundamental question remains: What should the law be? Numerous philosophers and jurists (legal scholars) have attempted to answer this question.

Definition of Law

The American jurists and Supreme Court Justices Oliver Wendell Holmes and Benjamin Cardozo defined law in a functional sense as predictions of the way that a court will decide specific legal questions. The English jurist Black-

5

stone, on the other hand, defined law as "a rule of civil conduct prescribed by the supreme power in a state, commanding what is right, and prohibiting what is wrong."

Roscoe Pound, a distinguished American jurist and former dean of the Harvard Law School, stated that law may mean any of three things:

> First, we may mean the legal order, that is, the régime of ordering human activities and relations through systematic application of the force of politically organized society, or through social pressure in such a society backed by such force. We use the term "law" in this sense when we speak of "respect for law" or for the "end of law."
>
> Second, we may mean the aggregate of laws or legal precepts; the body of authoritative grounds of judicial and administrative action established in such a society. We may mean the body of received and established materials on which judicial and administrative determinations proceed. We use the term in this sense when we speak of "systems of law" or of "justice according to law."
>
> Third, we may mean what Mr. Justice Cardozo has happily styled "the judicial process." We may mean the process of determining controversies, whether as it actually takes place, or as the public, the jurists, and the practitioners in the courts hold it ought to take place.

Legal Sanctions

Sanction—means of enforcing legal judgments

A primary function of the legal system is to ensure that legal rules are enforced. Sanctions are the means by which the decisions of the courts are enforced. Laws without sanctions would be ineffectual and unenforceable.

An example of a sanction in a civil (noncriminal) case is the seizure and sale of a debtor's property. Moreover, under certain circumstances the court may enforce its orders by finding an offender in contempt of court and sentencing him to jail until he obeys the court's order. In criminal cases, the principal sanctions are fines, imprisonment, and capital punishment.

The mere existence of sanctions is not enough. Individuals in the community must also be willing to submit to law. Important attitudes that make the law respected and obeyed without the necessity of the government's invoking legal sanctions include public sentiment and opinion, habits of obedience to law, and a desire to conform to societal standards.

Laws and Morals

Although the law is greatly affected by moral concepts, morals and law are not the same. They may be considered as two intersecting circles (See Figure 1-1). The shaded area common to both circles includes the vast body of ideas that are both moral and legal. For instance, "Thou shall not kill" and Thou shall not steal" are both moral precepts and legal constraints.

On the other hand, the part of the legal circle not intersecting the morality circle (the unshaded portion) includes many rules of law that are completely unrelated to morals, such as the rules that you must drive on the right side of the road and that you must register before you can vote. Likewise, the part of the morality circle not intersecting the legal circle includes moral precepts not enforced by law, such as that you should not silently stand by and watch a blind man walk off a cliff or that you should not foreclose a poor widow's mortgage. For a contrary view see Law in the News on page 7.

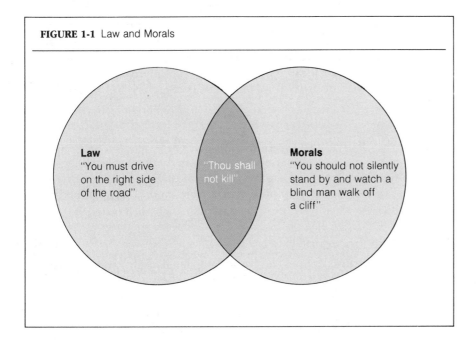

FIGURE 1-1 Law and Morals

Law
"You must drive on the right side of the road"

"Thou shall not kill"

Morals
"You should not silently stand by and watch a blind man walk off a cliff"

Law and Justice

The law is no guarantee of justice—these terms represent separate and distinct concepts. Justice is an ideal which good law continually strives to achieve. However, without law and order there can be no justice.

Law In The News

Minnesota Law Mandates Bystander Help in Crises

ST. PAUL, Aug. 2 (AP)—Being a "Good Samaritan" is now a duty, not an option, in Minnesota, where a new provision in state statutes provides up to a $100 fine for people who fail to aid in an emergency.

The amendment to an older law went into effect Monday. It is designed to prevent incidents such as one last week in St. Louis, where a 13-year-old girl was raped over 40 minutes by two youths as several people stood by. Police finally were summoned by an 11-year-old boy.

Previously, an expert lifeguard "could watch a 6-month-old baby crawl into the river and drown and sit by and do nothing about it and nothing would happen," said State Representative Randy Staten, an author of the measure. "That is totally unacceptable conduct for civilized society."

Many states have "Good Samaritan" laws that relieve a person of liability when they render aid in an emergency. The amendment to Minnesota's law goes a step further by making it a duty to assist.

Linda Close, division manager of public safety and litigation in the Minnesota Attorney General's office, said the amended statute "creates a duty to help somebody if a person is exposed to 'grave physical harm.'"

Mr. Staten, a Minneapolis Democrat, says he believes the statute is the first of its kind in the country, and he said officials from other states appear interested in enacting similar laws. The amendment was prompted by incidents far from Minnesota, he said, citing the rape of a woman on a pool table in New Bedford, Mass., as a group of people watched, and the Kitty Genovese case of many years ago, in which the Queens, N.Y., woman was fatally stabbed as people watched from apartment windows.

If the law is regarded as the sum total of governmental rules in a society, the difference between law and justice becomes clear. Law is inseparable from a politically organized society. In a dictatorship the laws might be oppressive, harsh, and intended chiefly to maintain the domination of the dictator. A rule, regulation, edict, or order is no less a law because it is harsh, unwise, or unjust.

Classification of Law

Because the study of law is vast, it is helpful to classify the law into categories. This can be done in a number of ways, but the most useful categories are (1) substantive and procedural, (2) public and private, and (3) civil and criminal (see Figure 1-2).

Substantive and Procedural Law

Substantive law–the basic law creating rights and duties

Procedural law–rules for enforcing substantive law

Substantive law creates, defines, and regulates legal rights and obligations. Thus, the rules of contract law that determine when a binding contract is formed are rules of substantive law. On the other hand, procedural law sets forth the rules for enforcing those rights which exist by reason of the substantive law. Thus procedural law defines the method by which to obtain a remedy in court.

Public and Private Law

Public law–the law dealing with the relationship between government and individuals

Private law–the law involving relationships among individuals and legal entities

Public law is that branch of substantive law which deals with the government's rights and powers and its relationship to individuals or groups. Public law consists of constitutional, administrative, and criminal law. Private law is that part of substantive law which governs individuals and legal entities (such as corporations) in their relationships with one another. Business law is primarily private law.

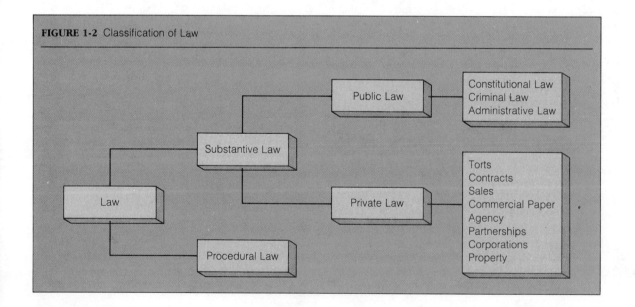

FIGURE 1-2 Classification of Law

Civil and Criminal Law

The civil law defines duties the violation of which constitutes a wrong against the party injured by the violation. In contrast, the criminal law establishes duties the violation of which is a wrong against the whole community. Civil law is a part of private law, whereas criminal law is a part of public law. In a civil action the injured party **sues** to recover *compensation* for the damage and injury that he has sustained as a result of defendant's wrongful conduct. The party bringing a civil action (the **plaintiff**) has the burden of proof which he must sustain by a **preponderance** (greater weight) **of the evidence.** The purpose of the civil law is to compensate the injured party, not to punish the wrongdoer as in the case of criminal law. The principal forms of relief afforded by the civil law are a judgment for money damages and a decree ordering the defendant to specifically perform a certain act or to desist from specified conduct. Figure 1-3 compares civil and criminal law.

A **crime** is any act or omission prohibited by public law in the interest of protection of the public and made punishable by the government in a judicial proceeding brought **(prosecuted)** by it. The government must prove criminal guilt **beyond a reasonable doubt,** which is a significantly higher burden of proof than that required in a civil action. Crimes are prohibited and **punished** on the ground of public policy, which may include the protection and safeguarding of government, human life, or private property. Additional purposes of the criminal law include deterrence and rehabilitation.

Within recent times the scope of the criminal law has increased substantially. Traditional crimes have been augmented by a multitude of regulations and laws to which are attached criminal penalties. These pertain to nearly every phase of modern living. Typical examples in the field of business law are those concerning the licensing and conduct of a business, the laws governing the sale of securities, and antitrust law. Criminal law is more fully discussed in Chapter 4.

Civil law–the law dealing with the rights and duties of individuals among themselves

Criminal law–the law that involves offenses against the entire community

Sue–to begin a lawsuit in a court

Defendant–the person against whom a legal action is brought

Plantiff–the person who initiates a civil suit

Preponderance of the evidence greater weight of the evidence; standard used in civil cases

Prosecute–to bring a criminal proceeding

Beyond a reasonable doubt–evidence which is entirely convincing

---

FIGURE 1-3 Comparison of Civil and Criminal Law

	Civil Law	Criminal Law
Commencement of action	Aggrieved individual (plaintiff) sues	State or Federal government prosecutes
Purpose	Compensation Deterrence	Punishment Deterrence Rehabilitation Preservation of peace
Burden of proof	Preponderance of the evidence	Beyond a reasonable doubt
Principal sanctions	Monetary damages Equitable remedies	Capital punishment Imprisonment Fines

Sources of Law

The sources of law in the American legal system are the Federal and State constitutions, Federal treaties, interstate compacts, Federal and State statutes, the ordinances of countless local municipal governments, Federal and State executive orders, the rules and regulations of Federal and State administrative agencies, and an ever-increasing volume of reported Federal and State court decisions.

The **supreme law** of the land is the United States Constitution. The Constitution also provides that treaties made under the authority of the United States shall be the supreme law of the land. Federal treaties are, therefore, paramount to State constitutions and statutes. Federal legislation is of next significance as a source of law. The importance and complexity of new bills enacted at each congressional session result from the interplay of tremendous economic and social forces within this nation. Other Federal actions having the force of law are executive orders by the President and rules and regulations set by Federal administrative officials, agencies, and commissions. The Federal courts also contribute considerably to the body of law in the United States.

The same pattern exists in every State. The paramount law of each State is contained in its written constitution. Subordinate to this are the statutes enacted by its legislature and the case law developed by its judiciary. Likewise, rules and regulations of State administrative agencies have the force of law, as do executive orders issued by the Governor. In addition, cities, towns, and villages have limited legislative powers within their respective municipal areas to pass ordinances and resolutions.

We will discuss these sources of law in the following sections. In addition, we will consider constitutional and administrative law more fully in Chapter 3.

Constitutional Law

Constitution–fundamental law of a government establishing its powers and limitations

A constitution—the fundamental law of a particular level of government— serves a number of critical functions. It establishes the governmental structure and allocates power among the levels of government, thereby defining political relationships. One of the fundamental principles on which our government is founded is that of separation of powers. As incorporated into our Constitution this means that there are three distinct and independent branches of government—the Federal judiciary, the Congress, and the Executive branch.

A constitution also restricts the powers of government and specifies the rights and liberties of the people. For example, the Constitution of the United States not only specifically states what rights and authority is vested in the people's creation—the national government—but also specifically enumerates certain rights and liberties of the people. Moreover, the Ninth Amendment to the U.S. Constitution makes it clear that this enumeration of rights does not in any way deny or limit other rights which are retained by the people. Alexander Hamilton, a co-author of *The Federalist*, put it this way: "Here in strictness the people surrender nothing; and as they retain everything, they have no need of particular reservations."

Judicial review–authority of the courts to determine the constitutionality of legislative and executive acts

All other law in the United States is subject to the Federal Constitution. No law, Federal or State, is valid if it violates the Federal Constitution. The final arbiter as to constitutionality is the Supreme Court of the United States. This principle of **judicial review** is one of the basic ideas incorporated in the

Federal Constitution, which the British statesman William Gladstone once characterized as "the greatest [document] ever struck off at one time by the brain and the purpose of man."

Judicial Law

The American legal system is a **common law system** first developed in England, that relies heavily on the judiciary as a source of law and on the **adversary** method for settling disputes. In an adversary system the parties, not the court, must initiate and conduct litigation. This approach is based on the belief that the truth is more likely to emerge from the investigation and presentation of evidence by two opposing parties, both motivated by self-interest, than from judicial investigation motivated only by official duty. The common law system is also used in other English-speaking countries, including England, Canada, and Australia.

In distinct contrast to the common law system are **civil law systems** (as opposed to civil or noncriminal law), which are based on Roman law. These systems depend on comprehensive legislative enactments (called Codes) and the **inquisitorial** method of determining disputes. In the inquisitorial approach, the judiciary initiates litigation, investigates pertinent facts, and conducts the presentation of evidence. The civil law system prevails in most of Europe, Scotland, the State of Louisiana, the province of Quebec, Mexico and South America.

Common Law   The courts in common law systems have developed a body of law that serves as precedent for determination of later controversies. This law is called case law, judge-made law, or common law. In this sense, common law is distinguished from other sources of law, such as legislation and administrative rulings.

The principle of **stare decisis** ("to stand by the decisions"), whereby rules of law announced and applied by courts in prior decisions are later adhered to and relied on in deciding cases of a similar nature, upholds the stability of the common law. Judicial decisions have two uses: first, to determine with finality the case being decided; and second, to indicate how similar cases will be decided if and when they arise. Thus, as defined by the jurist Jerome Frank, the law "as to any given situation is either (a) actual law, i.e., a specific past decision, as to that situation, or (b) probable law, i.e., a guess as to a specific future decision."

Stare decisis does not preclude correction of erroneous decisions or judicial choice among conflicting precedents. Thus, the doctrine allows sufficient flexibility for the common law to change. Justice Musmanno of the Supreme Court of Pennsylvania paid tribute to the doctrine of *stare decisis* when he stated:

> Without *stare decisis,* there would be no stability in our system of jurisprudence.
> *Stare decisis* channels the law. It erects lighthouses and flys the signals of safety. The ships of jurisprudence must follow that well-defined channel which, over the years, has been proved to be secure and trustworthy. But it would not comport with wisdom to insist that, should shoals rise in a heretofore safe course and rocks emerge to encumber the passage, the ship should nonetheless pursue the original course, merely because it presented no hazard in the past. The principle of *stare decisis* does not demand that we follow precedents which shipwreck justice.

Common law system— body of law originating in England and derived from judicial decisions

Adversary system—system in which opposing parties initiate and present their case

Civil law system—body of law derived from Roman law and based upon comprehensive legislative enactments

Inquisitorial system— system in which the judiciary initiates, conducts and decides cases

Stare decisis—principle that courts should apply rules decided in prior cases in deciding substantially similar cases

Stare decisis is not an iron mold into which every utterance by a Court—regardless of circumstances, parties, economic barometer and sociological climate—must be poured, and, where, like wet concrete, it must acquire an unyielding rigidity which nothing later can change.

The history of law through the ages records numerous inequities pronounced by courts because the society of the day sanctioned them. Reason revolts, humanity shudders, and justice recoils before much of what was done in the past under the name of law. Yet, we are urged to retain a forbidding incongruity in the law simply because it is old.

While age adds venerableness to moral principles and physical objects, it sometimes becomes necessary, and it is not sacrilegious to do so, to scrape away the moss of the years to study closely the thing which is being accepted as authoritative, inviolable, and untouchable. When a rule offends against reason, when it is at odds with every precept of natural justice, and when it cannot be defended on its own merits, but has to depend alone on a discredited genealogy, courts not only possess the inherent power to repudiate, but, indeed, it is required, by the very nature of judicial function, to abolish such a rule.

The strength of the common law is its ability to adapt to change without losing its sense of direction. As Justice Cardozo said: "The inn that shelters for the night is not the journey's end. The law, like the traveler, must be ready for the morrow. It must have a principle of growth."

Equity   As the common law developed in England, it became overly rigid and beset with technicalities. As a consequence, in many cases no remedies were provided because the judges insisted that a claim be within the scope of one of the recognized forms of action. Moreover, courts of common law could provide only limited remedies; the principal type of relief obtainable was a money judgment. Consequently, individuals who could not obtain adequate relief from monetary awards began to petition the king directly for justice. He, in turn, came to delegate these petitions to his chancellor.

Gradually, there evolved what was in effect a new and supplementary system of needed judicial relief for those who could not receive adequate remedies through the common law. This new system, called **equity,** was administered by a Court of Chancery presided over by the chancellor. The chancellor, deciding cases on "equity and good conscience," provided relief in many instances in which the common law judges refused to act or where the remedy at law was inadequate. Thus, there grew up, side by side, two systems of law administered by different tribunals, the common law courts and courts of equity.

An important difference between law and equity is that the chancellor could order a defendant to do or refrain from doing a specific act. If the defendant did not comply with this order called a **decree,** he could be held in contempt of court and punished by fine or imprisonment. This power of compulsion available in a court of equity opened the door to many needed remedies not available in a court of common law.

While courts of equity in some cases recognized rights that were enforceable at common law, they provided more effective remedies. For example, for breach of a land contract the buyer could obtain a decree of **specific performance** in a court of equity. The defendant seller would be commanded to perform his part of the contract by transferring title to the land. Another powerful and effective remedy available only in the courts of equity was the

Equity–body of law based upon principles distinct from common law and providing remedies not available at law

Decree–decision of a court of equity

Specific performance–decree ordering a party to perform a contractual duty

injunction, a court order requiring a party to do or refrain from doing a specified act. No comparable remedies were available in the common law courts. Another remedy in courts of equity not available elsewhere was the remedy of **reformation,** where, upon the ground of mutual mistake, an action could be brought to reform or change the language of a written agreement to conform to the actual intention of the contracting parties. An action for **rescission** of a contract, which allowed a party to invalidate a contract under certain circumstances, was another remedy.

Although courts of equity provided remedies not available in courts of law, they granted them only at their discretion, not as a matter of right. This discretion was exercised according to the general legal principles, or **maxims,** formulated by equity courts over the years.

In nearly every jurisdiction in the United States there has been a union of courts of common law and equity into a single court that administers both systems of law. However, vestiges of the old division continue. For example, the right to a trial by jury applies only to actions at law and not to suits filed in equity.

Restatements of Law   The common law of the United States results from the independent decisions of the State and Federal courts. The rapid increase in the number of decisions by these courts led to the establishment of the American Law Institute (ALI) in 1923. The ALI was composed of a distinguished group of lawyers, judges, and law teachers who set out to prepare "an orderly restatement of the general common law of the United States, including in that term not only the law developed solely by judicial decision, but also the law that has grown from the application by the courts of statutes that were generally enacted and were in force for many years."

The Restatements cover many of the important areas of the common law, including torts, contracts, agency, property, and trusts. Although not law by themselves, they are highly persuasive, and courts have frequently used them to support their opinions. The Restatements are regarded as the authoritative statement of the common law of the United States. Because they provide a concise and clear statement of much of the common law, relevant portions of the Restatements are frequently relied on in this book.

Injunction–a decree ordering a party to do or refrain from doing a specified act

Reformation–equitable remedy rewriting a contract to conform with the original intent of the contracting parties

Rescission–an equitable remedy invalidating a contract

Maxim–a general legal principle

FIGURE 1-4 Comparison of Law and Equity

	Law	Equity
Remedy	Judgment	Decree
Availability	Primarily	Secondarily if remedy at law is inadequate
Jury	If either party demands	None
Formality	Technical	Relaxed
Precedents	*Stare decisis*	Equitable maxims

Legislative Law

Since the end of the nineteenth century, legislation has become the primary source of new law and ordered social change in the United States. The annual volume of legislative law is enormous. Justice Felix Frankfurter's remarks to the New York City Bar in 1947 are even more appropriate today:

> . . . Inevitably the work of the Supreme Court reflects the great shift in the center of gravity of law-making. Broadly speaking, the number of cases disposed of by opinions has not changed from term to term. But even as late as 1875 more than 40 percent of the controversies before the Court were common-law litigation, fifty years later only 5 percent, while today cases not resting on statutes are reduced almost to zero. It is therefore accurate to say that courts have ceased to be the primary makers of law in the sense in which they "legislated" the common law. It is certainly true of the Supreme Court that almost every case has a statute at its heart or close to it.

This emphasis on legislative or statutory law has occurred because common law, which develops evolutionarily and haphazardly, is not well suited for making drastic or comprehensive changes. Moreover, although courts tend to be hesitant about overruling prior decisions, legislatures commonly repeal prior enactments. In addition, legislatures are independent and able to choose the issues they wish to address, but courts may deal only with those issues presented by actual cases. As a result, legislatures are better equipped to make the dramatic, sweeping, and relatively rapid changes in the law that are needed to respond to technological, social, and economic innovations.

Some business law topics, such as contracts, agency, property, and trusts, remain governed principally by the common law. But most areas of commercial law have become largely statutory, including partnerships, corporations, sales, commercial paper, secured transactions, insurance, securities regulation, antitrust, and bankruptcy. Because most States enacted their own statutes dealing with these branches of commercial law, a great diversity developed among the States and hampered the conduct of commerce on a national scale. The increased need for greater uniformity brought about the codification of large parts of business or commercial law.

The most successful example is the **Uniform Commercial Code** (UCC), which was prepared under the joint sponsorship and direction of the National Conference of Commissioners on Uniform State Laws and the American Law Institute. The entire Official Text of the Code is set forth in the Appendix of this book. All fifty States (although Louisiana has adopted only Articles 1, 3, 4 and 5), the District of Columbia, and the Virgin Islands have adopted the Uniform Commercial Code. The underlying purposes and policies of the Code are:

1. to simplify, clarify and modernize the law governing commercial transactions;

2. to permit the continued expansion of commercial practices through custom, usage and agreement of the parties;

3. to make uniform the law among the various jurisdictions.

Other uniform laws include the Uniform Partnership Act, the Uniform Limited Partnership Act, the Model Business Corporation Act, and the Uniform Probate Code.

Administrative Law

Administrative law is the branch of public law that deals with the various regulatory functions and activities of the government in its executive capacity as performed, supervised, and regulated by public officials, departments, boards, and commissions. It also involves controversies arising between individuals and these public officials and agencies. Administrative functions and activities concern in general matters of public health, safety, and welfare including the establishment and maintenance of military forces, police, citizenship and naturalization, taxation, the coinage of money, elections, environmental protection, the regulation of transportation, interstate highways, waterways, television, radio, and trade and commerce.

Administrative law–law dealing with the establishment, duties and powers of agencies in the executive branch of government

Because of the increasing complexity of the social, economic, and industrial life of the nation, the scope of administrative law has expanded enormously. Justice Jackson stated that "the rise of administrative bodies has been the most significant legal trend of the last century, and perhaps more values today are affected by their decisions than by those of all the courts, review of administrative decisions apart." This is evidenced by the great increase in the number and activities of Federal government boards, commissions, and other agencies. Certainly, agencies create more legal rules and decide more controversies than all the legislatures and courts combined.

Legal Analysis

Decisions in State trial courts are not generally reported or published. The weight of the precedent set by a trial court is not sufficient to warrant permanent reporting. Except in New York and a few other States where selected opinions of trial courts are published, decisions in trial courts are simply filed in the office of the clerk of the court, where they are available for public inspection.

Decisions of courts of appeals are published in volumes called "reports", which are numbered consecutively. Most State court decisions are found in the State reports of that State. In addition, State reports are published in a regional reporter published by West Publishing Company called the National Reporter System, composed of the following: Atlantic (A. or A.2d); South Eastern (S.E. or S.E.2d); South Western (S.W. or S.W.2d); New York Supplement (N.Y.S. or N.Y.S.2d); North Western (N.W. or N.W.2d); North Eastern (N.E. or N.E.2d); Southern (So. or So.2d); and Pacific (P. or P.2d). After they are published, these opinions or "cases" are referred to ("cited") by giving the name of the case, the volume, name, and page of the official State report, if any, in which it is published; the volume, name, and page of the particular set and series of the National Reporter System; and the volume, name, and page of any other selected case series. For instance, the case of Lefkowitz v. Great Minneapolis Surplus Store, Inc., 251 Minn. 188, 86 N.W.2d 689 (1957), indicates that the opinion in this case may be found in Volume 251 of the official Minnesota Reports at page 188; and in Volume 86 of the Northwestern Reporter, Second Series, at page 689. The Federal Court decisions are found in the Federal Reporter (Fed. or F.2d); Federal Supplement (F.Supp.); Federal Rules Decisions (F.R.D.); and United States Supreme Court Reports (U.S.), Supreme Court Reporter (S.Ct.), and Lawyers Edition (L.Ed.).

In reading the title of a case, such as "Jones v. Brown," the "v." or "vs." means versus or against. In the trial court, Jones is the **plaintiff,** the person who filed the suit, and Brown is the **defendant,** the person against whom the suit was brought. When the case is appealed, some, but not all, courts of appeals or appellate courts place the name of the party who appeals, or the **appellant,** first, so that "Jones v. Brown" in the trial court becomes, if Brown loses and is the appellant, "Brown v. Jones" in the appellate court. But because some appellate courts retain the trial court order of names, it is not always possible to determine from the title itself who was the plaintiff and who the defendant. You must carefully read the facts of each case and clearly identify each party in your mind in order to understand the discussion by the appellate court.

Appellant–party who appeals

Study of the reported cases requires an understanding and application of legal analysis. Normally, the reported opinion in a case sets forth (a) the essential facts, the nature of the action, the parties, what happened to bring about the controversy, what happened in the lower court, and what pleadings are material to the issues; (b) the issues of law or fact; (c) the legal principles involved; (d) the application of these principles; and (e) the decision.

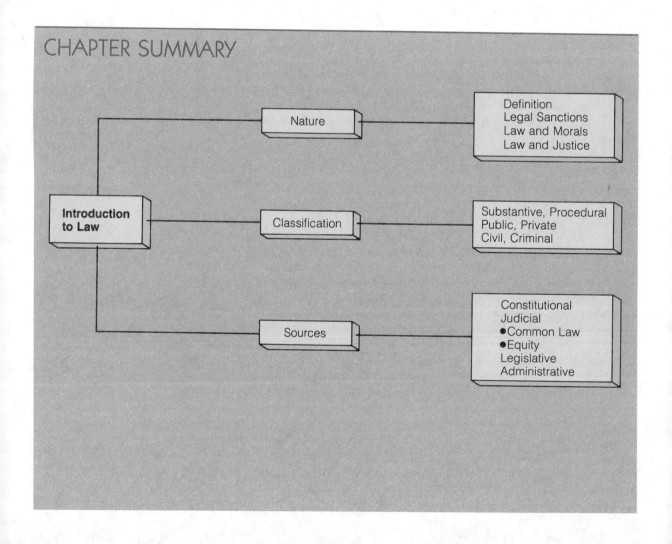

CHAPTER SUMMARY

Introduction to Law

Nature — Definition / Legal Sanctions / Law and Morals / Law and Justice

Classification — Substantive, Procedural / Public, Private / Civil, Criminal

Sources — Constitutional / Judicial / ●Common Law / ●Equity / Legislative / Administrative

KEY TERMS

Sanction
Substantive law
Procedural law
Public law
Private law
Civil law
Criminal law
Sue
Plaintiff

Defendant
Preponderance of the evidence
Prosecute
Beyond a reasonable doubt
Supreme law
Constitution
Judicial review
Common law system
Adversary system

Civil law system
Inquisitorial system
Stare decisis
Equity
Decree
Specific performance
Injunction
Reformation
Rescission

2

THE JUDICIAL SYSTEM

As we discussed in Chapter 1, substantive law sets forth the rights and duties of individuals and other legal entities, whereas procedural law determines how these rights are asserted. Procedural law attempts to accomplish two competing objectives—to be fair and impartial; to operate efficiently. The judicial process in the United States represents a balance between these two objectives as well as a commitment to the adversary system.

In the first part of this chapter we describe the structure and function of the Federal and State court systems. The second part deals with jurisdiction, and the final section covers the procedure in civil lawsuits.

The Court System

Courts are impartial tribunals (seats of judgment) established by governmental bodies to settle disputes. A court may render a binding decision only when it has jurisdiction over the dispute and the parties to that dispute, that is, when it has a right to hear and make a judgment in a case. The United States has a dual court system: the Federal government has its own system, as does each of the fifty States and the District of Columbia.

The Federal Courts

Article III of the United States Constitution states that the judicial power of the United States shall be vested in one Supreme Court and such lower courts as Congress may establish. Congress has established a Federal court system consisting of a number of special courts, district courts, courts of appeals, and the Supreme Court. Judges in the Federal court system are appointed for life by the President, subject to confirmation by the Senate. The structure of the Federal court system is illustrated in Figure 2-1.

District Courts   The district courts are trial courts of general jurisdiction in the Federal system; they can hear and decide most legal controversies. Most Federal cases begin in the district court, and it is here that issues of fact are decided. The district court is generally presided over by *one* judge, although in certain cases three judges preside. In a few cases, an appeal from a judgment or decree of a district court is taken directly to the Supreme Court. In most

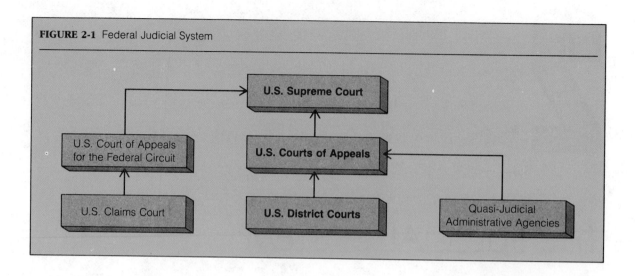

FIGURE 2-1 Federal Judicial System

cases, however, appeals go to the Circuit Court of Appeals of the appropriate circuit, the decision of which is in most cases final.

Congress has established judicial districts, each of which is located entirely in a particular State. All States have at least one district, while certain States contain more than one district. For instance, New York has four districts, Illinois has three, and Wisconsin has two, while a number of less populated States each make up a single district.

Court of Appeals   Congress has established twelve judicial circuits (eleven numbered circuits plus the D.C. circuit), each having a court known as the Court of Appeals, which primarily hears appeals from the district courts located within its circuit (see Figure 2-2). In addition, they review orders of certain administrative agencies. The United States Courts of Appeals generally hear cases in panels of *three* judges.

The Courts of Appeals exercise no original jurisdiction (the right to hear a case first) being solely courts of review. Accordingly, they do *not* hear witnesses. Their function is to examine the record of a case on appeal and to determine whether the trial court committed prejudicial error (error substantially affecting the appellant's rights and duties). If so, the appellate court will reverse or modify the judgment of the lower court and if necessary **remand** or send it back to the lower court for further proceeding. If there is no prejudicial error, the appellate court will affirm the decision of the lower court.

The Supreme Court   The nation's highest tribunal is the United States Supreme Court, which consists of nine justices (a Chief Justice and eight Associate Justices) who sit as a group in Washington, D.C. Although the United States Supreme Court has original jurisdiction in certain types of cases, the Court's principal function is to review decisions of the Federal Courts of Appeals and, in some instances, those of the highest State courts or other tribunals. Cases reach the Supreme Court under its appellate jurisdiction by one of two routes. A relatively few come by way of **appeal by right.** The Court must hear these cases if one of the parties requests the review. Appeal by

Appeal by right—mandatory review by a higher court

FIGURE 2-2 The Thirteen Federal Judicial Circuits

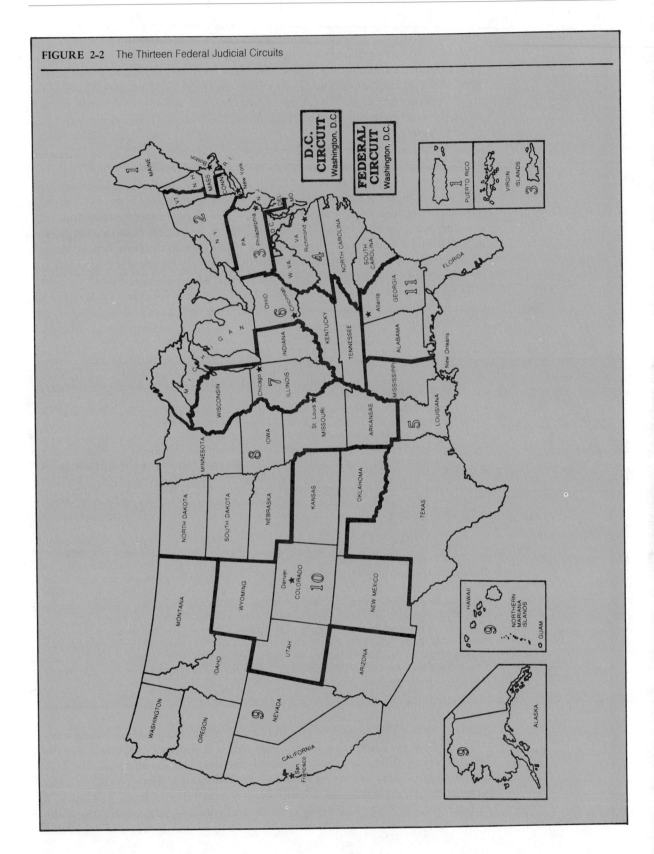

right to the United States Supreme Court can be made if a United States *Court of Appeals* declares a State statute to be in violation of the Constitution, treaties, or laws of the United States. Appeal by right from the highest court of a *State* is available in two situations: (1) the State court declares a Federal statute or treaty invalid or (2) the State court upholds the validity of a State statute against a challenge that it is in violation of the Constitution, treaties, or laws of the United States.

The second way in which a decision of a lower court may be reviewed by the Supreme Court is by the discretionary **writ of *certiorari*,** which requires a lower court to produce the records of a case it has tried. The great majority of cases reaching the Supreme Court come to it by means of writs of *certiorari*. The Court grants writs when there is a Federal question of substantial importance or a conflict in the decisions of the U.S. Circuit Courts of Appeals and if four Justices vote to hear the case. However, only a small percentage of the petitions to the Supreme Court for review by *certiorari* are granted, as the Court uses the writ as a device to choose which cases it wishes to hear. The following case describes some of the criteria the Supreme Court uses in deciding whether to grant review by *certiorari* as well as explaining the effect of a denial.

Writ of certiorari—discretionary review by a higher court

MARYLAND v. BALTIMORE RADIO SHOW, INC.

Supreme Court of the United States, 1950.
338 U.S. 912, 70 S.Ct. 252, 94 L.Ed. 562.

FACTS: Eugene James was arrested for the brutal slaying of a young girl who was dragged from her bicycle and stabbed to death in Baltimore. On the night of his arrest, Baltimore Radio Show broadcasted over much of Maryland a sensational and devastating account disclosing that James had confessed to the crime, that he had a long criminal record, and that he returned to the scene with the police and dug up the knife he had used. As a result, the Criminal Court of Baltimore found Baltimore Radio Show guilty of contempt for obstructing justice because its broadcast had prevented James from exercising his right to an impartial jury trial. However, the Maryland Court of Appeals reversed this contempt conviction based on its interpretations of the U.S. Supreme Court's recent decisions concerning freedom of speech and the press. The State of Maryland then asked the U.S. Supreme Court to issue a writ of *certiorari* to review the decision of the Maryland Court of Appeals.

DECISION: *Certiorari* denied. Petitions for review on writ of *certiorari*, particularly from a State court, may be denied for technical reasons such as the review is sought too late or the judgment to be reviewed is not from a State court of last resort. In addition, *certiorari* may be denied on the basis of judicial policy. For example, a case may raise an important question but the record may be too cloudy or it may be desirable to have the lower courts further examine different aspects of an issue. For *certiorari* to be granted, four or more Justices must think that *certiorari* is necessary as a "matter of sound judicial discretion." Moreover, if *certiorari* is denied, no written explanation is required. Most important, a denial carries absolutely no implication of the court's views of the merits of the case which it has declined to review. Here, fewer than four Justices thought review of the Court of Appeals' reversal would have been proper, so *certiorari* was denied. The denial does not decide whether either of the lower courts correctly decided the legal issues involved in the case.

Special Courts   The special courts in the Federal judicial system include the U.S. Claims Court, the Tax Court, and the U.S. Court of Appeals for the Federal Circuit. These courts have jurisdiction over particular areas. The U.S. Claims Court hears claims against the United States. The Tax Court has jurisdiction over certain cases involving Federal taxes. The U.S. Court of Appeals for the Federal Circuit reviews decisions of the Claims Court, the

Patent and Trademark Office, the United States Court of International Trade, and the Merit Systems Protection Board.

State Courts

Each of the fifty States and the District of Columbia has its own court system. In most States judges are elected by the voters for a stated term. State courts have general jurisdiction—they can hear and decide all cases arising under the common law and under the statutes of the State, as well as most cases arising under Federal law. Although the structure of State court systems varies from State to State, Figure 2-3 shows a typical system.

A State's highest tribunal is a reviewing court that is generally called the Supreme Court of the State. Except for those cases in which review by the U.S. Supreme Court is available, the decision of the highest State tribunal is final. Most States have also created intermediate appellate courts to handle the large volume of cases in which review is sought. Review by such a court is usually by right. Further review is in most cases a matter of the highest court's discretion.

Jurisdiction

Jurisdiction simply means the power or authority of a court to hear and decide a given case. To proceed with a lawsuit, a court must have two kinds of jurisdiction. The first is jurisdiction over the **subject matter** of the lawsuit. Where a court lacks jurisdiction over the subject matter of a case, any action it takes in the case will not have legal effect.

The second kind of jurisdiction is over the **parties** to a lawsuit. A court usually may obtain jurisdiction over the defendant in a lawsuit if the defendant lives or is present in the court's territory or the transaction giving rise to the case has a substantial connection to the court's territory. The court obtains jurisdiction over the plaintiff when the plaintiff voluntarily submits to the court's power through filing his complaint with the court.

> Jurisdiction—authority of a court to hear and decide a case

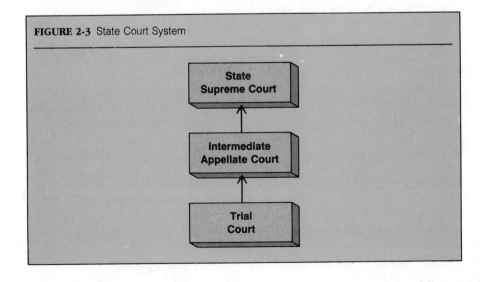

FIGURE 2-3 State Court System

State Supreme Court

Intermediate Appellate Court

Trial Court

A valid exercise of jurisdiction also requires that the parties to the dispute be given fair notice and a reasonable opportunity to be heard. This overriding limitation is imposed on the Federal and State courts by the U.S. Constitution.

Subject Matter Jurisdiction

Subject matter jurisdiction—authority of a court to decide a particular kind of case

Subject matter jurisdiction refers to the authority of a particular court to judge a controversy of a particular kind. Federal courts have *limited* subject matter jurisdiction. Article III, Section 2(1), of the Federal Constitution sets forth the subject matter jurisdiction of the Federal courts as follows:

> The judicial Power shall extend to all Cases, in Law and Equity, arising under this Constitution, the Laws of the United States, and Treaties made, or which shall be made, under the Authority,—to all Cases affecting Ambassadors, other public Ministers and Consuls;—to all Cases of admiralty and maritime Jurisdiction;—to Controversies to which the United States shall be a party—to Controversies between two or more States;—between a State and Citizens of another State;—between Citizens of different States;—between Citizens of the same State claiming Lands under Grants of different States, and between a State, or the Citizens thereof, and foreign States, Citizens or Subjects.

State courts have jurisdiction over *all* matters that have not been exclusively given to the Federal courts or expressly taken away by the Constitution or Congress.

Exclusive jurisdiction jurisdiction that permits only one court to hear a case

Exclusive Federal Jurisdiction   The Federal Courts have exclusive jurisdiction over Federal criminal prosecutions, admiralty, bankruptcy, antitrust, patent, trademark and copyright cases, suits against the United States, and cases arising under certain Federal statutes that expressly provide for exclusive Federal jurisdiction.

Concurrent jurisdiction—authority of more than one court to hear the same case

Concurrent Federal Jurisdiction   All instances of Federal jurisdiction other than exclusive are concurrent; this means that they may be heard by either State or Federal courts. Federal concurrent jurisdiction may be classified into two basic categories. The first arises when the Federal courts do not have exclusive jurisdiction over a Federal question and the amount in controversy exceeds $10,000. (In many instances, however, Congress has eliminated the jurisdictional dollar requirement.) A **Federal question** is any case arising under the Constitution, statutes, or treaties of the United States.

Federal question—any case arising under the Constitution, statutes or treaties of the United States

The second type of concurrent Federal jurisdiction occurs in a civil suit where there is diversity of citizenship and the amount in controversy exceeds $10,000. **Diversity of citizenship** exists (1) when the plaintiffs are citizens of a State or States different from the State or States of which the defendants are citizens; (2) when a foreign country brings an action against citizens of the United States; *or* (3) when the controversy is between citizens of the United States and citizens of a foreign country. See Law in the News. The citizenship of an individual litigant (party in a lawsuit) is the State of his residence or domicile, whereas that of a corporate litigant is both the State of incorporation and the State where its principal place of business is located. For example, if the amount in controversy exceeds $10,000, then diversity of citizenship jurisdiction would be satisfied if A, a citizen of California, sues B, a citizen of Idaho. However, if W, a citizen of Virginia, and X, a citizen of North Carolina, sue Y, a citizen of Georgia, and Z, a citizen of North Carolina, there is *not* diversity of citizenship, because both X, a plaintiff, and Z, a defendant, are citizens of North Carolina.

The next case explains the general rules for determining whether the $10,000 jurisdictional requirement has been satisfied.

FACTS: Mariana Deutsch worked as a knitwear mender and attended a school for beauticians. The sink in her apartment collapsed on her foot fracturing her big toe and making it painful for her to stand. She claims that as a consequence of the injury she was compelled to abandon her plans to become a beautician because that job requires standing for long periods of time. She also asserts that she was unable to work at her current job for a month. She filed a tort claim against Hewes Street Realty for negligence in failing properly to maintain the sink. She brought the suit in Federal district court, claiming damages of $25,000. Her medical expenses and actual loss of salary were less than $1,500; the rest of her alleged damages were for loss of future earnings as a beautician. Hewes Street moved to dismiss the suit on the basis that Deutsch's claim fell short of the $10,000 jurisdictional requirement and, therefore, the Federal court lacked subject matter jurisdiction over her claim.

DECISION: Judgment for Deutsch. The general rule for determining the $10,000 jurisdictional amount in controversy requirement is that an amount alleged in good faith to exceed $10,000 will satisfy the requirement, unless it appears to be a legal certainty that the claim is really for less than $10,000. However, the court may look beyond the face of the complaint to determine the validity of the alleged amount. For example, the court may dismiss a suit for lack of jurisdiction (1) if the damages claimed are not recoverable at all under applicable law, or (2) if the damages that are recoverable cannot as a matter of law exceed $10,000, or (3) if the amount of damages was inflated solely to gain access to the Federal courts.

In this case, Deutsch's claim for unliquidated damages of $25,000 for her loss of future earnings as a beautician satisfies the jurisdictional requirement. Although it may seem unlikely that she could actually prove $25,000 in damages, it cannot be said with legal certainty that the damages do not exceed $10,000. Therefore, she should have an opportunity to have her claim decided on its merits in a Federal court.

DEUTSCH v. HEWES STREET REALTY CORP.

United States Court of Appeals, Second Circuit, 1966.
359 F.2d 96.

When a Federal district court hears a case solely under diversity of citizenship jurisdiction, no Federal question is involved, and accordingly the Federal courts must apply State law.

In any case involving concurrent jurisdiction, the plaintiff has the choice of bringing the action in either an appropriate Federal court or State court. However, if the plaintiff brings the case in a State court, the defendant usually may have it removed (shifted) to a Federal court for the district in which the State court is located.

Exclusive State Jurisdiction   The State courts have exclusive jurisdiction over *all other matters.* All matters not granted in the Constitution or not exercised by Congress are solely within the jurisdiction of the States. Accordingly, exclusive State jurisdiction would include cases involving a Federal question or diversity of citizenship but where the amount in controversy is $10,000 or less and this amount has not been statutorily waived by Congress. In addition, the State courts have exclusive jurisdiction over all cases to which the Federal judicial power does not reach, including, but by no means limited to, property, torts, contract, agency, commercial transactions, and most crimes.

The jurisdiction of the Federal and State courts is illustrated in Figure 2-4.

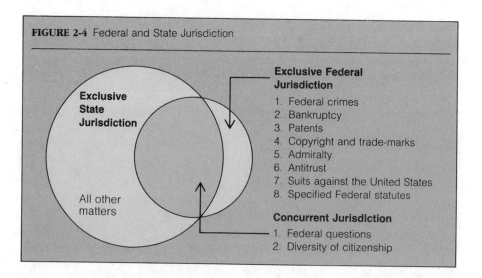

FIGURE 2-4 Federal and State Jurisdiction

Exclusive State Jurisdiction

All other matters

Exclusive Federal Jurisdiction

1. Federal crimes
2. Bankruptcy
3. Patents
4. Copyright and trade-marks
5. Admiralty
6. Antitrust
7. Suits against the United States
8. Specified Federal statutes

Concurrent Jurisdiction

1. Federal questions
2. Diversity of citizenship

Stare Decisis in the Dual Court System   The doctrine of *stare decisis* presents certain problems when there are two parallel court systems. As a consequence, in the United States *stare decisis* works approximately as follows (see also Figure 2-5):

1. The United States Supreme Court has never held itself to be rigidly bound by its own decisions, and lower Federal courts and State courts have followed that course in respect to their own decisions.

2. A decision of the U.S. Supreme Court on Federal questions is binding on all other courts, Federal or State.

3. Although a decision of a Federal court other than the Supreme Court may be persuasive in a State court on a Federal question, it is nevertheless not binding.

4. A decision of a State court may be persuasive in the Federal courts, but it is not binding except where Federal jurisdiction is based on diversity of citizenship. In such a case the Federal courts must apply local State law as determined by the highest State tribunal and not by a trial or intermediate appellate court.

5. Decisions of the Federal courts (other than the U.S. Supreme Court) are not binding on other Federal courts of coordinate rank or inferior rank, unless the latter owe obedience to the deciding court. For example, a decision of the Fifth Circuit Court of Appeals binds district courts in the fifth circuit but no other Federal court.

6. A decision of a State court is binding on all courts inferior to it in its jurisdiction. Thus, the decision of the supreme court in a State binds all other courts in that State.

7. A decision of a State court is not binding on courts in another State except where the latter courts are required to apply the law of the first State as determined by the highest court in that State. For example, if a North Carolina court is required to apply Virginia law, it must follow decisions of the Virginia Supreme Court.

Averting a Bhopal Legal Disaster

By Douglas J. Besharov
And Peter Reuter

Five months ago a gas leak at a Union Carbide Corp. chemical plant in Bhopal, India, killed an estimated 1,700 Indians and injured as many as 200,000 more. The scale of death and suffering made this a singular human disaster. Now it seems that the outcome of the resulting litigation will be another disaster: Either the victims will receive grossly inadequate (and much delayed) compensation or U.S. firms operating overseas will face uniquely onerous legal liability, further handicapping them in competing with foreign firms. But with leadership from both governments, the interests of all parties can be reconciled.

Most lawsuits are settled, and probably, so will be this one. Union Carbide Chairman Warren Anderson accepted "moral responsibility" for the tragedy, and the company has already pledged $7 million to survivors for "immediate interim relief." But no legal settlement is likely before we know where the case would be tried. Why? The possibility of punitive damages.

The recent legal jockeying comes down to the simple question of forum: Will the Bhopal victims persuade some U.S. trial court to accept jurisdiction over their claims? So central is this issue to the outcome of the case that the Indian government, in joining the suit, has also asked that the case be handled in the U.S.

Only in the U.S.

Two factors bring the Bhopal case to U.S. shores. First, Indian courts do not seem to be equipped for a case of this magnitude. U.S. courts have developed proce-

dures, however cumbersome, for handling cases with very large numbers of plaintiffs and complicated legal and scientific issues. In fact, many experts believe that, should the effort to bring litigation in the U.S. fail, no suit will ever be filed in India. Instead, Union Carbide would settle for negligible amounts per victim.

Second, unbounded damages to "punish" defendants, a uniquely U.S. invention, could be awarded. They are not available anywhere else in the world. To punish wrongdoers, other societies rely on criminal prosecution or other governmental sanctions. In recent years, however, U.S. judges have progressively expanded the old English common law concept of punitive damages (originally limited to narrowly circumscribed situations in which ordinary damages were deemed inadequate) so that they can be awarded against any defendant whose behavior suggests a reckless or wanton disregard for safety—allegations already made against Union Carbide. Punitive awards of between $1 million and $5 million are no longer unusual. Recognize that those were awards in favor of individual plaintiffs and one sees why these claims are in the billions.

The magnified liability Union Carbide would face in U.S. courts will undoubtedly lead it to argue that the suits belong in India. U.S. judges retain discretion to dismiss lawsuits that, although falling under their formal jurisdiction, should be brought elsewhere. Is it more convenient, given the witnesses and documents, to have it heard in the U.S. or in India? Union Carbide will emphasize the failure of local operators; the victims, design defects and corporate responsibility.

There is a nasty element of Russian roulette here. If the plaintiffs prevail on the forum issue, they win big. Union Carbide could be pushed to bankruptcy. If the company can persuade U.S. courts to dismiss the suits, the victims would lose most of their bargaining power, and they would be compelled to settle for far less than they could get now.

Furthermore, the outcome of this gamble will not be known for three or four years at best. The forum issue cannot be definitively decided until appeals are exhausted. In the meantime, the victims will be left waiting.

The vast disparity in the likely outcomes in U.S. and Indian courts is what makes an early compromise unlikely. Union Carbide, with its public image and the prospect of unbounded punitive damages in mind, should be willing to settle for an amount approximating the actual damages inflicted. But it will see little reason to offer more than an appropriate premium for early settlement until the imposition of punitive damages seem probable.

A very rough calculation can be made of the probable compensatory (not punitive) award. Based on a recent Rand Corp. study of wrongful-death awards in Chicago, an American's life is worth about $500,000. But in setting monetary value on the damage inflicted, U.S. courts will take into account the differences between U.S. and Indian costs and standards of living. Indian per capita gross national product is only about 1.7% of the U.S. figure ($256 compared with $15,000). Thus a U.S. court might award only $8,500 for an Indian's death. Multiplied by 17,000 deaths, this would come to about $14.5 million. For the 200,000 injured—

Averting Disaster continued

some very seriously, some only slightly—we base our estimate on a Rand study of asbestos litigation. The average payment to asbestos victims, a population with similarly varied injuries, was $64,000. Using the same adjustment for Indian income, we project an average of $1,100 for each injury, which would total $220 million. In all, Union Carbide might expect an offer of between $200 million and $300 million to receive serious consideration, if punitive damages were not a factor.

The U.S. lawyers representing the victims, sensing the possibility of an astronomical award of punitive damages, will have little incentive to settle for compensatory damages. Since their contingency fees will be relatively modest unless the damages are bolstered by a punitive award, they will go for double or nothing. Actually, it is more likely tenfold or nothing.

The fate of the Bhopal victims should not hinge on such an outrageous gamble. There is only one way to break the present deadlock and ensure prompt and adequate payment to the victims: The question of compensation must be separated from the question of punishment.

The Indian and U.S. governments should establish a special, bilateral tribunal to handle the claims. By agreement among them, Union Carbide and any other responsible parties (there may be more defendants) should be required to provide full and prompt compensation for the victims. A government - to - government agreement is needed to prevent the plaintiffs' U.S. lawyers from

challenging the settlement in court. Although congressional action would be preferable, such a claims tribunal could probably be established by executive order, as was the one created by President Carter as part of the Iranian hostage settlement.

Punitive damages should be excluded. This quintessentially American delegation of law-enforcement powers to private litigants is not needed to meet the pressing needs of the victims. The Indian government, like the victims, should be willing to trade off the long-term possibility of a windfall gain for the certainty of immediate payment of satisfactory compensation. (Such practical compromises frequently resolve domestic litigation when the possibility of unbounded damages is balanced against questionable liability.) If the Indian government thinks that punitive action is needed, it can bring the appropriate criminal prosecution—in India.

Besides being fair to the victims, such an agreement would be in the U.S.'s interest. As a society, it has decided to impose punitive liability on business to protect U.S. citizens. Many Americans, understandably, would like to hold U.S. business to the same levels of liability for its actions overseas. But doing so handicaps U.S. firms as they compete against foreign firms that do not carry similarly expensive liabilities. Whether the U.S. thinks other countries should do so is beside the point. It can't make them assume those liabilities, and the result will be the further loss of overseas markets for U.S. firms.

Sensitive to Accusations

Also, not every country can afford U.S. levels of liability. Even if other developed countries decided to adopt those other wonders of contemporary America—strict liability, punitive damages, contingency fees—it is not clear that the Third World would want to buy them, embedded in exports and investment. Countries like India may reasonably deem them unnecessary luxuries, just as an Indian OSHA might allow much laxer workplace safety than would its U.S. counterpart. It is not the U.S.'s place to impose its rules concerning safety and liability.

We harbor no illusions, though, about the eagerness of either government to pursue this seemingly sensible resolution. The U.S. government will be sensitive to accusations that it is protecting a major U.S. corporation and condoning the exploitation of Third World peoples.

The Indian government, too, will fear charges that it is kowtowing to an "imperialist" nation. Better to leave the matter in the courts and, if the outcome is no recovery for the victims, the "imperialists" can still be blamed.

Nevertheless, both governments have ample reason for concluding that a compensation-based settlement is in the interest of all concerned. If either government summons up the courage to pursue its enlightened self-interest—and the best interests of the victims—the other would be shortsighted to reject the offer.

Jurisdiction over the Parties

The second essential type of jurisdiction a court must have is the power of a court to bind the parties involved in the dispute. This type of jurisdiction is

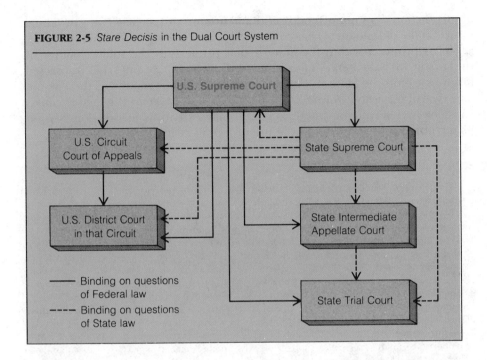

FIGURE 2-5 *Stare Decisis* in the Dual Court System

U.S. Supreme Court

U.S. Circuit Court of Appeals

State Supreme Court

U.S. District Court in that Circuit

State Intermediate Appellate Court

State Trial Court

——— Binding on questions of Federal law

- - - - Binding on questions of State law

called jurisdiction over the parties, and its requirements may be met in any of three ways: (1) *in personam* jurisdiction, (2) *in rem* jurisdiction, or (3) attachment jurisdiction. In addition, the exercise of jurisdiction must satisfy the constitutionally imposed requirements of reasonable notification and a reasonable opportunity to be heard. This means that the courts must exercise jurisdictional power in a manner consistent with the principle of "due process" of law as we discuss more fully in Chapter 3.

In Personam Jurisdiction   *In personam* jurisdiction or personal jurisdiction is jurisdiction of a court over the parties to a lawsuit in contrast to jurisdiction over their property. A court obtains *in personam* jurisdiction over a person either (1) by serving process on the party within the State in which the court is located or (2) by reasonable notification to a party outside the State in those instances where a "long-arm statute" applies. To *serve process* means to deliver a summons, which is an order to respond to a complaint lodged against a party. (The terms *summons* and *complaint* are more fully explained later in this chapter.)

Anyone personally served within a State, even a transient, is subject to personal jurisdiction of the courts within that State. For instance, Alison, a resident of Ohio, is served with a summons from a Texas court while driving her automobile through Texas. The Texas court has obtained personal jurisdiction over Alison because she was personally served within Texas. The same is true of Burt, a resident of New Jersey, who is served in Dallas when the airplane in which he is flying touches down for a brief stop.

In addition, most States have adopted **long-arm statutes** to expand their jurisdictional reach. These statutes allow courts to obtain jurisdiction over nonresident defendants under the following conditions, as long as the exercise

Jurisdiction over the parties —power of a court to bind the parties to a suit

In personam jurisdiction —jurisdiction based on claims against a person in contrast to jurisdiction over his property

of jurisdiction does not offend traditional notions of fair play and substantial justice: if the defendant (1) has committed a tort (civil wrong) within the State, (2) owns property within the State if that property is the subject matter of the lawsuit, (3) has entered into a contract within the State, or (4) has transacted business within the State if that business is the subject matter of the lawsuit. The case of *Clements v. Barney's Sporting Goods Store illustrates* the factors courts consider in determining whether a State may extend its jurisdiction beyond its territorial borders through the use of a long-arm statute.

CLEMENTS v. BARNEY'S SPORTING GOODS STORE

Appellate Court of Illinois, First District, Fifth Division, 1980.
84 Ill.App.3d 600, 40 Ill.Dec. 342, 406 N.E.2d 43.

FACTS: Plaintiff, Thomas Clements, brought this action to recover damages for breach of warranty against defendant, Signa Corporation. As we will discuss in Chapter 19, a warranty is an obligation that the seller of goods assumes with respect to the quality of the goods sold. Clements had purchased a motor boat from Barney's Sporting Goods, an Illinois corporation. The boat was manufactured by Signa Corporation, an Indiana corporation with its principal place of business in Decatur, Indiana. Signa has no office in Illinois and no agent authorized to do business on its behalf within Illinois. Clements saw Signa's boats on display at the Chicago Boat Show. In addition, literature on Signa's boats was distributed at the Chicago Boat Show. Several boating magazines, delivered to Clements in Illinois, contained advertisements for Signa's boats. Clements had also seen Signa's boats on display at Barney's Sporting Goods Store in Palatine, Illinois, where he eventually purchased the boat. A written warranty issued by Signa was delivered to Clements in Illinois. Although Signa was served with a summons, it failed to enter an appearance in this case. A default order was entered against Signa and subsequently a judgment of $6,220 was entered against Signa. Signa appealed.

DECISION: Judgment for Clements. Under Section 17 of the Illinois Long-Arm Statute, a non-resident corporation which transacts business within the State of Illinois is subject to personal jurisdiction in the Illinois State courts in any lawsuit arising out of such business. The assertion of personal jurisdiction, however, must satisfy the due process clause of the Fourteenth Amendment to the United States Constitution. Due process requires sufficient "minimum contacts" between Illinois and the non-resident corporation so that the exercise of personal jurisdiction is consistent with traditional notions of fair play and substantial justice.

By displaying its boats and distributing literature at the Chicago Boat Show, as well as by advertising in magazines which have Illinois subscribers and selling its boats to Illinois retailers, Signa Corporation satisfies the due process "minimum contacts" test and the Illinois Long-Arm Statute. Since it has intentionally and consistently engaged in practices designed to promote sales of its boats in Illinois, it would not violate traditional notions of fair play and justice for the Illinois State court to assert personal jurisdiction over Signa on a claim which arose out of the sale of one of its boats to an Illinois resident, Clements, in Illinois.

In rem jurisdiction—jurisdiction based on claims against property

In Rem Jurisdiction   Courts in a State have the jurisdiction to adjudicate claims to property situated within the State if the plaintiff gives reasonable notice and an opportunity to be heard to those persons who have an interest in the property. Such jurisdiction over property is called *in rem jurisdiction* from the Latin word *res*, which means "thing." For example, if A and B are involved in a lawsuit over property located in Kansas, then an appropriate court in Kansas would have *in rem* jurisdiction to adjudicate claims over this property as long as both parties are given notice of the lawsuit and a reasonable opportunity to contest the claim.

Quasi in rem jurisdiction—jurisdiction over property not based on claims against it

Attachment Jurisdiction   Attachment jurisdiction or **quasi in rem jurisdiction,** like *in rem* jurisdiction, is jurisdiction over property rather than over a person. But attachment jurisdiction is invoked by seizing the defendant's property located within the State to obtain payment of a claim against the defendant that is *unrelated* to the property seized. The basis of jurisdiction, therefore, is the State's connection with the property; it does not depend on any connection between the State and the defendant. Attachment jurisdiction differs from *in rem* jurisdiction in that the purpose of *in rem* jurisdiction is to resolve conflicting claims to the property; in attachment jurisdiction both parties accept that the property is owned by the defendant, but the plaintiff seeks to seize it to obtain payment for his claim against the defendant. For example, A, a resident of Ohio, has obtained a valid judgment in the amount of $20,000 against B, a citizen of Kentucky. A can attach B's automobile, which is located in Ohio, to satisfy his court judgment against B.

However, in attachment jurisdiction, as with all forms of jurisdiction, the State must have sufficient, minimum contacts with the controversy so that due process will not be violated. In the example above, the fact that A was a resident of Ohio satisfies this requirement. But if the automobile had been located in West Virginia it is doubtful that a court in West Virginia could assert attachment jurisdiction over B's automobile.

Venue   Venue, which is often confused with jurisdiction, deals with the location where a lawsuit *should* be brought. State rules of venue typically require that a suit be initiated in the county where one of the defendants lives. In matters involving real estate, most venue rules require that a suit be initiated in the county where the property is situated. However, a defendant may object to the venue for various reasons. For instance, a defendant may object to venue based on the principle of *forum non-conveniens*. This basically means that the presentation of the case in that court will create a hardship on the defendant or on relevant witnesses because of the great distance the individuals must travel. The court does not dismiss the case in such a situation. Rather, it shifts the case to a more convenient location.

Venue—particular geographical place where a court with jurisdiction may hear a case

Civil Procedure

Civil disputes that enter the judicial system must follow the rules of civil procedure. These are designed to resolve the dispute in a just, prompt, and inexpensive way.

To acquaint you with civil procedure, we will carry a hypothetical action through the trial court to the highest court of review in the State. Although there are technical differences in trial and appellate procedure among the States, the following illustration will give you a general understanding of the trial and appeal of cases. Assume that Pam Pederson, a pedestrian, while crossing a street in Chicago, is struck by an automobile driven by David Dryden. Pederson suffers serious personal injuries, incurs heavy medical and hospital expenses, and is unable to work for several months. She desires that Dryden pay her for the loss and damages she sustained. Attempts at settlement failing, Pederson brings an action at law against Dryden. Thus Pederson is the plaintiff and Dryden the defendant. Each is represented by a lawyer. Let us follow the progress of the case.

The Pleadings

The purpose of pleadings is to establish the issues of fact and law presented and disputed. An "issue of fact" is a dispute between the parties regarding the events that gave rise to the lawsuit. In contrast, an "issue of law" is a dispute between the parties as to what legal rules apply to these facts. Issues

Pleadings—series of responsive, formal, written statements by each side to a lawsuit

of fact are decided by the jury whereas issues of law are decided by the court. A lawsuit begins when Pederson, the plaintiff, files with the clerk of the trial court a **complaint** against Dryden that alleges: (1) the relevant facts, (2) the existence of a duty owing by the defendant to the plaintiff by reason of the facts, (3) a breach or violation of that duty by the defendant, and (4) loss and damage caused to the plaintiff proximately resulting from that breach. In addition, the complaint requests a judgment for money damages or another appropriate remedy.

Complaint–initial pleading by the plaintiff stating his case

The county sheriff or one of his deputies serves a summons and a copy of the complaint on Dryden, the defendant, commanding him to file his appearance and answer with the clerk of the court within a specific time, usually thirty days from the date the summons was served. The **summons** has the important function of notifying the defendant that a suit has been brought against him. Proper service of the summons establishes the court's jurisdiction over the person of the defendant.

Summons–notice given to inform a person of a lawsuit against him

In this example, Pederson's complaint alleges that while exercising due and reasonable care for her own safety, she was struck by Dryden's automobile, which was negligently being driven by Dryden, causing personal injuries and damages of $50,000, for which Pederson requests judgment.

At this point Dryden, the defendant, has several options. He may make **pre-trial motions** contesting the court's jurisdiction over him or asserting that the action is barred by the Statute of Limitations, which requires suits to be brought within a specified time. Dryden may also move, or request, that the complaint be made more definite and certain, or he may instead move that the complaint be dismissed for failure to state a claim on which relief may be granted. Such a motion is sometimes called a **demurrer;** it essentially asserts that even if all of Pederson's allegations are true, she would still not be entitled to the relief she seeks and therefore there is no need for a trial of the facts. The court rules on this motion as a matter of law. If it rules in favor of the defendant, the plaintiff may appeal the ruling.

Answer–defendant's initial pleading in response to the plaintiff's complaint.

More likely, however, Dryden will respond to the complaint by filing an **answer,** which may contain denials, admissions, affirmative defenses, and counterclaims. Dryden might answer the complaint by denying its allegations of negligence and stating that he was driving his car at a low speed and with reasonable care (a **denial**) when his car struck Pederson (an **admission**), who had dashed across the street in front of his car without looking in any direction to see whether cars or other vehicles were approaching; that, accordingly, Pederson's injuries were caused by her own negligence (an **affirmative defense**), and therefore she should not be permitted to recover any damages. Dryden might further state that Pederson caused damage to his car and request a judgment for $2,000 (a **counterclaim**). These pleadings create an issue of fact about whether Dryden or Pederson, or both, had failed to exercise due and reasonable care under the circumstances and were thus negligent and liable for their carelessness.

Reply–plaintiff's pleading in response to the defendant's answer

If the defendant counterclaims, the plaintiff must respond by a **reply,** which may also contain admissions, denials or affirmative defenses.

After the pleadings, either party may move for **judgment on the pleadings,** which requests the judge to rule as a matter of law whether the facts as alleged in the pleadings of the nonmoving party are sufficient to grant the requested relief.

Pretrial Procedure

In preparation for trial and even before completion of the pleadings stage, each party has the right to obtain evidence, or facts that may lead to evidence, from the other party. This procedure is known as **discovery.** It includes (1) pretrial *depositions* consisting of sworn testimony of the opposing party or other witnesses taken out of court; (2) sworn answers by the opposing party to *written interrogatories,* or questions; (3) *production* of documents and physical objects in the possession of the opposing party; (4) *examination* by a physician of the physical condition of the opposing party, as needed; and (5) admissions of facts set forth in a *request for admissions* submitted to the opposing party. By using discovery properly, each party may become fully informed of the evidence and avoid surprise at the trial. Another purpose of this procedure is to encourage and help settlements by giving both parties as much relevant information as possible.

Discovery—pretrial exchange of information between opposing parties to a lawsuit

The evidence disclosed by discovery may be so clear that a trial to determine the facts becomes unnecessary. If this is so, either party may move for a **summary judgment,** which requests the judge to rule that, because there are no issues of fact to be determined by trial, as a matter of law that party should prevail. The following case involving the famous actress Shirley MacLaine explains the rules courts use to determine whether to grant summary judgment.

FACTS: Shirley MacLaine Parker, a well-known actress, contracted with Twentieth Century-Fox Film Corporation in August, 1965 to play the female lead in Fox's upcoming production of "Bloomer Girl," a motion picture musical that was to be filmed in California. Fox agreed to pay Parker $750,000 for 14 weeks of her services. Fox decided to cancel its plans for "Bloomer Girl" before production had begun, and, instead, offered Parker the female lead in another film, "Big Country, Big Man," a dramatic western to be filmed in Australia. The compensation offered was identical, but Parker's right to approve the director and screenplay would have been eliminated or altered by the "Big Country" proposal. She refused to accept and brought suit to recover the $750,000 for Fox's breach of the "Bloomer Girl" contract. Fox's sole defense in its answer was that it owed no money to Parker because she had deliberately failed to mitigate or reduce her damages by unreasonably refusing to accept the "Big Country" lead. Parker filed a motion for summary judgment. Fox, in opposition to the motion, claimed, in effect, only that the "Big Country" offer was not employment different or inferior to that under the "Bloomer Girl" contract.

PARKER v. TWENTIETH CENTURY-FOX FILM CORP.

Supreme Court of California, 1970.
3 Cal.3d 176, 89 Cal.Rptr. 737, 474 P.2d 689.

DECISION: Summary judgment granted to Parker. The matter to be determined by the trial court on a motion for summary judgment is whether facts have been presented which give rise to a triable factual issue. The court may not pass upon the issue itself. Summary judgment is proper only if the affidavits or declarations in support of Parker, the moving party, would be sufficient to sustain a judgment in her favor and her opponent does not by affidavit show facts sufficient to present a triable issue of fact. The affidavits of the moving party are strictly construed, and doubts as to the propriety of summary judgment should be resolved against granting the motion. Such summary procedure is drastic and should be used with caution so that it does not become a substitute for the open trial method of determining facts.

Here, it is clear that the trial court correctly ruled that Parker's failure to accept Fox's tendered substitute employment could not be applied in mitigation of damages because the offer of the "Big Country" lead was of employment both different and inferior, and that no factual dispute was presented on that issue. Therefore, summary judgment in favor of Parker is granted for $750,000.

Trial

A party who desires a trial by jury, in cases where one is available, must file a written jury demand. Where there is no trial by jury, the court acts as the "trier of facts." Otherwise, the jury decides what facts are established by the evidence. If the demand for a jury is timely, the trial begins by selection of a jury. The jury selection process involves an examination by the parties' attorneys (or in some courts by the judge) of the potential jurors called **voir dire.** Each party has an unlimited number of **challenges for cause,** which allow a party to prevent a prospective juror from serving if he is biased or cannot be fair and impartial. In addition, each party has a limited number of **peremptory challenges** for which no cause is required to disqualify a prospective juror.

Voir dire—preliminary examination of potential jurors

After the jury has been selected, each attorney makes an **opening statement** about the facts that he expects to prove in the trial. The plaintiff and her witnesses then testify on **direct examination** by the plaintiff's attorney. Each is subject to **cross-examination** by the defendant's attorney. Pederson has her witnesses testify that the traffic light at the street intersection where she was struck was green for traffic in the direction in which she was crossing but changed to yellow when she was about one-third of the way across the street.

During the trial the judge rules on the admission and exclusion of evidence. If the judge does not allow certain evidence to be introduced or certain testimony to be given, the attorney must make an **offer of proof** to preserve for review on appeal the question of its admissibility. The offer of proof is not regarded as evidence, and the offer, which consists of oral statements of counsel or witnesses for the record to show the evidence that the judge has ruled inadmissible, is not heard by the jury.

After cross-examination, followed by redirect examination of each of her witnesses, Pederson rests her case. At this time Dryden may move for a **directed verdict** in his favor. If the judge concludes that the evidence introduced by Pederson, which is assumed to be true, would not be sufficient for the jury to find in favor of the plaintiff, then the judge will grant the directed verdict in favor of the defendant.

If the judge denies the motion for a directed verdict, however, the defendant then has the opportunity to present evidence. Dryden and his witnesses testify that he was driving his car at a low speed when it struck Pederson and that Dryden at the time had the green light at the intersection. After the defendant has presented his evidence and both parties have rested (concluded), then each party may move for a directed verdict. By this motion the party contends that the evidence is so clear that reasonable persons could not differ about the outcome of the case. If the judge grants the motion for a directed verdict, he takes the case away from the jury and enters a judgment for the party making the motion.

If these motions are denied, then Pederson's attorney makes an argument to the jury, reviewing the evidence and urging a verdict in favor of his client, Pederson, followed by the defendant's attorney, who summarizes the evidence in the light most favorable to his client, Dryden. Pederson's attorney is permitted to make a short argument in rebuttal.

The attorneys have previously given written **jury instructions** on the applicable law to the trial judge, who gives those which he approves to the jury and denies those which he considers incorrect. The judge may also give the jury instructions of his own. These instructions (called "charges" in some States) advise the jury of the particular rules of law that apply to the facts as the jury determines from the evidence. The jury then retires to the jury room to deliberate and to reach its **verdict** in favor of one party or the other. If the jury finds the issues in favor of Dryden, its verdict is that he is not liable. If, however, it finds the issues for Pederson and against Dryden, its verdict will be that the defendant is liable and will specify the amount of the plaintiff's damages. In this case the jury found that Pederson's damages were $35,000. On returning to the jury box, the foreman either announces the verdict or hands it in written form to the clerk to give to the judge, who reads the verdict in open court. The unsuccessful party may then file a written motion for a new trial or for **judgment notwithstanding the verdict** (also referred to as a judgment n.o.v.), which is similar to a motion for a directed verdict, only it is made after the jury's verdict. If the judge denies these motions, he enters judgment on, or confirms, the verdict for $35,000 in favor of the plaintiff.

Verdict—formal decision by the jury on questions submitted to it

If Dryden does not appeal, or if the reviewing court affirms the judgment if he does appeal, and Dryden does not pay the judgment, the task of enforcement remains. Pederson requests the clerk to issue a **writ of execution** demanding payment of the judgment, which is served by the sheriff on the defendant. If the writ is returned "unsatisfied," that is, if Dryden still does not pay, Pederson may post bond or other security and order a levy on and sale of specific nonexempt property belonging to the defendant which is then seized by the sheriff, advertised for sale, and sold at a public sale under the writ of execution. If the sale does not produce enough money to pay the judgment, Pederson's attorney may begin another proceeding in an attempt to locate money or other property belonging to Dryden. Pederson's attorney may also proceed by **garnishment** against Dryden's employer to collect from his wages or a bank in which he has an account in an attempt to collect the judgment.

Appeal

Let us assume that Dryden directs his attorney to appeal. The attorney files a notice of appeal with the clerk of the trial court within the prescribed time. Later Dryden, the party appealing or appellant, files in the reviewing court the record on appeal, which contains the pleadings, a transcript of the testimony, rulings by the judge on motions made by the parties, arguments of counsel, jury instructions, the verdict, posttrial motions, and the judgment from which the appeal is taken. In States where there is an intermediate court of appeals, it will usually be the reviewing court. In States where there are no intermediate courts of appeal, a party may appeal directly from the trial court to the State supreme court.

Dryden, as appellant, is required to prepare a condensation of the record, known as an abstract, or pertinent excerpts from the record, which he files together with a **brief** and argument with the reviewing court. His brief contains a statement of the facts, the issues, the rulings by the trial court that Dryden contends are erroneous and prejudicial, grounds for reversal of the judgment, a statement of the applicable law, and arguments on his behalf. Pederson, the appellee, files an answering brief and argument. Dryden may, but is not required to, file a reply brief. The case is now ready to be considered by the reviewing court.

The appellate court does not hear any evidence. It decides the case on the record, abstracts, and briefs. After **oral argument** by the attorneys, if the court elects to hear one, the court takes the case under advisement, or begins deliberations. The appellate court then makes a decision based on majority rule. The court prepares a written opinion containing the reasons for its decision, the rules of law that apply, and its judgment. The judgment may affirm the judgment of the trial court, or if the court finds that reversible error was committed, the judgment may be reversed or modified or returned to the lower court (remanded) for a new trial. The losing party may file a petition for rehearing, which is usually denied.

If the reviewing court is an intermediate appellate court, the party losing in that court may decide to seek a reversal of its judgment by filing within a prescribed time a notice of appeal, if the appeal is by right, or a petition for leave to appeal to the State supreme court, if the appeal is by discretion. This petition corresponds to a petition for a writ of *certiorari* in the United States Supreme Court. The party winning in the appellate court may file an answer to the petition for leave to appeal. If the petition is granted, or if the appeal is by right, the record is certified to the higher court, and each party files a new brief and argument in the supreme court. The supreme court may hear oral argument or simply review the record; it then takes the case under advisement. If the supreme court concludes that the judgment of the appellate court is correct, it affirms. If it decides otherwise, it reverses the judgment of the appellate court and enters a reversal or an order of remand. The unsuccessful party may again file a petition for a rehearing, which is likely to be denied. Barring the remote possibility of an application for still further review by the United States Supreme Court, the case has either reached its termination or, on remand, is about to start its second journey through the courts, beginning as originally in the trial court.

The various stages in civil procedure are illustrated in Figure 2-6.

Arbitration

Arbitration—nonjudicial proceeding where neutral third party selected by disputants renders a binding decision

As we have just seen litigation is complex, time consuming and expensive. Consequently, a number of non-judicial methods of dealing with disputes have developed. The most important of these alternatives to litigation is arbitration. In arbitration the parties select a neutral person or persons (arbitrators) who render a binding decision. Because the presentation of the case is less formal and the rules of evidence are more relaxed, arbitration usually takes less time and costs less than litigation. Moreover, in many arbitration cases the parties are able to select an arbitrator with special expertise concerning the subject of the dispute. Thus, the quality of the arbitrator's decision may be higher than that available through the court system.

There are two basic types of arbitration—consensual, which is by far the most common, and compulsory. **Consensual arbitration** occurs whenever the

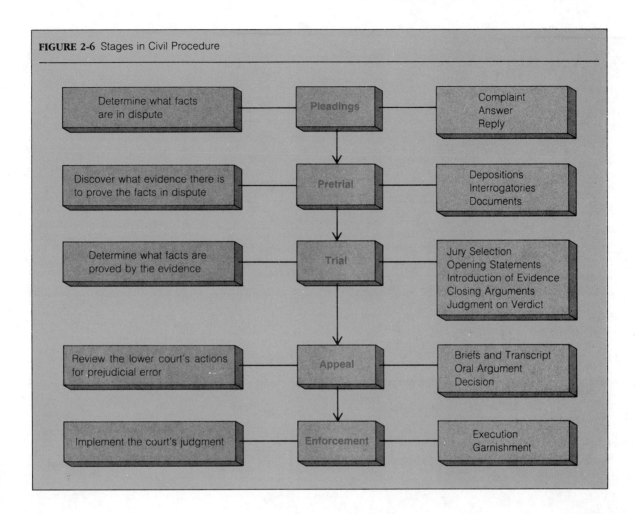

FIGURE 2-6 Stages in Civil Procedure

Determine what facts are in dispute	Pleadings	Complaint Answer Reply
Discover what evidence there is to prove the facts in dispute	Pretrial	Depositions Interrogatories Documents
Determine what facts are proved by the evidence	Trial	Jury Selection Opening Statements Introduction of Evidence Closing Arguments Judgment on Verdict
Review the lower court's actions for prejudicial error	Appeal	Briefs and Transcript Oral Argument Decision
Implement the court's judgment	Enforcement	Execution Garnishment

parties to a dispute agree to submit the controversy to arbitration. They may do this in advance by agreeing in their contract that disputes arising out of their contract will be resolved by arbitration. Or they may do so after a dispute arises by then agreeing to submit the dispute to arbitration. In either instance, such agreements are enforceable under the U.S. Arbitration Act and statutes in over forty States. In **compulsory arbitration,** which is relatively infrequent, a Federal or State statute requires arbitration for specific types of disputes such as those involving public employees like police officers or fire fighters.

The decision of the arbitrators, called an **award,** is binding on the parties. Nevertheless, it is subject to limited judicial review for such matters as illegality, fraud or other misconduct, lack of due process or excess of the arbitrators' powers. Historically, the courts were unfriendly to arbitration. However, as the next case illustrates, the courts have dramatically changed their attitude and now favor arbitration.

Award—the decision of an arbitrator

LaSTELLA v. GARCIA ESTATES, INC.

Supreme Court of New Jersey, 1975.
66 N.J. 297, 331 A.2d 1.

FACTS: La Stella leased property from Garcia for use as a golf course. A few years later, Garcia refused to allow La Stella to exercise the renewal option, so La Stella filed suit to compel renewal of the lease. The court submitted the issue to an arbitration proceeding as stipulated under the contract. The arbitration clause provided that all disputes arising under the lease would be settled by arbitration; that the landlord and tenant would each choose an arbitrator and the two arbitrators thus chosen would select a third arbitrator; and that the findings and award of the three arbitrators thus chosen would be final and binding on the parties.

The arbitrators reached a majority decision (2 to 1) in La Stella's favor. Garcia appealed claiming that under the common law the panel's decision must be unanimous to be binding.

DECISION: Judgment for La Stella. The modern rule is that a majority award by an arbitration panel is binding unless otherwise directed by the agreement to arbitrate. The old common law rule required unanimity unless otherwise indicated in the contract. This rule, however, often resulted in successive proceedings, excessive costs and unnecessary delays, thus frustrating the fundamental purposes of speed and efficiency in an arbitration proceeding. Therefore, since La Stella and Garcia did not expressly provide for a unanimous decision from the panel, unanimity should not be required. Consequently, the arbitration panel's 2-to-1 decision granting La Stella a lease renewal is binding upon Garcia.

CHAPTER SUMMARY

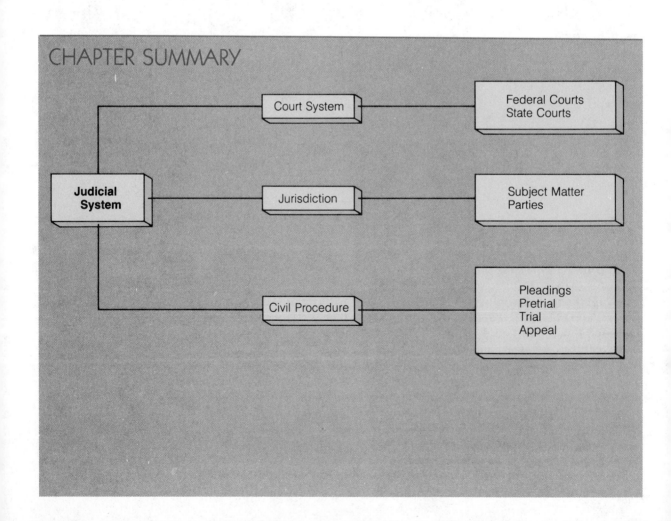

KEY TERMS

Appeal by right
Write of *certiorari*
Jurisdiction
Subject matter jurisdiction
Exclusive jurisdiction
Concurrent jurisdiction
Federal question
Jurisdiction over the parties

In personam jurisdiction
In rem jurisdiction
Quasi in rem jurisdiction
Venue
Pleadings
Complaint
Summons

Answer
Reply
Discovery
Voir dire
Verdict
Arbitration
Award

CONSTITUTIONAL AND ADMINISTRATIVE LAW

We mentioned in Chapter 1 that public law is the branch of substantive law which deals with the government's rights and powers and its relationship to individuals or groups. Public law consists of constitutional law, administrative law, and criminal law. We discuss the first two in this chapter, and we cover criminal law in the next chapter.

Public law has become increasingly important to the study of business. Significant areas of the regulation of business arise from public law. For example, bankruptcy, antitrust, employment law, and securities regulation are principally public law. Other areas of the law, such as products liability and warranties, unfair competition, and consumer protection are also greatly affected by public law.

Constitutional Law

You will recall from Chapter 1 that a constitution is the fundamental law of a particular level of government. It establishes the structure of government and defines political relationships within it. It also places restrictions on the powers of government and lists the rights and liberties of the people.

The Constitution of the United States was adopted on September 17, 1787, in Philadelphia by representatives of the thirteen newly created States. Its purpose is stated in the preamble:

> We the People of the United States, In Order to form a more perfect Union, establish Justice, insure domestic Tranquility, provide for the common defence, promote the general Welfare, and secure the Blessings of Liberty to ourselves and our Posterity, do ordain and establish this Constitution for the United States of America.

Although the framers of the U.S. Constitution stated precisely what rights and authority were vested in the new national government, they considered it unnecessary to list those liberties the people kept to themselves. Nonetheless, at the time of its adoption, all the representatives at the convention were agreed that the Constitution would contain a Bill of Rights that would guarantee protection of individuals from oppression by the newly formed Federal government. The Bill of Rights, which consists of the first ten amendments to the Constitution, was adopted on December 15, 1791. Its provisions were insisted on by the States as curbs and restrictions on the power and authority of the Federal government.

We are concerned in this Chapter with constitutional law as it applies to business and commerce. We begin by surveying some of the basic principles of constitutional law, and then we examine the allocation of power between the Federal and State governments with respect to the regulation of business. Finally, we discuss the constitutional restrictions imposed on the power of government to regulate business.

Basic Principles

A number of concepts are basic to constitutional law in the United States. These principles apply to analysis of both the powers of and the limitations on government. These principles are (1) Federal supremacy and preemption, (2) judicial review, (3) separation of powers, and (4) state action.

Federal Supremacy and Preemption

All other law in the United States, whether case law, statutory law, or administrative law, is subject to the Federal Constitution, which is the **"supreme law of the land."** Article VI of the United States Constitution states:

> This Constitution, and the Laws of the United States which shall be made in Pursuance thereof; and all Treaties made, or which shall be made, under the Authority of the United States, shall be the supreme Law of the Land; and the Judges in every State shall be bound thereby, any Thing in the Constitution or Laws of any State to the Contrary notwithstanding.

Accordingly, no law, Federal or State, is valid if it violates the Federal Constitution. In the landmark case of *McCulloch v. Maryland,* Chief Justice Marshall stated, "This great principle is, that the Constitution and the laws made in pursuance thereof are supreme; that they control the Constitution and laws of the respective states, and cannot be controlled by them."

Federal preemption—first right of the Federal government to regulate matters within its powers to the possible exclusion of State regulation

Whenever Congress exercises a power granted it by the Constitution—that is, when it passes legislation—any conflicting State legislation is **preempted** (overridden) by the Federal action. Even if a State regulation is not obviously in conflict, it must still give way if Congress has clearly intended that its action should preempt the State legislation. This intent may be specifically stated in the legislation or inferred from the scope of the legislation, the need for uniformity, or the danger of conflict between coexisting Federal and State regulation.

Where Congress has not acted, the fact that Congress has the power to act does not prevent the States from acting. Until Congress exercises its power to preempt, State regulation is *not* forbidden.

FACTS: Karen Silkwood was a laboratory analyst for Kerr-McGee Corporation at its Cimmaron plant in Oklahoma. The plant made plutonium fuel pins for use as reactor fuel in nuclear power plants. Accordingly, the plant was subject to licensing and extensive Federal regulation by the Nuclear Regulatory Commission (NRC), pursuant to the Atomic Energy Act, which preempts Oklahoma's regulation of the safety aspects of nuclear energy. During a three-day work period in 1974, Silkwood was contaminated by plutonium at the plant. After high levels of contamination were detected on her when she arrived at work on the third day, Kerr-McGee ordered a decontamination squad to Silkwood's apartment, resulting in the unavoidable destruction of many of her personal belongings. Silkwood was sent to the Los Alamos Scientific Laboratory to determine the extent of the contamination in her body's vital organs. A week later she returned to work but died that night in an unrelated automobile accident. Her father, as administrator of her estate, filed a claim against Kerr-McGee under Oklahoma tort law for Karen's personal injuries and property damage resulting from her contamination. On the basis of the jury's verdict, the trial court awarded Silkwood $505,000 ($500,000 for personal injuries and $5,000 for property damage) plus punitive damages of $10,000,000. Kerr-McGee claimed that the Federal government's extensive regulations and intrusion into the nuclear energy field preempted the Oklahoma State law allowing recovery of punitive damages.

DECISION: Judgment for Silkwood. The Federal preemption of State regulation of the safety aspects of nuclear energy does not extend to a State authorized award of punitive damages. Preemption concerning damages for radiation injuries should not be judged on the basis that the Federal government has so completely occupied the field of safety that State remedies are foreclosed. Rather, preemption depends on whether there is an irreconcilable conflict between the State and Federal standards or whether the imposition of a State standard in a damages suit would frustrate the objectives of the Federal law.

Here, there is no conflict between the payment of a punitive damages award under Oklahoma State law and a Federal fine imposed for an infraction of the NRC's standards. An examination of the statutory scheme and legislative history indicates that Congress did not intend to forbid the States from providing remedies for those suffering injuries from radiation in nuclear plants. Moreover, an award of punitive damages under State law does not hinder Congress' purpose of encouraging the development of atomic energy nor do such damages frustrate the goal of precluding dual regulation of radiation hazards. On the contrary, Congress believed that the NRC should have exclusive regulatory authority over the safety aspects of nuclear development while at the same time plaintiffs like Silkwood should have the right under State law to recover for injuries caused by nuclear hazards.

SILKWOOD v. KERR-McGEE CORPORATION

Supreme Court of the United States, 1984.
464 U.S. 238, 104 S.Ct. 615, 78 L.Ed.2d 443.

Judicial Review

A corollary to the basic principle of Federal supremacy is that of judicial review—that the Supreme Court of the United States is the final authority in determining the constitutionality of any law. Alexander Hamilton forcefully expressed the idea when he stated, "The interpretation of the laws is the proper and peculiar province of the courts. A constitution is, in fact, and must be regarded by the judges, a fundamental law. It therefore belongs to them to ascertain its meaning as well as the meaning of any particular act or proceeding from the legislative body. If there should happen to be an irreconcilable variance between the two, that which has the superior obligation and validity ought of course to be preferred; or, in other words, the Constitution ought to be preferred to the statute, the intention of the people to the intention of their agents."

Judicial review –power of the courts to determine the constitutionality of any legislative or executive act

Separation of Powers

The third basic principle on which our government is founded is that of separation of powers. In our Constitution this means that there are three distinct and independent branches of government—the executive, legislative, and judicial branches. The purpose of the doctrine of separation of powers is to prevent any branch of government from gaining too much power. The doectrine also permits each branch to function without interference from the other branch. Basically, the legislative branch is granted the power to make the law, the executive branch to enforce the law, and the judicial branch to interpret the law. However, the separation of power is not complete. For example, some administrative agencies exercise a judicial function when they hold hearings and also a legislative function when they issue regulations. Nevertheless, our government generally operates under a three-branch scheme providing for separation of powers with checks and balances on the power of each branch.

State Action

Most of the protections provided by the U.S. Constitution and its amendments apply only to governmental action, referred to as "state" action. Only the Thirteenth Amendment, which abolishes slavery or involuntary servitude, applies to the actions of private individuals. "State action" includes any actions of the Federal and State governments and their subdivisions, such as city or county governments and agencies.

In addition, if "private" individuals or entities engage in public functions, their actions may be considered state action subject to constitutional limitations. For example, in *Marsh v. Alabama,* 326 U.S. 501 (1946), it was held that a company town was subject to the First Amendment because the State had allowed the company to exercise all of the public functions and activities that usually were conducted by a town government. Since that case the Supreme Court has been less willing to find state action based upon private entities performing public functions. The next case, *Jackson v. Metropolitan Edison Co.,* illustrates this trend.

JACKSON v.
METROPOLITAN
EDISON CO.

Supreme Court of the United
States, 1974.
419 U.S. 345, 95 S.Ct. 449, 42
L.Ed.2d 477.

FACTS: Metropolitan Edison Company is a privately owned and operated Pennsylvania corporation subject to extensive regulation by the Pennsylvania Public Utility Commission. Under a provision of its general tariff filed with the Commission, Edison had the right to discontinue electric service to any customer on reasonable notice of non-payment of bills. Catherine Jackson had been receiving electricity from Metropolitan Edison when her account was terminated in 1970 because of her delinquency in payments. Edison later opened a new account for her residence in the name of James Dodson, another occupant of Jackson's residence. In August 1971, Dodson moved away and no further payments were made to the account. Finally, in October 1971, Edison disconnected Jackson's service without any prior notice. Jackson brought suit claiming that her electric service could not be terminated without notice and a hearing. She further argued that such action, allowed by a provision of Edison's tariff filed with the Commission, constituted "state action" depriving her of property in violation of the Fourteenth Amendment's guarantee of due process of law.

DECISION: Judgment for Metropolitan Edison. Deprivations of property without due process by the State are prohibited by the Fourteenth Amendment, but private actions depriving individuals of property are immune from the due process requirement. The test for classifying an action as state action is whether a sufficiently close "nexus" (connection) exists between the State and the challenged action so that it can be fairly attributed to the State itself for purposes of the

Fourteenth Amendment. Although Edison is closely regulated by the Commission and enjoys at least a partial monopoly in the area, it is nonetheless a privately owned utility which terminated Jackson's service in a manner which the Commission found to be permissible under State law. Under these circumstances, the State of Pennsylvania was not sufficiently connected with Edison's actions. Therefore, the termination of Jackson's service by Edison was a private action, immune from the Fourteenth Amendment's due process requirement.

Powers of Government

The U.S. Constitution created a Federal government of enumerated powers. Moreover, as the Tenth Amendment declares, "the powers not delegated to the United States by the Constitution, nor prohibited by it to the States, are reserved to the States respectively, or to the people." Therefore, as the Supreme Court has explained, "the sovereign powers vested in the State governments, by their respective constitutions, remained unaltered and unimpaired, except so far as they were granted to the government of the United States."

In this part of the chapter we examine the sources and extent of the powers of the Federal government—as well as the power of the States—to regulate business and commerce.

Federal Commerce Power

Article I, Section 8, of the U.S. Constitution provides in part that "the Congress shall have Power . . . To regulate Commerce with foreign Nations, and among the several States. . . ." This clause has two important effects: (1) it is a broad source of power for the Federal government to regulate the economy, and (2) it operates as a restriction on State regulations that obstruct or unduly burden interstate commerce. As the U.S. Supreme Court has stated: "The Clause is both a prolific sourc[e] of national power and an equally prolific source of conflict with legislation of the state[s]." We discuss the first of these effects below and discuss the second effect in the next section.

> **Commerce power**–exclusive power granted by the U.S. Constitution to the Federal government to regulate commerce with foreign countries and among the States

The U.S. Supreme Court interprets the commerce clause as granting virtually complete power to Congress to regulate the economy and business. A court may invalidate legislation enacted under the commerce clause for only two reasons: (1) if it is clear that the activity regulated by the Legislation does not affect interstate commerce, or (2) if it is clear that there is no reasonable connection between the regulatory means selected and the stated ends. For example, activities that are carried on solely in one State, such as the practice of law or real estate brokerage agreements, are subject to Federal antitrust laws under the power granted by the commerce clause provided that (1) the local activity substantially affects interstate commerce or (2) the local activity is in the flow of commerce.

The following civil rights case illustrates the operation of this test.

FACTS: The McClungs owned Ollie's Barbecue, a restaurant located a few blocks from the interstate highway in Birmingham, Alabama, with dining accommodations for whites only and a take-out service for Negroes. In the year preceding the passage of the Civil Rights Act of 1964, the restaurant had purchased a substantial portion of the food it served from outside the State. The restaurant has refused to serve Negroes since its original opening in 1927 and asserts that if it were required to serve Negroes it would lose much of its business. The McClungs sought

> **KATZENBACH v. McCLUNG**
>
> Supreme Court of the United States, 1964.
> 379 U.S. 294, 85 S.Ct. 377, 13 L.Ed.2d 290.

a declaratory judgment to render unconstitutional the application of the Civil Rights Act to its restaurant since its admitted racial discrimination did not restrict or significantly impede interstate commerce.

DECISION: Judgment declaring the Act constitutional and valid. The Commerce Clause of the Constitution empowers Congress to regulate interstate commerce and to make all laws necessary and proper for that purpose. Even if a business' activity is local it may be reached by Congress if the activity directly or indirectly burdens or obstructs interstate commerce. Title II of the Civil Rights Act passed by Congress in 1964 prohibits racial discrimination in a restaurant if it serves or offers to serve interstate travelers or if a substantial portion of the food it serves has moved in interstate commerce. Testimony introduced during the Congressional hearings on the Act revealed that racial discrimination by restaurants, especially in the South, has resulted in the sale of fewer interstate goods, obstructed interstate travel by Negroes, deterred new businesses from being established there, and has caused business in general to suffer. Consequently, there is a connection between discrimination by restaurants and the movement of interstate commerce.

Ollie's Barbecue purchases through interstate commerce a substantial portion of the food it serves, thereby at least indirectly burdening interstate commerce. Not only would the application of the Civil Rights Act to the McClungs' restaurant not violate any express constitutional limitations, it would also remain within the limits of the Commerce Clause. Therefore, as applied to restaurants like the McClungs', the Act is constitutionally valid.

Because of the broad and permissive interpretation of the commerce power, Congress currently regulates a vast range of activities. Many of the activities discussed in this text are regulated by the Federal government based on the commerce power, including: Federal crimes, consumer warranties, consumer credit transactions, electronic fund transfers, trademarks, unfair trade practices, consumer transactions, residential real estate transactions, consumer safety, employee safety, labor relations, civil rights in employment and transactions in securities. See Law in The News on page 47.

State Regulation of Commerce

The commerce clause, as we previously discussed, specifically grants to Congress the power to regulate commerce among the States. In addition to acting as a broad source of Federal power, the clause also restricts the States' power to regulate activities if the result obstructs or unduly burdens interstate commerce.

Regulations   The Supreme Court ultimately decides the extent of permissible State regulation affecting interstate commerce. In doing so, the Court weighs and balances several factors: (1) the necessity and importance of the State regulation, (2) the burden it imposes on interstate commerce, and (3) the extent to which it discriminates against interstate commerce in favor of local concerns. The application of these factors involves case by case analysis.

Taxation   The commerce clause in conjunction with the import-export clause also limits the power of the State to tax. The import-export clause provides: "No State shall, without the Consent of the Congress, lay any Imposts or Duties on Imports or Exports." Together, the commerce clause and the import-export clause exempt or immunize from State taxation goods that have entered the stream of commerce, whether they are interstate or foreign and whether as imports or exports. The purpose of this immunity is to protect goods in commerce from both discriminatory and cumulative State taxes. Once the goods enter the stream of interstate or foreign commerce, the power of the State to tax ceases and does not resume until the goods are delivered to

Nine for the seesaw

Arguments over the division of powers in a federal system are often fierce. They can indeed, as Americans know, lead to civil war. In normal times, however, they are resolved peacefully through the Supreme Court, one of whose tasks is to define the constitutional balance between the federal government and the states. In recent years the court has changed its mind so often and, in effect, so radically, that the definition has become a blur.

The latest change of mind came late in February, in a mundane case about whether a federal law on wages and working hours could constitutionally be applied to workers on the buses run by the city of San Antonio in Texas. The court ruled, by five votes to four, that the federal law applied. In so doing, it announced an important shift in the balance of power between the federal government and the states—in favour of Washington. At the same time, the decision broke one of the main ideological thrusts of Reaganism (about which, however, the Reagan administration has itself been ambivalent), and raised serious questions about the Supreme Court's own power.

The justices were interpreting two constitutional provisions. One is the commerce clause in article 1 of the constitution; it gives congress the power to regulate commerce between the states and with foreigners. Congressional control over interstate commerce has become the exception which swallows the general rule that, unless the constitution specifically grants congress authority over a subject, it is the states and not the federal government which have the power to legislate about it. Much, if not most, modern federal regulation of American life is based on the commerce clause—including, for

example, important parts of the civil-rights laws of the 1960s.

The other provision is the obscure 10th amendment, which declares that powers not specifically granted to the federal government or prohibited to the states "are reserved to the states respectively, or to the people." In the San Antonio case the Supreme Court ruled, in effect, that the 10th amendment did not interfere with congress's customary authority under the commerce clause, even though the workers involved in the case were local employees.

Nobody understands the 10th amendment, and it was ignored for 30 years after the court stopped resisting New Deal legislation in 1937. Nevertheless it is curious that in the San Antonio case the justices explicitly overruled a decision they had made only nine years before; decades usually pass before the court will overturn one of its precedents. But then the 1976 decision, also on a five-to-four vote, had itself overruled a decision made only in 1968.

Even more startling, though, was the view of federalism that the majority put forward to support its decision. The court could have made its ruling on a narrow technical ground. It did not. Justice Harry Blackmun, whose change of heart since 1976 was enough to shift the court, wrote in the majority opinion that the protection of the states from federal power "inhered principally in the workings of the national government itself," rather than in the constitution as interpreted by the Supreme Court. In other words, the states have some influence on congress and the president; if they do not succeed in using it to keep Washington from encroaching unduly on their powers, they should not expect the court to do

the job for them by declaring federal laws unconstitutional. This view, said one of the dissenting justices, Mr. Lewis Powell, "rejects almost 200 years of the understanding of the constitutional status of federalism."

It also called into question a central principle of the Supreme Court's own constitutional position. Since 1803 the court has claimed the authority, meekly submitted to by presidents and congresses ever since, to invalidate actions of the federal government if they conflict with the constitution. The San Antonio decision seems to suggest that the principle of judicial review does not apply to questions of federalism when congress acts under the commerce clause.

The implications of the decision are so remarkable that one dissenter, Justice William Rehnquist, contented himself with observing that he was confident the court would in time overrule itself yet again. The Reagan administration's department of labour, which wanted the ruling but on more modest grounds, professed itself baffled.

The states do not, of course, enjoy the independence and authority they once did; the flow of power to the federal government over the past half century has seen to that. But the authority remaining to the states has not been trivial; on some questions, education being perhaps the most important, the states still have a bigger say than Washington.

Congress has been careful not to intervene directly in matters that have traditionally belonged to the states. It has generally used the considerable power of the federal purse to persuade states to follow its policies (on a 55-mph speed limit, for example). As the court's

Nine for the seesaw continued

majority expects, congress will probably continue to be cautious. But the way is now open, in theory at least, for the federal government to bark orders at the states. Limits on federal action have long since been cicumvented by the commerce clause (everything these days affects interstate commerce). Now the Supreme Court seems to have declared that judicial enforcement of the constitutional position on federalism is at an end. *The Economist*, March 2, 1985.

the purchaser or the owner terminates the movement of the goods through interstate or foreign commerce.

Federal Fiscal Powers

The Federal government exerts a dominating influence over the national economy. Much of this impact results from the exercise of its regulatory powers under the commerce clause, as previously discussed. In addition, a substantial portion of its influence derives from powers arising independent of the commerce clause. These include (1) the power to tax and spend, (2) the power to borrow and coin money, and (3) the power of eminent domain.

The Federal government's power to tax, although extremely broad, has three major limitations: (1) direct taxes other than income taxes must be apportioned among the States, (2) all custom duties and excise taxes must be uniform throughout the United States and (3) no duties may be levied on exports from any State.

Besides raising revenues, taxes also have regulatory and socioeconomic effects. For example, import taxes and custom duties can protect domestic industry from foreign competition. Graduated or progressive tax rates and exemptions may further social policies of redistributing wealth. Tax credits encourage investment in favored enterprises to the disadvantage of unfavored businesses. Nevertheless, a tax will be upheld "so long as the motive of Congress and the effect of its legislative action are to secure revenue for the benefit of the general government . . ."

The Constitution authorizes the Federal government to pay debts and spend for the common defense and general welfare of the United States. The spending power of Congress is extremely broad and will be upheld so long as it does not violate a specific constitutional limitation on Federal power. Moreover, the power to spend is an important way in which the Federal government regulates the economy. In some cases this is accomplished directly as the level and type of government expenditure have a significant impact on economic cycles and activity. More indirectly, governmental expenditures may have as a condition that the recipients engage in or refrain from certain conduct. For instance, under an executive order issued in 1965, many contractors who enter into contracts with the Federal government must comply with affirmative action requirements in their employment practices. Whether directly or indirectly, the power of the Federal government to spend money represents an important regulatory force in the economy and significantly affects the general welfare of the United States.

Borrowing and Coining Money

Article I, Section 8, states: "The Congress shall have Power . . . To borrow money on the credit of the United States. . . ." The broad extent of this grant of power is shown by the current size of the

Federal deficit. Article I, Section 8, also states: "The Congress shall have Power . . . to coin Money, regulate the Value thereof, and of foreign Coin. . . ." The power to borrow and the power to coin money together have enabled the Federal government to establish a national banking system, the Federal Reserve System, and specialized Federal lending programs such as the Federal Land Bank. Through these and other institutions and agencies the Federal government wields extensive control over national fiscal and monetary policies and exerts considerable influence over interest rates, the money supply, and foreign exchange rates.

Eminent Domain   Supplementing the government's power to tax is its power to take private property for public use, known as the power of **eminent domain,** which is recognized as one of the inherent powers of government in the Federal Constitution and in the constitutions of the States. At the same time, however, the power is carefully limited. The Fifth Amendment to the Federal Constitution provides: "nor shall private property be taken for public use, without just compensation." This amendment applies to the States through the Fourteenth Amendment, which we discuss later. Moreover, similar or identical provisions are found in the constitutions of the States. There is, therefore, a direct constitutional prohibition against taking private property without just compensation and an implicit prohibition against taking private property for other than public use. Under both Federal and State constitutions, the individual is entitled to due process of law in connection with the taking. Eminent domain is discussed further in Chapter 45.

> **Eminent domain**–the power of a government to take private property for public use upon payment of fair compensation

Limitations on Government

The U.S. Constitution specifies certain powers that are granted to the Federal government. Other unspecified powers have been reserved to the States. However, the Constitution and its amendments impose limits on all these powers. In this part of the chapter we discuss those limitations most applicable to business: (1) the contract clause, (2) the First Amendment, (3) due process, and (4) equal protection.

Contract Clause

Article I, Section 10, of the Constitution provides: "No State shall . . . pass any . . . Law impairing the Obligation of Contracts. . . ." The Supreme Court has used this clause to restrict States from retroactively modifying public charters and private contracts. For example, the contract clause protects the charter of a corporation formed under a State incorporation statute against modification.

Incorporation and other enabling statutes commonly reserve to the State the power to prescribe such regulations, provisions, and limitations as it shall deem advisable, and to amend, repeal, or modify the statute at its pleasure. Because such reservations are actually written into the contract between the State and the other party, any amendment or modification does not impair the obligation of contract because it was expressly permitted by the contract or charter.

Moreover, the Supreme Court has held that the contract clause does *not* preclude the States from exercising eminent domain or their police powers. As the Supreme Court stated: "No legislature can bargain away the public health or the public morals."

First Amendment

The First Amendment states:

> Congress shall make no law respecting an establishment of religion, or prohibiting the free exercise thereof; or abridging the freedom of speech, or of the press; or the right of the people peaceably to assemble, and to petition the Government for a redress of grievances.

This amendment is the constitutional source of many of the civil and political rights enjoyed in the United States. Accordingly, it gives rise to a wide range of issues, far too broad for us to address fully in this text. We will examine the application of the First Amendment's guarantee of free speech to (1) commercial speech and (2) defamation.

Commercial speech
expression related to the economic interests of the speaker and its audience

Commercial Speech

Commercial speech is expression related to the economic interests of the speaker and its audience, such as advertisements of a product or service. Within the past decade, U.S. Supreme Court decisions have eliminated the doctrine that commercial speech is wholly outside the protection of the First Amendment. Instead the Court has established the principle that speech that does no more than propose a commercial transaction is entitled to a "lesser degree" of constitutional protection. This limited grant of protection is justified because of interest in the communication by the advertiser, consumer, and general public. Advertising and other such messages provide important information for the proper and efficient distribution of resources in our free market system. At the same time, commercial speech is less valuable and less vulnerable than other varieties of speech and therefore does not merit complete First Amendment protection.

These Supreme Court cases establish an *ad hoc* balancing test to determine the constitutional validity of governmental regulations that suppress commercial expression. The analysis weighs—with *close* scrutiny—the implicated First Amendment interests against the State's justification for its regulation, and focuses specifically on whether the regulation substantially furthers a legitimate state interest and whether a less drastic alternative is available. Although this standard is less rigorous than the traditional First Amendment test of *exacting* scrutiny, the commercial speech standard is far from undemanding.

Because the constitutional protection extended to commercial speech is based on the informational function of advertising, governments may regulate or suppress commercial messages that do not accurately inform the public about lawful activity. "The government may ban forms of communication more likely to deceive the public than to inform it, or commercial speech related to illegal activity." Therefore, governmental regulation of false and misleading advertising is permissible under the First Amendment.

Defamation–injury of a person's reputation by publication of false statements

Defamation

Defamation is a civil wrong or tort consisting of a communication that injures a person's reputation by disgracing him and diminishing the respect in which he is held. An example would be the publication of a statement that a person had committed a crime or had a loathsome disease. (Defamation is also discussed in Chapter 5.)

Because defamation involves a communication, the protection extended to speech by the First Amendment applies. But the Supreme Court has ruled in *New York Times Co. v. Sullivan* that a public official who is defamed in regard to his conduct, fitness, or role as public official may *not* recover in an action of defamation unless the statement was made with *actual malice*, which requires proof that the defendant had knowledge of the falsity of the communication or acted in reckless disregard of its truth or falsity. This restriction on the right to recover for defamation is based on "a profound national commitment to the principle that debate on public issues should be uninhibited, robust and wide-open, and that it may well include vehement, caustic and sometimes unpleasantly sharp attacks on government and public officials." The communication may deal with the official's qualifications for office and his performance in it, which would likely include most aspects of his character and his public conduct.

In addition, the Supreme Court has extended the same rule to candidates for public office and public figures. The Court, however, has not precisely defined the term *public figure*. Examples of persons held to be public figures include a well-known football coach of a State university and a retired army general who takes a prominent and controversial position regarding racial segregation. The Court has explained:

> For the most part [public figures are] those who attain this status [by assuming] roles of especial prominence in the affairs of society. Some occupy positions of such persuasive power and influence that they are deemed public figures for all purposes. More commonly, those classed as public figure have thrust themselves to the forefront of particular public controversies in order to influence the resolution of the issues involved.

Due Process

The Fifth and Fourteenth Amendments respectively prohibit the Federal and State governments from depriving any person of life, liberty, or property without due process of law. The Fifth Amendment provides that

> "No person shall be . . . deprived of life, liberty, or property, without due process of law;"

while the Fourteenth Amendment similarly states

> ". . . nor shall any State deprive any person of life, liberty, or property, without due process of law."

Due process has two different aspects: *substantive* due process and *procedural* due process. As we discussed in Chapter 1, substantive law creates, defines, or regulates legal rights, whereas procedural law establishes the rules for enforcing rights created by the substantive law. Accordingly, **substantive due process** concerns the compatibility of a law or governmental action with fundamental constitutional rights such as free speech. In contrast, **procedural due process** involves the review of the decision-making process that enforces substantive laws and results in depriving a person of life, liberty, or property.

Substantive Due Process   Substantive due process involves a court's determination of whether a particular governmental action is compatible with individual liberties. From 1885 until 1937 the Supreme Court viewed substantive due process as authorizing it to act as a "super legislature" and enabling it to invalidate any law it considered unwise. Since 1937 the Court has abandoned

Substantive due process—requirement that governmental action be compatible with individual liberties

this approach and no longer overturns legislation affecting economic and social interests so long as the legislation is rationally related to legitimate governmental objectives.

Where fundamental rights of individuals under the Constitution are affected, however, the Court will carefully scrutinize the legislation to determine that it is necessary to promote a compelling or over-riding state interest. Included among the fundamental rights that trigger the strict scrutiny standard of substantive due process are (1) the First Amendment rights of freedom of speech, religion, press, peaceful assembly, and petition; (2) the right to engage in interstate travel; (3) the right to vote; (4) the right to privacy; and (5) the right to marry.

Procedural Due Process   Procedural due process pertains to the governmental decision-making process that results in depriving a person of life, liberty, or property. As the Supreme Court has interpreted procedural due process, the government is required to provide persons with a fair procedure if, but only if, the person is faced with deprivation of life, liberty, or property. When governmental action adversely affects an individual but does not deny life, liberty, or property, the government is not required to give the person any hearing at all.

Procedural due process requirement that governmental action depriving a person of life, liberty or property be done through a fair procedure

Liberty for the purposes of procedural due process generally includes the ability of individuals to engage in freedom of action and choice regarding their personal lives. Any significant physical restraint is a deprivation of liberty that requires procedural safeguards. The most important and common example is criminal proceedings. Civil proceedings that result in depriving a person of freedom of action are also subject to the requirements of procedural due process.

Governmental action impairing a person's right to exercise fundamental constitutional rights is also considered a deprivation of liberty subject to due process. As mentioned above, these fundamental rights include the First Amendment rights of freedom of speech, religion, press, peaceful assembly, and petition; the right to engage in interstate travel; and the rights to vote, to privacy, and to marry. Other rights may also be protected by procedural due process.

Property for the purposes of procedural due process includes not only all forms of real and personal property but also certain benefits (entitlements) conferred by government, such as social security payments and food stamps. If a person is hired by the government and is assured continued employment or dismissal only for specified reasons, then there must be a fair procedure to discharge the employee. On the other hand, if the employment is terminable at any time by the government there is no property interest in the employee and, therefore, no requirement of procedural due process applies to a dismissal of the employee.

When applicable, procedural due process requires that the procedure be fair and impartial in the resolution of the factual and legal basis for the governmental actions that result in the deprivation of life, liberty, or property. Different situations will call for various types of procedures as is illustrated in the following case.

BOARD OF CURATORS
OF THE UNIVERSITY
OF MISSOURI v.
HOROWITZ

Supreme Court of the United
States, 1978.
435 U.S. 78, 98 S.Ct. 948, 55
L.Ed.2d 124.

FACTS: In the fall of 1971 Miss Horowitz was admitted as an advanced medical student at the University of Missouri-Kansas City. During the spring of 1972, several faculty members expressed dissatisfaction with Miss Horowitz's clinical performance noting that it was below that of her peers, that she was erratic in attendance at her clinical sessions, and that she lacked a critical concern for personal hygiene. Upon the recommendation of the school's Council on Evaluation, she was advanced to her second and final year on a probationary basis. After subsequent unfavorable reviews during her second year and a negative evaluation of her performance by seven practicing physicians, the Council recommended that Miss Horowitz be dismissed from the school for her failure to meet academic standards. The decision was approved by the Dean and later affirmed by the Provost after an appeal by Miss Horowitz. She brought suit against the school's Board of Curators claiming that her dismissal violated her right to procedural due process under the Fourteenth Amendment and deprived her of "liberty" by substantially impairing her opportunities to continue her medical education or to return to employment in a medically related field.

DECISION: Judgment for the Board of Curators. Oral or written notice and an opportunity for the student to present her side of the story at a "hearing" is only required for dismissals or suspensions based on disciplinary grounds. In contrast, a dismissal on academic grounds demands a less stringent procedure—merely an "informal give and take" between the student and administrative body which provides the student "the opportunity to characterize his conduct and put it in what he deems the proper context." Since the Council dismissed Miss Horowitz for failure to meet the school's academic standards, and not for disciplinary reasons, a hearing was not required. In this case the faculty fully informed Miss Horowitz of her unsatisfactory performance ratings and the dangers they posed to her timely graduation and continued enrollment. Furthermore, the Council went beyond the constitutionally required procedural due process by affording her the opportunity to be examined by independent physicians before reaching a final decision. Because the Council more than satisfied the constitutional requirement of procedural due process, its decision is upheld.

Equal Protection

The Fourteenth Amendment states that "nor shall any State . . . deny to any person within its jurisdiction the equal protection of the laws." Although this amendment applies only to the actions of State governments, the Supreme Court has interpreted the due process clause of the Fifth Amendment to subject Federal actions to the same standards of review. Basically, the guarantee of equal protection requires that similarly situated persons be treated similarly by governmental actions. Since 1937, when the Supreme Court abandoned substantive due process as a critical check on legislation, the equal protection guarantee has become the most important constitutional concept protecting individual rights.

When governmental action involves classification of people, the equal protection guarantee comes into play. In determining whether legislation satisfies the equal protection guarantee, the Supreme Court uses either of two standards of review: (1) the rational relationship test and (2) the strict scrutiny test.

Rational Relationship Test   This standard applies to economic legislation and simply requires that it is *conceivable* that the legislation bears some rational relationship to a legitimate governmental interest furthered by the legislation. Under this standard of review, the legislature is permitted to attack part of the evil to which the legislation is addressed. Moreover, there is a strong presumption that the legislation is constitutional. Therefore, the courts will overturn the legislation *only* if clear and convincing evidence shows that there is *no* reasonable basis justifying the legislation.

Strict Scrutiny Test   This test is far more exacting than the rational relationship test. Under the strict scrutiny test the courts do not defer to the legislature; rather they independently determine whether the classification is constitutionally permissible. This determination requires that the legislature's classification is necessary to promote a compelling or overriding governmental interest.

The strict scrutiny test is applied when the legislation affects fundamental rights or involves suspect classifications. Fundamental rights include most of the provisions of the Bill of Rights. Suspect classifications include those made on the basis of race or national origin. A classic and important example of strict scrutiny applied to classifications based upon race is the 1954 school desegregation case of *Brown v. Board of Education of Topeka* in which the Supreme Court ruled that segregated public school systems violated the equal protection guarantee. Subsequently, the Court has invalidated segregated public beaches, municipal golf courses, buses, parks, public golf courses, and courtroom seating.

BROWN v. BOARD OF EDUCATION OF TOPEKA Supreme Court of the United States, 1954. 347 U.S. 483, 74 S.Ct. 686, 98 L.Ed. 873.	FACTS: These are consolidated cases from Kansas, South Carolina, Virginia, and Delaware, each with a different set of facts and local conditions but also presenting a common legal question. Minors of the Negro race, through their legal representatives, sought court orders to obtain admission to the public schools in their community on a non-segregated basis. They had been denied admission to schools attended by white children under laws requiring or permitting segregation according to race. This Court had previously upheld such laws under the "separate but equal" doctrine which provides that there is equality of treatment of the races through substantially equal, even though separate, facilities. There were findings by the lower courts that the white schools and the Negro schools involved had been or were being equalized with respect to buildings, curricula, qualifications and salaries of teachers and other "tangible" factors. The Negro minors contended, however, that segregated public schools are not and cannot be made "equal" and that hence they have been deprived of the equal protection of the laws guaranteed by the Fourteenth Amendment. DECISION: Judgment for Brown and the other Negro children. Segregation of children in public schools solely on the basis of race generates a feeling of inferiority which diminishes their motivation to learn and affects "their hearts and minds in a way unlikely ever to be undone." Though the physical facilities and other "tangible" factors may be equal, segregation of the races with the sanction of law retards the educational and mental development of Negro children and deprives them of equal educational opportunities. Since separate educational facilities are inherently unequal, the "separate but equal" doctrine has no place in the field of public education. Therefore, segregation denies the Negro children the equal protection of the laws guaranteed by the Fourteenth Amendment.

Another important example of strict scrutiny is the "one person, one vote" rule based upon the fundamental right to vote. Chief Justice Warren formulated the rule as follows:

Legislators represent people, not trees or acres. . . . And, if a State should provide that the votes of citizens in one part of the State should be given two times, or five times, or ten times the weight of votes of citizens in another part of the State, it could hardly be contended that the right to vote of those residing in the disfavored areas had not been effectively diluted . . . the Equal Protection Clause requires that the seats in both houses of a bicameral state legislature must be apportioned on a population basis. *Reynolds v. Sims*, 377 U.S. 533 (1964).

Classifications based on sex have been subject to an intermediate standard of review. Under this test there must be a substantial relationship to an important governmental objective. The intermediate standard eliminates the strong presumption of constitutionality adhered to by the rational relationship test. For example, in *Orr v. Orr*, the Court invalidated an Alabama law which allowed courts to grant alimony awards only from husbands to wives and not from wives to husbands. Similarly, in *Reed v. Reed*, an Idaho statute gave preference to males over females in qualifying for selection as administrators of estates. The Court invalidated the statute because the preference did not bear a fair and substantial relationship to any legitimate objective of the legislation. On the other hand, not all legislation based upon gender is invalid. For example, the Court has upheld a California statutory rape law which imposed penalties only upon males as well as the Federal military selective service act which exempted women from registering for the draft.

Administrative Law

Administrative law is the branch of public law that deals with various regulatory functions and activities of the government in its executive capacity as performed, supervised, and regulated by public officials, departments, boards, and commissions, as well as with controversies arising between individuals and such public officials and agencies. Administrative functions and activities concern such important matters of national safety, welfare, and convenience as the establishment and maintenance of military forces, police, citizenship and naturalization, taxation, the coinage of money, elections, environmental protection, consumer protection, the regulation of transportation, interstate highways, labor relations, television, radio, trade and commerce, and in general, public health, safety, and welfare.

Because of the increasing complexity of the social, economic, and industrial life of the nation, the scope of administrative law has expanded enormously. Justice Jackson stated that "the rise of administrative bodies has been the most significant legal trend of the last century, and perhaps more values today are affected by their decisions than by those of all the courts, review of administrative decisions apart." This is evidenced by the great increase in the number and activities of Federal government boards, commissions, and other agencies. Certainly, agencies create more legal rules and adjudicate more controversies than all the legislatures and courts combined.

Among the more important boards and commissions in the States are those supervising and regulating banking, insurance, communications, transportation, public utilities, pollution control, and Worker's Compensation Boards for the administration of employers' liability laws.

Much of Federal, State, and local law in this country, therefore, is established by the countless administrative agencies. These agencies, which many label the "fourth branch of government," possess tremendous power and have long been criticized as being "in reality miniature independent governments

. . . [which are] a haphazard deposit of irresponsible agencies." In 1979 an article in *Fortune* magazine stated:

> In recent years, economists have joined the chorus of criticism, and have blamed excessive regulation for the nation's baffling troubles with innovation, productivity, shortages, unemployment, and inflation. The total cost of complying with government regulation, variously estimated at $50 billion to $150 billion a year, is now in the same league as industry's outlay on new plant and equipment.

Despite this criticism against administrative regulations, it is clear that these agencies play a significant and necessary role in our society. Administrative agencies serve the important function of relieving legislatures from the impossible burden of designing legislation that deals with every detail of the specific problem addressed. As a result, Congress can enact legislation, such as the Federal Trade Commission Act, that prohibits unfair and deceptive trade practices without having to define this phrase or anticipate all the particular problems that may arise. Instead, Congress created an agency—in this example, the Federal Trade Commission—to which it could delegate the power to issue rules, regulations, and guidelines to carry out the statutory mandate. In addition, the establishment of separate, specialized bodies enables administrative agencies to be staffed by individuals with expertise in the field being regulated. Moreover, a number of administrative agencies have responsibility to protect the public from powerful entities, such as large business corporations. For example, the Federal government has established the Consumer Product Safety Commission and the Environmental Protection Agency to safeguard the public against unreasonably dangerous consumer products and damage to the environment.

Federal Administrative Agencies

Federal administrative agencies can be classified as either independent or executive. Executive agencies are those agencies that are housed within the executive branch of government, whereas independent agencies are not. *All* agencies, whether executive or independent, receive their authority from the legislative branch.

Independent Agencies

The following are Federal independent agencies that have substantial impact upon business: Consumer Products Safety Commission (CPSC), Environmental Protection Agency (EPA), Equal Employment Opportunity Commission (EEOC), Federal Communication Commission (FCC), Federal Deposit Insurance Corporation (FDIC), Federal Reserve Board (Fed), Federal Trade Commission (FTC), Interstate Commerce Commission (ICC), National Labor Relations Board (NLRB), Securities and Exchange Commission (SEC), and the Small Business Administration (SBA). We discuss a number of these agencies in other parts of the text: the FTC in chapters 39 and 41, the Consumer Product Safety Commission in Chapter 41, the NLRB and EEOC in Chapter 27, and the SEC in Chapter 40.

Executive Agencies and Departments

A number of executive agencies also have a significant impact upon business and commerce. These include the Council of Economic Advisors, Department of Agriculture, Department of Commerce, Department of Defense, Department of Health and Human Services, Department of Labor, Department of Transportation and the Office of Management and Budget.

Operation

Most administrative agencies perform three basic functions: (1) making rules and regulations, (2) enforcing the law, and (3) adjudicating controversies. Thus, administrative agencies exercise powers that have been allocated by the Constitution to the three separate branches of government. More specifically, agencies exercise legislative power when they make rules, executive power when they enforce the statute and their rules, and judicial power when they adjudicate disputes. This concentration of power has raised questions regarding the propriety of having the same persons who establish the rules also act as prosecutor and as judge in determining whether the rules have been violated.

Rulemaking

Rulemaking is the process by which an administrative agency sets forth rules of law. Under the Administrative Procedure Act (APA), a rule is "the whole or a part of an agency statement of general or particular applicability and future effect designed to implement, interpret, or process law or policy." Once in force, rules apply to all parties. In many situations this is preferable to individual, case-by-case adjudication because all parties are treated equally. Moreover, the process of rulemaking puts all parties on notice that the proposed rule is being considered and provides concerned individuals with an opportunity to be heard.

Legislative rules must be promulgated (put in effect) in accordance with the APA. In addition, they may not involve an unconstitutional delegation of legislative power from the legislature to the agency. To be constitutionally permissible, the statute granting power to an agency must establish reasonable standards guiding the agency in implementing the statute. This requirement has been met by statutory language such as "unfair methods of competition," "fair and equitable," "public interest, convenience, and necessity," and other equally broad expressions. In any event, agencies may not exceed the actual authority granted by the enabling statute. The following case involves this issue.

Legislative rules–substantive rules issued by an administrative agency under the authority delegated to it by the legislature

---

FACTS: In May, 1976, the Federal Communications Commission issued rules requiring cable television systems of a designated size (1) to develop a minimum 20-channel capacity by 1986, (2) to make available on a first-come, non-discriminatory basis certain channels for access by third parties, and (3) to furnish equipment and facilities for such access. The purpose of these rules was to ensure public access to cable systems. Midwest Video Corporation claimed that the access rules exceeded the Commission's jurisdiction granted it by the Communications Act of 1934, because the rules infringe upon the cable systems' journalistic freedom by in effect treating the cable operators as "common carriers." A common carrier is one that "makes a public offering to provide [communication facilities] whereby all members of the public who choose to employ such facilities may communicate or transmit . . ." The Commission contended that its expansive mandate under the Communications Act to supervise and regulate broadcasting encompassed the access rules since they were intended to promote these broad objectives.

F.C.C. v. MIDWEST VIDEO CORP.

Supreme Court of the United States, 1979.
440 U.S. 689, 99 S.Ct. 1435,
59 L.Ed.2d 692.

DECISION: Judgment for Midwest Video. The Commission has the authority to issue rules to promote its long-established regulatory goals of increasing the number of outlets for local expression and diversifying programming. However, under the Communications Act of 1934 the Commission may not impose common carrier obligations on cable operators. This prohibition reflects a Congressional belief that the resulting intrusion upon the journalistic integrity of broadcasters would overshadow any benefits associated with increased public access. Since the access rules require cable operators to accept on a first-come, non-discriminatory basis those members of the general public who wish to use the system, the operators become essentially common carriers and their editorial freedom to control the content of programming is lost. The authority to compel cable operators to provide this type of public access must come specifically from Congress. Thus, the F.C.C.'s access rules went beyond the boundaries of its jurisdiction granted by the Communications Act of 1934 and are, therefore, set aside.

Interpretative rules statements issued by an administrative agency indicating its construction of its governing statute

Procedural rules–rules issued by an administrative agency establishing its organization, method of operation and rules of conduct for practice before it

To be distinguished from this type of rulemaking—which has the force of law—are interpretative and procedural rules. **Interpretative rules** are statements issued by the agency that provide guidance to the agency's construction of its governing statute. However, these rules, which are exempt from APA requirements, are *not* law in that they are not binding on the agency or the courts, although they are given substantial weight. **Procedural rules,** which are also exempt from the APA, establish the agency's organization, method of operation and rules of conduct for practice before the agency.

Enforcement

Agencies also have the power to determine whether their statutes or legislative rules have been violated. In carrying out this function the agencies have traditionally been given great discretion to require the disclosure of information. Accordingly, Congress has conferred on the agencies broad powers of investigation including the power to *subpoena* (command) the attendance of witnesses and the production of documents.

Adjudication

The activities of these administrative agencies have become so extensive that they are referred to in their entirety as the **administrative process.** This term is used in contrast to the term *judicial process.* The former term implies the administration of law by nonjudicial agencies; the latter, the administration of law by judicial bodies or courts. The courts have held that the agencies may adjudicate (by administrative process) subject to review by the courts.

The scope of judicial review of administrative agencies is limited to determining whether the agency has (1) exceeded its authority, (2) properly interpreted the applicable law, (3) violated any constitutional provision, (4) acted contrary to the procedural requirements of the law, (5) acted arbitrarily or capriciously, or (6) reached conclusions that are not supported by substantial evidence.

The procedures employed by the various administrative agencies to adjudicate cases are nearly as varied as the agencies themselves. Nevertheless, the APA does establish certain standards that Federal agencies covered by the act must follow. The hearing is presided over by an administrative law judge and is prosecuted by the agency. Thus, the agency serves as both the prosecutor and decision maker. In order to lessen this conflict of interest, the APA provides for the separation of functions between those engaged in investigation and prosecution from those involved in decision making.

CHAPTER SUMMARY

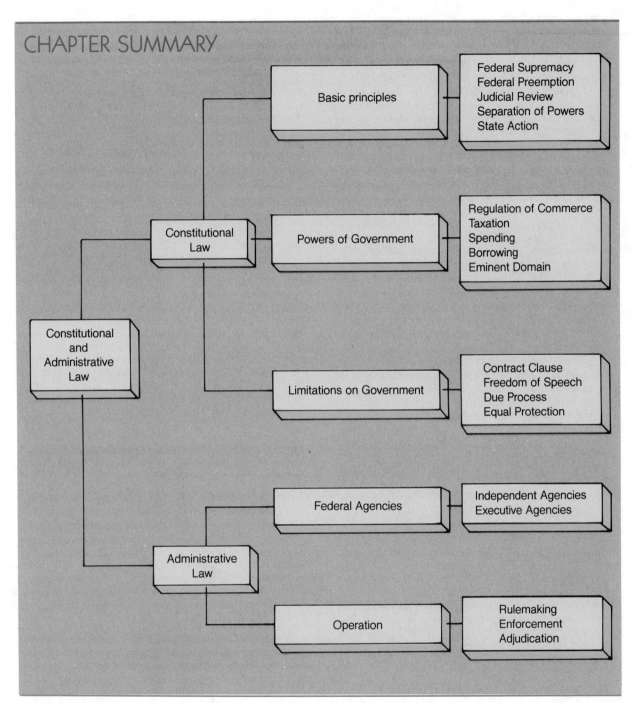

Basic principles → Federal Supremacy / Federal Preemption / Judicial Review / Separation of Powers / State Action

Constitutional Law

Powers of Government → Regulation of Commerce / Taxation / Spending / Borrowing / Eminent Domain

Constitutional and Administrative Law

Limitations on Government → Contract Clause / Freedom of Speech / Due Process / Equal Protection

Federal Agencies → Independent Agencies / Executive Agencies

Administrative Law

Operation → Rulemaking / Enforcement / Adjudication

KEY TERMS

Federal preemption
Judicial review
Separation of powers
State action
Commerce power

Eminent domain
Commercial speech
Defamation
Substantive due process

Procedural due process
Legislative rules
Interpretative rules
Procedural rules

PROBLEMS

1. In May, Patricia Allen left her automobile on the shoulder of a road in the city of Erewhon after the car stopped running. A member of the Erewhon city police department found the car later that day and placed on the car a sticker stating that unless the car were moved it would be towed. When after a week the car had not been removed, the police department authorized Baldwin Auto Wrecking Co. to tow it away and to store it on its property. Allen was told by a friend that her car was at Baldwin's. Allen asked Baldwin to allow her to take possession of her car, but Baldwin refused to relinquish the car until the $70 towing fee was paid. Allen could not afford to pay the fee and the car remained at Baldwin's for six weeks. At that time Baldwin requested the police department for a permit to dispose of the automobile. After the police department tried unsuccessfully to telephone Allen, the department issued the permit. In late July, Baldwin destroyed the automobile. Allen brings an action against the city and Baldwin for damages for loss of the vehicle, arguing that she was denied due process. Decision?

2. In 1967, large oil reserves were discovered in the Prudhoe Bay area of Alaska. As a result the State revenues increased from $124 million in 1969 to $3.7 billion in 1981. In 1980 the State legislature enacted a dividend program that would distribute annually a portion of these earnings to the State's adult residents. Under the plan, each citizen eighteen years of age or older receives one unit for each year of residency subsequent to 1959, the year Alaska became a State. Crawford, a resident since 1978, brings suit challenging the dividend distribution plan as violative of the equal protection guarantee. Decision?

3. Maryland enacted a statute prohibiting any producer or refiner of petroleum products from operating retail service stations within the State. The statute also required that any producer or refiner discontinue operating their company-owned retail service stations. Approximately 3,800 retail service stations in Maryland sell over twenty different brands of gasoline. However, no petroleum products are produced or refined in Maryland and only 5 percent of the total number of retailers are operated by a producer or refiner. Maryland enacted the statute because a survey conducted by the State Comptroller indicated that gasoline stations operated by producers or refiners had received preferential treatment during periods of gasoline shortage. Seven major producers and refiners brought an action challenging the statute on the ground that it discriminates against interstate commerce in violation of the commerce clause of the United States Constitution. Decision?

4. The Federal Aviation Act of 1958 provides that "The United States of America is declared to possess and exercise complete and exclusive national sovereignty in the airspace of the United States." The city of Orion adopted an ordinance which makes it unlawful for jet aircraft to take off from its airport between 11 P.M. of one day and 7 A.M. of the next day. The Jordan Airlines, Inc., is adversely affected by this ordinance and brings suit challenging it under the supremacy clause of the United States Constitution. Decision?

5. The Public Service Commission of State X issued a regulation completely banning all advertising that "promotes the use of electricity" by any electric utility company in State X. The Commission issued the regulation in order to conserve energy. Central Electric Corporation of State X challenges the order in the State courts, arguing that the commission had restrained commercial speech in violation of the First Amendment. Decision?

6. E-Z-Rest Motel is a motel with 216 rooms located in the center of a large city in State Y. It is readily accessible from two interstate highways and three major state highways. The motel solicits patronage from outside State Y through various national advertising media, including magazines of national circulation. It accepts convention trade from outside State Y, and approximately 75 percent of its registered guests are from out of State Y. An action under the Federal Civil Rights Act of 1964 has been brought against E-Z-Rest Motel alleging that the motel discriminates on the basis of race and color. The motel contends that the statute cannot be applied to it because it is not engaged in interstate commerce. Decision?

7. State Z enacted a Private Pension Benefits Protection Act requiring private employers with 100 or more employees to pay a pension funding charge on terminating a pension plan or closing an office in State Z. Acme Steel Company closed its offices in State Z, whereupon the State assessed the company $185,000 under the vesting provisions of the Act. Acme challenged the constitutionality of the Act under the contract clause (Article I, Section 10) of the U.S. Constitution. Decision?

8. In 1942 Congress passed the Emergency Price Control Act in the interest of national defense and security. The stated purpose of the Act was "to stabilize prices and to prevent speculative, unwarranted and abnormal increases in prices and rents. . . ." The Act established the Office of Price Administration, which was authorized to establish maximum prices and rents that were to be "generally fair and equitable and [were to] effectuate the purposes of this Act." Stark was convicted for selling beef at prices in excess of those set by the agency. Stark appeals on the ground that the Act was an unconstitutional delegation to the agency of the legislative power of Congress to control prices. Decision?

CRIMINAL LAW

As we discussed in Chapter 1, the civil law defines duties the violation of which constitutes a wrong against the injured party. In contrast, the criminal law establishes duties the violation of which is a wrong against the whole community. Civil law is a part of private law, whereas criminal law is a part of public law. In a civil action the injured party sues to recover compensation for the damage and injury that he has sustained as a result of the defendant's wrongful conduct. The party bringing a civil action (the plaintiff) has the burden of proof, which he must sustain by a preponderance (greater weight) of the evidence. The purpose of the civil law is to compensate the aggrieved party. Criminal law, on the other hand, is designed to prevent harm to society by declaring what conduct is criminal and establishing punishment for such conduct. Punishment for criminal conduct includes fines, imprisonment, and death. In a criminal case the defendant is prosecuted by the government. The government must prove the defendant's guilt beyond a reasonable doubt, which is a significantly higher burden of proof than that required in a civil action. Moreover, under Anglo-American law, guilt is never presumed. Indeed, the law presumes the innocence of the accused, and this presumption is not diminished by his failure to testify in his own defense. The government still has the burden of affirmatively proving the guilt of the accused beyond a reasonable doubt.

Of course, the same conduct may, and often does, constitute both a crime and a tort, which is a civil wrong. (Torts are discussed in Chapters 5 and 6). But an act may be criminal without being tortious, and by the same token an act may be a tort but not a crime.

In this chapter we cover the general principles of criminal law as well as the definitions of particular crimes under the following headings (1) nature of crimes, (2) offenses against the person, (3) offenses against property, (4) criminal defenses, and (5) criminal procedure.

Nature of Crimes

A crime is any act or omission forbidden by public law in the interest of protecting society and made punishable by the government in a judicial proceeding brought by it. Crimes are prohibited and punished on grounds of public policy, which may include the protection and safeguarding of government (as in treason), human life (as in murder), or private property (as in

Crime –an act or omission in violation of a public law and punishable by the government

larceny). Additional purposes of the criminal law include deterrence, rehabilitation, and retribution.

Within recent times the scope of the criminal law has increased greatly. Traditional crimes have been expanded by a great number of regulations and laws to which are attached criminal penalties. These pertain to nearly every phase of modern living. Typical examples in the field of business law are those laws concerning the licensing and conduct of a business, antitrust laws, and the laws governing the sales of securities.

Essential Elements

Actus reus–wrongful act

Mens rea–criminal intent

In general, a crime consists of two elements: (1) the wrongful or overt act (*actus reus*) and (2) the criminal intent (*mens rea*). For example, to support a larceny conviction it is not enough to show that the defendant stole another's goods; it must also be established that he intended to steal the goods. Conversely, criminal intent without an overt act is not a crime. For instance, Ann says to herself that she ought to rob the neighborhood grocery store and then really "live it up." Without more, Ann has committed no crime. Although most crimes do require intent, some statutory crimes do not. Most of these are regulatory statutes that deal with health and safety and impose only fines.

Criminal intent–desired or virtually certain consequences of one's conduct

Intent under criminal law has traditionally included both those consequences a person desires to cause as well as those consequences he knows, or should know, are virtually certain to result from his conduct. Thus, if Arthur shoots his rifle at Donna, who is seemingly out of gunshot range, with the desire to kill Donna and in fact does kill her, Arthur had the required criminal intent to kill Donna. Likewise, if B, desiring to poison P, places a toxic chemical in the water cooler in P's office and unwittingly poisons U and V, B will be found to have intended to kill U and V, regardless of B's feelings toward U and V.

One of the essential elements of most crimes is a guilty mind or criminal intent, and it has been argued that since a corporation is artificial, intangible, and incorporeal, it is therefore, incapable of committing a crime. The modern trend is to make corporations criminally responsible for the criminal conduct of their agents (such as employees) if the conduct is attributable to the corporation. The punishment necessarily is by fine and not imprisonment.

Classification

Historically, crimes were classified *mala in se* (wrongs in themselves or morally wrong, such as murder) or *mala prohibita* (not morally wrong but declared wrongful by law, such as the prohibition against making a U-turn).

Felony–serious crime

Misdemeanor–less serious crime

From the standpoint of the seriousness of the offense, crimes are also classified as a (1) *felony* (any crime punishable by death or imprisonment in the penitentiary or (2) *misdemeanor* (any crime punishable by a fine or imprisonment in a local jail). Federal law includes another category known as a (3) petty crime (any misdemeanor punishable by fine or imprisonment of six months or less).

White collar crime–corporate crime

An additional classification of crime called **white-collar crime** has been defined in various ways. The Justice Department defines it as nonviolent crime involving deceit, corruption, or breach of trust. It has also been defined as "crimes in the [corporate] suites" which includes crimes committed by individuals—such as embezzlement and forgery—as well as crimes committed on behalf of a corporation—such as commercial bribery, product safety and health crimes, and antitrust violations. A less precise definition is crime "committed by a person of respectability and high social status in the course of his occupation," while a more narrow definition is fraud or deceit practiced through misrepresentation, to gain an unfair advantage. Regardless of the definition of white-collar crime, it is clear that such crime costs society billions of dollars; estimates range from $40 billion to over $200 billion per year. See Law in the News—White Collar Crime Booming Again.

One special type of white-collar crime is computer crime. **Computer crime** involves the use of a computer to steal money or services, to remove personal or business information, or to tamper with information. Detection of crimes involving computers is extremely difficult. Also, computer crimes often are not reported because businesses do not want to give the impression that their security is lax. Losses due to computer crime are estimated to be in the tens of billions of dollars.

Offenses Against the Person

The more serious crimes against an individual include homicide, rape, and assault and battery. Although these crimes are rare in a business setting, an understanding of them is basic to understanding our criminal law system.

Homicide

Homicide is the unlawful taking of another's life. It can be classified into two categories—murder and manslaughter—each of which may be further classified. Murder is the more serious of the two.

Homicide–unlawful taking of another's life

Murder Murder has traditionally been defined as the unlawful killing of another with malice aforethought. Historically, *malice aforethought* meant that the perpetrator had an evil intent to kill and had planned the killing in advance; in short, it was a premeditated, intentional killing. Gradually this definition was expanded by the courts and legislatures to cover several additional types of murder: (1) murder with intent to cause serious bodily harm (2) gross recklessness murder, and (3) felony murder. The sentences for these different types of murder vary from State to State.

Murder–unlawful and premeditated taking of another's life

The first of these, murder with intent to cause serious bodily harm, involves a situation in which a person intends to cause serious bodily injury to another, without the intent to kill, but nonetheless does cause the death of the other. Thus, if Arthur intends to shoot Bob in the arm but misses and hits Bob in the heart and causes Bob's death, Arthur is guilty of the murder of Bob.

The second type of murder occurs when a person's conduct is grossly negligent or grossly reckless: although there is no actual intent to kill, the conduct creates an unreasonably high degree of risk of death or serious bodily injury to others and it does cause the death of another. Thus, if Tina drives her automobile at ninety miles per hour down Fifth Avenue in New York City on Friday at noon and "unintentionally" kills six people, Tina is guilty of gross recklessness murder.

Finally, the unintentional killing of another during the course of a felony is considered murder. Thus, if Tom, while burning a building which he believes is unoccupied, causes Jane, a child asleep in the building, to die by

Law in The News _____

White-Collar Crime: Booming Again

By Winston Williams

The business news lately has been reading like a drawn-out Hollywood script of corruption: Old line manufacturers exposed cheating the Pentagon. Venerable banks caught laundering money. A securities firm found fraudulently kiting checks. Once-respected businessmen and former government officials indicted—and jailed—for insider trading and fraud.

A corporate crime wave appears to be exploding across the nation. Not since the mid-1970's, when a series of foreign corporate bribes and illegal political contributions shocked the body politic, have there been so many deep gashes in corporate America's moral armor. The general public seems certain of the reason: There's only a fine line between business executive and crook, they say. But academics, executives and government officials are still trying to figure out what, exactly, is going on or how to stop it.

"These are the kinds of crimes that clearly involve a matter of choice," said D. Lowell Jensen, Deputy Attorney General of the United States. "These are cold, calculated crimes. It's not as though these are crimes of passion."

The business community's quasi-official leaders have remained dispassionate about the crimes. The last time the Business Roundtable, a group of some of the most prestigious businessmen in the country, made a major pronouncement on the subject of corporate ethics was a decade ago, when it published a compendium of ethical guidelines that companies drew up after the bribery and political payoff scandals. It has yet to consider, let alone take action on, the current cycle of mush-

rooming corporate crime. "We just haven't been doing that," said James Keogh, spokesman for the Roundtable.

But individually, businessmen are thinking about what is happening within corporate America. And their theories about the reasons for this latest bout of corporate criminality are as diverse as the crimes making headlines.

Some cite a breakdown in moral values throughout society. Others say that new pressure on managers to provide constantly rising earnings in an increasingly intense competitive environment has forced them into shady dealings. Still others say that the current Administration's laissez-faire attitude toward business has been interpreted by some as a green light to ignore regulations and some legal proscriptions.

And there are some who deny that crime is on the rise at all. They point to the number of ethics courses being offered by companies and business schools, as well as to the cottage industry of ethics consultants that has sprung into being. Corporate morality is on the the rise, they claim, and the scandals that have surfaced of late are merely coincidental.

* * *

"There's probably less corporate crime today than there has been in the past, but what there is, is getting more headlines," said Frank W. Considine, chairman of the National Can Corporation. "Ever since Watergate people have been looking under the bed for something."

If so, they have not had trouble finding what they seek, of late. Such once-venerable names as General Dynamics, General Electric, E.F. Hutton, E.M.S. Securities, and Bank of Boston have been

accused of criminal practices. Paul Thayer, former Deputy Secretary of Defense and a former chairman of LTV, and Jake Butcher, the Tennessee financier, are now convicted felons.

Significantly, both men have been sentenced to time in jail—four years for Mr. Thayer, and a hefty 20 years for Mr. Butcher. That fact may give pause to the overwhelming majority of citizens who believe sentences are far too lenient.

It certainly is pleasing those law enforcement officials who believe that white collar crime has been treated too lightly by the courts. "This kind of crime has been encouraged by not addressing it," said Mario Merola, the crusty Bronx District Attorney who indicted former Labor Secretary Raymond Donovan for fraud. (Mr. Donovan is charged with criminally manipulating a construction contract held by the Schiavone Construction Company, which he once headed.) "Because these guys commit their crimes with a pencil instead of a gun, there are people who are saying they should not go to jail," Mr. Merola said. "But I say differently. They should be prosecuted and sent to jail."

Actually, far more people echo Mr. Merola's view than he suggests. Perhaps the only point of unanimity among businessmen, consumer advocates and government officials these days is that more harsh sentences are needed to stem the wave of corporate crime. People as seemingly disparate as consumer advocate Ralph Nader and Deputy Attorney General Jensen say that stiff fines and jail sentences are needed. "The most effective deterrent is proper punishment of individual violators," Mr. Nader said.

White-Collar Crime continued

It is when the conversation leaves solutions and returns to causes that agreement falls apart. Gary Lynch, head of the Securities and Exchange Commission's enforcement division, sees little difference in the motivation of white collar criminals and street thugs. He states flatly that people guilty of insider trading "are motivated by greed and the belief that they aren't going to get caught."

But other proponents of wider reform in business see more complex motivations. They warn that too many companies are ignoring the issue of corporate morality, and thus fostering corporate cultures devoid of ethical values. That lack, coupled with an increasingly aggressive shareholder community and, in some cases, with corporate compensation plans that tie bonuses to divisional profits, leads to a surge of crimes in which the primary beneficiary is intended to be the corporate coffer, not an individual's wallet.

"A significant number of people are insecure enough in their jobs, or have an insecure boss," said Mr. Considine of National Can. "They will falsify something if there is a fear that their division or unit is not performing up to budget."

Lower-level employees often feel they are acting with top management's support, even if they are not under direct orders to indulge in unethical behavior. When E. F. Hutton pleaded guilty on May 1 to 2,000 felony counts of wire and mail fraud in an elaborate corporate check-kiting scheme, Robert Fomon, Hutton's chairman, said that none of the hundreds of employees involved knew the practice was illegal or against company policy. General Electric blamed "intentional errors" by lower-level management employees last month when it accepted responsibility for defrauding the Air Force by filing 108 false claims for payment.

* * *

Ralph Nader also dates the crime rise to 1981, but for a different reason: That was the year when President Reagan took office.

"The Reagan Administration has indicated that it is the friend of the business community and sensitive to it, and it has been looking the other way," he claimed. He sees other causes for growing illegalities, too—the ease of computer crime, and the temptations presented by increased military spending for example. But he says they pale in comparison to the impact of the "green signal" Mr. Reagan has given that "he's not going to be tough on corporate crime."

Mr. Nader is by no means alone in that view. "The atmosphere for the past several years has been to encourage people to get rich and not worry about the consequence," said Lloyd L. Weinreb, a professor at the Harvard Law School. "There's this notion you ought to do it on your own and you ought to get to keep what you've made. The more you encourage that, the more you encourage people to sail toward the edge."

The Administration has, in fact, trumpeted its friendliness to business. It opposes anti-foreign bribery laws, saying they hamstring American companies in international competition. Moreover, many of the agency heads appointed by Mr. Reagan had clear ties to the business community, a fact that alarmed many activists and academics who feared that regulations would not be even-handedly drawn or applied by the Administration. Many of the agency chiefs have since left under a cloud, and sometimes under criminal charges.

Rita LaVelle, former head of the Environmental Protection Agency's toxic waste cleanup effort, was recently jailed for perjury. And last month, Robert Rowland, director of the Occupational Safety and Health Administration, announced his resignation amid complaints of conflict of interest stemming from his ownership of stock in companies he was regulating.

But paradoxically this same Administration has produced the stepped-up enforcement that has shed light on shady business deals. It was the Securities and Exchange Commission's increased scrutiny of insider trading that felled Mr. Thayer. The Department of Defense has had a big part in exposing wrongdoing on the part of military contractors.

"It seems to me that the Reagan Administration is trying to root it out more than past administrations," said the American Management Association's Mr. Veal. "They've strengthened the procedures for discovering white collar crime, and they have put more emphasis on breaking it up."

Washington insiders, in fact, are outraged at charges of lax enforcement. "We have not slackened our enforcement or reduced our level of investigation," said Mr. Jensen, the deputy attorney general. "We've increased the number of FBI agents and we've increased the level of prosecution. It's difficult to get sophisticated measurements of the increases in crimes, but we're getting better at investigating and prosecuting."

* * *

Some chief executives say that society as a whole has been sending a muddled message about ethics. "There was a time when high standards of behavior were considered part of the American way of life. We had a consensus on val-

White-Collar Crime continued

ues and the importance of those values," said Sanford McDonnell, the chairman of McDonnell-Douglas, who laments what he perceives as a failure of families, schools and even churches to inculcate those values vigorously.

Mr. McDonnell, a former national president of the Boy Scouts of America, revised his corporate code two years ago along the lines of the boy scout code. He has invited ethics consultants in to meet with his top managers. And last June the top 19 officers of the company, Mr. McDonnell included, spent 13 hours in a seminar with professors from Stanford and Harvard discussing ethical corporate behavior.

McDonnell-Douglas has not remained untarred with charges of wrongdoing, however. The company has run afoul of the Pentagon for allegedly faulty workmanship, particularly on the F-18 fighter plane. Still, McDonnell-Douglas has so far avoided allegations of the serious ethical lapses of the sort that have embarrassed General Electric and General Dynamics.

Mr. McDonnell says that he will continue the ethics seminars throughout his company until everyone, including production workers, has been trained in corporate morality.

Allied Corp., Chemical Bank, Standard Oil of Ohio and Sears Roebuck have similar ethics programs. Allied acted after revelations that it was responsible for the contamination of Chesapeake Bay with kepone, a deadly chemical. And Sears started classes after it was charged with irregularities in the importation of television sets.

An even larger number of companies are strengthening their corporate credos. For example, Rueben F. Mettler, chairman of TRW, updated his company's ethical creed a few years ago, saying that the goal of the "highest legal and ethical standard of conduct" should "override all else." Analysts say TRW's vice chairman, Stanley C. Pace, was chosen to clean up the mess at General Dynamics largely because of TRW's reputation for integrity.

But "you need more than a legalistic code and a bunch of pious generalities," said David Schmidt, director of the Trinity Center for Ethics and Corporate Policy, a program sponsored by Trinity Church. Trinity, the Washington Ethics Center, as well as a host of business schools and independent consultants, are offering to send teams of ethical specialists to corporations to try to help senior managers find ways to integrate "organizational values" into their corporate culture.

Proponents of this approach say it is the only way to turn corporate behavior around and to change the public's perception of corporate morals. "You can't just write a code and hang it up on the wall," Mr. McDonnell said. "You have to keep reminding people what you stand for. Unless you stress that—especially with the emphasis in a corporation on making profits—its not always clear to people which way management wants them to go." And, he summed up, "If more corporations would do this across America, we would raise the trust of the man-in-the-street that's been lost by business, government and all institutions."

burning, Tom is guilty of a felony murder. Likewise, if during a robbery the robber ties up the victim and accidentally suffocates her, the robber is guilty of felony murder. Most jurisdictions now limit the scope of felony murder to prescribed felonies (e.g., those dangerous to life, common law felonies, or *mala in se* felonies) and/or to situations in which the death of the victim is foreseeable.

Manslaughter–unlawful taking of another's life without malice

Voluntary manslaughter–intentional killing of another under extenuating circumstances

Manslaughter   Manslaughter has traditionally been defined as the "unlawful killing of another without malice aforethought." Manslaughter has been divided into two types: voluntary and involuntary.

Voluntary manslaughter is generally defined as an intentional killing of another which, although not justified, is committed under extenuating circumstances, typically the defendant's heated passion provoked by the victim. To be manslaughter rather than murder, the provocation must be sufficient to cause a reasonable person to become enraged and there must be insufficient time between the provocation and the attack for a reasonable person to have calmed himself. For example, if a woman discovers her husband in the act of committing adultery and kills either her husband or his lover, she is guilty of voluntary manslaughter and not murder. However, if the woman takes a week to track down her husband after discovering the adultery, she would be guilty of murder and not voluntary manslaughter.

Involuntary manslaughter, on the other hand, involves a death caused during the course of a misdemeanor or by the defendant's criminal negligence. Criminal negligence is more than mere carelessness creating an unreasonable risk of harm but less than recklessness constituting murder. For example, an individual, who is aware that he is subject to relatively frequent epileptic seizures, suffers one while driving his car causing the car to run onto the sidewalk killing four small children, is guilty of involuntary manslaughter.

Likewise, as discussed in *Thiede v. State,* if one recklessly serves another an intoxicating liquor which by reason of its extreme potency or poisonous ingredients is dangerous to drink, such reckless serving may constitute involuntary manslaughter.

> **Involuntary manslaughter**–taking the life of another by criminal negligence or during the course of a misdemeanor

---

FACTS: Thiede and some friends of his had attempted to make some white whiskey in a homemade still. On the day in question, defendant, with Stromer and Forney, retrieved three jugs of the white whiskey, and he and Forney then went to the town of Prosser. In the course of an hour they returned with two girls. Stromer was found lying on the ground in a drunken stupor, with the jugs near him. At this time another, Nelson, was present and defendant gave him a drink from the jug. He testified that it tasted like hot acids and temporarily paralyzed him, and that, at the time of trial, he still felt the effects.

That night during a small, secret party in the woods, Thiede gave Knoll and others no more than two drinks each of the liquor. Later that evening, Knoll was completely helpless, unable to talk and vomiting. His brother took him home, placed him unconscious on the floor and called a doctor. Knoll died a few hours later. The doctor stated that alcoholic poisoning caused his death.

The Nebraska involuntary manslaughter statute makes it unlawful to "kill another without malice . . . or unintentionally, while the slayer is in the commission of some unlawful act." Thiede provided Knoll with the bootleg whiskey, an unlawful act, and Knoll died as a result. Thus, the trial court found Thiede guilty of involuntary manslaughter. Thiede appeals.

DECISION: New trial for Thiede. In this case where the act by its nature is not criminal, and in the commission of which the perpetrator of the act has no intent to do harm nor to injure another in his person or property the act is wrong only because prohibited. If in the commission of such an act, called malum prohibitum, a death results "the law will not convert the act, innocently done and done with no intent to injure and with no disregard for the safety of another, into a criminal act and pronounce the act of manslaughter." However, if, as the facts suggest, Thiede was aware of the danger of this particular batch of moonshine and was reckless in giving it to Knoll, he would be guilty of manslaughter. Therefore, the court's failure to instruct the jury on the issue of Thiede's recklessness entitled him to a new trial.

> **THIEDE v. STATE**
>
> Supreme Court of Nebraska, 1921.
> 106 Neb. 48, 182 N.W. 570.

Rape

At common law rape was defined as unlawful sexual intercourse with a woman against her will by force or threat of immediate force. The victim of a rape was limited to females, and a man could not be convicted of raping his wife. Today the crime of rape is statutorily defined and varies greatly from State

> **Rape**–unlawful and unconsented to sexual intercourse

to State. In addition, unforced sexual intercourse with a minor—*statutory rape*—is considered criminal rape.

Assault and Battery

Assault and battery are two distinct crimes, although frequently the word *assault* is used to cover both. Battery is the unlawful touching of another person. The touching may be direct, such as striking someone with one's fist or shooting someone, or indirect, such as placing poison in a person's drink. Assault is an unlawful attempt, together with the actual ability, to commit a battery. In addition, most States also classify as criminal assault intentional, threatening conduct that places the victim in reasonable fear of immediate bodily harm.

Offenses Against Property

Offenses against property greatly affect businesses and amount to losses in the hundreds of billions of dollars each year. In this section we cover the following crimes against property: (1) larceny, (2) embezzlement, (3) false pretenses, (4) robbery, (5) extortion and bribery, (6) burglary, (7) forgery, and (8) bad checks.

Larceny

The crime of larceny is the (1) trespassory (2) taking and (3) carrying away of (4) personal property (5) of another (6) with the intent to deprive the victim permanently of the goods. All six elements must be present for the crime to exist. Thus, if Barbara pays Larry $5,000 for an automobile that Larry agrees to deliver the following week and Larry does not do so, Larry is *not* guilty of larceny because he has not trespassed on Barbara's property. Larry has not taken anything from Barbara; he has simply refused to turn over the automobile to her. Larceny applies only when a person takes personal property from another without the other's consent. Here Barbara voluntarily paid the money to Larry. Larry has not committed larceny but has obtained the $5,000 by false pretenses (which is discussed below). Likewise, if Carol takes Dan's 1968 automobile without Dan's permission, intending to use it for a joyride and then to return it to Dan, Carol has not committed larceny because she did not intend to deprive Dan permanently of the automobile. On the other hand, if Carol left Dan's 1968 car in a junkyard after the joyride, Carol would most likely be held to have committed a larceny because of the high risk that Dan would be permanently deprived of the car.

Embezzlement

Embezzlement is the improper taking of an employer's property by an agent who through her employment was entrusted with receiving the money or property. This statutory crime was first enacted in response to a 1799 English case in which a bank employee was found not guilty of larceny for taking money given to him for deposit in the bank because the money had been voluntarily handed to him. Thus, embezzlement is a crime intended to prevent individuals who are lawfully in possession of property of another from taking the property for their own use. The key distinction between larceny and embezzlement, therefore, is whether the thief is in lawful possession of the property. In both there is a misuse of the property of another, but in larceny

---

Battery–unlawful touching of another

Assault–unlawful attempted battery

Larceny–trespassory taking and carrying away the goods of another with the intent to permanently deprive

Embezzlement–the taking in violation of a trust the property of one's employer

the thief unlawfully possesses the property whereas in embezzlement the thief lawfully possesses the property.

A second distinction between larceny and embezzlement is discussed in *United States v. Waronek*. Nonetheless in reading this case it should be noted that in order to constitute an embezzlement there must be a serious act of interference with the owner's rights to the property.

UNITED STATES v. WARONEK

United States Court of Appeals, Seventh Circuit, 1978.
582 F.2d 1158.

FACTS: Waronek owned and operated a trucking rig, transporting goods for L.T.L. Perishables, Inc. of St. Paul, Minnesota. He accepted an offer to haul a trailer load of beef from Illini Beef Packers, Inc. in Joslin, Illinois to Midtown Packing Company in New York City. After his truck was loaded with 95 forequarters and 95 hindquarters of beef in Joslin, Waronek drove north to his home in Watertown, Wisconsin rather than east to New York. While in Watertown, he asked employees of the Royal Meat Company to butcher and prepare four hindquarters of beef—two for himself and two for his friends. He also offered to sell ten hindquarters to one employee of the company at an alarmingly reduced rate. The suspicious employee contacted the authorities, who told him to proceed with the deal but to obtain information about Waronek. When he arrived in New York with his load short nineteen hindquarters, Waronek telephoned L.T.L. Perishables in St. Paul. He notified them "that he was short nineteen hindquarters, that he knew where the beef went, and that he would make good on it out of future settlements." L.T.L.. told him to contact the New York police but he failed to do so. Shortly thereafter, he was arrested by the Federal Bureau of Investigation and indicted for the embezzlement of goods moving in interstate commerce. Waronek appeals his conviction.

DECISION: Judgment of conviction affirmed. Waronek claims that the court erred by not instructing the jury that an essential element of embezzlement is the intent to permanently deprive the owner of the property. He contends that his intent to later pay for the beef proves that he did not intend to permanently deprive the owner of the goods. The offense of embezzlement of goods moving in interstate commerce has only two essential elements: (1) the act of embezzling or unlawfully taking goods moving in interstate commerce and (2) "doing such act willfully, knowingly, and unlawfully and with the intent to convert the goods or property to the use of the accused." Unlike the crime of larceny, the intent to permanently deprive the owner of his property is not required to complete an embezzlement. Here, Waronek intended to and did convert fourteen hindquarters to his own use. His professed desire to pay for them later is immaterial to he crime of embezzlement.

False Pretenses

False pretenses, like embezzlement, is a statutory crime enacted to close a loophole in the requirements of larceny. False pretenses is the crime of obtaining title to property of another by means of materially false representations of fact, with knowledge of their falsity, and made with the intent to defraud. Larceny does not cover this situation because the victim voluntarily transfers the property to the thief. For example, a con artist who goes door to door and collects money by saying he is selling stereo equipment, when indeed he is not, is committing the crime of false pretenses. The test of deception is *subjective*; if the victim is actually deceived the test is satisfied even though a reasonable person would not have been deceived by the defendant's lies. Therefore, gullibilty or lack of due care on the part of the victim is no defense.

False pretenses–intentional misrepresentation of fact in order to cheat another

Robbery

Under the common law as well as most statutes, robbery is a larceny with the additional elements that (1) the property is taken from the victim or in the immediate presence of the victim and (2) it is accomplished through either

Robbery–larceny from the person by force or threat of force

force or threat of force. The defendant's force or threat of force need not be against the person from whom the property is taken. For example, a robber threatens Sam that unless Sam relinquishes his wallet the robber will shoot Maria. Moreover, the victim's presence may be actual or constructive. By constructive presence it is meant that the victim is prevented from being present by either the defendant's actual or threatened force. For example, if the robber knocks the victim unconscious or ties her up, the victim is considered constructively present.

Many laws distinguish between simple robbery and aggravated robbery. **Aggravated robbery** is generally defined as (1) robbery with a deadly weapon, (2) robbery where the robber has the intent to kill or would kill if faced with resistance, (3) robbery that involves serious bodily injury, *or* (4) robbery by two or more persons.

Extortion and Bribery

Extortion—making threats to obtain property

Bribery—offering property to a public official to influence the official's decision

Although extortion and bribery are frequently confused, they are two distinct crimes. Extortion, or blackmail as it is sometimes called, is generally held to be the making of threats for the purpose of obtaining money or property. In a few jurisdictions, however, the crime of extortion occurs only if the defendant actually causes the victim to give up money or property.

Bribery, on the other hand, is the offer of money or property to a public official to influence the official's decision. The crime of bribery is committed when the illegal offer is made, whether accepted or not. Thus, if A offered M, the mayor of Town Y, a 20 percent interest in A's planned real estate development if M would use her influence to have the development proposal approved, A would be guilty of criminal bribery. In contrast, if M had threatened A that unless she received a 20 percent interest in A's development she would use her influence to prevent the approval of the development, M would be guilty of criminal extortion. Bribery of foreign officials is covered in the Foreign Corrupt Practices Act discussed in Chapter 40.

Some jurisdictions have gone beyond the general bribery law and have adopted statutes that make commercial bribery illegal. Commercial bribery is the use of bribery to acquire new business, obtain secret information or processes, or obtain kickbacks.

Burglary

Burglary—breaking and entering the home of another at night with intent to commit a felony

At common law, burglary was defined as a breaking and entering of a dwelling house at night with the intent to commit a felony. Of these elements the three that caused the greatest degree of confusion were (1) breaking, (2) entering, and (3) dwelling house. Breaking required that the defendant had to create the breach or opening; the opening could not have been created by the resident. Therefore, a person would not be guilty of common law burglary if she entered another's home in the night through an *open* window to steal jewelry. Moreover, the crime of burglary would not be committed even if the defendant had to open the window further in order to climb into the house. On the other hand, the common law was extremely lenient with respect to entry and required only that any part of the defendant's body enter the house, regardless of the length of the entry. For example, Kathy punches in a window of a dwelling house at night to gain entry and steal a television. When she reaches her hand in the broken window she triggers the burglar alarm and flees. Kathy has committed a burglary. Finally, the dwelling house of another means that it is someone's residence, regardless of whether the tenant is present at the time of the burglary.

Modern statutes are very different from the common law definition. Many of them simply require that there be (1) an entry (2) into a building (3) with the intent to commit a felony in the building. Thus, these statutory definitions omit three elements of the common law crime—the building need not be a dwelling house, the entry need not be at night, and the entry need not be a technical breaking. The modern statutes vary so greatly it is impossible to generalize, except that each of the statutes include some, but not all, of the common law elements.

Forgery

Forgery is the intentional falsification or false making of a document with the intent to defraud. Accordingly, if William prepares a false certificate of title to a stolen automobile, he is guilty of forgery. Likewise, if an individual alters some receipts in order to increase her income tax deductions, she has committed the crime of forgery.

Forgery–intentional falsification of a document with intent to defraud

Bad Checks

A statutory crime that has some relation to both forgery and false pretenses is the passing of "bad" checks—that is, writing a check when there is not enough money in the account to cover the check. All jurisdictions have now enacted laws making it a crime to issue bad checks; however, these statutes vary greatly from jurisdiction to jurisdiction. Most jurisdictions simply require that the check be issued; they do not require that the issuer receive anything in return for the check. Also, most jurisdictions require that the defendant issue a check with knowledge that she does not have enough money to cover the check. A few jurisdictions require only that there be insufficient funds.

Bad checks–issuing a check with insufficient funds to cover the check

Criminal Defenses

Even though a defendant is found to have committed a criminal act, he will not be convicted if he has a valid defense. Most criminal law defenses are valid against both crimes against the person and crimes against property. The one exception to this rule is that the defense of person or property (see below) serves only as a defense to crimes against the person.

Defense of Person or Property

Individuals may use reasonable force to protect themselves, other individuals, and their property. These defenses enable a person to commit without any criminal liability what would otherwise be considered the crime of assault, battery, manslaughter, or murder. The law gives this privilege to further important societal interests.

Self-Defense   An individual need not submit to force or violence against his person but may use force to protect himself. More specifically, an individual may use *reasonable* force to protect himself against an attack if he reasonably believes that he is in immediate danger of unlawful bodily harm and that the use of force is necessary to protect himself from such harm. Accordingly, even though an individual acts on the mistaken belief that he is defending himself against an unlawful attack, so long as the belief is based on reasonable

Self-defense–reasonable force to protect oneself against attack.

grounds, he is entitled to the same defense as if the attack had been as he believed. An individual who acts in self-defense has a complete defense against any crime based on him causing physical harm to the aggressor.

What constitutes "reasonable force" has given rise to a great deal of litigation and considerable commentary. As a general rule, a person may use *non-deadly* force to protect herself against unlawful bodily harm and *deadly* force to protect herself against an attack threatening death or serious bodily harm. Thus, Alan may not shoot Betty in order to protect himself against a punch in the mouth. On the other hand, if Betty attacked Alan with a knife, Alan could properly defend himself by shooting Betty, even if Betty's knife was in fact plastic, so long as Alan reasonably believed it to be real. A minority of States and the Model Penal Code require a person to retreat before using deadly force provided that he can safely do so. The objective of this rule is to protect human life even though it requires the avoidance of confrontation. Most States, however, do not require retreat, based on the view that a person should not be forced to take "cowardly" action against a criminal aggressor. Moreover, even in the jurisdictions following the minority rule, retreat is not required before a person may reasonably use deadly force in his own home.

Defense of Another   Generally, an individual has a complete defense against criminal prosecution if he uses reasonable force in defense of another provided he reasonably believes the other to be in immediate danger of unlawful bodily harm and that use of such force is necessary to prevent this harm. Most States permit this defense to be used by an individual in defense of *any* other person, even a stranger, although some States limit its use to the defense of individuals who have some defined relationship to the person who intervened. Moreover, some States limit the rule's application by permitting the defense only when the original victim had the right of self-defense. In other words, these States place the intervenor in the shoes of the party whom he is assisting. Under this rule, therefore, if one goes to the aid of the original aggressor in a fight the intervenor would not enjoy the privilege of defense of another.

Defense of Property   An individual also has the right to use reasonable force to protect her property. Under the majority rule, deadly force is *never* reasonable to protect property because life is deemed more important than the protection of property. For this reason, an individual cannot use a deadly mechanical device, such as a spring gun, to protect her property.

Incapacity

Under some circumstances an individual is declared incapable of forming criminal intent. Thus, even though that person commits a criminal act, he will not be held liable because of the lack of criminal intent. In these situations the person has a complete criminal defense based on his incapacity. The criminal capacity of persons will be discussed in the following order (1) insanity, (2) infancy, and (3) intoxication.

Insanity   The extent to which insanity should be a defense to criminal conduct has long troubled the legal system. Although it is difficult to conceive how any "sane" person could commit a brutal murder or a rape, it is not in that sense that the term **criminally insane** is used. The criminal law defense of insanity is directed at those for whom criminal sanctions are not appropriate. Those who are found "not guilty by reason of insanity" are generally not allowed to go free but are typically committed to a mental institution for treatment.

The traditional and most common test for insanity is the *McNaughton* test. Under this test a defendant is *not* criminally responsible for her conduct if, at the time of committing the act, she did not understand the nature and quality of her act or she could not distinguish between right or wrong. For example, if Alex axed Betty believing that Betty was a tree trunk that he was splitting for firewood, Alex would be found to be not guilty by reason of insanity.

Some States have added another test to the *McNaughton* test—the irresistible impulse test. Under this test a defendant is freed of criminal responsibility if he had a mental disease that prevented him from controlling his conduct, even though he understood the nature of his act and that it was wrong. For example, A killed B, although he knew it to be illegal and wrong, because he believed God's messenger had ordered him to do so. Under the irresistible impulse test, A would be not guilty by reason of insanity.

A third test of insanity has been accepted by some States and incorporated into the American Law Institute's Model Penal Code. This test provides:

1. A person is not responsible for criminal conduct if at the time of such conduct as a result of mental disease or defect he lacks substantial capacity either to appreciate the criminality (wrongfulness) of his conduct or to conform his conduct to the requirements of law.

2. As used in this Article, the terms "mental disease or defect" do not include an abnormality manifested only by repeated criminal or otherwise antisocial conduct.

Infancy   Under the common law and most modern statutes, a child under the age of seven is conclusively presumed to be incapable of committing a crime. From the ages of seven to fourteen there is a rebuttable presumption that the **child is incapable of committing** a crime. Above the age of fourteen there is a rebuttable presumption that the child is capable of committing a crime. The common law defense of infancy has been rendered moot, however, by the enactment of juvenile court acts, which require that all individuals below a certain age—varying among States between fourteen and eighteen—be brought before a juvenile, and not a criminal, court. Juvenile courts are not criminal in nature; rather they attempt to deal with the welfare of the youth and decide if the youth is a delinquent.

Intoxication   The great majority of the States follow what is commonly known as the voluntary/involuntary test, which makes voluntary intoxication *not* a defense. Thus, if Andy commits a burglary while so intoxicated as not to know what he is doing, Andy would *not* be guilty of criminal burglary if he involuntarily drank the alcohol because Jose forced him to against his free will. On the other hand, as pointed out in *Coots v. Commonwealth,* if Andy had drunk the liquor voluntarily, he would not have the defense of intoxication.

COOTS v. COMMONWEALTH Court of Appeals of Kentucky, 1967. 418 S.W.2d 752.	**FACTS:** Felix Coots, Jr., was convicted of rape and sentenced to ten years in prison. At trial, the victim testified unequivocally that Coots forced her with threats of physical injury to have sexual intercourse with him. Coots denied that he had sexual intercourse with her and stated that he was so drunk that he was unable to do so. Coots appeals his conviction. **DECISION:** Judgment for the Commonwealth. "Ordinarily, voluntary intoxication constitutes no excuse or justification for the commission of crime. Whenever an act constitutes the offense, drunkeness is no defense to its commission." Coots' intoxication therefore did not excuse his guilt for rape.

Other Defenses

Criminal duress–coercion by threat of serious bodily injury

Duress   A person who is threatened with immediate, serious bodily harm to himself or another unless he engages in criminal activity has a valid defense to criminal conduct other than murder. For example, Ann threatens to kill Ben if Ben does not assist her in committing larceny. Ben complies. Ben would not be guilty of the larceny because of duress. However, if Ann threatens Ben with death unless Ben kills Carol, Ben would *not* be relieved of the crime of homicide, although the crime may be reduced from murder to manslaughter. The Model Penal Code has rejected the "murder limitation" and relieves a person of all criminal responsibility if "a person of reasonable firmness would have been unable to resist."

Mistake of Fact   If a person reasonably believes the facts to be such that his conduct would not constitute a crime, then the law will treat the facts as he reasonably believed. Accordingly, an honest and reasonable mistake of fact will justify the defendant's conduct. For example, if Ann gets into a car which she reasonably believes to be hers—the car is the same color, model, and year as hers, is parked in the same parking lot and is started by her key—she will be relieved of criminal responsibility for taking Ben's automobile.

Entrapment–induced into committing a crime by a government official

Entrapment   The defense of entrapment arises when a law enforcement official induces a person to commit a crime when that person would not have done so otherwise. The rationale behind the rule is to prevent law enforcement officials from provoking crime and from engaging in reprehensible conduct. The doctrine is only aimed at government officials and agents and does not apply to private individuals. For example, if Paul, a police officer, entices Robert to commit a robbery, Robert would possess the valid defense of entrapment; if Paul were a private citizen, Robert would be guilty of criminal robbery.

Criminal Procedure

Each of the States and the Federal government has procedures for initiating and coordinating criminal prosecutions. In addition, the U.S. Constitution guarantees many defenses and rights of an accused. The Fourth Amendment prohibits unreasonable searches and seizures to obtain incriminating evidence. The Fifth Amendment requires indictment for capital crimes by a grand jury, prevents double jeopardy and self-incrimination, and prohibits deprivation of life or liberty without due process of law. The Sixth Amendment requires a speedy and public trial by jury, and that the accused be informed of the nature of the accusation, be confronted with the witnesses who testify against him, be given the power to obtain witnesses in his favor, and have the right to competent counsel for his defense. The Eighth Amendment prohibits excessive bail, excessive fines, and cruel or unusual punishment.

Most State constitutions have similar provisions protecting the rights of accused persons.

We will first discuss the steps in a criminal prosecution; then we will focus on the major constitutional protections for the accused in our system of criminal justice.

Steps in Criminal Prosecution

Although the particulars of criminal procedure vary from State to State, the following provides a basic overview. After arrest, the accused is booked and appears before a magistrate, commissioner, or justice of the peace, where formal notice of the charges is given, he is given advice of his rights, and bail is set. Next, a preliminary hearing is held to determine whether there is probable cause to believe the defendant is the one who committed the crime. The defendant is entitled to be represented by counsel.

For less serious crimes, prosecution begins by issuing a warrant, which is served on the accused together with an "information" of the charge at the time of his arrest. Serious crimes are prosecuted by an indictment or "true bill" after being presented to a grand jury, which determines only whether a criminal action should be brought. A grand jury consists of not less than sixteen and not more than twenty-three people. If there is sufficient evidence, the grand jury "indicts" the accused. Information, which is used in most misdemeanor cases and some felony cases, is a formal accusation of a crime brought by a prosecuting officer and not a grand jury.

At the arraignment the accused is informed of the charge against him and he enters his plea. The arraignment must be held promptly after the indictment or information has been filed. If his plea is "not guilty," he must stand trial. He is entitled to a jury trial, but if he chooses, he may have his guilt or innocence determined by the court sitting without a jury, which is called a "bench trial."

The trial begins with the selection of the jury and the opening statements by the prosecutor and the attorney for the defense. The prosecution presents evidence first; then the defendant presents his. At the conclusion of the testimony, closing statements are made and the jury is instructed as to the applicable law and retires to arrive at a verdict. In most States the verdict must be unanimous. If the verdict is "not guilty," the matter ends there. The State has no right to appeal from an acquittal; and the accused, having been placed in "jeopardy," cannot be tried a second time for the same offense. If the verdict is "guilty" and a judgment is entered, the defendant has further recourse. He may make a motion for a new trial, asserting that prejudicial error occurred at the trial, thus requiring a retrial of the case. Or he may assert that the evidence was insufficient to establish guilt *beyond any reasonable doubt* and ask for his discharge. He may appeal to a reviewing court, alleging error by the trial court and asking for either his discharge or a remandment of the case for a new trial. In addition, there may be other proceedings in a criminal case, including, for example, a request for probation.

Beyond a reasonable doubt–proof to a moral certainty of evidence, criminal law standard

Fourth Amendment

The Fourth Amendment protects all individuals against unreasonable searches and seizures.

This Amendment is designed to protect the privacy and security of individuals against arbitrary invasions by government officials. Although the Fourth Amendment directly applies only to the Federal government, the Fourteenth Amendment makes it applicable to the States as well.

When there is a violation of the Fourth Amendment the general rule prohibits the introduction of the illegally seized evidence. The purpose of this **exclusionary rule** is to discourage illegal police conduct and to protect individual liberty, not to hinder the search for the truth. In 1914, the United States Supreme Court stated:

> If letters and private documents can thus be seized and held and used in evidence against a citizen accused of an offense, the protection of the Fourth Amendment declaring his right to be secure against such searches and seizures is of no value, and, so far as those thus placed and concerned, might as well be stricken from the Constitution. The efforts of the courts and their officials to bring the guilty to punishment, praiseworthy as they are, are not to be aided by the sacrifice of those great principles established by years of endeavor and suffering which have resulted in their embodiment in the fundamental law of the land.

Nonetheless, in recent years the Supreme Court, as shown in *United States v. Leon*, has limited the exclusionary rule.

Exclusionary rule–prohibition of illegally obtained evidence

UNITED STATES v. LEON

Supreme Court of the United States, 1984.
— U.S. —, 104 S.Ct. 3405,
— L.Ed.2d —.

FACTS: Officer Cyril Rombach of the Burbank Police Department, an experienced and well-trained narcotics officer, applied for a warrant to search several residences and automobiles for cocaine, methaqualone and other narcotics. Rombach supported his application with information given to another police officer by a confidential informant of unproven reliability. He also based the warrant application on his own observations made during an extensive investigation—known drug offenders visiting the residences and leaving with small packages as well as a suspicious trip to Miami by two of the suspects. A state superior court judge issued a search warrant to Rombach based on this information. Rombach's searches netted large quantities of drugs and other evidence which produced indictments of several suspects on charges of conspiracy to possess and distribute cocaine. The defendants' moved to suppress the evidence on the grounds that the search warrant was defective in that Rombach had failed to establish the informant's credibility and that the information provided by the informant about the suspect's criminal activity was fatally stale. The court declared that the searches lacked probable cause, that the warrant was invalid, and that the obtained evidence must be excluded from the prosecution's case under the Fourth Amendment's exclusionary rule.

DECISION: Judgment for the United States. The Fourth Amendment contains no express provision mandating the exclusion of evidence obtained by an unlawful search and seizure. Consequently, an unlawful search and seizure will not automatically grant an individual a constitutional right to have the unlawfully obtained evidence excluded. When law enforcement officers act in good faith, reasonable reliance upon a facially valid search warrant issued by a detached, neutral magistrate, the evidence obtained should not be excluded, even if the warrant is subsequently declared defective. To exclude such evidence would punish law enforcement officers whose conduct is objectively reasonable for a magistrate's error. It may also result in permitting some guilty defendants to go free or receive reduced sentences, simply because of a technical flaw in the application. These considerations weigh heavily in favor of recognizing a good faith exception to the exclusionary rule.

To obtain a search warrant of a particular person, place, or thing, the law enforcement official must demonstrate to a magistrate that he has probable cause to believe that the search will reveal evidence of criminal activity. Probable cause means that "the apparent facts set out in the affidavit [of the requesting authority] are such that a reasonably discreet and prudent man would be led to believe that there was a commission of the offense charged . . . ."

Even though the Fourth Amendment requires that a search and seizure generally be made after a valid search warrant has been obtained, in some instances a search warrant is not necessary. For example, it has been held that a warrant is not necessary where (1) there is hot pursuit of a fugitive, (2) voluntary consent is given, (3) an emergency requires such action, (4) there has been a lawful arrest, (5) evidence of a crime is in plain view of the law enforcement officer, or (6) delay would present a significant obstacle to the investigation.

Fifth Amendment

The Fifth Amendment protects persons against self-incrimination, double jeopardy, and being charged with a capital or infamous crime except by grand jury indictment.

The prohibitions against self-incrimination and double jeopardy, but not the grand jury clause, also apply to the States through the Due Process Clause of the Fourteenth Amendment.

The privilege against self-incrimination extends only to testimonial evidence and not to physical evidence. The Fifth Amendment "privilege protects an accused only from being compelled to testify against himself, or otherwise provide the State with evidence of a testimonial or communicative nature." Therefore, a person can be forced to stand in a lineup for identification purposes, provide a handwriting sample, or take a blood test. Most significantly, the Fifth Amendment does not protect business records—it applies only to papers of individuals.

The following case is the landmark decision outling the defendant's privileges against self-incrimination.

MIRANDA v. ARIZONA

Supreme Court of the United States, 1966.
384 U.S. 436, 86 S.Ct. 1602,
16 L.Ed.2d 694.

FACTS: Four separate cases involving similar fact situations were consolidated since they presented the same constitutional question. In each case, police officers, detectives or prosecuting attorneys took a defendant into custody and interrogated him in a police station to obtain a confession. In none of these cases did the officials fully and effectively advise the defendant of his rights at the outset of the interrogation. Police interrogations produced oral admissions of guilt from each defendant, as well as signed statements from three of them which were used to convict them at their trials. The defendants appeal, arguing that the officials should have warned them of their constitutional rights and the consequences of waiving them before the questionings began. It was contended that to permit any statements obtained without such a warning violated their Fifth Amendment privilege against self-incrimination.

DECISION: Judgment for Miranda and other defendants. The long-standing Fifth Amendment privilege against self-incrimination applies to police interrogations of defendants in custody as well as in the courtroom. It guarantees the accused "the right to remain silent unless he chooses to speak in the unfettered exercise of his own will." Frequently, custodial interrogations by law enforcement officials involve intimidation, trickery, violence and other coercive measures that tend to deprive the defendant of his free will. Therefore, to safeguard the Fifth Amendment privilege, law enforcement officials must inform the defendant prior to an interrogation that: (1) he has the right to remain silent and anything he says might be used against him in court; (2) he has the right to consult with a lawyer and to have the lawyer present during the interrogation and; (3) if he is indigent, a lawyer will be appointed to represent him. If prior to or during the interrogation, the defendant indicates that he wishes to remain silent, the questioning must cease. If he states that he wants an attorney, the questioning must cease until the attorney is present. If statements are obtained following the defendant's waiver of his rights, the government has a heavy burden to prove that the waiver was given knowingly and intelligently. If the officials fail to follow this procedure, any statements obtained during the interrogation are inadmissible.

In each of these cases, the law enforcement officials did not inform the defendants of their Fifth Amendment privileges before their interrogations. The defendant's right to remain silent and protection from self-incrimination were not adequately protected, making their confessions inadmissible in court. Therefore, their convictions were reversed.

The Fifth Amendment and the Fourteenth Amendment also guarantee due process of law, which is basically the requirement of a fair trial. Every person is entitled to have charges or complaints against him, whether in civil or criminal proceedings, made publicly and in writing, and be given the opportunity to defend against them. In criminal prosecutions, it includes the right to counsel, to confront and cross-examine adverse witnesses, to testify in his own behalf if desired, to produce witnesses and offer other evidence, and to be free from any and all prejudicial conduct and statements.

Sixth Amendment

The Sixth Amendment provides that the Federal government shall provide the accused with a speedy and public trial by an impartial jury, to be informed of the nature and cause of the accusation, to be confronted with the witnesses against him, to have compulsory process for obtaining witnesses in his favor, and to have the assistance of counsel for his defense. The Fourteenth Amendment extends these guarantees to the States.

The Supreme Court has explained the purpose of guaranteeing the right to a trial by jury as follows: "[T]he purpose of trial by jury is to prevent oppression by the Government by providing a safeguard against the corrupt or overzealous prosecutor and against the compliant, biased, or eccentric judge . . . [T]he essential factors of a jury trial obviously lie in the interposition between the accused and his accuser of the common sense judgment of a group of laymen." Nevertheless, a defendant may give up his right to a jury trial.

Historically, juries consisted of twelve jurors, but in the Federal courts and in the courts of certain States the number has been reduced to six. The Supreme Court has held that the use of a six-member jury in a criminal case does not violate a defendant's right to a jury trial under the Sixth Amendment. The Supreme Court recognized that there was no observable difference between the results reached by a jury of twelve or by a jury of six, nor was there any evidence to suggest that a jury of twelve is more advantageous to a defendant. The jury needs only be large enough "to promote group deliberation, free from outside attempts at intimidation, and to provide a fair possibility for obtaining a representative cross section of the community." Moreover, State court jury verdicts need not be unanimous provided the vote is sufficient to assure adequate deliberations. Thus, the Supreme Court has upheld jury votes of 11–1, 10–2, and 9–3 but rejected as insufficient a 5–1 vote.

CHAPTER SUMMARY

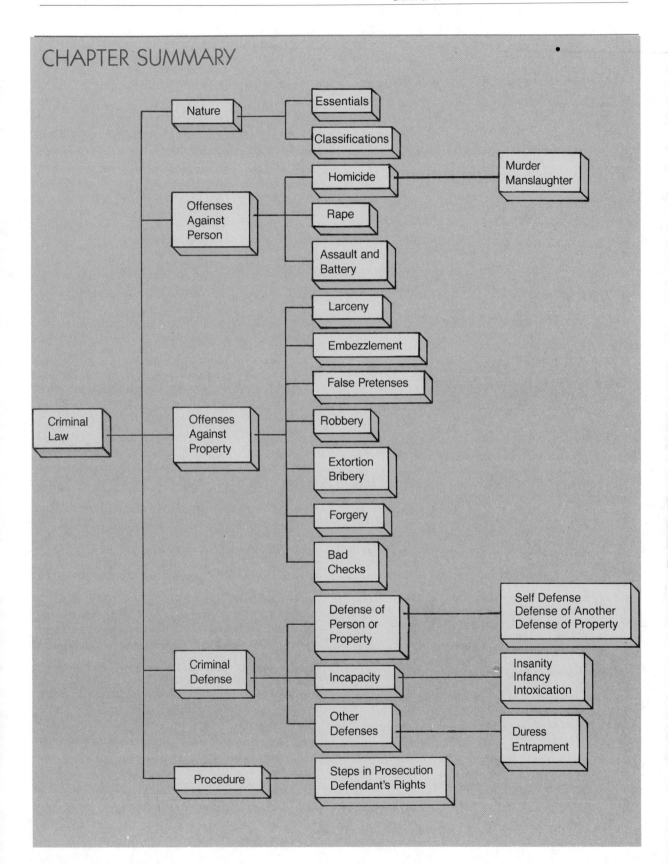

KEY TERMS

Crime	Manslaughter	Self-defense
Beyond a reasonable doubt	Voluntary manslaughter	Incapacity
Prosecutor	Involuntary manslaughter	Defense of another
Defendant	Criminal negligence	Defense of property
Actus Reus	Rape	Insanity
Mens Rea	Assault	McNaughton test
Intent	Battery	Infancy
Mala in se	Larceny	Intoxication
Mala prohibita	Embezzlement	Duress
Felony	False pretenses	Mistake of fact
Misdemeanor	Robbery	Entrapment
White-collar crime	Aggravated robbery	Grand jury
Petty crime	Extortion	Indictment
Computer crime	Bribery	Arraignment
Homicide	Commercial bribery	Exclusionary rule
Murder	Burglary	Probable cause
Malice aforethought	Forgery	Self-incrimination
Premeditated	Bad Check	Double jeopardy

PROBLEMS

1. X said to Y, "B is going to sell me a good used car next Monday and then I'll deliver it to you in exchange for your microcomputer, but I'd like to have the computer now." Relying on this statement, Y delivered the computer to X. X knew B had no car, would have none in the future, and had no such arrangement with B. The appointed time of exchange passed and X failed to deliver the car to Y. Has a crime been committed? Discuss.

2. X, a lawyer, drew a deed for Y by which Y was to convey land to B. The deed was correct in every detail. Y examined and verbally approved it but did not sign it. X erased B's name and substituted his own. Y signed the deed with all required legal formalities without noticing the change. Was X guilty of forgery? Discuss.

3. A took B's watch before B was aware of the theft. B discovered his loss immediately and pursued A. A pointed a loaded pistol at B, who, in fear of being shot, allowed A to escape. Was A guilty of robbery? Of any other crime?

4. X and Y were on trial, separately, for larceny of a $1,000 bearer bond (payable to the holder of the bond not a named individual) issued by A, Inc. The Commonwealth's evidence showed that the owner of the bond had dropped it accidentally in the street enclosed in an envelope bearing his name and address;

that X found the envelope with the bond in it; that X could neither read nor write; that X presented the envelope and bond to Y, an educated man, and asked Y what he should do with it; that Y told X that the finder of lost property becomes the owner of it; that Y told X that the bond was worth $100 but that the money could only be collected at the issuer's home office; that X then handed the bond to Y, who redeemed it at the corporation's home office and received $1,000; that Y gave X $100 of the proceeds. What rulings?

5. Truck drivers for a hauling company, while loading a desk, found a $100 bill that fell out of the desk. They agreed to get it exchanged for small bills and divide the proceeds. En route to a bank, one of them changed his mind and refused to proceed with the scheme, whereupon the other pulled a knife and demanded the bill. A police officer intervened. It turned out that the bill was counterfeit money. What crimes have been committed?

6. W was judged legally insane and committed as an inmate of a State hospital. Six months after his commitment he escaped and met his friend R. After R and W had several drinks of hard liquor, they rode to a liquor store in a car driven by W. In accordance with a previous plan W waited in the car while R held up the proprietor of the liquor store. W and R were later apprehended and are now being prosecuted for robbery. W pleaded not guilty by reason of insanity and intoxication and on the further ground that he did not enter the building or receive any part of the stolen property. Discuss and decide.

7. P, an undercover police agent, was trying to locate a laboratory where it was believed that methamphetamine or "speed"—a controlled substance—was being manufactured illegally. P went to D's home and said that he represented a large organization that was interested in obtaining methamphetamine. P offered to supply a necessary ingredient for the manufacture of the drug, which was very difficult to obtain, in return for one-half of the drug produced. D agreed and processed the chemical given to him by P in P's presence. Later P returned with a search warrant and arrested D. D was charged with various narcotics law violations. D asserted the defense of entrapment. Decision?

8. The police obtained a search warrant based on an affidavit that contained the following allegations: (a) D was seen crossing a State line on four occasions during a five-day period and going to a particular apartment; (b) telephone records disclosed that the apartment had two telephones; (c) D had a reputation as a bookmaker and as an associate of gamblers; and (d) the FBI was informed by a "confidential reliable informant" that D was conducting gambling operations. When a search was made based on the warrant, evidence was obtained that resulted in D's conviction of violating certain gambling laws. D challenged the constitutionality of the search warrant. Decision?

9. A national bank was robbed by a man with a small strip of tape on each side of his face. An indictment was returned against D. D was then arrested, and counsel appointed to represent him. Two weeks later, without notice to D's lawyer, an FBI agent arranged to have the two bank employees observe a lineup, including D and five or six other prisoners. Each person in the lineup wore strips of tape, as had the robber, and each was directed to repeat the words "Put the money in the bag," as had the robber. Both of the bank employees identified D as the robber. At D's trial he was again identified by the two, in the courtroom, and the prior lineup identification was elicited on cross examination by D's counsel. D's counsel moved the court either to grant a judgment of acquittal, or alternatively to strike the courtroom identifications, on the grounds that the lineup had violated D's Fifth Amendment privilege against self-incrimination and his Sixth Amendment right to counsel. Decision?

INTENTIONAL TORTS

All forms of liability are either (1) voluntarily assumed, as by contract, or (2) involuntarily imposed by law. Tort liability is of the second type. Tort law protects a person from civil wrongs or injuries to his person, property, and economic interests. A tort is committed when (1) a duty owing by one person to another (2) is breached and (3) proximately causes (4) injury or damage to the owner of a legally protected interest.

Tort–a civil wrong causing injury to a person, her property or her economic interests

Each person is legally responsible for the damages that are proximately caused by his tortious conduct. Moreover, as we discuss in Chapter 28, businesses that employ agents to conduct their business activities are also liable for the torts committed by their agents in the course of employment. The tort liability of employers makes the study of tort law essential to business managers.

In a tort action the injured party *sues* to recover *compensation* for the damage and injury that she has sustained as a result of the defendant's wrongful conduct. The purpose of tort law is to compensate the injured party, not to punish the wrongdoer as in the case of criminal law.

Of course, the same conduct may, and often does, constitute both a crime and a tort. An example is an assault and battery committed by A against B. For the commission of this crime, the State may take appropriate action against A. In addition, A has violated B's right to be secure in his person, and so has committed a tort against B. B, regardless of the criminal action by the State against A, may bring a civil tort action against A for damages. But an act may be criminal without being tortious; by the same token, an act may be a tort but not a crime. The closest that tort law comes to an implementation of the objectives of the criminal law is in certain cases where courts may award **punitive** or "exemplary" damages. Where the defendant's tortious conduct has been intentional and deliberate, showing malice or a fraudulent or evil motive, many courts permit a jury to award damages over and above the amount necessary to compensate the plaintiff. The allowance of punitive damages is designed to punish and make an example of the defendant and thus deter others from similar conduct.

Punitive damages–damages awarded in excess of normal compensation to punish a defendant for a serious civil wrong

Harms or injuries may be inflicted (1) intentionally, (2) negligently, or (3) without fault (strict liability). We discuss intentional torts in this chapter and cover negligence and strict liability in Chapter 6.

Tort law is primarily common law, and as we mentioned in Chapter 1, the Restatements, prepared by the American Law Institute, give an orderly presentation of many important areas of the common law, including torts. You will recall that although they are not law by themselves, they are highly persuasive in the courts. The first Restatement of Torts was adopted by the American Law Institute from 1934 to 1939. Since then, it has served as a vital force in shaping the law of torts. Between 1965 and 1978 the institute adopted a revised edition of the Restatement of Torts, which takes the place of the First Restatement. The revised Restatement will be referred to simply as the Restatement.

Intent

Intent–desire to cause the consequences of an act or knowledge that the consequences are substantially certain to result from the act

Intent, as used in tort law, does not require a hostile or evil motive. Rather, it means that the actor desires to cause the consequences of his act, or that he believes that the consequences are substantially (almost) certain to result from it. The following examples should help you understand the definition of intent: (1) If A fires a gun in the middle of the Mojave Desert, he intends to fire the gun, but when the bullet hits B, who is in the desert without A's knowledge, A does not intend that result. (2) A throws a bomb into B's office in order to kill B. A knows that C is in B's office and that the bomb is substantially certain to injure C, although A has no desire to do so. A is, nonetheless, liable to C for any injury caused C. A's intent to injure B is *transferred* to C.

Infants (i.e., persons who have not reached the age of majority) are held liable for their intentional torts. The infant's age and knowledge, however, are critical in determining whether the infant had sufficient intelligence to form the required intent. Incompetents, like infants, are generally held liable for their intentional torts.

Injury or Damage to the Person

The most common intentional torts involve an interference with personal rights. They include battery, assault, false imprisonment, infliction of emotional distress, defamation, and invasion of privacy. We discuss these torts in that order.

Battery

Battery–intentional infliction of harmful or offensive bodily contact

Battery is an intentional infliction of **harmful or offensive bodily contact.** It may cause serious injury, as a gunshot wound or a blow on the head with a club. Or it may cause little or no physical injury, such as knocking a hat off of a person's head or flicking a glove in another's face, as shown in the case of *Fisher* v. *Carrousel Motor Hotel.* Bodily contact is offensive if it would offend a reasonable person's sense of dignity. Bodily contact may be accomplished by the use of objects, such as Gustav's throwing a rock at Hester with the intention of hitting her. If the rock hits Hester or any other person, Gustav has committed a battery.

FISHER v. CARROUSEL
MOTOR HOTEL, INC.

Supreme Court of Texas,
1967.
424 S.W.2d 627.

FACTS: Fisher, a Black, attended a business meeting held at the Carrousel Motor Hotel. The meeting included a buffet luncheon. While he stood in the buffet line, a hotel employee approached Fisher and snatched the plate from his hand, shouting that no Negro could be served in the hotel. Fisher was not actually touched by the employee nor was he in apprehension of physical injury, but he was highly embarrassed by the incident which occurred in the presence of his business associates. He brought an action for battery against Carrousel based on the employee's conduct, seeking to recover actual damages for his humiliation and indignity plus punitive damages.

DECISION: Judgment for Fisher. Battery may consist of the offensive invasion of a person's dignity without any actual physical harm inflicted upon his body. The essence of battery for offensive contact is "the unpermitted and intentional invasion of the inviolability of [the plaintiff's] person." Therefore, the intentional snatching of an object from a person's hand constitutes a battery if the object is so intimately connected with the person's body as to be considered a part of it. The plate in Fisher's hand was such an object and the employee's intentional and unpermitted snatching of it was a battery. Accordingly, Carrousel must compensate Fisher for the invasion of his personal dignity caused by the employee's conduct, even though Fisher suffered no actual physical injury.

Assault

Assault is intentional conduct by one person directed at another that places him in **apprehension** of immediate bodily harm or offensive contact. It is usually committed immediately before a battery, but if the intended battery fails, the assault remains. The person in danger of immediate bodily harm must have *knowledge* of the danger and be apprehensive of its imminent threat to his safety. For example, A aims a loaded gun at B's back but is subdued by C before B becomes aware of the danger. A has not committed an assault on B.

Assault–intentional infliction of apprehension of immediate bodily harm or offensive contact

False Imprisonment

The tort of false imprisonment is the intentional **confining** of a person within fixed boundaries if the person is conscious of the confinement or harmed by it. As in the *Peterson* case, merely obstructing a person's freedom of movement is not false imprisonment so long as there is a reasonable alternative exit available.

False imprisonment–intentional interference with a person's freedom of movement by unlawful confinement

Merchants occasionally have a problem with potential liability for false imprisonment when they seek to question a suspected shoplifter. If the merchant detains an innocent person, she may face a lawsuit for false imprisonment. Most States have statutes protecting the merchant, provided she detains the suspect in a reasonable manner, for not more than a reasonable time, and with probable cause.

PETERSON v. SORLIEN

Supreme Court of Minnesota,
1980.
299 N.W.2d 123.

FACTS: Susan Jungclaus Peterson was a 21 year-old student at Moorehead State College who had lived most of her life on her family farm in Minnesota. A dean's list student during her first year, her academic performance declined after she became deeply involved in an international religious cult organization known locally as The Way of Minnesota, Inc. The cult demanded an enormous psychological and monetary commitment from Susan. Near the end of her junior year, her parents became alarmed by the changes in Susan's physical and mental well-being and concluded that she had been "reduced to a condition of psychological bondage by The Way."

They sought help from Kathy Mills, a self-styled "deprogrammer" of minds brainwashed by cults.

On May 24, 1976, Norman Jungclaus, Susan's father, picked up Susan from Moorehead State. Instead of returning home, they went to the residence of Veronica Morgel, where Kathy Mills attempted to deprogram Susan. For the first few days of her stay, Susan was unwilling to discuss her involvement. She lay curled in a fetal position in her bedroom, plugging her ears and hysterically screaming and crying while her father pleaded with her to listen. By the third day, however, Susan's demeanor changed completely. She became friendly and vivacious and communicated with her father. Susan also went roller skating and played softball at a nearby park over the following weekend. She spent the next week in Columbus, Ohio with a former cult member who had shared her experiences of the previous week. While in Columbus she spoke daily by telephone with her fiance, a member of The Way, who begged her to return to the cult. Susan expressed the desire to get her fiance out of the organization, but a meeting between them could not be arranged outside the presence of other members of The Way. Her parents attempted to persuade Susan to sign an agreement releasing them from liability for their actions but Susan refused. After nearly 16 days of "deprogramming" Susan left the Morgel residence and returned to her fiance and The Way. Upon the direction of The Way ministry, she brought this action against her parents for false imprisonment.

DECISION: Judgment for Mr. and Mrs. Jungclaus. "If a person is aware of a reasonable means of escape that does not present a danger of bodily or material harm, a restriction is not total and complete and does not constitute unlawful imprisonment." Also, a person cannot recover damages for any period of detention to which she voluntarily consents. For the final 13 days of the 16-day period Susan willingly remained in the company of her parents. She also had several reasonable and safe opportunities to escape while playing softball, roller skating and during her trip to Ohio. Given that the conditioning of the cult may have impaired her free will prior to her "deprogramming," it is reasonable to infer from her subsequent consent that she would have consented to the first three days' detention if she had her full capacity. Furthermore, parents may place limitations on their adult child's mobility, if they have a good faith reasonable belief that the child's judgmental capacity has been seriously affected by a cult and if she at some point assents to the limitations. Thus, Susan's assent during the 13-day period relieved her parents of liability for false imprisonment.

Infliction of Emotional Distress

Infliction of emotion distress–extreme and outrageous conduct intentionally or recklessly causing severe emotional distress

The law is not static, and the most recent type of tort is that of intentional infliction of emotional distress. One who by extreme and **outrageous conduct** intentionally or recklessly causes severe emotional distress to another is liable for such emotional distress as well as any resulting bodily harm.

This cause of action does not protect a person from abusive language or rudeness, but rather from atrocious, intolerable conduct beyond all bounds of decency. Examples of this tort include leading to a person's home, when he is present, a noisy demonstrating mob yelling threats to lynch him unless he leaves town, or placing a rattlesnake in another's bed as a practical joke.

SAMMS v. ECCLES

Supreme Court of Utah, 1961.
11 Utah 2d 289, 358 P.2d 344.

FACTS: Marcia Samms, a respectable married woman, claimed that David Eccles had repeatedly and persistently called her at various hours, including late at night, from May to December 1957, soliciting her to have illicit sexual relations with him. She also claimed that on one occasion Eccles came over to her residence to again solicit sex and indecently exposed himself to her. Mrs. Samms said she had never encouraged Eccles but had continuously repulsed his "insulting, indecent, and obscene" proposals. She brought suit against Eccles, claiming she suffered great anxiety and fear for her personal safety and severe emotional distress, demanding actual and punitive damages.

DECISION: Judgment for Samms. The recent judicial trend recognizes a cause of action for severe emotional distress, even though not accompanied by bodily impact or physical injury, where the defendant engaged in intentional conduct aimed at the plaintiff (1) with the purpose of inflicting emotional distress or (2) where any reasonable person should have known that emotional distress would result. In addition, the conduct must be outrageous and intolerable according to general community standards of decency and morality.

Usually, solicitation to sexual intercourse alone will not be actionable even though it may be offensive to the offeree. This is based on the customary assumption that "there is no harm in asking." Under the circumstances of this case, however, Eccles' conduct constitutes more than a mere solicitation, considering that it persisted for eight months and also involved indecent exposure. These aggravating circumstances are sufficient to give Samms a cause of action based solely on her severe emotional distress.

Defamation

The tort of defamation is a communication that injures a person's reputation by disgracing him and diminishing the respect in which he is held. An example would be the publication of a statement that a person had committed a crime or had a loathsome disease.

If the defamatory communication is handwritten, typewritten, printed, pictorical, or in any other form with similar communicative power, such as television or radio, it is designated **libel.** If it is spoken or oral, it is designated **slander.** In either case it must be communicated to a person or persons other than the one who is defamed. This is referred to as its *publication.* Thus, if Maurice writes a defamatory letter about Pierre's character that he hands or mails to Pierre, this is not a publication because it is intended only for Pierre.

Truth and *privilege* are complete defenses to defamation. In most States, truth is a complete defense no matter what the purpose or intent in publishing the defamation. There are three types of privileges: absolute, conditional, and constitutional.

As with the defense of truth, **absolute privilege** protects the defendant regardless of his motive or intent. Absolute privilege has been confined to those few situations where public policy clearly favors complete freedom of speech and includes: (1) statements made during a judicial proceeding; (2) statements made by members of Congress on the floor of Congress; (3) statements made by certain executive officers while performing their governmental duty; and (4) statements made between spouses when they are alone.

Conditional or qualified privilege depends on proper use of the privilege. A person has conditional privilege to publish defamatory matter to protect his own legitimate interests, or in some cases the interests of another. Conditional privilege also extends to many cases where the publisher and the recipient have a common interest, as with letters of reference. Conditional privilege, however, is forfeited by the publisher if she acts in an excessive manner, without probable cause, or for an improper purpose.

The First Amendment to the United States Constitution guarantees freedom of speech and freedom of the press. The courts have applied these rights to the law of defamation by extending a form of **constitutional** privilege to comment about public officials or public figures so long as it is done without *malice.* For these purposes "malice" is not ill will but proof of the publisher's knowledge of falsity or reckless disregard of the truth. See Law in the News on page 88.

Defamation–injury to a person's reputation by publication of false statements

Libel–defamation communicated by writing, television, radio or the like

Slander–oral defamation

Law In The News

The Libel Law at Work
The tangled legal doctrine is still under attack.

While both Time and Ariel Sharon suffered from their days in court, the battered but unbowed American law of libel shone brighter than it had for a long time. Unnecessarily complicated and academic to a fault, the 20-year-old law seemed for a moment positively rejuvenated and far less the tangled doctrine whose reform has been urgently recommended in recent months. "The lesson," said First Amendment lawyer Floyd Abrams, "is that [the law] can work. A conscientious judge can lead a conscientious jury to successfully focus on difficult issues."

In the short run, the Sharon verdict may change the style, but not the substance, of libel law. U.S. district judge Abraham D. Sofaer's clever directive to the jury requiring them to move cautiously through their deliberations, announcing one decision at a time, will undoubtedly be copied in future cases. Sofaer's move was a variation on what lawyers call a "special verdict"—a step-by-step process of decision-making juries are asked to follow in complicated cases. By making each incremental verdict public, the judge ensured that the jurors would keep to their appointed course rather than get hopelessly tangled in the laws' conundrums. "In my experience, judges have not instructed juries to report back the answer to each separate question," says Dallas libel lawyer Charles Babcock. "You can bet that in the future I will ask judges to give instructions much like those given by Sofaer."

Still, there are broad objections to current law that, while unaffected by *Sharon v. Time*, cannot be overruled indefinitely. Twenty years ago the U.S. Supreme Court tried to give the press some breathing space for public-affairs reporting by creating a new defense against libel suits brought by public officials. Under the ruling in *New York Times Co. v. Sullivan*, the press won the freedom to print or broadcast stories critical—even defamatory—of officeholders without fear of legal reprisal, unless the subject of such a story can show that it is both false and published with knowledge of its falsity or with "reckless disregard" for its truth or falsity. The decision was a bold and unprecedented step for the court, hailed at the time by legal philosopher Alexander Meiklejohn as an occasion for "dancing in the streets."

That euphoria has long since disappeared. While *Sullivan* has protected some First Amendment interests, it has not worked out quite as its advocates had hoped. Much of the criticism has focused on two points. First, jurors in libel cases tend to have trouble following the court's legal formulation, which uses the label "actual malice" to refer to publication or broadcast of falsehoods with either knowledge of falsity or reckless disregard. This has nothing to do with malice as lay people understand it—as a term connoting hostility or ill will. Judge Sofaer took great pains to explain this concept to the jury, using 20 pages of his 66-page charge to explain the ineptly labeled concept. In recent years, plaintiffs have won jury verdicts that were later reversed because of mistaken applications of "malice."

Second, *Sullivan* became an invitation for angry plaintiffs to poke through the editorial process: if an aggrieved official had the heavy burden of proving reckless disregard for the truth, the court held nearly six years ago in *Herbert v. Lando*, they were entitled to explore the editorial state of mind. That in turn has led to extensive and expensive pretrial fights in which journalists must explain and defend their editorial processes and judgments. Sharon's pretrial battle, in which the general's lawyers unearthed alleged breakdowns in Time's journalistic processes, gave him the ammunition to sustain the two-and-a-half-month courtroom war.

Expensive Litigation: Despite the difficulties it imposes on a plaintiff, *Sullivan* has not proved a deterrent to libel suits such as those brought by Mobil Oil president William Tavoulareas against The Washington Post and Gen. William C. Westmoreland against CBS—both of which survived pretrial motions that would have resulted in dismissal. In *Sullivan*, three of the justices were willing to take the radical step of barring libel suits by public officials outright but couldn't get a majority to vote with them. Now legal specialists like columnist Anthony Lewis and groups like the American Civil Liberties Union are reviving the idea. "The answer," says ACLU staff counsel Charles Sims, "is more speech, not lawsuits." Otherwise, the argument runs, a press fearful of expensive litigation and large damage awards will fall into timid self-censorship. That is particularly true of small, lower-budget publications that cannot afford to do legal battle with the wealthy or powerful.

But that approach shortchanges the traditional notion that

Libel Law continued

a person may seek to redeem in court his or her good name. By taking office, does a public servant forfeit this right? Should it depend on how effectively the charge might be answered in other arenas? Or on how inseparable the official is from a policy ripe for attack—a controversial military strategy, for example?

Stanford law Prof. Marc Franklin, who calls the current libel system "a hodge-podge at best," thinks he has a workable compromise. He would ban all punitive damages, limiting awards to compensatory amounts. Under Franklin's plan, plaintiffs could bring actions solely to restore their reputations, but only after the publisher or broad-

caster had been given an opportunity to retract the story publicly. The loser in most suits would have to pay his foe's attorney's fees. This wouldn't solve all the dilemmas but, as we have learned with *Sullivan*, nothing will.

ARIC PRESS with ANN McDANIEL
Copyright 1985, by Newsweek, Inc. All Rights Reserved. Reprinted by Permission.

FACTS: In March 1975, William Proxmire, a United States Senator from Wisconsin, initiated the "Golden Fleece of the Month Award" to publicize what he believed to be wasteful government spending. The second of these awards was given to the Federal agencies that had for seven years funded Dr. Hutchinson's research on stress levels in animals. The award was made in a speech Proxmire gave in the Senate; the text was also incorporated into an advance press release that was sent to 275 members of the national news media. Proxmire also referred to the research again in two subsequent newsletters sent to 100,000 constituents and during a television interview. Hutchinson then brought this action alleging defamation resulting in personal and economic injury. The District Court granted summary judgment for Proxmire and the Court of Appeals affirmed based on (1) absolute privilege under the Speech or Debate Clause of the U.S. Constitution and (2) constitutional privilege. Hutchinson (plaintiff) then brought this appeal.

DECISION: Grant of summary judgment for Proxmire reversed. Neither the advance news release, the newsletters, nor the comments made by Senator Proxmire during the television interview are protected by the absolute immunity provided members of Congress. That protection is not intended to create an absolute privilege from liability for defamatory statements made outside of Congress. Therefore, while a speech made by Proxmire in the Senate would be wholly immune, as would its reproduction in the Congressional Record, the press release and the newsletters do not receive this protection because neither was essential to the deliberations of the Senate.

Moreover, Senator Proxmire's news release and newsletters are not protected by the constitutional privilege provided by the First Amendment to defamatory comments made concerning public figures. Hutchinson was not a public figure merely because he accepted Federal funds or because some newspapers and wire services reported his response to the award. Rather, any public notoriety he achieved came as a result of the alleged defamation and, therefore, cannot serve as a basis for Proxmire's defense.

HUTCHINSON v.
PROXMIRE

Supreme Court of the United
States, 1979.
443 U.S. 111, 99 S.Ct. 2675.

Invasion of Privacy

The invasion of a person's right to privacy actually consists of four distinct torts: (1) appropriation of a person's name or likeness; (2) unreasonable intrusion on the seclusion of another; (3) unreasonable public disclosure of private facts; (4) unreasonable publicity that places another in a false light in the public eye.

It is entirely possible and not uncommon for a person's right of privacy to be invaded in such a way that two or more of these related torts are committed. For example, A forces his way into B's hospital room, takes a photograph of B, and publishes it to promote A's cure for B's illness along with false statements about B that would be highly objectionable to a reasonable person. B would be entitled to recover on any or all of the four torts comprising invasion of privacy.

Appropriation–unauthorized use of another person's name or likeness for one's own benefit

Appropriation   Appropriation is the use of another person's name or likeness for one's own benefit, as for example in promoting or advertising a product or service. The tort of appropriation seeks to protect the individual's right to the exclusive use of his identity and is also known as the "right of publicity." In the example above, A's use of B's photograph to promote A's business constitutes the tort of appropriation. The following case involving Johnny Carson also is an example of appropriation.

CARSON v. HERE'S JOHNNY PORTABLE TOILETS, INC.

United States Court of Appeals, Sixth Circuit, 1983. 698 F.2d 831.

FACTS: Plaintiff, John W. Carson, is the host and star of "The Tonight Show," a well-known television program broadcast by the National Broadcasting Company. Carson also appears as an entertainer in night clubs and theaters around the country. From the time he began hosting "The Tonight Show" in 1962, he has been introduced on the show each night with the phrase "Here's Johnny." The phrase "Here's Johnny" is generally associated with Carson by a substantial segment of the television viewing public. In 1967, Carson began authorizing use of this phrase by outside business ventures.

Defendant, Here's Johnny Portable Toilets, Inc., is a Michigan corporation engaged in the business of renting and selling "Here's Johnny" portable toilets. Defendant's founder was aware at the time he formed the corporation that "Here's Johnny" was the introductory slogan for Carson on "The Tonight Show." He indicated that he coupled the phrase with a second one, "The World's Foremost Commodian," to make "a good play on a phrase." Carson brought suit for invasion of privacy.

DECISION: Judgment for Carson. The right of privacy involves four distinct torts, one of which is the appropriation of a person's name or likeness. This tort, also known as the "right of publicity," protects the commercial interests of celebrities in exploiting their identities.

In this case there would have been no violation of Carson's right of publicity if the defendant had used Carson's actual name, such as "J. William Carson Portable Toilet" or the "John William Carson Portable Toilet" or the "J.W. Carson Portable Toilet." The reason is that, though literally using the plaintiff's "name," the defendant would not have appropriated Carson's identity as a celebrity. Here there was an appropriation of Carson's identity without using his "name," because of the public's association of Carson with the phrase "Here's Johnny."

Intrusion–unreasonable and highly offensive interference with the seclusion of another

Intrusion   This type of invasion of privacy is the unreasonable and highly offensive interference with the solitude or seclusion of another. Such unreasonable interference includes improper entry into another's dwelling, unauthorized eavesdropping on another's private conversations, and unauthorized examination of another's private papers and records. The intrusion must be offensive or objectionable to a reasonable person and must involve private matters. Thus, there is no liability if the defendant examines public records or observes the plaintiff in a public place. This form of invasion of privacy is committed once the intrusion occurs—publicity is not required.

Public disclosure of private facts–offensive publicity given to private information about another person

Public Disclosure of Private Facts   The law of privacy imposes liability for offensive *publicity* given to private information about another. As with intrusion, this tort applies only to private, not public, information about an individual, but unlike intrusion it requires publicity. The publicity required differs in degree from "publication" as used in the law of defamation. Under this tort the private facts must be communicated to the public at large or become public knowledge, whereas publication of a defamatory statement need only be made to a single third party. Thus A, a creditor of B, will not invade B's privacy by writing a letter to B's employer informing the employer of B's failure to pay the debt, but A would be liable if she posted in the window of her store a statement that B will not pay a debt owed to A. Also unlike defamation, this tort applies to truthful private information if the matter published would be offensive and objectionable to a reasonable person of ordinary sensibilities.

False Light   This invasion of privacy imposes liability for highly offensive *publicity* placing another in a false light if the defendant *knew* that the matter publicized was false or acted in *reckless disregard* of the truth. For example, Edgar includes Jason's name and photograph in a public "rogues' gallery" of convicted criminals. Jason has never been convicted of any crime. Edgar is liable to Jason for placing him in a false light.

False light–offensive publicity placing another in a false light

As with defamation, the matter must be untrue, but unlike defamation it must be "publicized," not merely "published." Although the matter must be objectionable to a reasonable person, it need not be defamatory. In many instances, the same facts will give rise to both an action for defamation and false light.

Defenses   *Absolute, conditional,* and *constitutional* privilege apply to the same extent to the torts of disclosure of private facts and false light as they do to defamation.

The following case deals with both public disclosure of private facts and false light as well as with constitutional privilege.

FACTS: Bill Kinsey was charged with murdering his wife while working for the Peace Corps in Tanzania. After waiting six months in jail he was acquitted at a trial which attracted wide publicity. Five years later, while a graduate student at Stanford University, Kinsey had a brief affair with Mary Macur. He abruptly ended the affair by telling Macur he would no longer be seeing her because another woman, Sally Allen, was coming from England to live with him. A few months later, Kinsey and Allen moved to Africa and were subsequently married. Soon after Bill ended their affair, Macur began a letter writing campaign designed to expose Bill and his mistreatment of her. Macur sent several letters to both Bill and Sally Kinsey, their former spouses, their parents, their neighbors, their parents' neighbors, members of Bill's dissertation committee, other faculty and the President of Stanford University. The letters contained statements accusing Bill of murdering his first wife, spending six months in jail for the crime, being a rapist, and other questionable behavior. The Kinseys brought an action for invasion of privacy, seeking damages and a permanent injunction.

DECISION: Judgment for the Kinseys. The tort of invasion of privacy includes four separate torts, two of which are involved here: (1) the public disclosure of true, embarrassing private facts concerning the plaintiff and (2) publicity which places the plaintiff in a false light in the public eye. In both of these torts there must be a communication to the general public or a large number of people as opposed to private communications. In this case, Macur sent the letters to approximately twenty people. However, the recipients were such a diverse group, living in several different States and totally unconnected either socially or professionally, that her campaign satisfied this requirement.

Macur claims that even if she invaded Kinsey's privacy, it was privileged because he was a public figure by virtue of his participation in the Peace Corps and his widely publicized murder trial. The definition of a public figure is not clear but membership in the Peace Corps is not sufficient to make a person a public figure. Moreover, once Kinsey had been acquitted at his trial, he was no longer a public figure and should be allowed "to melt into the shadows of obscurity" once again.

KINSEY v. MACUR

Court of Appeals of California, First District, 1980.
107 Cal.App.3d 265, 165 Cal.Rptr. 608.

Interference With Property Rights

In addition to protecting against intentional interference with the person, the law also provides protection against invasions of a person's interests in property. Intentional interference with property rights includes the torts of (1) trespass to real property, (2) nuisance, (3) trespass to personal property and (4) conversion.

Real Property

Real property–land and anything attached to it

Real property is land and anything attached to it, such as buildings, trees, and minerals. The law protects the rights of the possessor of land to its exclusive use and quiet enjoyment.

Trespass to real property–wrongful entry onto another's land

Trespass   A person is liable for trespass if he intentionally (1) enters or remains on land in the possession of another, (2) causes a thing or a third person to do so, or (3) fails to remove from the land a thing that he is under a duty to remove. Liability exists even though no actual damage is done to the land.

It is no defense that the intruder acted on the mistaken belief of law or fact that he was not trespassing. If the intruder intended to be on the particular property, it is irrelevant that he reasonably believed that he owned the land or had permission to enter on the land. An intruder is not liable if his presence on the land of another is not caused by his own actions. For example, if A is thrown onto B's land by C, A is not liable to B for trespass, but C is.

A trespass may be committed on, beneath, or above the surface of the land, although the law regards the upper air, above the prescribed minimum altitude of flight, as a public highway. There is no trespass unless the aircraft enters into the lower reaches of the air space and substantially interferes with the landowner's use and enjoyment.

Nuisance–nontrespassory invasion of another's interest in the private use and enjoyment of his land

Nuisance   A nuisance is a nontrespassory invasion of another's interest in the private use and enjoyment of land. In contrast to trespass, nuisance does not require interference with another's right to exclusive possession of land, but rather imposes liability for significant harm to another's use or enjoyment of land. Examples of nuisances include the emission of unpleasant odors, smoke, dust, or gas as well as the pollution of a stream, pond, or underground water supply.

Personal Property

Personal property any property other than an interest in land

Personal property is any type of property other than an interest in land. The law protects a number of interests in the possession of personal property, including an interest in the property's physical condition and usability, an interest in the retention of possession, and an interest in the property's availability for future use.

Trespass to personal property–intentional dispossession or unauthorized use of the personal property of another

Trespass   Trespass to personal property consists of the intentional dispossession or unauthorized use of the personal property of another. The interference with the right to exclusive use and possession may be direct or indirect, but liability is limited to instances in which the trespasser (1) dispossesses the other of the property, (2) substantially impairs the condition, quality, or value of the property, or (3) deprives the possessor of the use of the property for a substantial time. For example, A parks his car in front of his house. Later, B pushes A's car around the corner. A subsequently looks for his car but cannot find it for several hours. B is liable to A for trespass.

Conversion   Conversion is the intentional exercise of dominion or control over another's personal property that so seriously interferes with the other's right of control as justly to require the payment of full value for the property. Conversion may consist of the intentional destruction of the personal property or the use of the property in an unauthorized manner. For example, A entrusts an automobile to B, a dealer, for sale. B drives the car 8,000 miles on his own business. B is liable to A for conversion. On the other hand, in the example above in which B pushed A's car around the corner, B would *not* be liable to A for conversion.

> Conversion–intentional exercise of dominion or control over another's personal property

A major distinction between trespass to personal property and conversion is the measure of damages. In trespass, the possessor recovers damages for the actual harm to the property or for the loss of possession. In conversion, the possessor recovers the full value of the property, and the convertor takes possession of it on payment of the judgment.

Interference With Economic Interests

A third set of interests protected by the law against intentional interference is economic interests. The following are covered under this heading: (1) interference with contractual relations, (2) disparagement, and (3) fraudulent misrepresentation.

Interference with Contractual Relations

This tort consists of the intentional and improper interference with the performance of a contract by inducing one of the parties not to perform the contract. (Contracts are discussed extensively in Part Two of this text.) The injured party may recover the economic loss resulting from the breach of the contract. Similar liability is imposed for intentional and improper interference with another's prospective contractual relation.

> Interference with contractual relations–intentionally causing one of the parties to a contract not to perform the contract

In either case, the rule applies whenever a person acts with the purpose or motive of interfering with another's contract or with the knowledge that such interference is substantially certain to occur as a natural consequence of her actions. The interference may be by prevention through the use of physical force or by threats. Frequently, it is accomplished by inducement, such as the offer of a better contract. For instance, A may offer B, an employee of C, a yearly salary of $5,000 per year more than the contractual arrangement between B and C. If A is aware of the contract between B and C and that his offer to B interferes with that contract, then A is liable to C for intentional interference with contractual relations. However, if the employment contract between B and C was at will (that is, of no definite duration), there would be no tort, for C had no legal right to have the relation continued.

Disparagement

The tort of disparagement or injurious falsehood imposes liability for the publication of a false statement which results in harm to another's monetary interests if the publisher knows that the statement is false or acts in reckless disregard of its truth or falsity. This tort most commonly involves intentionally false statements casting doubt on the right of ownership or quality of another's property or products. Thus Simon, while contemplating the purchase of a stock of merchandise that belongs to Marie, reads an advertisement in a newspaper in which Ernst falsely asserts he owns the merchandise. Ernst has

> Disparagement–publication of false statements resulting in harm to another's monetary interests

disparaged Marie's property in the goods. Absolute, conditional, and constitutional privilege apply to the same extent to the tort of disparagement as they do to defamation.

Fraudulent Misrepresentation

Fraudulent misrepresentation–false statement made with knowledge of its falsity and intent to mislead

One who intentionally makes a misrepresentation of fact for the purpose of inducing another to act is liable for monetary loss caused by justifiable reliance on the misrepresentation. For example, A misrepresents to B that a tract of land in Texas is located in an area where drilling for oil had recently commenced. A made this statement knowing it was not true. In reliance upon the statement B purchased the land from A. A is liable to B for fraudulent misrepresentation. Although intentional, or fraudulent, misrepresentation is a tort action, it is closely connected with contractual negotiations and is discussed in Chapter 9.

Defenses to Intentional Torts

Even though the defendant has intentionally invaded the interests of the plaintiff, the defendant will not be liable if such conduct was privileged. A defendant's conduct is privileged if it furthers an interest of such social importance that the law grants immunity from tort liability for damage to others. Examples of privilege include self-defense, defense of property, and defense of others. In addition, the plaintiff's consent to the defendant's conduct is a defense to intentional torts.

FIGURE 5-1   Intentional Torts

Interest Protected	Tort
Person	
Freedom from contact	Battery
Freedom from apprehension	Assault
Freedom of movement	False imprisonment
Freedom from distress	Infliction of emotional distress
Reputation	Defamation
Privacy	Appropriation
	Intrusion
	Publicity of private facts
	False Light
Property	
Real	Trespass
	Nuisance
Personal	Trespass
	Conversion
Economic	
Contracts	Interference with contractual rights
Good will	Disparagement
Freedom from deception	Fraudulent misrepresentation

Consent

If a person consents to conduct resulting in damage or harm done to his own person, property, or economic interests, there is generally no liability for the intentional infliction of injury. Consent to an act is the willingness that it shall occur. It may be shown expressly or impliedly, by words or by conduct. For example, Lorenzo states that he wishes to kiss Wanda. Although Wanda does not wish Lorenzo to do so, she does not object or resist by word or act. Lorenzo kisses Wanda. Lorenzo is not liable to Wanda for battery because Wanda has impliedly consented to Lorenzo's conduct.

Consent must be given by an individual with capacity to do so. Consent given by a minor, mental incompetent, or intoxicated individual is invalid if he is not capable of understanding the nature, extent, or probable consequences of the conduct to which he has consented.

The defendant's privilege is limited to the conduct to which the plaintiff consents. For example, A consents to an exploratory operation by B, a surgeon, but refuses to have any further operation performed. While A is under ether, B discovers a condition indicating that an operation is needed and proceeds to operate. B is liable to A, even though the operation is properly and successfully performed, because B exceeded the consent given.

Consent to Participate in a Game

By agreeing to participate in a game, a person consents to encounter such bodily contact and limitations on freedom of movement as is permitted by or general to the game. However, such consent does not extend to intentional acts of violence or restrictions beyond the rules and usages of the game. Thus, if A participates in a game of ice hockey, he does not consent to be intentionally attacked by B, another player, wielding his hockey stick as a weapon.

Consent to a Criminal Act

The jurisdictions are divided as to whether consent to criminal conduct is a valid defense to an intentional tort. However, if conduct is made criminal in order to protect a certain class of persons, the consent of members of that class will *not* be effective as a defense to a tort action. For example, a statute makes it a crime to sell alcoholic beverages to a person who is intoxicated. Dwight sells liquor to Mark in violation of the statute. Mark consumes the liquor and suffers physical injury from it. Mark's consent in purchasing the liquor does not bar his suit against Dwight.

Privilege

In this section we deal with that form of privilege which entitles an individual to injure another's person without that person's consent. These privileges are created by law to enable an individual to protect himself, others or his property against tortious interference. By virtue of these privileges an individual may inflict or impose what would otherwise constitute battery, assault or false imprisonment. In this section we cover the following privileges: (1) self-defense, (2) defense of others, and (3) defense of property.

Self-Defense

The law permits an individual to take appropriate action to prevent harm to herself where time does not allow resort to the law. A person is privileged to use reasonable force, not intended or likely to cause death or serious bodily harm, to defend herself against a threatened harmful or offensive contact or confinement. The privilege of self-defense exists whether or not the danger actually exists, provided that the defendant reasonably believed that self-defense was necessary. The reasonableness of the defendant's actions is based on what a person of average courage would have thought under the circumstances.

Self-defense is warranted even if the defendant reasonably believed that she could avoid the threatened contact or confinement by retreating. However, the defendant is not privileged to retaliate, because revenge is not self-defense. The defendant, to protect herself from offensive or nonserious bodily contact, is limited to reasonable force, which is proportionate in extent to the harm from which the defendant is seeking to protect herself.

The defendant is privileged to defend by the use of force intended or likely to cause death or serious bodily harm if she reasonably believes that the plaintiff is about to inflict death, serious bodily harm, or ravishment on the defendant. Most States limit the right to use deadly force in self-defense to those situations in which the defendant does not have a completely safe means of escape. If the defendant, however, has the slightest reasonable doubt about the safety of her escape, she may stand her ground. One may also stand her ground and use deadly force if the attack occurs in her own residence, even though a reasonable means of escape exists.

Defense of Others

An individual is privileged to defend third persons from harmful or offensive contact to the same extent that he is privileged to protect himself, provided that the defendant correctly or reasonably believes that the third person possesses the privilege of self-defense and that the defendant's intervention is necessary for the safety of the third person. For example, A sees B about to strike A's friend C. B is, in fact, privileged to do so to repel C's attack. A has no reason to suspect that C is the aggressor and intercedes to assist C. A is privileged to use reasonable force to assist C against B.

Defense of Property

A possessor of property is permitted to use reasonable force, not intended or likely to cause death or serious bodily harm, to protect his real and personal property. Such force can be employed only if the possessor reasonably believes that the intrusion can only be terminated or prevented by use of force and the intruder has disregarded requests to cease. For example, A sees B walking across his vacant lot. A is not privileged to use even the mildest of force to eject B until A has requested B to leave and B has disregarded the warning. Once reasonable force has been used, the defendant may use such greater force as is necessary to protect himself and his property. The intruder is not entitled to invoke the privilege of self-defense.

A person may not through indirect means, such as mechanical devices, employ deadly force to protect his property unless he would, if present, have been privileged to employ such force. This applies to spring guns, electrified fences, and other traps that are intended or likely to cause death or serious bodily harm.

FACTS: The Brineys (defendants) owned a large farm on which was located an abandoned farmhouse. For a ten-year period the house had been the subject of several trespassings and house breakings. In an attempt to stop the intrusions, Briney boarded up the windows and doors and posted "no trespassing" signs. After one break-in, however, Briney set a spring gun in a bedroom. It was placed over the bedroom window so that the gun could not be seen from outside, and no warning of its presence was posted. The gun was set to hit an intruder in the legs. Briney loaded the gun with a live shell, but he claimed that he did not intend to injure anyone.

Katko (plaintiff) and a friend, McDonough, had broken into the abandoned farmhouse on an earlier occasion to steal old bottles and fruit jars for their antique collection. They returned for a second time after the spring gun had been set, and Katko was seriously wounded in the leg when the gun discharged as he entered the bedroom. He then brought this action for damages.

DECISION: Judgment for Katko. Katko and McDonough committed a felony when they broke into and entered Briney's farmhouse. Although Briney is privileged to use reasonable force in the protection of his property, he could not use such means of force as would take human life or inflict great bodily injury. A spring gun is such a means of force. Its use is permitted only if the trespasser is committing a felony of violence or a felony punishable by death or where the trespasser is endangering human life by his act. In other cases, such as in that of Katko's theft in an abandoned farmhouse, the law places a higher value on human safety than upon mere property rights. As such, Briney's use of a spring gun here constituted excessive force in the defense of property and is not justifiable.

KATKO v. BRINEY

Supreme Court of Iowa,
1971.
182 N.W.2d 657.

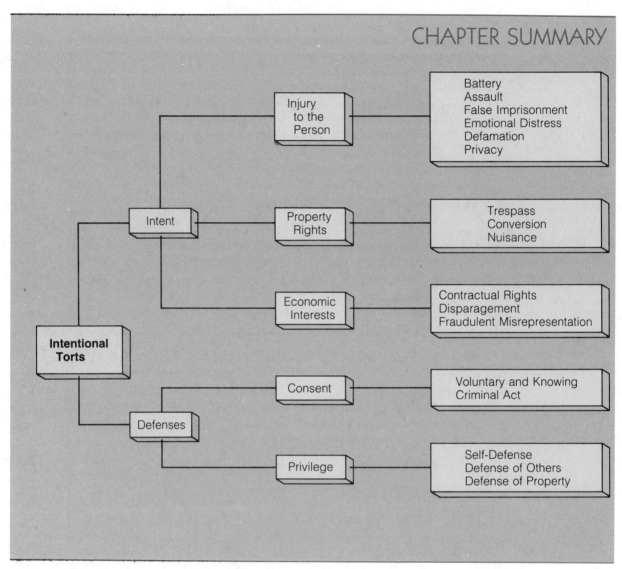

KEY TERMS

Tort
Punitive damages
Intent
Battery
Assault
False imprisonment
Infliction of emotional distress
Defamation
Libel

Slander
Appropriation
Intrusion
Public disclosure of private
    facts
False light
Real property
Trespass to real property

Nuisance
Personal property
Trespass to personal property
Conversion
Interference with contractual
    relations
Disparagement
Fraudulent misrepresentation

PROBLEMS

1. The Penguin intentionally hits Batman with his umbrella. Batman, stunned by the blow, falls backwards, knocking Robin down. Robin's leg is broken in the fall, and he cried out, "Holy broken bat bones! My leg is broken." Who, if anyone, has liability to Robin? Why?

2. For the purpose of frightening N.C. Kure, Bob comes up behind Kure in the desert and sounds a buzzer which is an excellent imitation of a rattlesnake. Kure, believing that he is about to be bitten, is frightened but suffers no bodily harm. May Kure recover from Bob for (a) the tort of assault? (b) the tort of intentional infliction of mental distress?

3. A kisses B while she is asleep but does not waken or harm her. B sues A for battery. Decision?

4. Cole Lect, a creditor, seeking to collect a debt, calls on Over Due and demands payment in a rude and insolent manner. When Due says that he cannot pay, Cole calls Due a deadbeat and says that he will never trust Due again. Is Cole liable to Due? If so, for what tort?

5. A, a ten-year-old child, is run over by a car negligently driven by B. A, at the time of the accident, was acting reasonably and without negligence. C, a newspaper reporter, photographs A while she is lying in the street in great pain. Two years later, D, the publisher of a newspaper, prints C's picture of A in his newspaper as a lead to an article concerning the negligence of children. The caption under the picture reads: "They ask to be killed." A, who has recovered from the accident, brings suit against C and D. What result?

6. In 1963 the Saturday Evening Post featured an article entitled "The Story of a College Football Fix," characterized in the subtitle as "A Shocking Report of How Wally Butts and Bear Bryant Rigged a Game Last Fall." Butts was athletic director of the University of Georgia, and Bryant was head coach of the University of Alabama. The article was based on a claim by one George Burnett that he had accidentally overheard a long distance telephone conversation between Butts and Bryant in the course of which Butts divulged information on plays Georgia would use in the upcoming game against Alabama. The writer assigned to the story by the Post was not a football expert and did not interview either Butts or Bryant, nor did he personally see the notes Burnett had made of the telephone conversation. Butts admitted that he had a long distance telephone conversation with Bryant but denied that any advance information on prospective football plays was given. Butts brought a libel suit against the Post. Decision?

7. A is a patient confined in a hospital with a rare disease that is of great interest to the public. B, a television reporter, requests A to consent to an interview. A refuses, but B, nonetheless, enters A's room over her objection and photographs her. A brings a suit against B. Decision?

8. Prop T. Owner has a place on his land where he piles trash. The pile has been there for a period of three months. John, a neighbor of Prop and without Prop's consent or knowledge, throws trash onto the trashpile. Prop learns that John has done this and sues him. What tort, if any, has John committed?

9. Chris leaves her car parked in front of a store. There are no signs that say Chris cannot park there. The store owner, however, needs the car moved to enable a delivery truck to unload. He releases the brake and pushes Chris's car three or four feet, doing no harm to the car. Chris returns and sees that her car has been moved and is very angry. She threatens to sue the store owner for trespass to her personal property. Can she recover?

10. N. O. Carr borrowed John's brand new Ford for the purpose of going to the store. He told John he would be right back. N. O. then decided, however, to go to the beach while he had the car. Can John recover from N. O. the value of the automobile? If so, for what tort?

NEGLIGENCE AND STRICT LIABILITY

Negligence involves conduct that creates an **unreasonable** risk of harm, whereas intentional torts deal with conduct that has a substantial certainty of causing harm. The failure to exercise reasonable care under the circumstances for the safety of another person or his property, which proximately causes injury to such person or damage to his property, or both, is the basis of liability for negligence. Thus, if the driver of an automobile intentionally runs down a person, she has committed the intentional tort of battery. However, if the driver hits and injures a person while driving unreasonably for the safety of others, she is negligent.

Strict liability is not based on the negligence or intent of the defendant but rather on the nature of the activity in which he is engaging. Both negligence and strict liability are the subject matter of this chapter.

Negligence

The Restatement defines negligence as "conduct which falls below the standard established by law for the protection of others against unreasonable risk of harm." The standard established by law is the conduct of a **reasonable man** acting prudently and with due care under the circumstances.

Negligence–failure to exercise reasonable care under the circumstances

A person is not liable for injury caused to another by an unavoidable accident—an occurrence that was not intended and could not have been prevented by the exercise of reasonable care. Thus, no liability results from the sudden loss of control of an automobile because the driver is suddenly and unforeseeably stricken with a heart attack, stroke, or fainting spell. If the driver, however, had warning of the imminent heart attack or other infirmity, it would be negligent for him to drive at all.

An action for negligence consists of four elements, each of which must be proved by the plaintiff:

1. that a legal duty required the defendant to conform to the standard of conduct established by law for the protection of others,

2. that the defendant failed to conform to the required standard of conduct,

3. that the injury and harm sustained by the plaintiff was proximately caused by the defendant's failure to conform to the required standard of conduct, and

4. that the injury and harm is protected against negligent interference.

We discuss the first two elements under the heading "Duty of Care," the third under "Proximate Cause," and the last under "Injury."

Duty of Care

The duty of care imposed by law is measured by the degree of carefulness that a reasonable man would exercise in a given situation.

Reasonable Man Standard

Reasonable man standard–duty of care required to avoid being negligent; one who is careful, diligent and prudent

The reasonable man is a fictitious individual who is always careful and prudent and never negligent. What the judge or jury determines that a reasonable man would have done in the light of the facts brought out by the evidence in a particular case sets the standard of conduct for that case. The reasonable man standard is thus external and *objective*.

Children The standard of conduct to which a child must conform to avoid being negligent is that of a reasonable person of like age, intelligence, and experience under like circumstances. The law applies an individualized test because children do not have the judgment, intelligence, knowledge, and experience of an adult. Moreover, children as a general rule do not engage in activities entailing high risk to others, and their conduct does not involve the same magnitude of harm. However, a child who engages in an adult activity, such as flying an airplane or driving a boat or car, is held to the standard of care applicable to adults.

Physical Disability If a person is ill or otherwise physically disabled, the standard of conduct to which he must conform to avoid being negligent is that of a reasonable man under like disability. Thus a blind man must act as a reasonable man who is blind.

Mental Deficiency The law makes no allowance for the insanity or other mental deficiency of the defendant in a negligence case, and he is held to the standard of conduct of a reasonable man who is *not* mentally deficient even though it is, in fact, beyond his capacity to conform to the standard.

Superior Skill or Knowledge Persons who are qualified and who practice a profession or trade that requires special skill and expertise are required to use the same care and skill normally possessed by members of their profession or trade. This standard applies to such professionals as physicians, surgeons, dentists, attorneys, pharmacists, architects, accountants, and engineers and to such skilled trades as airline pilots, electricians, carpenters, and plumbers. If a member of a profession or skilled trade possesses greater skill than that common to the profession or trade, she is required to exercise that skill. See Law in the News on page 103.

Emergency–sudden, unexpected event calling for immediate action

Emergencies In determining whether a defendant's conduct is reasonable, the fact that he was at the time confronted with a sudden emergency is taken into consideration. An emergency is a sudden, unexpected event that calls

Next, Clerical Malpractice?

In the practice of the ministry, American clergy are answerable to God, conscience and congregation, but—because of the First Amendment—not to the state. Now that constitutional protection is under challenge in a Los Angeles courtroom. Four clergymen are being sued for malpractice—an action that, if successful, could render every minister, priest and rabbi in the United States vulnerable to state supervision.

The case involves the pastors of Grace Community Church, with almost 4,500 fulltime members the third largest congregation in Los Angeles County, whose fundamentalist tenets call for "Biblical counseling" of troubled parishioners. In 1979 one of their clients was Ken Nally, 24, a convert studying at the church's seminary who had tried to take his own life and had subsequently received counseling from several Grace pastors. But two weeks after the suicide attempt, he did kill himself. Now, Nally's Roman Catholic parents are suing the pastors, alleging that they were negligent in failing to investigate seriously the young man's suicidal tendencies; in withholding information from them and from doctors about his desire to kill himself, and in not referring him to a psychiatrist. "I blame the church because they filled him up with guilt, guilt, guilt so that when he had troubles he thought . . . he had sinned," Walter Nally said of his son several years ago.

Suicide: In the trial, which reaches the halfway point this week, one central issue is in dispute. The Nallys say that the ministers are opposed to psychiatry and actively discouraged their son from seeing a professional after his first suicide attempt. The pastors say they sent him for therapy to several professionals—one unlicensed psychologist, a medical doctor and an osteopath who told the parents that their son should see a psychiatrist. Their lawyers are expected to argue that it was the father who ignored advice to commit him to a psychiatric hospital and that Ken Nally himself was partially to blame for resisting professional help.

Whatever the facts, the issues involve bedrock principles of church-state separation. If the court finds for the parents, it will have to spell out what standards of pastoral counseling the state can impose on clergy—something no court has ever dared attempt. "Psychologists and psychiatrists are held accountable," argues Edward Barker, attorney for the Nallys. "Why can pastors hide behind the First Amendment? Some pastors do a lot of good, but others are . . . uneducated and can do a lot of harm." That's the price of constitutional protection, counters Samuel Ericsson, attorney for the pastors: "Are the courts going to tell the church how to run their counseling service, who's competent to counsel and what kind of problems they can deal with? . . .

We are talking about clergymen's professional beliefs in the application of the Bible."

In practice, thousands of pastoral counselors do acknowledge the problem of competence, at least implicitly, by taking degrees in psychotherapy along with theology. Many of them are certified by the American Association of Pastoral Counselors (AAPC), which requires both ordination and supervised training in therapeutic work for membership. And, as of last month, it provides members with clergy-malpractice insurance. "Our concern is that there are a lot of ministers who aren't trained to handle their parishioners' psychotherapy," says James Ewing, executive director of the AAPC. "This is the kind of case that can clarify a pastoral counselor's accountability to the church and to the state."

The pastors of Grace Community Church, however, recognize no accountability to the state or to psychiatry, and no cure for the soul except Scripture. "The Bible is on trial, Biblical counseling is on trial," Grace senior pastor John MacArthur declared outside the court last week. It is a hard case, and if Justice Holmes was right to say that great and difficult cases make bad law, not much good can come of it either way.

KENNETH L. WOODWARD with JANET HUCK
Copyright 1985, by Newsweek, Inc. All Rights Reserved. Reprinted by Permission.

for immediate action and does not permit time for deliberation. The standard is still that of a reasonable man under the circumstances—the emergency is simply part of the circumstances. However, an emergency is not helpful to a defendant if his own negligent or tortious conduct created the emergency.

Violation of Statute The reasonable man standard of conduct may be established by legislation. Some statutes expressly impose civil liability on violators.

Without such a provision, courts may adopt the requirements of the statute as the standard of conduct if the statute is intended to protect a class of persons that includes the plaintiff against the particular hazard and kind of harm that resulted. If the statute is found to apply, the great majority of the courts hold that an unexcused violation is **negligence *per se;*** that is, it is conclusive on the issue of negligent conduct. In a minority of States the violation is considered merely evidence of negligence. In either event, the plaintiff must also prove legal causation and injury.

Negligence per se–conclusive on the issue of negligence (duty of care and breach)

For example, a statute enacted to protect employees from injuries requires that all factory elevators be equipped with specified safety devices. A, an employee in B's factory, and C, a business visitor to the factory, are injured when the elevator falls because of the failure to install the safety devices. The court may adopt the statute as a standard of conduct as to A, and hold B negligent *per se* to A, but not as to C, because A, and not C, is within the class of persons intended to be protected by the statute. C would have to establish that a reasonable person in the position of B under the circumstances would have installed the safety device.

VANCE v. UNITED STATES

United States District Court, D. Alaska, 1973.
355 F.Supp. 756.

FACTS: Vance was served liquor while he was an intoxicated patron of the Clear Air Force Station Non-Commissioned Officers' Club. He later injured himself as a result of his intoxication. An Alaska State statute makes it a crime to give or to sell liquor to intoxicated persons. Vance has brought this action seeking damages for the injuries suffered. He argues that the United States was negligent *per se* by its employee's violation of the statute.

DECISION: Judgment for Vance. An unexcused violation of a statute or regulation is negligence in itself, termed negligence *per se,* if the court adopts the statute as defining the conduct of a reasonable man. And even if the statute is not so adopted, a violation may still be considered as evidence of negligence.

A court will adopt a statute as the minimum standard of care if its purpose is at least in part: (1) to protect a class of persons that includes the one whose interest is invaded; (2) to protect the particular interest that is invaded; (3) to protect that interest against the kind of harm that resulted; and (4) to protect that interest against the particular hazard from which the harm resulted.

Applying these criteria to the statute in question, it is clear that all of the requirements are satisfied. The statute unquestionably is designed to protect against personal injuries caused by intoxication. And while the statute's principal purpose may be to protect third parties from the negligence of an intoxicated consumer, the purpose is also, at least in part, to protect the consumer himself.

Duty of Affirmative Action

Except in special circumstances, no one is required to aid another in peril. For example, Adolf, an adult standing along the edge of a steep cliff, observes a baby carriage with a crying infant in it slowly heading toward the edge and certain doom. Adolf could easily prevent the baby's fall at no risk to his own safety. Nonetheless, Adolf does nothing, and the baby falls to its death. Adolf is under no legal duty to act and therefore incurs no liability for failing to do so. However, special relations between the parties may exist that impose a duty on the defendant to aid or protect the other. Thus, if Adolf were the baby's parent or babysitter, Adolf would be under a duty to act and would therefore be liable for not taking action.

A duty of affirmative action is also imposed on those whose conduct, whether tortious or innocent, has injured another and left him helpless and in danger of further harm. For example, A drives her car into B, who is rendered unconscious. A leaves B lying in the middle of the road, where he is run over by a second car driven by C. A is liable to B for the additional injuries inflicted by C. Moreover, a person incurs a duty to exercise care by voluntarily coming to the assistance of another in need of aid. In such instance, the actor is liable if his failure to exercise reasonable care increases the risk of harm, causes harm to be suffered by reliance on the undertaking, or leaves the other in a worse position. For example, A finds B drunk and stumbling along a dark sidewalk. A leads B halfway up a steep and unguarded stairway, where he abandons B. B attempts to climb the stairs but trips and falls, suffering serious injury. A is liable to B for having left him in a worse position.

Special Duties of Possessors of Land

The duty of a possessor of land to persons who come on the land depends on whether that person is a trespasser, a licensee, or an invitee.

Duty to Trespassers   A trespasser is a person who enters or remains on the land of another without permission or privilege to do so. The lawful possessor of the land is *not* liable to trespassers for her failure to maintain the land in a reasonably safe condition. Nonetheless, the trespasser is not a criminal, and the lawful possessor is not free to inflict intentional injury on him. Some courts have held that the lawful possessor is required to exercise reasonable care for the safety of the trespasser on discovery of his presence on the land.

> **Trespasser**–person who enters or remains on the land of another without permission or privilege to do so

The law, however, extends greater protection to a child who trespasses by imposing on a possessor of land the liability for physical harm caused by artificial conditions upon the land if:

1. the place where the condition exists is one the possessor knows or has reason to know that children are likely to trespass;

2. the condition involves an unreasonable risk of death or serious bodily harm to children;

3. the children do not realize the risk involved;

4. the burden of eliminating the danger is slight as compared with the risk to children involved; and

5. the possessor fails to exercise reasonable care to eliminate the danger or otherwise to protect the children.

The Restatement provides the following illustration: "A has on his land a small artificial pond full of goldfish. A's land adjoins a nursery in which children from two to five years of age are left by their parents for the day, and such children are, as A knows, in the habit of trespassing on A's land and going near the pond. A could easily prevent this by closing and locking his gate. A does not do so. B, a child three years of age, trespasses, enters the pond to catch goldfish, and is drowned. A is subject to liability for the death of B."

Duty to Licensees   A licensee is a person who is privileged to enter or remain on land only by virtue of the consent of the lawful possessor. Licensees include members of the possessor's household and **social guests.** A licensee, however,

> **Licensee**–person privileged to enter or remain on land by virtue of the consent of the lawful possessor

will become a trespasser if he enters a portion of the land to which he is not invited or remains on the land after his invitation has expired.

The possessor owes a higher duty of care to licensees than to trespassers. The possessor must warn the licensee of dangerous activities and conditions of which the possessor has knowledge and which the licensee does not and is not likely to discover. If he is not warned, the licensee may recover if the activity or dangerous condition resulted from the possessor's failure to exercise reasonable care to protect him from the danger. To illustrate: Henry invites a friend, Anne, to his place in the country at eight o'clock on a winter evening. Henry knows that a bridge in his driveway is in a dangerous condition which is not noticeable in the dark. Henry does not inform Anne of this fact. The bridge gives way under Anne's car, causing serious harm to Anne. Henry is liable to Anne.

Invitee–person invited upon land for a business purpose

Duty to Invitees   An invitee is either a **public invitee** or a **business visitor.** A person is a public invitee if she enters on land that is open to the public, such as a public park, beach, or swimming pool or a governmental facility where business with the public is transacted openly, such as a post office or an office of the Recorder of Deeds. A business visitor is a person who enters on the premises to engage in private business, such as one who enters a store or a worker who enters a residence to make repairs.

The duty of the possessor of land to invitees with respect to the condition of the premises is to exercise reasonable care to protect them against dangerous conditions they are unlikely to discover. For example, A's store has a large glass front door that is well lighted and plainly visible. B, a customer, mistakes the glass for an open doorway and walks into the glass, injuring himself. A is not liable to B. If, on the other hand, the glass was difficult to see and it was foreseeable that a person might mistake the glass for an open doorway, then A would be liable to B if B crashed into the glass while exercising reasonable care.

These three kinds of duties are illustrated in Figure 6–1.

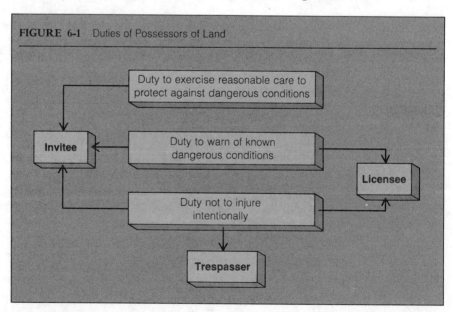

FIGURE 6-1   Duties of Possessors of Land

Duty to exercise reasonable care to protect against dangerous conditions

Invitee

Duty to warn of known dangerous conditions

Licensee

Duty not to injure intentionally

Trespasser

YANIA v. BIGAN

Supreme Court of
Pennsylvania, 1959.
397 Pa. 316, 155 A.2d 343.

FACTS: Joseph Yania and Boyd Ross visited a coal strip-mining operation owned by John Bigan to discuss a business matter with Bigan. On Bigan's property there were several cuts and trenches which he had dug to remove the coal underneath. While there, Bigan asked the two men to help him pump water from one of these cuts in the earth. This particular cut contained water 8 to 10 feet in depth with side walls or embankments 16 to 18 feet in height. The two men agreed and the process began with Ross and Bigan entering the cut and standing at the point where the pump was located. Yania stood at the top of one of the cut's side walls. Apparently, Bigan taunted Yania into jumping into the water from the top of the side wall—a height of 16 to 18 feet. As a result, Yania drowned. His widow brought a negligence action against Bigan. She claims that Bigan was negligent "(1) by urging, enticing, taunting and inveigling Yania to jump into the water; (2) by failing to warn Yania of a dangerous condition on the land . . . [and] (3) by failing to go to Yania's rescue after he jumped into the water."

DECISION: Judgment for Bigan. Taunting and enticement will only constitute actionable negligence if directed "at a child of tender years or a person mentally deficient." Therefore, Bigan's taunting of Yania, who was an adult in full possession of his mental faculties, is not negligence.

In addition, the owner of land ordinarily has, at the least, a duty to warn invitees of known or discoverable dangers which the owner should realize involve an unreasonable risk of harm to them. This warning is required only if the owner has no reason to believe the invitee will discover the condition or realize the risk of harm. Here, however, the dangers of the water-filled trench were "obvious and apparent to Yania," who was also a coal strip-mine operator. Accordingly, Bigan is not negligent in failing to warn Yania of the obvious.

Finally, despite Bigan's tauntings, Yania jumped into the water of his own accord. Bigan was not legally responsible, in whole or in part, for placing Yania in his perilous and fatal position. Therefore, although he may have had a moral responsibility, Bigan did not have a legal responsibility to rescue Yania, who died of his own foolhardiness.

Res Ipsa Loquitur

A rule has developed that permits the jury to infer *both* negligent conduct and causation from the mere occurrence of certain types of events. This rule is called *res ipsa loquitur*, which means "the thing speaks for itself," and it applies when the event is of a kind that ordinarily does not occur in the absence of negligence and other possible causes are sufficiently eliminated by the evidence. For example, Camille rents a room in Leo's motel. During the night a large piece of plaster falls from the ceiling and injures Camille. In the absence of other evidence the jury may infer that the harm resulted from Leo's negligence in permitting the plaster to become defective. Leo is permitted, however, to introduce evidence to contradict the inference of negligence. The following case involving the New York Mets explains the requirements of *res ipsa loquitur*.

Res ipsa loquitur–"the thing speaks for itself"; permits the jury to infer both negligent conduct and causation

UZDAVINES v.
METROPOLITAN
BASEBALL CLUB, INC.

Civil Court of the City of
New York, Queens County,
1982.
115 Misc.2d 343, 454
N.Y.S.2d 238.

FACTS: A foul ball struck Marie Uzdavines on the head while she was watching the Metropolitan Baseball Club ("The Mets") play the Philadelphia Phillies at "The Mets'" home stadium in New York. The ball came through a hole in a screen designed to protect spectators sitting behind home plate. The screen contained several holes which had been repaired with baling wire, a lighter weight wire than that used in the original screen. Although the manager of the stadium makes no formal inspections of the screen, his employees do try to repair the holes as they find them. Weather conditions, rust deterioration, and baseballs hitting the screen are the chief causes of these holes. The owner of the stadium, the City of New York, leases the stadium to "The Mets" and replaces the entire screen every two years. Uzdavines sued "The Mets" for negligence under the doctrine of *res ipsa loquitur*.

DECISION: Judgment for Uzdavines. Under *res ipsa loquitur* Uzdavines must show that: (1) the event is of a kind that ordinarily does not occur in the absence of someone's negligence; (2) "The

Mets" had exclusive control over the instrumentality (the protective screen) that caused the event; (3) the event was not due to any voluntary action or contribution on her part; and (4) evidence explaining the incident is more readily available to "The Mets" than to her. On these facts it is clear that the first, third and fourth requirements have been met. To prove that "The Mets" exercised "exclusive control," Uzdavines need only establish that they exercised "a degree of domination sufficient to identify defendant with probability as the party responsible" for her injuries.

Both "The Mets" and the City of New York owed an independent duty to a spectator which requires that "the Mets" exercise strict control of the screen, assuring the public that they may rely on the implied safety of sitting in that area. Since the "Mets" were under a duty to maintain and control the protective screening, the exclusive control requirement of *res ipsa loquitur* is satisfied and the doctrine applies to this case.

Proximate Cause

One of the requirements of imposing liability for the negligent conduct of a defendant is that the conduct not only caused injury to the plaintiff but was also the proximate cause of the injury. Most simply expressed, proximate cause consists of the judicially imposed limitations on a person's liability for the consequences of his negligence. As a matter of social policy, legal responsibility has not been permitted to follow all the consequences of a negligent act. Responsibility has been limited to those persons and results that are closely connected with the negligent conduct.

Causation in Fact

To support a finding that the defendant's negligence was the proximate cause of the plaintiff's injury, it is first necessary to show that the defendant's conduct was the *actual cause* of the injury. A widely applied test for causation in fact is the **but for rule:** A person's conduct is a cause of an event if the event would not have occurred *but for* the person's negligent conduct. Under this test, an act or omission to act is *not* a cause of an event if that event would have occurred regardless of the act or omission. For instance, A fails to erect a barrier around an excavation. B is driving a truck when its accelerator becomes stuck. A's negligence is not a cause in fact of B's death if the runaway truck would have crashed through the barrier even if it had been erected. Similarly, failure to install a proper fire escape to a hotel is not the cause in fact of the death of a person who is suffocated by the smoke while sleeping in bed.

The "but for" test, however, is not useful where there are two or more forces actively operating, each of which is sufficient to bring about the harm in question. For example, A accidentally stabs C with a knife while B negligently fractures C's skull with a rock. Either wound would be fatal, and C dies from both. Under the " but for" test, either A or B, or both, could argue that C would have died from the wound inflicted by the other and therefore he is not liable. The **substantial factor test** addresses this problem by stating that negligent conduct is a legal cause of harm to another if the conduct is a substantial factor in bringing about the harm. Under this test the conduct of both A and B would be found to be a cause in fact of C's death.

Limitations on Causation in Fact

As a matter of policy, the law imposes limitations on the causal connection between the defendant's negligence and the plaintiff's injury. Two of the factors that are taken into consideration in determining such limitations are (a) unforeseeable consequences and (b) superseding causes.

Unforeseeable Consequences   The liability of a negligent defendant for unforeseeable consequences has proved to be troublesome and controversial. The Restatement and a majority of the courts have adopted the following position. Even if the defendant's negligent conduct is a cause in fact of harm to the plaintiff, the defendant is *not* liable to the plaintiff *unless* the defendant could have reasonably anticipated injuring the plaintiff or a class of persons of which the plaintiff is a member. Proximate cause involves a recognition of the risk of harm to the plaintiff individually or to a class of persons of which the plaintiff is a member.

For example, A, while negligently driving an automobile, collides with a car carrying dynamite. A is unaware of the contents of the other car and had no reason to know about it. The collision causes the dynamite to explode, shattering glass in a building a block away. The shattered glass injures B, who is inside the building. The explosion also injures C, who is walking on the sidewalk near the collision. A would be liable to C because A should have realized that his negligent driving might result in a collision that would endanger pedestrians nearby, and the fact that the actual harm resulted in an unforeseeable manner does not affect his liability. B, however, was beyond the zone of danger, and A is therefore not liable to B. A's negligent driving is not deemed to be the "proximate cause" of B's injury because, looking back from the harm to A's negligence, it appears highly extraordinary that A's conduct should have brought about the harm to B.

FACTS: Palsgraf was on the railroad station platform buying a ticket when a train stopped at the station. As it began to depart, two men ran to catch it. After the first was safely aboard, the second jumped onto the moving car. When he started to fall, a guard on the train reached to grab him and another guard on the platform pushed the man from behind. They helped the man to regain his balance, but in the process they knocked a small package out of his arm. The package, which contained fireworks, fell onto the rails and exploded. The shock from the explosion knocked over a scale resting on the other end of the platform, and it landed on Mrs. Palsgraf. She then brought this action against the railroad to recover for the injuries she sustained.

DECISION: Judgment for the railroad. Negligence is not actionable unless it involves the invasion of a legally protected interest or the violation of a right. In other words, in order for a given act to be held negligent, it must be shown that the charged party owed a duty to the complaining individual, the observance of which would have averted or avoided the injury.

Here, then, Palsgraf cannot recover because the railroad, although perhaps negligent as to the man carrying the package, was not negligent as to her. This was because the harm to her was not foreseeable. She cannot recover for injuries sustained merely because the railroad's agents were negligent as to the man they assisted.

PALSGRAF v. LONG ISLAND RAILROAD CO.

Court of Appeals of New York, 1928.
248 N.Y. 339, 162 N.E. 99.

FACTS: The MacGilvray Shiras was a ship owned by the Kinsman Transit Company. During the winter months when Lake Erie was frozen, the ship and others moored at docks on the Buffalo River. As oftentimes happened, one night an ice jam disintegrated upstream, sending large chunks of ice downward. Chunks of ice began to pile up against the Shiras which at that time was without power and manned only by a shipman. The ship broke loose when a negligently constructed "deadman" to which one mooring cable was attached pulled out of the ground. The "deadman" was operated by Continental Grain Company. The ship began moving down the S-shaped river stern first and struck another ship, the Tewksbury. The Tewksbury also broke

PETITION OF KINSMAN TRANSIT CO.

United States Court of Appeals, Second Circuit, 1964.
338 F.2d 708.

loose from its mooring, and the two ships floated down the river together. Although the crew manning the Michigan Avenue Bridge downstream had been notified of the runaway ships, they failed to raise the bridge in time to avoid a collision because of a mixup in the shift changeover. As a result, both ships crashed into the bridge and were wedged against the bank of the river. The two vessels substantially dammed the flow of the river, causing ice and water to back up and flood installations as far as three miles upstream. The injured parties brought this action for damages against Kinsman, Continental and the City of Buffalo.

DECISION: Judgment for the injured parties. A ship insecurely moored in a fast-flowing river is a known danger to the owners of all ships and structures down the river and to persons upon them. Kinsman and Continental, then, owed a duty of care to all within the foreseeable reach of the ship's destructive path. Similarly, the city is liable to those who foreseeably could have been injured by its negligent failure to raise the bridge in time to prevent the collision. Finally, although the exact type of harm that occurred was not foreseeable this does not prevent liability. The damage resulted from the same physical forces whose existence required the exercise of greater care than was displayed and was of the same general type that was foreseeable. In short, the unforeseeability of the exact developments and of the extent of the loss will not limit liability where the persons injured and the general nature of the damage done was foreseeable.

Superseding Cause   A superseding cause is an *intervening* event or act that occurs after the defendant's negligent conduct and relieves him of liability for harm to the plaintiff caused in fact by both the defendant's negligence and the intervening event or act. For example, Gerald negligently runs down a cow, which is left lying stunned in the road. Several minutes later the cow regains consciousness, takes fright, and charges into Tina, a bystander. The cow's conduct is an intervening, but *not* a superseding, cause of harm to Tina because it is a normal consequence of the situation caused by Gerald's negligence. Therefore, Gerald is liable to Tina. In contrast, William negligently leaves an excavation in a public sidewalk into which Jack intentionally hurls Jill. William is not liable to Jill because Jack's conduct is a superseding cause that relieves William of liability.

Injury

The plaintiff must prove that the defendant's negligent conduct caused harm to a legally protected interest. Certain interests receive little or no protection from negligent interference, while others receive full protection. The extent of protection for a particular interest is determined by the courts as a matter of law on the basis of social policy and expediency. For example, negligent conduct that is the proximate cause of harmful contact with the person of another is actionable. Thus, if A negligently runs into B, a pedestrian, who is carefully crossing the street, A is liable for physical injuries sustained by B as a result of the collision. On the other hand, if A's careless conduct causes only offensive contact with B's person, A is not liable.

The courts have traditionally been reluctant to allow recovery for negligently inflicted emotional distress. This view has gradually changed during this century, and the majority of courts now hold a person liable for negligently causing emotional distress if bodily harm results from the distress. However, if the defendant's conduct merely results in emotional disturbance without bodily harm, the defendant is not liable.

Defenses

Although a plaintiff has established by the preponderance of the evidence all the required elements of a negligence action, he may nevertheless be denied recovery if the defendant proves a valid defense. As a general rule, any defense to an intentional tort is also available in an action in negligence. In addition, there are defenses available in negligence cases that are not defenses to intentional torts.

Contributory Negligence

Contributory negligence is defined as conduct on the part of the *plaintiff* that falls below the standard to which he should conform for his own protection and that is a legal cause of the plaintiff's harm. If negligence of the plaintiff together with negligence of the defendant proximately caused the injury and damage sustained by the plaintiff, he cannot recover *any* damages from the defendant. It does not matter whether the plaintiff's contributory negligence was slight or extensive.

> **Contributory negligence**–failure of a plaintiff to exercise reasonable care that legally causes the plaintiff's harm

Notwithstanding the contributory negligence of the plaintiff, if the defendant had a **last clear chance** to avoid injury to him but did not avail himself of such chance, the contributory negligence of the plaintiff does not bar his recovery of damages. For example, Kenneth negligently stops his car on the highway. Susan, who is driving along, sees Kenneth's car in sufficient time to stop. However, Susan negligently puts her foot on the accelerator instead of the brake and runs into Kenneth's car. Because Susan had the last clear chance to stop her car before striking Kenneth's car, Kenneth's contributory negligence does not bar his recovery from Susan.

Comparative Negligence

The harshness of the contributory negligence doctrine has caused an increasing majority of the States to reject the all-or-nothing rule of contributory negligence and to substitute the doctrine of comparative negligence. Under comparative negligence, damages are divided between the parties in proportion to the degree of fault or negligence found against them. For instance, B negligently drives his automobile into A, who is crossing against the light. A sustains damages in the amount of $10,000 and sues B. If the trier of fact (the jury or judge, depending on the case) determines that B's negligence contributed 70 percent to A's injury and that A's contributory negligence contributed 30 percent to her injury, then A would recover $7,000.

> **Comparative negligence**–doctrine dividing damages between the plaintiff and defendant where the negligence of each has caused the harm

Most States that have adopted the doctrine of comparative negligence have enacted statutes that do not permit the plaintiff any recovery if his contributory negligence was as great as or greater than that of the defendant. Thus, in the example above, if the trier of fact determined that B's negligence contributed 40 percent to A's injury and A's contributory negligence contributed 60 percent to her injury, then A would not recover anything from B.

Assumption of Risk

A plaintiff who has *voluntarily* and *knowingly* assumed the risk of harm arising from the negligent or reckless conduct of the defendant cannot recover from such harm. Basically, assumption of risk is the plaintiff's express or implied consent to encounter a known danger. Thus a spectator entering a baseball park may be regarded as consenting that the players may proceed with the game without taking precautions to protect him from being hit by the ball. The following case involves both contributory negligence and assumption of risk.

> **Assumption of risk**–plaintiff's express or implied consent to encounter a known danger

**FALGOUT v.
WARDLAW**

Court of Appeal of
Louisiana, Second Circuit,
1982.
423 So.2d 707.

FACTS: Carolyn Falgout accompanied William Wardlaw as a social guest to Wardlaw's brother's
camp. After both parties had consumed intoxicating beverages, Falgout walked onto a pier that
was then only partially completed. Wardlaw had requested that she not go on the pier. However,
Falgout said "don't tell me what to do," and proceeded to walk on the pier. Wardlaw then asked
her not to walk past the completed portion of the pier. She ignored his warnings and walked
to the pier's end. When returning to the shore, her shoe got caught between the boards. She
fell, hanging by her foot, with her head and arms in the water. Wardlaw rescued Falgout who
had seriously injured her knee and leg. She sued Wardlaw for negligence.

DECISION: Judgment for Wardlaw. A plaintiff's conduct may constitute both assumption of
risk and contributory negligence. To have assumption of risk, the plaintiff must have actual,
subjective knowledge of the damages involved. It is not enough that she is merely in a position
to make observations which would reveal the dangers. Only when she has actually made the
observations and should then have reasonably known of the particular risk can she be held to
have voluntarily assumed it. On the other hand, contributory negligence is determined by an
objective, "reasonable man" standard. If the plaintiff's conduct falls below the standard, she is
contributorily negligent. Both defenses relieve the defendant of liability due to the plaintiff's
fault.

   Here, Falgout actually observed the wide spacings in the pier when she walked to its end.
Also, Wardlaw warned her not to go out on it. These two facts establish that Falgout both saw
and understood the risks of walking on the pier and, yet, she voluntarily assumed them. Her
conduct also constituted contributory negligence. Either defense relieves Wardlaw of liability to
Falgout.

Strict Liability

In some instances a person may be held liable for injuries he has caused even
though he has not acted intentionally or negligently. Such liability is called
strict liability, absolute liability, or liability without fault. The courts have
determined that certain types of otherwise socially desirable activities pose
sufficiently high risks of harm regardless of how carefully they are conducted,
and therefore those who carry on these activities should bear the cost of all
harm they cause. The doctrine of strict liability is *not* based on any particular
fault of the defendant, but rather on the nature of the activity in which he is
engaging. In effect, strict liability makes those who conduct these activities
insurers of all who may be harmed by the activity.

Activities Giving Rise to Strict Liability

Abnormally Dangerous Activities

Strict liability is imposed for harm resulting from extraordinary, unusual,
abnormal, or exceptional activities, as determined in light of the place, time,
and manner in which the activity is conducted. Activities to which the rule
has been applied include collecting water in such quantity and location as to
make it dangerous; storing explosives or flammable liquids in large quantities;
blasting or pile driving; crop dusting; drilling for or refining oil in populated
areas; and emitting noxious gases or fumes into a settled community. On the
other hand, courts have refused to apply the rule where the activity is a
"natural" use of the land, such as drilling for oil in the oil fields of Texas,
collecting water in a stock watering tank, and transmitting gas through a gas
pipe or electricity in electric wiring.

   Whether strict liability is imposed for abnormally dangerous activities is
determined by considering a number of factors, including

FIGURE 6-2   Defenses to a Negligence Action

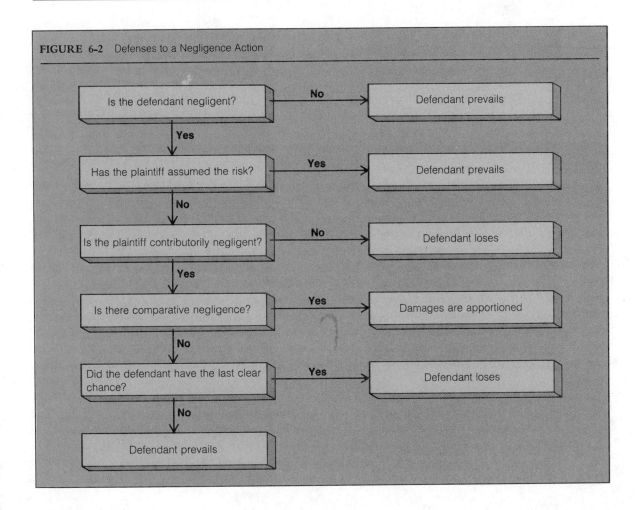

1. whether the activity involves a high degree of risk of harm;

2. whether the gravity of the harm is likely to be great;

3. whether the activity is a matter of common usage;

4. whether the activity is inappropriate to the place where it is carried on; and

5. the value of the activity to the community.

Keeping of Animals

Strict liability for harm caused by animals existed at common law and continues today with some modification. As a general rule, those who possess animals for their own purposes do so at their peril and must protect against harm to people and property.

Trespassing Animals   Keepers of animals are generally held liable for any damage done if their animals trespass on the property of another. There are three exceptions to this rule: (1) keepers of cats and dogs are liable only for negligence; (2) keepers of animals are not strictly liable for animals straying from a highway on which they are being lawfully driven, although the owner may be liable for negligence if he fails to control them properly; and (3) in some western States keepers of farm animals, typically cattle, are not strictly liable for harm caused by their trespassing animals that are allowed to graze freely.

Nontrespassing Animals   Keepers of wild animals are strictly liable for harm caused by such animals, whether or not they are trespassing. **Wild animals** are defined as those that in the particular region are known to be likely to inflict serious damage and that cannot be considered safe no matter how domesticated. Animals included in this category are bears, lions, elephants, monkeys, tigers, deer, and raccoons.

Domestic animals are those animals that are traditionally devoted to the service of mankind and that as a class are considered safe. Examples of domestic animals are dogs, cats, horses, cattle, and sheep. Keepers of domestic animals are liable if they knew, or should have known, of the animal's dangerous propensity. As in the next case, the dangerous propensity of the animal must be the cause of the harm. For example, a keeper is not liable for a dog that bites a human merely because he knows that the dog has a propensity to engage in combat with other dogs. On the other hand, if a person's 150-pound sheep dog has a propensity to jump enthusiastically on visitors, the animal's keeper would be liable for any damage done by the dog's playfulness.

ALLEN v. WHITEHEAD

Supreme Court of Alabama, 1982.
423 So.2d 835.

FACTS: Two year old David Allen was bitten by Joseph Whitehead's dog while he was playing on the porch at the Allen residence. Allen suffered facial cuts, a severed muscle in his left eye, a hole in his left ear, and scarring over his forehead. He sued Whitehead, claiming that, as owner, Whitehead is responsible for his dog's actions. Whitehead admitted that (1) the dog was large, mean looking and frequently barked at neighbors; (2) the dog was allowed to roam wild; and (3) the dog frequently chased and barked at cars. However, he stated that (1) the dog was friendly and often played with Whitehead's and other neighbors' children; (2) he had not received previous complaints about the dog; (3) the dog was neither aggressive nor threatening; and (4) the dog had never bitten anyone before this incident.

DECISION: Judgment for Whitehead. The common law rule is that a dog owner is not liable for the acts of his dog unless he knows or has reason to know of the dog's vicious propensities. In addition, the owner's liability is limited to the particular risks of which he has prior notice. The evidence shows only that Whitehead's "dog was large and mean looking, chased and barked at cars, and frequently barked at neighbors." These facts are not proof that the dog had vicious propensities. Moreover, Whitehead's previous knowledge of his dog's playfulness with children does not prove that he knew or had reason to know that the dog would attack and bite a child. Therefore, Whitehead is not liable to Allen for the injuries caused by the dog.

Products Liability

A recent and important trend in the law is the imposition of strict liability on manufacturers and merchants who sell goods in a defective condition unreasonably dangerous to the user or consumer. Liability is imposed regardless of the seller's due care and applies to all merchant sellers. We cover this topic in Chapter 19.

Defenses

Contributory Negligence

Because the strict liability of one who carries on an abnormally dangerous activity, keeps animals, or sells products is not based on his negligence, the ordinary contributory negligence of the plaintiff is *not* a defense to such liability. The law in imposing strict liability places the full responsibility for preventing harm on the defendant. For example, Sharon negligently fails to observe a sign on a highway warning of a blasting operation conducted by Nick. As a result Sharon is injured by these operations. Sharon may nonetheless recover from Nick.

Comparative Negligence

Despite the rationale that disallows contributory negligence as a defense to strict liability, some States apply the doctrine of comparative negligence to some types of strict liability, in particular, products liability.

Assumption of Risk

Voluntary assumption of risk *is* a defense to an action based on strict liability. If the owner of an automobile knowingly and voluntarily parks the vehicle in a blasting zone, he may not recover for harm to his automobile. The assumption of risk, however, must be voluntary. If blasting operations are established, the possessor of nearby land is not required to move away and may recover for harm suffered.

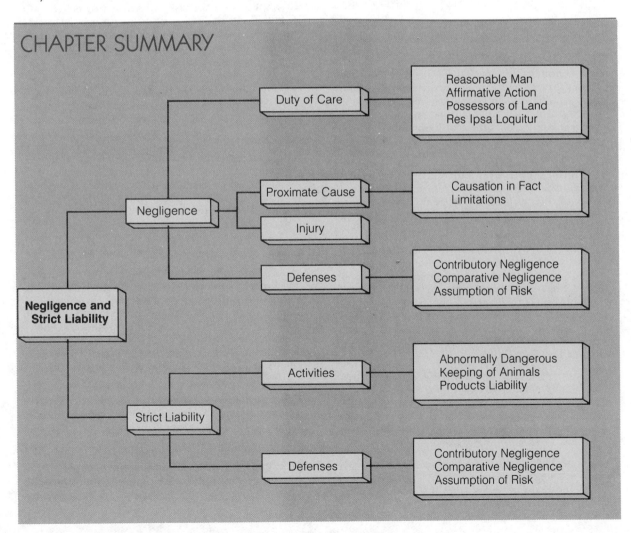

CHAPTER SUMMARY

KEY TERMS

Negligence
Reasonable man standard
Duty of care
Emergency
Negligence *per se*
Trespasser

Licensee
Invitee
Res ipsa loquitur
Proximate cause
Causation in fact
Contributory negligence

Comparative negligence
Assumption of risk
Strict liability
Abnormally dangerous
    activities

PROBLEMS

1. A statute that requires railroads to fence their tracks is construed as intended solely to prevent injuries to animals straying onto the right of way. B & A Railroad Company fails to fence its tracks. Two of C's cows wander onto the track. Nellie is hit by a train. Elsie is poisoned by weeds growing beside the track. For which cows, if any, is B & A Railroad Company liable to C? Why?

2. Martha invites John to come to lunch. Martha knows that her private road is dangerous to travel, having been guttered by recent rains. She doesn't warn John of the condition, reasonably believing that he will notice the gutters and exercise sufficient care. John's attention, while driving over, is diverted from the road by the screaming of his child, who has been stung by a bee. He fails to notice the condition of the road, hits a gutter, and skids into a tree. If John is not contributorily negligent, is Martha liable to John?

3. N is run over by a car and left lying in the street. Samaritan Sam, seeing N's helpless state, takes him in his car for the purpose of taking him to the hospital. Sam drives negligently into a ditch, causing additional injury to N. Is Sam liable to N?

4. Led Foot drives his car carelessly into another car. The second car contains dynamite, about which Led had no way of knowing. The collision causes an explosion which shatters a window of a building half a block away on another street. The flying glass inflicts serious cuts on Sally, who is working at a nearby desk. The explosion also harms Vic Jones, who is walking on the sidewalk near the point of the collision. Toward whom is Led Foot liable?

5. A statute requires all vessels traveling on the Great Lakes to provide lifeboats. One of W Steamship Company's boats is sent out of port without a lifeboat. P, a sailor, falls overboard in a storm so heavy that had there been a lifeboat it could not have been launched. P drowns. Is W liable to P's estate?

6. L is negligently driving an automobile at excessive speed. R's negligently driven car crosses the center line of the highway and scrapes the side of L's car, damaging its fenders. As a result, L loses control of his car, which goes into the ditch, wrecking the car and causing personal injuries to L. What can L recover?

7. (a) E, the owner of a baseball park, is under a duty to the entering public to provide a reasonably sufficient number of screened seats to protect those who desire it against the risk of being hit by batted balls. E fails to do so. F, a customer entering the park is unable to find a screened seat and, although fully aware of the risk, sits in an unscreened seat. F is struck and injured by a batted ball. Is E liable?

(b) G, F's wife, has just arrived from Germany and is viewing baseball for the first time. Without asking any questions, she follows F to a seat. After the batted ball hits F, it caroms into G, injuring her. Is E liable to G?

8. CC Railroad is negligent in failing to give warning of the approach of its train to a crossing and thereby endangers L, a blind man who is about to cross. M, a bystander, in a reasonable effort to save L, rushes onto the track to push L out of danger. Although M acts as carefully as possible, she is struck and injured by the train.

(a) Can M recover from L?

(b) Can M recover from CC Railroad?

9. S, constructing a building, operates pile-driving machinery that causes excessive vibrations abnormally dangerous to buildings in the vicinity. Cy, in an adjoining building, is conducting scientific experiments with extremely delicate instruments. Although the vibration causes no other harm to Cy or to the building, it ruins the instruments and prevents the experiments. Is S liable for the harm caused Cy?

10. T keeps a pet chimpanzee that is thoroughly tamed and accustomed to playing with its owner's children. The chimpanzee escapes, despite every precaution to keep it on the owner's premises. It approaches a group of children. W, the mother of one of the children, erroneously thinking the chimpanzee is about to attack the children, rushes to her child's assistance; in her hurry and excitement, she stumbles and falls, breaking her leg. Can W recover for her personal injuries?

PART TWO
CONTRACTS

PART TWO

CONTRACTS

PUBLIC POLICY, SOCIAL ISSUES AND BUSINESS ETHICS

Contract law, like the law as a whole, is not static. It has undergone—and is still undergoing—enormous changes. In the nineteenth century almost total freedom in forming contracts was the rule. As the noted legal scholar Samuel Williston wrote: "Economic writers adopted the same line of thought. Adam Smith, Ricardo, Bentham and John Stuart Mill successfully insisted on freedom of bargaining as the fundamental and indispensable requisite of progress; and imposed their theories on the educational thought of their times with a thoroughness not common in economic speculation." Although there was great freedom in forming contracts, there were also many technicalities involved. Contract liability was imposed only when the parties complied strictly with the required formalities. Once properly formed, however, a contract bound the parties tightly. It was enforced according to its terms, and neither party would be lightly excused from performing it.

This view was consistent with the philosophy of governmental *laissez-faire* that was dominant at the time. As Professor Friedmann in *Law in a Changing Society* explained it, "[t]he idea that the state on behalf of the community should intervene to dictate or alter terms of contracts in the public interest, is, on the whole, alien to the classical theory of common-law contract." Consequently, the watch-word of the day was *caveat emptor*—let the buyer beware. The following excerpt further describes the nineteenth-century doctrines as well as outlining the social forces and policies that brought about their decline:

The general principle that the buyer should and could look after himself had its roots in the idea that a system of robust trading was a good system in which the final outcome with respect to resource allocation and income distribution was desirable. This attitude was itself supported by three ideas. The value judgment was widespread that if a fool and his money were soon parted then that was no more than was to be expected and was 'right': just as a tone-deaf person could not expect a career as a professional musician, so a fool could not expect to engage in other than foolhardy actions. The second idea which consolidated the *caveat emptor* approach was the Adam Smith argument that a free market led to the best resource use. The third idea, running parallel to the second, was that if a buyer and seller made a 'contract' then, save for such cases as overt fraud, that contract was sacred.

If contracts, voluntarily entered into, were not going to be supported by the courts, then it was believed that fewer people would trade and so there would be less benefit from specialization and division of labor. This whole system of ideas seemed to be interlocking whole—and what is more a sensible way of running society, for it was also consistent with the notion of individual freedom and individual responsibility.

This system of values thus gave a low priority to consumer protection. The rising role of consumer protection law is an example of the point that—whatever lawyers claim—the law is not an immutable system but manmade. Changes in the law are largely the result of men perceiving the world differently from hitherto.

A least four reasons may be found for the rise of consumer protection law and the associated consumer lobbies. First, *caveat emptor* makes much sense in a primitive society where there is little trade but much self-reliance within the family and the village and what trade there is concerns goods such as farm produce where both buyer and seller might be equally knowledgeable. The buyer at the occasional fair or market would indeed be expected to take care, since he might never see the itinerant seller again. In many cases, the value of the sale would in any event be less than the likely transaction costs of going to court.

The twentieth-century consumer lives in a very different world. A far greater proportion of the family consumption of goods and services is bought and the average consumer is at some disadvantage compared to the retailer and manufacturer of electrical goods, consumer durables, and so forth—*that is, information is asymmetrically distributed*. This means that the concept of a bargain struck between equals is quite inappropriate and so, as in the case of monopoly legislation, attempts are made to defend the weaker party against any unfortunate outcomes of the bargains into which he freely enters—because he may have entered them innocently. It should be said that in many trivial transactions the costs of going to court far outweigh the losses and so many breaches of the letter or the spirit of the law go unpunished. The disgruntled shopper simply takes his business elsewhere in future.

If one reason for the attack on *caveat emptor* is because the world is more complex, and the distribution of information and bargaining power unequal, a second reason is that free market systems have come to be seen, at least technically, as not necessarily leading to the optimal use of resources. A third reason is that the value judgment implicit in the "devil take the hindmost" attitude to the parting of a fool from his money is now much less widely held. People are commonly seen as the products of their own history and environment rather than as responsible in any direct sense for their own foolhardiness, J.M. Oliver, *Law and Economics*, 82—83 (1979).

As a result of these forces, contract law has experienced tremendous changes during this century. As we discuss in the next ten chapters, many of the formalities of contract formation have been relaxed. Today contractual obligations are usually recognized whenever the parties clearly intend to be bound. In addition, an increasing number of promises are now enforced in certain circumstances even though they do not comply strictly with the basic requirements of a contract (see Chapter 10). Although in the past contract liability was absolute and there were few, if any, escapes from liability once assumed, presently the law allows a party to be excused from contractual

duties where fraud, duress, undue influence, mistake, unconscionability (unfairness), or impossibility is present. The nineteenth century's narrow view of contract damages has been expanded to grant equitable remedies and restitution for breach of contract. The older doctrine of privity of contract, which sharply restricted which parties could enforce contracts rights, has given way to the current view that permits intended third-party beneficiaries to sue in their own right. Earlier contract theory did not require good faith and fair dealing among contracting parties who dealt as arm's length. As Grant Gilmore in *The Death of a Contract* noted:

It seems apparent to the twentieth century mind, as perhaps it did not to the nineteenth century mind, that a system in which everybody is invited to do his own thing, at whatever cost to his neighbor, must work ultimately to the benefit of the rich and powerful, who are in a position to look after themselves and to act, so to say, as their own self-insurers. As we look back on the nineteenth century theories, we are struck most of all, I think, by the narrow scope of social duty which they implicitly assumed. No man is his brother's keeper; the race is to the swift; let the devil take the hindmost. For good or ill, we have changed all that. We are now all cogs in a machine, each dependent on the other. The decline and fall of the general theory of contract and, in most quarters, of laissez-faire economics may be taken as remote reflections of the transition from nineteenth century individualism to the welfare state and beyond.

Today, the duty of good faith is imposed on parties to a contract and the doctrine of unconscionability protects against grossly unfair dealings.

In brief, the twentieth century has left its mark on contract law by limiting the absolute freedom of contract and, at the same time, by relaxing the requirements of contract formation. The external, objective, and formal contract model of the nineteenth century has been replaced by one that is more individualized, subjective, and informal. Accordingly, we can say that now it is considerably easier both to get into a contract and to get out of one.

7

INTRODUCTION TO CONTRACTS

Every business enterprise, whether large or small, must enter into contracts with its employees, its suppliers of goods and services, and its customers in order to conduct its business operations. Thus contract law is an important subject for the business manager. Contract law is also basic to fields of law treated in other parts of this book, such as agency, sales of personal property, commercial paper, and secured transactions.

Even the most common transaction may involve many contracts. In a typical contract for the sale of land, the seller promises to transfer title, or right of ownership, to the land, and the buyer promises to pay an agreed-upon purchase price. In addition, the seller may promise to pay certain taxes, and the buyer may promise to assume a mortgage on the property or to pay the purchase price to a creditor of the seller. The buyer may pay part of the purchase price with a check, which is a contract containing the buyer's written order to his bank to pay a sum certain in money. If the parties have lawyers, they very likely have contracts with them. If the seller deposits the proceeds of the sale in a bank, he enters into a contract with the bank. If the buyer rents the property, he enters into a contract with the tenant. When one of the parties leaves his car in a parking lot to attend to any of these matters, he assumes a contractual relationship with the owner of the lot. In short, nearly every business transaction is based on contract and the expectations created by the agreed-upon promises. It is, therefore, essential that you know the legal requirements for making a promise or set of promises binding.

Development of the Law of Contracts

Common Law

Contracts are primarily governed by State common law. An orderly presentation of this law is found in the Restatements of the Law of Contracts. The first Restatement was adopted on May 6, 1932, by the American Law Institute. On May 17, 1979, the Institute adopted a revised edition of the Restatement— the Restatement, Second, Contracts—which will be referred to as the Restatement. For more than fifty years the Restatements have been regarded as a valuable authoritative reference work and extensively relied on and quoted in reported judicial opinions.

The Uniform Commercial Code

The sale of personal property is a large part of commercial activity. Article 2 of the Uniform Commercial Code (the Code or U.C.C.) governs such sales in all States except Louisiana. A sale is a contract involving the transfer of title to goods from seller to buyer for a price. The Code essentially defines goods as tangible personal property. **Personal property** is any property other than an interest in land. For example, the purchase of a television set, an automobile, or a textbook is a sale of goods. All such transactions are governed by Article 2 of the Code, but, where general contract law has not been specifically modified by the Code, the common law of contracts continues to apply. In other words, the law of sales is a specialized part of the general law of contracts, and the law of contracts governs unless specifically displaced by the Code.

Prior to the U.C.C., sales of personal property were governed by State laws which varied from State to State. Since such sales are an important part of commercial activity, and since much of that activity takes place across State lines, the diversity of laws created difficulties. The Code has been successful in bringing uniformity to the commercial laws of forty-nine of the fifty States.

Types of Contracts Outside the Code

General contract law governs all contracts outside the scope of the Code. Such contracts play a significant role in commercial activities. For example, the Code does *not* apply to employment contracts, service contracts (as in the next case), insurance contracts, contracts involving **real property** (land and anything attached to it, including buildings), and contracts for the sale of intangibles such as patents and copyrights. These transactions continue to be governed by general contract law. Figure 7–1 summarizes what law governs contracts.

Sale–transfer of ownership from seller to buyer

Goods–tangible personal property

Personal property–property other than an interest in land

Real property–land and anything attached to it

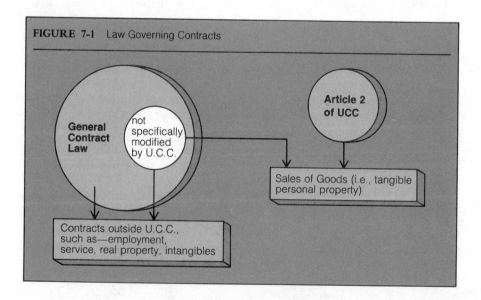

FIGURE 7-1   Law Governing Contracts

FACTS: St. Charles Drilling Co. contracted with Osterholt to install a well and water system which would produce a specified quantity of water. The water system failed to meet its warranted capacity and Osterholt sued for breach of contract.

DECISION: The U.C.C. does not apply to contracts primarily for services. The test for inclusion is whether the contract's predominant purpose is the rendition of services with goods incidentally involved, or whether it is a sale of goods with labor incidentally involved. In this case the contract to install a water system was a service transaction and, therefore, not within the scope of the U.C.C. for two reasons. First, the parties had no agreement as to what specific component parts were to be installed, but rather the contractor undertook to install a system of indefinite description and of warranted capacity. Second, the language of the contract itself indicated that the arrangement was a service contract rather than a sale.

OSTERHOLT v. ST. CHARLES DRILLING CO.

United States District Court, E.D. Missouri, 1980. 500 F.Supp. 529.

Definition of Contract

Put simply, a contract is a binding agreement that the courts will enforce. The Restatement more precisely defines a contract as "a promise or a set of promises for the breach of which the law gives a remedy, or the performance of which the law in some way recognizes a duty." A promise is a manifestation or demonstration of the intention to act or refrain from acting in a specified manner. Only those promises that meet *all* of the essential requirements of a binding contract will be enforced. All other promises are *not* contractual, and no legal remedy is available for a **breach** (a failure to perform properly) of these promises. Thus, a promise may be binding (contractual) or not binding (non-contractual). In other words, all contracts are promises, but not all promises are contracts (see Figure 7–2).

Breach–failure properly to perform a contractual obligation

For example, a contract must have a lawful purpose to be binding. If A promises to pay B $5,000 in return for B's promise to burn down C's factory,

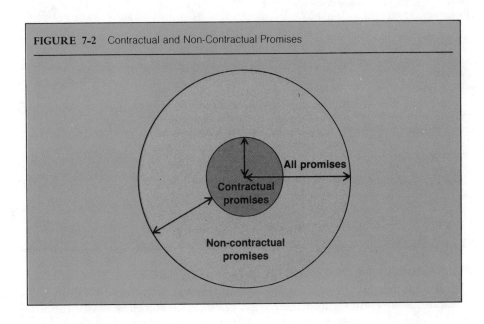

FIGURE 7-2   Contractual and Non-Contractual Promises

All promises

Contractual promises

Non-contractual promises

neither promise is binding because they are for an illegal purpose. As a result, the law will not provide a remedy to B for A's failure to fulfill his promise. A is not under any contractual or legal obligation to perform his promise.

Essentials of a Contract

The four essential ingredients of a binding promise are:

1. Manifestation of mutual assent.
2. Consideration.
3. Legality of object.
4. Capacity of the parties.

In addition, in a limited number of instances, a contract must be in writing to be enforceable, although in most cases an oral contract is binding and enforceable. As the following case shows, if all of these essentials are present, the promise is contractual and legally binding. If any of them is lacking, the promise is noncontractual. We consider these essentials separately in succeeding chapters.

STEINBERG v. CHICAGO MEDICAL SCHOOL

Illinois Court of Appeals, 1976.
41 Ill.App.3d 804, 354 N.E.2d 586.

FACTS: Robert Steinberg applied for admission to the Chicago Medical School as a first-year student and paid an application fee of $15. The school, a private educational institution, rejected his application. Steinberg brought an action against the school, claiming that it did not evaluate his and other applications according to the academic entrance criteria printed in the school's bulletin. Instead, he argues, the school based its decisions primarily on non-academic considerations, such as the applicant's family relationship to the school's faculty and members of its board of trustees, and the ability of the applicant or his family to donate large sums of money to the school. Steinberg asserts that by evaluating his application according to these unpublished criteria, the school breached the contract it had created when it accepted his application fee.

DECISION: Judgment for Steinberg. A contract is a promise or set of promises for the breach of which the law gives a remedy. "A contract's essential requirements are: competent parties, valid subject matter, legal consideration, mutuality of obligation and mutuality of agreement." Generally, parties may contract in any situation where there is no legal prohibition. However, to be binding, the terms must be "reasonably certain and definite." The contract must also be supported by consideration. Defined in its most general terms, consideration is some benefit accruing to one party or some detriment undertaken by the other, such as the payment of or promise to pay money. In addition, the parties must mutually agree to the contract's essential terms and conditions to make the contract binding. Mutual consent is gathered from the language employed by the parties or manifested by their words or acts.

In this situation, the school's promise to evaluate the applications according to academic standards is stated in a "definitive manner" in its bulletin. Steinberg accepted this in good faith and his $15 application fee served as valid consideration. When the school accepted this money it bound itself to honor the obligations stated in its bulletin. Therefore, its failure to use the stated academic criteria in evaluating applications constituted a breach of its contractual obligation to Steinberg.

Classification of Contracts

Contracts can be classified from various standpoints, such as their method of formation, their content, and their legal effect. The standard classifications are: (1) formal or informal contracts; (2) express or implied contracts;

(3) unilateral or bilateral contracts; (4) void, voidable, or unenforceable contracts; (5) executed or executory contracts.

Formal and Informal Contracts

A formal contract is legally binding because of its particular form or mode of expression. For example, at common law a promise under **seal,** a particular symbol that authenticates a document, is enforceable. (We discuss promises under seal in Chapter 10.) Another formal contract is a **negotiable instrument,** such as a check, which has certain legal attributes because of its special form. We cover negotiable instruments in Chapters 22–26. **Recognizances,** formal acknowledgments of indebtedness made in court, are another example of formal contracts. All other contracts, whether oral or written, are informal contracts, because they do not depend on mere formality for their legal validity.

> **Formal contract** –agreement which is legally binding because of its particular form or mode of expression

> **Informal contract** –all oral or written contracts other than formal contracts

Express and Implied Contracts

Parties to a contract may indicate their assent either in words or by conduct implying such willingness. For instance, a woman might pick up an item at a drug store, show it to the clerk, and walk out. This is a perfectly valid contract. The clerk knows from the customer's conduct that she is buying the item at the specified price and wants it charged to her account. Her actions speak as effectively as words. A contract in which the parties manifest assent in words is called an express contract; a contract formed by conduct is an implied (or more precisely, an **implied in fact**) contract. Both are generally genuine contracts, equally enforceable. The difference between them is merely the manner in which assent is manifested.

> **Express contract** –agreement of parties that is expressed in words either in writing or orally

> **Implied in fact contract** –contract where agreement of the parties is inferred from their conduct

---

FACTS: Richardson hired J.C. Flood Company, a plumbing contractor, to correct a stoppage in the sewer line of her house. The plumbing company's "snake" device, used to clear the line leading to the main sewer, became caught in the underground line. To release it, the company excavated a portion of the sewer line in Richardson's backyard. In the process, the company discovered numerous leaks in a rusty, defective water pipe which ran parallel with the sewer line. To meet public regulations, the water pipe, of a type no longer approved for such service, had to be replaced then or later when the yard would have to be redug for that purpose. The plumbing company proceeded to repair the water pipe. Richardson inspected the company's work daily and did not object to the extra work involved in replacing the water pipe. However, she refused to pay any part of the total bill after the company completed the entire operation. J.C. Flood Company then sued Richardson for the costs of labor and material it had furnished. Richardson argues that she only requested correction of a sewer obstruction but had never agreed to the replacement of the water pipe.

DECISION: Judgment for J.C. Flood Company. Contracts are either expressed or implied—expressed when their terms are stated by the parties, implied when arising from a mutual agreement not set forth in words. An implied contract "may be presumed from the acts and conduct of the parties as a reasonable man would view them under all the circumstances." Here, Richardson made daily inspections yet failed to object to the replacement of the water pipe until after the work was completed. Although she did not expressly agree to this extra work, her acts and conduct indicate her consent to it. Therefore, she created an implied (in fact) contract obligating her to pay for the reasonable value of the company's services.

RICHARDSON v. J.C. FLOOD CO.

District Court of Appeals, 1963.
190 A.2d 259.

Unilateral and Bilateral Contracts

In the typical contractual transaction, each party makes at least one promise. For example, Adelle says to Byron, "If you promise to mow my lawn, I will give you ten dollars," and Byron agrees to mow Adelle's lawn. Adelle and Byron have made mutual promises, each agreeing to do something in exchange for the promise of the other. When a contract is formed by the exchange of promises, each party is under a duty to the other. This kind of contract is called **bilateral,** because each party is both a **promisor** (a person making a promise) and a **promisee** (the person to whom a promise is made) (see Figure 7–3).

But suppose that only one of the parties makes a promise. Adelle says to Byron, "If you will mow my lawn, I will give you ten dollars." A contract will be formed when Byron has finished mowing the lawn and not before. At that time Adelle becomes contractually obligated to pay ten dollars to Byron. Adelle's offer was in exchange for Byron's act of mowing the lawn, and not for a promise of Byron to mow it. Byron was under no duty to mow the lawn. This is a **unilateral** contract because only *one* of the parties has made a promise (see Figure 7–4).

Thus, a bilateral contract results from the exchange of a promise for a return promise. A unilateral contract results from the exchange of a promise for an act or for a refrainment from acting. Where it is not clear whether a unilateral or bilateral contract has been formed, the courts presume that the parties intended a bilateral contract. Thus, if Adelle says to Byron, "if you will mow my lawn, I will pay you ten dollars," and Byron replies "O.K., I will mow your lawn," a bilateral contract is formed.

Void, Voidable, and Unenforceable Contracts

By definition a contract is an enforceable promise or agreement. Thus, a **void** contract is no contract at all. It is merely a promise or agreement that has no legal effect. An example of a void agreement is an agreement entered into by a person whom the courts have declared incompetent.

A **voidable** contract, on the other hand, is not wholly lacking in legal effect. It is a contract, but because of the manner or method in which it was formed, the law permits one or more of the parties to avoid the legal duties created by the contract. For instance, through intentional misrepresentation (*fraud*), A induces B to enter into a contract. B may, upon discovery of the fraud, notify A that by reason of the misrepresentation she will not perform her promise, and the law will support B. The contract induced by fraud is

Bilateral contract–contract in which both parties exchange promises

Promisor–person making a promise

Promisee–person to whom a promise is made

Unilateral contract–contract in which only one party makes a promise

Void–without legal effect

Voidable–capable of being made void

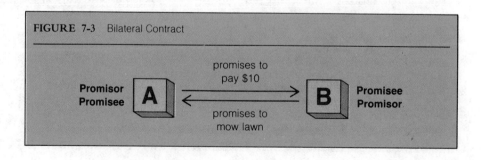

FIGURE 7-3   Bilateral Contract

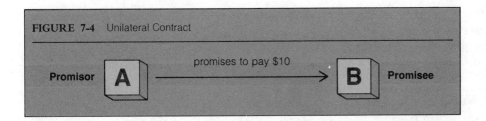

FIGURE 7-4 Unilateral Contract

Promisor **A** — promises to pay $10 → **B** Promisee

not void, but is voidable at the election of B, the defrauded party. A, the fraudulent party, has no such election.

Although a contract may be neither void nor voidable, it may be unenforceable. An **unenforceable** contract is one for the breach of which the law does not provide a remedy. For example, a contract may be unenforceable because of a failure to satisfy the requirements of the Statute of Frauds, which requires that certain kinds of contracts be in writing to be enforceable. Also, a party may not have the right to bring a lawsuit for breach of contract because of time limitations specified in the Statute of Limitations. After that period of time has passed, the contract is referred to as unenforceable, rather than void or voidable.

Unenforceable contract contract for the breach of which the law does not provide a remedy

Executed and Executory Contracts

A contract that has been fully carried out by all of the parties is an **executed** contract. Strictly, an executed contract is no longer a contract, because all duties under it have been performed, but it is useful to have a term for the completed contract. The term **executory** applies to contracts that are still partially or entirely unperformed by one or more of the parties.

Executed contract fully performed by all of the parties

Executory contract–contract partially or entirely unperformed by one or more of the parties

Quasi Contracts

In addition to express and implied-in-fact contracts, there are implied-in-law contracts or **quasi contracts,** which were not included in the previous classification of contracts for the reason that a quasi (meaning "as if") contract is not a contract at all.

Quasi contract–obligation *not* based upon contract that is imposed to avoid injustice

A quasi contract is not a contract because it is not based either on an express or an implied promise. For example, Willard by mistake delivers to Roy a plain, unaddressed envelope containing $100 intended for Lucia. Roy is under no contractual obligation to return it. However, Willard is permitted to recover the $100 from Roy. The law imposes an obligation on Roy in order to prevent his unjust enrichment at the expense of Willard.

One court has summarized the doctrine of quasi contract in the following manner:

> Quasi contracts are not contracts at all, although they give rise to obligations more akin to those stemming from contract than from tort. The contract is a mere fiction, a form imposed in order to adapt the case to a given remedy. . . . Briefly stated, a quasi-contractual obligation is one imposed by law where there has been no agreement or expression of assent, by word or act, on the part of either party involved. The law creates it, regardless of the intention of the parties, to assure a just and equitable result. Bradkin v. Leverton, 26 N.Y.2d 192, 309 N.Y.S.2d 192, 257 N.E.2d 643 (1970).

PUTTKAMMER v. MINTH

Supreme Court of Wisconsin, 1978.
83 Wis.2d 686, 266 N.W.2d 361.

FACTS: Minth is the owner of the Hiawatha Supper Club, which he leased during 1972 and 1973 to Piekarski. During the period of the lease Piekarski contracted with Puttkammer for the resurfacing of the access and service areas of the supper club. The work, including labor and materials, had a reasonable value of $2,540, but Puttkammer was never paid because Piekarski went bankrupt. Puttkammer (plaintiff) now brings this action against Minth (defendant) to recover the amount owed.

DECISION: Judgment for Minth. In order to establish a cause of action for unjust enrichment, Puttkammer must be able to demonstrate that (1) a benefit was conferred on Minth by Puttkammer; (2) Minth knew of or appreciated the benefit; and (3) Minth accepted or retained the benefit under circumstances making it inequitable for Minth to retain the benefit without paying for its value. Here, the first and second elements have been satisfied but not the third.

An action for unjust enrichment is based on the moral principle that one who has received a benefit has the duty to reimburse the other when to retain that benefit would be unjust. But it is not enough that the benefit was conferred and retained; the retention must also be unjust. Here, Puttkammer does not claim or imply that Minth ordered or ratified the work, that he performed the work expecting to be paid by Minth, that he was prejudiced by any misconduct or fault on Minth's part, or that Minth's interests were so intertwined with those of Piekarski that the contract could be said to have been executed on Minth's behalf. Rather, all that Puttkammer has alleged is that Minth knowingly acquiesced in the performance of the work.

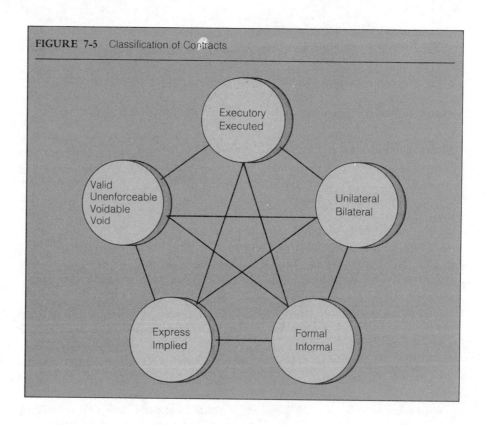

FIGURE 7-5 Classification of Contracts

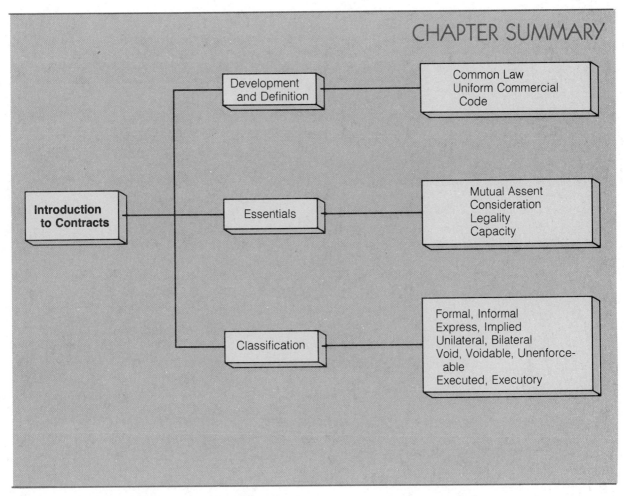

CHAPTER SUMMARY

Introduction to Contracts

- Development and Definition → Common Law, Uniform Commercial Code
- Essentials → Mutual Assent, Consideration, Legality, Capacity
- Classification → Formal, Informal; Express, Implied; Unilateral, Bilateral; Void, Voidable, Unenforceable; Executed, Executory

KEY TERMS

Sale
Goods
Personal property
Real property
Breach
Formal contract
Informal contract

Express contract
Implied in fact
    contract
Bilateral contract
Promisor
Promisee
Unilateral contract

Void
Voidable
Unenforceable contract
Executed contract
Executory contract
Quasi contract

MUTUAL ASSENT

Although each of the four requirements for the formation of a contract is essential to its existence, mutual asset is so basic that frequently a contract is referred to as an agreement between the parties. When the contract is enforced, it is the agreement that is enforced. The agreement between the parties is the very core of the contract.

A contractual agreement always involves either a promise exchanged for a promise (*bilateral contract*) or a promise exchanged for an act or forbearance to act (*unilateral contract*) as shown by what the parties communicate to one another. The way in which parties usually show mutual assent is by offer and acceptance.

To form a contract the agreement must be objectively manifested. The important thing is what the parties indicate to one another by spoken or written words or by conduct. The law applies an **objective** standard and is therefore concerned only with the assent, agreement, or intention of a party as it reasonably appears from his words or actions. The law of contracts is not concerned with what a party may have actually thought or the meaning that he intended to convey, insofar as his subjective understanding or intention differed from the meaning objectively manifested. For example, if Joanne offers to sell to Bruce her Chevrolet automobile but intends to offer and believes that she is offering her Ford automobile, and Bruce accepts the offer reasonably believing it was for the Chevrolet, a contract has been formed for the sale of the Chevrolet. Subjectively, there is no agreement as to the subject matter, but objectively there is a manifestation of agreement, and this is binding.

Offer

An offer is a definite proposal or undertaking made by one person to another indicating a willingness to enter into a bargain. The person making the proposal is the **offeror.** The person to whom it is made is the **offeree.** When it is received, the offer confers on the offeree the power of acceptance, which is an expression of willingness to comply with the terms of the offer.

Offer–indication of willingness to enter into a contract

Offeror–person making the offer

Offeree–recipient of the offer

Essentials of an Offer

An offer need not take any particular form to have legal effect. However, (1) it must be communicated to the offeree; (2) it must manifest an intent to enter into a contract; and (3) it must be sufficiently definite and certain. If these essentials are present, an offer that has not terminated grants the offeree the power to form a contract by accepting the offer. The communication of an offer to an offeree does not of itself confer any rights or impose any duties on either of the parties. The offeror, by making an offer, had simply conferred upon the offeree a power to create a contract between the parties by duly accepting the offer. Until the offeree exercises this power, the outstanding offer creates neither rights nor liabilities.

Communication

To have the mutual assent required to form a contract the offeree must know about the offer, and the offer must have been communicated by the offeror. An offeree cannot agree to something that he does not know about.

For example, Oscar signs a letter containing an offer to Ellen and leaves it on top of the desk in his office. Later that day, Ellen, without prearrangement, goes to Oscar's office, discovers that he is away, notices the letter on his desk, reads it, and then writes on it an acceptance that she dates and signs. No contract is formed because the offer never became effective because it was never communicated by Oscar to Ellen.

Not only must the offer be communicated to the offeree, but the communication must also be made or authorized by the offeror. If Jones tells Black that she is going to offer $600 to White for a piano, and Black promptly informs White of Jones's intention, no offer has been made. There was no authorized communication of any offer by Jones to White. By the same token, if David should offer to sell to Lou his diamond ring, an acceptance of this offer by Tia would not be effective, as David made no offer to Tia.

An offer need not be stated or communicated by words. Conduct from which a reasonable person may infer a promise in return for either an act or a promise amounts to an offer.

An offer may be made generally or to the public. However, no person can accept such an offer until and unless he knows that the offer exists. For example, if a person, without knowledge of the existence of an advertised reward for information leading to the arrest of a particular criminal, gives information leading to the arrest, he is not entitled to the reward. His act was not an acceptance of the offer because he could not accept something of which he had no knowledge.

Intent

To have legal effect an offer must further show an intent to enter into a contract. Some proposals lack such intent and are therefore not deemed offers. As a result, a purported acceptance does not bring about a contract but operates only as an offer.

Invitations Seeking Offers

It is important to distinguish language that constitutes an offer from that which merely solicits or invites offers. Communications between the parties in many cases take the form of preliminary negotiations. The parties are either requesting or supplying the terms of an offer that may or may not be given. A statement that may indicate a willingness to offer is not itself an offer. If Brown writes to Young, "Will you buy my automobile for $3,000?" and Young replies "Yes," there is no contract. Brown has not made an offer to sell her automobile to Young for $3,000. The offeror, as further shown in *Owen v. Tunison*, must manifest an intent to enter into a contract and not merely a willingness to enter into negotiation.

FACTS: Owen sent a letter to Tunison asking him to sell his property in Bucksport, Maine for $6,000. Tunison replied with a letter to Owen stating: "Because of improvements [to the property] . . . it would not be possible for me to sell it unless I was to receive $16,000 in cash." Owen quickly wired Tunison the following message: "Accept your offer for Bradley block Bucksport Terms sixteen thousand cash send deed to Eastern Trust and Banking Co. Bangor Maine Please Acknowledge." Four days later, Tunison notified Owen that he did not wish to sell the property. Owen sues for damages, claiming Tunison unjustly refused to complete the sale after his written offer and Owen's acceptance.

DECISION: Judgment for Tunison. In order for a buyer's acceptance to create a binding contract there must first exist a clear offer to sell. Here, Tunison's response to Owen's offer of $6,000 for his property merely indicated his interest to open negotiations that might lead to a sale. It was not a clear offer or proposal to sell, such as "I offer to sell to you."

OWEN v. TUNISON

Supreme Judicial Court of Maine, 1932.
131 Me. 42, 158 A. 926.

A businessperson who wants to sell merchandise is interested in informing potential customers about the goods, the terms of sale, and price. But if he makes widespread promises to sell to each person on his mailing list, it is conceivable that the number of acceptances and resulting contracts might exceed his ability to perform. Consequently, he might refrain from making offers by merely announcing that he has goods for sale, describing the goods, and quoting prices. He is inviting his customers and, in the case of published advertisements, the public, to make offers to him to buy the goods. His advertisements, circulars, quotation sheets, and display of merchandise are *not* offers because (1) they do not contain a promise, and (2) they leave unexpressed many terms that would be necessary to the making of a contract. Accordingly, the responses are not acceptances because no offer to sell has been made.

Nonetheless, a seller is not free to advertise goods at one price and then raise the price once demand has been stimulated. Although as far as contract law is concerned no offer has been made, such conduct is prohibited by the Federal Trade Commission as well as legislation in most States. Moreover, in some circumstances a public announcement or advertisement may constitute an offer. This is so if the advertisement or announcement contains a definite promise of something in exchange for something else and confers a power of acceptance on a specified person or class of persons. The typical offer of a reward is an example as is the landmark *Lefkowitz* case, which follows.

FACTS: On April 6, 1956, Great Minneapolis Surplus Store (defendant) published an advertisement in a Minneapolis newspaper reporting that "Saturday, 9:00 A.M. sharp; 3 brand new fur coats worth to $100; first come, first served, $1 each." Lefkowitz was the first to arrive at the store, but the store refused to sell him the fur coats because the "house rule" was that the offers were intended for women only and sales would not be made to men. The following week, Great Minneapolis published a similar advertisement for the sale of two mink scarves and a black lapin stole. Again Lefkowitz was the first to arrive at the store on Saturday morning, and once again the store refused to sell to him, this time because Lefkowitz knew of the house rule.

DECISION: Judgment for Lefkowitz. Whether a newspaper advertisement constitutes an offer, rather than a mere invitation to make an offer, depends upon the intention of the parties and

LEFKOWITZ v. GREAT MINNEAPOLIS SURPLUS STORE, INC.

Supreme Court of Minnesota, 1957.
251 Minn. 188, 86 N.W.2d 689.

the surrounding circumstances. If the facts show that some performance was promised in positive terms in return for something requested, then a newspaper advertisement addressed to the general public may lead to a binding obligation. Here the newspaper advertisements were clear, definite, explicit, and left nothing open for negotiation. Lefkowitz was the first to arrive at the store and to offer to purchase the furs and, therefore, was entitled to performance on the part of the store.

Objective Standard for Intent   Occasionally, a person exercises his sense of humor by speaking or writing words that taken literally and without regard to context or surrounding circumstances could be construed as an offer. However, the promise is intended as a joke, and the promisee as a reasonable man understands it to be such. Therefore it is not an offer. It does not create a sense of reasonable expectancy in the mind of the person to whom it is made because he realizes that it is not made in earnest. There is no contractual intent on the part of the promisor, and the promisee is or reasonably ought to be aware of that fact. However, if the intended jest, as in *Lucy v. Zehmer,* is so successful that the promisee as a reasonable person under all the circumstances reasonably believes that it has been made as an offer, and so believing accepts, the objective standard applies, and the parties have entered into a contract.

Objective standard
what a reasonable man under the circumstances would believe

LUCY v. ZEHMER

196 Va. 493, 84 S.E.2d 516 (1954).

FACTS: On December 20, 1952, Lucy and Zehmer met while having drinks in a restaurant. During the course of their conversation Lucy apparently offered to buy Zehmer's 471.6-acre farm for $50,000 cash. Although Zehmer claims that he thought that the offer was made in jest, he wrote the following on the back of a pad: "We hereby agree to sell to W. O. Lucy the Ferguson Farm complete for $50,000, title satisfactory to buyer." Zehmer then signed the writing and induced his wife Ida to do the same. She claims, however, that she signed only after Zehmer assured her that it was only a joke. Finally, Zehmer claims that he was "high as a Georgia pine" at the time but admits that he was not too drunk to make a valid contract.

DECISION: Judgment for Lucy. An agreement or mutual assent is essential to the formation of a valid contract. The mental assent of the parties is not a requisite, however, unless one party's undisclosed intentions are made known to the other party. If they are not, then the words and acts of the parties are judged by an objective standard to see if they manifest an intention to agree. Thus, Zehmer cannot claim that he was merely jesting when his conduct and words would warrant a reasonable person in believing that he intended a real agreement. Zehmer's response to Lucy's offer, therefore, whether made in earnest or in secret jest constituted a binding contract.

A promise made under circumstances of obvious excitement or emotional strain is likewise not an offer. For example, Sara, after having her month-old Cadillac break down for the third time in two days, screams in disgust, "I will sell this car to anyone for ten dollars." Larry hears Sara and hands her a ten-dollar bill. Under the circumstances, Sara's statement was not an offer, if a reasonable person in Larry's position would not have considered it one.

Definiteness

The terms of a contract must be clear enough to provide a court with a basis for determining the existence of a breach and for giving an appropriate remedy. It is a fundamental policy that contracts should be made by the parties and not by the courts; accordingly, remedies for breach must have a basis in the parties' contract. Recently a lawsuit has been filed for $14 billion involving whether a definite contract was formed or whether the parties merely "shook hands," see Law in the News on page 136.

However, where the parties have intended to form a contract, the courts will attempt to find a basis for granting a remedy. Missing terms may be supplied by course of dealing, usage of trade, or by inference. Thus, uncertainty as to incidental matters will seldom be fatal so long as the parties intend to form a contract. A court, as shown in the following case, will nevertheless not rescue a contract in which the parties cover a term but leave it vague or indefinite.

FACTS: Walker leased a small lot to Keith for ten years at $100 a month, with a right for Keith to extend the lease another 10-year term under the same terms except as to rent. The renewal option provided:

> rental will be fixed in such amount as shall actually be agreed upon by the lessors and the lessee with the monthly rental fixed on the comparative basis of rental values as of the date of the renewal with rental values at this time reflected by the comparative business conditions of the two periods.

Keith sought to exercise the renewal right and, when the parties were unable to agree on the rent, brought suit against Walker.

DECISION: Judgment for Walker. For the renewal right to be enforceable, the material terms of the renewal must be stated in the lease with sufficient certainty and definiteness. The amount of rental payments is a material term in a rental agreement. If Walker and Keith had agreed upon a specific method for determining the new rent, such as by computation, the application of a formula, or an arbitrator's decision, the renewal option would be enforceable. However, the renewal option stated a mere agreement to agree upon the amount of rent. "An agreement to agree simply does not fix an enforceable obligation." Furthermore, the option's reference to "comparative business conditions" as a standard for determining the new rent lacked the necessary certainty. It is not clear whether the parties meant "local conditions, national conditions, or conditions affecting [Keith's] particular business." Therefore, the lack of definiteness of this material term renders the renewal option unenforceable.

WALKER v. KEITH
Supreme Court of Kentucky, 1964.
382 S.W.2d 198.

Open Terms Under the Code   With respect to agreements for the sale of goods, the Uniform Commercial Code provides standards by which omitted terms may be determined, provided the parties intended to enter into a binding contract. The Restatement has adopted an approach similar to the Code's in supplying terms omitted in the parties' contract.

Under the Code, an offer for the purchase or sale of goods may leave open particulars of performance to be specified by one of the parties. Any such specification must be made in good faith and within limits set by commercial reasonableness. **Good faith** is defined as honesty in fact in the conduct or transaction concerned. **Commercial reasonableness** is a standard measured by the business judgment of reasonable persons familiar with the customary practices in the type of transaction involved and with regard to the facts and circumstances of the case.

Output, Requirements, and Exclusive Dealings   An agreement of a buyer to purchase the entire output of a seller's factory for a stated period, or an agreement of a seller to supply a buyer with all his requirements of certain

Law In The News

Pennzoil-Texaco Fight Is Question of Honor
Tradition Tested in $14 Billion Suit Over Buyout of Getty

By Bryan Burrough
Staff Reporter of
The Wall Street Journal
HOUSTON—J. Hugh Liedtke, one of the wiliest deal makers in the oil patch, was jubilant after making the biggest deal of his life. Standing in a sumptuous suite in New York's Pierre hotel, Mr. Liedtke, chairman of Pennzoil Co., shook hands and hoisted a glass of champagne with Gordon P. Getty, toasting an apparent decision by Getty Oil Co.'s board under which Pennzoil would assume management control of Getty Oil in a $5.3 billion leveraged buyout.

Forty-eight hours later, the party was over. Before Mr. Liedtke had the chance to complete a definitive contract, Mr. Getty made an abrupt about-face and agreed to sell the Getty family trust's 40.2% stake in Los Angeles-based Getty Oil to giant Texaco Inc. Within a day of that January 1984 agreement, Getty's board approved the company's sale to Texaco for about $10 billion. "They used to say that the oil business was built upon a handshake," Mr. Liedtke would soon tell Pennzoil shareholders. "Should it now require handcuffs?"

Next month, a state court jury here will begin hearing testimony on whether Mr. Liedtke had a contract with Getty Oil and whether Texaco induced Getty Oil to break it. Pennzoil, in its lawsuit against Texaco, is demanding a whopping $14 billion in damages, and a Delaware judge has said that Mr. Liedtke has a strong case.

But the suit represents much more than an opportunity for Pennzoil to reap a huge award for damages. It is one of the highest-stakes battles ever over the definition of a contract. And some

veteran deal makers in oil, where a man's word was always considered as good as his signature, view such disputes these days as a final stand against an erosion of traditional oil patch values in an era of mega-mergers engineered by slick Wall Street lawyers and investment bankers.

"If we keep breaking these agreements, handshakes won't be worth a damn, say-sos won't be worth a damn, and contracts won't be worth a damn," says Michel T. Halbouty, a legendary Houston independent oil man. "Where is the morality in business anymore?"

Texaco lawyers view the talk of handshakes, etiquette and honor as a smoke screen put up by Pennzoil to mask its ineptitude in the transaction. Moreover, they dismiss the discussion of morality as the product of a bygone era.

"That stuff won't get you to first base in New York," says Richard B. Miller, Texaco's lead lawyer in the case. "The crux of the matter is that Pennzoil doesn't have a written agreement of any kind with Getty." Mr. Miller likens the validity of Pennzoil's agreement with Getty Oil to a scene from the 1940 movie "Boom Town," in which two oil men decide ownership of their company by flipping a coin.

Pennzoil's Mr. Liedtke has lived by the code of the oil patch for more than 30 years. He treasures his membership in the All-American Wildcatters, an industry group whose motto is, "My word is my bond."

"Texaco evidently thinks it is rich enough and strong enough and powerful enough to walk over people with callous disregard," Mr. Liedtke said in a deposition. Texaco, he added, "reminds me of the

gorilla who sleeps where the gorilla wants to."

For a case that supposedly involves questions of honor and gentlemanliness, neither quality has been abundant in the proceedings so far. The only attempt to settle out of court took place in a meeting of Mr. Liedtke and Texaco Chairman John McKinley in Washington, D.C., during which Mr. Liedtke threatened to use all his "influence" on Capitol Hill unless Pennzoil was allowed to take part in the Getty transaction, according to a deposition given by Mr. McKinley. The Texaco chairman declined, but offered to sell Pennzoil part of Texaco's 35% interest in the bountiful Hueso oil field off the California coast, a Pennzoil official testified. But Mr. Liedtke, noting that *hueso* is Spanish for "bone," replied, "We're not interested in being thrown any bones," according to Pennzoil court documents.

Texaco, too, has played tough. After learning that a Pennzoil lawyer, Joe Jamail, had given a $10,000 campaign contribution to state court judge Anthony J. P. Ferris, who is presiding in the case, Texaco accused Mr. Jamail of impropriety and unsuccessfully moved to have the judge withdraw from the case. Another judge found no reason for Judge Ferris to withdraw.

Mr. Jamail, a personal-injury lawyer, says he intends to make an issue in the trial of Texaco's reputation for dealing heavy-handedly with suppliers and partners—an image the company has been working to correct. "The difference between Texaco's reputation and Hugh Liedtke's reputation is the difference between chicken manure and chicken salad,"

Pennzoil-Texaco continued

Mr. Jamail claims.

Contract law, which is taught to every first-year law student, is fraught with twists and turns, as this case demonstrates. Even though Mr. Liedtke never obtained any signed documents spelling out the agreement with Getty Oil, his lawyers are preparing to argue that a binding contract can be formed before all the papers are signed.

For one thing, Pennzoil says Getty's board, meeting in a marathon session to consider the proposed leveraged buyout, approved the bid in a 14–1 vote. Not so, says Texaco. Several former Getty directors said in depositions that the vote was on the price of the offer, not on whether to accept it.

Exactly what the board decided may never be known for certain, however. Getty Oil's counsel, Ralph Copley, destroyed his handwritten notes of the meeting a week later, three days after the litigation began. His were the only original minutes of the meeting. Mr. Copley says he often destroys such notes. The surviving minutes were edited three times on a word processor.

If any doubt existed over the board's action, Pennzoil also will argue, it disappeared the following morning, Jan. 4, when Getty Oil issued a news release proclaiming that it had reached an agreement in principle with Pennzoil on the buyout. In Los Angeles, an attorney for Mr. Getty

in another case stood up in a courtroom and called the transaction "an agreement which has been entered into after extremely careful consideration." In New York, as Messrs. Liedtke and Getty toasted the agreement, they discussed plans to meet with and reassure Getty Oil employees.

Were these events tantamount to a contract? "The evidence is as strong as an acre of garlic," says Mr. Jamail, the Pennzoil lawyer. Texaco will counter that news releases and handshakes don't count as contracts and that the transaction was subject to a definitive agreement.

A Delaware judge's opinion last year seems to favor Pennzoil, however. "I am convinced that Pennzoil has demonstrated a likelihood that it will be able to establish . . . that a contract came into being," wrote the judge, ruling in an unsuccessful attempt by Pennzoil to block the Texaco-Getty Oil merger. The judge noted a wide body of law holding that "a binding contract can be formed despite material open issues."

But Pennzoil won't have an easy time proving that Texaco induced Getty Oil to break a contract, if one existed. The Delaware judge termed this issue "a close call." Indeed, Goldman, Sachs & Co., shopping to obtain the best deal for Getty Oil, invited a bid from Texaco during a break in the Getty board meeting. Two days later, when Texaco's chairman called a top executive of Getty to ask

whether the company was still for sale, he was assured that, "The fat lady hasn't sung." Messrs. McKinley and Getty spent the night working out details of Texaco's better offer, and the rest is history.

Mr. Liedtke would be busy managing Getty Oil today instead of the court case if he had obtained a contract from Getty Oil in addition to the handshake from Mr. Getty. Some lawyers close to the case suggest that Pennzoil's longtime Houston law firm, Baker & Botts, simply didn't move quickly enough to put the agreement in writing after the Getty board meeting. Delays by Getty Oil lawyers also interfered with negotiations for a definitive agreement, lawyers on both sides agree. At one point after Texaco entered the picture, Getty Oil lawyers kept the Pennzoil legal team waiting an entire afternoon.

But as the trial nears, Texaco lawyers aren't underestimating Mr. Liedtke, a law graduate himself who personally structured the Pennzoil-Getty transaction and who has assumed a personal stake in the outcome of the litigation. Referring to Mr. Liedtke, Texaco's Mr. Miller says: "If you think a guy who graduated from Amherst, Harvard Business School and the University of Texas and who's been CEO of a major oil company for 20 years is a simple country boy—well, maybe he is. We'll find out."

goods used in his business operations, may appear to lack definiteness and mutuality of obligation. The exact quantity of goods is not specified; moreover, the seller may have some degree of control over his output and the buyer over his requirements. However, under the Code and the Restatement such agreements are enforceable by the application of an objective standard based on good faith of both parties. Thus the seller cannot operate her factory twenty-four hours a day and insist that the buyer take all of the output when she operated it only eight hours a day before the agreement was made. Nor can the buyer expand his business abnormally and insist that the seller supply all of his requirements.

A valid agreement between buyer and seller for exclusive dealing in goods, unless otherwise agreed, imposes an obligation on the seller to use her best efforts to supply the goods and on the buyer to use his best efforts to promote the sale of the goods.

Duration of Offers

An offer confers upon the offeree a power of acceptance, which continues until the offer terminates. The ways in which an offer may be terminated, other than by acceptance, are: (1) lapse of time; (2) revocation; (3) rejection; (4) counteroffer; (5) death or incompetency of the offeror or offeree; (6) destruction of the specific subject matter to which the offer relates; and (7) subsequent illegality of the type of contract contemplated by the offer.

Lapse of Time

The offeror may specify the time within which the offer is to be accepted, just as he may specify any other term or condition in the offer. Unless otherwise terminated, the offer remains open for the **specified** time period. After the expiration of that time, the offer no longer exists and cannot be accepted.

If no time is stated in the offer within which the offeree may accept, the offer will terminate after a **reasonable** period of time. What is a reasonable period of time is a question of fact, depending on the nature of the contract proposed, the usages of business, and other circumstances of the case. For instance, an offer to sell a perishable good would be open for a shorter period of time than an offer to sell undeveloped real estate.

Revocation

Revocation—cancellation of an offer by an offeror

Prior to its acceptance the offeror generally may cancel or revoke an offer at any time. If the offeror originally promises that the offer will be open for thirty days but after five days wishes to terminate it, he may do so merely by giving the offeree notice—explicitly or implicitly, as in *Hoover Motors* which follows—that he is withdrawing the offer. This notice may be given by any means of communication and effectively terminates the offer when *received* by the offeree. However, an offer made to the general public is revoked only by giving publicity to the revocation equivalent to that given the offer.

HOOVER MOTOR EXPRESS CO. v. CLEMENTS PAPER CO.

Supreme Court of Tennessee, 1951.
193 Tenn. 6, 241 S.W.2d 851.

FACTS: On November 19, 1949, Hoover Motor Express Company sent to Clements Paper Company a written offer to purchase certain real estate. Some time in December, Clements authorized Williams to accept. Williams, however, attempted to bargain with Hoover to obtain a better deal, specifically that Clements would retain easements on the property. In a telephone conversation on January 13, 1960, Williams first told Hoover of his plan to obtain the easements. Hoover replied: "Well, I don't know if we are ready. We have not decided, we might not want to go through with it." On January 20, Clements sent a written acceptance of Hoover's offer. Hoover refused to sell, claiming it had revoked its offer through the January 13 phone conversation. Clements then brought suit to compel the sale or obtain damages.

DECISION: Judgment for Hoover. Express notice of revocation before acceptance of an offer is not required. The offeror may implicitly revoke his offer through acts or communications to the offeree that are inconsistent with its continuance. If the offeree has knowledge of this inconsistent interest before he has accepted then the offer is revoked.

Here, Williams knew through the January 13 phone conversation that Hoover "thought they might not go through with it." This communication by Hoover to Williams effectively revoked its offer. Therefore, Clements' acceptance on January 20 came too late to bind Hoover to the sale.

Notice of revocation may be indirectly communicated to the offeree, as where he receives reliable information from a third person that the offeror has disposed of the property he has offered for sale or has otherwise placed himself in a position indicating an unwillingness or inability to perform the promise contained in the offer. For example, A offers to sell his portable television set to B and tells B that he has ten days in which to accept. One week later B observes the television set in C's house and is informed that C purchased it from A. The next day B sends to A an acceptance of the offer. There is no contract, because A's offer was effectively revoked when B learned of A's inability to sell the television set to B by reason of his having sold it to C.

Certain limitations, however, have been imposed on the offeror's power to revoke the offer at any time prior to its acceptance. These limitations apply to the following four situations.

Option Contracts   An option is a contract by which the offeror is bound to hold open an offer for a specified period of time. It must comply with all of the requirements of a contract, including **consideration** being given to the offeror by the offeree. For example, if in consideration of $500 paid to Alan by Barry, Alan gives Barry an option to buy Blackacre at a price of $80,000, exercisable at any time within thirty days, Alan's offer is irrevocable. Alan is legally bound to keep the offer open for thirty days, and any communication by Alan to Barry of notice of withdrawal of the offer is ineffective. Barry is not bound to accept the offer, but the option contract entitles him to thirty days in which to consider acceptance.

> Option –contract which provides that an offer stay open for a specified period of time

Firm Offers Under the Code   The Code provides that a *merchant* is bound to keep an offer to buy or sell **goods** open for a stated period not over three months, if the merchant gives assurance in a **signed writing** that it will be held open. The Code, therefore, makes a merchant's written promise not to revoke an offer for a stated period of time enforceable even though no consideration is given the offeror for that promise. A **merchant** is defined as a person (1) who is a dealer in the goods, or (2) who by his occupation holds himself out as having knowledge or skill peculiar to the goods or practices involved, or (3) who employs an agent or broker whom he holds out as having such knowledge or skill.

> Firm offer –irrevocable offer to sell or buy goods by a merchant in a signed writing which gives assurance that it will not be rescinded for up to three months

Statutory Irrevocability   Certain offers are made irrevocable by statute, such as bids for the construction of a building or some public work made to the State, municipality, or other governmental body. Another example is preincorporation stock subscription agreements, which are irrevocable for a period of six months under many State corporation statutes.

Irrevocable Offers of Unilateral Contracts   Where the offer contemplates a *unilateral* contract, that is, a promise for an act, injustice to the offeree may result if revocation is permitted after the offeree has started to perform the act requested in the offer and has substantially but not completely accomplished it. Traditionally, such an offer is not accepted and no contract is formed until the offeree has completed the requested act. By starting performance the offeree does not bind himself to complete performance and historically did not bind the offeror to keep the offer open. Thus the offeror could revoke the offer at any time before the offeree's completion of performance. For example, Jorden offers Karlene $300 if Karlene will climb to the top of the flagpole in the center of campus. Karlene starts to climb, but when she is five feet from the top, Jorden yells to her, "I revoke."

The Restatement deals with this problem by providing that where the performance of the requested act necessarily requires time and effort to be expended by the offeree, the offeror is obligated not to revoke the offer for a reasonable time. This obligation arises when the offeree begins the invited performance and the offeror's duty of performance is conditional on completion of the invited performance according to the terms of the offer. It is reasoned that the offeree's commencement of performance is equivalent to consideration being given to keep the offer open. However, if the offeror does not know of the offeree's performance and has no adequate means of learning of it within a reasonable period of time, the offeree must exercise reasonable diligence to notify the offeror.

Rejection

Rejection—the refusal to accept an offer

An offeree is at liberty to accept or reject the offer as he sees fit. If he decides not to accept it, he is not required to reject it. If he does reject the offer, it is thereby terminated. Just as the acceptance of an offer is a manifestation of the willingness of the offeree to accept, a rejection of an offer is a manifestation by the offeree of his unwillingness to accept. The power of acceptance is terminated by a communicated rejection. From the effective moment of rejection, which is the **receipt** of the rejection by the offeror, the offeree may no longer accept the offer. Rejection by the offeree may consist of express language or may be implied from language or conduct.

Counteroffer

Counteroffer—counterproposal to an offer

A counteroffer is a counterproposal from the offeree to the offeror and indicates a willingness to contract with reference to the subject matter of the offer but on terms or conditions different from those contained in the offer. It is not an unequivocal acceptance, and by indicating an unwillingness to agree to the terms of the offer, it operates as a rejection. See *Zeller v. First National Bank & Trust* below. To further illustrate, assume that Worthy writes Joanne a letter stating that he will sell to Joanne a secondhand color television set for $300. Joanne replies that she will pay Worthy $250 for the set. This is a counteroffer that, on **receipt** by Worthy terminates the original offer. However, if Joanne in her reply states that she wishes to consider the $300 offer but is willing to pay $250 at once for the set, that is a counteroffer that does *not* terminate Worthy's original offer. In the first instance, after making the $250 counteroffer, Joanne may not accept the $300 offer. In the second instance she may do so, as the counteroffer was stated in such a manner as not to indicate an unwillingness to accept the original offer, and Joanne therefore did not terminate it.

FACTS: On December 23, Wyman, a lawyer representing the First National Bank & Trust (defendant), wrote to Zeller (plaintiff) stating that he had been instructed to offer a building to Zeller for sale that Zeller had expressed an interest in purchasing for $240,000. The letter also set forth details concerning interest rates and loan fees.

After receiving the letter, Zeller instructed his attorney, Jamma, to send Wyman a written counteroffer of $230,000 with varying interest and loan arrangements. Jamma sent the written counteroffer as instructed on January 10. On the same day Jamma telephoned Wyman and informed him of the counteroffer. Jamma then tried to telegraph acceptance of the original offer to Wyman. When Wyman refused to sell the property to him, Zeller brought this action to seek enforcement of the alleged contract.

DECISION: Judgment for First National Bank. In order for an acceptance to create a binding contract, it must comply strictly with the terms of the offer. An acceptance requesting modification or containing terms which vary from those offered constitutes a rejection of the original offer and becomes a counteroffer which must be accepted by the original offeror before a valid, binding contract is formed. Here, in a telephone conversation on January 10 Jamma told Wyman of the $230,000 counteroffer. This counter-proposal operated as a rejection of the original offer and terminated Zeller's power of acceptance.

Finally, it matters not that the counteroffer was communicated orally in response to a written offer. If an offer requires a written acceptance, no other form will do. Here, however, no particular form of response was required, so the oral counteroffer was an effective rejection. As such, it is irrelevant that the written acceptance arrived prior to the written counteroffer since the oral counteroffer preceded them both.

ZELLER v. FIRST NATIONAL BANK & TRUST

Appellate Court of Illinois, First District, 1979. 79 Ill.App.3d 170, 34 Ill.Dec. 473, 398 N.E.2d 148.

Another common type of counteroffer is the **conditional acceptance.** A conditional acceptance claims to accept the offer but expressly makes the acceptance conditional on the offeror's assent to additional or different terms. Nonetheless, it is a counteroffer and generally terminates the original offer. However, a mere inquiry about the possibility of obtaining different or new terms is not a counteroffer and does not terminate the offer. The Code's treatment of acceptances containing terms that vary from the offer are discussed later in this chapter.

Conditional acceptance—an acceptance of an offer based upon the acceptance of an additional or different term

Death or Incompetency

The death or incompetency of either the offeror or the offeree ordinarily terminates an offer. On his death or incompetency the offeror no longer has the legal capacity to enter into a contract, and thus all outstanding offers are terminated. Death or incompetency of the offeree likewise terminates the offer, because an ordinary offer is not assignable and can be accepted only by the person to whom it was made. When the offeree dies or ceases to have legal capability to enter into a contract, there is, in effect, no one who can accept the offer. Therefore, the offer necessarily terminates.

The death or incompetency of the offeror or offeree, however, does *not* terminate an offer contained in an option.

Destruction of Subject Matter

Destruction of the specific subject matter of an offer terminates the offer. The impossibility of performance prevents a contract from being consummated and thus terminates all outstanding offers with respect to the destroyed property. Suppose that Sarah, owning a Buick, offers to sell the car to Barbara, and allows Barbara five days in which to accept. Three days later the car is destroyed by fire. On the following day Barbara, in ignorance of the destruction of the car, notifies Sarah that she accepts Sarah's offer. There is no contract. Sarah's offer was terminated by the destruction of the car. Clearly, there can be no agreement made concerning a specific car which is no longer in existence.

Subsequent Illegality

One of the four essential ingredients of a contract, as we previously mentioned, is legality of purpose or subject matter. If performance of a valid contract is subsequently made illegal, the obligations of both parties under the contract are discharged. Illegality taking effect after the making of an offer but prior to acceptance has the same effect. The offer is legally terminated.

Acceptance of Offer

Acceptance–manifestation of a willingness to enter into a contract on the terms of the offer

The acceptance of an offer is essential to the formation of a contract. Acceptance of an offer for a bilateral contract is some overt act by the offeree that manifests his assent to the terms of the offer, such as speaking or sending a letter, a telegram, or other communication to the offeror. If the offer is for a unilateral contract, acceptance is the performance of the requested act with the intention of accepting. For example, if Joy publishes an offer of a reward to anyone who returns the diamond ring that she has lost (a unilateral contract offer), and Bob with knowledge of the offer finds and returns the ring to Joy, Bob has accepted the offer. However, if Bob returns the ring to Joy but in doing so disclaims the reward and says that he does not accept the offer, there is no contract. Merely doing the act requested by the offeror is not sufficient to form a contract where it is not done with the intention of accepting the offer.

Once an acceptance has been given, the contract is formed.

Definiteness

Mirror image rule–an acceptance cannot deviate from the terms of the offer

An acceptance must be *positive* and *unequivocal*. It may not change any of the terms of the offer, nor add to, subtract from, or qualify in any way the provisions of the offer. It must be the **mirror image** of the offer. Except as modified by the Code, any communication by the offeree that attempts to modify the offer is not an acceptance but a mere counteroffer.

The common law "mirror image" rule, by which the acceptance cannot vary or deviate from the terms of the offer, is modified by the Code. This modification is necessitated by the realities of modern business practices. A vast number of business transactions use standardized business forms. For example, a buyer sends to the seller on the buyer's order form a purchase order for 1,000 dozen cotton shirts at sixty dollars per dozen with delivery by October 1 at the buyer's place of business. On the reverse side of this standard form are twenty-five numbered paragraphs containing provisions generally favorable to the buyer. When the seller receives the buyer's order, he sends to the buyer on his acceptance form an unequivocal acceptance of the offer. However, despite the fact that the seller agrees to the buyer's quantity, price, and delivery terms on the back of his acceptance form, the seller has thirty-two numbered paragraphs generally favorable to himself and in significant conflict with buyer's form. Under the common law's *mirror image* rule no contract would exist, for there has not been an unequivocal acceptance of all of the material terms of the buyer's offer.

The Code alleviates this **Battle of the Forms** problem by focusing on the intent of the parties. If the seller definitely and seasonably expresses his acceptance of the offer and does not expressly make his acceptance conditional on the buyer's assent to the additional or different terms, a contract is formed. The issue then becomes whether the seller's different or additional terms become part of the contract. If both buyer and seller are merchants, additional terms will be part of the contract if they do not materially alter the agreement and are not objected to either in the offer itself or within a reasonable period of time. If both of the parties are not merchants, then the additional terms are merely construed as proposals for addition to the contract. Different terms proposed by the offeree will not become part of the contract unless accepted by the offeror.

The following case deals with a situation involving whether additional terms become a part of the contract.

FACTS: The Brewers contracted to purchase Dower House from McAfee. Then, several weeks before the May 7, settlement date for the purchase of the house, the two parties began to negotiate for the sale of certain items of furniture in the house. On April 30, McAfee sent the Brewers a letter containing a list of the furnishings to be purchased at specified prices; a payment schedule including a $3,000 payment due on acceptance; and a clause reading: "If the above is satisfactory please sign and return one copy with the first payment."

On June 3, the Brewers sent a letter to McAfee stating that enclosed was a $3,000 check; that the original contract had been misplaced and could another be furnished; that they planned to move into Dower House on June 12; and that they wished that the red desk be included in the contract. McAfee then sent a letter dated June 8 to the Brewers listing the items of furniture purchased.

The Brewers moved into Dower House in the middle of June. Soon after they moved in, they tried to contact McAfee at his office to tell him that there had been a misunderstanding relating to their purchase of the listed items. They then refused to pay him any more money, and he brought this action to recover the balance outstanding.

DECISION: Judgment for McAfee. Under the U.C.C., a definite expression of acceptance, if sent within a reasonable time, is effective even though it states terms additional to or different from those offered or agreed upon, unless acceptance is expressly made conditional on assent to the additional or different terms. The additional terms should be construed as proposals for addition to the contract.

Here, McAfee did not indicate in his April 30 letter to the Brewers that a particular manner of acceptance was required. Therefore, the Brewer's letter of June 3, together with the enclosed $3,000 check, the amount due upon acceptance of the contract, manifested their assent to the items listed in the April 30 letter from McAfee. The June 3 letter was both definite and seasonable, and the reference to the red writing desk was not expressed in language making acceptance conditional upon inclusion of the desk. This item, then, was merely a proposal for an addition to the contract. Finally, although the Brewers did not sign and return one copy of the contract as McAfee requested, they did send a letter of their own. This was reasonable under the circumstances since they had misplaced the contract and, therefore, the letter constituted an effective acceptance of McAfee's offer.

McAFEE v. BREWER

Supreme Court of Virginia,
1974.
214 Va. 579, 203 S.E.2d 129.

Effective Moment

As we discussed previously, an offer, a revocation, a rejection, and a counteroffer are effective when they are *received*. An acceptance, as shown in the following case, is generally effective upon **dispatch.** This is true unless the offer specifically provides otherwise or the offeree uses an unauthorized means of communication.

CUSHING v. THOMSON

Supreme Court of New Hampshire, 1978.
118 N.H. 292, 386 A.2d 805.

FACTS: Cushing filed an application with the office of the Adjutant General of the State of New Hampshire for the use of the Portsmouth Armory to hold a dance on the evening of April 29, 1978. The application, made on behalf of the Portsmouth Area Clamshell Alliance, was received by the Adjutant General's office on or about March 30, 1978. On March 31 the Adjutant General mailed a signed contract offer agreeing to rent the armory for the evening requested. The agreement required acceptance by the renter's affixing his signature to the agreement and then returning the copy to the Adjutant General within five days after receipt. Cushing received the contract offer, signed it on behalf of the Alliance, and mailed it on April 3. At 6:30 on the evening of April 4, Cushing received a telephone call from the Adjutant General revoking the rental offer. Cushing stated during the conversation that he had already signed and mailed the contract. The Adjutant General sent a written confirmation of the withdrawal on April 5. On April 6 the Adjutant General's office received by mail the signed contract dated April 3 and postmarked April 5.

DECISION: Judgment for Cushing. When the parties to a contract are at a distance and the offer is sent by mail, the reply accepting the offer may be sent through the same medium. Moreover, the contract becomes complete and binding when the acceptance is mailed, properly addressed to the party making the offer, and is beyond the sender's control. Once the offer has been accepted by posting in the mail, the offer cannot be revoked by the offeror.

Cushing claims that he signed the contract and placed it in the outbox for mailing on April 3. Furthermore, it was customary practice for letters to be collected from the outbox daily and then placed in the U.S. mail. Since this occurred before the attempted revocation of the offer by the Adjutant General on April 4, the revocation was ineffective, and the contract is binding and enforceable.

Authorized Means

Historically, an authorized means of communication was the means expressly authorized by the offeror in the offer, or if none was authorized, it was the means used by the offeror. As in the above case of *Cushing v. Thomson,* if in reply to an offer by mail, the offeree places in the mail a letter of acceptance properly stamped and addressed to the offeror, a contract is formed at the time and place that the offeree mails the letter. This assumes, of course, that the offer at that time was open and had not been terminated by any of the methods previously discussed. The reason for this rule is that the offeror, by using the mail, impliedly authorized the offeree to use the same channel of communication, and his mailing of an acceptance is an overt act of manifestation of assent. It is immaterial if the letter of acceptance goes astray in the mails and is never received.

The Restatement and the Code both now provide that where the language in the offer or the circumstances do not otherwise indicate, an offer to make a contract shall be construed as authorizing acceptance in any **reasonable** manner. These provisions are intended to allow flexibility of response and the ability to keep pace with new modes of communication.

Unauthorized Means

When the medium of communication used by the offeree is unauthorized, the traditional rule is that acceptance is effective when dispatched provided that it is received within the time the authorized means would have arrived.

Stipulated Provisions in the Offer

If the offer specifically stipulates the means of communication to be used by the offeree, the acceptance must conform to that specification. Thus, if an offer states that acceptance must be made by registered mail, any purported acceptance not made by registered mail would be ineffective. Moreover, the rule that an acceptance is effective when dispatched or sent does not apply where the offer provides that the acceptance must be received by the offeror. If the offeror states that a reply must be received by a certain date or that he must hear from the offeree, or uses other language indicating that the acceptance must be received by him, the effective moment of the acceptance is when it is received by the offeror and not when it is sent or dispatched by the offeree.

Acceptance Following a Prior Rejection

After dispatching a rejection, an acceptance is not effective when sent by the offeree, but only when and if received by the offeror prior to his receipt of the rejection. Thus, when an acceptance follows a prior rejection, the *first communication* received by the offeror is the effective one. For example, Carlos in New York sends by air mail to Paula in San Francisco an offer that is expressly stated to be open for one week. On the fourth day Paula sends to Carlos by air mail a letter of rejection which is delivered on the morning of the sixth day. At noon on the fifth day Paula dispatches a telegram of acceptance that is received by Carlos before the close of business on that day. A contract was formed when Paula's telegram of acceptance was received by Carlos.

Defective Acceptances

A late acceptance or defective acceptance does not create a contract. After the offer has expired, it cannot be accepted. However, a late or defective acceptance does manifest a willingness on the part of the offeree to enter into a contract and therefore constitutes a new offer. In order to create a contract

---

FIGURE 8-1   Offer and Acceptance

	Time Effective	Effect
Communications by Offeror		
Offer	Received by offeree	Creates power to form a contract
Revocation	Received by offeree	Terminates power
Communications by Offeree		
Rejection	Received by offeror	Terminates offer
Counter-offer	Received by offeror	Terminates offer
Acceptance	Sent by offeree	Forms a contract
Acceptance after prior rejection	Received by offeror	If received before rejection, forms a contract

based on this offer, the original offeror must accept the new offer by manifesting his assent to the original offeree.

Mode of Acceptance

Silence as Acceptance

An offeree is generally under no legal duty to reply to an offer. Silence or inaction is therefore *not* an acceptance of the offer. However, by custom, usage, or course of dealing, silence or inaction by the offeree may operate as an acceptance.

Salespeople employed by a manufacturing company or by a distributor to solicit orders for its merchandise from its customers frequently have no authority to bind their employer by contract. The order forms often recite that no contract is formed until the order of the buyer is accepted at the home office of the seller. On receipt of purchase orders, however, the manufacturer or distributor is under a duty to notify the customer within a reasonable time of its nonacceptance in the event of its inability or unwillingness to ship the merchandise ordered. Silence or inaction by the soliciting company *is* treated as an acceptance of the order.

Furthermore, if an offeror sends unordered or unsolicited merchandise to a person with an offer stating that the goods are sent for examination, that the addressee may purchase the goods at a specified price, and that unless the goods are returned within a stated period of time the offer will be deemed to have been accepted, the offer is one for an inverted unilateral contract (i.e., an act for a promise). However, this practice led to abuse, which has prompted the Federal government as well as most States to enact statutes providing that in such cases the offeree-recipient of the goods may keep them as a gift and is under no obligation either to return them or to pay for them.

Contract Formed by Conduct

A contract may be formed by conduct. Thus there may be no definite offer and acceptance, or definite acceptance of an offer, yet a contract exists if both of the parties have acted in a manner that manifests a recognition by each of them of the existence of a contract. Recognition may result from the cumulative effect of a number of occurrences or events indicating the reliance of both parties on the existence of a contract. Thus it may be impossible to determine the exact moment when such a contract formed by conduct was made.

Auction Sales

The auctioneer at an auction sale does not make offers to sell the property being auctioned but invites offers to buy. The classic statement by the auctioneer is, "How much am I offered?" The persons attending the auction may make progressively higher bids for the property, and each bid or statement of a price or a figure is an offer to buy at that figure. If the bid is accepted, which is customarily indicated by the fall of the hammer in the hands of the auctioneer, a contract results. A bidder is free to withdraw his bid at any time prior to its acceptance. The auctioneer is likewise free to withdraw the goods from sale *unless* the sale is advertised or announced to be without reserve.

If the auction sale is advertised or announced in explicit terms to be **without reserve,** the auctioneer may not withdraw an article or lot put up for

Without reserve–auctioneer may not withdraw the goods from the auction sale unless no bid is made within a reasonable time. Unless so advertised or announced, the sale is with reserve. Whether with or without reserve, a bidder may retract his bid at any time prior to acceptance by the auctioneer. Such retraction does not revive any previous bid.

Under the Code, if the auctioneer knowingly receives a bid by or on behalf of the seller, and notice has not been given that the seller reserves the right to bid at the auction sale, any such bid by or on behalf of the seller gives the bidder to whom the goods are sold an election either (1) to avoid the sale or (2) to take the goods at the price of the last good faith bid.

CHAPTER SUMMARY

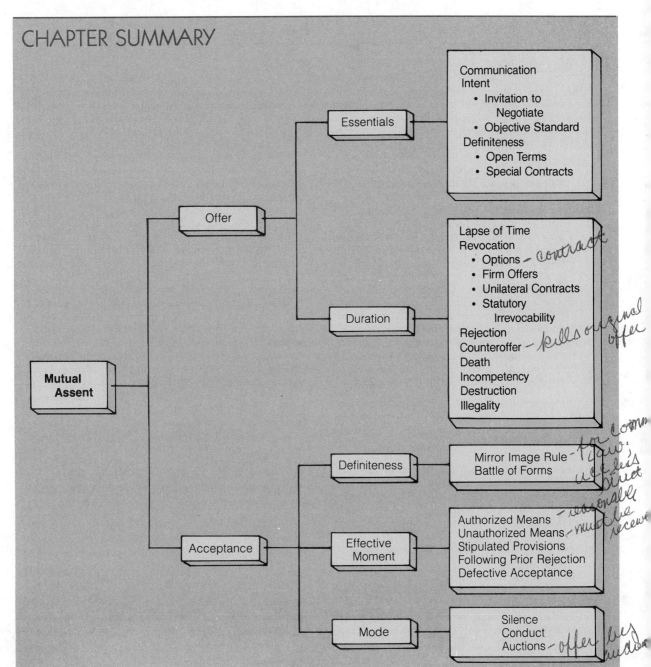

KEY TERMS

Offer	Firm offer	Battle of forms
Offeror	Merchant	Standardized contract
Offeree	Rejection	Authorized means
Objective standard	Counteroffer	Unauthorized means
Revocation	Conditional acceptance	Without reserve
Option	Mirror image rule	

PROBLEMS

1. Ames, seeking business for his lawn maintenance firm, posted the following notice in the meeting room of the Antlers, a local lodge: "To the members of the Antlers—Special this month. I will resod your lawn for two dollars per square foot using Fairway brand sod. This offer expires July 15."

The notice also included Ames's name, address, and signature and specified that the acceptance was to be in writing.

Bates, a member of the Antlers, and Cramer, the janitor, read the notice and became interested. Bates wrote a letter to Ames saying he would accept the offer if Ames would use Putting Green brand sod. Ames received this letter July 14 and wrote to Bates saying he would not use Putting Green sod. Bates received Ames's letter on July 16 and promptly wrote Ames that he would accept Fairway sod. Cramer wrote to Ames on July 10, saying he accepted Ames's offer.

By July 15, Ames had found more profitable ventures and refused to resod either lawn at the specified price. Bates and Cramer brought an appropriate action against Ames for breach of contract. Decision as to the respective claims of Bates and Cramer?

2. Justin owned four speedboats named Porpoise, Priscilla, Providence, and Prudence. On April 2, Justin made written offers to sell the four boats in the order named for $4,200 each to Charles, Diane, Edward and Fran, respectively, allowing ten days for acceptance. In which, if any, of the following four situations described was a contract formed?

(a) Five days later, Charles received notice from Justin that he had contracted to sell Porpoise to Mark. The next day, April 8, Charles notified Justin that he accepted Justin's offer.

(b) On the third day, April 5, Diane mailed a rejection to Justin that reached Justin on the morning of the fifth day. At 10 A.M., on the fourth day, Diane sent an acceptance by telegram to Justin, who received it at noon the same day.

(c) Edward, on April 3, replied that he was interested in buying Providence but declared the price

asked appeared slightly excessive and wondered if, perhaps, Justin would be willing to sell the boat for $3,900. Five days later, having received no reply from Justin, Edward accepted Justin's offer by letter, and enclosed a certified check for $4,200.

(d) Fran was accidently killed in an automobile accident on April 9. The following day, the executor of her estate mailed an acceptance of Justin's offer to Justin.

3. Alpha Rolling Mill Corporation, by letter dated June 8, offered to sell Brooklyn Railroad Company 2,000 to 5,000 tons of fifty-pound iron rails on certain specified terms and added that, if the offer was accepted, Alpha Corporation would expect to be notified prior to June 20. Brooklyn Company, on June 16, by telegram, referring to Alpha Corporation's offer of June 8, directed Alpha Corporation to enter an order for 1,200 tons of fifty-pound iron rails on the terms specified. The same day, June 16, Brooklyn Company, by letter to Alpha Corporation, confirmed the telegram. On June 18, Alpha Corporation, by telegram, declined to fulfill the order. Brooklyn Company, on June 19, telegraphed Alpha Corporation: "Please enter an order for 2,000 tons rails as per your letter of the eighth. Please forward written contract. Reply." To Brooklyn Company's repeated inquiries whether the order for 2,000 tons of rails had been entered, Alpha denied the existence of any contract between Brooklyn Company and itself. Thereafter, Brooklyn Company sues Alpha Corporation for breach of contract. Decision?

4. On April 8, Crystal received a telephone call from Akers, a truck dealer, who told Crystal that a new model truck in which Crystal was interested would arrive in one week. Although Akers initially wanted $10,500, the conversation ended after Akers agreed to sell and Crystal to purchase the truck for $10,000, with $1,000 down payment and the balance on delivery. The next day, Crystal sent Akers a check for $1,000, which Akers promptly cashed.

One week later, when Crystal called Akers and inquired about the truck, Akers informed Crystal he had several prospects looking at the truck and would not sell for less than $10,500. The following day Akers sent Crystal a properly executed check for $1,000 with the following notation thereon: "Return of down payment on sale of truck."

After notifying Akers that she will not cash the check, Crystal sues Akers for damages. Decision?

5. On November 15, I. Sellit, a manufacturer of crystalware, mailed to Benny Buyer a letter stating that Sellit would sell to Buyer 100 crystal "A" goblets at $100 per goblet and that "the offer would remain open for fifteen (15) days." On November 18, Sellit, noticing the sudden rise in the price of crystal "A" goblets, decided to withdraw his offer to Buyer and so notified Buyer. Buyer chose to ignore Sellit's letter of revocation and gleefully watched as the price of crystal "A" goblets continued to skyrocket. On November 30, Buyer mailed to Sellit a letter accepting Sellit's offer to sell the goblets. The letter was received by Sellit on December 4. Buyer demands delivery of the goblets. What result?

6. On May 1, Melforth Realty Company offered to sell Greenacre to Dallas, Inc., for $1,000,000. The offer was made by telegraph and stated that the offer would expire on May 15. Dallas decided to purchase the property and sent a registered letter to Melforth on May 10, accepting the offer. Due to unexplained delays in the postal service, the letter was not received by Melforth until May 22. Melforth wishes to sell Greenacre to another buyer, who is offering $1,200,000 for the tract of land. Has a contract resulted between Melforth and Dallas?

7. Rowe advertised in newspapers of wide circulation and otherwise made known that she would pay $5,000 for a complete set consisting of ten volumes of certain rare books. Ford, not knowing of the offer, gave Rowe all but one of the set of rare books as a Christmas present. Ford later learned of the offer, obtained the one remaining book, tendered it to Rowe, and demanded the $5,000. Rowe refused to pay. Is Ford entitled to the $5,000?

8. Scott, manufacturer of a carbonated beverage, entered into a contract with Otis, owner of a baseball park, whereby Otis rented to Scott a large signboard on top of the center field wall. The contract provided that Otis should letter the sign as desired by Scott and would change the lettering from time to time within forty-eight hours after receipt of written request from Scott. As directed by Scott, the signboard originally stated in large letters that Scott would pay $100 to any ball player hitting a home run over the sign.

In the first game of the season, Hume, the best hitter in the league, hit one home run over the sign. Scott immediately served written notice on Otis instructing Otis to replace the offer on the signboard with an offer to pay fifty dollars to every pitcher who pitched a no hit game in the park. A week after receipt of Scott's letter, Otis had not changed the wording on the sign, and on that day Perry, a pitcher for a scheduled game, pitched a no hit game and Todd, one of his teammates, hit a home run over Scott's sign.

Scott refuses to pay any of the three players. What are the rights of Scott, Hume, Perry, and Todd?

9. B accepted C's offer to sell to him a portion of C's coin collection. C forgot that his prized twenty-dollar gold piece at the time of the offer and acceptance was included in the portion that he offered to sell to B. C did not intend to include the gold piece in the sale. B, at the time of inspecting the offered portion of the collection, and prior to accepting the offer, saw the gold piece. Is B entitled to the twenty-dollar gold piece?

10. Small, admiring Jasper's watch, asked Jasper where and at what price he had purchased it. Jasper replied: "I bought it at West Watch Shop about two years ago for around $85, but I am not certain as to that." Small then said: "Those fellows at West are good people and always sell good watches. I'll buy that watch from you." Jasper replied: "It's a deal." The next morning Small telephoned Jasper and said he had changed his mind and did not wish to buy the watch.

Jasper sued Small for breach of contract. In defense, Small has pleaded that he made no enforceable contract with Jasper because (a) the parties did not agree on the price to be paid for the watch and (b) the parties did not agree on the place and time of delivery of the watch to Small. Are either, or both, of these defenses good?

CONDUCT INVALIDATING ASSENT

In Chapter 8 we considered one of the essential requirements of a contract, namely, the objective manifestation of mutual assent by each party to the other. This chapter deals with situations in which the manifested consent by one of the parties to the contract is not effective because it was not knowingly and voluntarily given. We consider five such situations in this chapter: duress, undue influence, fraud, misrepresentation, and mistake.

Duress

A person should not be held to an agreement that he has not entered into voluntarily. Accordingly, the law will not enforce any contract induced by duress, which consists of improper physical or mental coercion. There are two basic types of duress. The first occurs when a party is compelled to manifest assent to contract through actual **physical force,** such as pointing a gun at a person or taking a person's hand and compelling him to sign a written contract. This type of duress is extremely rare, but it renders the agreement **void,** as in the next case.

Duress–improper physical or mental coercion

Physical duress–coercion involving physical force or the threat of physical force

STATE v. ROLLINS

Supreme Court of Rhode Island, 1976.
116 RI 528, 359 A.2d 315.

FACTS: Rollins and Marchetti, two inmates of the Adult Correctional Institution in Rhode Island, led a takeover of one of the prison's cellblocks. In the process, they locked Picard, a uniformed correctional officer, in one of the emptied cells. With the cellblock completely overrun and Picard a hostage, Rollins made several demands upon prison officials, threatening possible bloodshed if the State Police were called in. Travisano, the director of the Department of Corrections, out of fear for the safety of Officer Picard, agreed to meet all but two of the prisoners' list of nine demands. Picard was then released by the prisoners. Rollins and Marchetti were subsequently convicted of assault, extortion and kidnapping and sentenced each to 20 years. They appeal, claiming that during the hostage negotiations Travisano, acting in his capacity as Director of the Department of Corrections, had promised them immunity from prosecution.

DECISION: Judgment for the State. Travisano's promise of immunity was extorted by Rollins and Marchetti using Officer Picard as a hostage and threatening bloodshed. His promise, extorted through violence and coercion (physical duress), is no promise at all. The promise is void from the beginning and unenforceable as a matter of public policy.

The second type of duress involves the use of **improper threats** or acts, including economic and social coercion, to compel a person to enter into a contract. The threat may be explicit or it may be inferred from the words or conduct. This type of duress makes the contract **voidable** at the option of the coerced party. For example, if A, a landlord, induces B, an infirm bedridden tenant, to enter into a new lease on the same apartment at a greatly increased rent by wrongfully threatening to terminate B's lease and evict her, B can avoid the new lease by reason of duress exerted on her. The next case illustrates how economic duress venders a contract voidable.

INTERNATIONAL UNDERWATER CONTRACTORS, INC. v. NEW ENGLAND TELEPHONE AND TELEGRAPH COMPANY Appeals Court of Massachusetts, Suffolk, 1979. 8 Mass.App. 340, 393 N.E.2d 968.	**FACTS:** International Underwater Contractors, Inc. (IUC) entered into a written contract with New England Telephone and Telegraph Company (NET) to assemble and install certain conduits under the Mystic River for a lump sum price of $149,680. Delays caused by NET forced IUC's work to be performed in the winter months instead of during the summer as originally bid, and as a result a major change had to be made in the system from that specified in the contract. NET repeatedly assured IUC that it would pay the cost if IUC would complete the work. The change cost IUC an additional $811,810.73; nevertheless, it signed a release settling the claim for a total sum of $575,000. IUC, which at the time was in financial trouble, now seeks to recover the balance due arguing that the signed release is not binding because it was signed under economic duress. **DECISION:** Judgment for IUC. A release signed under economic pressure illegally or immorally applied is not binding. To prove that the release was signed under economic duress, IUC must show that: (1) one side involuntarily accepted the terms of the other; (2) the circumstances permitted no other alternative; and (3) the circumstances were the result of the coercive acts of the other party. Merely taking advantage of another's financial difficulty is not duress; rather, the party claiming duress must show that its financial difficulty was contributed to or caused by the one accused of coercion. Here NET insisted on the change in the contract and repeatedly assured IUC that it would pay the substantial additional cost if IUC would complete the work. Furthermore, NET refused to make payments for almost a year, which in turn caused IUC's financial difficulties. Other factors also indicate the existence of economic duress including the unequal bargaining power of the two parties and the dispartiy among IUC's actual costs ($811,816.73), the amount NET's engineers had recommended for settlement ($775,000), and the final amount offered on a take-it-or-leave-it basis with the release ($575,000).

In the second and more common type of duress, the fact that the act or threat would not affect a person of average strength and intelligence is not important if it places the particular person in fear and induces an action against his will. The test is **subjective,** and the question is, did the threat actually induce assent on the part of the person claiming to be the victim of duress. Threats that would suffice to induce assent by one person may not suffice to induce assent by another. All circumstances must be considered, including the age, background, and relationship of the parties.

Ordinarily, the acts or threats constituting duress are themselves crimes or torts. But this is not true in all cases. The acts need not be criminal or tortious in order to be *wrongful;* they merely need be contrary to public policy or morally reprehensible. For example, if the threat involves a breach of a contractual duty of good faith and fair dealing or the use of the civil process in bad faith, it is improper.

Moreover, it has generally been held that contracts induced by threats of criminal prosecution are voidable, regardless of whether the coerced party had committed an unlawful act. Similarly, a threat of criminal prosecution of a close relative, as in the case of *Great American Indemnity Co. v. Berryessa*, is also duress. To be distinguished are threats to resort to ordinary civil remedies in order to recover a debt due from another. It is not wrongful to threaten to bring a civil suit against an individual to recover a debt. What is prohibited is the use of a threat of criminal prosecution to induce a contract.

GREAT AMERICAN INDEMNITY CO. v. BERRYESSA

Supreme Court of Utah, 1952.
122 Utah 243, 248 P.2d 367.

FACTS: Frank Berryessa stole funds from his employer, the Eccles Hotel Company. His father, W. S. Berryessa, learned of his son's trouble and, thinking the amount involved was about $2000, gave the hotel a promissory note for $2,186 to cover the shortage. In return, the hotel agreed not to publicize the incident nor to notify the bonding company. (A bonding company is paid a premium for agreeing to reimburse an employer for thefts by an employee.) However, before this note became due, the hotel discovered that Frank had actually misappropriated $6,865. The hotel then notified its bonding company, Great American Indemnity Company, to collect the entire loss. W. S. Berryessa claims that the agent for Great American told him that unless he paid them $2,000 in cash and signed a note for the remaining $4,865 that Frank would be prosecuted. Berryessa agreed, signed the note and gave the agent a cashier's check for $1,500 and a personal check for $500. He requested that the agent not cash the personal check for about a month. Subsequently, Great American sued Berryessa on the note. He defends against the note on the grounds of duress and counterclaims for the return of the $1,500 and the cancellation of the uncashed $500 check.

DECISION: Judgment for Berryessa on the $4,865 note; judgment for Great American on the two checks. Berryessa gave the $4,865 note to Great American in return for its promise to refrain from criminal prosecution of his son. The note was therefore obtained by duress and voidable by Berryessa. On the other hand, Berryessa had given the hotel the note for $2,186 voluntarily, with no coercion or threat of his son's prosecution. Since the $1,500 and $500 checks substituted for that note, Berryessa is not entitled to recover them under a claim of duress.

Undue Influence

Undue influence is taking unfair advantage of a person by reason of a dominant position based on a relationship of trust and confidence. The law has traditionally scrutinized very carefully contracts between those in a relationship of trust and confidence that is likely to permit one party to exert unfair persuasion on the other. Examples are the relationships of guardian and ward, trustee and beneficiary, principal and agent, husband and wife, parent and child, attorney and client, physician and patient, and clergyman and parishioner.

Where one party is under the domination of another, or because of the relationship between them is justified in assuming that the other party will not act in a manner inconsistent with his welfare, a transaction induced by unfair persuasion on the part of the latter is induced by undue influence and is **voidable.** The ultimate question in undue influence cases is whether the transaction was induced by dominating the mind or emotions of a submissive party. The weakness or dependence of the person persuaded is a strong circumstance tending to show that persuasion may have been unfair. For example, Abigail, a person without business experience, has for years been accustomed to rely in business matters on the advice of Boris, who is experienced in business. Boris, without making any false representations of fact, induces Abigail to enter into a contract with Boris' confederate, Cassius, that

Undue influence–taking unfair advantage of a person by reason of a dominant position based on a relationship of trust and confidence

is disadvantageous to Abigail, as both Boris and Cassius knew. The transaction is voidable on the grounds of undue influence.

SCHANEMAN v. SCHANEMAN

Supreme Court of Nebraska, 1980.
206 Neb. 113, 291 N.W.2d 412.

FACTS: Conrad Schaneman is a Russian immigrant who can neither read nor write the English language. In 1975, Conrad deeded (conveyed) a farm he owned to his eldest son, Laurence, for $23,500 which was the original purchase price of the property in 1945. The value of the farm in 1975 was between $145,000 and $160,000. At the time he executed the deed, Conrad was an 82 year old invalid, severely ill and completely dependent on others for his personal needs. He weighed between 325 and 350 pounds, had difficulty breathing, could not walk more than 15 feet and needed a special jackhoist to get in and out of the bathtub. Conrad enjoyed a long-standing, confidential relationship with Laurence, who was his principal advisor and handled Conrad's business affairs. Laurence also obtained a power of attorney from Conrad and made himself a joint owner of Conrad's bank account and $20,000 certificate of deposit. Conrad brought this suit to cancel the deed, claiming it was the result of Laurence's undue influence over Conrad.

DECISION: Judgment for Conrad Schaneman. A confidential or fiduciary relationship exists between two persons if one has gained the confidence of the other and purports to act or advise with the other's interest in mind. In such a relationship the court will scrutinize critically any transaction between the two parties, especially where age, infirmity, and instability are involved, to see that no injustice has occurred.

Here, the evidence shows that a confidential relationship existed between Conrad and Laurence, and that due to age and physical infirmities, Conrad was, for all intents and purposes, an invalid at the time of the conveyance. It further supports a finding that Conrad's mental acuity was impaired at times and that he sometimes suffered from disorientation and lapse of memory. Conrad was subject to the influence of Laurence, who was acting in a confidential relationship; that the opportunity to exercise undue influence existed; that there was a disposition on the part of Laurence to exercise such undue influence; and that the conveyance appears to be the effect of such influence. Accordingly, the deed is cancelled for undue influence.

Fraud

Another factor affecting the validity of consent manifested by a contracting party is fraud. Fraud prevents the assent from being knowingly given. There are two distinct types of fraud: fraud in the execution and fraud in the inducement.

Fraud in the Execution

Fraud in the execution misrepresentation that deceives the other party as to the nature of a document evidencing the contract

This type of fraud, which is extremely rare, consists of a misrepresentation deceiving the defrauded person as to the very nature of the contract. In this situation the innocent party is entirely unaware that he is entering into a contract and has no intention of doing so. For example, A delivers a package to B, requests B to sign a receipt for it, holds out a simple printed form headed "Receipt," and indicates the line on which B is to sign. This line appears to B to be the bottom line of the form, but instead it is the bottom line of a promissory note cleverly concealed underneath the receipt. B signs where directed without knowing that he is signing a note. This is fraud in the execution. The note is **void** and of no legal effect. The reason is simply that, although the signature is genuine and appears to be a manifestation of assent to the terms of the note, there is no actual assent. The nature of A's fraud precluded consent to the signing of the note because it prevented B from knowing what he was signing.

Fraud in the Inducement

Fraud in the inducement, generally referred to as fraud or deceit, is an intentional misrepresentation of material fact by one party to the other who consents to enter into a contract in reliance on the misrepresentation. For example, Alice, in offering to sell her dog to Bob, tells Bob that the dog won first prize in its class in the recent National Dog Show. In fact, the dog had not even been entered in the show. This statement induces Bob to accept the offer and pay a high price for the dog. There is a contract, but it is **voidable** by Bob because Alice's fraud induced his assent.

The requisite elements of fraud in the inducement are:

1. a false representation
2. of a fact
3. that is material
4. and made with knowledge of its falsity and the intention to deceive
5. that is justifiably relied on.

False Representation   A basic element of fraud is a false representation. There must be some positive statement or conduct that misleads. As a general rule, silence alone does *not* amount to fraud. There is generally no obligation on the part of a seller to tell a purchaser everything he knows about the subject of the sale, although if there is a latent (hidden) defect of a substantial character, one that would not be discovered by an ordinary examination, the seller is obliged to reveal it.

There are other situations in which the law imposes a duty of disclosure. For example, a person may have a duty of disclosure because of prior representations innocently made that are later discovered to be untrue before making a contract. Thus, A makes a true statement of his financial condition, intending that its substance be published to B's subscribers. B summarizes the information and transmits the summary to C, a subscriber. Shortly thereafter, A's financial condition becomes seriously impaired, but he does not disclose this to B. C makes a contract to lend money to A. A's failure to disclose is equivalent to an assertion that his financial condition is not seriously impaired, and this assertion is a misrepresentation.

Another instance in which silence may constitute fraud is a transaction involving a fiduciary. A **fiduciary** is a person who owes a duty of trust, loyalty, and confidence to another. For example, an agent owes a fiduciary duty to his principal, as does a trustee to the beneficiary of the trust and a partner to her copartners. A fiduciary may not deal at *arm's length* but rather owes a duty to make full disclosure of all relevant facts when he enters into a transaction with the other party to the relationship. In contrast, in most business transactions the parties deal at arm's length, that is, on equal terms. Accordingly neither party is required to make disclosures to the other.

Active **concealment** can likewise form the basis for fraud, as where a seller puts heavy oil or grease in a car engine to conceal a knock. Truth may be suppressed by concealment quite as much as by active misrepresentation. An express denial of knowledge of a fact that a party knows to exist, or the statement of misleading half-truth, can be fraudulent. Such conduct is clearly

Fraud in the inducement–misrepresentation regarding the subject matter of a contract and inducing the other party to enter into it

Fiduciary–person who owes a duty of trust, loyalty and confidence to another

more than mere silence and is considered the equivalent of a false representation.

Fact   The basic element of fraud is the misrepresentation of a material fact; actionable fraud can rarely be based on what is merely a statement of **opinion.** A representation is one of opinion if it expresses only the belief of the representor as to the existence of a fact or his judgment as to quality, value, authenticity, or other matters of judgment. The line between fact and opinion is not an easy one to draw and in close cases presents an issue for the jury. Suppose that Ellen induces Dan to purchase shares in a company unknown to Dan at a price of $100 per share by stating that she had paid $150 per share for them the preceding year, when in fact she had paid only $50 per share. This is a representation of a past event, definitely ascertainable, verifiable, and therefore fraudulent. If, on the other hand, Ellen said to Dan that

Law In The News

Realty and reality
Must toxic dump be revealed?

By Cheryl Frank

William Jackson and his wife and family were ready to settle down in Gloucester Township, N.J. He says they told their real estate agent they wanted to keep their children far from poisonous chemicals but were shocked to discover—even after a favorable property inspection report—that they were sold a home near a toxic landfill.

They refused to move in, and the case has gone to court.

"It [toxic wastes on or near property] is a growing area of concern. We are getting an increasing number of reports or complaints" from people who own homes near such sites, said William North, counsel to the National Association of Realtors in Chicago.

Duty to 'disclose facts'

North said the duties of real estate agents and brokers are not always clear. For example, he asked, who should test the soil and

decide when wastes are at a toxic level?

Last year California's First District Court of Appeal held that a real estate agent had a duty "to conduct a reasonably competent and diligent inspection" and "to disclose material facts" and "adverse factors" that the agent "should have known" (*Easton v. Strassburger,* 199 Cal.Rptr. 383).

Jackson said his home inspection report was enthusiastic. The couple put $1,000 down.

But they refused to move in after a neighbor told them about the nearby landfill operated by Gloucester Environmental Management Systems, or GEMS. The lending bank and several other plaintiffs sued the Jacksons for backing out of the deal. The Jacksons countersued, claiming that agents, inspectors and others failed to disclose information on the environmental hazard.

"Naturally, I'm very angry," Jackson said. "The banker used

the state's money to defraud me." State officials are looking into how its mortgage money is spent, he said.

'Is it fraud?'

The lawsuits have been consolidated and may plow new legal ground, said Jackson's lawyer, Arnold Feldman of Camden. He said the bank and others "knew or should have known" of the landfill. His complaint alleges that "material facts" were concealed (*ATCO National Bank v. Jackson v. Watson,* No. C-3489-83, Camden County Superior Court).

Asks Feldman: "What is the duty of a seller in disclosing latent defects? Does the duty extend to latent property defects, and is it fraud for an appraiser to exclude a toxic waste dump from her appraisal when it is 1,000 feet from the property?"

.   *   *   *

the shares were "a good investment," she is merely stating her opinion, and in the usual case Dan ought to regard it as no more than that. Suppose, however, that Ellen said the company "had a good year last year," when in fact it failed to show a profit. Is this opinion or fact? It is difficult, if not impossible, to decide without additional evidence. The solution will often depend on the knowledgeability of the person making the statement and the information available to the other party. If the representor is a professional broker advising a client, the courts are more likely to regard an untrue statement of opinion as actionable. It is the expression of opinion of one holding himself out as having **expert** knowledge, and the tendency is to grant relief to those who have sustained loss by reasonable reliance on expert evaluation, as in the next case.

FACTS: Mrs. Audrey E. Vokes, a widow of fifty-one years and without family, purchased fourteen separate dance courses from J. P. Davenport's Arthur Murray, Inc., school of dance. The fourteen courses totaled in the aggregate 2,302 hours of dancing lessons at a total cost to Mrs. Vokes of $31,090.45. Mrs. Vokes was induced continually to reapply for new courses by representations made by Mr. Davenport that her dancing ability was improving, that she was responding to instructions, that she had excellent potential, and that they were developing her into an accomplished dancer. In fact, she had no dancing ability or aptitude and had trouble "hearing the musical beat." Mrs. Vokes brought this action to have the contracts set aside.	**VOKES v. ARTHUR MURRAY, INC.** District Court of Appeal of Florida, 1968. 212 So.2d 906.

DECISION: Judgment for Mrs. Vokes. Ordinarily, for a misrepresentation to be actionable, it must be one of fact rather than of opinion. Where, as here, however, a statement is made by a party having superior knowledge, that statement may be taken as one of fact although it would be considered as one of opinion if the parties were dealing on equal terms. Here it could be said that Mr. Davenport had superior knowledge as to Mrs. Voke's dancing potential and as to her degree of improvement and that he set those "facts" forth in a greatly exaggerated fashion to induce her to enter into new contracts. Even in contractual situations where a party to a transaction owes no duty to disclose facts within his knowledge or to answer inquiries as to those facts, if he undertakes to speak, he must disclose the whole truth.

The distinction between statements of fact and opinion is also considered in connection with sales of goods. Statements of **value,** such as "This is the best car for the money in town" or "This deluxe model will give you twice the wear of a cheaper model," are not grounds for the avoidance of a contract. Such exaggerations and commendations of articles offered for sale are to be expected from dealers who are merely **puffing** their wares with "sales talk."

Also to be distinguished from a representation of fact is a **prediction** of the future. Predictions are closely akin to opinions, as one cannot know with certainty what will happen in the future, and normally they are not regarded as factual statements. Likewise, promissory statements ordinarily do not constitute a basis of fraud, as a breach of promise does not necessarily indicate that the promise was fraudulently made. However, a promise which the promisor at the time of making had no intention of keeping is fraudulent as a misrepresentation of fact. Most courts take the position that the state of a person's mind, which is being misrepresented, "is as much a fact as the state of a person's digestion." If a dealer promises, "I will service this machine free for the next year," but at the time has no intention of doing so, his conduct is actionable if the other elements of fraud are present.

Misrepresentations of **law** are also generally distinguished from those of fact. Suppose that the seller of land induces a sale by misrepresenting that a certain zoning classification will permit the type of commercial activity contemplated by the purchaser or that the zoning ordinance is unconstitutional as applied to the property. Has he made a misrepresentation of fact? Practically all courts will agree that he has not. Rather, he has misrepresented the state of the law, and since everyone is presumed to know the law, the purchaser is not justified in relying on the seller's representation of this type, and the sale is not fraudulent. There are, however, a few exceptions to this rule. If the seller occupies a fiduciary or confidential relationship with the purchaser, the latter will be able to avoid the transaction. A misrepresentation by one who is learned in the law, as a practicing attorney, may under certain circumstances be fraudulent.

The next case shows that the basic requirement in a fraud case is a misrepresentation of fact.

TRUSTEES OF COLUMBIA UNIVERSITY v. JACOBSEN

Superior Court of New Jersey, Appellate Division, 1959.
53 N.J.Super. 574, 148 A.2d 63.

FACTS: Columbia University brought suit against Jacobsen on two notes signed by him and his parents, representing the balance of tuition he owed the University. Jacobsen counterclaimed for money damages due to Columbia's deceit or fraudulent misrepresentation. Jacobsen argues that Columbia fraudulently misrepresented that it would teach wisdom, truth, character, enlightenment and similar virtues and qualities. He specifically cites as support the Columbia motto: "*in lumine tuo videbimus lumen*" (In your light we shall see light"); the inscription over the college chapel: "Wisdom dwelleth in the heart of him that hath understanding"; and various excerpts from its brochures, catalogues, and a convocation address made by the University's president. Jacobsen, a senior who was not graduated because of poor scholastic standing, claims that the University's failure to meet its promises made through these quotations constituted fraudulent misrepresentation or deceit.

DECISION: Judgment for Columbia University. The necessary elements of an action for deceit are: (1) a false representation; (2) knowledge or belief on the part of the person making the representation that it is false; (3) an intention that the other party act thereon; (4) reasonable reliance by such party in so doing; and (5) resultant damage to him. Here, the quotations in the University's brochures and catalogues, inscriptions over its buildings, and speech by its president merely indicated Columbia's objectives, desires, and hopes together with factual statements as to the nature of some of the courses included in its curricula. There is nothing in these statements to establish that Columbia represented that it would teach wisdom. Jacobsen's interpretation of them as a representation, express or implied, that it could or would teach wisdom and the like is entirely subjective and irrational. Wisdom is not a subject that can be taught and no reasonable person would accept such a claim made by any man or institution. Therefore, there is no false representation upon which to base an action in deceit.

Material–of substantial importance

Materiality   In addition to the requirement that the misrepresentation be one of fact, it is necessary that it be material. It must relate to something of sufficient substance to induce reliance. In the sale of a race horse it may not be material whether the horse was ridden in its most recent race by a certain jockey, but its running time for the race probably would be. In determining the materiality of a representation, courts look to the impression made on the mind of the party to whom it was made. It is usually material if, but for the representation, he would not have entered into the transaction. Most courts deem the misrepresentation to be material if, to a substantial degree, it influenced the making of a decision, even though it was not the decisive factor.

Knowledge of Falsity and Intention to Deceive   To establish fraud the misrepresentation must have been known by the one making it to be false and must be made with an intention to deceive. This element of fraud is called **scienter.** Knowledge of falsity can consist of (a) actual knowledge, (b) lack of belief in the statement's truthfulness, or (c) reckless indifference as to its truthfulness.

Fraud–misrepresentation known to be false and intended to mislead

Scienter–guilty knowledge

Justifiable Reliance   A person is not entitled to relief unless he has justifiably relied on the misrepresentation to his detriment or injury. If the complaining party's decision was in no way influenced by the misrepresentation, he must abide by the terms of the contract. He is not deceived if he does not rely. Moreover, if the complaining party knew or should have known that the representation of the defendant was untrue, but still entered into the contract, he has not justifiably relied. For example, Paul, seeking to purchase a six-passenger car, was told by the salesman that a two-seat sports car was appropriate and took Paul for a test drive. If Paul, nevertheless, relied on the salesman's statement, such reliance would not be justified, and Paul would not have been legally defrauded.

GARDNER v. MEILING

Supreme Court of Oregon, 1977.
280 Or. 665, 572 P.2d 1012.

FACTS: In February 1976, Gardner, a school teacher with no experience in running a tavern, entered into a contract to purchase for $40,000 the Punjab Tavern from Meiling. The contract was contingent upon Gardner's obtaining a five year lease for the Tavern's premises and a liquor license from the State. Prior to the formation of the contract Meiling had made no representations to Gardner concerning the gross income of the tavern. Approximately three months after the contract was signed, Gardner and Meiling met with an inspector from the Oregon Liquor Control Commission (OLCC) to discuss transfer of the liquor license. Meiling reported to the agent, in Gardner's presence, that the Tavern's gross income figures for February, March, and April, 1976, were $5,710, $4,918, and $5,009 respectively. The OLCC granted the required license, the transaction was closed, and Gardner took possession on June 10, 1976. After discovering that the Tavern's income was very low and had very few female patrons, Gardner contacted Meiling's bookkeeping service and learned that the actual gross income for those three months had been approximately $1,400 to $2,000. Gardner then sued for rescission of the contract based on Meiling's fraudulent misrepresentation of fact.

DECISION: Judgment for Meiling. To sustain a case of fraudulent misrepresentation, the injured party must prove that he actually relied upon the false representation, causing him to enter into the bargain. Meiling's only representations concerning the Tavern's gross income were made months after the contract was formed. Since these misrepresentations came after the binding agreement of February, they could not have been relied upon by Gardner in making the agreement. Therefore, rescission of the contract is not permitted.

Nonfraudulent Misrepresentation

At common law it was necessary for the injured party in a fraud action, whether seeking rescission or damages, to prove an intention by the defendant to deceive. Hence the necessity for showing knowledge of the falsity, or at least culpable ignorance. Today, a majority of courts permit a rescission for negligent or innocent (non-negligent) misrepresentation, provided, of course, that all of the remaining elements of fraud are present. Thus, a contract induced by negligent or innocent misrepresentation is **voidable.** Moreover, some courts also permit the recovery of damages for nonfraudulent misrepresentation.

Negligent misrepresentation–misrepresentation made without due care in ascertaining its falsity

Innocent misrepresentation–misrepresentation made without knowledge of its falsity but with due care

WHIPP v. IVERSON

Supreme Court of Wisconsin, 1969.
43 Wis.2d 166, 168 N.W.2d 201.

FACTS: Iverson owned Iverson Motor Company, an enterprise engaged in repair as well as the sale of Oldsmobile, Rambler, and International Harvester Scout automobiles. Forty percent of the business's sales volume and net earnings came from the Oldsmobile franchise.

Whipp contracted to buy Iverson Motors, which Iverson said included the Oldsmobile franchise. After the sale, however, General Motors refused to transfer the franchise to Whipp. Whipp then returned the property to Iverson and brought this action seeking rescission of the contract.

DECISION: Judgment for Whipp. Historically, an action for fraud required that the injured party show that the misrepresentation upon which it detrimentally relied was made with the speaker's knowledge of its falsity or with reckless disregard for the truth or falsity of the statement. Today, however, a cause of action may be based on an innocent misrepresentation. Here, Iverson represented that the Oldsmobile franchise was transferable when, in fact, it was not. That misrepresentation, even though innocently made, is voidable.

Mistake

Mistake is an understanding or belief that is not in accord with existing fact. An elusive branch of the law if that which is concerned with the effect of "mistake" on the formation of a contract. Certain problems have been settled, but many have not been. There is, however, one concept that runs through the cases and that will at least help to place the issues in a meaningful context as well as assist in predicting results. In Chapter 8, we gave attention to the standard by which the assent of the parties is to be tested. The courts favor an objective approach. A person is bound by the reasonable impression he has created in the mind of the other party, even if this differs from his own subjective intention.

An illustration is an offer in language manifesting an intention different from that actually intended by the offeror, a mistake resulting from carelessness, inattention, or failure to double check. This occurred in the case of A's offer to sell her Chevrolet when she intended to offer her Ford automobile. If the offer is accepted before it is corrected, A is bound by the intention that she manifested. In the absence of duress, fraud, or breach of fiduciary duty by the buyer, she has no legal remedy.

> **Mutual mistake**–where both parties have a common but erroneous belief forming the basis of a contract

The problem is, how far can the objective theory be extended in mistake cases? At what point is there a lack of "real consent"? The law grants relief in a situation involving mistake only where there has been a **mutual mistake of material fact** by both parties to the contract.

Existence or Identity of Subject Matter

Suppose A offers to sell B a certain boat but unknown to both parties the boat has been destroyed. If B accepts, is he entitled to damages on A's failure to deliver the boat as promised? He is not. The Code provides that, where the contract requires for its performance goods identified when the contract is made, and the goods suffer casualty without fault of either party before the risk of loss passes to the buyer, then, if the loss is total, the contract is avoided.

The rationale of this rule is based on the presumed intention of the parties in ordinary transactions; that is, *no subject matter, no contract.* To be distinguished is the case in which the parties are mutually mistaken, but the contract contemplates an assumption of the risk. For instance, a ship at sea may be sold "lost or not lost." In such case the buyer is liable whether the ship was lost or not lost at the time of the making of the contract. There is no mistake; instead, there is a conscious allocation of risk.

Possibly the most famous decision involving mutual mistake is *Raffles v. Wichelhaus*, 2 Hurlstone & Coltman 906 (1864), popularly known as the "Peerless Case." A contract of purchase was made for 125 bales of cotton to arrive on the Peerless from Bombay. It happened, however, that there were two ships by the name of "Peerless," each sailing from Bombay, one in October and the other in December. The buyer had in mind the ship that sailed in October, while the seller reasonably believed the agreement referred to the Peerless sailing in December. Neither party was at fault, but both believed in good faith that a different ship was intended. The English court held that no contract existed. The Restatement is in accord. There is no manifestation of mutual assent where the parties attach materially different meanings to their manifestations *and* neither party knows or has reason to know the meaning attached by the other. However, if blame can be ascribed to either party, he will be held responsible. Thus, if the seller knew of the sailing from Bombay of two ships by the name of Peerless, then he would be at fault, and the contract would be for the ship sailing in October as the buyer expected. If *neither* is to blame or *both* are to blame, there is **no** contract at all.

FACTS: Beginning in 1971, Treasure Salvors and the State of Florida entered into a series of four annual contracts governing the salvage of the *Nuestra Senora de Atocha*. The *Atocha* is a Spanish galleon which sank in 1622, carrying a treasure now worth well over $250 million. Both parties had contracted under the impression that that the seabed on which the *Atocha* lay was land owned by Florida. Treasure Salvors agreed to relinquish twenty-five percent of the items recovered in return for the right to salvage on State lands. In accordance with these contracts, Treasure Salvors delivered to Florida its share of the salvaged artifacts. In 1975, the United States Supreme Court held that the part of the continental shelf on which the *Atocha* was resting had *never* been owned by Florida. Treasure Salvors then brought suit to rescind the contracts and to recover the artifacts it had delivered to the State of Florida. **DECISION:** Judgment for Treasure Salvors. Both parties based their contracts upon the erroneous assumption that the State of Florida owned the land in question. But for this belief neither party would have entered into the agreements. The contracts are therefore voidable under the doctrine of mutual mistake of fact. Accordingly, Treasure Salvors may rescind the contracts and recover the artifacts delivered to the State of Florida.	**STATE OF FLORIDA, DEPARTMENT OF STATE v. TREASURE SALVORS, INC.** United States Court of Appeals, Fifth Circuit, 1980. 621 F.2d 1340.

Nature of Subject Matter

If Florence contracts to purchase Henry's automobile under the belief that she can sell it at a profit to Edmund, she obviously is not excused from liability if she is mistaken in this belief. Nor can she rescind the agreement simply because she was mistaken as to her estimate of what the automobile was worth. These are the ordinary risks of business, and courts do not undertake to relieve against them. But suppose that the parties contract on the assumption that the automobile is a 1984 Cadillac with 15,000 miles of use, when in fact the engine is that of a cheaper model and has been run in excess of 50,000 miles? Here, a court would likely allow a rescission because of mutual mistake respecting a material fact. Another example of mutual mistake of fact was presented in a California case where a noted violinist purchased two violins from a collector for $8,000, the bill of sale reading: ". . . I have on this date sold to Mr. Efrem Zimbalist one Joseph Guarnerius violin and one Stradivarius violin dated 1717." Actually, unknown to either party, neither violin was genuine. Taken together they were worth no more than $300. The sale was **voidable** by the purchaser for mutual mistake.

The foregoing cases are to be contrasted with situations in which the parties are aware that they do not know the character or value of the item sold. For example, the Supreme Court of Wisconsin refused to set aside the sale of a stone for which the purchaser paid one dollar, but which was subsequently discovered to be an uncut diamond valued at $700. The parties did not know at the time of sale what the stone was and knew they did not know. Each consciously assumed the risk that the value might be more or less than the selling price.

A mistake unknown to the party making it, however, becomes voidable if the other party recognizes it as a mistake. For example, suppose a building contractor submits a bid for a job that is one-half of what it should be, because he made a serious error in his computations. If the other party knows that he made such an error, or reasonably should have known of it, he cannot, as a general rule, take advantage of the other's mistake and accept the offer. In one such case the plaintiff, in computing his bid on a city sewer project, by mistake omitted the cost of one item, the steel. Accordingly, his bid was substantially lower than the others. He bid $429,444.20; the next higher bid was $671,600. All other bids were even higher. An estimate made by the city engineers, undisclosed to the bidders prior to the submission of the bids, was $632,000. The plaintiff received a sympathetic ear from the Oregon Supreme Court, which stated in the course of its opinion: "It is our belief that although the plaintiff alone made the mistake, the City was aware of it. When it accepted the plaintiff's bid, with knowledge of the mistake, it sought to take an unconscionable advantage of an inadvertent error." *Rushlight Automatic Sprinkler Co. v. City of Portland,* 189 Or. 194, 219 P.2d 732 (1950). Some courts refer to a case of this type as one of **palpable unilateral mistake,** to distinguish it from the situation where the other had no suspicion nor any good reason to suspect that an error had been committed. In the latter type of case no judicial relief from the unilateral mistake is available.

Unilateral mistake–erroneous belief on the part of only one of the parties to a contract

Failure to Read Document

As a general proposition, a party is held to what she signs. Her signature authenticates the writing, and she cannot repudiate that which she has voluntarily approved. As a Louisiana court expressed it: "Signatures to obligations are not mere ornaments." Generally, one who assents to a writing is presumed to know its contents and cannot escape being bound by its terms merely by contending that she did not read them; her assent is deemed to cover unknown as well as known terms. However, there are instances where one is relieved of obligations to which she has apparently assented; namely, where the character of the writing was misrepresented by the other party or where the writing was such that a reasonable person would not think it contained contractual provisions. An example of the latter would be a coat-check stub containing in fine print a limitation of the proprietor's liability in case of loss or damage to the item checked. Ordinarily, stubs of this type are used for identification purposes only; hence, in the usual case one is not held to have assented to the limitation of proprietor liability merely by accepting the stub.

Mistake of Law

In the absence of fraud, one cannot obtain a release from contractual liability on the ground that he did not understand the legal effect of the contract. Courts will not grant relief from a mistake of law. By the majority view in this country, one paying money to another under a mistake of law cannot recover that money even though it was not legally due, provided the payee's claim was asserted in good faith. There are, however, some exceptions. Payments made by governmental agencies or payments made to a court or court official under mistake of law are recoverable. The general reluctance to grant relief for mistake of law has been subjected to serious criticism and has been changed by statute in some States. In these States relief for mistake of law is placed upon the same basis as mutual mistake of a material fact.

FIGURE 9-1   Conduct Invalidating Assent

Conduct	Effect
Duress by physical force	Void
Duress by improper threats	Voidable
Undue influence	Voidable
Fraud in the execution	Void
Fraud in the inducement	Voidable
Non-Fraudulent Misrepresentation	Voidable
Mutual mistake of fact	Voidable

CHAPTER SUMMARY

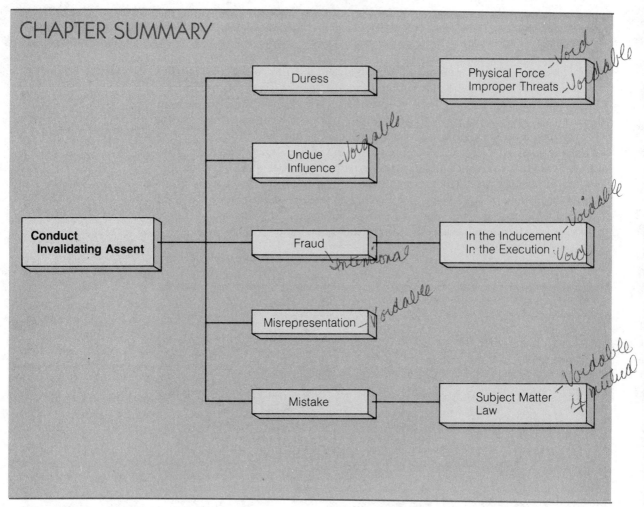

KEY TERMS

Duress

Physical duress

Undue influence

Fraud in the execution

Fraud in the inducement

Fiduciary

Material

Reliance

Fraud

Scienter

Negligent misrepresentation

Innocent misrepresentation

Mutual mistake

Unilateral mistake

Mistake of fact

Mistake of law

PROBLEMS

1. A and B were negotiating, and A's attorney prepared a long and carefully drawn contract that was given to B for examination. Five days later and prior to its execution, B's eyes became so infected that it was impossible for him to read. Ten days thereafter and during the continuance of the illness A called on B and urged him to sign the contract, telling him that time was running out. B signed the contract despite the fact he was unable to read it. In a subsequent action by A, B claimed that the contract was not binding on him because it was impossible for him to read and he did not know what it contained prior to his signing it. Decision?

2. (a) A tells B that he paid $150,000 for his farm in 1983, and that he believes it is worth twice that at the present time. Relying on these statements, B buys the farm from A for $225,000. A did pay $150,000 for the farm in 1983, but its value has increased only slightly, and it is presently not worth $300,000. On discovering this, B offers to reconvey the farm to A and sues for the return of his $225,000. Result?

(b) Modify the facts in (a) by assuming that A had paid $100,000 for the property in 1983. What result?

3. On September 1, A in Portland, Oregon, wrote a letter to B in New York City offering to sell to B 1,000 tons of chromite at forty-eight dollars per ton, to be shipped by S.S. Malabar sailing from Portland, Oregon, to New York City via the Panama Canal. Upon receiving the letter on September 5, B immediately mailed to A a letter stating that she accepted the offer. There were two ships by the name of S.S. Malabar sailing from Portland to New York City via the Panama Canal, one sailing in October and the other sailing in December. At the time of mailing her letter of acceptance B knew of both sailings and further knew that A knew only of the December sailing. Is there a contract? If so, to which S.S. Malabar does it relate?

4. A owes B, a police captain, $500. A threatens B that unless B gives him a discharge form the debt, A will disclose the fact that B has on several occasions become highly intoxicated and has been seen in the company of certain disreputable persons. B, induced by fear that such a disclosure would cost him his position or in any event lead to social disgrace, gives A a release, but subsequently sues to set it aside and recover on his claim. Decision?

5. A owned a farm that was worth about $600 an acre. By false representations of fact A induced B to buy the farm at $1,500 an acre. Shortly after taking possession of the farm, B discovered oil under the land. A, on learning this, sues to have the sale set aside on the ground that it was voidable because of fraud. Decision?

6. On February 2, A induced B to purchase from her fifty (50) shares of stock in the XYZ Corporation for $10,000, representing that the actual book value of each share was $200. A certificate for fifty (50) shares was delivered to B. On February 16, B discovered that the book value was only $50 per share on February 2. Thereafter, B sues A. Decision?

7. D mistakenly accused P's son, S, of negligently burning down D's barn. P believed that his son, S, was guilty of the wrong, and that he, P, was personally liable for the damage, since S was only fifteen years old. Upon demand made by D, P paid D $2,500 for the damage to D's barn. After making this payment, P learned that his son, S, had not caused the burning of D's barn and was in no way responsible for its burning. P then sued D to recover the $2,500 that he had paid D. Decision?

8. Jones, a farmer, found an odd-looking stone in his fields. He went to Smith, the town jeweler, and asked him what he thought it was. Smith said he did not know but thought it might be a ruby. Jones asked Smith what he would pay for it, and Smith said two hundred dollars; whereupon Jones sold it to Smith for $200. The stone turned out to be an uncut diamond worth $3,000. Jones brought an action against Smith to recover the stone. On trial, it was proved that Smith actually did not know the stone was a diamond when he bought it, but thought it might be a ruby. Decision?

9. Decedent, a bedridden, lonely woman of eighty-six years, owned outright Greenacre, her ancestral estate. F, her physician and friend, visited her weekly and was held in the highest regard by Decedent. Decedent was extremely fearful of pain and suffering and depended on F to ease her anxiety and pain. Several months before her death Decedent deeded Greenacre to F for $5,000. The fair market value of Greenacre at this time was $125,000. Decedent was survived by two children and six grandchildren. Decedent's children challenge the validity of the deed. Decision?

10

CONSIDERATION

To be binding, a promise or agreement must satisfy the requirement of legally sufficient consideration. If there is no consideration, neither party can enforce the promise or agreement. The doctrine of consideration has been used to ensure that promises are enforced only where the parties have exchanged something of value in the eye of the law. **Gratuitous** (gift) promises, accordingly, are not legally enforceable.

Consideration is whatever is given in exchange for something else. It is present only when the parties intend an exchange, whether it is a promise exchanged for a promise, a promise exchanged for an act, or a promise exchanged for a forbearance to act. Thus consideration has two basic elements: (1) legal sufficiency (something of value) and (2) bargained-for exchange. Both must be present to satisfy the requirement of consideration.

Legal Sufficiency

The doctrine of consideration requires that the promises or performance of *both* parties be legally sufficient. If the consideration is not mutual, the contract is void. To be legally sufficient, the promise must be something of "value in the eye of the law," either a benefit to the promisor **or** a detriment to the promisee.

Legal sufficiency–benefit to promisor or detriment to promisee

Definition

The definition of legal sufficiency is technical, and in certain cases its application produces an artificial result. To be legally sufficient, the consideration for the promise must be either a legal detriment to the promisee **or** a legal benefit to the promisor.

Legal detriment means (1) the doing (or undertaking to do) that which the promisee was under no prior legal obligation to do **or** (2) the refraining from doing (or undertaking to refrain from doing) that which he was previously under no legal obligation to refrain from doing. On the other hand, **legal benefit** means the obtaining by the promisor of that which he had no prior legal right to obtain.

Legal detriment–doing an act not legally obligated to do or not doing an act which one has a legal right to do

Legal benefit–obtaining something one had no legal right to

Unilateral Contracts

In unilateral contract a promise is exchanged for an act or a forbearance to act. Accordingly one party is the promisor and the other party is the promisee.

Promisor–person making a promise

167

Promisee–person receiving a promise

For example, A promises to pay B $500 if B paints A's house. B paints A's house.

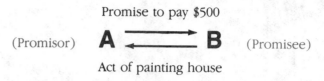

Promise to pay $500

(Promisor)   **A**   **B**   (Promisee)

Act of painting house

A's promise is binding only if it supported by consideration consisting of either a legal detriment to B, the promisee, or a legal benefit to A, the promisor. B's painting the house is a legal detriment to B, the promisee, because she was under no prior legal duty to paint A's house. Also, B's painting of A's house is a legal benefit to A, the promisor, because A had no prior legal right to have his house painted by B.

A unilateral contract may also consist of a promise exchanged for a forbearance. To illustrate, A negligently injures B, for which B may recover damages in a tort action. A promises B $5,000 if B forbears from bringing suit. B accepts by not filing suit.

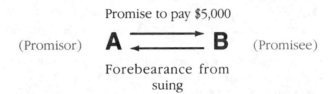

Promise to pay $5,000

(Promisor)   **A**   **B**   (Promisee)

Forebearance from
suing

A's promise to pay B $5,000 is binding because it is supported by consideration; B, the promisee, has incurred a legal detriment by refraining from bringing suit, which he was under no prior legal obligation to refrain from doing. A, the promisor, has received a legal benefit because she had no prior legal right to B's forbearance from bringing suit.

To illustrate further, suppose that Andrew promises Bonnie, a high school graduate, that if Bonnie will attend and graduate from XYZ College, Andrew will pay to Bonnie the entire cost of her college education when she graduates. Bonnie enters XYZ College and duly graduates. The college education she received is an actual benefit to Bonnie, but legally she suffered a detriment in graduating from XYZ College because she gave up her freedom to attend any other college, or to not attend college at all, in consideration for Andrew's promise. Consequently, the consideration that Bonnie, the promisee, gave for Andrews's promise, although not actually detrimental, was legally detrimental to Bonnie. It is therefore legally sufficient, and Andrew's promise is enforceable by Bonnie. Furthermore, Andrew, the promisor, may have received no actual benefit from Bonnie's having obtained a college education at XYZ College, yet Andrew received a legal benefit in that he obtained from Bonnie something that he had no previous right to have—Bonnie's attendance at XYZ College and her graduation. Although this legal benefit may be of no value or usefulness to Andrew, nevertheless his promise allowed him to obtain a performance from her that he was not otherwise entitled to have. Thus, in this illustration the promisor (Andrew) received a legal benefit and the promisee (Bonnie) suffered a legal detriment, although **either** one of these would satisfy the test of legal sufficiency.

Bilateral Contracts

In a bilateral contract each party is *both* a promisor and a promisee. Thus, if A promises to purchase an automobile from B for $10,000 and B promises to sell the automobile to A for $10,000, the following relationship exists:

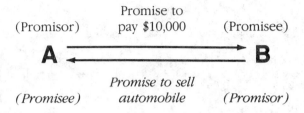

(Promisor)   Promise to pay $10,000   (Promisee)

A   B

(Promisee)   *Promise to sell automobile*   *(Promisor)*

A's promise to pay B $10,000 is binding if that promise is supported by legal consideration, which may consist of either a legal detriment to B, the *promisee*, or a legal benefit to A, the *promisor*. B's promise to sell A the automobile is a legal detriment to B because he was under no prior legal duty to sell the automobile to A. Moreover, B's promise is also a legal benefit to A because A had no prior legal right to that automobile. Consequently, A's promise to pay $10,000 to B **is** supported by consideration and is binding.

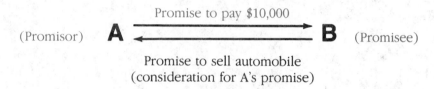

Promise to pay $10,000

(Promisor)   A   B   (Promisee)

Promise to sell automobile
(consideration for A's promise)

For **B's promise** to sell the automobile to A to be binding, it likewise must be supported by consideration, which may be either a legal detriment to A, the *promisee,* or a legal benefit to B, the *promisor.* A's promise to pay B $10,000 is a legal detriment to A because he was under no prior legal duty to pay $10,000 to B. At the same time, A's promise is also a legal benefit to B because B had no prior legal right to the $10,000. Thus, B's promise to sell the automobile **is** supported by consideration and is binding.

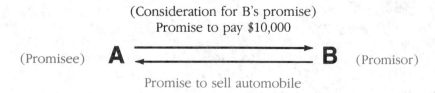

(Consideration for B's promise)
Promise to pay $10,000

(Promisee)   A   B   (Promisor)

Promise to sell automobile

To summarize, for *A's promise* to B to be binding, it must be supported by legally sufficient consideration, which requires that the promise or forbearance received from B in exchange provide either a legal benefit to A *(the promisor)* or a legal detriment to B *(the promisee)*. In most cases where there is legal detriment to the promisee, there is also a legal benefit to the promisor.

However, as the following case demonstrates, the presence of *either* one is sufficient. In a bilateral contract where B makes a return promise to A, that *promise* must also be supported by consideration.

COLLINS v. PARSONS COLLEGE

Supreme Court of Iowa, 1973.
203 N.W.2d 594.

FACTS: Ben Collins was a full professor with tenure at Wisconsin State University in 1966. In March of 1966, Parsons College, in order to lure Dr. Collins from Wisconsin State offered him a written contract promising him the rank of full professor with tenure and a salary of $25,000 for the 1966–67 academic year. The contract further provided that the College would increase his salary by $1000 each year for the next five years. In return, Collins was to teach two trimesters of the academic year beginning in October, 1966. In addition, the contract stipulated, by reference to the College's faculty by-laws, that tenured professors could only be dismissed for just cause and after written charges were filed with the Professional Problems Committee. The two parties signed the contract and Collins resigned his position at Wisconsin State.

In February of 1968, the college tendered a different contract to Collins to cover the following year. This contract reduced his salary to $15,000 with no provision for annual increments, but left his rank of full professor intact. It also required that Collins waive any and all rights or claims existing under any previous employment contracts with the College. Collins refused to sign this new contract and Parsons College soon notified him that he would not be employed the following year. The College did not give any grounds for his dismissal nor file charges with the Problems Committee. As a result, Collins was forced to take a teaching position at the University of North Dakota at a substantially reduced salary. He sued to recover the difference between the salary Parsons College promised him until 1971 and the amount he earned.

DECISION: Judgment for Collins. The College's promise to employ Collins permanently (with tenure), at a specified salary with increments to 1971, must be supported by consideration from Collins to be enforceable. Collins did not promise to serve permanently or even until 1971 in exchange for the College's promise. However, consideration may consist of a detriment to the promisee (Collins) and benefit need not move to the promisor (the College). Parsons College promised Collins tenure, knowing that he would have to resign his permanent, tenured position at Wisconsin State. Therefore, Collins' surrender of his former position to accept the College's offer constituted binding consideration.

Adequacy

Legal sufficiency has nothing to do with adequacy of consideration. The items or actions that the parties agree to exchange do not need to have the same value. The law will regard the consideration as adequate if the parties have freely agreed to the exchange. The requirement of legally sufficient consideration is, therefore, *not* at all concerned with whether the bargain was good or bad, or whether one party received disproportionately more or less than what he gave or promised in exchange for it. Such an inquiry might be relevant if a question of fraud, duress, or undue influence were involved. However, the requirement of legally sufficient consideration is simply (1) that the parties have agreed to an exchange and (2) that with respect to each party the subject matter exchanged, or promised in exchange, either imposed a legal detriment on the promisee or conferred a legal benefit on the promisor.

Mutuality of Obligation

A contract is enforceable only if **both** parties to a contract give consideration. Each promise is the consideration for the other, and the parties are mutually obligated to perform their respective promises. This presents some problems in instances involving illusory promises, output and requirement contracts, and exclusive dealing contracts. The first destroys the mutuality of consideration whereas the last two do not.

Illusory Promises It is fundamental to the formation of a bilateral contract that if one party is not bound, neither party is bound. A promise by its literal terms may impose no obligation on the promisor. Thus a promise to purchase such quantity of goods as the promisor may "desire" or "want" or "wish to buy" imposes no obligation to buy any goods, because its performance is entirely optional. Thus, if Exxon offers to sell to Getty as many barrels of oil as Getty shall choose at forty dollars per barrel, there is no contract for lack of consideration. An offer containing such a promise, although accepted by the offeree, does not create a contract because the promise is illusory—performance is entirely optional with Getty, and no constraint is placed on his freedom. He is not bound to do anything, nor can Exxon reasonably expect him to do anything. Thus, Getty, by his promise, suffers no legal detriment and confers no legal benefit. Consequently Getty's promise does not provide legally sufficient consideration for Exxon's promise, and thus Exxon's promise is not binding on it. The following case provides a much more difficult case of whether the promise was illusory. Do you agree with the court's decision?

FACTS: In 1934 Baker entered into an oral agreement with Healey, the state distributor of Ballantine & Son's liquor products, that Ballantine would supply Baker with its products on demand and that Baker would have the exclusive agency for Ballantine within a certain area of Connecticut. Shortly thereafter the agreement was modified to give Baker the right to terminate at will. Eight months later, when Ballantine & Sons revoked his agency, Baker sued to enforce the oral agreement.

DECISION: Judgment for Ballantine & Sons. To agree to do something and reserve the right to cancel the agreement at will is no agreement at all. By the valid addition to their oral agreement, Baker had an unconditional right to terminate the contract at will. His promise under the agreement, then, was merely illusory. As such, it was insufficient consideration to support Ballantine's promise of an exclusive agency to Baker.

R. F. BAKER & CO., INC.
v. P. BALLANTINE &
SONS

Supreme Court of Errors of
Connecticut, 1941.
127 Conn. 680, 20 A.2d 82.

Output and Requirement Contracts An agreement to sell the entire production of a particular plant, factory, or mine is called an output contract. It gives the seller an assured market for her product. An agreement to purchase all the materials of a particular kind that the purchaser needs is called a requirements contract. It assures the buyer of a ready source of inventory or supplies. These contracts when made may or may not include an estimate of the quantity to be sold or purchased. Nevertheless, they are *not* illusory. The buyer under a requirements contract does not promise to buy as much as she desires to buy, but rather to buy as much as is *needed*. Similarly, under an output contract the seller promises to sell to the buyer the seller's entire production, not merely as much as the seller desires.

Furthermore, the Code as well as the Restatement imposes a good faith limitation on the quantity to be sold or purchased under an output or requirements contract. Thus an output or requirements contract means such actual output or requirements as may occur in good faith, except that no quantity unreasonably different from any stated estimate or, in the absence of a stated estimate, any normal prior output or requirements may be demanded. Therefore, after contracting with Smith to sell to Smith its entire output, Miles company cannot increase its production from one eight-hour shift per day to three eight-hour shifts per day.

Output contract –agreement to sell all of one's production

Requirement contract agreement to buy all of one's needs

Exclusive dealing–sole
right to sell goods in a defined market

Exclusive Dealing Contracts   Where a manufacturer of goods grants an exclusive franchise or license to a distributor to sell its products in a designated territory, unless otherwise agreed, an implied obligation is imposed on the manufacturer to use its best efforts to supply the goods and on the distributor to use her best efforts to promote their sale. The obligations which arise on acceptance of the exclusive franchise are sufficient consideration to bind both parties to the contract.

Conditional Contracts   The fact that the obligation to perform a contract may not arise until a specified event occurs does not invalidate the contract. This is so even though the specified event may never occur. Mutuality of obligation still exist because neither party need perform if the event does not occur. This is also true where the obligation to perform terminates on the occurrence of a specified event.

Thus, if Joanne offers to pay Barry $8,000 for Barry's automobile, provided that Joanne receives such amount as an inheritance from the estate of her deceased uncle, and Barry accepts the offer, the duty of Joanne to pay $8,000 to Barry is *conditioned* on her receiving $8,000 from her deceased uncle's estate. The consideration moving from Barry to Joanne is the transfer of title to the automobile. The consideration moving from Joanne to Barry is the promise of $8,000 subject to the condition. Although the contract is conditional, it is complete, definite, and certain. If the stated condition is an event that could not possibly occur, then no contract would exist because the agreement would be illusory.

Pre-existing Public Obligation

The law does not regard the performance of or promise to perform a pre-existing public duty as either a legal detriment or as a legal benefit. A public duty is one that does not arise out of a contract but is imposed on members of society by force of the common law or by statute. Illustrations are found in the law of torts, such as the duty not to commit an assault, battery, false imprisonment, or defamation. The criminal law also imposes many public duties on everyone. Thus, if Norton promises to pay Holmes, the village ruffian, $100 not to abuse him physically, Norton's promise is unenforceable because Holmes is under a pre-existing public obligation imposed by both tort and criminal law to refrain from such abuse.

Public officials, such as the mayor of a city, members of a city council, policemen (see *Denny v. Reppert,* below) and firemen, are under a pre-existing obligation to perform their duties by virtue of their public office. If Smith's house catches fire and Smith telephones the chief of the city fire department and promises him $500 if he will immediately send a fire truck and firemen to Smith's house to put out the fire, and he does so, the promise is not enforceable. A public official is not allowed to gain privately by performing his duty.

Pre-existing Contractual Obligation

The performance of a pre-existing contractual duty, which is neither doubtful nor the subject of honest dispute, is also legally insufficient consideration because the doing of what one is legally bound to do is neither a detriment to a promisee nor a benefit to the promisor. For example, if Anita employs Ben for one year at a salary of $1,000 per month, and at the end of six months promises Ben that in addition to the salary she will pay Ben $3,000 if Ben remains on the job for the remainder of the period originally agreed on, Anita's promise is not binding for lack of legally sufficient consideration. However, if Ben's duties were by agreement changed even to a small extent in nature or amount, Anita's promise would be binding.

The following case deals with both pre-existing public and contractual obligations.

FACTS: In June three armed men entered and robbed the First State Bank of Eubank, Kentucky, of $30,000. Acting on information supplied by four employees of the bank, Denney, Buis, McCollum and Snyder, three law enforcement officials apprehended the robbers. Two of the arresting officers, Godby and Simms, were State policemen, and the third, Reppert, was a deputy sheriff in a neighboring county. Now all claim the reward for the apprehension and conviction of the bank robbers.

DECISION: Judgment for Reppert. In general, when a reward is offered to the general public for the performance of some specified act, the reward may be claimed by the person who performs that act unless that person is an agent, employee, or public official acting within the scope of his employment or official duties. For this reason the bank employees cannot recover. At the time of the robbery, they were under a duty to protect the bank's resources and to safeguard the institution furnishing them employment. Thus, in assisting the police officers in apprehending the bank robbers, the bank employees were merely doing their duty and, therefore, are not entitled to share in the reward.

Similarly, the State policemen, Godby and Simms, were exercising their duty as police officers in arresting the bank robbers and, thus, are not entitled to share in the reward. Reppert, on the other hand, was out of his jurisdiction at the time and, thus, was under no legal duty to arrest the bank robbers.

DENNY v. REPPERT

Court of Appeals of Kentucky, 1968.
432 S.W.2d 647.

Modification of a Pre-existing Contract   Under the common law, a modification of an existing contract must be supported by mutual consideration to be enforceable. In other words, the modification must be supported by some new consideration beyond that which is already owing. For example, Diane and Fred agree that Diane shall put in a gravel driveway for Fred at a cost of $2,000. Subsequently, Fred agrees to pay an additional $1,000 if Diane will blacktop the driveway. Since Diane was not bound by the original contract to provide blacktopping, she would incur a legal detriment in doing so and is therefore entitled to the additional $1,000. Likewise, as in the following case, consideration may consist of the promisee refraining from exercising a legal right.

FACTS: Plaintiff, Brenner, entered into a contract with the defendant, Little Red School House, Ltd., which stated that in return for a nonrefundable tuition of $1,080 Brenner's son could attend defendant's school for a year. When Brenner's ex-wife refused to enroll their son, plaintiff sought and received a verbal promise of a refund. Defendant now refuses to refund plaintiff's money for lack of consideration.

DECISION: Judgment for Brenner. A contract modification must be supported by consideration to be binding. Such consideration can be found in the promisee refraining from doing anything

BRENNER v. LITTLE RED SCHOOL HOUSE, LIMITED

Court of Appeals of North Carolina, 1982.
295 S.Ed.2d 607.

which he has a legal right to do in exchange for the modification. Here, Brenner relinquished the right to have his son attend the Little Red School House. This detriment constituted sufficient consideration to support the school's promise to refund his money.

The Code has modified the common law rule by providing that a contract for the sale of goods can be effectively modified by the parties without new consideration, provided they wish to do so and act in good faith. Moreover, the Restatement has moved toward this position by providing that a modification of an executory contract is binding if it is fair and equitable in light of the surrounding facts that were not anticipated by the parties when the contract was made.

Settlement of an Undisputed Debt   An "undisputed" debt is an uncontested obligation to pay a certain sum in money or to pay an amount that can be reduced to a certain sum in money. If the debtor has made an express promise to pay a specific sum of money, for example, $100, the debt is **liquidated** or certain in amount. If she has agreed to pay three dollars per bushel for apples delivered and fifty bushels of apples have been delivered, the debt is liquidated in the amount of $150.

Liquidated debt–certain in amount

Under the common law, the payment of a lesser sum of money than is owed in consideration of a promise to discharge a fully matured undisputed debt is legally insufficient to support the promise of discharge. To illustrate, assume that B owes A $100, and in consideration of B's paying A $50, A agrees to accept the lesser sum in full satisfaction of the debt. In a subsequent suit by A against B to recover the remaining $50, at common law A is entitled to a judgment for $50 on the ground that A's promise of discharge is not binding because B's payment of $50 was no legal detriment to the promisee, B, as he was under a *pre-existing legal obligation* to pay that much and more. By the same token, the receipt of $50 was no legal benefit to the promisor A. Consequently, the consideration for A's promise of discharge was legally insufficient, and A is not bound by his promise. However, if A had accepted from B any new or different consideration, such as the sum of $40 and a fountain pen worth $10 or less or even the fountain pen with no payment of money, in full satisfaction of the $100 debt, the consideration moving from B would be legally sufficient because B was under no legal obligation to give a fountain pen to A. In this example, consideration would also exist if A had agreed to accept $50 *before* the debt became due, in full satisfaction of the debt. B was under no legal obligation to pay any of the debt before its due date. Consequently, B's early payment is a legal detriment to B as well as a legal benefit to A. The law is not concerned with the amount of the discount, because that is simply a question of adequacy. Likewise, B's payment of a lesser amount on the due date at an agreed-upon different place of payment would be legally sufficient consideration.

Settlement of a Disputed Debt   A disputed debt is an obligation whose existence or amount is contested. Implied contracts frequently create obligations to pay uncertain amounts. For example, where a person has requested professional services from a doctor or a dentist and no agreement was made about the amount of the fee to be charged, the doctor or dentist is entitled to receive from her patient a reasonable fee for the service performed. Because no definite amount was agreed on, the patient's obligation is uncertain or **unliquidated.** The patient has a legal obligation to pay the reasonable worth of the services that were performed. When the doctor or dentist sends the patient a bill for her services, the amount stated in the bill is her estimate of the reasonable value of the services, but the debt does not in this manner become liquidated until and unless the patient agrees to pay the amount of the bill. If the patient honestly disputes the amount that is owing and offers in full settlement an amount less than the bill, acceptance of the lesser amount by the creditor discharges the debt. Thus, if Andy sends to Bess, an accountant, a check for $120 in payment of his debt to Bess for services rendered, which services Andy considered worthless but for which Bess billed Andy $600, Bess' acceptance (cashing) of the check releases Andy from any further liability. Andy has given up his right to further dispute the billing, and Bess has forfeited her right to further collection. Thus, there is mutuality of consideration.

> **Unliquidated debt**—uncertain or contested in amount

For the giving up of a disputed claim to constitute legally sufficient consideration, the dispute must be *honest* and not frivolous. Where the dispute is based on contentions without merit or not made in good faith, giving up such contentions by the debtor is not a legal detriment.

FACTS: Hilda Boehm, an unmarried typist, became pregnant while she was dating Louis Fiege. Boehm told Fiege that he was the father of her child and proposed an agreement to provide support for it. Before the child was born, Fiege agreed to pay all her medical and miscellaneous expenses; to compensate her for her loss of salary due to the child's birth; and to pay her $10 per week for child support until it reached the age of 21. In return, Boehm promised not to institute bastardy proceedings against him. Boehm had the child and three years later placed it for adoption, claiming $2,895 total expenses to be paid by Fiege under the agreement. Fiege paid $480 of that sum, but ceased payments when blood tests revealed that the child could not have been his. Boehm instituted bastardy proceedings, but Fiege was acquitted, based largely on the evidence of the blood tests. She then sued to recover the remainder of the expenses Fiege had agreed to pay under their previous agreement. Fiege claims that their "alleged" contract was not supported by consideration since Boehm's promise not to prosecute was not based on a valid claim.

FIEGE v. BOEHM

Court of Appeals of Maryland, 1956.
210 Md. 352, 123 A.2d 316.

DECISION: Judgment for Boehm. A promise not to assert an invalid claim by one who does not have an honest and reasonable belief in its possible validity is not sufficient consideration. However, if the claim has an objectively reasonable basis for support, in fact or in law, and the surrender of it is made with a good faith belief in its validity, then their is adequate consideration.

Here, Boehm's bastardy suit against Fiege was a lawful claim with an objectively reasonable basis for support. Even though her claim proved unsubstantiated, she entered into the agreement not to prosecute in good faith and with reasonable belief as to its validity. Therefore, it is sufficient consideration and renders Fiege's promise to pay child support enforceable.

Substituted Contracts Distinguished   A substituted contract occurs when the parties to a contract mutually agree to rescind or withdraw their original contract and enter into a new one. Substituted contracts are perfectly valid and effective to discharge the original contract and to impose obligations under the new contract. The rescission is binding in that each party by giving up his rights under the original contract has provided consideration to the other, as long as each party still has rights under the original contract.

Bargained-For Exchange

Bargain—negotiated exchange

The central idea behind consideration is that the parties have intentionally entered into a bargained exchange with each other and have each given to the other something in exchange for her promise or performance. "Bargain" as used in this context does not mean making an advantageous deal or buying something at a price less than its fair market value. As used in the phrase "bargained-for exchange," it means simply that the parties have negotiated and mutually agreed upon the terms of what each party is giving to the other party in exchange for what he is receiving. Thus, a promise to give someone a birthday present is without consideration, because the promisor received nothing in exchange for her promise of a present.

Past Consideration

The element of exchange is absent where a promise is given for a past transaction. Hence, past consideration is no consideration. A promise made on account of something that the promisee has already done is not enforceable. For example, Donna gives emergency care to Tim's adult son while the son is ill. Tim subsequently promises to reimburse Donna for her expenses. Tim's promise is not binding because there is no bargained-for exchange. Consideration is the inducement for a promise or performance. Therefore, unbargained-for past events are not consideration, despite their designation as "past consideration."

Moral Obligation

A promise made in order to satisfy a pre-existing moral obligation is likewise unenforceable for lack of consideration. Instances involving such moral obligation include promises to pay for board and lodging previously furnished to a needy relative of the promisor, promises to pay debts owed by a relative of the promisor, and the promise made in the following case.

HARRINGTON v. TAYLOR

Supreme Court of North Carolina, 1945.
225 N.C. 690, 36 S.E.2d 227.

FACTS: Taylor assaulted his wife, who then took refuge in Ms. Harrington's house. The next day, Mr. Taylor entered the house and began another assault on his wife. Taylor's wife knocked him down and, while he was lying on the floor, attempted to cut his head open or decapitate him with an axe. Harrington intervened, to stop the bloodshed and was hit by the axe as it was descending. The axe fell upon her hand, mutilating it badly, but sparing Taylor his life. Afterwards, Taylor orally promised to compensate Harrington for her injury. He payed a small sum but nothing more. Harrington sued to enforce Taylor's promise.

DECISION: Judgment for Taylor. Taylor may have a moral obligation to honor his promise but not a binding contractual one. Harrington's humanitarian act "voluntarily performed, is not such consideration as would entitle her to recover at law."

Third Parties

Consideration to support a promise may be given to a person other than the promisor if the promisor bargains for that exchange. For example, A promises to pay B fifteen dollars if B delivers a specified book to C.

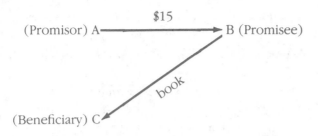

A's promise is binding because B incurred a legal detriment by delivering the book to C, as B was under no prior legal obligation to do so. A's promise to pay fifteen dollars is also consideration for B's promise to give C the book.

Conversely, consideration may be given by some person other than the promisee. For example, A promises to pay B twenty-five dollars in return for D's promise to give A a radio.

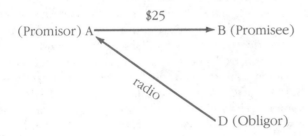

A's promise to pay twenty-five dollars is consideration for D's promise to give A a radio and *vice versa*.

Contracts Without Consideration

Certain transactions are enforceable even though they are not supported by consideration. These transactions include the following.

Promise to Pay Debt Barred by the Statute of Limitations

Every State has statutes stating that actions to enforce debts must be brought within a prescribed period of time after the debts become due. Actions not begun within the specified time period will be dismissed. The time periods vary among the States and also with the nature of the claim. These statutes are known as **Statutes of Limitations.**

A new promise by the debtor to pay the debt renews the running of the Statute of Limitations for a second statutory period. This new promise requires no consideration. The following facts operate as a sufficient promise unless circumstances indicate otherwise: (1) a voluntary, unqualified admission that the debt is owing; (2) a partial payment of the debt; or (3) a statement that the Statute of Limitations will not be pleaded as a defense.

Statute of limitation–
time period in which a lawsuit must be initiated

Promise to Pay Debt Discharged in Bankruptcy

A promise to pay a debt that has been discharged in bankruptcy is also enforceable without consideration. The Bankruptcy Reform Act of 1978, however, imposes a number of requirements before a promise to pay a debt discharged in bankruptcy may be enforced:

1. The debtor's promise must be made before the discharge of the debt is granted;

2. The debtor does not revoke the promise within thirty days after the promise becomes enforceable;

3. The debtor, if an individual, must be informed by the bankruptcy court of his legal rights and the effects of his new promise; and

4. The debtor's promise, if the debtor is an individual and the debt is a consumer obligation, must be approved by the bankruptcy court as being in the best interest of the debtor.

Promissory Estoppel

A person may make a promise under circumstances that lead the promisor to expect that the promisee will act or refrain from acting based on the promise. If the promisee does take such action or forbearance the promisor is estopped, or prohibited, from denying the promise. The basis of the promisor's liability is the doctrine of promissory estoppel, and consideration for the promise is not required. This does not mean that every promise given without consideration is binding simply because it is followed by a change of position on the part of the promisee. Liability is created by the change of position in justifiable reliance on the promise if injustice can be avoided only by the enforcement of the promise. For example, Ann promises Larry not to foreclose on a mortgage Ann owns on Larry's land for a period of six months. Larry then spends $100,000 on a building constructed on the land. Ann's promise not to foreclose is binding on her under the doctrine of promissory estoppel.

> **Promissory estoppel**– prohibited from denying one's promise based upon equity

The most common application of the doctrine of promissory estoppel is to charitable subscriptions. Numerous churches, memorials, college buildings, stadiums, hospitals, and other structures used for religious, educational, or charitable purposes have been built with the assistance of contributions made through fulfillment of pledges or promises to contribute to particular worthwhile causes. Although the pledgor regards herself as making a gift for a charitable purpose and gift promises are generally not enforceable, the courts have generally enforced charitable subscription promises. Although various reasons and theories have been advanced in support of liability, the one most commonly accepted is that the subscription has induced a change of position by the promisee (the church, school, or charitable organization) in reliance on the promise. The Restatement, moreover, has relaxed the reliance requirement for charitable subscriptions so that actual reliance need not be shown; the probability of reliance is sufficient.

Contracts Under Seal

Under the common law, when a person desired to bind himself by bond, deed or solemn promise, he executed his promise under seal. He did not have to sign the document. His delivery of a document to which he had affixed his seal was sufficient. No consideration for his promise was necessary. In some States a promise under seal is still binding without consideration.

Nevertheless, most States have abolished by statute the distinction between contracts under seal and written unsealed contracts. In these States the seal is no longer recognized as a substitute for consideration. The Code has also adopted this position and specifically eliminates the use of seals in contracts for the sale of goods.

Other Promises Which Require No Consideration

Renunciation   Under both the Code and the Restatement, any claim or right arising out of an alleged breach of contract can be discharged in whole or in part without consideration by a written waiver or renunciation signed and delivered by the aggrieved party.

Firm Offer   Under the Code a written offer signed by a merchant offeror to buy or sell goods is not revocable for lack of consideration during the time stated that it is open, not to exceed three months, or if no time is stated, for a reasonable time.

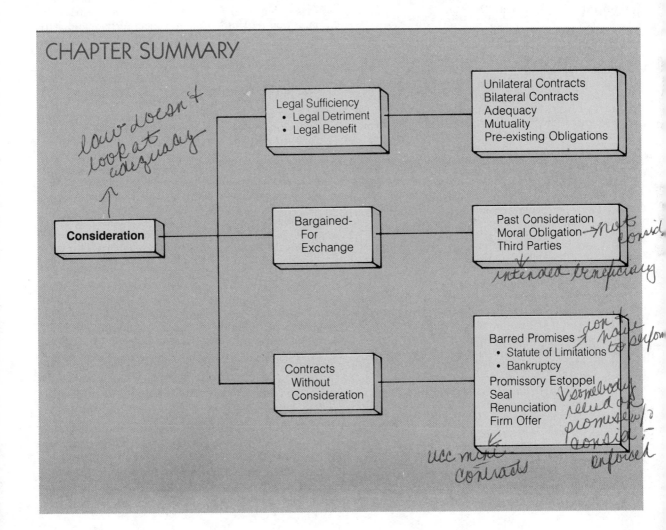

CHAPTER SUMMARY

KEY TERMS

Consideration
Gratuitous
Legal sufficiency
Bargained-for exchange
Legal detriment

Legal benefit
Illusory promise
Output contract
Required contract

Excusive dealing contract
Liquidated debt
Unliquidated debt
Statute of limitations

PROBLEMS

1. In consideration of $800 paid to him by Joyce, Hill gave Joyce a written option to purchase his house for $80,000 on or before April 1. Prior to April 1, Hill verbally agreed to extend the option until July 1. On May 18, Hill, known to Joyce, sold the house to Gray, who was ignorant of the unrecorded option. Joyce brought suit against Hill. Decision?

2. Ann owed $500 to Barry for services Barry rendered to Ann. The debt was due June 30, 1985. In March 1986, the debt was still unpaid. Barry was in urgent need of ready cash and told Ann that if she would pay $150 on the debt at once, Barry would release her from the balance. Ann paid $150 and stated to Barry that all claims had been paid in full. In August 1986, Barry demanded the unpaid balance and subsequently sued Ann for $350. Decision?

3. (a) Modify the facts in (2) by assuming that Barry gave Ann a written receipt stating that all claims had been paid in full. Result?
   (b) Modify the facts in (2) by assuming that Ann owed Barry the $500 on Ann's purchase of motorcycle from Barry. Result?

4. A owed B $800 on a personal loan. Neither the amount of the debt nor A's liability to pay the $800 was disputed. B had also rendered services as a carpenter to A without any agreement as to the price to be paid. When the work was completed, an honest and reasonable difference of opinion developed between A and B with respect to the value of B's services. Upon receiving B's bill for the carpentry services for $600, A mailed in a properly stamped and addressed envelope his check for $800 to B. In an accompanying letter, A stated that the enclosed check was in full settlement of both claims. B indorsed and cashed the check. Thereafter, B unsuccessfully sought to collect from A an alleged unpaid balance of $600. B then sued A for $600. Decision?

5. The Snyder Mfg. Co., being a large user of coal, entered into separate contracts with several coal companies, in each of which it was agreed that the coal company would supply coal during the year 1986 in such amounts as the manufacturing company might

desire to order, at a price of forty-nine dollars per ton. In February 1986, the Snyder Company ordered 1,000 tons of coal from Union Coal Company, one of the contracting parties. Union Coal Company delivered 500 tons of the order and then notified Snyder Company that no more deliveries would be made and that it denied any obligation under the contract. In an action by Union Coal to collect forty-nine dollars per ton for the 500 tons of coal delivered, Snyder files a counterclaim, claiming damages of $1,500 for failure to deliver the addition 500 tons of the order and damages of $4,000 for breach of agreement to deliver coal during the balance of the year. Decision?

6. On February 5, D entered into a written agreement with P whereby P agreed to drill a well on D's property for the sum of $5,000 and to complete the well on or before April 15. Before entering into the contract, P made test borings and had satisfied himself as to the character of the subsurface. After two days of drilling P struck hard rock. On February 17, P removed his equipment and advised D that the project had proved unprofitable and that he would not continue. On March 17, D went to P and told P that he would assume the risk of the enterprise and would pay P $100 for each day required to drill the well, as compensation for labor, the use of P's equipment, and P's services in supervising the work, provided P would furnish certain special equipment designed to cut through hard rock. P said that the proposal was satisfactory. The work was continued by P and completed in an additional fifty-eight days. Upon completion of the work D failed to pay, and P brought an action to recover $5,800. D answered that he had never become obligated to pay $100 a day and filed a counterclaim for damages in the amount of $500 for the month's delay based on an alleged breach of contract by P. Decision?

7. Discuss and explain whether there is valid consideration for each of the following promises:
   (a) A and B entered into a contract for the purchase and sale of goods. A subsequently promised to pay a higher price for the goods when B refused to deliver at the contract price.
   (b) A promised in writing to pay a debt, which was

due from B to C, on C's agreement to extend the time of payment for one year.

(c) A executed a promissory note to her son, B, solely in consideration of past services rendered to A by B, for which there had been no agreement or request to pay.

8. Alan purchased shoes from Barbara on open account. Barbara sent Alam a bill for $10,000. Alan wrote back that 200 pairs of the shoes were defective and offered to pay $6,000 and give Barbara his promissory note for $1,000. Barbara accepted the offer, and Alan sent his check for $6,000 and his note in accordance with the agreement. Barbara cashed the check, collected on the note, and, one month later, sued Alan for $3,000. Decision?

9. B owed A $1,500, but A did not initiate a lawsuit to collect the debt within the time period prescribed by the Statute of Limitations. Nevertheless, B promises A that she will pay the barred debt. Thereafter, B refuses to pay. A brings suit to collect on this new promise. Decision?

ILLEGAL BARGAINS

An essential requirement of a binding promise or agreement is that the objective is legal. When the formation or performance of an agreement is criminal, tortious, or otherwise contrary to public policy, the agreement is illegal and **unenforceable.** The law does *not* provide a remedy for the breach of an unenforceable agreement and thus "leaves the parties where it finds them." It is preferable to use the term "illegal bargain" or "illegal agreement" rather than "illegal contract," because the word "contract," by definition, denotes a legal and enforceable agreement. The illegal bargain is made unenforceable (1) to discourage the undesirable conduct in the future and (2) to avoid the inappropriate use of the judicial process in carrying out the socially undesirable bargain.

In this chapter we discuss this subject in terms of agreements (a) in violation of a statute and (b) contrary to public policy.

Violations of Statutes

An agreement declared illegal by statute will not be enforced by the courts. For example, "wagering or gambling contracts" are specifically declared unenforceable in most States. Likewise, an agreement induced by criminal conduct will not be enforced. For example, if Alice enters into an agreement with Brent Co. through the bribing of Brent Co.'s purchasing agent, the agreement would be unenforceable.

Licensing Statutes

Every jurisdiction has laws requiring a license for those who engage in certain trades, professions, or businesses. Common examples are licensing statutes that apply to lawyers, doctors, dentists, accountants, brokers, plumbers, and contractors. Whether a person may recover for services rendered if he has failed to comply with a licensing requirement depends on the terms or type of licensing statute.

The statute itself may expressly provide that an unlicensed person engaged in a business or profession for which a license is required shall not recover for services rendered. Where there is no such statutory provision, the courts commonly distinguish between **regulatory** statutes or ordinances and those that are enacted merely to raise **revenue.** If the statute is regulatory, a

License–formal authorization to engage in certain practices

Regulatory license–measure to protect the public interest

Revenue license–measure to raise money

person cannot recover for professional services unless he has the required license as long as the public policy behind the regulatory purpose clearly outweighs the person's interest in being paid for his services. However, if the law requiring a license is for revenue purposes only, agreements for such services are enforceable.

A regulatory measure is one designed to protect the public against unqualified persons. Examples are statutes prescribing standards for those who seek to practice law or medicine. A revenue measure, on the other hand, does not seek to protect against the incompetent or unqualified, but simply seeks to raise money. An example is a statute requiring a license of plumbers but not establishing standards of competence for those who seek to follow the trade. The courts regard this as a taxing measure lacking any expression of legislative intent to prevent unlicensed plumbers from enforcing their business contracts.

TOVAR v. PAXTON COMMUNITY MEMORIAL HOSP.

Appellate Court of Illinois, Fourth District, 1975.
29 Ill.App.3d 218, 330 N.E.2d 247.

FACTS: Tovar applied for the position of resident physician in Paxton Community Memorial Hospital. The hospital examined his background and licensing and assured him that he was qualified for the position. Relying upon the hospital's promise of permanent employment, Tovar resigned from his job and began work at the hospital. He was discharged two weeks later, however, because he did not hold a license to practice medicine in Illinois as required by State law. He had taken the examination but had never passed it. Tovar claims that the hospital promised him a position of permanent employment and that by discharging him it breached their employment contract.

DECISION: Judgment for Paxton Hospital. The purpose of the licensing statute is not to generate revenue but rather to protect the public by assuring them of adequately trained physicians. Since the purpose of the licensing requirement is to protect the public from unqualified persons, any contract relating to the licensed activity and entered into with an unlicensed person is illegal. The contact between the hospital and Tovar was illegal, and therefore is unenforceable as against public policy.

Gambling Statutes

In a wager the parties stipulate that one shall win and the other lose depending on the outcome of an event in which their only "interest" is the possibility of such gain or loss.

All States have legislation on gambling, and American courts generally refuse to recognize the enforceability of a gambling agreement. Thus, if Smith makes a bet with Brown on the outcome of a ball game, the agreement is unenforceable by either party. Some States, however, now permit certain kinds of regulated gambling; these include State-operated lotteries.

What are the contractual rights and obligations of the parties involved in the following Law in the News excerpt on the Tulane basketball scandal?

Sunday Statutes

Blue law–prohibition of certain types of commercial activity on Sunday

At common law a valid contract may be entered into on Sunday as on any other day. Some States have legislation called **Blue Laws** that modify this common law rule and prohibit certain types of commercial activity on Sunday. The modern tendency is to permit weekday "ratification" or "adoption" of a contract executed on Sunday. Even in a State that prohibits contracts on Sunday, a court will enforce a subsequent weekday ratification. Blue Laws usually do not apply to activities of "necessity" and "charity."

"The Fix Is On"

Tulane basketball is out

New Orleans Lawyer Ned Kohnke was stunned at dinner last month when his brother mentioned a rumor: a Tulane basketball player had told friends before a recent game, "The fix is on." Kohnke, a Tulane alumnus, benefactor and basketball fan, agonized for several days before contacting Orleans Parish District Attorney Harry Connick.

So began the unraveling of a two-month-old point-shaving conspiracy, a cocaine-distribution arrangement and an unrelated but long-standing recruiting-payments scheme. Last week, to confront "the questions of moral values and academic integrity," University President Eamon Kelly announced plans to abolish Tulane's basketball program, permanently.

As an indictment filed last week tells it, the point-shaving plan was hatched on Feb. 2, the day of a game with Southern Mississippi; Tulane was favored by 10½ points. Students Gary Kranz, 21, Mark Olensky, 21, and David Rothenberg, 22, all members of Alpha Epsilon Pi fraternity, decided to see whether some of the players would agree to hold the team under the point spread. Kranz allegedly had already given cocaine to

Senior forwards Clyde Eads and Jon Johnson. When he offered them a piece of the proceeds from bets on the game, Eads and Johnson were not only interested but recruited Guards David Dominique and Bobby Thompson and Star Center John ("Hot Rod") Williams into the deal. Tulane beat Southern Mississippi by a single point. Two Saturdays later the players allegedly conspired to fix the Virginia Tech game, but the plan apparently misfired. Four days after that, they went into the tank again. Tulane, which finished the season with a mediocre 15-13 record, lost to Memphis State by eleven points, more than the four-point margin the betting line had predicted.

For their lack of effort, the five players are said to have made at least $19,500. Eads and Johnson, having helped bring the three others into the scam, proceeded to negotiate immunity from prosecution for their testimony. Those they have implicated face up to 30 years in prison if convicted.

The ease with which the players apparently fell to cheating may be partially explained by the climate of exploitation that has long pervaded college sports. In particular, Williams, a potential first-

round pro draft pick, knows the temptations. A high school star from rural Sorrento, La., he reportedly told prosecutors that after he agreed to attend Tulane, a former assistant coach gave him a shoe box containing $10,000 in cash, and that he had received weekly envelopes from Coach Ned Fowler containing $100 stipends. Such payments, while not criminal, violate N.C.A.A. rules. Fowler and two of his assistants (who were not involved in the point shaving or any of the drug incidents) resigned last week after disclosure of the weekly payments.

The "commercialization" of college sports, Kelly said, "has eroded many of the positive values that come with athletic programs." To stanch the flow of under-the-table money to collegiate athletes, the N.C.A.A. Presidents' Commission voted last week to urge that athletic department budgets be overseen by college administrators. Easy attitudes toward drugs, betting and corner cutting to make big-time money call for hard lessons. They should reverberate beyond Tulane.

—By Michael S. Serrill.

Usury Statutes

Historically, every State had a "usury law," a statute establishing a maximum rate of permissible interest that may be contracted for between a lender and borrower of money. Recently, however, the trend is to limit or relax usury statutes. Maximum rates permitted vary greatly from State to State and among types of transactions. These statutes typically are general in their application, although certain types of transactions are exempted. For example, many States impose no limit on the rate of interest that may be charged on loans to corporations. Furthermore, some States permit the parties to contract for any

Usury law—establishes a maximum rate of interest

rate of interest on loans made to individual proprietorships or partnerships for the purpose of carrying on a business.

In addition to the exceptions accorded certain designated types of borrowers, a number of States have exempted specific lenders. For example, the majority of the States have enacted installment loan laws, which permit eligible lenders a higher return on installment loans than would otherwise be permitted under the applicable general interest statute. These specific lender usury statutes, which have all but abrogated the general usury statute, vary greatly but have generally encompassed small consumer loans, corporate loans, loans by small lenders, real estate mortgages, and numerous other transactions.

General usury statutes have traditionally exempted credit terms granted by vendors. Nevertheless, vendor credit has been covered by the judicially created time-price doctrine. The **time-price** doctrine provides that sellers may have two prices for their merchandise—a cash price and a credit or "time price," and that the credit price may exceed the cash price by more than the statutorily allowed interest on the cash price. Today, most States have rendered the time-price doctrine moot by adopting state retail installment sales acts, which apply specific usury statutes to specific consumer transactions and are beyond the scope of the general usury statutes.

For a transaction to be usurious, courts usually require evidence of the following factors: (a) a loan (b) of money (c) that is repayable absolutely and in all events (d) for which an interest charge is exacted in excess of the interest rate allowed by law. Transactions that are really loans may not be clothed with the trappings of a sale for the purpose of avoiding the usury laws.

Assuming that it is established that the arrangement is for a loan, certain expenses or charges are permitted in addition to the maximum legal interest. Payments made by a borrower to the lender for expenses incurred or for services rendered in good faith in making a loan or in obtaining security for its repayment are generally not included in determining whether the loan is usurious. Commonly permissible expenses by the lender include costs of examining title, investigating the credit rating of the borrower, drawing necessary documents, and inspecting the property. If not excessive, they are not considered in determining the rate of interest under the usury statutes. However, as shown in the following case, payments made to the lender or from which he derives an advantage if they exceed the reasonable value of services actually rendered are considered.

ABRAMOWITZ v. BARNETT BANKS OF WEST ORLANDO

Florida Court of Appeals, 1981.
394 So.2d 1033.

FACTS: Abramowitz obtained a one year mortgage loan from Barnett Bank for $400,000 at 9% interest with a 1% "point" or service fee. The maximum lawful rate of interest on such a loan is 10%. The bank deducted the $4000 service fee from the loan proceeds actually disbursing only $396,000 to Abramowitz. During the one year term of his loan, Abramowitz was charged and he paid $36,347.78 in interest. He claims the loan was usurious since the $4000 "service fee" plus the $36,347 interest charge exceeded the 10% limit on total interest.

DECISION: Judgment for Abramowitz. If the $4000 was "interest", Abramowitz paid more than $40,000, or 10% on his $400,000 loan, in total interest charges. If the loan was a "discount" loan, with interest paid in advance, then the rate should be properly gauged on the amount of principal actually disbursed to Abramowitz plus the legitimate expenses incurred by the bank. These expenses must be actual, reasonable expenses of making this particular loan, and may not include the general overhead of the bank. The only reasonable, legitimate expense the bank suffered in making this loan amounted to $300. Thus, the lawful amount of interest on Abramowitz's loan is $39,630 (10% of $396,300—the actual principal disbursed plus the $300).

The legal effect of a usurious loan varies from State to State. In a few States the lender forfeits both principal and interest. In some jurisdictions the lender can recover the principal but forfeits all interest. In other States only that portion of interest exceeding the maximum permitted is forfeited. In several States the amount forfeited is a multiple (double or treble) of the interest charged. How the usurious interest already paid is disposed of also varies. Some States do not allow the borrower to recover any of the usurious interest paid; others allow a recovery of the usurious interest paid or a multiple of it.

Violations of Public Policy

The reach of a statute may extend beyond its language. Sometimes the courts, by analogy, use the statute and the policy it embodies as a guide in determining the private contract rights of a person. In addition, the courts must frequently express the "public policy" of the State without significant help from statutory sources. This judicially declared public policy is very broad in scope, it often being said that agreements which have "a tendency to be injurious to the public or the public good" are contrary to public policy. In the following sections we consider examples of agreements that (1) involve tortious conduct, (2) restrain trade, (3) tend to obstruct the administration of justice, (4) tend to corrupt public officials or impair the legislative process, (5) exempt a party from liability for his own negligence, or (6) are unconscionable.

The following case of *Marvin v. Marvin* provides a general overview of the nature and extent of public policy.

MARVIN v. MARVIN

Supreme Court of California, 1976.
18 Cal.3d 660, 134 Cal.Rpt. 815, 557 P.2d 106.

FACTS: In 1964, Michelle Marvin and Lee Marvin began living together, holding themselves out to the general public as man and wife without actually being married. The two orally agreed that while they lived together they would share equally any and all property and earnings accumulated as a result of their individual and combined efforts. In addition, Michelle promised to render her services as a "companion, homemaker, housekeeper and cook" to Lee. Shortly thereafter, she gave up her lucrative career as an entertainer in order to devote her full time to being Lee's companion, homemaker, housekeeper and cook. In return, he agreed to provide for all of her financial support and needs for the rest of her life. In 1970, Lee compelled Michelle to leave his household, but continued to provide for her support. However, in late 1971, he refused to provide further support. Michelle sued to recover support payments and half of their accumulated property. Lee contends that their agreement is so closely related to the supposed "immoral" character of their relationship that its enforcement would violate public policy. The trial court granted Lee's motion for judgment on the pleadings.

DECISION: Judgment for Michelle Marvin. Adults who voluntarily live together and engage in sexual relations can, nonetheless, make arrangements concerning their earnings and property rights. However, they cannot contract to pay for the performance of sexual services; such a contract is essentially an agreement for prostitution and illegal.

Here, the Marvins' agreement does not rest, explicitly or entirely, upon a promise of sexual services or any other illicit consideration. The allocation of their finances and property rights as they choose does not violate public policy. Therefore, their agreement furnishes a suitable basis upon which a trial court can render relief.

Tortious Conduct

An agreement that requires a person to commit a tort is an illegal agreement and thus unenforceable. The courts will not permit contract law to violate the law of torts. Any agreement attempting to do so is considered contrary to public policy. For example, Ada and Bernard enter into an agreement under which Ada promises Bernard that in return for $5,000 she will disparage the product of Bernard's competitor Cone in order to provide Bernard with a competitive advantage. Ada's promise is to commit the tort of disparagement and is unenforceable as contrary to public policy.

Common Law Restraint of Trade

At early common law any restraint on an individual's right to engage in his trade or calling was illegal. Such restraints were viewed with disfavor because the courts believed that they would diminish the individual's means of earning a living, deprive the public of useful services, adversely affect competition, and otherwise be harmful to the welfare of the community. But this strict view has been modified so that **reasonable** restraints of trade are enforceable.

Today an agreement to refrain from a particular trade, profession, or business is enforceable if (1) the purpose of the restraint is to protect a property interest of the promisee and (2) the restraint is no more extensive than is reasonably necessary to protect that interest. Restraints typically arise in two situations: (a) the sale of a business and (b) employment contracts.

Sale of a Business   As part of an agreement to sell a business, the seller frequently promises not to compete in the particular business in *a defined area* for a stated period of *time*. To protect the business's good will, an asset that the buyer has purchased, the buyer must be allowed to enforce such a covenant (promise) by the seller not to compete with the purchaser within reasonable limitations. Most litigation on this subject has involved the requirement that the restraint be no greater than is reasonably necessary. The reasonableness of the restraint depends on the geographic area covered and the time period for which the restraint is to be effective.

Covenant–promise

For example, the promise of a person selling a service station business in Detroit not to enter the service station business in Michigan for the next twenty-five years is unreasonable, both as to area and time. The business interest to be protected would not include the entire State, so it is not necessary to the protection of the purchaser that the seller be prevented from engaging in the service station business in the entire State or perhaps, for that matter, the entire city of Detroit. Limiting the area to the neighborhood or within a radius of a few miles would probably be adequate protection. If the business was citywide, such as a laundry or cleaning establishment with neighborhood outlets, a covenant restraining competition anywhere in the city might well be reasonable.

The same type of inquiry must be made about time limitations. In the sale of a service station twenty-five years would be unreasonable, but one year probably would not. Each case must be considered on its own facts, with the court determining what is reasonable under the particular circumstances.

HAYNES v. MONSON

Supreme Court of Minnesota, 1974.
301 Minn. 327, 224 N.W.2d 482.

FACTS: Haynes sold Monson a business known as Haynes Bookkeeping and Tax Service located in Austin, Minnesota. As part of the sale, Haynes agreed not to engage in the business of bookkeeping, accounting, or tax practice within fifty miles of Austin. After working for Monson for eighteen months after the sale, Haynes opened a new office in Red Wing, a town 100 miles from Austin. He did not sell his Austin residence, however, nor did he disconnect his telephone service, and, therefore, he was able to maintain contact with his former clients. Under this arrangement Haynes continued to furnish bookkeeping and tax service for forty-five residents of Austin and filed tax returns for them from his new office. Monson claims that Haynes breached their contract by violating his covenant not to compete.

DECISION: Judgment for Monson. The covenant not to compete which accompanied the sale of the business protected a legitimate interest and was reasonable in time and area. it is unnecessary to show active solicitation to prove that the covenant not to compete was breached. Haynes conducted the business in the same area for many years and had built a sizable clientele. Under these circumstances his solicitation by mere reputation and past business practice is sufficient to constitute competing for the business of his former customers in violation of the restrictive covenant.

Employment Contracts   Salespeople, management personnel, and other employees are frequently required to sign employment contracts prohibiting them from competing with their employers during the time of employment and for some additional stated period after termination. The courts readily enforce a covenant not to compete during the period of employment. But the promise not to compete after termination of employment is subjected to an even stricter test of reasonableness than that applied to non-competition promises included in a contract for the sale of a business. A court order enjoining (prohibiting) the former employee from competing in a described territory for a stated period of time is the usual way an employer seeks enforcement of an employee's promise not to compete. Before the courts will grant such injunctions, the employer must demonstrate the restriction is *necessary* to protect his legitimate interests, such as trade secrets or customer lists. Because the injunction may have the practical effect of placing the employee out of work, the courts must carefully balance the public policy favoring the employer's right to protect his business interests against the public policy favoring full opportunity for individuals to gain employment.

Thus one court has held unreasonable a covenant in a contract that a travel agency employee after termination of her employment would not engage in a like business in any capacity in either of two named towns or within a radius of sixty miles of the towns for a period of two years. There was no indication that the employee had enough influence over customers to cause them to move their business to her new agency nor was not shown that any trade secrets were involved. The following case provides another example of an invoked restriction.

POST v. MERRILL LYNCH, PIERCE, FENNER & SMITH, INC.

New York Court of Appeals, 1979.
48 N.Y.2d 84, 397 N.E.2d 358, 421 N.Y.S.2d 847.

FACTS: Merrill Lynch employed Post and Maney as account executives beginning in April 20, 1959 and May 15, 1961, respectively. Both men elected to be paid a salary and to participate in the firm's pension and profit-sharing plans rather than take a straight commission. Merrill Lynch terminated the employment of both Post and Maney on August 30, 1974. On September 4, 1974, both began working for Bache & Company, a competitor of Merrill Lynch. Merrill Lynch then informed them that all of their rights in the company-funded pension plan had been forfeited pursuant to a provision of the plan which permitted forfeiture in the event that an employee directly or indirectly competed with the firm.

DECISION: Judgment for Post and Maney. Employment contracts prohibiting competition create a tension between the freedom of individuals to contract and the reluctance to see one barter away his freedom. Nevertheless, the State will enforce limited restraints on an employee's employment mobility where a mutuality of obligation is freely bargained for by the parties. An essential aspect of that relationship, however, is the employer's continued willingness to employ the party while he does not compete. Where the employer terminates the employment relationship without cause, his action necessarily destroys the mutuality of obligation on which the covenant rests as well as the employer's ability to impose a forfeiture. Thus the forfeiture of the pension benefits is unreasonable as a matter of law, and Post and Maney are entitled to the benefits due.

Obstructing the Administration of Justice

Agreements that are harmful to the administration of justice are illegal and unenforceable. For example, a promise by an employer not to press criminal charges against an embezzling employee who restores the stolen funds is not enforceable. Similarly, a promise to conceal evidence or to give false testimony tends to obstruct the administration of justice and for that reason is illegal and unenforceable.

Corrupting Public Officials

Agreements that may adversely affect the public interest through the corruption of public officials or the impairment of the legislative process are unenforceable. Examples are improper means to influence legislation, to secure some official action, or to procure a government contract.

For example, a bargain by a candidate for public office to make a certain appointment following his election is illegal. In addition, an agreement to pay a public officer something extra for performing his official duty, such as a promise to a policeman for strictly enforcing the traffic laws on his beat, is illegal. The same is true of an agreement in which a citizen promises to perform, or to refrain from performing, duties imposed on her by citizenship. Thus, a promise by Carl to pay fifty dollars to Rachel if she will register and vote is opposed to public policy and illegal.

Exculpatory Clauses

Exculpatory clause—excusing oneself from fault or liability

Some contracts for services contain an exculpatory clause that excuses one party from liability for his own tortious conduct. The courts generally regard this type of clause with disfavor because it is public policy to discourage overreaching and to assure that wrongdoers will pay the damages caused by their negligence. Accordingly, an exculpatory clause on the reverse side of a parking lot claim check that attempts to relieve the parking lot operator of liability for negligently damaging the customer's automobile is unenforceable. On the other hand, the policy of freedom of contract is also a factor in determining the validity of contractual clauses exempting a party from liability for his negligence, and thus not all such clauses are held to be against public policy.

HENRIOULLE v. MARIN VENTURES, INC.

Supreme Court of California, 1978.
20 Cal.3d 512, 573 P.2d 465, 143 Cal.Rptr. 247.

FACTS: Henrioulle was an unemployed widower with two children and received public assistance in the form of a rent subsidy. He entered into a lease agreement with Marin Ventures that provided "INDEMNIFICATION: Owner shall not be liable for any damage or injury to the tenant, or any other person, or to any property, occurring on the premises, or any part thereof, and Tenant agrees to hold Owner harmless for any claims for damages no matter how caused." Henrioulle fractured his wrist when he tripped over a rock on a common stairway in the apartment building. At the time of the accident the landlord had been having difficulty keeping the common areas of the apartment building clean.

DECISION: Judgment for Henrioulle. The criteria used to identify when an exculpatory clause is invalid as against public policy include whether: (1) it concerns a business of a type generally thought suitable for public regulation; (2) the party seeking exculpation is engaged in performing a service of great importance to the public, which is often a matter of practical necessity for some members of the public; (3) the party seeking exculpation is in a superior bargaining position; (4) the exculpatory clause is part of a standard adhesion contract in which the terms of the contract are put on a "take-it-or-leave-it" basis. Here, the transaction, a residential rental agreement, meets these criteria, and therefore, the exculpatory clause is invalid as contrary to public policy. Accordingly, Henrioulle is entitled to recover for his injuries.

Unconscionable Contracts

The Uniform Commercial Code provides that every contract for the sale of goods may be scrutinized by the court to determine whether in its commercial setting, purpose, and effect it is unconscionable or unfair. The court may refuse to enforce an unconscionable contract or any part of the contract it finds to be unconscionable.

The Code denies or limits enforcement of an unconscionable contract for the sale of goods in the interest of fairness and decency and to correct harshness in contracts resulting from unequal bargaining positions of the parties. Although the principle is not novel, its embodiment in a statute dealing with commercial transactions is novel.

Unconscionable contract—unfair or unduly harsh

In many cases a contract between a buyer in pressing need who is in an unequal bargaining position with the seller has been held unconscionable because the seller has put an exorbitant price on his goods. In one case, a price of $749 ($920 on time) for a vacuum cleaner that cost the seller $140 was held unconscionable. In another case the buyers, welfare recipients, purchased by a time payment contract a home freezer unit for $900 that, when added to the time credit charges, credit life insurance, credit property insurance, and sales tax, amounted to $1,235. The purchase resulted from a visit to the buyer's home by a salesman representing Your Shop At Home Service, Inc., and the maximum retail value of the freezer unit at time of purchase was $300. The court held the contract unconscionable and reformed it by reducing the price to the total payment ($620) made by the buyers. Another landmark case follows:

WILLIAMS v. WALKER-THOMAS FURNITURE CO.

United States Court of Appeals, District of Columbia Circuit, 1965.
350 F.2d 445.

FACTS: Between 1957 and 1962, Williams purchased a number of household items on credit from Walker-Thomas Furniture Co., a retail furniture store. Walker-Thomas retained the right in its contracts to repossess an item if Williams defaulted on an installment payment. Each contract also provided that each installment payment by Williams would be credited *pro rata* to all outstanding accounts or bills owed by Walker-Thomas. As a result of this provision, an unpaid balance would remain on every item purchased until the entire balance due on all items, whenever purchased, was paid in full. Williams defaulted on a monthly installment payment in 1962, and Walker-Thomas sought to repossess all the items that Williams had purchased since 1957. Williams claimed that the contracts were unconscionable and therefore unenforceable.

DECISION: Judgment for Williams. In general, one who signs an agreement without knowledge of its terms is bound and is held to have assumed the risk that the bargain was one-sided. But if a party with little bargaining power and, therefore, no meaningful choice enters into a commercially unreasonable contract with little or no knowledge or understanding of its terms, one cannot say that the supposed acceptance was an objective manifestation of assent to all of the terms of the contract. In cases involving allegedly unconscionable terms, the court will examine the reasonableness or fairness of the term at the time that the contract was entered into to determine whether it should be enforced. Generally, the suspect term is evaluated in light of general commercial background and the particular reason for the term's inclusion. If the term is found to be so extreme as to be unconscionable, enforcement of that term should be denied. The contract provision as to prorating each payment on all purchases whenever made is unconscionable and therefore unenforceable.

Effect of Illegality

Unenforceable–neither party can recover under the contract

With few exceptions, illegal contracts are unenforceable. In most cases, neither party to an illegal agreement can sue the other for breach or recover for any performance rendered. It is often said that where parties are *in pari delicto* (in equal fault), a court will leave them where it finds them. The law will provide neither with any remedy.

This strict rule of unenforceability is subject to certain exceptions, however, which we discuss below.

Party Withdrawing Before Performance

Under some circumstances a party to an illegal agreement may, before performance, withdraw from the transaction and recover whatever she has contributed. A common example is recovery of money left with a stakeholder for a wager before it is paid over to the winner, but the rule has also been applied to more serious misconduct.

Party Protected by Statute

Sometimes an agreement is illegal because it violates a statute designed to protect persons who by their actions take the position of one of the parties. For example, State "Blue Sky Laws" prohibiting the sale of unregistered securities are designed primarily to protect investors. In such case, even though there is an unlawful agreement, the statute usually expressly gives the purchaser a right to withdraw the sale and recover the money paid.

Party Not Equally at Fault

Where one of the parties is less at fault than the other, he will be allowed to recover payments made or property transferred. For example, this exception would apply where one party is induced to enter into an illegal bargain through the fraud, duress, or undue influence of the other party.

Party Ignorant of Facts Making Bargain Illegal

An agreement that appears to be entirely permissible on its face may nevertheless be illegal because of facts and circumstances of which one of the parties is completely unaware. For example, a man and woman make mutual promises to marry, but unknown to the woman, the man is already married. This is an agreement to commit the crime of bigamy. It is illegal, and the marriage, if entered into, is void. In such a case the courts permit the party who is ignorant of the illegality to bring a lawsuit against the other party for damages.

Partial Illegality

Ordinarily, the entire agreement is unenforceable if any part of it is illegal. For example, a promise to pay $1,000 for the delivery of two different kinds of goods, one type legal and the other illegal, is unenforceable. The seller may not recover payment for any of the goods delivered. But if the agreement allocates separate prices for the different goods, say $250 for the legal and $750 for the illegal, the seller may recover for the legal goods costing $250. Even though the agreement is tainted with illegality, the courts tend to disregard this if the legal and illegal portions can be "severed" and to permit recovery for the legal portion.

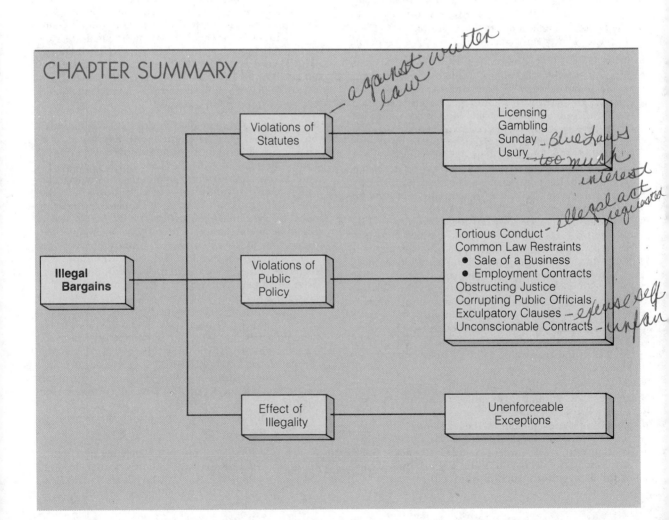

CHAPTER SUMMARY

Illegal Bargains

- Violations of Statutes → Licensing, Gambling, Sunday, Usury *— against written law* *— Blue Laws — too much interest*
- Violations of Public Policy → Tortious Conduct *— illegal act requested*, Common Law Restraints (• Sale of a Business • Employment Contracts), Obstructing Justice, Corrupting Public Officials, Exculpatory Clauses *— excuse self*, Unconscionable Contracts *— unfair*
- Effect of Illegality → Unenforceable, Exceptions

KEY TERMS

License	Blue law	Covenant not to compete
Regulatory statute	Sunday law	Unconscionable contracts
Revenue statute	Usury	Unenforceable
Gambling	Exculpatory clause	

PROBLEMS

1. A and B were the principal shareholders in XYZ Corporation located in the city of Jonesville, Wisconsin. This corporation was engaged in the business of manufacturing paper novelties, which were sold over a wide area in the Midwest. The corporation was also in the business of binding books. A purchased B's shares of the XYZ Corporation and, in consideration thereof, B agreed that for a period of two years he would not: (a) manufacture or sell in Wisconsin any paper novelties of any kind that would compete with those sold by the XYZ Corporation or (b) engage in the bookbinding business in the city of Jonesville. Discuss the validity and effect, if any, of this agreement.

2. Wilkins, a Texas resident licensed by that State as a certified public accountant, rendered service in his professional capacity in Louisiana to Coverton Cosmetics Company. He was not registered as a certified public accountant in Louisiana. His service under his contract with the cosmetics company was not the only occasion on which he had practiced his profession in that State. The company denied liability and refused to pay him, relying on a Louisiana statute declaring it unlawful for any person to perform or offer to perform services as a CPA for compensation until he has been registered by the designated agency of the State and holds an unrevoked registration card. The statute provides that a CPA certificate may be issued without examination to any applicant who holds a valid unrevoked certificate as a CPA under the laws of any other State. The statute provides further that rendering services of the kind performed by Wilkins, without registration, is a misdemeanor punishable by a fine or imprisonment in the county jail, or by both fine and imprisonment. Wilkins brought action against Coverton seeking to recover a fee in the amount of $1,500 as the reasonable value of his services. Decision?

3. A is interested in promoting the passage of a bill in the State legislature. He agrees with B, an attorney, to pay B for her services in writing the required bill, obtaining its introduction in the legislature, and making an argument for its passage before the legislative committee to which it will be referred. B renders these services. Subsequently, on A's refusal to pay B, B sues A for damage for breach of contract. Decision?

4. Anthony promises to pay McMoore $10,000 if McMoore reveals to the public that Washington is a communist. Washington is not a communist and never has been. McMoore successfully persuades the media to report that Washington is a communist and now seeks to recover the $10,000 from Anthony, who refuses to pay. McMoore initiates a lawsuit against Anthony. What results?

5. The Dear Corporation was engaged in the business of making and selling harvesting machines. It sold everything pertaining to the business to the HI Company, agreeing "not again to go into the manufacture of harvesting machines anywhere in the United States." The Dear Corp. had a national and international goodwill in its business. It now begins the manufacture of such machines contrary to its agreement. Should the court stop it from doing so?

6. Charles Leigh, engaged in the industrial laundry business in Central City, employed Tim Close, previously employed in the home laundry business, as a route salesman on July 1, 1986. Leigh rents linens and industrial uniforms to commercial customers; the soiled linens and uniforms are picked up at regular intervals by the route drivers and replaced with clean ones. Every employee is assigned a list of customers whom he or she services. The contract of employment stated that in consideration of being employed, on termination of the employment, Close would not "directly or indirectly engage in the linen supply business or any competitive business within Central City, Illinois, for a period of one year from the date when his employment under this contract ceases." On May 10 of the following year, Close's employment was terminated by Leigh for valid reasons. Close then accepted employment with Ajax Linen Service, a direct competitor of Leigh in Central City. He began soliciting former customers whom he had called on for Leigh and obtained some of them as customers for Ajax.

Leigh brings an action to enforce the provisions of the contract. Decision?

7. On July 5, 1980, Billy and Nancy entered into a bet on the outcome of the 1980 presidential election. On January 28, 1982, Nancy, who bet on Ronald Reagan, approached Billy seeking to collect the $3,000 Billy had wagered on Jimmy Carter. Billy paid Nancy the wager and now seeks to recover the funds from Nancy. Result?

8. C, a salesman for S, comes to B's home and sells him a complete set of "gourmet cooking utensils" that are worth approximately $300. B, an eighty-year-old man, lives alone in a one-room efficiency apartment. B signs a contract to buy the utensils for $1,450 plus a credit charge of $145 and to make payment in ten equal monthly installments. Three weeks after C leaves with the signed contract, B decides he cannot afford the cooking utensils and has no use for them. What can B do?

9. A rents a bicycle from B. The bicycle rental contract A signed provides that B is not liable for any injury to the renter caused by any defect in the bicycle or the negligence of B. A is injured when she is involved in an accident due to B's improper maintenance of the bicycle. A sues B for her damage. Decision?

12

CONTRACTUAL CAPACITY

A binding promise or agreement requires that the parties to the agreement have contractual capacity. Everyone is regarded as having such capacity unless the law for public policy reasons holds that the individual lacks such capacity. We consider this essential ingredient of a contract by discussing those classes and conditions of persons who are legally limited in their capacity to contract: minors, incompetent persons, and intoxicated persons.

Minors

A minor, also called an infant, is a person who has not attained the age of legal majority. At common law a minor was an individual who had not reached the age of twenty-one years. Today the age of majority has been changed in nearly all jurisdictions by statute, usually to age eighteen. Almost without exception a minor's contract is **voidable** at his option. Even an "emancipated" minor, one who because of marriage or other reasons is no longer subject to strict parental control, may avoid contractual liability in most jurisdictions. Consequently, businesspeople deal with minors at their peril.

Minor—under full legal age

Voidable—can be terminated by one or more of the parties

Liability for Necessaries

Contractual immunity does not excuse a minor from an obligation to pay for necessaries, those things that suitably and reasonably supply his personal needs, such as food, shelter, and clothing. Even here, however, the minor is contractually liable not for the agreed price but for the reasonable value of the items furnished. Recovery is based on quasi contract. Thus, if a clothier sells a minor a suit that the minor needs, the clothier can successfully sue the minor and recover the reasonable value of the suit. The clothier is limited to this amount even if it is much less than the selling price.

Necessary—items to maintain one's station in life

Determining what are necessaries is a difficult problem. In general, the States regard as necessary those things that the minor needs to maintain himself in his particular station in life. Items necessary for subsistence and health, such as food, lodging, clothing, medicine, and medical services, are obviously included. But other less essential items such as textbooks, school instruction, and legal advice, may be included as well. Further, some States enlarge the concept of necessaries to include articles of property and services that a minor needs to earn the money required to provide the necessities of life for himself and his dependents. Moreover, many States limit necessaries to items that are not provided to the minor. Thus, if a minor's guardian provides her with an adequate wardrobe, a blouse the minor purchased would *not* be considered a necessity.

The following is the leading case on the rights and obligations of minors for the purchase of "necessaries."

GASTONIA PERSONNEL CORP. v. ROGERS

Supreme Court of North Carolina, 1970.
276 N.C. 279, 172 S.E.2d 19.

FACTS: Rogers was a nineteen-year-old (the age of majority then being twenty-one) high school graduate pursuing a civil engineering degree when he learned that his wife was expecting a child. As a result he quit school and sought assistance from Gastonia Personnel Corporation in finding a job. Rogers signed a contract with the employment agency providing that he would pay the agency a service charge if it obtained suitable employment for him. The employment agency found him such a job, but Rogers refused to pay the service charge asserting that he was a minor when he signed the contract. Gastonia sued to recover the agreed upon service charge from Rogers.

DECISION: Judgment for Gastonia Personnel Corporation. In general, a contract with a minor is voidable by the minor unless the contract is for necessaries. The law is based on the idea that society has a moral obligation to protect the interests of minors from overreaching adults. In its effort to protect "older minors" from improvident or unfair contracts, however, the law should not deny them the opportunity and the right to obligate themselves for articles of property or services that are reasonably necessary to enable them to provide for the proper support of themselves and their dependents. Since the service provided by the employment agency in finding Rogers a suitable job qualifies as such a service, the contract is not voidable, and the agency can recover the service charge.

Ordinarily, luxury items, such as cameras, tape recorders, phonographs, television sets, and motorboats, do not qualify as necessaries. Whether automobiles and trucks are necessaries has caused considerable controversy, but some courts have recognized that under certain circumstances an automobile may be a necessary where it is used by the minor for his business activities. The following case should be compared with *Halbman v. Lemke* on page 199 and *Robertson v. King* on page 200.

ROSE v. SHEEHAN BUICK, INC.

Florida Court of Appeals, 1967.
204 So.2d 903.

FACTS: Rose, a minor, bought a new Buick Riviera from Sheehan Buick. Seven months later, while still a minor, he attempted to disaffirm the purchase. Sheehan Buick refused to accept the return of the car or to refund the purchase price. Rose, at the time of the purchase, gave all the appearance of being of legal age. The car had been used by him to carry on his school, business, and social activities.

DECISION: Judgment for Sheehan Buick. The car is a necessity for Rose in order to carry out his schooling, business, and other activities. Therefore, he cannot avoid the obligation.

Liability on Contracts

A minor's contract is not entirely void and of no legal effect; rather, it is voidable at the minor's option. He has a power of avoidance. His exercise of this power is called a **disaffirmance,** and he is released from any liability on the contract. On the other hand, after the minor becomes of age, he may choose to adopt or **ratify** the contract, in which case he becomes bound.

Disaffirmance–avoidance of the contract

Disaffirmance   As we stated earlier, a minor's contract is voidable at his option; he thus has the power to avoid liability. He may exercise his power to disaffirm a contract through words or conduct showing an intention not to abide by it. We consider aspects of this power in the following order: (1) When can the minor disaffirm? (2) How can she disaffirm? (3) What, if anything, must she do upon a disaffirmance?

In general, a minor may disaffirm a contract at any time, either before or within a reasonable time after he becomes of age. A notable exception is that a sale of land by a minor cannot be disaffirmed until after he reaches his majority. But must he disaffirm immediately upon becoming an adult? In the case of a sale of land, there is a strong precedent that the minor may wait until the expiration of the period of the Statute of Limitations if there are no questions of fairness and equity involved. This is not the case with other types of contracts. There he must disaffirm either during his minority or within a reasonable time after reaching majority, the precise time period varying with the circumstances and local law.

Disaffirmance may be either *express* or *implied*. No particular form of words is essential, so long as they show an intention not to be bound. This intention may be manifested by acts or by conduct. For example, a minor agrees to sell property to Andy and then sells the property to Betty. The sale to Betty constitutes a disaffirmance of the contract with Andy.

A troublesome yet important problem in this area pertains to the minor's duty upon disaffirmance. The courts do not agree on this question. The majority, as demonstrated in *Halbman v. Lemke,* hold that the minor must only return any property he has received from the other party, provided he has it in his possession at the time of disaffirmance. Nothing more is required. If the minor disaffirms the purchase of an automobile and the vehicle has been wrecked, he need only return the wrecked vehicle. A few States, however, either by statute or common law, recognize a duty on the part of the minor to make *restitution*, that is, to return an equivalent of what has been received so that the seller will be in approximately the same position he would have occupied had the sale not occurred. Other States require at least the payment of a reasonable amount for the use of the property or the amount of its depreciation while in the hands of the minor.

HALBMAN v. LEMKE

Supreme Court of Wisconsin, 1980.
99 Wis.2d 241, 298 N.W.2d 562.

FACTS: Halbman, a minor, purchased a 1968 Oldsmobile from Lemke for $1,250. Under the terms of the contract, Halbman would pay $1,000 down and the balance in $25 weekly installments. Upon making the down payment, Halbman received possession of the car, but Lemke retained the title until the balance was paid. After Halbman had made his first four payments, a connecting rod in the car's engine broke. Lemke denied responsibility, but offered to help Halbman repair it if Halbman would provide the parts. Halbman, however, placed the car in a garage where the repairs cost $637.40. Halbman never paid the repair bill.

Hoping to avoid any liability for the vehicle, Lemke transferred title to Halbman even though Halbman never paid the balance owed. Halbman returned the title with a letter disaffirming the contract and demanded return of the money paid. Lemke refused. Since the repair bill remained unpaid, the garage removed the car's engine and transmission and towed the body to Halbman's father's house. Vandalism during the periods of storage rendered the car unsalvageable. Several times Halbman requested Lemke to remove the car. Lemke refused. Halbman sued Lemke for the return of his consideration and Lemke countersued for the amount still owed on the contract.

DECISION: Judgment for Halbman. Halbman, as a minor, had an absolute right to disaffirm the contract for the purchase of the car, since it is not a necessary item. In addition, he is entitled to recover all consideration he has conferred incident to the transaction. As a disaffirming minor, he is under an enforceable duty to return only that much of the consideration as remained in his possession; he need not make restitution for that which he does not possess. If there was a misrepresentation by Halbman or willful destruction of the car, Lemke could have recovered damages in tort. But absent these factors, to require a disaffirming minor to make restitution for diminished value is, in effect, to bind the minor to a part of the obligation which by law he is privileged to avoid.

Finally, can a minor disaffirm and recover property that he has sold to a buyer who in turn has sold it to a good faith purchaser for value? Traditionally, the minor could avoid the contract and recover the property, despite the fact that the third person gave value for it and had no notice of the minority. However, the Uniform Commercial Code has changed this principle in connection with sales of goods. The Code provides that a person with voidable title (e.g., the person buying goods from a minor) has power to transfer valid title to a good faith purchaser for value. For example, a minor sells his car to an individual who resells it to a use-car dealership, a good faith purchaser for value. The used-car dealer would acquire legal title even though he bought the car from a seller who had only voidable title. The case of *Robertson v. King* discusses what the minor would be entitled to receive once the automobile can no longer be obtained through disaffirmance. In the case of the sale of real estate, however, the traditional rule applies, and a minor's deed of conveyance may be taken back even against a good faith purchaser of the land who did not know of the minority.

ROBERTSON v. KING

Supreme Court of Arkansas, 1955.
225 Ark. 276, 280 S.W.2d 402.

FACTS: L. D. Robertson bought a pickup truck from King and Julian, doing business as the Julian Pontiac Company. Robertson, at the time of purchase was 17 years old, living at home with his parents and driving his father's truck around the county to different construction jobs. According to the sales contract, he traded in a passenger car for the truck and was given $723 credit toward the truck's $1,743 purchase price, agreeing to pay the remainder in monthly installments. After he paid the first month's installment, the truck caught fire and was rendered useless. The insurance agent, upon finding that Robertson was a minor, refused to deal with him. Consequently, Robertson sued to exercise his right as a minor to rescind the contract and to recover the purchase price he had already paid ($723 credit for the car plus the one month's installment). The defendants argue that Robertson, even as a minor, cannot rescind the contract since it was for a necessary item.

DECISION: Judgment for Robertson. A minor may rescind a contract to purchase where the property involved is not a necessary. There was no evidence that Robertson, who lived at home with his parents, needed the truck in connection with any work he was doing. Since the defendants failed to prove that the truck was a necessary item, Robertson, as a minor, may rescind.

Upon avoidance of the contract the plaintiff was then entitled to recover the car traded in on payment for the truck, but the defendants had already disposed of it. Robertson was therefore entitled to receive the actual value of the traded-in car. Nonetheless, the actual value of a trade-in may be more or less than the value stated in the contract, neither party is bound by the contract value. Thus, Robertson is entitled to recover the reasonable market value of the car at the time of purchase ($350), rather than the value stated in the contract ($723).

Ratification–affirmation of the contract

Ratification   Suppose that a minor makes a contract to buy property from an adult. The contract is voidable by the minor, and she can escape liability. But suppose that after reaching her majority, she promises to go through with the purchase. Her promise is binding, and the adult can sue for breach if she fails to carry out the terms of the contract. She has *expressly* ratified the contract entered into when she was a minor.

Ratification makes the contract binding *ab initio*. That is, the result is the same as if the contract had been valid and binding from the beginning. Ratification, once effected, is final and cannot be withdrawn.

Ratification must be in total; it must validate the entire contract. The minor can ratify the contract only as a whole, both as to burdens and benefits. He cannot, for example, ratify so as to retain the consideration he received and escape payment or other performance on his part.

FACTS: Langstraat, age seventeen, owned a motorcycle which he insured against liability with Midwest Mutual Insurance Company. He signed a notice of rejection attached to the policy indicating that he did not desire to purchase uninsured motorists coverage from the insurance company. Later he was involved in an accident with another motorcycle owned and operated by a party who was uninsured. Langstraat now seeks to recover from the insurance company asserting that his rejection was not a valid rejection because he is a minor.

DECISION: Judgment for Midwest Mutual Insurance Company. This is not a case in which the minor seeks to disaffirm a contract. What Langstraat seeks here is to ratify and retain the benefits of the policy but to avoid the one provision which has become burdensome. A minor is not permitted this selective choice. Ratification and disaffirmance go to the whole contract. Since Langstraat did not wish to disaffirm the insurance policy, the notice of rejection is valid, and he is not entitled to recover.

LANGSTRAAT v.
MIDWEST MUTUAL,
INS. CO.

Supreme Court of Iowa,
1974.
217 N.W.2d 570.

Ratification need not be express; it may be *implied* from a person's conduct. Suppose that the minor, after attaining her majority, uses the property, undertakes to sell it to someone else, or performs some other act showing an intention to affirm the contract. She may not thereafter disaffirm the contract but is bound by it. Perhaps the most common form of implied ratification occurs when the minor, after attaining her majority, continues to use the property that she purchased as a minor. This use is obviously inconsistent with the nonexistence of the contract. Whether the contract is performed or still partly executory, the continued use of the property amounts to a ratification and prevents a disaffirmance by the minor. Simply keeping the goods for an unreasonable time after attaining majority has also been construed as a ratification. Although the courts are divided on this issue, payments by the minor either on principal or interest or on the purchase price of goods have been held to amount to a ratification. Some courts require some additional evidence of an intention to abide by the contract, such as an express promise to that effect or the actual use of the subject matter of the contract.

Note that a minor has *no* power to ratify a contract while he remains a minor. A ratification *cannot* be based on words or conduct occurring while he is still underage, for his ratification at that time would be no more effective than his original contractual promise. The ratification must take place after the individual has acquired contractual capacity by attaining his majority.

Liability for Misrepresentation of Age

The States do not agree whether a minor who fraudulently misrepresents her age when entering into a contract has the power to disaffirm. Suppose a minor says that she is eighteen years of age (or twenty-one if that is the year of attaining majority) and actually looks that old or even older? By the prevailing view in this country the minor may nevertheless disaffirm the contract. However, some States prohibit disaffirmance if a minor misrepresents her age and the adult, in good faith, reasonably relied on the misrepresentation. Other States, including Colorado as shown in the following case, not following the majority rule either (a) require the minor to restore the other party to the position she occupied before making the contract or (b) allow the defrauded party to recover damages against the minor in tort.

KESER v. CHAGNON

Supreme Court of Colorado, 1966.
159 Colo. 209, 410 P.2d 637.

FACTS: On June 11, 1964, Chagnon bought a 1959 Edsel from Keser for $995. Chagnon, who was then a twenty-year-old minor, obtained the contract by falsely advising Keser that he was over twenty-one years old, the age of majority. On September 25, 1964, two months and four days after his twenty-first birthday, Chagnon disaffirmed the contract and, ten days later, returned the Edsel to Keser. He then brought suit to recover the money he had paid for the automobile. Keser counterclaims that he suffered damages as the direct result of Chagnon's false representation as to his age.

DECISION: Judgment for Keser. If a minor does not exercise his right to disaffirm a contract within a "reasonable time" after he reaches the age of majority, he loses that right. Here, however, Chagnon's disaffirmance just two months after reaching majority, was within a reasonable time. Once he returned the car—the only consideration in his possession—he was entitled to recover the full $995.

However, while a false representation as to his age does not destroy a minor's right to disaffirm, it does permit the seller to deduct from the buyer's compensation any damages which he suffered due to the false representation. The measure of damages for the seller is the difference between the reasonable value of the property on the date of delivery and its reasonable value on the date of its return. Since Chagnon obtained the contract by false representation as to his age, he will not recover his full $995. Instead, his recovery is decreased by the amount of Keser's damages—the loss of the Edsel's reasonable value.

Liability for Tort Connected with Contract

It is well settled that minors are generally liable for their torts. There is, however, a doctrine in the law that if a tort and a contract are so connected or "interwoven" that to enforce the tort action the court must enforce the contract, the minor is not liable in tort. Thus, if a minor rents an automobile from an adult, he enters into a contractual relationship obliging him to exercise reasonable care and diligence to protect the property from injury. By negligently damaging the automobile, he breaches that contractual undertaking. But his contractual immunity protects him from an action by the adult based on the contract. Can the adult sue for damages on a tort theory? By the majority view he cannot. For, it is reasoned, a tort recovery would, in effect, be an enforcement of the contract and would defeat the protection that contract law gives the minor.

There is a different result, however, when the minor departs from the terms of the agreement, as by using a rental automobile for an unauthorized purpose and in so doing negligently causes damage to the automobile. In that event most courts would hold that the tort is independent, and the adult can collect from the minor. This would not involve the breach of a contractual duty, but rather the commission of a tort during the course of an activity that is a complete departure from the rental agreement.

Incompetent Persons

Person Under Guardianship

If a person is under guardianship by **court order,** her contracts are **void** and of no legal effect. A *guardian* is appointed by a court, generally under the terms of a statute, to control and preserve the property of a person (the *ward*) with impaired capacity to manage her own property. Nonetheless, a party dealing with an individual under guardianship may be able to recover the fair value of any necessaries provided to the incompetent. Moreover, the contracts of the ward may be ratified by her guardian during the period of guardianship or by herself on termination of the guardianship.

Guardianship–the relationship under which a person (the guardian) is appointed by a court to preserve and control the property of another (the ward)

Void–no contract

Mental Illness or Defect

Because a contract is a consensual transaction, the parties to a valid contract must have a certain level of mental capacity. If a person lacks such capacity, or is mentally incompetent, he may avoid liability under the agreement.

A person who is lacking in sufficient mental capacity to enter into a contract is one unable to comprehend the subject of the contract, its nature, and its probable consequences. He does not need to be proved permanently incompetent to avoid the contract, but his mental defect must be something more than a weakness of intellect or a lack of average intelligence. In short, a person is competent unless he is unable to understand the nature and effect of his act.

Mentally incompetent–unable to understand the nature and effect of one's acts

---

G.A.S. v. S.I.S.

Family Court of Delaware, New Castle County, 1978. 407 A.2d 253.

FACTS: G.A.S. married his wife, S.I.S., on January 19, 1957. His mental health problems began in 1970 when he was hospitalized at the Delaware State Hospital for eight weeks. Similar illnesses occurred in 1972 and the early part of 1974, with G.A.S. suffering from such symptoms as paranoia and loss of a sense of reality. In early 1975, G.A.S. was still committed to the Delaware State Hospital, attending a regular job during the day and returning to the hospital at night. It was during this time that he entered into a separation agreement prepared by his wife's attorney. G.A.S., however, never spoke with the attorney about the contents of the agreement, nor did he read it prior to signing. Moreover, G.A.S. was not independently represented by counsel when he executed this agreement. G.A.S. brings this action to rescind (disaffirm) the separation agreement.

DECISION: Judgment for G.A.S. Only competent persons can make a contract, and where there is no capacity to understand or agree, there can be no contract. Although G.A.S. was still under commitment to the Delaware State Hospital at the time of execution of the separation agreement, he had not been judicially judged mentally incompetent. The agreement, therefore, is not void but may be voidable. The mental incapacity sufficient to permit the cancellation of an agreement must render the afflicted individual incapable of understanding the nature and effect of the transaction and unable to properly, intelligently, and fairly protect and preserve his property rights. In this case G.A.S. was not able to understand or comprehend what he was signing, and hence the separation agreement is voidable.

As with minors and persons under guardianship, an incompetent person is liable for *necessaries* furnished on the principle of quasi contract, the amount of recovery being the reasonable value of the goods or services. Moreover, an incompetent person may *ratify* or *disaffirm* his **voidable** contracts when he becomes competent, or during a lucid period.

According to the predominant view in this country, an incompetent person's responsibility on disaffirmance varies somewhat from a minor's. If the contract is fair and the competent party had no reason to suspect the incompetency of the other, the incompetent must restore the competent party to the *status quo* by a return of the consideration received by the incompetent or its equivalent in money.

Intoxicated Persons

A person may *avoid* any contract that he enters into if the other party has reason to know that, because of intoxication, he is unable to understand the nature and consequences of his actions or unable to act in a reasonable manner. Such contracts are **voidable.** Although slight intoxication will not destroy one's contractual capacity, it is not essential that a person is so drunk that he is totally without reason or understanding.

The effect of intoxication on contractual capacity is generally the same as that given to contracts that are voidable because of incompetency. The options of *ratification* or *disaffirmance* remain, although the courts are even more strict with respect to the requirement of restitution on disaffirmance than they are in the area of an incompetent person's agreements. The rule is relaxed only where the person dealing with the intoxicated person fraudulently takes advantage of the intoxicated individual. As with incompetent persons, intoxicated persons are liable in quasi contract for necessaries furnished during their incapacity.

Figure 12-1 summarizes the effects of contracts made by persons with contractual incapacity.

FIGURE 12-1   Contractual Incapacity

Incapacity	Effect
Minority	Voidable
Mental illness or defect	Voidable
Guardianship for incompetency	Void
Intoxication	Voidable

CHAPTER SUMMARY

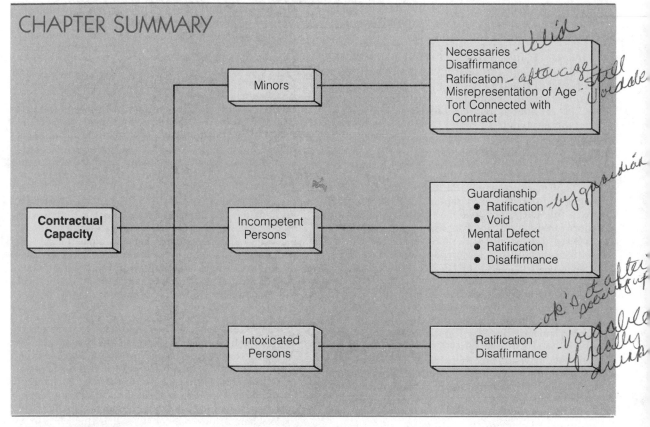

Minors — Necessaries, Disaffirmance, Ratification — *aftercare* (handwritten: *valid*, *aftercare still voidable*), Misrepresentation of Age, Tort Connected with Contract

Contractual Capacity — Incompetent Persons — Guardianship: Ratification (handwritten: *by guardian*), Void; Mental Defect: Ratification, Disaffirmance

Intoxicated Persons — Ratification, Disaffirmance (handwritten: *ok's it after sobering up*, *voidable if really drunk*)

KEY TERMS

Capacity	Ratification	Guardian
Minor	Disaffirmance	Ward
Voidable	Mentally Incompetent	Void
Necessary	Guardianship	Intoxicated person

PROBLEMS

1. M, a minor, operates a one-man automobile repair shop. A, having heard of M's good work on other cars, takes her car to M's shop for a thorough engine overhaul. M, while overhauling A's engine, carelessly fits an unsuitable piston ring on one of the pistons, with the result that A's engine is seriously damaged. M offers to return the sum that A paid him for his work, but refuses to make good the damage. A sues M in tort for the damage to her engine. Decision?

2. (a) On March 20, Andy Small became seventeen years old, but he appeared to be at least eighteen (the age of majority). On April 1, he moved into a rooming house in Chicago and orally agreed to pay the land-lady $300 a month for room and board, payable at the end of each month.

(b) On April 4, he went to Honest Al's Car-feteria and signed a contract to buy a used car on time with a small down payment. He made no representation as to his age, but Honest Hal represented the car to be in top condition, which it subsequently turned out not to be.

(c) On April 7, Andy sold and conveyed to Adam Smith a parcel of real estate that he owned.

On April 30, Andy refused to pay his landlady for his room and board for the month of April; he returned the car to Honest Hal and demanded a refund of his down payment; and he demanded that Adam

Smith reconvey the land although the purchase price, which Andy received in cash, had been spent in riotous living. Decisions as to each claim?

3. Jones, a minor, owned a 1984 automobile. She traded it to Stone for a 1985 car. Jones went on a three-week trip and found that the 1985 car was not as good as the 1984 car. She asked Stone to return the 1984 car but was told that it had been sold to Tate. Jones thereupon sued Tate for the return of the 1984 car. Decision?

4. On May 7, Roy, a minor, a resident of Smithton, purchased an automobile from Royal Motors, Inc., for $7,750 in cash. On the same day he bought a motor scooter from Marks, also a minor, for $750 and paid him in full. On June 5, two days before attaining his majority, Roy disaffirmed the contracts and offered to return the car and the motor scooter to the respective sellers. Royal Motors, Inc. and Marks each refused the offers. On June 16, Roy brought separate appropriate actions against Royal Motors, Inc., and Marks to recover the purchase price of the car and the motor scooter. By agreement on July 30, Royal Motors, Inc., accepted the automobile. Royal filed a counterclaim against Roy for the reasonable rental value of the car between June 5 and July 30. The car was not damaged during this period. Royal knew that Roy lived twenty-five miles from his place of employment in Smithton and that he would probably use the car, as he did, for necessary transportation. Decision as to (a) Roy's action against Royal Motors, Inc., and its counterclaim against Roy; (b) Roy's action against Marks?

5. On October 1, George Jones, who was then a minor, entered into a contract with Johnson Motor Company, a dealer in automobiles, to buy a car for $7,600. He paid $1,100 down and agreed to make monthly payments thereafter of $325 each. Although he made the first payment on November 1, he failed to make any more payments. Jones was seventeen years old at the time he made the contract. He represented to the company that he was twenty-one years old because he was afraid that the company would not sell the car to him if it knew his real age. His appearance was that of a man of twenty-one years of age. On December 15, the company repossessed the car under the terms provided in the contract. At that time, the car had been damaged and was in need of repairs. On December 20, George Jones became of age and at once disaffirmed the contract and demanded the return of

the $1,425 paid on the contract. When the company refused to do so, Jones brought an action to recover the $1,425, and the company set up a counterclaim for $1,500 for expenses to which it was put in repairing the car. Decision?

6. A entered into a written contract to sell certain real estate to M, a minor, for $80,000, payable $4,000 on the execution of the contract and $400 on the first day of each month thereafter until paid. M paid the $4,000 down payment and eight monthly installments before attaining her majority. Thereafter, M made two additional monthly payments and caused the contract to be recorded in the county where the real estate was located. M was then advised by her attorney that the contract was voidable. After being so advised, M immediately tendered the contract to A, together with a deed reconveying all of M's interest in the property to A. Also, M demanded that A return the money which she had paid under the contract. A refused the tender and declined to repay any portion of the money paid to him by M. M then brought an action to cancel the contract and recover the amount paid to A. Decision?

7. A sold and delivered an automobile to B, a minor. B, during his minority, returned the automobile to A, saying that he disaffirmed the sale. A accepted the automobile and said she would return the purchase price to B the next day. Later in the day, B changed his mind, took the automobile without A's knowledge, and sold it to C. A had not returned the purchase price when B took the car. On what theory, if any, can A recover from B?

8. N, who in 1984 had been found innocent of a criminal offense because of insanity, was released from the hospital for the criminally insane during the summer of 1985 and since that time has been a reputable and well-respected citizen and businessman. On February 1, 1986, N and S entered into a contract in which N would sell his farm to S for $100,000. N seeks to void the contract. S insists that N is fully competent and has no right to avoid the contract. Who will prevail? Why?

9. D, while under the influence of alcohol, agreed to sell his 1983 automobile to B for $8,000. The next morning when B went to D's house with the $8,000 in cash, D stated that he did not remember the transaction but "a deal is a deal." One week after completing the sale, D decides that he wishes to avoid the contract. What result?

CONTRACTS IN WRITING

An **oral** contract, that is, one not in writing, is in every way as enforceable as a written contract unless otherwise provided by statute. Although most contracts do not need to be in writing to be enforceable, it is highly desirable that significant contracts be written. Written contracts avoid many problems inevitably involved in proving the terms of oral contracts. The process of setting down the contractual terms in a written document also tends to clarify the terms and bring to light a number of problems the parties might not otherwise foresee. Moreover, the terms of a written contract do not change over time, whereas the parties' recollections of the terms might.

When the parties do reduce their agreement to a complete and final written expression, the law (the parol evidence rule) honors this document by not allowing the parties to introduce any evidence in a lawsuit that would alter, modify, or vary the terms of the written contract. Nevertheless, the parties may differ as to the proper or intended meaning of language contained in the written agreement where such language is ambiguous or susceptible to different interpretations. To determine the proper meaning requires an interpretation, or construction, of the contract. The rules of construction permit the parties to introduce evidence to resolve ambiguity and to show the meaning of the language employed and the sense in which both parties used it.

In this chapter we examine (1) the types of contracts that must be in writing to be enforceable, (2) the parol evidence rule, and (3) the rules of contractual interpretation.

Statute of Frauds

The Statute of Frauds requires that certain designated types of contracts be in a particular form to be enforceable. The original statute became law in 1677 when the English Parliament adopted "An Act for Prevention of Frauds and Perjuries," commonly referred to as the Statute of Frauds. From the early days of American history practically every State has and continues to have a Statute of Frauds patterned on the original English statute.

Statute of frauds–contracts that must be in writing

Contracts Within the Statute of Frauds

Many more types of contracts are not subject to the Statute of Frauds than are subject to it. Most oral contracts, as previously indicated, are as enforceable and valid as a written contract. However, if a given contract is subject to the

Statute of Frauds, the contract is said to be **"within"** the Statute, and to be enforceable it must comply with the requirements of the Statute. All other types of contracts are said to be "not within" or "outside" the Statute and need not comply with its requirements to be enforceable.

The following five types of contracts are within the original English Statute and remain within most State statutes. Compliance requires a writing signed by the party to be charged (the party seeking to avoid the contract).

1. Promises to answer for the duty of another;

2. Promises of an executor or administrator to answer personally for a duty of the decedent whose funds he is administering;

3. Agreements upon consideration of marriage;

4. Agreements for the sale of an interest in land; and

5. Agreements not to be performed within one year.

A sixth type of contract within the Statute applied to contracts for the sale of goods. The enforceability of contracts of this type is now governed by the Uniform Commercial Code.

In addition to those contracts specified in the original statute, some modern statutes require that others be written. Examples are a contract to make a will, to authorize an agent to sell real estate, or to pay a commission to a real estate broker. Moreover, the UCC requires that a contract for the sale of securities and contracts creating certain types of security interests be in writing.

Suretyship Provision

Suretyship–guarantee to pay debts of another

Surety–promisor who secures the debt of another

Principal debtor–person whose debt is being supported

Collateral–secondarily liable, only liable if the party with primary liability does not perform

The suretyship provision applies to a contractual promise by a *promisor* (called a **surety**) to a **creditor** (*promisee*) to perform the duties or obligations of a third person **(principal debtor)** if the principal/debtor does not perform. Thus, if a mother tells a merchant to extend $1,000 worth of credit to her son and says, "If he doesn't pay, I will," the promise must be in writing to be enforceable. The factual situation can be reduced to the simple "If X doesn't pay, I will." The promise is said to be **collateral,** in that the promisor is not the one who is primarily liable. She does not promise to pay in any event; her promise is to pay only if the one primarily obligated defaults.

(son) **Principal Debtor** — (1) $1,000 Debt credit → **Promisee/Creditor** (merchant)

(2) Pay $1,000 Debt if Principal Debtor does not

(mother) **Promisor/ Surety**

The rule applies only to cases where three parties and two contracts are involved. The primary contract is between the principal debtor and the creditor and creates the indebtedness. The collateral contract is made by the third person (surety) directly with the creditor, whereby she promises to pay the debt to the creditor in case the principal debtor (son) fails to do so. For a complete discussion of suretyship see Chapter 37.

Promise Must Be Collateral   It is sometimes difficult to determine whether a promise is "collateral" ("I'll pay if X doesn't") or whether the promisor undertakes to become primarily liable, or, as the courts say, makes an **original** promise ("I'll pay"). For example, a father tells a merchant to deliver certain items to his daughter and says, "I will pay $400 for them." The Statute of Frauds does not apply, and the promise may be oral. Here, the father is not promising to answer for the debt of another, but rather he is making the debt his own. It is to the father, and to the father alone, that the merchant extends credit and may look for payment. The following case further illustrates the distinction.

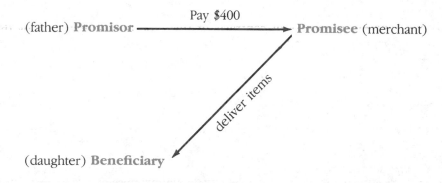

SHANE QUADRI v. GOODYEAR SERVICE STORES

Court of Appeals of Indiana, Third District, 1980. 412 N.E.2d 315.

FACTS: The defendant, Shane Quadri, contacted Dan Hoffman, an employee of defendant Al J. Hoffman & Co., to procure car insurance. Later, Quadri's car was stolen on October 25 or 26, 1977. Quadri contacted Hoffman who arranged with Budget Rent-a-Car, a plaintiff in this case, for a rental car for Quadri until his car was recovered. Hoffman authorized Budget Rent-a-Car to bill the Hoffman Agency. Later, when the stolen car was recovered, Hoffman telephoned plaintiff, Goodyear, and arranged to have four new tires put on Quadri's car to replace those damaged during the theft. The plaintiffs (Budget and Goodyear) sued the defendants (Quadri and Hoffman) for payment for the car rental and tires.

DECISION: Judgment for Budget and Goodyear against Hoffman and judgment for Quadri. Although the Statute of Frauds makes unenforceable oral contracts to pay the debts of a third person, it does not apply to original promises to pay for services rendered to a third person. Hoffman initiated the transactions with both Budget and Goodyear by telephone, indicating that Quadri was insured and authorized the billing of the Hoffman Agency. By signing the rental agreement and tire invoice, Quadri merely obtained the benefits of the transactions authorized by Hoffman. Since credit was extended solely to the Hoffman Agency, the statute does not apply to Hoffman's oral promises. Thus, they are enforceable against Hoffman.

Main Purpose Doctrine   The courts have developed an exception to the suretyship provision based on the purpose or object of the promisor, called the "main purpose doctrine" or "leading object rule." Where the object of the promisor is to obtain an economic benefit that he did not previously have, the promise is *not* within the Statute. Suppose that a supply company has refused to furnish materials on the credit of a building contractor. Faced with

Main purpose–object of promisor/surety is to provide an economic benefit for herself

a possible slowdown in construction of his building, the owner of the land promises the supplier that if he will extend credit to the contractor, the owner will pay if the contractor does not. Here, the purpose of the promisor was to serve an economic interest of his own, even though the performance of the promise would discharge the duty of another. The intent to benefit the contractor was at most incidental, and courts will uphold oral promises of this type. Another application of the rule is provided in the following case:

STUART STUDIO, INC. v. NATIONAL SCHOOL OF HEAVY EQUIPMENT, INC.

Court of Appeals of North Carolina, 1975.
25 N.C.App. 544, 214 S.E.2d 192.

FACTS: Stuart Studios, an art studio, prepared a new catalog for a school run by Gilbert and Donald Shaw. When the art work was virtually finished, Gilbert Shaw requested Stuart Studios to purchase and supervise the printing of 25,000 catalogs. Shaw told the art studio that payment of the printing costs would be made within ten days after billing and that if the "National School would not pay the full total that he would stand good for the entire bill." Shaw was chairman of the Board of Directors of the school and he owned 100 percent of its voting stock and 49 percent of its Class B stock. The school became bankrupt, and Stuart Studios was unable to recover the sum from the school. Stuart Studios then brought this action against Shaw on the basis of his promise to stand good for the bill. The trial court granted Shaw's motion for a directed verdict and Stuart Studios brought this appeal.

DECISION: Judgment for Stuart Studio. The Statute of Frauds requires promises to answer for the duties of another to be in writing to be enforceable. However, where the promise is collateral and it appears that the promisor's main purpose in guaranteeing the obligation was to secure an advantage or economic benefit for himself, the promise is enforceable even though it was not in writing. The benefit accruing to a party merely by virtue of his position as a stockholder, officer, or director of a corporation alone is not such personal, immediate, and economic benefit as to invoke the main purpose rule. Rather, the court will examine the surety's position and ownership interest in the corporation to determine whether he has enough control of the corporation to benefit directly. Here, Gilbert Shaw exercised sufficient control over the National School to render his oral promise enforceable.

Promise Made to Debtor   Courts do not regard promises made to a *debtor* as being within the Statute. For example, D owes a debt to C. S promises D to pay her debt. Since the promise of S was made to the debtor, not the creditor, the promise may be oral.

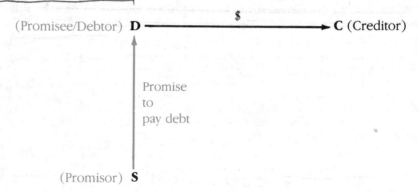

Executor-Administrator Provision

The executor-administrator provision applies to promises of an executor of a decedent's will, or the administrator of the estate if there is no will, to answer personally for a duty of the decedent. An executor or administrator is a person appointed by a court to carry on, subject to order of court, the administration of the estate of a deceased person. If the will of a decedent nominates a certain person as executor, the court usually appoints that person. If an executor or administrator promises to answer personally for a duty of the decedent, the promise is unenforceable unless in writing. For example, A, who is B's son and executor of B's will, recognizes that B's estate will not have enough funds to pay all of the decedent's debts. He orally promises C, one of B's creditors, that he will personally pay all of his father's debts in full. A's oral promise is not enforceable.

Marriage Provision

The notable feature of the marriage provision is that it does not apply to mutual promises to marry. The provision, as shown in the case which follows, applies only if a promise to marry is made in consideration for some promise other than a mutual promise to marry. Therefore, this provision covers and renders unenforceable the ordinary "marriage settlement," as for example, where a man orally promises a woman to convey title to a certain farm to her if she accepts his proposal of marriage.

MILLER v. GREENE

Supreme Court of Florida, 1958.
104 So.2d 457.

FACTS: Ethel Greenberg acquired the ownership of the Carlyle Hotel on Miami Beach but had little experience in the hotel business. She asked Miller to participate in and counsel her operation of the hotel, which he did. Because his efforts produced a substantial profit, he claims that Ethel made an oral agreement for the continuation of his services. Miller alleges that in return for his services, Ethel promised to marry him and to share the net income resulting from the operation of the hotel. Miller agreed and rendered his services to Ethel in reliance upon her promises, and the couple planned to wed in the fall of 1955. Ethel, due to physical illness, decided not to marry.

DECISION: Judgment for Ethel Greenberg. Any oral promise or agreement made in consideration of marriage, other than a mutual promise to marry, is within the Statute of Frauds. If the marriage is not the real end or purpose of the agreement but a mere incident or condition, then the statute is not applicable. However, the statute applies in full force and effect when, despite other inducements, marriage is in whole or in part the real consideration for the agreement.

In this case, the oral agreement was supported by two promises by Ethel—to marry and to share the net income of the hotel. Her promise of marriage was an essential element of the indivisible contract and cannot be removed without destroying the parties' intentions. Since the consideration of marriage was not merely incidental but was the real consideration for their agreement, the statute applies. Thus, their oral agreement is unenforceable.

Land Contract Provision

The land contract provision covers promises to transfer "any interest in land," which includes any right, privilege, power, or immunity in real property. Thus all promises to transfer, buy, or pay for an interest in land, including ownership interests, leases, mortgages, options, and easements, are within the provision.

Interest in land–any right, privilege, power or immunity in real property

The land contract provision does not include contracts to transfer an interest in personal property. It also does not cover short-term leases, which by statute in most States are those for one year or less.

Moreover, an oral contract for the transfer of an interest in land may be enforced if the party seeking enforcement has so changed his position in reasonable reliance on the contract that injustice can be prevented only by enforcing the contract. For example, Jane orally agrees to sell land to Jack for $30,000. With Jane's consent, Jack takes possession of the land, pays Jane $10,000, builds a house on the land, and occupies it. Several years later Jane repudiates the contract. The courts will enforce the contract against Jane. On the other hand, courts will not enforce the promise unless equity so demands.

BURNS v. McCORMICK

Court of Appeals of New York, 1922.
233 N.Y. 230, 135 N.E. 273.

FACTS: In June, 1918, Halsey, a widower, was living, without family or housekeeper, in his house in Howell, New York. Burns and his wife claim that Halsey invited them to give up their house and business in Andover, New York, to live in his house and care for him. In return, they allege, he promised them the house and its furniture upon his death. Acting upon this proposal, the Burnses left Andover, moved into Halsey's house and cared for him until he died five months later. No deed, will, or memorandum exists to authenticate Halsey's promise. McCormick, the administrator of the estate, claims the oral promise is unenforceable under the Statute of Frauds.

DECISION: Judgment for McCormick. In general, a contract to convey an interest in land must be in writing to satisfy the Statute of Frauds. As an exception, equity will sometimes enforce an oral agreement affecting rights in land if the one who will gain the interest has partially performed his promise under the agreement. However, to satisfy this exception, the partial performance must be "unequivocally referable" to the agreement—such as possession or improvement of the promised land.

Here, the Burnses never occupied the land as owners or under claim of present right. As boarders, they did not even have possession. Halsey maintained possession, they were merely his personal servants or guests. Though likely to have been rewarded in some fashion, their services to Halsey are not unequivocally referable to his promise to convey the land. Therefore, in the absence of a writing confirming it, his promise is unenforceable.

One Year Provision

The Statute requires that all contracts that **cannot** be fully performed within one year of the making of the contract be in writing.

The Possibility Test

The test here is not whether the agreement is likely to be performed within one year from the date it was formed or whether the parties think that performance will be within the year, but whether it is *possible* for the contract to be performed within a year. The enforceability of the contract does not depend on probabilities or on the actuality of subsequent events. For example, an oral contract between Alice and Bill for Alice to build a bridge, which should reasonably take three years, is enforceable if it is possible, although extremely unlikely and difficult, for Alice to perform the contract in one year. Similarly, if Alice agrees to employ Bill for life, the contract is not within the Statute of Frauds. It is possible that Bill may die within the year, in which case the contract would be completely performed. The contract is therefore one that is *fully performable* within a year. However, an oral contract to employ another person for thirteen months could not possibly be performed within a year and is unenforceable.

FACTS: In September 1961, Tanenbaum entered into an oral employment contract with the Biscayne Osteopathic Hospital. According to the agreement, the hospital would employ Tanenbaum as an osteopathic radiologist for a period of five years terminable only after that period and then only upon 90 days written notice by either party. To accept the job, Tanenbaum resigned his former position with another hospital in Pennsylvania, moved his family to Florida and purchased a house. Approximately seven months later, the hospital fired Tanenbaum apparently for reasons having no relation to his competence as a radiologist. Tanenbaum sued to recover damages for the hospital's breach of their oral agreement.

DECISION: Judgment for Biscayne Osteopathic Hospital. The Statute of Frauds renders unenforceable oral contracts not to be performed within one year. The employment contract between the hospital and Tanenbaum was for a five-year period, with the option to cancel arising only after that period; it could not be performed within one year and is within the Statute. Therefore, since there is no writing to confirm the oral agreement, it is unenforceable.

TANENBAUM v. BISCAYNE OSTEOPATHIC HOSPITAL, INC.

District Court of Appeal of Florida, Third District, 1965. 173 So.2d 492.

Computation of Time   The year runs from the time the *agreement is made*, not from the time when the performance is to begin. For example, on January 1, 1986, Sam hires Jean to work for eleven months starting on April 1, 1986, under the terms of an oral contract. That contract will be fully performed on March 31, 1987, which is more than one year after January 1, 1986, the date the contract was made. Consequently, it is *within* the Statute of Frauds and unenforceable because it is oral.

A and B enter into oral contract	B commences performance	Oral contract must be completed to be enforceable	B finishes performance
Jan. 1, 1984	April 1, 1984	Jan. 1, 1985	March 31, 1985

Similarly, a contract for a year's performance that is to begin three days from the date of the making of the contract is within the Statute and if oral, is unenforceable. If, however, the performance is to begin the following day or under the terms of the agreement could have begun the following day, it is not within the Statute and need not be in writing:

FACTS: Dean was hired on February 12, 1962 as a sales manager of the Co-op Dairy for a minimum period of one year with the Dairy agreeing to pay his moving expenses. By February 26, 1962, Dean had signed a lease, moved his family from Oklahoma to Arizona, and reported for work. After he worked for a few days, he was fired. Dean then brought this action against the Dairy for his salary for the year, less what he was paid. The Dairy argues that enforcement of the oral contract is barred by the Statute of Frauds because the contract was not to be performed within one year.

DECISION: Judgment for Dean. A contract of employment to start in the future and to continue for one year is within the Statute of Frauds because the one-year period runs from the date the contract is made, not the date when performance is to begin. However, a contract for one year's employment to commence the day following the making of the contract is not within the Statute of Frauds. The contract here did not prohibit Dean from commencing work until he had moved from Oklahoma. Since he could have reported to work the next day, there was the possibility

CO-OP DAIRY, INC. v. DEAN

Supreme Court of Arizona, In Division, 1968. 102 Ariz. 573, 435 P.2d 470.

that the contract could have been performed within one year. The Statute of Frauds is not applicable if there is the slightest possibility that the contract can be fully performed within one year. Therefore, Dean can recover on the contract even though it was not in writing.

Full Performance by One Party   Where a contract has been fully performed on one side, most courts hold that the promise of the other party is enforceable even though by its terms its performance was not possible within the period of a year. For example, Jane borrows $4,800 from Tom. Jane orally promises to pay Tom $4,800 in three annual installments of $1,600. Jane's promise is enforceable, notwithstanding the one-year provision, because Tom has fully performed by making the loan.

Sales of Goods

Goods—tangible personal property

The original Statute of Frauds applied to contracts for the sale of goods and has been used as a prototype for the UCC Article 2 Statute of Frauds provision. The UCC provides that a contract for the sale of goods for the price of **$500 or more** is not enforceable unless there is some writing sufficient to indicate that a contract for sale has been made between the parties. *Goods*, as previously indicated, are defined as tangible personal property. The definition expressly includes growing crops and unborn animals.

Other UCC Statute of Frauds Provisions

Sale of Securities   The Code, in Article 8, contains a separate Statute of Frauds applying to contracts for the sale of securities (stocks and bonds). There is no minimum price involved; therefore every contract for the sale of securities is within the Statute and must be in writing to be enforceable.

Security Interest in Personal Property   As we discuss in Chapter 37, the UCC requires that agreements that create or provide a nonpossessory security interest in personal property be contained in a signed writing to be effective.

Sale of Other Kinds of Personal Property   The UCC also contains a catchall Statute of Frauds provision applicable to contracts for the sale of personal property other than goods, securities, or security agreements, in amount or value beyond $5,000. This provision makes such contracts unenforceable unless there is some writing indicating that a contract for sale has been made between the parties. This section of the Code covers contractual rights, royalty rights, patent rights, and "general intangibles."

A summary of the contracts within and the exceptions to the Statute of Frauds is provided in Figure 13-1.

Modification or Rescission of Contracts Within the Statute of Frauds

Oral contracts modifying previously existing contracts are unenforceable if the resulting contract is within the Statute of Frauds. The reverse is also true: an oral modification of a prior contract is enforceable if the new contract is not within the Statute of Frauds.

Thus, an oral promise to guarantee additional duties of another and an oral agreement to substitute different land for that described in the original contract are both examples of unenforceable oral contracts. On the other

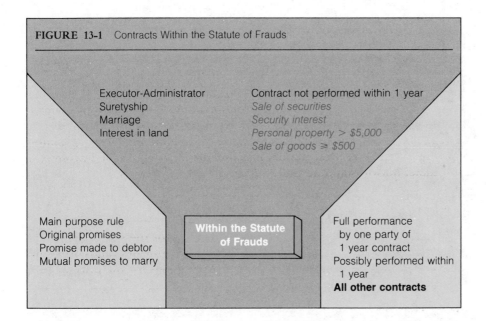

FIGURE 13-1   Contracts Within the Statute of Frauds

hand, an oral agreement to modify an employee's contract from two years to six months at a higher salary is not within the Statute of Frauds and is enforceable.

By extension, an oral rescission is effective and discharges all unperformed duties under the original contract. For example Jones and Brown enter into a written contract of employment for a two-year term. Later they orally agree to rescind the contract. The oral agreement is effective and the written contract is rescinded. However, where land has been transferred, an agreement to rescind the transaction is a contract to retransfer the land and is within the Statute of Frauds.

Under the UCC, if the parties enter into an oral contract to sell a motorcycle for $450 to be delivered to the buyer and later, prior to delivery, orally agree that the seller shall paint the motorcycle and install new tires and the buyer pay a price of $550, the modified contract is unenforceable. Conversely, if the parties have a written contract for the sale of 200 bushels of wheat at a price of $4 per bushel and later, on oral agreement, decrease the quantity to 100 bushels at the same price per bushel, the agreement, as modified, is enforceable.

Figure 13-2 summarizes the enforceability of modifications to contracts.

Methods of Compliance

The most common way to satisfy the Statute of Frauds is for the parties to enter into a written agreement; nevertheless there are several other methods by which the parties may comply with the statutory mandates.

A Writing or Memorandum

General Contract Provisions   The original Statute of Frauds and most modern Statutes of Frauds require that the agreement be in writing to be enforceable. Such writing or memorandums must:

FIGURE 13-2   Modification of Contracts

Original Contract	Modification/ Rescission	New Contract	Result
2 year oral employment contract	*Oral:* Shorten contract by 1½ years, increase salary	Employment contract for 6 months	Modification and new contract are binding, original contract was not binding
2 year written employment contract	*Oral:* Rescission of contract	None	Rescission of written employment contract is effective
Sale of land	*Oral:* Rescission of contract	Retransfer of land	Rescission of original contract must be in writing to be enforceable
$450 for Motorcycle	*Oral:* $100 for new tires and paint job	$550 for motorcycle with new tires and paint job	Modification must be in writing to be enforceable
Written: $800 for 200 bushels of wheat ($4.00/ bushel)	*Oral:* Decrease contract by 100 bushels ($4.00/ bushel)	$400 for 100 bushels of wheat ($4.00/ bushel)	Modification and new contract are binding

1. be signed by the party to be charged or by her agent;

2. specify the parties to the contract; and

3. specify with reasonable certainty the subject matter and the essential terms of the unperformed promises.

The note or memorandum may be formal or informal; all that is necessary is that it contain the required information and be signed by the party to be charged (the person seeking to avoid the contract). The "signature" may be by initials or even typewritten or printed so long as the party intended it to authenticate the writing. Furthermore, the "signature" need not be at the bottom of the page or at the customary place for a signature.

The memorandum may be such that the parties view it as having no legal significance whatever. For example, a personal letter between the parties, an interdepartmental communication, an advertisement, or the record books of a business may serve as a memorandum. The writing need not have been delivered to the party who seeks to take advantage of it, and it may even contain a repudiation of the oral agreement. For example, Sid and Gail enter into an oral agreement that Sid will sell Blackacre to Gail for $5,000. Sid subsequently receives a better offer and sends Gail a signed letter, which begins by reciting all the material terms of the oral agreement. The letter concludes with: "Since my agreement to sell Blackacre to you for $5,000 was oral, I am not bound by my promise. I have since received a better offer and will accept that one." Sid's letter constitutes a sufficient memorandum for Gail to enforce Sid's promise to sell Blackacre. However, because Gail did not sign the memorandum, the writing does not bind her. Thus a contract may be enforceable against only one of the parties.

The memorandum may consist of *several* papers or documents, none of which would be sufficient by itself. The several memoranda, however, must together satisfy all of the requirements of a writing to comply with the Statute of Frauds and must clearly indicate that they relate to the same transaction. The latter requirement can be satisfied if (a) the writings are physically attached, (b) the writings refer to each other, or (c) an examination of the writings shows them to be in reference to each other.

UCC Provisions   The Statute of Frauds provisions under the UCC are more liberal. For a sale of goods or securities the Code, as evidenced in *Alice v. Robett Manufacturing Co.*, requires merely some writing: (a) sufficient to indicate that a contract has been made between the parties; (b) signed by the party against whom enforcement is sought or by her authorized agent or broker; and (c) specifying the **quantity** of goods or securities to be sold. The writing is not insufficient because it omits or incorrectly states a term agreed on, but the contract in the situation where the quantity term is misstated can be enforced only to the extent of the quantity shown in the writing.

ALICE v. ROBETT MANUFACTURING CO.

United States District Court, District of Georgia, 1970. 328 F.Supp. 1377.

FACTS: Alice solicited an offer from Robett Manufacturing Company to manufacture certain clothing which Alice intended to supply to the Government. Alice contends that in a telephone conversation Robett made an oral offer which he immediately accepted. He then received the following letter from Robett which, he claims confirmed their agreement:

> Confirming our telephone conversation, we are pleased to offer the 3,500 shirts at $4.00 each and the trousers at $3.80 each with delivery approximately ninety days after receipt of order. We will try to cut this to sixty days if at all possible.
> This, of course, as quoted f.o.b. Atlanta and the order will not be subject to cancellation, domestic pack only.
> Thanking you for the opportunity to offer these garments, we are
>   Very truly yours,
>   ROBETT MANUFACTURING CO., INC.

Alice sued to enforce this agreement.

DECISION: Judgment for Robett Manufacturing Company. Since the alleged transaction involved a sale of goods for more than $500, the memorandum must satisfy the statute of frauds. Under the Uniform Commercial Code the memorandum need not contain all the terms of the agreement. However, it must (1) evidence a contract for the sale of goods between the parties; (2) be signed by the party to be charged; and (3) specify a quantity.

Here, Robett admits the signing of the letter and that the letter specifies a quantity. Nevertheless, the writing does not evidence a contract for the sale of goods, it merely constitutes an offer to sell. Hence, the memorandum does not satisfy the minimum requirements of the statute of frauds and the agreement is unenforceable.

As with general contracts, several related documents may satisfy the writing requirement. Moreover, the "signature" may be by initials or even typewritten or printed so long as the party intended to authenticate the writing.

Other Methods of Compliance Under the UCC

An oral contract for the *sale of goods* is enforceable in the following instances.

Written Confirmation As between merchants, a written confirmation that is sufficient against the sender is also sufficient against the recipient of the confirmation unless the recipient gives written notice of his objection within ten days after receiving the confirmation. Thus, the Code provides relief to a merchant who has confirmed an oral agreement for the sale of goods by letter or signed writing to the other party if he too is a *merchant*.

CAMPBELL v. YOKEL

Appellate Court of Illinois, Fifth District, 1974.
20 Ill.App.3d 702, 313 N.E.2d 628.

FACTS: Yokel, a grower of soybeans, had sold soybeans to Campbell Grain and Seed Company and other grain companies in the past. Campbell entered into an oral contract with Yokel to purchase soybeans from him. Promptly after entering into the oral contract, Campbell signed and mailed to Yokel a written confirmation of the oral agreement. Yokel received the written confirmation but did not sign it or object to its content. Campbell now brings this action against Yokel for breach of contract upon Yokel's failure to deliver the soybeans. The trial court ruled in favor of the defendant, Yokel, on the ground that the defendant is not a "merchant" within the meaning of the Code.

DECISION: Judgment for Campbell. Under the Code a written confirmation between merchants satisfies the Statutes of Frauds provision of the Code against the recipient as well as the sender unless the recipient gives written notice of his objection within ten days after receiving the confirmation. Yokel, however, insists that he is not a "merchant" within the meaning of the Code, and, therefore, the written confirmation provision is not applicable. The term "merchant" means a person who deals in goods of the kind sold, or otherwise by his occupation holds himself out as having knowledge or skill particular to the practices or goods involved. Yokel is a dealer in soybeans and hence is a merchant within the meaning of the Code. The written confirmation to which Yokel failed to object, therefore, satisfies the Statute of Frauds provision of the Code.

Admission The Code permits an oral contract for the sale of goods to be enforced against a party who in his pleading, testimony, or otherwise in court admits that a contract was made, but limits enforcement to the quantity of goods he admits.

Specially Manufactured Goods The Code permits enforcement of an oral contract for goods specially manufactured for the buyer only if evidence indicates that the goods were made for the buyer and the seller can show that he has made a *substantial beginning* of their manufacture before receiving any notice of repudiation. If the goods, although manufactured on special order, are readily marketable in the ordinary course of the seller's business, this exception does not apply.

Delivery or Payment and Acceptance Before the UCC was in force, delivery and acceptance of part of the goods or payment and acceptance of part of the price made enforceable the entire oral contract against the buyer who had received part delivery or against the seller who had received part payment. Under the Code, such "partial performance," as a substitute for the required memorandum, validates the contract only for the goods that have been accepted or for which payment has been accepted. To illustrate, Liz orally agrees to buy 1,000 watches from David for $15,000. David delivers 300 watches to Liz, who receives and accepts the watches. The oral contract is enforceable to the extent of 300 watches ($4,500)—those received and accepted; but is unenforceable to the extent of 700 watches ($10,500).

But what if the contract is indivisible, such as one for the sale of an automobile, so that if part payment is made there is only a choice between not enforcing the contract or enforcing the contract as a whole? Presently, there is a division of authority on this issue, although the better rule appears to be that such part payment and acceptance makes the entire contract enforceable.

A summary of methods of compliance with the Statute of Frauds is presented in Figure 13-3.

Effect of Noncompliance

The original Statute provided that "no action shall be brought" on a contract to which the Statute of Frauds applied *and* which did not comply with its requirements. The Code states that the contract "is not enforceable by way of action or defense." Despite the difference in language, the basic legal effect is the same: a contracting party has a defense to an action by the other for

FIGURE 13-3   Methods of Compliance

Type of Contract	Applicable Method of Compliance					
	Written memos	Full performance by both parties	Written confirmation	Admission	Specially manufactured	Delivery or payment and acceptance
General Contracts						
Executor—Administrator	●	●		?		
Suretyship	●	●		?		
Marriage	●	●		?		
Interest in land	●	●		?		
One-year	●	●		?		
UCC						
Sale of goods ≥ $500	●	●	●	●	●	●
Sale of securities	●	?	●	●	●	●
Security interest	●					
Personal property > $5,000	●					

enforcement of an oral contract that is within the Statute and does not comply with its requirements. In short, the oral contract is **unenforceable.**

If Kirkland, a painter, and Riggsbee, a home owner, make an oral contract under which Riggsbee is to give Kirkland a certain tract of land in return for the painting of Riggsbee's house, the contract is unenforceable under the Statute of Frauds. It is a contract for the sale of an interest in land. Either party can repudiate and has a defense to an action by the other to enforce the contract.

However, after *all* the promises of an oral contract have been *performed* by all the parties, the Statute of Frauds no longer applies.

If the painter has already performed a *part* of the work, is she completely without a remedy? Clearly, she cannot enforce the contract, but courts may still permit a recovery in quasi contract to prevent an unjust enrichment. The remedy of restitution allows the painter to recover damages equal to the amount of the benefit that she has conferred on the home owner. Thus, all may not be lost to a party unable to enforce an oral contract. However, this possibility should prompt a contracting party to use the utmost caution to assure compliance with the Statute. Only by complying with the Statute of Frauds can one be reasonably certain of obtaining the benefit of the bargain that has been made.

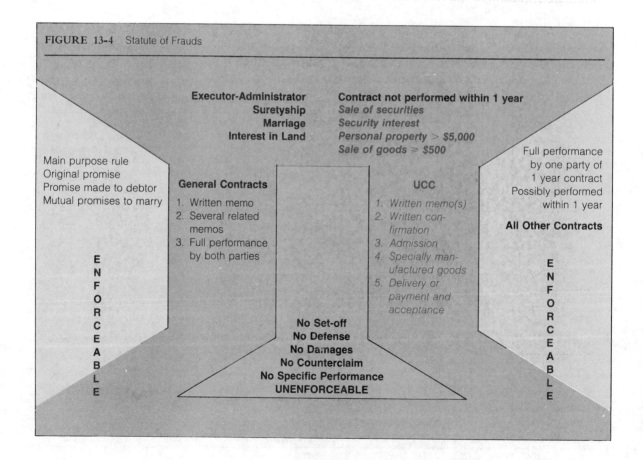

FIGURE 13-4 Statute of Frauds

Parol Evidence Rule

A contract reduced to writing and signed by the parties is frequently the result of many conversations, conferences, proposals, counterproposals, letters, and memoranda and sometimes the product of negotiations conducted, or partly conducted, by agents of the parties. At some state in the negotiations tentative agreements may have been reached on a certain point or points that were superseded (or so regarded by one of the parties) by subsequent negotiations. Offers may have been made and withdrawn, either expressly or by implication, or lost sight of in the give-and-take of negotiations. Ultimately a final draft of the written contract is prepared and signed by the parties. It may or may not include all of the points that were discussed and agreed upon in the course of the negotiations. However, by signing the agreement, the parties have declared it to be their contract, and the terms as contained in it represent the contract they have made. As a rule of substantive law, neither party is later permitted to show that the contract which they made is different from the terms and provisions that appear in the written agreement. This rule is called the "parol evidence" rule.

The Rule

When a contract is expressed in a writing that is intended to be the complete and final expression of the rights and duties of the parties, parol evidence of (1) **prior** oral or written negotiations or agreements of the parties or (2) their **contemporaneous** oral agreements that **vary** or **change** the written contract are not admissible. The world *parol* means literally "speech" or "words." The term **parol evidence** refers to any evidence, whether oral or in writing, that is outside the written contract and not incorporated into the contract either directly or by reference.

The parol evidence rule applies only to an **integrated** contract, that is, one in which the parties have assented to a certain writing or writings as the statement of the complete agreement or contract between them. When there is such an integration of a contract, parol evidence of any prior agreement will not be permitted to vary, change, alter, or modify any of the terms or provisions of the written contract.

The reason for the rule is that the parties, by reducing their entire agreement to writing, are regarded as having intended the writing that they signed to include the whole of their agreement. The terms and provisions contained in the writing are there because the parties intended them to be in their contract. Any provision not in the writing is regarded as having been omitted because the parties intended that it should not be a part of their contract. The rule excluding evidence that would tend to change, alter, vary, or modify the terms of the written agreement is therefore a rule safeguarding the contract as made by the parties. The rule applies to all integrated written contracts and deals with what terms are part of the contract. The rule differs from the Statute of Frauds, which governs what contracts must be in writing to be enforceable.

Situations To Which The Rule Does Not Apply

The parol evidence rule, in spite of its name, is not an exclusionary rule of evidence, nor is it a rule of construction or interpretation. It is a rule of

Parol evidence–oral evidence, but now includes prior to and contemporaneous, oral and written evidence not incorporated into the contract

Integrated contract–complete and total agreement

substantive law that defines the limits of a contract. Bearing this in mind, as well as the reason underlying the rule, you will readily understand that the rule does **not** apply to any of the following situations:

1. A contract that is *partly written* and partly oral, that is, the parties do not intend the writing to be their entire agreement.

2. A clerical or *typographical error* that obviously does not represent the agreement of the parties. Where a written contract for the services of a skilled mining engineer provides that his rate of compensation is to be $2.00 per day, a court of equity would permit reformation (correction) of the contract to correct the mistake if both parties intended the rate to be $200 per day.

3. The lack of *contractual capacity* of one of the parties, such as proof of minority or mental incompetency. Such evidence would not tend to vary, change, or alter any of the terms of the written agreement, but merely to show that the written agreement was voidable or void.

4. A *defense* of fraud, misrepresentation, duress, undue influence, mistake, or illegality. Evidence establishing any of these defenses would not claim to vary, change, or alter any of the terms of the written agreement, but merely to show such agreement to be voidable, void, or unenforceable.

5. A *condition precedent* agreed on orally at the time of the execution of the written agreement and to which the entire agreement was made subject. Such evidence does not tend to vary, alter, or change any of the terms of the agreement, but merely to show whether the entire written agreement, unchanged and unaltered, ever became effective.

6. A *subsequent mutual rescission* or *modification* of the written contract. Parol evidence of a later agreement does not tend to show that the integrated writing did not represent the contract between the parties at the time it was made.

Supplemental Evidence

Under the Restatement and the Code, although a written agreement may not be contradicted by evidence of a prior agreement or of a contemporaneous oral agreement, a written contract may be explained or supplemented by (1) course of dealing between the parties, (2) usage of trade, (3) course of performance, or (4) evidence of consistent additional terms unless the writing was intended by the parties as a complete and exclusive statement of their agreement.

Course of dealing–previous conduct between the parties

Usage of trade–practice engaged in by the trade or industry

Course of performance–conduct between the parties concerning performance of the particular contract

A **course of dealing** is a sequence of previous conduct between the parties to an agreement that may be fairly regarded as establishing a common basis of understanding for interpreting their expressions and other conduct.

A **usage of trade** is a practice or method of dealing regularly observed and followed in a place, vocation, or trade.

Course of performance refers to the manner and extent to which the respective parties to a contract have accepted successive tenders of performance by the other party without objection.

The Restatement and the Code permit *supplemental consistent evidence* to be introduced into a court proceeding. Such evidence is admissible only if it does not contradict a term or terms of the original agreement and would probably not have been included in the original contract.

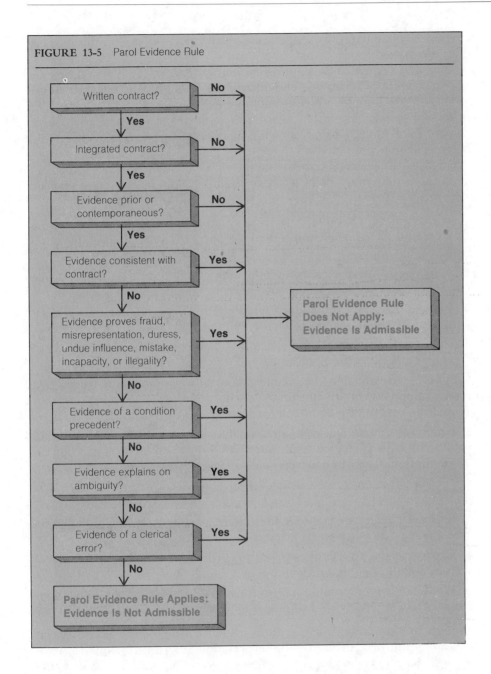

FIGURE 13-5   Parol Evidence Rule

Interpretation of Contracts

Although the written words or language in which the parties embodied their agreement or contract may not be changed by parol evidence, the ascertainment (determination) of the meaning to be given to the written language is outside the scope of the parol evidence rule. The written words embody the terms of the contract. However, words are but symbols. If their meaning is not clear, it may be made clear by the application of rules of interpretation or construction and by the use of extrinsic (external) evidence for this purpose where necessary.

Interpretation–construction or meaning of the contract

The Restatement defines **interpretation** as the ascertainment of the meaning of a promise or agreement or a term of the promise or agreement. Where the language in a contract is clear and unambiguous, extrinsic evidence tending to show a meaning different from that which the words clearly convey will not be accepted by a court. It is the function of the court to interpret and construe written contracts and documents. The court adopts rules of interpretation to apply a legal standard to the words contained in the agreement by which to determine their sense or meaning. Among the rules that aid interpretation are:

1. Words and other conduct are interpreted in the light of all the circumstances, and if the principal purpose of the parties is ascertainable, it is given great weight.

2. A writing is interpreted as a whole, and all writings that are part of the same transaction are interpreted together.

3. Unless a different intention is manifested, where language has a commonly accepted meaning, it is interpreted in accordance with that meaning.

4. Unless a different intention is manifested, technical terms and words of art are given their technical meaning.

5. Wherever reasonable, the manifestations of intention of the parties to a promise or agreement are interpreted as consistent with each other and with any relevant course of performance, course of dealing, or usage of trade.

6. An interpretation that gives a reasonable, lawful, and effective meaning to all the terms is preferred to an interpretation which leaves a part unreasonable, unlawful, or of no effect.

7. Specific terms and exact terms are given greater weight than general language.

8. Separately negotiated or added terms are given greater weight than standardized terms or other terms not separately negotiated.

9. Express terms, course of performance, course of dealing, and usage of trade are weighted in that order.

10. Where a term or promise has several possible meanings it will be interpreted against the party who supplied the contract or the term.

Through the application of the parol evidence rule, where it is properly applicable, and the above rules of interpretation and construction, it may be observed that the law not only enforces a contract but in doing so exercises great care that the contract being enforced is the one which the parties made, and that the sense and meaning of the intentions of the parties are carefully ascertained and given effect.

CHAPTER SUMMARY

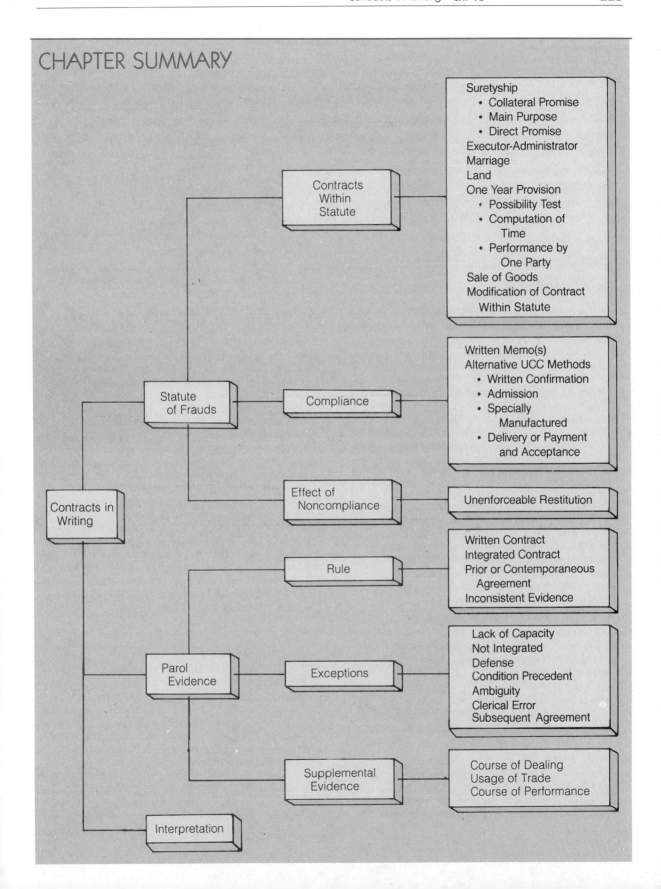

Contracts in Writing

Statute of Frauds

Contracts Within Statute
- Suretyship
  - Collateral Promise
  - Main Purpose
  - Direct Promise
- Executor-Administrator
- Marriage
- Land
- One Year Provision
  - Possibility Test
  - Computation of Time
  - Performance by One Party
- Sale of Goods
- Modification of Contract Within Statute

Compliance
- Written Memo(s)
- Alternative UCC Methods
  - Written Confirmation
  - Admission
  - Specially Manufactured
  - Delivery or Payment and Acceptance

Effect of Noncompliance
- Unenforceable Restitution

Parol Evidence

Rule
- Written Contract
- Integrated Contract
- Prior or Contemporaneous Agreement
- Inconsistent Evidence

Exceptions
- Lack of Capacity
- Not Integrated
- Defense
- Condition Precedent
- Ambiguity
- Clerical Error
- Subsequent Agreement

Supplemental Evidence
- Course of Dealing
- Usage of Trade
- Course of Performance

Interpretation

KEY TERMS

Statute of Frauds
Suretyship
Surety
Principal debtor
Creditor
Collateral agreement
Main purpose
Direct promise
Interest in land

Possibility test
Computation of time
Goods
Written Confirmation
Admission
Specially Manufactured
Unenforceable
Restitution
Parol evidence

Parol evidence rule
Integrated contract
Prior or contemporaneous
    agreement
Course of dealing
Usage of trade
Course of performance
Supplemental evidence
Interpretation

PROBLEMS

1. A was the principal shareholder in X Corporation, and as a result, he received the lion's share of X Corporation's dividends. X Corporation was anxious to close an important deal for iron ore products to use in its business. A written contract was on the desk of Z Corporation for the sale of the iron ore to X Corporation. Z Corporation, however, was cautious about signing the contract, and it was not until A called Z Corporation on the telephone and stated that if X Corporation did not pay for the ore, he would, that Z Corporation signed the contract. Business reverses struck X Corporation and it failed. Z Corporation sues A. What defense, if any, has A? Decision?

2. Green was the owner of a large department store. On Wednesday, January 26, he talked to Smith and said, "I will hire you to act as sales manager in my store for one year at a salary of $18,000. You are to begin work next Monday." Smith accepted and started work on Monday January 31. At the end of three months, Green discharged Smith. On May 15, Smith brings an action against Green to recover the unpaid portion of the $18,000 salary. Decision?

3. Dan, while driving, ran into Joanne, injuring her and rendering her unconscious. There was some doubt as to who was at fault. Dan took Joanne to a hospital, where she remained unconscious for twenty-four hours. On arriving at the hospital, Dan told the official in charge to treat Joanne for her injuries and stated that he would pay the bill. Joanne was duly treated and cured by the hospital, but Dan refused to pay the bill. On being sued by the hospital, Dan pleads the Statute of Frauds as a defense. Decision?

4. Ames, Bell, Cain, and Dole each orally ordered color television sets from Marvel Electronics Company, which accepted the orders. Ames's set was to be specially designed and encased in an ebony cabinet. Bell, Cain, and Dole ordered standard sets described

as "Alpha Omega Theatre." The price of Ames's set was $1,800, and the sets ordered by Bell, Cain, and Dole were $700 each. Bell paid the company $75 to apply on his purchase; Ames, Cain, and Dole paid nothing. The next day, Marvel sent Ames, Bell, Cain, and Dole written confirmations captioned "Purchase Memorandum," numbered 12345, 12346, 12347, and 12348, respectively, containing the essential terms of the oral agreements. Each memorandum was sent in duplicate with the request that one copy be signed and returned to the company. None of the four purchasers returned a signed copy. Ames promptly sent the company a repudiation of the oral contract, which it received before beginning manufacture of the set for Ames or making commitments to carry out the contract. Cain sent the company a letter reading in part, "Referring to your Contract No. 12347, please be advised I have cancelled this contract. Yours truly, (Signed) Cain." The four television sets were duly tendered by Marvel to Ames, Bell, Cain, and Dole, all of whom refused to accept delivery. Marvel brings four separate actions against Ames, Bell, Cain, and Dole for breach of contract.

Decide each claim.

5. A and B enter into an oral contract by which A promises to sell and B promises to buy Blackacre for $10,000. A repudiates the contract by writing a letter to B in which she states accurately the terms of the bargain, but adds "our agreement was oral. It, therefore, is not binding upon me, and I shall not carry it out." Thereafter, B sues A for specific performance of the contract. A interposes the defense of the Statute of Frauds, arguing that the contract is within the Statute and hence unenforceable. Decision?

6. On March 1, Lucas called Craig on the telephone and offered to pay him $90,000 for a house and lot that Craig owned. Craig accepted the offer immediately on the telephone. Later in the same day, Lucas told Annabelle that if she would marry him, he would convey to her the property then owned by Craig that was the subject of the earlier agreement. On March 2, Lucas called Penelope and offered her $16,000 if she would work for him for the year commencing March 15, and she agreed. Lucas and Annabelle were married on June 25. By this time Craig had refused to convey the house to Lucas. Thereafter, Lucas renounced his promise to convey the property to Annabelle. Penelope, who had been working for Lucas, was discharged without cause on July 5; Annabelle left Lucas and instituted divorce proceedings in July.

What rights, if any, have (a) Lucas against Craig for his failure to convey the property; (b) Annabelle against Lucas for failure to convey the house to her; (c) Penelope against Lucas for discharging her before the end of the agreed term of employment?

7. A orally promises B to sell him five crops of potatoes to be grown on Blackacre, a farm in Idaho, and B promises to pay a stated price for them on delivery. Is the contract enforceable?

8. A leased an apartment to B for the term May 1, 1986, to April 30, 1987, at $250 a month "payable in advance on the first day of each and every month of said term." At the time the lease was signed, B told A that he received his salary on the 10th of the month, and that he would be unable to pay the rent before that date each month. A replied that would be satis-

factory. On June 2, B not having paid the June rent, A sued B for the rent. At the trial, B offered to prove the oral agreement as to the date of payment each month. Decision?

9. Ann bought a car from the Used Car Agency under a written contract. She purchased the same in reliance on Used's agent's oral representations that the car had never been in a wreck and could be driven at least 2,000 miles without adding oil. Thereafter Ann discovered that the car had, in fact, been previously wrecked and rebuilt, that it used excessive quantities of oil, and that Used's agent was aware of these facts when the car was sold. Ann brings an action to rescind the contract and recover the purchase price. Used objects to the introduction of oral testimony concerning representations of its agent, contending that the written contract alone governed the rights of the parties. Decision on the objection?

10. In a contract drawn up by X Company, it agreed to sell and Y Contracting Company agreed to buy wood shingles at $650. After the shingles were delivered and used, X Company billed Y Company at $650 per bunch of 900 shingles. Y Company refused to pay because it thought the contract meant $650 per thousand shingles. X Company brought action to recover on the basis of $650 per bunch. The evidence showed that there was no applicable custom or usage in the trade and that each party held its belief in good faith. Decision?

RIGHTS OF THIRD PARTIES

In prior chapters we considered situations that essentially involved only two parties. In this chapter we deal with the rights of third parties, namely, persons who are not parties to the contract but have acquired a right to its performance. These rights arise either because of (1) an assignment of the rights of a party to the contract, or (2) the express terms of a contract entered into for the benefit of a third person. We consider these two situations in that order.

Assignment of Rights and Delegation of Duties

It is important to distinguish between an **assignment** of rights and a **delegation** of duties. Every contract creates both rights and duties. For instance, A promises to sell to B an automobile for which B promises to pay $10,000 in monthly installments over the next three years. A's right under the contract is to receive payment from B, whereas A's duty is to deliver the automobile. B's right is to receive the automobile; his duty is to pay for the automobile.

An assignment of rights is the voluntary transfer to a third party of the rights arising from the contract. In the above example, if A were to transfer his right under the contract (the installment payments due from B) to C for $8,500 in cash, this would constitute a valid **assignment of rights.** In this case, A would be the **assignor,** C would be the **assignee,** and B would be the **obligor.**

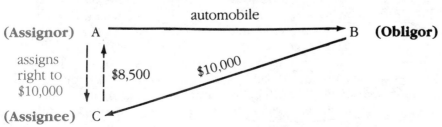

Assignment of rights— voluntary transfer to a third party of the rights arising from a contract

Assignor—party making an assignment

Assignee—party to whom contract rights are assigned

Obligor—party owing a duty (to the assignor) under the original contract

An effective assignment cancels the assignor's right to performance by the obligor. After an assignment *only* the assignee has a right to the obligor's performance.

On the other hand, if A agreed with D that D should deliver the automobile to B, this would constitute a **delegation,** not an assignment, **of duties.** In this instance, A would be the **delegator,** D would be the **delegatee,** and B would be the obligee.

Delegation of duty–transfer to a third party of a contractual obligation

Delegator–party delegating his duty to a third party

Delegatee–third party to whom the delegator's duty is delegated

Obligee–party to whom a duty of performance is owed (by the delegator and delegatee)

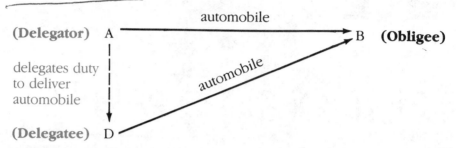

A delegation of duty, however, does *not* extinguish the delegator's obligation to perform. Rather, an additional party (the delegatee) is also obligated to perform. A delegation of duties results in **both** the delegator and delegatee being held liable for performance of the contractual duty to the obligee.

Assignment of Rights

At early common law an assignment of a contractual right was not allowed. At that time the law regarded the personal relationship between the parties to the contract as a vital part of the agreement. It could not be changed by one party any more than any other term of the contract. As commerce increased, the need to sell contract rights also increased. In response, courts of equity began to enforce assignments. Relief was allowed in equity so consistently that ultimately courts of law began to enforce assignments. Because this gave assignees an adequate remedy, courts of equity no longer were called upon to grant relief for assignments.

Requirements of an Assignment

The Restatement defines an assignment of a right as a manifestation of the assignor's intention to transfer it so that the assignor's right to performance by the obligor is extinguished in whole or in part and the assignee acquires the right to such performance.

What Amounts to an Assignment   No special form or particular words are necessary to create an assignment. Any words that fairly indicate an intention to make the assignee the owner of the right are sufficient, and the assignment, unless otherwise provided by statute, may be oral or written.

Consideration is *not* required for an effective assignment. Consequently, gratuitous assignments are valid and enforceable. However, a gratuitous assignment is revocable by the assignor and is terminated by the assignor's death, incapacity, or subsequent assignment of the right, *unless* an effective delivery of the assignment has been made by the assignor to the assignee, as in the case of *Speelman v. Pascal.* Such delivery can be accomplished by transferring a deed or other document evidencing the right, such as a stock certificate or savings passbook. Delivery may also consist of physically delivering a signed, written assignment of the contract right. A gratuitous assignment is also made irrevocable if, before the attempted revocation, the donee-assignee has received payment of the claim from the obligor, has obtained a judgment against the obligor, or has obtained a new contract of the obligor. For example, Nancy owes Howard $50,000. Howard signs a written statement granting Paul a gratuitous assignment of his rights from Nancy. Howard dies prior to delivering to Paul the signed, written assignment of the contract right. The assignment is terminated and therefore ineffective. On the other hand, had Howard delivered the signed, written assignment to Paul before Howard died, the assignment would have been effective and irrevocable.

FACTS: In 1952, the estate of George Bernard Shaw granted to Gabriel Pascal Enterprises, Limited the exclusive rights to produce a musical play and a motion picture based on Shaw's play "Pygmalion." The agreement contained a provision terminating the license if Gabriel Pascal Enterprises did not arrange for well-known composers, such as Lerner and Loewe, to write the musical and produce it within a specified period of time. George Pascal, owner of 98% of the Gabriel Pascal Enterprise's stock, attempted to meet these requirements, but died in July, 1954 before negotiations had been completed. However, in February, 1954, while the license had two years yet to run, Pascal sent a letter to Kingman, his executive secretary, granting to her certain percentages of his share of the profits from the expected stage and screen productions of "Pygmalion." Subsequently, Pascal's estate arranged for the writing and production of the highly successful "My Fair Lady," based on Shaw's "Pygmalion." Kingman then sued to enforce Pascal's gift assignment of the future royalties.

DECISION: Judgment for Kingman. Assignments to rights to sums which are expected to become due to the assignor are enforceable. To make a gift of such an assignment, the donor need only demonstrate a present intent to transfer irrevocably his right to the donee. Although at the time of the delivery of the letter there was no musical play or motion picture in existence, Pascal's letter was intended to transfer irrevocably by assignment a percentage of the royalties from the future productions to Kingman. Therefore, the assignment is enforceable as a valid gift.

SPEELMAN v. PASCAL

Court of Appeals of New York, 1961.
10 N.Y.2d 313, 178 N.E.2d 723.

Partial Assignments   A partial assignment is a transfer of a portion of the contractual rights to one or more assignees, as in the case above. At early common law, partial assignments were not enforceable because it was believed that they could increase the burden on the obligor. For instance, it was argued that the obligor who had a valid defense for not performing the contract would have to relitigate the issue with each and every assignee. Today, partial assignments are permitted and are enforceable. However, the obligor may require all the parties entitled to the promised performance to litigate the matter in one action. This ensures that all parties are present and avoids the undue hardship of multiple suits. For example, B owes A $2,500. A assigns $1,000 to C. Neither A nor C can maintain an action against B if B objects, unless the other is joined in the proceeding against B.

Partial assignment—transfer of a portion of contractual rights to one or more assignees

Rights That Are Assignable

As a general rule most contract rights, including rights under an option contract, are assignable. So long as the assignment merely substitutes the assignee for the assignor and does not materially increase the burden or risk on the obligor, the assignment is effective and valid, as in the next case involving Billy Cunningham. The most common contractual right which may be assigned is the right to the payment of money such as wages due or an account receivable. The right to other property like land or goods is frequently assignable.

MUNCHAK CORPORATION v. CUNNINGHAM

United States Court of Appeals, Fourth Circuit, 1972.
457 F.2d 721.

FACTS: While under contract to play professional basketball for the Philadelphia 76ers, Billy Cunningham negotiated a three year contract with the Carolina Cougars, another pro basketball team. The contract with the Cougars was to begin at the expiration of the contract with the 76ers. In addition to a signing bonus of $125,000, Cunningham was to receive under the new contract a salary of $100,000 for the first year, $110,000 for the second, and $120,000 for the third. The contract also stated that Cunningham "had special, exceptional and unique knowledge, skill and ability as a basketball player" and therefore that Cunningham agreed that the Cougars could enjoin him from playing basketball for any other team for the term of the contract. In addition, the contract contained a clause prohibiting its assignment to another club without Cunningham's consent. In 1971, the ownership of the Cougars changed and Cunningham's contract was assigned to Munchak Corporation, the new owners, without his consent. When Cunningham refused to play for the Cougars, Munchak Corporation sought to enjoin his playing for any other team. Cunningham asserts that his contract was not assignable.

DECISION: Judgment for Munchak. Generally, the right to performance of a personal service contract requiring special skills and based upon the personal relationship between the parties cannot be assigned without the consent of the party rendering those services. However, such contracts may be assigned when the character of the performance and the obligation will not change following the assignment. Although the contract required his special skills as a ballplayer, Cunningham was not obligated to perform any differently for Munchak than for the original owners. Moreover, the contract prohibited its assignment to another *club* without his consent but did not prohibit assignment to another owner of the same club. Therefore, under these facts, his contract is assignable.

Rights That Are Not Assignable

In order to protect the obligor, some contract rights are not assignable. These nonassignable contract rights include those that (a) materially increase the risk or burden upon the obligor, (b) transfer highly personal contract rights, (c) are validly prohibited by the contract, or (d) are prohibited by law.

Assignments That Materially Increase the Risk or Burden   An assignment is ineffective where performance by the obligor to the assignee would be materially different from performance to the assignor, that is, where the assignment would significantly change the nature or extent of the obligor's duty. Thus, an automobile liability insurance policy issued to A is not assignable by A to B. The risk assumed by the insurance company was liability for A's negligent operation of the automobile. Liability for operation of the same automobile by B would be an entirely different risk and one that the insurance company had not assumed. Similarly, A would not be allowed to assign her contractual right to have B paint her small, two-bedroom house to C, the owner of a twenty-five room mansion. Clearly, such an assignment would materially increase B's duty of performance. By comparison, the right to receive monthly payments under a contract may be assigned, for it costs no more to mail the check to the assignee than it does to mail it to the assignor.

Assignments of Personal Rights   Where the rights under a contract are of a highly personal nature, they are not assignable. An extreme example of such a contract is an agreement of two persons to marry one another. The prospective groom obviously can not transfer the prospective bride's promise to marry to some third party. A more common example of contracts of a personal character is a contract for the personal services of one of the parties.

SCHUPACK v. McDONALD'S SYSTEM, INC.

Supreme Court of Nebraska, 1978.
200 Neb. 485, 264 N.W.2d 827.

FACTS: McDonald's granted to Copeland a franchise in Omaha, Nebraska. In a separate letter, it also granted him a Right of First Refusal for future franchises to be developed in the Omaha-Council Bluffs area. Copeland then sold all rights in his six McDonald's franchises to Schupack. When McDonald's offered a new franchise in the Omaha area to someone other than Schupack, he attempted to exercise the Right of First Refusal. However, McDonald's would not recognize the Right in Schupack, claiming that it was personal to Copeland and, therefore, non-assignable without its consent. Schupack brought an action for specific performance requiring McDonald's to accord Schupack the Right of First Refusal.

DECISION: Judgment for McDonald's. Contracts for personal services or involving relations of personal confidence and trust are not assignable without the consent of the other party to the contract. Whether the Right of First Refusal is personal and, therefore, not assignable depends on the intent of the parties to the original contract. The evidence shows that it is the "basic and undeviating policy of McDonald's to retain the rigid and absolute control over *who* receives new franchises." Here, the Right was granted solely to Copeland and independently of the franchise contract. Furthermore, McDonald's granted the Right on the basis of the personal confidence and trust that it placed in Copeland. The intent and purpose of the letter granting the Right was to look to the personal performance of Copeland. These factors indicate that McDonald's intended the Right of First Refusal to be personal to Copeland and non-assignable without its consent.

Express Prohibition Against Assignment   At common law the courts enforced contracts containing express prohibitions against an assignment of the rights created under it. Such prohibitions, however, are now strictly construed; most courts interpret a general prohibition against assignments as a mere promise not to assign. As a consequence, the prohibition, if violated, gives the obligor a right to damages for breach of the terms forbidding assignment but does *not* render the assignment ineffective.

The Restatement and Article 2 of the Code provide that, unless circumstances indicate the contrary, a contract term prohibiting assignment of the *contract* bars only the delegation to the assignee (delegatee) of the assignor's (delegator's) *duty* of performance and not the assignment of *rights*. Thus, Norman and Lucy contract for the sale of land by Lucy to Norman for $30,000 and provide in their contract that Norman may not assign his rights under it. Norman pays Lucy $30,000 and thereby fully performs his obligations under the contract. Norman then assigns his rights to George. George is entitled to receive the land from Lucy (the obligor) despite the contractual prohibition of assignment.

Assignments Prohibited by Law   Various Federal and State statutes, as well as public policy, prohibit or regulate the assignment of certain types of contract rights. For instance, assignments of future wages are subject to statutes. Some statutes prohibit them altogether; others require them to be in writing and subject to certain restrictions. An assignment that violates public policy will be unenforceable even in the absence of a prohibiting statute.

Rights of the Assignee

Obtains Rights of Assignor   The general rule is that an assignee **stands in the shoes** of the assignor. He acquires the rights of the assignor but *no* new rights and takes the assigned right with all of the defenses, defects, and infirmities to which it would be subject in an action against the obligor by the assignor. Thus, in an action brought by the assignee against the obligor, the obligor may plead fraud, duress, undue influence, failure of consideration, breach of contract, or any other defense against the assignor that arose before the obligor was notified of the assignment. The obligor may also assert rights of set-off or counterclaim arising out of entirely separate matters that he may have against the assignor, as long as they arose before he had notice of the assignment.

The Code permits the buyer under a contract of sale to agree as part of the contract that he will not assert against an assignee who takes an assignment for value and in good faith any claim or defense that the buyer may have against the seller. Such a provision in an agreement gives greater marketability to the rights of the seller. The Federal Trade Commission, however, has invalidated such waiver of defense provisions in consumer credit transactions. This rule is discussed more fully in Chapter 24.

Notice   A valid assignment does not require that notice be given to the obligor. However, it is advisable that such notice be given because an assignee will lose his rights against the obligor if the obligor pays the assignor without notice of the assignment. It would be unfair to compel an obligor to pay a claim a second time when she has already paid it to the only person whom she knew to be entitled to receive payment. Also, as already indicated, defenses to the contract as well as set-offs and counterclaims of the obligor that arise out of entirely separate matters cannot be used against the assignee if they arise *after* the notice has been given.

Implied Warranties of Assignor

In the absence of an express intention to the contrary, an assignor who receives value makes the following implied warranties to the assignee with respect to the assigned right:

1. that he will do nothing to defeat or impair the assignment;

2. that the assigned right actually exists and is subject to no limitations or defenses other than those stated or apparent at the time of the assignment;

3. that any writing evidencing the right delivered to the assignee or exhibited to him as an inducement to accept the assignment is genuine and what it purports to be; and

4. that he has no knowledge of any fact that would impair the value of the assignment.

Thus, Eric has a right against Julia and assigns it for value to Gwen. Later Eric gives Julia a release. Gwen may recover damages from Eric.

The assignor is further bound by any specific express warranties he makes to the assignee about the right assigned. However, unless explicitly stated, the assignor does *not* guarantee that the obligor will pay the assigned debt or otherwise perform.

Successive Assignments of the Same Right

The owner of a right could conceivably make successive assignments of the same claim to different persons. Although this action is morally and legally

Set-off–claim by obligor against assignor arising out of an entirely separate transaction

Implied warranty–obligation imposed by law upon the transferor of property or contract rights

Express warranty–explicitly made contractual promise regarding property or contract rights transferred

inappropriate, it raises the question of what rights successive assignees have. Assume that B owes A $1,000. On June 1, A for value assigns the debt to C. Thereafter, on June 15, A assigns it to D, who in good faith gives value and has no knowledge of the prior assignment by A to C. The majority rule in the United States is that the **first assignee in point of time** (C) prevails over later assignees. In England and in a minority of the States, the first assignee that notifies the obligor prevails.

BOULEVARD NATIONAL BANK OF MIAMI v. AIR METAL INDUSTRIES

Supreme Court of Florida, 1965.
176 So.2d 94.

FACTS: Tompkins-Beckwith, as the contractor on a construction project, entered into a subcontract with a division of Air Metal Industries. Air Metal procured American Fire and Casualty Company to be surety on certain bonds in connection with contracts it was performing for Tompkins-Beckwith and others. As security for these bonds, on January 3, 1962, Air Metal executed an assignment to American Fire of all accounts receivable under the Tompkins-Beckwith subcontract. On November 26, 1962, Boulevard National Bank lent money to Air Metal. To secure the loans, Air Metal purported to assign to the bank certain accounts receivable it had under its subcontract with Tompkins-Beckwith.

In June, 1963 Air Metal defaulted on various contracts bonded by American Fire. On July 1, 1963, American Fire served formal notice on Tompkins-Beckwith of Air Metal's assignment. Tompkins-Beckwith acknowledged the assignment and agreed to pay. In August, 1963, Boulevard National Bank notified Tompkins-Beckwith of its assignment. Tompkins-Beckwith refused to recognize the bank's claim and, instead, paid all remaining funds which had accrued to Air Metal to American Fire. The bank then sued to enforce its claim under Air Metal's assignment.

DECISION: Judgment for Air Metal and American Fire. There are two rules of priority concerning successive assignments of the same contract right. The American rule gives priority to the first assignee in point of time of the assignment without regard to notice to the debtor. In contrast, the English rule gives preference to the assignment of which the debtor was first given notice. The court in this case chose to follow the English or minority rule. It reasoned that intangible accounts receivables are subject to secret, fraudulent conveyances. Notice to the debtor of the assignment fixes the accountability of the debtor to the assignee instead of the assignor and enables all involved to deal more safely. Therefore, since American Fire was the first assignee to give proper notice to the debtor Tompkins-Beckwith, its claim takes precedence over the bank's claim.

Delegation of Duties

As we indicated earlier, contractual **duties** are *not* assignable, but their performance may generally be *delegated* to a third person. For example, A has entered into a contract with B to deliver to B a specified amount of copper for $5,000. A may properly delegate the performance of this contract to C. The courts, however, will examine a delegation more closely than an assignment because with a delegation the nondelegating party to the contract (the obligee) is being compelled to receive performance from a party with whom she has not dealt.

A delegation will not be permitted if: (a) the nature of the duties are personal; (b) the performance is expressly made nondelegable; or (c) the delegation is prohibited by statute or public policy. For example, a school teacher may not delegate her performance to another teacher, even if the substitute is equally competent, for this contract is personal in nature. On the other hand, where performance by a party involves no special skill and where no personal trust or confidence is involved, he may delegate performance of his duty. The next case deals with this question.

MACKE COMPANY v.
PIZZA OF
GAITHERSBURG, INC.

Court of Appeals of
Maryland, 1970.
259 Md. 479, 270 A.2d 645.

FACTS: In 1966, Pizza of Gaithersburg and The Pizza Shops contracted with Virginia Coffee Service to have vending machines installed in each of their pizza establishments. One year later, The Macke Company purchased Virginia's assets and the vending machine contracts were assigned to Macke. When the Pizza Shops attempted to terminate their contracts for vending services, Macke brought suit for damages for breach of contract. The Pizza Shops argued that they had dealt with Macke before but had chosen Virginia because they preferred the way it conducted its business. They contended that since there was a material difference between the performance of Virginia and that of Macke, they were justified in refusing to recognize Virginia's delegation of its duties to Macke.

DECISION: Judgment for Macke Company. A contractual duty may be delegated and the promisee cannot rescind the contract, if the quality of the performance remains materially the same. Here, the original contract was for the installation, maintenance and stocking of a vending machine. It involved either a license granted to Virginia by the Pizza Shops or a lease of a portion of their premises. It did not involve a contract for personal services. Since the quality of performance remained substantially the same under Macke, Virginia's delegation of its duties was entirely permissible and enforceable.

Novation–contract substituting a new promisor for an existing promisor and to which the promisee is a party

Even when permitted, a delegation of a duty to a third person leaves the delegator bound to perform. If the delegator desires to be discharged of the duty, it may be possible for her to enter into an agreement obtaining the consent of the obligee to substitute a third person (the delegatee) in her place. This is a **novation** whereby the delegator is discharged and the third party becomes directly bound on his promise to the obligee. Nevertheless, unlike an assignment that extinguishes the assignor's rights under the original contract or a novation that extinguishes the duties of the original obligor, a **delegation** leaves **both** the delegator and delegatee **liable** for proper performance of the original contractual duty. A delegation, therefore, amounts to no more than an authorization for a third party to perform the duty for the delegator.

Since a delegatee becomes liable for performance, the delegatee must agree to the delegation. But if A and C agree to an assignment of A's contract with B, does this include both an assignment of rights and a delegation of duties? The common law rule is unclear because there is a division of authority among the jurisdictions. The Restatement and the Code clearly resolve this conflict by providing that, unless the language or circumstances indicate the contrary, an assignment of "the contract" or of "all my rights under the contract" or an assignment in similar general terms is an assignment of rights **and** a delegation of performance of the duties of the assignor, and its acceptance by the assignee constitutes a promise by her to perform those duties. For example, Cooper Oil Company has a contract to deliver oil to Halsey. Cooper makes a written assignment to Lowell Oil Company "of all Cooper's rights and duties under the contract." Lowell is under a duty to Halsey to deliver the oil called for by the contract, and Cooper is liable to Halsey if Lowell does not perform. You should also recall that the Restatement and the Code provide that a clause prohibiting an assignment of "the contract" is to be construed as barring only the delegation to the assignee (delegatee) of the assignor's (delegator's) performance, unless the circumstances indicate the contrary.

Third-Party Beneficiary Contracts

A contract in which a party (the **promisor**) promises to render a certain performance not to the other party (the **promisee**) but to a third person (the **beneficiary**) is called a third-party beneficiary contract. The third person is not a party to the contract but is merely a beneficiary of the contract. Such contracts may be divided into two types: (1) **intended** beneficiary contracts and (2) **incidental** beneficiary contracts. An intended beneficiary is intended by the two parties to the contract (the promisor and promisee) to receive a benefit from the performance of their agreement. Accordingly, the courts generally enforce the intended beneficiary type of third-party contracts. For example, A promises B to deliver an automobile to C if B promises to pay $10,000. C is the intended beneficiary.

Third party beneficiary contract – contract in which one party promises to render a performance to a third person

Intended beneficiary – third party intended by the two contracting parties to receive a benefit from their contract

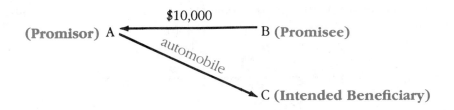

However, where the third party incidentally and not intentionally is to receive a benefit under the contract, no court will enforce the third party's right to the benefits of the contract. For example, A promises to purchase and deliver to B an automobile for $10,000. In all probability A would acquire the automobile from D. D would be an incidental beneficiary.

Incidental beneficiary – third party whom the two parties to a contract have no intention of benefitting by their contract

(Promisor) A ← $10,000 — **B (Promisee)**

automobile

D (Incidental Beneficiary)

Intended Beneficiary

Gift Promise

A third party is an intended beneficiary if the promisee's purpose in bargaining for and obtaining the agreement with the promisor was to make a gift to the beneficiary. The ordinary life insurance policy is an illustration of this type of intended beneficiary third-party contract. The insured (the promisee) makes a contract with an insurance company (the promisor), which promises, in consideration of premiums paid to it by the insured, to pay upon the death of the insured a stated sum of money to the named beneficiary, who is an **intended donee beneficiary**.

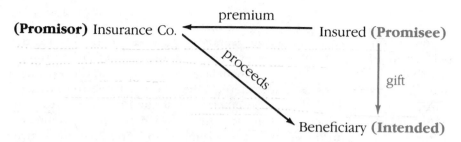

Creditor Beneficiary

A third person is also an intended beneficiary if the promisee intends the performance of the promise to satisfy a legal duty owed to the beneficiary, who is a creditor of the promisee. The contract involves consideration moving from the promisee to the promisor in exchange for the promisor's engaging to pay some debt or discharge some obligation of the promisee to the third person.

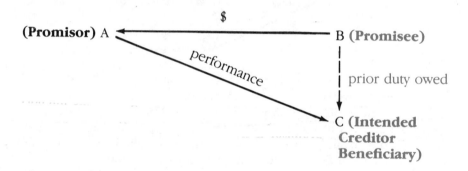

To illustrate: in the contract for the sale by Wesley of his business to Susan, she promises Wesley that she will pay all of his outstanding business debts, as listed in the contract. Wesley's creditors are creditor beneficiaries.

The making of the contract, however, does not (as with delegation of duties) in any way change or affect any previous obligation of the promisee to the beneficiary. The beneficiary in this situation has **both** rights against the promisee based on the original obligation and rights against the promisor based on the third-party beneficiary contract. If neither performs, the third person can maintain separate suits against both and obtain judgments against both, although he can collect his debt only once.

LAWRENCE v. FOX

Court of Appeals of New York, 1859.
20 N.Y. 268.

FACTS: Holly loaned Fox $300 in consideration for Fox's promise to pay that sum to Lawrence, a creditor of Holly's. Fox failed to pay Lawrence, who sued Fox for the $300.

DECISION: Judgment for Lawrence, who may recover as a third party creditor beneficiary to the contract between Holly and Fox. Where a party to a contract promises to render performance, not to the promisee but to a third party who is a creditor of the promisee, the third party is a creditor beneficiary of the promise and may maintain an action for breach of contract.

Rights of Intended Beneficiary

A promise in a contract creates a duty by the promisor to perform the promise to an intended beneficiary, and the intended beneficiary may enforce this duty. Generally, the rights of an intended beneficiary begin at the time of the making of the contract, whether she has knowledge of it or not. However, within a reasonable time after learning of the contract's existence, the intended beneficiary may reject the promised benefit.

A provision in a contract between the promisor and promisee stating that its terms may not be varied without the consent of the beneficiary will be upheld. If there is not such a provision, the parties to the contract may rescind or vary the contract unless the intended beneficiary has brought an action on the promise or has changed her position in reliance on it.

An intended *donee* beneficiary may sue the promisor only. He cannot maintain an action against the promisee since the promisee was under no legal obligation to him. An intended *creditor* beneficiary, however, may sue either or both parties.

In an action by the intended beneficiary of a third-party contract to enforce the promise, the promisor may assert any defense that would be available to him if the action had been brought by the promisee. The rights of the third party are based on the promisor's contract with the promisee. Thus the absence of mutual assent or consideration, lack of capacity, fraud, mistake, and the like may be asserted by the promisor against the intended beneficiary. But claims and defenses of the promisor against the promisee arising out of *separate* transactions do not affect the rights of the intended beneficiary unless the contract so provides. Likewise, the right of the intended beneficiary against the promisor is not subject to the promisee's claims or defenses against the beneficiary.

FACTS: The International Association of Machinists (the union) was the bargaining agent for the employees of Powder Power Tool Corporation. On August 24, 1953, the union and the corporation executed a collective bargaining agreement providing for retroactive increased wage rates for the corporation's employees effective as of April 1, 1953. Three employees were working for Powder before and for several months after April 1, 1953, but were not employed by the corporation when the agreement was executed on August 24, 1953. They were paid to the time their employment terminated at the old wage scale. The three employees assigned their claims to Springer who brought this action against the corporation for the extra wages.

DECISION: Judgment for Springer. An employee may sue his employer to collect benefits accruing to the employee under a collective bargaining agreement made between his employer and the union. The employee is considered an intended third-party beneficiary of the labor agreement. Here, the agreement stated unequivocally that the wage increase became effective on April 1, 1953 and it did not limit the retroactive increase to employees who were employed at the time of the agreement's execution on August 24. Therefore, the agreement grants increased wages to employees for work done after April 1, regardless of whether they are employed on August 24.

SPRINGER v. POWDER POWER TOOL CORPORATION

Supreme Court of Oregon, 1960.
348 P.2d 1112.

Incidental Beneficiary

An incidental third-party beneficiary is a person whom the parties to a contract did not intend to benefit but who nevertheless would derive some benefit by its performance. For instance, a contract to raze an old, unsightly building and replace it with a costly modern house would benefit the owner of the adjoining property by increasing his property's value. However, he would have no rights under the contract, as the benefit to him is unintended and incidental.

A third person who may be incidentally benefited by the performance of a contract to which he is not a party has no rights under the contract. It was not the intention of either the promisee or the promisor that the third person benefit. Assume that for a stated consideration Charles promises Madeline that he will purchase and deliver to Madeline a new Sony television of the latest model. Madeline performs. Charles does not. Reiner, the local exclusive Sony dealer, has no rights under the contract, although performance by Charles would produce a sale from which Reiner would derive a benefit. Reiner is only an incidental beneficiary.

The following case further illustrates that incidental beneficiaries may not enforce contracts.

JACKSON, LEWIS, SCHNITZLER & KRUPMAN v. LOCAL 100, TRANSPORT WORKERS UNION OF AMERICA

Supreme Court, Special Term, Queens County, New York, 1981.
108 Misc.2d 458, 437 N.Y.S.2d 895.

FACTS: On April 1, 1980, members of Local 100, Transport Workers Union of America (TWU) began an 11-day mass transit strike which paralyzed the life and commerce of the City of New York. Jackson, Lewis, Schnitzler & Krupman, a Manhattan law firm, brought a class action suit against the TWU for the direct and foreseeable damages it suffered as a result of the union's illegal strike. The law firm sought to recover as a third-party beneficiary of the collective bargaining agreement between the union and New York City. The agreement contains a no-strike clause and states that the TWU agreed to cooperate with the City to provide a safe, efficient, and dependable mass transit system. The law firm argues that its members are a part of the general public that depends on the mass transit system to go to and from work. Therefore, they are in the class of persons for whose benefit the union has promised to provide dependable transportation service.

DECISION: Judgment for the Transit Workers Union. A person not a party to a contract may sue for damages resulting from non-performance if the contract's primary intent was to benefit that person. That is not the case here. The City of New York contracted with the TWU for services which it had no obligation to provide to the public. In addition, the agreement does not clearly make the union answerable to a member of the general public for its breach. Consequently, no duty can be found against the union on behalf of a member of the general public. Therefore, the law firm cannot recover as a third-party beneficiary because it is only an incidental beneficiary.

CHAPTER SUMMARY

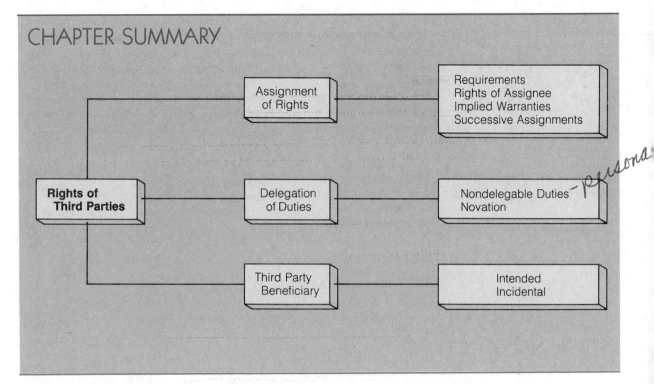

KEY TERMS

Assignment	Delegatee	Express warranty
Assignor	Obligee	Novation
Assignee	Partial assignment	Third party beneficiary
Obligor	Personal rights	Intended donee beneficiary
Delegation	Set-off	Intended creditor beneficiary
Delegator	Implied warranty	Incidental beneficiary

PROBLEMS

1. On December 1, A, a famous singer, contracted with B to sing at B's theater on December 31 for a fee of $25,000 to be paid immediately after the performance.

(a) A, for value received, assigns this fee to C.

(b) A, for value received, assigns this contract to sing to D, an equally famous singer.

(c) B sells his theater to E, and assigns his contract with A to E.

State the effect of each of these assignments.

2. The Smooth Paving Company entered into a paving contract with the city of Chicago. The contract contained the clause "contractor shall be liable for all damages to buildings resulting from the work performed." In the process of construction one of the bulldozers of the Smooth Paving Company struck and broke a gas main, causing an explosion and a fire that destroyed the house of John Puff. Puff brought an appropriate action against the Smooth Paving Company to recover damages for the loss of this house. Decision?

3. A, who was unemployed, registered with the X Employment Agency. A contract was then made under which A, in consideration of such position as the

Agency would obtain for A, agreed to pay the Agency one-half of her first month's salary. The contract also contained an assignment by A to the Agency of one-half of her first month's salary. Two weeks later, the Agency obtained a permanent position for A with the B Co. at a monthly salary of $900. The agency also notified the B Co. of the assignment by A. At the end of the first month, the B Co. paid A her salary in full. A then quit and disappeared. The Agency now sues the B Co. for $450 under the assignment. Decision?

4. B purchased an option on Blackacre from S for $1,000. The option contract contained a provision by which B promised not to assign the option contract without S's permission. B, without S's permission, assigns the contract to A. A seeks to exercise the option, and S refuses to sell Blackacre to him. Decision?

5. B contracts to sell to A, an ice cream manufacturer, the amount of ice A may need in his business for the ensuing three years to the extent of not more than 250 tons a week at a stated price per ton. A makes a corresponding promise to B to buy such an amount of ice. A sells his ice cream plant to C and assigns to C all A's rights under the contract with B. On learning of the sale, B refused to furnish ice to C. C sues B for damages. Decision?

6. Brown enters into a written contract with Ideal Insurance Company under which, in consideration of the payment of the premiums, the Insurance Company promises to pay XYZ College the face amount of the policy, $100,000, on Brown's death. Brown pays the premiums until her death. Thereafter, XYZ College makes demand for the $100,000 of Insurance Company, which refuses to pay on the ground that XYZ College was not a party to the contract. Decision?

7. A and B enter into a contract binding A personally to do some delicate cabinet work. A assigns his rights and delegates performance of his duties to C. On being informed of this, B agrees with C, in cosideration of C's promise to do the work, that B will accept C's work, if properly done, instead of the performance promised by A. Later, without cause, B refuses to allow C to proceed with the work, though C is ready to do so, and makes demand on A that A perform.

A refuses. Can C recover damages from B? Can B recover from A?

8. A, a homeowner, enters into a valid written contract with B, a carpenter, for the construction of various bookshelves and cabinets in A's house. Prior to beginning the work B assigns his interest in the contract to C, another carpenter. A refuses to permit C to do the work, employs another carpenter, and brings an action against B claiming as damages the difference between the contract price and the cost to employ the other carpenter. Decision?

9. S hired G in the spring, as she had for many years, to set out in beds the flowers S had grown in her greenhouses during the winter. The work was to be done in S's absence for $300. G became ill the day after S departed and requested his friend, B, to set out the flowers, promising to pay him $250 when he was paid. B agreed. On completion of the planting, an agent of S's, who had authority to dispense the money, paid G, and G paid B. Within two days it became obvious that the planting was a disaster. Everything set out by B had died of water rot, because he did not operate S's automatic watering system properly.

May S recover damages from B? May S recover damages from G, and, if so, does G have an action against B?

10. Caleb, operator of a window-washing business, dictated a letter to his secretary addressed to Apartments, Inc., stating: "I will wash the windows of your apartment buildings at $4.10 per window to be paid on completion of the work." The secretary typed the letter, signed Caleb's name and mailed it to Apartments, Inc. Apartments, Inc. replied: "Accept your offer."

Caleb wrote back: "I will wash them during the week starting July 10 and direct you to pay the money you will owe me to my son, Bernie. I am giving it to him as a wedding present." Caleb sent a signed copy of the letter to Bernie.

Caleb washed the windows during the time stated and demanded payment to him of $8,200 (2,000 windows at $4.10 each), informing Apartments, Inc., that he had changed his mind about having the money paid to Bernie.

What are the rights of the parties?

PERFORMANCE, BREACH AND DISCHARGE

The subject of discharge of contracts concerns the termination of contractual duties. In earlier chapters we have seen how parties may become bound to their promises by a contract. It is also important to know how a person may become unbound from a contract. When a contract is made, neither party intends that the duties created will exist forever. Contractual promises are made for a purpose, and the parties reasonably expect this purpose to be fulfilled by performance. However, performance of a contractual duty is only one method of discharge.

Whatever causes a binding promise to cease to be binding is a discharge of the contract. In general, there are four types of discharge: (1) by performance of the parties, (2) by breach of the parties, (3) by agreement of the parties, and (4) by operation of law. In addition, each type of discharge may occur in various ways.

Moreover, many contractual promises are not absolute and unconditional promises to perform but rather are conditional promises. The obligation to perform conditional promises depends on the happening or nonhappening of a specific event. We will discuss the subject of conditions briefly.

Conditions

A condition is an event whose happening or nonhappening affects a duty of performance under a contract. Some conditions must be satisfied before any duty to perform arises; others terminate the duty to perform; still others either limit or modify the duty to perform. A condition is therefore the natural enemy of a promise. It is inserted in a contract to protect and benefit the promisor. The more conditions to which a promise is subject, the less content the promise has. A promise to pay $8,000 provided that such sum is realized from the sale of an automobile, provided the automobile is sold within sixty days, and provided that the automobile, which has been stolen, can be found, is clearly different from and worth considerably less than an unconditional promise by the same promisor to pay $8,000.

There is a fundamental difference between the breach or nonperformance of a promise and the failure or nonhappening of a condition. A breach

Condition–an uncertain event which affects the duty of performance

243

of contract subjects the promisor to liability. It may or may not, depending on its materiality, excuse nonperformance by the other party, the promisee, of his duty under the contract. The happening or nonhappening of a condition, on the other hand, either prevents the promisee from acquiring a right or deprives him of a right, but subjects neither party to any liability.

Conditions may be either (1) express, (2) implied-in-fact, or (3) implied-in-law. They are also classified as (4) conditions concurrent, (5) conditions precedent, and (6) conditions subsequent.

Express Conditions

Express condition—performance is contingent on the happening or nonhappening of a stated event

A condition is express when it is set forth in language usually preceded by such words as *provided that, on condition that, while, after, upon,* or *as soon as.* Although no particular form of words is necessary to create an express condition, the event to which the performance of the promise is made subject is in some manner clearly expressed. An illustration is the provision frequently found in building contracts that before the owner is required to pay, the builder shall furnish the architect's certificate stating that the building has been constructed according to the plans and specifications. The price is being paid for the building, not for the certificate, yet before the owner is obliged to pay, he must have both the building and the certificate. The duty of payment was made expressly conditional on the presentation of the certificate. This condition is excused if the architect dies, becomes insane, or capriciously refuses to give a certificate or if there is collusion between the owner and the architect.

Satisfaction—express condition making performance contingent upon one of the party's approval of the other's performance

The parties to a contract may also agree that performance by one of them shall be to the **satisfaction** of the other, who will not be obligated to pay for it unless he is satisfied. This is an express condition to the duty to pay for the performance. It is a valid condition. Assume that tailor Ken contracts to make a suit of clothes to Dick's satisfaction, and that Dick promises to pay Ken $250 for the suit if he is satisfied with it when completed. Ken completes the suit using materials ordered by Dick. The suit fits Dick beautifully, but Dick tells Ken that he is not satisfied with it and refuses to accept or pay for it. Ken is not entitled to recover $250 or any amount from Dick because the express condition did not happen. This is so even if the dissatisfaction of Dick, although honest and sincere, is unreasonable. Where satisfaction relates to a matter of personal taste, opinion, or judgment, the law applies the *subjective* standard, and the condition has not occurred if the promisor is actually dissatisfied. However, if the contract does not clearly indicate that satisfaction is subjective, or if the performance contracted for relates to mechanical fitness or utility, the law would assume an *objective* standard of satisfaction. For example, the objective standard of satisfaction would be applied in the sale of a building or goods; it would be assumed that the satisfaction standard applies to the marketability, utility, or mechanical fitness of the item being sold. In such cases, the question would not be whether the promisor was actually satisfied with the performance by the other party, but whether as a reasonable man, he ought to be satisfied.

Implied-in-Fact Conditions

Implied-in-fact condition—contingency understood but not expressed by the parties

Implied-in-fact conditions are similar to express conditions in that they are understood by the parties to be part of the agreement even though they are not stated in express language. They are necessarily inferred from the promise contained in the contract. Thus, if Edna for $750 contracts to paint Sy's house any color desired by Sy, it is necessarily implied in fact that Sy will inform Edna of the desired color before Edna begins to paint. The notification of choice of color is an implied-in-fact condition, an operative event that must occur before Edna is subject to the duty of painting the house.

Implied-in-Law Conditions

A condition implied-in-law differs from an express condition and a condition implied-in-fact in that it is not contained in the language of the contract or necessarily implied from the contract but is imposed by law in order to accomplish a just and fair result. For example, A contracts to sell a certain tract of land to B for $18,000, but the contract is silent as to the time of delivery of the deed and payment of the price. According to the law, the contract implies that payment and delivery of the deed are not independent of each other. The courts will treat the promises as mutually dependent and will therefore hold that a delivery or tender of the deed by A to B is a condition to the duty of B to pay the price. Conversely, payment or tender of $18,000 by B to A is a condition to the duty of A to deliver the deed to B. However, if the contract specifies a sale on credit, giving B thirty days after delivery of the deed within which to pay the price, these conditions are not implied by law, because the parties by their contract have expressly made their respective duties of performance independent of each other.

> **Implied-in-law condition**—contingency that arises from operation of law

Concurrent Conditions

Concurrent conditions are performances by two mutual promisors that are to take place at the same time. As we indicated in the section above, in the absence of agreement to the contrary, the law assumes that the respective performances under a contract are concurrent conditions. See *K & G Construction Co. v. Harris* on p. 247 for an illustration of mutually dependent, concurrent conditions.

> **Concurrent conditions** performance by the parties are to occur simultaneously

Condition Precedent

A condition precedent is an operative event that must occur before performance is due under a contract. In other words, the immediate duty of one party to perform is subject to the condition that some event must first occur. For instance, Steve is to deliver shoes to Nancy on June 1, and Nancy is to pay for the shoes on July 15. Steve's delivery of the shoes is a condition precedent to Nancy's performance. Similarly, if Rachel promises to buy Justin's land for $50,000, provided Rachel can obtain financing in the amount of $40,000 at 12 percent or less for thirty years within sixty days of signing the contract, Rachel's obtaining the specified financing is a condition precedent to her duty. If the condition is met, Rachel is bound to perform; if it does not occur, she is not bound to perform. Rachel, however, is under an implied-in-law duty to use her best efforts to obtain financing under these terms.

> **Condition precedent**—an event which must occur or not occur before performance is due

Condition Subsequent

A condition subsequent is an operative event that terminates an existing duty. Where goods are sold under terms of "sale or return," the buyer has the right to return the goods to the seller within a stated period but is under an immediate duty to pay the price unless credit has been agreed on. The duty to

> **Condition subsequent** an event which terminates a duty of performance

pay the price is terminated by a return of the goods, which operates as a condition subsequent.

Discharge by Performance

Discharge–termination of contractual duty

Performance–fulfillment of one's contractual obligations

Tender–offer of performance

Discharge by performance is undoubtedly the most frequent method of discharging a contractual duty. If a promisor exactly performs his duty under the contract, he is no longer subject to that duty. Substantial but less than exact performance does not fully discharge a promisor, although under the common law, substantial performance by one party deprives the other party of an excuse for nonperformance of his promise.

Where the contract is bilateral, a *tendered* or offered performance by one party to the other that is refused or rejected may be treated as a repudiation excusing or discharging the tendering party from further duty of performance under the contract. However, a tender of payment of a debt past due does not discharge the debt if the creditor refuses to accept the tender; instead, further accumulation of interest on the debt will stop.

Discharge by Breach

Breach by One Party as a Discharge of the Other

Breach–wrongful failure to perform the terms of a contract

Breach of contract always gives rise to a cause of action for damages by the aggrieved (injured) party. It may, however, have a more important effect. Because of the rule that one party need not perform unless the other party performs, an uncured (uncorrected) **material** breach by one party operates as an excuse for nonperformance by the other party and discharges the aggrieved party from any further duty under the contract. If the breach, on the other hand, is nonmaterial, the aggrieved party is not discharged from the contract, although she may recover money damages.

Material breach–nonperformance which significantly impairs the aggrieved party's rights under the contract

Material Breach   An unjustified failure to perform *substantially* the obligations promised in a contract is a material breach. The key is whether the aggrieved party obtained substantially what he bargained for. A material breach discharges the aggrieved party from his duty of performance. For instance, Joe orders a specially made, tailored suit from Peggy to be made of wool, but Peggy makes the suit of cotton instead. Peggy has materially breached the contract. Consequently, Joe is discharged from his duty to pay for the suit. Joe may also sue for money damages.

Although there are no clear-cut rules as to what constitutes a material breach, several basic principles can be applied. First, partial performance is a material breach of a contract if it omits some essential part of the contract. Second, the courts will consider a breach material if it is quantitatively or qualitatively serious. Third, an *intentional* breach of contract is generally held to be material. Fourth, a failure to perform promptly a promise is a material breach if time is of the essence, that is, if the parties have clearly indicated that a failure to perform by the stated time is material; otherwise, the aggrieved party may recover damages only for loss caused by the delay. Finally, the parties to a contract may, within limits, specify what breaches are to be considered material.

FACTS: K & G Construction Co. was the owner and general contractor for a housing subdivision project. Harris contracted with it to do excavating and earth-moving work on the project. Certain provisions of the contract stated that: (1) K & G was to make monthly progress payments to Harris; (2) no such payments were to be made until Harris obtained liability insurance; and (3) all of Harris's work on the project must be performed in a workmanlike manner. On August 9, a bulldozer operator, working for Harris, drove too close to one of K & G's houses, causing the collapse of a wall and other damage. When Harris and his insurance carrier denied liability and refused to pay for the damage, K & G refused to make the August monthly progress payment. Harris, nonetheless, continued to work on the project until mid-September when it ceased its operations due to K & G's refusal to make the progress payment. K & G had another excavator finish the job at an added cost of $450. It then sued Harris for the bulldozer damage, alleging negligence, and also for the $450 damages for breach of contract. Harris claims that K & G defaulted first, having no legal right to refuse the August progress payment.

DECISION: Judgment for K & G Construction Co. Contractual obligations are either independent of each other or mutually dependent. They are independent if the parties intend that performance by each of them is in no way conditioned upon performance by the other. Failure of one party to perform its independent promise does not excuse the other's non-performance. On the other hand, promises are concurrent conditions and mutually dependent if the parties intend performance by one to be conditioned upon performance by the other. A material breach of a mutually dependent promise by one party excuses the other's performance of his contractual obligations. The modern rule is that there is a presumption that mutual promises are concurrent and dependent, and are to be so regarded, whenever possible.

Here, the bulldozer operator's negligent damage to the house was a material breach of Harris's promise to perform in a workmanlike manner. Under a reasonable interpretation of the circumstances and the contract, the progress payment was conditioned upon Harris's non-negligent workmanlike performance. Hence, the promises are concurrent and mutually dependent. K & G then had a right to refuse making the progress payment without cancelling the contract, based upon Harris's negligence.

*K & G
CONSTRUCTION CO.
v. HARRIS*

Court of Appeals of
Maryland, 1960.
223 Md. 305, 164, A.2d 451.

The Code greatly alters the common law doctrine of material breach by adopting what is known as the **perfect tender rule.** This rule, which we discuss more fully in Chapter 20, essentially provides that *any* deviation from the promised performance in a sales contract under the Code constitutes a material breach of the contract and discharges the aggrieved party of his duty of performance.

Perfect tender –performance must strictly comply with contractual duties, U.C.C. standard

Substantial Performance

If a party substantially, but not completely, performs her obligations under a contract, the courts will generally allow that party to obtain the other party's performance less any damages caused by the partial performance. If no harm is caused, as in *Walker & Co. v. Harrison*, the breaching party will obtain the other party's full contractual performance. Thus, in the specially ordered suit illustration, if Peggy, the tailor, improperly used black buttons instead of blue, she would be permitted to collect from Joe the contract price of the suit less the damage, if any, caused to Joe by the substitution of the wrongly colored buttons. The doctrine of substantial performance assumes particular importance in the construction industry in cases where a structure is built on the aggrieved party's land. Consider the following: A builds a $300,000 house for B but deviates from the specifications, causing B $10,000 worth of damages. If the courts considered this breach material, then B would not have to pay for the house that is now on her land. However,

Substantial performance –performance that is incomplete but does not defeat the purpose of the contract

this would clearly be unjust. Therefore, because A's performance has been substantial, the courts would probably not deem the breach material. As a result, A would be able to collect $290,000 from B.

WALKER & CO. v. HARRISON

Supreme Court of Michigan, 1957.
347 Mich. 630, 81 N.W.2d 352.

FACTS: Walker & Co. contracted to provide a sign for Harrison to place above his dry cleaning business. According to the contract, Harrison would lease the sign from Walker, making monthly payments for 36 months. In return, Walker agreed to maintain and service the sign at its own expense. Walker installed the sign in July, 1953 and Harrison made the first rental payment. Shortly thereafter, someone hit the sign with a tomato. Harrison also claims he discovered rust on its chrome and little spider cobwebs in its corners. Harrison repeatedly called Walker for the maintenance work promised under the contract, but Walker did not respond. Harrison then telegraphed Walker that due to Walker's failure to perform the maintenance services he held Walker in material breach of the contract and thus repudiated the contract.

DECISION: Judgment for Walker & Co. Repudiation may be used by an injured party if the other party has committed a material breach. Here, however, the cobwebs and rust were within easy reach of Harrison and could have been remedied by him with little difficulty. The tomato stain, while not within his reach, also caused Harrison little damage since it was faded and partially washed away. Furthermore, Walker did send a service crew a week after Harrison's telegram. While the delay may have been irritating to Harrison it provided Walker with the essence of what he contracted for and was not sufficient to constitute a material breach on Walker's part. Therefore, Walker substantially performed the contract and Harrison was the breaching party.

Prevention of Performance

One party's substantial interference with or prevention of performance by the other generally constitutes a material breach that discharges the other party to the contract. For instance, A prevents an architect from giving a certificate that is a condition to A's liability to pay B a certain sum of money. A may not use B's failure to produce a certificate as an excuse for nonpayment. Likewise, if A has contracted to grow a certain crop for B, and after A has planted the seed, B plows the field and destroys the seedling plants, his interference with A's performance discharges A from his duty under the contract. It does not, however, discharge B from his duty under the contract. The following case further illustrates the point.

JACOBS v. JONES

Supreme Court of Colorado, 1967.
161 Colo. 505, 423 P.2d 321.

FACTS: Jacobs, owner of a farm, entered into a contract with Earl Walker in which Walker agreed to paint the buildings on the farm. Walker purchased the paint from Jones. Before the work was completed, Jacobs ordered Walker to stop because she was dissatisfied with the results. Offers were made by Jones and Walker to complete the job, but Jacobs declined to permit Walker to fulfill his contract. Jones and Walker bring this action against Jacobs for breach of contract.

DECISION: Judgment for Jones and Walker. By her order to Walker to cease work and by refusing to permit either Walker or Jones to complete the work, which they were willing to do, Jacobs breached the contract and excused further performance on the part of Walker. Under the circumstances the law implies a promise on the one party not to prevent, hinder, or delay the performance of the other party. Under the facts, Jones was entitled to be paid for the value of the paint furnished and used upon Jacobs's barns and house, and Walker was entitled to recover for the reasonable value of the work completed by him in accordance with the contract.

Anticipatory Repudiation

A breach of contract is simply a failure to perform the terms of the contract. It is logically and physically impossible to fail to perform a duty before the date that performance is due. A party, however, may announce before the due date that she will not perform, or she may commit an act that makes her unable to perform. Either of these acts is a repudiation of the contract, which notifies the other party that a breach is imminent. Such repudiation before the date fixed by the contract for performance is called an anticipatory breach. The courts, as shown in the leading case which follows, allow it to be treated as a breach and permit the nonrepudiating party to bring suit immediately as if it were a breach. Nonetheless, under the concept of election the non-breaching party may wait until the time of performance to see if the repudiator will retract his repudiation and perform his contractual duties. If the "repudiator" does perform then there is a discharge by performance, if he does not perform there is a material breach.

Anticipatory repudiation–breach of a contract before it is due by announcing that one will not perform or by committing an act which makes it impossible to perform

---

FACTS: On April 12, 1852, Hochster contracted with De La Tour to serve as a guide for De La Tour on his three-month trip to Europe, beginning on June 1 at an agreed upon salary. On May 11, De La Tour notified Hochster that he would not need Hochster's services. He also refused to pay Hochster any compensation. Hochster brings this action to recover damages for breach of contract.

DECISION: Judgment for Hochster. Hochster may treat the repudiation by De La Tour as a breach of contract and immediately bring suit. Otherwise, Hochster would have to remain ready to perform and to refrain from accepting other employment in order to tender his services on June 1. It is far more rational, upon repudiation of the contract by one of the parties, to allow the other party to consider his performance under the contract as excused and seek other employment while retaining his right to sue for damages.

HOCHSTER v. De La TOUR

2 Ellis and Blackburn Reports 678 (Q.B. 1853) (England)

Material Alteration of Written Contract

An unauthorized alteration or change of *any* of the material terms or provisions of a written contract or document is a discharge of the *entire* contract. To be a discharge, the alteration must be material and fraudulent and must be the act of a party to the contract or someone acting on his behalf. An unauthorized change in the terms of a written contract by a person who is not a party to the contract does not discharge the contract.

Discharge by Agreement of the Parties _____

Mutual Rescission

A rescission is an agreement between the parties to terminate their respective duties under the contract. It is a contract to end a contract. All of the essentials of a contract must be present. Each party, as shown in the following case, furnishes consideration in giving up their rights under the contract in exchange for the other party's relinquishment of their rights under the contract. Although, as indicated in the article reproduced in Law in the News on page 251, one of the parties sometimes gives additional consideration to be relieved of his contractual duties.

Rescission–termination of contractual duties

WATTS
CONSTRUCTION CO.
v. CULLMAN COUNTY

Supreme Court of Alabama,
1980.
382 So.2d 520.

FACTS: In May 1976, Watts was awarded a construction contract, based on its low bid, by the Cullman County Commission. The contract provided that it would not become effective until approved by the State Director of the Farmers Home Administration. In September construction still had not been authorized and Watts wrote to the County Commission requesting a 5 percent price increase to reflect seasonal and inflationary price increases. The County Commission countered with an offer of 3.5 percent. Watts then wrote the Commission insisting on a 5 percent increase and stating that if this was not agreeable, it was withdrawing its original bid. The Commission obtained another company to perform the project and on October 14, 1976 informed Watts that it had accepted the withdrawal of the bid. Watts sued for breach of contract.

DECISION: Judgment for Cullman County. Watts's letter withdrawing his bid and the Commission's letter accepting that withdrawal effectively rescinded any contract that might have existed. Parties to a contract may by mutual consent and without other consideration rescind the contract. Once the contract between Watts and Cullman County had been rescinded, Watts cannot recover damages for breach of contract.

A contract containing a provision that is contrary to or inconsistent with a provision in a prior contract between the same parties is a mutual rescission of the inconsistent provision in the prior contract. Whether the later contract completely supersedes and discharges all of the provisions of the prior contract is a matter of interpretation.

Substituted Contracts

Substituted contract–an agreement between the parties to rescind their old contract and replace it with a new contract

A substituted contract occurs when the parties to a contract mutually agree to rescind their original contract and enter into a new one. Substituted contracts are perfectly valid and effective to discharge the original contract and to impose obligations under the new contract.

Accord and Satisfaction

Accord and satisfaction–substituted performance under a contract (accord) and the discharge of the prior contractual obligation by performance of the new duty (satisfaction)

An *accord* is a contract between a promisee and promisor by which the promisee agrees to accept and the promisor agrees to give a substituted performance in *satisfaction* of an existing contractual duty. Thus, if Dan owes Sara $500 and the parties agree that Dan will paint Sara's house in satisfaction of the debt, the agreement is an executory accord. The debt, however, is not discharged until Dan performs the accord by painting Sara's house; the $500 debt is then discharged by accord and satisfaction.

Novation

Novation–substituted contract involving a new third party promisor or promisee

A novation is a substituted contract that involves an agreement among *three* parties to substitute a new promisee for the existing promisee or to replace the existing promisor with a new one. A novation discharges the old obligation because it creates a new contract in which there is either a new promisee or a new promisor. Thus, if B owes A $500, and A, B, and C agree that C will pay the debt and B will be discharged, the novation is the substitution of the new debtor C for B. Alternatively, if the three parties agree that B will pay $500 to C instead of to A, the novation is the substitution of a new creditor C for A. In each instance the debt owed by B to A is discharged.

Rozier to Jump Leagues After Buying Out Contract

Associated Press
PHILADELPHIA—Running back Mike Rozier, the 1983 Heisman Trophy winner who signed with the United States Football League, is jumping to the National Football League's Houston Oilers under a four-year contract worth an estimated $2 million, his agent said Monday.

Attorney Art Wilkinson said at a news conference that the former University of Nebraska All-American had bought out his multi-year contract with the USFL's Jacksonville Bulls to join the Oilers. Wilkinson, who said Rozier was visiting with his parents in southern New Jersey, said his client will sign with Houston this week.

In New York, NFL spokesman Dick Maxwell said Rozier is free to sign with the Oilers immediately because "we have reviewed his case . . . and found that he is free of any contract obligation."

The Oilers and Rozier have been awaiting NFL clearance to sign before an Aug. 1 guideline date designed to ensure that USFL players were free of other contractual obligations.

Houston obtained NFL rights to Rozier in a 1984 supplemental draft of USFL players. He was the No. 2 pick behind Brigham Young quarterback Steve Young of the Los Angeles Express, who was chosen by the Tampa Bay Buccaneers.

Wilkinson said Jacksonville attempted to retain Rozier with an offer that included $1 million in real estate.

"The down payment was $400,000 to $500,000. The issue was not enough cash," Wilkinson said.

The agent said it was decided to go with the "safe money" from Houston.

Wilkinson said Rozier "felt glad about the opportunity to play in the USFL this year and prove he could play. He did that. He feels like he can come in and be every bit as good a running back as Earl Campbell was at Houston and he was at Nebraska."

Campbell, a former Heisman winner from the University of Texas, led the NFL in rushing his first three seasons and spent more than six seasons with the Oilers before a 1984 trade to New Orleans.

Wilkinson admitted that Rozier had turned down a $3.2 million Oilers' offer in 1984, "because it involved a deferred payment schedule with the final payment in 1999.

"It was not acceptable because we would have had to buy out our contract with Pittsburgh [of the USFL] for $1 million. The [Pittsburgh] Maulers still were in existence at the time."

Rozier, 24, of Camden. N.J., won the Heisman, Maxwell and Walter Camp trophies in 1983, when he set Nebraska and Big Eight Conference rushing records. He then signed with the Maulers and played with them in 1984, under a personal service contract with team owner Edward D. DeBartolo Sr.

Wilkinson said DeBartolo owed Rozier $1.4 million under their personal services contract and they finally convinced DeBartolo to buy out the pact "for a bit less than $750,000."

He denied reports that Rozier bought the contract from DeBartolo.

Used By Permission of The Associated Press.

Discharge by Operation of Law

Subsequent Illegality

The performance of a contract that was legal when formed may become illegal or impractical because of a subsequently enacted law. In such a case the duty of performance is discharged. For example, Linda contracts to sell and deliver to Carlos ten cases of a certain whiskey each month for one year. A subsequent prohibition law makes the manufacture, transportation, or sale of intoxicating liquor unlawful. The duties in the contract that are still unperformed by Linda are discharged.

Impossibility

Impossibility–perfor-
mance cannot be done

It may be impossible for a promisor to perform his contract because he is financially unable or because he personally lacks the capability or competence. This is the situation presented in *Christy v. Pilkinton* and is *subjective* impossibility and does not excuse the promisor from liability for breach of contract. On the other hand, performance may be impossible not because the particular promisor is unable to perform, but because no one is able to perform. This is **objective** impossibility and generally will be held to excuse the promisor or discharge his duty to perform. Thus, the death or illness of a person who has contracted to render personal services is a discharge of his contractual duty. Furthermore, if a jockey contracts to ride a certain horse in the Kentucky Derby and the horse dies prior to the Derby, the contract is discharged. It is objectively impossible for this or any other jockey to perform the contract. Also, if Ken contracts to lease to Karlene a certain ballroom for a party on a scheduled future date, destruction of the ballroom by fire without Ken's fault before the scheduled event discharges the contract. Destruction of the subject matter or of the agreed-upon means of performance of a contract is excusable impossibility.

CHRISTY v. PILKINTON

Supreme Court of Arkansas, 1954.
224 Ark 407, 273 S.W.2d 533.

FACTS: The Christys entered into a written contract to purchase an apartment house from Pilkinton for $30,000. Pilkinton tendered a deed to the property and demanded payment of the unpaid balance of $29,000 due on the purchase price. As a result of a decline in Christy's used car business, the Christys did not possess and could not borrow the unpaid balance and, thus, asserted that it was impossible for them to perform their contract. This suit was brought by Pilkinton to enforce the sale of the apartment house.

DECISION: Judgment for Pilkinton. There is an important distinction between objective impossibility, which amounts to saying, "the thing cannot be done," and subjective impossibility— "I cannot do it." The latter, which is well illustrated by a promisor's financial inability to pay, does not discharge the contractual duty.

Frustration of purpose
purpose of the contract
cannot be fulfilled

Where the purpose of a contract has been frustrated by unexpected circumstances that deprive the performance of the value attached to it by the parties, although performance is not impossible, the courts generally regard the frustration as a discharge. This rule developed from the so-called coronation cases. When Edward VII became King of England on the death of his mother Queen Victoria, impressive coronation ceremonies were planned, including a procession along a designated route through London. Owners and lessees of buildings along the route made contracts to permit the use of rooms on the day scheduled for the procession. The King became ill, and the procession did not take place. Consequently the rooms were not used. Numerous suits were filed, some by landowners seeking to hold the would-be viewers liable on their promises, and some by the would-be-viewers seeking to recover money they had paid in advance for the rooms. The principle involved was novel, but from these cases evolved the **frustration of purpose** doctrine, under which a contract is discharged if supervening circumstances make fulfillment of the purpose that both parties had in mind impossible, unless one of the parties contractually assumed that risk.

The Restatement and Code view of impossibility conform to and expand this position by providing that performance need not be actually or literally impossible, but that **commercial impracticability** will excuse nonperformance. This does not mean mere hardship or that the cost of performance would be more than expected. A party will be discharged from performing his duty only when his performance is made impracticable by a supervening event. Moreover, the nonoccurrence of the subsequent event must have been a "basic assumption" made by both parties when entering into the contract.

Commercial impracticability–performance can only be accomplished at unforeseen and unjust hardship

FACTS: Northern Corporation entered into a contract with Chugach in August 1966 to repair and upgrade the upstream face of Cooper Lake Dam in Alaska. The contract required Northern to obtain rock from a quarry site at the opposite end of the lake and to transport the rock to the dam during the winter across the ice on the lake. In December 1966, Northern cleared the road on the ice to permit deeper freezing, but thereafter water overflowed on the ice preventing its use. Northern complained of unsafe conditions of the lake ice, but Chugach insisted on performance. In March 1967, one of Northern's loaded trucks broke through the ice and sank. Northern continued to encounter difficulties and ceased operations with the approval of Chugach. On January 8, 1968 Chugach notified Northern that it would be in default unless all rock was hauled by April 1. After two more trucks broke through the ice, causing the deaths of the drivers, Northern ceased operations and notified Chugach that it would make no more attempts to haul across the lake. Northern advised Chugach it considered the contract terminated for impossibility of performance and commenced suit to recover the cost incurred in attempting to complete the contract.

DECISION: Judgment for Northern. Northern's contract to perform was discharged by impossibility of performance. The particular method of performance specified in the contract presupposed the existence of ice frozen to sufficient depth to permit hauling of rock across the lake. This expectation by both parties was never fulfilled. A party is discharged from its contractual obligation, even if it is technically possible to perform, if the cost of performance would be so greatly disproportionate to that reasonably contemplated by the parties that performance would be commercially impracticable. In addition, a serious risk to life or health will excuse nonperformance.

NORTHERN CORP. v. CHUGACH ELECTRICAL ASSOCIATION

Supreme Court of Alaska, 1974.
518 P.2d 76.

Bankruptcy

Bankruptcy is a method of discharge of a contractual duty by operation of law available to a debtor who, by compliance with the requirements of the Bankruptcy Act, obtains an order of discharge by the bankruptcy court. It applies only to obligations that the Act provides are dischargeable in bankruptcy. We treat the subject of bankruptcy in Chapter 38.

Statute of Limitations

At common law a plaintiff was not subject to any time limitation within which to bring an action. Now, however, all States have statutes providing such a limitation. Although the courts hold that the running of the period of the Statute of Limitations does not operate as a discharge, it does bar the remedy. The debt is not discharged, but the creditor cannot maintain an action against the debtor after the Statute has run.

For a summary of discharge of contracts, see Figure 15–1.

FIGURE 15-1   Discharge of Contracts

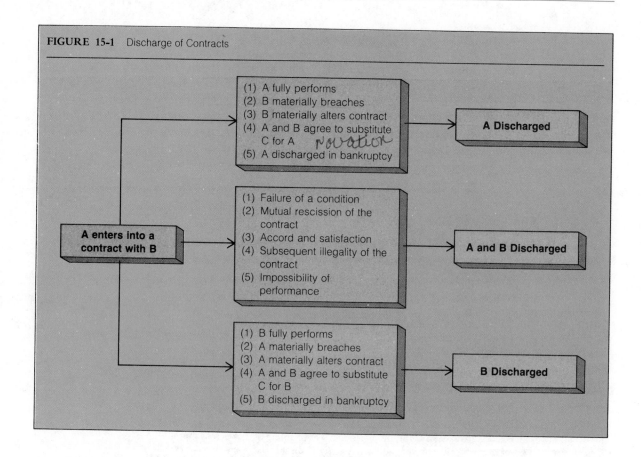

CHAPTER SUMMARY

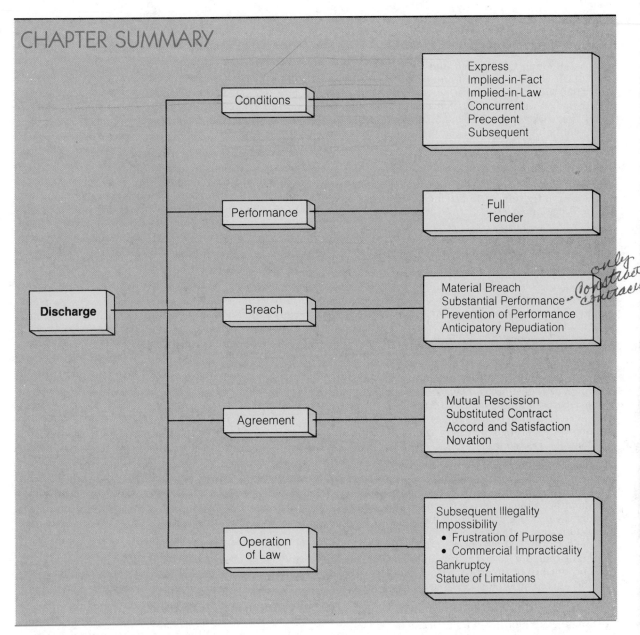

KEY TERMS

Condition
Express condition
Satisfaction
Implied-in-fact condition
Implied-in-law condition
Concurrent condition
Condition precedent
Condition subsequent
Performance

Discharge
Tender
Material breach
Perfect tender
Substantial performance
Anticipatory repudiation
Prevention of performance
Rescission
Substituted contract

Accord
Satisfaction
Accord and satisfaction
Novation
Illegality
Impossibility
Frustration of purpose
Commercial impracticality

PROBLEMS

1. A-1 Roofing Co. entered into a written contract with Jaffe to put a new roof on the latter's residence for $900 with a specified type of roofing, and to complete the job without unreasonable delay. A-1 undertook the work within a week thereafter, and when all the roofing material was at the site and the labor 50 percent completed, the premises were totally destroyed by fire caused by lighting. A-1 submitted a bill to Jaffe for $600 for materials furnished and labor performed up to the time of the destruction of the premises. Jaffe refused to pay the bill, and A-1 sued Jaffe. Decision?

2. By contract dated January 5, 1986, A agreed to sell to B and B agreed to buy from A a certain parcel of land then zoned commercial. The specific intent of B, which was known to A, was to erect a storage plant on the land. The contract stated that the agreement was conditioned on B's ability to construct a storage plant on the land. The closing date for the transaction was set for April 1, 1986. On February 15, 1986, the city council rezoned the land from commercial to residential, which precluded the erection of the storage plant intended by B. As the closing date drew near, B made it known to A that she did not intend to go through with the purchase because the land could no longer be used as intended. On April 1, A tendered the deed to B, who refused to pay A the agreed purchase price. A brought an action against B for breach of contract. Decision?

3. The Perfection Produce Company entered into a written contract with Hiram Hodges for the purchase of 200 tons of potatoes to be grown on Hodge's farm in Maine at a stipulated price per ton. The land would ordinarily produce 1,000 tons. Although the planting and cultivation were properly done, Hodges was able to deliver only 100 tons because an unprecedented drought caused a partial crop failure. Hodges sued the produce company to recover an unpaid balance of the agreed price for 100 tons of potatoes. The produce company, by an appropriate counterclaim against Hodges, sought damages for his failure to deliver the additional 100 tons. Decision?

4. On November 23, S agreed to sell to B her Pontiac automobile for $7,000, delivery and payment to be made on December 1. On November 26, B informed S that he wished to rescind the contract and would pay S $350 if S agreed. S agreed and took the $350 cash. On December 1, B tendered to S $6,650 and demanded that S deliver the automobile. S refused and B initiated a lawsuit. Decision?

5. S dealt in automobile accessories at wholesale. Although manufacturing a few items in his own factory, among them windshield wipers, S purchased most of his supplies from a large number of other manufacturers. In January, S entered into a written contract to sell B 2,000 windshield wipers for $1,900, delivery to be made June 1. In April, S's factory burned to the ground, and S failed to make delivery on June 1. B, forced to buy windshield wipers elsewhere at a higher price, brings an action against S for breach of contract. Decision?

6. On May 15, the Hughes Electric Company and the Moss Coal Company entered into a written contract whereby the coal company agreed to sell and deliver to the electric company 500 tons of coal at a stipulated price, on or before November 1. By September 1, the market price of coal had increased considerably and, on that date, the coal company notified the electric company that it would not make delivery of the coal, as agreed. By its reply, mailed on September 2, the electric company notified the coal company that it would expect performance in full by the coal company on November 1. On September 30, the electric company closed its plant temporarily because of a slump in the sales of electric equipment. On November 1, the coal company delivered 500 tons of coal to the electric company. The electric company refused to accept any part of the coal delivered. Thereafter, the coal company sued the electric company for damages for breach of contract. Decision?

7. Green owed White, $3,500, which was due and payable on June 1. White owed Brown $3,500, which was due and payable on August 1. On May 25, White received a letter signed by Green stating: "If you will cancel my debt to you, in the amount of $3,500, I will pay, on the due date, the debt you owe Brown, in the amount of $3,500." On May 28, Green received a letter signed by White stating: "I received your letter and agree to the proposals recited therein. You may consider your debt to me canceled as of the date of this letter." On June 1, White, needing money to pay his income taxes, made a demand upon Green to pay him the $3,500 due on that date. Is Green obligated to pay the money demanded by White?

8. By written contract Ames agreed to build a house on Bowen's lot for $45,000, commencing within ninety days of the date of the contract. Prior to the date for beginning construction, Ames informed Bowen that he was repudiating the contract and would not perform. Bowen refused to accept the repudiation and demanded fulfillment of the contract. Eighty days after the date of the contract, Bowen entered into a new contract with Curd for $42,000. The next day, without knowledge or notice of Bowen's contract with Curd, Ames began construction. Bowen ordered Ames from the premises and refused to allow him to continue.

Ames sued Bowen for damages. Decision?

9. A agreed in writing to work for B for three years as Superintendent of B's manufacturing establishment and to devote herself entirely to the business, giving it her whole time, attention, and skill, for which she was to receive $24,000 per annum, in monthly installments of $2,000. A worked and was paid for the first twelve months, when through no fault of her own or B's, she was arrested and imprisoned for one month. It became imperative for B to employ another, and he treated the contract with A as breached and abandoned, refusing to permit A to resume work on her release from jail. What rights, if any, does A have under the contract?

10. The Park Plaza Hotel awarded the valet and laundry concession to Larson for a three-year term. The contract contained the following provision: "It is distinctly understood and agreed that the services to be rendered by Larson shall meet with the approval of the Park Plaza Hotel, which shall be the sole judge of the sufficiency and propriety of the services." After seven months, the hotel gave a month's notice to discontinue services based on the failure of the services to meet its approval. Larson brought an action against the hotel, alleging that its dissatisfaction was unreasonable. The hotel defended on the ground that subjective or personal satisfaction may be the sole justification for termination of the contract. Decision?

16

REMEDIES

When one party to a contract breaches the contract by failing to perform his contractual duties, the law provides a remedy for the injured party. The primary objective of contract remedies is to compensate the injured party for the loss resulting from the breach. However, it is impossible for any remedy to equal the promised performance. The only relief that any court can give the injured party is what it regards as an equivalent of the promised performance. Even a decree of *specific performance* (a court order requiring the breaching party to perform his contractual duties) does not give the injured party what he was entitled to receive by the terms of the contract because the remedy comes at the end of a lawsuit many months or even years after the performance was due.

In this chapter we examine the most common remedies available for breach of contract: (1) monetary damages, (2) the equitable remedies of specific performance and injunction, and (3) restitution. Sales of goods are governed by Article 2 of the Uniform Commercial Code, which provides specialized remedies that we discuss in Chapter 21.

Monetary Damages

Compensatory Damages

The right to recover compensatory money damages for breach of contract is always available to the injured party. As we previously mentioned, the purpose in allowing damages is to provide compensation to the injured party that will, to the extent possible, place him in as good a position as if the other party had performed under the contract. The amount of damages is generally the **loss of value** to the injured party caused by the other party's failure to perform or by his deficient performance. Damages are not recoverable for loss beyond an amount that the injured party can establish with reasonable certainty.

In general, the loss of value is the *difference between the value of the promised performance* of the breaching party *and the value of the actual performance* rendered by the breaching party. If no performance is rendered at all, then the loss of value is the value of the promised performance. If defective or partial performance is rendered, the loss of value is the difference between the value that full performance would have had and the value of the performance actually rendered. Thus, where there has been a breach of warranty, the injured party may recover the difference between the value of the goods if

Compensatory damages—contract damages placing the injured party in as good a position as if the other party had performed

259

they had been as warranted and the value of the goods in their actual condition when received by the buyer. To illustrate, Jacob sells an automobile to Juliet and expressly warrants that it will get forty-five miles per gallon, but the automobile gets only twenty miles per gallon. The automobile would have been worth $8,000 if as warranted but is worth only $6,000 as delivered. Juliet would recover $2,000 in damages for loss of value.

Incidental damages damages arising directly out of a breach of contract

The injured party may *also* recover for all other loss actually suffered, subject to the limitation of foreseeability discussed below. These damages include incidental and consequential damages. **Incidental damages** are damages that arise directly out of the breach, such as costs incurred to acquire the nondelivered performance from some other source. For example, A employs B for nine months for $20,000 to supervise construction of a factory. A fires B without cause after three weeks. B spends $350 in reasonable fees attempting to find comparable employment. B may recover $350 in incidental damages in addition to any other actual loss suffered. **Consequential damages** include lost profits and injury to person or property resulting from defective performance. Thus, if Tracy leases to Sean a defective machine that causes $4,000 in property damage and $12,000 in personal injuries, Sean may recover, in addition to damages for loss of value and incidental damages, $16,000 as consequential damages.

Consequential damages—damages not arising directly out of a breach but as a foreseeable result of the breach

The recovery by the injured party, however, is reduced by any cost or loss she has avoided by not having to perform. For example, A agrees to build a hotel for B for $1,250,000 by September 1. A breaches by not completing construction until October 1. As a consequence, B loses revenues for one month in the amount of $10,000 but saves operating expenses of $6,000. B may recover damages for $4,000. Similarly, in a contract in which the injured party has not fully performed, the injured party's recovery is reduced by the value to the injured party of the performance promised by the injured party but not rendered. For example, A agrees to convey land to B in return for B's promise to work for A for two years. B repudiates the contract before A has conveyed the land to B. A's recovery for loss from B is reduced by the value to A of the land.

To summarize, the amount of **compensatory damages** an injured party may recover for breach of contract is computed as follows:

Value of performance of party in default
+ Incidental damages
+ Consequential damages
− Loss or cost avoided by injured party

Compensatory damages

Nominal damages—a small sum awarded where a contract has been breached but the loss is negligible or unproved

An action to recover damages for breach of contract may be maintained even though the plaintiff has not sustained or cannot prove any injury or loss resulting from the breach. In such case he will be permitted to recover **nominal damages**—a small sum fixed without regard to the amount of loss. Such a judgment may also include an award of court costs.

Reliance Damages

Reliance damages—contract damages placing the injured party in as good a position as he would have been in had the contract not been made

Instead of seeking compensatory damages, the injured party may seek reimbursement for loss caused by his reliance on the contract. The result of this remedy is to place the injured party in as good a position as he would have been in had the contract *not been made*. Damages for reliance include expenses incurred in preparing to perform, in actually performing, or in foregoing opportunities to enter into other contracts. An injured party may prefer damages for reliance to compensatory damages when he is unable to establish his lost profits with reasonable certainty or when the contract is itself unprofitable. For example, Donald agrees to sell his retail store to Gary. Gary spends $50,000 in acquiring inventory and fixtures. Donald then repudiates the contract, and Gary sells the inventory and fixtures for $35,000. Neither party can establish with reasonable certainty what profit Gary would have made. Gary may recover from Donald as damages the loss of $15,000 he sustained on the sale of the inventory and fixtures plus any other costs he incurred in entering into the contract.

Foreseeability of Damages

A contracting party is generally expected to consider those risks that are foreseeable at the time he entered into the contract. Therefore, compensatory or reliance damages are recoverable only for loss that the party in breach had reason to foresee as a *probable* result of a breach when the contract was made. The breaching party is not liable in the event of a breach for loss that was not foreseeable at the time of entering into the contract. The test of foreseeability is an **objective** test based on what the breaching party had reason to foresee. Loss may be foreseeable as a probable result of a breach because it follows from the breach (a) in the ordinary course of events or (b) as a result of special circumstances, beyond the ordinary course of events, that the party in breach had reason to know about.

Foreseeable damages – loss that the party in breach had reason to know of when the contract was made

A leading case on the subject of foreseeability of damages is *Hadley v. Baxendale*, decided in England in 1854.

FACTS: The plaintiffs operated a flour mill at Gloucester. They had to stop operating the mill because of a broken crankshaft attached to the steam engine that furnished power to the mill. It was necessary to send the broken shaft to a foundry in Greenwich so that a new shaft could be made. The plaintiffs delivered the broken shaft to the defendants, who were common carriers, for immediate transportation from Gloucester to Greenwich, but did not inform the defendants that the mill had ceased operating because of the broken crankshaft. The defendants received the shaft, collected the freight charges in advance, and promised the plaintiffs to deliver the shaft at Greenwich the following day. The defendants neglected to make prompt delivery as promised. As a result the plaintiffs could not operate the mill for several days, thus losing profits that they otherwise would have received. The defendants contended that the loss of profits was too remote, and therefore unforeseeable, to be recoverable. In awarding damages to the plaintiffs, the jury was permitted to consider the loss of these profits.

DECISION: Judgment for defendants. The appellate court reversed the decision and ordered a new trial on the ground that the special circumstances that caused the loss of profits, namely, the continued stoppage of the mill while awaiting the return of the new crankshaft, had never been communicated by the plaintiffs to the defendants. A common carrier would not reasonably foresee that the plaintiff's mill would be shut down as a result of delay in transporting the broken crankshaft. Damages for "breach of contract should be such as may fairly and reasonably be considered either arising naturally, i.e., according to the usual course of things, from such breach . . . or such as may reasonably be supposed to have been in the contemplation of both parties at the time they made the contract, as the probable result of the breach of it."

HADLEY v. BAXENDALE

Court of Exchequer, 1854. 9 Ex. 341, 156 Eng.Rep. 145.

On the other hand, if the defendants in *Hadley v. Baxendale* had been informed that the shaft was necessary for the operation of the mill, or otherwise had reason to know this fact, they would be liable to the plaintiffs for loss of profit during the period of shutdown caused by their delay. Under these circumstances the loss would be the "foreseeable" and "natural" result of the breach in accordance with common experience. The plaintiffs' loss of profit would be the probable result of the defendants' delay in transporting the shaft and would be recoverable from the defendants.

But what if the plaintiff's expected profit should be extraordinarily large? The general rule, as stated above, is that the breaching party will be liable for such extraordinary loss only if he had reason to know of the special loss. In any event the plaintiff may recover for any ordinary loss resulting from the breach. Thus, if A breaches a contract with B, causing B, due to special circumstances, $10,000 in damages where ordinarily such a breach would only result in $6,000 in damages, A would be liable to B for $6,000, not $10,000, so long as A was unaware of the special circumstances causing B the unusually large loss.

Damages for Misrepresentation

Out-of-pocket damages–difference between the value received and the value given

Benefit-of-the-bargain damages–difference between the value received and the value of the fraudulent party's performance as represented

Fraud   A party who has been induced to enter into a contract by fraud may recover damages in a tort action. The minority of States allow the injured party to recover only **"out of pocket"** damages equal to the difference between the value of what she has received and the value of what she has given for it. The great majority of States, however, permit the intentionally defrauded party to recover damages under the **"benefit-of-the-bargain"** rule that are equal to the difference between the value of what she has received and the value of the fraudulent party's performance as represented. The Restatement of Torts provides the fraudulently injured party with the option of either out-of-pocket or benefit-of-the-bargain damages. To illustrate, Emily intentionally misrepresents the capabilities of a printing press and thereby induces Melissa to purchase the machine for $20,000. The value of the press as delivered is $14,000, but if the machine had performed as represented, it would be worth $24,000. Under the out-of-pocket rule Melissa would recover $6,000, whereas under the benefit-of-the-bargain rule she would recover $10,000.

Nonfraudulent Misrepresentation   Where the misrepresentation is not fraudulent, the Restatement of Torts permits out-of-pocket damages but expressly excludes recovery of benefit-of-the-bargain damages.

Punitive Damages

Punitive damages are monetary damages in addition to compensatory damages awarded a plaintiff in certain situations involving willful, wanton, or malicious conduct. Their purpose is to punish the defendant and thus discourage him and others from similar wrongful conduct. The purpose of allowing contract damages, on the other hand, is to compensate the plaintiff for the loss he sustained because of the defendant's breach of contract. In a case where the plaintiff has established a breach of contract and evidence of loss or damage, the court will award him a judgment in an amount it deems sufficient to place him in the position where he would have been if the defendant had not breached the contract. Accordingly, the Restatement provides that punitive damages are *not* recoverable for a breach of contract unless the conduct constituting the breach is also a tort for which punitive damages are recoverable.

Liquidated Damages

A contract may contain a provision by which the parties agree in advance to the damages to be paid in event of breach. Such a liquidated damages provision will be enforced if it amounts to a reasonable forecast of the loss that may result from the breach. If, however, the sum agreed on as liquidated damages does not bear a reasonable relationship to the amount of probable loss, it is unenforceable as an invalid penalty. This is because the objective of contract remedies is compensatory not punitive. The courts will look at the substance of the provision, the nature of the contract, and extent of probable harm to the promisee that may reasonably be expected to be caused by a breach in order to determine whether the agreed amount is proper as liquidated damages or unenforceable as a penalty. It is immaterial what name or label the parties to the contract attach to the provision. If a liquidated damages provision is not enforceable, the injured party is nevertheless entitled to the ordinary remedies for breach of contract.

Liquidated damages—reasonable damages agreed to in advance by the parties to a contract

CITY OF RYE v. PUBLIC SERVICE MUTUAL INSURANCE CO.

Court of Appeals of New York, 1974.
34 N.Y.2d 470, 358 N.Y.S.2d 391, 315 N.E.2d 458.

FACTS: Developers under a plan approved by the city of Rye had constructed six luxury cooperative apartment buildings and were to construct six more. In order to obtain certificates of occupancy for the six completed buildings, the developers were required to post a bond with the city to insure completion of the remaining buildings. The developers posted a $100,000 bond upon which the defendant, Public Service Mutual Insurance Company, as guarantor or surety, agreed to pay $200 for each day after April 1, 1971 that the remaining buildings were not completed. More than 500 days passed without completion of the buildings within the time limit. The city sued the developers and the insurance company to recover $100,000 on the bond.

DECISION: Judgment for the insurance company. A contract may contain a liquidated damage provision, but the sum agreed upon must be a reasonable measure of the anticipated harm. The amount of the bond was not a reasonable estimate of probable monetary harm or damage to the city but rather was a penalty. The harm which the city contends it would suffer is minimal and speculative. Since the agreement to pay $200 a day was actually a penalty provision, the court will not enforce it.

Mitigation of Damages

When a breach of contract occurs, the injured party is required to take reasonable action to lessen or mitigate the damages that he may sustain. The injured party may not recover damages for loss that he could have avoided without undue risk, burden, or humiliation. Thus, where Earl is under a contract to manufacture goods for Karl and Karl repudiates the contract after Earl has begun performance, Earl will not be allowed to recover for losses he sustains by continuing to manufacture the goods, if to do so would increase the amount of damages. The amount of loss that could reasonably have been avoided is deducted from the amount that would otherwise be recoverable as damages. On the other hand, if the goods were almost completed when Karl repudiated the contract, the completion of the goods might reduce the damages, because the finished goods may be resalable whereas the unfinished goods may not.

Mitigation of damages—requirement that the injured party take reasonable steps to lessen or avoid damages

Similarly, a buyer who does not receive goods or services promised to him under a contract cannot recover damages resulting from his doing without such goods or services where it is possible for him to substitute goods or services that he can obtain elsewhere. Likewise, if A contracts to work for B for one year for a weekly salary and after two months is wrongfully discharged by B, A must use reasonable efforts to mitigate his damages by seeking other employment. If he cannot obtain other employment of the same general character, he is entitled to recover full pay for the contract period that he is unemployed. He is not obliged to accept a radically different type of employment or to accept work at a distant place. For example, a person employed as a school teacher or accountant who is wrongfully discharged is not obliged to accept employment as a chauffeur or truck driver. The next case involving Shirley MacLaine turns on whether acting in a western is equivalent employment to singing and dancing in a musical.

PARKER v. TWENTIETH CENTURY-FOX FILM CORP.

Supreme Court of California, 1970.
3 Cal.3d 176, 89 Cal.Rptr. 737, 474 P.2d 689.

FACTS: Shirley MacLaine Parker, a well known actress, contracted with Twentieth Century-Fox Film Corporation in August, 1965 to play the female lead in Fox's upcoming production of "Bloomer Girl," a motion picture musical that was to be filmed in California. The contract provided that Fox would pay Parker a minimum "guaranteed compensation" of $750,000 for 14 weeks of Parker's services, beginning May 23, 1966. By letter dated April 4, 1966, Fox notified Parker of its intention not to produce the film and, instead, offered to employ Parker in the female lead of another film entitled "Big Country, Big Man," a dramatic western to be filmed in Australia. The compensation offered and most of the other provisions in the substitute contract were identical to the "Bloomer Girl" provisions, except that Parker's right to approve the director and screenplay would have been eliminated or reduced under the "Big Country" contract. Parker refused to accept and brought suit against Fox to recover $750,000 for breach of the "Bloomer Girl" contract. Fox contended that it owed no money to Parker because she had deliberately failed to mitigate or reduce her damages by unreasonably refusing to accept the "Big Country" lead.

DECISION: Judgment for Parker. A wrongfully discharged employee generally has a duty to mitigate her damages by either attempting to, or actually, finding substitute employment. The measure of recovery is typically the amount of salary promised under the original contract minus the amount which the employer proves the employee has earned, or with reasonable effort might have earned, from other, "substantially similar" employment. The employee's rejection of or failure to seek other employment of a different or inferior kind cannot be used to mitigate damages.

"Bloomer Girl" was to be a musical review calling upon Parker's talents as a dancer as well as an actress and was to be filmed in Los Angeles. On the other hand, "Big Country, Big Man" was a straight acting, "western type" motion picture taking place in an opal mine in Australia. In addition, Parker would have had her right to approve the director and screenplay eliminated or impaired by the "Big Country" contract. Such disparities between the two render the substitute "Big Country" lead of a kind different and inferior to the "Bloomer Girl" role. Therefore, Parker need not accept or seek such inferior employment and could reject Fox's substitute offer with no reduction in her award for failure to mitigate.

Remedies in Equity

The remedies of specific performance and injunction are forms of equitable relief that may be available as alternatives to damages as means of enforcing contracts. The remedies of specific performance and injunction are not a matter of right but rest largely in the discretion of the court. Consequently, they will not be granted where there is an adequate remedy at law; where it is impossible to enforce them, as where the seller has already transferred the subject matter of the contract to an innocent third person; where the contract is without consideration; where the consideration is grossly inadequate; or where the contract is tainted with fraud, duress, undue influence or other defect. Also, the plaintiff must be ready and able to perform in full on his part. This can usually be shown by a tender of the full purchase price into court.

Specific Performance

As a general principle, a contract creates enforceable rights, courts will enforce contracts, and a remedy is the means of enforcing rights. These statements are substantially correct, but as to the vast majority of contracts they are not literally correct. Ordinarily, a contract will not be enforced by courts in the sense that they will require the breaching party literally to carry out his contractual obligations. The usual remedy for breach of contract, as we have seen, is an action at law for money damages by way of compensation for the loss. Suppose, for example, that A contracts to sell and deliver coal to B, and that A wrongfully refuses to deliver the coal to B. No court will force A to deliver the coal to B. B can buy the coal elsewhere. However, if B suffers a loss by having to pay a higher price than the contract price, he has his remedy at law: an action against A for money damages to compensate B for his loss. A judgment for money damages is the only remedy that a court of law can award. And, in most cases, it is a just and adequate remedy. Cases, however, occasionally arise where an award of money damages is wholly inadequate as a remedy. Since this is the only remedy a court of law can grant, the injured party is without an adequate remedy at law. In such a case, his remedy is a suit in equity for specific performance of the contract. See *Tamarind Lithography Workshop v. Sanders.*

Specific performance, in one sense, is the actual performance by the defaulting party of her contractual obligations as decreed by a court of equity. Primarily, the term is used to indicate the equitable remedy which compels the performance of a contract according to its terms. Ordinarily, as we have seen, in case of breach by the seller of her contract for the sale of personal property, the buyer has a sufficient remedy at law. Where, however, the property contracted for is rare or *unique*, this remedy is inadequate. Examples are a famous painting or statue, the original manuscript or a rare edition of a book, a patent, a copyright, shares of stock in a close corporation, a relic or an heirloom. Articles of this kind cannot be purchased elsewhere, nor do they have a market value. Clearly, on breach by the seller of her contract for the sale of any such article, money damages will not adequately or completely compensate the buyer. Consequently, in these cases the buyer may avail himself of the equitable remedy of specific performance.

Specific performance– court decree ordering breaching party to render promised performance

While it is only in exceptional circumstances that courts of equity will grant specific performance in connection with contracts for the sale of personal property, they will always grant it in case of breach of contract for the sale of *real property*. The reason for this is that any particular parcel of land is regarded as unique and as differing from any other parcel. Consequently, if the seller refuses to convey title to the real estate contracted for, the buyer may seek the aid of a court of equity to compel the seller to convey the title. As to real estate contracts, the remedy is mutual. Court of equity will likewise compel the buyer to perform at the suit of the seller.

Courts of equity will not grant specific performance of contracts for personal services. In the first place, there is the practical difficulty, if not impossibility, of enforcing a decree in any such case. In the second place, it is against the policy of the courts to force one person to work for or serve another against his will, even though he has contracted to do so. Such enforcement would probably amount to involuntary servitude. For example, if A, an accomplished concert pianist, agrees to appear at a certain time and place to play a specified program for B, upon A's refusal to appear a court would not issue a decree of specific performance.

TAMARIND LITHOGRAPHY WORKSHOP v. SANDERS

Court of Appeal of California, Second District, 1983.
143 Cal.App.3d 571, 193 Cal.Rptr. 409.

FACTS: In 1969, Sanders agreed in writing to write, direct and produce a motion picture on the subject of lithography for the Tamarind Lithography Workshop. After the completion of this film, "Four Stones for Kanemitsu," litigation arose concerning the parties' rights and obligations under their 1969 agreement. Tamarind and Sanders resolved this dispute by a written settlement agreement, whereby Tamarind promised to provide Sanders a screen credit stating: "A Film by Terry Sanders." However, Tamarind did not comply with this agreement and failed to include a screen credit for Sanders in the prints it subsequently distributed. In the ensuing litigation Sanders seeks damages for Tamarind's breach of the settlement agreement, and specific performance to compel Tamarind's compliance with its obligation to provide a screen credit.

DECISION: Decision for Sanders granting specific performance. To obtain specific performance Sanders must show: (1) the inadequacy of his legal remedy; (2) an underlying contract that is both reasonable and supported by adequate consideration; (3) the existence of mutuality of remedies; (4) contractual terms which are sufficiently definite; and (5) a substantial similarity of the requested performance to that promised in the contract. Sanders' legal remedy is inadequate here because: first, an accurate assessment of damages for lost public acclaim is far too difficult and requires too much speculation; and second, any future showings of the film might be deemed a further breach creating "the danger of an untold number of lawsuits." The remedy of specific performance avoids these difficulties and provides Sanders with the contracted for public acclaim. Since the other requisites for granting specific performance have been met, Sanders is entitled to a writ of specific performance requiring Tamarind to add a screen credit to the film.

Injunctions

Injunction—court order prohibiting a party from doing a specific act

The injunction, as used as a contract remedy, is a formal court order enjoining (commanding) a person to refrain from doing a specific act or engaging in a specific conduct. A person who violates an injunctive order may be held guilty of contempt of court and fined or imprisoned until released by the court.

A court of equity, at its discretion, may grant an injunction against breach of a contractual duty where damages for a breach would be inadequate. For example, Clint enters into a written agreement to give Janice the right of first refusal on a tract of land owned by Clint. However, Clint subsequently offers the land to Blake without first offering it to Janice. A court of equity may properly enjoin Clint from selling the land to Blake. Similarly, valid covenants not to compete may be enforced by an injunction.

An employee's promise of exclusive personal services may be enforced by an injunction against serving another employer as long as the probable result will not be to leave the employee without other reasonable means of making a living. Suppose, for example, that A makes a contract with B, a famous singer, under which B agrees to sing at A's theater on certain dates for an agreed fee. Before the date of the first performance, B makes a contract with C to sing for C at his theater on the same dates. A cannot obtain specific performance by B of his contract, as already discussed. A court of equity will, however, on suit by A against B, issue an injunction against B ordering B not to sing for C. This is the situation in the case of *Madison Square Garden Corp., Ill. v. Carnera*. Where the services contracted for are *not* unusual or extraordinary in character, the injured party cannot obtain injunctive relief. His only remedy is an action at law for damages.

FACTS: Carnera (defendant) agreed with Madison Square Garden (plaintiff) to render services as a boxer in his next contest with the winner of the Schmeling-Stribling contest for the heavyweight championship title. The contract also provided that prior to the match Carnera would not engage in any major boxing contest without the permission of Madison Square Garden. Without obtaining such permission, Carnera contracted to engage in a major boxing contest with Sharkey. Madison Square Garden brought suit requesting an injunction against Carnera's performing his contract to box Sharkey.

DECISION: Judgment for Madison Square Garden. Specific performance will not be ordered to compel Carnera to render personal services, but the court will specifically enforce a negative covenant by injunctive order where damages are not readily ascertainable.

MADISON SQUARE GARDEN CORP., ILL. v. CARNERA

Circuit Court of Appeals, Second Circuit, 1931. 52 F.2d 47.

Restitution

One of the remedies that may be available to a party to a contract is restitution. Restitution is a return to the aggrieved party of the consideration, or its value, that he gave to the other party. The purpose of restitution is to restore the injured party to the position he was in before the contract was made. Therefore, the party seeking restitution must return what he has received from the other party.

Restitution is available in several contractual situations: (1) as an alternative remedy for a party injured by breach, (2) for a party in default, (3) for a party who may not enforce the contract because of the Statute of Frauds, and (4) on avoidance of a voidable contract.

Restitution – restoration of the injured party to the position he was in before the contract was made

Party Injured by Breach

A party is entitled to restitution if the other party totally breaches the contract by nonperformance or repudiation. For example, Benedict agrees to sell land to Beatrice for $60,000. Beatrice makes a partial payment of $15,000. Benedict wrongfully refuses to transfer title. As an alternative to damages or specific performance, Beatrice may recover the $15,000 in restitution.

Party in Default

Where a party, after having partly performed, commits a breach by nonperformance or repudiation that discharges the other party's duty to perform, the party in default is entitled to restitution for any benefit she has conferred in excess of the loss she has caused by her breach. For example, A agrees to sell land to B for $60,000, and B makes a partial payment of $15,000. B then repudiates the contract. A sells the land to C in good faith for $55,000. B may recover from A in restitution the part payment of the $15,000 *less* the $5,000 damages A sustained because of B's breach, which equals $10,000.

Statute of Frauds

Parties to a contract that is unenforceable because of the Statute of Frauds may, nonetheless, have acted in reliance on the contract. In such a case each party may recover in restitution the benefits conferred on the other in relying on their unenforceable contract. Thus, if Wilton makes an oral contract to furnish services to Rochelle that are not to be performed within a year and Rochelle discharges Wilton after three months, Wilton may recover as restitution the value of the services rendered during the three months.

Voidable Contracts

A party who has avoided a contract for lack of capacity, duress, undue influence, fraud, misrepresentation, or mistake is entitled to restitution for any benefit he has conferred on the party. For example, A fraudulently induces B to sell land for $60,000. A pays the purchase price, and B conveys the land. B then discovers the fraud. B may disaffirm the contract and recover the land as restitution. Generally, the party seeking restitution must return any benefit that he has received under the agreement; however, this is not always the case, as we discussed in Chapter 12, which dealt with contractual capacity.

Figure 16–1 summarizes the remedies for breach of contract.

Limitations on Remedies

Election of Remedies

If a party is injured by a breach of contract and has more than one remedy available to him, his manifestation of a choice of one of them by bringing suit or otherwise does not prevent him from seeking another remedy unless the remedies are inconsistent and the other party materially changes his position in reliance on the manifestation. For example, a party who seeks specific performance, an injunction, or restitution may be entitled to incidental damages, such as delay in performance. However, damages for total breach are inconsistent with the remedies of specific performance, injunction, and restitution. Likewise, the remedy of specific performance or an injunction is inconsistent with that of restitution.

HEAD & SEEMAN, INC. v. GREGG

Court of Appeals of Wisconsin, 1981.
104 Wis.2d 156, 311 N.W.2d 667.

FACTS: Bettye Gregg offered to purchase a house from Head & Seeman, Inc. (seller). She represented in writing that she had $15,000 to $20,000 of equity in another home that she would pay to the seller after she sold the other home. She knew that she did not have such equity. In reliance upon these intentionally fraudulent representations the seller accepted Gregg's offer and the parties entered into a land contract. After taking occupancy, Gregg failed to make any of the contract payments. The seller's investigations then revealed the fraud. Head & Seeman then brought suit seeking rescission of the contract, return of the real estate and restitution. Restitution was sought for the rental value for the five months of lost use of the property and the seller's out-of-pocket expenses made in reliance upon the bargain. Gregg contends that under the election of remedies doctrine the seller cannot both rescind the contract and recover damages for its breach.

DECISION: Judgment for Head & Speelman. The election of remedies doctrine bars a plaintiff from maintaining inconsistent theories or forms of relief. Its purpose is to prevent a double recovery for the same wrong. Under the doctrine a defrauded party must choose either (1) to rescind or (2) to affirm the contract and seek damages. This rule applies where the defrauded party is seeking benefit-of-the-bargain damages. It does not, however, prevent a defrauded party from rescinding and recovering "restorative" damages that put the defrauded party back in his position prior to the making of the contract. Rescission and restitutionary (restorative) damages are consistent remedies and are not subject to the election of remedies doctrine.

Here, the restoration of the rental value and out-of-pocket expenses works consistently with rescission of the contract to restore Head & Speelman to its pre-contract position. There is no possibility of the corporation obtaining an inconsistent or double recovery. Therefore, the election of remedies does not apply.

FIGURE 16-1   Contract Remedies

Monetary	**Equitable**	**Restitution**
Compensatory	Specific performance	Return of consideration
Reliance	Injunctions	
Liquidated		

The Code liberalizes the common law concerning contracts for the sale of goods by not restricting a defrauded party to an election or remedies. That is, he may both rescind the contract by restoring the status quo and, in addition, recover damages or obtain any other remedy available under the Code.

Loss of Power of Avoidance

A party with a power of avoidance for lack of capacity, duress, undue influence, fraud, misrepresentation, or mistake may lose that power if (1) she affirms the contract, (2) she delays unreasonably in exercising the power of disaffirmance, or (3) the rights of third parties intervene.

Affirmance   A party who has the power to avoid a contract for lack of capacity, duress, undue influence, fraud, misrepresentation, or mistake will lose that power by affirming the contract. Affirmance occurs where the party, with full knowledge of the facts, either declares his intention to proceed with the contract or takes some other action from which such intention may reasonably be inferred. Thus, suppose that A was induced to purchase a ring from B through B's fraudulent misrepresentation. If, after learning the truth, A undertakes to sell the ring to C or does something else that is consistent only with his ownership of the ring, he may no longer rescind the transaction. In the case of incapacity, duress, or undue influence, affirmance is effective only after the circumstances that made the contract voidable cease to exist. Where there has been fraudulent misrepresentation, the defrauded party may affirm only after he knows of the misrepresentation, whereas if the misrepresentation is nonfraudulent or there is a mistake, only after he knows or should know of the misrepresentation or mistake.

Delay   The power of avoidance may be lost if the party who has the power does not rescind within a reasonable time. What is a reasonable time depends on all the circumstances, including the extent to which the delay enables the party with the power of avoidance to speculate at the other party's risk. To illustrate, a defrauded purchaser of stock cannot wait unduly to see if the market price or value of the stock appreciates sufficiently to justify retaining the stock. A reasonable time does not begin until the circumstances that made the contract voidable have ceased to exist.

Rights of Third Parties   The power of avoidance and the accompanying right to restitution are further limited by the intervening rights of third parties. In a transaction that is voidable by A, if A transfers property to B and B sells the property to C, a good faith purchaser for value, before A exercises her power of avoidance, A will lose the right to recover the property.

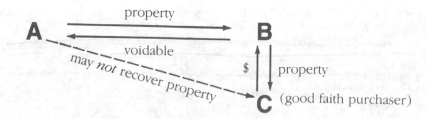

Thus, if a third party, a good faith purchaser (C) acquires an interest in the subject matter of the contract before A has elected to rescind, no rescission is permitted. Because the transaction is voidable, B acquires a voidable title to the property. Upon a sale of the property by him to C, who is a purchaser in good faith and for value, C obtains good title and is allowed to retain the property. Since both A and C are innocent, the law will not disturb the title held by C, the good faith purchaser. In this case, as in all cases where rescission is not available, A's only recourse is against B.

The one notable exception to this rule is the situation involving a sale by a minor who subsequently wishes to avoid a transaction, *other than for a sale of goods*, from a good faith purchaser. Under this special rule a good faith purchaser is deprived of the protection generally provided. Therefore, the third party in a transaction not involving goods is no more protected from the minor's disaffirmance than is the person dealing directly with the minor.

CHAPTER SUMMARY

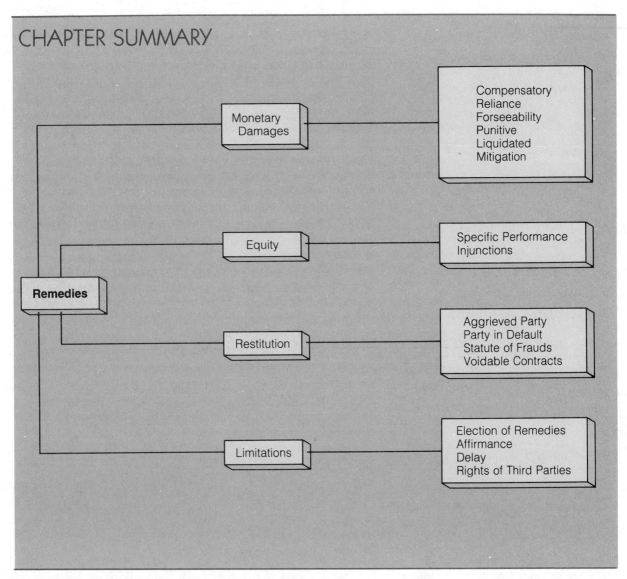

KEY TERMS

Compensatory damages	Foreseeable damages	Specific performance
Incidental damages	Out-of-pocket damages	Injunction
Consequential damages	Benefit-of-the-bargain damages	Restitution
Nominal damages	Liquidated damages	Election of remedies
Reliance damages	Mitigation of damages	

PROBLEMS

1. A contracted to buy 1,000 barrels of sugar from B. B failed to deliver, and because A could not buy any sugar in the market, he was forced to shut down his candy factory. (a) What damages is A entitled to recover? (b) Would it make any difference if B had been told by A that he wanted the sugar to make candies for the Christmas trade and that he had accepted contracts for the delivery by certain dates?

2. A agreed to erect an apartment building for B for $750,000, A to suffer deduction of $1,000 per day for every day of delay. A was twenty days late in finishing the job, losing ten days because of a strike and ten days because the material suppliers were late in furnishing A with materials. A claims that he is entitled to payment in full (a) because the agreement as to $1,000 a day is a penalty; (b) because B had not shown that he has sustained any damage. Discuss each contention and decide.

3. A contracted with B, a shirtmaker, for 1,000 shirts for men. B manufactured and delivered 500 shirts, which A paid for. At the same time, A notified B that she could not use or dispose of the other 500 shirts and directed B not to manufacture any more under the contract. Nevertheless, B made up the other 500 shirts and tendered them to A. A refused to accept the shirts. B then sued for the purchase price. Decision?

4. A contracts to act in a comedy for B and to comply with all theater regulations for four seasons. B promises to pay A $800 for each performance and to allow A one benefit performance each season. It is expressly agreed that "A shall not be employed in any other production for the period of the contract." A and B, during the first year of the contract, had a terrible quarrel. Thereafter, A signed a contract to perform in C's production and ceased performing for B. B seeks (a) to prevent A from performing for C and (b) to require A to perform his contract with B. What result?

5. A leases a building to B for five years at a rental of $1,000 per month, commencing July 1, 1985. B is to deposit $10,000 as security for performance of all her promises in the lease, to be retained by A in case of any breach on B's part, otherwise to be applied in payment of rent for the last ten months of the term of the lease. B defaulted in the payment of rent for the months of May and June 1986. After proper notice to B of the termination of the lease for nonpayment of rent, A sued B for possession of the building and recovered a judgment for possession. Thereafter, B sues A to recover the $10,000 less the amount of rent due A for May and June 1986. Decision?

6. (a) A and B enter into a written agreement under which A agrees to sell and B agrees to buy 100 shares of the 300 shares outstanding of the capital stock of the Infinitesimal Steel Corporation, whose shares are not listed on any exchange and are closely held, for ten dollars per share. A refused to deliver when tendered the $1,000, and B sues in equity for specific performance, tendering the $1,000. Decision?

(b) Modifying (a) above, assume that the subject matter of the agreement is stock of the United States Steel Corporation, which is traded on the New York Stock Exchange. Decision?

(c) Modifying (a) above, assume that the subject matter of the agreement is undeveloped farm land of little commercial value. Decision?

7. On March 1, A sold to B fifty acres of land in Oregon that A at the time represented to be fine black loam, high, dry, and free of stumps. B paid A the agreed price of $40,000 and took from A a deed to the land. B subsequently discovered that the land was low, swampy, and not entirely free of stumps. B, nevertheless, undertook to convert the greater part of the land into cranberry bogs. After one year of cranberry culture, B became entirely dissatisfied, tendered the land back to A, and demanded from A the return of the $40,000. On A's refusal to repay the money, B brings an action at law against him to recover the $40,000. What judgment?

8. A contracts to make repairs to B's building in return for B's promise to pay $12,000 on completion of the repairs. After partially completing the repairs, A is unable to continue. B hires another builder, who completes the repairs for $5,000. The building's value to B has increased by $10,000 as a result of the repairs, but B has lost $500 in rents because of the delay caused by A's breach. A sues B. How much, if any, may A recover in restitution from B?

9. L induced S to enter into a purchase of a stereo amplifier by intentionally misrepresenting the power output to be sixty watts R.M.S. at rated distortion when in fact it only delivered twenty watts. S paid $450 for the amplifier. Amplifiers producing twenty watts generally sell for $200. Amplifiers producing sixty watts generally sell for $550. S decides to keep the amp and sue for damages. How much may S recover in damages from L?

10. M induced N to sell N's boat to M by misrepresentation of material fact on which N reasonably relied. M promptly sold the boat to P, who paid fair value for it and knew nothing concerning the transaction between M and N. Upon discovering the misrepresentation, N seeks to recover the boat. What are N's rights against M and P?

PART THREE
SALES

PART THREE

SALES

PUBLIC POLICY, SOCIAL ISSUES AND BUSINESS ETHICS

Part Three of the text deals with sales—the most common and important of all commercial transactions. In an exchange economy such as ours, sales are the essential means by which the various units of production exchange their outputs, thereby providing the opportunity for specialization and enhanced productivity. An advanced, complex, industrialized economy with highly coordinated manufacturing and distribution systems requires a reliable mechanism for assuring that *future* exchanges can be entered into today and fulfilled at a later time. The critical role of the law of sales is to establish a framework in which these essential present and future exchanges may take place in a predictable, certain, and orderly fashion with a minimum of transaction costs.

Until the early 1900s sales transactions were completely governed by general contract law. In 1906 the Uniform Sales Act was promulgated and eventually adopted by thirty-six States. By the end of the 1930s, however, dissatisfaction with this and other uniform commercial statutes brought about the development of the Uniform Commercial Code. Article 2 of the Code deals with transactions in sales. Nevertheless, the law of sales still remains in large measure a part of general contract law:

The law of sales is a branch of the more general law of contracts. Therefore, rules of law applicable to contracts generally are applicable to contracts for the sale of goods unless those rules have been displaced by the Code. Nordstrom, *Law of Sales*, 80–81.

One of the most significant ways in which the Code has displaced common law is the Code's movement away from formalistic rules to an emphasis on the intent of the parties. Under the common law, parties intending to enter into a binding sale often discovered that they had not done so due to an inadvertent failure to comply with one or another formality. Such an outcome is much less likely under the Code. The rules for contract formation have been greatly relaxed by the Code and thus it is far easier for parties to form a binding sales contract. This approach achieves two important policies of sales law: to add predictability to the use of sales contracts by recognizing contracts where the parties intend to be bound, and to reduce the transaction costs of sales. It also promotes a third objective of modernizing the law governing business transactions. Accordingly, the Code not only responds more closely than the common law to the intention of the parties, but it also reflects the needs, practices, and usages of the market place. As Section 1-102 states, one of the underlying purposes and policies of the Code is "to permit the continued expansion of commercial practices through custom, usage and agreement of the parties."

The Code has also modified general contract law by providing that an agreement of the parties does not fail merely because it does not state all the material terms of the contract. The drafters of the Code realized that the parties may intentionally omit a term—such as price—in order to ensure themselves of a contract while at the same time not binding themselves to a specific price in a widely fluctuating market. The Code has explicitly adopted the policy of permitting the parties to a sales contract to use such "open terms" by systematically supplying its own terms to fill the omitted terms. The Code does so on the assumption that the parties intended to be bound by terms that are commercially reasonable.

To counterbalance the relaxed rules of contract formation, the Code has statutorily established two overriding regulatory requirements on all sales transactions—unconscionability and good faith. Under the doctrine of unconscionability, courts may invalidate a contract, or any part of a contract, that is so one-sided as to be unconscionable. This doctrine recognizes that the parties to a contract may not be of relatively equal bargaining power and, therefore, that the laissez-faire principle of freedom of contract must be modified to reflect this reality of the modern world. For example, although standardized contracts are widely used today, they are usually nonnegotiable and incomprehensible to the typical consumer. Therefore, the Code has provided the potent device of unconscionability to prevent oppression and unfair surprise.

The other policing device established by the Code is the obligation imposed on all parties to contracts formed under the Code to act in good faith. The significance of this provision to business ethics has been explained by Robert Summers:

It is natural for two parties to assume that each will act in good faith toward the other throughout the course of their contractual dealings. Moreover, morals obligate them to act this way. Yet, in one sense their interests will remain essentially antagonistic, for each will be expecting to get something from the other on advantageous terms. And, in a given case, misunderstandings may arise, unforeseen events occur, expected gains disappear or dislikes develop which may motivate one party to act

in bad faith. If, however, such a party is legally as well as morally obligated to act in good faith, he will be significantly less likely to break faith.

The Uniform Commercial Code continues and expands upon the public policy of contract law to place the aggrieved party in as good a position as if the other party had fully performed. The Code accomplishes this by providing an impressive array of cumulative remedies for both the buyer and seller. At the same time the Code deplores economic waste and requires commercially reasonable actions by the aggrieved party to mitigate damages.

Intertwined with the Code's enhanced remedies is its strengthened warranty provisions. As Professor Friedrich Kessler stated:

Modern sales law, in its desire to protect the buyer and his expectations as to quality, is adopting the position that the seller is responsible for the qualities which the buyer is entitled to expect in the light of all surroundings circumstances, including the purchase price. . . . Indeed, the conviction is gaining ground that the function of warranty law is to establish a "subjective" equivalence between price and quality.

Since information is one sided and frequently not available to the consumer, it is important to ensure a certain minimum level of quality and safety, an objective that has been greatly furthered by both the warranty provisions in sales law and strict liability in tort law.

While reading the five chapters in this part, you should consider the overall purpose and policy of the law governing sales: to provide a predictable, certain, and orderly system by which exchanges of goods may take place in a complex, highly interdependent exchange economy. General contract law supplies the greater part of this system but Article 2 of the Code has refined it considerably by simplifying, clarifying, and modernizing the law governing sales transactions.

17

INTRODUCTION TO SALES

Of all business and legal transactions, the sale is without question the most common. The manufacture and distribution of goods involve numerous sales transactions and practically everyone in our economy is a purchaser of both durable and consumable goods. Originally part of the Law Merchant, the law of sales was absorbed into the common law and codified in Article 2 of the Uniform Commercial Code, which has been adopted in all States—except Louisiana—plus the District of Columbia and the Virgin Islands.

In this chapter we discuss the nature and formation of sales contracts.

Nature of Sales Contracts

The law of sales, which governs contracts involving the sale of goods, is a specialized branch of both the law of contracts (discussed in Chapters 7–16) and the law of personal property (discussed in Chapter 42). This relationship is illustrated by Figure 17–1. This section will cover the definition of a sales contract and the fundamental principles of Article 2 of the Code.

Definition

The Code defines a sale as the transfer of title to goods from seller to buyer for a price. The price can be money, other goods, real estate, or services. **Goods** are essentially defined as **movable, tangible, personal property.** For example, the sale of a bicycle, stereo set, or this textbook is considered a sale of goods. "Goods" also include the unborn young of animals, growing crops, and, if removed by the seller, timber, minerals, or a building attached to real property.

Sale-transfer of ownership from seller to buyer for a price

Goods-tangible personal property

Governing Law

Sales transactions are governed by Article 2 of the Code, but where general contract law has not been specifically modified by the Code, contract law continues to apply. In other words, the law of sales is a specialized part of the general law of contracts, and the law of contracts continues to govern unless specifically displaced by the Code.

General contract law also continues to govern all contracts outside the scope of the Code. Transactions not within the scope of Article 2 include employment contracts, service contracts, insurance contracts, contracts involving real property, and contracts for the sale of intangibles such as stocks, bonds, patents, and copyrights. For an illustration of this relationship, see Figure 7–1 and *Osterholt v. Charles Drilling Co.* in Chapter 7. The following two cases deal with the question of when electricity is considered a good for the purposes of Article 2.

HELVEY v. WABASH COUNTY REMC

Court of Appeals of Indiana, First District, 1972.
151 Ind.App. 176, 278 N.E.2d 608.

FACTS: On March 4, 1970 Helvey brought suit against REMC for breach of implied and express warranties. He alleged that REMC furnished electricity in excess of 135 volts to Helvey's home, causing damage to his 110 volt household appliances. This incident occurred on January 10, 1966. In defense, REMC pleads that the Uniform Commercial Code's Article 2 statute of limitations of 4 years has passed thereby barring Helvey's suit. Helvey argues that providing electrical energy is not a transaction in goods under the U.C.C. but rather a furnishing of services that would make applicable the general contract statute of limitations of six years.

DECISION: Judgment for REMC. To be within the U.C.C.'s definition of a good electricity must be (1) a thing, (2) existing, and (3) movable, with (2) and (3) occurring simultaneously. Electricity can be measured in order to establish a purchase price by the amount of current which passes through the meter, thus fulfilling the existing and movable requirements. Also, it is legally considered personal property, subject to ownership, and may be bartered, sold, and, in fact, stolen. Therefore, the sale of electricity is a sale of goods subject to Article 2's statute of limitations.

NAVARRO COUNTY ELECTRIC CO-OP, INC. v. PRINCE

Court of Appeals of Texas, 1982.
640 S.W.2d 398.

FACTS: While adjusting a television antenna beside his mobile home and underneath a high voltage electric transmission wire, Prince received an electric shock resulting in personal injury. He claims the high voltage electric current jumped from the transmission wire to the antenna. The wire, which carried some 7200 volts of electricity, did not serve his mobile home but ran directly above it. Prince sued the Navarro County Electric Co-Op, the owner and operator of the wire, for breach of implied warranty of merchantability under the Uniform Commercial Code. He contends that the Code's implied warranty of merchantability extends to the container of a product—in this instance the wiring—and that the escape of the current shows that the wiring was unfit for its purpose of transporting electricity. The electric company argues that the electricity passing through the transmission wire was not being sold to Prince and, therefore, there was no sale of goods to Prince.

DECISION: Judgment for Navarro County Electric Co-Op. The court held that the sale of electricity is more fittingly termed the rendition of a service. Thus, the transmission of electrical energy along high tension power lines which eventually leads to a transformer is not goods within the meaning of the U.C.C. Furthermore, the 7200 volts of electricity being transmitted through the wire was not the subject of a sale of electricity to Prince. The U.C.C.'s implied warranty of merchantability, therefore, does not apply.

Nonsales Transactions in Goods

Bailment–transfer of possession but not title of personal property by the owner or rightful possessor

A number of transactions that are not sales significantly affect goods. For example, a **bailment** is a transfer of the possession of personal property by the owner or rightful possessor (**bailor**) to another (**bailee**) for a determinable period of time *without* a transfer of title. For example, A (the bailor) creates a bailment when he delivers his soiled laundry to the XYZ Laundry Company (the bailee) for cleaning. Other examples of bailments include delivery of goods to a repairman, a carrier, or a warehouse man. In contrast, transfer of title is essential to a sale, although transfer of possession is not.

Lease–transfer of possession but not title by owner of property

A **lease** of goods is a contract whereby the owner of the goods (the **lessor**) agrees with another person (the **lessee**) that he will transfer to the lessee the possession and right to use the goods for a period of time in consideration

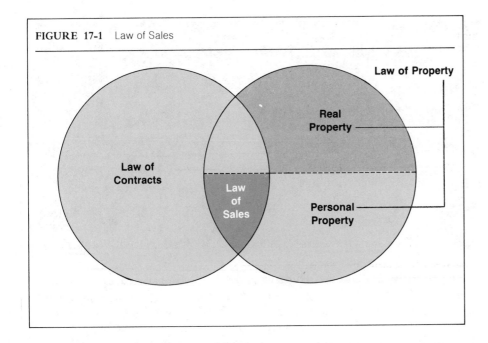

FIGURE 17-1   Law of Sales

of a specified payment. A lease of goods does not involve a transfer of title to the goods.

A **gift** is a transfer of property from one person to another without consideration. The lack of any consideration is the basic distinction between a gift and a sale. A promise to make a gift is not binding. Because a gift involves no consideration or compensation, to be effective it must be completed by delivery of the gift. There must also be intent on the part of the maker (the **donor**) of the gift to make a present transfer, and there must be acceptance by the recipient (the **donee**) of the gift. In a sale, delivery of the property is not necessary to transfer title.

A sale is distinguished from a **security interest** in that a sale transfers to the buyer all of the ownership rights of the seller in the goods, whereas under a security agreement both the **creditor** and the **debtor** have ownership rights in the goods. The right of the secured creditor in the goods is to take possession of the goods in the event of default by the debtor.

Although Article 2 governs sales, the drafters of the Article have invited the courts to extend Code principles to nonsale transactions in goods. To date a number of courts have accepted this invitation and have applied Code provisions by analogy to other transactions in goods not expressly included within the Article, most frequently to leases and bailments. The Code has also greatly influenced the Restatement, Second, Contracts, which, as we discussed in Chapter 7, has great effect on all contracts. In these ways the policies and principles of the Code have been extended to nonsales transactions.

Figure 17–2 summarizes the various transactions in goods.

Fundamental Principles of Article 2

The purpose of Article 2 is to modernize, clarify, simplify, and make uniform the law of sales. Furthermore, the Article is to be interpreted according to

Gift–transfer of ownership of property from one person to another without consideration

Security interest–right in personal property securing payment or performance of an obligation

FIGURE 17-2   Transactions in Goods

	Transfer of Title	Transfer of Possession	Governing Law
Sale	Yes	Usually, but not necessarily	Article 2
Gift	Yes	Yes	Common law
Bailment	No	Yes	Common law
Lease	No	Yes	Common Law
Non-possessory Security Interest	No	No	Article 9

these principles and not according to some abstraction such as the passage of title. The Code "is drawn to provide flexibility so that, since it is intended to be a semi-permanent piece of legislation, it will provide its own machinery for expansion of commercial practices. It is intended to make it possible for the law embodied in this Act to be developed by the courts in the light of unforeseen and new circumstances and practices. However, the proper construction of the Act requires that its interpretation and application be limited to its reason." This open-ended drafting includes the following fundamental concepts.

Good Faith

Good faith–honesty in fact in conduct or a transaction

All parties who enter into a contract or duty within the scope of the Code must perform their obligations in good faith. The Code defines good faith as "honesty in fact in the conduct or transaction concerned." In the case of a merchant (defined below), good faith also requires the observance of reasonable commercial standards of fair dealing in the trade. For instance, if the parties agree that the seller is to set the price term, the seller must establish the price in good faith.

Unconscionability

Every contract of sale may be scrutinized by the court to determine whether in its commercial setting, purpose, and effect it is unconscionable. The court may refuse to enforce an unconscionable contract or any part of it found to be unconscionable. The Code does not define *unconscionable;* however, the term is defined in the *Oxford Universal Dictionary* (3rd ed.) as: "monstrously extortionate, harsh, showing no regard for conscience."

The Code denies or limits enforcement of an unconscionable contract for the sale of goods in the interest of fairness and decency and to correct harshness or oppression in contracts resulting from unequal bargaining position of the parties. Although the principle is not novel, its embodiment in a statute dealing with commercial transactions is. The following case illustrates the application of this doctrine as does *Williams v. Walker-Thomas Furniture Co.* in Chapter 10.

FACTS: Frank's Maintenance and Engineering, Inc. orally ordered steel tubing from C. A. Roberts Co. for use in the manufacture of motorcycle front fork tubes. Since these front fork tubes bear the bulk of the weight of a motrocycle, the steel used must be of high quality. Roberts Co. sent an acknowledgment with conditions of sale including one which limited consequential damages and restricted remedies available upon breach by requiring claims for defective equipment to be promptly made upon receipt. The conditions were located on the back of the acknowledgment. The legend "conditions of sale on reverse side" was stamped over so that on first appearance it read "No conditions of sale on reverse side." Roberts delivered the order in December, 1975. The steel had no visible defects. However, when Frank's Maintenance began using the steel in its manufacture in the Summer of 1976, it discovered that the steel was pitted and cracked beyond repair. Frank's Maintenance informed Roberts Co. of the defects, revoked its acceptance of the steel, and sued for breach of warranty of merchantability.

DECISION: Judgment for Frank's Maintenance. The U.C.C. provides that consequential damages may be limited or excluded unless it is unconscionable. Unconscionability can be procedural or substantive. It is procedural if it consists of some impropriety during the process of forming the contract, depriving a party of a meaningful choice. Provisions limiting liability must have been bargained for, brought to the other party's attention, or be conspicuous. Substantive unconscionability concerns the question whether the terms themselves are commercially reasonable. Parties may not limit remedies in an unreasonable or unconscionable way; there must be a fair quantum of remedy left for breach.

Here, the limiting clause was on the reverse side of the acknowledgment which was made to seem irrelevant by the stamp on the front. It was not conspicuous and was not known to Frank's Maintenance at the time the contract was made. Furthermore, the defects in the steel allegedly were latent and could not have been discovered promptly after acceptance. Thus, it would have been impossible to make a claim at that time as required by the limiting clause. Therefore, the clause is unconscionable.

FRANK'S
MAINTENANCE AND
ENGINEERING, INC. v.
C. A. ROBERTS CO.

Appellate Court of Illinois,
First District, Fourth
Division, 1980.
86 Ill.App.3d 980, 42 Ill.Dec.
25, 408 N.E.2d 403.

Expansion of Commercial Practices

An underlying policy of the Code is "to permit the continued expansion of commercial practices through custom, usage and agreement of the parties." In particular, the Code places great emphasis on course of dealings and usage of trade in interpreting agreements.

A **course of dealing** is a sequence of previous conduct between the parties that may fairly be regarded as establishing a common basis of understanding for interpreting their expressions and agreement.

A **usage of trade** is a practice or method of dealing regularly observed and followed in a place, vocation, or trade. To illustrate: Connie contracts to sell Ward 1,000 feet of San Domingo mahogany. By usage of dealers in mahogany, known to Connie and Ward, good figured mahogany of a certain density is known as San Domingo mahogany, though it does not come from San Domingo. Unless otherwise agreed, the usage is part of the contract.

Course of dealing–sequence of previous conduct between parties establishing a basis for interpreting their agreement

Usage of trade–practice or method of dealing regularly observed and followed in a place, vocation or trade

Sales By and Between Merchants

A novel feature of the Code is the establishment of separate rules that apply to transactions between merchants or involving a merchant as a party. A merchant is defined as a person (1) who is a dealer in the goods, or (2) who by his occupation holds himself out as having knowledge or skill peculiar to the goods or practices involved, or (3) who employs an agent or broker whom he holds out as having such knowledge or skill.

Various sections of the Code contain special rules that apply solely to transactions between merchants or to transactions in which a merchant is a

Merchant–dealer in goods or person who by his occupation holds himself out as having knowledge or skill peculiar to the goods

party. These rules exact a higher standard of conduct from merchants because of their knowledge of trade and commerce and because merchants as a class generally set the standards.

Liberal Administration of Remedies

The Code provides that its remedies shall be liberally administered in order to place the aggrieved party in as good a position as if the defaulting party had fully performed. However, the Code does make it clear that remedies are limited to compensation and may not include consequential or punitive damages, unless specifically provided by the Code. Nevertheless, the Code provides that even in cases where the Code does not expressly provide a remedy for a right or obligation, the courts should provide an appropriate remedy.

Freedom of Contract

Most of the Code's provisions are not mandatory but permit the parties to vary or displace them altogether. The effect of provisions of the Code may be varied by agreement, except as otherwise provided and except that the obligations of good faith, diligence, reasonableness, and care prescribed by the Code may not be disclaimed by agreement. However, the parties may by agreement determine the standards by which the performance of such obligations is to be measured, so long as these standards are not obviously unreasonable. This approach of the Code not only maximizes freedom of contract but also permits the continued expansion of commercial practices through private agreement.

Validation and Preservation of Sales Contracts

One of the requirements of commercial law is the establishment of rules that determine when an agreement is valid. The Code's approach to this is to reduce formal requisites to the bare minimum and attempt to preserve agreements whenever the parties manifest an intent to enter into a contract.

Formation of a Sales Contract

The Code's basic approach to validation is to recognize contracts whenever the parties manifest such an *intent.* This is so whether or not the parties can identify a precise moment at which they formed the contract.

As already noted, the law of sales is a subset of the general law of contracts and is governed by general contract law unless particular provisions of the Code displace the general law. Although the Code leaves the great majority of issues of contract formation to general contract law, it has modified the general law of contract formation in several significant respects. These modifications were made to modernize contract law, to relax the validation requirements of contract formation, and to promote fairness.

Manifestation of Mutual Assent

Definiteness of an Offer

The Code provides that even though one or more terms to a contract may have been omitted, the contract need not fail for indefiniteness. The Code provides standards by which omitted essential terms may be ascertained and supplied, provided the parties intended to enter into a binding agreement. The more terms left open, however, the more likely the parties did not intend to enter into a binding contract.

Open Price The parties may enter into a contract for the sale of goods even though they have reached no agreement on the price. Under the Code the price is a reasonable one at the time for delivery where the agreement (1) says nothing as to price, (2) provides that the parties shall agree later as to the price and they fail to so agree, or (3) fixes the price in terms of some agreed market or other standard or as set by a third person or agency and the price is not so set.

An agreement that the price is to be fixed by the seller or buyer means that it must be fixed in good faith. If the price is to be fixed other than by agreement and is not so fixed through the fault of one of the parties, the other party has an option to treat the contract as canceled or to fix a reasonable price in good faith for the goods. However, where the parties intend not to be bound unless the price is fixed or agreed upon as provided in the agreement, and it is not so fixed or agreed upon, the Code in accordance with the parties' intent provides that there is no contract.

Open Delivery Unless otherwise agreed the place of delivery is the seller's place of business. Moreover, the delivery, if unspecified, must be made within a reasonable time period and in a single delivery.

Open Quantity: Output and Requirement Contracts An agreement of a buyer to purchase the entire output of a seller for a stated period, or an agreement of a seller to supply a buyer with all her requirements of certain goods used in her business operations, may appear to lack definiteness and mutuality of obligation. The exact quantity of goods is not specified, and the seller may have some degree of control over his output and the buyer over her requirements. However, such agreements are enforceable by the application of an objective standard based on the good faith of both parties, and the quantities may not be disproportionate to any stated estimate or the prior output or requirements. For example, the seller cannot operate his factory twenty-four hours a day and insist that the buyer take all of the output when he operated the factory only eight hours a day at the time the agreement was made. Nor can the buyer triple the size of her business and insist that the seller supply all of her requirements.

Other Open Terms Where the parties do not agree, the Code further provides rules as to the terms of payment, duration, and the particulars of performance.

Firm Offers

The Code provides that a merchant is bound to keep an offer open for a maximum of three months if the merchant gives assurance in a signed writing that it will be held open. The Code, therefore, makes a merchant's written promise not to revoke an offer for a stated period of time enforceable even though no consideration is given the merchant-offeror for that promise.

Variant Acceptances

The common law **"mirror image"** rule, by which the acceptance can not vary or deviate from the terms of the offer, is modified by the Code. This modification is necessitated by the realities of modern business practices. A vast number of businesses use standardized business forms. For example, a buyer sends to the seller on the buyer's order form a purchase order for 1,000 dozen cotton shirts at sixty dollars per dozen with delivery by October 1 at the buyer's place of business. On the reverse side of this standard form are twenty-five numbered paragraphs containing provisions generally favorable to the buyer. When the seller receives the buyer's order, he sends to the buyer on his acceptance form an unequivocal acceptance of the offer. However, despite the fact that the seller agrees to the buyer's quantity, price, and delivery terms, on the back of his acceptance form the seller has thirty-two numbered paragraphs generally favorable to himself and in significant conflict with the buyer's form. Under the common law's "mirror image" rule no contract would exist, for there has not been an unequivocal acceptance of all of the material terms of the buyer's offer.

The Code addresses this **battle of the forms** problem by focusing on the intent of the parties. If the seller definitely and seasonably expresses his acceptance of the offer and does not expressly make his acceptance conditional on the buyer's assent to the additional or different terms, a contract is formed. The issue then becomes whether the seller's different or additional terms become part of the contract. If both buyer and seller are merchants, **additional** terms will be part of the contract if they do not materially alter the agreement and are not objected to either in the offer itself or within a reasonable period of time. If neither of the parties are merchants, or if the terms materially alter the offer, then the additional terms are merely construed as proposals for addition to the contract. **Different** terms proposed by the offeree **also** will not become part of the contract unless specifically accepted by the offeror. See Figure 17–3.

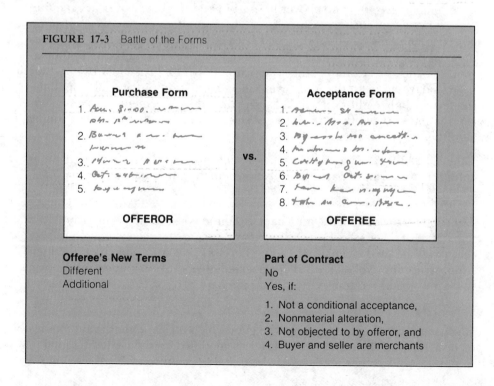

FIGURE 17-3   Battle of the Forms

Purchase Form vs. **Acceptance Form**

OFFEROR · OFFEREE

Offeree's New Terms
Different
Additional

Part of Contract
No
Yes, if:

1. Not a conditional acceptance,
2. Nonmaterial alteration,
3. Not objected to by offeror, and
4. Buyer and seller are merchants

FACTS: Dorton, as a representative for the Carpet Mart, purchased carpets from Collins & Aikman that were supposedly manufactured of 100% Kodel polyester fiber but were, in fact, made of cheaper and inferior fibers. Dorton then brought suit for compensatory and punitive damages against Collins & Aikman for its fraud, deceit, and misrepresentation in the sale of the carpets. Collins & Aikman moved for a stay pending arbitration, claiming that Dorton was bound to an arbitration agreement printed on the reverse side of Collins & Aikman's printed sales acknowledgment form. A provision printed on the face of the acknowledgment form stated that its acceptance was "subject to all of the terms and conditions on the face and reverse side thereof, including arbitration, all of which are accepted by buyer." Holding that there existed no binding arbitration agreement between the parties, the District Court denied the stay. Collins & Aikman appeals.

DECISION: Judgment for Collins & Aikman; case remanded to District Court for further findings of fact. The Uniform Commercial Code recognizes some contracts in which an acceptance or confirmation contains additional or different terms from the offer. To do so, however, the offeree's intent to accept must be definitely expressed and the acceptance must not be made expressly conditional on the offeror's assent to the additional or different terms. If these two stipulations are met, then a contract is formed and the additional or different terms are treated as "proposals" to the contract. If the transaction is between merchants, then the additional terms become part of the contract unless they materially alter it.

Here, the provision on the face of the Collins and Aikman acknowledgment form made acceptance conditional upon the additional or different terms, not upon Dorton's assent to those terms. Since it was not made expressly conditional upon Dorton's assent, the acknowledgment form constituted an acceptance and created a binding contract. In addition, Dorton did not object to the arbitration agreement. Therefore, unless it materially alters the terms of Dorton's original oral offer, the arbitration clause is part of the binding contract. The case is remanded to the trial court to determine whether the arbitration clause materially altered the contract.

DORTON v. COLLINS & AIKMAN CORP.

United States Court of Appeals, Sixth Circuit, 1972. 453 F.2d 1161.

Manner of Acceptance

The Code provides that where the language in the offer or the circumstances do not otherwise clearly indicate, an offer to make a contract invites acceptance in any manner and by any medium reasonable in the circumstances. The Code therefore allows flexibility of response and the ability to keep pace with new modes of communication.

An offer to buy goods for prompt or current shipment may be accepted either by a prompt promise to ship or by prompt shipment. However, acceptance by performance requires notice within a reasonable time, or the offer may be treated as lapsed.

Auctions

The Code provides that if an auction sale is advertised or announced in explicit terms to be **without reserve,** the auctioneer may not withdraw the article put up for sale unless no bid is made within a reasonable time. Unless the sale is advertised as being without reserve, the sale is **with reserve,** and the auctioneer may withdraw the goods at any time until he announces completion of the sale. Whether with or without reserve, a bidder may retract his bid at any time prior to acceptance by the auctioneer. Such a retraction, however, does not revive any previous bid.

If the auctioneer knowingly receives a bid by or on behalf of the seller, and notice has not been given that the seller reserves the right to bid at the auction sale, the bidder to whom the goods are sold can either avoid the sale or take the goods at the price of the last good faith bid before the sale. For example, A advertises a sale of his household furniture without reserve. An article of furniture is put up for sale without a contrary announcement and B is the highest *bona fide* bidder. A, however, is dissatisfied with the bidding and accepts a higher, fictitious bid from an agent employed for that purpose. A is obligated to sell the article to B at the price B bid.

Consideration

Contractual Modifications

The Code has abandoned the common law rule requiring that a modification of an existing contract be supported by consideration in order to be valid. The Code provides that a contract for the sale of goods can be effectively modified without new consideration, provided the modification is made in good faith.

Discharge of Claim After Breach

Any claim of right arising out of an alleged breach of contract can be discharged in whole or in part without consideration by a written waiver or renunciation signed and delivered by the aggrieved party.

Firm Offers

As previously noted, a firm offer is not revocable for lack of consideration.

Form of the Contract

Statute of Frauds

Section 17 of the original Statute of Frauds applied to contracts for the sale of goods and has been used as a prototype for the Article 2 Statute of Frauds provision, which applies to a contract for the sale of goods costing **$500 or more.**

Modification of Contracts Within the Statute of Frauds
An agreement modifying a contract must be in writing if the resulting contract is within the Statute of Frauds. Conversely, if a contract that was previously within the Statute of Frauds is modified so as to no longer fall within it, the modification is enforceable even if it is oral. Thus, if the parties enter into an oral contract to sell a dining room table for $450 to be delivered to the buyer and later, prior to delivery, *orally* agree that the seller shall stain the table and the buyer pay a price of $550, the modified contract is unenforceable. In contrast, if the parties have a written contract for the sale of 150 bushels of wheat at a price of $4.50 per bushel and later orally agree to decrease the quantity to 100 bushels at the same price per bushel, the agreement, as modified, is enforceable. See Figure 13–2 in Chapter 13.

Written Compliance
The Statute of Frauds compliance provisions under the Code are more liberal than the rules under general contract law. The Code requires merely some writing (1) sufficient to indicate that a contract has been made between the parties, (2) signed by the party against whom enforcement is sought or by her authorized agent or broker, and (3) including a term specifying the quantity. The Code's noninsistence that the writing contain all of the terms, other than quantity, is consistent with other provisions of the Code that contracts may be enforced even though material terms are omitted. Nevertheless, the contract is enforceable only to the extent of the quantity

stated. Given proof that a contract was intended and a signed writing describing the goods, the quantity of goods, and the names of the parties, the court, under the Code, can supply omitted terms such as price and particulars of performance. Moreover, several related documents may satisfy the writing requirement.

As between merchants, a written confirmation, if sufficient against the sender, is also sufficient against the recipient of the confirmation unless the recipient gives written notice of her objection within ten days after receiving the confirmation.

Alternative Methods of Compliance A contract that does not satisfy the writing requirement but is otherwise valid is enforceable in the following instances.

The Code permits an oral contract for the sale of goods to be enforced against a party who in his pleading, testimony, or otherwise in courts **admits** that a contract was made, but the Code limits enforcement to the quantity of goods he admits. This provision recognizes that the policy behind the Statute of Frauds does not apply when the party seeking to avoid the oral contract admits under oath the existence of the contract.

The Code also permits enforcement of an oral contract for goods **specially manufactured** for the buyer. Nevertheless, if the goods are readily marketable in the ordinary course of the seller's business, even though they were manufactured on special order, the contract is not enforceable unless in writing.

Prior to the Code, in most States, delivery and acceptance of part of the goods or payment of part of the price and acceptance of the payment made the entire oral contract enforceable against the buyer who had received part delivery or against the seller who had received partial payment. Under the Code, such "partial performance" validates the contract only for the goods that have been **delivered and accepted** or for which **payment** has been **accepted.** Receipt and acceptance either of the goods or of the price constitutes an admission by both parties that some contract exists between them. If the court can make a just apportionment, the agreed price of any goods delivered under an oral contract can be recovered; if the price has already been paid, the seller can be forced to deliver an apportionable part of the goods.

Parol Evidence

Contractual terms that are set forth in a writing intended by the parties as a final expression of their agreement may not be contradicted by evidence of any prior agreement or of a contemporaneous oral agreement but may be explained or supplemented by (a) course of dealing, usage of trade, or course of performance; and (b) evidence of consistent additional terms, unless the writing was intended as the complete and exclusive statement of the terms of the agreement.

Seal

The Code makes seals inoperative with respect to contracts for the sale of goods or an offer to buy or sell goods.

CHAPTER SUMMARY

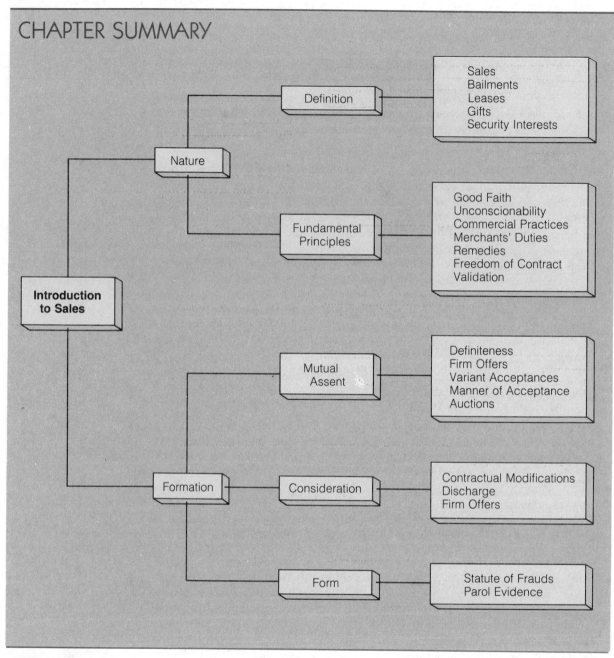

		Sales
	Definition	Bailments
		Leases
		Gifts
		Security Interests
Nature		
		Good Faith
		Unconscionability
	Fundamental	Commercial Practices
	Principles	Merchants' Duties
		Remedies
		Freedom of Contract
		Validation
Introduction to Sales		
		Definiteness
		Firm Offers
	Mutual	Variant Acceptances
	Assent	Manner of Acceptance
		Auctions
		Contractual Modifications
Formation	Consideration	Discharge
		Firm Offers
		Statute of Frauds
	Form	Parol Evidence

KEY TERMS

Sale	Security interest	Merchant
Goods	Good faith	Open price
Bailment	Unconscionability	Firm offer
Lease	Course of dealing	Battle of forms
Gift	Usage of trade	

PROBLEMS

1. A orders 1,000 widgets at five dollars per widget from International Widget to be delivered within sixty days. After the contract is consummated and signed, A requests that International deliver the widgets within thirty days rather than sixty days. International agrees. Is the contractual modification binding?

2. In question 1 what affect, if any, would the following telegram have:

> International Widget:
>
> In accordance with our agreement of this date you will deliver the 1,000 previously ordered widgets within thirty days. Thank you for your cooperation in this matter.
>
> (signed) A

3. A, a San Francisco company, orders from U.S. Electronics, a New York company, 10,000 electronic units. A's order form provides that any dispute would be resolved by an arbitration panel located in San Francisco. U.S. Electronics executes and delivers to A its acknowledgment form accepting the order and containing the following provision: "All disputes will be resolved by the State courts of New York." A dispute arose concerning the workmanship of the parts, and A wishes the case to be arbitrated in San Francisco. What result?

4. Would the result change in problem 3 if the U.S. Electronics' form contained the following provisions:

(a) "The seller's acceptance of the purchase order to which this acknowledgment responds is expressly made conditional on the buyer's assent to any or different terms contained in this acknowledgment"?

(b) "The seller's acceptance of the purchase order is subject to the terms and conditions on the face and reverse side hereof and which the buyer accepts by accepting the goods described herein"?

(c) "The seller's terms govern this agreement— this acknowledgment merely constitutes a counter-offer"?

5. A executed a written contract with B to purchase an assorted collection of shoes for $3,000. A week before the agreed shipment date, B called A and said, "We cannot deliver at $3,000; unless you agree to pay $4,000, we will cancel the order." After considerable discussion, A agreed to pay $4,000 if B would ship as agreed in the contract. After the shoes had been delivered and accepted by A, A refused to pay $4,000 and insisted on paying only $3,000. Decision?

6. On November 23, A, a dress manufacturer, mailed to B a written and signed offer to sell 1,000 sundresses at fifty dollars per dress. The offer stated that "it would remain open for ten days and that it could not be withdrawn prior to that date."

Two days later, A, noting a sudden increase in the price of sundresses, changed his mind. A therefore sent B a letter revoking the offer. The letter was sent on November 25 and received by B on November 28.

B chose to disregard the letter of November 25; instead, she happily continued to watch the price of sundresses rise. On December 1, B sent a letter accepting the original offer. The letter, however, was not received by A until December 9, due to a delay in the mails.

B has demanded delivery of the goods according to the terms of the offer of November 23, but A has refused. Decision?

7. H and W, an elderly immigrant couple, agree to purchase from B a refrigerator with a fair market value of $450 for twenty-five monthly installments of $60 per month. H and W now wish to void the contract, asserting that they did not realize the exorbitant price they were paying. Result?

TRANSFER OF TITLE
AND RISK OF LOSS

Historically, the principle of title governed nearly every aspect of the rights and duties of the buyer and seller arising out of a sales contract. In an attempt to add greater precision and certainty to sales contracts, however, the Code has abandoned the common law's reliance on title. Instead, the Code approaches each legal issue arising out of a sales contract on its own merits and provides separate and specific rules to control various transactional situations.

Transfer of Title and Other Property Rights

In addition to de-emphasizing the significance of the passage of title, the Code makes use of other property rights in its transactional approach to the law of sales. These other property rights include the special property as well as insurable interests and security interests. Nevertheless, the determination of who has title to the goods does retain some significance. In this section we explore these topics in addition to the circumstances under which the seller has the right or power to transfer title to the buyer.

Passage of Title

A sale of goods is defined as the transfer of title from the seller to the buyer for a consideration known as the price. Transfer of title is, therefore, fundamental to the existence of a sale of goods.

Title passes when the parties *intend* it to pass as in the case of *Meinhard-Commercial Corp. v. Hargo Woolen Mills*. In many cases, however, such intention is difficult to ascertain because of conflicting testimony or because the negotiation between the parties leading to formation of the contract involved no discussion or mention of title. Where the parties have no explicit agreement as to transfer of title, the Code provides rules that determine when title passes to the buyer.

Physical Movement of the Goods

When delivery is to be made by moving the goods, title passes at the time and place where the seller completes his performance with reference to delivery of the goods. A contract involving movement of goods is either a shipment contract or a destination contract.

Shipment Contract

Shipment contract–seller is required to tender delivery of the goods to a carrier for delivery to buyer who bears the expense and risk of loss

A "shipment contract" requires or authorizes the seller to send the goods to the buyer but does not require the seller to deliver them to a particular destination. Under a shipment contract title passes to the buyer at the time and place that the seller delivers the goods to the carrier for shipment to the buyer.

Destination Contract

Destination contract seller is required to tender delivery of the goods at a particular destination; seller bears the expense and risk of loss

A "destination contract" requires the seller to deliver the goods to a particular destination, and title passes to the buyer on tender of the goods at that destination. For example, under a destination contract specifying the destination as the buyer's place of business, title passes at the time the goods are tendered to the buyer at her place of business.

No Movement of the Goods

When delivery is to be made without moving the goods, title passes: (a) on delivery of a document of title where the contract calls for delivery of such document (documents of title are documents which evidence a right to receive specified goods; they are discussed more fully in Chapter 43); or (b) at the time and place of contracting where the goods at that time have been identified by either the seller or the buyer as the goods to which the contract refers and no documents are to be delivered.

MEINHARD-COMMERCIAL CORP. v. HARGO WOOLEN MILLS

Supreme Court of New Hampshire, 1972.
112 N.H. 500, 300 A.2d 321.

FACTS: Shabry Trading Company shipped twenty-four bales of card waste to Hargo, a manufacturer of woolen cloth. Although Shabry had supplied card waste to Hargo for many years, Hargo had not ordered the present shipment, nor did it wish to purchase it. Hargo intended to return the card waste, but Shabry, in order to avoid the cost of warehouse storage, offered to let Hargo retain possession of the bales with the option to buy as much as Hargo would give notice that it intended to use. Hargo agreed and accordingly marked and stored Shabry's card waste separately from its other goods. On one occasion Hargo notified Shabry that it would use eight bales of waste, and Shabry invoiced the goods to Hargo accordingly. The sixteen remaining bales were kept separately stored until a receiver appointed for Hargo took possession of them. Shabry claimed that it was the owner of the bales and requested their return.

DECISION: Judgment for Shabry. Whether or not a transaction is a sale is determined by the intent of the parties. Hargo and Shabry did not contemplate passage of title to the card waste until Hargo notified Shabry of its intention to use the goods. Only then would Shabry invoice the goods to Hargo. Hargo was never obligated to purchase the goods, and Shabry could have sold them to other buyers. The mere delivery of goods to the premises of a prospective buyer does not create a sale if neither party intended that one take place. Rather, the parties agreed only to store the card waste with Hargo for their mutual benefit, and Hargo was only a bailee with an option to buy the goods. Therefore, title never passed to Hargo.

Other Property Rights

Special Property

The Code created a new property interest in goods that did not exist at common law. It is a "special property" right that the buyer obtains by the **identification** of existing goods as goods to which the contract of sale refers. After forming a contract, it is normal for the seller to take steps to obtain, manufacture, prepare, or select goods with which to fulfill her obligation under the contract. At some stage in the process the seller will have identified the goods that she intends to ship, deliver or hold for the buyer. These goods may or may not conform to the contract, but in either case the identification of goods to the contract immediately creates for the buyer a special property right in the goods identified. This Code-created interest gives the buyer an insurable interest in the goods, as well as a number of specific remedies that we discuss in Chapter 21.

Identification may be made by either the seller or the buyer and can be made at any time and in any manner agreed on by the parties. In the absence of explicit agreement, identification takes place as follows:

1. if the contract is for goods already existing and identified, when the contract is made;

2. if the contract is for crops to be grown within twelve months or the next normal harvest, or for the offspring of animals to be born within twelve months, when the crops are planted or become growing, or when the young animals are conceived; or

3. if the contract is one for all other future goods, when the seller ships, marks, or otherwise designates the goods as those to which the contract refers.

Insurable Interest

For a contract or policy of insurance to be valid, the insured must have an insurable interest in the subject matter. At common law only a person with title or a lien (a legal claim on property) could insure his interest in specific goods. The Code, as previously noted, extends this right to a buyer's interest in goods that have been identified as those to which the contract refers. This interest enables the buyer to purchase insurance protection on goods that he does not presently own but that he will own when delivered by the seller.

So long as he has title to them or any security interest in them, the seller also has an insurable interest in the goods. Nothing prevents both seller and buyer from simultaneously carrying insurance on goods in which they both have a property interest, whether it is title, a security interest, or a special property.

Insurable interest –interest in property that may be insured against loss

Lien –a nonconsensual claim against property

Security Interest

A "security interest" is defined in the Code as an interest in personal property or fixtures that secures payment or performance of an obligation. Any reservation by the seller of title to goods delivered to the buyer is limited in effect to a reservation of a security interest. Security interests in goods are governed by Article 9 of the Code and are discussed in Chapter 37.

Power to Transfer Title

It is important to understand under what circumstances a seller has the right or power to transfer title or other property rights to a buyer. If the seller is the rightful owner of goods or is authorized to sell the goods for the rightful owner, then the seller has the **right** to transfer title. But when a seller possesses goods that he neither owns nor has authority to sell, then the sale is not rightful. However, in some situations nonowner sellers may have the **power** to transfer good title to certain buyers. This section pertains to such sales by a person in possession of goods that he neither owns nor has authority to sell.

The rule of property law protecting existing ownership of goods is the starting point and background in any discussion of a sale of goods by a nonowner. It is elementary that a purchaser of goods obtains such title as his transferor had or had power to transfer, and the Code expressly states this. Likewise, the purchaser of a limited interest in goods acquires rights only to the extent of the interest that he purchased. By the same token, no one can transfer what he does not have. A purported sale by a thief or finder or ordinary bailee of goods does not transfer title to the purchaser.

The reasons underlying the policy of the law in protecting existing ownership of goods are obvious. A person should not be required to retain possession at all times of all the goods that he owns in order to maintain his ownership of them. One of the valuable incidents of ownership of goods is the freedom of the owner to make a bailment of his goods as he pleases, and the mere possession of goods by a bailee does not authorize the bailee to sell them.

A policy of the law that conflicts with the policy protecting existing ownership is protection of the good faith purchaser based on the importance in trade and commerce of protecting the security of good faith transactions in goods. To encourage and make secure good faith acquisitions of goods it is necessary that *bona fide* (good faith) purchasers for value under certain circumstances be protected. A **good faith purchaser** is defined as one who acts honestly, gives value, and takes the goods without notice or knowledge of any defect in the title of his transferor.

Good faith purchaser— buyer who acts honestly, gives value, and takes the goods without notice or knowledge of any defect in the title of his transferor

You should consider the problems presented in this section and the rules for their solution in the light of these two competing policies of the law. Both policies are sound, beneficial, and worthy of enforcement. One protects existing property rights; the other protects the stability of good faith transactions in the marketplace. In the area of sales of goods by a nonowner, these policies come into conflict. In every such conflict only one may prevail. As between these two innocent parties, the law must either protect existing ownership and defeat the interest of the *bona fide* purchaser for value, or vice versa.

Void and Voidable Title to Goods

A void title is no title. A person claiming ownership of goods by an agreement that is void obtains no title to the goods. Thus, a person who acquires goods by physical duress or from someone under guardianship, or a thief or a finder of goods, has no title to them and can transfer none.

A voidable title is one acquired under circumstances that permit the former owner to rescind the transfer and revest herself with title, as in the case of mistake, common duress, undue influence, fraud in the inducement, or sale by a person without contractual capacity (other than an individual under guardianship). In these situations, the buyer has acquired legal title to the goods of which he may be divested by action taken by the seller. However, if the buyer should resell the goods to a *bona fide* purchaser for value and without notice of any infirmity in his title before the seller has rescinded the transfer of title, the right of rescission in the seller is cut off, and the *bona fide* purchaser acquires good title.

The distinction between a void and voidable title is, therefore, extremely important in determing the rights of *bona fide* purchasers of goods. The *bona fide* purchaser always believes that she is buying the goods from the owner or from one with authority to sell. Otherwise she would not be acting in good faith. In each situation the party selling the goods appears to be the owner, whether his title is valid, void, or voidable. As between two innocent persons, the true owner who has done nothing wrong and the *bona fide* purchaser who has done nothing wrong, the law will not disturb the legal title but will rule in favor of the one who has it. Thus, where A transfers possession of goods to B under such circumstances that B acquires no title or a void title, and B thereafter sells the goods to C, a *bona fide* purchaser for value, B has nothing except possession to transfer to C. In a lawsuit between A and C involving the right to the goods, A will win because she has the legal title. C's only recourse is against B for breach of warranty of title which we discuss in Chapter 19. (See Figure 18–1.) However, if B acquired a voidable title from A and resold the goods to C, in a suit between A and C over the goods, C would win. In this case, B had title, although it was voidable, which she transferred to the *bona fide* purchaser. The title thus acquired by C will be protected. The voidable title in B is title until it has been avoided. After transfer to a *bona fide* purchaser, it may not be avoided. A's only recourse is against B for restitution or damages. (See Figure 18–2.)

The Code enlarges this doctrine by providing that a good faith purchaser for value obtains valid title from one possessing voidable title even if that person's voidable title was obtained by (1) fraud as to his identity, (2) delivery of a subsequently dishonored check, (3) an agreement that the transaction was to be a cash sale and the sale price has not been paid, or (4) criminal fraud punishable as larceny.

Another way in which the Code has expanded the rights of *bona fide* purchasers is with respect to sales by **minors.** The common law permitted a minor seller of goods to disaffirm the sale and to recover the goods from a third person who had purchased them in good faith from the party who acquired the goods from the minor. The Code had changed this rule and does not permit a minor seller to prevail over a *bona fide* purchaser for value.

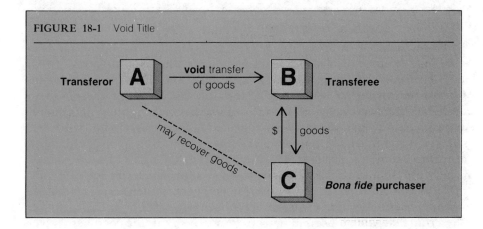

FIGURE 18-1   Void Title

Transferor   **A**   **void** transfer of goods   **B**   Transferee

may recover goods

$ goods

C   *Bona fide* purchaser

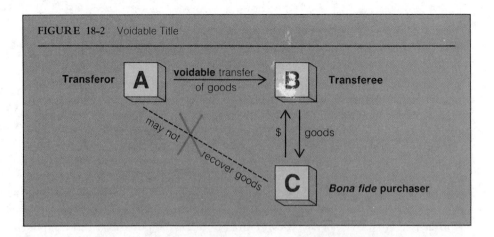

FIGURE 18-2   Voidable Title

UNITED ROAD MACHINERY CO. v. JASPER	FACTS:

UNITED ROAD MACHINERY CO. v. JASPER

Court of Appeals of Kentucky, 1978.
568 S.W.2d 242.

FACTS: United Road Machinery Company, a dealer in heavy road equipment (including truck scales supplied by Thurman Scale Company), received a telephone call on July 21, 1975, from James Durham, an officer of Consolidated Coal Company, seeking to acquire truck scales for his coal mining operation. United and Consolidated entered into a twenty-four-month lease-purchase arrangement. United then notified Thurman that Consolidated would take possession of the scales directly. United paid for the scales and Consolidated took possession of them, but the latter never signed and returned the contract papers forwarded to it by United. Consolidated also never made any of the rental payments ($608/month) due under the lease. On September 20, 1975, Consolidated, through its officer Durham, sold the scales to Kentucky Mobile Homes for $8,500. Kentucky's president, Ethard Jasper, checked the county records prior to the purchase and found no lien or encumberance on the title; likewise, he denied knowledge of the dispute between Consolidated and United. On September 22, 1975, Kentucky sold the scales to Clyde Jasper, individually, for $8,500. His search also failed to disclose any lien on the title to the scales, and he denied knowledge of the dispute between Consolidated and United. United brought suit to recover the scales from Jasper.

DECISION: Judgment for Jasper. If Consolidated had good title to the scales, Jasper, as purchaser, in turn acquired good title. Furthermore, if Consolidated had only voidable title, Jasper, as good faith purchaser for value, took good title. Jasper is a good faith purchaser for value because he took by purchase with sufficient consideration to support a simple contract and with honesty in the transaction.

Entrusting of Goods to a Merchant

The Code establishes a broad rule protecting good faith buyers of goods in the ordinary course of business from merchants who deal in goods of that kind, where the owner has entrusted possession of the goods to the merchant. Any such entrusting of possession bestows on the merchant the power to transfer all rights of the entruster to a buyer in the ordinary course of business. For example, A brings his stereo for repair to B, who also sells both new and used stereo equipment. C purchases A's stereo from B in good faith and in the ordinary course of business. The Code protects the rights of C and defeats the rights of A. A's only recourse is against B. (See Figure 18–3.)

The Code, however, does not go so far as to protect the *bona fide* purchaser from a merchant to whom the goods have been entrusted by a thief or finder or by a completely unauthorized person. It merely grants the good faith buyer in the ordinary course of business the rights of the entruster.

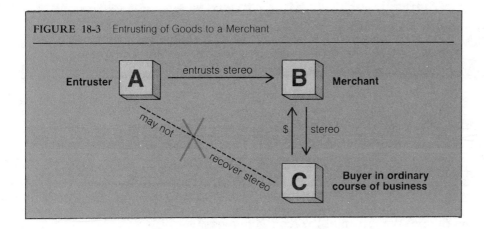

FIGURE 18-3 Entrusting of Goods to a Merchant

The Code defines **buyer in ordinary course of business** as a person who in good faith and without knowledge that the sale to him is in violation of the ownership rights or security interest of another buys the goods in the ordinary course of business from a person in the business of selling goods of that kind, other than a pawnbroker.

Where a buyer of goods to whom title has passed leaves the seller in possession of the goods, the buyer has "entrusted the goods" with the seller. If that seller is a merchant and resells and delivers the goods to a *bona fide* purchaser for value, this second buyer acquires good title to the goods. Thus, Dennis sells certain goods to Sylvia, who pays the price but allows possession to remain with Dennis. Dennis thereafter sells the same goods to Karen, a *bona fide* purchaser for value without notice of the prior sale to Sylvia. Karen takes delivery of the goods. Sylvia does not have any rights against Karen or to the goods. Sylvia's only remedy is against Dennis.

> **Buyer in ordinary course of business** – person who buys in ordinary course, in good faith, and without knowledge that the sale to him is in violation of anyone's ownership rights

---

FACTS: Porter, the owner of a collection of art works, had a number of art transactions with Harold Von Maker who used, among other names, that of Peter Wertz. In 1973, Porter permitted Von Maker to have temporarily a painting by Maurice Utrillo, "Chateau de Lion-sur-Mer," and to hang it in his home until he decided whether to purchase it. A few months later, Porter sought the return of the Utrillo painting but was unable to reach Von Maker. Porter subsequently discovered that he was not dealing with Peter Wertz but with Harold Von Maker, a man with an extensive criminal record, including a conviction for defrauding the Chase Manhattan Bank. When Porter finally reached him, Von Maker claimed the Utrillo was on consignment with a client. Von Maker then agreed in writing either to return the painting to Porter within 90 days or to make compensation for it. At the time he entered this agreement, Von Maker had already sold the painting. He had used the real Peter Wertz, a delicatessen employee and acquaintance, to effect the sale of the Utrillo to Feigen for $20,000. Feigen, an art dealer, then sold the painting to Brenner and it is now somewhere in Venezuela. Porter brought suit against Feigen, and the others involved, to recover possession of the Utrillo or its value.

DECISION: Judgment for Porter. The entrustment provision of the UCC empowers a merchant entrusted with possession of goods in which he deals to transfer the rights of the entruster to a "buyer in the ordinary course of business." To apply in this case, Feigen must fit the definition of a buyer in the ordinary course of business. The Code defines such a buyer as a "person who in good faith and without knowledge that the sale to him is in violation of the ownership rights . . . of a third party in the goods buys in ordinary course from a person in the business of selling goods of that kind." Feigen bought the painting from the real Wertz, who was a delicatessen

PORTER v. WERTZ

Supreme Court of New York,
Appellate Division, 1979.
68 A.D.2d 141, 416 N.Y.S.2d
254.

employee, not an art dealer "in the business of selling goods of that kind." In addition, Feigen made no investigation to verify Wertz as the true owner or an art dealer. Accordingly, Feigen did not act in good faith. Therefore, the Code's entrustment provision does not apply, and Porter is entitled to possession of the Utrillo painting or its value.

Risk of Loss

Risk of loss–placement of loss between seller and buyer where the goods have been damaged, destroyed or lost

Risk of loss, as the term is used in the law of sales, means the placement of the loss between seller and buyer where the goods have been damaged, destroyed, or lost *without the fault* of either the seller or the buyer. If placed on the buyer, he is under a duty to pay the price for the goods even though they were damaged or he never received them. If placed on the seller, he has no right to recover the purchase price from the buyer, although he does have the right to the return of the damaged goods.

In determining who has the risk of loss the Code provides definite rules for specific situations, a sharp departure from the common law concept of risk of loss, which was determined by ownership of the goods and depended on whether title had been transferred. In its transactional approach the Code is necessarily detailed and for this reason is probably more understandable and meaningful than the common law's reliance on the abstract concept of title.

For the most part, the Code attempts to place the risk of loss on the party who is more likely to have greater control over the goods, is more likely to insure the goods, or is better able to prevent the loss. However, this approach is not followed where one party has breached the contract. Accordingly, the Code has adopted separate rules for determining the risk of loss in the absence of breach from those that apply where there has been a breach of the sales contract.

Risk of Loss in Absence of a Breach

Agreement of the Parties

The parties by agreement may not only shift the allocation of risk of loss but may also divide the risk between them. Such agreement is controlling. Thus, the parties may agree that a seller shall retain the risk of loss even though the buyer is in possession of the goods or has title to them. Furthermore, the agreement may provide that the buyer bears 60 percent of the risk and the seller bears 40 percent.

Trial Sales

Sale on approval–transfer of possession without title to buyer for trial period

Sale on Approval   In a sale on approval, possession, but not title to the goods, is transferred to the buyer for a stated period of time or, if none is stated, for a reasonable time, during which period the buyer may use the goods to determine whether she wishes to buy them. Both title and risk of loss remain with the *seller* until "approval" or acceptance of the goods by the buyer.

Use of the goods consistent with the purpose of approval by the buyer is not acceptance, but failure of the buyer within a reasonable period of time to notify the seller of her election to return the goods is an acceptance. The buyer's approval may also be manifested by exercising any dominion or control over the goods inconsistent with the seller's ownership. On approval, risk of loss and title passes to the buyer, who then becomes liable to the seller for the purchase price of the goods. If the buyer decides to return the goods and notifies the seller, the return is at the seller's risk and expense.

Sale or Return   In a sale or return, the goods are sold and delivered to the buyer with an option to return them to the seller. The risk of loss is on the *buyer,* who also has title until she revests it in the seller by a return of the goods. The return of the goods is at the buyer's risk and expense.

> Sale or return –sale where buyer has option to return goods to seller

It is frequently difficult to determine from the facts of a particular transaction whether the parties intended a sale on approval or a sale or return. The consequences are drastically different with respect to transfer of title and risk of loss. Thus the Code provides a neat, sensible, and easily applied test; unless otherwise agreed, if the goods are delivered primarily for the buyer's use, the transaction is a sale on approval; if they are delivered primarily for resale by the buyer, it is a sale or return.

Consignment   A consignment is a delivery of possession of personal property to an agent for sale by the agent. Under the Code, a sale on consignment is regarded as a sale or return. Therefore, creditors of the consignee (the agent who receives the merchandise for sale) prevail over the consignor and may obtain possession of the consigned goods, provided the consignee maintains a place of business where he deals in goods of the kind involved under a name other than the name of the consignor. Nevertheless, the consignor will prevail if she (a) complies with applicable State law requiring a consignor's interest to be evidenced by a sign, or (b) establishes that the consignee is generally known by his creditors to be substantially engaged in selling the goods of others, or (c) complies with the filing provisions of Article 9 (Secured Transactions).

> Consignment –delivery of possession of personal property to an agent for sale

Contracts Involving Carriers

If the contract does not require the seller to deliver the goods at a particular destination but merely to the carrier (a shipment contract), risk of loss passes to the buyer when the goods are delivered to the carrier. If the seller is required to deliver them to a particular destination (a destination contract), risk of loss passes to the buyer at destination when the goods are tendered to the buyer.

Sales contracts frequently contain terms indicating the agreement of the parties as to delivery. These terms designate whether the contract is a shipment contract or a destination contract and, by implication, when the risk of loss passes.

Shipment Contracts   The initials *F.O.B.* mean "free on board"; *F.A.S.* means "free alongside." Under the Code these are delivery terms even though used only in connection with the stated price. When the contract provides that the sale is **F.O.B. place of shipment** or **F.A.S. port of shipment,** then the contract is a shipment contract. For example, A, whose place of business is in New York, enters into a contract with B, the buyer, who is located in San Francisco. The contract calls for delivery of the goods F.O.B. New York. This is a shipment contract.

> F.O.B. –free on board
>
> F.A.S. –free alongside

The initials **C.I.F.** mean "cost, insurance, and freight"; **C. & F.** means simply "cost and freight." Under a C.I.F. contract, in consideration for an

> C.I.F. –cost, insurance, and freight
>
> C. & F. –cost, insurance, and freight

agreed unit price for the goods the seller pays all costs of transportation, insurance, and freight to destination. The amount of the agreed unit price of the goods will, of course, reflect these costs. The unit price in a C. & F. contract is less than in a C.I.F. contract because it does not include the cost of insurance. Under the Code, *both* C.I.F. and C. & F. contracts are regarded as shipment contracts, not destination contracts.

Under any of these shipment contracts, when the seller has delivered the goods to the carrier under a proper contract of shipment, title and risk of loss pass to the buyer.

C.O.D.–collect on delivery

The initials **C.O.D.** mean "collect on delivery" and are instructions to the carrier not to deliver the goods at a destination until it has collected the price and transportation charges from the buyer. In this manner the seller retains control over the possession of the goods by preventing the buyer from obtaining delivery unless he pays the price. A C.O.D. contract is generally a shipment contract, and title and risk of loss pass to the buyer on delivery to the carrier.

Destination Contracts   Where the contract provides that the sale is **F.O.B. place of destination,** the seller must at his own expense and risk transport the goods to that place and there tender delivery of them to the buyer. These are destination contracts. For example, if the buyer is in Boston and the seller in Chicago, a contract providing F.O.B. Boston is a destination contract under which the seller must deliver the goods to the designated place in Boston, at his own expense and risk.

Ex-ship–from the ship

Where the contract provides for delivery **"ex-ship,"** or "from the ship," it is a destination contract and risk of loss does not pass to the buyer until the goods are unloaded from the carrier at destination.

Finally, where the contract contains terms **"no arrival, no sale,"** the title and risk of loss do not pass to the buyer until the seller makes a tender of the goods after their arrival at destination. The major significance of the "no arrival, no sale" term is that it excuses the seller from any liability to the buyer for failure of the goods to arrive, unless the seller has caused their nonarrival.

The following case deals with the question of when the risk of loss passes where the parties have no specific provision nor any delivery term.

PESTANA v. KARINOL

District Court of Appeals of Florida, Third District, 1979. 367 So.2d 1096.

FACTS: Nahim Amar B. contracted with Karinol for the purchase of electronic watches. The contract contained no explicit provisions specifying who would bear the risk of loss while the watches were in the carrier's possession. Nor were there any F.O.B., F.A.S. or C & F terms in the contract. However, it did contain a notation stating Chetumal, Mexico as the destination. Karinol delivered the watches to its agent for delivery to Amar. Karinol's carrier obtained insurance for the two cartons of watches, naming Karinol as the insured. The goods were then shipped by air to Belize where they were to be shipped by truck to Chetumal. Upon their arrival in Belize, Amar paid Pestana the balance due on the contract. However, when customs officials and an agent of Amar opened the cartons in Belize for customs clearance, they found the packages were empty.

Pestana, the executor of Amar's estate, contends that the "send to Chetumal, Mexico" notation made the contract a destination contract. Therefore, he argues, Karinol should bear the loss of the watches since its carrier had not yet tendered delivery of them in Chetumal.

DECISION: Judgment for Karinol. In a destination contract, the seller bears the risk of loss of the goods until tender of delivery to the buyer. On the other hand, in a shipment contract, risk of loss passes to the buyer when the seller delivers the goods to the carrier. The parties must explicitly agree to a destination contract; otherwise, it is considered a shipment contract.

Here, there were no specific provisions in the contract allocating the risk of loss of the goods while in transit and no delivery terms, such as F.O.B. Chetumal. The "send to" term, common to all contracts requiring the delivery of goods, by itself is not enough to convert a shipment contract into a destination contract. The contract, therefore, was a shipment contract with Amar bearing the risk of loss after Karinol delivered the watches to its carrier. Thus, Amar may not recover the purchase price of the watches from Karinol.

Goods in Possession of Bailee

In some sales the goods at the time of the contract are held by a bailee and are to be delivered without being moved. For instance, a seller may contract with a buyer to sell grain that is located in a grain elevator and that the buyer intends to leave in the same elevator. In such situations the risk of loss passes to the buyer when one of the following occurs:

1. If a negotiable document of title (discussed in Chapter 43) is involved, when the buyer *receives* the document.

2. If a non-negotiable document of title is used by the bailee as a receipt for storage of the seller's goods, when the document is tendered to the buyer, unless the buyer objects within a reasonable time.

3. If no documents of title are employed, either (a) when the seller tenders to the buyer written directions to the bailee to deliver the goods to the buyer, unless the buyer seasonably objects, or (b) when the bailee acknowledges the buyer's right to possession of the goods.

All Other Sales

If the contract of sale is not on approval and does not provide expressly for the passage of risk of loss and if the goods were not to be shipped by carrier, and were not in the possession of a bailee, the situation is one of frequent occurrence in which a seller is required to tender or deliver the goods to the buyer. In such case risk of loss depends on whether the seller is a merchant. If the seller is a **merchant,** risk of loss passes to the buyer on the buyer's receipt of the goods. If the seller is **not a merchant,** it passes on tender of the goods from the seller to the buyer.

Suppose Ted goes to Jack's furniture store, selects a particular set of dining room furniture and pays Jack the agreed price of $800 for it on Jack's agreement to stain the set a darker color and deliver it. Jack stains the furniture and notifies Ted that he may pick up the furniture. That night it is accidentally destroyed by fire. Ted can recover the $800 payment from Jack. The risk of loss is on seller Jack because he is a merchant and the goods were not received by Ted but were only tendered to him.

On the other hand, suppose X, an accountant, having moved to a different city, contracts to sell her household furniture to Y for $3,000 by a written agreement signed by Y, and notifies Y that the furniture is available for Y to pick up. Y delays picking up the furniture several days, and in the interim the furniture is stolen from X's residence through no fault of X's. X may recover the $3,000 purchase price from Y. The risk of loss is on buyer Y because seller X is not a merchant and tender is sufficient to transfer the risk.

MARTIN v.
MELLAND'S INC.

Supreme Court of North
Dakota, 1979.
283 N.W.2d 76.

FACTS: Martin entered into a written agreement with Melland's, a farm implement dealer, to purchase a truck and attached haystack mover. According to the contract, Martin was to trade-in his old truck and haystack mover unit; to mail or bring the certificate of title to the old unit to Melland's within a week; and to retain the use and possession of the old unit until Melland's had the new one ready. The contract contained no provision allocating the risk of loss of the trade-in unit. After Martin mailed the certificate to Melland's, but while he still had possession of the trade-in unit itself, the unit was destroyed by fire. Martin then sued to compel Melland's to bear the loss of the trade-in, claiming that title had passed to Melland's before the destruction of the old unit.

DECISION: Judgment for Melland's. Under the Code, the passage of title is irrelevant to the determination of who bears the risk of loss. The risk of loss is determined by specific provisions of the Code. The provision applicable here states: "The risk of loss passes to the buyer on his receipt of the goods if the seller is a merchant; otherwise the risk passes to the buyer on tender of delivery." Because Martin was the original owner of the trade-in unit, he is considered the seller of it. Moreover, Martin, by his own admission, is not a merchant seller. Thus, the risk of loss would shift to Melland's only after Martin had tendered delivery of the unit. Since both parties agreed that Martin would keep the old unit until the new one was ready, tender of delivery had not been made when the unit was destroyed. Consequently, Martin must bear the loss.

Risk of Loss Where There is a Breach

Breach by the Seller

If the seller ships goods to the buyer that do not conform to the contract, the risk of loss remains on the seller until the buyer has accepted the goods or the seller has remedied the defect.

Where the buyer has accepted nonconforming goods, and thereafter by timely notice to the seller rightfully revokes his acceptance (discussed in Chapter 20), he may treat the risk of loss as resting on the seller from the beginning to the extent of any deficiency in the buyer's effective insurance coverage. For example, S delivers to B nonconforming goods, which B accepts. Subsequently, B discovers a hidden defect in the goods and rightfully revokes his prior acceptance. If the goods are destroyed through no fault of either party, and B has insured the goods for 60 percent of their fair market value of $10,000, then the insurance company will cover $6,000 of the loss and S will bear the loss of $4,000. If the buyer's insurance coverage had been $10,000, then the seller would not bear any of the loss.

Breach by the Buyer

Where conforming goods have been identified to a contract that the buyer repudiates or breaches before risk of loss has passed to him, the seller may treat the risk of loss as resting on the buyer "for a commercially reasonable time" to the extent of any deficiency in the seller's effective insurance coverage. For example, S agrees to sell 40,000 pounds of plastic resin to B, F.O.B. B's factory, delivery by March 1. On February 1, B wrongfully repudiates the contract by telephoning S and telling her that he does not want the resin. S immediately seeks another buyer, but before she is able to locate one, and within a commercially reasonable time, the resin is destroyed by a fire through no fault of S's. The fair market value of the resin is $35,000. S's insurance covers only $15,000 of the loss. B is liable for $20,000.

Sales of Goods in Bulk

A sale of goods in bulk occurs when a merchant sells all or a major portion of his inventory all at once. Creditors have an obvious interest in such a disposal of the bulk of merchandise made not in the ordinary course of business. The danger to creditors is that the debtor may secretly liquidate all or a major part of his tangible assets by a bulk sale and conceal or divert the proceeds of the sale without paying his creditors. The central purpose of bulk sales law is to deal with two common forms of commercial fraud. These occur when (a) the merchant, owing debts, sells out his stock in trade to a friend for a low price, pays his creditors less than he owes them, and hopes to come back into the business through the back door some time in the future; and (b) the merchant, owing debts, sells out his stock in trade to any one for any price, pockets the proceeds, and disappears without paying his creditors.

Article 6 of the Code applies to such sales and defines a bulk transfer as "any transfer in bulk and not in the ordinary course of the transferor's business of a major part of the materials, supplies, merchandise, or other inventory." The transfer of a substantial part of the equipment is a bulk transfer only if made in connection with a bulk transfer of inventory. The enterprises subject to Article 6 of the Code are those whose principal business is the sale of merchandise from stock, including those who manufacture what they sell.

Bulk transfer–transfer not in the ordinary course of the transferor's business of a major part of his inventory

Requirements of Article 6

The Code provides that a bulk transfer of assets is ineffective against any creditor of the transferor, unless the following four requirements are met:

1. The transferor furnishes to the transferee a sworn list of his existing creditors, including those whose claims are disputed, stating names, business addresses, and amounts due and owing when known.

2. The transferor and transferee prepare a schedule or list of the property being transferred.

3. The transferee preserves the list of creditors and schedule of property for six months and permits inspection by any creditor of the transferor.

4. The transferee gives the notice of the proposed transfer in bulk to each creditor of the transferor at least ten days before the transferee takes possession of the goods or makes payment for them. This notice must specify (a) that a bulk transfer is about to be made, (b) the names and business addresses of the transferor in bulk and transferee in bulk, and (c) whether all debts of the transferor in bulk are to be paid in full as a result of the transaction, and if so, the address to which creditors should send their bills.

Exempted Bulk Transfers

Certain transfers in bulk are exempt and need not comply with Article 6 of the Code. They include:

1. Transfers by way of security;

2. General assignments for the benefit of all the creditors of the transferor in bulk;

3. Transfers in settlement or realization of a lien or security interest;

4. Sales by executors, administrators, receivers, trustees in bankruptcy, or any public officer under judicial process;

5. Sales in the course of proceedings for the dissolution or reorganization of a corporation in a court proceeding where notice is given to creditors;

6. Transfers to a person who maintains a known place of business in the State who agrees to become bound to pay in full the debts of the transferor in bulk, gives public notice of that fact, and who is solvent after becoming so bound;

7. Transfers to a new business enterprise organized to take over and continue the business of the transferor in bulk, if public notice is given and the new enterprise assumes the debts of the transferor, who receives nothing from the transaction except an interest in the new enterprise that is subordinate to the claims of creditors;

8. Transfers of property that is exempt from execution under exemption statutes.

Effect of Failure to Comply with Article 6

The effect of a failure to comply with the requirements of Article 6 of the Code is that the goods in the possession of the transferee continue to be subject to the claims of unpaid creditors of the transferor. These creditors may proceed against the goods by levy or attachment and by sheriff's sale, or by causing the involuntary bankruptcy of the transferor and the appointment of a trustee in bankruptcy to take over the goods from the transferee.

Where the title of the transferee is subject to the defect of noncompliance with the Code, a *bona fide* purchaser of the goods from the transferee who pays value in good faith and takes the property without notice of such defect acquires the goods free of any claim of creditors of the transferor. A purchaser of the property from the transferee who pays no value or who takes them with notice of noncompliance acquires the goods subject to the claims of creditors of the transferor.

Application of the Proceeds

In the case of bulk transfers for which new consideration is payable, except those made at auction sales, the Code imposes in an optional section a personal duty on the transferee to apply the new consideration to the payment of the debts of the transferor and if it is insufficient to pay them in full, to make a proportional distribution to the creditors.

In States that do not adopt the optional section of the Code, the transferee owes no duties to the creditors of the transferor. If there has been noncompliance with Code, except for sales at auction, the creditors merely proceed to enforce their claims against the transferred property as though it belonged to the transferor. This is what is meant by the language of the Code that the bulk transfer "is ineffective against any creditor of the transferor." The transferee loses the property but does not assume any obligation to pay the debts of the transferor.

The optional section provides that the transferee may discharge her duty to pay the creditors of the transferor out of the proceeds by payment of the consideration into court within ten days after taking possession of the goods, and by giving notice to all of the creditors that such payment has been made and that they should file their claims with the court.

CHAPTER SUMMARY

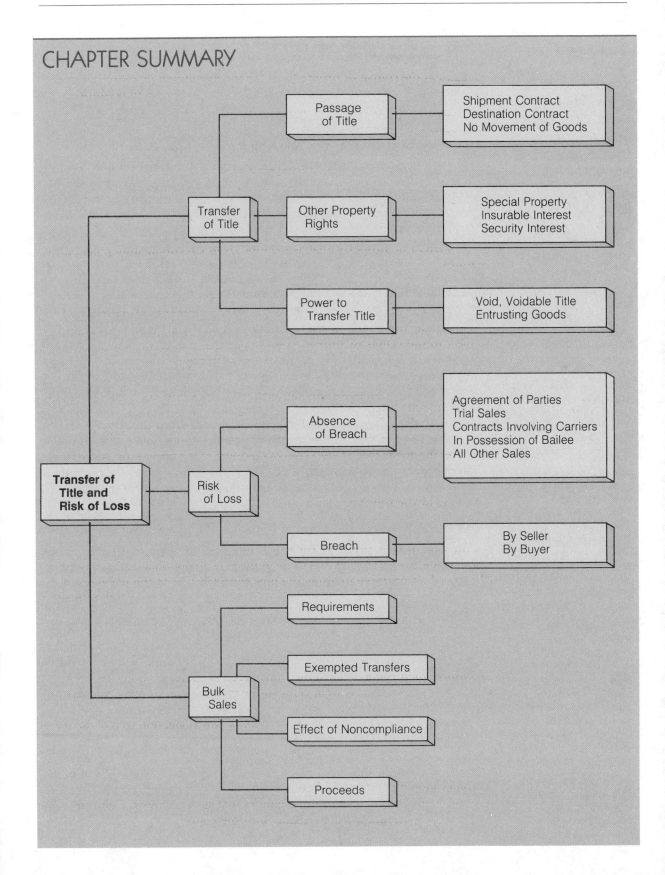

KEY TERMS

Transfer of title	Good faith purchaser	F.O.B.
Shipment contract	Entrustment	F.A.S.
Destination contract	Buyer in ordinary course of	C.I..F
Special property	business	C. & F.
Identification	Risk of loss	C.O.D.
Insurable interest	Sale on approval	Ex-ship
Lien	Sale or return	No arrival, no sale
Security interest	Consignment	Bulk transfer

PROBLEMS

1. Stein, a mechanic, and Beal, a life insurance agent, entered into a written contract for the sale of Stein's tractor to Beal for $2,800 cash. It was agreed that Stein would tune the motor on the tractor. Stein fulfilled this obligation and on the night of July 1 telephoned Beal that the tractor was ready to be picked up on making payment. Beal responded, "I'll be there in the morning with the money." On the next morning, however, Beal was approached by an insurance prospect and decided to get the tractor at a later date. On the night of July 2, the tractor was destroyed by fire of unknown origin. Neither Stein nor Beal had any fire insurance. Who must bear the loss?

2. Regan received a letter from Chase, the material portion of which stated: "Chase hereby places an order with you for fifty cases of Red Top Tomatoes. Ship them C.O.D." As soon as he received the letter, Regan shipped the tomatoes to Chase. While en route, the railroad car carrying the tomatoes was wrecked. When Chase refused to pay for the tomatoes, Regan started an action to recover the purchase price. Chase defended on the ground that because the shipment was C.O.D., neither title to the tomatoes nor risk of loss passed until their delivery to Chase. Decision?

3. On May 10, the A Company, acting through Brown, entered into a contract with C for the installation of a milking machine at C's farm. Following the enumeration of the articles to be furnished, together with the price of each article, the written contract provided: "This outfit is subject to thirty days free trial and is to be installed about June 1." Within thirty days after installation the entire outfit, except for the double utility unit, was destroyed by fire through no fault of C's. The A Company sued C to recover the value of the articles destroyed. Decision?

4. A contracted to buy sixty cases of X Brand canned corn from B at a contract price of $600. Based on the contract, B selected and set aside sixty cases of X Brand canned corn and tagged them "For A." The contract required B to ship the corn to A via T Railroad, F.O.B. Toledo. Before B delivered the corn to the railroad the sixty cases were stolen from B's warehouse.

(a) Who is liable for the loss of the sixty cases of corn, A or B?

(b) Suppose B had delivered the corn to the railroad in Toledo. After the corn was loaded on a freight car, but before the train left the yard, the car was broken open and its contents, including the corn, were stolen. Who is liable for the loss, A or B?

(c) Would your answer in question (b) be the same if this contract were F.O.B. A's warehouse, all other facts remaining the same?

5. A owned a quantity of corn that was stored in a corn crib located on A's farm. On March 12, A wrote a letter to B stating that he would sell to B all of the corn in this crib, which he estimated at between 900 and 1,000 bushels, for $3.60 per bushel. B received this letter on March 13 and immediately wrote and mailed on the same day a letter to A stating that he would buy the corn. The corn crib and contents were accidentally destroyed by a fire that broke out about 3:00 A.M. on March 14. What are the rights of the parties? What difference, if any, in result if A were a merchant?

6. A, a New York dealer, purchased twenty-five barrels of specially graded and packed apples from a producer at Hood River, Oregon. He afterward resold the apples to B under a contract that specified an agreed price on delivery at B's place of business in New York. The apples were shipped to A from Oregon but, through no fault of either A or B, were totally destroyed before reaching New York. Does any liability rest on A?

7. Smith was approached by a man who introduced himself as Brown of Brown and Co. Smith did not know Brown, but Smith asked Dun & Bradstreet for a credit report on Brown. He thereupon sold Brown some expensive gems and billed Brown & Co. "Brown" turned out to be a clever jewel thief, who later sold the gems to Brown & Co. for valuable consideration. Brown & Co. was unaware of "Brown's" transaction with Smith. Smith sued Brown & Co. for the return of the gems or the price as billed to Brown & Co. Decision?

8. Z, the owner of a new Cadillac automobile, agreed to loan the car to Y for the month of February while she (Z) went to Florida for a winter vacation. It was understood that Y, who was a small-town Cadillac dealer, would merely place Z's car in his showroom for exhibition and sales promotion purposes. While Z was away, Y sold the car to B. When Z returned from Florida, she sued to recover the car from B. Decision?

9. A offered to sell his used automobile to B for $2,600 cash. B agreed to buy the car, gave A a check for $2,600, and drove away in the car. The next day B sold the car for $3,000 to C, a bona fide purchaser. The bank returned B's $2,600 check to A because of insufficient funds in B's account. A brings an action against C to recover the automobile. What judgment?

10. B told S he wished to buy S's automobile. He drove the car for about ten minutes, returned to S, stated he wanted to take the automobile to show it to his wife, and then left with the automobile and never returned. B sold the automobile in another State to T and gave him a bill of sale. S sued T to recover the automobile. Decision?

PRODUCT LIABILITY: WARRANTIES AND STRICT LIABILITY

In this chapter we consider the liability of manufacturers and sellers of goods to buyers, users, consumers, and bystanders for damages caused by defective products. The rapid and expanding development of case law has established product liability as a separate and distinct field of law, combining and enforcing rules and principles of contracts, sales, negligence, torts, and statutory law.

One reason for the expansion of such liability has been the modern practice of sales. Today the retailers serve principally as a conduit of prepackaged goods in sealed containers that are widely advertised by the manufacturer or distributor. This has hastened the extension of product liability coverage to include manufacturers and other parties within the chain of distribution. The extension of product liability to manufacturers, however, has not noticeably lessened the liability of a seller to his immediate purchaser. Rather, it has broadened and extended the base of liability by the development and application of new principles of law.

Currently, the liability of manufacturers and sellers of goods for a defective product, or its failure to perform adequately, may be based on one or more of the following: (1) negligence, (2) misrepresentation, (3) violation of statutory duty, (4) warranty, and (5) strict liability in tort. We covered the first three of these causes of actions in Chapters 6 and 9. In this chapter we explore the last two.

Warranties

The concept of warranty as an obligation of the seller to the buyer concerning the title, quality, condition, or performability of goods sold or to be sold is an ancient one. Historically, the remedy of the buyer for breach of warranty was an action in tort for deceit. However, today the liability of a seller for breach of warranty is universally recognized as contractual, and it has been codified by the Uniform Commercial Code.

The liability of a seller for the quality of goods sold has long presented many legal problems. The traditional concept of *caveat emptor*—"let the buyer

Caveat emptor–let the buyer beware

309

beware"—was premised on the principle that the buyer and seller were each attempting to obtain the best bargain possible. Because each had relatively equal bargaining power, the law did not interfere. Today, however, this is not the case; the consumer generally possesses far less bargaining power than the seller. Consequently, the law of sales has abandoned the doctrine of *caveat emptor* and employs warranties to protect the buyer.

Warranty–obligation of the seller to the buyer concerning title, quality, characteristics or condition of goods

A warranty creates a duty on the part of the seller to assure that the goods he sells will conform to certain qualities, characteristics, or conditions. A warranty may arise out of any affirmation of fact or promise to the buyer (an express warranty) or the circumstances under which the sale is made (an implied warranty). If the seller breaches his warranty, the buyer may recover a judgment against the seller for damages. In addition, by timely notice, the buyer may reject or revoke acceptance of the goods.

A seller is not required to warrant the goods, and in general he may, by appropriate words, disclaim, exclude, negate, or modify a particular warranty or even all warranties. Moreover, he may carefully refrain from making an express warranty. However, he must act affirmatively and in the manner prescribed by the Code to effectively disclaim liability for implied warranties.

In this section we examine the various types of warranties, as well as the obstacles to a cause of action for breach of warranty.

Types of Warranties

Express Warranties

An express warranty is an explicit declaration by the seller about the quality, description, condition, or performability of the goods. The declaration may consist of **affirmations** or statements of **fact** or **promises.** For example, a statement made by the seller that a camera has automatic focus is an express warranty. The Code does not require that the affirmation by the seller be relied on by the buyer but only that it constitutes a part of the *basis of the bargain.* If it is basic to the bargain, reliance by the buyer is presumed.

To create an express warranty, the seller does not need to have a specific intention to make a warranty or use formal words such as "warrant" or "guarantee." Moreover, it is not necessary that a seller have knowledge of the falsity of a statement made by her in order to be liable for breach of express warranty; the seller may be acting in good faith. To be liable for fraud, on the other hand, a person must make a misrepresentation of fact with knowledge of its falsity.

Express warranty–affirmation of fact or promise about the goods or a description, including sample, of goods which becomes part of the basis of the bargain

Affirmations of fact by the seller about the goods are frequently part of the **description** of the goods. If so, the seller expressly warrants that the goods will conform to the description. The use of a **sample** or model is another means of describing the goods, and the seller expressly warrants that the entire lot of goods sold will conform to the sample or model.

Statements or promises made by the seller to the buyer before the sale may be express warranties because they may form a part of the basis of the bargain just as much as statements made at the time of the sale. Therefore, statements in advertisements, catalogs, and the like may constitute an express warranty. Under the Code, statements or promises made by the seller after the contract of sale may become express warranties even though no new consideration is given. Thus, a statement or promise of assurance concerning the goods made by the seller to the buyer at the time of delivery may be a binding modification of the prior contract of sale and held to be an express warranty as basic to the bargain.

The Code further provides that a mere statement of the value of the goods or a statement purporting merely to be the seller's *opinion* of the goods does *not* create a warranty. Such statements are not factual and do not deceive the ordinary buyer. They are accepted merely as opinions or as **puffery** (sales talk). If the seller genuinely believes that the goods are more valuable than the stated price, she probably would not sell them. However, a statement of *value* may be an express warranty in situations where the seller states the price at which the goods were purchased from a former owner, or where she gives market figures relating to sales of similar goods. These are affirmations of facts. They are statements of events and not mere opinions, and the seller is liable for breach of warranty if they are untrue.

Although a statement of opinion by the seller is not ordinarily a warranty, if the seller is an *expert* and gives her opinion as such, she may be liable for breach of warranty. Thus, if an art expert states that a certain painting is a genuine Rembrandt, and this becomes part of the basis of the bargain, then the expert warrants the accuracy of her professional opinion. A seller may also be liable if she misrepresents her opinion. A seller may say, "This car is in excellent mechanical condition," or "In my opinion, this car is in excellent mechanical condition." In the first instance she has made an express warranty of the mechanical soundness of the car. In the second, she has made no warranty as to the mechanical soundness of the car but has warranted that she believes the car to be mechanically sound. Thus, if she knew at the time that the car was mechanically unsound, she has misrepresented her opinion as a factual matter. This is not only fraud but also a breach of warranty.

Warranty of Title

Under the Code the seller implicitly warrants that (1) the title conveyed is good and its transfer rightful and (2) the goods have no security interest or other lien (another's right in the property) of which the buyer had no knowledge at the time of contracting.

For example, Steven acquires goods from Nancy in a transaction that is void and then sells the goods to Rachel. Nancy brings an action against Rachel and recovers the goods. Steven has breached the warranty of title due to the fact that Steven did not have good title to the goods and his transfer of the goods to Rachel was not rightful. Accordingly, Steven is liable to Rachel for damages.

The Code, however, does not label the warranty of title as an implied warranty, even though it arises out of the sale and not from any particular words or conduct. Instead, the Code has a separate disclaimer provision for warranty of title; thus the Code's general disclaimer provision for implied warranties does not apply. Nevertheless, a seller of goods does implicitly warrant title to those goods.

Implied Warranties

An implied warranty, unlike an express warranty, is not a specific affirmation or promise by the seller; it is not found in the language of the sales contract.

Puffery–sales talk

Warranty of title–ownership without any lien

W of Title is separate from other warrantees

Implied warranty–arises out of certain circumstances

Instead, it exists by operation of law. An implied warranty arises out of the circumstances under which the parties enter into their contract and depends on such factors as the type of contract or sale entered into, whether the seller is a merchant, the conduct of the parties, and the applicability of other Federal or State statutes. Implied warranties have been developed by the law, not as something to which the parties have agreed, but as a departure from the early rule of *caveat emptor*.

Merchantability–merchant seller guarantees that the goods are fit for their ordinary purpose

Merchantability   At early common law a seller was not held to any implied warranty concerning the quality of the goods. However, under the Code a **merchant seller** does make an implied warranty of the merchantability of goods that are of the kind in which he deals. The implied warranty of merchantability is an obligation of the merchant seller that the goods are reasonably fit for the **ordinary** purposes for which they are manufactured and sold, and also that they are of fair, average quality. *Vlasis v. Montgomery Ward and Company* on the bottom of this page provides an example.

The official Comments to the Code further provide that a contract for the sale of secondhand goods "involves only such obligation as is appropriate to such goods for that is their description." It has been held that "such obligation" includes an implied warranty of merchantability. In defining this warranty, the price, age, and condition of the goods are considered.

Fitness for Particular Purpose

Fitness for a particular purpose–goods are fit for a stated purpose provided the seller selects the product knowing the buyer's intended use and that the buyer is relying on the seller's judgment

Any seller, whether or not he is a merchant, makes an implied warranty that the goods are reasonably fit for the **particular** purpose of the buyer for which the goods are required, if at the time of contracting the seller has reason to know the particular purpose and that the buyer is relying on the seller's skill and judgment to furnish suitable goods. In contrast to the implied warranty of merchantability, the implied warranty of fitness for a particular purpose pertains to a specific purpose, rather than the ordinary purpose, of the goods. A particular purpose may be a specific use or may relate to a special situation in which the buyer intends to use the goods. Thus, if the seller has reason to know that the buyer is purchasing a pair of shoes for mountain climbing and that the buyer is relying on the seller's judgment to furnish suitable shoes for this purpose, a sale of shoes suitable only for ordinary walking purposes would be a breach of this implied warranty.

The buyer need not specifically inform the seller of her particular purpose. It is sufficient if the seller has reason to know it. However, for the implied warranty to exist, the buyer must rely on the seller's skill or judgment to select or furnish suitable goods.

Frequently, as in the case which follows, a seller's conduct may involve both the implied warranty of merchantability and the implied warranty of fitness for a particular purpose.

VLASES v. MONTGOMERY WARD & COMPANY, INC.

United States Court of Appeals, Third Circuit, 1967. 377 F.2d 846.

FACTS: Vlases, a coal miner who had always raised small flocks of chickens, spent two years building a new two-story chicken coop large enough to house 4,000 chickens. After its completion, he purchased 2,200 one-day old chicks from Montgomery Ward for the purpose of producing eggs for sale. He had selected them from Ward's catalogue, which stated that these chicks, hybrid Leghorns, were noted for their excellent egg production. Vlases had equipped the coop with brand new machinery and had taken further hygiene precautions for the chicks' health. Almost one month later, Vlases noticed that their feathers were beginning to fall off. A veterinarian's examination revealed signs of drug intoxication and hemorrhgic disease in a few of the chicks. Eight months later, it was determined that the chicks were suffering from visceral and ocular leukosis, or bird cancer, which reduced their egg-bearing capacity to zero. Avian leukosis may be transmitted either genetically or by unsanitary conditions. Subsequently, the disease infected the entire flock. Vlases then brought suit against Montgomery Ward for its breach of the implied warranties of merchantability and of fitness for a particular purpose. Ward claims that there was no way to detect the disease in the one-day old chicks nor is there medication available to prevent this disease from occurring.

DECISION: Judgment for Vlases. The implied warranty of merchantability and the implied warranty of fitness for a particular purpose are designed to protect the buyer from bearing the loss when the goods do not conform to normal commercial standards or meet the buyer's particular purpose. The seller is therefore liable for the breach of these warranties even if he is unable to discover the defect in the goods or cure the damage if it could be ascertained. However, under both warranties, the goods must be defective at the time of delivery to hold the seller liable.

Here, the avian leukosis definitely rendered the chicks commercially inferior and unmerchantable. They also were unfit for the purpose of laying eggs, for which Vlases had purchased them, relying on Ward's catalogue advertisement. Vlases had taken the necessary hygienic precautions in the handling, care and housing of the chicks. There is a strong inference, then, that the chicks had contracted the disease genetically rather than because of unsanitary conditions. Therefore, they were of inferior quality at the time of the delivery, although the disease was not discovered until 8 months later. Despite its inability to detect or prevent the leukosis in the one-day old chicks, Ward is liable for the breach of both warranties.

Obstacles to Warranty Actions

Disclaimer or Modification of Warranties

The Code calls for a reasonable construction of words or conduct to negate or limit warranties. In addition, it provides that remedies and recovery of damages for breach of warranty may be contractually limited.

Disclaimer–negation of warranty

The Code makes clear that the seller should not rely on a time-honored formula of words and expect to obtain a disclaimer that may go unnoticed by the buyer. To be effective, disclaimers should be positive, explicit, unequivocal, and conspicuous.

Express Exclusions

A **warranty of title** may be excluded or modified only by specific language or by certain circumstances, including a judicial sale or sales by sheriffs, executors, or foreclosing lienors. In the latter cases the seller is clearly offering to sell only such right or title as he or a third person might have in the goods, because it is apparent that the goods are not the property of the person selling them.

A seller can avoid making an **express warranty** by carefully refraining from making any promise or affirmation of fact relating to the goods, refraining from making a description of the goods, or refraining from using a sample or model in a sale. The seller may also negate an express warranty by *clear, specific, unambiguous* language. The Code, nevertheless, provides that words or conduct relevant to the creation of an express warranty and words or conduct tending to negate or limit a warranty shall be construed wherever reasonable as consistent with each other and that a negation or limitation has no effect if it is unreasonable. Thus, seller and buyer make a written contract in which the seller warrants that the camera he is selling to the buyer is free of defects. This express warranty nullifies another provision in the contract that attempts to disclaim liability for any repairs required by defects in the camera. The inconsistency between the two contractual provisions makes the disclaimer ineffective. Moreover, a general disclaimer attempting to negate "all express warranties" would be ineffective against the specific express warranty providing that the camera is free of all defects. Finally, oral warranties made before the execution of a written agreement that contains an express disclaimer are subject to the parol evidence rule. Thus, as discussed in Chapter 13, if the written contract is intended to be the final and *complete* statement of the agreement between the parties, parol evidence of warranties that *contradicts* the terms of the written contract is inadmissible.

CENTURY DODGE, INC. v. MOBLEY

Court of Appeals of Georgia, 1980.
155 Ga.App. 712, 272 S.E.2d 502.

FACTS: Mobley purchased from Century Dodge a car described as new in the contract. The contract also contained a disclaimer of all warranties, express or implied. Subsequently, Mobley discovered that the car, had, in fact, been involved in a previous accident. He then sued Century Dodge to recover damages, claiming it breached its express warranty that the car was new. Century Dodge argues that it had adequately disclaimed all warranties.

DECISION: Judgment for Mobley. Under the Uniform Commercial Code, words or conduct creating an express warranty and words or conduct negating or limiting warranties are to be construed as consistent with each other whenever reasonable. The negation or limitation, however, is inoperative to the extent that such construction is unreasonable.

Here, the description of the car as new in the contract was an express warranty, since it was part of the basis of the bargain. Mobley may have acknowledged the blanket disclaimer by signing the contract; nevertheless, it is unreasonable to allow the express warranty to be negated by the general disclaimer because the two provisions are not consistent with each other. Therefore, Century Dodge is liable for its breach of the express warranty if the car is not, in fact, new.

To exclude or modify an **implied warranty of merchantability,** the language of disclaimer of modification must mention *merchantability* and, in the case of a writing, must be *conspicuous*.

To exclude or to modify an **implied warranty of fitness** for the particular purpose of the buyer, the disclaimer must be in *writing* and *conspicuous*.

As is—disclaimer of implied warranties

All implied warranties, unless the circumstances indicate otherwise, are excluded by expressions like **"as is," "with all faults,"** or other language plainly calling the buyer's attention to the exclusion of warranties. Implied warranties may also be excluded by course of dealing, course of performance, or usage of trade.

O'NEIL v. INTERNATIONAL HARVESTER CO.

Colorado Court of Appeals, 1978.
40 Colo.App. 369, 575 P.2d 862.

FACTS: On August 22, 1975, O'Neil purchased a used diesel tractor-trailer combination from International Harvester. O'Neil claimed that International Harvester's salesman had told him that the truck had recently been overhauled and that it would be suitable for hauling logs in the mountains. The written installment contract signed by the parties provided that the truck was sold "AS IS WITHOUT WARRANTY OF ANY CHARACTER express or implied." O'Neil admitted that he had read the disclaimer clause but claimed that he understood it to mean that the tractor-trailer would be in the condition that International Harvester's salesman had promised.

O'Neil paid the $1700 down payment, but he failed to make any of the monthly payments. He claimed that he refused to pay because his employee had many problems with the truck when he took it to the mountains. Delays resulting from those problems, O'Neil argued, had caused him to lose his permit to cut firewood and, therefore, the accompanying business. An International Harvester representative agreed to pay for one-half of the cost of certain repairs, but the several attempts made to fix the truck were unsuccessful. O'Neil then tried to return the truck and to rescind the sale, but International Harvester refused to cooperate.

DECISION: The implied warranty of fitness for a particular purpose and the implied warranty of merchantability can be disclaimed by an As Is clause. As a result, O'Neil's admission that he had read the disclaimer provision in the written contract was enough effectively to disclaim the implied warranty of fitness for a particular purpose and the implied warranty of merchantability.

The alleged express warranty, however, presents a different question. If the words or conduct of a party give rise to an express warranty, then a provision in the written contract limiting that express warranty is inoperative to the extent that it cannot be construed consistently with the express warranty. At the same time, however, the parol evidence rule generally operates to exclude evidence of a prior agreement or a contemporaneous oral agreement if it appears that the parties intended the written contract to be a final expression of their agreement with respect to any warranty terms. In this case, however, in addition to the alleged oral warranty made prior to the written contract, the conduct of International Harvester (including a commitment to pay for certain repairs) tends to show that an express warranty was in fact given. A material issue of fact remains as to the actual final agreement between the parties and thus a trial on the issue of the express warranty is appropriate.

Buyer's Examination or Refusal to Examine   If the buyer inspects the goods, **implied** warranties do not apply to obvious defects that are apparent on examination. Moreover, there is no implied warranty on defects that an examination ought to have revealed not only where the buyer has examined the goods as fully as she desired, but also where the buyer has *refused* to examine the goods.

Federal Legislation Relating to Warranties of Consumer Goods   To protect purchasers of **consumer goods** (defined as "tangible personal property normally used for personal, family or household purposes"), the Congress enacted the **Magnuson-Moss Warranty Act.** The purpose of the Act is to prevent deception and to make sure consumer purchasers are adequately informed about warranties.

The Federal Trade Commission administrates and enforces the Act. The Commission's guidelines about the type of information that must be given in warranties of consumer products are aimed at providing the consumer with clear and useful information. More significantly, the Act provides that a seller who makes a written warranty cannot disclaim *any* implied warranty. For a more complete discussion of the Act see Chapter 41.

Privity of Contract

Because of the close association between warranties and contracts a principle of law became established in the nineteenth century that a plaintiff could not recover for breach of warranty unless he was in a contractual relationship with the defendant. This relationship is known as privity of contract.

Privity–contractual relationship

Under this rule a warranty by seller A to buyer B, who resells the goods to purchaser C under a similar warranty, gives C no rights against A. There is no privity of contract between A and C. In the event of breach of warranty, C may recover only from his seller B, who in turn may recover from A.

Horizontal Privity   Horizontal privity pertains to noncontracting parties who are injured by the defective goods; this group would include users, consumers, and bystanders who are not the contracting purchaser. Horizontal privity determines who benefits from a warranty and may therefore sue for its breach (see Figure 19–1).

Horizontal privity–who may bring a cause of action

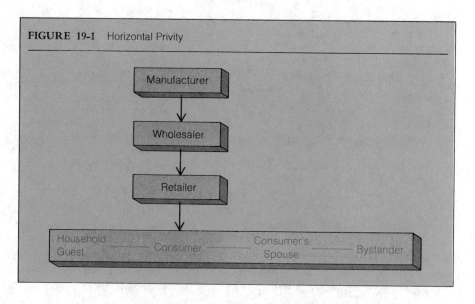

FIGURE 19-1 Horizontal Privity

Manufacturer

Wholesaler

Retailer

Household Guest —— Consumer —— Consumer's Spouse —— Bystander

The Code relaxes the requirement of horizontal privity of contract by permitting recovery on a seller's warranty to, at a minimum, members of the family or household of the buyer or guests in his home. The Code provides three alternative sections from which the States may select. Alternative A, the least comprehensive and most widely adopted of these legislative alternatives, provides that a seller's warranty, whether express or implied, extends to any natural person who is in the family or household of the buyer or who is a guest in his home if it is reasonable to expect that such person may use, consume, or be affected by the goods and who is injured in person by breach of the warranty. A seller may not exclude or limit the operation of this section. Alternative B extends Alternative A to "any natural person who may reasonably be expected to use, consume or be affected by the goods." Alternative C further expands the coverage of the section to any person, not just natural persons, and to property damage as well as personal injury.

Nonetheless, the Code was not intended to establish outer boundaries as to which third parties may recover for injuries caused by defective goods. Rather, it sets a minimum standard that the States may expand through case law. Most States have judicially accepted the Code's invitation to relax the requirements of horizontal privity and, for all practical purposes, have *eliminated* horizontal privity in warranty cases.

Vertical privity—who is liable to the plaintiff

Vertical Privity

Vertical privity pertains to remote sellers within the chain of distribution, such as manufacturers and wholesalers, with whom the consumer purchaser has not dealt (see Figure 19–2). Thus, vertical privity determines who is liable for breach of warranty. Although the Code adopts a neutral position regarding vertical privity, the courts in most States have eliminated the requirement of vertical privity in warranty actions.

Requirement of Notice of Breach

When a buyer has accepted a tender of goods that are not as warranted by the seller, she is required to notify the seller of any breach of warranty, express or implied, as well as any other breach, within a reasonable time after she has

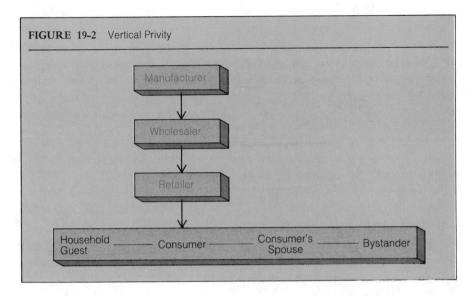

FIGURE 19-2   Vertical Privity

discovered or should have discovered it. If the buyer fails to notify the seller of any breach within a reasonable time, she is barred from any remedy against the seller.

Contributory Negligence

Because of the development of warranty liability in the law of sales and contracts, contributory negligence of the buyer is *no* defense to an action against the seller for breach of warranty. Contributory negligence is a tort concept and does not apply to contract actions.

Voluntary Assumption of Risk

If the buyer discovers a defect in the goods that may cause injury and nevertheless proceeds to make use of them, he will not be permitted to recover damages from the seller for loss or injuries caused by such use. This is not contributory negligence, but voluntary assumption of a known risk.

Some limits on this defense to an implied warranty cause of action is presented in the following case.

FACTS: Guarino and two others (plaintiffs) died of gas asphyxiation and five others were injured when they entered a sewer tunnel without masks to answer the cries for help of their crew leader Rooney. Rooney had left the sewer shaft and entered the tunnel to fix a water leakage problem. Having corrected the problem, Rooney was returning to the shaft when he apparently was overcome by gas because of a defect in his oxygen mask manufactured by Mine Safety Appliance Company (defendant). Plaintiffs brought this action against the defendant for breach of warranty and defendant raised the defense of plaintiffs' voluntary assumption of the risk.

DECISION: Judgment for Guarino. If a seller of goods through its negligence or breach of warranty places another person in a position of imminent peril, that seller may be held liable for any damages sustained by a rescuer in his attempt to aid the imperiled victim under the "danger invites rescue" doctrine. Here, Mine Safety Appliance Company, through its breach of warranty on the oxygen mask, placed Rooney in a position of imminent peril in the tunnel. The company, then, is liable for damages suffered by Rooney's attempted rescuers and cannot successfully plead the defense of voluntary assumption of risk.

GUARINO v. MINE SAFETY APPLIANCE CO.

Court of Appeals on New York, 1969.
25 N.Y.2d 460, 306 N.Y.S.2d 942, 255 N.E.2d 173.

Strict Liability in Tort

The most recent and far-reaching development in the field of product liability is that of strict liability in tort. All but a very few States have now accepted the concept, which is embodied in **Section 402A** of the Restatement, Second, Torts. It imposes liability only on a person who is in the *business* of selling the product involved. It does not apply to an occasional seller who is not in the business of selling the product, such as a person who trades in his used car or who sells his lawn mower to a neighbor. It is similar in this respect to the implied warranty of merchantability, which applies only to sales by a merchant of goods of the type in which he deals.

Nature of Strict Liability in Tort

Section 402A imposes liability on sellers for both personal injuries and property damage for selling the product in **a defective condition, unreasonably dangerous** to the user or consumer. Specifically, this section provides:

1. One who sells any product in a defective condition unreasonably dangerous to the user or consumer or to his property is subject to liability for physical harm thereby caused to the ultimate user or consumer, or to his property, if (a) the seller is engaged in the business of selling such a product, and (b) it is expected to and does reach the user or consumer without substantial change in the condition in which it is sold.
2. The rule stated in Subsection (1) applies although (a) the seller has exercised all possible care in the preparation and sale of his products, and (b) the user or consumer has not bought the product from or entered into any contractual relation with the seller.

We emphasize that negligence is not the basis of this liability; it applies even though the seller has exercised all possible care in the preparation and sale of his product. However, the seller is not an insurer of the goods that he manufactures or sells, and the essential requirements for this type of liability are: (1) that the defendant sold the product in a defective condition; (2) that the defendant was engaged in the business of selling such a product; (3) that the defective condition made the product unreasonably dangerous to the user or consumer or to his property; (4) that the defect in the product existed at the time it left the hands of the defendant; (5) that the plaintiff sustained physical harm or property damage by use or consumption of the product; and (6) that the defective condition was the proximate cause of this injury or damage.

This liability is imposed by law as a matter of public policy and does not depend on contract, either express or implied. It does not require reliance by the injured user or consumer on any statements made by the manufacturer or seller. The liability is not limited to persons in a relationship of buyer and seller; thus neither vertical nor horizontal privity is required. No notice of defect is required to have been given by the injured user or consumer. The liability, furthermore, is generally not subject to disclaimer, exclusion, or modification by contractual agreement. The liability is strictly in tort and arises out of the common law. It is not governed by the provisions of the Uniform Commercial Code. The majority of courts considering the question, however, have held that Section 402A imposes liability only for injury to person and damage to property but not for commercial loss (such as loss of bargain or profits), which is recoverable in an action for breach of warranty.

Although liability for personal injuries caused by defective goods is usually associated with sales of goods, this liability also exists on leases and bailments of defective goods. The extension of liability to lessors and bailors of goods is not surprising in view of the rationale developed by the courts in imposing strict liability in tort on manufacturers and sellers of products. The danger to which the public is exposed by defectively manufactured cars and trucks traveling on the highways is not greatly different from the hazards of defectively maintained cars and trucks leased to operators.

Defective Condition

In an action against a defendant manufacturer or seller to recover damages under the rule of strict liability in tort, the plaintiff must prove a defective condition in the product, but she is not required to prove how or why or in what manner the product became defective. In an action based on 402A liability, the reason or cause of the defect is not material. The plaintiff, however, must show that at the time she was injured the condition of the product was not substantially changed from what it was at the time it was sold by the defendant manufacturer or seller. The defect may arise through faulty manufacturing, through faulty product design, or through inadequate warning, labeling, or instructions.

Manufacturing Defect   A manufacturing defect occurs when the product is not properly made; that is, it fails to meet its own manufacturing specifications. For instance, suppose a chair is manufactured with legs designed to be attached by four screws and glue. If the chair were produced without inserting the appropriate screws, this would constitute a manufacturing defect.

Manufacturing defect–not produced according to specifications

Design Defect   A product contains a design defect when it is produced as specified but is dangerous or hazardous because its design is inadequate. Design defects can result from a number of causes, including poor engineering, poor choice of materials, and poor packaging. An example of a design defect that received great notoriety was the Ford Pinto. A number of courts found the car to be inadequately designed because the fuel tank had been placed too close to its rear axle, causing the fuel tank to rupture when the car was hit from the rear. For a more detailed discussion of the Ford Pinto controversy see the Wall Street Journal article reproduced in Law in the News on page 321.

Design defect–inadequate plans or specifications to insure the products safety

Another example involing an alleged design defect is provided in the following case.

FACTS: Heckman, an employee of Clark Equipment Company, severely injured his left hand when he caught it in a power press that he was operating at work. The press was manufactured by Federal Press Company and sold to Clark in 1970. It could be operated either by hand controls that required the use of both hands away from the point of operation, or alternatively by an optional foot pedal. When the foot pedal was used without a guard, nothing remained to keep the operator's hands from the point of operation. Federal Press did not provide safety appliances unless the customer requested them, but when it delivered the press to Clark with the optional pedal, it suggested that Clark install a guard. The press had a similar warning embossed on it. Clark did in fact purchase a guard for $100, but it was not mounted on the machine at the time of the injury nor was it believed to be an effective safety device.

HECKMAN v. FEDERAL PRESS CO.

United States Court of Appeals, Third Circuit, 1979. 587 F.2d 612.

Heckman argued that one type of guard, if installed, would have made the press safe in 95 percent of its customary uses. Federal, in turn, argued that the furnishing of guards was not customary in the industry; that the machine's many uses made it impracticable to design and install any one guard as standard equipment; that Clark's failure to obey Federal's warning was a superseding cause of the injury; and that State regulations placed responsibility for the safe operation of presses on employers and employees.

DECISION: Judgment for Heckman. A failure to provide proper safety devices constituted a design defect that subjected Federal to liability. The question as to whether Federal's guardless press created an unreasonable risk of harm to the user was a question for the jury to decide after considering such factors as: 1) the feasibility of incorporating safety features during manufacture; 2) the likelihood that users would not secure adequate protective devices; 3) whether the machine was of standard make or custom built; 4) the relative expertise of the manufacturer and the customer with regard to the product; 5) the extent of risk to the user; and 6) the seriousness of the injury which could be anticipated.

Inadequate Warning or Instructions   A seller has a duty to provide adequate warning of possible danger and to provide appropriate directions for safe use. Nevertheless, inadequate and dangerous products, regardless of their warning, will be held to be defective, especially if there are superior alternative designs or manufacturing procedures. Typically, warnings or instructions are needed to ensure that appropriately designed and manufactured products are properly used. Comment j to Section 402A provides that in some instances, "in order to prevent the product from being unreasonably dangerous, the seller may be required to give directions or warning, on the container, as to its use." For example, in one case a drug company was found liable for inadequately warning of the dangerous and not infrequent side effects of one of its drugs.

Almost any product may be used or misused in a manner that may cause physical harm. The blow of a poorly aimed hammer may crush a thumb. The inhaling of a feather may damage a lung. The use of a sled on a busy street may endanger the child using it. The excessive drinking of liquor is dangerous. Allowing children to play with firearms is also dangerous. These hazards arise when products are used in a way that they were not intended by the supplier to be used, and generally no duty is imposed on the manufacturer or seller to give warning against the possible dangers that might arise from such misuse of the product.

The duty to give a warning arises out of a foreseeable danger of physical harm arising out of the normal or probable use of the product and the likelihood that unless warned, the user or consumer will not ordinarily be aware of such danger or hazard.

In addition to warning of dangers, the seller must provide adequate directions for the safe and efficient use of the product. Furthermore, whenever a deviation from the directions may give rise to a serious danger to the user, the seller must provide warning of this danger.

Unreasonably Dangerous

Unreasonably danger-
ous–danger beyond that
which the ordinary con-
sumer contemplates

Section 402A liability only applies if the defective product is unreasonably dangerous to the user or consumer. An unreasonably dangerous product is one that contains a danger beyond that which would be contemplated by the ordinary consumer who purchases it with the common knowledge of its characteristics. Thus, Comment i to Section 402A states: "good whiskey is not

Why the Pinto Jury Felt Ford Deserved $125 Million Penalty

Film of Test Crash Is Stressed Along With Cost Savings; 'A Lousy, Unsafe Product'

SANTA ANA, Calif.—Andrew Quinn, a retired policeman, had to give up golf temporarily for jury duty. Ford Motor Co. wishes he had stayed on the links.

Last week, jury foreman Quinn read in state Superior Court here a verdict assessing $125 million in punitive damages against Ford in a case involving the rupture and explosion of the fuel tank on a 1972 Pinto. The car, stalled on a freeway, was struck in the rear by another car six years ago.

The verdict, reached in only a day and a half of jury deliberations after a six-month trial, is the largest punitive award ever made by a jury in a personal-injury case, according to lawyers who specialize in the field. "We came up with this high amount so that Ford wouldn't design cars this way again," says foreman Quinn, who describes the Pinto as "a lousy and unsafe product." The jury, he says, wanted a punishment severe enough to sting the big auto maker.

"It Won't Be Upheld"

It did. Ford calls the verdict "so unreasonable and unwarranted that it won't be upheld" and plans to ask the judge to overturn it. The award was so big that it even stunned attorneys for the plaintiff who won it: Richard Grimshaw, now 19 years old, who was burned over 90% of his body and lost his nose, left ear and much of his left hand in the flames. (He has undergone some 60 operations to alleviate the damage.) The Pinto's driver, 52-year-old Lily Gray, the only other person in the car, died of her burns. The jury awarded an additional $3.5 million in compensatory damages to Mr. Grim-

shaw and to Mrs. Gray's relatives, for a total of $128.5 million.

The massive punitive award may well be thrown out or trimmed back. But the reasoning used by the jurors in arriving at it, and their emotional reaction to evidence produced by Ford itself, suggest that manufacturers of all kinds of products may be in for an increasingly tough time in personal-injury cases.

Jurors mulled the results of five pre-1972 Ford fuel-tank tests; the tanks on experimentally crashed Pintos showed significant damage and leakage in each case. Juror C. V. Greene, a telephone-company dispatcher, was especially struck by a Ford film of a Pinto backed into a wall at 20 miles an hour in the final test before the Pinto was introduced to the public in 1970. The gas tank, filled with a nonflammable substance, ruptured with such force, Mr. Greene says, that "it looked like a fireman had stuck a hose inside the car and turned it on."

Mr. Greene wondered what would have happened if the fluid had been gasoline and passengers were inside. "In my mind," he says, "that film beat the Ford Motor Co."

Foreman Quinn was impressed by the testimony of a retired Ford designer, Harley Copp, who was called by plaintiffs' attorneys to explain how company executives balance safety and cost factors in designing a car. Mr. Copp, a critic of the Pinto fuel-tank design, referred to Ford documents indicating that the company could save $20.9 million if it delayed making tank improvements for two years.

Juror Drives One

All this convinced jurors that Ford had known the design was dangerous and retained it anyway

in order to save money. "Ford knew people would be killed," declares juror David Blodgett, who works for Western Electric Co. and who is the only member of the panel who drives a Pinto. (He says he'll keep his 1974 model anyway. Ford said in court that it has made several gas-tank changes in recent years; the most significant change was mandated by new federal standards taking effect with 1977 models.)

Ford's own records, obtained by the plaintiffs' attorneys in discovery proceedings, indicated that the company could have given the gas tank extra protection with metal and plastic for about $10 to $15 a car, but declined to do so for cost and weight-saving reasons.

Plaintiffs' attorneys argued that when Detroit introduced small cars to compete with cheaper, lighter-weight European models, it saved money by placing the gas tank behind the rear axle, making it vulnerable to even low-speed collisions. "The Pinto was the worst," says Mark Robinson Jr., one attorney for Mr. Grimshaw. "The tank was only 3¼ inches behind the differential housing, and in a crash the housing works like a can opener."

Ford's trial argument was that the Pinto was hit at 50 miles an hour, and that, at that speed, the fuel-system design of any subcompact car, including the Pinto, could not have withstood the impact. But jurors believed, instead, that the collision was at much lower speed, and that the victims would have escaped uninjured had it not been for the fire.

Judge Leonard Goldstein instructed the jurors that they could vote punitive damages only if they believed that the evidence showed

$125 Million Penalty continued

Ford had intentionally caused the injuries, or had willfully disregarded safety. By then most jurors had concluded that the auto maker belonged in the second category.

Plaintiffs' attorneys had asked for a punitive award of $100 million, the amount they estimated Ford had saved by retaining the allegedly defective design on Pintos and other small-car models from the time they were introduced until the federally mandated standards took effect on 1977 cars. In the first round of deliberations, two jurors were opposed to punitive damages, foreman Quinn says. Of the remainder, eight were "in the ballpark" of $100 million, one wanted to assess $20.9 million, and another $500 million.

Mr. Greene, impressed by that last juror's argument, recalls bringing up the $125 million figure himself. He reasoned that if Ford had saved $100 million by not installing safe tanks, an award matching that wouldn't really be punitive. So he added $25 million. Eight of the nine others voting for punitive damages agreed, and the jury's job was over; in California, only nine members of a panel need to agree on the amount of damages.

When Arthur Hews, an attorney for Mr. Grimshaw, heard the verdict, he was astounded. "I damn near cried. I was very proud of that jury," says Mr. Hews, who spent six years preparing and arguing the case.

Ford apparently didn't have much of a chance in the jury room. Juror Greene says he later told a Ford attorney that he had had a tough job. "I said, 'You can't plow a field with a one-legged mule.'"

Ford says that it has lost three other Pinto fuel-tank-fire cases in recent years—the largest, a $3 million 1976 award in Florida that is being appealed—but that the Grimshaw case is the first in which punitive damages have been levied.

A spokesman says the company is reviewing its insurance coverage in light of the Grimshaw verdict. Insurance-industry sources note, however, that coverage for punitive damages has been increasingly hard to secure. They suggested that, in any event, Ford's protection very likely wouldn't approach $125 million for a single case.

C. C. Clark, executive vice president of the Insurance Information Institute, a trade group, criticizes the verdict as being "not reflective of economic reality." T. Lawrence Jones, president of the American Insurance Association, calls it "cruel and unusual punishment" and says that where insurance does exist such verdicts only rebound against the consumer. The costs of big awards, he contends, are passed on by the insurer in the form of higher premiums and, eventually, by the insured in the form of higher product prices.

Ford is soon expected to report fourth quarter profits of $380 million to $395 million. Thus, the jury award is about equal to Ford's profit for one recent month.

Some of the jurors themselves concede that their verdict is likely to be pruned back, but they still feel that it was the proper one and that it was dictated by the evidence. "We wanted Ford to take notice," foreman Quinn says. "I think they've noticed."

[Authors' note: This verdict was subsequently lowered to 3.5 million dollars by the judge, holding that the larger figure was excessive as a matter of law.]

By Roy J. Harris Jr.
Reprinted by permission of The Wall Street Journal, © Dow Jones & Company, Inc. 1979. All Rights Reserved.

unreasonably dangerous merely because it will make some people drunk, and is especially dangerous to alcoholics; but bad whiskey, containing a dangerous amount of fuel oil, is unreasonably dangerous. Good tobacco is not unreasonably dangerous merely because the effects of smoking may be harmful; but tobacco containing something like marijuana may be unreasonably dangerous. Good butter is not unreasonably dangerous merely because, if such be the case, it deposits cholesterol in the arteries and leads to heart attacks; but bad butter, contaminated with poisonous fish oil, is unreasonably dangerous." Most courts have left the question of what a consumer reasonably expects to find to the jury.

Obstacles to Recovery

Disclaimers and Notice

Comment m to Section 402A provides that the basis of strict liability rests solely in tort and therefore is not subject to contractual defenses. The comment specifically states that strict product liability is not governed by the Code, that it is not affected by contractual limitations or disclaimers, and that it is not subject to any requirement that notice be given to the seller by the injured party within a reasonable time. Nevertheless, most courts have *allowed* clear and specific disclaimers of Section 402A liability in commercial transactions between merchants of relatively equal economic power.

Privity

Horizontal Privity   The strict liability in tort of manufacturers and other sellers extends not only to buyers, users, and consumers, but also to injured by-standers.

Vertical Privity   The rule of strict liability in tort, as formulated in Section 402A, imposes liability on the seller for physical harm to the ultimate user or consumer of the defective product. Such liability extends to any seller who is engaged in the business of selling the product, including a wholesaler or distributor as well as the manufacturer and retailer.

FACTS: Mrs. Embs went into Stamper's Cash Market to buy soft drinks for her children. She removed five bottles from an upright soft drink cooler, placed them in a carton, and then turned to move away from the display when a bottle of Seven-Up in a carton at her feet exploded, cutting her leg. Apparently several other bottles had exploded that same week. Stamper's Cash Market received its entire stock of Seven-Up from Arnold Lee Vice, the area distributor. Vice in turn received his entire stock of Seven-Up from Pepsi-Cola Bottling Co.

DECISION: Judgment for Embs. The doctrine of strict liability in tort extends not only to actual purchasers and users, but also to bystanders whose injury from a defective product is reasonably foreseeable. Moreover, as a matter of public policy, the retailer and the distributor as well as the bottler are liable for injuries resulting from defective products. These members of the marketing chain are best able to bear the loss and can distribute the risk among themselves by means of insurance and re-imbursement agreements.

In the present case the explosion of the bottle in the course of normal handling permitted the inference of a defect, particularly where there was evidence of similar explosions earlier in the week.

EMBS v. PEPSI-COLA BOTTLING CO. OF LEXINGTON, KENTUCKY, INC.

Court of Appeals of Kentucky, 1975.
528 S.W.2d 703.

The rule of strict liability in tort also applies to the manufacturer of a defective component part that is used in a larger product where no essential change has been made in it by the manufacturer of the finished product. The manufacturer of the defective component is not excused from liability because the manufacturer of the finished product failed to discover the defect by testing or inspection. The manufacturer of the finished product is also liable for damages caused by a defective condition of the goods resulting exclusively from a defective component part.

Finally, a growing number of jurisdictions recognize the applicability of strict liability in tort to merchant sellers of used goods. One court has stated in a case involving the sale of a used automobile. "The safety of the general public demands that when a used motor vehicle, for example, is sold for use as a *serviceable motor vehicle* (and not as junk parts), absent special circumstances, the seller be responsible for safety defects whether known or unknown at the time of sale, present while the machine was under his control."

Plaintiff's Conduct

Contributory Negligence　At common law in an action based on negligence, contributory negligence of the plaintiff completely barred recovery. Contributory negligence generally is immaterial in an action based on strict liability in tort, although a few States have held contributory negligence to be a valid defense. The minority view, however, which totally bars the plaintiff from recovery, is contrary to the principle of strict liability, and is contrary to Comment n to Section 402A.

Comparative Negligence　Many States have adopted the rule of comparative negligence in negligence actions. This rule diminishes the amount of a plaintiff's recovery in proportion to his fault. In response to the doctrinal difficulties and inequities of applying contributory negligence to strict liability in tort, a growing number of courts and legislatures have applied the principle of comparative negligence to strict liability in tort.

Voluntary Assumption of the Risk　Assumption of risk is a defense in an action based on strict liability in tort. The user or consumer who voluntarily uses the goods in an unusual, inappropriate, or improper manner for which they were not intended, and that under the circumstances is unreasonable, assumes the risk of injuries that result from such use.

To establish such defense the burden is on the defendant to show that (1) the plaintiff actually knew and appreciated the particular risk or danger created by the defect, (2) the plaintiff voluntarily encountered the risk while realizing the danger, and (3) the plaintiff's decision to encounter the known risk was unreasonable.

Misuse or Abuse of the Product　Closely connected to voluntary assumption of the risk is the valid defense of misuse or abuse of the product by the injured party. The major difference is that misuse or abuse includes actions that the injured party does not know to be dangerous, whereas assumption of the risk does not include such conduct. The courts, however, have significantly limited this defense by requiring that the misuse or abuse not be foreseeable by the seller. If a use is foreseeable, then the seller must take measures to guard against it. Thus, a manufacturer has been held liable for injuries to a stevedore who was injured while walking on cargo, for failing to package its cargo so as to avoid such injury. It was foreseeable that stevedores would indeed walk on the cargo.

Subsequent Alteration

Section 402A provides that liability only exists if the product reaches "the user or consumer without substantial change in the condition in which it is sold." Accordingly, most but not all courts would not hold a manufacturer liable for a faulty carburetor if the retailer had removed the part and made significant changes in it before reinserting it into the automobile.

KENNEDY v. CUSTOM ICE EQUIPMENT CO., INC.

Supreme Court of South Carolina, 1978.
271 S.C. 171, 246 S.E.2d 176.

FACTS:　Kennedy was fifteen years old and working his first job as an employee of Georgetown Ice Company. On his third day at work, he was instructed to empty ice storage bins which were fed by an overhead conveyor. The machinery had been designed and installed by Custom Ice Equipment Company. It was common for the ice to freeze and not fall out of the bins through the trap doors. Thus, it had to be physically dislodged. Georgetown had constructed a catwalk alongside the bins from which its employees would reach into them and break up the frozen ice with a garden hoe. Kennedy proceeded to dislodge the frozen ice with a hoe and was drawn into the conveyor by his left arm, which was then torn off. Kennedy brought suit against Custom for the amputation of his left arm, claiming strict liability in tort. Custom defends on the ground that Georgetown modified the conveyor when it constructed the catwalk, creating the defect and relieving Custom of liability.

DECISION: Judgment for Kennedy. The test of whether a product is defective when sold is whether the product is unreasonably dangerous to the consumer or user given the conditions and circumstances that will foreseeably attend the use of the product. The jury here determined that Custom had actual knowledge of the construction and use of similar catwalks in other ice plants and should have foreseen the use of a catwalk by Georgetown. The catwalk's use was a foreseeable circumstance that required the incorporation of protective shields in the design of the conveyer. The lack of these shields therefore rendered the product defective as designed by Custom and Custom is not relieved by the addition of the catwalk—a foreseeable alteration.

Figure 19–3 compares strict liability in tort with the implied warranty of merchantability.

FIGURE 19-3   Products Liability

	Warranty of Merchantability	Strict Liability in Tort
Condition of goods	Not Merchantable	Defective condition, unreasonably dangerous
Character of defendant	Seller who is a merchant with respect to the goods sold	Seller who is engaged in the business of selling such a product
Disclaimer	Permitted if: 1) specific 2) conspicuous 3) conscionable subject to Magnuson–Moss Act	None possible in consumer transaction; most courts allow in commercial transactions
Notice	Within reasonable time	None required
Causation	Required	Required
Protected Harm	Alt. A: To person of buyer, family or guests in home Alt. B: To person of anyone reasonably to be expected to use product Alt. C: To person reasonably to be expected to use product or to his property	Physical harm to person or property of the ultimate user or consumer; judicial trend towards including bystanders
Type of Transaction	Sales; some courts apply to leases and bailments	Sales, leases, and bailments

CHAPTER SUMMARY

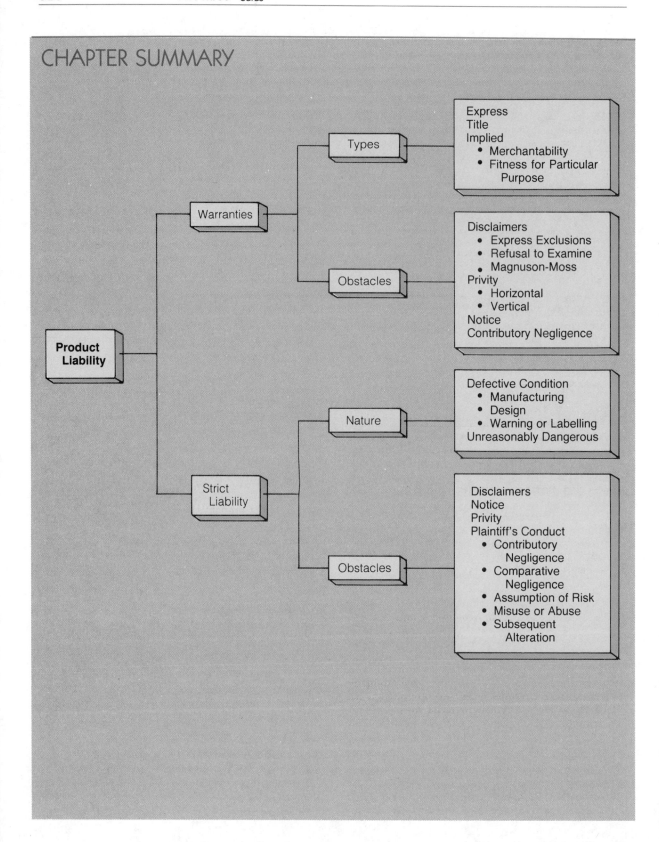

KEY TERMS

Warranty	Disclaimer	Strict liability in tort
Express warranty	As is	Defective condition
Caveat emptor	Magnuson-Moss Act	Manufacturing defect
Puffery	Privity	Design defect
Basis of the bargain	Horizontal privity	Inadequate labelling
Warranty of title	Vertical privity	Unreasonably dangerous
Implied warranty	Contributory negligence	Comparative negligence
Warranty of merchantability	Assumption of risk	Misuse or abuse
Warranty of fitness for a	Notice of breach	Subsequent alteration
particular purpose	402A	

PROBLEMS

1. At the start of the social season Aunt Lavinia purchased a hula skirt in Sadie's dress shop. The saleslady told her: "This superior garment will do things for a person." Aunt Lavinia's houseguest, her niece, Florabelle, asked and obtained her aunt's permission to wear the skirt to a masquerade ball. In the midst of the festivity, where there was much dancing, drinking, and smoking, the long skirt brushed against a glimmering cigarette butt. Unknown to Aunt Lavinia and Florabelle, its wearer, the garment was made of a fine unwoven fiber that is highly flammable. It burst into flames, and Florabelle suffered severe burns. Aunt Lavinia notified Sadie of the accident and of Florabelle's intention to recover from Sadie. Florabelle seeks to recover damages in an action against Sadie, the proprietor of the dress shop, and Exotic Clothes, Inc., the manufacturer from which Sadie purchased the skirt. Decision?

2. The X Company, manufacturer of a widely advertised and expensive perfume, sold a quantity of this product to Y, a retail druggist. A and B visited the store of Y, and A, desiring to make a gift to B, purchased a bottle of this perfume from Y, asking for it by its trade name. Y wrapped up the bottle and handed it directly to B. The perfume contained an injurious foreign chemical substance that upon the first use of the perfume by B, severely burned her face and caused a permanent facial disfigurement. What are the rights of B, if any, against A, Y, and the X Company?

3. Jane Doe, a housewife, purchased a bottle of "Bleach-All," a well-known brand, from Roe's combination service station and grocery store. When Jane Doe used the "Bleach-All," the clothes severely deteriorated due to an error made in mixing the chemicals

during manufacture of "Bleach-All." Jane Doe brings an action against Roe to recover damages. Decision?

4. A route salesman for Ideal Milk Company delivered a one-half gallon glass jug of milk to Allen's home. The next day when Allen grasped the milk container by its neck to take it out of his refrigerator, it shattered in his hand and caused serious injury. Allen paid Ideal on a monthly basis for the regular delivery of milk. Ideal's milk bottles each contained the legend "Property of Ideal—to be returned," and the route salesman would pick up the empty bottles when he delivered milk. Allen brought an action against Ideal Milk Company. Decision?

5. While Butler and his wife Wanda were browsing through Sloan's used car lot, Butler told Sloan that he was looking for a safe but cheap family car. Sloan said, "That old Cadillac hearse ain't hurt at all, and I'll sell it to you for $2,950." Butler said, "I'll have to take your word for it because I don't know a thing about cars." Butler asked Sloan whether he would guarantee the car, and Sloan replied. "I don't guarantee used cars." Then Sloan added, "But I have checked that Caddy over, and it will run another 10,000 miles without needing any repairs." Butler replied, "It has to because I won't have an extra dime for any repairs." Butler made a down payment of $400 and signed a printed form contract furnished by Sloan that contained a provision, "Seller does not warrant the merchandise's condition or performance of any used automobile described herein."

As Butler drove the car out of Sloan's lot, the left rear wheel fell off, and Butler lost control of the vehicle. It veered over an embankment, causing serious injuries to Wanda. What is Sloan's liability to Butler and Wanda?

6. John purchased for cash a Revenge automobile manufactured by Japanese Motors, Ltd., from an authorized franchised dealer in the United States. The dealer told John that the car had a "24 months—24,000 miles warranty." Two days after John accepted delivery of the car, he received an eighty-page manual in fine print that stated, among other things, on page 72:

> The warranties herein are expressly in lieu of any other express or implied warranty, including any implied-warranty of merchantability or fitness, and of any other obligation on the part of the company or the selling dealer.
>
> Japanese Motors, Ltd. and the selling dealer warrant to the owner each part of this vehicle to be free under use and service from defects in material and workmanship for a period of twenty-four months from the date of original retail delivery of first use, or until it has been driven for 24,000 miles, whichever first occurs.

Within nine months after the purchase, John has been forced to return the car for repairs to the dealer on thirty different occasions, and the car has been in the dealer's custody for over seventy days during these nine months. The dealer has been forced to make major repairs of the engine, transmission, and steering assembly. The car is now in the custody of the dealer for further major repairs, and John has demanded that it keep the car and refund his entire purchase price. The dealer has refused on the ground that it has not breached its contract and is willing to continue repairing the car during the remainder of the "24–24" period. What are the rights and liablities of the dealer and John?

7. Fred Lyon of New York, while on vacation in California, rented a 1985 model Home Run automobile from Hart's Drive-A-Car. The car was manufactured by the X Motor Company and was purchased by Hart's from Jammer, Inc., an automobile importer. Lyon was driving the car on a street in San Jose when, due to a defect in the steering mechanism, it suddenly became impossible to steer. The speed of the car at the time was thirty miles per hour, but before Lyon could bring it to a stop, the car jumped a low curb and struck Peter Wolf, who was standing on the sidewalk, breaking both of his legs and causing other injuries. Wolf sues Hart's Drive-A-Car, the X Motor Company, Jammer, Inc., and Lyon. Decisions?

8. Plaintiff brings this cause of action against a manufacturer for the loss of one leg below the hip. The leg was lost when caught in the gears of a screw auger machine sold and installed by the defendant. Shortly before the accident, plaintiff's co-employees had removed a covering panel from the machine by use of sledge-hammers and crowbars in order to do repair work. When finished, they replaced the panel with a single piece of cardboard instead of restoring the equipment to its original condition. The plaintiff stepped on the cardboard in the course of his work and fell, catching his leg in the moving parts. Decision?

9. The plaintiff, while driving a van manufactured by the defendant, was struck in the rear by another motor vehicle. Upon impact, the plaintiff's head was jarred backward against the rear window of the cab, causing the plaintiff serious injury. The van was not equipped with a headrest, and none was required at the time. Should the plaintiff prevail on a cause of action based upon strict liability in tort? Why?

10. Plaintiff, while dining at defendant's restaurant, ordered a chicken pot pie. While she was eating the food, she swallowed a sliver of chicken bone which became lodged in her throat, causing her serious injury. Plaintiff brings a cause of action. Should she prevail? Why?

20

PERFORMANCE

Performance of a contract is a realization of the expectations of the parties and a discharge of the duties created by the contract. The basic obligation of the seller in a contract for the sale of goods is to transfer and deliver the goods, and that of the buyer is to accept and pay for the goods in accordance with the contract.

The obligations of the parties are determined by their contractual agreement. Thus the contract of sale may expressly state whether the seller must deliver the goods before receiving payment of the price or whether the buyer must pay the price before receiving the goods. If the contract does not sufficiently cover the particulars of performance, these terms will be supplied by the Code, common law, course of dealings, usage of trade, and course of performance. In all events, both parties to the sales contract must perform their contractual obligations in good faith.

Before either party can maintain an action for nonperformance of the contract against the other, he must first put the other party in default. This is accomplished either by his (a) performance according to the contract, (b) tender of performance according to the contract, or (c) being excused from tender of performance. In this chapter we examine the performance obligations of the seller and the buyer as well as the circumstances under which they may be excused from performance of their contractual obligations.

Performance By The Seller

Unless the parties have agreed otherwise, the Code is explicit in requiring performance or tender of performance by one party as a condition to performance by the other party. Tender of conforming goods by the seller entitles him to acceptance of them by the buyer and to payment of the price according to the contract. The rights of the parties are fixed by the terms of the contract. For example, if the seller has agreed to sell goods on sixty or ninety days' credit, he is required to perform his part of the contract before the buyer performs.

Tender of delivery requires that the seller put and hold goods that conform to the contract at the buyer's disposition and that he give the buyer reasonable notification to enable him to take delivery. For example, Jim agrees to sell Joan a stereo system composed of a turntable, a receiver, a tape deck, and two speakers. Each component is specified by manufacturer and model

Performance–fulfillment of one's contractual obligations

Tender of delivery– seller makes available to buyer goods conforming to the contract and so notifies the buyer

329

number, and delivery is to be at Jim's store. Jim obtains the ordered equipment in accordance with the contractual specifications and notifies Joan that she may pick the system up at her convenience. Jim has now tendered and thus performed his obligations under the sales contract: he holds goods that conform to the contract, he has placed them at the buyer's disposition, and he has notified the buyer of their readiness.

Time and Manner of Delivery

Tender must be at a **reasonable** time, and the goods tendered must be kept available for the period reasonably necessary to enable the buyer to take possession of them. If no definite time for delivery is fixed by the terms of the contract, the seller is allowed a reasonable time after the making of the contract within which to deliver the goods to the buyer. Likewise, the buyer has a reasonable time within which to accept delivery. What length of time is reasonable depends on the facts and circumstances of each case. If the goods can be delivered immediately, a reasonable time would be very short. If the goods must be constructed or manufactured, however, a reasonable time would be longer and would depend on all the circumstances, including the usual length of time required to make the goods.

A contract is not performable piecemeal or in installments unless the parties so agree. All of the goods called for by a contract must be tendered in a single delivery, and payment is due on such tender.

Place of Tender

If the contract does not specify the place for delivery of the goods, the place for delivery is the **seller's place of business,** or if he has none, his residence. If the contract is for the sale of identified goods that the parties know at the time of making the contract are located elsewhere than the seller's place of business or residence, the *location* of the goods is then the place for delivery. For example, Arnold, a boat builder in Chicago, contracts to sell to Susan a certain yacht, which both parties know is anchored at Milwaukee. The place of delivery would be Milwaukee. On the other hand, if the contract provides that Arnold shall overhaul the motor at Arnold's shipyard in Chicago, Arnold would have to return the yacht to Chicago, and the place of delivery would be Arnold's Chicago shipyard.

As we discussed in Chapter 18, the parties frequently agree expressly on the place of delivery, typically by use of one of the various *delivery terms.* Such agreements determine the place where the seller must tender delivery of the goods.

Shipment Contracts

The delivery terms *F.O.B. place of shipment, F.A.S. seller's port, C.I.F., C.&F.,* and *C.O.D.* are all shipment contracts. Under a shipment contract the seller is required or authorized to send the goods to the buyer, but the contract does not obligate her to deliver them at a particular destination. In these cases the seller's tender of performance occurs at the **point of shipment,** provided the seller meets certain specified conditions designed to protect the interests of the absent buyer.

Under a shipment contract the seller is required to: (1) deliver the goods to a carrier; (2) make a contract for their transportation that is reasonable according to the nature of the goods and other circumstances of the case;

Shipment contract–seller is required to tender delivery of the goods to a carrier for delivery to buyer, buyer bears the expense and risk of loss

(3) obtain and promptly deliver or tender to the buyer any document necessary to enable the buyer to obtain possession of the goods from the carrier; and (4) promptly notify the buyer of the shipment.

Destination Contracts

The delivery terms *F.O.B. at city of buyer, ex-ship,* and *no arrival, no sale* are destination contracts. Since a destination contract requires the seller to tender *delivery* of conforming goods at a **specified destination,** the seller must place the goods at the buyer's disposition and give the buyer reasonable notice to enable him to take delivery. In addition, if the destination contract involves documents of title, the seller must tender the necessary documents.

> **Destination contract** – seller is required to tender delivery of the goods at a named destination, seller bears the expense and risk of loss

Goods Held by Bailee

Where goods are in the possession of a bailee and are to be delivered without being moved, in most instances the seller may either tender a document of title (symbol of ownership of the goods) or obtain an acknowledgment by the bailee of the buyer's right to possess the goods.

For a summary of performance by the seller, see Figure 20-1.

Quality of Tender

Perfect Tender Rule

The Code imposes on the seller the obligation that her tender of goods conform *exactly* to the requirements of the contract. The seller's tender cannot deviate in any way from the terms of the contract. If the goods or the tender of delivery fail in any respect to conform to the contract, the buyer may (1) reject the whole lot, (2) accept the whole lot, or (3) accept any commercial unit or units and reject the rest. A commercial unit means such a unit of goods as by commercial usage is a single unit and which, if divided, would materially impair its character or value.

> **Perfect tender rule** – seller's tender of performance must conform exactly to the contract

Thus, a buyer may rightfully reject the delivery of 110 dozen shirts under an agreement calling for delivery of 100 dozen shirts. The size or extent of the breach does *not* affect the right to reject. The following case further illustrates the perfect tender rule.

FACTS: Moulton Cavity & Mold Inc. agreed to manufacture twenty-six innersole molds to be purchased by Lyn-Flex. Moulton delivered the twenty-six molds to Lyn-Flex after Lyn-Flex allegedly approved the sample molds. Lyn-Flex rejected the molds, claiming that the molds did not satisfy the specifications exactly and denied that it had ever approved the sample molds. Moulton then sued, contending that Lyn-Flex wrongfully rejected the molds. Lyn-Flex argues that the Code's perfect tender rule permitted its rejection of the imperfect molds, regardless of Moulton's substantial performance.

DECISION: Judgment for Lyn-Flex. Under the Code's perfect tender provision, "if the goods or the tender of delivery fail in any respect to conform to the contract, the buyer may reject the whole." Therefore, Moulton's substantial performance does not obligate Lyn-Flex to accept the molds. If they failed to meet the contract's specifications in any respect, then Lyn-Flex was entitled to reject them without liability.

> **MOULTON CAVITY & MOLD INC. v. LYN-FLEX IND.**
>
> Supreme Court of Maine, 1979.
> 396 A.2d 1024.

Modifications of the Perfect Tender Rule

There are three basic modifications of the buyer's right to reject the goods if the seller fails to comply with the perfect tender rule: (1) agreement between

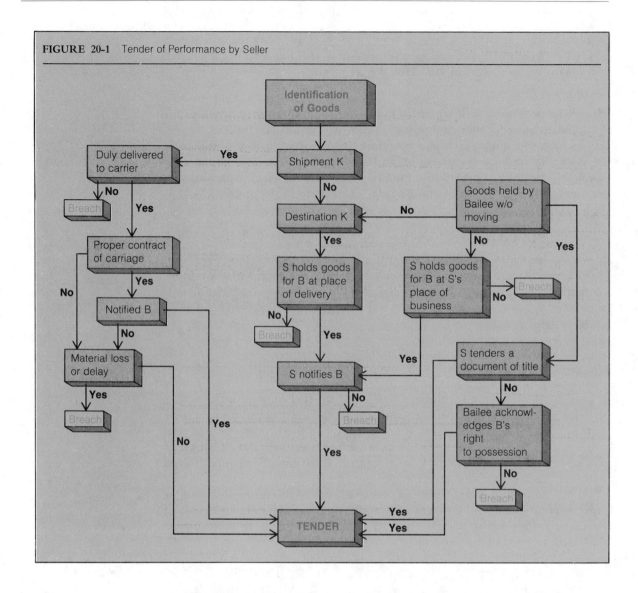

FIGURE 20-1   Tender of Performance by Seller

the parties limiting the buyer's right to reject nonconforming goods, (2) cure by the seller, and (3) installment contracts.

Agreement by the Parties   The parties may contractually agree to limit the operation of the perfect tender rule. For example, they may agree that the seller shall have the right to repair or replace any defective parts or goods. We discuss these contractual limitations in Chapter 21.

Cure by the Seller   Where the buyer refuses to accept a tender of goods that do not conform to the contract, the seller by acting promptly and within the time allowed for performance may make a proper tender or delivery of conforming goods and "cure" his defective tender or performance. For example, Neal is to deliver to Jessica twenty-five blue shirts and fifty white shirts by October 15. On October 1, Neal delivers twenty-nine blue shirts and forty-six white shirts which Jessica rejects as not conforming to the contract. Jessica notifies Neal of her rejection and the reasons for it. Neal has until October

Cure–remedy a nonconforming delivery (two methods)

15 to cure the defect by making a perfect tender if he seasonably notifies Jessica of his intention to do so.

The Code also provides the seller an opportunity to cure a nonconforming tender that the seller had reasonable grounds to believe would be acceptable with or without money allowance. If, on the buyer's notice of rejection, the seller seasonably notifies the buyer of his intention to cure, the seller is permitted a reasonable period of time to substitute a conforming tender. For example, Tim orders from Noel a model 110X television to be delivered on January 20. The 110X is unavailable, but Noel can obtain a model 110, which is last year's model of the same television and lists for 5 percent less than the 110X. On January 20, Noel delivers to Tim the 110 at a discount price of 10 percent less than the contract price for the 110X. Tim rejects the substituted television set. Noel promptly notifies Tim that she will obtain and deliver a model 110X. Noel will have a reasonable time beyond the January 20 deadline in which to deliver the 110X television set to Tim because under these facts Noel had reasonable grounds to believe the model 110 would be acceptable with the money allowance. See also *Wilson v. Scampoli* which follows.

FACTS: On November 4, 1965, Wilson purchased a color television set from Scampoli. When the set was delivered, installed, and turned on two days later, the picture had a reddish tinge. Scampoli's delivery man told Wilson's daughter, Mrs. Kolley, that he could not adjust the set but that a service representative would arrive in a couple of days to fix it. Mrs. Kolley then unplugged the set and did not use it.

On November 8, a service representative arrived but after an hour of work was unable to remove the red tinge from the picture. He told Mrs. Kolley that he would have to remove the chassis from the set and take it to his shop for a closer examination. Mrs. Kolley refused, demanding a brand new set rather than a repaired one. She then requested that her purchase price be returned. Scampoli refused, but he repeated his offer to repair the set, or if unable to do so, then to replace it.

DECISION: Judgment for Scampoli. When a buyer rejects a nonconforming tender that the seller had reasonable grounds to believe would be acceptable, the seller may, if he seasonably notifies the buyer, have a further reasonable time in which to substitute a conforming tender.

Here, Scampoli, a retail dealer, had reasonable grounds to believe that a television set arriving in its factory crate would be acceptable, and that if it was defective, then it would have the right to substitute conforming tender. Scampoli could cure the imperfect tender by repair, but only if that could be done without subjecting Wilson to any great inconvenience or loss. Since new televisions often must be removed for repairs, no such inconvenience was found, and Scampoli must be given an adequate opportunity to repair or to replace the set.

WILSON v. SCAMPOLI

District of Columbia Court of Appeals, 1967.
228 A.2d 848.

If the buyer refuses a tender of goods or rejects them as nonconforming without disclosing to the seller the nature of the defect, she may not assert such defect as an excuse for not accepting the goods or as a breach of contract by the seller if the defect is curable.

Installment Contracts Unless the parties have otherwise agreed, the buyer does not have to pay any part of the price of the goods until the entire quantity specified in the contract has been delivered or tendered to her. An installment contract is an instance where the parties have otherwise agreed. It expressly provides for delivery of the goods in separate lots or installments and usually for payment of the price in installments. If the contract is silent about payment, the Code provides that the price, if it can be apportioned, may be demanded for each lot.

Installment contract goods are delivered in separate lots

The buyer may reject any nonconforming installment if the nonconformity *substantially* impairs the value of that *installment* and cannot be cured. When the installment does substantially impair the value of the installment but not the value of the entire contract and the seller gives adequate assurance of the installment's cure, then the buyer cannot reject the installment. Whenever the nonconformity or default of one or more of the installments substantially impairs the value of the *whole contract*, the buyer can treat the breach as a breach of the whole contract.

Performance By The Buyer

A buyer is obliged to accept conforming goods and to pay for them according to the contract terms. Tender of payment or payments by the buyer, unless otherwise agreed, is a condition to the seller's duty to tender and to complete any delivery. Thus, if the buyer has agreed to pay for the goods in advance of delivery either to the seller or to a carrier, his duty to perform is not conditional on performance or a tender of performance by the seller. Tender of payment in the form of a check in the ordinary course of business is sufficient unless the seller demands cash and allows the buyer a reasonable time within which to obtain it.

Inspection

Inspection–examination of the goods to determine whether they conform to the contract

Unless otherwise agreed between the parties, the buyer has a right to inspect the goods before payment or acceptance. This enables him to satisfy himself that the goods tendered or delivered conform to the contract. If the contract requires payment before acceptance, such as where the contract provides for shipment C.O.D., payment must be made prior to inspection. However, payment in such case is not an acceptance of the goods.

The buyer is allowed a reasonable time to inspect the goods. He may lose the right to reject or revoke acceptance of nonconforming goods by failing to inspect them within a reasonable time. Although the expenses of inspection must be borne by the buyer, they may be recovered from the seller if the goods do not conform and are rejected.

Rejection

Rejection–manifestation of an unwillingness to accept the goods

Rejection is a manifestation by the buyer of his unwillingness to become owner of the goods. It must be made within a reasonable time after the goods have been tendered or delivered and is not effective unless the buyer seasonably notifies the seller.

Rejection of the goods may be rightful or wrongful, depending on whether the goods tendered or delivered conform to the contract. The buyer's rejection of nonconforming goods or tender is rightful under the perfect tender rule.

After the buyer has rejected the goods, any exercise of ownership of the goods by her is not allowed. If the buyer possesses the rejected goods but has no security interest in them, she is obliged to hold them with reasonable care for a time sufficient to permit the seller to remove them. The buyer who is not a merchant is under no further obligation with regard to goods rightfully rejected.

A merchant buyer of goods who has rightfully rejected them is obligated to follow reasonable instructions from the seller about disposing of the goods in her possession or control, when the seller has no agent or business at the place of rejection. If the merchant buyer receives no instructions from the seller within a reasonable time after notice of the rejection, and the rejected goods are perishable or threaten to decline in value speedily, she is obligated to make reasonable efforts to sell them for the seller's account. Otherwise, she may (1) store the goods for the seller's account, (2) reship them to the seller, or (3) resell them for the seller's account. Such action is not an acceptance of the goods.

CAN-KEY INDUSTRIES, INC. v. INDUSTRIAL LEASING CORP.

Supreme Court of Oregon, 1979.
286 Or. 173, 593 P.2d 1125.

FACTS: Can-Key Industries, Inc. manufactured a turkey hatching unit which it sold to Industrial Leasing Corporation (ILC), which leased it to Rose-A-Linda Turkey Farms. ILC conditioned its obligation to pay on Rose-A-Linda's acceptance of the equipment. Rose-A-Linda indicated its dissatisfaction with the equipment, and ILC refused to perform its obligations under the contract. Can-Key then brought suit against ILC for breach of contract. It argued that Rose-A-Linda accepted the equipment since it used it for fifteen months between March 1976 and May 1977. ILC contended that the equipment was unacceptable and asked that it be removed. It claimed that Can-Key refused and failed to instruct Rose-A-Linda to refrain from using the equipment. Therefore, ILC argued, Rose-A-Linda effectively rejected the turkey hatching unit, relieving ILC of its contractual obligations.

DECISION: Judgment for ILC. Since ILC's acceptance was conditioned upon the acceptance by its lessee, Rose-A-Linda, it was only obligated to pay for the unit if Rose-A-Linda accepted it. Under the Code, Rose-A-Linda accepted the unit only if it either: (1) failed to make an effective rejection after a reasonable opportunity to inspect it or (2) performed any act inconsistent with Can-Key's ownership of it. Rose-A-Linda twice notified Can-Key that the equipment was unacceptable and asked that it be removed, which constituted an effective rejection. Furthermore, the fifteen months' use related to Rose-A-Linda's initial inspection of the equipment and Can-Key's subsequent efforts to remedy the "bugs." During this time, Can-Key did not instruct Rose-A-Linda to refrain from using the equipment nor does it argue that Rose-A-Linda's own tests and modifications damaged the equipment in any way. Therefore, Rose-A-Linda did not perform any act inconsistent with Can-Key's ownership. Since Rose-A-Linda did not accept the turkey hatching unit, ILC is under no duty to pay.

When the buyer sells the rejected goods, she is entitled to reimbursement from the seller or out of the proceeds for the reasonable expenses of caring for and selling them and a reasonable selling commission not to exceed 10 percent of the gross proceeds.

Acceptance

Acceptance of goods means a willingness by the buyer to become the owner of the goods tendered or delivered to him by the seller. Acceptance of the goods precludes any rejection of the goods accepted. It includes overt acts or conduct that manifest such willingness. Acceptance may be indicated by express words, by the presumed intention of the buyer through his failure to act, or, as shown by the case which follows, by conduct of the buyer inconsistent with the seller's ownership of the goods. More specifically, acceptance occurs when the buyer, after a reasonable opportunity to inspect the goods, (1) signifies to the seller that the goods conform to the contract, (2) signifies to the seller that he will take the goods or retain them in spite of their nonconformity to the contract, or (3) fails to make an effective rejection of the goods.

Acceptance–willingness to become owner of the goods

IMPORT TRADERS,
INC. v. FREDERICK
MANUFACTURING
CORP.

Civil Court of the City of
New York, Kings County,
1983.
117 Misc.2d 305, 457
N.Y.S.2d 742.

FACTS: Frederick Manufacturing Corp. ordered 500 dozen units of Import Traders' rubber pads for $2,580. The order indicated that the pads should be "as soft as possible." Import Traders delivered the rubber pads to Frederick Manufacturing on November 19, 1981. Frederick failed to inspect the goods upon delivery even though the parties recognized that there might be a problem with the softness. Frederick finally complained about the nonconformity of the pads in April, 1982, when Import Traders requested the contract price for the goods. Import Traders then sued Frederick to recover the contract price.

DECISION: Judgment for Import Traders. Under the Code the contract price may be recovered by a seller when a buyer accepts the goods. Here, acceptance occurred when Frederick failed to make an effective rejection after having had a reasonable opportunity to inspect the pads. Its five-month silence after receiving the goods, which at the time of ordering were of questionable quality, constituted acceptance. Therefore, Import Traders is entitled to recover the $2,580 contract price for the rubber pads.

The buyer must pay at the contract rate for any goods accepted but may recover damages for any nonconformity of the goods, provided the buyer reasonably notifies the seller of any breach.

Acceptance of any part of a commercial unit is acceptance of the entire unit.

Revocation of Acceptance

**Revocation of accept-
ance**–rescission of one's
acceptance of goods based
upon the nonconformity of
the goods which substan-
tially impairs their value

The buyer may revoke his acceptance of goods that do not conform to the contract if the nonconformity *substantially* impairs the value of the goods to him, provided that his acceptance was: (1) premised on the reasonable assumption that the nonconformity would be cured by the seller, and it was not seasonably cured; or (2) made without discovery of the nonconformity, and such acceptance was reasonably induced by the difficulty of discovery before acceptance or by assurances of the seller. The test of substantial impairment of the value to the buyer of nonconforming goods is *subjective* rather than objective.

Revocation of acceptance is not effective until notification is given to the seller. This must be done within a reasonable time after the buyer discovers or should have discovered the grounds for revocation and before the goods have undergone any substantial change not caused by their own defects. On revocation of acceptance, the buyer is in the same position with respect to the goods and has the same rights and duties with regard to them as if she had rejected them.

The following case summarizes the right of revocation of acceptance.

PECKHAM v. LARSEN
CHEVROLET

Supreme Court of Idaho,
1978.
99 Idaho 675, 587 P.2d 816.

FACT: On March 17, 1976, Peckham bought a new car from Larsen Chevrolet for $6,400.85. During the first one-and-one-half months after the purchase, Peckham discovered that the car's hood was dented, its gas tank contained no baffles, its emergency brake was inoperable, the car did not have a jack or a spare tire, and neither the clock nor the speedometer worked. Larsen claimed that Peckham knew of the defects at the time of the purchase. Peckham, on the other hand, claimed that despite his repeated efforts the defects were not repaired until June 11, 1976. Then, on July 15 the car's dashboard caught fire, leaving the car's interior damaged and the car itself inoperable. Peckham then returned to Larsen Chevrolet and told Larsen that he had to repair the car at its own expense or he, Peckham, would either rescind the contract or demand a new automobile. Peckham also claimed that at the end of their conversation he notified Larsen

Chevrolet that he was electing to rescind the contract and demanded the return of the purchase price. Larsen denied having received that oral notification. On October 12, 1976, Peckham sent a written notice of rescission to Larsen.

DECISION: Judgment for Peckham. Although Peckham sought the common law remedy of rescission, the relief sought was equivalent to the Code concept of revocation of acceptance. For Peckham to revoke his acceptance, he had to show 1) that the car was nonconforming; 2) that the nonconformity substantially impaired the value of the car; 3) that if Peckham knew of the defects when he accepted delivery of the car, then he acted under a reasonable assumption that they would be repaired and they were not; 4) that if he did not know of the defects when he accepted delivery of the car, then he must show that his acceptance was reasonably induced either by the difficulty of discovering the defects before acceptance or by Larsen's assurances; 5) that his revocation of acceptance occurred within a reasonable time after he discovered or should have discovered the defect and before any substantial change in the condition of the car not caused by its own defects; and 6) that he notified Larsen Chevrolet of the revocation, at which time the revocation became effective.

Obligation of Payment

The terms of the contract may expressly state the time and place that the buyer is obligated to pay for the goods. If so, these terms are controlling. In the absence of agreement, payment is due at the time and place where the buyer is to receive the goods even though the place of shipment is the place of delivery. This rule is understandable in view of the right of the buyer to inspect the goods before being obliged to pay for them in the absence of agreement to the contrary.

Where the sale is on credit, the buyer is not obligated to pay for the goods when he receives them. The credit provision in the contract will control the time of payment.

Excuses For Nonperformance

Contracts for the sale of goods necessarily involve risks that future events may or may not occur. In some instances the parties explicitly allocate these risks, but in most instances they do not. The Code contains three sections that allocate these risks when the parties fail to do so themselves. Each provision, when applicable, relieves the parties from the obligation of full performance under the sales contract.

Casualty to Identified Goods

If goods are destroyed before an offer to sell or buy them is accepted, the offer is terminated by general contract law. But what if the goods are destroyed after the sales contract is formed? With one exception, the rules for the passage of risk of loss apply: if the contract is for goods that are identified when the contract was made, and these goods are totally lost or damage without fault of either party and before the risk of loss passes to the buyer, the contract is avoided. This means that the seller is no longer obligated to deliver and the buyer need not pay the price. Each party is excused from his performance obligation under the contract.

In the case of a partial destruction or deterioration of the goods, the buyer has the option to avoid the contract or to accept the goods with due allowance or deduction from the contract price for the deterioration or de-

Identified goods–designated goods as a part of a particular contract

ficiency in quantity. Thus, A agrees to sell to B a specific lot of wheat containing 1,000 bushels at a price of four dollars per bushel. Without the fault of A or B fire destroys 300 bushels of the wheat. B does not have to take the remaining 700 bushels of wheat, but he has the option to do so upon paying $2,800, the price of 700 bushels.

If the destruction or casualty to the goods, whether total or partial, occurs after risk of loss has passed to the buyer, the buyer must pay the entire contract price of the goods.

Non-Happening of Presupposed Condition

The ability to perform a contract for the sale of goods is subject to a number of possible hazards, such as strikes, lockouts, unforeseen shutdown of sources of supply, and loss of plant or machinery by fire or other casualty. Ordinarily these do not operate as an excuse on the ground of impossibility of performance, unless the contract expressly so provides. However, both parties may have understood at the time the contract was made that its performance depended on the existence of certain facilities or that the purpose of the contract and the value of performance depended entirely on the happening of a specific future contemplated event. In such a case the seller is excused from her duty of performance on the nonoccurrence of presupposed conditions that were a basic assumption of the contract, unless the seller has expressly assumed the risk.

Increased production cost alone does not excuse performance by the seller, nor does a collapse of the market for the goods excuse the buyer. However, a contract for the sale of programs for a scheduled Superbowl that is called off, for the sale of tin horns for export that become subject to embargo, or for the production of goods at a designated factory that becomes damaged or destroyed by fire would be an excuse for nonperformance.

Although the seller may be relieved of her contractual duty by the non-happening of presupposed conditions, if the contingency affects only a part of the seller's capacity to perform, she must to the extent of her remaining capacity allocate delivery and production among her customers.

Substituted Performance

The Code provides that where neither party is at fault and the agreed manner of delivery of the goods becomes commercially impracticable, for example, because of the failure of loading or unloading facilities, or the unavailability of an agreed type of carrier, a substituted manner of performance, if commercially reasonable, must be tendered and accepted. Neither seller nor buyer is excused on the ground that delivery in the express manner provided in the contract is impossible where a practical alternative or substitute exists.

If the means or manner in which the buyer is to make payment becomes impossible because of subsequent governmental regulation, the seller may withhold or stop delivery of the goods unless the buyer provides payment that is commercially a substantial equivalent to that required by the contract. If delivery has already been made, payment as provided by the governmental regulation discharges the buyer unless the regulation is discriminatory, oppressive, or predatory.

CHAPTER SUMMARY

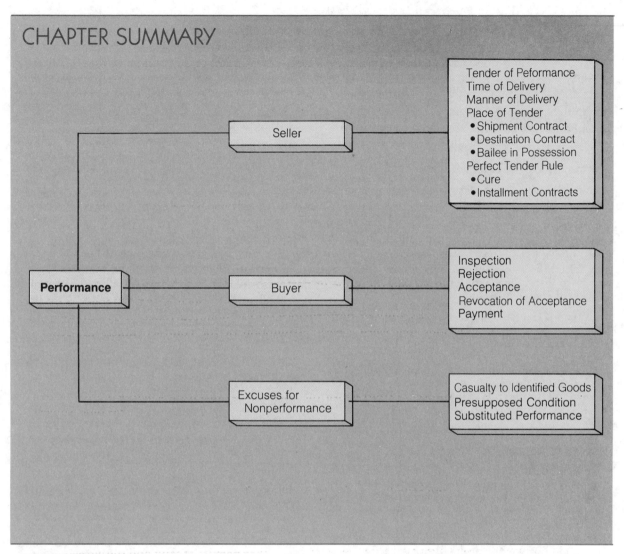

Performance

Seller
- Tender of Peformance
- Time of Delivery
- Manner of Delivery
- Place of Tender
  - Shipment Contract
  - Destination Contract
  - Bailee in Possession
- Perfect Tender Rule
  - Cure
  - Installment Contracts

Buyer
- Inspection
- Rejection
- Acceptance
- Revocation of Acceptance
- Payment

Excuses for Nonperformance
- Casualty to Identified Goods
- Presupposed Condition
- Substituted Performance

KEY TERMS

Performance
Tender of delivery
Shipment contract
Destination contract
Bailee
Perfect tender rule

Commercial unit
Cure
Installment contract
Inspection
Rejection
Acceptance

Revocation of acceptance
Casualty
Identified goods
Presupposed condition
Substituted performance

PROBLEMS

1. A contracted with B to manufacture, sell, and deliver to B and put in running order a certain machine. A set up the machine and put it in running order. B found it unsatisfactory and notified A that she rejected the machine. She continued to use it for three months, but continually complained of its defective condition. At the end of the three months she notified A to come and get it. Has B lost her right (a) to reject the machine? (b) to revoke acceptance of the machine?

2. Smith, having contracted to sell to Beyer thirty tons of described fertilizer, shipped to Beyer by carrier thirty tons of fertilizer that he stated conformed to the contract. Nothing was stated in the contract as to time to payment, but Smith demanded payment as a condition of handing the fertilizer over to Beyer. Beyer refused to pay unless he were given the opportunity to inspect the fertilizer. Smith sues Beyer for breach of contract. Decision?

3. A and B entered into a contract for the sale of 100 barrels of flour. No mention was made of any place of delivery. Thereafter, B demanded that A should deliver the flour at B's place of business, and A demanded that B should come and take the flour from A's place of business. Neither party acceded to the demand of the other. Has either one a right of action against the other?

4. A, a manufacturer of air conditioning units, made a written contract with B to sell and deliver to B forty units at a price of $200 each and to deliver them at a certain apartment building owned by B for installation by B. On the arrival of A's truck for delivery at the apartment building, B examined the units on the truck, counted only thirty units, and asked the driver if that was the total delivery. The driver replied that it was as far as he knew. B told the driver that she would not accept delivery of the units. The next day A telephoned B and inquired why delivery was refused. B stated that the units on the truck were not what she ordered in that she ordered forty units and that only thirty were tendered, and that she was going to buy air conditioning units elsewhere. In an action by A against B for breach of contract, B defends on the ground that the tender of thirty units was improper as the contract called for delivery of forty units. Is this a valid defense?

5. S sells a sofa to B for $800. S and B both know that the sofa is in S's warehouse located approximately ten miles from B's home. The contract did not specify the place of delivery, and B insists that the place of delivery is either B's house or S's store. Is B correct?

6. On November 4, S contracted to sell to B 500 sacks of flour at four dollars each to be shipped in November to B in X City. On November 27, S shipped the flour. By December 5, when the car arrived, containing only 450 sacks, the market price of flour had fallen. The usual time required for shipment was five to twelve days. B refused to accept delivery or to pay. S shipped 50 more sacks of flour, which arrived December 10. B refused delivery. S resold the flour for three dollars per sack. What are S's rights against B?

7. A and B entered into a written contract whereby A agreed to sell and B to buy 6,000 bushels of wheat at $3.75 per bushel, deliverable at the rate of 1,000 bushels a month commencing June 1, the price for each installment being payable ten days after delivery thereof. A delivered and received payment for the June installment. A defaulted by failing to deliver the July and August installments. By August 15, the market price of wheat had increased to four dollars per bushel. B thereupon entered into a contract with C to purchase 5,000 bushels of wheat at four dollars per bushel deliverable over the ensuing four months. In late September, the market price of wheat started to decline and by December 1 was $3.25 per bushel. B brings an action against A for breach of contract. Decision?

8. Bain ordered from Marcum a carload of lumber, which he intended to use in the construction of small boats for the U.S. Navy pursuant to contract. The order specified that the lumber was to be free from knots, wormholes, and defects. The lumber was shipped, and immediately on receipt Bain looked into the door of the fully loaded car, ascertained that there was a full carload of lumber, and acknowledged to Marcum that the carload had been received. On the same day Bain moved the car to his private siding and sent to Marcum full payment in accordance with the terms of the order.

A day later the car was moved to the work area and unloaded in the presence of the Navy inspector, who refused to allow three-fourths of it to be used because of excessive knots and wormholes in the lumber. Bain then informed Marcum that he was rejecting the order and requested refund of the payment and directions as to disposition of the lumber. Marcum replied that since Bain had accepted the order and unloaded it, he was not entitled to return of the purchase price. Bain thereupon brought an action against Marcum to recover the purchase price. Decision?

21

REMEDIES

A contract for the sale of goods may be completely performed at one time or performed in stages, according to the agreement made. At any stage one of the parties may breach or repudiate the contract or become insolvent. Breach may occur when the goods are in the possession of the seller while identified to the contract, in the possession of a bailee of the buyer, in transit to the buyer, or in the possession of the buyer. Moreover, the goods may conform or may not conform to the contract. The buyer may have justifiably or unjustifiably rejected the goods on tender or delivery or revoked his acceptance of them. Remedies, therefore, are necessary to address not only the type of breach of contract but also the factual situation with respect to the goods. Consequently, the Code provides separate and distinct remedies for the seller and for the buyer, each specifically keyed to the factual situation.

In all events, the purpose of the Code is to put the aggrieved party in as good a position as if the other party had fully performed. Therefore the Code has rejected the doctrine of election of remedies. Essentially, the Code provides that remedies for breach are cumulative. Whether one remedy bars another depends entirely on the facts of the individual case.

Remedies of the Seller

When a buyer defaults in any of his contractual obligations, the seller has been deprived of the rights for which he bargained. The buyer's default may consist of any of the following acts: the buyer wrongfully rejects the goods; the buyer wrongfully revokes acceptance of the goods; the buyer fails to make a payment due on or before delivery; or the buyer repudiates the contract in whole or in part. The Code catalogs the seller's remedies for each of these defaults. These remedies are:

1. to withhold delivery of the goods;
2. to stop delivery of the goods by a carrier or other bailee;
3. to identify conforming goods to the contract not already identified;
4. to resell the goods and recover damages;
5. to recover damages for nonacceptance of the goods or repudiation of the contract;

6. to recover the price;

7. to recover incidental damages;

8. to cancel the contract; and

9. to reclaim the goods on the buyer's insolvency.

It is useful to note that the first three and the ninth remedies indexed above are **goods oriented**—that is, they relate to the seller's exercising control over the goods. The fourth through seventh remedies are **money oriented** because they provide the seller with the opportunity to recover monetary damages. The eighth remedy is **obligation oriented** because it allows the seller to avoid his obligation under the contract.

Moreover, if the seller delivers goods on credit and the buyer fails to pay the price when due, the seller's sole remedy, unless the buyer is insolvent, is to sue for the unpaid price. If, however, the buyer received the goods on credit while insolvent, the seller may be able to reclaim the goods. **Insolvency** is defined by the Code to include both its equity meaning and its bankruptcy meaning. The **equity** meaning of insolvency is the inability of a person to pay his debts in the ordinary course of business or as they become due. The **bankruptcy** meaning is that total liabilities exceed the total value of all assets.

As noted, the Code's remedies are **cumulative.** Thus, by way of example, an aggrieved seller may (1) identify goods to the contract, *and* (2) withhold delivery, *and* (3) resell or recover damages for nonacceptance or recover the price, *and* (4) recover incidental damages, *and* (5) cancel the contract.

Insolvency (equity) –inability to pay debts in ordinary course of business or as they become due

Insolvency (bankruptcy) –total liabilities exceed total value of assets

To Withhold Delivery of the Goods

A seller may withhold delivery of the goods to a buyer who has wrongfully rejected or revoked acceptance of the goods, who has failed to make a payment due on or before delivery, or who has repudiated the contract. This right is essentially that of a seller to withhold or discontinue performance of her side of the contract because of the buyer's breach.

Where the contract calls for installments, any breach of an installment that impairs the value of the *whole* contract will permit the seller to withhold the entire undelivered balance of the goods. In addition, on discovery of the buyer's insolvency, the seller may refuse to deliver the goods except for cash, including payment for all goods previously delivered under the contract.

To Stop Delivery of the Goods

An extension of the right to withhold delivery is the right of an aggrieved seller to stop delivery of the goods in transit to the buyer or in the possession of a bailee. The seller accomplishes this by timely notification to the carrier or other bailee to stop delivery of the goods. After this notification the carrier or bailee must hold and deliver the goods according to the directions of the seller, who is liable to the carrier or bailee for any charges or damages incurred.

If the seller discovers that the buyer is insolvent, then the seller may stop *any* delivery. If the buyer is not insolvent but repudiates or otherwise breaches the contract, the seller may stop carload, truckload, planeload, or larger shipments.

The right of the seller to stop delivery ceases when (1) the buyer receives the goods; or (2) the bailee of the goods, except a carrier, acknowledges to the buyer that he holds them for the buyer; or (3) the carrier acknowledges to the buyer that he holds them for the buyer by reshipment or as warehouser;

or (4) a negotiable document of title covering the goods is negotiated to the buyer.

To Identify Goods to the Contract

On a breach of the contract by the buyer, the seller may proceed to identify to the contract conforming goods in her possession or control that were not so identified at the time she learned of the breach. Furthermore, the seller may resell any unfinished goods that have demonstrably been intended for fulfillment of the particular contract. The seller may either complete the manufacture of unfinished goods and identify them to the contract or cease their manufacture and resell the unfinished goods for scrap or salvage value. In so deciding, the seller must exercise reasonable judgment to minimize her loss.

To Resell the Goods and Recover Damages

Under the same circumstances that permit the seller to withhold delivery of goods to the buyer (i.e., wrongful rejection or revocation, repudiation, or failure to make timely payment), the seller may resell the goods concerned or the undelivered balance of the goods. If the resale is made in good faith and in a commercially reasonable manner, the seller may recover from the buyer the **difference between the resale price and the contract price,** *together* with any incidental damages (discussed below), *less* expenses saved in consequence of the buyer's breach. For example, A agrees to sell goods to B for a contract price of $8,000 due on delivery. B wrongfully rejects the goods and refuses to pay A anything. A resells the goods in strict compliance with the Code for $6,000 and incurs incidental damages for sales commissions of $500 but saves $200 in transportation costs. A would recover from B the contract price ($8,000) minus the resale price ($6,000) plus incidental damages ($500) minus expenses saved ($200) which equals $2,300.

The resale may be a public or private sale, and the goods may be sold as a unit or in parcels. The goods resold must be identified as those related to the contract, but it is not necessary that the goods be in existence or that they have been identified to the contract before the buyer's breach.

Where the resale is a private sale, the seller must give the buyer reasonable notice of his intention to resell. Where the resale is at a public sale, only identified goods can be sold except where there is a recognized market for a public sale of future goods of the kind involved. The public sale must be made at a usual place or market for public sale if one is reasonably available. The seller must give the buyer reasonable notice of the time and place of the resale unless the goods are perishable or threaten to decline in value speedily. Prospective bidders at the sale must be given an opportunity for reasonable inspection of the goods before the sale. The seller may be a purchaser of the goods at the public sale.

The seller is not accountable to the buyer for any profit made on any resale of the goods. Moreover, a *bona fide* purchaser at a resale takes the goods free of any rights of the original buyer, even though the seller has failed to comply with one or more of the requirements of the Code in making the resale.

To Recover Damages for Nonacceptance or Repudiation

The seller, in the event of the buyer's repudiation, failure to make timely payment, or wrongful rejection or revocation, may recover damages from the buyer measured by the **difference between the market price** at the time and place of tender of the goods **and the unpaid contract price,** *plus* incidental damages, *less* expenses saved in consequence of the buyer's breach. This remedy is an alternative to the remedy of reselling the goods.

For example, Joyce in Seattle agrees to sell goods to Maynard in Chicago for $20,000 F.O.B. Chicago, delivery on June 15. Maynard wrongfully rejects the goods. The market price would be ascertained as of June 15 in Chicago because F.O.B. Chicago is a destination contract in which the place of tender would be Chicago. The market price of the goods on June 15 in Chicago is $15,000. Joyce incurred $1,000 in incidental expenses while saving $500 in expenses. Joyce's recovery from Maynard would be the contract price ($20,000), minus the market price ($15,000), plus incidental damages ($1,000), minus expenses saved ($500), which equals $5,500.

If the difference between the market price and the contract price will not place the seller in as good a position as performance would have, then the measure of damages is the profit, including reasonable overhead, that the seller would have realized from full performance by the buyer, plus any incidental damages less expenses saved in consequence of the buyer's breach. For example, A, an automobile dealer, enters into a contract to sell a large, fuel inefficient luxury car to B for $22,000. The price of gasoline increases 20 percent, and B repudiates. The market value of the car is still $22,000, but because A cannot sell as many cars as he can obtain, A's sales volume has decreased by one due to B's breach. Therefore, A would be permitted to recover the profits he lost on the sale to B (computed as the contract price minus what the car costs A plus an allocation of overhead), plus any incidental damages. The following case explains the computation of lost profits.

**TERADYNE, INC. v.
TELEDYNE
INDUSTRIES, INC.**

United States Court of Appeals, First Circuit, 1982. 676 F.2d 865.

FACTS: Teledyne Industries, Inc. entered into a contract with Teradyne, Inc. to purchase a T-347A transistor test system for the list and fair market price of $98,400 less a discount of $984. After the system was packed for shipment, Teledyne cancelled the order, offering to purchase a Field Effects Transistor System for $65,000. Teradyne refused the offer. Teradyne then sold the T-347A to another purchaser pursuant to an order that was on hand prior to cancellation. Teradyne then sued Teledyne for breach of contract.

DECISION: Judgment for Teradyne permitting recovery of lost profits. The Code permits an aggrieved seller to recover the difference between the unpaid contract price and the market price. Under this rule, Teradyne would recover nothing because the market price exceeded the contract price. However, the Code also states that this rule does *not* apply if it is inadequate to put the seller in as good a position as performance would have done. In such an instance the measure of damages is the expected profit on the broken contract. Here, Teradyne would have made the sale to the resale purchaser even if Teledyne had not breached its contract. Teradyne is a "lost volume seller" and thus entitled to recover from Teledyne its expected profit (including reasonable overhead) on the broken contract despite the resale.

The formula for determining lost profit is the contract price minus the direct costs of producing and selling the goods, provided that all variable expenses are identified. Here, Teradyne paid wages (including fringe benefits equal to 12 percent of wages) to its testers, shippers, installers and other employees who directly handled the T-347A. These costs are not considered part of Teradyne's overhead. Rather, they are "direct costs" and, therefore, should be deducted from the contract price to determine Teradyne's recovery of lost profit.

To Recover the Price

Under the common law an action by the seller to recover the price depended on a transfer of title to the buyer. The Code permits the seller to recover the price in three situations: (1) where the buyer has accepted the goods; (2) where conforming goods have been lost or damaged after the risk of loss has passed to the buyer; and (3) where the goods have been identified to the contract and there is no ready market available for their resale at a reasonable price.

A seller who sues for the price must hold for the buyer any goods that have been identified to the contract and are still in her control. If resale becomes possible, the seller may resell the goods at any time before the collection of the judgment, and the net proceeds of such resale must be credited to the buyer. Payment of the judgment entitles the buyer to any goods not resold.

FACTS: On March 22 and 25, French bid on and bought eight antique guns from Sotheby & Co., a London-based auctioneer, for 10,480 pounds. On May 6, French made a payment on the account of 1571 pounds leaving a balance due of 8909 pounds. She did not take possession of the guns, however, and subsequently refused to pay the balance due. Sotheby & Co. brought this action for the balance due on the sale price.

DECISION: Judgment for French. When French wrongfully rejected the guns, Sotheby & Co. had the option of recovering damages for nonacceptance or, in a proper case, maintaining an action for the price. Sotheby & Co. elected to pursue the latter alternative. An action for the price, however, is available only when the goods were accepted, were lost after risk of loss passed to the buyer, or the seller was unable to resell them at a reasonable price. Passage of title is irrelevant in this regard. Here, however, Sotheby & Co. failed to show any of these alternatives and thus could not maintain an action for the price. Rather, its available remedy was limited to recovering damages for nonacceptance.

FRENCH v. SOTHEBY & CO.

Supreme Court of Oklahoma, 1970.
470 P.2d 318.

To Recover Incidental Damages

In addition to recovering damages for the difference between the resale price and the contract price, or recovering damages for nonacceptance or repudiation, or recovering the price, the seller may also recover in the same action her incidental damages. Incidental damages are defined to include any commercially reasonable charges, expenses, or commissions incurred in stopping delivery; in the transportation, care, and custody of goods after the buyer's breach; in connection with return or resale of the goods; or otherwise resulting from the breach.

Incidental damages–expenses directly resulting from breach

To Cancel the Contract

Where the buyer wrongfully rejects or revokes acceptance of the goods, or fails to make a payment due on or before delivery, or repudiates the contract in whole or in part, the seller may cancel the part of the contract that concerns the goods directly affected. If the breach is of an installment contract and it substantially impairs the whole contract, the seller may cancel the entire contract.

The Code defines cancellation as the putting an end to the contract by one party by reason of a breach by the other. The obligation of the canceling

Cancellation–putting an end to a contract by one party because of a breach by other party

party for any future performance under the contract is discharged, although he retains any remedy for breach of the whole contract or any unperformed balance. Thus, if the seller has the right to cancel, he may recover damages for breach without having to tender any further performance.

To Reclaim the Goods upon the Buyer's Insolvency

In addition to the right of an unpaid seller to withhold and stop delivery of the goods, he may reclaim them from an insolvent buyer by demand made to the buyer within ten days after the buyer has received the goods. Moreover, where the buyer has committed fraud by a misrepresentation of her solvency made to the seller in writing within three months prior to delivery of the goods, the ten-day limitation does not apply.

The seller's right to reclaim, however, is subject to the rights of a purchaser of the goods from the buyer in ordinary course of business or other good faith purchaser. If a seller successfully reclaims the goods from an insolvent buyer, he is excluded from all other remedies with respect to those goods.

Remedies of the Buyer

There are basically three different ways in which a seller may default: he may repudiate; he may fail to deliver the goods without repudiation; or he may deliver or tender goods that do not conform to the contract. The Code provides remedies for each of these breaches. Some remedies are available for all of these types of breaches, whereas others are available only for certain types. Moreover, some remedies must be triggered by certain actions taken by the buyer. For example, if the seller tenders nonconforming goods, the buyer may reject or accept them. If the buyer rejects them, he can choose from a number of remedies. On the other hand, if the buyer accepts the nonconforming goods and does not justifiably revoke his acceptance, he limits himself to recovering damages.

Where the seller fails to make delivery or repudiates, or the buyer rightfully rejects or justifiably revokes acceptance, the buyer may with respect to any goods involved, or with respect to the whole if the breach goes to the whole contract, (1) cancel *and* (2) recover payments made. In addition, the buyer may (3) "cover" and have damages *or* (4) recover damages for nondelivery. Where the seller fails to deliver or repudiates, the buyer where appropriate may also (5) recover identified goods if the seller is insolvent, *or* (6) "replevy" the goods, *or* (7) obtain specific performance. Moreover, on rightful rejection or justifiable revocation of acceptance, the buyer (8) has a security interest in the goods. Where the buyer has accepted goods and given notification to the seller of their nonconformity, the buyer may (9) recover damages for breach of warranty. Finally, in addition to the remedies listed above, the buyer may, where appropriate, (10) recover incidental damages and (11) recover consequential damages.

It may be observed that the first remedy catalogued above is **obligation oriented;** the second through fourth and ninth through eleventh are **money oriented;** and the fifth through eighth are **goods oriented.**

To Cancel the Contract

Where the seller fails to make delivery or repudiates the contract, or where the buyer rightfully rejects or justifiably revokes acceptance of goods tendered or delivered to him, the buyer may cancel the contract with respect to any goods involved, and if the breach by the seller concerns the whole contract, the buyer may cancel the entire contract.

The buyer must give the seller notice of his cancellation of the contract and is not only excused from further performance or tender on his part but also may "cover" and have damages or recover damages from the seller for nondelivery of the goods.

To Recover Payments Made

The buyer, on the seller's breach, may also recover as much of the price as he has paid. For example, A and B enter into a contract for a sale of goods for a contract price of $3,000, and B, the buyer, has made a down payment of $600. A delivers nonconforming goods to B, who rightfully rejects them. B may cancel the contract and recover the $600 plus whatever other damages he may prove.

To Cover

On the seller's breach the buyer may protect herself by obtaining "cover." This means that the buyer may in good faith and without unreasonable delay proceed to purchase goods or make a contract to purchase goods in substitution for those due under the contract from the seller. This right enables the buyer to assure herself of the needed goods.

On making a reasonable contract of cover the buyer may recover from the seller the **difference between the cost of cover and the contract price,** *plus* any incidental and consequential damages *less* expenses saved in consequence of the seller's breach. For example, Phillip, whose factory is in Oakland, agrees to sell goods to Edith, in Atlanta, for $22,000 F.O.B. Oakland. Phillip fails to deliver and Edith covers by purchasing substitute goods for $25,000, incurring $700 in sales commissions. Edith suffered no other damages as a consequence of Phillip's breach. Shipping costs from Oakland to Atlanta for the goods are $1,300. Edith would recover the cost of cover ($25,000), less the contract price ($22,000), plus incidental damages ($700 in sales commissions), minus expenses saved ($1,300 in shipping costs Edith need not pay under the contract of cover), which equals $2,400.

The buyer is not required to obtain "cover," and his failure to do so does not bar him from any other remedy provided by the Code. However, the buyer may not recover consequential damages that he could have prevented by cover.

Cover–buyer's purchase of goods in substitution for those not delivered by breaching seller

BIGELOW-SANFORD, INC. v. GUNNY CORP.

United States Court of Appeals, Fifth Circuit, Unit B, 1981. 649 F.2d 1060.

FACTS: The plaintiff, Bigelow-Sanford, Inc., contracted with defendant Gunny Corp. for the purchase of 100,000 linear yards of jute at $.64 per yard. Gunny delivered 22,228 linear yards in January 1979. The February and March deliveries required under the contract were not made, and 8 rolls (each roll containing 66.7 linear yards) were delivered in April. With 72,265 linear yards undelivered Gunny told Bigelow-Sanford that no more would be delivered. In mid-March Bigelow-Sanford then turned to the jute spot market to replace the balance of the order at a price of $1.21 per linear yard. Since several other companies had also defaulted on their jute contracts with Bigelow-Sanford, the plaintiff purchased a total of 164,503 linear yards on the spot market. Plaintiff sues defendant to recover losses sustained as a result of the breach of contract.

DECISION: Judgment for Bigelow-Sanford. The Code permits a buyer to "cover" his damages due to the seller's breach by purchasing goods in substitution for those due from the seller. However, the buyer must make the substitute purchases in good faith and without unreasonable delay. If he does so, the buyer may recover as damages the difference between the cost of cover and the contract price (plus any incidental damages but less expenses saved in consequence of the seller's breach).

Here, Gunny breached when it notified Bigelow-Sanford in February that no more jute would be delivered. Bigelow-Sanford made its first spot market purchases to cover by mid-March. Thus, Bigelow-Sanford covered without undue delay. Since its purchases were also reasonable and made in good faith, Bigelow-Sanford is entitled to damages. Bigelow did not specifically allocate the spot market replacements to the individual sellers' accounts. Therefore, it is reasonable to determine the cost of cover by multiplying the average cost of the spot market purchases times the amount of jute Gunny had failed to deliver.

To Recover Damages for Nondelivery or Repudiation

If the seller repudiates the contract or fails to deliver the goods, or if the buyer rightfully rejects or justifiably revokes acceptance of the goods, the buyer is entitled to recover damages from the seller measured by the **difference between the market price** at the time when the buyer learned of the breach **and the contract price,** together *with* incidental and consequential damages, *less* expenses saved in consequence of the seller's breach. The market price is to be determined as of the place for tender, or in the event that the buyer has rightfully rejected the goods or has justifiably revoked his acceptance of them, the market price is to be determined as of the place of arrival.

For example, A agrees to sell goods to B for $7,000 C.O.D., with delivery by November 15. A fails to deliver. As a consequence, B suffered incidental damages of $1,500 and consequential damages of $1,000. In the case of nondelivery or repudiation, market price is determined as of the place of tender. Since C.O.D. is a shipment contract, the place of tender would be the seller's city. Therefore, the market price must be determined in the seller's city and on November 15, when B learned of the breach. At this time and place the market price is $8,000. B would recover the market price ($8,000), minus the contract price ($7,000), plus incidental damages ($1,500), plus consequential damages ($1,000), less expenses saved ($0 in this example), which equals $3,500.

In the example above, if A had instead delivered nonconforming goods that B rejected, then the market price would be determined at B's place of business; if instead A repudiated the contract on November 1, then the market price would be determined on that date.

To Recover Identified Goods on the Seller's Insolvency

Where existing goods are identified to the contract of sale, the buyer acquires a **special property** in the goods. This special property exists even though the goods are nonconforming and the buyer has the right to return or reject them. Identification of the goods to the contract may be made either by the buyer or by the seller.

The Code gives the buyer a right, which does not exist at common law, to recover from an insolvent seller the goods in which the buyer has a special property and for which he has paid a part or all of the price. This right exists where the seller, who is in possession or control of the goods, becomes insolvent within ten days after receipt of the first installment of the price. To exercise it the buyer must tender to the seller any unpaid portion of the price. If the special property exists by reason of an identification made by the buyer, he may recover the goods only if they conform to the contract for sale.

To Sue for Replevin

Replevin is a form of action at law to recover specific goods in the possession of a defendant that are being unlawfully withheld from the plaintiff. The buyer may maintain against the seller an action for replevin for goods that have been identified to the contract where the seller has repudiated or breached the contract, if (1) the buyer after a reasonable effort is unable to obtain cover for such goods, or (2) the goods have been shipped under reservation of a security interest in the seller and satisfaction of this security interest has been made or tendered.

Replevin—legal action to recover specific goods unlawfully held by seller

To Sue for Specific Performance

Other than the limited right of replevin, in an action at law the buyer may recover only a money judgment against a seller who refuses or fails to perform. Ordinarily, compensatory money damages are an adequate remedy. However, where the contract is for the purchase of a unique item such as a work of art, a famous racehorse, or an heirloom, money damages may not be an adequate remedy. In such a case a court of equity has jurisdiction to order the seller specifically to deliver to the buyer the goods described in the contract on payment of the price. In addition, the Code provides that a decree for specific performance may include terms and conditions as to payment of the price, damages, or other relief.

To Enforce a Security Interest in the Goods

A buyer who has rightfully rejected or justifiably revoked acceptance of goods that remain in her possession or control has a security interest in these goods to the extent of any payment of the price that she has made and for any expenses reasonably incurred in their inspection, receipt, transportation, care, and custody. The buyer may hold such goods and resell them in the same manner as an aggrieved seller may resell goods. In the event of resale the buyer is required to account to the seller for any excess of the net proceeds of the resale over the amount of her security interest.

To Recover Damages for Breach in Regard to Accepted Goods

Where the buyer has accepted nonconforming goods and has given timely notification to the seller of the breach of contract, the buyer is entitled to maintain an action at law to recover from the seller the damages resulting in the ordinary course of events from the seller's breach. In a proper case incidental and consequential damages may also be recovered.

In the event of breach of warranty, the measure of damages is the **difference** at the time and place of acceptance **between the value of the goods which have been accepted and the value** that the goods would have had if they had been **as warranted,** unless special circumstances show proximate damages of a different amount. In addition, incidental and consequential damages, where appropriate, may also be recovered.

The contract price of the goods does not figure in this computation, because the buyer is entitled to the benefit of his bargain, which is to receive goods that are as warranted. For example, Eleanor agrees to sell goods to Timothy for $1,000. The value of the goods accepted is $800, but if they had been as warranted, their value would have been $1,200. The buyer's damages for breach of warranty are $400, which he may deduct from any unpaid balance due on the purchase price on notice to the seller of his intention to do so. The following case further illustrates this rule.

STATE v. TRAVELERS
INDEM. CO.

Supreme Court of Oregon,
1968.
250 Or. 356, 442 P.2d 612.

FACTS: Hawkins-Hawkins Company, an unpaid seller of materials used in a highway construction project, brought an action to recover the contract price of $31,916. The purchaser paid $24,143 into the court, alleging that Hawkins-Hawkins had substituted inferior materials for those called for in the contract.

DECISION: Judgment for the purchaser. The purchaser did not reject the materials supplied even though it protested the invoices and asserted that there were defects in the materials. Thus, the correct measure of the purchaser's damages is the difference between the value of the goods as accepted and the value of the goods as warranted. The purchaser may deduct this amount from the contract price.

To Recover Incidental Damages

In addition to such remedies as covering, recovering damages for nondelivery or repudiation, or recovering damages for breach of warranty, the buyer may recover incidental damages. The buyer's incidental damages resulting from the seller's breach include expenses reasonably incurred in inspection, receipt, transportation, and care and custody of goods rightfully rejected; any commercially reasonable charges, expenses, or commissions in connection with obtaining cover; and any other reasonable expense connected to the delay or other breach. For example, the buyer of a racehorse justifiably revokes acceptance because the horse does not conform to the contract. The buyer will be allowed to recover as incidental damages the cost of caring for the horse from the date the horse was delivered until it is returned to the seller.

To Recover Consequential Damages

In many cases the remedies discussed above will not fully compensate the aggrieved buyer for her losses. For example, nonconforming goods that are accepted may explode and destroy the buyer's warehouse and its contents. Undelivered goods may have been the subject of a lucrative contract of resale, the profits from which are lost. The Code responds to this problem by providing the buyer with the opportunity to recover consequential damages resulting from the seller's breach, including (1) any loss resulting from the buyer's requirements and needs of which the seller at the time of contracting had reason to know and which could not reasonably be prevented by cover or otherwise; and (2) injury to person or property proximately resulting from any breach of warranty.

Consequential damages—damages resulting from buyer's requirements of which seller had reason to know at the time of contracting as well as injury to person or property proximately resulting from breach of warranty.

A summary of the remedies for breach available to both buyer and seller is given in Figure 21-1.

Contractual Provisions Affecting Remedies

Within specified limits, the Code permits the parties to a sales contract to modify, exclude, or limit by agreement the remedies or damages that will be available for breach of that contract. Two basic types of contractual provisions affect remedies: (1) liquidation or limitation of damages and (2) modification or limitation of remedy.

FIGURE 21-1   Remedies for Breach

Buyer's Breach	Seller's Breach
1) B wrongfully rejects	1) B rightfully rejects
2) B wrongfully revokes acceptance	2) B justifiably revokes acceptance
3) B fails to make payment	3) S fails to deliver
4) B repudiates	4) S repudiates
	5) B accepts non-conforming goods

Seller's Remedy / **Buyer's Remedy**

Obligation Oriented

(1–4)	Cancel	Cancel	(1–4)

Goods Oriented *— equitable*

(1–4)	Withhold delivery of goods	Recover payments made	(1–4)
(3)	Reclaim goods upon B's insolvency	Recover identified goods if S is insolvent	(3,4)
(1–4)	Stop delivery of goods by carrier or bailee	Have security interest	(1,2)
(1–4)	Identify conforming goods to contract		

Money Oriented *— legal remedy*   *— contract $ – FMV*   *— cover : contract – buying price*

(1–4)	Resell and recover damages	Cover and recover damages	(1–4)
(1–4)	Recover damages for non-acceptance	Recover damages for non-delivery	(1–4)
		Recover damages for breach of warranty	(5)

Specific Performance *— equitable*

(1–4)	Recover price *"the price"* *"action for the price"*	Replevy goods	(3,4)
	only when $ damages don't work	Obtain specific performance	(3,4)

Liquidation or Limitation of Damages

The parties may provide for liquidated damages in their contract by specifying the amount or measure of damages that either party may recover in the event of a breach by the other party. The amount of such damages must be reasonable and commensurate with the anticipated or actual loss resulting from a breach. A provision in a contract fixing unreasonably large liquidated damages is void as a penalty.

FACTS: Equitable Lumber Corporation entered into a contract with IPA Land Development Corporation, a builder and developer, in which Equitable agreed to supply lumber and building materials to IPA. The contract contained a provision entitling Equitable to recover the reasonable value of attorney's fees incurred as a result of a breach by IPA. It liquidated the amount recoverable for the attorney's fees at 30% of the total damages recovered by Equitable. IPA accepted deliveries of lumber and materials from Equitable, but subsequently refused to pay for them, claiming they were not of merchantable quality. Equitable then brought suit to recover the purchase price of the materials and the attorney's fees as stipulated in the contract. The district court determined that the amount of actual damages was $3,936.42 and that Equitable could recover the reasonable value of the attorney's fees. However, it refused to enforce the provision for a 30% fee. Instead,

EQUITABLE LUMBER CORP. v. IPA LAND DEVELOPMENT CORP.

Court of Appeals of New York, 1976.
38 N.Y.2d 516, 344 N.E.2d 391.

the court determined that the reasonable value of the attorney's fees was $450 (approximately 11% of the amount recovered). Equitable appeals to recover attorney fees of 30%.

DECISION: Judgment for Equitable; remanded for further factual findings. A liquidated damages provision is valid if reasonable with respect to either (1) damages anticipated at the time of contracting or (2) the actual damages caused by the breach. Nevertheless, such a provision may be invalidated if it is so unreasonably large that it serves as a penalty rather than a good faith attempt to pre-estimate damages. Furthermore, a liquidated damages clause may be unconscionable and, therefore, unenforceable.

Here, since the attorney's fees were incapable of estimation at the time of contracting, the liquidated damages scheme was appropriate. Equitable and IPA were two businesses dealing at arms' length and with relatively equal bargaining power. Thus, the provision is not void due to unconscionability. The 30% fee may be reasonable in relation to the anticipated damages equivalent to the normal contingent fee an attorney would charge for such a case. On the other hand, the provision may also be upheld if it corresponds to the actual arrangement between Equitable and its attorney. In either case, the time spent by Equitable's attorney in obtaining collection is not necessarily the correct measure of damages. Even if it meets these two tests for reasonableness, however, the 30% fee may be struck down if it is unreasonably large in relation to anticipated damages so as to be a penalty to IPA. These are questions of fact to be decided by the trial court on remand.

Modification or Limitation of Remedy by Agreement

The contract between the seller and buyer may expressly provide for remedies in addition to or instead of those provided in the Code and may limit or change the measure of damages recoverable in the event of breach. For instance, the contract may validly limit the remedy of the buyer to a return of the goods and a refund of the price, or to the replacement of nonconforming goods or parts.

A remedy provided by the contract, however, is deemed optional unless it is expressly agreed to be exclusive of other remedies, in which event it is the sole remedy. Moreover, where circumstances cause an exclusive or limited remedy to fail in its essential purpose, resort may be had to the remedies provided by the Code, as in the next case.

The contract may expressly limit or exclude consequential damages unless such limitation or exclusion would be unconscionable. Limitation of consequential damages for personal injuries resulting from breach of warranty in the sale of consumer goods is always unconscionable, whereas limitation of such damages where the loss is commercial is not.

WILSON TRADING CORP. v. DAVID FERGUSON, LIMITED

Court of Appeals of New York, 1968.
23 N.Y.2d 398, 297 N.Y.S.2d 108, 244 N.E.2d 685.

FACTS: Wilson Trading Corp. agreed to sell David Ferguson a specified quantity of yarn for use in making sweaters. The written contract provided that notice of defects to be effective had to be received by Wilson before knitting or within ten days of receipt of the yarn. When the knitted sweaters were washed, the color of the yarn "shaded" (i.e., variations in color from piece to piece appeared). David Ferguson immediately notified Wilson of the problem and refused to pay for the yarn, claiming that the defect made the sweaters unmarketable.

DECISION: Judgment for Ferguson. Ordinarily, a buyer who accepts goods has a reasonable time after he discovers or should have discovered a breach to notify the seller of the breach. At the same time, however, parties can within limits modify or exclude warranties and fashion their own remedies for the breach of those warranties. Nevertheless, if the remedies available are limited in an unconscionable manner, the limiting terms are subject to being replaced by the general remedial provisions of the U.C.C. Since the notice provision in effect precluded buyers from giving notice of latent defects, the provision failed in its essential purpose and left David Ferguson without a remedy. To that extent the contract provision was displaced by the rule that Ferguson had a reasonable time to notify Wilson of the defect.

CHAPTER SUMMARY

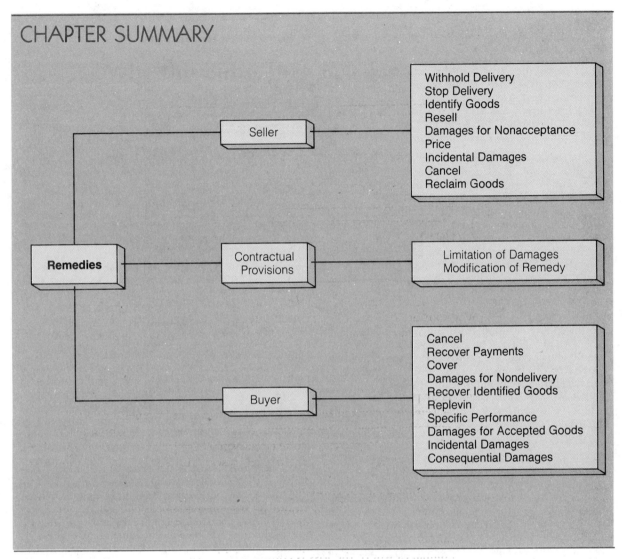

Remedies

Seller
- Withhold Delivery
- Stop Delivery
- Identify Goods
- Resell
- Damages for Nonacceptance
- Price
- Incidental Damages
- Cancel
- Reclaim Goods

Contractual Provisions
- Limitation of Damages
- Modification of Remedy

Buyer
- Cancel
- Recover Payments
- Cover
- Damages for Nondelivery
- Recover Identified Goods
- Replevin
- Specific Performance
- Damages for Accepted Goods
- Incidental Damages
- Consequential Damages

KEY TERMS

Insolvency (equity)
Insolvency (bankruptcy)
Incidental damages (seller)

Cancellation
Cover
Replevin

Specific performance
Incidental damages (buyer)
Consequential damages

PROBLEMS

1. A contracts to sell 1,000 bushels of wheat to B at $4.00 per bushel. Just before A was to deliver the wheat, B notified her that he would not receive or accept the wheat. A sold the wheat for $3.60 per bushel, the market price, and later sued B for the difference of $400. B claims he was not notified by A of the resale and hence not liable. Decision?

2. On December 15, 1984, A wrote a letter to B stating that he would sell to B all of the mine-run coal that B might wish to buy during the calendar year 1985 for use at B's factory, delivered at the factory at a price of $40 per ton. B immediately replied by letter to A stating that he accepted the offer, that he would purchase all of his mine-run coal from A, and that he would need 200 tons of coal during the first week in January 1985. During the months of January, February, and March, A delivered to B a total of 700 tons of coal, for all of which B made payment to A at the rate of $40 per ton. On April 10, B ordered 200 tons of mine-run coal from A, who replied to B on April 11 that he could not supply A with any more coal except at a price of $48 per ton delivered. B thereafter purchased elsewhere at the market price, namely $48 per ton, all of the requirements of his factory of mine-run coal for the remainder of the year, amounting to a total of 2,000 tons of coal. B now brings an action against A to recover damages at the rate of $8 per ton for the coal thus purchased, amounting to $16,000. Decision?

3. On January 10, B, of Emanon, Missouri, visited the show rooms of the X Piano Company in St. Louis and selected a piano. A sales memorandum of the transaction signed both by B and by the salesman of the X Piano Company read as follows: "Sold to B one new Andover piano, factory number 46832, price $3,300 to be shipped to the buyer at Emanon, Missouri, freight prepaid, before February 1. Prior to shipment seller will stain the case a darker color in accordance with buyer's directions and will make the tone more brilliant." On January 15, B repudiated the contract by letter to the X Piano Company. The Company subsequently stained the case, made the tone more brilliant, and offered to ship the piano to B on January 26. B persisted in her refusal to accept the piano. In an action by the X Piano Company against B to recover the contract price, what judgment?

4. Sims contracted in writing to sell Blake 100 electric motors at a price of $100 each, freight prepaid to Blake's warehouse. By the contract of sale Sims expressly warranted that each motor would develop twenty-five brake horsepower. The contract provided that the motors would be delivered in lots of 25 per week beginning January 2, that Blake should pay for each lot of 25 motors as delivered, but that Blake was to have right of inspection on delivery.

Immediately on delivery of the first lot of 25 motors on January 2, Blake forwarded Sims a check for $2,500, but on testing each of the 25 motors Blake determined that none of them would develop more than fifteen brake horsepower.

State all of the remedies available to Blake.

5. A and B entered into a written contract whereby A agreed to sell and B agreed to buy a certain automobile for $3,500. A drove the car to B's residence and properly parked it on the street in front of B's house, where he tendered it to B and requested payment of the price. B refused to take the car or pay the price. A informed B that he would hold him to the contract; but before A had time to enter the car and drive it away, a fire truck, answering a fire alarm and traveling at a high speed, crashed into the car and demolished it. A brings an action against B to recover the price of the car. Who is entitled to judgment? Would there be any difference in result if A were a dealer in automobiles?

6. A sells and delivers to B on June 1 certain goods and receives from B at the time of delivery B's check in the amount of $900 for the goods. The following day B is petitioned into bankruptcy, and the check is dishonored by B's bank. On June 5, A serves notice on B and the trustee in bankruptcy that she reclaims the goods. The trustee is in possession of the goods and refuses to deliver them to A. What are the rights of the parties?

7. The ABC Company, located in Chicago, contracted to sell a carload of television sets to Dodd in St. Louis, Missouri, on sixty-days credit. ABC Company shipped the carload to Dodd. On arrival of the car at St. Louis, Dodd paid the freight charges and reshipped the car to Hines of Little Rock, Arkansas, to whom he had previously contracted to sell the television sets. While the car was in transit to Little Rock, Dodd went bankrupt. ABC Company was informed of this at once and immediately telegraphed XYZ Railroad Company to withhold delivery of the television sets. What should the XYZ Railroad Company do?

8. S in Chicago entered into a contact to sell certain machines to B in New York. The machines were to be manufactured by S and shipped F.O.B. Chicago not later than March 25. On March 24, when S was about to ship the machines, he received a telegram from B wrongfully repudiating the contract. The machines cannot readily be resold for a reasonable price because they are a special kind used only in B's manufacturing processes. S sues B to recover the agreed price of the machines. What are the rights of the parties?

PART FOUR
COMMERCIAL PAPER

PART FOUR

COMMERCIAL PAPER

PUBLIC POLICY, SOCIAL ISSUES AND BUSINESS ETHICS

Commercial paper includes checks, promissory notes, drafts, and certificates of deposit. These instruments, as they are commonly called, are crucial to the sale of goods and services as well as the financing of most businesses. The use of commercial paper has increased to such an extent that payments made with these instruments, particularly checks, far outnumber payments made with cash. In fact, currency is now primarily used for smaller transactions. Accordingly, the vital importance of commercial paper as a method of payment cannot be overstated:

A reliable payment system is crucial to the economic growth and stability of the nation. The smooth functioning of markets for virtually every good and service is dependent upon the smooth functioning of banking and financial markets, which in turn is dependent upon the integrity of the nation's payment mechanism. History tells us—all too vividly—that fragility of a country's payment system can precipitate or intensify a general economic crisis. *Federal Reserve Bulletin*, September, 1984.

To accomplish these social and economic objectives, the payment system must be quick, sure, and efficient. The use of cash can never satisfy all of these requirements because (1) it is inconvenient to maintain large quantities of cash, (2) the risk of loss or theft is far too great, (3) the risk in sending cash is likewise too high, as is the cost of postage and insurance in shipping cash over long distances, and (4) the costs to the Federal government of maintaining an adequate supply of currency

would be prohibitive. In addition, commercial paper used for payment provides a convenient receipt as well as a record for accounting and tax purposes. Although commercial paper acts as a very close approximation of cash for the purpose of payment, it is not the exact equivalent of cash because, for example, commercial paper is more susceptible to forgery, it may be drawn on insufficient funds, payment may be stopped, or the instrument may be materially altered. Nevertheless, these risks (which are real but very infrequent—over 99 percent of all checks are paid), assume small proportions compared to the advantages that commercial paper provides for payment. Consequently, a major policy objective of the law of commercial paper and the bank collection process is to reduce these risks by increasing the safety, soundness, and operating efficiency of the entire payment system.

Because commercial paper plays a central role in the payment system, it is important that you are aware of the social and ethical issues arising out of the use of commercial paper. Many of these issues involve the relationship between customers and their bank. For instance, should a customer have the right to stop payment on a check? If so, under what conditions? At whose expense? How long should a stop payment order be effective? What effect do stop payment orders have on public confidence in the payment system? Who should bear the loss for forgeries: the bank or the customer? With the enormous volume of checks written daily, can a bank be expected to "know" the signatures of all of its customers? These are just some of the public policy questions concerning customer/bank relations that you should consider in studying this part of the text.

Equally important are the ethical issues concerning the forthrightness of banks in informing their customers of their rights as depositors. What obligations should a financial institution have to inform its customers of their rights? What responsibility should the customer have to inform himself of his rights? Should the State of Federal governments be involved in resolving these issues?

Closely related is the ethical question of what essential services financial institutions should provide and how much they should charge for their services. It has been argued that with the deregulation of the financial services industry, current customer service fees greatly favor large customers at heavy financial cost to lower-income households. Should such unequal treatment be permitted? Who should be responsible for monitoring such developments?

Another significant ethical question that various legislative and administrative bodies are now addressing concerns the right of banks to "hold" deposited checks before making the funds available to their depositors. In order to determine the validity of checks, some banks hold checks for up to fifteen days before permitting customers to use the funds. The banks use the funds during this delay, but depositors cannot. Some States are now restricting the time period during which financial institutions may hold checks.

Overall, the current payment system has transformed the United States into a virtually cashless society. The advent and technological advances of computers make it likely that electronic fund transfer systems will bring about a checkless society in the forseeable future. Such a system could increase the speed and efficiency of the payment system by eliminating the cumbersome process of moving paper. However, there are important, and to date unanswered, questions about the safety of electronic fund transfer systems. Moreover, it is not yet clear how, if at all, such a system would be able to perform all of the various functions now accomplished by checks.

While studying Part Four you should consider these and other social, ethical, and policy issues in order to determine the reasonableness, appropriateness, and above all, the fairness of the legal principles of commercial paper.

22

FORM AND CONTENT

Modern business could not be conducted without the use of commercial paper—checks, drafts, promissory notes, and certificates of deposit. A tremendous number of transactions involve the writing of one or more checks. Drafts, of which checks are a specialized form, provide an important monetary and credit function in the business world, both inside and outside the banking system. Promissory notes serve an important business purpose, not only in areas of high finance, but at the level of the small businessperson and consumer as well. In recent years certificates of deposit have been increasingly used by individuals instead of savings accounts. The various forms of commercial paper, commonly referred to as instruments, may or may not have the unique characteristic of negotiability, although the term "commercial paper" is usually used to refer to negotiable instruments. The way rights and obligations are acquired in commercial paper is important because of the huge volume of daily transactions in promissory notes, certificates of deposit, drafts, and checks.

Negotiability

The law gives the quality of negotiability to commercial paper. The concept was devised by the law to meet the needs of traders, merchants, and businesspeople who wanted promises and orders to pay money to circulate freely in the marketplace, not as money, but as a ready substitute for money in business transactions. The concept of negotiability applies not only to commercial paper, which is governed by Article 3 of the Code, but also to documents of title (governed by Article 7 and discussed in Chapter 43) and investment securities (governed by Article 8 and discussed in Chapter 34).

Commercial paper–drafts, checks, promissory notes, and certificates of deposits

Negotiable–instruments that meet certain specific requirements

   The starting point for an understanding of negotiable instruments is to recognize that four or five centuries ago in England a contract right to the payment of money was not assignable. The reason was that a contractual promise ran to the promisee. Performance could be rendered to him and to no one else. This was a hardship on the owner of the right because it prevented him from selling or disposing of it. Eventually, the law permitted recovery on an assignment by the assignee against the obligor, although the assignee acquired no new rights but only those of his assignor.

   An innocent assignee bringing an action against the obligor was subject to all defenses available to the obligor. Such an action would result in the

359

same outcome regardless of whether it was brought by the assignee or assignor. Thus a contract right became assignable but not very marketable, because merchants had no interest in buying into a possible lawsuit. This remains the law of assignments: the **assignee stands in the shoes of his assignor.**

With the flourishing of trade and commerce it became essential to develop means to exchange contractual rights for money. For example, a merchant who sells goods for cash may use the cash to buy more goods for resale. If he makes a sale on credit in exchange for a promise to pay money, why shouldn't he be permitted to sell that promise to someone else for cash with which to carry on his business? One difficulty was that the buyer of the goods gave the seller only a promise to pay money to him. He was the only person to whom performance or payment was promised. However, if the seller obtained from the buyer a promise in writing to pay money to anyone in possession (**bearer**) of the writing (**paper** or **instrument**) or to anyone the seller (*payee*) designated, then the duty of performance would run directly to the bearer of the paper or to the person to whom the payee ordered payment to be made. This is one of the essential distinctions between negotiable and nonnegotiable instruments. Although there are other formal requirements of a negotiable instrument, this particular one eliminates the limitations of a promise to pay money only to a named promisee.

Moreover, if the promise to pay were not subject to all of the defenses available against the assignor, then a transferee such as the bearer or the person to whom the payee *ordered* payment to be made, would not only be more willing to acquire the promise but also would also pay more for it. The law of negotiable instruments accordingly developed the concept of **holder in due course,** whereby certain good faith transferees who gave value acquired the right to be paid free of most of the defenses to which an assignee would be subject. Thus, by reason of this doctrine such a transferee of a negotiable instrument acquires *greater* rights than his transferor had, whereas an assignee would acquire *only* the rights of his assignor.

With these two basic innovations, negotiable instruments enabled merchants to sell their contractual rights more readily and thereby keep their capital working.

Negotiability invests commercial paper with a high degree of marketability and commercial utility. It allows commercial paper to be freely transferable and enforceable by a person with the rights of a holder in due course against any person obligated on the paper, subject only to a limited number of defenses. To illustrate, let it be assumed that A sells and delivers goods to B for $500 on sixty days' credit and that, a few days later, A assigns this account to C. Unless B is duly notified of this assignment, he may safely pay the $500 to A on the due date without incurring any liability to C, the assignee. Assume next that the goods were defective and that B accordingly has a defense against A to the extent of $200. Assume also that C duly notified B of the assignment. The result is that C can recover only $300 from B and not $500, because B's defense against A is equally available against A's assignee, C. In other words, an assignee of contractual rights merely "steps into the shoes" of his assignor and hence acquires only the same rights as his assignor had—and no more.

Assume instead, that on the sale by A to B, B executed and delivered his negotiable note to A for $500 payable to A's order in sixty days, and that, a

Bearer–person in possession of an instrument

Instrument–commercial paper (check, draft, promissory note, or certificate of deposit)

short time later, A duly negotiates the note to C. In the first place, C is not required to notify B that he has acquired the note from A. One who issues a negotiable instrument is charged with knowledge that the instrument may be negotiated from hand to hand and is obligated to pay the holder of the instrument. In the second place, assuming that C acquired the note in good faith for value and had no knowledge of B's defense against A, B's defense is not available against C. C, therefore, is entitled to hold B at maturity for the full face amount of the note, namely, $500. In other words, C, by the negotiation of the note to him acquired greater rights than A had, since A, had he kept the note, could have recovered only $300 because B could have successfully asserted the defense to the amount of $200 against A.

To have the full benefit of negotiability, commercial paper must not only meet the requirements of negotiability under the Code, but must also be acquired by a "holder in due course." This chapter and the three chapters that follow discuss in order: (1) form and content, (2) transfer and negotiation, (3) holder in due course, and (4) liability of the parties.

Types of Commercial Paper

There are four types of commercial paper: drafts, checks, notes, and certificates of deposit. The first two each contain **orders** to pay money; the last two contain **promises** to pay money.

Order to Pay

Drafts A draft involves three parties, each in a distinctly different capacity. One party, the **drawer, orders** a second party, the **drawee,** to pay a sum certain in money to a third party, the **payee** (see Figure 22–1). The same party may appear in more than one capacity; for instance, the drawer may also be the payee.

Drafts may be either "time" or "sight." A **time** draft is one payable at a specified future date, whereas a **sight** draft is payable immediately on presentation to the drawee.

Checks A check is a specialized form of draft, namely, an order to pay money drawn on a **bank** and payable on **demand.** Once again, there are parties involved in three distinct capacities: the **drawer,** who orders the **drawee,** a bank, to pay the **payee** on demand (see Figure 22–2).

Draft –order to pay

Drawer –issuer of an order to pay (draft or check)

Drawee –party ordered to pay a draft or a check

Payee –person to receive payment on any instrument

Check –draft drawn on a bank and payable on demand

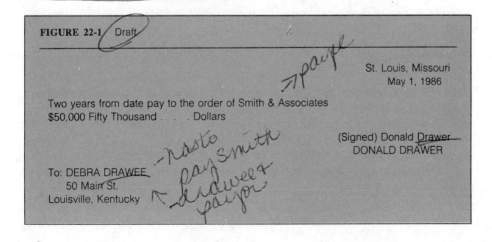

FIGURE 22-1 Draft

St. Louis, Missouri
May 1, 1986

Two years from date pay to the order of Smith & Associates
$50,000 Fifty Thousand . . . Dollars

(Signed) Donald Drawer
DONALD DRAWER

To: DEBRA DRAWEE
50 Main St.
Louisville, Kentucky

FIGURE 22-2   Check

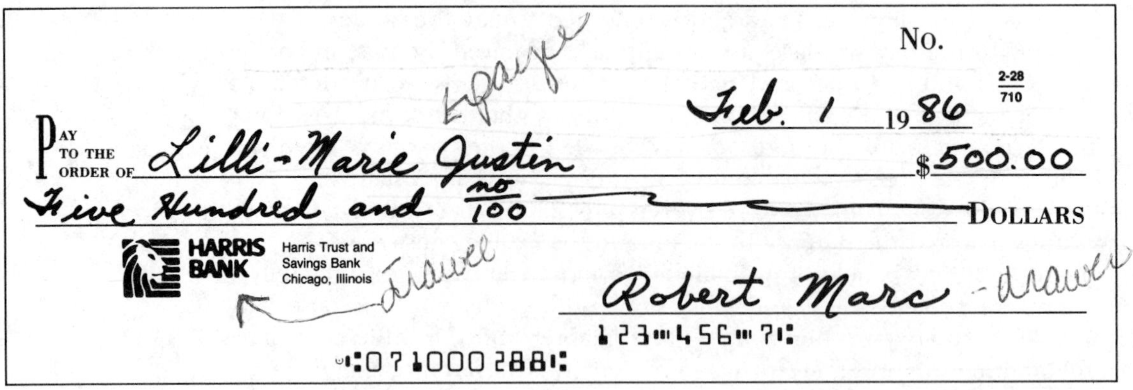

A *cashier's check* is a check drawn by a bank on itself to the order of a named payee.

Promises to Pay

Promissory note–a written promise by a maker to pay a payee

Notes   A promissory note is an instrument involving two parties in two capacities. One party, the **maker, promises** to pay to the order of a second party, the **payee,** a stated sum of money, either on demand or at a stated future date (see Figure 22–3).

Maker–issuer of a promissory note or certificate of deposit

Certificates of Deposit   A certificate of deposit is a specialized form of *promise* to pay money given by a **bank** or thrift association. It is a written acknowledgment by a bank of the receipt of a specific sum of money that it engages to pay on demand or at a stated future date, with interest at a stated rate, to a person named in the certificate, and according to the terms stated in the certificate. The issuing party, the **maker,** which is always a bank or thrift association, promises to pay a second party, the **payee** (see Figure 22–4).

Certificate of deposit–a specialized note given by a bank or thrift association

Form of Commercial Paper

To perform its function in the business community effectively, commercial paper must be capable of passing from hand to hand freely. This is made

FIGURE 22-3 Note

$10,000	Albany, N.Y.	July 7, 1986

Six months from date I promise to pay to the order of Pat Payee ten thousand dollars.

(signed) Matthew Maker

FIGURE 22-4 *(Certificate of Deposit)*

The Mountain Bank *— maker*
1200 Central Avenue, Mountain, Illinois 70040

CERTIFICATE OF DEPOSIT
No. 13900
Date August 3, 1986 Soc. Sec. No. 123-5-7809

..... John Payee .... HAS DEPOSITED IN THIS BANK

..... One Thousand .... $ 1,000 ....

_____ DOLLARS _____

This Certificate shall be payable to the Registered Holder(s) or to the survivor(s) in current funds upon surrender property endorsed by the Registered Holder(s) on August 3, 1987 with interest at 14 per cent per annum.

This Certificate of Deposit constitutes a contract whereby the depositor agrees that no part of the deposit may be withdrawn before maturity. In the event the Bank at its option permits payment of any part or all of this deposit prior to the maturity thereof Federal laws and regulations require that three month/six months of interest hereon be forfeited. In case of the Depositor's death or mental incompetency the bank is required to honor a request for withdrawal prior to maturity without penalty.

NOT SUBJECT TO CHECK
Member F.D.I.C.

Bill Bank *(maker)*
AUTHORIZED SIGNATURE

possible because **negotiability** is wholly a matter of form. Within the four corners of the instrument must be all the information required to determine whether it is negotiable. No reference to any other source is required or permitted. For this reason a negotiable instrument is called a "courier without luggage."

An instrument must satisfy the following formal requirements to be negotiable:

1. it must be in writing, *(no pictures)*
2. it must be signed,
3. it must contain a promise or order to pay,
4. it must be unconditional, *(no conditions)*
5. it must be for a sum certain in money, *-- only one amount*
6. it must contain no other promise or order,
7. it must be payable on demand or at a definite time, and
8. it must be payable to order or to bearer. *→ name on check & holding check* *↳ can pay someone else*

If these requirements are not met, the instrument is not negotiable, and the rights of the parties are governed by the law of assignment discussed in Chapter 14.

Negotiable instrument commercial paper or certain other instruments that satisfy the requirements of negotiability

FIRST STATE BANK AT GALLUP v. CLARK

Supreme Court of New Mexico, 1977.
91 N.M. 117, 570 P.2d 1144.

FACTS: Horne executed a $100,000 note in favor of R. C. Clark. On the back of the instrument was a restriction stating that the note could not be transferred, pledged, or otherwise assigned without Horne's written consent. As part of the same transaction between Horne and Clark, Horne gave Clark a separate letter authorizing Clark to pledge the note as collateral for a loan of $50,000 that Clark intended to secure from First State Bank. Clark did secure the loan and pledged the note, which was accompanied by Horne's letter authorizing Clark to use the note as collateral. First State contacted Horne and verified the agreement between Horne and Clark as to using the note as collateral, but when First Bank later attempted to collect on the note, Horne refused to pay, and this suit was instituted.

DECISION: Judgment for First State Bank, even though the note in question is not a negotiable instrument. In order for a note to be classified as a negotiable instrument, one must be able to ascertain from the instrument itself and without reference to other documents that the instrument: (1) is signed by the maker or drawer; (2) contains an unconditional promise or order to pay a sum certain in money; (3) and contains no other promise by the maker or drawer except as authorized by law; (4) is payable on demand or at a definite time; and (5) is payable to order or bearer. The note executed by Horne failed to meet the requirements of negotiability because the promise to pay was not payable to order or bearer. Rather, a transfer of the note was conditioned on the holder's obtaining Horne's written consent. This limitation, although it appeared only on the back of the instrument, was part of the instrument and destroyed its negotiability. Furthermore, that flaw could not be overcome by the accompanying letter from Horne to Clark. In order to facilitate the transfer of notes, the party receiving the note must be able to determine its validity and negotiability from the face of the note. Thus, the note was assigned and is governed by the law of assignments.

Writing

The requirement that the instrument be a writing is broadly construed. Printing, typewriting, or any other intentional reduction to tangible form is sufficient to satisfy the requirement. Most negotiable instruments, of course, are written on paper, but this is not required.

Signed

A note or certificate of deposit must be signed by the maker; a draft or check must be signed by the drawer. As in the case of a writing, extreme latitude is granted in determining what constitutes a signature. Any symbol executed or adopted by a party with the intention to authenticate a writing is sufficient. Moreover, it may consist of any word or mark used in place of a written signature, such as initials, an *X*, or a thumb print. It may be a trade name or assumed name. Even the location of the signature on the document is unimportant. Normally, a maker or drawer signs in the lower right-hand corner of the instrument, but this is not required.

Promise or Order to Pay

A negotiable instrument must contain a promise to pay money, in the case of a note or certificate of deposit, or an order to pay, in the case of a draft or check.

A promise is an undertaking and must be more than the mere acknowledgment or recognition of the existing obligation. The so-called due bill or I.O.U. is not a promise but a mere acknowledgment of indebtedness. Accordingly, an instrument stating "due Adam Brown $100" or "I.O.U., Adam Brown, $100" is not negotiable because it does not contain a promise to pay.

An order is a direction to pay that must be more than an authorization or request and must identify the person to pay with reasonably certainty. The usual way to express an order is by use of the word "pay:" "*Pay* to the order of John Jones" or "*Pay* bearer."

Unconditional

The requirement that the promise or order be unconditional is to prevent the inclusion of any provision that could diminish the obligation. The currency and credit functions of negotiable instruments would be defeated by conditions limiting the promise. Costly and time-consuming investigations would become necessary to determine the degree of risk imposed by the condition. Moreover, if the **holder** (person in possession of the instrument) had to take an instrument subject to certain conditions, her risk factor would be substantial, and this would lead to limited transferability. Substitutes for money must be capable of rapid circulation at minimum risks.

A promise or order is conditional if (a) the instrument states that it is subject to or governed by any other agreement, or (b) the instrument states that it is to be paid only out of a particular fund or source.

Reference to Other Agreements   The restriction against reference to another agreement is to enable any person to determine the right to payment provided by the instrument without having to look beyond its four corners. If such right is made subject to the terms of another agreement, the instrument is nonnegotiable.

A distinction is to be made between a mere recital of the *existence* of a separate agreement (this does not destroy negotiability) and a recital that makes the instrument *subject* to the terms of another agreement (this does destroy negotiability).

A statement in a note such as

> This note is given in partial payment for a color TV set to be delivered two weeks from date in accordance with a contract of this date between the payee and the maker

does not impair negotiability. It merely is a description of the transaction giving rise to the note and describes the consideration. The promise is not made subject to any implied or constructive condition. Added words that *would* impair negotiability are:

> and the seller is subject to all of the terms of said agreement.

The following case provides another example of words that render the instrument conditional and thus nonnegotiable.

FACTS: Holly Hill Acres, Ltd., executed and delivered a promissory note and a purchase money mortgage to Rogers and Blythe. The note provided that it was secured by a mortgage on certain real estate and that the terms of that mortgage "are by this reference made a part hereof." Rogers and Blythe then assigned the note to Charter Bank, and the Bank now seeks to foreclose on the note and mortgage. Holly Hill Acres refuses to pay and claims that it was defrauded by Rogers and Blythe.

DECISION: Judgment for Holly Hill Acres. A note that states that it is subject to or governed by any other agreement does not contain an unconditional promise to pay, and, therefore, it is

HOLLY HILL ACRES, LIMITED v. CHARTER BANK OF GAINESVILLE

District Court of Appeals of Florida, Second District, 1975.
314 So.2d 209.

not a negotiable instrument. Here, the note executed by Holly Hill Acres provided that it was secured by a mortgage on real estate. This is a common commercial practice, and such a reference does not in itself destroy the negotiability of the note. In addition, however, the note also states that the terms of the mortgage are by reference made a part of the note. This condition on the promise to pay renders the note nonnegotiable because it depends on terms not appearing on the face of the instrument. And since the note, therefore, is nonnegotiable, Charter Bank, as the assignee of a mortgage securing a nonnegotiable note, must take subject to all defenses available against Rogers and Blythe.

The Particular Fund Doctrine   An order or promise to pay out of a particular fund is conditional and destroys negotiability because payment depends on the existence and sufficiency of the particular fund. On the other hand, a promise or order to pay, coupled with a mere indication of a particular fund out of which reimbursement is to be made or a particular account to be debited with the amount, does not impair negotiability, because the drawer's or maker's general credit is relied on and charging a particular account is merely a bookkeeping entry to be followed after payment. Thus, there is a difference between an instrument stating, "Sixty days after date pay to the order of John Jones $500 out of the proceeds of the sale of the contents of freight car No. 1234" and one stating, "Sixty days after date pay to the order of John Jones $500 and charge to proceeds of sale of the contents of freight car No. 1234." In the first case, payment would be made only if the contents of the freight car were sold and then only to the extent of the proceeds. In the second case, the instrument contains an unqualified order to pay with merely bookkeeping instructions to the drawee of the draft.

Sum Certain in Money

The holder must be able to determine from the face of the instrument the amount that he is entitled to receive in any event, so that he can ascertain the present and future value of the instrument.

Money-medium of exchange issued by a governmental body

Money   The term "money" means a medium of exchange authorized or adopted by a domestic or foreign government as part of its currency. Consequently, even though local custom may make gold dust or uncut diamonds a medium of exchange, an instrument payable in such commodities would be nonnegotiable because the government does not sanction these articles as legal tender. On the other hand, a sum certain payable in French francs, German marks, Italian lira, Japanese yen, or other foreign currency would not impair its negotiability.

Sum Certain   The requirement that payment be of a "sum certain" must be considered from the point of view of the holder, not the maker or drawer. The holder must be assured of a determinable minimum payment, although provisions of the instrument may increase the amount of recovery under certain circumstances. Thus, a frequent provision of a note is that the maker will pay, in addition to the face amount and specified interest, costs of collection and attorney's fees on default in payment. Such a provision is designed to make the paper more attractive without lessening the certainty of the amount due.

An instrument payable with a stated rate of interest is an obligation for a sum certain. The rates may be different before and after default, or before and after a specified date. However, if interest is payable "at the current rate" (which means the current banking rate), it is nonnegotiable because this is *not* a matter that can be determined without reference to any outside source.

A sum payable is a sum certain even though it is payable in installments, or with a fixed discount if paid before maturity, of a fixed addition if paid after maturity. This is so because it is always possible to make the necessary computations from the face of the instrument to determine the amount due at any given time.

No Other Promise or Order

A negotiable instrument must contain a promise or order to pay money, but it may not contain any other promise, order, obligation, or power given by the maker or drawer, except as specifically authorized under the Code. Accordingly, if an instrument contains an order or promise to do an act in addition to the payment of money, it is not negotiable. For example, a promise to pay $100 "and a ton of coal" is nonnegotiable.

The UCC sets out a list of terms and provisions that may be included in instruments without affecting negotiability. Among these are (1) a promise or power to maintain, protect, or increase collateral and to sell it in case of a default in payment of the instrument; (2) a term authorizing confession of judgment (written authority by the debtor to allow the holder to enter judgment against the debtor in favor of the holder) on the instrument if it is not paid when due; (3) a term purporting to waive the benefit of any law intended for the advantage or protection of any obligor; and (4) a term in a draft providing that the payee, by indorsing or cashing it, acknowledges full satisfaction of an obligation of the drawer. It is important to note that the UCC does not render any of these terms legal or effective; it merely provides that their inclusion will not affect negotiability.

Payable on Demand or at a Definite Time

A negotiable instrument must "be payable on demand or at a definite time." This requirement, like the other formal requisites of negotiability, is designed to promote certainty in determining the present value of a negotiable instrument.

Demand paper always has been considered sufficiently certain as to time of payment to satisfy the requirements of negotiability, because it is the holder who makes the demand and thus sets the time for payment. An instrument such as a check in which no time for payment is stated is payable on demand. An instrument qualifies as being payable on demand if it is payable "at sight" or "on presentation."

Demand paper–payable on request

Instruments payable at a definite time, other than on demand, are called **time paper.** An instrument that by its terms is payable only on an act or event whose time of occurrence is uncertain is *not* payable at a definite time, even though the act or event has occurred. Familiar examples include instruments providing for payment to the payee or order "thirty days after my marriage" or "when the payee is twenty-one years old." Such promises in otherwise negotiable instruments destroy their negotiability. The instruments are not payable at a definite time. Nor does the fact that the maker or drawer may marry or the payee becomes twenty-one years of age change the result. Negotiability is determined from the face of the instrument.

Time paper–payable at definite time

Various types of provisions are regarded as fixing a definite time for payment of an instrument. We discuss these provisions below.

"On or Before" Clauses   An instrument is payable at a definite time if it is payable "on or before a stated date." The holder is thus assured that she will have her money by the maturity date at the latest, although she may receive it sooner. This right of anticipation enables the obligor, at his option, to pay before the stated maturity date (prepayment) and thereby stop the further accrual of interest or, if interest rates have gone down, to refinance at a lower rate of interest. Nevertheless, it constitutes sufficient certainty so as not to impair negotiability.

At a Fixed Period after a Stated Date   Frequently, instruments are made payable at a fixed period after a stated date. For example, the instrument may be made payable "thirty days after date." This means it is payable thirty days after the date of issuance given on the instrument. Such an instrument is payable at a definite time, for its exact maturity date can be determined by simple arithmetic.

An undated instrument payable "thirty days after date" is not payable at a definite time, because the date of payment cannot be determined from its face. It is therefore nonnegotiable until a date is added.

At a Fixed Period after Sight   This clause is frequently used in drafts. An instrument payable at a fixed period after sight is negotiable, for it means a fixed period after acceptance, and therefore a slight mathematical calculation makes the maturity date certain.

At a Definite Time Subject to Acceleration   An instrument payable at a fixed time subject to acceleration by the holder satisfies the requirement of being payable at a definite time. Indeed, such an instrument would seem to have a more certain maturity date than a demand instrument because it at least states a definite maturity date.

At a Definite Time Subject to Extension   A provision permitting the obligor of an instrument to extend the maturity date to a further *definite* time does not affect negotiability. For example, a provision in a note, payable one year from date, that the maker may extend the maturity date six months does not impair negotiability. However, if the obligor is given an option to extend the maturity of the instrument for an *indefinite* period of time, his promise is illusory, and there is no certainty of time of payment. Such an instrument is nonnegotiable. If the obligor's right to extend is limited to a definite time, the extension clause is no more indefinite than an acceleration clause with a time limitation. Moreover, a provision in an instrument granting the *holder* an option to extend the maturity of the instrument for an indefinite period does not impair its negotiability.

Payable to Order or to Bearer

A negotiable instrument must contain words indicating that the maker or drawer intends that it may pass into the hands of someone other than the payee. The "magic words" of negotiability are thus *"to the order of"* or *"to bearer,*" but other words that mean the same as these will also fulfill this requirement. The use of synonyms, however, only invites trouble.

This requirement should not be confused with the requirement that the instrument contain an order or promise to pay. An order to pay is a direction to a third party to pay the instrument as drawn. An "order instrument," on the other hand, pertains to the transferability of the instrument rather than specifying which party is to pay.

Payable to Order In addition to the eminently correct "Pay to the order of Jane Jones," the maker or drawer may state: "Pay to Jane Jones or her order"; or "Pay to Jane Jones or her assigns." Moreover, in every instance the person to whose order the instrument is payable must be designated with reasonable certainty. Within this limitation a broad range of payees is possible, including an individual, the maker or drawer, the drawee, two or more payees, an office, an estate, trust or fund, a partnership or unincorporated association, and a corporation.

> Order paper–names person to be paid or to whomever else that person identifies to be paid

Payable to Bearer An instrument fulfills the requirements of being payable to bearer if by its terms it is payable (1) to bearer or the order of bearer; (2) to a specified person or "bearer"; or (3) to "cash" or to the order of "cash" or any other indication that does not designate a specific payee. It should be noted, however, that an instrument made payable both to order and to bearer is payable to order unless the words "payable to bearer" are handwritten or typewritten on a printed form.

> **BROADWAY MANAGEMENT CORP. v. BRIGGS**
>
> Court of Appeals of Illinois, 1975.
> 30 Ill.App.3d 403, 332 N.E.2d 131.

FACTS: Broadway Management Corporation obtained a judgment by confession against Briggs. The note on which the confession of judgment was based reads in part: "Ninety Days after date, I, we, or either of us, promise to pay to the order of Three Thousand Four Hundred Ninety Eight and 45/100––––––––––Dollars." (The underlined words and symbols were typed in; the remainder was printed.) There were no blanks on the face of the instrument, any unused space having been filled in with hyphens. The note contains clauses permitting acceleration in the event the holder deems itself insecure and authorizes confession of judgment "if this note is not paid at any stated or accelerated maturity." Briggs appeals, claiming that the note, as negotiable order paper, did not authorize Broadway to exercise the judgment and, therefore, it is void.

DECISION: Judgment for Briggs. Under the UCC, to be payable to the bearer, the instrument, by its terms, must be made payable to: (a) bearer or the order of bearer; (b) a specified person or bearer; or (c) "cash" or the order of "cash" or any other indication which does not purport to designate a specific payee. However, a negotiable instrument made payable "to the order of _____" is not bearer paper, but an incomplete order instrument, unenforceable until a payee's name is inserted.

Here, neither the acceleration clause nor the confession of judgment clause destroys the negotiability of the note. Because the wording of the negotiable instrument implied that the payee's name was to be inserted between the promise and the amount, the note is order paper, not bearer paper. Thus, since the holder could not be determined from the face of the instrument, Broadway could not exercise the right of a holder to invoke the confession of judgment.

Moreover, it should be remembered that indorsements can not create or destroy negotiability and that negotiability must be determined from the "Face" of the instrument.

IN RE LEVINE

United States Bankruptcy
Court, S.D. New York, 1982.
23 B.R. 410.

FACTS: On September 2, 1976, Levine executed a mortgage bond under which she promised to pay the Mykoffs a preexisting obligation of $54,000. On October 14, 1979, the Mykoffs transferred the mortgage to Bankers Trust Co., indorsing the instrument with the words "Pay to the Order of Bankers Trust Company Without Recourse." The Lincoln First Bank, N.A., brought this action asserting that the Mykoffs' mortgage is a nonnegotiable instrument because it is not payable to order or bearer, thus it is subject to Lincoln's defense that the mortgage was not supported by consideration since antecedent debt is not consideration.

DECISION: Judgment for Lincoln First Bank. Antecedent debt is sufficient consideration to support a negotiable instrument, but not a nonnegotiable one. Under the UCC, a writing, to be negotiable, must "be payable to order or to bearer." Since the mortgage did not contain such language, it was not a negotiable instrument. The Mykoffs' indorsement could not change the instrument to a negotiable one. Therefore, the mortgage bond is nonnegotiable and unenforceable because it lacks legal consideration. Bankers Trusts' claim is unsecured in that, as assignee, Bankers Trust is subject to the defense of lack of consideration (its position can be no better than that of its assignor, the Mykoffs).

Terms and Omissions and Their Effect on Negotiability

The negotiability of an instrument may be questioned because of an omission of certain provisions or ambiguity of language. Problems may also arise in connection with interpretation of instruments whether or not negotiability is called into question. The Code contains rules of construction that apply to every instrument.

Absence of Statement of Consideration   Consideration is required to support a contract. However, as stated in *In re Levine*, the negotiability of an instrument is *not* affected by the omission of a statement of consideration.

Absence of Statement of Where the Instrument is Drawn or Payable   To determine what law applies to the issuance and form of an instrument, the place of issue must be known. To determine the law applicable to matters of payment, the place of payment must be known. But the omission of a statement of either of these on the face of the instrument does not affect its negotiability.

Sealed Instruments   The fact that an instrument is under seal has no effect on its negotiability, whatever other effect the seal might have under common law.

Dating of the Instrument   The negotiability of an instrument is not affected by the fact that it is *undated,* antedated, or postdated.

If the instrument is *antedated,* that is, it carries a date prior to its actual issue, the stated date controls. Hence, a note dated October 1, 1986, payable thirty days after date, and issued on November 1, 1986, is due and payable the day before its issue.

If the instrument is *postdated,* that is, it carries a date later than the day on which it was issued, the date stated on the instrument is conclusive. A demand instrument, therefore, by postdating becomes a time instrument. For example, if on January 2, 1986, the drawer issues a check and dates it January 21, 1986, the drawer's bank is not authorized to pay the instrument until January 21.

Incomplete Instruments   Occasionally a party will sign a paper that is clearly intended to be an instrument but is incomplete in some necessary way, such as the omission of promise or order, designation of the payee, amount payable, or time for payment. Such an instrument is not negotiable until completed.

Ambiguous Instruments   Rather than commit the parties to the use of parol evidence to establish the interpretation of an instrument, the Code establishes rules to resolve common ambiguities. This promotes negotiability by providing a degree of certainty to the holder.

Where it is doubtful whether the instrument is a draft or note, the holder may treat it as either and present it for payment to the drawee or the person signing it. For example, an instrument reading

To X: On demand I promise to pay $500 to the order of Y.

/s/Z

may be presented for payment to X as a draft or to Z as a note.

An instrument naming no drawee but stating

On demand, pay $500 to the order of Y

/s/Z

although in the form of a draft, may be treated as a note and presented to Z for payment.

If a printed form of note or draft is used and the party signing it inserts handwritten or typewritten language that is inconsistent with the printed words, the handwritten words control the typewritten and the printed words, and the typewritten words control the printed.

If the amount payable is set forth on the face of the instrument in both figures and words, and the amounts differ, the words control the figures. It is presumed that the maker or drawer would be more careful with words.

Figure 22–5 shows examples of nonnegotiable and negotiable instruments.

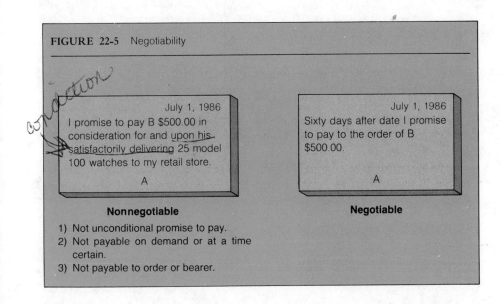

FIGURE 22-5   Negotiability

July 1, 1986
I promise to pay B $500.00 in consideration for and upon his satisfactorily delivering 25 model 100 watches to my retail store.

A

Nonnegotiable

1) Not unconditional promise to pay.
2) Not payable on demand or at a time certain.
3) Not payable to order or bearer.

July 1, 1986
Sixty days after date I promise to pay to the order of B $500.00.

A

Negotiable

CHAPTER SUMMARY

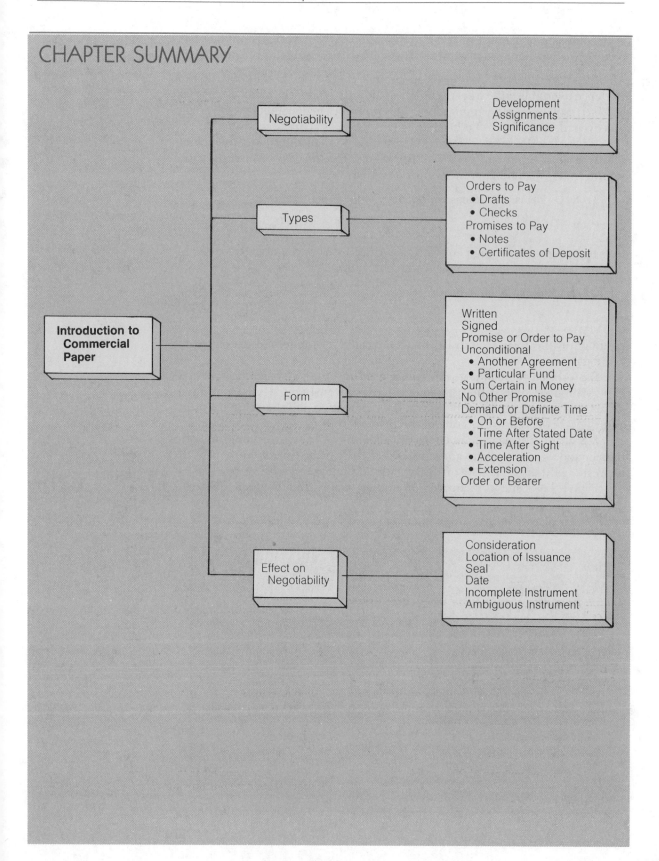

KEY TERMS

Commercial paper	Promissory note	Money
Negotiable	Maker	Sum certain
Negotiable instrument	Certificate of deposit	Demand paper
Bearer	Holder	Time paper
Instrument	Writing	On or before
Draft	Signed	On sight
Drawer	Promise to pay	Acceleration clause
Drawee	Order to pay	Extension clause
Payee	Unconditional	Pay to order
Check	Particular fund doctrine	Pay to bearer
Cashier's check	Subject to	

PROBLEMS

1. State whether the following provisions impair or preclude negotiability, if the instruments are otherwise in proper form. Answer each statement with either the word "Negotiable" or "Nonnegotiable," and explain why.

(a) A note for $2,000 payable in twenty monthly installments of $100 each, providing: "In case of death of maker all payments not due at date of death are canceled."

(b) A note stating, "This note is secured by a mortgage of even date herewith on personal property located at 351 Maple Street, Smithton, Illinois."

(c) A certificate of deposit reciting, "John Jones has deposited in the Citizens Bank of Emanon, Illinois, Two Thousand Dollars, to the credit of himself, payable upon the return of this instrument properly indorsed, with interest at the rate of 12¾ percent per annum from date of issue upon ninety days written notice."

(d) An instrument reciting "I.O.U., Mark Noble, $1,000.00."

(e) A note stating "In accordance with our contract of December 13, 1986, I promise to pay to the order of Sam Stone $100 on March 13, 1987."

(f) A draft drawn by Brown on the Acme Publishing Company for $500, payable to the order of the Sixth National Bank of Erehwon, directing the bank to "Charge this draft to my royalty account."

(g) A note executed by Pierre Janvier, a resident of Chicago, for $2,000, payable in Swiss francs.

(h) An undated note for $1,000 payable "six months after date."

(i) A note for $500 payable to the order of Ray Rodes six months after the death of Albert Olds.

(j) A note for $500 payable to the assigns of Levi Lee.

2. State whether the following provisions in a note impair or preclude negotiability, if the instruments are otherwise in proper form. Answer each statement with either the word "Negotiable" or "Nonnegotiable" and explain why.

(a) A note signed by Henry Brown in the trade name of the Quality Store.

(b) A note for $450, payable to the order of TV Products Company, "If, but only if, the color television set for which this note is given proves entirely satisfactory to me."

(c) A note executed by Adams, Burton, and Cady Company, a partnership, for $1,000, payable to the order of Davis, payable only out of the assets of the partnership.

(d) A note promising to pay $500 to the order of Leigh and to deliver ten tons of coal to Leigh.

(e) A note for $10,000 executed by Eaton payable to the order of the First National Bank of Emanon in which Eaton promises to give additional collateral if the bank deems itself insecure and demands additional security.

(f) A note reading, "I promise to pay to the order of Richard Roe $2,000 on January 31, 1986, but it is agreed that if the crop of Blackacre falls below ten bushels per acre for the 1985 season, this note shall be extended indefinitely."

(g) A note payable to the order of Ray Rogers fifty years from date but providing that payment shall be accelerated by the death of Silas Hughes to a point of time four months after his death.

(h) A note for $4,000 calling for payments of installments of $250 each and stating, "In the event any installment hereof is not paid when due this note shall immediately become due at the holder's option."

(i) An instrument dated September 17, 1986, in the handwriting of John Henry Brown which reads in full: "Sixty days after date, I, John Henry Brown, promise to pay to the order of William Jones $500."

(j) A note reciting; "I promise to pay Ray Reed $100 on December 24, 1986."

3. On March 10, Tolliver Tolles, also known as Thomas Towle, delivered to Alonzo Craig and Abigail Craig the following instrument, written by him in pencil:

> For value received, I, Thomas Towle, promise to pay to the order of Alonzo Craig or Abigail Craig One Thousand Seventy-Five ($1,000.75) Dollars six months after my mother, Alma Tolles, dies with interest at the rate of 12 percent from date to maturity and after maturity at the rate of 14 percent. I hereby waive the benefit of all laws exempting real or personal property from levy or sale.

Is this instrument negotiable? Explain.

4. Henry Hughes, who operates a department store, executed the following instrument:

> $2,600   Chicago, March 5, 1986
> On July, 1, 1986, I promise to pay Daniel Dalziel, or order, the sum of Twenty-Six Hundred Dollars for the privilege of one framed advertising sign, size 24 × 36 inches, at one end of each of two hundred sixty motor coaches of the New Omnibus Company for a term of three months from May 15, 1986.
>
>   Henry Hughes.

Is this instrument negotiable? Explain.

5. P agreed to lend M $500. M made and delivered his note for $500 payable to P or order "ten days after my marriage." Shortly thereafter M was married. Is the instrument negotiable? Explain.

6. On June 1, A executed a note for $1,000 payable to the order of B. The note contained the clause:

"This note is payable when this year's corn crop is harvested." Is the instrument negotiable? Explain.

7. M employs A to work for her for one year from January 1, 1986, to December 31, 1986, at a salary of $1,000 a month payable monthly. On January 2, M delivers to A twelve promissory notes in otherwise negotiable form, maturing respectively on the last day of successive calendar months throughout the year 1986. On the first note there is the statement "For January 1986 salary"; on the second note "For February 1986 salary"; and so on for each note. On January 3, 1986, A sold and indorsed the twelve notes to XYZ Bank and on January 4, 1986, quit work. Are these notes negotiable? Explain.

8. For the balance due on the purchase of a tractor Henry Brown executed and delivered to Jane Jones his promissory note containing the following language:

> January 1, 1986, I promise to pay to the order of Jane Jones the sum of $7,000 to be paid only out of my checking account at the XYZ National Bank in Pinckard, Illinois, in two installments of $3,500 each, payable on May 1, 1986, and on July 1, 1986, provided that if I fail to pay the first installment on the due date, the entire sum shall become immediately due. (Signed) Henry Brown.

Is the note negotiable? Explain.

9. Sam Sharpe executed and delivered to Don Dole the following instrument:

>   Knoxville, Tennessee
>   May 29, 1986
> Thirty days after date I promise to pay Don Dole or order, Five Thousand Dollars. The holder of this instrument shall have the election to require the assignment and delivery to him of my 100 shares of Brookside Iron Works Corporation stock in lieu of the payment of Five Thousand Dollars in money.
>
>   (Signed) Sam Sharpe.

Is this instrument negotiable? Explain.

23

TRANSFER

The primary advantage of commercial paper is its ease of transferability. Both negotiable and nonnegotiable instruments are transferable by assignment, but only a transferee of a negotiable instrument can become a holder. This distinction is highly significant. If the transferee of a negotiable instrument is by its terms entitled to payment, he is a holder of the instrument. Only holders may be holders in due course and thus entitled to greater rights in the instrument than the transferor may have possessed. These rights are discussed in the next chapter and are the reason why negotiable instruments move freely in the marketplace. In this chapter we discuss the methods by which commercial paper may be transferred.

Transfer and Negotiation

Whether a transfer is by *assignment* or *negotiation*, the transferee acquires the rights his transferor had. The transfer need not be for value; if the instrument is transferred as a gift, the donee acquires all the rights of the donor. If the transferor was a holder in due course, the transferee acquires the rights of a holder in due course, which he in turn may transfer. This rule, which is sometimes referred to as the **shelter rule**, existed at common law and exists under the Uniform Commercial Code.

Shelter rule–transferee gets rights of transferor

Negotiation is the transfer of a negotiable instrument in such a manner that the transferee becomes a holder of it. A **holder** is defined as "a person who is in possession of an instrument drawn, issued or indorsed to him or to his order or to bearer on in blank." Accordingly, to qualify as a holder a person must have possession of an instrument that runs to him. Because *bearer paper* (an instrument payable to bearer) runs to whoever is in possession of it, a finder or a thief of bearer paper would be a holder even though he did not receive possession by voluntary transfer. For example, P loses an instrument payable to bearer that M issued to him. F finds it and sells and delivers it to B, who thus receives it by negotiation and is a holder. F also qualified as a holder because he was in possession of bearer paper. As a holder, F had the power to negotiate the instrument, and the transferee (B) may be a holder in due course if he meets the Code's requirements for such a holder. (See Figure 23–1 for an illustration of this example.)

Negotiation–transferee becomes a holder

Holder–possessor of instrument properly drawn or indorsed to her or to bearer

Thus, a **bearer instrument** is transferred by mere *possession* and is therefore comparable to cash. On the other hand, if the instrument is **order paper**

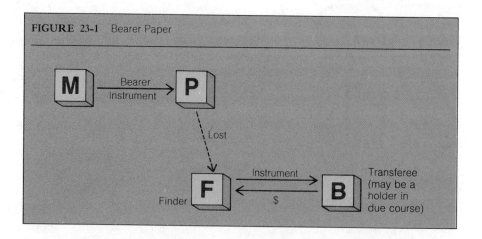

FIGURE 23-1   Bearer Paper

(an instrument payable to order), both *possession* and *indorsement* by the appropriate parties are necessary for the transferee to become a holder (see Figure 23–2).

Any transfer for value of an instrument not payable to bearer gives the transferee the specifically enforceable right to have the unqualified indorsement of the transferor, unless the parties otherwise agreed. The parties may agree that the transfer is to be an assignment rather than a negotiation, in which case no indorsement is required. If there is no such agreement, the courts presume that negotiation was intended when value is given, and if the instrument is not payable to bearer, the right of the transferee to an unqualified indorsement is enforceable by court order. Where a transfer is not for value, the transaction is normally not commercial; thus the courts do not make such a presumption.

Until the necessary indorsement has been supplied, the transferee has nothing more than the contract rights of an assignee. Negotiation takes effect only when a proper indorsement is made, because it is not until then, notwithstanding possession, that the transferee of order paper becomes a holder of the instrument.

Indorsements

Indorsement–signature of a payee, drawee, holder, or third party on the instrument

An indorsement is the signature of a payee, drawee, accommodation indorser, or holder of an instrument. An indorsement must be written on the instrument

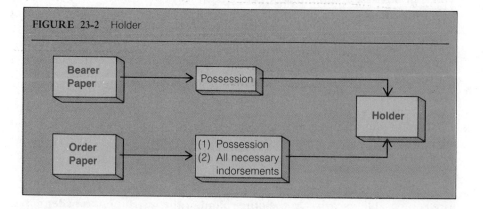

FIGURE 23-2   Holder

or on a paper, called an **allonge,** so firmly affixed to the instrument as to become a part of it. The use of an allonge is required when there are so many indorsements that there is no room for additional signatures or when the indorsement is too lengthy to fit on the instrument. A purported indorsement on a separate piece of paper, clipped or pinned to the instrument, is not valid, while a piece of paper stapled to the instrument is generally valid.

Allonge–piece of paper firmly affixed to the instrument

FACTS: The drawer Commercial Credit Corporation issued two checks payable to Rauch Motor Company. Rauch indorsed the checks in blank, deposited them to its account in University National Bank and received a corresponding amount of money. The Bank stamped "pay any bank" on the checks and initiated collection. However, the checks were dishonored and returned to the Bank with the notation "payment stopped." Rauch, through subsequent deposits, repaid the bank. Later, to compromise a lawsuit, the Bank executed a special two-page indorsement of the two checks to Lamson. Lamson then sued the Corporation for the face value of the checks, plus interest. The Corporation contends that Lamson was not a holder of the checks because the indorsement was not in conformity with the UCC in that it was stapled to the checks.

DECISION: Judgment for Lamson. The Bank indorsed the checks to Lamson by name, thus qualifying as a special indorsement. However, the UCC requires that an indorsement must be written on the instrument or "on a paper so firmly affixed thereto as to become a part thereof." Since it was physically impossible to place all of the language on the two small checks, the indorsement was typed on two separate sheets of paper and stapled to the checks. Such an attachment is called an allonge. Paper clipping the allonge to the checks would not have satisfied the UCC's "firmly affixed" requirement. Nevertheless, stapling is a sufficiently permanent attachment of the allonge to the checks to meet the UCC standard. Since Lamson possessed the Bank's special indorsement, stapled to the checks and written in his behalf, he was a holder. Therefore, he was entitled to payment unless the Corporation establishes a valid defense.

LAMSON v. COMMERCIAL CREDIT CORP.

Supreme Court of Colorado, 1975.
187 Colo. 382, 531 P.2d 966.

Customarily, indorsements are made on the back or reverse side of the instrument, starting at the top and continuing down the back. The order of the indorsement and the liability of indorsers, unless otherwise agreed, is presumed to be the order in which their signatures appear. An indorsement showing that the signer is not in the chain of title is notice of its **accommodation** character. An accommodation indorser receives no money or value for her indorsement but signs in order to add her liability and thereby accommodate, or assist, another party who might otherwise be unable to obtain funds.

Accommodation indorser–signer not in the chain of title

An indorsement may be complex or simple. It may be dated and may indicate where it is made, but neither date nor place is required. The simplest type is merely the signature of the indorser. Since the indorser undertakes certain obligations, as explained later, an indorsement consisting of merely a signature may be said to be the shortest contract known to the law. A forged or otherwise unauthorized signature necessary to negotiation is inoperative and thus breaks the chain of title to the instrument.

An indorsement conveying less than the entire instrument or any unpaid balance is not a negotiation. For example, an indorsement containing a direction to pay Ann "one-half of the note" or "$500 of the note," or to pay "two-thirds to Ann, one-third to Bob" constitutes only an assignment, and neither Ann nor Bob becomes a holder. But an indorsement "to Art and Bess" is effective as a negotiation because it transfers the entire interest to Art and Bess. Words such as "I hereby assign all my right, title, and interest in the within note" are also sufficient as a negotiation.

The type of indorsement used in negotiating an instrument affects its subsequent negotiation. Every indorsement is (1) either blank or special, (2) either restrictive or nonrestrictive, and (3) either qualified or unqualified. These indorsements are not mutually exclusive. Indeed, all indorsements may be sorted into three of these six categories, because all indorsements disclose three things: (1) the method to be employed in making subsequent negotiations (this depends on whether the indorsement is blank or special); (2) the kind of interest that is being transferred (this depends on whether the indorsement is restrictive or nonrestrictive); and (3) the liability of the indorser (this depends on whether the indorsement is qualified or unqualified). For instance, an indorser who merely signs her name on the back of an instrument is making a blank, nonrestrictive, unqualified indorsement.

Blank Indorsements

Blank indorsement–no indorsee is specified

A blank indorsement specifies no indorsee and may consist of merely the signature of the indorser or her authorized agent. A blank indorsement converts order paper into **bearer paper.** Thus, an instrument indorsed in blank may be negotiated by delivery alone without further indorsement. Hence, the holder should treat it with the same care as cash. See *Palmer & Ray Dental Supply of Abilene, Inc. v. First National Bank* at page 380. He may protect himself, however, by converting the blank indorsement to a special indorsement by writing over the signature of the indorser any contract consistent with the character of the indorsement. For example, on the back of a negotiable instrument appears the blank indorsement "Sally Seller." Harry Holder, who received the instrument from Seller, may convert this bearer instrument into order paper by inserting above Seller's signature "Pay Harry Holder" or other similar words.

Special Indorsements

Special indorsement designates an indorsee to be paid

A special indorsement specifically designates the person to whom or to whose order the instrument is to be payable **(order paper).** Thus, if P, the payee of a note, indorses it with the words "Pay to the order of A" or even "Pay A," the indorsement is special because it names the transferee. Words of negotiability are not required in an indorsement and any further negotiation of the instrument requires A's indorsement or that of A's authorized agent.

CASAREZ v. GARCIA

Court of Appeals of New Mexico, 1983.
99 N.M. 508, 660 P.2d 598.

FACTS: Arthur and Lucy Casarez contracted with Blas Garcia, who purported to be a representative of the Albuquerque Fence Company, for the construction of a new home. Blas introduced the Casarezes to Cecil Garcia, who agreed to make a loan to them to be used as a down payment on the project. Cecil then obtained a loan from Rio Grande Valley Bank ("the Bank") in the form of a $25,000 cashier's check payable to himself, which he indorsed over to Lucy Casarez. Lucy indorsed the check: "Pay to the order of Albuquerque Fence Company, Lucy N. Casarez," and delivered it to Blas Garcia. Claiming he was following Cecil's instructions, Blas indorsed the check: "Alb. Fence Co." and gave the check to Cecil. Cecil signed his own name under "Alb. Fence Co." and presented the check to the Bank in exchange for $25,000. The Casarezes soon learned that Blas and Cecil Garcia had never been in any way affiliated or employed by the Albuquerque Fence Company. Lucy then brought suit against the Bank, claiming that the unauthorized signatures of Blas and Cecil Garcia invalidated the special indorsement to Albuquerque Fence Company and that therefore the Bank negligently cashed the check, rendering the Bank liable to Lucy for the amount of the check.

DECISION: Judgment for Lucy Casarez. A special indorsement specifies to whom or to whose order it makes the instrument payable. If it is specially indorsed to an organization, only one authorized by the organization may indorse it. Here, Lucy specially indorsed the check to the Albuquerque Fence Company. Blas indorsed it without proper authority from the Company, rendering Lucy's special indorsement ineffective to pass title to Cecil and preventing its further negotiation. Cecil, having knowledge of Lucy's special indorsement and Blas' lack of authority, could gain no more authority to indorse than Blas had. Thus, Lucy remained the owner of the check. The Bank, therefore, is liable to Lucy, the owner of the cashier's check, since it negligently failed to check the validity of the indorsements.

Restrictive Indorsements

As the term implies, a restrictive indorsement attempts to restrict the rights of the indorsee in some fashion. The UCC defines four types of indorsements as restrictive: conditional indorsements, indorsements prohibiting further transfer, indorsements for deposit or collection, and indorsements in trust. An unrestrictive indorsement does not attempt to restrict the rights of the indorsee.

Restrictive indorsement–limits the rights of the indorser

Conditional Indorsements   In a conditional indorsement the indorser makes the rights of the indorsee subject to the happening or nonhappening of a specified event. Suppose Mark makes a note payable to Pat's order. Pat indorses it "Pay Adam, but only if the good ship Jolly Jack arrives in Chicago harbor by November 15, 1986." If Mark had used this language in the instrument, it would be nonnegotiable, because her promise to pay must be unconditional to satisfy the formal requisites of negotiability. But indorsers *are* permitted to condition the rights of their indorsees without destroying negotiability.

If the good ship Jolly Jack does not arrive in Chicago harbor by November 15, 1986, Adam has no rights in the instrument. If he presents the instrument to Mark for payment, Mark must dishonor the instrument or be required to pay it again to Pat. Mark is not discharged when he pays an instrument that has been restrictively indorsed, unless he pays in a manner consistent with the indorsement.

Indorsements Prohibiting Further Transfer   To be negotiable, an instrument not payable to bearer must be payable to the order of a payee. If the instrument reads merely "Pay A," it is not negotiable, and the only possible method of transfer is by assignment. The requirements of negotiability, however, are not imposed on indorsements. An indorsement reading "Pay A" or even "Pay A only" is interpreted as meaning "Pay to the order of A." Such indorsements, or any other purporting to prohibit further transfer, are designed to be a restriction on the rights of the indorsee. To remove any doubt as to the effect of such a provision the Code provides that *no* restrictive indorsement prevents further transfer or negotiation of the instrument. The net result of this provision is that an indorsement that purports to prohibit further transfer of the instrument is given the same effect as an unrestricted indorsement.

Indorsements for Deposit or Collection   The most frequently used form of restrictive indorsement is that designed to lodge the instrument in the banking system for deposit or collection. Indorsements of this type include those "for collection," "for deposit," and "pay any bank." Such indorsements *effectively limit* further negotiation to those consistent with its limitation and put all nonbanking persons on notice as to who has a valid interest in the paper. The following two cases should be contrasted.

PALMER & RAY DENTAL SUPPLY OF ABILENE, INC. v. FIRST NATIONAL BANK

Court of Civil Appeals of Texas, 1972.
477 S.W.2d 954.

FACTS: Mrs. Wilson was employed as the office manager of Palmer & Ray Dental Supply. Soon after an auditor discovered a discrepancy in the company's inventory, Mrs. Wilson confessed to cashing thirty-five checks that she was supposed to deposit on behalf of the company. Palmer & Ray Dental Supply used a rubber stamp to indorse checks. The stamp listed the company name and address but did not read "for deposit only." Mrs. Wilson was authorized by the company president, James Ray, to indorse checks with this stamp. All checks were cashed at First National Bank. Palmer & Ray Dental Supply now claims that First National converted the company's funds by giving Mrs. Wilson cash instead of depositing the checks into the company bank account. Summary judgment was granted in favor of First National and Palmer & Ray brought this appeal.

DECISION: Judgment for the First National Bank. A blank indorsement is one that specifies no particular indorsee and that may consist of a mere signature. A restrictive indorsement, on the other hand, includes one that uses the words "for deposit." The rubber stamp used by Mrs. Wilson to indorse the checks on the company's behalf was a blank indorsement, as it only stated the company name and its address. Moreover, Mrs. Wilson indorsed the checks under the actual implied or apparent authority granted by Mr. Ray, the company president. Accordingly, when First National Bank delivered cash to Mrs. Wilson instead of depositing the proceeds from the checks into the company account, the bank acted in conformity with the indorsement.

FULTZ v. FIRST NATIONAL BANK IN GRAHAM

Supreme Court of Texas, 1965.
388 S.W.2d 405.

FACTS: Mrs. McCoy, as employee of Fultz, secured cash in the amount of $13,060 from checks she deposited on Fultz's behalf and misappropriated the funds to her personal use. The full indorsement which was stamped on the back of each check read: "Pay to order of the First National Bank, Graham, Texas—For deposit only—W. B. Fultz." Mrs. McCoy had not signed a signature card at the bank and was not authorized by Fultz to indorse checks or to withhold cash amounts from the deposits made on his behalf. Fultz now brings this suit against First National to recover the cash received by Mrs. McCoy on the "for deposit only" transactions.

DECISION: Judgment for Fultz. All of the checks deposited by Mrs. McCoy were indorsed for deposit only. This represented an unqualified direction to the bank to place the full amount of the check into Fultz's account. Fultz had established a regular deposit routine including the restrictive indorsement, and he had no further duty to inquire if the bank had followed his instructions. Furthermore, Fultz had no actual knowledge of the bank's disbursement of cash to Mrs. McCoy, and he in no way misled the bank as to Mrs. McCoy's authority since he neither filed a signature card for her nor authorized her to indorse checks for him or withdraw funds on his behalf. The bank, then, is liable to Fultz for not following the instructions of the restrictive indorsement.

Indorsements in Trust   Another common kind of restrictive indorsement is that in which the indorser creates a trust for the benefit of himself or others. If an instrument is indorsed "Pay T in trust for B" or "Pay T for B" or "Pay T for account of B" or "Pay T as agent for B," T is a fiduciary (trustee), subject to liability for any breach of his obligation. Trustees commonly and legitimately sell trust assets, and as a consequence, a trustee has power to negotiate an instrument. The first taker under an indorsement to him in trust (T in the above examples) is under the duty to pay or apply all funds given by him consistently with the indorsement or risk having to pay twice. Subsequent indorsees or transferees are not bound by such indorsement unless they have knowledge that the negotiation to the first taker was in breach of fiduciary duty.

Qualified Indorsements

Indorsers, except those indorsing without recourse, promise that they will pay the instrument according to its terms at the time of their indorsement to the holder or to any subsequent indorser. In short, an **unqualified** indorser guarantees payment of the instrument if certain conditions are met.

An indorser may disclaim her liability on the contract of indorsement, but only if the indorsement declares this intention and it is written on the instrument. The customary manner of disclaiming liability is to add the words **"without recourse"** before or after the signature. An indorsement "without recourse" is called a **qualified** indorsement. A qualified indorsement and delivery is a negotiation and transfers legal title to the indorsee, but the indorser does *not* guarantee payment of the instrument. A qualified indorsement does not destroy negotiability or prevent further negotiation of the instrument. For example, assume that an attorney receives a check payable to her order in payment of a client's claim. She may indorse the check to the client without recourse, thereby disclaiming liability as a guarantor of payment of the check. The qualified indorsement plus delivery would transfer title to the client.

Figure 23–3 illustrates the classification of indorsements.

Qualified indorsement without recourse, limiting one's liability on the instrument

---

FIGURE 23-3   Indorsements

Indorsement	Type of Indorsement	Interest Transferred	Liability of Indorser
1. "John Doe"	Blank	Nonrestrictive	Unqualified
2. "Pay to Richard Roe, John Doe"	Special	Nonrestrictive	Unqualified
3. "Without recourse, John Doe"	Blank	Nonrestrictive	Qualified
4. "Pay to Richard Roe, without recourse, John Doe"	Special	Nonrestrictive	Qualified
5. "For collection only, without recourse, John Doe"	Blank	Restrictive	Qualified
6. "Pay to XYZ Bank, for collection only, John Doe"	Special	Restrictive	Unqualified

CHAPTER SUMMARY

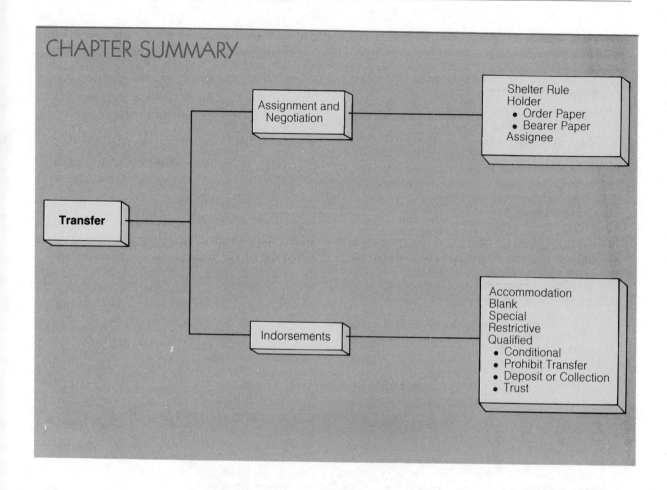

KEY TERMS

Assignment

Transfer

Negotiation

Shelter rule

Holder

Assignee

Indorsement

Allonge

Accommodation indorser

Blank indorsement

Special indorsement

Restrictive indorsement

Unrestrictive indorsement

Conditional indorsement

Unconditional indorsement

For deposit only

Indorsement in trust

PROBLEMS

1. Roy Rand executed and delivered the following note to Sue Sims: "Chicago, Illinois, June 1, 1986. I promise to pay to the order of Sue Sims or bearer, on or before July 1, 1986, the sum of $7,000. This note is given in consideration of Sims's transferring to the undersigned title to her 1984 Buick automobile. (signed) Roy Rand." Rand and Sims agreed that delivery of the car be deferred to July 1, 1986. On June 15, Sims sold and delivered the note, without indorsement, to Karl Kaye for $6,200. What rights, if any, has Kaye acquired?

2. Lavinia Lane received a check from Wilmore Enterprises, Inc., drawn on the Citizens Bank of Erehwon, in the sum of $10,000. Mrs. Lane indorsed the check "Mrs. Lavinia Lane for deposit only, Account of Lavinia Lane," placed it in a "bank by mail" envelope addressed to the First National Bank of Emanon, where she maintained a checking account, and placed the envelope over a tier of mailboxes in her apartment building along with other letters to be picked up by the postman the next day.

Flora Fain stole the check, went to the Bank of X, where Mrs. Lane was unknown, represented herself to be Lavinia Lane, and cashed the check. Has Bank X taken the check by negotiation? Why or why not?

3. What types of indorsements are the following:
(a) "Pay to M without recourse."
(b) "Pay to A for collection."
(c) "I hereby assign all my rights, title, and interest in this note to F in full."
(d) "Pay to the Southern Trust Company."
(e) "Pay to the order of the Farmers Bank of Nicholasville for deposit only."

Indicate whether the indorsement is (1) blank or special, (2) restrictive or nonrestrictive, and (3) qualified or unqualified.

4. Explain whether the following transactions result in a valid negotiation:
(a) A gives a negotiable check payable to bearer to B without indorsing it.

(b) G indorses a negotiable promissory note payable to the order of G, "Pay to M and N, (signed) G."
(c) X lost a negotiable check payable to his order. Y found it and indorsed the back of the check: "Pay to Z, (signed) Y."
(d) C indorsed a negotiable promissory note payable to the order of C, "(signed) C," and delivered it to D. D then wrote above C's signature, "Pay to D."

5. Alpha issues a negotiable check to Beta payable to the order of Beta in payment of an obligation Alpha owed Beta. Beta delivers the check to Gamma without indorsing it in exchange for 100 shares of General Motors stock owned by Gamma. How has Beta transferred the check? What rights, if any, does Gamma have against Beta?

6. M executed and delivered to P a negotiable promissory note payable to the order of P as payment for 100 bushels of wheat P had sold to M. P indorsed the note "Pay to R only, (signed) P" and sold it to R. R then sold the note to S after indorsing it "Pay to S, (signed) R." What rights, if any, does S acquire in the instrument?

7. Simon Sharpe executed and delivered to Ben Bates a negotiable promissory note payable to the order of Ben Bates for $500. Bates indorsed the note, "Pay to Carl Cady upon his satisfactorily repairing the roof of my house, (signed) Ben Bates," and delivered it to Cady as a downpayment on the contract price of the roofing job. Cady then indorsed the note and sold it to Timothy Tate for $450. What rights, if any, does Tate acquire in the promissory note?

8. Debbie Dean issued a check to Betty Brown payable to the order of Cathy Cain and Betty Brown. Betty indorsed the check "Pay to Elizabeth East, (signed) Betty Brown." What rights, if any, does Elizabeth acquire in the check?

24

HOLDER IN DUE COURSE

The unique and most significant aspect of negotiability is the concept of the holder in due course. While a mere holder acquires a negotiable instrument subject to all claims and defenses to it, a holder in due course, in a *nonconsumer* credit transaction, takes the instrument free of all claims of other parties and free of all defenses to the instrument except for a very limited number specifically set forth in the Uniform Commercial Code. The law has conferred this preferred position on the holder in due course to encourage the free negotiability of commercial paper by minimizing the risks assumed by an innocent purchaser of the instrument. In this chapter we discuss how a transferee becomes a holder in due course and the benefits conferred on a holder in due course.

Requirements of a Holder in Due Course

To acquire the preferential rights of a holder in due course, a person must meet the requirements of the Code or must "inherit" these rights under the shelter rule. To satisfy the requirements a holder in due course must:

1. be a holder of a negotiable instrument;
2. take it for value;
3. take it in good faith; and
4. take it without notice
   (a) that it is overdue or has been dishonored, or
   (b) of any defense against or claim to it on the part of any person.

Figure 24-1 illustrates the various steps in becoming a holder in due course.

Holder

The transferee must be a holder before he can become a holder in due course. As previously discussed, a holder is a person who possesses a negotiable instrument that is drawn or issued either to his order or to bearer and is either indorsed to him or in blank. In other words, by the terms of the instrument the holder is entitled to payment. Whether or not the holder is the owner of

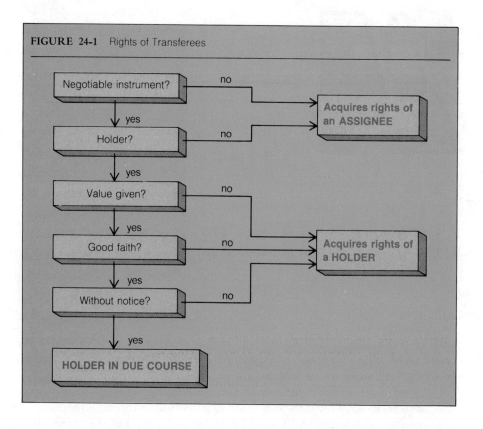

FIGURE 24-1   Rights of Transferees

the instrument, he may transfer it, negotiate it, discharge it, or enforce payment in his own name.

The significance of being a holder is brought out in the following factual situation, which is illustrated in Figure 24-2. Poe indorsed her paycheck in blank and cashed it at a tavern where she was a well-known customer. Shortly thereafter, a burglar stole the check from the tavern. The owner of the tavern immediately notified Poe's employer, who gave the drawee bank a stop payment order. The burglar indorsed the check in a false name and passed it to a grocer, who took it in good faith and for value. The check was dishonored on presentment to the drawee bank. The paycheck became bearer paper when Poe indorsed it in blank. It retained this character in the hands of the tavern owner, in the hands of the burglar, and in the hands of the grocer, who became a holder in due course even though he had received it from a thief who had indorsed it with a false name. An indorsement is not necessary to the negotiation of bearer paper. The forged indorsement was therefore immaterial. The thief was a holder of the check and as such could negotiate it. Accordingly, one who, like the grocer, takes from a holder for value, in good faith, and without notice becomes a holder in due course and can collect the amount of the check from the drawer.

This rule does not apply to a stolen order instrument. In the example above assume that the thief had stolen the paycheck from Poe prior to indorsement. The thief then forged Poe's signature and passed the check to the grocer, who again took it in good faith, for value, and without notice.

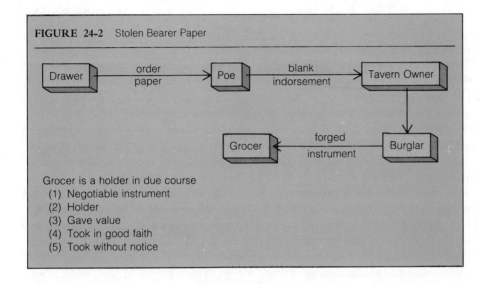

FIGURE 24-2   Stolen Bearer Paper

Grocer is a holder in due course
(1) Negotiable instrument
(2) Holder
(3) Gave value
(4) Took in good faith
(5) Took without notice

Negotiation of an order instrument requires a valid indorsement by the person to whose order the instrument is payable, in this case Poe. A forged indorsement is not valid. Consequently, the grocer has not taken the instrument with all necessary indorsements, and he could not be a holder or a holder in due course. Figure 24-3 illustrates this example.

Value

The law requires a holder in due course to have given value. An obvious case of failure to give value is where the holder makes a gift of the instrument to a third person.

The concept of value in the law of negotiable instruments is not the same as that of consideration under the law of contracts. An executory promise, clearly valid consideration to support a contract, is not the giving of value to support holder-in-due course status. A purchaser of a note or draft who has not yet given value may rescind the transaction and avoid it through a valid defense. A person who has given value, however, needs and deserves the

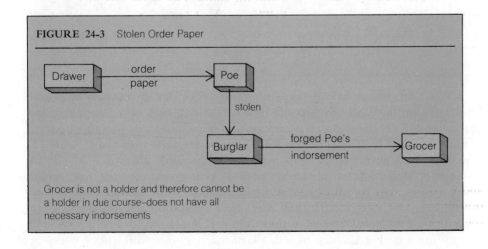

FIGURE 24-3   Stolen Order Paper

Grocer is not a holder and therefore cannot be
a holder in due course–does not have all
necessary indorsements

protection given to a holder in due course. Thus, as demonstrated in *Korzenik v. Supreme Radio, Inc.*, a holder takes an instrument for value only to the extent that the agreed consideration has been *given*, provided the consideration was given before the holder learned of any defense or claim to the instrument.

For example, M executes and delivers a $1,000 note payable to the order of P, who negotiates it to H, who promises to pay P for it a month later. During the month, H learns that M has a defense against P. H can rescind the agreement with P and return the note to P. This makes him whole, and he has no need to cut off M's defense. Assume, on the other hand, that H has paid P for the note before he learns of M's defense. It may not be possible for H to recover his money from P. H then needs the holder-in-due course protection that permits him to recover on the instrument from M. Further, assume that H had agreed to pay P $850 for the note. If H had paid P $600, he could be a holder in due course only to the extent of $600, and if a defense were available, it would be valid against him only to the extent of the balance. When H paid the $250 balance to P, he would become a holder in due course as to the full $1,000 face value of the note, provided payment was made prior to H's discovery of M's defense. If the $250 payment was made after discovery of the defense or claim, H would be a holder in due course only to the extent of $600. A holder in due course, to give value, is not required to pay the face amount of the instrument, but only the amount he agreed to pay.

> **Value**–the performance of legal consideration, the forgiveness of an antecedent debt, the giving of a negotiable instrument, or the giving of an irrevocable commitment to a third party

KORZENIK v. SUPREME RADIO, INC.

Supreme Judicial Court of Massachusetts, 1964.
347 Mass. 309, 197 N.E.2d 702.

FACTS: Supreme Radio, Inc. issued to Southern New England Distributing Corporation two notes worth $1,900. The two notes and others, all of a total face value of about $15,000, were transferred to Korzenik, an attorney, by their client Southern "as a retainer for services to be performed" by Korzenik. Although Korzenik was unaware of the fact, Southern had obtained the notes by fraud. Southern retained Korzenik on October 25, in connection with certain antitrust litigation, and the notes were transferred on October 31. The value of the services performed by Korzenik during that time is unclear. Korzenik now brings this action against Supreme Radio to recover $1,900 on the notes.

DECISION: Judgment for Supreme Radio. In order to qualify as a holder in due course, a holder of an instrument must take for value. A holder takes an instrument for value (a) to the extent that the agreed consideration has been performed or that he acquires a security interest in or a lien on the instrument otherwise than by legal process; or (b) when he takes the instrument in payment of or as security for an antecedent claim against any person whether or not the claim is due; or (c) when he gives a negotiable instrument for it or makes an irrevocable commitment to a third person. Value is divorced from consideration, and except as is provided in (c), an executory promise to give value is not value. Here, Korzenik has failed to show the extent to which the agreed consideration has been performed and, hence, the value that has been given.

The Code, as noted in the above case, provides an exception to the executory promise rule in two situations: (1) the giving of a negotiable instrument and (2) the making of an irrevocable commitment to a third party. Suppose that M makes a note for $1,000 payable to the order of P, which P indorses and delivers to H, who gives P her personal check for $1,000 in exchange for it. H met the requirement of giving value for the note when she gave P her check, not when the check was paid by the drawee bank. Value would likewise be given if H made any other irrevocable commitment, if the commitment was to a *third party* rather than to P. An example of an irrevocable commitment is the issuance by a bank of a letter of credit, under which it agrees to pay amounts advanced to the person to whom it is issued, up to a stated limit. The bank has no way of stopping payment on such a letter of credit.

Where an instrument is given as security for an obligation, the lender is also regarded as having given value to the extent of his security interest. For example, P is the holder of a $1,000 note payable to his order, executed by M, and due in twelve months. P uses the note as security for a $700 loan made to him by H. Because H has advanced $700, he has met the requirement of value to this extent.

Finally, under general contract law an **antecedent debt** is not sufficient consideration to support a promise to pay the debt or a lesser amount in full satisfaction. However, under the Code a holder does give value when she takes an instrument in payment of or as security for an antecedent debt. Thus, M makes and delivers a note for $1,000 to the order of P, which P sells by indorsement and delivery to H in payment of or security for a debt owing to H by P. H has met the value requirement. Similarly, see *St. Paul Fire & Marine Ins. Co. v. State Bank of Salem* below.

Antecedent debt–preexisting obligation

Good Faith

The Code defines good faith as "honesty in fact in the conduct or transaction concerned." The test is **subjective:** it measures good faith by what the purchaser knows or believes. He may be empty-headed, but if his heart is pure, he can pass muster on good faith grounds. Under this test, if the purchaser was actually innocent, he is held to have bought the paper in good faith, even though a prudent man under the circumstances would have known that something was wrong.

Good faith–honesty in fact

Lack of Notice

To become a holder in due course, a holder must also take the instrument without notice that it is overdue, dishonored, or subject to any defense or claim. Notice of any of these matters should alert the purchaser that she may be buying a lawsuit and therefore should refuse to take the instrument. To be effective, notice must be received at such a time and way that will give the recipient a reasonable opportunity to act on it.

Notice of a Claim or Defense   A purchaser has notice of a claim or defense if the instrument so bears visible evidence of forgery or alteration, or is so irregular as to call its validity into question. For example, D draws a check on the First National Bank for $100, payable to the order of P. P crudely raises the amount of the check to $1,000 and negotiates it to H. H cannot be a holder in due course. The instrument is irregular, and the alteration is so obvious that H would be held to have notice of it. Nonetheless, as the following case demonstrates, the courts vary greatly on how irregular the alteration must be to rule that a holder had notice of it.

FACTS: Stephens delivered 184 bushels of corn to Aubrey for which he was to receive $478.23. Aubrey issued a check with $478.23 typewritten in numbers and on the line customarily used to express the amount in words appeared "$100478 and 23 cts" imprinted in red with a check-writing machine. Before Stephens cashed the check, someone crudely typed "100" in front of the typewritten $478.23. When Stephens presented this check to the State Bank of Salem, Anderson, the manager, questioned Stephens. Anderson knew that Stephens had just declared bankruptcy and was not accustomed to making such large deposits. Stephens told Anderson he

ST. PAUL FIRE AND MARINE INSURANCE CO. v. STATE BANK OF SALEM

Court of Appeals of Indiana, First District, 1980. 412 N.E.2d 103.

had bought and sold a large quantity of corn at a great profit. Anderson accepted the explanation, applied the monies to nine promissory notes, an installment payment, and accrued interest owed by Stephens. Stephens also received $2000 in cash with the balance deposited in his checking account.

Later that day, Anderson reexamined the checks and discovered the suspicious appearance of the typewriting. He then contacted Aubrey who said a check in that amount was suspicious, whereupon Anderson froze the transaction. When Aubrey stopped payment on the check, the Bank sustained a $28,193.91 loss, because Stephens could not be located. The Bank then sued Aubrey for the loss. As defenses, Aubrey claims that the Bank did not take the check for value and that the typed "100" put the Bank on notice of Aubrey's defense. Thus, Aubrey contended that the Bank was not a holder in due course and did not possess a valid claim against Aubrey.

DECISION: Judgment for State Bank of Salem. Under the UCC, value is given for an instrument when the instrument is taken in payment for an antecedent debt. Moreover, when credit is drawn upon, value is given to that extent. Value is also given to the extent that the funds represented by the check are applied to an overdrawn account. Here, the Bank's application of funds made available by the Aubrey check to Stephens' indebtedness and the surrender of the notes constituted taking the instrument for value.

Furthermore, the Bank took the check without notice of Aubrey's defense. In case of ambiguity, typewritten terms control printed terms and words control figures. The court determined that the impressions made by the check imprinter were not "printed" terms. However, they should be considered "words", since they were on the line typically used for expressing the amount in words, not figures. Moreover, Aubrey did not prove that Anderson violated customary banking standards by not comparing the two amounts. Consequently, Anderson's reliance upon the amount expressed by the check imprinter was reasonable. In addition, the typed figure "100", was not such visible evidence of an alteration of the check as to put the Bank on notice of Aubrey's defense.

Finally, the circumstances surrounding such a transaction may be so irregular as to put a reasonably prudent banker on notice of a defense or claim. However, Anderson's knowledge of Stephens' questionable general financial position, by itself, is insufficient to defeat the Bank's holder in due course status. Thus, the Bank can enforce the check against Aubrey to the extent it gave value for it.

Suppose, however, there is an obvious change on the face of the instrument that does not normally indicate wrongdoing. For instance, the date may be changed from January 2, 1985, to January 2, 1986. It would be reasonable to assume that the drawer, out of force of habit, wrote "1985" rather than "1986." This would not be considered a material alteration that would give notice of a defense or claim.

Additionally, a purchaser has notice of a claim or defense if the purchaser has notice that the obligation of any party is *voidable* or that *all* parties to the instrument have been discharged. The fact that the holder knows that one or more but not all the parties have been discharged does not prevent the holder from being a holder in due course with respect to the nondischarged parties. For example, M issues a negotiable promissory note to P, who indorses it in blank and delivers it to Arthur. The instrument then passes by blank indorsements to Bob, Clara, and Diane. Diane strikes out Clara's indorsement and negotiates it for value to H. H would have notice that Clara's liability had been discharged. This would not prevent H from being a holder in due course with respect to M, P, Arthur, Bob, and Diane because their liability is not discharged.

Notice an Instrument is Overdue   To be a holder in due course the purchaser must take the instrument without notice that it is overdue. This requirement is based on the idea that overdue paper conveys a suspicion that something is wrong. Thus, if an instrument is payable on July 1, a purchaser cannot become a holder in due course by buying it on July 2, provided that July 1 was a business day.

Demand paper is not overdue for purposes of preventing one from becoming a holder in due course unless the purchaser has notice that she is taking it after demand has been made, or until it has been outstanding an unreasonable length of time. Although the UCC does not state what a reasonable time is, in the case of a demand note it is usually about sixty days. The time is somewhat shorter for drafts, and with regard to checks a reasonable time is presumed to be thirty days. However, the particular situation, business custom, and other relevant factors must be considered in making the determination, and no hard and fast rules are possible.

Notice an Instrument Has Been Dishonored   If a transferee has notice that an instrument has been dishonored by the refusal of a party to pay or accept it, he cannot become a holder in due course. He knows the instrument may not be paid.

Holder in Due Course Status

A Payee May Be a Holder in Due Course

The Code provides that a payee may be a holder in due course. This does not mean that the payee will always be a holder in due course but merely that he *may* if he satisfies all the requirements for a holder to become a holder in due course. For example, if a seller delivers goods to a buyer and accepts a current check in payment, the seller will be a holder in due course if he acted in good faith and had no notice of defenses or claims. However, the seller takes the check **subject to** all claims and defenses because a holder in due course takes instruments free of defenses only from persons he has *not* dealt with.

In a number of situations, however, the payee is not an immediate party to the transaction and therefore will not be subject to claims and most defenses if he meets the requirements of a holder in due course. For example, Robin, after purchasing goods from Paul, fraudulently obtains a check from Chris payable to the order of Paul and forwards it to Paul. Paul takes it for value and without any knowledge that Robin had defrauded Chris into issuing the check. In such a case, the payee, Paul, is held to be a holder in due course and takes the instrument free and clear of Chris's defense of fraud in the inducement. There are a number of other ways in which a payee may be a holder in due course, but they are rather infrequent. In every instance there are three parties involved in the transaction, and the defense exists between the parties other than the payee.

FACTS: Eldon's Super Fresh Stores, Inc., is a corporation engaged in the retail grocery business. William Drexler was the attorney for and the corporate secretary of Eldon's and was also the personal attorney of Eldon Prinzing, the corporation's president and sole shareholder. From January 1969 through January 1970, Drexler maintained an active stock trading account in his name with Merrill Lynch. Eldon's had no such account. On August 12, 1969, Drexler purchased 100 shares of Clark Oil & Refining Company stock through his Merrill Lynch stockbroker. He paid for the stock with a check drawn by Eldon's made payable to Merrill Lynch and signed by Prinzing. On August 15, 1969, Merrill Lynch accepted the check as payment for Drexler's stock purchase. There was no communication between Eldon's and Merrill Lynch until November 1970, fifteen months after the issuance of the check. At that time Eldon's inquired of Merrill

ELDON'S SUPER FRESH STORES, INC. v. MERRIL LYNCH, PIERCE, FENNER & SMITH, INC.

Supreme Court of Minnesota, 1933.
296 Minn. 130, 207 N.W.2d 282.

Lynch as to the whereabouts of the stock certificate and asserted a claim as to its ownership. It then brought this action, claiming that it gave the check to Drexler to be delivered to Merrill Lynch for Eldon's benefit.

DECISION: Judgment for Merrill Lynch. A payee may be a holder in due course if it can be shown that it took the instrument for value, in good faith, and without notice that the instrument was overdue or had been dishonored or of any defense against or claim to it on the part of any person. At issue here is whether Merrill Lynch took the instrument without notice of a defense to it by Eldon's. Merrill Lynch did not have actual knowledge of the claim, nor did it have "inferable knowledge" from the fact that Drexler settled his account with a check drawn by Eldon's. The bank check was delivered to Merrill Lynch by Eldon's agent, Drexler, with the consent and knowledge of Eldon's president; it contained no restrictions or designations as to its use; and Eldon's had no trading account with Merrill Lynch; therefore, Merrill Lynch took the check without notice of Eldon's claims and became a holder in due course of the check free from Eldon's claim of wrongful delivery.

The Shelter Rule

The transferee of an instrument, as previously noted, acquires the same rights in the instrument that the transferor had. Therefore, even if a holder does not comply with all the requirements for being a holder in due course, she nevertheless acquires all the rights of that status if some previous holder of the instrument had been a holder in due course. Thus, P induces M by fraud to make a note payable to her order and then negotiates it to A, a holder in due course. After the note is overdue, A gives it to B, who has notice of the fraud. B is not a holder in due course, since he has taken the instrument when overdue, did not pay value, and has notice of M's defense. Nonetheless, through the operation of the shelter rule B acquires A's rights as a holder in due course, and M cannot successfully assert his defense against B. The purpose of the shelter provision is not to benefit the transferee but to assure the holder in due course of a free market for commercial paper he acquires.

The rule, however, states that a person who is not a holder in due course cannot obtain the rights of one by reacquiring it from a subsequent holder in due course or a person having the rights of one. For example, P induces M by fraud to make an instrument payable to the order of P. P subsequently negotiates the instrument to H, a holder in due course, and later reacquires it from H. P does not succeed to H's rights as a holder in due course and remains subject to the defense of fraud.

The Preferred Position of a Holder in Due Course

In a **nonconsumer** transaction, a holder in due course takes the instrument free from all claims on the part of any person and free from all defenses of any party with whom he has not dealt except for a limited number of defenses which are available against anyone, including a holder in due course. Such defenses are referred to as **real** defenses, as opposed to defenses that may not be asserted against a holder in due course, which are referred to as **personal** or **contractual** defenses (see Figure 24-4).

Real Defenses

The real defense available against **all** holders, including holders in due course, are:

1. minority to the extent that it is a defense to a simple contract;

Real defenses–defenses that are valid against all holders, including holders in due course

Personal defenses–contractual defenses which are good against holders but not holders in due course

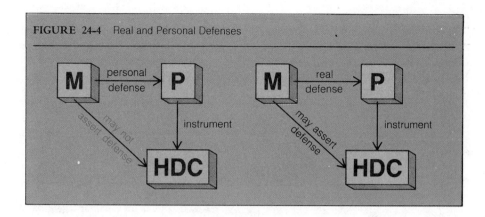

FIGURE 24-4   Real and Personal Defenses

2. any incapacity, duress, or illegality of the transaction that renders the obligation of the party void;

3. fraud in the execution;

4. discharge in insolvency proceedings;

5. any other discharge that the holder has notice of when he takes the instrument;

6. forgery; and

7. material alteration.

Minority   All States have a firmly entrenched public policy of protecting minors from persons who might take advantage of them through contractual dealings. The UCC does not state when minority is available as a defense or the conditions under which it may be asserted. Rather, it provides that minority is a defense available against a holder in due course to the extent that it is a defense to a simple contract under the laws of the State involved.

Void Obligations   Where the obligation on an instrument originates in such a way that under the law of the State involved it is *void*, the UCC authorizes the use of this defense against a holder in due course. This follows from the fact that where the party was never obligated, it is unreasonable to permit an event over which he has no control—negotiation to a holder in due course—to make a void obligation into a valid claim against him.

Incapacity, duress, and illegality of the transaction are defenses that may render the obligation of a party voidable or void, depending on the law of the State and how it is applied to the facts of a transaction. To the extent the obligation is rendered void, the defense may be asserted against a holder in due course. To the extent it is voidable only, which is generally the case, the defense (other than minority) is not available against a holder in due course.

Fraud in the Execution   Fraud in the execution of the instrument renders the instrument void and therefore is a defense valid against a holder in due course. The Code describes this type of fraud as misrepresentation that induced the party to sign the instrument with neither knowledge nor reasonable opportunity to obtain knowledge of its character or its essential terms. For example, Mary is asked to sign a receipt and does so without realizing or having the opportunity of learning that her signature is going on a form of promissory note cleverly concealed under the receipt. Mary's signature has been obtained by fraud in the execution, and Mary would have a valid defense against a holder in due course. The fraud, however, as previously indicated and as shown in the following case must preclude the deceived party from knowing or having a reasonable opportunity to know what she was signing.

EXCHANGE INTERNATIONAL LEASING CORP. v. **CONSOLIDATED BUSINESS FORMS CO.** United States District Court, W.D. Pennsylvania, 1978. 462 F.Supp. 626.	**FACTS:** Consolidated Business Forms leased a Phillips business computer from Benchmark. Benchmark subsequently transferred the lease and promissory note to Exchange International Leasing Corporation. Consolidated stopped making rental payments when the computer malfunctioned, and Exchange International brought this suit to recover the payments due on the promissory note. Consolidated defends on the grounds that Benchmark prevented its agent, Mr. Spohn, from examining the contents of the agreement between the two companies and further represented that the computer would be removed with a complete refund if it failed to operate properly. **DECISION:** Judgment for Exchange International. Exchange International by virtue of the negotiation of the instrument attained the status of a holder in due course. Accordingly, Exchange International took the instrument free from all defenses of any party to the instrument with whom it had not dealt unless the party had a real defense. To establish the real defense of fraud in the execution one must not only have no knowledge of the document's character or essential terms but also have had no reasonable opportunity to acquire such knowledge. Here, even if the Benchmark employee represented to Consolidated's agent, Mr. Spohn, that the computer would be removed with a complete refund if it malfunctioned, it cannot be said that Spohn lacked a reasonable opportunity to acquire knowledge of the essential terms of the agreement. Moreover, the misrepresentation allegedly made by Benchmark is an example of fraud in the inducement, which is not a defense to a claim by a holder in due course.

Discharge in Insolvency Proceedings   If a party's obligation on an instrument is discharged in a bankruptcy proceeding, he has a valid defense in any action brought against him on the instrument, including one by a holder in due course.

Discharge of Which the Holder Has Notice   Any holder, including a holder in due course, takes the instrument subject to *any* discharge of which she has notice when she takes the instrument. As previously noted, if a holder acquires an instrument with notice that *all* prior parties have been discharged, she cannot become a holder in due course. However, if only some, but not all, of the parties to the instrument have been discharged, the purchaser can still become a holder in due course. Discharged parties possess a real defense, however, against a holder in due course who has notice of their discharge.

Forgery and Unauthorized Signature   A person's signature on an instrument is a forgery when it is made without actual (express, implied, or apparent) authority. A person whose signature is forged cannot be held liable on the instrument in the absence of estoppel or ratification, even if the instrument is negotiated to a holder in due course. He has not made a contract. Similarly, if Frank's signature were forged on the back of an instrument, Frank could not be held as an indorser. Frank has not made a contract. Thus, any unauthorized signature is totally invalid as that of the person whose name is signed unless he ratifies it or is precluded from denying it; the unauthorized signature operates only as the signature of the unauthorized signer.

It is well settled that a person may be **estopped** or precluded from asserting a defense because his conduct in the matter has caused reliance by a third party to his loss or damage. Suppose Don's son forges Don's name to a check, which the drawee bank cashes. When the returned check reaches Don, he learns of the forgery. Rather than subject his son to trouble, possibly criminal prosecution, Don says nothing. Thereafter, Don's son continues to forge checks and cash them at the drawee bank. The bank may be suspicious of the signature, but the fact that Don has not complained may induce it to believe that the signatures are proper. Finally, Don does complain, seeking to compel the bank to recredit his account for all the forged checks. Don will not succeed, because he is estopped by his conduct from denying that his son had authority to sign his name.

A party is similarly precluded from denying the validity of his signature if his **negligence** substantially contributes to the making of the unauthorized signature. The most obvious case is that of the drawer who makes use of a mechanized or other automatic signing device and is negligent in looking after it. In such an instance the drawer would not be permitted to assert the unauthorized signature as a defense against a holder in due course.

An unauthorized signature may be **ratified** and thereby become valid as a signature. Thus, Oscar forges Sarah's indorsement on a promissory note and negotiates it to Rachel. Sarah subsequently ratifies Oscar's act. As a result Oscar is no longer liable to Rachel on the note, although Sarah is liable. Nonetheless, Sarah's ratification does *not* relieve Oscar from civil liability to Sarah nor does it in any way affect Oscar's criminal liability for the forgery.

Material Alteration   Any alteration that changes the contract of any party to the instrument in any way is material. Against any person *other* than a subsequent holder in due course,

Material alteration –any change that changes the contract of any party to the instrument.

1. an alteration by the holder that is *both* fraudulent and material discharges any party whose contract is thereby changed, unless that party assents to the change or is precluded from asserting the defense;

2. no other alteration discharges any party, and the instrument may be enforced according to its original tenor (that is, its original terms) or for incomplete instruments according to the authority given to the holder by the issuing party (e.g., an authorization to fill in an amount on a check for the amount of a purchase).

A subsequent holder in due course may always enforce the instrument according to its original tenor, and when an incomplete instrument has been completed, she may enforce it as completed.

Because an alteration is material only when it changes the contract of a party to the instrument, the addition or deletion of words that do not in any way affect the contract of any previous signer is not material. For example, where there is a discrepancy between words and figures on a check, the words stating "twenty-five hundred dollars" and the figures "$25," a correction of the figures to $2,500 is not a material change. But even a slight change in the contract of a party is a material alteration; the addition of one cent to the amount payable or an advance of one day in the date of payment will operate as a discharge if it is fraudulent.

A material alteration, as previously stated, does not discharge any party unless it is made for a fraudulent purpose. Thus, there is no discharge where a blank is filled in the honest belief that it is as authorized. Likewise, if the alteration is not material there is no discharge, and the instrument may be enforced according to its original tenor. Where blanks are filled in or an incomplete instrument is otherwise completed, there are no original tenors, but the instrument may be enforced according to the authority actually given.

Thus, a party is discharged from liability on a negotiable instrument to any holder, other than a holder in due course, by an alteration if the alteration is (1) made by a holder (2) with fraudulent intent and (3) is material. If any of these requirements is not met, no party is discharged, and a holder may recover the original tenor of the altered instrument or the authorized amount where the instrument was incomplete. In keeping with the preferential position accorded a holder in due course, he may enforce any altered instrument according to its original terms and may enforce an incomplete instrument as completed (see Figure 24-5).

Material alterations frequently are made possible by the **negligent** manner in which the instrument is drawn or made. Suppose that M makes a note,

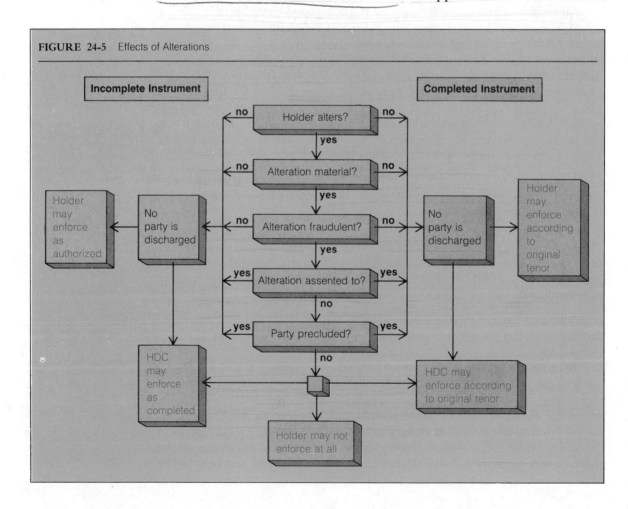

FIGURE 24-5   Effects of Alterations

writing it out in lead pencil. A party raises the amount. M will be precluded from raising the defense of material alteration due to his own negligence that allowed the alteration. Assent to an alteration given before or after it is made also prevents the party from asserting the defense.

The following examples, illustrated in Figure 24-6, may explain the operation of these rules.

1. M executes and delivers a note to P for $2,000, which P subsequently indorses and transfers to A for $1900. A intentionally and skillfully raises the note to $20,000 and then negotiates it to B who takes it in good faith and without notice of any wrongdoing for $19,000. B is a holder in due course and therefore can collect the amount of the original tenor ($2,000) from M or P and the full amount ($20,000) from A, less the amount paid by the other parties.

FIGURE 24-6   Material Alteration

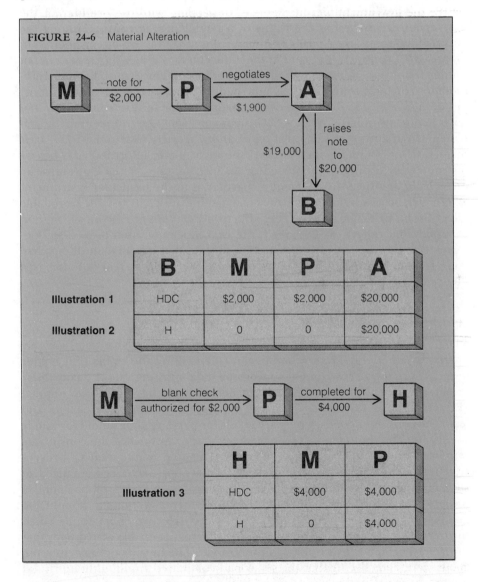

	B	M	P	A
Illustration 1	HDC	$2,000	$2,000	$20,000
Illustration 2	H	0	0	$20,000

	H	M	P
Illustration 3	HDC	$4,000	$4,000
	H	0	$4,000

2. Assume the facts in (1) except that B is not a holder in due course, M and P are both discharged by A's fraudulent and material alteration. B's only recourse is against A for the full amount ($20,000).

3. M issues his blank check to P, who is to complete it when the exact amount is determined. P wrongfully fills in $4,000 when the correct amount should be $2,000. P then negotiates the check to H. If H is a holder in due course, she can collect the amount as completed ($4,000) from either M or P. However, if H is not a holder in due course, she has no recourse against M but may recover the full amount ($4,000) from P.

Personal Defenses

Defenses to an instrument may arise in many ways, either at the time it is issued or later. In general, defenses to liability on a negotiable instrument are similar to those that may be raised in the case of any action for breach of contract. They are numerous and are available against any holder of the instrument unless he has the rights of a holder in due course. Among the personal defenses are: (1) lack of consideration; (2) failure of consideration; (3) breach of contract; (4) fraud in the inducement; (5) illegality that does not render the transaction void; (6) duress, undue influence, mistake, misrepresentation, or incapacity that does not render the transaction void; (7) set-off or counterclaim; (8) discharge of which the holder in due course does not have notice; (9) nondelivery of an instrument, whether complete or incomplete; (10) unauthorized completion of an incomplete instrument; (11) payment without obtaining surrender of the instrument; (12) theft of a bearer instrument or a properly indorsed order instrument; (13) lack of authority of a corporate officer or an agent or partner as to the particular instrument, where such officer, agent, or partner had general authority to issue negotiable paper for his principal or firm. These thirteen situations are the most common examples, but others exist. Indeed, the UCC does not attempt to detail defenses that may be cut off. It is content to state that a holder in due course takes free and clear of all defenses except those listed as real defenses (see Figure 24-7).

Limitations on Rights of Holder in Due Course

The preferential position enjoyed by a holder in due course has been severely limited by a Federal Trade Commission rule limiting the rights of a holder in due course of an instrument concerning a debt arising out of a **consumer credit contract,** which includes negotiable instruments. The rule, entitled "Preservation of Consumers' Claims and Defenses," applies to sellers and lessors of consumer goods, which are goods for personal, household, or family use. It also applies to lenders who advance money to finance the consumer's purchase of consumer goods or services. The rule is intended to prevent situations in which consumer purchase transactions have been financed in such manner that the purchaser is legally obligated to make full payment of the price to a third party, although the dealer from whom she bought the goods had committed fraud or the goods were defective. This occurs when the purchaser executes and delivers to the seller a negotiable instrument that the seller negotiates to a holder in due course. The buyer's defense that the goods were defective or that the seller had committed fraud, although valid against the seller, is not valid against a holder in due course of the instrument.

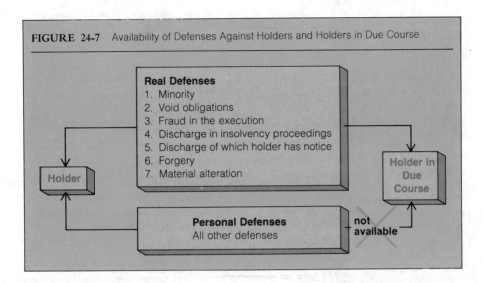

FIGURE 24-7 Availability of Defenses Against Holders and Holders in Due Course

Real Defenses
1. Minority
2. Void obligations
3. Fraud in the execution
4. Discharge in insolvency proceedings
5. Discharge of which holder has notice
6. Forgery
7. Material alteration

Holder

Holder in Due Course

Personal Defenses
All other defenses

not available

In order to correct this situation the Federal Trade Commission rule preserves claims and defenses of consumer buyers and borrowers against holders in due course. The rule states that no seller or creditor can take or receive a consumer credit contract unless the contract contains this conspicuous (bold face) provision:

This credit contract finances a purchase. All legal rights which the buyer has against the seller arising out of this transaction, including all claims and defenses, are also valid against any holder of this contract. The right to recover money from the holder under this provision is limited to the amount paid by the buyer under this contract.

A claim is a legally valid reason for suing the seller. A defense is a legally valid reason for not paying the seller. A holder is anyone trying to collect for the purchase.

The purpose of this conspicuous notice is to inform any holder that he takes the instrument subject to all claims and defenses that the buyer could assert against the seller. See *Jefferson Bank & Trust Co. v. Stamatiou* which follows. The effect of the rule is to place a holder in due course of the paper or negotiable instrument in the position of an assignee. Figure 24-8 illustrates the rights of holders in due course under the FTC rule.

JEFFERSON BANK & TRUST CO. v. STAMATIOU

Supreme Court of Louisiana, 1980.
384 So.2d 388.

FACTS: Stamatiou purchased a truck from Key Dodge, Inc., apparently for use in his tow truck business. Stamatiou and an agent of Key Dodge signed an instrument designated Sale and Chattel Mortgage with a promissory note at the bottom of the same page. The note portion contained an unconditional promise to pay the entire purchase price on prescribed terms. The Sale and Chattel Mortgage portion included a provision preserving for the purchaser his defenses against a future holder of the note. Also included was a provision by which the purchaser acknowledged that the note secured by the Sale and Chattel Mortgage would be assigned to Jefferson Bank and Trust Company "as assignee and CREDITOR within the meaning of the "applicable Federal law." Nowhere did the instrument designate the intended purpose for which the truck was purchased. Finally, Stamatiou signed the instrument at the end of the Sale and Chattel Mortgage and again at the end of the promissory note.

Key Dodge did, in fact, transfer the contract to Jefferson Bank and Trust Company; Stamatiou ceased making payments a short time later, however, and notified both Key Dodge and

Jefferson that the truck had become inoperable and unusable, and he demanded rescission of the contract. Jefferson Bank brought this action to collect on Stamatiou's promissory note.

DECISION: Judgment for Stamatiou. The Federal Trade Commission requires that all "consumer credit contracts" for the sale of goods or services include a provision such as that present in the Sale and Chattel Mortgage here that preserves for the purchaser his defenses against a future holder of the instrument. A consumer credit contract is one in which credit is extended to a purchaser who is acquiring an item or services for personal, family, or household use. This regulation is designed to prevent the seller in a consumer credit transaction from separating the buyer's duty to pay from the seller's duty to perform as promised. The seller could otherwise accomplish this by negotiating the buyer's promissory note to a financing institution as against whom, because of its status as a holder in due course, defenses would otherwise not be available.

But whether this contract is a consumer credit contract to which the Federal regulation applies is irrelevant. Here, the preservation of defenses provision was included in the contract and, thus, became a part of the contract whether or not it was required to be a part of the contract. Furthermore, the provision appeared on the face of the contract, thus placing any assignee/holder on notice that Stamatiou retained all defenses against the assignee that he retained against the seller, Key Dodge. As such, Stamatiou's claims and defenses take precedence over any rights that Jefferson Bank otherwise would have been legally entitled to as a holder in due course.

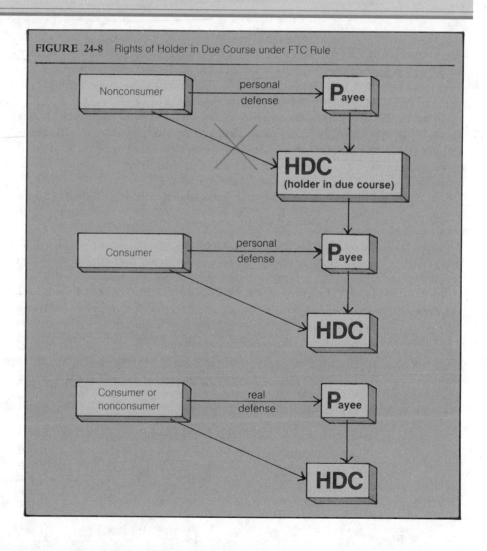

FIGURE 24-8   Rights of Holder in Due Course under FTC Rule

CHAPTER SUMMARY

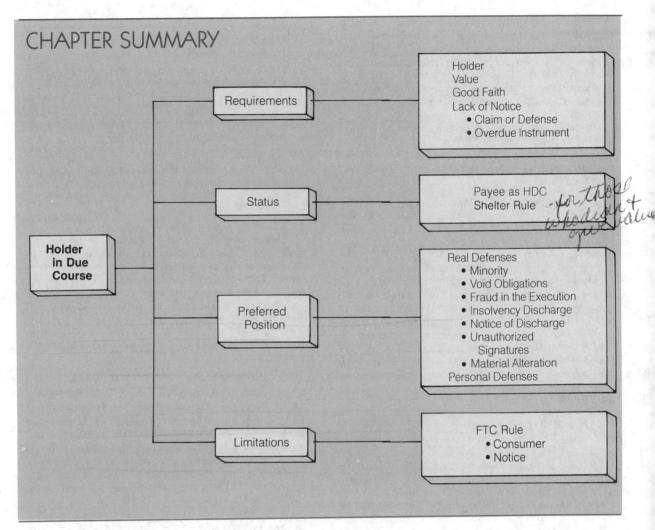

Holder in Due Course

Requirements — Holder
Value
Good Faith
Lack of Notice
• Claim or Defense
• Overdue Instrument

Status — Payee as HDC
Shelter Rule

for those who don't give value

Preferred Position — Real Defenses
• Minority
• Void Obligations
• Fraud in the Execution
• Insolvency Discharge
• Notice of Discharge
• Unauthorized Signatures
• Material Alteration
Personal Defenses

Limitations — FTC Rule
• Consumer
• Notice

KEY TERMS

Holder in due course	Lack of notice	Personal defenses
Holder	Shelter rule	FTC rule
Value	Real defenses	Material alteration
Good faith		

PROBLEMS

1. On November 1, P installed a burglar alarm system in M's store. M executed and delivered to P a negotiable promissory note payable to the order of P for $1,100, the purchase price, due on December 1. On November 8, P returned to M's store and told M that he needed money and would accept $1,000 as payment in full. M immediately paid P $1,000 but forgot to obtain the note from P.

On November 10, P indorsed the note in blank and transferred it to H for value. Two days later, H learned that M had already paid P for the note, whereupon he gave the note to X, his mother-in-law, as a going away present without further indorsement. X was not aware of M's prior payment of the note.

What are the rights of X, if any, against M? Explain.

2. M issues a negotiable promissory note payable to the order of P for the amount of $3,000. P raises the amount to $13,000 and negotiates it to H for $12,000.

(a) If H is a holder in due course, how much can she recover from M? How much from P? If M's negligence substantially contributed to the making of the alteration, how much can H recover from M and P, respectively?

(b) If H is not a holder in due course, how much can she recover from M? How much from P? If M's negligence substantially contributed to the making of the alteration, how much can H recover from M and P, respectively?

3. On December 2, 1986, Miles executed and delivered to Proctor a negotiable promissory note for $1,000, payable to Proctor or order, due March 2, 1987, with interest at 14 percent from maturity, in partial payment of a printing press. On January 3, 1987, Proctor, in need of ready cash, indorsed and sold the note to Hughes for $800. Hughes paid $600 in cash to Proctor on January 3 and agreed to pay the balance of $200 one week later, namely, on January 10. On January 6, Hughes learned that Miles claimed a breach of warranty by Proctor and, for this reason, intended to refuse to pay the note when it matured. On January 10, Hughes paid Proctor $200, in conformity with their agreement of January 3. Following Mile's refusal to pay the note on March 2, 1987, Hughes sues Miles for $1,000. Decision?

4. X fraudulently represented to D that he would obtain for her a new car to be used in D's business for $7,800 from P Motor Company. D thereupon executed her personal check for $7,800, payable to the order of P Motor Company, and delivered the check to X, who immediately delivered it to the Motor Company in payment of his own prior indebtedness. The Motor Company had no knowledge of the representations made by X to D. X now brings an action to recover the amount of the check from P Motor Company contending a failure of consideration on P's part. Decision?

5. Adams reads with difficulty. He arranged to borrow $200 from Bell. Bell prepared a note, which Adams read laboriously. As Adams was about to sign it, Bell diverted Adams's attention and substituted the following paper, which was identical with the note Adams had read except that the amounts were different:

> On June 1, 1986, I promise to pay Ben Bell or order Two Thousand Dollars with interest from date at 16 percent. This note is secured by certificate No. 13 for 100 shares of stock of Brookside Mills, Inc.

Adams did not detect the substitution, signed as maker, handed the note and stock certificate to Bell, and received from Bell $200. Bell indorsed and sold the paper to Fore, a holder in due course, who paid

him $1,800. Fore presented the note at maturity to Adams, who refused to pay. What are Fore's rights, if any, against Adams?

6. On January 2, 1986, Martin, seventeen years of age, as a result of Dealer's fraudulent misrepresentation bought a used motorboat to use in his fishing business for $2,000 from Dealer, signed an installment contract for $1,500, and gave Dealer the following instrument as down payment:

> Dated:........1986
> I promise to pay to the order of Dealer, six months after date, the sum of $500 without interest. This is given as a down payment on an installment contract for a motorboat.
>
> (signed) Martin

Dealer, on July 1, sold his business to Henry and included this note in the transaction. Dealer wrote on the back of the note the following: "Collection guaranteed. (signed) Dealer" and handed it to Henry. Henry left the note in his office safe. On July 10, Sharpie, an employee of Henry, stole the note and sold it to Bert for $300, indorsing the note "Sharpie." At the time, in Bert's presence, Sharpie filled in the date on the note as February 2, 1986. Bert demanded payment from Martin, who refused to pay.

What are Bert's rights against Martin?

7. M borrowed $1,000 from A. A, disturbed about M's ability to pay, demanded security. M indorsed and delivered to A a negotiable promissory note executed by T for $1,200 payable to M's order in twelve equal monthly installments. The note did not contain an acceleration clause, but it recited that the consideration for the note was M's promise to paint and shingle T's barn. At the time M transferred the note to A, the first installment was overdue and unpaid. A was unaware that the installment had not been paid. T did not pay any one of the installments on the note. When the last installment became due, A presented the note to T for payment. T refused on the ground that M had not painted or reshingled her barn.

What are A's rights, if any, against T on the note?

8. M purchased a refrigerator for his home from P Appliance Store for $700. M paid $200 in cash and signed an installment contract for $500, which in its entirety stated:

> January 15, 1986
> I promise to pay to the order of P Appliance Store the sum of $500 in ten equal monthly installments.
>
> (signed) M

P negotiated the installment contract to H, who took the instrument for value in good faith and without notice of any claim or defense of any party. After M had paid two installments, the refrigerator ceased operating. M wishes to recover his down payment, his first two monthly payments, and to discontinue further payments. What outcome?

9. Joseph Higbee executed and delivered to Robert Dudley the following instrument:

> On September 19, 1986, I promise to pay $15,000 to Robert Dudley.
>
> (signed) Joseph Higbee

This note was secured by a mortgage on Higbee's real property. Dudley altered the note and mortgage by changing the amount to $25,000 and the date to September 17, 1986. Dudley then sold the note and mortgage for $25,000 less 2 percent discount to Citizens Bank, which was unaware of the alterations. Dudley assigned the mortgage to Citizens Bank and signed the reverse side of the note as follows: "I hereby assign this note to the order of Citizens Bank. (signed) Robert Dudley."

On September 18, 1986, Citizens Bank demanded payment of the note from Higbee. Higbee refused. On September 22, Citizens Bank notified Higbee that the note was in default and demanded payment from him. Higbee again refused. Citizens Bank thereupon brought an action against Higbee to recover $25,000 on the note. No action was taken by Citizens Bank to foreclose the mortgage.

What defenses, if any, may Higbee properly assert in this action?

10. Adams, by fraudulent representations, induced Barton to purchase 100 shares of the capital stock of the Evermore Oil Company. The shares were worthless. Barton executed and delivered to Adams a negotiable promissory note for $5,000 dated May 5, in full payment for the shares, due six months after date. On May 20, Adams indorsed and sold the note to Cooper for $4,800. On October 21, Barton, having learned that Cooper now held the note, notified Cooper of the fraud and stated he would not pay the note. On December 1, Cooper negotiated the note to Davis, who, while not a party, had full knowledge of the fraud perpetrated on Barton. When Barton refused to pay the note, Davis sued Barton for $5,000. Decision?

25

LIABILITY OF PARTIES

In the preceding chapters we discussed the negotiability of commercial paper, the transfer of negotiable instruments, and the preferred position of a holder in due course. In this chapter we examine the liability of parties arising out of negotiable instruments and the ways in which liability may be terminated.

Two types of potential liability are associated with commercial paper: contractual liability and warranty liability. The basis for contractual liability, as provided in the Code, is that "[n]o person is liable on an instrument unless his signature appears thereon." The law imposes contractual liability on those who sign a negotiable instrument. Some parties to a negotiable instrument never sign it and consequently never assume contractual liability.

Warranty liability, on the other hand, is not based on a signature; thus it may be imposed on both signers and nonsigners. Warranty liability applies (1) to persons who transfer an instrument and (2) to persons who receive payment or acceptance of an instrument.

Contractual Liability

All parties whose **signatures** appear on a negotiable instrument incur certain contractual obligations, unless they disclaim liability. The *maker* of a promissory note and the *acceptor* of a draft assume an absolute obligation (**primary liability**) to pay according to the tenor of the instrument when they sign it. *Drawers* of drafts and checks and *indorsers* of all instruments incur **secondary liability** if the instrument is not paid. A *drawee* assumes **no** liability on the instrument until he *accepts* it. The contractual obligations of the maker, drawer, drawee, indorser, and acceptor are codified by the UCC, as illustrated in Figure 25–1.

Primary liability–absolute obligation to pay the instrument

Secondary liability–obligation to pay is subject to the conditions of presentment, dishonor, notice of dishonor, and sometimes protest

Signature

The word "signature," as discussed in Chapter 22, is broadly defined to include any name, word, or mark, whether handwritten, typed, printed, or in any other form, made with the intention of authenticating the instrument. The

FIGURE 25-1   Contractual Liability

	Maker	Drawee	Acceptor	Drawer	Indorser
Primary Liability	●		●		
Secondary Liability				●	●

signature may be made by the individual herself or on her behalf by the individual's authorized agent.

Authorized Signatures

Authorized agents often execute negotiable instruments on behalf of the makers or drawers (the principals). The agent is not liable if the instrument is executed properly (e.g., "P, principal, by A, agent") and the agent is authorized to execute the instrument. Only the principal is liable. Occasionally, however, the agent, although fully authorized, uses an inappropriate form of signature, and holders or prospective holders may be misled as to the identity of the obligor. (For a comprehensive discussion of the principal-agent relationship see Chapters 27 and 28.)

Although there are many incorrect forms of signatures by agents, they can be conveniently sorted into three groups. The first type occurs when an agent signs only his own name to an instrument. He does not indicate that he is signing in a representative capacity and he does not state the name of the principal. For example, Adams, the agent of Prince, makes a note on behalf of Prince but signs it "Adams." The signature does not indicate that Adams has signed in a representative capacity or that he has made the instrument on behalf of Prince. In this situation only the agent is liable on the instrument. Although Prince may be liable to Adams or to a third party because of other factors, he is not liable on the instrument because his name does not appear on it.

The second type of incorrect form occurs when an authorized agent indicates that he is signing in a representative capacity but does not disclose the name of his principal. For example, Adams, executing an instrument on behalf of Prince, merely signs it "Adams, agent." In this case, Prince is liable if the payee is an immediate party to the instrument and knows that Adams represents Prince. However, if any subsequent payee does not know that Adams represents Prince, Prince is not liable. Adams alone is personally liable.

The third type of inappropriate signature occurs when an agent reveals both his and his principal's name, but does not indicate that he has signed in a representative capacity. For example, Adams, signing an instrument on behalf of Prince, signs it "Adams and Prince." Because a subsequent holder might well think that Adams and Prince were co-makers, Adams is fully liable. However, if a party knew or should have known that Adams was acting on behalf of Prince without intending to incur personal liability, Adams may prove this fact by other evidence including, as the following case demonstrates, the type of instrument and notations on the instrument, and avoid liability.

FACTS: On October 21, 1977, Cook, the treasurer of Arizona Auto Auction and R. V. Center, Inc., issued three corporate checks to Central Motors Company. The checks were boldly imprinted at the top "Arizona Auto Auction, Inc." Also, "Arizona Auto Auction, Inc." was imprinted above the signature line appearing at the lower right-hand corner. Cook's signature appeared under the imprinted name of Arizona Auto Auction without any designation of her office or capacity. Central Motors deposited these three checks in its corporate account held by Valley National Bank, Sunnymead (the Bank). However, pursuant to a stop payment order, Arizona Auto Auction's drawee bank dishonored each of these checks. The checks were returned to the Bank, and the account of Central Motors was charged back for the amount of the checks—$9,795. The Bank, unable to recover this amount from Central Motors, brought suit against Arizona Auto Auction, Cook, and her spouse. The Bank claims that Cook is personally liable for the checks.

DECISION: Judgment for Cook. While it may be common for creditors of small corporations to demand that corporate officers personally obligate themselves on corporate notes, it would be highly unusual to demand the individual obligation of an officer on corporate checks. One's signature on a corporate check, without including their representative capacity, should not subject one to personal liability. Therefore, since Cook made no personal guaranty of these checks or any other corporate obligation, she is not personally liable.

VALLEY NATIONAL BANK, SUNNYMEAD v. COOK

Arizona Court of Appeals, Division One, 1983. 136 Arizona 232, 665 P.2d 576.

Unauthorized Signatures

Unauthorized signatures include both forgeries and signatures made by an agent without proper power to do so. An unauthorized signature is generally not binding on the person whose name appears on the instrument, but it is binding on the unauthorized signer whether or not her own name appears on the instrument. Thus, if Adams, without authority, signed Prince's name to an instrument, Adams, not Prince, would be liable on the instrument. The rule therefore is an exception to the principle that only those whose names appear on a negotiable instrument can be liable on it.

There is an important exception to this rule that an unauthorized signature does not bind the person whose name is signed: any person who by his **negligence** substantially contributes to the making of an unauthorized signature may not assert the lack of authority as a defense against a holder in due course or a person who pays for the instrument in good faith and according to reasonable commercial standards. For example, Jones employs a signature stamp to sign his checks and carelessly leaves it accessible to third parties. Brown discovers the stamp and uses it to write a number of checks with Jones' unauthorized signature as the drawer. Howard, a subsequent holder in due course of one the checks, will *not* be subject to Jones' defense of unauthorized signature and will be able to recover the amount of the check from Jones.

Liability of Primary Parties

There is a primary party on every note: the *maker*. The maker's commitment is unconditional. No one, however, is primarily liable on a draft or check as issued. The *drawee* is *not* liable on the instrument unless he accepts it. He is free to pay or accept it as he sees fit, although by refusing to accept or pay it he may be liable to the drawer for breach of contract. For example, a bank is not obligated to pay any check drawn on it. To do so would be to obligate a bank to pay an instrument regardless of whether the drawer had an account at that bank or sufficient funds in his account. On the other hand, if the drawer does have sufficient funds to cover the check, the drawee may still refuse to honor the instrument, but this would constitute a breach of its contract of deposit with the drawer.

The drawee's refusal to pay or accept the draft causes the *drawer* to become liable on the instrument after receiving proper notice of dishonor. If, on the other hand, the drawee accepts the draft, after which he is known as the *acceptor,* he becomes primarily liable on the instrument. **Acceptance,** or in the case of a check, certification, is the drawee's signed engagement to honor the draft as presented to him.

Acceptance–a drawee's signed commitment to honor the instrument

Makers

Makers guarantee that they will pay the instrument according to its terms when made or, in the case of an incomplete instrument, as completed.

Acceptors

Acceptor–drawee upon acceptance of an instrument

A drawee has no liability on the instrument until she accepts it, at which time she becomes an acceptor and, like a maker, primarily liable. The acceptor becomes liable on the draft according to its terms at the time of the acceptance or as completed if an incomplete instrument.

An acceptance must be written on the instrument. No writing separate from the draft and no oral statement or conduct of the drawee will convert the drawee into an acceptor. The acceptance may take many forms. It may be printed on the face of the draft, ready for the drawee's signature. It may consist of a rubber stamp, with the signature of the drawee added. It may be the drawee's signature, preceded by a word or phrase such as "Accepted," "Certified," or "Good." It may consist of nothing more than the drawee's signature. Normally, but by no means necessarily, an acceptance is written vertically across the face of the draft. It must not, however, contain any words indicating an intent to refuse to honor the draft. Accepted checks are said to be certified. **Certification** is the drawee bank's promise to honor the check when presented for payment. The bank, however, has no obligation to certify a check. The order on the bank is to *pay* the check, and if the bank is willing to pay, refusal to certify is not a dishonor of the check.

Certification–acceptance of a check by a drawee bank

Where a check is certified at the request of the holder, the drawer and all prior indorsers are discharged. The liability of indorsers after certification is not affected. When the bank certifies an instrument, it should withhold sufficient funds from the drawer's account to pay the check. Because the bank is primarily liable on its certification and has the funds and the drawer does not, the discharge is reasonable.

Certification at the request of the drawer does not, however, relieve the drawer of secondary liability on the instrument. For example, the drawer may have a check certified before using it to close a business transaction, such as the purchase of a house. Because the drawer is then obtaining the benefit of the transaction, she should bear the risk of the bank's credit, rather than the payee.

Liability of Secondary Parties

The drawer, the payee (if he indorses), and other indorsers of an instrument are secondarily liable, because their liability is subject to the conditions of presentment, dishonor, notice of dishonor, and sometimes protest. They do not unconditionally promise to pay the instrument, but expect the drawee-acceptor or maker to pay.

Indorsers and Drawers

If the instrument is not paid by a primary party and the conditions precedent to the liability of secondary parties are satisfied (discussed below), a secondary party who is not a qualified drawer or qualified indorser is liable. The **drawer** engages that she will pay the amount of the draft to the holder or any indorser who takes it up, unless she has disclaimed this liability by drawing it without recourse. Unless the indorsement otherwise specifies, as by using such words as "without recourse," every **indorser** promises that she will pay the holder or any subsequent indorser of the instrument according to its tenor at the time of her indorsement.

Conditions Precedent to Liability

Conditions precedent to the liability of secondary parties are presentment, dishonor, prompt notice of dishonor, and in some situations, protest. Drawers and indorsers face quite different consequences, however, for failing to comply with the conditions precedent.

Conditions precedent–events (presentment, dishonor, notice of dishonor and sometimes protest) which must occur to hold a secondary party liable

Presentment Presentment is a demand for acceptance or payment made by the holder on the maker, acceptor, or drawee. If there are two or more makers, acceptors, or drawees, presentment to one is sufficient.

Presentment–demand for payment or acceptance

Presentment may be made in any reasonable manner. An instrument with a specified maturity date is due for presentment on that date or, if the specified date is not a full business day, on the next full business day. In any other case presentment is due within "a reasonable time." What is "a reasonable time" depends on all the facts of the particular case. For an uncertified check, a reasonable time for presentment for payment is *presumed* to be: (a) with respect to the liability of the *drawer, thirty days* after date or issue, whichever is later; and (b) with respect to the liability of an *indorser, seven days* after his indorsement.

A delay in presentment *discharges* the **indorsers.** However, the **drawer** is discharged only to the extent of any *loss* suffered because of the delay. The discharge of one indorser, of course, does not mean that all are discharged. Assume that D draws a check payable to the order of P on March 1. P indorses it to A on March 3, and A indorses it to B on March 6. B must present the check by March 10 to hold P liable and must present it by the 13th to hold A liable. If he waits until after the 13th, both indorsers are discharged unless B can show that the presentment was made within a reasonable time. However B has until March 31 to present the check to hold D liable, because a reasonable time for presentment with regard to the drawer is presumed to be thirty days. If B did not present the check for payment until after March 31, D would be discharged *only* to the extent of any loss he might have suffered as the result of the delay, but not otherwise. The indorsers P and A, however, would be completely discharged by B's failure to make presentment within a reasonable time, whether or not they had any loss.

Notice of Dishonor An instrument is **dishonored** when (1) presentment has been duly made, and acceptance or payment is refused or cannot be obtained

Dishonor–refusal to pay or accept an instrument upon proper presentment

within the prescribed time, or (2) presentment is excused and the instrument is not duly accepted or paid. Return for lack of a proper indorsement is not dishonor.

On proper presentment and dishonor, and subject to any necessary notice of protest, the holder has an immediate right of recourse against drawers and indorsers after giving them timely notice of presentment and dishonor. Such notice is necessary to charge any indorser. Notice also must be made to the drawer, the acceptor of a draft payable at a bank, or the maker of a note payable at a bank, but failure to give such notice discharges these parties only if the bank becomes insolvent, thus depriving them of funds they maintained at the bank to cover the instrument.

Notice of dishonor is normally given by the holder or by an indorser who has himself received notice. For example, M makes a note payable to the order of P; P indorses it to A; A indorses it to B; and B indorses it to H, the last holder. H presents the note to M within a reasonable time, but M refuses to pay. H may give notice of dishonor to all the secondary parties: P, A, and B. If he is satisfied that B will pay him, he may only notify B. B then must see to it that A or P is notified, or B will have no recourse. B may notify either or both. If he notifies A only, A will have to see to it that P is notified, or A will have no recourse.

If, in this hypothetical problem, H notifies P alone, A and B are discharged. P cannot complain, because he has no claim against A or B, who indorsed the note after he did. It cannot matter to P that he is compelled to pay H rather than A. Therefore, subsequent parties are permitted to skip intermediate indorsers if they want to discharge them and are willing to look solely to prior indorsers for recourse.

Any necessary notice must be given by a *bank* before midnight on the first banking day after the banking day when it receives notice of dishonor. Any *nonbank* must give notice before midnight of the third business day after dishonor or receipt of notice of dishonor. Written notice is effective when sent, regardless of whether it is received. For instance, D draws a check on Y bank payable to the order of P; P indorses it to A; A deposits it to her account in X bank; and X bank properly presents it to Y bank, the drawee. Y bank dishonors the check because the drawer, D, has insufficient funds on deposit to cover it. Y bank has until midnight of the following day to notify X bank, A, P, or D of the dishonor. X bank has until midnight of the day after receipt of notice of dishonor to notify A, P, or D of the dishonor. That is, if X received the notice of dishonor on Monday, it would have until midnight on Tuesday to notify A, P, or D. If it failed to notify A, it could not charge the item back to her. A has until midnight of the third business day after receipt of notice of dishonor to notify P or D. If she received notice on Tuesday, she would have until midnight on Friday to notify P or D. P would also have three business days in which to notify D.

HANE v. EXTEN

Court of Appeals of
Maryland, 1969.
255 Md. 668, 259 A.2d 290.

FACTS: On August 10, 1964, Theta Electronic Laboratories, Inc., executed a promissory note to George and Marguerite Thomson. Three other individuals, Gerald Exten, Emil O'Neil, and James Hane, and their wives also indorsed the note. The note was then transferred to Hane by the Thomsons on November 26, 1965. Although a default occurred at this time, it was not until

April 1967, eighteen months later, that Hane gave notice of the dishonor and made a demand for payment on the Extens as indorsers.

DECISION: Judgment for the Extens. Unless an indorsement otherwise specifies (as by words such as "without recourse"), every indorser agrees that upon presentment, dishonor, and any necessary notice of dishonor he will pay the instrument according to its terms at the time of his indorsement to the holder or to any subsequent indorser who pays it. Generally, presentment for payment and notice of any dishonor are necessary to charge any indorser and unless either is waived or excused, an unreasonable delay will discharge the indorser.

Here, Hane waited for an unreasonable period of eighteen months until he gave notice of the dishonor and presented the note to the Extens for payment. This was far beyond the requirement that notice of dishonor be given by persons other than banks before midnight of the third business day after dishonor or receipt of notice of dishonor.

Frequently, notice of dishonor is given by returning the unpaid instrument with a stamp, ticket, or memorandum attached stating that the item was not paid and requesting that the recipient make good on it. But since the purpose of notice is to give knowledge of dishonor and to inform the secondary party that he may be held liable on the instrument, any kind of notice informing the recipient of his potential liability is sufficient. No formal requisites are imposed—notice may be given in any reasonable manner. An oral notice is sufficient, but is inadvisable because it may be difficult to prove.

Protest   A protest is a certificate of dishonor made under the hand and seal of a United States consul or vice-consul or a notary public or other person authorized to certify to a dishonor by the law of the place where the dishonor occurred. It must identify the instrument and certify either that due presentment has been made or the reason why it is excused and that the instrument has been dishonored by nonacceptance or nonpayment. The protest may also certify that notice of dishonor has been given to all parties or to specified parties. Protest, or the noting for protest, must be made within the time allowed for giving notice of dishonor. Protest is required only if the draft is drawn or payable *outside* the United States.

Protest—certification of dishonor

Delay in Presentment, Notice, or Protest Excused   The Code excuses *a delay* in presentment, notice, or protest in two situations. The first excuses a delay where the holder does not have notice that the instrument is due; for example, an instrument may provide that its maturity shall be automatically accelerated on the happening of a particular event. If the holder does not know that this event has happened, she is excused from presentment until she learns of the acceleration, and secondary parties are not discharged because of the delay. Once the holder learns that the event has occurred she must present the note within a reasonable time and give prompt notice of dishonor to hold the indorsers liable.

The second situation excuses the holder's delay where it is caused by circumstances beyond his control. For example, suppose the holder cannot present the instrument to the primary party because a storm has disrupted all means of communication and transportation. The circumstances need not make presentment impossible. It is enough if they are of the degree and character that would deter persons of ordinary prudence, energy, and courage from encountering them in the pursuit of business.

Presentment, Notice, or Protest Excused

The Code *entirely* excuses the holder from presentment, notice, or protest if the party to be charged has himself dishonored the instrument or has countermanded payment, or if the holder otherwise has no reason to expect the instrument to be accepted or paid. If, for example, D draws a check on a bank where he has no account, or if he has closed his account or stopped payment on the check, he is not entitled to a due presentment and notice of dishonor. These matters are entirely excused so far as he is concerned. But they would not be excused for intermediate indorsers who did not have any reason to expect that the instrument would not be accepted or paid.

The Code also entirely excuses a presentment, notice, or protest, as the case may be, if these things cannot be accomplished by reasonable diligence. For example, if the maker of a note has "departed for places unknown" and cannot be located by reasonable diligence, the holder has no way of making a presentment to him. In such case, presentment is entirely excused, and the holder should treat the instrument as dishonored and give prompt notice of dishonor to the indorsers. Likewise, if one of the indorsers cannot be located by reasonable diligence, notice of dishonor would not have to be given to him—it would be entirely excused.

Presentment Excused

The Code sets out some specific situations in which presentment is *entirely* excused. These situations, which do not excuse notice or protest, include the following: (1) the maker, acceptor, or drawee is dead or in insolvency proceedings; or (2) payment of acceptance is refused for reasons not relating to proper presentment, making it clear that a subsequent presentment would be useless.

Waiver of Presentment, Notice, or Protest

Presentment, notice, or protest may also be waived either before or after it is due. Waivers are of two types, express and implied.

Disclaimer of Liability by Secondary Parties

Both drawers and indorsers *may* disclaim their normal secondary liability by drawing or indorsing instruments **"without recourse."** The use of the qualifying words "without recourse" is understood in commercial circles to place purchasers on notice that they may not rely on the credit of the person using this language, but may look only to the other parties to the instrument. A person drawing or indorsing an instrument in this manner does not incur the normal contractual liability of a drawer or indorser to pay the instrument, but he may nonetheless be liable for breach of warranty under certain circumstances.

Liability of Accommodation Parties

Accommodation parties are those who sign a negotiable instrument for the purpose of lending their credit to another party. They may be makers or co-makers, drawers or co-drawers, or indorsers. An indorsement indicating that the party is not in the chain of title is notice of the party's accommodation.

Frequently, one or more persons indorse an instrument to accommodate another party, rather than sign as maker or drawer. Suppose M wants to borrow money from P, and P insists that M procure the signatures of A, B, C, and D before the loan is made. M asks these parties to accommodate him and makes the note, and A, B, C, and D sign their names on the back of it in that order. Because A, B, C, and D have signed the note, they are liable to P as indorsers. M is liable to P and to A, B, C, and D, if these accommodating parties pay the instrument.

Suppose M becomes insolvent so that the reimbursement rights that A, B, C, and D have against him are meaningless. Suppose further that P enforces the note against D. Can D pass the loss on to C? May C shift it to B? Would A ultimately be out-of-pocket simply because she signed first? Parol evidence would be admissible to show that the indorsers had agreed to share the loss equally or in some other proportion, if that is the case. If they made no agreement among themselves, the rule that indorsers are liable in the order in which they signed does *not* apply. The law of suretyship, which applies to accommodation parties, is based on concepts of equity and fairness that would not be consistent with having the rights of these sureties among themselves depend on the order in which they signed the instrument. Although each is liable to the holder for the full amount, they should share the loss equally, and one who is required to pay more than his share is entitled to recover proportionately from the others. See Chapter 37 for a further discussion of suretyship.

Liability of Parties for Conversion

Conversion is a tort whereby a person becomes liable in damages because of his wrongful control over the personal property of another. The Code provides that a conversion occurs in three situations: (a) when a drawee to whom a draft is delivered for acceptance refuses to return it on demand; (b) when any person to whom an instrument is delivered for payment refuses on demand either to pay or to return it; and (c) when an instrument is paid on a forged indorsement. Situations (a) and (b) involve willful action on the part of the party guilty of the conversion, whereas in situation (c) the payor's action was in all probability completely innocent—his dominion over the instrument resulted from an unrecognized break in the chain of title. Nevertheless, liability is the same in all three cases. Good faith is completely immaterial, and the person wrongfully exercising dominion over the instrument is liable for damages.

Special Situations Affecting Liability

If a drawee of a draft or check pays it, the drawer is generally under a duty to make reimbursement. Usually, the drawer has funds in the hands of the drawee, and the drawee, honoring a draft or check, reimburses itself immediately by charging the drawer's account or her funds. The drawee can be reimbursed, however, only if it acts in accordance with the drawer's *order* as it appears on the instrument. Thus, if Davis draws a check to the order of Jones, the drawee bank to whom the instrument is addressed acquires no right or reimbursement by paying Roe, unless Jones has indorsed the check to Roe. In short, the drawee must determine whether the person presenting the item for payment or acceptance has rights in it. If it pays the wrong party, it is the drawee's loss and not the drawer's. Two situations involving these principles that are especially troublesome have been specifically modified by the Code.

The Impostor Rule

Usually, this rule comes into play in situations involving a confidence man who impersonates a respected citizen and who deceives a third party into delivering a negotiable instrument to the impostor in the name of the respected citizen. For instance, John Doe, falsely representing himself as Richard Doe, a creditor of Ray Davis, induces Davis to draw a check payable to the order of Richard Roe and to deliver it to him. Doe then forges Roe's name to the check and presents it to the drawee for payment. The drawee pays it. Subsequently, the drawer denies the drawee's right of reimbursement on the ground that the drawee did not pay in accordance with his order: the drawer ordered payment to Roe or to Roe's order. Roe did not order payment to anyone; therefore, the drawee would not acquire a right of reimbursement against the drawer Davis. This is the argument in favor of the drawer and is supported by the general rule governing unauthorized signatures.

Nevertheless, the Code provides that the indorsement of the impostor or of any other person in the name of the named payee is **effective** if the impostor has induced the maker or drawer to issue the instrument to him or his confederate using the name of the payee. It is as if the named payee had indorsed the instrument. The reason for this rule is that the drawer or maker is to blame for failing to detect the impersonation by the impostor. Thus, as in the above example and the case which follows, the drawee would be able to debit the drawer's account.

PHILADELPHIA TITLE INSURANCE CO. v. FIDELITY-PHILADELPHIA TRUST CO.

Supreme Court of Pennsylvania, 1965.
419 Pa. 78, 212 A.2d 222.

FACTS: Edmund Jezemski, estranged and living apart from his wife, Paula, was administrator and sole heir-at-law of his deceased mother's estate, one asset of which was real estate in Philadelphia. Without Edmund's knowledge or consent, and with the assistance of John M. McAllister, an attorney, and Anthony DiBenedetto, a real estate broker, Paula arranged for a mortgage on the property through Philadelphia Title Insurance Company. Shortly before settlement, Paula represented to McAllister and DiBenedetto that her husband would be unable to attend the closing on the mortgage. She appeared at McAllister's office in advance of the closing, accompanied by a man, whom she introduced to McAllister and DiBenedetto as her husband. She and this man, in the presence of McAllister and DiBenedetto, executed a deed conveying the property from the estate to her husband and herself as tenants by the entireties and also executed the mortgage. McAllister and DiBenedetto were witnesses. Thereafter, McAllister, DiBenedetto and Paula met at the office of the Title Company on the closing date, produced the signed deed and mortgage, and Paula obtained from Title Company its check for the mortgage loan proceeds of $15,640.82, payable to the order of Edmund Jezemski and Paula Jezemski individually and to Edmund as administrator.

Paula cashed the check, bearing the purported indorsements of all the payees, at Penns Grove National Bank and Trust Company. Edmund received none of the proceeds, either individually or as administrator. His purported indorsements were forgeries. In the collection process the check was presented to and paid by the drawee bank, Fidelity-Philadelphia Trust Company, and charged against the drawer Title Company's account. Upon discovery of the existence of the mortgage, Edmund brought an action which resulted in the setting aside of the deed and mortgage and the repayment of the amount advanced by the mortgagee. Title Company thereupon sued the drawee bank (Fidelity) to recover the amount of the check, $15,640.82.

DECISION: Judgment for Fidelity-Philadelphia Trust Co. The UCC makes an imposter's indorsement in the name of a named payee effective if the impostor, "by use of the mails or otherwise," induces the maker or drawer to issue the instrument. This "Imposter Rule" applies irrespective of whether the impersonation was accomplished in a face-to-face transaction, through the mails, or by telephone. Paula's mystery accomplice induced Title Company to issue the mortgage check by impersonating Edmund. He acted through McAllister and DiBenedetto and had no direct contact with the Title Company. Nonetheless, the Impostor Rule operates to make his unauthorized indorsement effective. Consequently, the Title Company, as the drawer, must suffer the loss and it cannot recover the $15,640 from Fidelity-Philadelphia Trust Company.

The Fictitious Payee Rule

The second situation is similar to the imposter situation, but it involves a faithless agent rather than an impostor. For instance, the drawer's agent falsely tells the drawer that money is owed to X, and the drawer writes a check payable to the order of X and hands it to the agent for delivery to X. The agent forges X's name on the check and obtains payment from the drawee bank. The drawer then denies the bank's claim to reimbursement on the ground that the bank did not comply with her order; that the drawer had ordered payment to X or order; that the drawee did not make payment either to X or as ordered by X, inasmuch as the forgery of X's signature is wholly inoperative; that the drawee paid in accordance with the scheme of the faithless agent and not in compliance with the drawer's order.

Once again, the drawee bank will be able to debit the drawer's account. An indorsement by any person in the name of a named payee is **effective** if an agent or employee of the maker or drawer has supplied her with the name of the payee for fraudulent purposes. The risk of employee fraud presents business risks that the Code imposes on the party employing the agent.

The rule also applies to the similar situation in which a person signs as or on behalf of a maker or drawer and does not intend the payee to have an interest in the instrument. In such situations any person's indorsement in the name of the named payee is **effective.** For instance:

FACTS: While assistant treasurer of Travco Corporation, Frank Mitchell caused two checks, each payable to a fictitious company, to be drawn on Travco's account with Brown City Savings Bank. In each case Mitchell indorsed the check in his own name and then cashed it at Citizens Federal Savings & Loan Association of Port Huron. Both checks were cleared through normal banking channels and charged against Travco's account with Brown City. Travco subsequently discovered the embezzlement, and after its demand for reimbursement was denied, it brought this suit against Citizens.

DECISION: Judgment for Travco. An indorsement by any person in the name of a named payee is effective if an agent or employee of the maker or drawer has supplied him with the name of the payee intending the latter to have no such interest. Here, however, although Mitchell was an employee of the drawer, Travco, and had supplied the drawer with the names of fictitious payees, neither check was indorsed in the name of the named payee. Instead, Mitchell indorsed them in his own name, and as a consequence the indorsements were not effective against Travco, and Citizens therefore is liable.

TRAVCO CORPORATION v. CITIZENS FEDERAL SAVINGS & LOAN ASSOCIATION OF PORT HURON

Michigan Court of Appeals, 1972.
42 Mich. App. 291, 201 N.W.2d 675.

Liability Based on Warranty

A negotiable instrument is not only the written evidence of contract liability but also a kind of property intended for trading and having marketability. Just as certain implied warranties under the Code are attached to the sale of goods, certain warranties imposed by the Code are attached to the *sale* of commercial paper. These warranties are effective whether or *not* the transferor or presenter signs the instrument, although, as you will see, the extent of the warranty to subsequent holders does depend on whether they have indorsed the instrument. There are two types of warranties: (a) transferor's warranties and (b) presenter's warranties. Like other warranties, these may be disclaimed by agreement between immediate parties. In the case of an indorser, his disclaimer of transfer warranties must appear in the indorsement itself.

Warranties on Transfer

Transferor's warranty– warranties given by any person who transfers an instrument and receives consideration

Any person who transfers an instrument, whether by negotiation or assignment, and receives *consideration* makes certain warranties. Warranties on transfer run to the immediate transferee only if transfer is by delivery alone. If the transfer is made by indorsement, whether qualified or unqualified, the warranty runs to "any subsequent holder who takes the instrument in good faith" (see Figure 25–2). The warranties of the transferor are as follows.

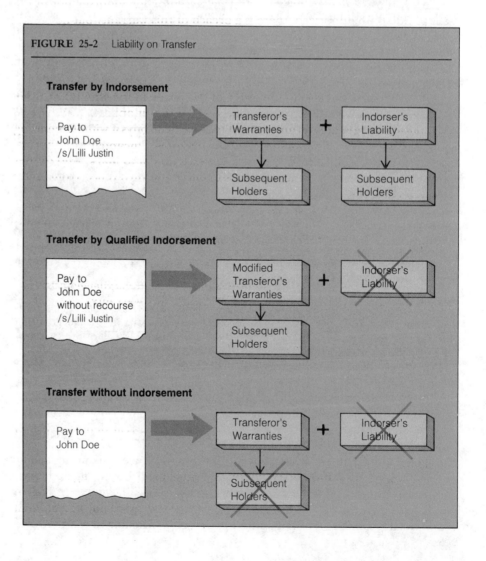

FIGURE 25-2 Liability on Transfer

Good Title

The first warranty that the Code imposes on a transferor is that the transferor has good title to the instrument or is authorized to obtain payment or acceptance on behalf of one who has good title, and the transfer is otherwise rightful. We illustrate this rule with the following example. M makes a note payable to the order of P. A thief steals the note from P, forges P's indorsement, and sells the instrument to Karen. Karen does not have good title, because the break in the indorsement chain prevents her from acquiring title. If Karen indorses the instrument to Ben for value, Ben can hold Karen liable for breach of warranty. The warranty action is important to Ben, because it enables him to hold Karen liable, even if Karen indorsed the note "without recourse."

Signatures Genuine

In the example above the second warranty imposed by the Code, that **all** signatures are genuine or authorized, would also be breached. However, if the signature of a maker, drawer, drawee, acceptor, or indorser not in the chain of title is unauthorized, there is a breach of this warranty but no breach of the warranty of good title.

No Material Alteration

A third warranty is the warranty against material alteration. Suppose that Mark makes a note payable to the order of the payee in the amount of $100. The payee, without authority, alters the note so that it appears to be drawn for $1,000 and negotiates the instrument to Alice, who buys it without knowing of the alteration. Alice, indorsing "without recourse," negotiates the instrument to Barry for value. Barry presents the instrument to Mark, who refuses to pay more than $100 on it. Barry can collect the difference from Alice. Although Alice is not liable to Barry on the indorsement contract because of her qualified indorsement, she is liable to him for breach of warranty. If Alice had not qualified her indorsement, Barry would be able to recover against Alice on either the basis of warranty or the indorsement contract.

No Defenses

The fourth transferor's warranty imposed by the Code is that *no defense* of any party is good against the transferor. Under this warranty, a transferor who indorses "without recourse" stands in a better position than an unqualified indorser. His warranty is only that he has *no knowledge* of any such defense. Suppose that M, a minor, a resident of a State where minors' contracts for nonnecessaries are void, makes a note payable to bearer in payment of a motorcycle. Paul, the first holder, negotiates it to Alan by mere delivery. Alan indorses it "without recourse" (qualified indorsement) and negotiates it to Betty, and Betty unqualifiedly indorses it to Henry. Henry cannot recover on the instrument against M because of M's minority (a real defense). Henry therefore recovers against Betty on either the breach of warranty that no valid defenses exist to the instrument or the indorsement contract, provided Henry gave Betty prompt notice of dishonor. Betty cannot recover against Alan because of Alan's qualified indorsement. Can Betty hold Alan for breach of warranty? Because Alan indorsed without recourse, he does not warrant that the instrument is without defense; he only warrants that he knows of no defense that is good against him. Assuming that Alan did not know that M was a minor, Betty cannot hold Alan for breach of warranty. Can Betty hold Paul? Paul is not liable as an indorser, because he did not indorse the instrument. Although Paul as a transferor warrants that there are no defenses good against him, this warranty extends only to his immediate transferee, Alan. Therefore, Betty cannot hold Paul. This illustration shows the interplay between indorsement and warranty liability. It also shows the relationship between the liability imposed under the various warranties and the individuals who can or cannot claim protection under a particular warranty.

No Knowledge of Insolvency

Any person who transfers a negotiable instrument warrants that he has no knowledge of any insolvency proceedings instituted by the maker, acceptor, or drawer of an unaccepted instrument. Thus, if M makes a note payable to bearer, and the first holder, P, negotiates it without indorsement to A, who then negotiates it by qualified indorsement to B, both P and A make a warranty that they do not know that M is in bankruptcy. However, B could not hold P for breach of warranty, because P's warranty runs only in favor of her immediate transferee, A, since P transferred the instrument without indorsement. If B should hold A liable on her warranty, A could then hold P, her immediate transferor, liable.

Warranties on Presentment

Presenter's warranty— warranties given to any payor or acceptor of an instrument

All parties called on to pay or accept an instrument must do so strictly in compliance with the order given. The drawee bank agrees to pay checks as ordered by the drawer so long as his account is sufficient to cover them. If the bank pays without the drawer's order, it cannot charge the payment to the drawer's account.

If a drawee pays an instrument that has been forged or altered, he has the initial loss, for he cannot charge this amount to the drawer. May the drawee shift this loss to the person who received the payment? For instruments on which the drawer's signature has been forged, the general answer is no. The drawee can, however, recover from a person to whom it made payment for any loss incurred because of a forged indorsement or an alteration of the instrument.

For example, suppose D's (drawer's) name is forged to a check, making it appear that it was drawn by her. If the bank pays this check, it cannot charge D's account and cannot recover from a *holder in due course* or a person who in *good faith* has changed his position in reliance on the forged instrument. Similarly, if a drawee pays a draft purportedly drawn by D, it cannot seek reimbursement from D if D's signature is forged. The justification for the rule is that the drawee is supposed to know the drawer's signature. On the other hand, if D draws a check to P or order, and P's indorsement is forged, the bank does not follow D's order in paying such an item, and hence cannot charge her account (except in the impostor or faithless employee situations discussed above). The bank, however, can recover from the person who obtained payment of the check from it. The bank should not be required to bear this loss, because it should not be expected to know the signature of payees of checks, although it should know the signatures of its own customers.

The same rationale applies to raised instruments. If D makes a check to P's order in the amount of $3 and it is raised so as to appear to be in the amount of $300, the bank cannot charge the $300 it pays out on such an item to the drawer's account. It can charge the account only $3, because that is all the drawer ordered it to pay. On the other hand, the bank can charge back the difference against the presenting party who received payment from it.

The examples to this point have involved drawees. The maker of a note obviously cannot recover payment he made on a forged maker's signature to a holder in due course or a good faith taker who changed his position in reliance; he should know his own signature. But suppose that the maker of a note pays on a forged indorsement or an altered item. The maker, like the drawee, cannot know everyone's signature, and where the indorser's signature is forged, the maker can recover any money paid to the presenting party. The situation is different where the amount of the note has been raised. Suppose that the maker makes a note in the amount of $300, and it is raised to $3,000. If he pays this note, he is not permitted to recover from an innocent presenting party, because the maker—unlike a drawee—has a way of knowing the original amount of the instrument. Similarly, suppose that a check or draft is raised *after* it has been accepted or certified by the drawee. If the acceptor pays the raised amount to an innocent presenting party, the acceptor is not entitled to recover the amount by which the instrument was raised because the innocent holder has no way of knowing the proper amount while the acceptor does.

Presenter's warranties run not only *from* the person who obtains payment or acceptance, but also from *any* prior transferor. These presentment warranties are as follows.

Good Title

Presenters give the same warranty of good title to persons who pay or accept that is granted to transferees under the transferor's warranty. More significantly, as demonstrated in the example above, the warranty extends to the genuineness of the indorser's signatures, but *not* to the signature of the drawer or maker.

Genuineness of Signature of Maker and Drawer

The presenter warrants that he has no *knowledge* that the signature of the maker or drawer is unauthorized. To protect a person who takes an instrument in good faith and later learns it was forged, certain exceptions to this warranty are specified in the Code. A holder in due course acting in good faith does not give such a warranty to (1) the maker with respect to his own signature; (2) the drawer with respect to his own signature; and (3) an acceptor of a draft with respect to the drawer's signature if such holder took the draft after acceptance or obtained the acceptance without knowledge of the unauthorized signature. These exceptions are available only to a holder in due course.

No Material Alteration

The presenter, as shown above, also gives a warranty against material alteration, but again it is not given by a holder in due course acting in good faith to a maker or drawer, whether or not the drawer is also the drawee. Further, the holder in due course does not give this warranty to the acceptor of a draft or check when an alteration was made before it was accepted if the holder received the instrument after acceptance, even though the acceptance included a term such as "payable as originally drawn." The acceptor had the first opportunity to detect the alteration. To permit the acceptor to shift the responsibility for a prior material alteration to a subsequent party would defeat the entire purpose of acceptance and certification. An acceptance or certification must constitute a definite commitment to honor a definite instrument.

This rule should not be confused with that which applies where the alteration is made *after* the acceptance or certification. In such a situation the drawee knows the amount of the original acceptance or certification, and she should not be able to charge back against an innocent party if she pays out more than that amount. Hence, a holder in due course does not warrant against alterations made after acceptance.

Figure 25–3 illustrates the various types of liability based on warranty.

Termination of Liability

Eventually, every commercial transaction must end, with the potential liabilities of the parties to the instrument terminated. Except for the presentment

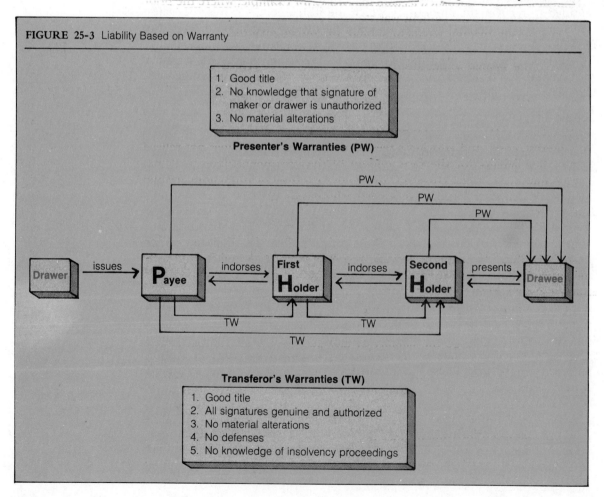

FIGURE 25-3 Liability Based on Warranty

1. Good title
2. No knowledge that signature of maker or drawer is unauthorized
3. No material alterations

Presenter's Warranties (PW)

Drawer —issues→ **P**ayee —indorses→ **First Holder** —indorses→ **Second Holder** —presents→ Drawee

Transferor's Warranties (TW)

1. Good title
2. All signatures genuine and authorized
3. No material alterations
4. No defenses
5. No knowledge of insolvency proceedings

warranties, a holder in due course has no further liability to an acceptor or payor after acceptance or payment: the payment or acceptance is *final*. The payor or acceptor cannot subsequently recover even though she discovers she has paid or accepted an instrument with a forged drawer's or maker's signature, or she has paid a check over a stop order. These provisions, as previously noted, also favor a person who in good faith has changed her position in reliance on the payment or acceptance.

The Code specifies the various methods and extent by which the liability of any party, primary or secondary, and of all parties is discharged. However, no discharge of a party is effective against a subsequent holder in due course unless she has knowledge of the discharge when she takes the instrument.

Payment or Satisfaction

The most obvious way for a party to discharge liability on an instrument is to pay the holder. Such a payment results in a discharge even though it is made with knowledge of the claim of another person to the instrument, unless such other person either supplies adequate indemnity or obtains an injunction in a proceeding to which the holder is made a party. The person making payment is not required to decide at his peril whether the claim to the instrument is valid or not. Such a claim may arise, for example, where the prior holder contends the instrument was stolen from him.

The person making payment should, of course, take the instrument or have it canceled so that it cannot pass into the hands of a subsequent holder in due course against whom his discharge would not be effective.

Tender of Payment

Any party liable on an instrument who makes tender of full payment to a holder when or after payment is due is discharged from all subsequent liability for interest, costs, and attorney's fees. However, her tender does not relieve her of her liability for the face amount of the instrument or any interest accrued until that time. However, the holder's refusal of full tender has the effect of wholly discharging every party who has a right of recourse against the party making tender. For example, a note executed by M in favor of P is negotiated by indorsement successively to A, B, and H. M defaults, and H asserts her rights against indorsers P, A, and B. If P tenders full payment to H and H refuses to accept it, desiring to collect from M, A and B are wholly discharged. The reason is that both A and B would have rights of recourse against P if they were required to pay.

Cancellation and Renunciation

A holder may discharge the liability of any party to an instrument in any manner apparent on the face of the instrument or the indorsement, such as by canceling the instrument or the signature of the party or parties to be discharged by destruction or mutilation, or by striking out a party's signature.

Because the instrument itself constitutes the obligation, intentional cancellation of it by the holder results in a discharge of all parties. Accidental destruction of an instrument does not have such an effect, nor does cancellation in any form by anyone other than the holder.

If the holder wishes to discharge one, but not all parties, he may merely strike out that party's signature. He must be careful, however, that he does not discharge other parties as well by impairing their rights of recourse, as discussed below.

A holder may also renounce his rights by a writing, signed and delivered, or by surrender of the instrument to the party to be discharged. As in the case of other discharges, however, a written renunciation is of no effect against a subsequent holder in due course who has no knowledge of the renunciation.

Cancellation or renunciation is effective even without consideration.

Impairment of Recourse or Collateral

If the holder collects the amount of an instrument from an indorser, the indorser normally has a right of recourse against parties primarily liable, prior indorsers, if any, and the drawer in the case of a draft or check. At the time the indorser accepted the instrument, she relied on the credit of the prior parties, the strict nature of their liability, and, in the case of an instrument secured by collateral, on the value of that collateral.

If any of these rights is adversely affected by the action or inaction of the holder, the indorser should not be required to pay the instrument, because when she subsequently seeks reimbursement, she will not possess the rights she bargained for when she accepted the instrument. The same rule applies to an accommodation party or acceptor who is known by the holder as an acceptor.

The Code, therefore, provides that the holder discharges any party to the instrument to the extent that without her consent the holder

1. releases or agrees not to sue any person against whom such party, to the knowledge of the holder, has a right of recourse;

2. agrees to suspend the right to enforce against such person the instrument or collateral;

3. otherwise discharges such person; or

4. unjustifiably impairs any collateral for the instrument given by or on behalf of the party or any person against whom such party has a right of recourse.

Other Methods of Discharge

As we discussed earlier, other methods by which a party's liability may be discharged include (1) fraudulent and material alteration; (2) discharge of the drawer and prior indorsers by certification of a check procured by a holder; and (3) unexcused delay in presentment, notice of dishonor, or protest. Also, any party may be discharged from liability against another party by agreeing to pay money in exchange for discharge.

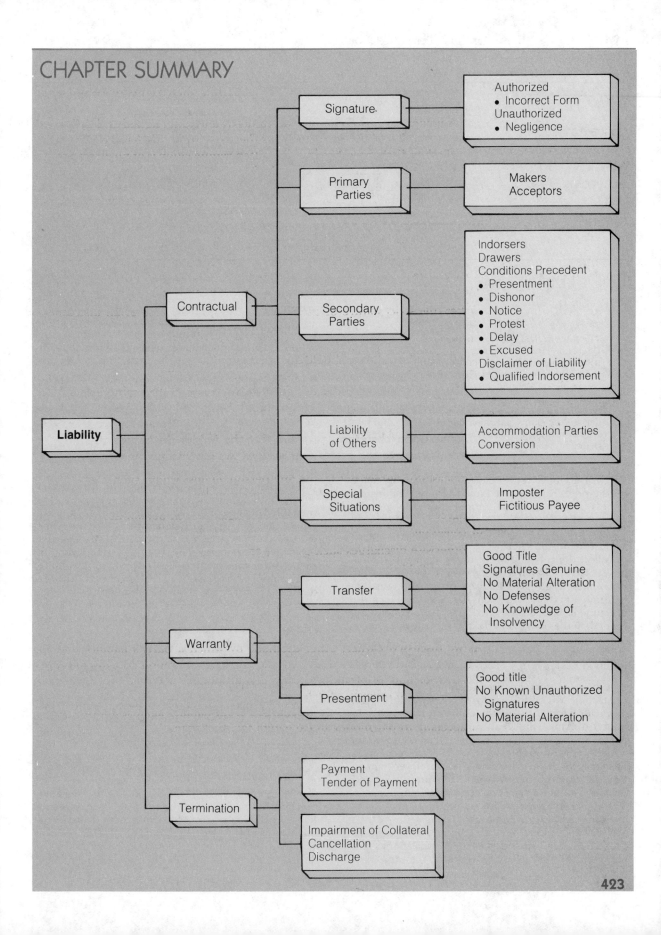

KEY TERMS

Contractual liability

Primary liability

Secondary liability

Acceptance

Certification

Acceptor

Condition precedents to liability

Presentment

Dishonor

Notice of dishonor

Protest

Conversion

Imposter rule

Fictitious payee rule

Warranty liability

Transferor's warranty

Presenter's warranty

Termination of liability

PROBLEMS

1. $800.00

Smalltown, Illinois
November 15, 1985

The undersigned promises to pay to the order of John Doe, Nine Hundred Dollars with interest from date of note. Payment to be made in five monthly installments of One Hundred Eighty Dollars, plus accrued interest beginning on December 1, 1985. In the event of default in the payment of any installment or interest on installment date, the holder of this instrument may declare the entire obligation due and owing and proceed forthwith to collect the balance due on this instrument.

(signed) Acton, agent

On December 18, no payment having been made on the note, Doe indorsed and delivered the instrument to Todd to secure a pre-existing debt in the amount of $800.

On January 18, 1986, Todd brought an action against Acton and Phi Corporation, Acton's principal, to collect the full amount of the instrument with interest. Acton defended on the basis that he signed the instrument in a representative capacity and that Doe had failed to deliver the consideration for which the instrument had been issued. Phi Corporation defended on the basis that it did not sign the instrument and that its name does not appear on the instrument.

For what amount, if any, are Acton and Phi Corporation liable?

2. Cole was supervisor of the shipping department of Machine Mfg., Inc. In February, Cole found herself in need of funds and at the end of that month submitted to Ames, the treasurer of the corporation, a payroll listing including the name, Ben Day, to whom was allegedly owed $800 for services rendered during February. Actually, there was no employee named Day. Relying on the word of Cole, Ames drew and delivered to her a series of corporate payroll checks drawn on the corporate account in the Capital Bank, one of which was made payable to the order of Ben Day for $800. Cole took the check, indorsed on its back "Ben Day," cashed it at the Capital Bank, and pocketed the proceeds. She repeated the same procedure at the end of March, April, and May. In mid-June, Machine Mfg., Inc., learned of Cole's fraudulent conduct, fired her, and brought an appropriate action against Capital Bank seeking a judgment for $3,200. Decision?

3. While employed as a night watchman at the place of business of A. B. Cate Trucking Company, Fred Fain observed that the office safe had been left unlocked. It contained fifty payroll checks that were ready to be distributed to employees two days later. The checks had all been signed by the sole proprietor, Cate. Fain removed five of the checks and also took two blank checks that were in the safe. Fain forged the indorsements of the payees on the five payroll checks and cashed them at local supermarkets. He then filled out one of the blank checks, making himself payee, and forged Cate's signature as drawer. After cashing that check at a supermarket, Fain departed by airplane to Jamaica. The six checks were promptly presented for payment to the drawee bank, the Bank of Emanon, which paid each of the checks. Shortly thereafter Cate learned about the missing payroll checks and forgeries, and demanded that the Bank of Emanon credit his account with the amount of the six checks.

Must the bank comply with Cate's demand? What are the bank's rights, if any, against the supermarkets? You may assume that the supermarkets cashed all of the checks in good faith.

4. A negotiable promissory note executed and delivered by B to C passed in due course to and was indorsed in blank by C, D, E, and F. G, the present holder, strikes out D's indorsement. What is the liability of C, D, E, and F on their respective indorsements?

5. On June 15, 1981, J, for consideration, executed a negotiable promissory note for $10,000 payable to R on or before June 15, 1986. J subsequently suffered financial reverses. During January, 1984, R on two occasions told J that he knew that J was having a difficult time and that he, R, did not need the money and the debt should be considered as completely canceled, with no other act or payment being required. These conversations were witnessed by three persons, including L. On March 15, 1986, R changed his mind and indorsed the note for value to L. The note was not paid by June 15, 1986, and L sued J for the amount of the note. J defended on the ground that R had canceled the debt and renounced all rights against J and that L had notice of this fact. Decision?

6. Tate and Fitch were longtime friends. Tate was a man of considerable means; Fitch had encountered financial difficulties. In order to bolster his failing business, Fitch desired to borrow $6,000 from Farmers Bank of Erehwon. To accomplish this, he persuaded Tate to help him make a promissory note by which it would appear that Tate had the responsibility of maker, but with Fitch agreeing to pay the instrument when due. Accordingly, they executed the following instrument:

> December 1, 1985
>
> Thirty days after date and for value received, I promise to pay to the order of Frank Fitch the sum of $6,600.
>
> /s/ Timothy Tate

On the back of the note, Fitch indorsed, "Pay to the order of Farmers Bank of Erehwon /s/ Frank Fitch" and delivered it to the bank in exchange for $6,000.

When the note was not paid at maturity, the bank, without first demanding payment by Fitch, brought an action on the note against Tate. (a) Decision? (b) If Tate voluntarily pays the note to the Bank, may he then recover on the note against Fitch, who appears as an indorser?

7. Alpha orally appointed Omega as his agent to find and purchase for him a 1930 Dodge automobile in good condition. Omega located such a car. The car's owner, Roe, agreed to sell and deliver the car on January 10, 1986, for $9,000. To evidence the purchase price, Omega mailed to Roe the following instrument:

> December 1, 1985
>
> $9,000.00
>
> We promise to pay to the order of bearer Nine Thousand Dollars with interest from date of this instrument on or before January 10, 1986. This note is given in consideration of John Roe's transferring title to and possession of his 1930 Dodge automobile.
>
> (signed) Omega, agent

Smith stole the note from Roe's mailbox, indorsed Roe's name on the note, and promptly discounted it with Sunset Bank for $8,700. Not having received the note, Roe sold the car to a third party. On January 10, 1986, the bank, having discovered all the facts, demanded payment of the note from Alpha and Omega. Payment was refused by both.

What are Sunset Bank's rights with regard to Omega? Its rights with regard to Roe and Smith?

8. In payment of the purchase price of a used motorboat that had been fraudulently misrepresented, Y signed and delivered to A his negotiable note in the amount of $2,000 due October 1, with S as an accommodation co-maker. Y intended to use the boat for his fishing business. A indorsed the note in blank preparatory to discounting it. T stole the note from A and delivered it to M on July 1 in payment of a past-due debt owing by T to M in the amount of $600, with M making up the difference by giving T his check for $800 and an oral promise to pay T an additional $600 on October 1.

When M demanded payment of the note on December 1, both Y and S refused to pay the note because it had not been presented for payment on its due date and because A had fraudulently misrepresented the motorboat for which the note had been executed.

What are M's rights, if any, against Y, S, T, and A, respectively?

9. On July 1, A sold D, a jeweler, a necklace containing imitation gems that A fraudulently represented to be diamonds. In payment for the necklace D executed and delivered to A her promissory note for $25,000 dated July 1 and payable on December 1 to A's order with interest at 14 percent per annum.

The note was thereafter successively indorsed in blank and delivered by A to B, B to C, and by C to S, who became a holder in due course on August 10. On November 1, D discovered A's fraud and immediately notified A, B, C, and S that she would not pay the note when it became due. B, a friend of S, requested that S release him from liability on the note, and S, as a favor to B and for no other consideration, struck out B's indorsement.

On November 15, S, who was solvent and had no creditors, indorsed the note to the order of F, his father, and delivered it to F as a gift. At the same time, S told F of D's statement that D would not pay the note when it became due. F presented the note to D for payment on December 1, but D refused to pay. Thereafter F gave due notice of dishonor to A, B, and C.

What are F's rights, if any, against A, B, C, and D on the note?

26

BANK DEPOSITS AND COLLECTIONS

In today's society, most goods and services are bought and sold without a physical transfer of cash. Credit cards, charge accounts, and various deferred payment plans have made cash sales increasingly rare. But even credit sales must ultimately be settled—when they are, payment is usually made by check rather than cash. If the parties to a sales transaction happen to have accounts at the same bank, a transfer of credit is easily accomplished. In most cases, however, the parties do business at different banks. Then the buyer's check must journey from the seller-payee's bank (the **depositary** bank), where the check is deposited by the seller for credit to his account, to the buyer-drawer's bank (the **payor** bank) for payment. In this collection process the check frequently passes through one or more other banks (**intermediary** banks) so that it may be collected and the appropriate entries recorded. Any bank handling the item for collection other than the payor bank (that is, any intermediary or depositary bank) is also referred to as a **collecting** bank.

Our banking system has developed a network to handle the collection of checks and other instruments. Article 4 of the Uniform Commercial Code, entitled "Bank Deposits and Collections," provides the principal rules governing the bank collection process. Since items in the bank collection process are essentially those covered by Article 3, "Commercial Paper," and to a lesser extent by Article 8, "Investment Securities," these Articles may apply to a bank collection problem.

Collection of Items

When a person deposits a check in his bank (the depositary bank), the bank credits his account by the amount of the check. This is **provisional** credit. Normally, a bank does not permit a customer to draw funds against a provisional credit, but if it does permit its customer to draw against the credit it has given value and may be a holder in due course. Under the customer's contract with his bank, the bank must make a reasonable effort to obtain payment of all checks deposited for collection. When the amount of the check has been collected from the payor bank (the drawee), the credit becomes **final.**

If the payor bank does not pay the check for some reason, such as a stop payment order or insufficient funds in the drawer's account, the depositary bank reverses the provisional credit to the customer's account, debits his ac-

Depositary bank –the bank of the payee or holder

Provisional credit –tentative credit for the deposit of an instrument until final credit is given

Final credit –payment of the instrument by the payor

Payor bank –drawee bank

427

count for that amount, and returns the check to him with a statement of the reason for nonpayment. If, in the meantime, he has been permitted to draw against the provisional credit, the bank may recover the payment from him.

In some cases the bank involved is both the depositary bank—the bank in which the payee or holder deposited the check for credit to his account—and the payor bank—the bank on which the drawer wrote his check. In most cases, however, the depositary and payor banks are different, and the bank collection aspects of Article 4 come into play. Where the depositary and payor banks are different, a check must pass from one bank to the other, either directly through a clearinghouse or through one or more "intermediary banks," as illustrated in Figure 26–1.

Collecting Banks

In the usual situation where the depositary and payor banks are different, the depositary bank gives a provisional credit to its customer, transfers the item to the next bank in the chain, receiving a provisional credit or "settlement" from it, and so on to the payor bank, which then debits the drawer's account. When the check is paid, all the provisional settlements given by the respective banks in the chain become final, and the transaction has been completed. No adjustment is necessary on the books of any of the banks involved. This procedure simplifies the bookkeeping processes of all the banks involved because only one entry is necessary if the check is paid.

If the payor bank does not pay the check, however, it returns the check, and each intermediary or collecting bank reverses the provisional settlement or credit it previously gave to its forwarding bank. Ultimately, the depositary bank will charge the account of its customer that deposited the item, and he must seek recovery from the indorsers or the drawer.

Intermediary bank–a bank involved in the collection process other than the depositary or payor bank

Collecting bank–any bank handling the item for payment except the payor bank

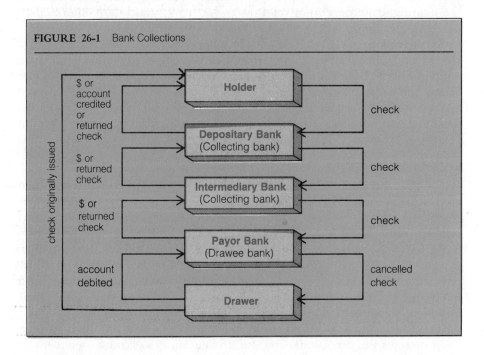

FIGURE 26-1   Bank Collections

A collecting bank is an **agent** or subagent of the owner of the check until the settlement becomes final. Clearly, then, unless otherwise provided, any credit given for the item initially is provisional. Once it is finally settled, the agency relationship changes to one of debtor-creditor. The effect of this agency rule is that the risk of loss remains with the owner and any chargebacks go to her, not to the collecting bank.

All collecting banks have certain responsibilities and duties in collecting checks and other types of commercial paper. We discuss these below. For a discussion of ways which this system has been abused see *Law in the News* on page 430.

Duty of Care   A collecting bank must use ordinary care in handling an item transferred to it for collection. The steps it takes in presenting an item or sending it for presentment are particulary important. It must act within a reasonable time after receipt of the item and must choose a reasonable method of forwarding the item for presentment.

Duty to Act Seasonably   Closely related to the collecting bank's duty of care is its duty to act seasonably. A collecting bank acts seasonably in any event if it takes proper action, such as forwarding or presenting an item before its "midnight deadline" following receipt of the item, notice, or payment. If the bank adheres to this standard, the timeliness of its action cannot be challenged. Although a reasonably longer time may be seasonable, the bank bears the burden of proof in such cases. The **midnight deadline** means midnight of the banking day following the banking day on which it receives an item. Thus, if a bank receives a check on Monday, it must take proper action by midnight on the next banking day, or Tuesday. A banking day means that part of any day on which a bank is open to the public for carrying on its primary banking functions.

Midnight deadline-midnight of the next banking day after receiving an item

Because it takes time to process an item through a bank—whether depositary, intermediary, or payor bank—the midnight deadline presents a problem. If the various steps involved in a day's transaction are to be completed without overtime work, the bank must either close early or fix an earlier cutoff time for the day's work. Recognizing this problem, the Code provides that for the purpose of allowing time to process items, prove balances, and make the necessary entries on its books to determine its position for the day, a bank may fix an afternoon hour of 2:00 P.M. or later as a cutoff hour for the handling of money and items and the making of entries on its books. Items received after the cutoff hour fixed as the close of the banking day are considered to have been received at the opening of the next banking day, and the time for taking action and for determining the bank's midnight deadline begins to run from that point.

Recognizing that if an item is not paid, everyone involved will be greatly inconvenienced, the Code provides that unless otherwise instructed, a collecting bank in a good faith effort to secure payment may, in the case of specific items, waive, modify, or extend the time limits, but not in excess of one additional banking day.

Indorsements   When an item is restrictively indorsed with words such as "pay any bank," it is locked into the bank collection system, and only a bank may acquire the rights of a holder. When a bank forwards an item for collection,

Law In The News _____

What Did Hutton's Managers Know—and When Did They Know It?

When trading in E. F. Hutton & Co.'s stock was halted early on May 2, New York Stock Exchange traders assumed that a buyout of the widely respected brokerage giant was imminent. Instead, over the ticker came the shocking news that Hutton was pleading guilty to 2,000 separate counts of mail and wire fraud. Hutton agreed to pay $2 million in fines—the maximum penalty and the largest imposed on a brokerage house in memory. "We were very surprised," says a veteran executive at a rival firm. "The Street generally viewed Hutton like Caesar's wife—beyond suspicion."

But after a three-year investigation headed by the Justice Dept., Hutton admitted to fraudulently obtaining the use of more than $1 billion in interest-free funds by systematically overdrawing checking accounts at some 400 banks. By pleading guilty, Hutton avoided a long, public trial. But the highly publicized episode has tarnished the company's reputation and embarrassed both Hutton Chairman Robert M. Fomon and Securities & Exchange Commission Chairman John S. R. Shad, who was vice-chairman of Hutton when the abuses started. Moreover, both Justice's complaint and the company's own 40-page explanation of what happened skirt the explosive issue of what role Hutton senior management might have played in the scheme. Executives at other Wall Street firms say it is hard to believe that Hutton's senior management did not know what was going on.

Repercussions.

Justice intends the Hutton case to be a warning to corporate America. Prosecutors do not feel that the overtly abusive practices that prompted criminal charges against Hutton are widely used. But the department also filed a civil complaint against the firm over procedures it believes to be fairly common and that it considers illegal under the Comprehensive Crime Control Act passed by Congress last year. The most important: drawing checks against uncollected funds without a written agreement from the bank.

The Hutton bombshell has already had wide-ranging repercussions. Companies in all sorts of industries began scrambling to make sure their cash management procedures conform to the law. William S. Wire II, chief financial officer at Genesco Inc., an apparel and shoe manufacturer, interrupted his Florida vacation to place an urgent call to the company's Nashville headquarters. "I got right on the phone with our treasurer and said, 'Double-check everything, and make sure we're perfectly legal.'"

Under its agreement with Justice, Hutton promised to cover the $750,000 cost of the government's investigation and make restitution to the banks it defrauded. The company set up reserves of $8 million during the course of 1984 and contends that these will be sufficient to cover all claims against it. However, government prosecutors estimate that the firm could be liable for as much as $20 million, which would put a sizable dent in Hutton's future earnings. Last year the company earned $52.7 million on $2.8 billion in revenues.

The damage to Hutton's reputation is likely to prove more costly, though difficult to quantify. Most securities industry observers do not expect many of Hutton's retail customers to pull their accounts, because the scheme did not harm them. But Hutton's guilty plea put the firm's army of 6,000 brokers on the defensive, anyway. "This will hurt my business," says an assistant branch manager. "It's difficult to prospect with Hutton's name all over the newspapers."

The fallout could be worse in investment banking, where Hutton is locked in fierce rivalry for corporate and municipal clients. Only hours after Hutton's announcement, New York Mayor Edward I. Koch dropped the firm as a co-manager of an upcoming $586 million bond issue, which in turn caused Hutton to be bounced from a separate $125 million New York City housing deal. "Every time I try to talk to a public official now, first they want to talk about Hutton," says the top public finance specialist at a leading underwriting firm.

Although Hutton has settled with Justice, it could still face SEC sanctions. In return for agreeing to cooperate with any SEC investigation of fraudulent practices, Hutton received a 180-day waiver from a law that would automatically disqualify it from acting as an investment adviser or as the principal underwriter for mutual funds and unit investment trusts—both important businesses for the firm. The SEC is considering Hutton's request that this exemption be made permanent. Chairman Shad will not take part in the decision.

Hutton's Managers continued

In the end, how much Hutton is damaged depends on the extent to which the company's senior management knew about or participated in the scheme. The Justice Dept. did not name a single individual in its charges, prompting swift criticism from Mayor Koch and 15 prominent Senate Democrats, who called on Attorney General Edwin Meese III to explain what they termed "blatant failure to find individual liability."

Prosecutors said that as many as 25 Hutton employees were involved, nearly half of whom were granted immunity by Justice in the course of its investigation. Meese has said that the government decided not to prosecute individuals because it would involve lengthy litigation and because the fraud "was a corporate scheme rather than a group of individual criminals operating together."

Hard to Swallow.

Fomon also refused to identify any of the employees involved. But he said in a press conference that with the completion of Justice's investigation, the firm would take "appropriate" action against individual employees. He conceded

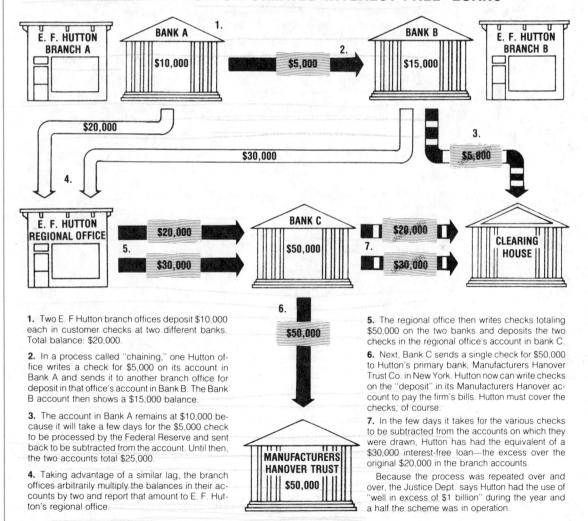

HOW E. F. HUTTON CREATED INTEREST-FREE 'LOANS'

1. Two E. F Hutton branch offices deposit $10,000 each in customer checks at two different banks. Total balance: $20,000.

2. In a process called "chaining," one Hutton office writes a check for $5,000 on its account in Bank A and sends it to another branch office for deposit in that office's account in Bank B. The Bank B account then shows a $15,000 balance.

3. The account in Bank A remains at $10,000 because it will take a few days for the $5,000 check to be processed by the Federal Reserve and sent back to be subtracted from the account. Until then, the two accounts total $25,000.

4. Taking advantage of a similar lag, the branch offices arbitrarily multiply the balances in their accounts by two and report that amount to E. F. Hutton's regional office.

5. The regional office then writes checks totaling $50,000 on the two banks and deposits the two checks in the regional office's account in bank C.

6. Next, Bank C sends a single check for $50,000 to Hutton's primary bank, Manufacturers Hanover Trust Co. in New York. Hutton now can write checks on the "deposit" in its Manufacturers Hanover account to pay the firm's bills. Hutton must cover the checks, of course.

7. In the few days it takes for the various checks to be subtracted from the accounts on which they were drawn, Hutton has had the equivalent of a $30,000 interest-free loan—the excess over the original $20,000 in the branch accounts.

Because the process was repeated over and over, the Justice Dept. says Hutton had the use of "well in excess of $1 billion" during the year and a half the scheme was in operation.

Hutton's Managers continued

fault, along with other managers, for failing to impose controls adequate to prevent branch officers from using cash management tactics that were "not consistent with either the policy or the standards of this firm." As soon as senior management saw what was going on, says Fomon, the abuses were halted. He refused to speak to BUSINESS WEEK for this story, however.

Many Wall Streeters found Fomon's explanation hard to swallow. "The probability that there was some kind of a branch office conspiracy that headquarters did not know about is very, very low," says an expert in securities industry management systems. "Cash management has been centralized at every brokerage firm. One desk knows where every dollar is all the time."

Adds Jon M. Burnham, an executive vice-president of Drexel Burnham Lambert Inc. and the chief administrator of its retail system: "I found it hard to believe when Mr. Fomon blamed it on the branch managers. If I was a branch manager at Hutton, I'd be mad as hell."

At issue are the techniques Hutton used to transfer funds from its local branches to its central account in New York. Because banks do not pay interest on commercial deposits, most companies try to keep their checking account balances to a minimum and put idle cash to work as fast as possible.

Banks keep track of two balances for each account: the "ledger" balance, including total deposits, and the "collected" balance, limited to those checks the bank has actually cleared. Banks often permit corporate clients to use uncollected funds—the float—but charge for the privilege.

By shuffling $10 billion from one account to another, Hutton obtained the interest-free use of more than $1 billion in uncollected funds from July, 1980, through February, 1982, a period during which short-term interest rates often were in the 18%-to-20% range. The government contends, in large part, that these abuses resulted from the overzealous response to bonuses offered to branch and regional managers to encourage "aggressive" and "creative" cash management.

For its part, Hutton says the system was set up to capture its fair share of the float, rather than leaving all to the banks. The company used a formula for the temporary overdrafting of its branch and regional accounts. The overdrafts were covered by depositing checks drawn against central Hutton accounts in which the company was not required to keep any money on hand. Only when checks on these zero-balance accounts were actually presented for payment did the company wire cash into the account. Therefore, the company got a few precious days to see the float interest-free.

Lax Oversight?

But Hutton's technique did not merely capture float, it created float. Hutton says that 20 branches created overdrafts far in excess of that permitted under the firm's formulas simply by making up numbers. An additional 83 branches manufactured float by transferring funds back and forth among other branches (illustration, ["How E. F. Hutton Created Interest-Free 'Loans' "]). The government's criminal charges are based on these deliberate attempts to mislead banks.

Hutton's senior management claims it did not learn that the system was being abused until a small bank in Batavia, N.Y., bounced a large check. But closing the loop on the scheme required sizable cash transfers into the zero-balance accounts at Hutton's central banks to prevent checks from bouncing. Those transfers presumably required the approval of someone at headquarters.

It may well be that Fomon and his lieutenants are guilty of nothing worse than lax oversight—a grievous enough failing at a brokerage house. But the cloud over E. F. Hutton is likely to linger until the company or the government starts naming names.

By Anthony Bianco and G. David Wallace in New York, with Daniel B. Moskowitz and Peter Philipps in Washington

Reprinted from the May 20, 1985 issue of *Business Week* by special permission. © 1985 by McGraw-Hill, Inc.

it normally indorses it "pay any bank," irrespective of the type of indorsement, if any, that the item carried at the time of receipt. This serves to protect the collecting bank by making it impossible for the item to stray from regular collection channels.

If the item had no indorsement when received by the depositary bank, it may supply any indorsement of its customer that is necessary to title unless the item contains the words "payee's indorsement required" or the like. The depositary bank must examine the item for prior restrictive indorsements. Subsequent intermediary banks and the payor bank need check only the indorsement of its transferor and may rely on the fact that the depositary bank performed its required function.

Warranties   Customers and collecting banks give basically the same warranties as those given by parties under Article 3 of the Code on presentment and transfer, which were discussed in Chapter 25. Each customer or collecting bank who **transfers** an item and receives a settlement or consideration warrants to his transferee and subsequent transferees that: (1) he has good title (that is, the transferor is the true owner or is an authorized agent of the owner); (2) *all* signatures are genuine or authorized; (3) the item has not been materially altered; (4) no defense of any party is good against him; and (5) he has no knowledge of any insolvency proceeding involving the maker or acceptor or the drawer of an unaccepted instrument. Moreover, each customer or collecting bank who obtains payment or acceptance, as well as all prior customers and collecting banks, warrants to the *payor* bank on **presentment** that: (1) she has good title or is authorized to obtain payment; (2) she has no knowledge that the signature of the maker or drawer is unauthorized; and (3) the item has not been materially altered.

Final Payment   The provisional settlements made in the collection chain are all directed toward final payment of the item by the payor bank. This is one end of the collection process—the turn-around point from which the proceeds of the item begin the return flow and provisional settlements become final. For example, a customer of the California Country State Bank may deposit a check drawn on the State of Maine Country National Bank. The check may then take a course such as follows: from the California Country State Bank to a correspondent bank in San Francisco, to the Federal Reserve Bank of San Francisco, to the Federal Reserve Bank of Boston, to the payor bank. Provisional settlements were made at each step. When the payor bank finally paid the item, the proceeds began a return flow over the same course.

The critical question, then, is the point in time when the item has been **paid** by the payor bank, because this not only starts the payment process but also affects questions of priority between the item on the one hand and actions such as the filing of a stop payment order against the item. It is clear that final payment occurs at some moment during the processing of the item by the payor bank; however, this moment may be difficult to ascertain.

Under the Code, final payment occurs when the payor bank does any of the following, whichever happens first: (1) pays an item in cash; (2) settles and does not reserve the right to revoke the settlement, or does not have such right through agreement, statute, or clearinghouse rule; (3) makes a provisional settlement and does not revoke it in the time and manner permitted by statute, clearinghouse rule, or agreement; or (4) completes the process of posting the item to the account of the drawer. Posting is normally completed after the following steps have been taken: (a) verifying any signature; (b) ascertaining that sufficient funds are available; (c) affixing a "paid" or other stamp; (d) entering a charge or entry to a customer's account; and (e) correcting or reversing an entry or erroneous action on the item.

Payor Banks

The payor or drawee, under its contract of deposit with the drawer, agrees to pay to the payee or his order checks issued by the drawer provided the order is not countermanded and that there are sufficient funds in the drawer's account.

Due to the tremendous increase in volume of bank collections as well as the improved methods of processing items by payor banks, it has become necessary to adopt production-line methods for handling checks to assure an even flow of items on a day-to-day basis. This is necessary if work is to be conducted without abnormal peak loads and overtime. The solution has been the institution of deferred posting procedures whereby items are sorted and proved on the day they are received, but are not posted to customers' accounts or returned until the next banking day. The UCC not only approves this procedure but also sets up specific standards to govern its application to the actions of payor banks.

When a payor bank that is not also a depositary bank receives a demand item other than for immediate payment over the counter, it must either return the item or give its transferor a provisional settlement before midnight of the banking day on which the item is received. Otherwise it becomes liable to its transferor for the amount of the item unless it has a valid defense.

If it gives the provisional settlement as required, it then has until its midnight deadline to return the item or, if it is held for protest or is otherwise unavailable for return, to send written notice of dishonor or nonpayment. After doing this, it is entitled to revoke the settlement and recover any payment made. If the payor bank fails to return the item or send notice before its midnight deadline, it becomes accountable for the amount of the item unless it has a valid defense for its inaction.

There are many reasons why a bank may dishonor an item and return it or send notice. The following situations are the most common. The drawer or maker may have no account or may have insufficient funds to cover the item; a signature on the item may be forged; or payment of the item may have been stopped by the drawer or maker.

Relationship Between Payor Bank and Its Customer

Payment of an Item

When a payor bank receives an item properly payable from a customer's account but there are insufficient funds in the account to pay it, the bank may (1) dishonor the item and return it or (2) pay the item and charge its customer's account even though an overdraft is created as a result. The item authorized or directed the bank to make the payment and hence carries with it an enforceable implied promise to reimburse the bank. Further, the customer may be liable to the bank to pay a service charge for the bank's handling of the overdraft or may be liable to pay interest on the amount of the overdraft.

A check or draft, however, is not an assignment of funds in the hands of the drawee available for its payment, and the drawee is not liable on an instrument until it is accepted. The holder of a check has no right to require the drawee bank to pay it, whether or not there are sufficient funds in the drawer's account. But if an item is presented to a payor bank and the bank improperly refuses payment, it will incur a liability to its customer from whose account the item should have been paid. If the item is not more than six months old and regular in form, if the customer has adequate funds on deposit and there is no other valid basis for the refusal to pay, the bank is liable to its customer for any reasonably expectable damages that the customer incurs.

A payor bank is under no obligation to its customer to pay an uncertified check that is over six months old. This rule reflects the usual banking practice of consulting a depositor before paying an old item on her account. The bank, as shown in the case which follows, is not required to dishonor such an item and if payment is made in good faith, it may charge the amount of the item to its customer's account.

FACTS: Advanced Alloys, Inc., issued a check in the amount of $2,500 to Sergeant Steel Corporation. The check was presented for payment fourteen months later to the Chase Manhattan Bank. Chase Manhattan made payment on the check and charged Advanced Alloy's account. Advanced Alloy now seeks to recover the payment made on the check.

DECISION: Judgment for Chase Manhattan. A bank is under no obligation to a customer having a checking account to pay a check, other than a certified check, which is presented more than six months after its date, but it may charge its customer's account for a payment made thereafter in good faith. Good faith is defined as honesty in fact in the conduct or transaction concerned. Chase Manhattan acted in good faith when it paid the check presented fourteen months after its issuance without inquiry of the depositor Advanced Alloys because it did not know that Advanced Alloys did not want the check paid.

ADVANCED ALLOYS, INC. v. SERGEANT STEEL CORP.

Civil Court of the City of New York, Queens County, 1973.
72 Misc.2d 614, 340 N.Y.S.2d 266.

Stop Payment Orders

A check drawn on a bank is an order to pay a sum of money and an authorization to charge the amount to the drawer's account. The drawer may countermand this order, however, by means of a stop payment order. If the order does not come too late, the bank is bound by it. If the bank inadvertently pays a check over a valid stop order, it is liable to the customer, but only to the extent of the customer's loss resulting from the payment. The burden of establishing the fact and amount of loss is on the customer.

To be effective, a stop payment order must be received by the bank in time to give it a reasonable opportunity to act on it. See *Siniscalchi v. Valley Bank New York* which follows. An oral stop order is binding on the bank for only fourteen calendar days. Therefore, the normal practice is for a customer to confirm an oral stop order in writing; this order is effective for six months and may be renewed in writing.

Stop payment–order for a drawee not to pay an instrument

FACTS: On Tuesday, June 11, Siniscalchi issued a $200 check on the drawee Valley Bank. On Saturday morning, June 15, the check was cashed. This transaction, as well as others taking place on that Saturday morning, was not recorded or processed through the bank's bookkeeping system until Monday, June 17. On that date Siniscalchi arrived at the bank at 9 A.M. and asked to place a stop payment order on the check. A bank employee checked the bank records which at that time indicated that the instrument had not cleared the bank. At 9:45 A.M. she gave him a printed notice confirming his request to stop payment. Siniscalchi now seeks to recover the $200 paid on the check.

DECISION: Judgment for Valley Bank. A customer has a right to stop payment on a check, but the stop payment order must be received at such time and in such manner as to afford the bank a reasonable opportunity to act on the stop payment. Here, the check was cashed before the stop payment order was issued, and hence the stop payment order did not effectively bind Valley Bank.

SINISCALCHI v. VALLEY BANK OF NEW YORK

District Court, Nassau County, Second District, 1974.
79 Misc.2d 64, 359 N.Y.S.2d 173.

The fact that a drawer has filed a stop payment order does not automatically relieve her of liability. If the bank honors the stop payment order and returns the check, the holder may bring an action against the drawer. If the holder qualifies as a holder in due course, personal defenses that the drawer might have to such an action would be of no avail.

Customer's Duties

The Code imposes certain affirmative duties on bank customers and fixes time limits within which they must assert their rights. The duties arise and the time starts to run from the time the bank either sends or makes available to its customer a statement of account accompanied by the items paid against the account. The customer is required to exercise reasonable care and promptness to examine the bank statement and items to discover his unauthorized signature or any alteration on an item. Because he is not presumed to know the signatures of payees or indorsers, this duty of prompt and careful examination applies only to his own signature and alterations, both of which he should be able to detect immediately. If he discovers an unauthorized signature or an alteration, he must notify the bank promptly.

If the customer fails to carry out these duties of prompt examination and notice, he may not assert against the bank his unauthorized signature or any alteration if the bank can show that it suffered a loss because of the customer's failure to carry out these duties promptly.

Furthermore, the customer will lose his rights in a potentially more important situation. Occasionally a forger carries out a series of transactions involving the account of the same individual. Perhaps he is an employee who has access to his employer's checkbook. He may forge one or more checks each month until he is finally detected. The bank on the other hand, having paid one or more of the customer's checks with the false signatures without objection, may be lulled into a false sense of security. Suddenly the forgery is detected by the customer after many months or even years. Under the Code, the bank is not held liable for all such items. The customer must examine the statement and items within a reasonable period, which in no event may exceed fourteen calendar days and may under the circumstances be less, and notify the bank. Any alterations or unauthorized signatures on instruments by the same wrongdoer and paid by the bank during that period will still be the responsibility of the bank, but any paid thereafter but before the customer notifies the bank may not be asserted against it. This rule is based on the concept that the loss involved is directly traceable to the customer's negligence and as a result he should stand the loss.

The bank must, of course, exercise ordinary care in paying the items involved. If it does not, it loses its right to require prompt action on the part of its customer. But whether the bank exercised due care or not, the customer must always report an alteration or his unauthorized signature within one year from the time the statement and items were made available to him or be precluded from asserting them against the bank. Any unauthorized indorsement must be asserted within three years from the time the bank statements and items containing such indorsements are made available to the customer.

Electronic Fund Transfers

We mentioned earlier that the use of commercial paper for payment has transformed the United States into a virtually cashless society. The advent and technological advances of computers make it likely that in the foreseeable future electronic fund transfer systems (EFTs) will bring about a checkless society. Financial institutions seek to substitute EFTs for checks for two principal reasons. The first is to eliminate the ever-increasing paperwork involved in processing the billions of checks that are issued annually. The second is to eliminate the "float" that a drawer of a check currently enjoys as a result of maintaining the use of his funds during the check-processing period between issuing the check and final payment.

An EFT has been defined as "any transfer of funds, other than a transaction originated by check, draft, or similar paper instrument, which is initiated through an electronic terminal, telephonic instrument, or computer or magnetic tape so as to order, instruct or authorize a financial institution to debit or credit an account." For example, with EFTs, Carl in New York would be able to pay a debt he owes to Joanne in Illinois by entering into his computer an order to his bank to pay Joanne. The drawee bank would then instantly debit Carl's account and transfer the credit to Joanne's bank, where Joanne's account would immediately be credited in that amount. The entire transaction would be completed in minutes.

Electronic fund transfer –a transaction with a financial institution by means of computer, telephone or electronic instrument

Although EFTs are still fairly new, their use has brought about considerable confusion concerning the legal rights of customers and financial institutions. A partial solution to these legal issues was provided in 1978 by Congress when it enacted the Electronic Fund Transfer Act, which we discuss below. However, many important legal problems remain. Currently, a committee of the Permanent Editorial Board of the Uniform Commercial Code is in the process of drafting a New Payments Code to deal with EFTs.

Types of Electronic Fund Transfers

Although it is highly probable that a number of new EFTS will appear in the coming years, at the moment there are principally four types of EFTs in use: (1) automated teller machines, (2) point-of-sale systems, (3) direct deposit and withdrawal of funds and (4) pay-by-phone systems.

Automated Teller Machines   Automated teller machines (ATM) are rapidly becoming available throughout the country. ATMs permit customers to conduct various transactions with their bank through the use of electronic terminals. After activating an ATM with a plastic identification card and a secret number, customers can deposit and withdraw funds from their accounts, transfer funds between accounts, obtain cash advances from bank credit card accounts, and make payments on loans.

Do ATMs constitute branch banks? If so, what does this do to the future utilization of such machines? The following recent case deals directly with the first of these questions.

FACTS: Wegmans, a chain grocery store, had installed automated teller machines (ATMs) in 31 of its stores to attract customers and support a high-volume grocery business. In January 1983, the federally chartered Marine Midland Bank entered into an agreement with Wegmans that permitted Marine depositors to use the ATM located in the Wegmans Canandaigua store. Canandaigua has a population of approximately 11,000 and is the principal office of the Canandaigua National Bank. The ATM in the Canandaigua store has Wegmans' logo on it, is under Wegmans' control and is a shared ATM, that is, it may be used by several financial institutions. Marine's account-holders may use the ATM to make deposits and cash withdrawals, obtain cash advances against credit cards, transfer funds between accounts, pay bills and obtain account balances. Wegmans is obligated under the agreement to load the machine with cash, provide

INDEPENDENT BANKERS ASSOCIATION OF NEW YORK STATE, INC. v. MARINE MIDLAND BANK, N.A.

United States Court of Appeals, Second Circuit, 1985.
757 F.2d 453 (1985).

deposit envelopes and other customer forms, issue transaction receipts and provide security, insurance and maintenance services.

The Independent Bankers Association, of which Canandaigua National Bank is a member, brought suit against Marine Midland Bank. The Association claims that Marine's use of Wegmans' ATM constitutes branch banking which violates Federal law. Federal law, the McFadden Act, incorporates the state law prohibiting a bank from opening a branch in any community with a population of 50,000 or less that is the principal office of another bank (home office protection). Marine contends that ATM is not a "branch" under the Act.

DECISION: Judgment for Marine Midland Bank. A particular facility must be established and operated by a national bank to be deemed a branch under the McFadden Act. The question of whether an automated teller machine is a branch does not rest entirely upon whether the machine is a "place of business . . . at which deposits are received [and] checks paid." Rather, the determinative consideration is whether the machine is "owned or rented" by the particular national bank.

Here, Wegmans decided to install the ATM to attract customers to the store, it owns the machine and maintains it, and Wegmans apparently decides whether to allow customers of different banks to use the machine. Moreover, the transaction fees which Marine pays Wegmans for each customer's use of the machine does not constitute rent. These fees do not grant Marine, or any other participating bank, any proprietary or lease-hold interest in the ATM, even temporarily. Instead, they are analogous to a charge incurred for a phone call. Therefore, Marine's use of Wegmans' ATM does not constitute the establishment of a "branch bank" within the meaning of the McFadden Act.

Point-of-Sale Systems   Point-of-sales (POS) systems permit consumers to transfer funds from their bank account to a merchant automatically. The POS machines are located within the merchant's store and are activated by the consumer's identification card and code. The computer will then instantaneously debit the consumer's account and credit the merchant's account.

Direct Deposits and Withdrawals   Another type of EFTs involves direct deposits made to a customer's account through an electronic terminal when the deposit has been authorized in advance by the consumer. Examples include direct payroll deposits, deposits of Social Security payments, and deposits of pension payments. Conversely, automatic withdrawals are preauthorized electronic fund transfers from the customer's account for regular payments to some party other than the financial institution where the funds are deposited. Automatic withdrawals to pay insurance premiums, utility bills, or automobile loan payments are common examples of this type of EFT.

Pay-by-Phone Systems   Recently some financial institutions have instituted a service that permits customers to pay bills by telephoning the bank's computer system and directing transfer of funds to a designated third party. This service also permits customers to transfer funds between accounts.

Electronic Fund Transfer Act

In 1978 Congress determined that the use of electronic systems to transfer funds provided the potential for substantial benefits to consumers. However, due to the unique characteristics of such systems, the application of existing consumer protection legislation was unclear, leaving the rights and obligations of consumers and financial institutions undefined. Accordingly, Congress enacted the Electronic Fund Transfer Act to "provide a basic framework establishing the rights, liabilities, and responsibilities of participants in electronic fund transfers" with primary emphasis on "the provision of individual consumer rights." The Act is similar in many respects to the Fair Credit Billing Act (see Chapter 41), which applies to credit card transactions. The Act is administered by the Board of Governors of the Federal Reserve System, which is authorized to make regulations to carry out the purposes of the Act.

Disclosure   The Act requires that the terms and conditions of electronic fund transfers involving a consumer's account be disclosed at the time the consumer contracts for such services in readily understandable language. Included among the required disclosure are the consumer's liability for unauthorized transfers, the types of EFTs allowed, any charges for transfers or the right to make transfers, the consumer's right to stop payment of preauthorized EFTs, the consumer's right to receive documentation of EFTs, and the financial institution's liability to the consumer under the Act.

Documentation and Periodic Statements   The Act requires the financial institution to provide the consumer with written documentation of each transfer made from an electronic terminal at the time of the transfer. The documentation must clearly state the amount involved, the date, the type of transfer, the identity of the consumer's accounts involved, the identity of any third party involved, and the location of the terminal involved. In addition, the financial institution must provide each consumer with a periodic statement for each account of the consumer that may be accessed by means of an EFT.

Preauthorized Transfers   A preauthorized transfer *from* a consumer's account must be authorized in advance by the consumer in *writing,* and a copy of the authorization must be provided to the consumer when made. A consumer may stop payment of a preauthorized EFT by notifying the financial institution orally or in writing at any time up to three business days before the scheduled date of the transfer. The financial institution may require the consumer to provide written confirmation within fourteen days of an oral notification.

Error Resolution   The consumer has sixty days after the financial institution sends a periodic statement in which to notify the financial institution of any errors that appear on that statement. The financial institution is required to investigate and report the results within ten business days. If the financial institution needs more than ten days to investigate, it may take up to forty-five days, provided it recredits the consumer's account for the amount alleged to be in error. If it determines that an error did occur, it must properly correct the error. Failure to investigate in good faith makes the financial institution liable to the consumer for treble damages (that is, three times the amount of provable damages).

Consumer Liability   A consumer's liability for unauthorized electronic fund transfer is limited to a maximum of $50 if the consumer notifies the financial institution within *two days* after he learns of the loss or theft. If the consumer does not report the loss or theft within two days he is liable for losses up to $500. If the consumer fails to report the unauthorized use within *sixty days* of transmittal of a periodic statement, he is liable for losses resulting from *any* unauthorized EFT that appeared on the statement if the financial institution can show that the loss would not have occurred but for the failure of the consumer to report the loss within sixty days.

Liability of Financial Institution   A financial institution is liable to a consumer for all damages proximately caused by its failure to make an EFT according to the terms and conditions of an account, in the correct amount or in a timely manner when properly instructed to do so by the consumer. However, there are some exceptions. The financial institution will not be liable if

1. the consumer's account has insufficient funds through no fault of the financial institution,

2. the funds are subject to legal process,

3. such transfer would exceed an established credit limit,

4. an electronic terminal has insufficient cash, or

5. circumstances beyond the financial institution's control prevents the transfer.

The financial institution is also liable for failure to stop payment of a preauthorized transfer from a consumer's account when instructed to do so in accordance with the terms and conditions of the account.

CHAPTER SUMMARY

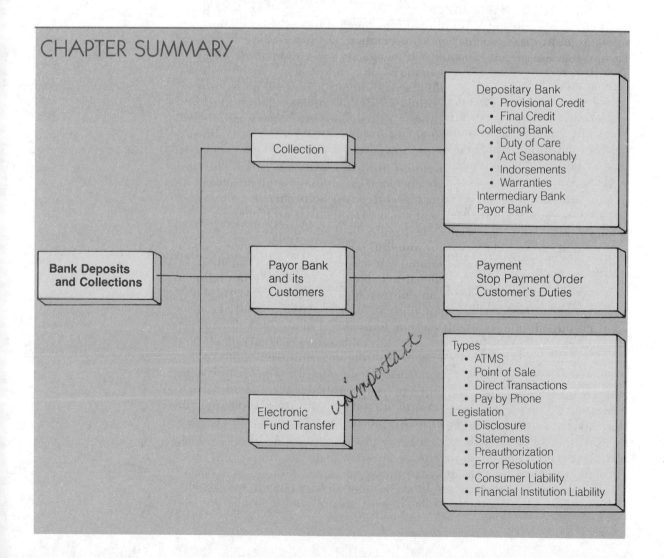

KEY TERMS

Depositary bank
Provisional credit
Final credit
Intermediary bank
Collecting bank

Payor bank
Midnight deadline
Stop payment order
Electronic fund transfer

ATM
Point-of-sale
Direct transaction
Pay-by-phone

PROBLEMS

1. On December 9, Jane Jones writes a check for $500 payable to Ralph Rodgers in payment for goods to be received later in the month. Before the close of business on the 9th, Jane notifies the bank by telephone to stop payment on the check. On December 19 Ralph gives the check to Bill Briggs for value and without notice. On the 20th, Bill deposits the check in his account at Bank A. On the 21st, Bank A sends the check to its correspondent Bank B. On the 22nd, Bank B presents the check through the clearinghouse to Bank C. On the 23rd, Bank C presents the check to Bank P, the payor bank. On December 28 the payor bank makes payment of the check final. Jane Jones sues the payor bank. Decision?

2. Howard Harrison, a long-time customer of Western Bank, operates a small department store, Harrison's Store. Because his store has few experienced employees, Harrison frequently travels throughout the United States on buying trips, although he also runs the financial operations of the business. On one of his buying trips Harrison purchased a gross of sport shirts from Well-Made Shirt Company and paid for the transaction with a check on his store account with Western Bank in the amount of $1,000. Adams, an employee of Well-Made who deposits its checks in Security Bank, sloppily raised the amount of the check to $10,000 and indorsed the check, "Pay to the order of Adams from Pension Plan Benefits, Well-Made Shirt Company by Adams." He cashes the check and cannot be found. The check is processed and paid by the Western Bank and is sent to Harrison's Store with the monthly statement. After brief examination of the statement, Harrison leaves on another buying trip for three weeks.

(a) Assuming the bank acted in good faith and the alteration is not discovered and reported to the bank until an audit conducted thirteen months after the statement was received by Harrison's Store, who must bear the loss on the raised check?

(b) Assuming that Harrison, because he was unable to examine his statement promptly due to his buying trips, left instructions with the bank to carefully examine and to notify him of any item over

$5,000 to be charged to his account and the bank paid the item anyway in his absence, who bears the loss if the alteration is discovered one month after the statement was received by Harrison's Store?

3. Tom Jones owed Bank Y $10,000 on a note due November 17, with 1 percent interest due the bank for each day delinquent in payment. Tom Jones issued a $10,000 check to Bank Y and deposited it in the night vault the evening of November 17. Several days later he received a letter saying he owed one day's interest on the payment because of one-day delinquency in payment. Jones refused because he said he had put it in the vault on the November 17. Decision?

4. Assume that D draws a check on Y Bank payable to the order of P; that P indorses it to A; that A deposits it to her account in X Bank; that X Bank presents it to Y Bank, the drawee; and that Y Bank dishonors it because of insufficient funds. X Bank receives notification of the dishonor on Monday. X Bank fails to notify A until Wednesday. What result?

5. Jones, a food wholesaler whose company has an account with B Bank in New York City, is traveling in California on business. He finds a particularly attractive offer and decides to buy a carload of oranges for delivery in New York. He gives S, the seller, his company's check for $25,000 to pay for the purchase. S deposits the check, with others he received that day, with his bank, the C Bank. C Bank sends the check to D Bank in Los Angeles, which in turn deposits it with the Los Angeles Federal Reserve Bank. The L.A. Fed. sends the check, with others, to the N.Y. Fed. The N.Y. Fed. forwards the check to B Bank, Jones's bank, for collection.

(a) Is B Bank a depository bank? A collecting bank? A payor bank?

(b) Is C Bank a depository bank? A presenting bank?

(c) Is the N.Y. Fed. an intermediary bank?

(d) Is D Bank a collecting bank?
Explain.

6. On April 1, M gave P a check properly drawn by M on Z Bank for $500 in payment of a painting to be framed and delivered the next day. P immediately indorsed the check and gave it to Y Bank as payment in full of his indebtedness to the bank on a note he previously had signed. Y Bank canceled the note and returned it to P.

On April 2, on learning that the painting had been destroyed in a fire at P's studio, M promptly went to Z Bank, signed a printed form of stop payment order, and gave it to the cashier. Z Bank refused payment on the check on proper presentment by Y Bank.

(a) What are the rights of Y Bank against Z Bank?

(b) What are the rights of Y Bank against M?

(c) Assuming that Z Bank by inadvertence had paid the amount of the check to Y Bank and debited M's account, what are the rights of M against Z Bank?

7. As payment in advance for services to be performed, Acton signed and delivered the following instrument:

December 2, 1985

LAST NATIONAL BANK
MONEYVILLE, ILLINOIS
Pay to the order of Olaf Owen $1,500.00 _____
Fifteen Hundred Dollars _____For services to be performed by Olaf Owen starting on December 7, 1985.
(signed) Arthur Acton

Owen requested and received Last National Bank's certification of the check even though Acton had only $900 on deposit. Owen indorsed the check in blank and delivered it to Dan Doty in payment of a pre-existing debt.

When Owen failed to appear for work, Acton gave a written stop payment order to the bank ordering the bank not to pay the check. Doty presented the check to Last National Bank for payment. The bank refused payment.

What are the Bank's rights and liabilities relating to the transactions described?

8. Jones drew a check for $1,000 on The First Bank and mailed it to the payee, T, Inc. C stole the check from T, Inc., chemically erased the name of the payee, and inserted the name of H as payee. C also increased the amount of the check to $10,000 and, by using the name of H, negotiated the check to W. W then took the check to The First Bank and obtained its certification on the check. W then negotiated the check to G who deposited the check in The Second National Bank for collection. The Second National forwarded the check to the D Trust Company for collection from The First Bank, which honored the check. G exhausted her account in the Second National Bank, and the account was closed. Shortly thereafter, The First Bank learned that it had paid an altered check.

What are the rights of each of the parties? Assume that all parties (except C) are respectively holders in due course.

PART FIVE
AGENCY AND EMPLOYMENT

PART FIVE

AGENCY AND EMPLOYMENT

PUBLIC POLICY, SOCIAL ISSUES AND BUSINESS ETHICS

In considering Part Five, Agency and Employment, you should keep in mind the importance of the agency relationship in permitting business enterprises—proprietorships, partnerships, and corporations—to expand their business activities. Agency, as we fully explore in the next two chapters, is a relationship between two persons whereby one of them (the agent) is authorized to act for and on behalf of the other (the principal). Within the scope of the authority granted to her by her principal, the agent may negotiate the terms of contracts with others and bind her principal to such contracts. An agent may be an employee of the principal, but this is not necessary.

If the law were to require each party to a business transaction to participate personally and directly in carrying out the transaction, the ability of any person to conduct a business enterprise would be limited by the number of transactions that he could *personally* negotiate. This would severely curtail the size and operation of every business unit and practically paralyze commercial activity. Furthermore, it would make the conduct of business by a corporation impossible, because as an artificial legal entity a corporation can act only through its agents, officers, and employees. Moreover, it would radically change the fundamental rule of the law of partnership that every partner is an agent of the partnership with respect to the conduct of its business. The agency concept is therefore indispensable to modern trade and commerce. Through the use of agents, one person may enter into any number of business

transactions with the same effect as if done by him personally, and in no more time than he would normally require to negotiate a single contract. A person may thus multiply and expand his business activities.

Because of the enormous economic significance of agency, it is important to consider the social costs that may be imposed by the use of agents and the public policy considerations that determine the allocation of these costs among those who use agents, the agents themselves, third parties with whom they deal, and society at large.

Because of the power an agent has to bind her principal in contracts, the law imposes a number of obligations on the agent, including the duties of loyalty, diligence, and obedience. For example, the duty of loyalty requires an agent to devote her actions exclusively to her principal and to promote the interests of her principal. However, what if her principal is engaged in unlawful conduct such as selling adulterated food or polluting a stream? Should the agent's duty of loyalty to her principal control, or is there a higher duty owed to society that requires the agent to disclose the criminal activities? If the agent does disclose publicly may the principal discharge the agent? The long-standing rule has been that if the agency or employment relationship is not for a definite term, the principal or employer is free to terminate the relationship for cause, no cause, or "bad" cause. Some courts, however, have made an exception to this rule where the agent's disclosure protects the public interest, especially where there is a definite violation of a criminal statute by the principal or employer.

What if an agent, while pursuing her principal's business, tortiously injures a third party? Who should bear the responsibility for the loss? The principal would argue that he did not cause the harm and that the responsibility is solely the agent's. The third party would assert that the agent would not have caused the harm had she not been engaged in carrying on the principal's business. The law has imposed civil liability for the loss on the agent *and,* when the agent was acting within the scope of her employment, *also* on the principal. The liability of the principal is vicarious and called *respondeat superior.* William Prosser and W. Page Keeton, eminent authorities on the law of torts, have explained the policy reasons for this doctrine:

What has emerged as the modern justification for vicarious liability is a rule of policy, a deliberate allocation of a risk. The losses caused by the torts of employees, which as a practical matter are sure to occur in the conduct of the employer's enterprise, are placed upon that enterprise itself, as a required cost of doing business. They are placed upon the employer because, having engaged in an enterprise, which will on the basis of all past experience involve harm to others through the torts of employees, and sought to profit by it, it is just that he, rather than the innocent injured plaintiff, should bear them; and because he is better able to absorb them, and to distribute them, through prices, rates or liability insurance, to the public, and so to shift them to society, to the community at large. Added to this is the makeweight argument that an employer who is held strictly liable is under the greatest incentive to be careful in the selection, instruction and supervision of his servants, and to take every precaution to see that the enterprise is conducted safely. Notwithstanding the occasional condemnation of the entire doctrine which used to appear in the past, the tendency is clearly to justify it on such grounds, and gradually to extend it.

Similar issues are raised by the question of whether a principal should be held *criminally* liable for an agent's violation of the criminal law. When the principal has actually authorized the agent to commit the crime the answer is simple: both the principal and the agent are criminally liable. But when the principal has not expressly authorized the criminal act the question is much more difficult, because imposing vicarious criminal liability raises distinctly different policy considerations than imposing vicarious civil liability. The purposes of the criminal law are to punish and deter offensive conduct; tort law attempts to compensate injured parties and redistribute loss. Accordingly, as a general rule a principal is not ordinarily liable for the unauthorized criminal acts of his agents. However, there has been a trend to impose a criminal penalty on an employer where the criminal act is that of an advisory or managerial person acting in the scope of employment. Moreover, where a crime does not require intent, a principal may be held subject to a penalty for acts of agents acting within the scope of employment.

Finally, to what extent should an agent have the power to bind his principal contractually to third parties? The answer to this question constitutes the keystone of the law of agency and is addressed in detail in Chapter 28. The competing policy interests are clear: the principal wishes to be bound only to those contracts he actually authorized the agent to form, whereas third parties want the principal bound to all contracts that the agent negotiates on the principal's behalf. The law of agency has chosen an intermediate outcome—the principal is bound to those contracts he actually authorized *plus* those the principal has by word or conduct *apparently* authorized the agent to negotiate.

27

AGENCY AND
EMPLOYMENT RELATIONSHIP

The law of agency, like the law of contracts, is basic to almost every other branch of business law. Practically every form of contract or business transaction can be created or conducted through an agent. Therefore, the place and importance of agency in the practical conduct and operation of business cannot be overemphasized, particularly in the case of partnerships and corporations. Partnership is founded on the agency of the partners. Each partner is an agent of the partnership and as such has the authority to represent and bind the partnership in all usual transactions pertaining to the partnership business. Corporations must function through the agency of its officers and employees. Thus, practically and legally, agency is an integral part of partnerships and corporations. Agency, however, is not limited to these business associations. Sole proprietors may also employ agents in the operation of their business. Business, in other words, is very largely conducted, not by the proprietors of business, but by their representatives or agents.

In short, agency is as essential to the operation of modern business as electrical power is to the operation of modern society. By using agents, one person (the principal) may enter into any number of business transactions as though he had carried them out personally. A person may thus multiply and expand his business activities. Although there is some overlap, the law of agency divides broadly into two main parts: the internal and external parts. An agent can function as an agent only by dealing with third persons. It is in this way that legal relations are established between the principal and third persons. These relations are the external part of agency law, which we discuss in the next chapter. In this chapter, however, we consider the nature and function of agency, as well as other topics of the internal part of the law of agency.

Agency is primarily governed by State common law. An orderly presentation of this law is found in the Restatements of the Law of Agency. The first Restatement was adopted on June 30, 1933, by the American Law Institute. On April 11, 1958, the Institute adopted a revised edition of the Restatement, the Restatement, Second, Agency, which will be referred to as the Restatement. The Restatements have been regarded as a valuable authoritative reference work and extensively cited and quoted in reported judicial opinions.

In addition to the law of agency, the relationship between employer and employee is also governed by a number of Federal and State statutes addressing specific aspects of the employment relationship, including concerted activities by employees (strikes and picketing, for example), discrimination by employers, and employee safety. In the second part of this chapter we examine the law regulating the employment relationship.

Agency Relationship

In this section of the chapter we cover the internal part of the law of agency governing the relationship between principal and agent, including the nature of agency, how an agency is created, the duties of agent to principal, the duties of principal to agent, and the termination of agency.

Nature of Agency

Agency is the relation existing between two persons known as **principal** and **agent** through which the agent is the business representative of the principal. An agent is therefore one who represents another, the principal, in business dealings with third persons. Three persons are involved in the operation of agency: the principal, the agent, and a third person. In dealings with a third person, the agent acts for and in the name and place of the principal. The parties to the transaction, which is usually contractual, are the principal and the third person. The agent is not a party but simply an intermediary. The result of the agent's functioning is exactly the same as if the principal had dealt directly with the third person and without the intervention of an agent. When the agent is dealing with the third person, the principal, in legal effect, is present in the person of the agent.

Definition

Agency –relationship authorizing one party (agent) to act for and on behalf of the other (principal)

Agency is therefore a relationship between two persons whereby one of them (the agent) is authorized to act for and on behalf of the other (the principal). Within the scope of the authority granted to her by her principal, the agent may negotiate the terms of contracts with others and bind her principal to such contracts. Moreover, the negligence of an agent in conducting the business of her principal exposes the principal to tort liability for injury and loss to third persons. A duly authorized agent may effect a transfer of her principal's title to real estate or personal property. The old maxim *"Qui facet per alium, facet per se"* ("Who acts through another, acts himself") accurately describes the relationship between principal and agent.

MURPHY v. HOLIDAY INNS, INC.

Supreme Court of Virginia, 1975.
216 Va. 490, 219 S.E.2d 874.

FACTS: Murphy, while a guest at a motel operated by the Betsy-Len Motor Hotel Corporation, sustained injuries from a fall allegedly caused by negligence in maintaining the premises. At that time, Betsy-Len was under a license agreement with Holiday Inns, Inc. The license contained provisions permitting Holiday Inns to regulate the architectural style of the buildings as well as the type and style of the furnishings and equipment. In return, Betsy-Len used the trade name, "Holiday Inns," and paid a fee for use of the license and Holiday Inns' national advertising. Murphy sued Holiday Inns, claiming Betsy-Len was its agent.

DECISION: Judgment for Holiday Inns. The license agreement between Holiday Inns and Betsy-Len was a franchise contract. The degree of control which the franchisor (Holiday Inns) exerts over the franchisee (Betsy-Len) determines whether a principal-agent relationship exists. Holiday Inns enjoyed some regulatory control over Betsy-Len under the franchise contract. However, the contract did not grant Holiday Inns the power to control the day-to-day operations of Betsy-Len's motel, to fix customer rates, or to demand a share of the profits. Betsy-Len could hire and fire its employees, determine wages and working conditions, supervise employee work routine, and discipline its employees. Thus, the regulatory provisions of the franchise contract did not constitute sufficient control to establish an agency relationship.

Scope of Agency Purposes

As a general rule, whatever business activity a person may accomplish personally, he may do through an agent. Conversely, whatever he cannot legally do himself, he cannot authorize another to do for him. Thus a person may not validly authorize another to commit on his behalf an illegal act or crime. Any such agreement is illegal and therefore unenforceable. Also, a person may not appoint an agent to perform acts that are so personal that their performance may not be delegated to another, as in the case of a contract for personal services. For example, P, a painter, contracts to paint a portrait of Y. P has one of his students execute the painting and tenders it to Y. This is not a valid tender as the duty to paint Y's portrait is not delegable.

Other Legal Relations

Two other legal relationships are closely related to agency: employer-employee and principal-independent contractor. In the **employment** relationship (historically referred to as the master-servant relationship), the employer has the right to *control* the physical conduct of the employee. In contrast, a person who engages an **independent contractor** to do a specific job does *not* have the right to control the conduct and activities of the independent contractor in the performance of his contract. The latter simply contracts to do a job and is free to choose the method and manner to perform the job. For example, a full-time chauffeur is an employee, whereas a taxicab driver hired to carry a person to the airport is an independent contractor of the passenger.

Employment relationship—one in which employer has right to control the physical conduct of employee

Independent contractor—person who contracts with another to do a particular job and is *not subject* to the control of the other

This distinction is extremely important because a person is usually liable for the torts committed by an employee within the scope of his employment but not for torts committed by an independent contractor. We discuss this liability further in Chapter 28.

For example, A and B, a building contractor, enter into a contract under which B agrees to build a house for A according to certain plans and specifications at an agreed cost. If in the course of the work one of B's workers, C, should injure T, a third person, T cannot recover damages from A because C is not an employee of A. T may, however, recover from C, because a person is always liable for his own torts, whether he commits them in the capacity of an employee, agent, or otherwise. T could, of course, trace liability through C to B, because of the relationship of employer and employee between B and C. However, because B is neither the agent nor employee of A, T cannot trace liability through B to A. B, as an independent contractor, insulates A from liability.

Creation of Agency

Agency is a **consensual** relationship that may be formed by contract or agreement between the principal and agent. Because the relationship of principal and agent is consensual and not necessarily contractual, it may exist without consideration. However, agency by contract is the most usual method of creating the relationship and must satisfy all of the requirements of a contract.

Formalities

As a general rule, no particular formality is required in a contract of agency. In most cases the contract may be oral. In some cases, however, the contract must be in writing. The appointment of an agent for a period of more than a year comes within the one-year clause of the Statute of Frauds and thus must be in writing. In some States, the authority of an agent to sell land must be in writing and signed by the principal. Where the authority of an agent will require him to execute an instrument under seal, this authority must be granted in an instrument executed under seal by the principal.

Power of attorney—written, formal appointment of an agent

A power of attorney is a formal appointment of an agent, who is known as an attorney in fact. Under a power of attorney, for example, a principal may appoint an agent not only to execute a contract for the sale of the principal's real estate but also to execute the deed conveying title to the real estate to the third party. In such cases, the agent executes the contract, deed, or other instrument in the following manner: John Preston, by Peter Ames, his attorney in fact.

Capacity

Capacity to Be a Principal   The capacity to act through an agent depends on the capacity of the principal to do the act herself. For example, contracts entered into by a minor or an incompetent not under a guardianship are voidable. Consequently, the appointment of an agent by a minor or an incompetent not under a guardianship and any resulting contracts are voidable, regardless of the agent's contractual capacity.

voidable by minor

Capacity to Be an Agent   Because the act of the agent is considered the act of the principal, the incapacity of an agent to bind himself by contract does *not* disqualify him from making a contract that is binding on his principal. Thus, minors and incompetents not under a guardianship may act as agents. Although the contract of agency may be voidable, the contract between the principal and the third person who dealt with the agent is valid. Nonetheless, some mental capacity is necessary in an agent; therefore, very young minors and mental incompetents may not have the capacity to act as agents in certain situations.

Duties of Agent to Principal

Because the relation of principal and agent is ordinarily created by contract, the duties of the agent to the principal are determined by the provisions of the contract. In addition to the contractual duties assumed by the agent, he is subject to various other duties imposed by law. Normally, a principal selects an agent based on the agent's ability, skill and integrity. Moreover, the principal not only authorizes and empowers the agent to bind him on contracts with third persons, but in many cases he also places the agent in possession of his money and other property. As a result, the agent is in a position, either through negligence or dishonesty, to injure the principal by involving him in detrimental liabilities or obligations to third persons or by wrongfully using or disposing of the property committed to his care. Accordingly, an agent owes his principal the duties of obedience, diligence, providing information, providing an accounting, and loyalty as a fiduciary, that is, as a person in a position of trust and confidence. Moreover, an agent is liable for any loss caused to the principal for breach of any of these duties.

Duty of Obedience

The duty of obedience requires the agent to act in the principal's affairs only as authorized by the principal and to obey all reasonable instructions and directions of the principal. The agent may be subject to liability to his principal for breach of this duty (1) because he entered into an unauthorized contract for which his principal is liable; (2) because he has improperly delegated his authority; or (3) because he has committed a tort for which the principal is liable. Thus, if an agent sells on credit in violation of the explicit instructions of the principal, the agent has breached the duty of obedience and is liable to the principal for any amounts not paid by the purchaser.

Duty of Diligence

An agent must act with reasonable care and skill in performing the work for which he is employed. He must also exercise any special skill that he may have. If an agent does not exercise the required care and skill, he is liable to the principal for any resulting loss. For example, P appoints A as his agent to sell goods in markets where the highest price can be obtained. A sells goods in a market which is glutted and obtains a low price, although a higher price would have been obtained in a nearby market if A had used care in obtaining information which was available to him. A is subject to liability to P for breach of the duty of diligence.

Duty to Inform

An agent must use reasonable efforts to give the principal information that is relevant to the affairs entrusted to her and that, as the agent knows or should know, the principal would desire to have. This duty is made essential by the rule of agency providing that notice to an agent is notice to his principal. Some examples of information that an agent has been held under a duty to communicate to his principal are that a customer of the principal has become insolvent; that a debtor of the principal has become insolvent; that one of the partners of a firm with which the principal has previously dealt, and with which the principal or agent is about to deal, has withdrawn from the firm; or that the principal's property that the principal has authorized the agent to sell at a specified price can be sold at a higher price.

Duty to Account

The agent is under a duty to maintain and provide the principal with a true and complete account of money or other property that the agent has received or expended on behalf of the principal. An agent must also keep the principal's property separate from his own.

☆ Fiduciary Duty

A fiduciary duty is one that arises out of a relationship of trust and confidence. It is a duty imposed by law and is owed by a trustee to a beneficiary of a trust, an officer or director of a corporation to the corporation and its shareholders, a lawyer to his clients, an employee to his employer, and an agent to his principal. Fiduciary duties are not limited to these situations but exist in every relationship where the law authorizes one person to place trust and confidence in another.

Fiduciary duty—duty of utmost loyalty and good faith owed by agent to principal

The fiduciary duty is one of **utmost loyalty and good faith.** An agent must act solely in the interest of his principal and not in his own interest or in the interest of another. An agent may not represent his principal in any transaction in which he has a personal interest. An agent may not take a position in conflict with the interest of his principal, unless the principal, with full knowledge of all of the facts, consents. The agent owes his principal at all times the duty of full disclosure. He does not deal with his principal at arm's length.

The fiduciary duty of an agent prevents him from competing with his principal or acting on behalf of a competitor or for persons whose interests conflict with those of the principal. Moreover, an agent who is employed to buy may not buy from himself without the principal's consent. Thus, P employs A to purchase for her a site suitable for a shopping center. A owns one which is suitable and sells it to P at the fair market value. A does not disclose to P that A had owned the land. P may rescind the transaction. An agent who is employed to sell may not become the purchaser, nor may he act as agent for the purchaser. The agent's loyalty must be undivided, and his actions must be devoted exclusively to represent and promote the interests of his principal.

An agent may not use information obtained in the course of the agency for his own benefit and contrary to the interest of his principal. For example, if an agent in the course of his employment discovers a defect in his principal's title to certain property, he may not use the information to acquire the title for himself. Or, if an employee prior to the expiration of his employer's lease secretly obtains a lease of the property for his own benefit, he may be compelled to transfer it to his employer.

An agent is not permitted to make a secret profit out of any transaction subject to the agency. All such profits belong to the principal. Thus, if an agent authorized to sell certain property of his principal for $1,000 sells it for $1,500, he may not secretly pocket the additional $500. Further, suppose Michael employs real estate broker Doris to sell his land for a commission of 6 percent of the sale price. Doris, knowing that Michael is willing to sell for $20,000, agrees secretly with a prospective buyer who is willing to pay $22,000 for the land that she will endeavor to obtain the consent of Michael to sell for $20,000, in which event the buyer will pay Doris $1,000, or one-half of the amount the buyer believes she is saving on the price. The broker has violated her fiduciary duty, and she must pay the $1,000 to Michael. Furthermore, Doris loses the right to any commission on the transaction. The result is that the seller, who willingly sold the land for $20,000, expecting to pay a commission of $1,200 and net $18,800, receives $21,000 free of commission. Doris's breach of fiduciary duty produces an unexpected windfall for Michael. However, this is incidental to the deterrent purpose of the rule that requires a faithless fiduciary to account for any gain or profit from his acts of disloyalty.

SIERRA PACIFIC
INDUSTRIES v.
CARTER

Court of Appeal, First
District, Division 3, 1980.
104 Cal.App.3d 579, 163
Cal.Rptr. 764.

FACTS: Sierra Pacific Industries purchased various areas of timber and six other pieces of real property including a ten-acre parcel on which five duplexes and two single-family units were located. Sierra Pacific requested the assistance of Joseph Carter, a licensed real estate broker, in selling the non-timberland properties. It commissioned him to sell the property for an asking price of $85,000, of which Sierra Pacific would receive $80,000 and Carter would receive $5,000 as a commission. Carter was unable to find a prospective buyer, and finally he sold the property to his daughter and son-in-law for $85,000 and retained the $5,000 commission without informing Sierra Pacific of his relationship to the buyers. After learning of these facts, Sierra Pacific brought this action for fraud against Carter.

DECISION: Judgment for Sierra Pacific. An agent owes a fiduciary duty to his principal which requires the disclosure of all information in the agent's possession that is relevant to the subject matter of the agency. An agent may not compete with the principal, nor may he act as agent for another whose interests conflict with those of the principal. A real estate agent must refrain from dual representation in a transaction unless he obtains the consent of both principals after full disclosure. Under most circumstances, then, if the agent is related to the buyer in a way that suggests a reasonable possibility that the agent himself could be acquiring an interest in the property, the relationship is a material fact that must be disclosed. Therefore, Sierra Pacific may recover the $5,000 commission paid to Carter plus any actual and proximately caused loss on the price it received for the property.

Duties of Principal to Agent

Although both principal and agent have rights and duties arising out of the agency relationship, more emphasis is placed on the duties of the agent. This is necessarily so because of the nature of the agency relationship. First, the acts and services to be performed, both under the agency contract and as may be required by law, are to be performed mostly by the agent. Second, the agent is a fiduciary and is subject to the duties of loyalty and good faith, as discussed earlier. Nonetheless, an agent has certain rights against the principal, both under the contract and by the operation of the law. Connected to these rights are certain duties that the principal owes to the agent. The duties are based in contract and tort law.

Contractual Duties

As with any party to a contract, a principal is under a duty to perform his part of the contract according to its terms. The most important duty of the principal, from the standpoint of the agent, is to compensate the agent as specified in the contract. As you will see, the duty to compensate, if not expressed, will be implied. It is also the duty of the principal not to terminate the agency wrongfully. Whether the principal must furnish the means of employment or opportunity for work will depend on the particular case. A bank, on employing a teller, must obviously furnish the opportunity and usual facilities for work by which the teller can carry on the employment. A principal who employs an agent to sell his goods must supply the agent with the goods. If the contract specifies the quality of the goods, the principal must not furnish inferior or defective goods. In other cases, the agent must create his own opportunity for work, as in the case of a broker employed to procure a buyer for his principal's house. How far, if at all, the principal must assist or cooperate with the agent will depend on the particular agency. Usually, cooperation on the part of the principal is more necessary where the agent's compensation is contingent on the success of his efforts than where the agent is paid a fixed salary regularly over a period of permanent employment.

Compensation   A principal has a duty to compensate her agent unless the agent has agreed to serve gratuitously. If the agreement does not specify a definite amount or rate of compensation, a principal is under a duty to pay the reasonable value of authorized services performed for her by her agent. A principal also has a duty to maintain and provide the agent a true and complete account of money or property due from her to the agent.

Reimbursement   A principal is under a duty to reimburse his agent for authorized payments made by the agent on behalf of the principal and for authorized expenses incurred by the agent. For example, an agent who reasonably and properly pays a fire insurance premium for the protection of her principal's property is entitled to reimbursement for the payment.

Indemnification   The principal is under a duty to indemnify the agent for losses incurred or suffered while acting as directed by the principal in a transaction that is not illegal or not known by the agent to be wrongful. To indemnify is to make good or pay a loss, as in insurance. Suppose that P, the principal, has in his possession goods belonging to X. P directs A, his agent, to sell these goods. A, believing P to be the owner, sells the goods to T. X then sues A for the conversion of his goods, and recovers a judgment which A pays to X. A is entitled to payment from P for his loss, including the amount reasonably expended by A in defense of the lawsuit brought by X.

Tort Duties

In addition to his contractual duties, an employer owes certain tort duties to his employees. Among these is the duty to provide an employee with reasonably safe conditions of employment and to warn the employee of any unreasonable risk involved in the employment. An employer is also liable to his employees for injury caused by the negligence of other employees and of other agents doing work for him. We discuss these duties more fully in the second part of this chapter.

Termination of Agency

Because the authority of an agent is based on the consent of the principal, the agency is terminated when such consent is withdrawn or otherwise ceases to exist. On revocation by the principal, the power of the agent to bind the principal to contracts with third persons with whom the agent has previously dealt will continue until such persons have been notified or have knowledge of the revocation. On termination of the agency the agent's actual authority ends, and she is not entitled to compensation for services subsequently rendered, although her fiduciary duties may continue. Termination of the agent's authority may take place by acts of the parties or by operation of law.

Acts of the Parties

Termination by the acts of the parties may be by the acts of both principal and agent or by the act of either one of them. The methods of termination by acts of the parties are as follows.

Reimbursement–duty owed by principal to pay back authorized payments agent has made on principal's behalf

Indemnification–duty owed by principal to agent to pay agent for losses incurred while acting as directed by principal

Lapse of Time   Authority conferred upon an agent for a specified time terminates at the expiration of that period. If no time is specified, authority terminates at the end of a reasonable period. For example, P authorizes A to sell a tract of land for him. Ten years pass without communication between P and A. A purports to sell the tract. A's authorization has terminated due to lapse of time and the purported sale is not binding upon P.

Mutual Agreement of the Parties   The agency relationship is created by agreement and may be terminated at any time by mutual agreement of the principal and the agent.

Fulfillment of Purpose   The authority of an agent to perform a specific act or to accomplish a particular result is terminated when the act is performed or the result is accomplished by the agent. Thus, if A authorizes B to sell or lease A's land, and B leases the land to C, B's authority is terminated, and he may not thereafter sell or lease the land without new authorization.

Revocation of Authority   A principal may revoke an agent's authority at any time. However, if such revocation constitutes a breach of contract by the principal, as in the next case, the agent may recover damages from the principal.

FACTS: Harvey Hilgendorf was a licensed real estate broker acting as the agent of the Hagues in the sale of eighty acres of farmland. The Hagues, however, terminated Hilgendorf's agency before the expiration of the listing contract when they encountered financial difficulties and decided to liquidate their entire holdings of land at one time. Hilgendorf brought this action for breach of the listing contract. The Hagues maintain that Hilgendorf's duty of loyalty requires him to give up the listing contract. **DECISION:** Judgment for Hilgendorf. Since agency is a consensual relationship, a principal has the power to terminate an agency which is not coupled with an interest even though the term of the agency has not yet expired. However, without a legal reason for doing so, the principal does not have the right to terminate an unexpired agency contract and may subject himself to liability for doing so. Although an agent's duty of loyalty does require him to place the principal's interests first in dealing with third parties, in the contract of agency itself between the agent and the principal, each is acting in his own behalf. The Hagues' financial difficulties did not give them the legal right to terminate the agency relationship, and Hilgendorf was under no duty to relinquish his role as their agent simply because the principal encountered financial problems. Therefore, Hilgendorf may recover damages for breach of the listing contract.	HILGENDORF v. HAGUE Supreme Court of Iowa, 1980. 293 N.W.2d 272.

Renunciation by the Agent   The agent also has the power to put an end to the agency by notice to the principal that she renounces the authority given her by the principal. However, if the parties have contracted that the agency continue for a specified time, an unjustified renunciation prior to the expiration of the time is a breach of contract.

Operation of Law

An agency relationship may also be terminated by operation of law. Although one of the parties may suffer a loss, in any such case, he has no rights against the other regarding the loss, because the agency was terminated by law. Thus, where the agency is terminated by the death of the principal, the agent has no claim against the deceased principal's estate for any loss he suffers because the agency was terminated. As a matter of law, agency is ordinarily terminated by the occurrence of any of the following events.

Bankruptcy Bankruptcy is a proceeding in a Federal court affording relief to financially distressed debtors. The filing of the petition in bankruptcy, which initiates the proceedings, usually terminates all the debtor's existing agency relationships. Moreover, if the credit standing of the agent is important to the agency relationship, then it will be terminated by the bankruptcy of the agent. Thus, A is appointed by P, an investment house, to act as its agent in advising P's local clients as to investments. A becomes bankrupt. A is no longer authorized to act for P.

can't just be insolvency

Death The death of the principal terminates the authority of the agent. For example, P employs A to sell P's line of goods under a contract which specifies A's commission and that the employment is to continue for a year even if P should die before then. Without A's knowledge P dies. A has no authority to sell P's goods. Similarly, the authority given to an agent by a principal is strictly personal, and the agent's death terminates the agency.

Incapacity Incapacity of the principal that occurs after the formation of the agency terminates the agent's authority. To illustrate: P authorizes A to sell in the next 10 months an apartment complex for not less than $2 million. P is adjudicated incompetent two months later without A's knowledge. A's authority to sell the apartment complex is terminated. Likewise, subsequent incapacity of an agent to perform the acts authorized by the principal terminates the agent's authority.

Change in Business Conditions The authority of an agent is terminated by notice or knowledge of a change in the value of the subject matter or of a change in business conditions from which the agent should reasonably infer that the principal would not consent to an exercise of the authority given him. For example, A authorizes B to sell his eighty acres of farm land for $800 per acre. Subsequently, oil is discovered on nearby land and A's land greatly increases in value. B knows of this, but A does not. B's authority to sell the land is terminated.

Loss or Destruction of the Subject Matter Where the authority of the agent relates to a specific subject matter that becomes lost or destroyed, her authority is thereby terminated. This corresponds to the rule that loss or destruction of the subject matter of an offer terminates the offer. For example, P authorizes A to make a contract for the sale of P's residence. The next week the residence burns completely, as A is aware. A's authority is terminated.

Loss of Qualification of Principal or Agent When the authority given the agent relates to the conduct of a certain business for which a license from the government or a regulatory agency is required, the failure to acquire or the loss of this license terminates the authority of the agent. Thus, A, who holds a retail liquor license, employs B to sell liquor at retail in A's store. A's license is revoked. B's authority to sell A's liquor at retail is terminated.

Disloyalty of Agent If an agent, without the knowledge of her principal, acquires interests that are adverse to those of the principal or otherwise breaches her duty of loyalty to the principal, her authority to act on behalf of the principal is terminated. Thus, A employs B, a realtor, to sell A's land. Unknown to A, B has been authorized by C to purchase this land from A. B is not authorized to sell the land to C.

Change of Law   A change in the law that takes effect after the employment of the agent may cause the performance of the authorized act to be illegal or criminal. Such a change in the law terminates the authority of the agent. Thus, A directs his agent B to ship young elm trees from State X to State Y. In order to control elm disease, a quarantine is established by State X on the shipment of elm trees to any other State, and any such shipment is punishable by fine. B's authority to ship the elm trees is terminated.

Outbreak of War   Where the outbreak of war places the principal and agent in the position of alien enemies, the authority of the agent is terminated because its exercise is illegal. Where the principal and agent are citizens of the same country and the outbreak of war or a revolution makes the originally authorized transaction unexpectedly hazardous or impracticable, the agent's authority is terminated.

Irrevocable Agencies

In the foregoing discussion of the various ways in which the authority of an agent may be terminated, the agency relationship was assumed to be the ordinary one in which the agent does not have a security interest in the power conferred on him by the principal. Where the **agency is coupled with an interest** of the agent in the subject matter, as where the agent has advanced funds on behalf of the principal and his power to act is given as security for the loan, the authority of the agent may *not* be revoked by the principal. In addition, the death, incapacity, or bankruptcy of the principal will not terminate the authority or power of the agent.

Employment Relationship

The common law governed the relationship between employer and employee in terms of tort and contract duties. This common law has been supplemented—and in some instances replaced—by statutory enactments, principally at the Federal level. In fact, the balance and working relationship between employers and employees are now greatly affected by government regulation. First, the general framework in which management and labor negotiate and bargain over the terms of employment is regulated by Federal statutes designed to promote both labor-management harmony and the welfare of society at large. Second, Federal law has been enacted to prohibit discrimination in employment based upon race, sex, religion, age, handicap, or national origin. Finally, Congress, in response to the changing nature of American industry and the tremendous number of industrial accidents, has intervened by mandating that employers provide their employees with a safe and healthy work environment. Moreover, all of the States have adopted Worker's Compensation Acts to provide compensation to employees injured during the course of employment.

This part of the chapter will focus upon these three categories of government regulation of the employment relationship: (1) labor law, (2) employment discrimination law, and (3) employee safety.

Labor Law

Traditionally, labor law did not favor concerted activities by workers (such as strikes, picketing, and refusals to deal with certain employers) to obtain higher wages and better working conditions. At various times these concerted activities were found to constitute criminal conspiracy, tortious conduct, and violation of antitrust law. Eventually public pressure in response to the adverse treatment accorded labor forced Congress to intervene.

Norris-La Guardia Act

The Norris-LaGuardia Act, which was enacted in 1932, withdrew from the Federal courts the power to issue injunctions in nonviolent labor disputes. The term **labor dispute** was broadly defined to include any controversy concerning terms or conditions of employment or union representation regardless of whether the parties stood in an employer-employee relationship. More significantly, the Act declared it to be the policy of the United States that labor was to have full freedom to form labor unions without interference by the employer.

Labor dispute–any controversy concerning terms or conditions of employment or union representation

National Labor Relations Act

The National Labor Relations Act, or **Wagner Act,** was enacted in 1935 and marked an affirmative effort by the Federal government to support collective bargaining and unionization. The Act provided that "the right to self-organization, to form, join or assist labor organizations, to bargain collectively through representatives of their own choosing, and to engage in concerted activities for the purpose of collective bargaining or other mutual aid or protection" is a Federally protected right. Moreover, the Act seeks to enforce this right by prohibiting certain conduct by employers as **unfair labor practices.** Under the Act, the following activities by employers are unfair labor practices: (1) to interfere with the employees' rights to unionize and bargain collectively; (2) to dominate the union; (3) to discriminate against union members; and (4) to refuse to bargain in good faith with the duly established representatives of the employees.

The Act also established the **National Labor Relations Board** (NLRB) to monitor and administer these employee rights. The NLRB is empowered to order employers to remedy their unfair labor practices and to supervise elections by secret ballot so that employees can freely select a representative organization.

Labor-Management Relations Act

Following the passage of the National Labor Relations Act, the country underwent a tremendous increase in union membership and labor unrest. In response to this trend Congress passed the Labor-Management Relations Act **(Taft-Hartley Act)** in 1947. The Act prohibits certain **union unfair practices** and separates the NLRB's prosecutorial and adjudicative functions. More specifically, the Act forbids secondary boycotts, jurisdictional strikes over work assignments, refusal to bargain in good faith, featherbedding (causing an employer to pay for work not performed), and strikes to force an employer to discharge or discriminate against a nonunion employee. In addition to prohibiting unfair union practices the Act also limited the scope of unfair *employer* labor practices in order to enhance "employer free speech." The Act declared that no *employer* unfair labor practice could be based upon any statement of opinion or argument which contained no threat of reprisal. Finally, the Act reinstated the availability of civil injunctions in labor disputes, but only against an unfair labor practice and at the request of the NLRB.

Labor-Management Reporting and Disclosure Act

This Labor-Management Reporting and Disclosure Act, also known as the **Landrum-Griffin Act,** was aimed at eliminating corruption in labor unions. The Act, which was passed in 1959, attempts to deal with the problem of corruption by establishing an elaborate reporting system and the enactment of a union "bill of rights" designed to make unions more democratic. Under the latter union members have the right to nominate candidates for union offices, to vote in elections, to attend membership meetings, to participate in union business, to have free expression at union meetings and conventions, and to be given a full and fair hearing before the union takes any disciplinary action against them.

Employment Discrimination Law

A number of Federal statutes prohibit discrimination in employment on the basis of race, sex, religion, national origin, age, and handicap. The cornerstone of Federal employment discrimination law is Title VII of the 1964 Civil Rights Act, but the Equal Pay Act, the Age Discrimination in Employment Act of 1967, the Rehabilitation Act of 1973, and various executive orders are also significant. In addition, most States have enacted similar laws prohibiting discrimination based on race, sex, religion, national origin, and handicap.

Equal Pay Act

The Equal Pay Act prohibits an employer from discriminating between employees on the basis of **sex** by paying unequal wages for the same work. The Act forbids an employer from paying wages at a rate less than the rate at which he pays wages to employees of the opposite sex for equal work at the same establishment. Once the employee has demonstrated that the employer pays unequal wages for *equal* work to members of the opposite sex, the burden shifts to the employer to prove that the pay differential is based on a seniority system, a merit system, a system that measures earnings by quantity or quality of production, or any factor except sex. Remedies include recovery of back pay and enjoining the employer from further unlawful conduct.

Civil Rights Act of 1964

Title VII of the Civil Rights Act of 1964 prohibits **discrimination** on the basis of race, color, sex, religion, or national origin in hiring, firing, compensating, promoting, training, or otherwise. The Act applies to employers engaged in an industry affecting commerce and having fifteen or more employees. The following case illustrates one type of discriminatory conduct prohibited by the Act.

GRIGGS v. DUKE POWER CO.

Supreme Court of the United States, 1971.
401 U.S. 424, 91 S.Ct. 849, 28 L.Ed.2d 158.

FACTS: During the years prior to the passage of the Civil Rights Act, Duke Power openly discriminated against Blacks by allowing them to work only in the Labor Department of the plant's five departments. The highest paying job in the Labor Department paid less than the lowest paying jobs in the other four "operating" departments in which only whites were employed. In 1955 the company began requiring a high school education for initial assignment to any department except Labor. When Duke Power stopped restricting Negroes to the Labor Department in 1965, it made completion of high school a prerequisite to transfer from Labor to any other department. However, white employees hired before the high school education requirement was adopted continued to perform satisfactorily and achieve promotions in the "operating" departments.

In 1965, the company also began requiring new employees in the departments other than Labor to register satisfactory scores on two professionally prepared aptitude tests, in addition to having a high school education. In September, 1965, Duke Power began to permit employees to qualify for transfer to another department from Labor by passing two tests, neither of which was directed or intended to measure the ability to learn to perform a particular job or category of jobs. Griggs brought suit against Duke Power, claiming that the high school education and testing requirements were discriminating and therefore prohibited by the Civil Rights Act of 1964.

DECISION: Judgment for Griggs. The objective of the Civil Rights Act of 1964 is to achieve equality of employment opportunities and remove barriers which have operated to favor white employees over other employees. The Act proscribes not only overt discrimination but also practices, procedures, and tests that are fair in form, but discriminatory in operation. The standard is business necessity. If an employment practice operates to exclude Negroes and is not related to job performance, the practice is prohibited.

Here, employees who had not completed high school nor taken the tests nonetheless continued to perform satisfactorily and make progress in those departments which used these criteria. Neither high school completion nor the general intelligence test was shown to bear a demonstrable relationship to successful job performance. Rather, these requirements served a covert discriminatory function and are, therefore, prohibited by the Civil Rights Act of 1964.

The enforcement agency is the **Equal Employment Opportunity Commission** (EEOC). The EEOC has the power and responsibility to (1) file legal actions in its own name or intervene in actions filed by third parties; (2) attempt to resolve alleged violations through informal means prior to bringing suit; (3) investigate all charges of discrimination; and (4) issue guidelines and regulations concerning enforcement policy.

The Act provides three basic defenses: (1) a *bona fide* seniority or merit system, (2) a professionally developed ability test, and (3) a *bona fide* occupational qualification. Remedies for violation of the Act include enjoining the employer from engaging in the unlawful behavior, appropriate affirmative action, and reinstatement of employees and award of back pay from a date not more than two years prior to the filing of the charge with the EEOC. **Affirmative action** generally means the active recruitment of minority applicants, although courts have used the remedy of affirmative action to impose numerical hiring ratios and hiring goals based on race and sex. The following case explores the permissible limits of affirmative action plans.

Affirmative action—active recruitment of minority applicants

UNITED STEELWORKERS OF AMERICA v. WEBER

Supreme Court of the United States, 1979.
443 U.S. 193, 99 S.Ct. 2721, 61 L.Ed.2d 480.

FACTS: In 1974, the United Steelworkers of America and Kaiser Aluminum entered into a master collective-bargaining agreement covering terms and conditions of employment at 15 Kaiser plants. The agreement contained an affirmative action plan designed to eliminate conspicuous racial imbalances in Kaiser's then almost exclusively white craftwork forces. Black craft-hiring goals were set for each Kaiser plant equal to the percentage of blacks in the respective local labor forces. To meet these goals, on-the-job training programs were established to teach unskilled production workers—blacks and white—the skills necessary to become craftworkers. The plan reserved for black employees 50% of the openings in these newly created in-plant training programs.

Pursuant to the national agreement, Kaiser altered its craft-hiring practice in its Gramercy, Louisiana plant by establishing a program to train its production workers to fill craft openings. Selection of craft trainees was made on the basis of seniority. However, at least 50% of the new trainees were to be black until the percentage of black skilled craftworkers in the Gramercy plant approximated the percentage of blacks in the local labor force. During the first year of the operation of this affirmative action plan, 13 craft trainees (seven black, six white) were selected from Gramercy's productions work force. The most senior black selected had less seniority than several white production workers who were denied admission to the program. Weber, one of these white employees, brought suit claiming that the affirmative action plan discriminated against white employees and therefore violated the Civil Rights Act of 1964.

DECISION: Judgment for United Steelworkers of America. The Civil Rights Act of 1964 was primarily intended to open employment opportunities to Negroes in occupations which have been traditionally closed to them. It is not intended to prohibit the private sector from implementing voluntary, private affirmative action plans to accomplish this purpose.

Here, the Kaiser-USWA affirmative action plan promotes the Act's goal of providing equal employment opportunities to Negroes without unnecessarily trammelling the interests of the white employees. It did not require the discharge of the white workers and their replacements with new black hires. Nor did the plan create an absolute bar to the advancement of white employees in that half of those trained in the program were white. Furthermore, the plan was a temporary measure to eliminate manifest racial imbalance. Therefore, the Kaiser-USWA affirmative action plan did not violate the Civil Rights Act.

Age Discrimination in Employment Act of 1967

The Age Discrimination in Employment Act prohibits discriminating in hiring, firing, salaries, or otherwise on the basis of age. It applies the substantive language of Title VII to benefit individuals between the ages of forty and seventy years. The Act applies to private employers having 20 or more employees and to all governmental units regardless of size. The Act also prohibits the mandatory retirement of most employees under the age of seventy.

The major statutory defenses include: (1) a *bona fide* occupational qualification; (2) a *bona fide* seniority system; and (3) any other reasonable action. Remedies include back pay, injunctive relief, and affirmative action.

See Law in the News on page 462.

Rehabilitation Act of 1973

The Rehabilitation Act of 1973 attempts to assist the handicapped in obtaining rehabilitation training, access to public facilities, and employment. The Act requires Federal contractors and Federal agencies to take affirmative action to hire qualified handicapped persons. It also prohibits discrimination on the basis of handicap in Federal programs and programs receiving Federal financial assistance.

Executive Order

In 1965 President Johnson issued an executive order prohibiting discrimination by Federal contractors on the basis of race, color, sex, religion, or national origin in employment on *any work* performed by the contractor during the period of the Federal contract. Federal contractors must also take affirmative action in recruiting. The Secretary of Labor, **Office of Federal Contract Compliance Programs** (OFCCP) administers enforcement of the program.

Law In The News

The program applies to all contractors who enter into a contract to be performed in the United States with the Federal government and all of their subcontractors in excess of $10,000. Compliance with the affirmative action requirement differs for construction and nonconstruction contractors. All **nonconstruction** contractors with fifty or more employees or with contracts for more than $50,000 must have a written affirmative action plan in order to be in compliance. The plan must include a work-force analysis, planned corrective action, if necessary, with specific goals and timetables, and procedures for auditing and reporting. The Director of the OFCCP periodically issues goals and timetables for each segment of the **construction** industry for each region of the country. As a condition precedent to bidding on the Federal contract, the contractor must agree to make a good faith effort to achieve current published goals.

Employee Safety

Occupational Safety and Health Act

In 1970 Congress enacted the Occupational Safety and Health Act to assure, as far as possible, every worker a safe and healthful working environment. The Act established the **Occupational Safety and Health Administration** (OSHA) to develop standards, conduct inspections, monitor compliance, and institute enforcement actions against those who are not in compliance.

The Act imposes upon each employer a general duty to provide a work environment that is "free from recognized hazards that are causing or likely to cause death or serious physical harm to his employees." In addition to this general duty the employer is required to comply with specific safety risks promulgated by OSHA. The Act also requires employees to comply with all OSHA rules and regulations. Finally, the Act prohibits any employer from discharging or discriminating against an employee who exercises his rights under the Act as in *Whirlpool Corp. v. Marshall.*

Penalties for violations are both civil and criminal and may be as high as $1,000 per violation per day, while a $10,000 criminal penalty may be imposed for certain willful violations. In cases involving civil penalties, serious violations require that a penalty be proposed, while in nonserious violation cases penalties are rarely proposed. The Secretary of Labor is further empowered by the Act to obtain temporary restraining orders in situations where regular OSHA procedures cannot be effective to shut down business operations that create imminent dangers of death or serious injury.

WHIRLPOOL CORP. v. MARSHALL

Supreme Court of the United States, 1980.
445 U.S. 1, 100 S.Ct. 883, 63 L.Ed.2d 154.

FACTS: At Whirlpool's manufacturing plant in Ohio, overhead conveyors transported household appliance components throughout the plant. A wire mesh screen was positioned below the conveyors in order to catch falling components and debris. Maintenance employees frequently had to stand on the screens to clean them. In 1973, Whirlpool began installing heavier wire because several employees had fallen partly through the old screens and one had fallen completely through to the plant floor. At this time, the company warned workers to walk only on the frames beneath the wire but not on the wire itself. Before the heavier wire had been completely installed a worker fell to his death through the old screen. A short time after this incident, Deemer and Cornwell, two plant employees, met with the plant safety director to discuss the mesh, to voice their concerns, and to obtain the name, address, and telephone number of the local Occupational Safety and Health Administration (OSHA) representative. The next day the two employees refused to clean a portion of the old screen. They were then ordered to punch out for the remainder of the shift without pay and also received written reprimands, which were placed in their employment files. Secretary of Labor Marshall brought suit, claiming that Whirlpool's actions against Deemer and Cornwell constituted discrimination in violation of the Occupational Safety and Health Act.

DECISION: Judgment for Marshall. The fundamental objective of the Occupational Safety and Health Act is to prevent occupational deaths and serious injuries. The Act does not expressly grant the employee the right to walk off the job because of unsafe conditions at the workplace. However, in certain situations the employee may justifiably believe that his express rights under the Act will not protect him from death or serious injury. Such a situation may arise when (1) the employee is ordered to work under conditions which he reasonably believes pose an imminent risk of death or serious bodily injury, and (2) he has reason to believe that there is not sufficient time or opportunity either to seek effective redress from his employer or apprise OSHA of the danger. Under these circumstances, the employee has an implied right to refuse to expose himself to the dangerous condition without being subjected to "subsequent discrimination" by his employer.

Here, Deemer and Cornwell were faced with a potentially life-threatening work condition without time or opportunity to get assistance from OSHA or seek adequate redress against Whirlpool. Their justified refusal was an exercise of a right implied by the Act. Therefore, Whirlpool's measures against them for exercising this right were discriminatory and in violation of the Act.

start again

↓ ## Worker's Compensation

At common law the basis of most actions by an injured employee against his employer is the failure of the employer to use reasonable care under the circumstances for the safety of the employee. However, in such an action the employer has several well-established defenses available to him at common law. These include the defense of the fellow servant rule, contributory negligence on the part of the employee, and the doctrine of assumption of risk by the employee.

The **fellow servant rule** is that an employer is not liable for injuries sustained by an employee caused by the negligence of a fellow employee. Another common law defense is **contributory negligence.** If an employer establishes that the negligence of an injured employee contributed to the injury he sustained in the course of his employment, in many jurisdictions the employee cannot recover damages from the employer. At common law an employer is not liable to an employee for harm or injury caused by the unsafe condition of the premises if the employee, with knowledge of the facts and understanding the risks involved, voluntarily enters into or continues in the employment. This is regarded as a **voluntary assumption of risk** by the employee.

In order to provide speedier and more certain relief to injured employees, all States have adopted Worker's Compensation Acts. These statutes create commissions or boards that determine whether an injured employee is entitled to receive compensation and if so, how much. The common law defenses discussed above are *not* available to employers in proceedings under these statutes. Such defenses are abolished, and the only requirement is that the employee be injured and that the injury arise out of and in the course of his employment. The amounts recoverable are fixed by statute for each type of injury and are normally less than a court or jury would award in an action at common law. However, actions at law are not permitted against employers to injured employees who come within the Worker's Compensation Acts. The courts do not have jurisdiction over such cases except to review decisions of the board or commission, and then only to determine whether such decisions are in accordance with the statute. However, if a third party causes the injury, the employee may bring a tort action against that third party.

Fellow servant rule–common law defense relieving employer for liability to an employee for injuries caused by negligence of fellow employee

Contributory negligence–failure of injured party to exercise reasonable care that also legally causes his own harm

Assumption of risk–injured party's consent to encounter a known danger

matter of struct liability

can sue employer for intentional tort
- *medical*
- *disability*
- *death*

Fair Labor Standards Act

The Fair Labor Standards Act (FLSA) regulates the employment of child labor outside of agriculture. The Act prohibits the employment of anyone under fourteen years in nonfarm work except for newspaper deliverers and child actors. Fourteen- and fifteen-year-olds may be employed for a limited number of hours outside of school hours, under specific conditions, in certain *nonhazardous* occupations. Sixteen- and seventeen-year-olds may work in any *nonhazardous* job; persons eighteen years old or older may work in *any* job whether it is hazardous or not. The Secretary of Labor determines which occupations are considered hazardous.

In addition, the FLSA imposes wage and hour requirements on covered employers. The Act provides for a minimum hourly wage (currently $3.35) and overtime pay of time and a-half for hours worked in excess of forty hours per week. Certain jobs are exempted from both the FLSA's minimum wage and overtime provisions, including the following: professionals, managers, and outside salespersons.

Social Security and Unemployment Insurance

Social Security was enacted in 1935 in an attempt to provide limited retirement and death benefits to certain employees. Since then the Federal Social Security system has expanded to cover almost all employees and to increase greatly the benefits offered. The system now contains four major benefit programs: (1) Old-Age and Survivors Insurance (OASI) (providing retirement and survivor benefits); (2) Disability Insurance (DI); (3) Hospitalization Insurance (Medicare); and (4) Supplemental Security Income (SSI).

The system is financed by contributions (taxes) paid by employers, employees, and self-employed individuals. Employees and employers pay matching contributions. These contributions are calculated by multiplying the social security tax (a fixed percentage) times the employee's wages up to a specified maximum. Both the basic tax rate and the maximum dollar amount are subject to change by Congress. It is the employer's responsibility to withhold the employee's contribution and to forward the full amount of the tax to the Internal Revenue Service. Contributions made by the employee are not tax deductible by the employee, while those made by the employer are tax deductible.

Self-employed persons are also required to report their own taxable income and pay the Social Security tax. Currently, the tax paid by self-employed individuals is greater than that paid by either the employer or employee, but less than the combined employer/employee contribution.

The Federal **unemployment insurance** system was initially created by Title IX of the Social Security Act of 1935. Subsequently, Title IX was supplemented by the Federal Unemployment Tax Act as well as numerous other (FUTA) Federal statutes. This complex system depends upon the cooperation of State and Federal programs. Federal law provides the general guidelines, standards, and requirements, while the States handle the administration of the program under their own employment laws. The system is funded by taxes imposed on employers with Federal taxes generally paying the administrative costs of the program and State contributions paying for the actual benefits. The purpose of the tax is to provide unemployment compensation to workers who have lost their jobs and cannot find other employment. Payments generally are made weekly and are based on the particular State's formula.

CHAPTER SUMMARY

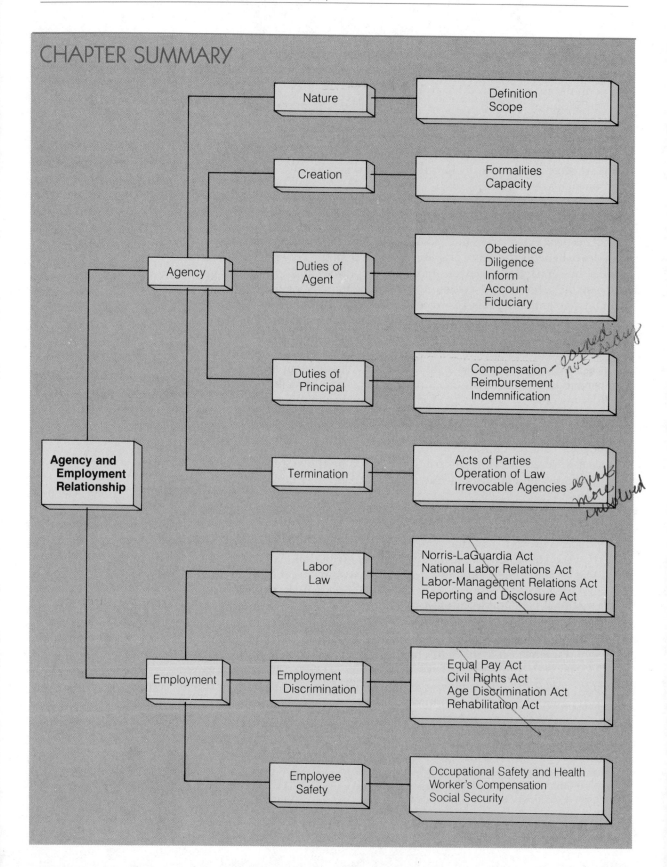

Agency and Employment Relationship

Agency
- Nature — Definition, Scope
- Creation — Formalities, Capacity
- Duties of Agent — Obedience, Diligence, Inform, Account, Fiduciary
- Duties of Principal — Compensation, Reimbursement, Indemnification
- Termination — Acts of Parties, Operation of Law, Irrevocable Agencies

Employment
- Labor Law — Norris-LaGuardia Act, National Labor Relations Act, Labor-Management Relations Act, Reporting and Disclosure Act
- Employment Discrimination — Equal Pay Act, Civil Rights Act, Age Discrimination Act, Rehabilitation Act
- Employee Safety — Occupational Safety and Health, Worker's Compensation, Social Security

KEY TERMS

Agency
Principal
Agent
Employment relationship
Independent contractor
Power of attorney
Duty of obedience

Duty of diligence
Fiduciary duty
Reimbursement
Indemnification
Agency coupled with an interest
Labor dispute

Unfair labor practice
Union unfair practices
Affirmative action
Fellow servant rule
Contributory negligence
Assumption of risk

PROBLEMS

1. A, the owner of certain unimproved real estate in Chicago, employed B, a real estate agent, to sell the property for a price of $25,000 or more and agreed to pay B a commission of 6 percent for making a sale. B negotiated with C who was interested in the property and willing to pay as much as $28,000 for it. B made an agreement with C that if B could obtain A's signature to a contract to sell the property to C for $25,000, C would pay B a bonus of $1,000. B prepared and A and C signed a contract for the sale of the property to C for $25,000. C refuses to pay B the $1,000 as promised. A refuses to pay B the 6 percent commission. In an action by B against A and C, what judgment?

2. P employed A to sell a parcel of real estate at a fixed price without knowledge that D had previously employed A to purchase the same property for him. P gave A no discretion as to price or terms, and A entered into a contract of sale with D on the exact terms authorized by P. After accepting a partial payment, P discovered that A was employed by D and brought an action to rescind. D resisted on the ground that admittedly P had suffered no damage for the reason that A had been given no discretion and the sale was made on the exact basis authorized by P. Decision?

3. P owned and operated a fruit cannery in Southton, Illinois. He stored a substantial amount of finished canned goods in a warehouse in East St. Louis, Illinois, owned and operated by A in order to have goods readily available for the St. Louis market. On March 1, he had 10,000 cans of peaches and 5,000 cans of apples on storage with A. On the day named, he borrowed $5,000 from A, giving A his promissory note for this amount due June 1 together with a letter authorizing A, in the event the note was not paid at maturity, to sell any or all of his goods on storage, pay the indebtedness, and account to him for any surplus. P died on June 2 without having paid the note. On June 8, A told T, a wholesale food distrib-

utor, that he had for sale as agent of the owner 10,000 cans of peaches and 5,000 cans of apples. T said he would take the peaches and would decide later about the apples. A contract for the sale of 10,000 cans of peaches for $6,000 was thereupon signed. "A, agent for P, seller; T, buyer." Both A and T knew of the death of P. Delivery of the peaches and payment were made on June 10. On June 11, A and T signed a similar contract covering the 5,000 cans of apples, delivery and payment to be made June 30. On June 23, P's executor, having learned of these contracts, wrote A and T stating that A had no authority to make the contracts, demanding that T return the peaches, and directing A not to deliver the apples. Discuss the correctness of the contentions of P's executor.

4. Green, a licensed real estate broker in Illinois, and Jones, also an Illinois resident, while both were in New York, signed a contract whereby Green agreed to endeavor to find a buyer for certain real estate located in Illinois owned by Jones, who agreed to pay Green a commission of $10,000 in the event of a sale. Green found a buyer, a resident of New York, to whom the land was sold. Thereafter, Jones refused to pay the commission. Green commenced an action in Illinois to recover the commission. Jones defended on the sole ground that the brokerage contract was unenforceable because Green was not a licensed real estate broker in New York.

Relevant provisions of the applicable New York statute forbid any person from holding himself out or acting temporarily as a real estate broker or salesman without first procuring a license. A violation is declared to be a misdemeanor, and the commission of a single prohibited act is a violation for which the statute provides a penalty. For whom should judgment be rendered?

5. B made a valid contract with A under which A was to sell B's goods on commission during the period from January 1 to June 30. A made satisfactory sales up to May 15 and was then about to close an unusually large order when B suddenly and without notice revoked A's authority to sell. Can A continue to sell B's goods during the unexpired term of her contract?

6. A Electric Co. gave a list of delinquent accounts to B, an employee, with instructions to discontinue electric service to delinquent customers. Among those listed was C Hatchery, which was then in the process of hatching chickens in a large, electrically heated incubator. C Hatchery told B that it did not consider its account delinquent, but B nevertheless cut the wires leading to the hatchery. Subsequently, C Hatchery recovered a judgment of $5,000 against B in an action brought against B for the loss resulting from the interruption of the incubation process. B has paid the judgment and brings a cause of action against A Electric Co. Decision?

7. In October 1981, Black, the owner of the Grand Opera House, and Harvey entered into a written agreement leasing the Opera House to Harvey for five years at a rental of $30,000 a year. Harvey engaged Day as manager of the theater at a salary of $175 per week plus 10 percent of the profits. One of Day's duties was to determine the amounts of money taken in each night and, after deducting expenses, to divide the profits between Harvey and the manager of the particular attraction playing at the theater. In September 1986, Day went to Black and offered to rent the Opera House from Black at a rental of $37,500

per year, whereupon Black entered into a lease with Day for five years at this figure. When Harvey learned of and objected to this transaction, Day offered to assign the lease to him for $60,000 per year. Harvey refused and brought an appropriate action seeking to have Day declared a trustee of the Opera House on behalf of Harvey. Decision?

8. Erwick was dismissed from her job at the C&T Steel Company because she was "an unsatisfactory employee." At the time Erwick was active in an effort to organize a union at C&T. Is the dismissal valid?

9. Johnson, president of the First National Bank of A, believes that it is only appropriate to employ female tellers. Hence, First National refuses to employ Ken Baker as a teller but does make him an offer to be a maintenance man at the same salary. Baker brings a cause of action against First National Bank. Decision?

10. Janet, a twenty-year-old woman, applied for a position driving a truck for Federal Trucking, Inc. Janet, who is 5'4" tall and weighs 135 lbs., was denied the job because the company requires that all employees be at least 5'6" tall and weigh at least 150 lbs. Federal justified this requirement on the basis that its drivers frequently were forced to move heavy loads in order to make pick-ups and deliveries. Janet brings a cause of action. Decision?

28

RELATIONSHIP WITH THIRD PARTIES

The purpose of an agency relationship is to allow the principal to extend his business activities by authorizing agents to enter into contracts with third persons on the principal's behalf. So long as the agent operates within his authority, actual or apparent, the principal and third party become bound to each other, each acquiring contractual rights and liabilities, while the agent assumes neither. In some circumstances, however, the agent will himself have contractually created obligations or rights or both. Moreover, in the course of an agency, third parties may suffer injuries from the tortious conduct of the agent. As a consequence, the principal and agent may incur tort liability to these injured parties.

Relationship of Principal and Third Persons

In this section we first consider the contract liability of the principal; then we examine the principal's potential tort liability.

Contract Liability of the Principal

The **authority** of an agent is his power or capacity to change the legal status of his principal. Thus, whenever an agent, acting within his authority, makes a contract for his principal, he creates new rights or liabilities of his principal and thus changes his principal's legal status. This authority of an agent to act for his principal in business transactions is the basic factor in agency. Without it the agency relation could not exist.

Authority–power of an agent to change the legal status of his principal

It is fundamental that a principal is liable on contracts made for her by her agent acting with actual or apparent authority, including those contracts in which her identity is not disclosed. Conversely, she is not liable in contract for unauthorized acts of an agent unless she subsequently ratifies them. The other party to a contract made by an agent acting within his actual or apparent authority is liable to the principal as if he had contracted directly with the principal.

Types of Authority

There are two basic types of authority: actual and apparent. **Actual authority** occurs when the principal gives actual consent to the agent. It may be either

Actual authority–power conferred upon agent by actual consent given by principal

469

express or implied. In either case it is binding and gives the agent both the power and the right to create or affect legal relations of the principal with third persons. **Apparent authority** is based on acts or conduct of the principal that show a third person that the agent has actual authority and on which the third person *justifiably* relies. This manifestation may consist of words or actions of the principal as well as other facts and circumstances that induce the third person reasonably to rely on the existence of an agency relationship. To the extent that things are as represented, there is both actual and apparent authority. Whether the authority of an agent is actual (express or implied) or apparent, it is effective to bind the principal in contract by acts of the agent or supposed agent within its scope (see Figure 28-1).

Apparent authority–
power conferred upon agent by acts or conduct of principal that reasonably lead a third party to believe that agent has such power

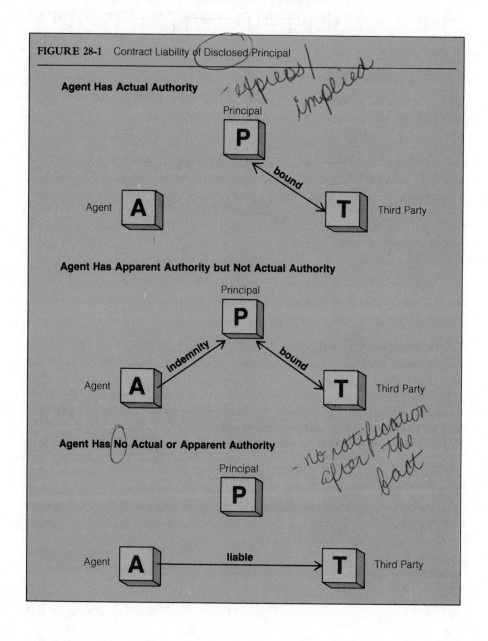

FIGURE 28-1   Contract Liability of Disclosed Principal

Agent Has Actual Authority

Agent Has Apparent Authority but Not Actual Authority

Agent Has No Actual or Apparent Authority

Actual Express Authority   The express authority of an agent is found in the words of the principal, spoken or written, and communicated to the agent. It is actual authority embodied in language directing or instructing the agent to do something specific. Thus, if Lee orally or in writing requests his agent Anita to sell Lee's automobile for $6,500, Anita's authority to sell the car for this sum is actual and express.

Actual Implied Authority   Implied authority is not found in express or explicit words of the principal, but is inferred from words or conduct manifested to the agent by the principal. Authority granted to an agent to accomplish a particular purpose necessarily includes authority to employ means reasonably required for its accomplishment. For example, Helen authorizes Clyde to manage her eighty-two-unit apartment complex. Nothing is said by Helen about expenses. In order to manage the building, however, Clyde must employ a janitor, purchase fuel for heating, and arrange for ordinary maintenance. The authority to incur these expenses, while not expressly granted, is implied from the express authority to manage the building, because they are required for its proper management. The agent has implied authority to do what is reasonably necessary to complete the task assigned.

Certain rules have been developed to determine what authority is implied in particular types of agencies. Unless otherwise agreed, authority to buy or to sell property for the principal includes authority to agree on the terms, to demand or make the usual representations and warranties, to receive or execute the instruments usually required, to pay or receive as much of the purchase price as is to be paid at the time of the transfer, and to receive possession of the goods if a buying agent, or to surrender possession of them if a selling agent.

General authority to manage or operate a business for a principal confers, unless otherwise agreed, implied authority on the agent (1) to buy and sell property for the principal; (2) to make contracts that are incidental or reasonably necessary to such business; (3) to acquire equipment and supplies; (4) to make repairs; (5) to employ, supervise, and discharge employees; (6) to receive payments due the principal and to pay debts due from the principal; and (7) to direct the ordinary operations of the business.

Apparent Authority   Apparent authority is authority that arises out of words or conduct of a **disclosed** principal manifested to third persons by which they are reasonably induced to rely on the assumption that actual authority exists. Apparent authority confers on the agent or supposed agent the **power** to bind the principal in contracts with third persons and precludes the principal from denying the existence of actual authority.

For example, A writes a letter to B authorizing her to sell his automobile and sends a copy of the letter to C, a prospective purchaser. On the following day, A writes a letter to B revoking the authority to sell the car, but does not send a copy of the second letter to C, who is not otherwise informed of the revocation. Although B has no actual authority to sell the car, she continues to have apparent authority with respect to C. Or, suppose that B, in the presence of A, tells C that B is A's agent to buy lumber. Although this statement is not true, A does not deny it, as he could easily have done. C, in reliance on the statement, ships lumber to A on B's order. A must pay for the lumber because B had apparent authority to act on A's behalf. However, this apparent authority of B exists only with respect to C. If B were to give D an order for a shipment of lumber to A, D would not be able to hold A liable. No actual authority existed, and as to D there was no apparent authority.

Thus, when there is apparent authority but not actual authority, the principal is nonetheless bound by the act of the agent. However, by exceeding his actual authority the agent has violated his duty of obedience and is liable to the principal for any loss sustained as a result of his acting in excess of his actual authority.

SCHOENBERGER v. CHICAGO TRANSIT AUTHORITY

Appellate Court of Illinois, First District, First Division, 1980.
84 Ill.App.3d 1132, 39 Ill.Dec. 941, 405 N.E.2d 1076.

FACTS: Schoenberger applied for and interviewed concerning a position with the Chicago Transit Authority (C.T.A.). He met several times with Frank ZuChristian, who was in charge of recruiting for the C.T.A. Data Center. At the third of these meetings, ZuChristian informed Schoenberger that he wanted to employ him at a salary of $19,800, and that he was making a recommendation to that effect. When the formal offer was made by the Placement Department, however, the salary was stated at $19,300. Schoenberger did not accept the offer immediately, but instead called ZuChristian for an explanation of the salary difference. After making inquiries, ZuChristian informed Schoenberger that a clerical error had been made and that it would take some time to correct. He urged Schoenberger to accept the job at $19,300 and said that he would see that the $500 was made up to him at one of the salary reviews in the following year. When the increase was not given, Schoenberger resigned and filed this suit to recover damages.

DECISION: Judgment for Chicago Transit Authority. ZuChristian had neither the actual nor the apparent authority to bind CTA for the additional $500.

The actual authority of an agent may only come from the principal and must be founded on the words or acts of the principal and not on the acts or words of the agent. Apparent authority, in contrast, is such authority as the principal knowingly permits the agent to assume or which he holds his agent out as possessing. It is such authority as a reasonable, prudent man, exercising diligence and discretion, in view of the principal's conduct, would naturally suppose the agent to possess.

Here, two of ZuChristian's superiors testified that he had no actual authority to make an offer of a specific salary to Schoenberger or to make any promise of additional compensation. Moreover, ZuChristian did not have the apparent authority to do either. The mere fact that he was allowed to interview prospective employees does not establish that CTA held him out as possessing the authority to hire or to set salaries, and Schoenberger was told that the formal offer would be made by the Placement Department.

Delegation of Authority

The appointment of an agent reflects confidence and reliance of the principal on the agent's personal skill, integrity, and other qualifications. The agent has been selected because of her fitness to perform the task assigned to her and therefore ordinarily has no power to delegate her authority or to appoint a subagent. Thus, Donna employs Harold to collect her accounts. Harold may not delegate this authority to Davis, as Donna reposed trust and confidence in Harold and not in Davis.

However, in certain situations it is clear that the principal intended to permit the agent to delegate the authority granted to her. Such an intention may be gathered from the express authorization of the principal, the character of the business, the usages of trade, or the prior conduct of the parties. For example, if a check is deposited in a bank for collection at a distant place, the bank is impliedly authorized to employ another bank at the place of payment.

If an agent is authorized to appoint or select other persons, called **subagents,** to perform or assist in the performance of the agent's duties, the acts of the subagent are binding on the principal to the same extent as if they had been done by the agent. The subagent is an agent of both the principal and the agent and owes a fiduciary duty to each.

If no authorization exists to delegate the agent's authority, but the agent nevertheless does so, the acts of the subagent do not impose any obligations or liability on the principal to third persons. Likewise, the principal acquires no rights against such third persons.

Subagent–person appointed by agent to perform agent's duties

Effect of Termination of Agency on Authority

On the termination of an agency, the agent's actual authority ceases. When the termination is by death or incapacity of the principal or agent, the agent's apparent authority also expires. Notice of such termination to third persons is *not* required. Thus, in a case where T, a tenant of the principal P, paid rent to P's agent A in ignorance of P's death, and A failed to account for the payment, T is liable to P's estate for payment of the amount of the rent. The same holds where an authorized transaction is made impossible of performance.

In other cases, apparent authority continues with respect to third parties with whom the agent had previously dealt until they receive **actual notice.** Actual notice requires a communication to the third party, either oral or written. All other third parties need only be given **constructive notice,** such as publication in a newspaper of general circulation in the area where the agency is regularly carried on. To illustrate: A is the general agent of P, who carries on business in Chicago. X knows of the agency, but has never dealt with A. Y sells goods on credit to A, as agent of P. P revokes A's authority and publishes a statement to that effect in a newspaper of general circulation published in Chicago. X does not see the statement and deals with A in reliance upon the former agency. Y also does not see the statement and has no knowledge of the revocation. Y sells more goods to A, as the agent of P. P has given sufficient notice of revocation as to X and, therefore, A's apparent authority has terminated with respect to X. On the other hand, P has not given sufficient notice of revocation as to Y and P is bound to Y by the contract of sale made on P's behalf by A.

Actual notice–knowledge actually and expressly communicated

Constructive notice–knowledge imputed by law

FACTS: Raymond Zukaitis was a physician practicing medicine in Douglas County, Nebraska. Aetna issued a policy of professional liability insurance to Zukaitis through its agent, the Ed Larsen Insurance Agency. The policy covered the period from August 31, 1969 through August of the following year. On August 7, 1971, Dr. Zukaitis received a written notification of a claim for malpractice that occurred on September 27, 1969. Dr. Zukaitis notified the Ed Larsen Insurance Agency immediately and forwarded the written claim to them. The claim was then mistakenly referred to St. Paul Fire and Marine Insurance Company, the company that currently insured Dr. Zukaitis. Apparently without notice to Dr. Zukaitis, the agency contract between Larsen and Aetna had been canceled on August 1, 1970, and St. Paul had been replaced as the insurance carrier. When St. Paul discovered it was not the carrier on the date of the alleged wrongdoing, it notified Aetna and withdrew from Dr. Zukaitis's defense. Aetna, however, refused to represent Dr. Zukaitis, contending that it was relieved of its obligation to Dr. Zukaitis because he had not notified Aetna immediately of the claim. Dr. Zukaitis then secured his own attorney to defend against the malpractice claim and brought this action against Aetna to recover the attorney's fees and other expenses incurred in the defense.

ZUKAITIS v. AETNA CASUALTY AND SURETY CO.

Supreme Court of Nebraska, 1975.
195 Neb. 59, 236 N.W.2d 819.

DECISION: Judgment for Dr. Zukaitis. Aetna is responsible for the defense of Dr. Zukaitis. The notice given by Dr. Zukaitis to Larsen, the agent of Aetna, constitutes notice to Aetna and obligates it to carry out the terms of its insurance contract with Dr. Zukaitis. A revocation of the agent's authority does not become effective as between the principal and third persons until they receive notice of the termination. More specifically, when an insurer terminates the agency contract, it is its duty to notify third persons, such as the insureds with whom the agent dealt, and inform them of such termination. If it does not do so and such third persons or insureds deal with the agent without notice or knowledge of the termination and in reliance on the apparently continuing authority of the agent, the insurer is bound by the acts of the former agent. Therefore, the notice given by Zukaitis to Larsen, the agent of Aetna, obligates Aetna to carry out the terms of its insurance contract with Dr. Zukaitis and to provide for his defense against the malpractice claim.

Ratification

Ratification–confirmation of a prior unauthorized act

Ratification is the confirmation or affirmance by one person of a prior act that another, without authority, has done as his agent. The ratification of such act or contract binds the principal and the third party as if the agent had been initially authorized.

Ratification may relate to the acts of an agent that have exceeded the authority granted to him, as well as to acts that a person without any authority makes on behalf of an alleged principal. To be ratified, however, the act must indicate to the third person that it is on behalf of the alleged principal. Thus, A without any authority, contracts to sell to T an automobile belonging to P. A states to T that the auto is A's. T promises to pay $5,500 for the automobile. P affirms. There is *no* ratification and P is not a party to the contract because A did not purport to act on P's behalf. There can be no ratification by a principal who is undisclosed.

To effect a ratification the principal must show an intent to do so with knowledge of all material facts concerning the transaction. However, the principal does not need to communicate this intent either to the purported agent or to the third person. It may be manifested by express language or implied from conduct of the principal. Thus, if A, without authority, contracts in P's name for the purchase of goods from T on credit, and P, having learned of A's unauthorized act, accepts the goods from T, he thereby impliedly ratifies the contract and is bound on the contract. In express ratification the principal gives notice of affirmance of the unauthorized act to the third person. In any event, the principal must ratify the entire act or contract.

A ratification relates back to the time of performance of the unauthorized act. For example, Jeffrey, without authority from Robin, represents to Bart that he is Robin's agent and on June 1 enters into a bilateral executory contract with Bart on behalf of Robin. Jeffrey acted without authority, and neither Robin nor Bart is bound to the supposed contract. On June 15, Robin ratifies the act of Jeffrey. Both Robin and Bart thereupon become bound to the contract, effective as of June 1, to which date the ratification relates. However, suppose that on June 12, Bart learned of Jeffrey's lack of authority and notified Robin that he withdrew from the contract. Robin's ratification of June 15 would not cause a contract to be formed. To be effective, ratification must occur before the third person gives notice to the principal or agent of his withdrawal.

If the affirmance of a transaction occurs at a time when the situation has so materially changed that it would be inequitable to subject the third party to liability on the transaction, the third party may elect to avoid liability. For example, A has no authority but, purporting to act for P, A contracts to sell P's house to T. The next day the house burns down. P then affirms. T is not bound.

Finally, for ratification to be effective the purported principal must have been in existence when the act was done. For example, a promoter of a corporation not yet in existence may enter into contracts on behalf of the corporation. In the vast majority of States these acts cannot be *ratified* by the corporation because it did not exist when the contracts were made.

Once made, a valid ratification is irrevocable. Ratification is equivalent to prior authority, which means that the effect of ratification is substantially the same as though the purported agent had been a duly authorized agent when he performed the act. The respective rights, duties, and remedies of P and T are the same as if A had originally possessed due authority. Both P and A are in the same position as they would have been if the act had been originally authorized by P. A is entitled to his due compensation and is freed from liability to P for acting as his agent without authority or for exceeding his authority, as the case may be. Between A and T, A is released from any liability he may have been under to T by reason of his having induced T to enter into the contract without P's authority. If, however, in the course of his dealings with T, A committed a tort against T, A remains liable on the tort to T, whether or not P ratified the tort.

FACTS: Serges is the owner of a retail meat marketing business. His managing agent borrowed $3,500 from David on Serges's behalf and for use in Serges's business. Serges paid $200 on the alleged loan and on several other occasions told David that the full balance owed would eventually be paid. He then disclaimed liability on the debt, asserting that he had not authorized his agent to enter into the loan agreement. David brought this action to collect on the loan.

DECISION: Judgment for David. Serges's partial payment and his promise to pay off the loan constituted a ratification of his agent's action. Ratification is the principal's affirmance of a prior act by the agent that would not otherwise have been binding on the principal. Its effect is to bind the principal as if the agent's act had been authorized.

DAVID v. SERGES

Supreme Court of Michigan, 1964.
373 Mich. 442, 129 N.W.2d 882.

Tort Liability of the Principal

In addition to contract liability to third persons, a principal may be liable in tort to third persons as a consequence of the acts of her agent. Tort liability may arise directly or indirectly from authorized or unauthorized acts of the agent.

Direct Liability of Principal

All individuals are liable for their own tortious conduct. Consequently, a principal may be held liable in damages for his own negligence or recklessness in carrying on an activity through employees or agents. Such negligence or recklessness may result from giving improper or ambiguous orders, using improper persons or instruments, or providing inadequate supervision. For example, if Larry lends to his employee, Molly, a company car to run a business errand knowing that Molly is incapable of driving the vehicle, Larry would be liable for his own negligence to anyone injured by Molly's negligent driving.

Vicarious Liability of Principal for Authorized Acts of Agent

Vicarious liability–indirect legal responsibility for the act of another

A principal who authorizes his agent to commit a tortious act concerning the property or person of another is liable for the injury or loss sustained by that person. The authorized act is that of the principal. Thus, if A directs his agent, B, to enter on C's land and cut timber, which neither A nor B has any right to do, the cutting of the timber is a trespass, and A is liable to C. Or, suppose A instructs his agent B to make certain representations as to A's property that B is authorized to sell. A knows these representations are false, but B does not. Such representations by B to C, who buys the property in reliance on them, is a deceit for which A is liable to C.

Vicarious Liability of Principal for Unauthorized Acts of Agent

Respondeat superior–let the superior (employer) respond

A principal may be liable for an unauthorized tort committed by his agent, even one that is in flagrant disobedience of his instructions, if the tort was committed by the agent in the course of her employment. This is a form of liability without fault and is based on the doctrine of *respondeat superior,* ("let the superior respond"). The rationale of this doctrine is that a person who carries out his business activities through the use of agents and employees should be liable for their negligence in carrying out the business purposes for which they were employed. It is the price the employer pays for enlarging the scope of his business activities. It does not matter how carefully the employer selected the employee, if in fact the latter negligently injured a third person while engaged in the business of the employer. Consequently, an undisclosed principal is likewise liable for the torts committed by his agent within the scope of the agent's employment. Also, a principal is liable for the torts committed by an unauthorized agent in connection with a transaction that the purported principal, with full knowledge of the tort, subsequently ratifies. Needless to say, cases involving unauthorized but ratified torts are rare.

The Doctrine of *Respondeat Superior* The liability of the principal under *respondeat superior* is vicarious or derivative and depends on proof of wrongdoing by the agent *in the course of his employment*. Frequently both principal and agent are defendants in the same suit. If the agent is not held liable, the principal is not liable. A principal who is held liable for her agent's tort has a right of **indemnification** against the agent, which is the right to be reimbursed for the amount that she was required to pay as a result of the agent's wrongful act. However, frequently an agent is not able to reimburse his employer, and the principal must bear the brunt of the liability.

The wrongful act of the agent or employee must be connected with his employment and within its scope if the principal is to be held liable for resulting injuries or damage to third persons. For example, Hal is delivering gasoline for Martha. He lights his pipe and negligently throws the blazing match into a pool of gasoline that has dripped on the ground during the delivery. The gasoline ignites. For the resulting harm, Martha is subject to liability because the negligence of the employee delivering the gasoline relates directly to the manner in which he is handling the goods in his custody. However, if a chauffeur while driving his employer's car on an errand for his employer suddenly decided to use his pistol and shoot at pedestrians on the sidewalk for target practice, the employer would not be liable to the pedestrians. This willful and intentional misconduct is not related to the performance of the services for which the chauffeur was employed.

The same rule applies to negligent misconduct of an employee unrelated to his employment. If A employs B to deliver merchandise to A's customers in a given city, and while driving a delivery truck in going to or returning from a place of delivery B negligently causes the truck to hit and injure C, A is liable to C for injuries sustained. But if, after making the scheduled deliveries, B drives the truck to a neighboring city to visit a friend and while so doing negligently causes the truck to hit and injure D, A is not liable. In such case, B is said to be on a "frolic of his own." He has deviated from the purpose of his employment and was using A's truck to accomplish his own purposes, not those of his employer. Of course, in all of these situations the wrongdoing agent is personally liable to the injured persons because he committed a tort.

The tort liability of principal and agent are illustrated in Figure 28–2.

FACTS: Sherwood negligently ran into the rear of Austen's car which was stopped at a stoplight. As a result, Austen received bodily injuries and her car was damaged. Sherwood, arts editor for the *Mississippi Press Register,* was en route from a Louis Armstrong concert he had covered for the newspaper. When the accident occurred he was on his way to spend the night at a friend's house. Austen sued Sherwood and—under the doctrine of *respondeat superior*—Sherwood's employer, the *Mississippi Press Register.*	AUSTEN v. SHERWOOD

Court of Appeal of Louisiana, Fifth Circuit, 1983. 425 So.2d 818. |

DECISION: Judgment for Austen against Sherwood; *Mississippi Press Register* not liable. Under the doctrine of *respondeat superior*, the negligent acts of an employee on his way to and from work are not generally imputed to his employer. The determination of liability depends upon whether the employee's conduct is more closely related to his employment duties or to purely personal considerations separate from the employer's interests.

Here, Sherwood was on his way from work to visit a friend. This excursion in no way benefitted his employer nor was it related to his employment duties. It did not occur within the course and scope of Sherwood's employment. Therefore, his employer, the *Mississippi Press Register,* is not liable.

Torts of Independent Contractor An independent contractor is not the agent or employee of the person for whom he is performing work or rendering services. Hence, the doctrine of *respondeat superior* does not apply to torts committed by an independent contractor such as an attorney, broker or rental agent. For example, P authorizes A, his broker, to sell land for him. P, T and A meet in T's office. A arranges the sale to T. While A is preparing a deed for P to sign, he negligently knocks over an inkstand and ruins a valuable rug belonging to T. A but *not* P is liable to T. Similarly, P employs A, a roofer, as an independent contractor to repair P's roof. A drops a hammer upon T, a pedestrian walking by on the public sidewalk. A but not P is liable to T.

Nevertheless, certain duties imposed by law are nondelegable, and a person may not escape the consequences of their nonperformance by contracting with an independent contractor. For example, a landowner who permits an

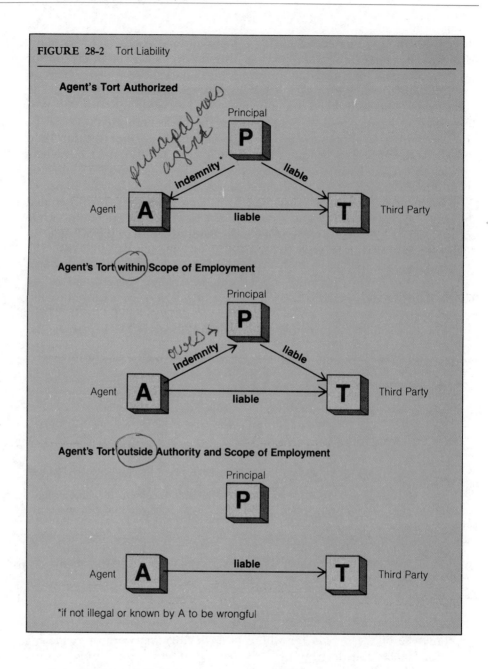

FIGURE 28-2 Tort Liability

Agent's Tort Authorized
Principal
P
indemnity*
liable
Agent
A
liable
T
Third Party
Agent's Tort within Scope of Employment
Principal
P
indemnity
liable
Agent
A
liable
T
Third Party
Agent's Tort outside Authority and Scope of Employment
Principal
P
liable
Agent
A
T
Third Party

*if not illegal or known by A to be wrongful

independent contractor to maintain a dangerous condition on his premises, such as an excavation that adjoins a public sidewalk and is unprotected by a guard rail or by lights at night, is liable to a member of the public who is injured as a result of falling into the excavation.

Moreover, the principal may be liable if he should know that there is an undue risk that the agent will be negligent and harm others. Thus, Melanie employs Gordon as an independent contractor to repair her roof. Melanie knows that Gordon is an alcoholic. Gordon attempts the repairs while heavily intoxicated and drops a fifty pound bundle of shingles upon Eric, a pedestrian walking by on the public sidewalk. Both Gordon and Melanie are liable to Eric.

Criminal Liability of the Principal

A principal is liable for the authorized criminal acts of his agents only if the principal directed, participated in or approved of the act. Otherwise, a principal is not ordinarily liable for the unauthorized criminal acts of his agents. One of the elements of a crime is a guilty mind, and this element is not present, so far as criminal responsibility of the principal is concerned, where the act of the agent was not authorized. However, an employer may be subject to a criminal penalty for the act of an advisory or managerial person acting in the scope of employment.

Moreover, a principal may be liable for penalties under criminal law for certain unauthorized acts of his agent whether the agent is managerial or not. Even under the common law some crimes do not require intent. In addition, many regulatory statutes do not require intent to violate them, or even knowledge of the act which causes the conduct to be illegal. In such cases, a principal may be held subject to a penalty for conduct of agents acting on his behalf in doing acts or in conducting transactions of the kind for which they are employed. Examples include the publication of a criminal libel in a newspaper, the sale of liquor to minors or to intoxicated persons, or the sale of unwholesome or adulterated food.

Relationship of Agent and Third Persons

The function of an agent is to assist in the conduct of the principal's business by carrying out his orders. The agent is not normally a party to the contract that she makes with a third person on behalf of a **disclosed** principal. The third person is generally aware of the fact that he is dealing with an agent who is not personally undertaking to perform the contract that she is negotiating on behalf of her principal. The resulting contract, if within the agent's actual or apparent authority, is between the third person and the principal. The agent ordinarily incurs no liability on the contract to either party. Thus, A who has actual authority to sell circuit boards manufactured by P writes to T: "On behalf of P, I offer to sell you 5,000 circuit boards for $15,000." T accepts. There is a contract between T and P. A is not a party to that contract and has no liability to P or T.

An agent, however, may be personally liable to the third person in certain situations:

1. by acting without authority or exceeding the scope of the authority granted;
2. by entering into a contract on behalf of an undisclosed or partially disclosed principal;
3. by knowingly entering into a contract on behalf of a nonexistent principal;
4. by guaranteeing performance of a contract by the principal; or
5. by committing a tortious or wrongful act.

In this section we cover these five situations, as well as the circumstances under which an agent may acquire rights against third persons.

Contract Liability of Agent

Unauthorized Contracts

If an agent exceeds his actual and apparent authority, the principal is not bound. However, the fact that the principal is not bound does not of itself make the agent a party to the contract. The agent's liability, if any, arises from express or implied representations about his authority that he makes to a third party.

Agent's Implied Warranty of Authority   A person who undertakes to contract as agent makes an implied warranty that he is in fact authorized to make the contract on behalf of the party whom he claims to represent. If the agent does not have authority to bind the principal, the agent is liable to the third party for damages unless the principal ratifies the contract. However, no implied warranty exists if the contract expressly provides that the agent shall not be responsible for any lack of authority, or if the agent, acting in good faith, discloses to the third person all of the facts on which his authority rests. For example, agent Larson has received an ambiguous letter of instruction from his principal Dan. He shows it to Carol, stating that it represents all of the authority that he has to act, and both Larson and Carol rely on its sufficiency. In this case there is no implied or express warranty by Larson to Carol of his authority.

Misrepresentation   If a purported agent falsely represents to a third person that he has authority to make a contract on behalf of a principal whom he has no power to bind, he is liable in a tort action to the third person for the loss sustained in reliance on the misrepresentation.

Undisclosed or Partially Disclosed Principal

Undisclosed principal—one whose existence and identity are not known

An agent acts for an undisclosed principal when she appears to be acting in her own behalf and the third person with whom she is dealing has no knowledge that she is acting as an agent. The instructions of the principal to the agent are to conceal not only the identity of the principal but also the agency relationship. Thus the third person is dealing with the agent as though she were a principal. A partially disclosed principal is one whose existence is known but whose identity is unknown. Thus, the third person is aware that the agent is acting on behalf of another, but he is not told the name or identity of the partially disclosed principal. The use of undisclosed or partially disclosed principals may be helpful where the third party might inflate the price of property he was selling if he knew the identity of the principal.

Partially disclosed principal—one whose existence is known but whose identity is not known

Liability of the Parties   The agent is personally liable on a contract that she enters into with a third person on behalf of an undisclosed principal or a partially disclosed principal, unless the third person after discovering the existence and identity of the principal chooses to hold the principal to the contract. The reason for the liability of the agent is that the third person has placed reliance on the agent individually and has accepted the agent's personal undertaking to perform the contract. Obviously, where the principal is wholly undisclosed, the third person does not know of the interest of anyone in the contract other than himself and the agent. The reason for the liability of the undisclosed or partially disclosed principal is that the concealment by the agent follows the instructions of the principal, and having received the benefits of the agent's acts, she should also assume and be responsible for the burdens.

After the third person has become informed of the identity of the undisclosed or partially disclosed principal, he may hold either the principal or the agent to performance of the contract, but not both. Having once made an election, he is bound by it and cannot change his decision. However, the third person may bring suit against both principal and agent so that he does not incur the risk that in a trial the evidence may fail to establish the agency relationship. In most States, bringing suit and proceeding to trial against both is not an election, but before the entry of any judgment the third person is compelled to make an election, because he is not entitled to a judgment against both. If the agent is held liable by the third party, the agent has the right to be reimbursed by the principal.

VAN D. COSTAS, INC. v. ROSENBERG

District Court of Appeal of Florida, Second District, 1983. 432 So.2d 656.

FACTS: Costas entered into a contract to remodel the entrance of the Magic Moment Restaurant owned by Seascape Restaurants, Inc. Rosenberg, part owner and president of Seascape, signed the contract on the line under which was typed "Jeff Rosenberg, The Magic Moment." When a dispute arose over the performance and payment of the contract, Costas brought suit against Rosenberg for breach of contract. Rosenberg contends that he has no personal liability for the contract and that only Seascape, the owner of the restaurant, is liable. Costas claims that Rosenberg signed for an undisclosed principal and, therefore, is individually liable.

DECISION: Judgment for Costas. To avoid personal liability, an agent must disclose both that he is acting as an agent and the identity of his principal. If the contracting party knows the identity of the principal for whom the agent is acting, the principal is considered disclosed. However, it is not the contracting party's duty to seek out the identity of the principal.

Here, nothing indicates that Costas had ever heard of Seascape at the time the contract was signed. Moreover, use of a tradename (here Magic Moment) is not sufficient disclosure of the identity of the principal. Rosenberg knew that Seascape was the owner and he could have avoided personal liability by properly disclosing the identity of his principal. Since he did not, Rosenberg is personally liable.

Rights of Undisclosed or Partially Disclosed Principal An undisclosed or partially disclosed principal acquires rights and may maintain an action in his own name against the third person with whom the agent entered into a contract in the agent's name. However, if the agent represents to the third person that she is not acting on behalf of another but solely for herself as principal, the undisclosed principal would have have no rights on the contract.

Figure 28-3 illustrates the contract liability when the principal is undisclosed or partially disclosed.

Liability of Agent Where Principal is Nonexistent

A person who claims to act as agent for a fictitious or nonexistent principal is personally liable on a contract entered into with a third person on behalf of such a principal. A promoter of a corporation who enters into contracts with third persons in the name of a corporation to be organized is personally liable on such contracts. The corporation is not liable because it did not authorize the contracts. But if the corporation after coming into existence affirmatively adopts a preincorporation contract made on its behalf, it becomes bound along with the promoter. However, if the corporation enters into a

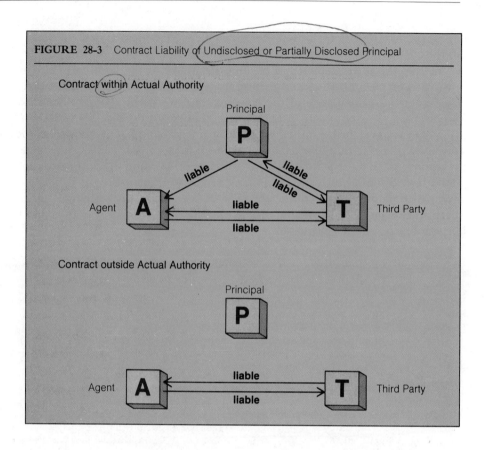

FIGURE 28-3   Contract Liability of Undisclosed or Partially Disclosed Principal

new contract with such a third person, the prior contract between the promoter and the third person is discharged, and the liability of the promoter is terminated. This is a novation.

Where an agent enters into a contract with a third person on behalf of a principal who, unknown to both the agent and the third person, had died prior to the making of the contract, it is generally held that the existence of the principal at the time of the making of the contract is an implied condition precedent to the contract, and that neither the agent, the third person, nor the estate of the decedent principal is liable on it.

Performance Guaranteed by Agent

An agent who guarantees that the principal will perform the contract between the third party and the principal will be liable to the third party if the principal fails to perform. The agent in this situation is acting as a surety and would have a right of reimbursement from the principal. For a more complete discussion of suretyship, see Chapter 37.

Tort Liability of Agent

An agent is personally liable for his tortious acts that injure third persons, whether or not such acts are authorized by the principal and whether or not the principal may also be liable.

An agent who commits a wrong at the direction or under instructions of his principal is also personally liable. For example, an agent is personally liable if he converts the goods of a third person to his principal's use. An agent is also liable for making representations that he knows to be fraudulent to a third person who suffers a loss because she relied on them.

Rights of Agent Against Third Person

An agent who makes a contract with a third person on behalf of a disclosed principal has no right of action against the third person for breach of contract. The agent is not a party to the contract. However, an agent for an undisclosed principal or partially disclosed principal may maintain in her own name an action against the third person for breach of contract. In such case the agent is also individually liable on the contract.

CHAPTER SUMMARY

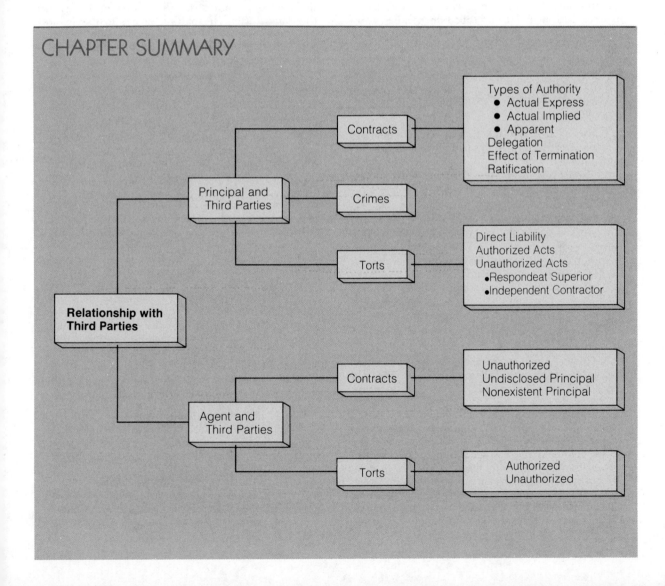

KEY TERMS

Authority	Subagent	Non-delegable duty
Actual authority	Actual notice	Indemnification
Apparent authority	Constructive notice	Implied warranty of authority
Actual express authority	Ratification	Undisclosed principal
Actual implied authority	Vicarious liability	Partially disclosed principal
Disclosed principal	Respondeat superior	Nonexistent principal

PROBLEMS

1. A was P's traveling salesperson and was also authorized to collect accounts. Before the agreed termination of the agency, P wrongfully discharged A. A then called on T, an old customer, and collected an account from T. He also called on X, a new prospect, as P's agent, secured a large order, collected the price of the order, sent the order to P, and disappeared with the collections. P delivered the goods to X as per the order.

(a) P sues T for his account. Decision?

(b) P sues X for the agreed price of the goods. Decision?

2. P instructed A, her agent, to purchase a quantity of hides. A ordered the hides from T in his own (A's) name and delivered the hides to P. T, learning later that P was the principal, sends the bill to P, who refuses to pay T. T sues P and A. Decision?

3. A sold goods to B in good faith, believing him to be a principal. B in fact was acting as agent for C and within the scope of his authority. The goods were charged to B, and on his refusal to pay, A sued B for the purchase price. While this action was pending, A learned of B's relationship with C. Nevertheless, thirty days after learning of that relationship, A obtained judgment against B and had an execution issued that was never satisfied. Three months after the judgment was made, A sued C for the purchase price of the goods. Decision?

4. X Grocery Company employed Jones as its manager and gave her authority to purchase supplies and goods for resale. Jones had conducted business for several years with Brown Distributing Company, although her purchases had been limited to groceries. Jones contacted Brown Distributing Company and had it deliver a color television set to her house. She told Brown Company that the set was to be used in promotional advertising to increase X Grocery Company's business. The advertising did not develop. Jones disappeared from the area, taking the television set with her. Brown Company sued X Company for the purchase price of the set. Decision?

5. Stone was the authorized agent to sell stock of the X Company at $10 per share and was authorized in case of sale to fill in the blanks in the certificates with the name of the purchaser, the number of shares, and the date of sale. He sold 100 shares to Barrie, and without the knowledge or consent of the company and without reporting to the company, he indorsed on the back of the certificate the following:

"It is hereby agreed that X Company shall, at the end of three years after the date, repurchase the stock at $11.00 per share on thirty days' notice. X Company, by Stone."

After three years, demand was made on X Company to repurchase, which was refused, and the company repudiated the agreement on the ground that the agent had no authority to make the agreement for repurchase. Barrie sued X Company. Decision?

6. Helper, a delivery boy for Gunn, delivered two heavy packages of groceries to Reed's porch. As instructed by Gunn, Helper rang the bell to let Reed know the groceries had arrived. Mrs. Reed came to the door and asked Helper if he would deliver the groceries into the kitchen because the bags were heavy. Helper did so, and on leaving he observed Mrs. Reed having difficulty in moving a cabinet in the dining room. He undertook to assist her, but being more interested in watching Mrs. Reed than the cabinet, he failed to observe a small, valuable antique table, which he smashed into with the cabinet and totally destroyed.

Does Reed have a cause of action against Gunn for the value of the destroyed antique?

7. Driver picked up Friend to accompany him on an out-of-town delivery for his employer, Speedy Service. A "No Riders" sign was prominently displayed on the windshield of the truck, and Driver violated specific instructions of his employer by permitting an unauthorized person to ride in the vehicle.

While discussing a planned fishing trip with Friend, Driver ran a red light and collided with an automobile driven by Motorist. Both Friend and Motorist were injured. Is Speedy Service liable to either Friend or Motorist for the injuries they sustained?

8. X Department Store advertises that it maintains a barber shop in its store managed by Y. Actually, Y is not an employee of the store but merely rents space in the store. Y, while shaving Z in the barber shop, negligently puts a deep gash, requiring ten stitches, into one of Z's ears. Z sues X Department Store for damages. Decision?

9. The following contract was executed on August 22:

> Ray agrees to sell and Shaw, the representative of Todd and acting on his behalf, agrees to buy 10,000 pounds of 0.32 × 1⅝ stainless steel strip type 410.
>
> (signed) Ray
(signed) Shaw

On August 26, Ray informs Shaw and Todd that the contract was in reality signed by him as agent for Upson. What are the rights of Ray, Shaw, Todd, and Upson in the event of a breach of the contract?

10. Harris, owner of certain land known as Red Bank, mailed a letter to Byron, a real estate broker in City X, stating: "I have been thinking of selling Red Bank. I have never met you, but a friend has advised me that you are an industrious and honest real estate broker. I therefore employ you to find a purchaser for Red Bank at a price of $35,000." Ten days after receiving the letter, Byron mailed the following reply to Harris: "Acting pursuant to your recent letter requesting me to find a purchaser for Red Bank, this is to advise that I have sold the property to Sims for $35,000. I enclose your copy of the contract of sale signed by Sims. Your name was signed to the contract by me as your agent."

Is Harris obligated to convey Red Bank to Sims?

PART SIX
PARTNERSHIPS

PART SIX

PARTNERSHIPS

PUBLIC POLICY, SOCIAL ISSUES AND BUSINESS ETHICS

Owners of businesses frequently decide to join forces with one or more associates, usually to gain additional and otherwise unavailable capital or expertise. Once this decision has been made, a second and just as significant decision must be reached—what form of business organization should be used? There are two general types of business associations: unincorporated and incorporated. In Part Six we discuss the three most common forms of unincorporated business associations: general partnerships, joint ventures, and limited partnerships. In Part Seven we cover incorporated business associations, which are usually referred to simply as corporations.

Although corporations today outnumber unincorporated business associations by almost two to one and generate greater revenues by twenty-two to one, unincorporated business associations are widely used in a number of areas. General partnerships have been used principally in finance, insurance, accounting, real estate, wholesale and retail trade, law, and other services. Joint ventures have enjoyed popularity among major corporations planning to engage in cooperative research; in the exploitation of land and mineral rights; in the development, promotion, and sale of patents, trade names, and copyrights; and in manufacturing operations in foreign countries. Limited partnerships have been widely used for enterprises such as real estate investment and development, motion picture and theater productions, oil and gas ventures, and equipment leasing.

Regardless of the particular form of business organization, three sets of basic policy issues are important. First, what rights and responsibilities should owners and managers of the business have among themselves? Second, what should the rights and responsibilities of the business unit and its members be with respect to the rest of society? Third, what should be the rights and responsibilities between the business organization and its employees? Unlike the first two policy issues, which vary considerably with the form of business organization, employee relations is independent of the type of business entity as we discussed in Chapter 27.

The first issue—the relationship of the owners and managers among themselves—involves several policy questions. For example, what limitations, if any, should be placed on the number or type of associates, the name they may use for the business, the purposes for which the business may be formed, the size of the entity, the powers it may exercise, or the property it may own? In addition, to what extent should the associates be allowed to vary by contract their rights and responsibilities? Conversely, how much automatic protection should the law provide for business associates who fail to make their own arrangements to set forth each associate's rights and responsibilities?

In the operation of the business, to what extent may the associates exert control over the management of the enterprise? How far may the majority go in advancing their own interests? May the minority have veto power over the will of the majority? What remedies should be available to the minority and to the majority? How should the financial gains and losses be divided among the owners?

When changes are made in the organization, should all the owners have control over choosing new associates and making fundamental changes in the business? Should a member be permitted to transfer his interest to outsiders or to withdraw his capital contribution? How long should the enterprise be permitted to exist, and who may bring about its termination?

The second set of basic policy issues involves the relationship of the business unit and its members to the rest of society—suppliers, customers, creditors, parties injured by civil wrongs committed by members, employees and agents of the business, and society at large if the enterprise or one of its members commits a crime. How these issues of external liability are resolved affect the ease by which capital can be raised and the extent to which financially risky enterprises use a particular form of business organization. External liability for a business arises in a variety of ways, but for most enterprises the crucial and most commonly occurring causes of loss consist of tort and contract liability. The first results from some act or omission that falls below the standard of care that society demands of all its members. Losses from contract liability can occur as a result of incorrect judgments about market conditions and constrictions in cash flow that render the firm unable to meet its debt service, as well as any number of other problems.

A critical social issue is whether a person with a tort or contract claim should be limited to proceeding against the property of the enterprise or whether he may seek satisfaction of his court judgment from property of the individual members of the business organization.

A less common but still important issue is the extent to which the organization and its members should be held accountable for the criminal conduct of the business' employees, members, and agents.

As we indicated above, the resolution of these questions varies considerably among the different types of business organizations. Consequently, when choosing which form of organization is most appropriate, business associates should consider these factors as well as questions of taxation. This decision, however, cannot be made in any general way. It depends entirely on the particular circumstances of the given group of associates:

Apart from the ever changing problems of taxation, . . . there are certain ponderables and imponderables which must be weighed in the choice of a business association. Continuity of existence of the business, centralization of control, legitimate devices to obtain and keep control, limited or unlimited liability of the associates, the possibility of death, bankruptcy, insanity, inadequate performance or poor health and old age of the associates, probability of expansion and the necessity of obtaining capital from outside sources, the ease or difficulty of holding and disposing of property both personal and real, of bringing suit and defending the same, of the use of authority or the abuse of it by the associates, of the amount of "red tape" involved in making reports to governmental agencies, of complying with state and federal securities acts, and of the expense involved in setting up the particular business association, should be analyzed and weighed before determining what business form should be recommended. N. Lattin, *The Law of Corporations* 3–4 (1971).

In Part Six we examine how the law resolves these public policy issues for unincorporated business associations. These legal resolutions have a significant impact on business persons in organizing, financing, operating, and dissolving their business organizations.

29

NATURE AND FORMATION

A business enterprise may be operated or conducted by a sole proprietor, a general partnership, a limited partnership, a corporation, or by some other form of business organization. The owner or owners of the enterprise determine which form of business unit to use. Various factors, not the least of which are Federal and State income tax laws, affect the decision to use one medium rather than another. Other factors include ease of formation, capital requirements, flexibility of management and control, extent of external liability, and the duties imposed by law on management. For a concise comparison of general partnerships, limited partnerships and corporations, see Figure 33-2 in Chapter 33.

In Chapters 29 through 31 we examine general partnerships, commonly called simply partnerships; in Chapter 32 we discuss limited partnerships and other types of unincorporated business associations. Part Seven covers corporations. In the three chapters dealing with general partnerships we make frequent reference to the Uniform Partnership Act (UPA), which, since its promulgation in 1914, has been adopted by forty-eight States, all except Georgia and Louisiana, and also by the District of Columbia, the Virgin Islands, and Guam.

Nature of Partnership

Definition of Partnership

A partnership, or copartnership as it is sometimes called, has been defined in various ways. The standard definition, however, is contained in the UPA: "A partnership is an association of two or more persons to carry on as co-owners a business for profit."

The UPA broadly defines "person" to include "individuals, partnerships, corporations, and other associations." A business is defined by the UPA to include every trade, occupation, or profession.

Partnership–an association of two or more persons to carry on as co-owners of a business for profit

Entity Theory

An entity is anything that possesses the quality of oneness and may, therefore, be regarded as a single unit. Thus a legal person or legal entity is a unit with the capacity of possessing legal rights and being subject to legal duties. A legal

Legal entity–an organization having a separate legal existence from its members entity may acquire, own, and dispose of property. It may enter into contracts, commit wrongs, sue, and be sued. Each human being is a legal entity of natural origin. Each business corporation is a legal entity having a distinct legal existence separate from its members.

Although a partnership is an association of persons that has the quality of oneness, it was regarded by the common law as an aggregation of individuals, not as an entity. The UPA, however, has basically, but not totally, rejected the common law view of partnerships. It treats partnerships as a legal entity for most purposes, although for some purposes it still treats them as an aggregate.

Partnership as a Legal Entity   A partnership is recognized as a legal entity in the following respects.

1. The assets, liabilities, and business transactions of the firm are treated as those of a business unit and are considered separate and distinct from the individual assets, liabilities, and nonpartnership business transactions of its members.

2. Under the doctrine of "marshalling of assets—which applies in cases of insolvency administered by a State court of equity—partnership creditors have a prior right to partnership assets, while creditors of the individual members have a prior right to the separate assets of their individual debtors.

3. Title to real estate may be acquired by a partnership in the partnership name. If acquired in this way, it can be transferred only in the partnership name.

4. Every partner is considered an agent of the partnership.

5. In certain States and in the Federal courts, a partnership may sue and be sued in the partnership name.

6. A partnership is defined as a person in such statutes as the Uniform Commercial Code and the Bankruptcy Reform Act.

This listing is by no means exhaustive. It may, therefore, be observed that a partnership is a unit and in most transactions is regarded as a business entity distinct from each of its component members.

HORN'S CRANE SERVICE v. PRIOR

Supreme Court of Nebraska, 1967.
182 Neb. 94, 152 N.W.2d 421.

FACTS: Horn's Crane Service furnished supplies and services under a written contract to a partnership engaged in operating a quarry and rock-crushing business. Horn brought this action against Prior and Cook, the individual members of the partnership, to recover a personal judgment against them for the partnership's liability under that contract. Horn has not sued the partnership itself, nor does he claim that the partnership property is insufficient to satisfy its debts.

DECISION: Judgment for Prior and Cook. A partnership is a legal entity distinct and apart from the members composing it. Therefore, in order to hold the individual partners liable, it is necessary for a creditor to show that the partnership property is insufficient to satisfy the debts of the partnership. The partnership relation is such that the separate property of a partner cannot be subjected to the payment of partnership debts until the property of the firm is exhausted. There are two reasons for this rule. First, since credit was extended to the partnership, the partnership property should be exhausted first. Second, to allow a partnership creditor to bypass the partnership's assets and exhaust the assets of an individual member would allow the other partners to profit unjustly at his expense.

Partnership as a Legal Aggregate   Because a partnership is considered an aggregate for some purposes, it can neither sue nor be sued in the firm name unless a statute specifically allows such suits. Similarly, the debts of the partnership are ultimately the debts of the individual partners, and any one partner may be held liable for the partnership's entire indebtedness. Thus, if Neal and Michele enter into a partnership that becomes insolvent, as does Neal, Michele is fully liable for the debts of the partnership.

Legal aggregate—a group of individuals not having a legal existence separate from its members

In addition, a partnership lacks continuity of existence: whenever any partner ceases to be associated with the partnership, it is dissolved. However, the UPA does grant partnership continuity of existence in certain circumstances.

Finally, the Internal Revenue Code treats a partnership as an aggregate. A partnership is not required to pay Federal income tax but must file an information return stating the name of each partner and the amount of income derived from the partnership. It is the responsibility of each partner to include his share of partnership income in his individual tax return and to pay the tax on his share. Partnership income is taxed to the individual partners regardless of whether the income is actually distributed.

Types of Partners

A **general partner** is a partner whose liability for partnership indebtedness is unlimited, who has full management powers, and who shares in the profits.

General partner—member of either a general or limited partnership with unlimited liability for its debts, full management powers and a right to share in the profits

A **special or limited partner** is one who, as a member of a limited partnership, is liable for firm indebtedness only to the extent of the capital that he has contributed or agreed to contribute. We discuss limited partners in Chapter 32.

Limited partner—member of a limited partnership with liability for its debts only to the extent of her capital contribution

A **silent partner** is a partner who has no voice and takes no part in the partnership business.

A **secret partner** is a partner whose membership in the firm is not disclosed to the public.

A **dormant partner** is a partner who is both a silent and a secret partner.

Formation of a Partnership

Association

The formation of a partnership is relatively simple and may be done consciously or unconsciously. A partnership may result from an oral or written agreement between the parties, from an informal arrangement, or from the conduct of the parties. Persons become partners by associating themselves in business together as co-owners. Whether their agreement is simple or elaborate, definite or indefinite, fully understood and fair, or obscure and inequitable is of importance principally to the partners. The legal existence of the relationship depends on the parties' explicit or implicit agreement and their association in business as co-owners, and not on the degree of care, intelligence, study, or investigation that preceded its formation.

Articles of Partnership   In the interest of achieving a more clear, definite, and complete understanding between the partners, it is preferable, although not usually required, that partners put their agreement in writing. A written agreement creating a partnership is referred to as the partnership agreement or articles of partnership and should include:

Articles of partnership—written partnership agreement

1. the firm name and the identity of the partners;
2. the nature and scope of the partnership business;
3. the duration of the partnership;
4. the capital contributions of each partner;
5. the division of profits and sharing of losses;
6. the duties of each partner in the management;
7. a provision for salaries, if desired;
8. restrictions, if any, on the authority of particular partners to bind the firm;
9. the right, if desired, of a partner to withdraw from the firm, and the terms, conditions, and required notice in the event of such withdrawal; and
10. a provision for continuation of the business by the remaining partners, if desired, in the event of the death of a partner or other dissolution, and a statement of the method or formula for appraisal and payment of the interest of the deceased or former partner.

When a well-drawn agreement is used, it can provide almost any conceivable arrangement of capital investment, control sharing, and profit distribution that the partners desire. In addition, it can provide for continuity of the partnership in the event of one member's death or retirement.

Figure 29-1 shows a sample partnership agreement.

Who May Become Partners   Any natural person having full *capacity* may enter into a partnership. Nonetheless, no person may become a member of a partnership without the consent of all the partners. To the extent that a minor has capacity to act as a principal or agent, she may become a partner, although she has the right both to disaffirm the partnership agreement at any time before reaching majority and to avoid personal liability to partnership creditors. On disaffirmance and withdrawal from the partnership, a minor is entitled to the return of her capital contribution and her accrued and unpaid share of the profits, except to the extent that such funds are necessary to pay partnership creditors.

The position of a nonadjudicated incompetent is basically the same as that of a minor except that his incompetency may afford his co-partners a ground for seeking dissolution by court decree. Since all contracts of an adjudicated incompetent are void, not voidable, a partnership agreement entered into by such an individual is null and void.

A corporation is defined as a "person" by the UPA and is therefore legally capable of entering into a partnership in those States whose incorporation statutes authorize a corporation to do so.

Incidence of Statute of Frauds   The Statute of Frauds does not specifically apply to a contract for the formation of a partnership, and therefore no writing is required to create the relationship. However, a contract to form a partnership to continue for a period longer than one year is **within** the Statute and requires a writing in order to be enforceable. Moreover, a contract for the transfer of an interest in real estate to or by a partnership is governed by the Statute of Frauds and requires a writing to be enforceable.

FIGURE 29-1   Sample Partnership Agreement

This agreement, made and entered into as of the [*Date*], by and among [*Names*] (hereinafter collectively sometimes referred to as "Partners").

WITNESSETH:

Whereas, the Parties hereto desire to form a General Partnership (hereinafter referred to as the "Partnership"), for the term and upon the conditions hereinafter set forth;

Now, therefore, in consideration of the mutual covenants hereinafter contained, it is agreed by and among the Parties hereto as follows:

Article I
BASIC STRUCTURE

§ 1.1   Form

The Parties hereby form a General Partnership pursuant to the Laws of [*Name of State*].

§ 1.2   Name

The business of the Partnership shall be conducted under the name of [*Name*].

§ 1.3   Place of Business

The principal office and place of business of the Partnership shall be located at [*Describe*], or such other place as the Partners may from time to time designate.

§ 1.4   Term

The Partnership shall commence on [*Date*], and shall continue for [*Number*] years, unless earlier terminated in the following manner:

(a) By the completion of the purpose intended, or

(b) Pursuant to this Agreement, or

(c) By applicable [*State*] law, or

(d) By death, insanity, bankruptcy, retirement, withdrawal, resignation, expulsion, or disability of all of the then Partners.

§ 1.5   Purpose—General

The purpose for which the Partnership is organized is _____.

Article II
FINANCIAL ARRANGEMENTS

§ 2.1   Initial Contributions of Partners

Each Partner has contributed to the initial capital of the Partnership property in the amount and form indicated on Schedule A attached hereto and made a part hereof. Capital contributions to the Partnership shall not earn interest. An individual capital account shall be maintained for each Partner.

§ 2.2   Additional Capital Contribution

If at any time during the existence of the Partnership it shall become necessary to increase the capital with which the said Partnership is doing business, then (upon the vote of the Managing Partner(s)):

Each party to this Agreement shall contribute to the capital of this Partnership within _____ days notice of such need in an amount according to his then Percentage Share of Capital as called for by the Managing Partner(s).

§ 2.3   Percentage Share of Profits and Capital

(a) The Percentage Share of Profits and Capital of each Partner shall be (unless otherwise modified by the terms of this Agreement) as follows:

Names	Initial Percentage Share of Profits and Capital

§ 2.4   Interest

No interest shall be paid on any contribution to the capital of the Partnership.

§ 2.5   Return of Capital Contributions

No Partner shall have the right to demand the return of his capital contributions except as herein provided.

FIGURE 29-1 continued

§ 2.6 Rights of Priority

Except as herein provided, the individual Partners shall have no right to any priority over each other as to the return of capital contributions except as herein provided.

§ 2.7 Distributions

Distributions to the Partners of net operating profits of the Partnership, as hereinafter defined, shall be made at (*least monthly/such times as the Managing Partner(s) shall reasonably agree.*) Such distributions shall be made to the Partners simultaneously.

For the purpose of this Agreement, net operating profit for any accounting period shall mean the gross receipts of the Partnership for such period, less the sum of all cash expenses of operation of the Partnership, and such sums as may be necessary to establish a reserve for operating expenses.

§ 2.8 Compensation

No Partner shall be entitled to receive any compensation from the Partnership, nor shall any Partner receive any drawing account from the Partnership.

Article III
MANAGEMENT

§ 3.1 Managing Partners

The Managing Partner(s) shall be [*Names*] [*or* "all partners"].

§ 3.2 Voting

The Managing Partner(s) shall have the right to vote as to the management and conduct of the business of the Partnership as follows:

Names   **Vote**

Article IV
DISSOLUTION

§ 4.1 Dissolution

In the event that the Partnership shall hereinafter be dissolved for any reason whatsoever, a full and general account of its assets, liabilities and transactions shall at once be taken. Such assets may be sold and turned into cash as soon as possible and all debts and other amounts due the Partnership collected. The proceeds thereof shall thereupon be applied as follows:

(a) To discharge the debts and liabilities of the Partnership and the expenses of liquidation.

(b) To pay each Partner or his legal representative any unpaid salary, drawing account, interest or profits to which he shall then be entitled and in addition, to repay to any Partner his capital contributions in excess of his original capital contribution.

(c) To divide the surplus, if any, among the Partners or their representatives as follows:

(1) First (to the extent of each Partner's then capital account) in proportion to their then capital accounts.

(2) Then according to each Partner's then Percentage Share of *Capital/Income*.

§ 4.2 Right To Demand Property

No Partner shall have the right to demand and receive property in kind for his distribution.

Witnesses   **Partners**

_____   _____

_____   _____

Dated: _____

Adopted from "West's Legal Forms," 2d ed. by Paul Lieberman. Copyright © 1981 by West Publishing Co. Reprinted with permission.

Firm Name In the interest of acquiring and retaining good will, a partnership should have a firm name. The name selected by the partners should not be identical with or deceptively similar to the name of any other existing business concern. It may be the name of the partners or of any one of them, or the partners may decide to operate the business under a fictitious or assumed name, such as "Peachtree Restaurant" or "Globe Theater" or "Paradise Laundry." A partnership may not use a name that would be likely to indicate to the public that it is a corporation.

Nearly all of the States have enacted statutes that require any person or persons conducting or transacting any business under an assumed or fictitious name to file in a designated public office a certificate setting forth the name under which the business is conducted and the real names and addresses of all persons conducting the business as partners or proprietors. The purpose of such a statute is to disclose and make available to the public the real names of all parties who choose to deal with the public under an assumed or fictitious name. When a person ceases to be a member of a partnership operating under an assumed name or a new member is added and the partnership continues to use the assumed name, a new certificate must be filed.

Tests of Partnership Existence

Partnerships can be formed without the slightest formality. Consequently, if two or more individuals share the control and profits of a business, the law may consider them partners without regard to how they might characterize their relationship. Thus, associates frequently discover, to their chagrin, that they have inadvertently formed a partnership and have thereby subjected themselves to the duties and liabilities of partners. The existence of a common interest for business purposes is the fundamental test of the existence of a partnership. By this it is meant that there exists a common interest in profits and losses, and a common authority to conduct the business operations. In short, there must be **co-ownership of a business.**

Business Element The UPA provides that co-ownership, whether it is joint tenancy, tenancy in common, tenancy by the entireties, joint property, common property, or part ownership, does not of itself establish a partnership, even though the co-owners share the profits derived from use of the property. For a partnership to exist, there must be a business in addition to the mere co-ownership of property. Because an intention to acquire profits is essential to the conduct of a business enterprise, it is clear that an unincorporated nonprofit association, such as a social club, a literary society, or a fraternal or political organization, is not a business and therefore not a partnership. Where persons are associated together for mutual financial gain on a temporary or limited basis involving a single transaction or relatively few isolated transactions, no partnership results because the parties are not engaged in a continuous series of commercial activities necessary to constitute a business. Co-ownership of the means or instrumentality of accomplishing a single business transaction or a limited series of transactions may result in a joint venture but not a general partnership. (We discuss joint ventures in Chapter 32.)

Joint venture–an association of two or more persons to carry on a single business enterprise for profit

For example, Emmett and Beth are joint owners of shares of the capital stock of a corporation, have a joint bank account, and have inherited or purchased real estate as joint tenants or tenants in common. They share the dividends paid on the stock, the interest on the bank account, and the net proceeds from the sale or lease of the real estate. Emmett and Beth are not partners. Although they are co-owners and share profits, they are not engaged in the carrying on of a business, and hence no partnership results. On the other hand, if Emmett and Beth were engaged in continuous transactions of buying and selling real estate over a period of time and were carrying on a business of trading in real estate, a partnership relation would exist between them, regardless of whether they regarded one another as partners.

In another example, A, B, and C each inherit an undivided one-third interest in a hotel and, instead of selling the property, decide by an informal and incomplete agreement to continue operation of the hotel. The operation of a hotel is a business, and, as co-owners of a hotel business, A, B, and C are partners and are subject to all of the rights, duties, and incidents arising from the partnership relation.

Co-ownership   Although co-ownership of *property* used in a business is neither a necessary nor a sufficient condition for the existence of a partnership, the co-ownership of a *business* is essential. In determining the element of co-ownership of a business, factors such as the sharing of profits, the sharing of losses, and the right to manage and control the business are important.

The receipt by a person of a share of the **profits** of a business is *prima facie* evidence that he is a partner in the business. However, the UPA provides that no inference of the existence of a partnership relation shall be drawn where such profits are received in payment:

1. of a debt by installments or otherwise;

2. of wages of an employee or rent to a landlord;

3. of an annuity to a widow or representative of a deceased partner;

4. of interest on a loan, though the amount of payment may vary with the profits of the business, or

5. as consideration for the sale of the good will of a business or other property by installments, or otherwise.

These transactions do not give rise to a presumption that the party is a partner because the law assumes it more likely that the creditor, employee, landlord, or other recipient of a share of the profits is not a co-owner. However, it is possible to establish that such a person was a partner by proof of other facts and circumstances. For example, the payment of money or the transfer of title to property in exchange for a share of the profits may be either the capital contribution of a partner or a loan or sale on credit by a creditor. Outside the usual incidents of a loan or a sale on credit, the test most frequently employed in doubtful situations is whether an obligation has been created to pay for the property received or to repay the money advanced in any event. If the party sought to be charged as a partner is entitled at some time to receive payment for the money or property that he advanced, he is generally not a partner but a creditor. Moreover, the sharing of *gross returns*, in contrast to profits, does *not* of itself establish a partnership. This is so whether or not the persons sharing the gross returns have a joint or common interest in any property from which the returns are derived.

An agreement to share in or contribute to the *losses* of a business, however, affords strong evidence of an ownership interest. Few jurisdictions insist on an express agreement of loss sharing for a partnership to exist, but all consider such an agreement compelling proof of the existence of a partnership.

By itself, evidence as to participation in the *management* or **control** of a business is not conclusive proof of a partnership relation. A voice in management and control of a business may be given, in a limited degree, to an employee, a landlord, or a creditor. On the other hand, one who is actually a partner may take no active part in the affairs of the firm and may, by agreement with his co-partners, forego all right to exercise any control over the ordinary affairs of the business. In any event, the right to participate in control is an important factor considered by the courts in conjunction with other factors, profit sharing in particular.

Figure 29-2 illustrates the tests for determining whether a partnership exists, as do the following two cases.

CHAIKEN v. EMPLOYMENT SECURITY COMMISSION

Superior Court of Delaware, 1971.
274 A.2d 707.

FACTS: Chaiken entered into separate but nearly identical agreements with Strazella and Spitzer to operate a barber shop. Under the terms of the "partnership" agreements, Chaiken would provide barber chairs, supplies, and licenses, while the other two would provide tools of the trade. The agreements also stated that gross returns from the partnership were to be divided on a percentage basis among the three men and that Chaiken would decide all matters of partnership policy. Finally, the agreements stated hours of work and holidays for Strazella and Spitzer and required Chaiken to hold and distribute all receipts. The Delaware Employment Security Commission, however, determined that Strazella and Spitzer were not partners of Chaiken but rather were his employees. The commission then brought this action to assess unemployment compensation contributions against Chaiken for the two barbers. Chaiken contends that they are not employees but partners pursuant to written partnership agreements. As partners, Chaiken would not be liable for unemployment compensation contributions.

DECISION: Judgment for the commission. A partnership is an association of two or more persons to carry on as co-owners a business for profit. However, the mere existence of a writing labeled "partnership" agreement and the characterization of its signatories as "partners" does not conclusively establish the existence of a partnership. Rather, the intention of the parties, as explained by the wording of the agreement, is controlling.

Here, several aspects of the agreements between Chaiken and the two barbers, when considered as a whole, negate the finding of a partnership arrangement. First, Chaiken reserved the exclusive right to determine partnership policy. Second, distribution of assets upon dissolution of a partnership is to occur only after all partnership liabilities have been satisfied. Here, however, there was no such condition placed on post-dissolution distributions to Strazella and Spitzer. Third, the agreements set forth holidays and hours of work for the two barbers, subjects not commonly found in partnership agreements. Finally, and of most importance, the agreements provide for a division of gross returns, not of net profits. The intent to divide profits is an indispensable requisite of a partnership. All of these factors taken together negate a finding of partnership intent here. Rather, Strazella and Spitzer are employees of Chaiken, and unemployment compensation contributions on their behalf must be paid.

CUTLER v. BOWEN

Supreme Court of Utah, 1975.
543 P.2d 1349.

FACTS: Cutler worked as a bartender for Bowen until they orally agreed that Bowen would have the authority and responsibility for the entire active management and operation of the tavern business known as the Havana Club. Each was to receive $100 per week, plus half of the net profits. The business continued under this arrangement for four years until the building was taken over by the Salt Lake City Redevelopment Agency. The agency paid $10,000 to Bowen as compensation for disruption. The business, however, was terminated after Bowen and Cutler failed to find a new, suitable location. Cutler, alleging a partnership with Bowen, then brought this action against him to recover one-half of the $10,000. Bowen contends that he is entitled to the entire $10,000 because he was the sole owner of the business and that Cutler was merely his employee. Cutler argues that although Bowen owned the physical assets of the business, she, as a partner in the business, is entitled to one-half of the compensation that was paid for the business's good will and going-concern value.

DECISION: Judgment for Cutler. Cutler was a partner and, therefore, is now entitled to one-half of the relocation compensation. A primary consideration in determining whether a partnership exists is the nature of the contribution that each party makes to the enterprise. It need not be in the form of tangible assets or capital but may be in the form of services and management. Cutler's efforts were largely responsible for the going-concern and good will value of the business. Further, Cutler's involvement in the business was such that she would have been liable for any losses that may have occurred in its operation. Therefore, as a partner, she is entitled to participate in any profits or advantages that inure to it, including the compensation paid by the Redevelopment Agency.

Partnership Capital

Partnership capital–total money and property contributed by partners for permanent use by the partnership

The total money and property contributed by the partners and dedicated to permanent use in the enterprise is the **partnership capital.** Unlike a corporation, a partnership is not required to have a minimum amount of capitalization before starting business. Nonetheless, no partner may withdraw any part of his capital contribution without the consent of all the partners, except when the partnership is dissolved.

Partnership property–sum of all of the partnership's assets

Partnership property, on the other hand, is the sum of all of the partnership assets (including capital contributions), and it may vary in amount, whereas partnership capital is a fixed amount, changed only by an amendment to the articles of partnership. All property originally brought into the partnership or subsequently acquired by the partnership is partnership property.

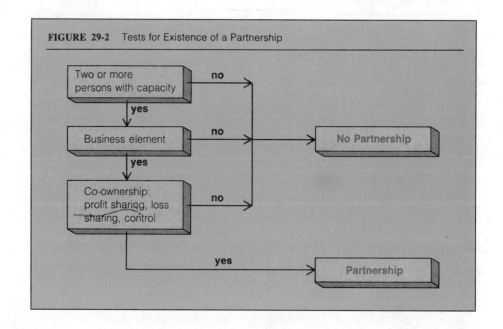

FIGURE 29-2   Tests for Existence of a Partnership

Unless the contrary intention appears, property acquired with partnership funds is also partnership property.

A partner, by the terms of the agreement, may contribute no capital but only his skill and services, or a partner may contribute the use of certain property rather than the property itself. For example, a partner who owns a store building may contribute to the partnership the use of the building but not the building itself. The building is therefore not partnership property, and the amount of capital contributed by this partner is the reasonable value of the rental of the building.

Although in accounting practice partnership profits are frequently included in the capital amount, a clear differentiation should be made between capital and profits. Likewise, a loan by a partner to the firm should be distinguished from capital. A partner is entitled to her share of the profits and to repayment of money advanced as a loan without any new agreement with her co-partners, but a withdrawal of capital requires a new agreement. Furthermore, on dissolution, a debt owed to a partner by the partnership has priority over the rights of partners to return of capital.

Title to real estate that is properly a partnership asset, as where purchased with partnership funds or specifically made a capital contribution, may stand in the name of the partnership, an individual partner, or a third party. The UPA alters the common law by permitting title to real estate to be conveyed to a partnership in the partnership name. Title so acquired may be conveyed only in the partnership name.

A question may arise whether property owned by a partner before formation of the partnership and used in the partnership business is a capital contribution and an asset of the partnership. Whether it is a partnership asset determines the rights of creditors and partners in the property. The fact that legal title to the property remains unchanged is not conclusive evidence that it has not become a partnership asset. An intention that property is partnership property may be inferred from any of the following facts: (1) the property was improved with partnership funds; (2) the property was carried on the books of the partnership as an asset; (3) taxes, liens, or expenses, such as insurance, were paid by the partnership; (4) income or proceeds of the property were treated as partnership funds; or (5) admissions or declarations by the partners.

GAULDIN v. CORN

Court of Appeals of Missouri, Southern District, Division One, 1980. 595 S.W.2d 329.

FACTS: In 1966, Gauldin and Corn entered into a partnership for the purpose of raising cattle and hogs. The two men were to share equally all costs, labor, losses, and profits. The business was started on land which was owned by Corn's parents but was later acquired by Corn and his wife. No rent was ever requested or paid for use of the land. Partnership funds were used to bulldoze and clear the land, to repair and build fences, and to seed and fertilize the land. In 1970, at a cost of $2,487.50, a machine shed was built on the land. In 1975, a Cargill unit was built on the land at a cost of $8,000. When the partnership dissolved in 1976, Gauldin paid Corn $7,500 for the "removable" assets. However, the two had no agreement regarding the distribution of the barn and the Cargill unit. Gauldin sues Corn, claiming he is entitled to one-half of the value of the two buildings.

DECISION: Judgment for Gauldin. The well-established rule is that improvements made upon lands owned by one partner, if made with partnership funds for purposes of the partnership business, are the property of the partnership. The non-landowning partner is then entitled to his proportionate share of the value of the improvements. However, this general rule only applies where there is no agreement between the partners controlling the disposition of the improvements.

Here, Gauldin and Corn had no agreement regarding the disposition of the fixed assets upon the partnership's dissolution. The barn and Cargill unit, acquired with partnership funds for the purpose of raising cattle and hogs, are such fixed assets. Therefore, Gauldin is entitled to his proportionate share (one-half) of the value of the two buildings at the time of the partnership's dissolution.

CHAPTER SUMMARY

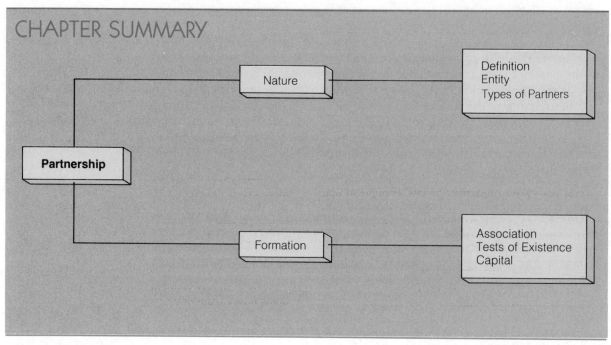

KEY TERMS

Partnership
Person
Legal entity
Aggregate
General partner

Limited partner
Silent partner
Secret partner
Dormant partner

Articles of partnership
Joint venture
Partnership capital
Partnership property

PROBLEMS

1. A and B are joint owners of shares of stock of a corporation, have a joint bank account, and have purchased and own as tenants in common a piece of real estate. They share equally the dividends paid on the stock, the interest on the bank account, and the rent from the real estate. Without the knowledge of A, B makes a trip to inspect the real estate and on his way runs over X. X sues A and B for his personal injuries, joining A as defendant on the theory that A was B's partner. Is A liable?

2. Smith, Jones, and Brown were creditors of White, who operated a grain elevator known as White's Elevator. White was heavily involved and about to fail when the three creditors mentioned agreed to take title to his elevator property and pay all the debts. It was also agreed that White should continue as manager of the business at a salary of $1,500 per month and that all profits of the business were to be paid to Smith, Jones, and Brown. It was further agreed that they could dispense with White's services at any time, and he was also at liberty to quit when he pleased. White accepted the proposition and continued to operate the business as before, buying and selling grain, incurring obligations, and borrowing money at the bank in his own name for the business. He did, however, tell the banker of the transaction with Smith, Jones, and Brown, and other former creditors of the business knew of it. It worked successfully and for several years paid substantial profits, enough so that Smith, Jones, and Brown had received back nearly all that they had originally advanced. Were Smith, Jones, and Brown partners? Explain.

3. A and B engaged in the grocery business as partners. In one year they earned considerable money, and at the end of the year, they invested a part of the profits in oil land. Title to the land was taken in their names as tenants in common. The investment was fortunate, for oil was discovered near the land, and its value increased many times. A died, leaving a wife and one child. Who owns the land? Why?

4. A owned an old roadside building that she believed could be easily converted into an antique shop. She talked to her friend B, an antique fancier, and they executed the following written agreement:

(a) A would supply the building, all utilities, and $10,000 capital for purchasing antiques.

(b) B would supply $3,000 for purchasing an-

tiques, A to repay her at the time the business terminates.

(c) B would manage the shop, make all purchases, and receive a salary of $100 per week plus 5 percent of the gross receipts.

(d) Fifty percent of the net profits would go into the purchase of new stock. The balance of the net profits would go to A.

(e) The business would operate under the name Roadside Antiques.

Business went poorly, and the result after one year is a debt of $4,000 owing to Old Fashioned, Inc., the principal supplier of antiques purchased by B in the name of Roadside Antiques. Old Fashioned, Inc., sues Roadside Antiques, and A and B as partners. Decision?

5. Clark owned a vacant lot. Bird was engaged in building houses. An oral agreement was entered into between Clark and Bird by which Bird was to erect a house on the lot. When the house and lot were sold, Bird was to have his money first. Clark was then to have the agreed value of the lot, and the profits were to be equally divided. Did a partnership exist?

6. X, Y, and Z formed a partnership for the purpose of betting on boxing matches. X and Y would become friendly with various boxers and offer them bribes to lose certain bouts. Z would then place large bets, using money contributed by all three, and would collect the winnings. After Z had accumulated a large sum of money, X and Y demanded their share, but Z refused to make any split. X and Y then brought suit in a court of equity to compel Z to account for the profits of the partnership. What decision?

7. A, B, C, and D, residents of State X, were partners doing business under the trade name of Morning Glory Nursery. A owned a one-third interest and B, C, and D, two-ninths each. The partners acquired three tracts of land in State X for the purpose of the partnership. Two of the tracts were acquired in the names of the four partners, "trading and doing business as Morning Glory Nursery." The third tract was acquired in the names of the individuals, the trade name not appearing in the deed. This third tract was acquired by the partnership out of partnership funds and for partnership purposes. Who owns each of the three tracts? Why?

RIGHTS AND DUTIES

The operation and management of a partnership involve interactions among the partners as well as with third persons. In this chapter we consider both of these relationships. The first part of the chapter focuses on the rights and duties of the partners among themselves, which are determined by the partnership agreement, the common law, and the Uniform Partnership Act. The second part of the chapter focuses on the relations of partners to third persons dealing with the partnership, which are governed by the law of agency and the UPA.

Relationships of Partners to One Another

When parties enter into a partnership or other business association, the law imposes certain obligations on the parties and also gives them specific rights. So long as the rights of third parties are not affected and standards of fairness are maintained, the parties may by agreement vary these rights and obligations.

The legal duties imposed on partners in their relationship among themselves are (1) the duty of loyalty (the fiduciary duty), (2) the duty of obedience, and (3) the duty of care. These duties correspond precisely with those duties owed by an agent to his principal and reflect the fact that a large part of the law of partnership is the law of agency.

Likewise, the law gives partners certain rights, which include: (1) rights in specific partnership property; (2) their interest in the partnership; (3) the right to share in distributions; (4) the right to participate in management; (5) the right to choose associates; and (6) enforcement rights.

These rights and duties remain in force until the partnership is terminated.

Duties Among Partners

Fiduciary Duty

A fiduciary relationship exists among the members of a partnership based on the high standard of trust and confidence that they have a right to place in one another. Each partner owes a duty of absolute and **utmost good faith** and **loyalty** to his partners. It is only on such basis that so intimate a business relationship can function.

The law of partnership has adopted as part of the fiduciary duty the requirement of the law of agency that a partner shall not make a profit other than his agreed compensation, shall not compete with the partnership, and shall not otherwise profit from the relationship at the expense of the partnership. The UPA states that every partner must account to the partnership for any benefit and hold as trustee for it any profits he made without the consent of the other partners from any transaction connected with the formation, conduct, or liquidation of the partnership or from any use by him of its property. A partner may not deal at arm's length with his partners. He may not prefer himself over the firm. His duty is one of undivided and continuous loyalty to his partners.

The extent of this fiduciary duty, which binds all fiduciaries and not just partners, has been most eloquently expressed by the often quoted words of Judge (later Justice) Cardozo:

> Joint adventures, like copartners, owe to one another, while the enterprise continues, the duty of the *finest loyalty*. Many forms of conduct permissible in a workaday world for those acting at arm's length, are forbidden to those bound by fiduciary ties. A trustee is held to something stricter than the morals of the market place. *Not honesty alone, but the punctilio of an honor the most sensitive, is then the standard of behavior.* As to this there has developed a tradition that is unbending and inveterate. Uncompromising rigidity has been the attitude of courts of equity when petitioned to undermine the rule of undivided loyalty by the "disintegrating erosion" of particular exceptions. Only thus has the level of conduct for fiduciaries been kept at a level higher than that trodden by the crowd. It will not consciously be lowered by any judgment of this court [emphasis added].

The next case illustrates how rigorously the courts enforce the fiduciary duty.

CLEMENT v. CLEMENT

Supreme Court of Pennsylvania, 1970.
436 Pa. 466, 260 A.2d 728.

FACTS: Charles and L. W. Clement are brothers who had formed a partnership lasting forty years. In 1964, Charles discovered that his brother, who was the brighter of the two and kept the partnership's books, had made several substantial personal investments with funds improperly withdrawn from the partnership. He then brought an action in equity seeking dissolution of the partnership, appointment of a receiver, and an accounting. The chancellor of the court of equity issued a decree in favor of Charles but the court *en banc* reversed his decision.

DECISION: Decree for Charles. There is a fiduciary relationship between partners such that a person does not have to deal with his partner as though he were the opposite party in an arm's length transaction. Where a partner commingles partnership funds with is own and generally deals loosely with partnership assets, he has the burden of proving that he did not breach his fiduciary duty. Here, L. W. dealt loosely with partnership funds. At various times he made substantial investments in his own name, but he is unable to explain where he got the funds to make those investments. The burden is on L. W. to show the source of the funds that have gone into his investments. L. W. has not satisfied that burden, and, therefore, Charles is entitled to recover even though he cannot trace the money invested by his brother dollar for dollar from the diverted partnership funds.

Duty of Obedience

A partner owes his partners a duty to act in obedience to the partnership agreement and to any business decisions properly made by the partnership.

A partner who violates this duty is individually liable for any resulting loss. For example, a partner who violates a specific agreement not to extend credit to relatives and advances money from partnership funds and sells goods on credit to an insolvent relative is personally liable to his partners for the unpaid debt.

Duty of Care

A partner must manage the partnership affairs without culpable negligence. **Culpable negligence** is something more than ordinary negligence, yet short of gross negligence. Thus, a partner does not breach her duty of care if she makes honest errors of judgment or fails to use ordinary skill in transacting partnership business so long as she is not culpably negligent. For example, a partner assigned to keep the partnership books uses a complicated system of bookkeeping and produces numerous mistakes. Since these errors result simply from poor judgment rather than fraud and are not intended to and do not operate to the personal advantage of the bookkeeping partner, the negligent partner is *not* liable to her copartners for any resulting loss.

> Culpable negligence–greater than ordinary negligence but less than gross negligence

Rights Among Partners

Rights in Specific Partnership Property

A partner's ownership interest in any specific item of partnership property is that of a **tenant in partnership.** This type of ownership, which exists only in a partnership, has the following principal characteristics:

> Tenancy in partnership–type of joint ownership that determines partners' rights in specific partnership property

1. Each partner has an equal right with his copartners to possess partnership property for partnership purposes, but he has no right to possess it for any other purpose without the consent of his copartners.

2. A partner may not make an individual assignment of his right in specific partnership property.

3. A partner's interest in specific partnership property is not subject to attachment or execution by his individual creditors. It is subject to attachment or execution only on a claim against the partnership.

4. Upon the death of a partner, his right in specific partnership property vests in the surviving partner or partners. Upon the death of the last surviving partner, his right in such property vests in his legal representative.

Partner's Interest in the Partnership

In addition to owning as a tenant in partnership every specific item of partnership property, each partner has an interest in the partnership that is defined as his share of the **profits** and **surplus** and is expressly stated to be personal property.

> Interest in partnership–partner's share in the partnership's profits and surplus

Assignability A partner may sell or assign her interest in the partnership, but this does not cause dissolution. The new owner does *not* become a partner, does not succeed to the partner's rights to participate in the management, and does not have access to the information available to a member of the firm as a matter of right. She is merely entitled to receive the share of profits and rights on liquidation to which the assigning partner would otherwise be entitled. The assigning partner remains a partner with all the other rights and duties of a partner.

Charging order–judicial lien against a partner's interest in the partnership

Creditors' Rights   A partner's interest is subject to the claims of that partner's creditors who may obtain a charging order (a type of judicial lien) against the partner's interest. A creditor who has charged the interest of a partner with a judgment debt may apply for the appointment of a receiver. The court may appoint a receiver for the partner's interest who will receive and hold for the benefit of the creditor the share of profits that ordinarily would be paid to the partner. Neither the judgment creditor nor the receiver becomes a partner, and neither is entitled to participate in the management or to have access to information.

Figure 30–1 compares a partner's rights in specific partnership property with his interest in the partnership, as does the next case.

BOHONUS v. AMERCO

Supreme Court of Arizona, 1979.
124 Ariz. 88, 602 P.2d 469.

FACTS: Amerco secured a personal judgment against Bohonus. The company now seeks to enforce that judgment by requesting a judicial sale of the assets and property of a partnership of which Bohonus is a member and in which he has an interest.

DECISION: Judgment for the partnership. The property rights of a partner include his rights in specific partnership property, his interest in the partnership, and his right to participate in the management. But only the partner's interest in the partnership—his share of the profits and surplus—can be charged and sold to satisfy the individual debt of that partner. In contrast, his right in specific partnership property is not subject to attachment or execution except on a claim against the partnership. Accordingly, a court cannot order the sale of partnership assets to satisfy the individual debt of Bohonus.

Right to Distributions

Distribution–transfer of partnership property from the partnership to a partner

A distribution is a transfer of partnership property from the partnership to a partner. Distributions include a division of profits, a return of capital contributions, a repayment of a loan or advance made by a partner to the partnership, and a payment made to compensate a partner for services rendered to the partnership.

FIGURE 30-1   Partnership Property Compared with Partner's Interest

	Partnership Property	**Partner's Interest**
Definition	Tenant in Partnership	Share of profits and surplus
Possession	For partnership purposes and not for individual purposes	Intangible, personal property right
Assignability	NO: unless all other partners assign their rights in the property	YES: but the assignee does not become a partner
Attachment	YES: but only for a claim against the partnership	YES: by a charging order
Inheritance	NO: goes to surviving partner(s)	YES: passes to the personal representative

Right to Share in Profits   Because a partnership is an association to carry on a business for profit, each partner is entitled, unless otherwise agreed, to a share of the profits. Conversely, each partner must contribute toward the losses. If the partners do not have an agreement about dividing the profits, the partners share the profits *equally*, regardless of the ratio of their financial contributions or their degree of participation in the management. Unless the partnership agreement provides otherwise, the partners bear losses in the *same proportion* in which they share profits. The agreement may, however, validly provide for bearing losses in some different proportion than that in which profits are shared.

Right to Return of Capital   After all partnership creditors have been paid, each partner is entitled to be repaid his capital contribution when the firm is terminated. Unless otherwise agreed, a partner is not entitled to interest on his capital contribution. His share of the profits of the partnership may be considered as earnings on his investment of capital. However, if there is a delay in return of his capital contribution, he is entitled to interest at the legal rate from the date when it should have been repaid.

Right to Return of Advances   If a partner makes advances (loans) over and above his agreed capital contribution, he is entitled to repayment of the advance plus interest on it. His position as a creditor of the firm, however, is subordinate to the claims of creditors who are not partners. In addition, a partner who has incurred personal liabilities in the ordinary and proper conduct of the business of the firm or who has made payments on behalf of the partnership is entitled to indemnification or repayment.

Right to Compensation   The UPA provides that, unless otherwise agreed, *no* partner is entitled to payment for acting in the partnership business. This represents the common law viewpoint that whatever a partner does for the partnership, he is doing for himself. If the partnership agreement states that one partner is to perform a substantial or disproportionate share of the work of conducting the business, that partner may, by agreement among all of the partners, receive a salary or an increased percentage of the profits. If the partners do not have such an agreement, he is entitled to no salary but only his share of the profits. The only exception to the rule is that a surviving partner is entitled to reasonable compensation for his services in winding up the partnership affairs.

Right to Participate in Management

Although each of the partners may have responsibility for a certain area of the business, they all, unless otherwise agreed, have an *equal* voice in its management. The majority generally governs the actions and decisions of the partnership, except that *all* the partners must consent to any actions that are contrary to the partnership agreement. There is conflict, however, among the authorities as to what should be done if there is an equal division of opinion resulting in a stalemate, as in the next case. Some courts hold that, in such cases, a partner is free to go ahead and deal with third parties. Others hold to the contrary.

**NATIONAL BISCUIT v.
C. N. STROUD**

Supreme Court of North
Carolina, 1959.
249 N.C. 467, 106 S.E.2d 692.

FACTS: Stroud and Freeman are general partners in Stroud's Food Center, a grocery store. Nothing in the articles of partnership restricts the power or authority of either partner to act in respect to the ordinary and legitimate business of the Food Center. In late 1955, however, Stroud informed National Biscuit that he would not be personally responsible for any more bread sold to the partnership. Then, in February 1956, at the request of Freeman, National Biscuit sold and delivered more bread to the Food Center. When payment was refused, National Biscuit brought this action against the partner Stroud and the partnership to recover the value of the bread delivered to the Food Center.

DECISION: Judgment for National Biscuit. Freeman's purchase bound both the partnership and his copartner Stroud. Freeman is a general partner with no restrictions on his authority to act within the scope of partnership business. Under the U.P.A., then, he had "equal rights in the management and conduct of the partnership business." Stroud could not restrict the power and authority of Freeman to buy bread for the partnership as a going concern, for such a purchase was an "ordinary matter connected with the partnership business," for the purpose of its business and within its scope. Such a restriction on Freeman's powers could only be implemented by a majority of the partners, which Stroud was not.

Right to Choose Associates

No partner may be forced to accept any person as a partner whom she does not choose. This is because of the fiduciary relationship between the parties, and because each partner has a right to take part in the management of the business, to handle the partnership assets for partnership purposes, and to act as an agent of the partnership. It is possible that a partner, by her negligence, injudiciousness, or dishonesty, may bring financial loss or ruin to her copartners. Because of the close relationship involved, partnerships must necessarily be founded on mutual trust and confidence. All this finds expression in the term **delectus personae,** which literally means, "choice of the person" and indicates the right one has to choose or select her partners. This principle is embodied in the UPA, which provides: "No person can become a member of a partnership without the consent of **all** the partners" (emphasis added).

Delectus personae–partner's right to choose who may become a member of the partnership

As we mentioned earlier, when a partner sells her interest, the purchaser does not become a partner and is not entitled to participate in the management. When the partnership terminates, he is entitled only to receive the profits and liquidation rights for the share that he bought.

Enforcement Rights

As we have discussed, the partnership relationship creates a number of duties and rights among the partners. Accordingly, partnership law provides the partners with the means to enforce these rights and duties. First, each partner is allowed to have access to all information concerning the partnership and its books. Second, under certain circumstances, a partner may obtain a judicially ordered and supervised accounting (a detailed statement of financial transactions, including a balance owed) in an action brought in a court of equity against the partnership or his partners.

Right to Information and Inspection of the Books   Each partner may demand to have full information about all partnership matters at any time, and each has a duty to supply other partners with the information that he possesses. The right to demand information extends also to the legal representative of a deceased partner for a reasonable time following the dissolution of the partnership.

Unless the partners agree otherwise, the books of the partnership are to be kept at the principal place of business at all times, and each partner has an absolute right to have access to them, to inspect them, and to copy any of them. This right may also be exercised by a duly authorized attorney or accountant on behalf of a partner.

Right to an Accounting   At common law and under the UPA, a partner is entitled to an accounting, which is an equitable proceeding for a comprehensive and effective settlement of all partnership affairs. An accounting is designed to produce and evaluate all testimony relevant to the various claims of the partners. A partner may invoke the power of a court of equity to decree an accounting whenever (1) he is wrongfully excluded from the partnership business or possession of its property by his copartners, (2) the partnership agreement provides, (3) a partner makes a profit in violation of his fiduciary duty, or (4) other circumstances render it just and reasonable. A partner is not permitted to sue the partnership at law, because he would be suing himself, but he may sue in equity in an action for an accounting.

Accounting–equitable proceeding for a complete settlement of all partnership affairs

---

CENTRAL TRUST & SAFE DEPOSIT CO. v. RESPASS

Court of Appeals of Kentucky, 1902.
112 Ky. 606, 66 S.W. 421.

FACTS: Respass and Sharp, as partners, owned and managed a racing stable and, in addition, were engaged in bookmaking, that is, accepting bets on race horses. When Sharp died, $4,724—representing the undistributed profits of the bookmaking business—was on deposit in Sharp's personal bank account. Respass brought suit against Central Trust & Safe Deposit Co., the executor of Sharp's will, for an accounting of profits from their gambling business. Respass claims he is entitled to one-half of those profits.

DECISION: Judgment for Central Trust denying an accounting of the gambling profits. When a partnership conducts an illegal business, no partner is entitled to an accounting of the profits gained by the illegal venture. Nor will the courts grant to any of the partners any recovery for losses, expenses, contribution, or reimbursement. Since gambling was illegal, Respass, a partner in the illicit business, cannot obtain an accounting to recover his half of the gambling profits.

Relationship Between Partners and Third Parties

In the course of doing business, partners may also acquire rights and incur duties to third parties. Under the law of **agency** a principal is liable on contracts made on his behalf by his duly authorized agents and is liable in tort for the wrongful acts his agents commit in the course of their employment. A large part of the law of partnership is the law of agency, and most problems arising between partners and third persons require the application of principles of agency law. This relationship is made explicit by the UPA, which states, "The law of agency shall apply under this act" and "Every partner is an agent of the partnership for the purpose of its business."

Contracts of Partnership

Contract Liability of Partners

The act of every partner binds the partnership on transactions *within* the scope of the partnership business unless the partner does not have actual or apparent authority to so act. If the partnership is bound, then each partner has **unlimited personal liability** for that partnership obligation. The UPA provides that partners are jointly liable on all debts and contract obligations

Joint liability–liability where creditor must sue all of the obligors as a group

of the partnership. As a consequence, any suit against the partners must name all the partners as defendants.

Authority to Bind Partnership

A partner may bind the partnership by her act (a) if she has actual authority, express or implied, to perform the act or (b) if she has apparent authority to perform the act. If the act is not apparently within the scope of the partnership business, then the partnership is bound only where the partner has actual authority. In these cases the third person dealing with the partner assumes the risk of the existence of such actual authority. See Figure 30–2.

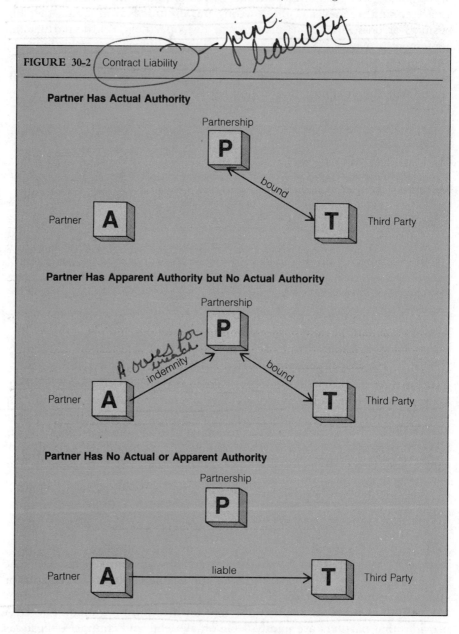

FIGURE 30-2 Contract Liability

Partner Has Actual Authority

Partnership
P
Partner A
bound
T Third Party

Partner Has Apparent Authority but No Actual Authority

Partnership
P
Partner A
indemnity
bound
T Third Party

Partner Has No Actual or Apparent Authority

Partnership
P
Partner A
liable
T Third Party

Actual Express Authority   The actual express authority of partners may be specifically set forth in the partnership agreement or in an additional agreement between the partners and may be written or oral. In addition, it may arise from decisions made by a majority of the partners regarding ordinary matters connected with the partnership business.

The UPA provides that the following acts do **not** bind the partnership unless authorized by **all** of the partners:

1. assignment of partnership property for the benefit of its creditors;

2. disposal of the good will of the business;

3. any act that would make it impossible to carry on the ordinary business of the partnership;

4. confession of a judgment;

5. submission of a partnership claim or liability to arbitration.

In addition, a partner who does not have actual authority from all of her partners may not bind the partnership by any of the following acts, which under ordinary circumstances are clearly outside the scope of the partnership: (1) execution of contracts of guaranty and suretyship in the firm name; (2) sale of partnership property not held for sale in the usual course of business; and (3) payment of individual debts out of partnership assets.

Actual Implied Authority   Actual implied authority is authority that is neither expressly granted nor expressly denied but is reasonably deduced from the nature of the partnership, the terms of the partnership agreement, or the relations of the partners. For example, a partner has implied authority to hire and fire employees whose services are necessary to carry on the business of the partnership. In addition, a partner has implied authority to purchase property necessary for the business.

Apparent Authority   Apparent authority (which may or may not be actual) is authority that may, in view of the circumstances and the conduct of the parties, be reasonably considered to exist by a third person who has no knowledge or notice of the lack of actual authority. For example, a partner has apparent authority to indorse checks and notes, to make representations and warranties in selling goods, and to enter into contracts for advertising. A third person may not rely on apparent authority in any situation where he is put on notice or already knows that the partner does not, or may not, have actual authority. In these situations, the third person must make sure of the actual authority of the partner or assume the risk of its absence.

Confession of judgment—written agreement by debtor authorizing creditor to obtain a court judgment in the event debtor defaults

FACTS: Hodge and Voeller, the managing partner of the Pay-Ont Drive-In Theatre, signed a contract for the sale of a small parcel of land belonging to the partnership. The parcel was not used in theater operations except for the last 20 feet, which was necessary for the theater's driveway. The agreement stated that it was between Hodge and the partnership with Voeller signing for the partnership. Voeller claims that he told Hodge before signing that a plat plan would have to be approved by the other partners before the sale. Hodge denies this and sues for specific performance, claiming that Voeller had actual and apparent authority to bind the partnership. The partners argue that Voeller had no such authority and that Hodge knew this.

HODGE v. GARRETT

Supreme Court of Idaho, 1980.
101 Idaho 397, 614 P.2d 420.

DECISION: Judgment for the partners. Under the UPA a partner may convey legal title to property held in the partnership name. However, the partnership may recover the property (except from a good faith purchaser) if (1) the conveying partner did not have apparent authority, or (2) he did not have any authority and the purchaser knew this fact.

Here, although Voeller was managing partner, selling the land adjacent to the theater is not in the usual course of the business of operating a theater. Therefore, Voeller did not have apparent authority to sell the land. Furthermore, there is no evidence that Voeller had sold property before on behalf of the partnership nor was the partnership engaged in the business of buying and selling real estate. Thus there was no actual authority to sell real property belonging to the partnership. In the absence of both apparent and actual authority, the contract is not binding on the partnership.

Partnership by Estoppel

Partnership by estoppel imposes partnership duties and liabilities on a non-partner who has either represented himself or consented to be represented as a partner. It extends to a third person to whom such a representation is made and who gives credit to the partnership in justifiable reliance on the representation.

For example, A and B are partners doing business as A and Company. A introduces C to T, describing C as a member of the partnership. Believing that C is a member of the partnership and relying on C's good credit standing, T sells goods on credit to A and Company. In an action by T against A, B, and C as partners to recover the price of the goods, C is liable even though he is not a partner in A and Company. T had justifiably relied on the representation that C was a partner in A and Company, to which C by his silence consented. However, if T at the time knew that C was not a partner, his reliance on the representation would not have been justified, and C would not be liable.

Torts of Partnership

The UPA provides that a partnership is liable for loss or injury caused by any wrongful act or omission of any partner while acting within the ordinary course of the business of the partnership or with the authority of his copartners. If the partnership is liable, then each partner has **unlimited personal liability** for the partnership obligation. The liability of partners for a tort or breach of trust committed by any partner or by an employee of the firm in the course of partnership business is joint and several, which means that all of the partners may be sued jointly in one action or separate actions may be maintained against each of them and separate judgments obtained. Judgments obtained are enforceable only against property of the defendant or defendants named in the suit. However, payment of any one of the judgments satisfies all of them.

Joint and several liability–liability where creditor may sue obligors jointly as a group or separately as individuals

This liability is comparable to the vicarious liability imposed on a principal for the torts of an agent by the doctrine of *respondeat superior*. The partner committing the tort is directly liable to the third party and must also **indemnify** the partnership for any damages it pays to the third party (see Figure 30–3). Tort liability of the partnership may include not only the negligence of the partners but also trespass, fraud, defamation, and breach of fiduciary duty, so long as the tort is committed in the course of partnership business. More-

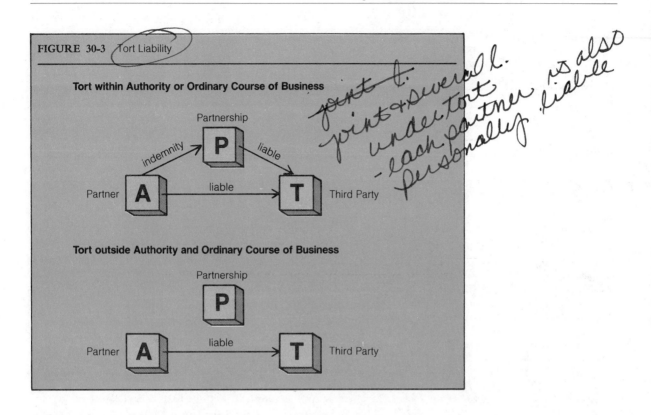

FIGURE 30-3 Tort Liability

Handwritten annotations: joint L. / joint & several l. / under tort / - each partner is also / personally liable

Tort within Authority or Ordinary Course of Business

Partnership

Partner A — indemnity → P — liable → T Third Party

A — liable → T

Tort outside Authority and Ordinary Course of Business

Partnership

P

Partner A — liable → T Third Party

over, the fact that a tort is intentional does not necessarily remove it from the course of business, but it is a factor to be considered, as in the case of *Vrabel v. Acri.*

FACTS: Michael and Florence Acri, then husband and wife, were joint proprietors of the Acri Cafe. On February 17, 1947, Vrabel and a friend were sitting quietly at the bar of the Acri Cafe enjoying a few drinks, when, for no apparent reason, Michael Acri shot and killed Vrabel's companion and viciously attacked Vrabel. Although Michael Acri had been treated on a number of occasions for mental disorders, he had never previously attacked or physically abused anyone, except his wife, Florence, when they experienced marital difficulties.

All licenses connected with the operation of the cafe had been issued in the name of Michael Acri alone. Moreover, Florence's operation and management of the cafe had been confined principally to those times when Michael was away on account of illness. In September, 1946 the couple permanently separated and Florence sued for divorce. Thereafter, she no longer had any direct connection with the Acri Cafe; Michael exercised sole management and control of the cafe to the exclusion of Florence. Vrabel brought suit against Florence for the injuries he suffered as a result of Michael's attack. He claims Florence was negligent in failing to protect the cafe's customers from Michael, her partner in the joint proprietorship.

DECISION: Judgment for Florence Acri. Generally, a partner is liable for another partner's tort if that partner is acting in the ordinary course of the business of the partnership or with the authority of his copartners. However, if the partner is not acting within the actual or apparent scope of the venture, the other partners are not liable unless they assent to, concur in, or ratify that partner's tortious conduct.

Here, Michael's attack on Vrabel was a clear departure from his employment. It was not within the scope of the business of operating the cafe to attack viciously its patrons. In addition, Florence had no reason to believe that Michael was a dangerous individual prone to assaulting

VRABEL v. ACRI

Supreme Court of Ohio, 1952. 156 Ohio St. 467, 103 N.E.2d 564.

the cafe's customers. Moreover, she had been excluded from control over the cafe's management for a long period prior to the incident. Therefore, Florence is not liable for Michael's assault on Vrabel.

Law in The News

FDIC Sues Peat Marwick for $130 Million Over Its Audit of Failed Penn Square Bank

OKLAHOMA CITY, Okla.—The Federal Deposit Insurance Corp. is suing Peat, Marwick, Mitchell & Co. for more than $130 million, charging that the accounting firm didn't conduct a proper audit of Penn Square Bank before the bank failed in 1982.

The FDIC complaint, filed as an addition to the agency's suit in federal court here against Penn Square officers, charges that the partners in Peat Marwick's Oklahoma City office compromised the firm's independence by accepting more than $1 million of loans, directly and indirectly, from Penn Square.

The FDIC's 83-page complaint also alleges that the accounting firm didn't properly evaluate Penn Square's lending policies, that the firm's audit team at Penn Square wasn't as large and as experienced as it should have been and that the team didn't prod the bank to set up a sufficiently large reserve against possible loan losses.

In New York, Peat Marwick said it would stand by its audit of Penn Square and said the loans to Peat Marwick officials were made before the firm was retained as the bank's accountant.

Although Peat Marwick partners aren't named as defendants in the FDIC suit, two partners are mentioned by name for taking loans from the bank. The two have since left Peat Marwick.

The complaint also alleges that all partners in Peat Marwick's Oklahoma City office in 1981, about 12 in all, were members of an Oklahoma general partnership called Doral Associates. The complaint says Doral Associates borrowed $566,501 from Penn Square and guaranteed a Penn Square loan of $1,650,000 to a Doral joint venture.

A. Marshall Snipes, who was a Peat Marwick partner until early 1983, had direct and indirect loans from Penn Square totaling $570,500, and another Peat Marwick partner, Richard K. Turner, got a $453,683 Penn Square loan as a general partner of BFD Investors, an investment partnership, the complaint alleges. Mr. Turner left Peat Marwick in November of last year. Messrs. Snipes and Turner couldn't be reached for comment.

The FDIC is seeking $65.8 million in actual damages and $65 million in punitive damages. The agency also is seeking interest on the damage claims. A source close to the FDIC said that the $65.8 million of actual damages stem only from losses on loans of more than $500,000. The plaintiff is asking for an additional payment from Peat Marwick to cover losses on loans of less than $500,000. The amount of such additional claims hasn't yet been determined.

A Peat Marwick attorney said he doubted that the punitive damages would be seriously consid-

ered. He said that Peat Marwick was confident that it had done its job properly and that the accounting firm had offered to have the dispute settled by binding arbitration or to have its work on Penn Square's loan-loss reserve reviewed by another major accounting firm. The FDIC declined both offers, he said.

The FDIC's decision to sue Peat Marwick continues a growing trend of shareholders and third parties holding big accounting firms liable for financial losses. It appears that recent court decisions are spurring the trend, accounting firms' attorneys say. For example, they interpret a decision by the New Jersey supreme court last year as "saying the existence of liability insurance justifies pursuing a claim against big accounting firms." The court decision established for the first time that auditors are liable to "third parties" for fraudulent information in audit reports.

Recent settlements by big accounting firms have totaled as much as $50 million, and that is likely to make their liability insurance rates jump by mid-1985, insurance companies say. Deductibles for such insurance already range from $1 million to $5 million, compared with $250,000 or less a decade ago.

Admissions of and Notice to a Partner

An admission or representation by any partner about partnership affairs, within the scope of his authority, may be used as evidence against the partnership. One person's admission that a partnership exists does not prove its existence. But once the partnership is established by competent evidence, the admission of one partner may be used against the partnership, provided the partner is acting within the scope of the partnership business.

A partnership is bound (1) by notice to any partner of any matter relating to partnership affairs, (2) by the knowledge of the partner acting in a particular matter acquired while he was a partner, and (3) by the knowledge of any other partner who reasonably could and should have communicated it to the acting partner.

A demand on one partner as a representative of the firm is a demand on the partnership.

Liability of Incoming Partner

A person admitted as a partner into an existing partnership is liable for **all** of the obligations of the partnership arising before his admission as though he had been a partner when such obligations were incurred, although this liability may be satisfied **only** out of partnership property. This means that the liability of an incoming partner for pre-existing debts and obligations of the firm is limited to his capital contribution. This restriction does not apply, of course, to obligations that arise after his admission into the partnership. His liability for these obligations is *unlimited*. For example, Nash is admitted to Higgins, Cooke and White Co., a partnership. Nash's capital contribution is $7,500 which was paid in cash upon her admission to the partnership. A year later the partnership is dissolved when liabilities of the firm exceed its assets by $40,000. Porter had lent the firm $15,000 eight months before Nash was admitted; Skinner lent the firm $20,000 two months after Nash was admitted. Nash has no liability to Porter *except* to the extent of her capital contribution. Nash is *personally* liable to Skinner.

Incoming Partner

Outgoing
- *must notify all creditors or be liable in future*
- *put notice in paper*

CHAPTER SUMMARY

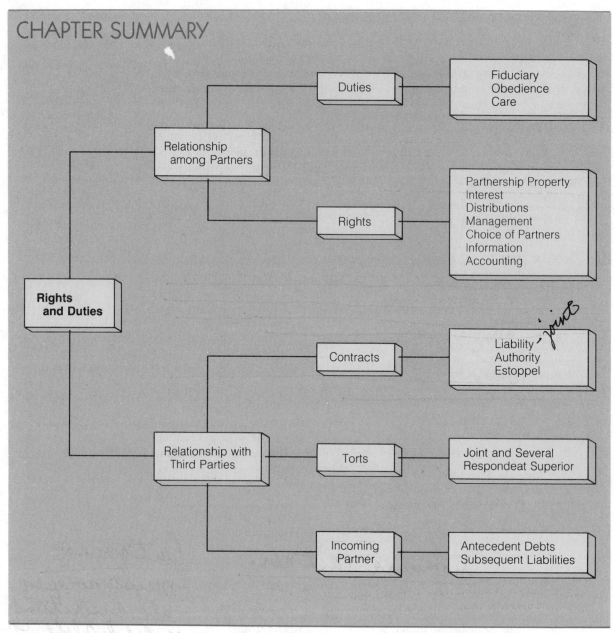

KEY TERMS

Fiduciary duty
Duty of obedience
Duty of care
Culpable negligence
Tenancy in partnership

Interest in the partnership
Charging order
Distributions
Delectus personae

Accounting
Joint liability
Partnership by estoppel
Several liability

PROBLEMS

1. A, B, and C own and operate the Roy Lumber Company. Each contributed one-third of the capital, and they share equally in the profits and losses. Their partnership agreement states that all purchases over $500 must be authorized in advance by two partners and that only A is authorized to draw checks. Unknown to A or C, B purchases on the firm's account a $2,500 diamond bracelet and a $5,000 forklift and orders $2,000 worth of logs, all from D, who operates a jewelry store and is engaged in various activities connected with the lumber business. Before B made these purchases, A told D that B is not the log buyer. A refuses to pay D for B's purchases. D calls at the mill to collect, and A again refuses to pay him. D calls A an unprintable name, and A then punches D in the nose. While D is lying unconscious on the ground, an employee of Roy Lumber Company negligently drops a log on D's leg, breaking three bones. The firm and the three partners are completely solvent.

What are the rights of D?

2. A, B, and C agree that A and B will form and conduct a partnership business and that C will become a partner in two years. C agrees to lend the firm $5,000 and take 10 percent of the profits in lieu of interest. Without C's knowledge, A and B tell X that C is a partner, and X, relying on C's sound financial status, gives the firm credit. Later the firm becomes insolvent, and X seeks to hold C liable as a partner. Should X succeed?

3. X and Y had been partners for many years in a mercantile business. However, their relationship deteriorated to the point where X threatened to bring an action for an accounting and dissolution of the firm. Y then offered to buy X's interest in the partnership for $25,000. X refused the offer and told Y that she would take no less than $36,000. A short time later, Z approached Y and informed him he had inside information that a proposed street change would greatly benefit the business and that he, Z, would buy the entire business for $100,000 or buy a one-half interest for $50,000. Y made a final offer of $35,000 to X for her interest. X accepted this offer, and the transaction was completed. Y then sold the one-half interest to Z for $50,000. Several months later, X learned for the first time of the transaction between Y and Z.

What rights, if any, does X have against Y?

4. A and B were partners doing business as the Petite Garment Company. C owned a dye plant that did much of the processing for the Company. A and B decided to offer C an interest in their company in consideration for which C would contribute his dye plant to the partnership. C accepted the offer and was duly admitted as a partner.

At the time he was admitted as a partner, C did not know that the partnership was on the verge of insolvency. A and B had incurred many debts that they were unable to meet. About three months after C was admitted to the partnership, a textile firm obtained a judgment against the partnership in the amount of $50,000. This debt represented an unpaid balance that had existed before C was admitted as a partner.

The textile firm brought an action to subject the partnership property, including the dye plant, to the satisfaction of its judgment. The complaint also requested that, in the event the judgment was unsatisfied by sale of the partnership property, C's home be sold and the proceeds applied to the balance of the judgment. A and B owned nothing but their interest in the partnership property.

What should be the result (a) with regard to the dye plant and (b) with regard to C's home?

5. Jones and Ray formed a partnership in October 1984 known as JR Construction Co. to engage in the construction business, each partner owning a one-half interest. On December 27, 1984, while conducting partnership business, Jones negligently injured Ware, who brought an action against Jones, Ray, and JR Construction Co. and obtained judgment for $25,000 against them on March 1, 1985. On April 15, 1985, Muir joined the partnership by contributing $10,000 cash, and by agreement each partner was entitled to a one-third interest. In July 1985, the partners agreed to purchase new construction equipment for the partnership, and Muir was authorized to obtain a loan from XYZ Bank in the partnership name for $20,000 to finance the purchase. On July 10, 1985, Muir signed a $20,000 note on behalf of the partnership, and the equipment was purchased.

In November 1985 the partnership was in financial difficulty, its total assets amounting to $5,000. The note was in default, with a balance of $15,000 owing to XYZ Bank. Muir has substantial resources, while Jones and Ray each individually have assets of $2,000.

What is the extent of Muir's personal liability and the personal liability of Jones and Ray as to (a) the judgment obtained by Ware, and (b) the debt owing to XYZ Bank?

6. A, B, and C were partners under a written agreement made in 1978 that it should continue for ten years. During 1985, C, being indebted to X, sold and conveyed his interest in the partnership to X. A and B paid X $5,000 as C's share of the profits for the year 1985 but refused X permission to inspect the books or to come into the managing office of the partnership. X brings an action setting forth the above facts and asks for an account of partnership transactions and an order to inspect the books and to participate in the management of the partnership business.

(a) Does C's action dissolve the partnership?

(b) To what is X entitled with respect to (1) partnership profits, (2) inspection of partnership books, (3) an account of partnership transactions, and (4) participation in the partnership management?

7. Adams, a consulting engineer, entered into a partnership with three others for the practice of their profession. The only written partnership agreement is a brief document specifying that Adams is entitled to 55 percent of the profits and the others to 15 percent each.

The venture is a total failure. Creditors are pressing for payment, and some have filed suit. The partners are in fundamental disagreement as to their future course of action.

How many of the partners must agree to achieve each of the following objectives:

(a) To add Jones, also an engineer, as a partner, Jones being willing to contribute a substantial amount of new capital.

(b) To sell a vacant lot held in the partnership name, which had been acquired as the site of a future office for the partnership.

(c) To move the offices of the partnership to less expensive quarters.

(d) To demand a formal accounting.

(e) To dissolve the partnership.

(f) To agree to submit certain disputed claims to arbitration, which Adams believes will prove less expensive than litigation.

(g) To sell all of the partnership personal property, Adams having what he believes to be a good offer for the property from a newly formed engineering firm.

(h) To alter the respective interests of the parties in the profits and losses by decreasing Adams's share to 40 percent and increasing the others' shares accordingly.

(i) To assign all the assets to a bank in trust for the benefit of creditors, hoping to work out satisfactory arrangements without formal bankruptcy.

8. A and B orally agreed to become partners in a small tool-and-die business. A, who had experience in tool-and-die work, was to operate the business. B was to take no active part but was to contribute the entire $50,000 capitalization. A worked ten hours a day at the plant, for which he was paid nothing. Despite A's best efforts, the business failed. The $50,000 capital was depleted, and the partnership owed $50,000 in debts. Before the business failed, B became personally insolvent so that the creditors of the partnership collected the entire $50,000 indebtedness from A, who was forced to sell his home and farm to satisfy the debt. B later regained his financial responsibility, and A brought an appropriate action against B for (a) one-half of the $50,000 he had paid to partnership creditors and (b) one-half of $18,000, the reasonable value of A's services during the operation of the partnership. Decision?

9. S refuses an invitation to become a partner of P and R in the retail grocery business. Nevertheless, P inserts an advertisement in the local newspaper representing S as their partner. S takes no steps to deny the existence of a partnership between them. X, who extended credit to the firm, seeks to hold S liable as a partner. Decision?

10. Hanover leased a portion of his farm to Brown and Black, doing business as the Colorite Hatchery. Brown went on the premises to remove certain chicken sheds that he and Black had placed there for hatchery purposes. Hanover thought Brown intended to remove certain other sheds that were Hanover's property, and an altercation occurred between them. Brown willfully struck Hanover and knocked him down. Then Brown ran to the Colorite truck, which he had previously loaded with chicken coops, and drove back to the hatchery. On the way, he picked up George, who was hitchhiking to the city to look for a job. Brown was in a hurry and was driving at seventy miles per hour down the highway. At an open intersection with another highway, Brown ran a stop sign and struck another vehicle at the intersection. The collision caused severe injuries to George. Brown and Black's partnership was dissolved directly after these incidents, and Brown was insolvent. Hanover and George each bring separate actions against Black as copartner for the alleged tort committed by Brown against each.

What judgments as to each?

DISSOLUTION, WINDING UP, AND TERMINATION

Three steps lead to the extinguishment of a partnership: (1) dissolution, (2) winding up or liquidation, and (3) termination. The Uniform Partnership Act defines dissolution as the change in the relation of the partners caused by any partner's ceasing to be associated in the carrying on, as distinguished from the winding up, of the business. After dissolution, the partnership is not terminated. It continues to wind up the partnership affairs by putting the business affairs in order, collecting receivables, making payments to creditors, and distributing the remaining assets to the partners. When liquidation has been completed, the partnership is terminated.

Dissolution

Causes of Dissolution

Dissolution may be brought about by (1) an act of the partners, (2) operation of law, or (3) court order. A number of events that were considered causes of dissolution under the common law are no longer considered so under the UPA. For example, the assignment of a partner's interest, a creditor's charging order on a partner's interest, and an accounting do *not* cause a dissolution.

Dissolution–change in the relation of partners caused by any partner's ceasing to be associated with the carrying on of the business

Dissolution by Act of the Partners   A partnership is a personal relationship, and a partner always has the *power* to dissolve it, but whether he has the *right* to do so is determined by the partnership agreement. A partner who has withdrawn in violation of the partnership agreement is liable to the remaining partners for damages resulting from the wrongful dissolution.

A partnership is **rightfully dissolved,** that is, without violation of the agreement between the partners, by the act of the partners:

1. when they specifically agree to dissolve the partnership;

2. when the period of time provided in the agreement has ended or the purpose for which the partnership was formed has been accomplished;

3. when a partner withdraws from a partnership at will, that is one with no definite term or specific undertaking, or

4. when a partner is expelled in accordance with a power to expel conferred by the partnership agreement.

Dissolution by Operation of Law   A partnership is dissolved by operation of law upon (1) the death of a partner; (2) the bankruptcy of a partner or of the partnership; or (3) the subsequent illegality of the partnership, which includes any event that makes it unlawful for the business of the partnership to be carried on or for the members to carry on the business in partnership form. For example, a partnership formed to manufacture liquor would be dissolved by a law prohibiting the production and sale of alcoholic beverages. A partnership of lawyers would be dissolved if one of its members was disbarred from the practice of law.

Dissolution by Court Order   After application by a partner, a court will order a dissolution if it finds that (1) a partner is incompetent or suffers some other incapacity that prevents him from functioning as a partner; (2) a partner is guilty of conduct prejudicial to the business or has willfully and persistently breached the partnership agreement; (3) the business can be carried on only at a loss; or (4) other circumstances render a dissolution equitable.

An assignee of a partner's interest or a partner's personal creditor who has obtained a charging order against the partner's interest may petition the court to dissolve a partnership. Application for a court-ordered dissolution may be made at any time if the partnership was at will when the interest was assigned or the charging order was issued but, if the partnership was not at will, only after the end of the specified term or particular undertaking.

Effects of Dissolution

On dissolution, the partnership is *not* terminated but continues until the winding up of partnership affairs is completed. Moreover, dissolution does *not* of itself discharge the existing liability of any partner. However, dissolution *does* bring about restrictions on the authority of partners to act for the partnership.

On Authority   On dissolution, the *actual* authority of a partner to act for the partnership terminates, except so far as may be necessary to wind up partnership affairs. Actual authority to wind up includes completing existing contracts, reducing partnership assets to cash, and paying partnership obligations.

Although actual authority terminates on dissolution, *apparent authority* persists and binds the partnership for acts within the scope of the partnership business unless notice of the dissolution is given to the third party. A third party who had extended credit to the partnership before dissolution may hold the partnership liable for any transaction that would bind the partnership if dissolution had not taken place, unless the third party has knowledge or actual notice of the dissolution. **Actual notice** requires a verbal statement to the third party or actual delivery of a written statement. On the other hand, a third party who knew of the partnership, but had not extended credit to it before its dissolution can hold the partnership liable unless he has knowledge, actual notice, or constructive notice of dissolution. **Constructive notice** consists of advertising a notice of dissolution in a newspaper of general circulation in the places at which partnership business was regularly conducted.

On Existing Liability   The dissolution of the partnership does not by itself discharge the existing liability of any partner. But in some instances the cause of dissolution may result in discharging an executory contract. For example, if the contract called for the personal services of one of the partners, the death of that partner usually will discharge the contract and also bring about the dissolution of the partnership.

A retiring partner may be discharged from his existing liabilities by a **novation** entered into with the continuing partners and the creditors. A creditor must agree to the novation, although his consent may be inferred from his course of dealing with the partnership after dissolution. Whether such dealings with the continuing partnership constitutes an implied novation is a factual question of intent.

Winding Up

Whenever a dissolved partnership is not to be continued, the partnership must be liquidated. The process of **liquidation** is called winding up and involves completing unfinished business, collecting debts, reducing assets to cash, taking inventory, auditing the partnership books, paying creditors, and distributing the remaining assets to the partners. During this period the fiduciary duties of the partners continue in effect.

liquidation

Winding up—completion of unfinished business, collecting debts, and distributing assets to creditors and partners

The Right to Wind Up

On dissolution, any partner has the right to insist on the winding up of the partnership unless the partnership agreement provides otherwise. However, a partner who has wrongfully dissolved the partnership or who has been rightfully expelled according to the terms of the partnership agreement cannot force the liquidation of the partnership. Unless otherwise agreed, all nonbankrupt partners who have not wrongfully dissolved the partnership have the right to wind up the partnership affairs, as illustrated in the next case. A court, on the petition of a partner, may appoint a receiver of all of the property and assets of the partnership. The receiver has authority to operate the business under the court's direction for such time as may be reasonably necessary. The appointment of a receiver is discretionary with the court, and its discretion may be exercised on such grounds as dissension among the partners or waste, fraud, mental incompetence, misconduct, or other breach of duty by a partner.

FACTS: Stark, Henning & Co., a partnership formed by Stark and Henning for the purpose of acting as sales representatives for various firms in upstate New York, contracted with Utica Screw Product, Inc. on June 19, 1975 to act as its sales representative for most of New York State. On October 22, 1976 Stark sent a letter to Henning terminating the partnership. A copy of this letter was also sent to the president of Utica. When Utica refused to pay commissions owed to the partnership for orders which the partnership had obtained for Utica between February 10, 1976 and October 20, 1976, Stark brought this action on behalf of the partnership to recover the commissions due. Utica contended that Stark had no standing to sue, because he had not received authority from his partner, Henning, to institute this action.

DECISION: Judgment for Stark. Upon dissolution of a partnership any partner has the right to participate in the winding up of the partnership. He needs no authority from his co-partners. On dissolution the partnership continues until the winding up of the partnership affairs is completed. The only way in which a partnership is wound up is through an accounting. After the dissolution of a partnership, a partner may bind the partnership by any appropriate action necessary to wind up the partnership affairs or to complete transactions unfinished at the time of dissolution.

STARK v. UTICA SCREW PRODUCTS, INC.

City Court of Utica, 1980. 103 Misc.2d 163, 425 N.Y.S.2d 750.

Here, Stark can sue Utica without Henning's permission. Any recovery will be for the benefit of the partnership, and not for himself individually. It would then be up to Stark and Henning to wind up the partnership through an accounting.

Distribution of Assets

After all the partnership assets have been collected and reduced to cash, they are then distributed to the creditors and partners. When the partnership has been profitable, the order of distribution is not critical; however, when liabilities are greater than assets, the order of distribution has great importance.

The UPA sets forth the rules to be observed in settling accounts between the parties after dissolution. It states that the liabilities of a partnership are to be paid out of partnership assets in the following order:

1. amounts owing to creditors other than partners;
2. amounts owing to partners other than for capital and profits; *loans*
3. amounts owing to partners in respect of capital contributions;
4. amounts owing to partners in respect of profits.

The partners may by agreement change the internal priorities of distribution (numbers 2, 3, and 4) but not the preferred position of third parties (1). This is the situation in the *Petersen* case below. The UPA defines partnership assets to include all partnership property as well as the contributions necessary for the payment of all partnership liabilities, which consist of 1, 2, and 3.

In addition, the UPA provides that, in the absence of any contrary agreement, each partner shall share equally in the profits and surplus remaining after all liabilities (1, 2, and 3) are satisfied and must contribute towards the losses, whether capital or otherwise, sustained by the partnership according to his share in the profits. Thus the proportion in which the partners bear losses, whether capital or otherwise, does not depend on their relative capital contributions. Rather, it is determined by their agreement. If there is no specific agreement, losses are borne in the same proportion in which profits are shared.

If the partnership is insolvent, the partners individually must contribute their respective share of the losses in order to pay the creditors. Furthermore, if one or more of the partners is insolvent or bankrupt or is out of the jurisdiction and refuses to contribute, the other partners must contribute the additional amount necessary to pay the firm's liabilities, in the relative proportions in which they share the profits. When any partner has paid an amount in excess of his proper share of the losses, he has a right of contribution against the partners who have not paid their share.

The following examples illustrate the operation of these rules.

Solvent Partnership   Assume that A, B, and C form the ABC Company, a partnership, with A contributing $6,000 capital, B contributing $4,000 capital, and C contributing services but no capital. A also loaned the partnership $3,000, which has not been repaid. There is no agreement as to the proportions in which profits and losses are to be shared. After a few years of operation, the partnership is liquidated. At this time the assets of ABC Company are $54,000, and its liabilities to creditors are $26,000. The partnership is thus solvent and has enjoyed a profit of $15,000, which is calculated by subtracting the total liabilities ($39,000) from the total assets ($54,000). The total liabilities consist of the amount owed to creditors ($26,000), the amount owed to partners other than for capital and profits ($3,000 owed to A for his loan), and the capital contributions of the partners ($6,000 from A and $4,000 from B). Because A, B, and C have not explicitly agreed on a profit-sharing ratio, they share the profits equally, in this case receiving $5,000 ($15,000 ÷ 3). After the creditors have been paid in full, A will receive $14,000 ($3,000 for repayment of the loan, $6,000 for capital and $5,000 for share of profits); B will receive $9,000 ($4,000 for capital and $5,000 for share of profits); and C will receive $5,000 (for share of profits).

Insolvent Partnership   Assume the same partnership had experienced financial adversity instead. It still owes creditors $26,000, but its total assets only amount to $12,000. In this case the partnership has sustained an aggregate loss of $27,000, which is calculated by subtracting the total liabilities ($39,000, calculated as in the example above) from the total assets ($12,000). If the agreement makes no other arrangement, the losses are shared as the profits are, which in this case is equally. Accordingly, each partner's share of the loss will be $9,000 ($27,000 ÷ 3). After the creditors are paid ($26,000), A will receive nothing ($3,000 owed for the loan plus $6,000 for capital *minus* $9,000 for his share of losses); B must make an additional *contribution* of $5,000 to make good his share of the loss ($4,000 owed for capital *minus* $9,000 for his share of losses); and C must contribute $9,000 (his share of losses).

Contribution of Partner on Insolvency   In the insolvent partnership example above, if A were individually insolvent, the results would not be changed, because A was not required to contribute any additional moneys. However, if A and B were solvent and C were individually insolvent, C would be unable to pay any of his share of the loss. Then A and B must contribute equally, because that is the relative proportion in which they share profits, in order to make good the amount of C's share. C's share of the loss is $9,000, and therefore A and B must each contribute an additional $4,500. This means that in total A will have to contribute $4,500 and B $9,500 in order to satisfy the unpaid claims of partnership creditors. On the other hand, if A and C were individually insolvent and B was solvent, B would be required to pay the entire balance of $14,000 due to partnership creditors, representing his unpaid share of the loss plus a contribution of the full amount of C's unpaid share of the loss.

PETERSEN v.
PETERSEN

Supreme Court of Minnesota,
1969.
284 Minn. 61, 169 N.W.2d
228.

FACTS: In 1946 Donald Petersen joined his father, William Petersen, in a chicken hatchery business which William had previously operated as a sole proprietorship. When the partnership was formed, William contributed the assets of the proprietorship which included cash, equipment, and inventory having a total value of $41,000. Donald contributed nothing. From 1946 until Donald's death in 1964, Donald took over the operation of the hatchery. This suit was brought on behalf of Donald's estate when William refused to distribute any of the partnership assets to the estate. William contended that the total value of the partnership property at the time of Donald's death was $18,572. He claimed the full amount on the theory that he was entitled to the return of his capital investment of $41,000 before Donald's estate could recover anything.

DECISION: Judgment for Donald's estate. According to the Uniform Partnership Act, the right of a partner to receive back the capital he contributed is subject to a contrary agreement among the partners. Such an agreement need not be written, but may be implied from the conduct of the partners.

Here, although Donald contributed no substantial capital to the business, he operated it with very little help from his father. Meanwhile, William continued to receive half of the income. The conduct of the parties makes it reasonable to infer that William put up the capital and Donald provided the labor under an agreement by which each was to own half of the business, including capital and profits. Donald's estate is therefore entitled to half of the value of the business.

Marshaling of Assets

Marshaling of assets— segregating the assets and liabilities of the partnership separately from the assets and liabilities of the individual partners

The doctrine of marshaling of assets applies *only* when the assets of a partnership and of its members are administered by a court of equity. Marshaling means segregating and considering the assets and liabilities of the partnership separately from the respective assets and liabilities of the individual partners. Partnership creditors are entitled to be satisfied first out of partnership assets. They have a right to recover any deficiency out of the individually owned assets of the partners, subordinate however to the rights of nonpartnership creditors to those assets.

Conversely, the nonpartnership creditors have first claim to the individually owned assets of their respective debtors; their claims to partnership assets are subordinate to claims of partnership creditors.

When a partner is insolvent, the order of distribution of his assets is as follows: (1) debts and liabilities owing to nonpartnership creditors; (2) debts and liabilities owing to partnership creditors; and (3) contributions owing to other partners who have paid more than their respective share of the firm's liabilities to partnership creditors.

This rule, however, is *no longer* followed if the partnership is a debtor under the Bankruptcy Reform Act of 1978. In a proceeding under the Federal bankruptcy law, a trustee is appointed to administer the estate of the debtor. If the partnership property is insufficient to pay all the claims against the partnership, then the trustee is directed by the Act to seek recovery of the deficiency first from the general partners who are not bankrupt. The trustee may then seek recovery against the estates of bankrupt partners on the same basis as other creditors of the bankrupt partner. This provision, although contrary to the UPA's doctrine of marshaling of assets, governs whenever the assets of a partnership are being administered by a bankruptcy court.

Continuation of Partnership After Dissolution

After a partnership has been dissolved one of two outcomes must follow: either the partnership is liquidated or the remaining partners continue the partnership. When a partnership is liquidated after dissolution, the value of a going concern is sacrificed. On the other hand, continuation of the partnership after dissolution avoids this loss. The UPA nonetheless gives each partner the right to have the partnership liquidated except in a limited number of instances where the partners have the right to continue the partnership.

Partners' Right to Continue Partnership

After dissolution the remaining partners have the right to continue the partnership (1) when the partnership has been dissolved in violation of the partnership agreement, (2) when a partner has been expelled in accordance with the partnership agreement, or (3) when all the partners agree to continue the business.

Continuation after Wrongful Dissolution   Because of the personal element in a partnership, courts will not decree specific performance of a partnership agreement. However, a partner who wrongfully withdraws cannot force the liquidation of the firm. The aggrieved partners have the option of either liquidating the firm and recovering damages for the breach of the partnership agreement or continuing the partnership by buying out the withdrawing partner. The withdrawing partner is entitled to realize his interest in the partnership less the amount of the damages that the other partners have sustained as the result of his breach. However, his interest is computed without considering the good will of the business. In addition, the remaining partners may use the capital contributions of the wrongdoing partner for the unexpired period of the partnership agreement. They must, however, indemnify the former partner against all present and future partnership liabilities.

Continuation after Expulsion   A partner expelled according to the partnership agreement cannot force the liquidation of the partnership. He is entitled only to be discharged from all partnership liabilities by either payment or a novation with the creditors and to receive in cash the net amount due him from the partnership.

Continuation per Agreement of the Parties   By far the best and most reliable way of assuring the preservation of a partnership business after dissolution is a continuation agreement. Continuation agreements are frequently used to ensure continuity in the event of death or retirement of one of the partners. A continuation agreement permits the remaining partners to keep the partnership property and carry on its business and to provide a specified settlement with the outgoing partners, as in the next case. Otherwise, when a partner dies or retires and the business is continued by the surviving partners, the retired partner or legal representative of the deceased partner is entitled to be paid the value of his interest as of the date of the dissolution as an ordinary creditor of the partnership. In addition, he is entitled to receive interest on this amount or, at his option, in lieu of interest, the profits of the business attributable to the use of his right in the property of the dissolved partnership. His rights, however, are subordinate to those of creditors of the dissolved partnership.

McCLENNEN v. COMMISSIONER OF INTERNAL REVENUE

United States Court of Appeals, First Circuit, 1943.
131 F.2d 165.

FACTS: George Nutter was a partner in the law firm of Nutter, McClennen & Fish. The partnership agreement provided that he was entitled to receive 8 percent of the firm's net profits and that on his death or retirement payments in the same percentage of net profits would continue to be made to Nutter or his estate for a period of eighteen months. The agreement expressly stated that the payments would be in full satisfaction of the deceased or retiring partner's interest in the capital, the assets, the receivables, and the good will of the firm.

When Nutter died in 1937, his partners continued the business and made the required payments totaling $34,070 to Nutter's estate, but the Federal estate tax return filed for the estate did not include an amount representing the value of Nutter's interest in the partnership. As a result the Commissioner of Internal Revenue filed this notice of deficiency for taxes due on $34,070, the value of Nutter's partnership interest.

DECISION: Judgment for the Commissioner. In the absence of a controlling agreement in the partnership articles providing otherwise, the death of a partner dissolves the partnership. The survivors then have a duty to wind up the partnership affairs with reasonable dispatch and distribute the partnership assets to the partners in accordance with their respective shares. But the representative of the deceased partner does not succeed to any right to specific partnership property. Instead, the deceased partner's share of the specific partnership assets vest in the surviving partners, and his estate is left with a right to receive a sum of cash.

Here, the partnership agreement provides a substitute arrangement under which the deceased partner's estate was to receive a share of the firm's net profits for eighteen months in lieu of a cash distribution equal to Nutter's interest in the partnership on dissolution. Nevertheless, the intent and the effect of the agreement was still to extract the value of Nutter's interest in the partnership but in a less drastic manner than by dissolution. Consequently, the amount of the eighteen monthly payments made to Nutter's estate should have been included in his gross estate for Federal estate tax purposes as the value of his interest in the partnership.

Rights of Creditors

Whenever a partnership is continued after dissolution, a new partnership is formed even though a majority of the old partners are present in the new combination. The creditors of the old partnership have claims against the new partnership and may also proceed to hold all of the members of the dissolved partnership personally liable. If a withdrawing partner has made arrangements with those who continue the business whereby they assume and pay all debts and obligations of the firm, the withdrawing partner is still liable to creditors whose claims arose prior to the dissolution. If she is compelled to pay such debts, the withdrawing partner has a right of indemnity against her former partners, who had agreed to pay the debts but failed to do so.

A withdrawing partner may protect herself against liability on contracts entered into by the firm after her withdrawal by giving notice that she is no longer a member of the firm. Otherwise, she is liable for debts thus incurred to a creditor who had no notice or knowledge of the partner's having withdrawn from the firm. Actual notice must be given to the persons with whom the partnership regularly does business, while notice by newspaper publication will be sufficient for the general business community.

CREDIT BUREAUS OF MERCED COUNTY, INC. v. SHIPMAN

District Court of Appeal, Third District, California, 1959.
334 P.2d 1036.

FACTS: Davis and Shipman founded a partnership in 1954 under the name of Shipman & Davis Lumber Company. On September 20, 1955, the partnership was dissolved by written agreement. Notice of the dissolution was published in a newspaper of general circulation in Merced County, where the business was conducted. No actual notice of dissolution was given to firms which had previously extended credit to the partnership. By the dissolution agreement, Shipman, who was to continue the business, was to pay all of the partnership's debts. He continued the business as a sole propietorship for a short time until he formed a successor corporation, Shipman Lumber Servaes Co. After the partnership's dissolution, two firms which had previously done business with the partnership extended credit to Shipman for certain repair work and merchandise. The partnership also had a balance due to Valley Typewriter Company owing for the prior purchase of a calculator. In 1956, two checks were drawn by Shipman Lumber Servaes Co. and accepted by Valley Typewriter as partial payment on this debt. Credit Bureaus of Merced County, as assignee of these three accounts, sued the partnership as well as Shipman and Davis individually. Davis argues that the dissolution of the partnership relieved him of personal liability for the accounts.

DECISION: Judgment for the Credit Bureaus. A retired partner may be relieved of liability for partnership debts incurred after his retirement if creditors receive appropriate notice of the partnership's dissolution. As to the firms having prior credit dealings with the partnership, actual notice is required.

Here, all three creditors had previously extended credit to the patnership. The publication of notice of the partnership's dissolution, by itself, is insufficient to show that these prior creditors received actual notice. Furthermore, the two checks do not, in themselves, prove that Valley

Typewriter entered into a novation to relieve Davis of liability for the account. Again, actual knowledge of the partnership's dissolution is required. Therefore, Davis remains liable for these debts.

Figure 31–1 summarizes the causes and consequences of dissolution of a partnership.

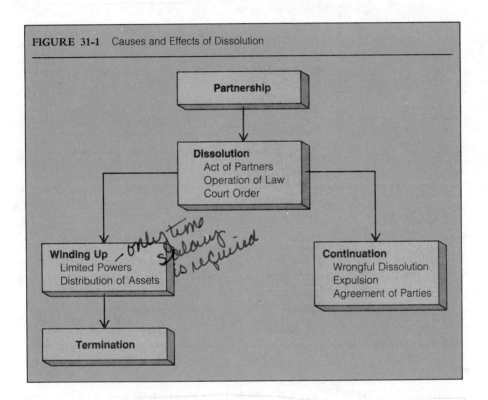

FIGURE 31-1   Causes and Effects of Dissolution

Partnership

Dissolution
Act of Partners
Operation of Law
Court Order

Winding Up
Limited Powers
Distribution of Assets

Continuation
Wrongful Dissolution
Expulsion
Agreement of Parties

Termination

CHAPTER SUMMARY

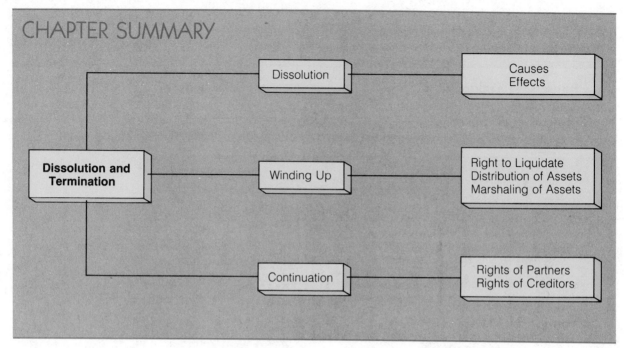

KEY TERMS

Dissolution	Rightful dissolution	Insolvent partnership
Winding up	Actual notice	Marshaling of assets
Liquidation	Constructive notice	Continuation
Termination	Solvent partnership	Wrongful dissolution

PROBLEMS

1. Simmons, Hoffman, and Murray were partners doing business under the firm name of Simmons & Co. The firm borrowed money from a bank and gave the bank the firm's note for the loan. In addition, each partner guaranteed the note individually. The firm became insolvent, and a receiver was appointed. The bank claims that it has a right to file its claim as a firm debt and also that it has a right to participate in the distribution of the assets of the individual partners before partnership creditors receive any payment from such assets.

  (a) Explain the principle involved in this case.

  (b) Is the bank correct?

2. A, B, and C form a partnership, A contributing $10,000, B $5,000, and C his time and skill. Nothing was said as to the division of profits. The firm becomes insolvent, and after payment of all firm debts owed to third parties $6,000 is left. A claims that she is entitled to the entire $6,000. B contends that the distribution should be $4,000 to A and $2,000 to B. C

claims the $6,000 should be divided equally among the partners. Who is correct? Explain.

3. Martin, Mark, and Marvin formed a retail clothing partnership named M Clothiers and conducted a business for many years, buying most of their clothing from Hill, a wholesaler. On January 15 Marvin retired from the business, but Martin and Mark decided to continue it. As part of the retirement agreement, Martin and Mark agreed in writing with Marvin that Marvin would not be responsible for any of the partnership debts, either past or future. A news item concerning Marvin's retirement appeared in the local newspaper on January 15.

  Before January 15, Hill was a creditor of M Clothiers to the extent of $10,000, and on January 30 he extended additional credit of $5,000. Hill was not advised and did not in fact know of Marvin's retirement and the change of the partnership. On January 30, Ray, a competitor of Hill, extended credit for the first time to M Clothiers in the amount of $3,000.

On February 1, Martin and Mark departed for parts unknown and left no partnership assets with which to pay the described debts. What is Marvin's liability, if any, (a) to Hill and (b) to Ray?

4. A, B, and C were partners sharing profits in proportions of one-fourth, one-third, and five-twelfths, respectively. Their business failed, and the firm was dissolved. At the time of dissolution no financial adjustments between the partners were necessary with reference to their respective capital contributions, but the firm's liabilities to creditors exceed its assets by $24,000. Without contributing any amount toward the payment of the liabilities, B moved to a destination unknown. A and C are financially responsible. How much must each contribute?

5. Indicate which of the following statements are true and which are false:

(a) Creditors having claims based on torts committed by partners in the course of business of the partnership are preferred over creditors with claims based on contracts.

(b) Partners who wish to continue the business have a prior right to purchase the assets.

(c) In the absence of a contract providing otherwise, the distribution to partners of accrued profits should be in equal parts regardless of the fact that the partners had contributed to the firm unequally.

(d) Advances in the nature of loans made by the various partners to the partnership share in the firm assets on the same basis as debts due other creditors.

(e) Between the partners, the assets of the partnership must be applied to pay the claims of partners with respect to capital ahead of the claims of partners with respect to profits.

(f) Debts owing to partners (other than for capital and profits) rank ahead of debts owing to partners with respect to capital and profits.

6. Ames, Bell, and Cole were equal partners in the ABC Construction Company. They had no formal or written partnership agreement. Cole died on June 30, 1985, and his widow, Cora Cole, qualified as executor of his will.

Ames and Bell continued the business of the partnership until December 31, 1985, when they sold all of the assets of the partnership. After paying all partnership debts, they distributed the balance equally among themselves and Mrs. Cole as executor.

Subsequently, Mrs. Cole learned that Ames and Bell had made and withdrawn a net profit of $20,000 during the period July 1 to December 31, 1985. The profit was made through new contracts using the partnership name and assets. Ames and Bell had concealed from Mrs. Cole the fact of such contracts and profit, and she learned about it from other sources. Immediately after acquiring this information, Mrs. Cole demand one-third of the profit of $20,000 from Ames and Bell. They rejected her demand.

What are the rights and remedies, if any, of Cora Cole as executor?

7. A and B were partners in Miami. C, a traveling salesman for D, called on them and on January 14 received from them an order for merchandise. The order was forwarded by C to D in New York on January 15; the partnership of A and B was dissolved by agreement between the partners on January 18. On January 19, D, without knowledge of the dissolution, acknowledged receipt of the order, accepted it, and shipped the goods the next day. B received them on January 23. On January 25, notice of dissolution of the partnership of A and B was duly published. D sues A and B for the purchase price of the merchandise sold. Decision?

8. The articles of partnership of the firm of Wilson and Company provide:

> William Smith to contribute $50,000; to receive interest thereon at 13 percent per annum and to devote such time as he may be able to give; to receive 30 percent of the profits.
> John Jones to contribute $50,000; to receive interest on same at 13 percent per annum; to give all of his time to the business and to receive 30 percent of the profits.
> Henry Wilson to contribute all of his time to the business and to receive 20 percent of the profits.
> James Brown to contribute all of his time to the business and to receive 20 percent of the profits.

There is no provision for sharing losses. After six years of operations, the firm has assets of $400,000 and liabilities to creditors of $420,000. Upon dissolution and winding up, what are the rights and liabilities of the respective parties?

9. Harold Fuller, Mary Warner, and Tom Clardy were copartners in a cattle-raising operation. Fuller and Clardy were both killed as the result of a common disaster. Mary Warner took charge of the partnership business and spent considerable time and effort in winding it up. In a suit brought for an accounting, Mary Warner made a claim for a reasonable allowance for services rendered in winding up the affairs of the partnership. The partnership agreement contained no provision for payment for services rendered in connection with the winding up of partnership affairs. What decision?

32

LIMITED PARTNERSHIPS

In this chapter we consider limited partnerships and other types of unincorporated business associations, including joint ventures and business trusts. These forms of organizations have developed to meet special business and investment needs. Each has its own set of characteristics that make it most appropriate for certain purposes.

Limited Partnerships

The limited partnership has proved itself to be an attractive vehicle for a variety of investments because of its tax advantages and the limited liability it confers on the limited partners. Before 1976 the governing statute in all States except Louisiana was the Uniform Limited Partnership Act (ULPA), which was promulgated in 1916. When the ULPA was adopted, most limited partnerships were small and had only a few limited partners. Today many limited partnerships are much larger and involve a small number of major investors and a relatively large group of widely distributed investors who purchase limited partnership interests. This type of limited partnership has evolved to attract substantial amounts of investment capital. However, the large scale and multistate operations of the modern limited partnership have severely burdened the framework established by the ULPA. These shortcomings prompted the National Conference of Commissioners on Uniform State Laws to develop a Revised Uniform Limited Partnership Act (RULPA), which was promulgated in 1976. According to its preface, the RULPA is "intended to modernize the prior uniform law while retaining the special character of limited partnerships as compared with corporations." Both the ULPA and RULPA are supplemented by the Uniform Partnership Act, which applies to limited partnership except where it is inconsistent with either Act. For a concise comparison of general and limited partnerships, see Figure 33–2 in Chapter 33.

In addition, limited partnership interests are considered to be securities, and their sale is subject to State and Federal regulation as discussed in Chapter 40.

way of avoiding unlimited liability

533

Definition

A limited partnership is one composed of one or more general partners and one or more limited partners. It differs from a general partnership in several respects, three of which are basic:

1. there must be a statute in effect providing for the formation of limited partnerships;
2. the limited partnership must fully comply with the requirements of such statute; and
3. the **liability** of a *limited* partner for partnership debts or obligations is **limited** to the extent of the capital that he has contributed or agreed to contribute.

Formation

Although the formation of a *general* partnership may be accomplished without special procedures, the formation of a *limited* partnership requires substantial compliance with the ULPA or RULPA. Failure to do so may result in the limited partners' loss of limited liability.

Filing of Certificate   The ULPA provides that two or more persons desiring to form a limited partnership shall sign and swear to a certificate, which shall contain the name of the partnership; the character of the business; the location of the principal place of business; the name and place of residence of each general and limited partner; the term for which the partnership is to exist; the amount of cash and any other property contributed by each limited partner; the additional contributions, if any, agreed to be made by each limited partner and the times at which or events on the happening of which they shall be made; the time, if agreed on, when the contribution of each limited partner is to be returned; and the share of the profits or the other compensation by way of income that each limited partner is entitled to receive. Figure 32–1 shows a sample limited partnership certificate.

The certificate must be filed in the office of a designated public official, usually in the county in which the principal office of the limited partnership is located. Some States also require that a copy of the certificate be filed with the Secretary of State. Under the RULPA, the certificate need only be filed in the office of the Secretary of State of the State in which the limited partnership has its principal office.

Name   The inclusion of the surname of a limited partner in the partnership name is prohibited unless it is also the surname of a general partner or unless the business had been carried on under that name before the admission of that limited partner. A violation of this provision renders the limited partner liable as a general partner to any creditor who did not know that he was a limited partner. The RULPA also prohibits a name that is deceptively similar to that of any corporation or other limited partnership. In addition, the name of the limited partnership must contain without abbreviation the words "limited partnership."

Contributions   Under the ULPA, the contribution of a limited partner may be cash or other property but *not* services. The RULPA, on the other hand, explicitly states that the contribution of a partner may be in cash, property,

FIGURE 32-1   Sample Limited Partnership Certificate

CERTIFICATE OF LIMITED PARTNERSHIP

The undersigned, desiring to form a Limited Partnership under the Uniform Limited Partnership Act of the State of _____ , make this certificate for that purpose.

§ 1.   Name.   The name of the Partnership shall be "_____ _____ ".

§ 2.   Purpose.   The purpose of the Partnership shall be to [*describe*].

§ 3.   Location.   The location of the Partnership's principal place of business is _____County, _____ .

§ 4.   Members and Designation.   The names and places of residence of the members, and their designation as General or Limited Partners are:

_____	[*Address*]	General Partner
_____	[*Address*]	General Partner
_____	[*Address*]	Limited Partner
_____	[*Address*]	Limited Partner

§ 5.   Term.   The term for which the Partnership is to exist is indefinite.

§ 6.   Initial Contributions of Limited Partners.   The amount of cash and a description of the agreed value of the other property contributed by each Limited Partner are:

[*Name*]   [*Describe*]
[*Name*]   [*Describe*]

§ 7.   Subsequent Contributions of Limited Partners.   Each Limited Partner may (but shall not be obliged to) make such additional contributions to the capital of the Partnership as may from time to time be agreed upon by the General Partners.

§ 8.   Profit Shares of Limited Partners.   The share of the profits which each Limited Partner shall receive by reason of his contribution is:

[*Name*]   _____ %
[*Name*]   _____ %

Signed _____ , 19_____

_____
_____
_____
_____

Signed and sworn before me, the undersigned authority, this _____ _____ , 19_____ .

Notary Public
_____County, _____

Source: Reprinted with permission from Edmund O. Belsheim's "Modern Legal Forms."
Copyright © 1971 by West Publishing Co.

or services rendered or in the form of a promissory note or other obligation to contribute cash or property or to perform services. A limited partner is liable to the partnership for the difference between the contribution she actually made and the amount that the certificate states that she made.

Defective Formation   The ULPA states that a person who has contributed to the capital of a business (an "equity participant"), erroneously believing that he has become a limited partner in a limited partnership, is not liable as a general partner provided that on discovering the mistake he promptly renounces his interest in the profits of the business. See *Vidricksen v. Grover* which follows. It is unclear whether the profits that must be renounced include past, current, or future profits. The RULPA clarifies this ambiguity by requiring the equity participant either to withdraw from the business and renounce *future* profits or to file an amendment curing the defect. In any event, the RULPA provides that the equity participant will be liable to any third party who transacted business with the enterprise before the withdrawal or amendment and in good faith believed that the equity participant was a general partner at the time of the transaction.

VIDRICKSEN v. GROVER United States Court of Appeals, Ninth Circuit, 1966. 363 F.2d 372.	**FACTS:** Dr. Vidricksen contributed $25,000 to become a limited partner in a Chevrolet car agency business with Thom, the general partner. Articles of limited partnership were drawn up, but no effort was made to comply with the State's statutory requirement of recording the certificate of limited partnership. In March 1961, Vidricksen learned that he may not have formed a limited partnership because of the failure to file. At this time the business developed financial difficulties and went into bankruptcy on September 11, 1961. Eight days later Vidricksen filed a renunciation of the business's profits. The trustee in bankruptcy now seeks to have Dr. Vidricksen adjudged a general partner for bankruptcy purposes. **DECISION:** Judgment for the trustee in bankruptcy. Vidricksen was a general partner with Thom in so far as their relationship with third party creditors is concerned. A person who has contributed to the capital of a business erroneously believing that he has become a limited partner will not be considered a general partner if, upon ascertainment of the mistake, he promptly renounces his interest in the business's profits. Although Vidricksen had filed a renunciation, his renunciation was not prompt because it was filed six months after he first learned that something was wrong with the organizational setup.

Rights

Because limited partnerships are organized according to statute, the rights of the parties are usually set forth with relative clarity in the articles of limited partnership. In addition, a general partner of a limited partnership has all the rights and powers of a partner in a partnership without limited partners.

Control   The general partners of a limited partnership have almost exclusive control and management of the limited partnership. A limited partner, on the other hand, cannot share in the management or control of the association; if he does so, he forfeits his limited liability. However, the ULPA does not define what constitutes "taking part in control," and the courts have permitted limited partners to consult and advise the general partners about the business.

FACTS: Weil organized Diversified Properties as a limited partnership with varying degrees of ownership in several apartment complexes and other real estate located in Maryland. The parties signed a formal written agreement in July 1967, and the partnership was properly registered in the District of Columbia. Weil was the only general partner and managed the partnership's affairs until May 1, 1968. At that time the partnership encountered cash flow problems, and to help matters, Weil gave up both his office and his salary. At a partnership meeting held the following week, two third parties, Rubenstein and Tempchin, were selected by the limited partners to manage the partnership properties on a commission basis in accordance with a proposal that Weil had advanced earlier. Weil began working for another real estate company as a vice-president, but he remained a general partner of Diversified Properties. Creditors of the partnership, therefore, turned to him with demands for payment of the partnership debts that had not been met. Weil claims that after he surrendered his office and his salary, he remained as the general partner but that his directions were ignored. He also claims that the limited partners at various times gave direct orders to Rubenstein and Tempchin as to how to manage the partnership's affairs. Accordingly, he brings this action seeking to have the limited partners declared general partners.

DECISION: Judgment for the limited partners. As a general rule, a limited partner shall not become liable as a general partner unless, in addition to the exercise of his rights and powers as a limited partner, he takes part in the control of the business. The rule is intended to protect creditors, and, therefore, it cannot be invoked by a general partner to change his relationship with his copartners or to enlarge their liability. And even if Weil, as a general partner, could hold his limited partners to account as general partners under certain circumstances, he cannot do so on the facts of this case. A limited partner is not by reason of that status precluded from continuing to have an interest in the affairs of the partnership, from giving advice and general suggestions to the general partner or his nominees, or from interesting himself in the specific aspects of the business. This is particularly true where, as here, the partnership is in financial trouble. Such casual advice does not constitute the active interference in the day-to-day management of the partnership business that Weil claims took place. Thus, for the foregoing reasons, Weil is not entitled to have the court declare the limited partners to be general partners.

WEIL v. DIVERSIFIED PROPERTIES, INC.

United States District Court, District of Columbia, 1970. 319 F.Supp. 778.

The RULPA specifies a number of activities in which a limited partner may engage without losing limited liability:

1. being a contractor for or an agent or employee of the limited partnership or of a general partner;

2. consulting with and advising a general partner about the business of the limited partnership;

3. acting as surety for the limited partnership (suretyship is discussed in Chapter 37);

4. approving or disapproving an amendment to the partnership agreement; and

5. voting on one or more of the following matters:
   a. the dissolution and winding up of the partnership;
   b. the sale, exchange, lease, mortgage, pledge, or other transfer of all or substantially all of the assets of the limited partnership other than in the ordinary course of its business;
   c. the incurrence of indebtedness by the limited partnership other than in the ordinary course of its business;
   d. a change in the nature of the business; or
   e. the removal of a general partner.

More significantly, the RULPA restricts the liability of a limited partner, whose participation is not substantially the same as the exercise of the powers of a general partner, to persons who transact business with the limited partnership with actual knowledge of his participation in control.

Choice of Associates   No person may be added as a general partner or a limited partner without the consent of **all** partners. After the formation of a limited partnership the admission of additional limited partners requires the written consent of all partners unless the partnership agreement provides otherwise. The admission of the new limited partner is not effective until the certificate of limited partnership has been amended to reflect that fact. After the formation of a limited partnership new general partners may be admitted *only* with the specific written consent of each partner.

Assignment of Interest   A limited partner may assign her interest. If she does so, the assignee may become a substituted limited partner if all the other partners consent or if the assigning partner, having such power provided in the certificate, grants the assignee this right.

Profit Sharing   Unless otherwise agreed, a limited partner is entitled to his share of the profits as stated in the certificate before the general partners receive their share of the profits. A limited partner does not share in the losses of the partnership beyond his capital contribution.

Under the RULPA, the profits and losses are allocated among the partners as provided in the partnership agreement. If the partnership agreement does not make such a provision, then the profits and losses are allocated on the basis of the value of contributions actually made by each partner. Nonetheless, limited partners are not liable for losses beyond their capital contribution.

Return of Contribution   A limited partner may rightfully demand the return of his contribution on dissolution of the limited partnership, on the date specified in the certificate for its return, or on six-months' written demand if no time is specified in the certificate for the return of the contribution or for dissolution. In all cases, a limited partner may not receive his capital contribution unless there are sufficient partnership assets to pay all liabilities owed to third party creditors and limited partners, other than their capital contributions.

Loans   Under the ULPA, limited partners may make unsecured loans to the partnership and are entitled to repayment of the loan on a proportional basis with creditors of the partnership. The ULPA, however, prohibits limited partners from receiving or holding any partnership property as security for a loan made to the partnership. General partners also may make unsecured loans to the partnership but are subordinated to all claims of limited partners and outside creditors.

Under the RULPA both general and limited partners may be secured or unsecured creditors of the partnership with the same rights as a person who is not a partner, subject to applicable State and Federal bankruptcy and fraudulent conveyance statutes.

Duties and Liabilities

The duties and liabilities of general partners in a limited partnership are quite different from those of a limited partner. A general partner is subject to all the duties and restrictions of a partner in a partnership without limited partners, whereas a limited partner is subject to few, if any, duties and enjoys limited liability.

Duties   A *general partner* of a limited partnership has a **fiduciary** relationship to her limited partners. This fiduciary duty imposed on the general partner has extreme importance to the limited partners because of the restricted role that a limited partner may play in the control and management of the business enterprise. Conversely, it remains unclear whether a limited partner stands in a fiduciary relation to his general partners or the limited partnership. Very limited judicial authority on this question exists, but it seems to point toward not placing such a duty on the limited partner.

As with fiduciary duty, the law does not distinguish between the duty of care owed by a general partner to a general partnership and that owed by a general partner to a limited partnership. This results in part from the UPA, which provides that "the act will apply to limited partnerships except insofar as it is inconsistent with the statutes relating to such partnerships." The general partner, as shown in *Wyler v. Feuer*, must exercise in good faith reasonable business judgment. On the other hand, a limited partner owes no duty of care to a limited partnership as long a she remains a limited partner.

WYLER v. FEUER

California Court of Appeal, Second District, Division 2, 1978.
85 Cal.App.3d 392, 149 Cal.Rptr. 626.

FACTS: Feuer and Martin, associated as Feuer and Martin Productions, Inc., (FMPI), had been successful producers of Broadway musical comedies. Their first motion picture "Cabaret" received eight Academy Awards in 1973. In 1972, FMPI bought the motion picture and television rights to Simone Berteaut's best-selling books about her life with her half-sister Edith Piaf. To finance a movie based on this novel, FMPI sought a substantial private investment from Wyler. In July, 1973, Wyler signed a final limited partnership agreement with FMPI. The agreement stated that Wyler would provide, interest free, 100 percent financing for the proposed $1.6 million project, in return for a certain portion of the profits, not to exceed 50%. In addition, FMPI would obtain $850,000 in production financing by September 30, 1973. The contract specifically provided that FMPI's failure to raise this amount by September 30, 1973 "shall not be deemed a breach of this agreement" and that Wyler's sole remedy would be a reduction in the producer's fee.

A year after its release in 1974, the motion picture proved less than an overwhelming success—costing $1.5 million with total receipts only $478,000. From the receipts, Wyler received $313,500 for his investment. FMPI had failed to obtain an amount even close to the required $850,000 for production financing. Wyler then sued Feuer, Martin and FMPI for mismanagement of the business of the limited partnership and to recover his $1.5 million as damages.

DECISION: Judgment for Feuer, Martin and FMPI. In a limited partnership, the limited partner restricts his liability to the amount of his capital investment. In return, the limited partner surrenders the right to manage and control the partnership business. The general partner owes to the limited partner a duty of reasonable care in his management of the business. However, the general partner may not be held liable to the limited partner for mistakes made or losses incurred in the good faith exercise of reasonable business judgment.

Here, Wyler proved only that the motion picture did not make money, was not sought after by distributors, and did not live up to its producer's expectations. He failed to show that Feuer and Martin's decisions and efforts breached the standards of good faith and reasonableness. Therefore, he cannot recover damages from Feuer and Martin for an investment which simply turned sour.

Limited liability–liability for partnership debts or obligations only to the extent of the capital that the limited partner contributed or agreed to contribute

Liabilities   One of the most appealing features of a limited partnership is the **limited personal liability** it offers to limited partners. Limited liability means that once a limited partner has paid her contribution she has no further liability to the limited partnership nor its creditors. Thus, if a limited partner buys a 25 percent share of a limited partnership for $50,000 and does not forfeit her limited liability, her liability is limited to the $50,000 contributed even if the limited partnership suffers losses of $500,000. However, this protection is subject to three conditions:

1. that a certificate of limited partnership has been filed;

2. that the surname of the limited partner does not appear in the partnership name; and

3. that the limited partner does not take part in control of the business.

In addition, if the certificate contains a false statement, any one who suffers loss by reliance on that statement may hold liable any party to the certificate who knew the statement to be false. As long as the limited partner abides by these conditions, his liability for any and all obligations of the partnership is limited to his capital contribution. At the same time, the general partners of a limited partnership have unlimited external liability.

Dissolution

As with a general partnership, there are three steps involved in the extinguishment of a limited partnership: (1) dissolution, (2) winding up or liquidation and (3) termination. The causes of dissolution and the priorities in the distribution of the assets, however, are somewhat different from those in a general partnership.

Causes   In a limited partnership the limited partners do *not* have the right or the power to dissolve the partnership, except by decree of the court. The death or bankruptcy of a limited partner does not dissolve the partnership. However, the retirement, death or insanity of a general partner dissolves the partnership unless the business is continued by the remaining general partners under a right to do so stated in the certificate or with the consent of all members. In addition, the ULPA grants a limited partner the right to have the partnership dissolved and its affairs wound up whenever he rightfully but unsuccessfully demands the return of his contribution. This rather drastic remedy has been eliminated by the RULPA, which specifies more precisely those events that will trigger a dissolution, after which the affairs of the partnership must be liquidated. These events are:

1. the expiration of the time period or the happening of events specified in the certificate;

2. the unanimous written consent of all the partners;

3. the withdrawal of a general partner, unless all partners agree to continue the business; or

4. a decree of judicial dissolution which may be granted whenever it is not practicable to carry on the business according to the partnership agreement.

Distribution of Assets   The ULPA states that the assets of a limited partnership shall be distributed in the following order:

1. To creditors, in the order of priority as provided by law, except those to limited partners on account of their contributions and to general partners;

2. To limited partners for their share of the profits and other income on their contributions;

3. To limited partners for their capital contributions;

4. To general partners other than for capital and profits; *- loans*

5. To general partners for profits;

6. To general partners for capital contributions.

A limited partner shares proportionately with general creditors for advances beyond her capital contribution.

    The ULPA's provisions for dissolution and liquidation are unclear, incomplete, and contrary to the normal expectations of partners. The RULPA not only remedies these deficiencies but also introduces greater flexibility by explicitly authorizing the partners to vary by agreement the internal priorities in distributing the assets of the partnership. The RULPA makes it clear that, to the extent that both general and limited partners are also creditors (other than in respect of their interests in the partnership), they share proportionately with other creditors. In addition, once the partnership's obligation to make a distribution to partners has accrued, it must be paid after monies owed to creditors but before any other distributions of equity. Finally, general and limited partners rank on the same level, except as otherwise provided in the partnership agreement, in sharing the return of their capital contributions and profits, in that order.

    Figure 32–2 provides a comparison of general and limited partners.

Other Types of Unincorporated Business Associations

Joint Venture

A joint venture or joint adventure is a form of temporary partnership organized to carry out a *single* or isolated business enterprise for profit. Usually,

joint venture–association of two or more persons to engage in a single business transaction for a profit

---

FIGURE 32-2 Comparison of General and Limited Partners

	General Partner	Limited Partner
Control	Has all the rights and powers of a partner in a partnership without limited partners	Has no right to take part in management or control
Liability	Unlimited	Limited, unless takes part in control or name used
Agency	Is an agent of the partnership	Is not an agent of the partnership
Fiduciary Duty	Yes	No
Duty of Care	Yes	No

although not necessarily, it is of short duration. It is an association of persons who combine their property, money, efforts, skill, and knowledge for the purpose of carrying out a single business operation for profit. An example is a securities underwriting syndicate. Another is a syndicate formed to acquire a certain tract of land for subdivision and resale. A third example is provided in *Florida Tomato Packers, Inc. v. Wilson*, which follows. A joint venture differs from a partnership, which is formed to carry on a business over a considerable or indefinite period of time. A joint venturer is *not* an agent of her co-venturers and does not necessarily have authority to bind them, although in a given case a joint venturer may have actual or apparent authority to bind her co-venturers. Usually the management and operation of the enterprise is placed by agreement in the hands of one member designated as manager. The death of a partner dissolves the partnership, whereas the death of a joint venturer does not necessarily dissolve the joint venture. A partner cannot sue a co-partner or the firm at law, but must go into equity for relief. On the other hand, a court of law will take jurisdiction over disputes between joint venturers. Except for these principal differences, a joint venture is generally governed by the law of partnerships.

FLORIDA TOMATO PACKERS, INC. v. WILSON

District Court of Appeal of Florida, Third District, 1974.

FACTS: On September 23, 1971, Campbell was driving a farm vehicle owned by Lytton which struck an automobile owned and operated by Willie Wilson. When the accident occurred, Campbell was employed as a farm hand by Lytton. Prior to the accident, Lytton, a tomato farmer, had entered into an arrangement with Florida Tomato Packers, Inc., a corporation engaged in the business of packing, selling, wholesaling and distributing tomatoes. According to this agreement, Lytton planted and raised the tomatoes, and transported them to Florida Tomato Packers' warehouse. Florida Tomato Packers paid all of Lytton's farming bills, including land and equipment rentals, equipment repair, gasoline and oil, seeds and fertilizer, and all labor. The corporation also packed, crated, shipped and sold the crop, after it arrived at the packing house. Any profits from the sale of the tomatoes were equally divided between Lytton and the corporation.

The Wilsons sued Florida Tomato Packers for the damages caused by the accident with Campbell.

DECISION: Judgment for the Wilsons. A joint venture is an association of persons or legal entities to carry out a single business for profit. Although a joint venture is a less formal relationship than a partnership, they both share several characteristics. The following elements must concur to create a joint venture: (1) a community of interest in the performance of the common purpose; (2) joint control or right of control; (3) a joint proprietary interest in the subject matter; (4) a right to share in profits; and (5) a duty to share in any losses which may be sustained. Here, the agreement provided that Lytton would provide the labor and Florida Tomato Packers would furnish funds and marketing. In such a case, a duty to share in losses may be implied. In addition, the two were to divide any profits equally. This arrangement is, therefore, a joint venture. Participants in a joint venture are each liable for the torts of the other or the other's servants in the joint undertaking. Since the accident occurred within the course and scope of Campbell's employment with Lytton, Florida Tomato Packers is also liable.

Joint Stock Company

Joint stock company--a general partnership with some corporate attributes

A joint stock company, or joint stock association as it is sometimes called, is technically a form of general partnership that has some of the characteristics of a corporation and differs in several important ways from the ordinary partnership. It is unlike a partnership in that:

1. its capital is divided into shares represented by transferable certificates;

2. its business and affairs are managed by directors or managers elected by the members, who alone have the authority to represent and bind it;

3. its members are not its agents; and

4. a transfer of shares by a member or his death, insanity, or other incapacity does not dissolve it or give grounds for dissolution.

It is similar to a partnership, but unlike a corporation, in that it is formed by contract and not by State authority.

Mining Partnerships

A mining partnership is an association of the several owners of the mineral rights in land for the purpose of operating a mine and extracting minerals of economic value for their mutual profit. Although mining partnerships are governed to a considerable extent by the law of general partnerships, there are certain important differences between them. For example, a mining partner has the right to sell his interest in the partnership, and the death of a partner does not dissolve a mining partnership.

Mining partnership–a specific type of partnership for the purpose of extracting raw minerals

Limited Partnership Associations

Limited partnership associations are permitted by statute in certain States. This type of organization is a legal hybrid. Although called a partnership association, it closely resembles a corporation. It is a legal entity separate and distinct from its members, who are not personally responsible for its debts, their liabilities being limited to their capital contribution, except in the event of violation of some statutory provision. An important difference between this kind of association and a corporation pertains to the transfer of shares. Although the shares in a limited partnership association are freely transferable, the transferee does not, however, become a member in the association unless so elected by the other members. If membership is refused, he may recover the value of his shares from the association.

Limited partnership association–a partnership which closely resembles a corporation

Business Trusts

A trust is a transfer of the legal title to certain specific property to one person for the use and benefit of another. Where an express trust results from contract, the agreement is commonly known as a declaration of trust. It customarily sets forth a designation of the property, the duration of the trust, the exact functions and duties of the trustees concerning the management of the property, the persons to whom the income of the trust is to be paid and the share to be received by each, the method of winding up the trust, and the person or persons entitled to share in the trust property on termination. See Chapter 46 for a more complete discussion of trusts.

Business trust–a trust (managed by a trustee for the benefit of a beneficiary) established to conduct a business for a profit.

Although trusts are almost as old as the law of equity itself, it was not until late in the nineteenth century that lawyers and business realized that the trust concept could be used as a method of conducting a commercial enterprise. The business trust, sometimes called a Massachusetts trust, was devised to avoid the burdens of corporate regulation and particularly the formerly widespread prohibition denying to corporations the power to own and deal in real estate. Like an ordinary trust between natural persons, a business trust may be created by a voluntary agreement without authorization or consent of the State.

A business trust has three distinguishing characteristics: (1) the trust estate is devoted to the conduct of a business; (2) by the terms of the agreement each beneficiary is entitled to a certificate evidencing his ownership of a beneficial interest in the trust that he is free to sell or otherwise transfer; and (3) the trustees must have the exclusive right to manage and control the business free from control of the beneficiaries. If the third condition is not met the trust may fail; the beneficiaries would then become personally liable for the obligations of the business as partners.

The trustees are personally liable for the debts of the business unless, in entering into contractual relations with others, it is expressly stated or definitely understood between the parties that the obligation is incurred solely on the responsibility of the trust estate. To escape personal liability on the contractual obligations of the business, the trustee must obtain the agreement or consent of the other contracting party to look solely to the assets of the trust. The personal liability of the trustees for their own torts or the torts of their agents and servants employed in the operation of the business stands on a different footing. While this liability cannot be avoided, the risk involved may be reduced substantially or eliminated altogether by insurance.

CHAPTER SUMMARY

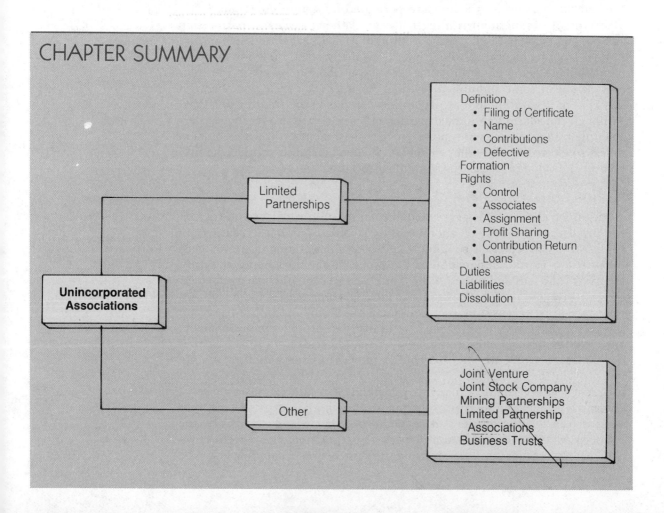

KEY TERMS

Limited partnership
Certificate of limited partnership
Defective formation
Control

Limited liability
Dissolution
Joint venture
Joint stock company

Mining partnership
Limited partnership association
Business trust

PROBLEMS

1. John Palmer and Henry Morrison formed the partnership of Palmer & Morrison for the management of the Huntington Hotel. The partnership agreement provided that Palmer would contribute $40,000 and be a general partner and Morrison would contribute $30,000 and be a limited partner. Palmer was to manage the dining and cocktail rooms, and Morrison was to manage the rest of the hotel. Nanette, a popular French singer, who knew nothing of the partnership affairs, appeared for four weeks in the Blue Room at the hotel and was not paid her fee of $8,000. Subsequently, Palmer and Morrison had a difference of opinion, and Palmer bought Morrison's interest in the partnership for $20,000. Palmer later went into bankruptcy. Nanette sued Morrison for $8,000. For how much, if anything, is Morrison liable?

2. A limited partnership was formed consisting of Webster as the general partner and Stevens and Stewart as the limited partners. The limited partnership was organized in strict compliance with the limited partnership statute. Stevens was employed by the partnership as a purchasing agent. Stewart personally guaranteed a loan made to the partnership. Both Stevens and Stewart consulted with Webster about partnership business, voted on a change in the nature of the partnership business, and disapproved an amendment to the partnership agreement proposed by Webster. The partnership experienced serious financial difficulties and its creditors seek to hold Webster, Stevens, and Stewart personally liable for the debts of the partnership. Decision?

3. Fox, Dodge, and Gilbey agreed to become limited partners in Palatine Ventures, a limited partnership. The certificate of limited partnership stated that each would contribute $20,000. Fox's contribution consisted entirely of cash; Dodge contributed $12,000 in cash and gave the partnership her promissory note for $8,000; and Gilbey's contribution was his promise to perform 500 hours of legal services to the partnership. What liability, if any, do Fox, Dodge, and Gilbey have to the partnership by way of capital contribution?

4. Madison and Tilson agree to form a limited partnership with Madison as general partner and Tilson as the limited partner, each to contribute $12,500 as capital. No papers were ever filed, and after ten months the enterprise fails with liabilities exceeding assets by $30,000. Creditors of the partnership seek to hold Madison and Tilson personally liable for the $30,000. Decision?

5. Kraft is a limited partner of Johnson Enterprises, a limited partnership. As provided in the limited partnership agreement, Kraft decided to leave the partnership and demanded that her capital contribution of $20,000 be returned. At this time the partnership assets were $150,000 and liabilities to all creditors totaled $140,000. The partnership returned to Kraft her capital contribution of $20,000. What liability, if any, does Kraft have to the creditors of Johnson Enterprises?

6. Gordon is the only limited partner in a limited partnership whose general partners are Daniels and McKenna. Gordon contributed $10,000 for his limited partnership interest and loaned the partnership $7,500. Daniels and McKenna each contributed $5,000 by way of capital. After a year the partnership is dissolved, at which time it owes $12,500 to its only creditor, Dickel, and has assets of $30,000. How should these assets be distributed?

7. A limited partner has which of the following rights or powers: (a) to assign his interest in the limited partnership, (b) to receive repayment of loans made to the partnership on a *pro rata* basis with general creditors, (c) to manage the affairs of the limited partnership, (d) to receive his share of the profits before the general partners receive their share of the profits, (e) to dissolve the partnership if he withdraws from the partnership.

PART SEVEN
CORPORATIONS

PART SEVEN

CORPORATIONS

PUBLIC POLICY, SOCIAL ISSUES AND BUSINESS ETHICS

Corporations are without question the major form of business organization in the United States. Corporate assets currently exceed $5 trillion, corporate revenues now exceed $4 trillion annually, and about 30 million persons directly own shares in corporations. In addition, another 100 million persons own shares indirectly through institutional investors, such as banks, insurance companies, pension funds, and investment companies. Moreover, corporations employ three-fourths of the nation's labor force.

There are two basic types of corporations—closely held and publicly held. Harry Henn and John Alexander describe the two forms in *Laws of Corporations:*

The closely-held corporation desires to function and does function very differently from the larger corporations with public shareholders. In the closely-held corporation, there are usually no public investors; its shareholders are active in the conduct and management of the business (with resulting coincidence of control and management); the insiders want to keep out outsiders (delectus personae), and the emphasis is on simplified and informal procedures with all participating, with attendant possible risk of deadlock. In short, its member or members desire to gain certain corporate advantages, such as limited liability and certain corporate tax consequences (with minimization of double taxation), at the same time preserving many of the internal attributes of an individual proprietorship or partnership.

In contrast with the closely-held corporation, larger corporations with public shareholders and other investors necessarily involve substantial separation of ownership and control, have a form of representative government-by-the-majority, with management delegated to a board of directors, following rather formal procedures, and operate in a relatively institutionalized and depersonalized manner, which is not susceptible to deadlock. The transfer of its shares is usually not only free from transfer restrictions but is facilitated by securities exchange listing or an active over-the-counter market.

Most incorporated business entities in the United States are closely held. Nonetheless, their special needs, which in many instances differ from those of publicly held corporations, have not until recently received any specific statutory attention. One of the difficulties in drafting such legislation is the great diversity of closely held corporations. Nevertheless, they do have one common problem: minority shareholders in closely held corporations are especially in need of protection from oppression exerted by other shareholders. The typical shareholder has a relatively large investment of his time and financial assets committed to the closely held corporation, and the need to protect his reasonable expectations is greater than that of a shareholder in a publicly held corporation. Although many forms of unfair treatment exist, there are two basic types of oppression in a closely held corporation. First, and probably most widespread, is the oppression of the minority shareholders by the majority shareholders. Without specific legal protection, the minority shareholders are essentially subject to the good will of the majority. The second type of oppression is that exercised by the minority on the majority shareholders, which can occur when minority shareholders who have a veto power over action desired by the majority misuse their power. Under these circumstances the majority needs an adequate remedy to resolve the deadlock. In the absence of special statutes for closely held corporations (only a dozen States have such legislation), the shareholders must provide their own protection through carefully drawn shareholder agreements and bylaws. While studying the corporate legal norms in the next four chapters, you should be alert to their failure to address the special requirements of the most common of corporations, the closely held corporation.

Whereas the shareholders of a closely held corporation need protection from oppression by other *shareholders,* those who own shares in a publicly held corporation need protection from unfair treatment by *management,* that is, the officers of the corporation who are supposedly selected by the board of directors who are elected by the shareholders. In *Taming the Giant Corporation,* Nader, Green, and Seligman state: "In reality, this legal image is virtually a myth. In nearly every large American business corporation, there exists a management autocracy. One man—variously titled the President, or the Chairman of the Board, or the Chief Executive Officer—or a small coterie of men rule the corporation. Far from being chosen by the directors to run the corporation, this chief exectutive or executive clique chooses the board of directors and, with the acquiescence of the board, controls the corporation." In a classic study published in 1932, Adolf Berle and Gardner Means concluded that great amounts of economic power had been concentrated in a relatively few large corporations, that the ownership of these corporations had become widely dispersed, and that the shareholders of these corporations had become far removed from active participation in manage-

ment. Since their original study these trends have steadily continued, and in 1981 the 500 largest U.S. industrial corporations had sales of $1,773.4 billion, profits of $84.2 billion, assets of $1,282.8 billion and 15,600,000 employees.

Thus vast amounts of wealth and power are now controlled by a small number of corporations, which are in turn controlled by a small group of corporate officers. In fact, the separation of ownership and control has widened so far that Myles Mace, a leading scholar in this area, has stated that boards of directors are so reluctant to discharge ineffective management that they fire a chief executive only when "the leadership of the [chief executive] was so unsatisfactory that even his mother thought he ought [to be removed] for the good of the company . . . before the board [of directors] reluctantly moved."

These developments raise a large number of social, policy, and ethical issues about how large publicly owned corporations are governed. These issues include the following: Who is actually running these corporations, and who should run them? To whom are they accountable, and to whom should they be accountable? What role should employees and shareholders have in corporate governance? Should the existing system of governance be changed, and if so, how? Is chartering by the States effective, or should these corporations be Federally chartered? The resolution of these and other issues is critical to dealing with a number of national policy issues affecting business, such as long-term economic prospects, employment policies, health and safety in the workplace, the quality of products, the effects of overseas operations, and environmental decisions. While reading the chapters on corporations, keep in mind the social, policy, and ethical concerns that have an impact on the operations of the large publicly held American business corporation.

NATURE AND FORMATION

A corporation is an entity created by law that exists separate and distinct from the individuals whose contributions of initiative, property, and control enable it to function. The corporation is the dominant form of business organization in the United States, accounting for 88 percent of the gross receipts of all business entities (see Figure 33–1). Domestic corporations currently doing business in the United States number well over 2 million and have annual revenues and assets in the trillions of dollars. Use of the corporation as an instrument of commercial enterprise has made possible the vast concentrations of wealth and capital that have largely transformed this country from an agrarian to an industrial economy. Due to its size, power, and impact, the business corporation is a key institution not only in the American economy but also in the world power structure.

In 1946 a committee of the American Bar Association after careful study and research submitted a draft of a Model State Business Corporation Act (MBCA). The Model Act has been amended frequently since then. The provisions of the Model Act do not become law until enacted by a State, but its influence has been widespread, and it has been adopted in whole or in part by a majority of the States. As a recommended model statute, it sets a standard for the statutory law of business corporations, and we will use it throughout the chapters on corporations in this text. Because a number of States have not amended their versions of the MBCA, the text will discuss the Model Act in both its amended and unamended forms. The Appendix of this text contains selected provisions of the MBCA as amended.

In 1983 a major revision of the Model Act was completed and distributed for comment. In 1984 it was approved by the Committee on Corporate Laws of the Section of Corporation, Banking and Business Law of the American Bar Association. It is "designed to be a convenient guide for revision of state business corporation statutes, reflecting current views as to the appropriate accommodation of the various commercial and social interests involved in modern business corporations." The Revised Act is the first complete revision of the Model Act in over 30 years although there had been numerous statutory amendments to it since it was first published. One of the tasks of the revision was to reorganize the provisions of the Model Act more logically and to revise

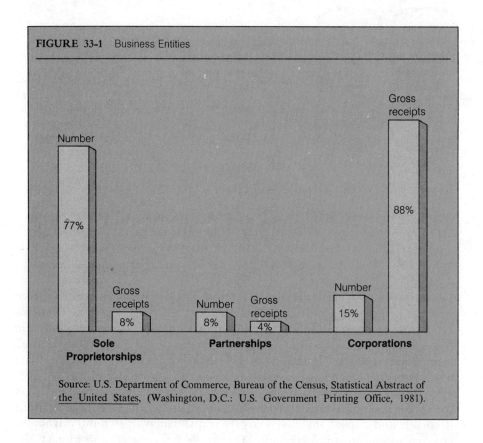

FIGURE 33-1   Business Entities

Source: U.S. Department of Commerce, Bureau of the Census, Statistical Abstract of the United States, (Washington, D.C.: U.S. Government Printing Office, 1981).

the language to make the Act more consistent. In addition, substantive changes were made in a number of areas. We will discuss those provisions of the Revised Act that have made significant changes in the Model Act as amended. We will refer to the revision as the Revised Act or the RMBCA.

Nature of Corporations

Corporations can be most readily understood by examining the common attributes and the various types of corporations. We discuss both of these topics in this section.

Corporate Attributes

The principal attributes of a corporation are that (1) it is a legal entity; (2) it owes its existence to a State, which also regulates it; (3) it provides limited liability to its shareholders; (4) its shares of stock are freely transferable; (5) it may have perpetual existence; (6) its management is centralized; and it is considered, for some purposes, (7) a person and (8) a citizen.

Legal Entity

Legal entity–an organization having a separate legal existence from its members

A corporation is a legal entity separate and apart from its shareholders, with rights and liabilities entirely distinct from theirs. It may sue or be sued by, as well as contract with, any other party, including any one of its shareholders. A transfer of stock in the corporation from one individual to another has no effect on the legal existence of the corporation. Title to corporate property belongs not to the shareholders but to the corporation. Even where a single individual owns all of the stock of the corporation, the shareholder and the corporation are not the same but have separate and distinct existences.

Creature of the State

A corporation may be formed only by compliance with a State incorporation statute. A corporation's charter and the provisions of the statute under which it is formed constitute a contract between it and the State. Article I, Section 10, of the United States Constitution provides that no State shall pass any law "impairing the obligation of contracts," and this prohibition applies to contracts between a State and a corporation.

To avoid the impact of this provision, incorporation statutes reserve to the State the power to prescribe such regulations, provisions, and limitations as it deems advisable and to amend, repeal, or modify the statute at its pleasure. This reservation is a material part of the contract between the State and a corporation formed under the statute, and amendments or modifications regulating or altering the structure of the corporation do not impair the obligation of contract because they are expressly permitted by the contract.

Limited Liability

A corporation is a legal entity and is therefore liable out of its own assets for its debts. Generally, the shareholders are *not personally liable* for the corporation's debts beyond the amount of their investment—although later in this chapter we discuss certain circumstances under which a shareholder may be personally liable. By the same token, the corporation is not liable for the personal obligations of its shareholders.

> **Limited liability**–liability limited to amount invested in a business enterprise

Free Transferability of Corporate Shares

In the absence of contractual restrictions, shares in a corporation may be freely transferred by sale, gift, or pledge. The ability to transfer shares is a valuable right and may enhance their market value. Transfers of shares of stock are governed by Article 8 of the Uniform Commercial Code, Investment Securities, and are discussed in Chapter 34.

Perpetual Existence

A corporation has perpetual existence unless a limited period of duration is stated in its articles of incorporation. As a consequence, the death or withdrawal of a shareholder, director, or officer does not terminate the existence of a corporation.

Centralized Management

The shareholders of a corporation elect the **board of directors,** which manages the business affairs of the corporation. The board must then appoint **officers** to run the day-to-day operations of the business. Because neither the directors nor the officers (collectively referred to as "management") need be shareholders, it is entirely possible, and in large corporations quite typical, for the ownership of the corporation to be separated from the management of the corporation. We discuss the management structure of corporations further in Chapter 35.

As a Person

Whether a corporation is a "person" within the meaning of a constitution or statute is a matter of construction based on the intent of the lawmakers in using the word. For example, a corporation is considered a person within the provision in the Fifth and Fourteenth Amendments to the Federal Constitution that no "person" shall be "deprived of life, liberty or property without due process of law" and in the provision in the Fourteenth Amendment that no State shall "deny to any person within its jurisdiction the equal protection of the laws." A corporation also enjoys the right of a person to be secure against unreasonable searches and seizures, as provided for in the Fourth Amendment. On the other hand, a corporation is not considered to be a person within the clause of the Fifth Amendment that protects a "person" against self-incrimination.

As a Citizen

A corporation is considered a citizen for some purposes but not for others. A corporation is not a citizen as the term is used in the Fourteenth Amendment, which provides "No state shall make or enforce any law which shall abridge the privileges or immunities of citizens of the United States."

A corporation, however, is regarded as a citizen of the State of its incorporation and of the State in which it has its principal office for the purpose of determining whether diversity of citizenship exists between the parties to a lawsuit as a basis for jurisdiction of the Federal courts.

Corporations differ from partnerships because of these and other attributes. Figure 33–2 further outlines the differences and similarities of general partnerships, limited partnerships, and corporations.

Classification of Corporations

Corporations may be classified as public or private, profit or nonprofit, domestic or foreign, closely held, and professional. As you will see, these classifications are not mutually exclusive. For example, a corporation may be a closely held, professional, private, profit, domestic corporation.

Public or Private

A public corporation is one that is created to administer a unit of local civil government, such as a county, city, town, village, school district, or park district or one created by the United States to conduct public business, such as the Tennessee Valley Authority or the Federal Deposit Insurance Corporation. Many public corporations are also referred to as municipal corporations.

A private corporation is one organized to conduct either a privately owned business enterprise for profit or a nonprofit corporation organized for community benefit or enjoyment.

Profit or Nonprofit

A profit corporation is one founded for the purpose of operating a business for profit from which payments are made to its shareholders in the form of dividends.

Although a nonprofit (or not-for-profit) corporation may make a profit, the profit may not be distributed to its members, directors, or officers but must be used exclusively for the charitable, educational, or scientific purpose

FIGURE 33-2   General Partnership, Limited Partnership, and Corporation Compared

	Partnership	Limited Partnership*	Corporation
Creation	By agreement of the parties	By statutory authorization	By statutory authorization
Entity	A legal entity for some but not all purposes	A legal entity for some but not all purposes	A legal entity
Duration	Dissolved by death, bankruptcy, or withdrawal of a partner	Limited partner may dissolve partnership only by decree of court	May be perpetual
Liability	Partners are subject to unlimited liability upon the contracts, debts, and torts of the partnership	Limited partners are not generally liable for the contracts, debts, or torts of the partnership	Shareholders are not generally liable for the contracts, debts, or torts of the corporation
Transferability	Interest of a partner in a partnership may be assigned but the assignee does not become a partner	Interest of a limited partner may be assigned and assignee may become a substituted limited partner if all members consent	Shares of stock in a corporation are freely transferable
Management	Each partner is entitled to an equal voice in the management and control of the business	Limited partner may not take part in control of the business	The business of the corporation is managed by a board of directors elected by the shareholders
Agency	Each partner is an agent of the partnership	Limited partner is not an agent of the partnership	A shareholder is neither a principal nor an agent of the corporation
Suits	In actions brought by or against the partnership all partners are generally necessary parties	Limited partners are not a necessary party except where suit is to enforce their rights against or liability to the partnership.	The corporation may sue and be sued in its own name

*A general partner of a limited partnership has all the rights, powers and liabilities of a partner in a general partnership.

for which it was organized. Examples of nonprofit corporations include private schools, library clubs, athletic clubs, fraternities, sororities, and hospitals.

Domestic or Foreign

A corporation is domestic in the State in which it is incorporated. It is foreign in every other State or jurisdiction. A corporation may not do business, except for acts in interstate commerce, in a State other than the State of its incorporation without the permission and authorization of the other State. Every State, however, provides for the issuance to foreign corporations of a certificate to do business within its borders and for the taxation of such foreign businesses. Obtaining a certificate (called "qualifying") usually involves filing certain information with the Secretary of State, the payment of prescribed fees, and designation of a resident agent. Conduct typically requiring a certificate of authority includes maintaining an office to conduct local intrastate business, selling personal property not in interstate commerce, entering into

Domestic corporation–corporation created under the laws of a given State

Foreign corporation–corporation created under the laws of any other State, government or country

contracts relating to local business or sales, and owning or using real estate for general corporate purposes. A single agreement or isolated transaction within a State does not constitute doing business, as in the next case.

A foreign corporation that transacts business without having first qualified may be subject to a number of penalties. Most statutes provide that an unlicensed foreign corporation doing business in the State shall not be entitled to maintain a suit in the State courts until it has obtained a certificate of authority. However, a failure to obtain a certificate of authority to transact business in the State does not impair the validity of a contract entered into by the corporation and does not prevent it from defending any action or proceeding brought against it in the State. In addition, many States impose fines on corporations that do not obtain certificates, and a few States also impose fines on the corporation's officers and directors, as well as holding them personally liable on contracts made within the State.

A State may also specify conditions under which a license or certificate of authority shall be revoked. In general, the statutes provide that a failure to pay taxes, file reports, or maintain a registered agent or registered office in the State will justify revocation of a license.

REISMAN v. MARTORI, MEYER, HENDRICKS, & VICTOR

Court of Appeals of Georgia, 1980.
155 Ga.App. 551, 271 S.E.2d 685.

FACTS: The plaintiff is an Arizona professional corporation consisting of approximately 18 lawyers. The defendant, Dr. Reisman, is a medical doctor and general surgeon practicing in Georgia. In November of 1977, Dr. Reisman engaged Edwin Hendricks, a member of the law firm, to provide legal advice and representation in a dispute between himself and the Floyd County Medical Center. Hendricks flew to Atlanta and hired local counsel with Dr. Reisman's approval. Hendricks represented Dr. Reisman in two hearings before the hospital and one court proceeding as well as negotiating a compromise between Dr. Reisman and the hospital. The total bill for the law firm's travel costs and professional services was $21,438.14 but Dr. Reisman refused to pay $6,438.14 of it. The law firm brought an action against Dr. Reisman for the balance owed and a jury awarded the firm the full amount of the unpaid portion of the bill. Dr. Reisman appealed arguing that the action should have been dismissed because the law firm failed to register as a foreign corporation in accordance with the Georgia Corporation Statute.

DECISION: Judgment for the law firm. In most jurisdictions, single or isolated transactions do not constitute doing business within the meaning of such registration statutes. Even if the transactions are part of the business which the corporation is organized to conduct, such isolated acts will not constitute doing business if they indicate no intent to engage in continuous business activity. The purpose of such statutes is to require registration of foreign corporations intending to conduct business within the State on a continuous basis, not as a temporary matter.

Here, the law firm's activities were concentrated in Arizona, although various attorneys in the firm handled litigation outside the State of incorporation. Furthermore, Hendricks had represented clients in Georgia on two prior occasions, but these had nothing to do with his representation of Dr. Reisman. The law firm's representation of Dr. Reisman amounted to an isolated transaction. Therefore, a certificate of authority was not required and the firm can collect from Dr. Reisman.

Closely Held

Closely held corporation–corporation that is owned by few shareholders and whose shares are not actively traded

A corporation is described as closely held when its outstanding shares of stock are held by a small number of persons, frequently family relatives or friends. In most closely held corporations the shareholders are active in the management and control of the business. Accordingly, the shareholders are concerned with who their fellow shareholders are, and therefore they typically enter into a buy-sell agreement with one another at the time of incorporation in order to prevent the stock from getting into the hands of persons outside the original group of shareholders. Although most corporations in the United States are closely held, they account for only a small fraction of corporate revenues and assets.

In most States closely held corporations are subject to the general incorporation statute that governs all corporations. The 1969 amendments to the MBCA included a number of liberalizing provisions for closely held corporations. Some States, however, have enacted special legislation to accommodate the needs of closely held corporations. Moreover, a Statutory Close Corporation Supplement to the MBCA has recently been promulgated.

Professional Corporations

All of the States have a "professional association act" that permits the practice of professions by duly licensed individuals under corporate form. Some statutes apply to all professions licensed to practice within the State, whereas others apply only to specified professions. The purpose of the statute in authorizing the formation of this type of corporation under specified limitations is to permit duly licensed professionals to obtain tax advantages not allowable to individuals or partnerships. Nonetheless, as a result of the Tax Equity and Fiscal Responsibility Act of 1982, which became effective in 1984, these tax advantages of the corporate form have in the main been eliminated.

Formation of a Corporation

Incorporation involves greater expense and formality than the formation of any other form of business organization. The formation of a corporation under a general incorporation statute requires the performance of several acts by various groups, individuals, and State officials. The procedure to organize a corporation begins with the promotion of the proposed corporation by its organizers, also known as **promoters,** who procure offers by interested persons known as **subscribers** to buy stock in the corporation when created and who also prepare the necessary incorporation papers. The articles of incorporation are then executed by the **incorporators** and filed with the Secretary of State, who issues the charter or certificate of incorporation. Finally, an organization meeting is held by the incorporators and shareholders or by the directors.

Organizing the Corporation

Promoters

A promoter is a person who brings about the "birth" of a corporation. The promoter arranges for the capital and financing of the corporation as well as assembling the necessary assets, equipment, licenses, personnel, leases, and services. He will also attend to the actual legal formation of the corporation. On incorporation, the promoter's organizational task is finished.

> Promoter–person who takes the preliminary steps to organize a corporation

Promoters' Contracts   In additional to procuring subscriptions and preparing the incorporation papers, promoters often enter into contracts in anticipation of the creation of the corporation. The contracts may be ordinary agreements necessary for the eventual operation of the business, such as leases, purchase orders, employment contracts, sales contracts, or franchises. If these contracts are executed by the promoter in her own name and there is no further action, the promoter is liable on such contracts, and the corporation, when created, is not liable. Moreover, a preincorporation contract made by promoters in the name of the corporation and on its behalf does not bind the corporation, except where so provided by statute. The promoter, in executing such contracts, may do so in the corporate name even though incorporation has not yet taken place. Before its formation a corporation has no capacity to enter into contracts or to employ agents or representatives. After its formation it is not liable at common law on any prior contract, even one made in its name, unless it adopts or ratifies the contract expressly, impliedly, or by knowingly accepting benefits under it.

A promoter who enters into a preincorporation contract in the name of the corporation usually remains liable on that contract even if the corporation adopts or ratifies the contract. This results from the rule of agency law that a principal must be in existence at the time a contract is made in order to ratify it. A promoter will be relieved of liability, however, if the contract itself provides that adoption shall terminate the promoter's liability or if the promoter, the third party, and the corporation enter into a novation substituting the corporation for the promoter.

Figure 33-3 summarizes the liability of the promoter and the corporation for preincorporation contracts.

Promoters' Fiduciary Duty   The promoters of a corporation occupy a fiduciary relationship among themselves as well as to the corporation, to its subscribers, and to its initial shareholders. This duty requires good faith, fair dealing, and full disclosure. Accordingly, the promoters are under a duty to account for any secret profit realized by them at the expense of those to whom this duty is owing. Failure to disclose may also violate Federal or State securities laws discussed in Chapter 40.

GOLDEN v. OAHE ENTERPRISES, INC.

Supreme Court of South Dakota, 1980.
295 N.W.2d 160.

FACTS: Oahe Enterprises was formed by the efforts of Emmick who acted as a promoter and contributed shares of Colonial Manors, Inc. (CM) stock in exchange for stock in Oahe. The CM stock had been valued by CM's directors for internal stock-option purposes at nineteen dollars per share. One month prior to Emmick's incorporation of Oahe Enterprises, however, CM's board reduced the stock value to $9.50 per share. Although Emmick knew of this reduction prior to the meeting to form Oahe Enterprises, he did not disclose this information to the Morrises, the other shareholders of the new corporation. Oahe Enterprises then brought this action to recover the shortfall.

DECISION: Judgment for Oahe Enterprises. As a promoter of Oahe Enterprises, Emmick stood in a fiduciary position to both Oahe and its shareholders, owing a duty to deal with them in the utmost good faith. He failed in this duty by not disclosing the information about the CM stock that he intended to transfer to Oahe for Oahe stock. His obtaining of a secret profit was a fraud on Oahe and its shareholders, and Emmick must account to the corporation for that profit.

Subscribers

Subscriber–person who agrees to purchase initial stock in a corporation

A **preincorporation subscription** is an offer to purchase capital stock in a corporation yet to be formed. The offeror is called a subscriber. Courts have traditionally viewed subscriptions in two ways. The majority regards a sub-

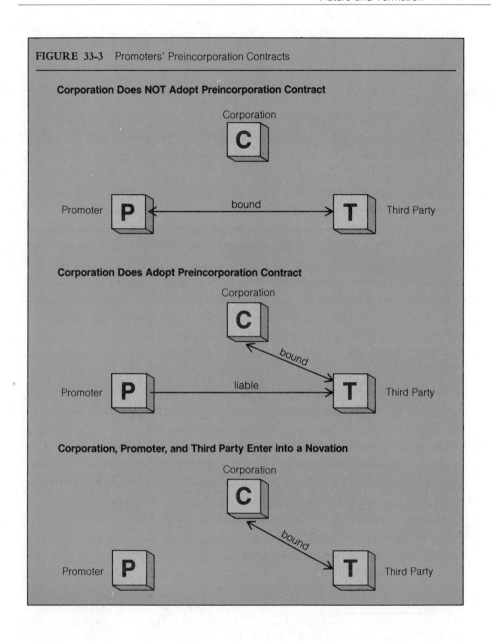

FIGURE 33-3   Promoters' Preincorporation Contracts

Corporation Does NOT Adopt Preincorporation Contract

Corporation

C

Promoter   **P** ←——— bound ———→   **T**   Third Party

Corporation Does Adopt Preincorporation Contract

Corporation

C

Promoter   **P** ——— liable ———→ **T**   Third Party

bound

Corporation, Promoter, and Third Party Enter into a Novation

Corporation

C

Promoter   **P**   **T**   Third Party

bound

scription as a continuing offer to purchase stock from a nonexisting entity, which is incapable of accepting the offer until created. Under this view a subscription may be revoked at any time prior to its acceptance. A minority of jurisdictions treat a subscription as a contract among the various subscribers, which makes it irrevocable except with the consent of all of the subscribers. Modern incorporation statutes have taken an intermediate position in resolving this issue. The MBCA provides that a subscription is irrevocable for a period of six months, unless otherwise provided in the subscription agreement or unless all of the subscribers consent to the revocation of the subscription. If the corporation accepts the subscription during the period of irrevocability, the subscription becomes a contract binding on both the subscriber and the corporation, as the following case explains.

LITTLE SWITZERLAND BREWING CO. v. OXLEY

Supreme Court of West Virginia, 1973.
156 W.Va. 800, 197 S.E.2d 301.

FACTS: Little Switzerland was incorporated on January 28, 1968. On February 18, Ellison and Oxley were made directors of the company after they purchased some stock. Then, on September 25, Ellison and Oxley signed stock subscription agreements to purchase 5,000 shares each. Under the agreement, they both issued a note which indicated that they would pay for the stock "at their discretion." In March 1970, the board of directors passed a resolution canceling the stock subscription agreements of Ellison and Oxley. The creditors of Little Switzerland brought this suit against Ellison and Oxley to recover the money owed under the subscription agreements.

DECISION: Judgment for the creditors. A subscriber to corporate stock is liable for his subscription regardless of any separate agreement between the subscriber and the corporation. Any person who permits the corporation to hold him out as a subscriber is estopped from denying the validity of the subscription as against creditors. Furthermore, the directors of the corporation did not have the authority to release Ellison and Oxley from liability on the agreements.

Selection of State for Incorporation

A corporation is usually incorporated in the State in which it is intended to be located and transact all or the principal part of its business. However, a corporation may be formed in one State and have its principal place of business and conduct all or most of its operations in another State or States by duly qualifying and obtaining a certificate of authority to transact business in such other States. The principal criteria useful in selecting a State for incorporation include the flexibility accorded management, the rights granted to shareholders, the limitations imposed on the issuance of shares, the restrictions placed on the payment of dividends, and the organizational costs such as fees and taxes.

Formalities of Incorporation

Although the procedure involved in organizing a corporation varies to some extent from State to State, typically the incorporators execute and deliver to the Secretary of State or another designated official, articles of incorporation in duplicate, which in effect are an application for a charter. The Model Act provides that after issuance of the certificate of incorporation, an organization meeting of the board of directors named in the articles of incorporation shall be held for the purpose of adopting bylaws, electing officers, and transacting such other business as may come before the meeting. After completion of these organizational details the life of the corporation is in the hands of its shareholders, and its business and affairs are managed by its board of directors and by its officers.

Selection of Name

Most general incorporation laws require that the name contain a word or words that clearly indicate that it is a corporation, such as "corporation," "company," "incorporated," "limited," "Corp.," "Co.," "Inc.," or "Ltd." Practically every incorporation statute provides that no corporate name shall be the same as, or deceptively similar to, the name of an existing corporation doing business within the State.

Incorporators

The incorporators are the persons who sign the articles of incorporation which are filed with the Secretary of State of the State of incorporation. Although they perform a necessary function, their services as incorporators are perfunctory and short-lived, ending with the organizational meeting of the initial board of directors following the issuance of the certificate of incorporation. Accordingly, modern statutes have greatly relaxed the qualifications of incorporators and reduced the number required. The Model Act, for example, provides that one or more persons or a domestic or foreign corporation may act as incorporators.

Articles of Incorporation

The articles of incorporation or **charter** is generally a rather simple document that includes:

Charter –a corporation's organizational document

1. the name of the corporation;
2. the location and address of the corporation;
3. the purpose for which the corporation is organized; — *intravires*
4. the period of duration, which may be perpetual;
5. the number of authorized shares and designations of classes of shares;
6. the number and names of the initial directors;
7. the name and address of each incorporator; and
8. any other provision consistent with the incorporation statute and other law.

Figure 33-4 shows a sample charter. After the charter is drawn up, it must be signed and filed with the Secretary of State. The articles of incorporation then become the basic governing document of the corporation, so long as its provisions are consistent with State and Federal law.

Organization Meeting

The Model Act requires that an organization meeting be held to adopt the bylaws, elect officers, and transact "such other business as may come before the meeting." Such business typically includes authorization to issue shares of stock, approval of preincorporation contracts made by promoters, and selection of a bank, as well as approval of a corporate seal and the form of stock certificate.

Bylaws *private documents*

The bylaws of a corporation are the rules and regulations that govern its internal management. They are necessary to its organization, and the adoption of bylaws is one of the first items of business at the organization meeting held promptly after incorporation. The bylaws may not contain anything contrary to or inconsistent with any provision in the incorporation statute or in the articles of incorporation. In contrast to the certificate of incorporation, which embodies the articles of incorporation, the bylaws do not have to be publicly filed and in many States may be changed without shareholder approval.

Bylaws –rules and regulations governing a corporation's internal management

FIGURE 33-4   Sample Articles of Incorporation

ARTICLES OF INCORPORATION OF [CORPORATE NAME]

The undersigned, acting as incorporator(s) of a corporation under the _____ Business Corporation Act, adopt(s) the following Articles of Incorporation for such corporation:

First: The name of the corporation is _____

_____

Second: The period of its duration is _____

Third: The purpose or purposes for which the corporation is organized are: _____

_____

Fourth: The aggregate number of shares which the corporation shall have authority to issue is _____

_____

Fifth: Provisions granting preemptive rights are:

Sixth: Provisions for the regulation of the internal affairs of the corporation are:

Seventh: The address of the initial registered office of the corporation is _____ and the name of its initial registered agent at such address is _____

_____ .

Eighth: The number of directors constituting the initial board of directors of the corporation is _____, and the names and addresses of the persons who are to serve as directors until the first annual meeting of shareholders or until their successors are elected and shall qualify are:

Name	**Address**
_____	_____
_____	_____
_____	_____

Ninth: The name and address of each incorporator is:

Name	**Address**
_____	_____
_____	_____
_____	_____

Dated _____, 19___ .

_____

_____

_____

Incorporator(s)

Source: Reprinted with permission from Henn & Alexander, Corporations, 3rd ed. Copyright © 1983 by West Publishing Co.

Recognition and Disregard of Corporateness

Business associates choose to incorporate to obtain one or more of the corporate attributes, primarily limited liability and perpetual existence. Because a corporation is a creature of the State, such corporate attributes are recognized when the enterprise complies with the State's requirements for incorporation. Although the formal procedures are relatively simple, errors or omissions sometimes occur. In some cases the mistakes may be trivial, such as an incorrect address of an incorporator; in other instances the error may be more significant, such as a complete failure to file the articles of incorporation. The consequences of noncompliance with the statutory incorporation procedure depend on the seriousness of the error. Conversely, even when a corporation has been formed in strict compliance with the incorporation statute, a court may disregard the corporateness of the enterprise if justice requires. In this section we address these two complementary issues.

Recognition of Corporateness

Corporation de Jure

A corporation *de jure* is one that has been formed in strict compliance with the incorporation statute and the required organizational procedure. Once formed, the existence of a *de jure* corporation may not be challenged by anyone, even the State in a direct proceeding for this purpose.

Corporation de Facto

A *de facto* corporation is a corporation that is not *de jure* due to a failure to comply substantially with the incorporation statute but nevertheless is recognized for most purposes as a corporation. A failure to form a *de jure* corporation may result in the formation of a *de facto* corporation if the following requirements are met: (1) the existence of a general corporation statute; (2) a *bona fide* attempt to comply with that law in organizing a corporation under the statute; and (3) the actual exercise of corporate power by conducting a business in the belief that a corporation has been formed. The existence of a *de facto* corporation can be challenged only by the State. If the corporation sues to collect a debt, it is no defense to such a suit that the plaintiff corporation is not *de jure*. Not even the State can collaterally (in a proceeding involving some other issue) question the *de facto* corporation's existence. The State must bring an independent suit against the corporation for this express purpose, known as an action of *quo warranto* ("by what right")".

The MBCA provides that a "certificate of incorporation shall be conclusive evidence that all conditions precedent required to be performed by the incorporators have been complied with and that the corporation has been incorporated under this Act, except as against this State."

Corporation by Estoppel

A person who has dealt with a defectively organized corporation may be precluded or estopped from denying its corporate existence where the necessary elements of holding out and reliance are present. The doctrine of corporation by estoppel is separate and distinct from that of corporation *de facto*. Estoppel does not create a corporation. It operates only to prevent a person or persons under the facts and circumstances of a particular case from raising the question of a corporation's existence or its capacity to act or to own property. The doctrine can be applied not only to third parties but also to the purported corporation as well as the associates who held themselves out as a corporation.

CRANSON v. INTERNATIONAL BUSINESS MACHINES CORP.

Court of Appeals of
Maryland, 1964.
234 Md. 477, 200 A.2d 33.

FACTS: In April 1961, Cranson was asked to invest in a new business corporation which was about to be created. He agreed to purchase stock and become an officer and director. After his attorney advised him that the corporation had been formed under the laws of Maryland, Cranson paid for and received a stock certificate evidencing his ownership of shares. The business of the new venture was conducted as if it were a corporation. Cranson was elected president and all transactions conducted by him for the corporation, including those with I.B.M., were made as an officer of the corporation. At no time did he assume any personal obligation or pledge his individual credit to I.B.M. Due to an oversight of the attorney, of which Cranson was unaware, the certificate of incorporation which had been signed and acknowledged prior to May 1, 1961, was not filed until November 24, 1961. Between May 1 and November 8, the "Corporation" purchased eight typewriters from I.B.M. After the corporation made only partial payment, I.B.M. brought suit against Cranson seeking to hold him personally liable for the balance due of $4,333.40.

DECISION: Judgment for Cranson. Two doctrines have been used to grant the corporate attribute of limited liability to an officer of a defectively incorporated association: the doctrine of *de facto* corporations and the doctrine of estoppel. The doctrine of *de facto* corporations applies when there is: (1) the existence of law authorizing incorporation; (2) an effort in good faith to incorporate under the existing law; and (3) actual exercise of corporate powers. The separate doctrine of estoppel applies when a person or legal entity deals with the association in such a manner as to recognize it as a corporate body. If so, the person or legal entity seeking to hold the officer personally liable is estopped from denying the corporation's existence. The doctrine of estoppel may apply even if the association is not a corporation *de facto*.

Here, the failure of the association to file its certificate may have prevented it from being a corporation *de jure* or *de facto*. Nevertheless, I.B.M. dealt with Cranson's business as if it were a corporation and relied on its credit rather than Cranson's. Therefore, I.B.M. is estopped to deny the corporate existence of the association. Cranson, then, is not personally liable.

Defective Corporation

If the associates who purported to form a corporation fail to comply with the requirements of the incorporation statute to such an extent that neither a *de jure* nor a *de facto* corporation is formed and the circumstances do not justify the application of the corporation by estoppel doctrine, then the courts generally deny the associates the benefits of incorporation. A defective corporation does not have the attribute of limited liability. The Model Act provides that all persons who assume to act as a corporation without authority to do so shall have joint and several unlimited liability for all debts and liabilities incurred as a result of so acting.

The Revised Act imposes liability only on persons who act as or on behalf of a corporation, *knowing that there was no incorporation*. This provision is analogous to the approach under the Uniform Limited Partnership Act discussed in Chapter 32. Consider the following two illustrations: First, A had been shown executed articles of incorporation some months before he invested in the corporation and became an officer and director. He was also told by the corporation's attorney that the articles had been filed, but in fact they had not been filed because of confusion in the attorney's office. Under the Revised Act and many court decisions A would not be held liable for the obligations of the defective corporation. Second, B represents that a corporation exists and enters into a contract in the corporate name when she knows that no corporation has been formed because no attempt has been made to file articles of incorporation. B would be held liable for the obligations of the defective corporations under the Model Act, the Revised Act and most court decisions involving similar situations.

Figure 33-5 illustrates the requirements and results of these degrees of corporateness.

Disregard of Corporateness

If a corporation is formed by substantial compliance with the incorporation statute so that a *de jure* or *de facto* corporation results, the general rule is that corporateness and its attendant attributes—including limited liability—will be recognized. However, the courts will disregard the corporate entity when it is used to defeat public convenience, commit a wrongdoing, protect fraud, or circumvent the law. Going behind the corporate entity in order to prevent its use by individuals seeking to insulate themselves from personal accountability and the consequences of their wrongdoing is referred to as **piercing the corporate veil.** Courts will pierce the corporate veil where deemed necessary to remedy wrongdoing. They have done so most frequently with closely held corporations and in parent-subsidiary relationships.

Closely Held Corporations

The joint and active management by all the shareholders of closely held corporations frequently results in a tendency to forgo adherence to all of the niceties of corporate formalities, such as holding meetings of the board and shareholders, while the small size of close corporations often results in creditors who are unable to satisfy fully their claims against the corporation. Accordingly, the frustrated creditor will likely invoke the court to disregard the organization's corporateness and impose personal liability for the corporate obligations on the shareholders. Courts have responded by piercing the corporate veil where the shareholders (1) have not conducted the business on a

FIGURE 33-5 Recognition of Corporate Attributes

Requirements		Result
Strict compliance with incorporation statute	**Corporation de Jure**	Corporate attributes, insulation from collateral and direct suits
• *Bona fide* attempt to comply with incorporation statute • Exercise of corporate powers	**Corporation de Facto**	Corporate attributes, insulation from collateral suits
• Holding out • Reliance • Equitable considerations	**Corporation by Estoppel**	Corporate existence may not be denied by the parties
Serious failure to comply with incorporation statute	**Defective Corporation**	Unlimited personal liability for associates

corporate basis or (2) have not provided an adequate financial basis for the business. Conducting the business on a corporate basis involves maintaining the corporation's funds separate from the shareholders' funds, maintaining separate financial records, holding regular directors' meetings, and generally observing corporate formalities. Adequate capitalization requires that the shareholders invest sufficient capital to meet the reasonably anticipated requirements of the enterprise.

UNITED STATES v. HEALTHWIN-MIDTOWN CONVALESCENT HOSPITAL

United States District Court, Central District of California, 1981.
511 F.Supp. 416.

FACTS: On September 14, 1971, Healthwin-Midtown Convalescent Hospital, Inc. was incorporated in California for the purpose of operating a health care facility. From that date until November 30, 1974, it participated as a provider of services under the Federal Medicare Act and received periodic payments from the United States Department of Health, Education and Welfare. Undisputed audits revealed that a series of overpayments had been made to Healthwin in the total amount of $30,481.00. The United States brought an action to recover this sum from the defendants, Healthwin and Zide. Zide was a member of the Board of Directors of the Healthwin Corporation, the administrator of its health care facility, its president and owner of fifty percent of its stock. Only Zide could sign the corporation's checks without prior approval of another corporate officer. In addition, Zide had a fifty percent interest in a partnership which owned both the realty in which Healthwin's health care facility was located and the furnishings used at that facility. The corporation was initially undercapitalized, and the liabilities of the corporation continued to exceed substantially its assets. Zide exercised his control over Healthwin causing its finances to become inextricably intertwined with both his personal finances and his other business holdings. The United States contends that the corporate veil should be pierced and that Zide should be held personally liable for the Medicare overpayments made to Healthwin.

DECISION: Judgment for the United States. Under the *alter ego* theory, the corporate veil may be pierced if: (1) there is such unity of interest and ownership that the personalities of the corporation and the individual no longer exist separately; and (2) if it would be inequitable to treat the acts as those of the corporation alone. It is not necessary that there is actual fraud; it is sufficient that the failure to pierce the corporation's veil would result in an injustice. Other factors the courts consider in determining whether the corporate veil should be pierced include: the inadequacy of the corporation's capitalization or its insolvency; the failure to observe corporate formalities; the absence of regular board meetings; the nonfunctioning of corporate directors; the commingling of corporate and noncorporate assets; the diversion of assets from the corporation to the detriment of creditors; and the failure of an individual to maintain an arm's length relationship with the corporation.

All these factors are present here. The corporation was under-capitalized; Healthwin consistently had outstanding liabilities in excess of $150,000, its initial capitalization was only $10,000. Zide exercised his control over Healthwin so as to cause its finances to become inextricably intertwined with both his personal finances and his other business holdings. Zide handled Healthwin's finances so as to accommodate his own business interests. Another factor present here is that the operations of Healthwin were marked by an essential disregard of corporate formalities. For example, board meetings were not regularly held. Furthermore, to leave Healthwin's corporate veil unpierced would result in an injustice. Healthwin's insolvency would subject all its creditors, including the United States, to inequitable risks regarding the corporation's debts. Therefore, Healthwin's corporate entity should be disregarded and Zide held personally liable.

Subsidiary corporation–corporation controlled by another corporation

Parent corporation–corporation which controls another corporation

Parent-Subsidiary

A corporation may choose to risk only a portion of its assets in a particular enterprise by forming a subsidiary corporation. A **subsidiary corporation is** one in which another corporation, **the parent corporation,** owns at least a majority of the subsidiary's shares and therefore has control over the subsidiary corporation. Courts will pierce the corporate veil and hold the parent liable for the debts of its subsidiary if

1. both corporations are not adequately capitalized, *or*

2. the formalities of separate corporate procedures are not observed, *or*

3. each corporation is not held out to the public as separate enterprises, *or*

4. the funds of the two corporations are commingled, *or* (shared)

5. the parent corporation completely dominates the operation of the subsidiary to advance only the parent's own interests.

So long as these pitfalls are avoided, the courts will generally recognize the separateness of the subsidiary even though the parent owns all the stock of the subsidiary and the two corporations have common directors and officers.

FACTS: Berger was planning to produce a fashion show in Las Vegas. In April 1965, Berger entered into a written licensing agreement with CBS Films, Inc., a wholly owned subsidiary of CBS, for presentation of the show. In 1966 Stewart Cowley decided to produce a fashion show similar to Berger's and entered into a contract with CBS. CBS broadcast Cowley's show and not Berger's show, and Berger brought this action against CBS to recover damages for breach of his contract with CBS Films. Berger claims that CBS is liable because CBS Films is its instrumentality or alter ego, and that the court should disregard the parent-subsidiary form. In support of this claim, Berger has shown that CBS Films' directors are employees of CBS, that CBS's organizational chart includes CBS Films, and that all lines of employee authority from CBS Films pass through employees of CBS to the chairman of the board of CBS. CBS, in turn, argues that Berger has failed to justify piercing the corporate veil and disregarding the corporate identity of CBS Films in order to hold CBS liable.

DECISION: Judgment for CBS. Generally, a corporation is a creature of the law, endowed with a personality separate and distinct from that of its owners. A principal reason that legal recognition is given to the separate corporate personality is to allow stockholders an opportunity to limit their personal liability. Therefore, in order to justify the application of the instrumentality rule holding the parent liable for the acts of its subsidiary, Berger must have shown 1) control and complete domination of the subsidiary by the parent; 2) use of such control to commit fraud or wrong; and 3) that the control and breach of duty is the proximate cause of the injury complained of. Here, the evidence does not sustain any finding that CBS completely dominated the finances, policy, and business practices of CBS Films. Therefore, the instrumentality rule is inapplicable, and the parent, CBS, cannot be held liable for any breach of contract by its subsidiary CBS Films.

BERGER v. COLUMBIA BROADCASTING SYSTEM, INC.

United States Court of Appeals, Fifth Circuit, 1972. 453 F.2d 991.

Corporate Powers

Because a corporation derives its existence and all of its powers from the State of incorporation, it has only those powers that the State has conferred on it. These powers are those expressly set forth in the statute and articles of incorporation and powers reasonably implied from them.

Sources of Corporate Powers

Statutory Powers

Typical of the general powers granted by incorporation statutes are those provided by the Model Act, which include the following:

1. to have perpetual succession;

2. to sue and be sued in its corporate name;

3. to acquire, own, mortgage, and dispose of real and personal property;

4. to lend money and use its credit to assist its employees;

5. to acquire, own, vote, and dispose of shares or obligations of other business entities;

6. to make contracts, incur liabilities, and issue notes, bonds, or other obligations;

7. to invest surplus funds and acquire its own shares;

8. to conduct its business and carry on its operations within or outside the State of incorporation;

9. to elect or appoint officers and agents, define their duties, and fix their compensation;

10. to make and alter bylaws for the administration and regulation of its affairs;

11. to make donations for the public welfare or for charitable, scientific, or educational purposes;

12. to establish pension, profit-sharing, and other incentive plans for its directors, officers, and employees;

13. to be a promoter, partner, member, associate, or manager of any partnership, joint venture, trust, or other enterprise;

14. to amend its articles of incorporation;

15. to merge or consolidate with one or more other corporations; and

16. to indemnify against personal liability officers, directors, employees, and agents of the corporation who act on behalf of the corporation in good faith and without negligence.

Express Charter Powers

The objects or purposes for which a corporation is formed are stated in its articles of incorporation, which outline in general language the type of business activities in which the corporation proposes to engage. This serves (1) to advise the shareholders of the nature and kind of particular business activity in which their investment is being risked, (2) to advise the officers, directors, and management of the extent of the corporation's authority to act; and (3) to inform any person who may contemplate dealing with the corporation of the extent of its legally authorized power.

The express powers must relate to a legitimate business activity or industry within the purview of the general statute.

Implied Powers

A corporation has the authority to take any action that is necessary or convenient to and consistent with the execution of any of its express powers and the operation of the business that it was formed to conduct. This power exists by implication and does not depend on express language in the charter or statute but on reasonable inference as to the proper scope and content of such language, taking into consideration the facts and circumstances of the particular case.

[handwritten margin note: acts like a person—can do anything]

The express powers of a corporation may and should be stated in general language, and it is not necessary to set forth in detail every particular type of act that the corporation has authority to perform. A general statement of corporate purpose or object is sufficient to give rise to all of the powers necessary, incidental, or convenient to accomplish that purpose. For instance, a corporation organized "to buy and sell goods, wares, and merchandise" has implied power to (a) purchase or lease store premises, (b) employ salespersons, (c) buy or rent trucks, (d) spend money for advertising, (e) open and manage a bank account, (f) employ buyers and pay their salaries and traveling expenses, and (g) purchase insurance on the lives of officers, as well as other powers necessary or incidental to such stated purpose.

Ultra Vires Acts

Because a corporation has authority to act only within the limitation of its express and implied powers, any action taken or contract made by it that goes beyond these powers is *ultra vires*. *Ultra vires* does not mean without power or capability, but rather without legal authorization because the act is not within the scope and type of acts that the corporation is legally empowered to perform.

The doctrine of *ultra vires* is of less significance today because modern statutes permit incorporation for any lawful purpose and most articles of incorporation do not limit the powers of the corporation. As a consequence, far fewer acts are *ultra vires*.

Effect of Ultra Vires Acts

Traditionally, *ultra vires* contracts were unenforceable as null and void. Under the modern approach, courts allow the *ultra vires* defense where the contract is wholly executory on both sides. A corporation having received full performance from the other party to the contract is not permitted to escape liability by a plea of *ultra vires*. Conversely, where a corporation is suing for breach of a contract that has been fully performed on its side, the other party may not use the defense of *ultra vires*. In any event, an illegal contract, whether *ultra vires* or not, is unenforceable on the basis of illegality.

Most statutes now have abolished the defense of *ultra vires* in an action by or against a corporation. The MBCA provides that "no act of a corporation and no conveyance or transfer of real or personal property to or by a corporation shall be invalid by reason of the fact that the corporation was without capacity or power to do such act or to make or receive such conveyance or transfer." This provision extends beyond contract actions and covers any corporate action including conveyances of property. Thus, it is not necessary for persons dealing with a corporation to examine its charter to discover any limitations upon its purposes or powers that may appear there. The provision does not, however, validate illegal corporate actions.

Remedies for Ultra Vires Acts

Although *ultra vires* under modern statutes may no longer be used defensively as a shield against liability, corporate activities that are *ultra vires* may be redressed in any of the three following ways, as provided by the Model Act:

1. in an injunction proceeding brought by a shareholder against the corporation to restrain and enjoin the commission of the *ultra vires* act if equitable and if all affected persons are party to the proceeding;

2. in a suit by the corporation or through shareholders in a representative suit against the officers or directors of the corporation for causing the corporation to engage in an *ultra vires* act; or

3. in a proceeding by the Attorney General of the State of incorporation to dissolve the corporation or to enjoin it from the transaction of unauthorized business.

Liability for Torts and Crimes

A corporation is liable for the torts and crimes committed by its agents in the course of their employment. The doctrine of *ultra vires*, even in those jurisdictions where it is permitted as a defense, has no application to wrongdoing by the corporation. The doctrine of **respondeat superior** imposes full liability on a corporation for the torts committed by its agents and employees during the course of their employment. For example, X, a truck driver employed by the ABC Corporation, while on a business errand, negligently runs over Y, a pedestrian. Both X and the ABC Corporation are liable to Y in an action by her to recover damages for the injuries sustained. A corporation may also be found liable for fraud, false imprisonment, malicious prosecution, libel, and other torts, but some States hold the corporation liable for *punitive* damages only if it authorized or ratified the act of the agent.

One of the essential elements of most crimes is a guilty mind or criminal intent, and it has been argued that since a corporation is artificial, intangible, and incorporeal, it cannot have either a mind or a soul and is therefore incapable of committing a crime. This is a tenuous argument and overlooks the fact that corporations do transgress laws that exist for the welfare and safety of the community and the State. The modern trend is to make corporations criminally responsible for the criminal conduct of their agents, if the conduct is attributable to the corporation. The Model Penal Code provides that a corporation may be convicted of a criminal offense for the conduct of its employees if:

1. the legislative purpose of the statute defining the offense is to impose liability on corporations and the conduct is within the scope of the agent's office or employment;

2. the offense consists of an omission to discharge a specific, affirmative duty imposed on corporations by law; *or*

3. the offense was authorized, requested, commanded, performed, or recklessly tolerated by the board of directors or by a high managerial agent of the corporation.

The punishment necessarily is by fine and not imprisonment.

CHAPTER SUMMARY

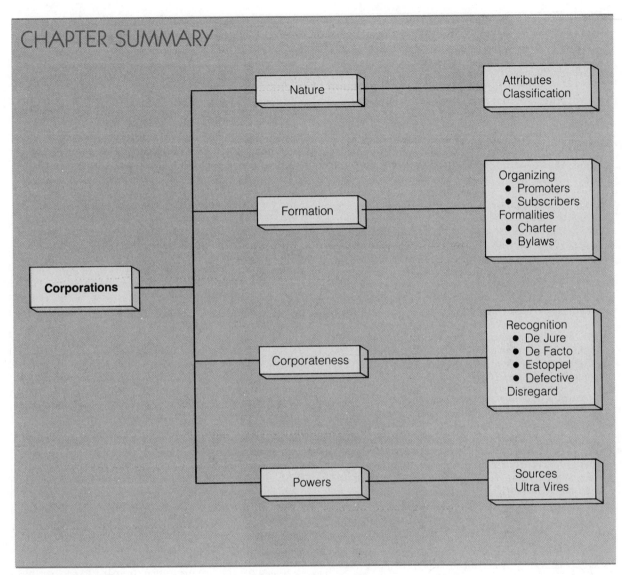

KEY TERMS

Corporation
Legal entity
Limited liability
Management
Public corporation
Private corporation
Profit corporation
Nonprofit corporation
Domestic corporation

Foreign corporation
Closely held corporation
Professional corporation
Promoter
Subscriber
Incorporator
Charter
Bylaws

Corporation de jure
Corporation de facto
Corporation by estoppel
Defective corporation
"Piercing the corporate veil"
Subsidiary corporation
Parent corporation
Ultra vires

PROBLEMS

1. After part of the shares of a proposed corporation had been successfully subscribed, A, the promoter, hired a carpenter to repair a building. The promoters subsequently secured subscriptions to the balance of the shares and completed the organization, but the corporation declined to use the building or pay the carpenter for the reason that it was not suitable to the purposes of the company. The carpenter brought suit against the corporation for the amount that the promoter agreed would be paid to him. Decision?

2. C. A. Nimocks was a promoter engaged in organizing the Times Printing Company. On September 12, on behalf of the proposed corporation, he made a contract with McArthur for her services as comptroller for the period of one year beginning October 1. The Times Printing Company was incorporated October 16, and on that date McArthur commenced her duties as comptroller. No formal action on her employment was taken by the board of directors or by any officer, but all the shareholders, directors, and officers knew of the contract made by Nimocks. On December 1, McArthur was discharged without cause. Has she a cause of action against the Times Printing Company?

3. A and B obtained an option on a building that was used for manufacturing pianos. They acted as the promoters for a corporation and turned the building over to the new corporation for $500,000 worth of stock. As a matter of fact, their option on the building called for a purchase price of only $300,000. The other shareholders desire to have $200,000 of the common stock canceled. Can they succeed in this action?

4. S signed a subscription agreement for ten shares of stock having a value of $100 per share of the proposed ABC Company. Two weeks later the company was incorporated. A certificate was duly tendered to S, but he refused to accept it. He was notified of all shareholders' meetings, but he never attended. A dividend check was sent to him, but he returned it. ABC Company brings action against S to recover $1,000. He defends on the ground that his subscription agreement was an unaccepted offer, that he had done nothing to ratify it, and that he was therefore not liable on it. Decision?

5. A, B, and C petitioned for a corporate charter for the purpose of conducting a retail shoe business. All the statutory provisions were complied with, except that they failed to have their charter recorded. This was an oversight on their part, and they felt that they had fully complied with the law. They operated the business for three years, after which time it became

insolvent. The creditors desire to hold the members personally and individually liable. May they do so?

6. A, B, C, and D decided to form a corporation for bottling and selling apple cider. A, B, and C were to operate the business, and D was to supply the necessary capital but was to have no voice in the management. They went to Jane Lawyer, who agreed to organize a corporation for them under the name A-B-C Inc., and sufficient funds were paid to her to accomplish the incorporation. Lawyer promised that the corporation would definitely be formed by May 3. On April 27, A telephoned Lawyer to inquire how the incorporation was progressing, and Lawyer said she had drafted the articles of incorporation and would send them to the Secretary of State that very day. She assured A that A-B-C Inc. would be incorporated before May 3.

Relying on Lawyer's assurance, A, with the approval of B and C, on May 4 entered into a written contract with Grower for his entire apple crop. The contract was executed by A in behalf of "A-B-C Inc." Grower delivered the apples as agreed. Unknown to A, B, C, D, or Grower, the articles of incorporation were never filed, through Lawyer's negligence. The business subsequently failed.

What are Grower's rights, if any, against A, B, C, and D as individuals?

7. The AB Corporation has outstanding 20,000 shares of common stock, of which 19,000 are owned by Peter B. Arson, 500 shares are owned by Elizabeth Arson, his wife, and 500 shares are owned by Joseph Q. Arson, his brother. These three individuals are the officers and directors of the corporation. The AB Corporation obtained a $250,000 fire insurance policy covering a certain building owned by it. Thereafter, Peter B. Arson set fire to the building, and it was totally destroyed. The corporation now brings an action against the fire insurance company to recover on the $250,000 fire insurance policy. What judgment?

8. A Corporation is formed for the purpose of manufacturing, buying, selling, and dealing in drugs, chemicals, and similar products. The corporation, under authority of its board of directors, contracted to purchase the land and building occupied by it as a factory and store. S, a shareholder, sues in equity to restrain the corporation from completing the contract, claiming that as the certificate of incorporation contained no provision authorizing the corporation to purchase real estate, the contract was *ultra vires*. Decision?

9. X Corporation, organized under the laws of State S, sends traveling salespersons into State M to solicit orders, which are accepted only at the Home Office of X Corporation in State S. D, a resident of State M, places an order that is accepted by X Corporation in State S. The Corporation Act of State M provides that "no foreign corporation transacting business in this state without a certificate of authority shall be permitted to maintain an action in any court of this state until such corporation shall have obtained a certificate of authority." D fails to pay for the goods, and when X Corporation sues D in a court of State M, D defends on the ground that X Corporation does not possess a certificate of authority from State M. Result?

FINANCIAL STRUCTURE

Capital is necessary for any business to function. Two of the principal sources of capital formation in corporations involve debt and equity investment securities. The sale of equity securities provides an initial and often continuing source of corporate funds. **Equity securities** represent an ownership interest in the corporation and include both common and preferred stock. In addition, corporations finance much of their continued operations through debt securities. **Debt securities,** or bonds, do not represent an ownership interest in the corporation but rather create a debtor-creditor relationship between the corporation and the bondholder. The third principal way in which a corporation may meet its financial needs is through retained earnings.

In this chapter we discuss debt and equity securities as well as the payment of dividends and other distributions. In addition, we examine the manner in which debt and equity investment securities are transferred.

Debt Securities

Corporations frequently find it advantageous to use debt as a source of funds. Debt securities (also called bonds) generally involve the corporation's promise to repay the principal amount of the loan at a stated time and to pay interest, usually at a fixed rate, while the debt is outstanding. In addition to bonds, a corporation may finance its operations through the use of other forms of debt, such as credit extended by its suppliers and short-term commercial paper.

Authority to Issue Debt Securities

The Model Act provides that "[e]ach corporation shall have power to . . . borrow money at such rates of interest as the corporation may determine, issue its notes, bonds and other obligations, and secure any of its obligations by mortgage or pledge of all or any of its property, franchise and income." Moreover, the board of directors may do so without the authorization or consent of the shareholders.

Types of Debt Securities

Debt securities can be classified into various types depending on their characteristics. However, there are a great number of variants and combinations of each type, limited only by the ingenuity of the corporation. Debt securities are typically issued under an *indenture* or debt agreement, which specifies in great detail the terms of the loan.

Unsecured Bonds

Debenture—unsecured bond

Unsecured bonds, usually called **debentures,** have only the obligation of the corporation behind them. Debenture holders are thus unsecured creditors and rank equally with other general creditors. To protect the unsecured bondholders, debenture agreements frequently impose limitations on the corporation's borrowing, payment of dividends, and its redemption and reacquisition of its own shares.

Secured Bonds

A secured creditor is one whose claim against the corporation not only is enforceable against the general assets of the corporation but is also a lien on specific property. Thus, secured bondholders enjoy the security of specific corporate property in addition to the general obligation of the corporation. After resorting to the specified security, the holder of secured bonds becomes a general creditor for any unsatisfied amount of the debt.

Income Bonds

Traditionally, debt securities bear a fixed interest rate that is payable without regard to the financial condition of the corporation. Income bonds, on the other hand, condition the payment of interest to some extent on corporate earnings. This provision lessens the burden of the debt on the issuer during periods of financial adversity. Nonetheless, some income bonds call for a stated percentage of return regardless of earnings with additional payments dependent on earnings.

Convertible Bonds

Convertible bonds may be exchanged, usually at the option of the holder, for other securities of the corporation at a specified ratio. For example, a convertible bond may provide that the bondholder shall have the right for a specified time to exchange each bond for twenty shares of common stock.

Callable Bonds

Callable bonds are bonds that are subject to a **redemption** provision that permits the corporation to redeem or call (pay off) all or part of the issue before maturity at a specified redemption price. This provision enables the corporation to reduce fixed costs, to improve its credit rating, to refinance at a lower interest rate, to free mortgaged property, or to reduce its proportion of debt.

Equity Securities

The shareholders of a corporation as owners of the equity occupy a position of greater financial risk than creditors, and changes in the corporation's fortunes and general economic conditions have a greater effect on shareholders than on any other class of investor. The market value of shares of stock should proportionately advance more in times of prosperity and decline more in times of adversity, and do either more rapidly, than should the market value of bonds, debentures, or any type of debt security.

Shares are a method of describing a proportionate proprietary interest in a corporate enterprise, but they do not in any way vest their owner with title to any property of the corporation. However, shares do confer on their owner a threefold interest in the corporation: (1) the right to participate in control, (2) the right to participate in the earnings of the corporation, and (3) the right to participate in the residual assets of the corporation on dissolution. The shareholder's interest is usually represented by a certificate of ownership and is recorded by the corporation.

Share–a proportionate ownership interest in a corporation

Issuance of Shares

Authority to Issue

The initial amount of shares to be issued is determined by the promoters or incorporators and is generally governed by practical business considerations and financial needs. A corporation, however, is limited to selling only the amount of shares that has been authorized in the articles of incorporation. Once the amount that the corporation is authorized to issue has been established and specified in the charter, it cannot be increased or decreased without amendment to the charter. This means that the shareholders have the residual authority over increases or decreases in the amount of authorized capital stock, because they must approve any amendment to the articles of incorporation. Consequently, it is common for articles of incorporation to specify more shares than are to be issued immediately. Unauthorized shares of stock that are purportedly issued by a corporation are void.

Qualification of Stock

All States now have statutes regulating the issuance and sale of corporate shares and other securities, popularly known as **Blue Sky Laws.** These statutes all have provisions prohibiting fraud in the sale of securities. In addition, a number of States require the registration of securities, and some States also regulate brokers, dealers, and others who engage in the securities business. In no case, however, does any State give any endorsement of the merits of the security by qualifying an issue of stock or other security for sale.

Blue Sky Laws–state laws regulating the issuance and sale of securities

In 1933, Congress passed the first Federal statute providing regulation of securities offered for sale and sold through the use of the mails or other instrumentalities of interstate commerce. This statute, often called the **Truth in Securities Act,** is administered by the Securities and Exchange Commission (SEC). The statute requires corporations to disclose certain information about a proposed security in a registration statement and in their prospectus (an offer made by corporations to interest people in buying stock). The SEC does not examine the merits of the proposed security but only the truthfulness, accuracy, and completeness of the information given.

Under certain conditions, a corporation may receive an exemption from the requirement of registration under the Blue Sky Laws of most States and the Securities Act of 1933 if it complies with the rules and regulations of the appropriate State agency and the SEC. If no exemption is available, a corporation offering for sale or selling its shares of stock or other securities, as well as any person selling such securities, is subject to court injunction, possible criminal prosecution, and civil liability in damages to the persons to whom securities are sold in violation of the regulatory statute. A more detailed discussion of Federal regulation of securities appears in Chapter 40.

Pre-emptive Rights

Pre-emptive right–shareholder's right to purchase a *pro rata* share of new stock offerings

At common law, a shareholder has the pre-emptive right to purchase a *pro rata* share of every new offering of stock by the corporation in order to preserve his proportionate interest in the equity. Pre-emptive rights do not apply to the reissue of previously issued shares, shares issued for noncash consideration, or shares issued in connection with a merger or consolidation. There is a division among the jurisdictions whether pre-emptive rights apply to originally authorized shares. Currently, most States expressly authorize the articles of incorporation to deny or limit pre-emptive rights. In some States pre-emptive rights exist unless denied by the charter; in other States they do not exist unless the charter so provides.

In the absence of a pre-emptive right, a shareholder may be unable to prevent a dilution of his ownership interest in the corporation. For example, Ken owns 200 shares of stock of the ABC Company, which has a total of 1,000 shares outstanding. The company decides to increase its capital stock to 2,000 shares. If Ken has pre-emptive rights, he and every other shareholder will be offered one share of the newly issued stock for every share they own. If he accepts the offer and buys the stock, he will have 400 shares out of a total of 2,000 outstanding, and his relative interest in the corporation will be unchanged. However, without pre-emptive rights he would have only 200 out of the 2,000 shares outstanding and would own 10 percent instead of 20 percent of the stock.

Amount of Consideration for Shares

Shares are deemed fully paid and nonassessable when the corporation receives full payment of the lawful consideration for which the shares are issued. The amount of consideration depends on the type of shares being issued.

Par Value Stock   Par value shares may be issued for any amount, not less than par, set by the board of directors or shareholders. The par value of a share of stock can be an arbitrary value selected by the corporation and may or may not reflect either the actual value of the share or the actual price paid to the corporation. It indicates only the *minimum price* that the corporation must receive for it. The par value of stock must be stated in the articles of incorporation.

The consideration received constitutes *stated capital* to the extent of the par value of the shares; any consideration in excess of par value constitutes *capital surplus*.

The 1979 amendments to the MBCA eliminated the concepts of par value, stated capital, and capital surplus. Under the MBCA as amended *all* shares may be issued for such consideration as authorized by the board of directors.

No Par Value Stock   Shares without par value may be issued for any amount set by the board of directors or shareholders. The entire consideration re-

[handwritten margin note: minimum par is $1.00]

[handwritten margin note: watered stock - issue below par value in consideration]

ceived constitutes *stated capital* unless the board of directors allocates a portion of the consideration to capital surplus within sixty days after the stock is issued. The directors are free to allocate any or all of the consideration received, unless the no par stock has a liquidation preference. In that event, only the consideration in excess of the amount of liquidation preference may be allocated to capital surplus. No par shares provide the directors with great latitude in establishing capital surplus, which can in some jurisdictions provide greater flexibility for subsequent distributions to shareholders.

Treasury Stock   Treasury stock are shares that a corporation buys back after it has issued them. Treasury shares are *issued but not outstanding,* in contrast to shares owned by shareholders, which are deemed issued *and* outstanding. A corporation may sell treasury shares for any amount the board of directors determines, even if the shares have a par value that is more than the sale price. Treasury shares do not have voting rights or pre-emptive rights. In addition, no dividend is paid on treasury stock.

Treasury stock–shares reacquired by a corporation

The 1979 amendments to the MBCA eliminated the concept of treasury shares. Under the MBCA as amended all shares reacquired by a corporation are authorized but unissued shares, unless the articles of incorporation prohibit reissue, in which event the authorized shares are reduced by the number of shares acquired.

Figure 34-1 illustrates the way authorized shares are categorized.

Payment for Newly Issued Shares

There are two major questions about payment for newly issued capital stock. First, what type of consideration may be validly accepted in payment for shares? Second, who shall determine whether valid consideration has been paid, and what limits are placed on the discretion of those making the decision?

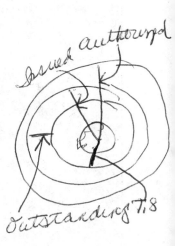

Type of Consideration   Consideration for the issuance of capital stock is defined in a more limited fashion than it is under contract law. Cash, property, and services actually rendered to the corporation are generally acceptable as valid consideration, but promissory notes and future services are not. The following case illustrates this requirement.

The Revised Act has greatly liberalized this rule by specifically validating contracts for future services and promissory notes as consideration for the issuance of shares. To guard against possible abuse, the Revised Act requires that corporations annually inform shareholders of all shares issued during the previous year for promissory notes or promises of future services.

Valuation of Consideration   The determination of the value to be placed on property exchanged for shares is the responsibility of the directors. The ultimate consequence of issuing stock for overvalued property may be to impose liability for the amount of the overvaluation on the shareholder to creditors or to other shareholders even though the stock is supposedly fully paid and nonassessable. The majority of jurisdictions hold that valuation is a matter of opinion and that, in the absence of fraud in the transaction, the judgment of the board of directors as to the value of the consideration received for shares shall be conclusive.

**UNITED STEEL
INDUSTRIES, INC. v.
MANHART**

Court of Civil Appeals of
Texas, 1966.
405 S.W.2d 231.

FACTS: United Steel issued stock to Hurt in exchange for future accounting services. United also issued shares to Griffitts in return for Griffitts's promise to convey land to United. Manhart, a shareholder of United, brought this action against the corporation, Hurt, and Griffitts, claiming that the shares were not issued for valid consideration and asking that the shares be declared void and canceled.

DECISION: Judgment for Manhart. A corporation may issue stock only in exchange for money paid, labor done, or property actually received. Neither the promise to perform services in the future nor the promise to convey land in the future constitutes payment for shares of stock. Therefore, the shares issued to Hurt and Griffitts were illegally issued and void.

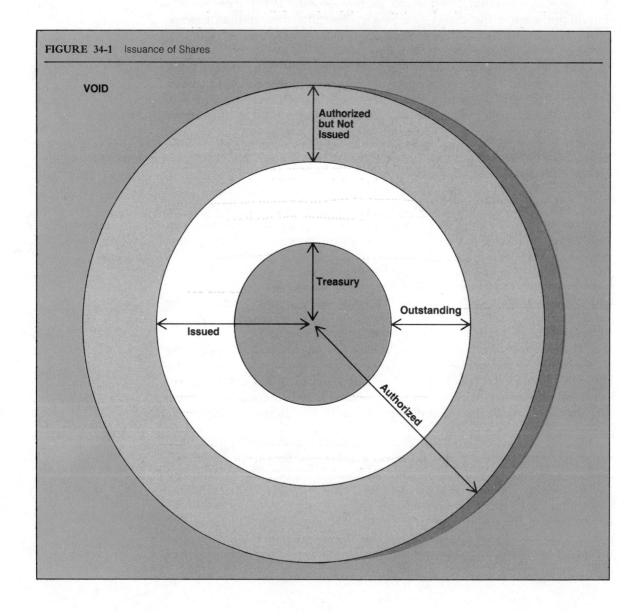

FIGURE 34-1   Issuance of Shares

Liability for Shares

A corporation is said to have issued **watered stock** when it issues fully paid up and nonassessable shares for consideration worth less than the full, lawful consideration for the shares. The liability of shareholders on watered stock is enforceable by both the corporation and its creditors. For example, assume that the directors of Corporation X authorize the issuance of 2,000 shares of common stock for five dollars per share to Kathy for property which the directors value at $10,000. The valuation is fraudulent and the property is actually worth $5,000. Kathy is liable to Corporation X and its creditors for $5,000. If, on the other hand, the valuation had been made by the directors without fraud and in good faith, then Kathy would not be liable even though the property is actually worth less than $10,000.

A transferee of watered stock is also liable for the balance due on the stock until the par or stated value of the stock has been fully paid, unless the certificate transferred to her recites that it is fully paid and nonassessable or she acquires the shares in good faith and without knowledge or notice that the shares are not fully paid. Under the Revised Act, if shares are issued for promissory notes or for contracts for services to be performed, a transferee of the shares is not liable for the unpaid balance but the transferor remains liable.

Classes of Shares

Corporations are generally authorized by statute to issue two or more classes of stock, which may vary with respect to their rights to dividends, their voting rights, and their right to share in the assets of the corporation on liquidation. The most usual classification of stock is into common and preferred shares.

Common Stock

Common stock does not have any special contract rights or preferences. Frequently it is the only class of stock outstanding. It generally represents the greatest proportion of the corporation's capital structure and bears the greatest risk of loss in the event of failure of the enterprise.

Common stock–stock not having any special contract rights

Preferred Stock

Stock is generally considered preferred if it has contractual rights superior to common stock with regard to dividends or assets on liquidation or both. Other types of special rights or privileges are not generally considered as removing a class of stock from the classification of common stock. The contractual rights and preferences of an issue of preferred stock must be provided for in the articles of incorporation.

Preferred stock–stock having contractual rights superior to common stock

Notwithstanding the special rights and preferences that distinguish preferred from common stock, both represent a contribution of capital. Preferred stock is no more a debt than common, and until a dividend is declared the holder of preferred shares is not a creditor of the corporation. Furthermore, the rights of preferred shareholders are subordinate to the rights of all of the creditors of the corporation.

Dividend Preferences   No dividend is payable on any class of stock, common or preferred, unless it has been declared by the board of directors. An issue of preferred stock with a dividend preference means that its holders will receive full dividends before any dividend may be paid to holders of common stock. Preferred stock may provide that dividends are cumulative, noncumulative, or cumulative-to-the-extent-earned.

For **cumulative** dividends, if the board does not declare regular dividends on the preferred stock, such omitted dividends cumulate, and no dividend may be declared on the common stock until all dividend arrearages on the preferred stock are declared and paid. If **noncumulative,** regular dividends do not cumulate on failure of the board to declare them, and all rights to a dividend for the period omitted are gone forever. Accordingly, noncumulative stock has a priority over common only in the fiscal period a dividend on common stock is declared. Unless the dividends on preferred stock are made expressly noncumulative, the courts generally hold them to be cumulative. **Cumulative-to-the-extent-earned** shares cumulate unpaid dividends only to the extent funds were legally available to pay such dividends in that fiscal period.

Preferred stock may also be **participating.** The nature and extent of such participation on a specified basis with the common stock must be stated in the articles of incorporation. For example, a class of participating preferred stock could be entitled to share at the same rate with the common in any additional distribution of earnings for a given year *after* provision has been made for payment of the prior preferred dividend and payment of dividends on the common at a rate equal to the fixed rate of the preferred.

Liquidation Preferences   When a corporation is dissolved, its assets liquidated, and claims of all of its creditors have been satisfied, the remaining assets are distributable *pro rata* among the shareholders according to their priority as provided in the articles of incorporation. If that preferred stock does not expressly provide for a preference of any kind on dissolution and liquidation, the holders of the preferred stock share *pro rata* with the common shareholders.

When a liquidation preference is provided, preferred stock usually has priority over common to the extent of the par value of the stock. In addition, if specified, preferred shares may participate beyond the liquidation preference in a stated ratio with other classes of shares. Such shares are called participating preferred with reference to liquidation. If not so specified, preferred shares do not participate beyond the liquidation preference.

ROTHSCHILD INTERNATIONAL CORP. v. LIGGETT GROUP, INC.

Court of Chancery of Delaware, 1983.
463 A.2d 642.

FACTS: GM Sub Corporation ("GM Sub"), a subsidiary of Grand Metropolitan Limited, acquired all outstanding shares of Liggett Group, Inc. a Delaware corporation. Rothschild International Corporation ("Rothschild") was the owner of 650 shares of the 7% Cumulative Preferred Stock of Liggett Group, Inc. According to Liggett's certificate of incorporation, the holders of the 7% Preferred were to receive $100 per share "in the event of any liquidation of the assets of the Corporation." GM Sub had offered $70 per share for the 7% Preferred, $158.63 for another class of preferred stock, and $69 for each common stock share. Liggett's board of directors approved the offer as being fair and recommended acceptance by Liggett's shareholders. As a result, 39.8% of the 7% Preferred shares was sold to GM Sub. In addition, GM Sub acquired 75.9% of the other preferred stock and 87.4% of the common stock. The acquisition of the overwhelming majority of these classes of stock—coupled with the fact that the 7% Preferred shareholders could not vote as a class on the merger proposal—gave GM Sub sufficient voting power to approve a follow-up merger. As a result, all remaining shareholders other than GM

Sub were eliminated in return for payment of cash for their shares. These shareholders received the same consideration ($70 per share) as offered in the tender offer.

   Rothschild brought suit against Liggett and Grand Metropolitan charging each with a breach of its duty of fair dealing owed to the 7% Preferred shareholders. Rothschild based both claims on the contention that the merger was a liquidation of Liggett insofar as the rights of the 7% Preferred stockholders were concerned. Therefore, those preferred shareholders were entitled to the liquidation preference of $100 per share, not $70 per share.

DECISION: Judgment for Liggett and Grand Met. Preference rights of preferred stock can be eliminated legally through the merger process. In addition, a merger is a separate and distinct process from a liquidation or a sale of assets. Thus, the 7% Preferred was always subject to defeasance by merger as the merger provisions of Delaware law are a part of Liggett's charter. The preferential rights attaching to shares of preferred stock are contractual in nature and governed by the express provisions of a corporation's charter. The holders of the 7% Preferred were entitled to be paid $100 per share only in the event of "any liquidation of the assets of the Corporation." However, the liquidation of the preferred shareholders' rights was not a liquidation of the corporation itself, since the corporation continued to operate as a legal entity. Because the merger did not activate the preferred shareholders' right to $100 per share, that right could not have been violated. Furthermore, the $70 price offered was a fair and adequate price as of the time of the tender offer and merger. Therefore, neither Liggett nor Grand Met breached a duty of fair dealing.

Additional Rights and Limitations   Preferred stock may have additional rights, designations, and limitations. For instance, it may be expressly denied voting rights if permitted by the incorporation statute, it may be redeemable by the corporation, or it may be convertible into shares of another class.

Stock Rights and Options

A corporation may create and issue rights or options entitling the holders of them to purchase from the corporation shares of a specified class or classes. Such rights or options state the terms, the time, and the price at which the shares may be purchased from the corporation. In the absence of fraud in the transaction, the judgment of the board of directors as to the adequacy of the consideration received for rights or options is conclusive. One of the uses of stock options is incentive compensation plans for directors, officers, and employees. Another is to assist in raising capital by making one class of securities more attractive by including rights to purchase shares in another class.

Stock option–contractual right to purchase stock from a corporation

Dividends and Other Distributions

The objective of every private, for-profit business corporation is to operate profitably, and it is a fundamental desire of most shareholders to share in the profits through the receipt of distributions, in particular dividends. In almost every State the declaration of distributions, including dividends, is within the discretion of the board of directors subject to certain restrictions and limitations.

   The conditions under which the earnings of a business may be paid out in the form of dividends or other distributions of corporate assets will depend on the contractual rights of the holders of the particular shares involved, the provisions in the charter and bylaws of the corporation, and the provisions of the State incorporation statute designed to protect creditors and shareholders from dissipation of corporate assets. More significant protection of creditors is provided by contractual restrictions typically included in their loan agreements, as well as by State fraudulent conveyance laws and Federal bankruptcy law.

Types of Dividends and Other Distributions

Distribution–transfer of property from a corporation to any of its shareholders

The Model Act defines a distribution as "a direct or indirect transfer of money or other property (except its own shares) or incurrence of indebtedness, by a corporation to or for the benefit of any of its shareholders in respect of any of its shares, whether by dividend or by purchase, redemption or other acquisition of its shares, or otherwise." We will discuss these distributions, as well as stock dividends and stock splits, which are not included in this definition.

Cash Dividends

The most customary type of dividend is the cash dividend declared and paid at regular intervals from legally available funds. These dividends may vary in amount depending on the policy of the board of directors and the earnings of the enterprise.

Property Dividends

Although dividends are almost always paid in cash, in a few instances a distribution of earnings has been made to shareholders in the form of property and has been termed a property dividend. On one occasion a distillery declared and paid a dividend in bonded whiskey.

Stock Dividends

A stock or share dividend is a ratable distribution of additional shares of the capital stock of the corporation to its shareholders. The practical and legal significance of a stock dividend differs greatly from a dividend payable in cash or property. Following the payment of a stock dividend, the assets of the corporation are no less than they were before, and the shareholder does not have any greater relative interest in the net worth of the corporation than he had before except possibly where the dividend is paid in shares of a different class. His shares will each represent a smaller proportionate interest in the assets of the corporation, but by reason of the increase in the number of shares his total investment will remain the same.

Stock Splits

A stock dividend should not be confused with a stock split. In a stock split, each of the issued and outstanding shares is simply broken up into a greater number of shares, each representing a proportionately smaller interest in the corporation. The usual purpose of a stock split is to lower the price per share to a more marketable price and thus increase the number of potential shareholders. As with a stock dividend, a stock split is *not* a distribution.

Liquidating Dividends

Although dividends are ordinarily identified with the distribution of profits, a distribution of capital assets to shareholders on termination of the business is considered a form of dividend and is referred to as a liquidating dividend. A distribution to common shareholders of paid-in surplus or capital surplus is also a liquidating dividend and should be specifically identified as such. Incorporation statutes usually require that the shareholder be informed when a distribution is a liquidating dividend.

Redemption of Shares

Redemption is the repurchase by the corporation of its own shares, usually at its own option. Shares of common stock ordinarily are not subject to redemption. Preferred shares, however, are frequently redeemable by the corporation at a **call** price stated in the stock certificate. This power of redemption must be expressly provided for in the articles of incorporation.

Acquisition of Shares

A corporation may acquire its own shares by purchase, gift, or otherwise. Such shares, unless canceled, are referred to as treasury shares. Under the MBCA as amended such shares are considered authorized but unissued. As with redemptions, acquisition of shares is a distribution to shareholders and has an effect similar to a dividend.

Legal Restrictions on Dividends and Other Distributions

The board of directors in its discretion determines when to declare distributions and dividends and in what amount. The corporation's working capital requirements, expectations of shareholders, tax consequences, and other factors influence the board in its formation of distribution policy. Nonetheless, a number of legal restrictions limit the amount of distributions the board may declare. All States have statutes restricting the funds that are legally available for dividends and other distributions of corporate assets. In many instances contractual restrictions imposed by lenders provide even more stringent limitations on the declaration of dividends and distributions.

States restrict in one way or another the payment of dividends and other distributions in order to protect creditors. All States impose the equity insolvency test, which prohibits the payment of any dividend or other distribution when the corporation is insolvent or when payment of the dividend or distribution would make the corporation insolvent. **Insolvent** means the inability of a corporation to pay its debts as they become due in the usual course of its business.

> Insolvent (equity) –inability to pay debts as they become due in the usual course of business

In addition, each State imposes further restrictions on what funds are legally available to pay dividends and other distributions. Some States permit dividends and other distributions to be paid only out of earned surplus; others are more permissive and allow dividends and other distributions to come from any kind of surplus. Moreover, some States permit dividends to be paid from current earnings even though there is no surplus. Such dividends are called "nimble dividends."

Definitions

The legal restrictions on the payment of dividends or other distributions involve the concepts of earned surplus, surplus, net assets, stated capital, and capital surplus (see Figure 34-2).

Earned surplus consists of the undistributed net profits, income, gains, and losses from the date of incorporation.

Surplus means the excess of the net assets of a corporation over its stated capital.

Net assets are the amount by which the total assets of a corporation exceed the total debts of the corporation.

Stated capital is defined as the sum of the consideration received by the corporation for its issued stock, except that part of the consideration properly

> Earned surplus –undistributed net profits, income, gains and losses
>
> Surplus –excess of net assets over stated capital
>
> Net assets –total assets minus total debts

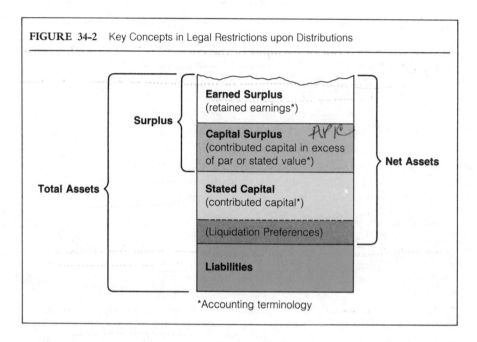

FIGURE 34–2   Key Concepts in Legal Restrictions upon Distributions

allocated to capital surplus, and including any amount transferred to stated capital when stock dividends are declared. In the case of par value shares, the amount of stated capital is the total par value of all the issued shares. In the case of no par stock, it is the consideration received by the corporation for all the no par shares that have been issued, except that amount allocated to an account designated as capital surplus or paid-in surplus in a manner permitted by law.

Capital surplus means the entire surplus of a corporation other than its earned surplus. It may result from an allocation of part of the consideration received for no par shares, or from any consideration in excess of par value received for par shares, or from a higher reappraisal of certain corporate assets.

Legal Restrictions on Cash Dividends

Earned Surplus Test   Unreserved and unrestricted earned surplus is available for dividends in all jurisdictions. Some States permit dividends to be paid *only* from earned surplus; dividends in these jurisdictions may not be paid out of capital surplus or stated capital. The MBCA used this test until 1979.

Surplus Test   A number of States are less restrictive and permit dividends to be paid out of any surplus—earned or capital. Some of these States express this test by prohibiting dividends that impair stated capital.

Net Asset Test   The Model Act now permits dividends to be paid unless the corporation's total assets after payment of the dividend would be less than the sum of its total liabilities and the maximum amount that then would be payable for all outstanding shares having preferential rights in liquidation.

Nimble Dividends   Although dividends in many States are properly payable only out of earnings or earned surplus and are generally not payable when the corporation has an accrued earned deficit, the statutes of a number of these States permit payment of dividends out of current earnings notwithstanding the existence of such deficit. Some States, such as Delaware, permit dividends to be paid out of earnings of the current or next preceding year, but shares having a liquidation preference may not be thus impaired. A board of directors in these States is permitted by timely action to declare a dividend in a year when the corporation has no earnings, provided it had earnings for the year immediately preceding. Because of the time limitation within which such dividends must be declared, they are sometimes called "nimble dividends."

Legal Restrictions on Liquidating Distributions

Even those States that do not permit cash dividends to be paid from capital surplus usually will permit distributions, or dividends, in partial liquidation from that source. A distribution paid out of such surplus is a return to the shareholders of a part of their investment.

No such distribution may be made, however, when the corporation is insolvent or would become insolvent by the distribution. Distributions from capital surplus are also restricted to protect the liquidation preference of preferred shareholders.

Unless provided for in the articles of incorporation, a liquidating dividend must be authorized not only by the board of directors but also by the affirmative vote of the holders of a majority of the outstanding shares of stock of each class.

The Model Act, as amended, does not distinguish between cash and liquidating dividends but imposes the same limitations discussed above under cash dividends.

Legal Restrictions on Redemptions and Acquisition of Shares

To protect creditors and holders of other classes of preferred shares, most States have statutory restrictions on redemption. A corporation may not redeem or purchase its redeemable shares when insolvent or when such redemption or purchase would render it insolvent or reduce its net assets below the aggregate amount payable on shares having prior or equal rights to the assets of the corporation on involuntary dissolution.

A corporation may purchase its own shares only out of earned surplus or, if the articles of incorporation permit or if the shareholders approve, out of capital surplus. As with redemption, no purchase of shares may be made at a time when the corporation is insolvent or when such purchase would make it insolvent.

The Model Act, as amended, permits the purchase, redemption, or other acquisition by a corporation of its own shares unless (1) the corporation's total assets after the distribution would be less than the sum of its total liabilities and the maximum amount that then would be payable for all outstanding shares having preferential rights in liquidation or (2) the corporation would be unable to pay its debts as they become due in the usual course of its business.

Declaration and Payment of Dividends

The board of directors of a corporation declares dividends, and this power may not be delegated. However, if the charter clearly and expressly provides for mandatory dividends, the board must comply with the provision. Nonetheless, such provisions are extremely infrequent, and any other attempt by shareholders to take over this power is ineffective, although it is in the shareholders' power to elect a new board. Moreover, it is well settled that there can be no discrimination in the declaration of dividends among shareholders of the same class.

A shareholder may not maintain an action at law against the corporation to recover a dividend until and unless the dividend has been formally declared by a resolution of the board of directors. A proper dividend so declared becomes a debt of the corporation and enforceable at law as any other debt.

Where the directors have failed to declare a dividend, a shareholder may bring a suit in equity against them and the corporation seeking a mandatory injunction requiring the directors to declare a dividend. Courts of equity are reluctant to order an injunction of this kind, which involves substituting the business judgment of the court for that of the directors elected by the shareholders. A court of equity will, however, grant an injunction and require the directors to declare a dividend where

1. a demand has been made on the directors before the suit was brought;

2. corporate earnings or surplus are available out of which a dividend may be legally declared;

3. the earnings or surplus is in the form of available cash; and

4. the directors have acted so unreasonably in withholding a dividend that their conduct clearly amounts to an abuse of discretion.

The existence of a large accumulated surplus does not by itself justify compelling the directors to distribute funds that, in their opinion, should be retained for *bona fide* corporate purposes. However, where the evidence shows noncorporate motives or personal animosity as the basis for a refusal to declare dividends, a court may require the directors to distribute what appears to be a reasonable portion of the earnings.

DODGE v. FORD MOTOR CO.

Supreme Court of Michigan, 1919.
204 Mich. 459, 170 N.W. 668.

FACTS: Ford Motor Company had made large profits for several years. Henry Ford, Ford's president and the dominant figure on the board of directors, declared that although it had paid special dividends in the past, Ford would not, as a matter of policy, pay any special dividends in the future but instead would reinvest the profits in the proposed expansion of the company. At the conclusion of Ford's most prosperous year, John and Horace Dodge, minority shareholders in Ford, brought this action against Ford's directors to compel the declaration of dividends and to enjoin the expansion of the business. The Dodges complain that the reinvestment of the profits is not in the best interests of Ford and its shareholders and that it is an arbitrary action of the directors.

DECISION: Judgment for Dodge. In general, it is not a violation of a corporation's charter to accumulate profits for reinvestment in the company. As the managers of a corporation, the directors are impliedly invested with discretionary power as to the time and manner of distributing the company's profits. But while the court is reluctant to substitute its judgment for that of the directors, their refusal to declare and pay special dividends in light of the large surplus was not an exercise of discretion but an arbitrary refusal to do what the circumstances required to be done.

The fact that a preferred shareholder has prior rights with respect to dividends does not make her position different from that of the holder of common shares with respect to the discretion of the directors as to the declaration of dividends. The holders of preferred stock, in the absence of special contractual or statutory rights, must likewise abide by the decision of the directors.

Once lawfully and properly declared, a cash dividend is considered a debt owing by the corporation to the shareholders. It follows from the debtor-creditor relationship created by the declaration of a cash dividend that, once declared, it cannot be rescinded as against nonassenting shareholders. However, a stock dividend may be revoked unless actually distributed.

The time, place, and manner of payment of dividends are at the discretion of the directors. It is not uncommon for the resolution declaring a dividend to fix a cutoff date by providing that the dividend shall be paid to the shareholders of record as of the close of business on a specified future date, usually about two weeks earlier than the date fixed for payment. Where the resolution declaring a dividend fixes a cutoff date, the shareholder of record as of that date is entitled to the dividend.

Liability for Improper Dividends and Distributions

The Model Act imposes joint and several liability on the directors of a corporation who vote for or assent to the declaration of a dividend or other distribution of corporate assets contrary to the incorporation statute or the articles of incorporation. The measure of damages is the amount of the dividend or distribution in excess of the amount that may have been lawfully paid. The directors may not escape liability by delegation of the power to declare dividends to an executive committee. The directors are not liable, however, if they rely in good faith on financial statements presented by the corporation's officers, public accountants, or finance committee.

The liability of directors is generally to the corporation or to its creditors. The Model Act expressly provides that the directors who vote for or assent to an illegal dividend or distribution are jointly and severally liable to the corporation.

The obligation of a shareholder to repay an illegally declared dividend depends on a variety of factors, which may include the good or bad faith on the part of the shareholder in accepting the dividend, his knowledge of the facts, the solvency or insolvency of the corporation, and in some instances, special statutory provisions. The existence of statutory liability on the part of directors does not relieve shareholders from the duty to make repayment.

A shareholder who receives illegal dividends either as a result of his own fraudulent act or with knowledge of their unlawful character is under a duty to refund them to the corporation. Where the corporation is insolvent, a dividend may not be retained by the shareholder even though received by him in good faith. Where an unsuspecting shareholder receives an illegal dividend from a solvent corporation, the majority rule is that he cannot be compelled to make a refund.

FRIED v. CANO

United States District Court, Southern District of New York, 1958. 167 F.Supp. 625.

FACTS: International Distributing Export Company (I.D.E.) was organized as a corporation on September 7, 1948 under the laws of New York, and commenced business on November 1, 1948. I.D.E. had formerly been in existence as an individual proprietorship. On October 31, 1948, the newly organized corporation had liabilities of $64,084.00. Its only assets, in the sum of $33,042, were those of the former sole proprietorship. However, the corporation set up an asset on its balance sheet in the amount of $32,000 for goodwill. As a result of this entry, I.D.E. had a surplus at the end of each of its fiscal years from 1949 until 1954. Cano, a shareholder, received $7,144 in dividends from I.D.E. during the period from 1950 to 1955. Fried, the trustee in bankruptcy of I.D.E., brought an action against Cano to recover the amount of these dividends paid to Cano, alleging that they had been paid when I.D.E. was insolvent or when its capital was impaired.

DECISION: Judgment for Cano. There was no evidence that the corporation was not paying its debts as they matured. The wrongful declaration of a dividend out of capital, in violation of the incorporation statute, is a wrong of those committing it. Innocent participants are not accomplices to its commission. In order to hold the stockholder who received the dividend liable, it is necessary to prove the stockholder's complicity in and knowledge of the wrong. Fried did not prove that Cano had knowledge that his dividends were paid out of I.D.E.'s capital, or that the dividends impaired I.D.E.'s capital. Therefore, Cano cannot be held liable.

Transfer of Investment Securities

Any investor has the right to transfer her securities by sale, gift, or pledge, just as she has the inherent right to transfer any other properties she may own. The right to transfer securities is a valuable one, and the ease with which it may be done adds to their value and marketability. The availability of a ready market for any security affords liquidity and makes the security attractive to investors and useful as collateral.

The statutory rules applicable to transfers of securities are contained in the Uniform Commercial Code, Article 8, Investment Securities, which establishes rules similar to those in Article 3, which concerns commercial paper. Article 8 applies not only to shares but also to bonds, debentures, voting trust certificates, certificates of beneficial interest in business trusts, and any other "interest in property of or an enterprise of the issuer or an obligation of the issuer" that is of a "class or series" and "issued or dealt in as a medium for investment."

A number of aspects of the transfer of securities are also regulated by Federal securities laws which we discuss in Chapter 40.

Ownership of Securities

Record Ownership

Certificated security—security represented by a certificate

Uncertificated security security not represented by a certificate

A security is intangible personal property and exists independently of a certificate. Article 8 permits the issuance and transfer of **uncertificated securities,** which are securities not represented by a certificate. The transfer of uncertificated securities is registered on books maintained for that purpose by or on behalf of the issuer.

The 1979 amendments to the MBCA provide that "the shares of a corporation shall be represented by certificates or shall be uncertificated shares." The rights and obligations of holders of uncertificated shares and certificated shares of the same class and series are identical.

Duty of Issuer to Register Transfer of Security

The issuing corporation is under a duty to register transfer of its certificated securities and issue new certificates to the new owner. The owner or purchaser is entitled to registration in order to vote and to receive dividends, notices, and periodic reports of the corporation and to receive a new certificate, because the only way that he can sell or pledge or dispose of the certificated securities is by a transfer of the certificate.

Lost, Destroyed, or Stolen Certificated Securities

If a certificated security has been lost, destroyed, or stolen, the owner is entitled to a new certificate to replace the missing one, provided she (1) requests it before the issuer has notice that the "missing" certificate has been acquired by a *bona fide* purchaser, (2) files a sufficient indemnity bond with the issuer, and (3) satisfies other reasonable requirements of the issuer, such as furnishing a sworn statement of the facts in connection with the loss.

The owner of a lost, destroyed, or stolen certificate may be deprived of the right to a replacement certificate by failing to notify the issuing corporation within a reasonable time after learning of the loss, if the corporation has registered a transfer of the certificate before receiving such notification.

Transfer of Securities

Manner of Transfer

Under the Code, a transfer of certificated securities is made by delivery of the certificate alone if it is in bearer form or indorsed in blank or, if in registered form, which is more usual, by delivery of the certificate with either (1) the indorsement on it by "an appropriate person," or (2) a separate document of assignment and transfer signed by "an appropriate person." The term "appropriate person" includes the person specified in the certificate or entitled to it by special indorsement, their successors in interest, or the authorized agent of a person so specified or so entitled. A transfer of uncertificated securities occurs at the time the transfer is registered.

Prior to presentment for registration of transfer of a certificated security in registered form, the corporation may treat the registered owner as the person entitled to vote, to receive notices, and otherwise to exercise all of the rights and powers of the owner.

The delivery of an unindorsed certificate by the owner with the intention of transferring title to the securities represented thereby gives the intended transferee as against the transferor complete rights in the certificate and in the certificated securities, including the right to compel indorsement. He becomes a *bona fide* purchaser of the certificated securities, however, only as of the time the indorsement is supplied.

Bona Fide Purchasers

like holder in due course

A "*bona fide* purchaser" is a purchaser for value in good faith and without notice of any adverse claim who takes delivery of a certificated security in bearer form or in registered form issued to her or indorsed to her or in blank. The negotiation and transfer of a security to a *bona fide* purchaser passes title to her free of all adverse claims not conspicuously noted on the certificate. Adverse claims include a claim that a transfer was or would be wrongful or that a particular adverse person is the owner of or has an interest in the security. Thus, the *bona fide* purchaser from a thief, finder, or other unauthorized person is protected.

Transfer Warranties

A person by transferring certificated securities to a purchaser for value warrants that

1. the transfer is effective and rightful;

2. the security is genuine and has not been materially altered; and

3. he knows of no fact that might impair the validity of the security.

A person who presents a certificated security for registration of transfer or for payment or exchange warrants to the issuer that he is entitled to the registration, payment, or exchange, but a purchaser for value and without notice of adverse claims who receives a new, reissued, or registered certificated security on registration of transfer warrants only that he has no knowledge of any unauthorized signature in a necessary indorsement.

Forged or Unauthorized Indorsement

The owner of securities represented by a certificate is not deprived of his title by a transfer of the certificate bearing a forged or unauthorized indorsement. The purchaser of a security bearing a forged or unauthorized indorsement who resells and transfers it to a *bona fide* purchaser is liable to him for the value of the securities at the time of sale, because he has breached his warranty that the transfer is effective and rightful. Neither party is owner of the securities, as title cannot be transferred through a forged or unauthorized indorsement.

Unless the owner has ratified an unauthorized indorsement or is otherwise prevented from asserting its ineffectiveness, he may assert its ineffectiveness against the issuer and against any purchaser other than a *bona fide* purchaser who has in good faith received a new, reissued, or reregistered certificated security on registration of transfer. An issuer who registers the transfer of a certificated security on an unauthorized indorsement is subject to liability for improper registration.

CHAPTER SUMMARY

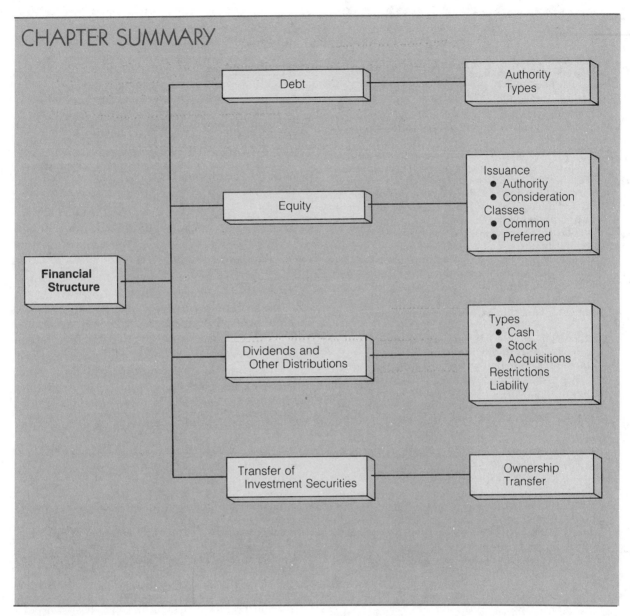

KEY TERMS

Equity securities
Debt securities
Debentures
Shares
Blue Sky Laws
Pre-emptive rights
Par value stock
Stated capital
Capital surplus

No par value stock
Treasury stock
Common stock
Preferred stock
Cumulative dividend
Noncumulative dividend
Stock options
Distribution
Stock dividend

Stock split
Liquidating dividends
Involvency test
Earned surplus
Surplus
Net assets
Uncertificated security
Certificated security

PROBLEMS

1. Frank McAnarney and Joseph Lemon entered into an agreement to promote a corporation to engage in the manufacture of farm implements. Before the corporation was organized, McAnarney and Lemon solicited subscriptions to the stock of the corporation and presented a written agreement for signatures of the subscribers.

The agreement provided that subscribers pay $100 per share for stock in the corporation in consideration of McAnarney's and Lemon's agreement to organize the corporation and advance the preincorporation expenses. Thomas Jordan signed the agreement, making application for 100 shares of stock. After the filing of the articles of incorporation with the Secretary of State, but before the charter to the corporation was issued, Jordan died. The administrator of Jordan's estate notified McAnarney and Lemon that the estate would not honor Jordan's subscription.

After the formation of the corporation, Franklin Adams signed a subscription agreement making application for 100 shares of stock. Before acceptance by the corporation, Adams informed the corporation that he was canceling his subscription.

(a) The corporation brings an appropriate action against Jordan's estate to enforce Jordan's stock subscription. Decision?

(b) The corporation brings an appropriate action to enforce Adams's stock subscription. Decision?

2. The XYZ Corporation was duly organized on July 10. Its certificate of incorporation provides for a total authorized capital of $100,000, consisting of 1,000 shares of common stock with a par value of $100 per share. The corporation issues for cash a total of fifty certificates, numbered one to fifty inclusive, representing various amounts of shares in the names of various individuals. The shares were all paid for in advance, so the certificates are all dated and mailed on the same day. The fifty certificates of stock represent a total of 1,050 shares. Certificate 49 for thirty shares was issued to Jane Smith. Certificate 50 for twenty-five shares was issued to William Jones. Is there any question concerning the validity of any of the stock thus issued? What are the rights of Smith and Jones?

3. D subscribed for 200 shares of 12 percent cumulative, participating, redeemable, convertible, preferred shares of the X Hotel Company with a par value of $100 per share. The subscription agreement provided that she was to receive a bonus of one share of common stock of $100 par value for each share of preferred stock. D fully paid her subscription agreement of $20,000 and received the 200 shares of preferred and the bonus stock of 200 shares of the par value common. The Hotel Company later becomes insolvent. R, the receiver of the corporation, brings

suit for $20,000, the par value of the common stock. What judgment?

4. The X Company has an authorized capital stock of 1,000 shares with a par value of $100 per share, of which 900 shares, all fully paid, are outstanding. Having an ample surplus, the X Company purchases from its shareholders 100 shares at par. Subsequently, the X Company, needing additional working capital, issues the 200 shares in question to S at $80 per share. Two years later the X Company is forced into bankruptcy. The trustee in bankruptcy now sues S for $4,000. Decision?

5. For five years B and C had been engaged as partners in building houses. They owned the necessary equipment to conduct the business and had an excellent reputation. In March, D, who had previously been in the same kind of business, proposed that B, C, and D form a corporation for the purposes of constructing medium-price houses. They engaged attorney A, who did all the work required and caused the business to be incorporated under the name of X Corp.

The certificate of incorporation authorized one hundred shares of $100 par value stock. At the organization meeting of the incorporators, B, C, and D were elected directors, and X Corp. issued a total of sixty-five shares of its stock. B and C each received twenty shares in consideration of transferring to X Corp. the equipment and good will of their partnership, which together had a value of over $4,000. D received twenty shares as an inducement to work for X Corp. in the future, and A received five shares as compensation for the legal services rendered in forming X Corp.

Later that year X Corp. had a number of financial setbacks and in December ceased operations. What rights, if any, does X Corp. have against B, C, D, and A in connection with the original issuance of its shares?

6. Paul Bunyan is the owner of noncumulative 8 percent preferred stock in the Broadview Corporation, which had no earnings or profits in 1983. In 1984 the corporation had large profits and a surplus from which it might properly have declared dividends. The directors refused to do so, but instead used the surplus to purchase goods necessary for their expanding business.

In view of the large profits made in 1984, the directors at the end of 1985 declared a 10 percent dividend on the common stock and an 8 percent dividend on the preferred stock without paying preferred dividends for 1984. The corporation earned a small profit in 1985.

(a) Is Bunyan entitled to dividends for 1983? For 1984?

(b) Is Bunyan entitled to a dividend of 10 percent rather than 8 percent in 1985?

7. A corporation has outstanding 400 shares of $100 par value common stock, which has been issued and sold at $105 per share for a total of $42,000. A is incorporated in State X, which has adopted the earned surplus test for all distributions. At a time when the assets of the corporation amount to $65,000 and the liabilities to creditors total $10,000, the directors learn that S, who holds 100 of the 400 shares of stock, is planning to sell her shares on the open market for $10,500. Believing that this will not be to the best interest of the corporation, the directors enter into an agreement with S to buy the shares for $10,500. About six months later, when the assets of the corporation have decreased to $50,000 and its liabilities, not including its liability to S, have increased to $20,000, the directors use $10,000 to pay a dividend to all of the shareholders. The corporation later becomes insolvent.

(a) Does S have any liability to the corporation or its creditors in connection with the corporation's reacquisition of the 100 shares?

(b) Was the payment of the $10,000 dividend proper?

8. Almega Corporation, organized under the laws of State S, has outstanding 20,000 shares of $100 par value nonvoting preferred stock calling for noncumulative dividends of $5.00 per year; 10,000 shares of voting preferred stock of par $50 value, calling for cumulative dividends of $2.50 per year; and 10,000 shares of no par common stock. State S has adopted the earned surplus test for all distributions. In 1981 the corporation had net earnings of $170,000; in 1982, $135,000; in 1983, $60,000; in 1984, $210,000; and 1985, $120,000. The board of directors passed over all dividends during the four years 1981–1984, since the company needed working capital for expansion purposes. In 1985 the directors declared a dividend of $5.00 per share on the noncumulative preferred shares, a dividend of $12.50 per share on the cumulative preferred shares, and a dividend of $30.00

per share on the common stock. The board submitted their declaration to the voting shareholders, and they ratified it. Before the dividends were paid, Payne, the record holder of 500 shares of the noncumulative preferred stock, brought an appropriate action to restrain any payment to the cumulative preferred or common shareholders until a full dividend for 1981–1985 was paid to noncumulative preferred shareholders. Decision?

9. Sayre learned that Adams, Boone, and Chase were planning to form a corporation for the purpose of manufacturing and marketing a line of novelties to wholesale outlets. Sayre had patented a self-locking gas tank cap but lacked the financial backing to market it profitably. He negotiated with Adams, Boone, and Chase, who agreed to purchase the patent rights for $5,000 in cash and 200 shares of $100 par value preferred stock in a corporation to be formed.

The corporation was formed and Sayre's stock issued to him, but the corporation has refused to make the cash payment. It has also refused to declare dividends, although the business has been very profitable because of Sayre's patent and has a substantial earned surplus with a large cash balance on hand. It is selling the remainder of the originally authorized issue of preferred shares, ignoring Sayre's demand to purchase a proportionate number of these shares. What are Sayre's rights, if any?

10. A bylaw of Betma Corporation provides that no shareholder can sell their shares unless they first offer them for sale to the corporation or its directors. The bylaw also states that this restriction shall be printed or stamped on each stock certificate and binds all present or future owners or holders. Betma Corporation did not comply with this latter provision. Shaw, having knowledge of the bylaw restriction, nevertheless purchased twenty shares of the corporation's stock from Rice, without having Rice first offer them for sale to the corporation or its directors. When Betma Corporation refused to effectuate a transfer of the shares to her, Shaw sued to compel a transfer and the issuance of a new certificate to her. Decision?

MANAGEMENT STRUCTURE

The corporate management structure, as designed by State incorporation statutes, is pyramidal. At the base of the pyramid are the **shareholders,** who are the residual owners of the corporation. Basic to their role in controlling the corporation is the right to elect representatives to manage the ordinary business matters of the corporation and the right to approve all extraordinary matters.

The **board of directors,** as the shareholders' elected representatives, are delegated the power to manage the business of the corporation. Directors exercise dominion and control over the corporation, hold positions of trust and confidence, and determine questions of operating policy. Directors are not ordinarily expected to devote full time to the affairs of the corporation and have broad authority to delegate power to officers and agents. The **officers** of the corporation hold their office at the will of the board. The officers, in turn, hire and fire all necessary operating personnel and run the day-to-day affairs of the corporation. The pyramid structure of corporate management is illustrated in Figure 35-1.

Role of Shareholders

The role of the shareholders in management is generally restricted to the election of directors, approval of certain extraordinary matters, and the right to bring suits to enforce these rights. At the same time, shareholders assume potential personal liability for defective incorporation, disregard of corporateness, and receipt of improper distributions.

Voting Rights of Shareholders

The shareholder's right to vote is fundamental to the concept of the corporation and its management structure. In most States today a shareholder is entitled to one vote for each share of stock that he owns, unless the articles of incorporation provide otherwise. In addition, incorporation statutes generally permit the issuance of one or more classes of nonvoting stock, as long as at least one class of shares has voting rights. The articles of incorporation may provide for more or less than one vote for any share.

Shareholders may exercise their voting rights at both annual and special shareholder meetings. **Annual meetings** are required and must be held at a

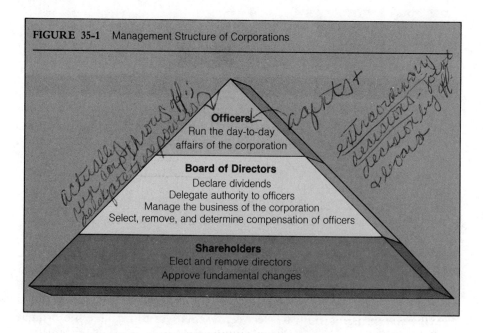

FIGURE 35-1   Management Structure of Corporations

Officers
Run the day-to-day
affairs of the corporation

Board of Directors
Declare dividends
Delegate authority to officers
Manage the business of the corporation
Select, remove, and determine compensation of officers

Shareholders
Elect and remove directors
Approve fundamental changes

time fixed by the bylaws. If the annual shareholder meeting is not held within a thirteen-month period, any shareholder may petition and obtain a court order requiring that a meeting be held. The Revised Act provides this right if the annual meeting is not held within the earlier of 6 months after the end of the corporation's fiscal year or 15 months after its last annual meeting.

Special meetings may be called by the board of directors, holders of at least 10 percent of the shares, or such other persons authorized in the articles of incorporation. The Revised Act reduces the 10 percent requirement to 5 percent. Written notice stating the place, day, and hour of the meeting and, in the case of a special meeting, the purposes for which it is called must be given in advance. Notice, however, may be waived in writing by any shareholder entitled to notice.

A quorum of shares must be represented at the meeting, either in person or by proxy. Unless otherwise provided in the articles of incorporation, a majority of shares entitled to vote constitutes a **quorum,** but under no circumstances may a quorum consist of less than one-third of the shares entitled to vote. Unissued shares and treasury stock may not be voted nor counted in determining whether a quorum exists. Decisions made at the meeting will have no effect if a quorum is not present. Once a quorum is present at a meeting, it is deemed present for the rest of the meeting despite the withdrawal of shareholders in an effort to break quorum.

Most States require shareholder actions to be approved by a majority of shares represented at the meeting and entitled to vote. Nonetheless, many States permit the articles of incorporation to increase the percentage of shares required to take any action subject to shareholder approval.

A number of States permit shareholders to conduct business without a meeting if all the shareholders consent in writing to the action taken. A few States, including Delaware, have further relaxed the formalities of shareholder action by permitting shareholders to act without a meeting with written consent of only the number of shares required to act on the matter.

Election and Removal of Directors

Directors are elected each year at the annual meeting of the shareholders. Most States provide that where the board consists of nine or more directors, the charter or bylaws may provide for a **classification** of directors, that is, a division into two or three classes to be as nearly equal in number as possible. If the directors are divided into two classes, the members of each class are elected once a year in alternate years for a two-year term; if into three classes, for three-year terms. This permits one-half of the board to be elected every two years, or one-third to be elected every three years, thus providing an element of continuity in the membership of the board. Moreover, where there are two or more classes of shares, each class may elect a specified number of directors if provided for in articles of incorporation.

Normally, each shareholder has one vote for each share owned and directors are elected by a *plurality* of the votes. However, in certain States, shareholders have the right of cumulative voting for the election of directors of the corporation. In most States cumulative voting is permissive and not mandatory. **Cumulative voting** entitles each shareholder, who has one vote for each share owned, to cumulate his votes and give one candidate as many votes as the number of directors to be elected multiplied by the number of shares owned, or to distribute his votes among as many candidates as he wishes. Cumulative voting permits a minority shareholder, or group of minority shareholders acting together, to obtain minority representation on the board if they own a certain minimum number of shares. Without cumulative voting, the holder or holders of 51 percent of the voting shares can elect all of the members of the board.

The formula for determining how many shares a minority shareholder with cumulative voting rights must own, or have proxies to vote, in order to secure representation on the board is as follows:

$$X = \frac{ac}{b + 1} + 1$$

a = number of shares voting

b = number of directors to be elected

c = number of directors desired to be elected

X = number of shares necessary to elect the number of directors desired to be elected

For example, Z corporation has two shareholders, A with 64 shares and B with 36 shares. The board of directors of Z corporation consists of three directors. Under "straight" or noncumulative voting, A could cast 64 votes for each of her three candidates, and B could cast 36 votes for his three candidates. As a result, all three of A's candidates would be elected. On the other hand, if cumulative voting were in force, B could elect one director:

$$X = \frac{ac}{b + 1} + 1$$

$$X = \frac{100 \, (1)}{3 + 1} + 1 = 26 \text{ shares}$$

Since B has the right to vote more than 26 shares, he would be able to elect one director. A, of course, with her 64 shares, could elect the remaining two directors:

$$X = \frac{ac}{b + 1} + 1$$

$$X = \frac{100 \, (2)}{3 + 1} + 1 = 51 \text{ shares}$$

To elect all three directors, A would need 76 shares $[100(3)/(3 + 1) + 1]$.

The effect of cumulative voting for directors may be diluted by classification or staggered election of the board of directors or by reducing the size of the board. For example, if nine directors are each elected annually, only 11 percent of the shares are needed to elect one director; if the nine directors are classified and three are elected annually, 26 percent of the shares are required to elect one director.

Shareholders may by a majority vote remove, with or without cause, any director or the entire board of directors in a meeting called for that purpose. However, in the case of a corporation having cumulative voting, removal of a director requires sufficient votes to prevent his election. We discuss removal of directors more fully later in this chapter.

Approval of Fundamental Changes

The board of directors manages the ordinary business affairs of the corporation. Extraordinary matters involving fundamental changes in the corporation require shareholder approval and include such matters as amendments to the articles of incorporation, a sale or lease of all or substantially all of the corporate assets not in the regular course of business, most mergers, consolidations, compulsory share exchanges, and dissolution. We discuss fundamental changes in Chapter 36.

Concentrations of Voting Power

Proxies A shareholder may vote either in person or by written proxy. A proxy is simply the authorization by a shareholder to an agent to vote his shares at a particular meeting or on a particular question. Generally, proxies must be in writing to be effective. The duration of proxies are typically limited by statute to no more than eleven months, unless the proxy specifically provides otherwise. Since a proxy is the appointment of an agent, it is revocable, as all agencies are, unless coupled with an interest, such as when shares are held as collateral. The solicitation of proxies by publicly held corporations is also regulated by the Securities Exchange Act of 1934 as we discuss in Chapter 40.

Proxy–authorization to vote another's shares at a shareholder meeting

direct voting

indirect

Voting Trusts Voting trusts, which are devices designed to concentrate corporate control in one or more persons, have been used in both publicly held and closely held corporations. A voting trust is a device by which one or more shareholders separate the voting rights of their shares from the ownership of them. Under a voting trust, all or part of the stock of a corporation may, by written agreement among the shareholders, be issued to a trustee or trustees who then holds legal title to the stock and has all of the voting rights possessed by the stock. In most States, voting trusts are permitted by statute, but are usually limited in duration to ten years.

Voting trust–transfer of corporate shares' voting rights to a trustee

Shareholder Agreements   In most jurisdictions, shareholders may agree in advance to vote in a specified manner for the election or removal of directors or on any matter subject to shareholder approval. Unlike voting trusts, shareholder agreements are not limited in duration. Shareholder agreements are used frequently in closely held corporations, especially in conjunction with restrictions on the transfer of shares, in order to provide each of the shareholders with greater control and *delectus personae* (the right to choose who become shareholders).

GALLER v. GALLER

Supreme Court of Illinois, 1965.
32 Ill.2d 16, 203 N.E.2d 577.

FACTS: In 1927, two brothers, Benjamin and Isadore Galler, incorporated the Galler Drug Co., a wholesale drug business that they had operated as equal partners since 1919. The company continued to grow, and in 1955, the two brothers and their wives, Emma and Rose Galler, entered into a written shareholder agreement to leave the corporation in equal control of each family after the death of either brother. Specifically, the agreement provided for the corporation to continue to provide income for the support and maintenance of their immediate families and for the parties to vote for directors so as to give the estate and heirs of a deceased shareholder the same representation as before.

Benjamin died in 1957, and shortly thereafter his widow Emma requested that Isadore, the surviving brother, comply with the terms of the agreement. When he refused and proposed that certain changes be made in the agreement, Emma brought this action seeking specific performance of the agreement. Isadore and his wife, Rose, defend on the ground that the shareholder agreement was against public policy and the State's corporation law.

DECISION: Judgment for Emma Galler. A close corporation is one in which the stock is held in a few hands and is rarely traded. In contrast to a shareholder in a public corporation, who may easily trade his shares on the open market when he disagrees with its management over corporate policy, the shareholder of a closely held corporation often has no ready market in which to sell his shares should he wish to do so. Moreover, the shareholder in a closely held corporation often has most of his capital invested in the corporation and, therefore, views himself as more than a mere investor, but also as a participant in the management of the business. Without a shareholder agreement subject to specific performance by the courts, the minority shareholder might find himself at the mercy of the controlling majority shareholder. In short, the detailed shareholder agreement is the only sound means by which the minority shareholder can protect himself. Therefore, since the agreement was reasonable in its scope and purpose of providing continuing support for the Galler brothers' families, it should be enforced.

Enforcement Rights of Shareholders

To protect a shareholder's interests in the corporation, the law provides shareholders with certain enforcement rights. These include the right to information, the right to sue the corporation directly or to sue on the corporation's behalf, and the right to dissent.

Right to Inspect Books and Records

Most States have enacted statutory provisions granting shareholders the right to inspect for a *proper purpose* books and records in person or by agent and to copy parts of them. A number of States, however, limit this right to shareholders who own a minimum number of shares or have been a shareholder for a minimum period of time. For example, the MBCA requires that a shareholder either must own 5 percent of the outstanding shares or must have owned his shares for at least six months. The Revised Act relaxes this rule and provides that *every* shareholder is entitled to examine specified corporate records upon prior written request if the demand is made in good faith and for a proper purpose. **Proper purpose** for inspection means a purpose that is reasonably relevant to that shareholder's interest in the corporation. Proper purposes include determining the financial condition of the corporation, the value of shares, the existence of mismanagement, or, as in the next case, the names of other shareholders in order to communicate with them about corporate affairs. The right of inspection is subject to abuse and will be denied a shareholder who is seeking information for an improper purpose. Examples of improper purpose are obtaining information for use by a competing company or obtaining a list of shareholders in order to offer it for sale.

APPLICATION OF LOPEZ

Supreme Court, Appellate Division, First Department, 1979.
420 N.Y.S.2d 225, 71 A.D.2d 976.

FACTS: Muller, a shareholder of SCM, brought an action against SCM over his unsuccessful negotiations to purchase some of SCM's assets overseas. He then formed a shareholder committee to challenge the position of SCM's management in that suit. In order to conduct a proxy battle for management control at the next election of directors, the committee sought to obtain the list of shareholders who would be eligible to vote. At the time, however, no member of the committee had owned stock in SCM for the six-month period required to gain access to such information. Then Lopez, a former SCM executive and a shareholder for over one year, joined the committee and demanded to be allowed to inspect the minutes of SCM shareholder proceedings and to gain access to the current shareholder list. His stated reason for making the demand was to solicit proxies in support of the committee's nominees for positions as directors. Lopez brings this action after SCM rejected this demand.

DECISION: Judgment for Lopez. Lopez's demand to inspect the shareholder list in order to conduct a proxy challenge to incumbent directors is for a valid purpose. When the demand is valid on its face, good faith on the part of the requesting party will be assumed. The burden then shifts to SCM to show that the demand was motivated by an improper purpose. The mere fact that Muller and his companies are engaged in litigation with SCM does not demonstrate a lack of good faith, nor would it be an improper purpose or in bad faith if communications with other shareholders discussed the litigation.

Shareholder Suits

The ultimate recourse of a shareholder, short of selling his shares, is to bring suit against or on behalf of the corporation. Shareholder suits are essentially of two types: direct suits or derivative suits.

Direct Suits   A direct suit may be brought by a shareholder to enforce a claim that the shareholder has *against* the corporation based on his ownership of shares. Any recovery in a direct suit goes to the shareholder plaintiff. Examples of direct suits include actions by a shareholder to compel payment of dividends properly declared, to enforce the right to inspect corporate records,

Direct suit–suit brought by a shareholder against the corporation based upon his ownership of shares to enforce the right to vote, to protect pre-emptive rights, and to compel dissolution.

Derivative Suits   A derivative suit is a cause of action brought by one or more shareholders on *behalf* of the corporation to enforce a right belonging to the corporation. It is brought when the board of directors refuses to take such action on behalf of the corporation. Recovery usually goes to the corporate treasury so that all shareholders can benefit proportionately. Examples of derivative suits are actions to recovery damages from an *ultra vires* act, to recover damages for a breach of duty by management, and to recover improper dividends. In many such situations the board of directors may be hesitant to bring suit against the corporation's officers or directors. Consequently, a shareholder derivative suit is the only recourse.

> **Derivative suit**–suit brought by a shareholder on behalf of the corporation to enforce a right belonging to the corporation

In most States a shareholder must have owned his shares at the time that the transaction complained of occurred in order to bring a derivative suit. In addition, the shareholder must first make demand on the board of directors to enforce the corporate right.

FACTS: Minority shareholders of Midwest Technical Institute Development Corporation, a closed-end investment company owning assets consisting principally of securities of companies in technological fields, brought a shareholder derivative suit against officers and directors of Midwest. The shareholders sought to recover on Midwest's behalf the profits realized by the officers and directors through dealings in stock held in Midwest's portfolio in breach of their fiduciary duty. Approximately three years after commencement of the action a new corporation, Midtex, was organized to acquire Midwest's assets. The shareholders now seek to add Midtex as a party defendant to their suit.

DECISION: Judgment for the shareholders. A stockholder derivative suit is an invention of equity designed to supply a remedy where none existed at law to redress breaches of fiduciary duty by corporate officers and directors. The action is a derivative or secondary one brought by a shareholder on the corporation's behalf. Thus, the stockholder may sue in the corporation's behalf only if he can show that the corporation refused to bring the action itself after a proper request or that such a request would be futile. Here, all of Midwest's assets were transferred to the newly organized corporation, Midtex, but this should not end the stockholders' right to seek relief. The stockholders of Midwest did not lose the right to recover for a breach of fiduciary duty simply because the assets were transferred to a new corporation.

McMENOMY v. RYDEN

Supreme Court of Minnesota,
1970.
286 Minn. 358, 176 N.W.2d
876.

Shareholder's Right to Dissent

A shareholder has the right to dissent from certain corporate actions that require shareholder approval. These actions include most mergers, consolidations, compulsory share exchanges, and a sale or exchange of all or substantially all the assets of the corporation not in the usual and regular course of business. We discuss the shareholder's right to dissent in Chapter 36.

Liability of Shareholders

As a general rule the liability of a shareholder is limited to his investment. However, as discussed in the previous chapter, a shareholder who has not fully paid the required consideration for his shares is liable for the deficiency. In addition, in several instances a shareholder who has fully paid for his shares may nonetheless have liability beyond his capital contribution.

Defective Incorporation

If a purported corporation is defectively formed, shareholders who actively participated may be personally liable for the enterprise's obligations.

Disregard of the Corporate Entity

Where justice requires, courts will "pierce the corporate veil" and impose liability on shareholders even though they have strictly complied with the required incorporation procedures.

Illegal Distributions

Shareholders who knowingly receive improperly declared dividends or other distributions are liable to return them to the corporation. Moreover, if the corporation is insolvent, the shareholders who received dividends must return them whether they knew they were improper or not.

Controlling Shareholders

Shareholders who own a sufficient number of shares to have effective control over the corporation are called controlling shareholders. In some instances, controlling shareholders are held to the same duties as directors and officers, which are discussed later in this chapter. Moreover, in close corporations some courts impose on *all* the shareholders a fiduciary duty similar to that imposed on partners.

PEPPER v. LITTON

Supreme Court of the United States, 1939.
308 U.S. 295, 60 S.Ct. 238, 84 L.Ed. 281.

FACTS: Litton, an officer and the dominant shareholder of Dixie Splint Coal Company, transferred the company's remaining assets to himself when the company came on the verge of bankruptcy. The transfer allegedly was in satisfaction of an accrued salary claim that Litton had not enforced until the company came into financial difficulty. The trustee in bankruptcy seeks to have Litton's claim disallowed.

DECISION: Judgment for the trustee in bankruptcy. As both a director and the dominant shareholder of Dixie Splint Coal, Litton's dealings with the corporation are subject to rigorous scrutiny. As a fiduciary, then, he must show not only that any challenged transaction was entered into in good faith, but also that it was fair. If the transaction does not appear to be the result of an arm's length transaction, then a court of equity will set it aside. Since under the circumstances it appears that Litton's actions were part of a planned and fraudulent scheme, his transfer of assets should be set aside.

A special problem arises when controlling shareholders sell their shares in a block because such a sale necessarily and unavoidably conveys control to the purchaser. The courts require that such sales be made with due care. The controlling shareholders must make a reasonable investigation so as not to transfer control to purchasers who wrongfully plan to convert or "loot" the assets of the corporation or to act contrary to the best interests of the corporation.

Additionally, purchasers are frequently willing to pay a premium for a block of shares that also conveys control. Although some courts require that this so-called control premium go to the benefit of the corporation, other courts permit the controlling shareholders to retain the full amount of the control premium. When the premium is recoverable, the courts are divided over whether to permit the corporation to retain the premium or to require the corporation to distribute the premium ratably among the shareholders.

Role of Directors and Officers

Management of a corporation is vested in its board of directors, which determines general corporate policy and appoints officers to execute that policy and to administer the day-to-day operations of the corporation. Both the directors and officers of the corporation owe certain duties to the corporate entity as well as to the corporation's shareholders and are liable for breaching these duties.

In the following sections we discuss the role of directors and officers of a corporation, including the function of the board of directors; the qualification, election, and tenure of directors; the exercise of directors' functions; officers; duties of directors and officers; and liabilities of directors and officers.

Function of the Board of Directors

Although the directors are elected by the shareholders to manage the corporation, they are neither trustees nor agents of the shareholders or the corporation. They are, however, fiduciaries who must perform their duties in good faith, in the best interests of the corporation, and with due care.

The Model Act states "[a]ll corporate powers shall be exercised by or under authority of, and the business and affairs of a corporation shall be managed under the direction of, a board of directors." In some corporations the board consists of members all of whom are actively involved in the management of the business. In these cases the corporate powers are exercised *by* the board of directors. On the other hand, in publicly held corporations a majority of the board members frequently are not actively involved in management. Here, the corporate powers are exercised *under* the authority of the board which formulates major management policy but does not involve itself in the day-to-day management. Under the Revised Act, a corporation having 50 or fewer shareholders may dispense with or limit the authority of a board of directors by describing in its articles of incorporation who will perform some or all of the duties of a board.

The board determines corporate policy in a number of areas, including (1) selecting and removing officers, (2) determining the capital structure, (3) initiating fundamental changes, (4) declaring dividends, and (5) setting management compensation.

Selection and Removal of Officers

In most States the board of directors has the responsibility to choose the corporate officers and may remove any officer at any time. Officers are agents of the corporation and are delegated their responsibilities by the board of directors.

Capital Structure

The board of directors determines the capital structure and financial policy of the corporation. For example, the board of directors has the power to

1. fix the selling price of newly issued par value shares at not less than par;

2. fix the stated value and selling price of no par shares, unless the power to do so is reserved to the shareholders by the articles of incorporation;

3. determine the value of the consideration in the form of property, labor, or services received by the corporation in payment for shares issued;

4. purchase, redeem, or otherwise acquire shares of the corporation's equity securities;

5. borrow money, issue notes, bonds, and other obligations, and secure any of the corporation's obligations by mortgage or pledge of any or all of the corporation's property; and

6. sell, lease, or mortgage assets of the corporation in the *usual* and *regular* course of business.

Fundamental Changes

The board of directors has the power to make, alter, amend, or repeal the bylaws, unless this power is reserved to the shareholders by the articles of incorporation. In addition, the board initiates a number of actions that are beyond its powers and require shareholder approval. For instance, the board must initiate proceedings to amend the articles of incorporation; to effect a merger, consolidation, compulsory share exchange, or the sale or lease of all or substantially all of the assets of the corporation other than in the usual and regular course of business; and to dissolve the corporation.

Dividends

The board of directors declares the amount and type of dividends, subject to restrictions in the State incorporation statute, the articles of incorporation, and corporate loan and preferred stock agreements. The board also provides for closing of stock transfer books and fixes a record date for the purpose of determining the shareholders who are entitled to receive dividends.

Management Compensation

The board of directors usually determines the compensation of officers. In addition, a number of States allow the board to fix the compensation of board members.

Qualification, Election, and Tenure of Directors

Qualification of Directors

The governing incorporation statute, articles of incorporation, and the bylaws determine the qualifications that individuals must possess in order to be eligible as directors of the corporation. The statute may require that directors be shareholders or residents of the State of incorporation, although most States have eliminated such requirements.

Election, Number, and Tenure of Directors

The initial board of directors is generally named in the articles of incorporation and serves until the first meeting of the shareholders. Thereafter, directors are elected at annual meetings of the shareholders and hold office for one year or until their successors are duly elected and qualified. If the shares represented at a meeting in person or by proxy are not sufficient to constitute a quorum, the incumbent board continues in office as "holdover" directors until a valid election can be held. State statutes traditionally required that each corporation have three or more directors, although the modern trend is to permit the board to consist of one or more members. Moreover, the number of directors may be increased or decreased, within statutory limits, by amendment to the bylaws or charter.

Vacancies and Removal of Directors

The Model Act provides that a vacancy in the board may be filled by the affirmative vote of a majority of the remaining directors, even though they constitute less than a quorum of the board, and the director so elected shall hold office for the unexpired term of his predecessor. A directorship to be filled because of an increase in the number of directors may be filled by the board for a term continuing until the next election of directors by the shareholders.

Some States have no statutory provision for removal of directors, although a common law rule permits removal for cause by action of the shareholders. The Model Act and an increasing number of other statutes permit removal of one or more of the directors or of the entire board by the shareholders, with or without cause, at a special meeting called for that purpose, subject to cumulative voting rights. The Revised Act permits the articles of incorporation to provide that directors may be removed only for cause.

Compensation of Directors

Traditionally, directors did not receive salaries for their services as directors, although it was usual for them to be paid a fee or honorarium for attendance at meetings. The Model Act and other incorporation statutes now specifically authorize the board of directors to fix the compensation of directors unless there is a contrary provision in the articles of incorporation.

Exercise of Directors' Functions

Meetings

Directors do not have the power to bind the corporation when acting individually but only when acting as a board. When an individual acts as a director, it is either at a meeting with other directors or by written consent by all of the directors, if written consent is authorized by the incorporation statute and not contrary to the charter or bylaws.

The board presumably represents the shareholders. Its members usually are people of experience in various fields of business and professions, who may represent and speak for diverse interests among the shareholders.

Meetings are held either at a regular time and place fixed in the bylaws or at special times as they are called. Notice of meetings must be given as prescribed in the bylaws. A director's attendance at any meeting is a waiver of such notice, unless the director attends for the express purpose of objecting to the transaction of any business on the ground that the meeting is not lawfully called or convened. Most modern statutes provide that meetings of the board may be held either in or out of the State of incorporation.

Quorum

A majority of the members of the board of directors constitutes a quorum, the minimum number of members necessary to be present at a meeting in order to transact business. The articles of incorporation or bylaws may, however, require a number greater than a simple majority. If a quorum is present at any meeting, the act of a majority of the directors in attendance at such meeting is the act of the board, unless the act of a greater number is required by the articles of incorporation or bylaws.

The Revised Act requires a quorum to be present when "a vote is taken," making it clear that the board may act only when a quorum is present. This rule is in contrast to the rule governing shareholder meetings: once a quorum of shareholders is obtained it *cannot* be broken by the withdrawal of shareholders. In any event, directors may not vote by proxy, although a number of States permit directors to participate in meetings by means of conference telephones.

Action Taken without a Meeting

The Model Act provides that, unless otherwise provided by the articles of incorporation or bylaws, any action required by the statute to be taken at a meeting of the board may be taken without a meeting if a consent in writing is signed by all of the directors. Such consent has the same effect as a unanimous vote.

Delegation of Board Powers

If provided for by the articles of incorporation or bylaws, the board of directors may by majority vote of the full board appoint executive and other committees, all of whose members must be directors. Committees may exercise all of the authority of the board except for certain matters specified in the incorporation statute, such as the declaration of dividends and other distributions, amending the bylaws, recommending fundamental changes to the shareholders, approving a merger not requiring shareholder approval, and authorizing the sale of stock. Delegation of authority to a committee does not relieve any board member of his duties to the corporation. Commonly used committees include executive committees, audit committees (to recommend and oversee independent public accountants), compensation committees, finance committees, nominating committees, and investment committees.

Directors' Inspection Rights

Directors have the right to inspect corporate books and records so they can competently and fully perform their duties.

Officers

The officers of a corporation are appointed by the board of directors to hold the offices provided in the bylaws, which sets forth the respective duties of each officer. Statutes generally require as a minimum that they consist of a president, one or more vice-presidents as prescribed by the bylaws, a secretary, and a treasurer. A person may hold more than one office, except that the same person may not hold the office of president and secretary at the same time. The Revised Act permits the same individual to hold *all* of the offices of a corporation.

Selection and Removal of Officers

Most State statutes provide that the officers are appointed by the board of directors and serve at the pleasure of the board. Accordingly, officers may be removed by the board with or without cause. Of course, if the officer has a valid employment contract for a specified period of time, removal of the officer without cause before the contract expires would constitute a breach of the employment contract. The board also determines the compensation of officers.

Role of Officers

The officers are, like the directors, fiduciaries to the corporation. On the other hand, unlike the directors, they are agents of the corporation. The roles of officers are set forth in the corporate bylaws. The following is a typical description drawn from model bylaws:

President   The president is the principal executive officer of the corporation and, subject to the control of the board of directors, in general supervises and controls all of the business and affairs of the corporation. He presides at all meetings of the shareholders and of the board of directors. He may sign for the corporation any deeds, mortgages, bonds, contracts, or other instruments that the board of directors has authorized to be executed.

Vice-President   In the absence of the president or in the event of his death, inability, resignation, or refusal to act, the vice-president shall perform the duties of the president and, when so acting, shall have all the powers of and be subject to all the restrictions on the president.

Secretary   The secretary keeps the minutes of the proceedings of the shareholders and of the board of directors; sees that all notices are duly given; is custodian of the corporate records and of the seal of the corporation; signs with the president certificates for shares of the corporation, the issuance of which shall have been authorized by resolution of the board of directors; and has general charge of the stock transfer books of the corporation.

The treasurer has charge and custody of and is responsible for all funds and securities of the corporation; he receives and gives receipts for and deposits money due and payable to the corporation.

Authority of Officers

The Model Act provides that all officers of the corporation shall have such authority as may be provided in the bylaws or as may be determined by resolution of the board of directors not inconsistent with the bylaws. As with other agents, the authority of an officer to bind the corporation may be (1) actual express, (2) actual implied or (3) apparent.

Actual Express Authority   Actual express authority results from the manifestation of assent by the corporation to the officer that the officer should act on the behalf of the corporation. Actual express authority arises from the incorporation statute, the articles of incorporation, the bylaws, and resolutions of the board of directors. The principal source of actual express authority is the resolutions of the board of directors.

Actual Implied Authority   Officers, as agents of the corporation, have implied authority to do what is reasonably necessary to perform their actual, delegated authority. In addition, the question arises whether officers possess implied authority merely by virtue of their positions. The courts have been cautious in granting such implied or inherent authority. Traditionally, the courts tended to hold that the president had no implied authority by virtue of his office, although the more recent decisions tend to recognize his authority to bind the corporation in ordinary business transactions. However, any act requiring board approval, such as issuing stock, is clearly beyond the implied authority of the president or any other officer. In most jurisdictions, implied authority of position does not extend to any officer other than the president.

Apparent Authority   Apparent authority arises from acts of the principal that lead third parties to believe reasonably and in good faith that an officer has the required authority. Apparent authority might arise when a third party relies on the fact that an officer has exercised the same authority in the past with the consent of the board of directors.

Ratification   A corporation may ratify the unauthorized acts of its officers. Ratification is equivalent to having granted the officer prior authority. Ratification relates back to the original transaction and may be express or implied from the corporation's acceptance of the benefits of the contract with full knowledge of the facts.

Duties of Directors and Officers

A corporation may not recover damages from its directors and officers for losses resulting from their poor business judgment or honest mistake of judgment. The directors and officers are not insurers of business success. They are required only to be obedient, reasonably diligent, and completely loyal. These duties of obedience, diligence, and loyalty are for the most part judicially imposed. State statutes supplement the common law by imposing liability on directors and officers for specific acts, but the common law still remains the most significant source of duties.

Duty of Obedience

Directors and officers must act within their respective authority. For any loss resulting to the corporation from their unauthorized acts, they are held absolutely liable in some jurisdictions; in others they are held liable only if they intentionally or negligently exceeded their authority.

Duty of Diligence

In the discharge of their duties, directors and officers must exercise ordinary care and prudence. Some States interpret this standard to mean that directors and officers must exercise "the same degree of care and prudence that men promoted by self-interest generally exercise in their own affairs." However, most States, as well as the MBCA, hold that the test requires that "[a] director shall perform his duties as a director . . . with such care as an ordinarily prudent person in a like position would use under similar circumstances."

So long as the directors and officers act in good faith and with due care, the courts will not substitute their judgment for the board's or officer's judgment—the so-called **business judgment rule.** Directors and officers will nevertheless be held liable for bad faith or negligent conduct. Moreover, they may be liable for failing to act. In one instance, a director of a bank who in the five and a-half years that he had been on the board had never attended a board meeting or made any examination of the books and records was held liable for the losses resulting from the unsupervised acts of the president and cashier, who had made various improper loans and had permitted large over-drafts.

Reliance on Others   Directors and officers, however, are permitted to entrust important work to others, and if they have selected employees with care, they are not personally liable for the negligent acts or willful wrongs of the employees. A reasonable amount of supervision is required, and an officer or director will be held liable for the losses resulting from an employee's carelessness, theft, or embezzlement if he knew or ought to have known or suspected that such losses were being incurred.

Directors may also rely on information provided them by officers and employees of the corporation. The Model Act provides:

> In performing his duties, a director shall be entitled to rely on information, opinions, reports or statements, including financial statements and other financial data, in each case prepared or presented by:
>
> (a) one or more officers or employees of the corporation whom the director reasonably believes to be reliable and competent in the matters presented,
>
> (b) counsel, public accountants or other persons as to matters which the director reasonably believes to be within such person's professional or expert competence, or
>
> (c) a committee of the board upon which he does not serve, duly designated in accordance with a provision of the articles of incorporation or the bylaws, as to matters within its designated authority, which committee the director reasonably believes to merit confidence
>
> but he shall not be considered to be acting in good faith if he has knowledge concerning the matter in question that would cause such reliance to be unwarranted.

An officer is also entitled to rely upon this information but this right may, in many circumstances, be more limited than a director's because of the officer's greater familiarity with the affairs of the corporation.

Business Judgment Rule   Directors are continuously called on to make decisions that require balancing the benefits and risks for the corporation. Although hindsight may reveal that some of these decisions were not the best, the business judgment rule precludes imposing liability on the directors for honest mistakes of judgment. To benefit from the business judgment rule, a director must

1. exercise due care;
2. act in good faith; and
3. act in a manner he reasonably believed to be in the best interests of the corporation.

This requires that the director make an informed decision without any conflict of interests and have a rational basis for making it. Moreover, where there is a failure to satisfy this standard of conduct, it must be shown that the directors' action (or inaction) is the proximate cause of damage to the corporation. The business judgment rule also applies to officers.

FRANCIS v. UNITED JERSEY BANK

Superior Court of New Jersey, 1978.
162 N.J.Super. 355, 392 A.2d 1233.

FACTS: Pritchard & Baird was a reinsurance broker. A reinsurance broker arranges contracts between insurance companies so companies that have sold large policies may sell participations in these policies to other companies in order to share the risks. According to the custom in the industry, the selling company pays the premium to the broker who deducts his commission and forwards the balance to the reinsuring company. Thus, the broker handles large amounts of money as a fiduciary for its clients. Pritchard and Baird was controlled for many years by Charles Pritchard, who died in December, 1973. Prior to his death, he brought his two sons, Charles, Jr. and William, into the business. The pair assumed an increasingly dominant role in the affairs of the business during the elder Charles' later years. However, "Charles, Jr. and William were extremely incompetent businessmen, almost totally devoid of any sense of self-restraint or morality." By the end of 1975, they had plunged Pritchard and Baird into hopeless bankruptcy. From 1970 until 1975, $10,355,376.91 was unlawfully paid out by the corporation of Pritchard & Baird to members of the Pritchard family. Most of the money went directly to William and Charles, Jr. These payments were designated as "loans" on the corporate books. Mrs. Lillian Pritchard, the widow of the elder Charles, was a member of the corporation's board of directors from April, 1959 until her resignation on December 3, 1975, the day before the corporation filed for bankruptcy. Francis, as trustee in the bankruptcy proceeding, brought suit against United Jersey Bank, the administrator of the estate of Charles, Sr. He also charged that Lillian Pritchard, as a director of the corporation, was personally liable for the misappropriated $10 million on the basis of negligence in discharging her duties as director.

DECISION: Judgment for Francis. Directors are responsible for the general management of the corporation. They have particular responsibility with respect to distributions of assets to shareholders and to loans to officers and directors. Moreover, even if a director does not actively participate in a wrongful diversion, she may still be liable if she should have known of the wrongdoing and acted to stop it. The issue is one of negligence. The inherent nature of a corporate director's job necessarily implies that she must have a basic idea of the corporation's activities. She should know what business the corporation is in, and she should have some broad idea of the scope and range of the corporation's affairs.

Here, Mrs. Pritchard should have known that Pritchard & Baird was in the reinsurance business as a broker and that it annually handled millions of dollars belonging to, or owing to, ceding companies and reinsurers. Charged with that knowledge, a director in Mrs. Pritchard's position had, at the bare minimum, an obligation to ask for and read the annual financial statements of the corporation. She would then have the obligation to react appropriately to what a reading of the statements revealed. The fact is that Mrs. Pritchard never knew what they were doing because she never made the slightest effort to discharge any of her responsibilities as a director of Pritchard & Baird. Financial statements were prepared annually which clearly reflected that the corporation had virtually no assets, vast liabilities, and that money was simply being stolen. Thus, Mrs. Pritchard was negligent in performing her duties and her estate is liable for the $10,355,736.91.

Duty of Loyalty

The officers and directors of a corporation owe a duty of loyalty (**fiduciary duty**) to the corporation and to its shareholders. The essence of a fiduciary duty is the subordination of self-interest to the interest of the person or persons to whom the duty is owing. It requires undeviating loyalty on the part of officers and directors to the corporation, which they both serve and control.

An officer or director is required to make full disclosure to the corporation of any financial interest that he may have in any contract or transaction to which the corporation is a party. This is a corollary to the rule that forbids fiduciaries from making secret profits. His business conduct must be insulated from self-interest, and he may not advantage of opportunities to advance his personal interest at the expense of the corporation. He may not represent

Are Outside Directors Put on Boards Just for Show?

Last month's firing of 10 Continental Illinois directors is reminiscent of the attention directed to the Penn Square debacle. A congressional hearing concerning the collapse of the "shopping center" bank in Oklahoma noted that the directors for the bank had insufficient expertise to question its practices. One House Banking Committee member is reported to have said that the testimony represented "an indictment of the regulatory system that placed too much reliance on outside directors who are lay persons."

As numerous groups, particularly regulators, have promoted the advantages of outside, "independent" directors, they have failed to stress the importance of getting qualified individuals for the job. Yet, in contrast to Penn Square, the list of the fired directors at Continental Illinois includes an impressive number of corporate chief executive officers. Despite the presence of these corporate chieftains, the FDIC pointed out that the Continental directors who served before 1980 permitted the disastrous management policies that eventually dragged the business down.

The attention directed at boards warrants reexamination of their responsibilities and suggestions for changing the approach to selecting board members.

Taking Committee Responsibilities Seriously. In recent years, board members' legal responsibilities have been increased. In fact, the New York Stock Exchange and actions by the Financial Executives Institute now require boards to maintain active audit committees. Directors on these committees are supposed to actively oversee control practices of both internal and external auditors' examinations. However, regular monthly exchanges of information between audit committees and external auditors is unusual, and regular review of even executive summaries of internal audit reports by audit committee members is virtually nonexistent. Regulators have been known to challenge directors—at Penn Square, for example—as to why they were not aware of the extent of troubled loans and the poor documentation practices of management with respect to new loans. Indeed, few professionals working with board members would expect any understanding of such detail by directors.

Even more interesting than an investigation of the depth of directors' oversight activities would be the polling of external auditors as to whether they believe that audit committees have been beneficial with respect to improving corporate governance. An informal survey I conducted has uncovered a split vote. The overriding concern is with the expertise of directors and the time that they reasonably can be expected to devote to oversight activities.

Board Members Should Complement Management. Inside directors are likely to be top-level generalists with substantial company experience. It is therefore desirable that outside directors should complement the insiders' experience. If the CEO's background is production, the outside directors should add finance and accounting expertise. Similarly, if the CEO's background is marketing or finance, getting an outside director with an engineering background makes sense. (All businesses seek counsel with attorneys and creditors, and these individuals have incentives to monitor operations without formally serving as directors.) The board should enlarge the pool of resources available to top management rather than merely replicating it.

Resist Hiring Local Celebrities. A review of annual reports quickly discloses a tendency for companies to bring "celebrity types" onto the board. These individuals can be telltale signs of managers wanting a rubber stamp rather than the advice of professionals with technical expertise.

Instead of focusing on highly visible presidents or deans of universities, companies ought to explore the potential candidates who have particular expertise in areas where detailed counsel is needed. A chemist, engineer, accountant, computer scientist, or marketing analyst who is active in state-of-the-art lines of inquiry can provide the technical expertise that may prove crucial when the economy slumps, industry-growth slows or controls fail. Similarly, other companies' line managers and technically oriented project managers may serve as far better complements to a board than other companies' CEOs. CPAs and internal auditors could offer obvious advantages to audit committees, just as compensation consultants could prove invaluable to compensation committees.

The Incentive System. The incentive for younger board members to more actively participate in boards' oversight functions is tied to their interest in signaling the labor market as to their capabilities. At the age of 65, a director faces very limited risk; it's not as though future livelihood and long-term professional reputation de-

Outside Directors continued

pend on his performance as a director. In contrast, a 40-year-old who imperils his or her reputation by performing poorly on a board can imperil a substantial amount of potential future income.

Increased incentives in the form of compensation may be needed, given that audit-committee membership (as one example) typically results in only $5,000 to $10,000 of incremental fees. On the other hand, the relative attractiveness of such income to professionals below the CEO income may increase the incentive for active monitoring by non-CEO-level directors.

Directors Must Adapt to Informatics. As microcomputers proliferate, tremendous data bases are available within seconds, and analytical tools are at the fingertips of all who are literate in computers and statistical techniques. Innovation yields benefits to professionals who undergo continuing education and imposes penalties on those who do not adapt. How many directors are comfortable with micros, large data bases, descriptive data, probability theory, simulation, statistical tests and modeling? Yet, use of these resources can provide powerful oversight capabilities for directors.

Avoid Rigid Prerequisites. I would no more encourage the total replacement of experience with technical expertise than I would endorse the current imbalance that seems to stress experience over innovative technical knowledge. A blend is needed. Directors must receive monthly financial statements, operating statistics, press releases, capital-expenditure plans, product developments, technical-innovation reports, and auditors' reports and have access to data bases on the industry and economy. Each board member should be prepared to provide timely advice, particularly with regard to his or her respective areas of expertise, and this advice ought to be tapped by managers.

By Wanda A. Wallace.

conflicting interests, and his duty is one of strict allegiance to the corporation.

The remedy for breach of fiduciary duty is a suit in equity by the corporation, or more often a derivative suit instituted by a shareholder, to require the fiduciary to pay to the corporation the secret profits that he obtained through breach of his fiduciary duty. It need not be shown that the corporation could otherwise have made the profits that the fiduciary realized. The object of the rule is to discourage breaches of duty by a fiduciary, and this is achieved by taking from the fiduciary all of the profits he has made. The enforcement of the rule may result in a windfall to the corporation, but this is incidental to the deterrent effect of the rule.

Conflict of Interests A contract between an officer or a director and the corporation is not void, but voidable. A rule that would not allow such a contract would be unreasonable because it would prevent directors from entering into contracts that are beneficial to the corporation. Therefore, if such a contract is honest and fair, it will be upheld.

In the case of contracts between corporations having an interlocking directorate, or having one or more persons who are members of both boards of directors, the courts subject the contracts to the severest scrutiny and are quick to set them aside unless the transaction is shown to have been entirely fair and entered into in good faith.

The Model Act addresses both of these related problems by providing that such transactions are neither void nor voidable if they are approved after full disclosure by either the board of disinterested directors or the shareholders or if they are fair and reasonable to the corporation. The Revised Act also makes this rule applicable to officers.

Loans to Directors The Model Act does not permit a corporation to lend money to its directors without authorization in each instance by its shareholders. The Revised Act permits such loans if the particular loan is approved (1) by a majority of disinterested shareholders or (2) by the board of directors after determining that the loan benefits the corporation.

Corporate Opportunity Directors and officers may not usurp any corporate opportunity that in all fairness should belong to the corporation. A corporate opportunity is an opportunity in which the corporation has a right, property interest, or expectancy, and it depends on the facts and circumstances of each case. For instance, a party proposes a business arrangement to X Corporation through its vice-president, who personally accepts it without offering it to the corporation. The vice-president has usurped a corporate opportunity. On the other hand, it would not generally include an opportunity that the corporation was unable to accept or one that the corporation specifically rejected by a vote of disinterested directors after full disclosure. In both of these instances a director or officer can take personal advantage of the opportunity.

Transactions in Shares The issuance of shares at favorable prices to management by excluding other shareholders will normally constitute a violation of the fidiciary duty. So might the issuance of shares to a director at a fair price if the purpose of the issuance is to perpetuate corporate control rather than to raise capital or serve some other interest of the corporation. Officers and directors have access to inside advance information not available to the public that may affect the future market value of the shares of the corporation. Federal statutes have attempted to deal with this trading advantage by prohibiting officers and directors from purchasing or selling shares of stock of their corporation without adequate disclosure of all material facts in their possession that may affect the value or potential value of the stock. Under the Securities Exchange Act of 1934, the Securities and Exchange Commission adopted Rule 10b-5, which requires disclosure in such purchases or sales where use has been made of the mails or an instrumentality of interstate commerce, such as the telephone or telegraph. In addition, Section 16(b) of the same statute requires insiders to give to the corporation any profit realized by their short-swing speculation in its stock. We discuss these matters more fully in Chapter 40.

Although State law has not consistently imposed liability on officers and directors for secret, profitable use of inside information, the trend is toward holding them liable for breach of fiduciary duty to shareholders from whom they purchase stock without making disclosure to them of facts that give the stock added potential value. They are also held liable to the corporation for profits realized on a sale of the stock when undisclosed conditions of the corporation make a substantial decline in value practically inevitable.

Duty Not to Compete As fiduciaries, directors and officers owe to the corporation the duty of undivided loyalty, which means that they may not compete with the corporation. Although directors and officers may engage in their own business interests, courts will closely scrutinize any interest that competes with the business of the corporation. Moreover, an officer or director may not use corporate personnel, facilities, or funds for his own benefit or disclose trade secrets of the corporation to others.

Liabilities of Directors and Officers

Directors and officers incur personal liability for breaching any of the duties they owe to the corporation and shareholders. As discussed above, most of these duties arise from court-made rules, with some supplementation by State and Federal statutory laws. Most of the potential liability applies to both officers and directors.

Under many modern incorporation statutes a corporation may indemnify a director or officer for liability incurred if he acted in good faith and in a manner he reasonably believed to be in the best interests of the corporation, so long as he has not been judged negligent or liable for misconduct. A corporation may purchase insurance to indemnify officers and directors for liability arising out of their corporate activities, including liabilities against which the corporation is not empowered to indemnify directly.

Breach of Duties to Corporation

Directors and officers are liable to the corporation for breach of any duty they owe the corporation. Where the breach is of the duty of obedience or diligence, the liability is for the loss resulting to the corporation from the *ultra vires*, unauthorized or negligent act. Where the breach is the duty of loyalty, the corporation may use a number of equitable remedies depending on the particular circumstances of the case. For instance, where a corporate opportunity has been usurped, the director or officer will be required to return the profits he has realized on the transaction, and the corporation may avail itself of the usurped opportunity. Where a conflict of interest is involved, the corporation may rescind the contract. A director or officer who breaches his fiduciary duty by competing with the corporation is liable for damages caused to the corporation. Whenever a director or officer breaches his fiduciary duty, he forfeits his rights to compensation during the period he engaged in the breach, as the following case demonstrates.

WILSHIRE OIL CO. OF TEXAS v. RIFFE

United States Court of Appeals, Tenth Circuit, 1969. 406 F.2d 1061.

FACTS: Riffe, while serving as an officer of Wilshire Oil Company, received a secret commission for work done on behalf of a competing corporation. Wilshire Oil brings this action against Riffe to recover these secret profits and, in addition, to recover the compensation paid to Riffe by Wilshire Oil during the period that he acted on behalf of the competitor.

DECISION: Judgment for Wilshire Oil Company. Riffe's actions in accepting the secret commission from a competing corporation constitute both a willful breach of his employment contract and a breach of his fiduciary duty to the corporation stemming from his position as a corporate officer. Either action alone is sufficient to justify denying Riffe compensation for the period of his misdealing. Riffe, then, is not only liable to the corporation for the profits realized but also most refund all compensation paid to him by the corporation during the period in which the breaches were committed.

Defective Incorporation

The MBCA imposes joint and several liability on those who assume to act as a corporation without authority for all debts and liabilities incurred as a result.

Some States impose liability on directors and officers for transacting business before the statutory minimum paid-in capital has been received.

Contracts

An officer who binds the corporation to a contract within his apparent authority but beyond his actual authority is liable to the corporation for any resulting loss. An officer who purports to contract with a third party in excess of his actual and apparent authority is personally liable to the third party for breach of implied warranty of authority.

Torts

Although officers and directors are insulated from personal liability on contracts of the corporation, unless outside the scope of their actual authority or *ultra vires,* they are subject to personal liability in tort for their intentional wrongdoing or negligent conduct even while engaged in corporate business activities.

Violation of State and Federal Statutes

Directors and officers may incur civil or criminal liability for violating State and Federal statutes. For example, failure to file required reports, denial of shareholders' inspection rights, violation of antitrust law (Chapter 39), and violation of securities laws (Chapter 40) may result in civil or criminal penalties or both.

Illegal Distributions

Directors are jointly and severally liable for issuing shares of the corporation at a discount and for declaring a dividend that is paid when the corporation is insolvent or in violation of the State incorporation statute. They are also liable for voting or assenting to a purchase by the corporation of its own shares in violation of the incorporation statute.

A director is not liable for any of the acts mentioned in the preceding paragraph if in assenting to them he acted in good faith and in reliance on information, reports, or financial statements of the corporation represented to him to be correct by an officer or employee of the corporation having charge of its books of account, or public accountant, or by a board committee. Nor is he liable if in good faith he considered the assets of the corporation to be of their book value in determining the amount available for a dividend or other distribution to shareholders.

CHAPTER SUMMARY

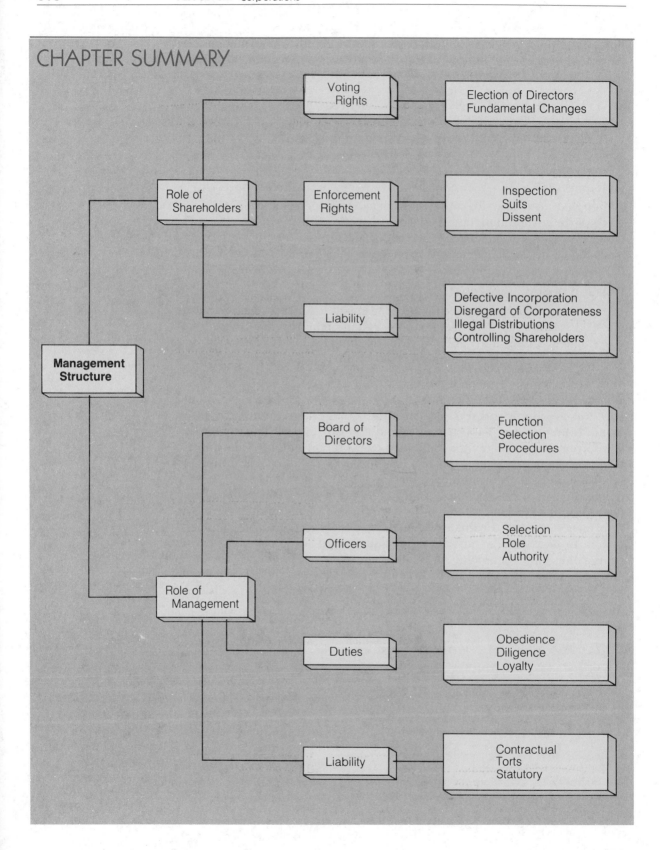

KEY TERMS

Quorum
Classification of directors
Cumulative voting
Proxy
Voting trusts

Shareholder agreements
Direct shareholder suit
Derivative shareholder suit
Right to dissent

Controlling shareholder
Board of directors
Business judgment rule
Corporate opportunity

PROBLEMS

1. Brown was the president and director of a corporation engaged in owning and operating a chain of motels. Brown was advised, on what seemed to be good authority, that a superhighway was to be constructed through the town of X, which would be a most desirable location for a motel. Brown presented these facts to the board of directors of the motel corporation and recommended that the corporation build a motel in the town of X at the location described. The board of directors agreed, and the new motel was constructed. It developed that the superhighway plans were changed after the motel was constructed. The highway was never built. Later, a packing house was built on property adjoining the motel, and as a result the corporation sustained a considerable loss.

The shareholders brought an appropriate action against Brown, charging that his proposal had caused a substantial loss to the corporation. Decision?

2. A, B, C, D, and E constituted the board of directors of the X Corporation. While D and E were out of town, A, B, and C held a special meeting of the board. Just as the meeting began, C became ill. He then gave a proxy to A and went home. A resolution was then adopted directing and authorizing the purchase by the X Corporation of an adjoining piece of land owned by S as a site for an additional factory building. A and B voted for the resolution, and A, as C's proxy, cast C's vote in favor of the resolution. A contract was then made by the X Corporation with S for the purchase of the land. After the return of D and E, another special meeting of the board was held with all five directors present. A resolution was then unanimously adopted to cancel the contract with S. S was so notified and now sues X Corporation for damages for breach of contract. Decision?

3. Bernard Koch was president of United Corporation, a closely held corporation. Koch, James Trent, and Henry Phillips made up the three-person board of directors. At a meeting of the board of directors, Trent was elected president, replacing Koch. At the same meeting, Trent attempted to have the salary of the president increased. He was unable to obtain board

approval of the increase because, although Phillips voted for the increase, Koch voted against it. Trent was disqualified from voting.

As a result, the directors, by a two-to-one vote, amended the bylaws to provide for the appointment of an executive committee composed of three reputable business persons to pass upon and fix all matters of salary for employees of the corporation. Subsequently, the executive committee, consisting of Jane Jones, James Black, and William Johnson, increased the salary of the president.

Koch brought an appropriate action against the corporation, Trent, and Phillips to enjoin them from paying the increased compensation to the president above that fixed by the board of directors. What decision?

4. Zenith Steel Company operated a prosperous business. In January 1986 its president, Roe, who is also a director, was voted a $100,000 bonus by the board of directors for his valuable services he provided to the company in 1985. Roe receives an annual salary of $85,000 from the company. Black, a minority shareholder in Zenith Steel Company, brings an appropriate action to enjoin the payment by the company of the $100,000 bonus. Decision?

5. (a) Smith, a director of the Sample Corporation, sells a piece of vacant land to the Sample Corporation for $25,000. The land cost him $10,000.

(b) Jones, a shareholder of the Sample Corporation, sells a used truck to the Sample Corporation for $2,800, although the truck was worth $2,400.

Raphael, a minority shareholder of the Sample Corporation, claims that these sales are void and should be annulled. Is he correct? Why?

6. The X Corporation manufactures machine tools. Its two principal competitors are Y Corporation and Z Corporation. The five directors of X Corporation are Black, White, Brown, Green, and Crimson. At a duly called meeting of the board of directors of X Corporation in January, all five directors were present. They transacted the following business and voted as indicated.

A contract for the purchase of $1 million worth of steel from the D Company, of which Black, White, and Brown are directors, was discussed and approved by a unanimous vote. There was a lengthy discussion about entering into negotiations for the purchase of Q Corporation, which allegedly was about to be sold for around $15 million. By a three-to-two vote it was decided not to open such negotiations.

Three months later Green purchased Q Corporation for $15 million. Shortly thereafter, a new board of directors for X Corporation took office.

X Corporation now brings actions to rescind its contract with D Company and to compel Green to assign to X Corporation his contract for the purchase of Q Corporation. Decisions as to each action?

7. Gore had been the owner of 1 percent of the outstanding shares of the Webster Company, a corporation, since its organization in 1963. Ratliff, the president of the company, was the owner of 70 percent of the outstanding shares. In April 1986, Ratliff used the shareholders' list to submit to the shareholders an offer of fifty dollars per share for their stock. Gore, on receiving the offer, called Ratliff and told him that the offer was inadequate and advised that she was willing to offer sixty dollars per share and for that purpose demanded a shareholders' list. Ratliff knew that Gore was willing and able to supply the funds necessary to purchase the stock, but he nevertheless refused to supply the list to Gore. Further, he did not offer to transmit Gore's offer to the shareholders of record. Gore then brought an action to compel the corporation to make the shareholders' list available to her. Decision?

8. M, N, O, and P, experts in manufacturing baubles, each owned fifteen out of one hundred authorized shares of Baubles, Inc., a corporation of State X that does not permit cumulative voting. On July 7, 1981, the corporation sold forty shares to Q, an investor, for $1,500,000, which it used to purchase a factory building. On July 8, 1981, M, N, O, and P contracted as follows:

> All parties will act jointly in exercising voting rights as shareholders. In the event of a failure to agree, the question shall be submitted to George Yost, whose decision shall be binding upon all parties.

Until a meeting of shareholders on April 17, 1986, when a dispute arose, all parties to the contract had consistently and regularly voted for N, O, and P as directors.

At that meeting Yost considered the dispute and decided and directed that M, N, O, and P vote their shares for the latter three as directors. N, O, and P so voted. M and Q voted for themselves and Q as directors.

(a) Is the contract of July 8, 1981, valid, and, if so, what is its effect?

(b) Who were elected directors of Baubles, Inc., at the meeting of its shareholders on April 17, 1986?

9. X Corporation's articles of incorporation require cumulative voting for the election of its directors. The board of directors of X Corporation consists of nine directors, each elected annually.

(a) A owns 25 percent of the outstanding shares of X Corporation. How many directors can he elect with his votes?

(b) If X Corporation were to classify its board into three classes, each consisting of three directors elected every three years, how many directors would A be able to elect?

36

FUNDAMENTAL CHANGES

Certain extraordinary changes affect a corporation in such a fundamental manner that they are outside the authority of the board of directors and require shareholder approval. Charter amendments, a sale or lease of all or substantially all the corporation's assets, mergers, consolidations, compulsory share exchanges, and dissolution are fundamental changes because they alter the basic structure of the corporation. Although each of these actions is authorized by State incorporation statutes that impose specific procedural requirements, they are also subject to equitable limitations imposed by the courts.

Since shareholder approval for fundamental changes does not usually need to be unanimous, such changes will frequently be approved despite opposition by minority shareholders. Shareholder approval means a majority (or some other specified fraction) of *all* votes entitled to be cast rather than a majority (or other fraction) of votes represented at a shareholders' meeting at which a quorum is present. In some instances minority shareholders have the right to dissent and recover the fair value of their shares if they follow the prescribed procedure. This right is called the **appraisal remedy.** We discuss the legal aspects of fundamental changes in this chapter.

Charter Amendments

Modern statutes permit the articles of incorporation to be amended freely. The amended articles of incorporation, however, may contain only those provisions that might be lawfully contained in the original articles of incorporation. The Model Act is comprehensive in its authorization for amendments and includes very broad powers. Several of the powers that the Model Act grants to corporations are as follows:

1. to change its corporate name;
2. to change its period of duration;
3. to change, enlarge, or diminish its corporate purposes;
4. to increase or decrease the number or par value of shares;
5. to reclassify shares and change the preferential rights of shares;
6. to create new classes of shares; and
7. to limit, deny, or grant pre-emptive rights.

621

Today, articles of incorporation rarely limit the duration or powers of the corporation, so the most common amendments relate to changes in the capital structure of the corporation.

Under modern statutes, the typical procedure for amending the articles of incorporation requires the board of directors to adopt a resolution setting forth the proposed amendment, which must then be approved by a majority vote of the shareholders entitled to vote, although some older statutes require a two-thirds shareholder vote. After the amendment is approved by the shareholders, articles of amendment are executed and filed with the Secretary of State. The amendment becomes effective on the issuance of the certificate of amendment by the Secretary of State but does not affect the existing rights of nonshareholders.

The Revised Act permits the board of directors to adopt certain amendments without shareholder action unless the articles of incorporation provide otherwise. These amendments include: (1) extension of the duration of the corporation, (2) splitting authorized shares if the corporation has only one class of shares, and (3) making minor name changes.

Under the Model Act *dissenting shareholders* are given an appraisal remedy *only* if an amendment materially and adversely affects the rights attached to the shares owned by the dissenting shareholders in one of the following ways:

1. the amendment alters or abolishes a preferential right of such shares;

2. the amendment creates, alters, or abolishes a right involving the redemption of such shares;

3. the amendment alters or abolishes a pre-emptive right of the holder of such shares; or

4. the amendment excludes or limits the right of the holder of such shares to vote on any matter or to cumulate his votes.

Under the Revised Act the required shareholder approval for an amendment depends upon the nature of the amendment. If the amendment would give rise to dissenters' rights, the amendment must be approved by a majority of all votes *entitled* to be cast on the amendment unless the Act or the charter require a greater vote. All other amendments must be approved by a majority of all votes *cast* on the amendment unless the Act or the charter require a greater vote.

Combinations

It may be desirable and profitable for a corporation to acquire all or substantially all of the assets of another corporation or corporations. This may be accomplished by (1) purchase or lease of the assets, (2) purchase of a controlling stock interest in other corporations, (3) merger with other corporations, or (4) consolidation with other corporations.

When any of these methods of combination involves the issuance of shares, proxy solicitations, or tender offers, it may be subject to Federal securities regulation, as discussed in Chapter 40. Moreover, when a combination may have a detrimental effect on competition, Federal antitrust laws, as discussed in Chapter 39, may apply.

Purchase or Lease of All or Substantially All of the Assets

When one corporation purchases or leases all or substantially all of the assets of another corporation, there is no change in the legal personality of either corporation. The purchaser or lessee corporation has simply acquired ownership or control of additional physical assets. The selling or lessor corporation, in exchange for its physical properties, receives cash, other property, or a stipulated rental. Each corporation continues its separate existence with only the form or extent of its assets altered (see Figure 36-1).

Generally, a corporation which purchase the assets of another corporation does not assume the other's liabilities unless: (1) the purchaser expressly or impliedly agrees to assume the liabilities of the seller; (2) the transaction amounts to a consolidation or merger of the two corporations; (3) the purchaser is a mere continuation of the seller; or (4) the sale is for the fraudulent purpose of avoiding the liabilities of the seller. Some courts, as in the next case, recognize a fifth exception (called the "product line" exception) which imposes strict tort liability upon the purchaser for defects in products manufactured and distributed by the seller corporation when the purchaser corporation continues the product line.

RAY v. ALAD CORP.

Supreme Court of California, 1977.
19 Cal.3d 22, 136 Cal.Rptr. 574, 560 P.2d 3.

FACTS: On March 24, 1969, Ray fell from a defective ladder while working for his employer. Ray brought suit in strict tort liability against the Alad Corporation (Alad II) which neither manufactured nor sold the ladder to Ray's employer. Prior to the accident, Alad II succeeded to the business of the ladder's manufacturer, the now dissolved "Alad Corporation" (Alad I), through a purchase of Alad I's assets for an adequate cash consideration. Alad II acquired Alad I's plant, equipment, inventory, trade name and good will and continued to manufacture the same line of ladders under the "Alad" name, using the same equipment, designs, and personnel. In addition, Alad II solicited through the same sales representatives with no outward indication of any change in the ownership of the business. The parties had no agreement, however, concerning Alad II's assumption of Alad I's tort liabilities.

DECISION: Judgment for Ray. Generally, a purchaser does not assume a seller's liabilities unless: (1) there is an express or implied agreement of such assumption; (2) the transaction is a consolidation or merger; (3) the purchasing corporation is a mere continuation of the seller; or (4) the transfer of assets to the purchaser is for the fraudulent purpose of escaping liability for the seller's debts. Here, there was no express or implied agreement of an assumption of tort liability nor were the assets transferred for a fraudulent purpose. Also, the second and third exceptions were not met, because the purchase of Alad I's assets did not amount to a consolidation or merger.

Since the general rule did not render Alad II liable, the court looked to the policy considerations underlying strict tort liability—the protection of otherwise defenseless victims of manufacturing defects and the spreading throughout society of the costs of compensating them. Justification for imposing strict liability upon Alad II rests upon (1) the virtual destruction of Ray's remedies against Alad I due to the purchase; (2) Alad II's ability to assume Alad I's risk-spreading role; and (3) the fairness of requiring Alad II to assume the responsibility for the defective product since it continued to enjoy Alad I's good will. The presence of these three factors renders Alad II strictly liable.

Regular Course of Business   If the sale or lease of all or substantially all of its assets is in the **usual and regular** course of business of the selling or lessor corporation, approval by its board of directors is required but shareholder

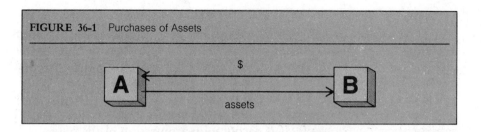

FIGURE 36-1   Purchases of Assets

authorization is not. In addition, a mortgage or pledge of any or all property and assets of a corporation—whether or *not* in the usual or regular course of business—also requires approval by just the board of directors.

Other Than in Regular Course of Business   Shareholder approval is necessary only if such a sale or lease is *not* in the usual and regular course of business. The selling corporation by liquidation of its assets or the lessor corporation by placing its physical assets beyond its control has significantly changed its position and perhaps its ability to carry on the type of business contemplated by its charter. For this reason, such sale or lease must be approved not only by action of the directors but also by the affirmative vote of the holders of a majority of its shares entitled to vote at a meeting of shareholders called for this purpose. In most States, *dissenting shareholders* of the selling corporation are given an appraisal remedy.

Purchase of Shares

An alternative to the purchase of the assets of another corporation is the purchase of its stock. When one corporation acquires all or a controlling interest of the stock of another corporation, there is no change in the legal existence of either corporation. The acquiring corporation acts through its board of directors, while the corporation that becomes a subsidiary does not act at all, because the sale of stock is a decision made by the individual shareholders. The capital structure of the subsidiary remains unchanged, and that of the parent is usually not altered unless required in connection with financing the acquisition of the stock. Because no formal shareholder approval of either corporation is required, there is *no* appraisal remedy (see Figure 36-2).

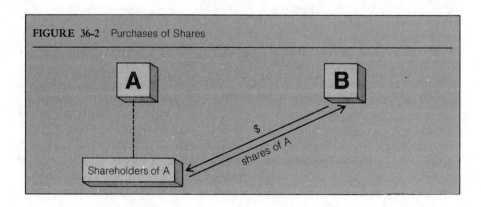

FIGURE 36-2   Purchases of Shares

Compulsory Share Exchange

The Model Act provides different procedures, however, where the share acquisition is through a compulsory share exchange, which is a transaction by which a corporation becomes the owner of *all* the outstanding shares of one or more classes of another corporation by an exchange that is *compulsory* on *all* owners of the acquired shares. The shares may be acquired with shares, obligations, or other securities of the acquiring corporation, or with other consideration. For example, if B corporation acquires all of the outstanding shares of A corporation through a compulsory exchange, then A becomes a wholly owned subsidiary of B. In all compulsory share exchanges, the separate existence of both corporate parties to the transaction is not affected by the exchange. Although producing results similar to a merger, as discussed below, compulsory share exchanges are used instead of mergers where it is desirable that the acquired corporation does not go out of existence as, for example, in the formation of holding company systems for insurance companies and banks.

A compulsory share exchange requires approval of the board of directors of each corporation and approval by the shareholders of the corporation whose shares are being acquired. The transaction need *not* be approved by the shareholders of the corporation acquiring the shares. After the compulsory share exchange plan is adopted and approved by the shareholders, it is binding on all holders of shares of the class to be acquired. Dissenting shareholders of the corporation whose shares are acquired are given an appraisal remedy.

Merger

A merger of two or more corporations is the combination of all of their assets. One of the corporations, known as the **surviving corporation,** receives title to all the assets. The other party or parties to the merger, known as the **merged corporation** or corporations, are merged into the surviving corporation and cease to exist as a separate entity. Thus, if A Corporation and B Corporation combine into the A Corporation, A is the surviving corporation and B the merged corporation. All debts and other liabilities of the merged corporation are assumed by the surviving corporation by operation of law, as in the next case. The shareholders of the merged corporation may receive stock or other securities issued by the surviving corporation or other consideration, as provided in the plan of merger (see Figure 36-3).

A merger requires the approval of the board of directors of each corporation, as well as the affirmative vote of the holders of a majority of the shares entitled to vote of each corporation that is involved in the merger. However, in a **short-form merger,** a corporation that owns at least *90 percent* of the outstanding shares of a subsidiary may merge the subsidiary into itself without approval by the shareholders of either corporation. Requiring the approval of the shareholders or board of directors of the subsidiary is unnecessary because the parent's 90 percent ownership assures that the plan of merger would be approved. All that is required is a resolution by the board of directors of the parent corporation.

The dissenting shareholders of the subsidiary have the right to obtain payment from the parent for their shares. The shareholders of the parent

Merger–combination of the assets of two or more corporations into one of the constituent corporations

Short-form merger–merger of a 90 percent subsidiary into its parent

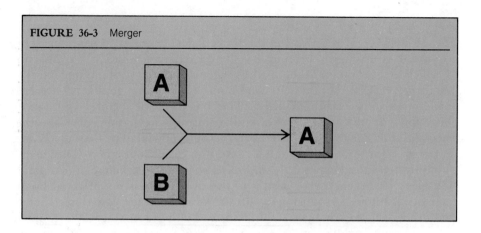

FIGURE 36-3   Merger

do not have this appraisal remedy because the transaction has not materially changed their rights. Instead of indirectly owning 90 percent of the subsidiary's assets the parent now directly owns 100 percent of the same assets.

TRETTER v. RAPID AMERICAN CORP.

United States District Court, Eastern District of Missouri, 1981.
514 F.Supp. 1344.

FACTS: Tretter alleged that his exposure over the years to asbestos products manufactured by Philip Carey Manufacturing Corporation caused him to contract asbestosis. Tretter brought an action against Rapid American Corporation which was the surviving corporation of a merger between Philip Carey and Rapid American. Rapid American denied liability claiming that immediately after the merger it had transferred its asbestos operations to a newly formed subsidiary corporation.

DECISION: Judgment for Tretter. "If the parties effect the transfer of a corporate enterprise through a merger, consolidation, or sale of stock, the transferee assumes its predecessor's liabilities, including product liability claims." Therefore, when Rapid American merged with Philip Carey, Rapid American assumed the liability for Tretter's claim. This fact was recognized in the "General Assignment & Assumption of Liabilities" agreement between Rapid American and its subsidiary. That document specifically referred to liabilities "to which Rapid American became subject as a result of the [merger between Rapid American and Philip Carey]." That Rapid American subsequently transferred this liability to its subsidiary does not defeat Tretter's cause of action; it merely gives Rapid American a claim for indemnity. Therefore, Rapid American, as the successor corporation, may be held for the liabilities of Philip Carey, its predecessor.

Consolidation

Consolidation–combination of two or more corporations into a new corporation

A consolidation of two or more corporations is the combination of all of their assets, title to which is taken by a newly created corporation known as the **consolidated corporation** (see Figure 36-4). Each of the constituent corporations ceases to exist, and all of their debts and liabilities are assumed by the new corporation. The shareholders of each of the constituent corporations receive stock or other securities, not necessarily of the same class, issued to them by the new corporation or other consideration provided in the plan of consolidation. A consolidation requires the approval of the boards of directors of each constituent corporation as well as the affirmative vote of the holders of a majority of the shares entitled to vote of each constituent corporation. Dissenting shareholders have an appraisal remedy. The Revised Act, however, has deleted all references to consolidations.

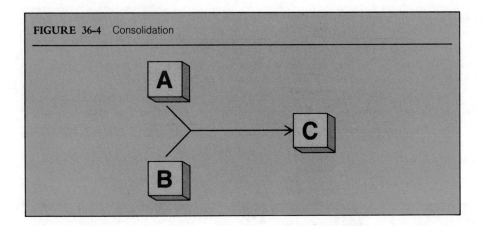

FIGURE 36-4   Consolidation

Dissenting Shareholders

The shareholder's right to dissent is a statutory right to obtain payment for his shares and is accorded to shareholders who object to certain fundamental changes in the corporation. Most States grant a right to dissent to any plan of *merger* or *consolidation* to which the corporation is a party as well as to a *sale or lease* of all or substantially all of the property or assets of the corporation not made in the usual or regular course of business. In addition to these three fundamental changes, the Model Act also provides a right to dissent to (1) any plan of compulsory share exchange to which the corporation is a party as the corporation the shares of which are to be acquired, (2) any amendment of the articles of incorporation that materially and adversely affects the rights appurtenant to the shares of the dissenting shareholder, and (3) any other corporate action taken pursuant to a shareholder vote with respect to which the articles of incorporation, the bylaws, or a resolution of the board of directors directs that dissenting shareholders shall have a right to obtain payment for their shares.

> **Dissenting share-holder**—one who opposes a fundamental change and has the right to receive the fair value of her shares

If a shareholder dissents and strictly complies with the provisions of the statute he is entitled to receive the fair value of his shares. In order to perfect his right to payment for his shares, a dissenting shareholder must:

1. file with the corporation a written objection to the proposed corporate action before the vote of the shareholders;

2. refrain from voting in favor of the proposed corporate action either in person or by proxy; and

3. make a written demand on the corporation on a form provided by that corporation within the time period set by the corporation, which may not be less than thirty days after the corporation mails the form.

Unless written demand is made within the prescribed time period, the dissenting shareholder is bound by the terms of the proposed corporate action.

A dissenting shareholder who complies with all of these requirements is entitled to an appraisal remedy, which is payment by the corporation of the fair value of his shares. The Model Act defines **fair value** to mean their value immediately before the corporate action to which the dissenter objects takes place, excluding any appreciation or depreciation in anticipation of such corporate action unless such exclusion would be inequitable. The next case explains how fair value is determined.

The purpose of the statutory procedure is to fix a reasonable time in which the corporation may know the number of shares for which it is required to pay cash in order to carry through the proposed corporate action. If enough dissenting shareholders demand to be paid, the lack of sufficient cash or the inability of the surviving or new corporation to raise funds for this purpose may mean that the proposed corporate action cannot be carried out at this time.

ENDICOTT JOHNSON CORP. v. BADE

Court of Appeals of New York, 1975.
37 N.Y.2d 585, 376 N.Y.S.2d 103, 338 N.E.2d 614.

FACTS: The shareholders of Endicott Johnson who had dissented from a proposed merger of Endicott with McDonough Corporation brought this proceeding to fix the fair value of their stock. At issue is the proper weight required to be given to the market price of the stock in fixing its fair value. The shareholders argue that the market value should not be considered because of McDonough's control of Endicott's stock and the stock's subsequent delisting from the New York Stock Exchange.

DECISION: Judgment for the shareholders. Shareholders who dissent from an impending merger are entitled to be paid the "fair value" of their stock. The elements to be considered in appraising the stock's value are its net asset value, investment value, and market value. However, all three elements should not be taken into account in every case. Here, it would be inappropriate to look at net asset value since the corporation was not being liquidated. Furthermore, the stock has no meaningful market value because McDonough controlled 70 percent of the outstanding shares and because the stock was delisted. The stock's investment value then is the only remaining determinant of its fair value in this case.

Dissolution

Although a corporation may have perpetual existence, its life may be terminated in a number of ways. Incorporation statutes usually provide both for dissolution without judicial proceedings and for dissolution with judicial proceedings. Dissolution does not terminate the corporation's existence but does require that the corporation **wind up** its affairs and **liquidate** its assets.

Nonjudicial Dissolution

Nonjudicial dissolution may be brought about by

1. an act of the legislature of the State of incorporation;

2. expiration of the period of time provided for in the articles of incorporation;

3. voluntary action on the part of all of the holders of all of the outstanding shares of stock; or

4. voluntary action by the corporation, pursuant to a resolution of the board of directors approved by the affirmative vote of the holders of a majority of the shares of the corporation entitled to vote at a meeting of the shareholders duly called for this purpose. No right to dissent and recover the fair value of shares is usually provided to shareholders objecting to dissolution. However, the Model Act grants dissenters' rights in connection with a sale or exchange of all or substantially all the assets not made in the usual or regular course

of business, *including* a sale in dissolution, but *excludes* such rights in sales by court order and sales for cash on terms requiring that all or substantially all of the net proceeds be distributed to the shareholders within one year.

Judicial Dissolution

Involuntary dissolution by judicial proceeding may be instituted by the State, the shareholders, or the creditors and may occur by:

1. court action taken at the instance of the attorney general of the State of incorporation when it is established that the corporation has failed to file its annual report with the Secretary of State, failed to pay its annual franchise tax, procured its articles of incorporation through fraud, continued to exceed or abuse the authority conferred upon it by law, failed for thirty days to appoint and maintain a registered agent in the State, or failed for thirty days after a change of its registered office or registered agent to file a statement of such change;

2. court action brought by shareholders when it is established that the directors are deadlocked in the management of the corporate affairs and the shareholders are unable to break the deadlock and that irreparable injury to the corporation is being suffered or is threatened; that the acts of the directors or those in control of the corporation are illegal, oppresive, or fraudulent; that the corporate assets are being misapplied or wasted; or that the shareholders are deadlocked and cannot elect directors; or

3. court action instituted by a creditor on showing that the corporation has become unable to pay its debts and obligations as they mature in the regular course of its business and either (a) the creditor has reduced his claim to a judgment and an execution issued on it has been returned unsatisfied or (b) that the corporation has admitted in writing that the claim of the creditor is due and owing.

CALLIER v. CALLIER

Appellate Court of Illinois,
Fifth District, 1978.
61 Ill.App.3d 1011, 18 Ill.
Dec. 941, 378 N.E.2d 405.

FACTS: All Steel Pipe and Tube is a closely held corporation engaged in the business of selling steel pipes and tubes. Leo and Scott Callier are its two equal shareholders. Leo, Scott's uncle, is one of the company's two directors and is president of the corporation. Scott is the general manager. Scott's father and Leo's grandfather, Felix, is the other director. Over the years, Scott and Leo have had differences of opinion about various aspects of the operation of the business. Despite the deterioration of their relationship, the company nonetheless flourished. Negotiations aimed at the redemption of Scott's shares by Leo began, but the parties could not reach an agreement. The discussion then turned to voluntary dissolution and liquidation of the corporation, but still no agreement could be reached. Finally, Leo fired Scott and began to wind down All Steel's business and formed a new corporation, Callier Steel Pipe and Tube. Leo then brought this action seeking a dissolution and liquidation of All Steel.

DECISION: Judgment for Scott. Corporations are creatures of statute and, therefore, can be dissolved only according to the applicable statute. Corporate dissolution is a drastic remedy, and it must not be lightly invoked. Its grant requires proof of an inalterable deadlock in the management and of irreparable injury to the corporation. The record here does not show such proof. Although Leo and Scott were not able to get along, this is not equivalent to an inability of the corporation to operate. In fact, All Steel continued to operate profitably during the disputes and the redemption negotiations, as both Scott and Felix refrained from interfering in the management of All Steel and allowed Leo to operate the company on his own. Accordingly, the requested order to dissolve All Steel must be denied.

Liquidation

Dissolution does not terminate the corporation's existence but does require that the corporation devote itself to winding up its affairs and liquidating its assets. After dissolution the corporation must cease carrying on its business except as is necessary to wind up. When a corporation is dissolved its assets are liquidated and used first to pay the expenses of liquidation and its creditors according to their respective contract or lien rights. Any remainder is distributed to shareholders proportionately according to their respective contract rights, and stock with a liquidation preference has priority over common stock. When liquidation is voluntary, it is carried out by the board of directors, who serve as trustees; when liquidation is involuntary, it is conducted by a receiver appointed by the court.

Protection of Creditors

The statutory provisions governing dissolution and liquidation usually prescribe procedures to safeguard the interests of creditors of the corporation.

FIGURE 36-5   Fundamental Changes

Change	Board of Director Resolution Required	Shareholder Approval Required	Shareholders' Appraisal Remedy Available
A amends its articles of incorporation	A: Yes	A: Yes	A: No, unless amendment materially and adversely affects rights of shares
A sells its assets in usual and regular course of business to B	A: Yes B: No	A: No B: No	A: No B: No
A sells its assets not in usual and regular course of business to B	A: Yes B: No	A: Yes B: No	A: Yes B: No
A voluntarily purchases shares of B	A: Yes B: No	A: No B: No, individual shareholders decide	A: No B: No
A acquires shares of B through a compulsory exchange	A: Yes B: Yes	A: No B: Yes	A: No B: Yes
A and B merge	A: Yes B: Yes	A: Yes B: Yes	A: Yes B: Yes
A merges its 90% subsidiary B into A	A: Yes B: No	A: No B: No	A: No B: Yes
A and B consolidate	A: Yes B: Yes	A: Yes B: Yes	A: Yes B: Yes
A voluntarily dissolves	A: Yes, unless unanimous shareholder consent	A: Yes	A: No usually

Such procedures typically include required mailing of notice to known creditors, general publication of notice, and preservation of claims against the corporation. For example, the Model Act provides that the dissolution of a corporation shall not impair any remedy available to or against the corporation, its directors, officers, or shareholders for any right or claim existing or any liability incurred before dissolution if suit is brought within two years after the date of dissolution. The Revised Act provides a five-year period for (1) a claimant who did not receive notice, (2) a claimant whose timely claim was not acted on, or (3) a claimant whose claim is contingent on an event occurring after dissolution.

CHAPTER SUMMARY

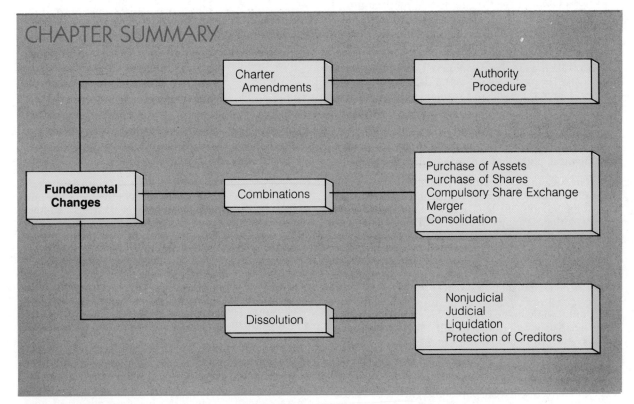

KEY TERMS

Charter amendments
Purchase of assets
Purchase of shares
Compulsory share exchange
Merger
Surviving corporation

Merged corporation
Short-form merger
Consolidation
Consolidated corporation
Dissenting shareholders
Appraisal remedy

Fair value
Dissolution
Nonjudicial dissolution
Judicial dissolution
Liquidation

PROBLEMS

1. The stock in Hotel Management, Inc., a hotel management corporation, was divided equally between two families. For several years the two families had been unable to agree or cooperate in the management of the corporation. As a result, no meeting of shareholders or directors had been held for five years. There had been no withdrawal of profits for five years, and last year the hotel operated at a loss. Although the corporation was not insolvent, such a state was imminent because the business was poorly managed and its properties were in need of repair. As a result the owners of half the stock brought an action in equity for dissolution of the corporation. What decision?

2. (a) When may a corporation sell, lease, exchange, mortgage, or pledge all or substantially all of its assets in the usual and regular course of its business?

(b) When may a corporation sell, lease, exchange, mortgage, or pledge all or substantially all of its assets other than in the usual and regular course of its business?

(c) What are the rights of a shareholder who dissents from a proposed sale or exchange of all or substantially all of the assets of a corporation other than in the usual and regular course of its business?

3. The X Company was duly merged into the Y Company. S, a shareholder of the former X Company, having paid only one-half of her subscription, is now sued by the Y Company for the balance of the subscription. S, who took no part in the merger proceedings, denied liability on the ground that, inasmuch as the X Company no longer exists, all her rights and obligations in connection with the X Company have been terminated. Decision?

4. Smith, while in the course of his employment with the Bee Corporation, negligently ran the company's truck into X, injuring him very severely. Subsequently, the Bee Corporation and the Sea Corporation consolidated, forming the SeaBee Corporation. X filed suit against the SeaBee Corporation for damages, and the SeaBee Corporation argued the defense that the injuries sustained by X were not caused by any of SeaBee's employees, that SeaBee was not even in existence at the time of the injury, and that the SeaBee Corporation was therefore not liable. What decision?

5. The Business Corporation Act of State X, after prescribing the procedure for the consolidation of two or more corporations, provides that "such surviving or new corporation shall thenceforth be responsible and liable for all the liabilities and obligations of each of the corporations so merged or consolidated."

The A Company, a corporation organized under the laws of State X, after proper authorization by the shareholders sold its entire assets to the B Company, also a State X corporation. T, an unpaid creditor of the A Company, sues the B Company on her claim. Decision?

6. Zenith Steel Company operates a prosperous business. In January 1986, the board of directors voted to spend $20 million of the surplus funds of the company to purchase a majority of the stock of two other companies—the Green Insurance Company and the Blue Trust Company. The Green Insurance Company is a thriving business whose stock is an excellent investment at the price at which it will be sold to Zenith Steel Company. The principal reasons for Zenith's purchase of the Green Insurance stock are as an investment of surplus funds and as a diversification of its business. The Blue Trust Company owns a controlling interest in Zenith Steel Company. The main purpose for Zenith's purchase of the Blue Trust Company stock is to enable the present management and directors of Zenith Steel Company to continue their management of the company.

Jones, a minority shareholder in Zenith Steel Company, brings an appropriate action to enjoin the purchase by Zenith Steel Company of the stock of either the Green Insurance Company or of the Blue Trust Company. Decision?

7. X, Y, and Z each own one-third of the stock of XYZ Corporation. On Friday, X received an offer to merge XYZ into Buyer Corporation. X agreed to call a shareholders' meeting to discuss the offer on the following Tuesday. X telephoned Y and Z and informed them of the offer and the scheduled meeting. Y agreed to attend. However, Z was unable to attend because he was leaving on a trip on Saturday and asked if the three of them could meet Friday night to discuss the offer. X and Y agreed. The three shareholders met informally Friday night and agreed to accept the offer only if they received preferred stock of Buyer Corporation for their shares. Z then left on his trip. On Tuesday, at the time and place appointed by X, X and Y convened the shareholders' meeting. After discussion, they concluded that the preferred stock payment limitation was unwise and passed a formal resolution to accept Buyer Corporation's offer without any such condition.

Z files suit to enjoin X, Y, and the XYZ Corporation from implementing this resolution. Decision?

PART EIGHT
DEBTOR AND CREDITOR RELATIONS

PART EIGHT

DEBTOR AND CREDITOR RELATIONS

PUBLIC POLICY, SOCIAL ISSUES AND BUSINESS ETHICS

In Part Eight we discuss debtor and creditor relations, an area of business that has assumed great importance. Today our economy literally runs on borrowed funds. In 1983 total net borrowing in the United States was over $600 billion. As of July 1984 there was $435 billion of consumer installment credit outstanding and almost $2,000 billion of mortgage debt outstanding.

This extensive use of credit has not always been the case. Shakespeare's well-known lines in *Hamlet* reflect the earlier view of debt: "Neither a borrower nor a lender be; For loan oft loses both itself and friend, And borrowing dulls the edge of husbandry." Professors Speidel, Summers, and White, in *Teaching Materials on Commercial Transactions,* have explained the longstanding historical opposition to debt:

It was once thought bad for a person to incur debts. In Plato's ideal legal system, debts were not to be incurred at all. It was thought even worse not to repay a debt. In early Rome, debtors who did not repay were dismembered: deprived of arms and legs and more. Not too long ago in Anglo-American law, they were thrown in jail where they might well rot. This was known as body execution on a live body. Even corpses were in jeopardy. Thus on July 7, 1816, Richard Brinsley Sheridan expired at the age of 65. "As his body lay in state in Great George Street, London, a bailiff, disguised as a mourner was admitted to have a last look. Once entered, he served the corpse with a warrant arresting it in the King's name for a debt of five hundred pounds. Only when Mr. Carring and Lord Sidmouth each satisfied the bailiff with a check for two-hundred and fifty pounds

did he release the body, so that the funeral could proceed."

Over time this attitude has changed dramatically, and today under our economic system borrowed funds are absolutely essential and entirely honorable. Without them units of production would be severely restricted in the goods and services they could provide, and consumers would be greatly limited in the quantities they could afford to purchase. The public policy and social issues to which the enormous use of debt gives rise are essentially fourfold. First, the means by which debt is created and transferred should be as simple and inexpensive as possible. Second, the risks to lenders should be reduced to the minimum level possible. Third, the lenders should have adequate means for collecting unpaid debts. Finally, debtors should have protection from overreaching and deception by lenders and, in some instances, from their own foolhardiness. The legal system's response to these needs constitutes the law of debtor and creditor relations.

The law governing the creation and transfer of debt is designed to make it as expeditious and efficient as possible. For the most part, this area of the law has been discussed elsewhere. For example, Article 3 of the Uniform Commercial Code (discussed in Part Four) deals with debt evidenced by commercial paper and Article 8 (discussed in Chapter 34) governs debt evidenced by investment securities such as bonds. The issuance and transfer of investment securities is also subject to State and Federal securities regulation, which we discuss in Chapter 39. In addition, the common law of contracts and sales law under Article 2 of the UCC provide simple methods of creating debt, although they do not provide very efficient means by which to transfer such debt, see Chapter 14 for a discussion of the assignment of contract rights.

A lender typically incurs two basic collection risks. The first is that the borrower is unwilling to repay the loan even though he is able to do so. The law has provided the lender with a considerable number of collection remedies that significantly reduce this risk, although these remedies are by no means without cost. We discuss a number of these remedies in Chapter 37.

The law has also sought to deal with the second and more significant collection risk: that the borrower may be *unable* to repay the loan. In addition to the remedies just mentioned, the law has developed several devices to maximize the likelihood that the loan will be repaid. The two most important of these are consensual security interests and sureties. A consensual security interest is an agreement by the borrower granting to the lender the right to reach specified property of the borrower to pay off the debt if the borrower fails to do so. If the property used as collateral is real property, the security is called a mortgage or a deed of trust, which we discuss in Chapter 44 in Part Ten. If the property is personal property, the security interest is governed by Article 9 of the Uniform Commercial Code, which we cover in Chapter 37.

The Official Comment to UCC Section 9-101 states: "The aim of this Article is to provide a simple and unified structure within which the immense variety of present-day secured financing transactions can go forward with less cost and with greater certainty." Article 9 establishes a comprehensive scheme for the regulation of security interests in personal property that supersedes prior law, which, although it had recognized a wide variety of security devices, did not keep pace with new types of collateral and financing that had de-

veloped. Moreover, the recognition of so many inconsistent devices had not only increased the costs to both lender and debtor but had also increased the uncertainty as to their rights. Article 9 replaced these distinct and diverse devices with a single "generic" security interest that applies to all transactions intended to create security interests in personal property. By doing so Article 9 has radically simplified the formal requirements for creating a security interest and has substituted a more rational system for the multiple filing systems of previous law. Both of these changes have reduced the cost of acquiring a security interest in personal property.

The other common device to reduce the risk of default is a surety. A surety is a person who promises the creditor that he will pay the debtor's obligation to the creditor if the debtor does not. If the debtor defaults, the creditor may proceed directly against the surety. The use of a surety with or without security can significantly reduce the collection risk to the lender.

The last important policy objective of debtor-creditor law is the protection of debtors against the overreaching of creditors as well as from the debtor's own foolhardiness. This problem is most acute where the creditor is a professional and the debtor is a consumer. Both State and Federal legislation has been enacted to address many of the particular problems faced by consumer debtors. We discuss these statutes in Chapter 41 in Part Nine.

In some instances debtors of all sorts—wage earners, sole proprietorships, partnerships, and corporations—accumulate debts far in excess of their assets or suffer financial reverses that make it impossible for them to meet their obligations as they become due. In such an event it is an important policy of the law to treat all creditors fairly and equitably. It is also necessary to provide the debtor with relief from these debts so that he may continue to function and contribute to society. These are the two basic purposes of the Federal bankruptcy law, which we discuss in Chapter 38.

37

SECURED TRANSACTIONS AND SURETYSHIP

A secured transaction includes two elements: (1) a debt or obligation to pay money and (2) an interest of the creditor in specific property of the debtor that secures performance of the obligation. An obligation or debt can exist without security; the vast amount of indebtedness is unsecured. In many situations, however, businesses or other individuals cannot obtain credit without giving adequate security. In other cases, an unsecured loan can be obtained, but giving security results in a lower interest rate. Financing transactions involving security in personal property are governed by **Article 9** of the Uniform Commercial Code, Secured Transactions. This Article provides a simple and unified structure within which the tremendous variety of current secured financing transactions can take place with less cost and with greater certainty. Moreover, the Article's flexibility and simplified formalities make it possible for new forms of secured financing to fit comfortably under its provisions. In the first part of this chapter we discuss secured transactions in personal property. Article 9 does not cover secured transactions involving real property, which we discuss in Chapter 45.

In addition to using security to reduce the risks involved in the extension of credit, creditors frequently require that one or more sureties be obtained. A surety is a person who promises the creditor that he will pay the debtor's obligation to the creditor if the debtor does not. Sureties are used *instead* of security interests when security is not available or the use of a secured transaction is too expensive or inconvenient. We cover the suretyship relation in the second part of this chapter.

Secured Transactions in Personal Property

Secured transactions in personal property are governed by Article 9 if the debtor *consents* to provide a security interest in personal property to secure the payment of a debt. Article 9 does *not* apply to security interests without consent that arise by operation of law, such as mechanic's or landlord's liens. A common type of consensual secured transaction covered by Article 9 occurs when a person who wants to buy goods does not have either the cash or sufficient credit standing to obtain the goods on open credit. The seller obtains a security interest in the goods to secure payment of all or part of the price.

Secured transaction –an agreement by which one party gets a security interest in the personal property of another

637

Alternatively, the buyer may borrow the purchase price from a third party and pay the seller in cash. The third-party lender may then take a security interest in the goods to secure repayment of the loan.

In every consensual secured transaction there is a debtor, a secured party, collateral, a security agreement, and a security interest. As defined in the Code, a **debtor** is a person who owes payment or performance of an obligation. A **secured party** is the creditor-lender, seller, or other person who owns the security interest in the collateral. **Collateral** is the property subject to the security interest. A **security agreement** is the agreement that creates or provides for a **security interest,** which in its broadest sense is an interest in personal property or fixtures that secures payment or performance of an obligation. Thus, a security interest is created when an automobile dealer sells and delivers a car to an individual *(debtor)* under a retail installment contract *(security agreement)* through which the dealer *(secured party)* obtains a *security interest* in the car *(collateral)* until the price is paid. A security interest in property cannot exist apart from the debt it secures, and once the debt is discharged in any way, the security interest in the property is terminated. Figure 37-1 illustrates the fundamental rights of the debtor and the secured party in a secured transaction.

Debtor–person who owes payment or obligation

Secured party–creditor who possesses a security interest in collateral

Collateral–personal property subject to security interest

Security agreement–agreement that grants a security interest

Security interest–right in personal property to insure payment of obligation

Classification of Collateral

The Code classifies collateral as (a) goods, (b) "indispensable paper," and (c) intangibles.

Goods

Goods–tangible personal property

Goods are tangible personal property that can be moved when the security interest in them becomes enforceable. Goods are subdivided into (1) consumer goods, (2) equipment, (3) farm products, (4) inventory, and (5) fixtures. An item of goods may fall into different classifications depending on its use or purpose. For example, a refrigerator purchased by a physician to store medicines in his office is classified as equipment, but the same refrigerator would be classified as consumer goods if it was purchased for use in his home. The refrigerator would be classified as inventory in the hands of a refrigerator dealer or manufacturer.

Consumer Goods

Consumer goods–goods primarily for personal, family, or household purposes

Goods are consumer goods if they are used or bought for use primarily for personal, family, or household purposes. Thus, Amos pur-

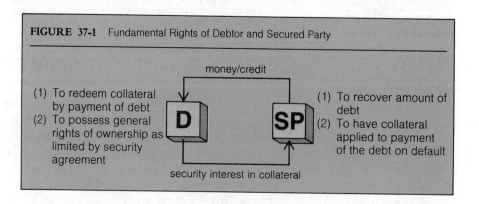

FIGURE 37-1   Fundamental Rights of Debtor and Secured Party

money/credit

(1) To redeem collateral by payment of debt
(2) To possess general rights of ownership as limited by security agreement

D   **SP**

(1) To recover amount of debt
(2) To have collateral applied to payment of the debt on default

security interest in collateral

chases a refrigerator for use in his house from an appliance dealer under a retail installment contract and grants the dealer a security interest in the refrigerator, this is an example of consumer goods.

Equipment   Goods are classified as equipment if they are used or purchased for use primarily in business (including farming or a profession), provided they are not included in the definition of inventory, farm products, or consumer goods. This category is broad enough to include a lawyer's library, a physician's office furniture, or machinery in a factory.

Equipment–goods used primarily in business

Farm Products   The Code defines farm products as "crops or livestock or supplies used or produced in farming operations or if they are products of crops or livestock in their unmanufactured states." Thus, farm products would include wheat growing on the farmer's land, the farmer's pigs, cows, hens and the hens' eggs.

Farm products–crops, livestock, or stock used or produced in farming

Inventory   Inventory includes goods held for sale or lease and raw materials, work in process, or materials used or consumed in a business. Thus, a retailer's or wholesaler's merchandise as well as a manufacturer's materials are inventory.

Inventory–goods held for sale or lease

Fixtures   Goods or personal property that have become so related to particular *real property* that an interest in them arises under real estate law are called fixtures. Thus, State law other than the Code determines whether and when goods become fixtures. In general terms, goods become fixtures when they are so firmly affixed or attached to real estate in such a way that they are considered part of the real estate, yet may be detached without destroying the structure. Examples are furnaces, air-conditioning units, and plumbing fixtures. See Chapter 42 for a further discussion of fixtures. A security interest under Article 9 may be created in goods that are fixtures, and under certain circumstances a perfected security interest in fixtures will have priority over a conflicting security interest or mortgage in the real property to which the goods have been attached.

Fixture–goods that are so firmly attached to real property that they are considered part of the real estate

Indispensable Paper

Three kinds of collateral involve rights evidenced by indispensable paper: (1) chattel paper, (2) instruments, and (3) documents.

Indispensable paper– chattel paper, instruments and documents

Chattel Paper   Chattel paper is a writing or writings that evidence both a monetary obligation and a security interest in or a lease of specific goods. Frequently, a secured party may borrow against or sell the security agreement of his debtor along with his interest in the collateral. The secured party's collateral in this type of transaction is called chattel paper. The Code provides the following illustration:

Chattel paper–writings that evidence both a debt and a security interest

> A dealer sells a tractor to a farmer on conditional sales contract or purchase money security interest. The conditional sales contract is a "security agreement," the farmer is the debtor, the dealer is the "secured party" and the tractor is the type of "collateral" defined . . . as "equipment." But now the dealer transfers the contract to his bank either by outright sale or to secure a loan. Since the conditional sales contract is a security agreement relating to specific equipment, the conditional sales contract is now the type of collateral called "chattel paper." In this

transaction between the dealer and his bank, the bank is the "secured party," the dealer is the "debtor," and the farmer is the "account debtor."

Instruments–negotiable instruments, stocks, bonds, and other investment securities

Instruments   Instruments include negotiable instruments, stocks, bonds, and other investment securities. An instrument is any writing that evidences a right to payment of money, that is transferable by delivery with any necessary indorsement or assignment, and that is not of itself a security agreement or lease.

Document–document of title

Documents   The term "document" includes documents of title, such as bills of lading and warehouse receipts, that may be either negotiable or nonnegotiable. A document of title is negotiable if by its terms the goods it covers are deliverable to bearer or to the order of a named person. Any other document is nonnegotiable.

Intangibles

The Code also recognizes two kinds of collateral that are neither goods nor indispensable paper, namely, accounts and general intangibles. These types of intangible collateral are not evidenced by any indispensable paper, such as a stock certificate or a negotiable bill of lading.

Intangibles–accounts and general intangibles

Account–account receivables

Accounts   The term "account" or "account receivable" refers to the right to payment for goods sold or leased or for services rendered that is not evidenced by an instrument or chattel paper, whether or not it has been earned by performance. The 1972 Code deletes the term "contract right" but includes contract rights in its expanded definition of account.

General intangible–catch-all category of collateral not otherwise covered

General Intangibles   The term "general intangibles" applies to any personal property other than goods, accounts, chattel paper, documents, instruments, and money. This is a catch-all category for interests not otherwise covered unless they are specifically excluded. It leaves room for the use of new kinds of collateral for financing purposes. It includes good will, literary rights, rights to performance of a contract, and interests in patents, trademarks, and copyrights to the extent they are not regulated by Federal statute.

Attachment

Attachment–security interest enforceable against the debtor

Attachment is the Code's terminology to describe a security interest that is **enforceable** against the debtor. Attachment is also a prerequisite to a security interest's enforceability against parties other than the debtor. Enforceability against third parties is called perfection and is discussed below. Until a security interest "attaches," it is ineffective against the debtor. The security interest created by a security agreement attaches to the described collateral once the following events have taken place:

1. the giving of value by the secured party;

2. the debtor's acquiring rights in the collateral; and

3. either the collateral is in the possession of the secured party according to agreement *or* the security agreement is in a writing that contains a description of the collateral and is signed by the debtor.

Value

Value–contract consideration, binding commitment to extend credit, or antecedent debt

The term "value" is broadly defined and includes consideration under contract law, a binding commitment to extend credit, and an antecedent debt. For example, Buyer purchases goods from Seller on credit. When Buyer fails to make timely payment, Seller and Buyer enter into a security agreement under which Seller is granted a security interest in the goods. Value has been given by the Seller, even though he does not provide any new consideration but instead relies on an antecedent debt—the original transfer of goods to Buyer. Moreover, Seller is not limited to acquiring a security interest in the goods he sold to Buyer but may also obtain a security interest in other personal property of the Buyer.

Debtor's Rights in Collateral

The concept of the debtor's rights in collateral is illusive and not specifically defined by the Code. Before 1972, the UCC attempted to provide rules for determining when a debtor acquired rights in certain types of collateral. The 1972 amendments eliminated these provisions because they were considered unnecessary, arbitrary, and confusing. It was decided that such questions were best left for the courts to determine. As a general rule, the debtor is deemed to have rights in collateral he owns or is in possession of as well as those items that he is in the process of acquiring from the seller. For example, if Julia borrows money from Nick and grants him a security interest in corporate stock that Julia owns, then Julia had rights in the collateral before entering into the secured transaction. If Susan sells goods to Peter on credit and Peter provides Susan a security interest in the goods, Peter will acquire rights in the collateral on identification of the goods to the contract.

Rights in collateral—personal property debtor owns, possesses, or in process of acquiring

Security Agreement

A security agreement cannot attach unless there is an agreement between the debtor and creditor granting, creating, or providing the creditor a security interest in the debtor's collateral. Moreover, unless the secured party is in possession of the collateral, the agreement must (1) be **in writing,** (2) be **signed** by the **debtor,** and (3) contain a **reasonable description** of the collateral. See *Matter of Amex-Protein Dev. Corp.* below. In addition, if the collateral is crops growing or to be grown or timber to be cut the agreement must contain a reasonable description of the land.

A sample security agreement is provided as Figure 37-2.

FACTS: Plant Reclamation Company sold equipment to Amex-Protein Development Corporation on an open account. Later Plant Reclamation substituted a promissory note for the open account indebtedness and caused a financing statement to be signed and filed that provided notice of the parties' intention to create a security interest in the property sold as collateral for the note. The note stated that it was secured by a security interest in the property "as per invoices." Amex-Protein subsequently declared bankruptcy, and the validity of Plant Reclamation's security interest in the property is now in issue. The trustee asserts that the promissory note does not constitute a valid security agreement and questions the adequacy of the description of the collateral contained in that instrument.

DECISION: Judgment for Plant Reclamation Corporation. The promissory note created a valid security agreement. No magic words or precise form are necessary to create a security interest if the minimum formal requirements of the Uniform Commercial Code are met. The aim of the liberal approach of the Code is to provide a simple and unified structure within which the immense variety of present-day secured transactions can take effect with less cost and with greater certainty. Since the promissory note executed by Amex-Protein satisfies these basic requirements, it qualifies as a security agreement that by its terms creates or provides for a security interest in the equipment.

MATTER OF AMEX-PROTEIN DEV. CORP.

United States Court of Appeals, Ninth Circuit, 1974. 504 F.2d 1056.

The description of the collateral contained in the promissory note is not very clear. There is no requirement, however, that a complete description appear in the security agreement itself, and an adequate description is provided through incorporation by reference of the subject invoices and through reference to the more specific description of the collateral contained in the financing statement.

FIGURE 37-2   Sample Security Agreement

SECURITY AGREEMENT

August 22, 1986

Daniel Debtor of 113 Hillsborough Street, City of Raleigh, County of Wake, State of North Carolina, hereinafter called the "Debtor," does hereby grant to S.P. & Assoc., Inc., of Raleigh, North Carolina, hereinafter called "S.P.," its successors and assigns, a security interest in the following described property, hereinafter called the "Collateral," to-wit:

    One (1) Deluxe Microcomputer
    Serial number VDL 16794321
    Manufacturer: Apex Mechanical
                  Equipment Co.
    Model 420A

to secure the payment of Debtor's note or notes of even date herewith in the aggregate principal or aggregate face amount of Seven Thousand Five Hundred Dollars ($7,500.00), together with interest and any renewal or extension thereof, in whole or in part, and any and all other debts, obligations, and liabilities of any kind of Debtor to S.P., however created, arising, or evidenced, whether direct or indirect, joint or several, whether as maker, indorser, surety, guarantor or otherwise, whether now or hereafter existing, whether due or not due, and however acquired by S.P. (all hereinafter called the "Obligations").

DEBTOR WARRANTS AND AGREES THAT:

1. Except for the security interest hereby granted, the Debtor will use the proceeds of advances made hereunder, which proceeds may be paid by the S.P. directly to the seller of the Collateral, to become the owner of marketable title to the Collateral free from any prior lien, security interest or encumbrance, and the Debtor will defend the Collateral against all claims and demands of all persons at any time claiming an interest therein.

2. The Collateral is and will be used primarily for personal, family, or household purposes, and the Debtor's residence is that shown at the beginning of this Agreement.

3. The Collateral will be kept at the Debtor's address shown at the beginning of this Agreement.

4. There are no financing statements covering any of the Collateral on file in any public office, and the Debtor has not executed in favor of other secured parties financing statements that could be placed on file prior to any of S.P.'s financing statements.

5. DEBTOR AGREES THAT:
A. He will pay to S.P. all amounts due on the note or notes mentioned above and the other Obligations secured hereby as and when same shall be due and payable, whether by maturity, acceleration, or otherwise, and will pay to S.P. reasonable

FIGURE 37–2, continued

attorney's fees incurred by S.P. in collection of said Obligations or enforcement of this Security Agreement.

B. He will maintain all mechanical equipment and machinery hereby covered in sound and efficient operating condition, including the procurement and installation of such new parts, attachments, and replacements as may be necessary or desirable to maintain said Collateral in proper operating condition.

C. He will maintain such insurance upon all of the Collateral as S.P. may require, payable to Debtor and S.P. as their interest may appear, in an amount not less than the actual value of the Collateral.

D. He will pay all insurance premiums and taxes, licenses, or other charges assessed against the Collateral or required to be paid in connection with the use and ownership of the Collateral. If Debtor shall fail to pay such insurance premiums, taxes, licenses, or other charges when they are due, S.P. at its opinion, may pay the cost thereof, and the amounts so paid and advanced shall be added to the indebtedness secured hereby and shall bear interest at the maximum rate permitted by Law.

E. He will not   (a) permit any liens or security interest to attach to any of the Collateral;   (b) permit any of the Collateral to be levied upon under any legal process;   (c) sell or dispose of any of the Collateral without prior written consent of S.P.;   (d) permit anything to be done that may impair the value of the Collateral or the security intended to be afforded by this Agreement.

F. He will immediately notify S.P. in writing of any change of the Debtor's place or residence, place or places of business, or the location of the Collateral.

G. He will not remove the Collateral from the State of North Carolina without prior written consent by S.P.

6. IT IS FURTHER AGREED THAT THE DEBTOR SHALL BE IN DEFAULT UNDER THIS AGREEMENT:

A. If the Debtor uses any of the Collateral in violation of any statute or ordinance or the Debtor is found to have a record or reputation for violating the laws of the United States or any State relating to liquor or narcotics; or

B. If the Debtor shall fail to perform any covenant or Agreement made by him herein; or

C. If the Debtor shall fail to make due and punctual payment of any of the Obligations secured hereby when and as any part or all of such Obligation becomes due and payable; or

D. If any warranty, representation, or statement made or furnished to S.P. by or on behalf of the Debtor in connection with this Agreement proves to have been false in any material respect when made or furnished; or

E. If the Collateral suffers material damage or destruction; or

F. If any bankruptcy or insolvency proceedings are commenced by or against the Debtor or any guarantor or surety for the Debtor; or

G. If the Debtor dies, becomes incompetent, is dissolved, or the Debtor's existence otherwise terminates.

Upon the happening of any of the above events of default or in the event that S.P., in good faith, deems itself insecure, S.P. may at its option, declare all Obligations secured hereby due and payable immediately and have, in addition to other rights and remedies, the rights and remedies of a secured party upon default under the North Carolina Uniform Commercial Code.

The waiver of any particular default of the Debtor hereunder shall not be a waiver of any other or subsequent default of the Debtor.

Any requirement of the North Carolina Uniform Commercial Code of reasonable notification of time and place of public sale, or the time on or after which private sale may be held, may be met by sending written notice by registered or certified mail to the above address of the Debtor at least five (5) days prior to public sale or the date after which private sale may be made.

The Debtor shall be and remain liable for any deficiency remaining after applying the proceeds of disposition of the Collateral first to the reasonable expenses of re-taking,

FIGURE 37–2, continued

holding, preparing for sale, selling, and the like, including the reasonable attorney's fees, incurred by S.P. in connection therewith, and then to satisfaction of the Obligations secured hereby.

This Agreement and all rights, remedies, and duties hereunder, including matters of construction, shall be governed by the laws of North Carolina.

This Agreement shall apply to, inure to the benefit of, and be binding upon the heirs, administrators, executors, and assigns of S.P. and the Debtor. This is the entire agreement of the parties, and no amendment, alteration, deletion, or addition hereto shall be effective and binding unless it is in writing and signed by the parties.

Debtor acknowledges that this Agreement is and shall be effective upon execution by the Debtor and delivery hereof to S.P., and it shall not be necessary for S.P. to execute or otherwise signify its acceptance hereof.

Signed and delivered on the day first above written.

_____ (SEAL)
Daniel Debtor

S.P. & Assoc., Inc.
(Secured Party)
By: _____

After-Acquired Property   A security agreement may provide a secured party with a security interest in after-acquired property. After-acquired property is property the debtor does not own or have rights to but may acquire at some time in the future. For example, after-acquired property clauses in a security agreement may include all present and subsequently acquired inventory, accounts, or equipment of the debtor. For example, this clause would provide the secured party with a valid security interest not only in the debtor's presently existing typewriter, desk, and file cabinet, but also in a personal computer subsequently purchased by the debtor. The concept of a "continuing general lien" or a "floating lien" is therefore accepted by Article 9. Nevertheless, it should be noted that no security interest may attach under an after-acquired property clause to **consumer goods** when given as additional security unless the debtor acquires rights in them within ten days after the secured party gives values.

> **After acquired property**–property the debtor may acquire at some time in the future

Proceeds   A secured party is necessarily interested in the use and control of the proceeds from the sale, exchange, collection, or other disposition of the collateral. These proceeds may be in the form of money, checks, deposit accounts, promissory notes, or other types of personal property. Unless otherwise agreed, a security agreement gives the secured party rights to proceeds.

> **Proceeds**–consideration for the sale, exchange, or other disposition of the collateral

Future Advances   The obligations covered by a security agreement may include future advances. Frequently a debtor will obtain a line of credit from a creditor for advances to be made at some later time. For instance, a manufacturer may provide a retailer with a $60,000 line of credit although the retailer initially uses only $20,000 of the credit. Nevertheless, the manufacturer may enter into a security agreement with the retailer granting the manufacturer a security interest in the retailer's inventory to secure not only the initial $20,000 advance but also any future advances.

Perfection

To be effective against third parties (including other creditors of the debtor, the debtor's trustee in bankruptcy, and transferees of the debtor), the security interest must be perfected. A security interest is perfected when it has attached *and* when all the applicable steps required for perfection have been taken.

    A security interest may be perfected:

1. by the secured party's filing a financing statement signed by the debtor;
2. by the secured party's taking or retaining possession of the collateral; or
3. automatically on the attachment of the security interest (see Figure 37-3).

Perfection–security interest enforceable against third parties

Filing a Financing Statement

Filing a financing statement is the general method of perfecting a security interest under Article 9. Filing may be used to perfect a security interest in any type of collateral with the exception of instruments. The form of the financing statement, which is filed to give public notice of the security interest, may vary from State to State. The **financing statement** does not contain details, but the names and addresses of the secured party and the debtor, a reasonable description of the collateral, and the signature of the debtor are required. Figure 37-4 shows a sample financing statement.

Financing statement– document filed by the secured party to provide notice of the security interest

    So that the terms of secured transaction between the parties can be determined, the security agreement or the collateral note or preferably both must be available. It is possible that neither the maturity date of the obligation nor the amount of the obligation secured will appear on the financing statement. Where no maturity date is stated on a financing statement, the statement is effective for *five years* from the date of filing. Moreover, if a **continuation statement** is filed by the secured party within six months prior to expiration, the effectiveness of the filing will be extended for another five-year period.

    In most States, security interests in **motor vehicles** must be perfected by a notation on the **certificate of title** rather than by filing a financing statement.

FIGURE 37-3 Requisites for Enforceability

I. Attachment
(against Debtor)

A. Agreement
   1) in writing (unless SP has possession)
   2) providing a security interest
   3) in described collateral
   4) signed by debtor,

B. Value given by secured party, and

C. Debtor has rights in collateral

II. Perfection
(against Third Parties)

A. Filing a financing statement, or

B. SP takes possession, or

C. Automatically

FIGURE 37-4   Sample Financing Statement

UNIFORM COMMERCIAL CODE—FINANCING STATEMENT
APPROVED FOR USE IN NORTH CAROLINA AND THE FOLLOWING STATES

Alabama	**Delaware**	**Maine**	**New Jersey**	**Tennessee**
Alaska	**Hawaii**	**Maryland**	**New Mexico**	**Virginia**
Arkansas	**Idaho**	**Massachusetts**	**North Dakota**	**West Virginia**
Arizona	**Indiana**	**Mississippi**	**Ohio**	**Wyoming**
Colorado	**Kansas**	**Montana**	**Oklahoma**	**District of Columbia**
Connecticut	**Kentucky**	**New Hampshire**	**South Carolina**	

UCC-1

This FINANCING STATEMENT is presented to a Filing Officer for filing pursuant to the Uniform Commercial Code.

No. of Additional Sheets Presented:

(1) Debtor(s) (Last Name First) and Address(es):

(2) Secured Party(ies) Name(s) and Address(es):

(3) (a) ☐ Collateral is or includes fixtures.
    (b) ☐ Timber, Minerals or Accounts Subject to G.S. 25·9·103(5) are covered
    (c) ☐ Crops Are Growing Or To Be Grown On Real Property Described in Section (5).
If either block 3(a) or block 3(b) applies describe real estate, including record owner(s) in section (5).

(4) Assignee(s) of Secured Party, Address(es):

For Filing Officer

(5) This Financing Statement Covers the Following types [or items] of property.

☐ Products of the Collateral Are Also Covered.

(6) Signatures: Debtor(s)   Secured Party(ies) [or Assignees]

(By) _____
Standard Form Approved by N.C. Sec. of State and other states shown above.

(1) Filing Officer Copy—Numerical

(By) _____
Signature of Secured Party Permitted in Lieu of Debtor's Signature:
(1) Collateral is subject to Security Interest In Another Jurisdiction and ☐
    ☐ Collateral Is Brought Into This State
    ☐ Debtor's Location Changed To This State
(2) For Other Situations See: G.S. 25·9·402 (2)

UCC-1

Nevertheless, in most States, certificate-of-title laws do not apply to motor vehicles that are held as inventory for sale by a dealer.

Where to File   The Code provides three alternative provisions regarding the proper place to file a financing statement. The alternatives differ as to which types of collateral are to be filed **locally** (in the county) or **centrally** (with the Secretary of State or another designated State official).

The first alternative, which has been adopted in only a few States, provides that where the collateral is fixtures, timber to be cut, or minerals to be extracted, then the financing statement should be filed locally in the office where a mortgage on real estate would be filed or recorded. All other filings are to be made centrally with the Secretary of State or another designated State official.

The second alternative, which is the most widely adopted, stipulates local filing for fixtures, farm products, consumer goods, timber, minerals, and farming equipment. All other filings are to be made in the office of the Secretary of State or another designated State official.

The third alternative is the same as the second except that where central filing is required, the secured party must *also* file locally if the debtor has a place of business in only one county or if the debtor has no place of business in the State but resides in the State.

Improper Filing   If a secured party fails to file the financing statement in the proper location or fails to file it in all the required locations, the filing is *ineffective,* subject to two exceptions. First, if the filing is made in good faith, it is effective for any collateral for which the filing complied with the requirements of Article 9. This exception applies to situations in which the filing covers a number of different types of collateral and is proper for some but not all of the collateral listed. Second, a filing made in good faith is also effective for collateral covered by the financing statement against any person who has knowledge of the contents of that financing statement. This exception has been limited by the 1972 amendments, which give a lien creditor priority over an unperfected security interest without regard to whether the lien creditor knew of the unperfected security interest.

Possession

A **pledge** or possessory security interest is the delivery of personal property to a creditor, or to a third party acting as an agent for the creditor, as security for the payment of a debt. Perhaps the most common pledge is that of a borrower who pledges corporate stock by delivery of the certificates to a bank in order to secure a loan. The delivery of the stock certificates (collateral) to the bank (secured party) is the essential element of the pledge. Since *delivery* is made, the security interest is "perfected" without filing. There is no pledge where the debtor retains possession of the collateral. In a pledge the debtor is not legally required to sign a written security agreement; an oral agreement granting the secured party a security interest is sufficient. In any situation other than a pledge, the Code requires a written security agreement.

Possession by the secured party may be used to perfect a security interest in goods (e.g., pawnbrokers), instruments, negotiable documents, or chattel

Pledge–possessory security interest

paper. A pledge cannot be used with items that are completely intangible. Subject to the limited exception of the twenty-one day temporary period of perfection discussed later in this chapter, possession is the *only* way to perfect a security interest in instruments. In addition, the usual and advisable method of perfecting a security interest in both negotiable documents and chattel paper is by possession. Although both of these types of collateral may be perfected by filing, it is not advisable to rely on filing because (a) the holder of a negotiable document of title that has been duly negotiated to him takes priority in the goods over an earlier security interest perfected by filing, and (b) a good faith purchaser in the ordinary course of business of chattel paper takes priority over an earlier security interest perfected by filing.

Field warehouse–secured party takes possession of the goods while the pledgor has access to the goods

One common type of pledge is the **field warehouse.** This common arrangement for financing inventory allows the debtor access to the pledged goods and at the same time gives the secured party control over the pledged property. In this arrangement, a professional warehouseman generally establishes a warehouse on the debtor's premises—usually by enclosing a portion of the premises and posting appropriate signs—to store the debtor's unsold inventory. Nonnegotiable receipts for the goods are then typically issued by the warehouseman to the secured party. The secured party may then authorize the warehouseman to release a portion of the goods to the debtor as the goods are sold, at a specified quantity per week, or at any rate agreed on by the parties. Thus the secured party legally possesses the goods but allows the debtor easy access to the inventory.

Automatic Perfection

Automatic perfection– perfection upon attachment

In some situations a security interest is automatically perfected on attachment. The two most important situations to which automatic perfection applies are (1) purchase money security interests in consumer goods and (2) temporary perfection for instruments, documents, and proceeds.

Purchase money secu-rity interest–a seller of goods who retains a security interest in goods purchased or a lender who obtains a security interest in goods purchased with the loaned money

Purchase Money Security Interest in Consumer Goods   A seller of goods who retains a security interest in them by a security agreement has a **purchase money security interest** (PMSI). Similarly, a third party who advances funds to enable the debtor to purchase goods has a purchase money security interest if he has a security agreement and the debtor in fact uses the funds to purchase the goods. A purchase money security interest in consumer goods, with the exception of motor vehicles, is perfected automatically on attachment without the necessity of filing a financing statement. For example, Don purchases a refrigerator from Carol on credit for Don's own personal, family, or household use. Don takes possession of the refrigerator and then grants Carol a security interest in the refrigerator according to a written security agreement. On Don's granting Carol the security interest in the refrigerator, Carol's security interest attaches and is automatically perfected. The same is also true if Don purchased the refrigerator for cash but borrowed the money from Laura, to whom Don granted a written security interest in the refrigerator. Laura's security interest attached and was automatically perfected when Laura received the security interest from Don.

Temporary Perfection   A security interest in *negotiable documents* or *instruments* is automatically perfected without filing or taking possession for **twenty-one days** from the time it attaches, to the extent that it arises for new value given under a written security agreement. However, the secured party runs the risk of loss or impairment of his security interest during the twenty-one-day period, for although his interest is temporarily perfected, a holder in due course of a negotiable instrument or a holder to whom a document has been duly negotiated will take priority over the security interest.

Figure 37-5 shows the methods of perfecting security interests.

Priorities

As we previously noted, a security interest must be perfected to be effective against other creditors of the debtor, the debtor's trustee in bankruptcy, and transferees of the debtor. Nonetheless, perfection of a security interest does *not* provide the secured party with a priority over *all* third parties with an interest in the collateral. On the other hand, even an unperfected security interest has priority over a limited number of third parties and is enforceable against the debtor. Article 9 establishes a complex set of rules that determine the relative priorities among these parties.

Priority–precedence in order of right

Against Unsecured Creditors

Once a security interest **attaches,** it has priority over claims of other creditors who do not have a security interest or a lien. This priority does not depend on perfection. However, an unperfected security interest is subordinate to a representative of unsecured creditors, such as an assignee for the benefit of creditors, a trustee in bankruptcy, or a receiver in equity.

Against Lien Creditors

A **perfected** security interest has priority over lien creditors who acquire their lien after perfection. An **unperfected** security interest is subordinate to the rights of a person who becomes a lien creditor before the security interest is perfected. However, if a secured party files with respect to a *purchase money*

FIGURE 37-5   Methods of Perfecting Security Interests

Collateral	Applicable Method of Perfection		
	Filing	Possession	Automatic
Goods			
Consumer	●	●	PMSI
Equipment	●	●	
Farm products	●	●	
Inventory	●	●	
Fixtures	●	●	
Indispensable Paper			
Chattel paper	●	●	
Instrument		●	21 days
Document	●	●	21 days
Intangibles			
Account	●		●
General intangibles	●		●

security interest within ten days after the debtor receives possession of the collateral, the secured party takes priority over the rights of a lien creditor that arise between the time the security interest attaches and the time of filing. A **lien creditor** means a creditor who has acquired a lien in the property by attachment *and* includes an assignee for the benefit of creditors as well as a **trustee in bankruptcy.** Nonetheless, a lien securing claims arising from services or materials furnished with respect to goods takes priority over a perfected security interest in those goods unless the lien is statutory and the statute specifically provides otherwise.

Lien creditor–a creditor who has acquired a lien on the property by attachment

Trustee in bankruptcy– representative of the estate in bankruptcy who is responsible for collecting, liquidating, and distributing the debtor's assets

Against Other Secured Creditors

The rights of a secured creditor against other secured creditors depend on which security interests are perfected, when they are perfected, and the type of collateral. Notwithstanding the rules of priority, it is possible for a secured party entitled to priority to subordinate her interest to that of another secured creditor. This may be done by agreement between the secured parties, and nothing need be filed.

Perfected versus Unperfected   A creditor with a **perfected** security interest has greater rights in the collateral than a creditor with an unperfected security interest.

Perfected versus Perfected   If two parties each have a **perfected** security interest, they rank according to priority in *time of filing or perfection.* Priority dates from the time a filing is first made covering the collateral or the time the security interest is first perfected, whichever is earlier, provided that there is no subsequent period when there is neither filing nor perfection. This rule gives special treatment to filing because it can occur prior to attachment and thus grants priority from a time which may precede perfection.

For example, D Store and S Bank enter into a loan agreement under the terms of which S agrees to lend $5,000 on the security of D's existing store equipment. A financing statement is filed, but no funds are advanced. One week later, D enters into a loan agreement with R Bank, and R Bank agrees to lend $5,000 on the security of the same store equipment. The funds are advanced, and a financing statement is filed. One week later, S Bank advances the agreed sum of $5,000. D Store defaults on both loans. Between S Bank and R Bank, S has priority. When both security interests are perfected by filing, priority is determined in the order of filing. R Bank could have checked the financing statements on file and would have learned that S bank claimed a security interest in the equipment. Once S's financing statement was on file, with no prior secured party of record, S was not required to check the files prior to advancing funds to D Store in accordance with its loan commitment.

To illustrate further, assume that X grants a security interest in a Chagall painting to S Bank, and according to the loan agreement the Bank advances funds to X. A financing statement is filed. Later X wishes more money and goes to C, an art dealer, who advances funds to X on a pledge of the painting. X defaults on both loans. Between S and C, S has priority because its security interest was filed before C's perfection by possession. By checking the financing statements on file, C could have discovered that S had a prior security interest in the painting.

Where there is a **purchase money security interest** in the collateral, the rules vary depending on whether the collateral is noninventory or inventory.

1. A purchase money security interest in **noninventory** collateral takes priority over a conflicting security interest if the purchase money security interest is perfected at the time the debtor receives possession of the collateral *or* within *ten days* of receipt.

For example, D Manufacturing Co. entered into a loan agreement with S Bank, which loaned money to D on the security of D's existing and future equipment. A financing statement was filed stating that the collateral is "all equipment presently owned and subsequently acquired" by D. At a later date, D buys new equipment from X Supply Co., paying 25 percent of the purchase price, with X retaining a security interest in the equipment to secure the remaining balance. If X files a financing statement within ten days of D's obtaining possession of the equipment, X's purchase money security interest in the new equipment has priority over S's interest. If X files on the eleventh day after D receives the equipment, X's interest is subordinate to S's interest.

FACTS: National Acceptance Company loaned Ultra Precision Industries $692,000, and to secure repayment of the loan Ultra executed a chattel mortgage security agreement on National's behalf on March 7, 1967. National perfected the security interest by timely filing a financing statement. Although the security interest covered specifically described equipment of Ultra's, both the security agreement and the financing statement contained an after-acquired property clause that did not refer to any specific equipment.

Later in 1967 and 1968, Ultra placed three separate orders for machines from Wolf Machinery Company. In each case it was agreed that after the machines had been shipped to Ultra and installed, Ultra would be given an opportunity to test them in operation for a reasonable period. If the machines passed inspection, Wolf would then provide financing that was satisfactory to Ultra. In all three cases, financing was arranged with Community Bank (Bank) and accepted, and a security interest was given in the machines. Furthermore, in each case a security agreement was entered into, and a financing statement was then filed by the secured parties within ten days. Ultra became bankrupt on October 7, 1969. National now claims that its security interest in the after-acquired machines should take priority over those of Wolf and Bank because their interests were not perfected by timely filed financing statements.

DECISION: Judgment for Wolf and Bank. Wolf and Bank provided funds for Ultra to purchase the machines and, therefore, had an interest classified as a purchase money security interest in equipment. National, on the other hand, had an ordinary secured interest in the equipment that it had properly perfected. As between these two conflicting interests, the purchase money security interest in the equipment has priority if it was perfected at the time that the debtor, Ultra, received possession of the collateral or within ten days thereafter. Here, Wolf and Bank filed financing statements long after the debtor Ultra received physical delivery of the machines but within ten days of when Ultra completed testing and secured financing and thereby incurred the obligation to purchase the machines. Only when Ultra executed and delivered the security agreements on the machines did it become a debtor. Therefore, since the financing statements were filed within ten days of that date, Wolf and Bank had properly perfected purchase money security interests in the machines that take priority over National's claims.

MATTER OF ULTRA PRECISION INDUSTRIES, INC.

United States Court of Appeals, Ninth Court, 1974.
503 F.2d 414.

---

2. A purchase money security interest in **inventory** has priority over conflicting security interests if the following requirements are met. The purchase money security holder must perfect his interest in the inventory at the time the debtor receives the inventory. Also, he must notify, in writing, all holders

of conflicting security interests who have filed a financing statement covering the same type of inventory of his acquisition of a purchase money security interest and must give a description of the secured inventory.

For example, D Store and S Bank enter into a loan agreement in which S agrees to finance D's entire inventory of stoves, refrigerators, and other kitchen appliances. A financing statement is filed, and S advances funds to D. Subsequently, D enters into an agreement in which R Stove Co. will supply D with stoves, retaining a purchase money security interest in this inventory. R will have priority on the inventory it supplies to D provided that a financing statement is filed and R notifies S that it is going to engage in this purchase money financing of the described stoves. If R fails to give the required notice or fails to file a financing statement, S will have priority over R on the stoves it supplies to D. The Code adopts a system of notice filing, and secured parties proceed at their peril in failing to check the financing statements on file.

Unperfected versus Unperfected   If neither security interest is perfected, then the first to attach has priority.

Against Buyers

A security interest continues in collateral even though it is sold, unless the secured party authorizes the sale. However, in some instances buyers of collateral sold without the secured party's authorization take it free of the security interest. Some of these purchasers take it free of even a perfected security interest; others take it free of only an unperfected security interest.

Buyers in the Ordinary Course of Business   A buyer in the ordinary course of business takes collateral free of any security interest created by *her* seller, even if the security interest is perfected and the buyer knows of its existence. This rule, however, does not apply to a person buying farm products from a person engaged in farming operations. A buyer in the ordinary course of business is a person who buys in good faith, without knowledge that the sale violates a security interest of a third party, and buys from a person in the business of selling goods of that kind. Thus, this rule applies primarily to purchasers of inventory. For example, a consumer who purchases a sofa from a furniture dealer and the dealer who purchases the sofa from another dealer are both buyers in the ordinary course of business. On the other hand, a person who purchases a sofa from a dentist who used the sofa in his waiting room or from an individual who used the sofa in his home is not a buyer in the ordinary course of business.

To illustrate further: a buyer in the ordinary course of business of an automobile from an automobile dealership will take free and clear of a security interest created by the dealer from whom he purchased the car. However, that same buyer in the ordinary course of business will *not* take clear of a security interest created by any person who owned the automobile prior to the dealer. A leading case on this point is National Shawmut Bank of Boston v. Jones, 108 N.H. 386, 236 A.2d 484 (1967). In that case Wever bought a 1964 Dodge Dart from Wentworth Motor Company for his own personal use and granted a security interest in the car to Wentworth. Wentworth later assigned the security interest to National Shawmut Bank which properly perfected it. Without Shawmut's consent, Wever sold the car to Hanson-Rock, another automobile dealer. Hanson-Rock then sold the car to Jones. Even

Buyer in the ordinary course of business–a person who buys in good faith, without knowledge that the sale violates a security interest, and from a merchant

though Jones is a buyer in the ordinary course of business from Hanson-Rock, he took the automobile subject to Shawmut's security interest since that interest had not been created by Jones' seller, Hanson-Rock. See also *Exchange Bank of Osceola v. Jarrett* which follows.

FACTS: On September 8, 1976, Daniel Holland purchased for his own use a tractor-scraper through the Exchange Bank of Osceola located in Kissimmee, Florida. The bank retained a security interest in the tractor for the full $13,000 purchase price and then perfected that security interest in Florida.

On February 1, 1977, Holland sold the tractor without the Exchange Bank's permission to C. B. and O. Equipment Company, a Council Bluffs, Iowa based farm implements merchant. The tractor arrived in Iowa on February 7, 1977, and on February 21, 1977, Jarrett, a Montana contractor, purchased it and transported it to Montana. Exchange Bank then properly filed a financing statement in both Iowa and Montana. When Holland subsequently defaulted on his obligation to Exchange Bank, the bank brought this action to foreclose on its security interest in the tractor.

DECISION: Judgment for Exchange Bank of Osceola. Exchange Bank perfected its security interest in the tractor when it filed the financing statement in Florida. Generally, a security interest continues in the collateral despite the debtor's sale or exchange of the collateral unless the secured party authorized the transfer in the security agreement or otherwise. Therefore, since Holland sold the tractor without Exchange Bank's permission, the purchaser C. B. and O. Equipment Company took the tractor subject to Exchange Bank's security interest.

Jarrett, moreover, did not take the tractor free of Exchange Bank's security interest. Although Jarrett was a buyer in the ordinary course of business because he purchased in good faith, without knowledge that the sale to him was in violation of Exchange Bank's security interest, in the ordinary course of business, and from a person in the business of selling tractors, a buyer in the ordinary course only takes free of security interests created by *his* seller. Here, Exchange Bank created the security interest which remained perfected, while C. B. and O. Equipment Company sold the tractor to Jarrett. Accordingly, Jarrett did not take free of Exchange Bank's security interest in the tractor, and the bank is entitled to foreclose due to Holland's default.

EXCHANGE BANK OF OSCEOLA v. JARRETT

Supreme Court of Montana,
1979.
588 P.2d 1006.

Buyers of Consumer Goods   In the case of consumer goods, a buyer who buys without knowledge of a security interest, for value, and for his own personal, family, or household use takes the goods free of any purchase money security interest automatically perfected, but takes the goods subject to a security interest perfected by filing. For example, Ann purchases on credit a refrigerator from Steve for use in her home and grants Steve a security interest in the refrigerator. Steve does not file a financing statement but has a perfected security interest by attachment. Ann subsequently sells the refrigerator to her neighbor, Nick, for use in Nick's home. Nick did not have knowledge of Steve's security interest and therefore takes the refrigerator free of Steve's interest. However, if Steve had filed a financing statement, Steve's security interest would continue in the collateral in the hands of Nick.

Other Buyers   An unperfected security interest is subordinate to the following rights: (1) in the case of goods, instruments, documents, and chattel paper, of a purchaser who gives value for the collateral, takes it without knowledge of the existing security interest, and before it is perfected; and (2) in the case of accounts and general intangibles, of a purchaser who takes the collateral for value, without knowledge of the security interest, and before perfection.

If either of these purchasers has knowledge of the unperfected security interest, he takes the collateral subject to the security interest.

A purchaser of chattel paper or an instrument who gives new value and takes possession of it in the ordinary course of his business has priority over a perfected security interest in the chattel paper or instrument if he acts without knowledge that the specific paper or instrument is subject to a security interest. A holder in due course of a negotiable instrument, a holder to whom a negotiable document of title has been duly negotiated, and a *bona fide* purchaser of an investment security take priority over an earlier security interest even though perfected. Filing under Article 9 does *not* constitute notice of the security interest to such holders or purchasers.

Default

After default, the rights and remedies of the parties are governed by the security agreement and by the applicable provisions of the Code. In general, the secured party may ask for a judgment or foreclosure or otherwise enforce the security interest by available judicial procedure. Unless the parties have agreed otherwise, the secured party may take possession of the collateral on default without judicial process if it can be done without a breach of the peace. See *Deavers v. Standridge* below. Or the secured party may make equipment unusable and dispose of it on the debtor's premises. Unless the debtor has waived his rights in the collateral after default, he has a right of **redemption** at any time before the secured party has disposed of the collateral or entered into a contract to dispose of it.

DEAVERS v. STANDRIDGE

Court of Appeals of Georgia, Division No. 2, 1978.
144 Ga.App. 673, 242 S.E.2d 331.

FACTS: Standridge purchased a 1965 Chevrolet automobile from Billy Deavers, an agent of Walker Motor Company. According to the sales contract, the balance due after trade-in allowance was $282.50, to be paid in 12 weekly installments. Standridge's version is that he was unable to make the second payment and that Billy Deavers orally agreed that he could make two payments the next week. The day after the double payment was due, Standridge still had not paid. That day, Ronnie Deavers, Billy's brother, went to Standridge's place of employment to repossess the car. Rather than consenting to the repossession, Standridge drove the car to the Walker Motor Company's place of business and tendered the overdue payments. The Deavers refused to accept the late payment and, instead demanded the entire unpaid balance. Standridge could not do so. The Deavers therefore "blocked-in" Standridge's car with another car and told him he could just "walk his _____ home." Standridge then brought suit, seeking damages for the Deavers' wrongful repossession of his car. The Deavers deny that they granted Standridge permission to make a double payment; that Standridge tendered the double payment, and that they rejected it. They claim that he made no payment and, therefore, they were entitled to repossess the car.

DECISION: Judgment for Standridge. Unless otherwise agreed in the contract, the secured party on default has the right to repossess the collateral without judicial process. Here, the sales contract specifically provided for repossession upon Standridge's default of any payments. The Deavers were then entitled to repossess without judicial process. However, the repossession must be done without breaching the peace. The jury determined that the Deavers' combined acts of blocking-in Standridge's car and speaking to him in offensive, insulting language were sufficiently provocative of violence to be a breach of the peace. Therefore, the Deaver's repossession was unlawful and Standridge is entitled to recover damages.

Sale of Collateral

The secured party may sell, lease, or otherwise dispose of any collateral in its existing condition at the time of repossession or following any commercially reasonable preparation or processing. The debtor is entitled to any surplus and is liable for any deficiency, except that in the case of a sale of accounts or chattel paper, he is not entitled to any surplus or liable for a deficiency unless the security agreement so provides.

The collateral may be disposed of at *public* or *private* sale, so long as all aspects of its disposition are "commercially reasonable." Unless the collateral is perishable or threatens to decline speedily in value or is of a type customarily sold on a recognized market, reasonable *notice* must be given to the debtor of a public sale or of the time after which a private disposition will be made and, except in the case of consumer goods, to other secured parties who have filed or who are known by the secured party to have security interests in the collateral.

The secured party may buy at a public sale and at a private sale if the collateral is customarily sold in a recognized market or is the subject of widely distributed standard price quotations.

Retention of Collateral

The secured party may, after default and repossession, send written notice to the debtor and, except in the case of consumer goods, to other secured parties that he proposes to retain the collateral in satisfaction of the obligation, and if no objection is received within twenty-one days, the secured party may retain the collateral. If there is objection within this period, however, the collateral must be disposed of as provided in the Code. In the case of **consumer** goods, if the debtor has paid *60 percent* of the obligation and has not, after default, signed a statement renouncing his rights, the secured party who has taken possession of the collateral must dispose of it by sale within ninety days after repossession, or the debtor may recover in conversion or under the Code not less than the credit service charge plus 10 percent of the principal amount of the debt or the time price differential plus 10 percent of the cash price.

Suretyship

It is common in many business transactions involving the extension of credit for the creditor to require that someone in addition to the debtor promise to fulfill the obligation. This promisor generally is known as a surety. Sureties are also frequently used by employers to protect against losses caused by embezzlement by employees, as well as in construction contracts for commercial buildings to bond the performance of the contract. Similarly, it is commonly required by statute that many contracts for work to be done for governmental entities have the added protection of a surety. Premiums for compensated sureties exceed $1 billion annually in the United States.

primary liability

Surety–promise to pay the debt of another, if that other party fails to perform

Nature and Formation

A **surety** promises to answer for the payment of a debt or the performance of a duty owed to one person (called the **creditor**) by another (the **principal debtor**) on the *failure* of the principal debtor to make payment or otherwise perform the obligation. Thus, the suretyship relationship involves three parties—the principal debtor, the creditor, and the surety—and three contractual obligations as illustrated by Figure 37-6. When there is more than one person bound for the same debt of a principal debtor, they are **cosureties.**

The creditor's rights against the principal debtor are determined by the contract between them. The creditor may also take action on any collateral securing the principal debtor's performance that the creditor or the surety holds. In addition, the creditor may proceed against the surety if the principal debtor defaults. If the surety is an **absolute surety,** then the creditor may hold the surety liable as soon as the principal debtor defaults. The creditor need *not* first proceed against the principal debtor. However, if the surety is a **conditional guarantor of collection,** he is liable only when the creditor exhausts his legal remedies against the principal debtor. Thus, a conditional guarantor of collection is liable if the creditor first obtains a judgment against the principal debtor and is unable to collect under the judgment.

A surety who is required to pay the creditor for the principal debtor's obligation is entitled to be **exonerated** (relieved of liability) and **reimbursed** by the principal debtor. In addition, the surety is **subrogated** to (assumes) the rights of the creditor and has a right of **contribution** from cosureties (see Figure 37-6). The rights of sureties are discussed more fully below.

Although in theory a distinction is drawn between a surety and a guarantor, the two terms are used almost synonymously in common usage. Strictly speaking, a **surety** is bound with the principal debtor as a primary obligor and usually, although not necessarily, on the same instrument, whereas the **guarantor** is separately or collaterally bound to pay if the principal debtor does not. For convenience, the term "surety" will be used to include both of

[handwritten margin notes: primary liability; secondary liability]

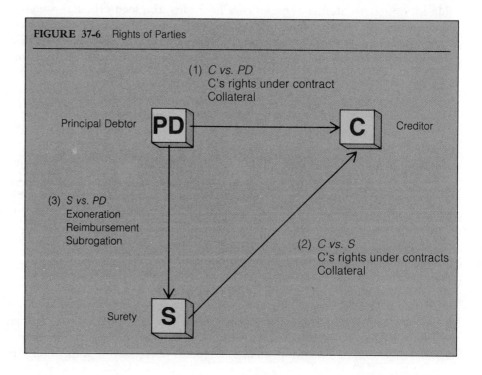

FIGURE 37-6   Rights of Parties

(1) *C vs. PD*
C's rights under contract
Collateral

Principal Debtor   **PD** ——————→ **C**   Creditor

(3) *S vs. PD*
Exoneration
Reimbursement
Subrogation

(2) *C vs. S*
C's rights under contracts
Collateral

Surety   **S**

these terms, because the rights and duties of a surety and a guarantor are almost indistinguishable.

Types of Sureties

A suretyship arrangement is frequently used by creditors seeking to reduce the risk of default by their debtors. For example, PD, a closely held corporation, applies to C, a lending institution, for a loan. After scrutinizing the assets and financial prospects of PD, the lender refuses to extend credit unless S, the sole shareholder of PD, promises to repay the loan if PD does not. S agrees and C makes the loan. S's undertaking is that of a surety. Similarly, PD wishes to purchase goods on credit from C, the seller, who agrees to extend credit to PD only if he obtains an acceptable surety. S agrees to pay C for the goods if PD does not. S is a surety. In each of these examples, the effect of the surety's promise is to give the creditor recourse for payment against two persons—the principal debtor and the surety—instead of one, thereby reducing the creditor's risk of loss.

Another common instance of a suretyship relation arises when an owner of property subject to a mortgage sells the property to a purchaser who **assumes the mortgage.** By assuming the obligation, the purchaser becomes the principal debtor and is personally obligated to pay the seller's debt to the lender. The seller nevertheless remains liable to the lender and is a surety on the obligation assumed by the purchaser (see Figure 37-7). If the purchaser does *not* assume the mortgage but simply takes the property **"subject to"** the mortgage, the purchaser is *not* personally liable for the mortgage nor is he a surety for the mortgage obligation. In this case, the purchaser's exposure to loss is limited to the value of the property. Although the mortgagee creditor may foreclose against the property, he may not hold the purchaser personally liable for the debt.

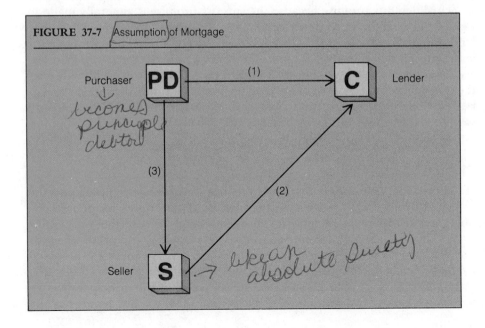

FIGURE 37-7   Assumption of Mortgage

In addition to the more common types of sureties, there are numerous specialized kinds of suretyship, the most important of which are (1) fidelity, (2) performance, (3) official, and (4) judicial. **Fidelity bonds** are undertakings by a surety to protect an employer against the dishonesty of an employee. **Performance bonds** guarantee the performance of the terms and conditions of a contract. These bonds are used frequently in the construction industry to protect the owner from losses that may result from the contractor's failure to perform the building contract. Statutes commonly require that a public officer furnish a bond for the faithful performance of her duties. Such bonds are called **official bonds** and obligate the surety for all losses caused by the officer's negligence or nonperformance of her duties. **Judicial bonds** are provided on behalf of a party to a judicial proceedings to cover losses caused by delay or deprivation of use of property resulting from the institution of the action. In criminal proceedings, the purpose of a judicial bond, called a **bail bond,** is to assure the appearance of the defendant in court.

Formation

The suretyship and guaranty relationship is contractual and must follow all the usual elements of a contract, including offer and acceptance, consideration, capacity of the parties, and legality of object, and it must also come within the provisions of the Statute of Frauds. Nonetheless, no particular words are required to constitute a contract of suretyship or guaranty.

As we discussed in Chapter 13, the contractual promise of a surety to the creditor must be in writing to be enforceable under the **Statute of Frauds.** This requirement applies only to collateral promises and is subject to the exception called the *main purpose doctrine.* Under this doctrine, if the leading object of the promisor (surety) is to obtain an economic benefit that he did not previously enjoy, then the promise is *not* within the Statute of Frauds.

The promise of a surety is *not* binding without **consideration.** The surety's promise is usually supported by the same consideration that supports the principal debtor's promise because the surety's promise is generally made to induce the creditor to confer a benefit on the principal debtor. Thus, if C lends money to PD on S's promise to act as a surety, PD's extension of credit is the consideration to support not only PD's promise to repay the loan but also S's suretyship undertaking. However, if the surety's promise is made *after* the principal debtor's receipt of the creditor's consideration, the surety's promise must be supported by new consideration. Accordingly, if C has already sold goods on credit to PD, a subsequent guaranty by S will not be binding unless new consideration is given.

Rights of Surety

If the principal debtor defaults, the surety has a number of rights against the principal debtor, third parties, and cosureties. These rights include (1) exoneration, (2) reimbursement, (3) subrogation, and (4) contribution. As discussed above, a surety or absolute guarantor has *no* right to compel the creditor to collect from the principal debtor or to take action on collateral provided by the principal debtor. Unless the contract of suretyship provides otherwise, the creditor is *not* required to give the surety notice of the principal debtor's default. A conditional guarantor of collection, on the other hand, has the right that the creditor first sue the principal debtor and exhaust his legal remedies of collection before resorting to the surety.

Exoneration

The ordinary expectation in a suretyship relation is that the principal debtor will perform the obligation and the surety will therefore not be required to perform. Therefore, the surety has the right that his principal debtor pay the creditor when the obligation is due. This right of the surety against the principal debtor is called the right of exoneration and is enforceable at equity. If the principal debtor fails to pay the creditor when the debt is due, the surety may obtain a decree ordering the principal debtor to pay the creditor. The surety's remedy of exoneration is against the principal debtor and in no way affects the creditor's right to proceed against the surety.

Exoneration–relieved of liability

A surety also has a right of exoneration against his cosureties. When the principal debtor's obligation becomes due, each surety owes every other cosurety the duty to pay her proportionate share of the principal debtor's obligation to the creditor. Accordingly, a surety may bring an action in equity against his cosureties for an order requiring them to pay their share.

Reimbursement

When a surety pays the creditor on the default of the principal debtor, the surety has the right of reimbursement against the principal debtor. The surety, however, has no right to reimbursement until he actually has made payment, and then only to the extent of the payment. Thus a surety who makes an advantageous negotiation of a defaulted obligation and settles it at a compromise figure less than the original sum may not recover from the principal debtor any more than he had to pay.

Subrogation

On the surety's payment of the principal debtor's *entire* obligation, the surety "steps into the shoes" of the creditor. This is called subrogation and confers on the surety all the rights the creditor has against or through the principal debtor. These include the creditor's rights

Subrogated–assumes the rights of the creditor

1. against the principal debtor, including the creditor's priorities in a bankruptcy proceeding;

2. in security of the principal debtor;

3. against third parties who are also obligated on the principal debtor's obligation, such as comakers; and

4. against cosureties.

Contribution

When there are more than one surety, the cosureties are *jointly and severally* liable for the principal debtor's default up to the amount of each surety's undertaking. The creditor may proceed against any or all of the cosureties and collect the entire amount of the default from any of them, limited to the amount that surety has agreed to guarantee. As a result, it is possible that one cosurety may pay the creditor the entire amount of the principal debtor's obligation.

Contribution–payment from cosureties of their proportionate share

When a surety pays her principal debtor's obligation, she is entitled to have her cosureties pay to her their proportionate share of the obligation paid. This right of contribution arises when a surety has paid more than her proportionate share of the debt even though the cosureties originally were not aware of each other or were bound on separate instruments. All that is required is that they are sureties for the same principal debtor and the same obligation. The right and extent of contribution is determined by the contractual agreement among the cosureties. If there is no such agreement, sureties obligated for equal amounts share equally; where they are obligated for varying amounts, the proportion of the debt that each surety must contribute is determined by proration according to each surety's undertaking. For example, if X, Y, and Z are cosureties for PD to C in the amounts of $5,000, $10,000, and $15,000 respectively, then X's share of the total is one sixth [$5,000/($5,000 + $10,000 + $15,000)], Y's share is one-third ($10,000/$30,000), and Z's share is one-half ($15,000/$30,000). The following case presents another example of contribution.

COLLINS v. THROCKMORTON

Supreme Court of Delaware, 1980.
425 A.2d 146.

FACTS: Throckmorton and Collins were the sole stockholders (as well as the officers and directors) in Central Ceilings, Inc. ("Central"). On March 26, 1973, Central borrowed $10,000 from the Wilmington Trust Company ("the bank"); a demand note was therefore executed by the corporate officers. On the back of the note, Throckmorton, Collins and their wives unconditionally guaranteed payment of the note. In August 1973, Collins left the employ of Central and ceased to be actively involved in management. By mid-1975, Central became insolvent. Central made no payments on the note after 1973 and the bank became concerned about Central's ability to repay. On May 30, 1975, Throckmorton and his wife took out a $15,402 loan, using $9,668.73 to satisfy the 1973 note. In return, the bank assigned its rights to Throckmorton. Throckmorton then sued both Collins and his wife each for one-quarter of the $9,668.73 plus interest and attorney's fees. The Collinses claim that Throckmorton's wife paid half of the total, or $4,834.16. Of the half that he paid, Throckmorton was only personally liable for half, $2,417.18, or one-quarter of the total. Therefore, he can recover only $2,417.18 total from the Collinses— the excess of the amount he personally paid—not $2,417.18 from each.

DECISION: Judgment for Throckmorton. The general rule governing contribution rights among co-guarantors is that "a surety who has discharged more than his proportionate share of the principal's duty is entitled to contribution from a co-surety." The undisputed facts showed that the 1973 note was guaranteed by four persons. Hence, each was liable for one-quarter of Central's default. The bank's assignment of the note to Throckmorton creates a reasonable inference that, as between him and his wife, he alone was entitled to seek contribution. Thus, Throckmorton can recover $2,417.18 from each of the Collinses. He cannot, however, recover the interest and attorney's fees.

Defenses of Surety ~ *likean expense*

The obligations owed to the creditor by the principal debtor and the surety both arise out of contracts. Accordingly, the usual contractual defenses are applicable, such as those that result from (1) the nonexistence of the principal debtor's obligation, (2) a discharge of the principal debtor's obligation, (3) a modification of the principal debtor's contract, or (4) a variation of the surety's risk. Some of these defenses are available only to the principal debtor, some only to the surety, and others to both parties (see figure 37-8).

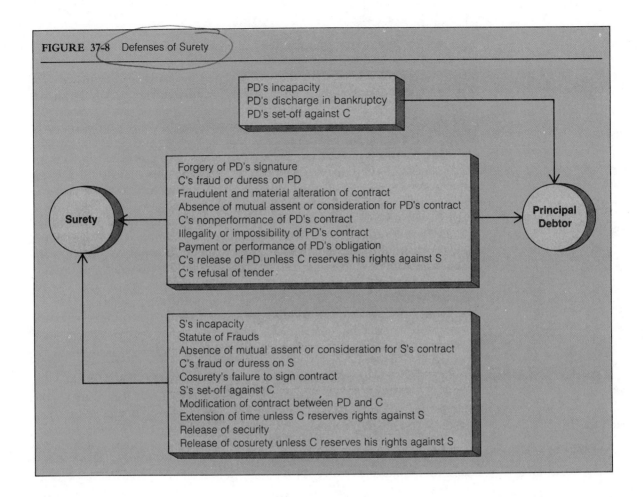

FIGURE 37-8 Defenses of Surety

PD's incapacity
PD's discharge in bankruptcy
PD's set-off against C

Forgery of PD's signature
C's fraud or duress on PD
Fraudulent and material alteration of contract
Absence of mutual assent or consideration for PD's contract
C's nonperformance of PD's contract
Illegality or impossibility of PD's contract
Payment or performance of PD's obligation
C's release of PD unless C reserves his rights against S
C's refusal of tender

S's incapacity
Statute of Frauds
Absence of mutual assent or consideration for S's contract
C's fraud or duress on S
Cosurety's failure to sign contract
S's set-off against C
Modification of contract between PD and C
Extension of time unless C reserves rights against S
Release of security
Release of cosurety unless C reserves his rights against S

Surety

Principal Debtor

Personal Defenses of Principal Debtor

Some defenses that a principal debtor may assert against the creditor are available *only* to him and thus are called personal defenses of the principal debtor. The principal debtor's **incapacity** due to infancy or mental incompetency is a defense for the principal debtor but may *not* be used by the surety. However, if the principal debtor disaffirms the contract *and* returns the consideration he received from the creditor, then the surety is discharged from his liability. A discharge of the principal debtor's obligation in **bankruptcy** also does not discharge the surety's liability to the creditor on that obligation. In addition, the surety may not use as a **set-off** any claim that the principal debtor has against the creditor.

Personal Defenses of Surety

Those defenses that only the surety may assert are called personal defenses of the surety. The surety may use his own **incapacity** as a defense as well as assert noncompliance with the **Statute of Frauds** or the absence of mutual assent and/or consideration. **Fraud** or **duress** practiced by the creditor on the surety is a defense for the surety. Although, as a general rule, nondisclosure of material facts by the creditor to the surety is not fraud, there are two important exceptions. If the prospective surety requests information, the creditor must disclose it, and concealment of material facts will constitute fraud. Second, if the creditor knows, or should know, that the surety is being deceived, the creditor is under a duty to disclose this information, and nondisclosure is considered fraud upon the surety. Fraud on the part of the principal debtor may *not* be asserted against the creditor if the creditor is unaware of the fraud. Similarly, duress exerted by the principal debtor on the surety is not a defense against the creditor.

A surety is not liable if an intended cosurety, as shown by the contract instrument, does not sign. A surety may set off his claims against the creditor if the creditor is solvent. If the creditor is insolvent, then the surety may use his claim against the creditor only if the principal debtor is also insolvent.

If the principal debtor and the creditor enter into a binding **modification** of their contract, the surety is discharged unless he assents to the modification. Most courts hold that even a modification that does not materially affect the surety's risk will discharge the surety. This rule applies to valid and binding extensions of the time of payment *unless* the creditor expressly reserves his rights against the surety. An extension of time with reservation is construed as only an agreement by the creditor not to sue the principal debtor for the period of the extension. Accordingly, the surety's rights of exoneration, reimbursement, and subrogation are *not* postponed. Thus, the surety's risk is not changed and he is not discharged.

As shown in the case below, if the creditor releases or impairs the value of the security, the surety is discharged to the extent of the value of the security released or impaired. Similarly, if the creditor releases a cosurety, the other cosureties are discharged to the extent of the contributive share of the surety released. However, if the creditor reserves his rights against the remaining cosureties, the release is considered a promise not to sue. As a result, the remaining cosureties are not discharged.

LANGEVELD v. L.R.Z.H. CORPORATION

Supreme Court of New Jersey, 1977.
74 N.J. 45, 376 A.2d 931.

FACTS: On March 10, 1972, L.R.Z.H. Corporation made and delivered to Langeveld its promissory note in the sum of $57,500. The indebtedness evidenced by the note was secured by a mortgage in the same amount on real property owned by the corporation. By an instrument of guaranty set forth at the bottom of the note, Higgins guaranteed performance of all obligations of the corporation under the note. The note became due on February 15, 1973 and was not paid. At this time Higgins discovered that Langeveld had never recorded the mortgage securing the note. Langeveld then recorded the mortgage on March 1, 1973. In the intervening year between execution of the mortgage and recordation, another mortgage and two liens in substantial amounts had been filed. Langeveld brought suit against Higgins on the guaranty. Higgins argues that the creditor, Langeveld, owed a duty to him as surety for the debt to protect the security and allow nothing to occur to impair its value. Since Langeveld failed to fulfill this duty, Higgins should be released from all liability on his guaranty.

DECISION: Judgment for Higgins. Generally, a release of collateral held by a creditor, or its impairment by improper action or inaction on his part, extinguishes the surety's obligation, at least to the extent of the value of the security released or impaired. This equitable doctrine is designed to protect the surety's right of subrogation. Upon paying the debt, the surety is as a matter of law, subrogated to all the creditor's rights against the principal debtor. He is also entitled to all benefits derivable from any security of the principal debtor that is in the creditor's possession.

Here, the failure to record the mortgage held as collateral-absent waiver, estoppel, or the like—was an instance of unjustifiable impairment. If the impairment of the collateral can be measured in monetary terms, then the calculated amount of the impairment will measure the extent of Higgins' discharge. However, if the prejudice Higgins sustained is incalculable in monetary terms, then he may be completely discharged.

Defenses of Both Surety and Principal Debtor

A number of defenses are available to both the surety and the principal debtor. Where the principal debtor's signature on an instrument is **forged** or the creditor has exerted **fraud** or **duress** on the principal debtor, neither the principal debtor nor the surety are liable. Likewise, if the contract instrument is fraudulently and **materially altered** by the creditor, both the principal debtor and the surety are discharged.

The absence of mutual assent or consideration to support the principal debtor's obligation is a defense for both the principal debtor and the surety. In addition, **illegality** and **impossibility** of performance of the principal debtor's contract are also defenses to both the surety and the principal debtor.

Payment or **performance** of the principal debtor's obligation discharges both the principal debtor and the surety. If the principal debtor owes several debts to the creditor and makes a payment to the creditor without directions as to which debt to apply payment, the creditor is free to apply it to any debt. For example, PD owes C two debts, one for $5,000 and another for $10,000. S is a surety on the $10,000 debt. PD sends C a payment in the amount of $3,500. If PD directs C to apply the payment to the $10,000 debt, C must apply it accordingly. Otherwise C may, if he pleases, apply the payment to the $5,000 debt.

If the creditor releases the principal debtor, then the surety is also discharged unless the surety consents to the release. However, if the creditor reserves his rights against the surety, the surety is *not* discharged. The release with reservation is construed as a promise not to sue, which leaves the surety's rights against the principal debtor unimpaired. Therefore, the surety is not discharged.

The creditor's refusal to accept tender of payment or performance by either the principal debtor or the surety completely discharges the surety. However, tender of payment by the principal debtor refused by the creditor does *not* discharge the principal debtor. The effect of such refusal is to stop further accrual of interest on the debt and to deprive the creditor of court costs on a subsequent suit by him to recover the amount due.

CHAPTER SUMMARY

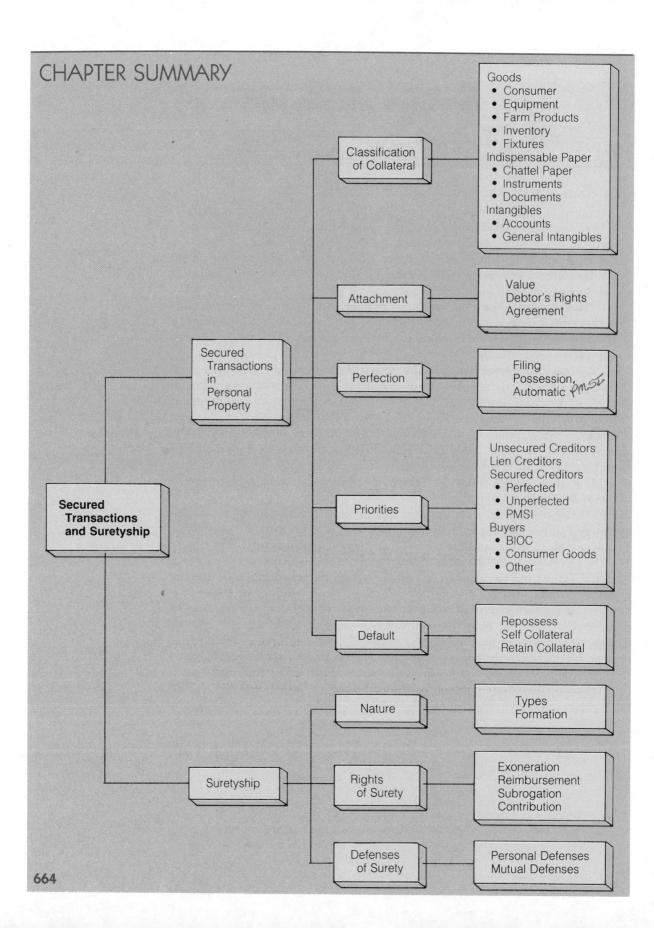

Goods
- Consumer
- Equipment
- Farm Products
- Inventory
- Fixtures

Indispensable Paper
- Chattel Paper
- Instruments
- Documents

Intangibles
- Accounts
- General Intangibles

Classification of Collateral

Attachment

Value
Debtor's Rights
Agreement

Perfection

Filing
Possession,
Automatic *PMSI*

Secured Transactions in Personal Property

Priorities

Unsecured Creditors
Lien Creditors
Secured Creditors
- Perfected
- Unperfected
- PMSI

Buyers
- BIOC
- Consumer Goods
- Other

Default

Repossess
Self Collateral
Retain Collateral

Secured Transactions and Suretyship

Nature

Types
Formation

Suretyship

Rights of Surety

Exoneration
Reimbursement
Subrogation
Contribution

Defenses of Surety

Personal Defenses
Mutual Defenses

KEY TERMS

Secured transaction	Value	Trustee in bankruptcy
Debtor	Debtor's rights in collateral	Buyer in ordinary course of business
Secured party	Agreement	Redemption
Collateral	After-acquired property	Surety
Security agreement	Proceeds	Principal debtor
Security interest	Future advance	Cosurety
Goods	Perfection	Absolute surety
Consumer goods	Filing	Conditional guarantor of collection
Equipment	Financing statement	Exoneration
Farm products	Continuation statement	Reimbursement
Inventory	Certificate of title	Subrogation
Fixture	Central filing	Contribution
Indispensable paper	Local filing	Assume mortgage
Chattel paper	Possession	Subject to mortgage
Instrument	Pledge	Fidelity bond
Document	Field warehouse	Performance bond
Intangible	Automatic perfection	Judicial bond
Account	Purchase money security interest	Official bond
General intangible	Temporary perfection	Bail bond
Attachment	Lien creditor	Personal defense

PROBLEMS

1. A sells to B a refrigerator under a conditional sales contract for $600 payable in monthly installments of $30 for twenty months. The refrigerator is installed in the kitchen of B's apartment. No financing statement is filed. Assume that after B has made the first three monthly payments:

(a) B moves from her apartment and sells the refrigerator in place to the new occupant for $350 cash. What are the rights of A?

(b) B is adjudicated bankrupt, and her trustee in bankruptcy claims the refrigerator. What are the rights of the parties?

2. On January 2, Burt asked Logan to loan him money "against my diamond ring." Logan agreed to do so if a credit check proved Burt to be solvent. To guard against intervening liens, Logan received permission to record his interest, and Burt and Logan signed a security agreement giving Logan an interest in the ring. Burt also signed a financing statement, which Logan properly filed on January 3. On January 4, Burt borrowed money from Tillo, pledging his ring to secure the debt. Tillo took possession of the ring and paid Burt the money on the same day. The next day, January 5, Logan received a favorable credit report on Burt and loaned him the money under the assumption that Burt still had the ring.

Who has priority, Logan or Tillo?

3. A takes a security interest in the equipment in X Store and files a financing statement claiming "equipment and all after-acquired equipment." B later sells X Store a cash register on conditional sale and (a) files nine days after X receives the register, or (b) files fifteen days after X receives the register. If X fails to pay both A and B and they foreclose their security interests, who has priority as to the cash register?

4. X Motor Company sells an automobile to A and retains a security interest in it. The automobile is insured, and X is named beneficiary. The automobile is totally destroyed in an accident, and three days later A files a petition in bankruptcy. Who is entitled to the insurance proceeds, X or A's trustee in bankruptcy?

5. On September 5, W, a widow who occasionally teaches piano and organ in her home, purchased an electric organ from M's music store for $4,800, trading in her old organ for $1,200 and promising in writing to pay the balance at $120 per month and granting to M a security interest in the property in terms consistent with and incorporating provisions of the UCC. A financing statement covering the transaction was also properly filled out and signed, and M properly filed it. W did not make the December or January payments, and M went to her home to collect the payments or take the organ. Finding no one home and the door unlocked, he went in and took the organ. Two hours later, T a third party and the present occupant of the house who had purchased the organ for his own use, stormed into M's store demanding return of the organ and exhibited a bill of sale from W to T dated December 15 that listed the organ and other furnishings in the house.

(a) What are the rights of M, T, and W?

(b) Would your answer change if M did not file a financing statement? Why?

6. On May 1, A lends B $20,000 and receives from B his promissory note for this amount due in two years and takes a security interest in the machinery and equipment in B's factory. A proper financing statement is filed with respect to the security agreement. On August 1, on A's request, B executes an addendum to the security agreement covering after-acquired machinery and equipment in B's factory. A second financing statement is filed covering the addendum. In September B acquires $5,000 worth of new equipment, which he installs in his factory. In December, C, a judgment creditor of B, causes an attachment to issue against the new equipment. What are the rights of the parties?

7. A bought a television set from B for her own personal use. B was out of conditional sales contracts and showed A a form B had executed with C, another consumer. A and B orally agreed to the terms of the form. A subsequently defaults on payment, and B seeks to repossess the television. Decision? Would the result differ if B had filed a financing statement?

8. A bought a television set for his own personal use from B. A properly signed a security agreement and paid B $25 down as required by their agreement. B did not file a financing statement, and subsequently A sells the television to C, A's neighbor, for $300 for C to use in her hotel lobby.

(a) When A fails to make the January and February payments, may B repossess the television from C?

(b) What if, instead of A's selling the television set to C, a judgment creditor levied (sought possession) of the television? Who would prevail?

9. Peter Diamond owes Carter $500,000 secured by a first mortgage on Diamond's plant and land. Stephens is a surety on this obligation in the amount of $250,000. After Diamond defaulted on the debt, Carter demanded and received payment of $250,000 from Stephens. Carter then foreclosed on the mortgage and sold the property for $375,000. What rights, if any, does Stephens have in the proceeds from the sale of the property?

10. Allen, Barker, and Cooper are cosureties on a $750,000 loan by Durham National Bank to Kingston Manufacturing Co., Inc. The maximum liability of the sureties is as follows: Allen, $750,000, Barker, $300,000, and Cooper, $150,000. If Kingston defaults on the entire $750,000 loan, what is the liability of Allen, Barker, and Cooper?

BANKRUPTCY

A debt is an obligation to pay money owed by a debtor to a creditor. Debts are created daily in countless purchases of goods at the consumer level; by retailers of goods in buying merchandise from a manufacturer, wholesaler, or distributor; and through the issuance and sale of debentures, corporate mortgage bonds, and other types of debt securities. An enormous volume of business transactions is entered into daily on a credit basis. Commercial activity would be restricted and greatly diminished if credit were not readily obtainable or needed funds not available for lending.

Fortunately, most debts are paid when due, thus justifying the extension of credit and encouraging its continuation. Defaults may create credit and collection problems, but normally the total amount in default represents a very small percentage of the total amount of outstanding indebtedness. Nevertheless, both individuals and corporations encounter financial crises and business misfortune. An individual or a business unit may be confronted by an accumulation of debts that exceeds total assets. Or it may have assets in excess of total indebtedness but have the assets in such noncash form that the debtor is unable to pay his debts as they mature. Relief from pressing debt and from the threat of impending lawsuits by creditors is frequently necessary for economic survival.

Various solutions to the conflict between creditor rights and debtor relief have developed, such as voluntary adjustments and compromises requiring payment in installments to creditors over a period of time during which they agree to withhold legal action. Other voluntary methods include compositions and assignments of assets by a debtor to a trustee or assignee for the benefit of creditors. Equity receiverships or insolvency proceedings are sometimes filed by creditors in a State court according to statute. Nonetheless, the most adaptable and frequently used method of debtor relief—one that also affords protection to creditors—is by a proceeding in a Federal court under the Bankruptcy Act.

Federal Bankruptcy Law

Bankruptcy legislation serves a dual purpose: (1) to bring about an **equitable distribution** of the debtor's property among her creditors, and (2) to **discharge** the debtor from her debts and enable her to rehabilitate herself

667

and start afresh. Other purposes are to provide uniform treatment of creditors, preserve existing business relations, stabilize commercial usages, and bring about a speedy, as well as equitable, distribution of the debtor's assets.

Article I of the Constitution of the United States states: "The Congress shall have power ... to establish ... uniform Laws on the subject of Bankruptcies throughout the United States." Under this power congress has enacted or substantially revised bankruptcy acts in 1800, 1841, 1867, 1898, and 1938. Federal bankruptcy law has generally superseded State insolvency laws.

In 1978 Congress again enacted a major revision of the Bankruptcy Act. The **Bankruptcy Reform Act of 1978,** which we will refer to as the Bankruptcy Act, became effective on October 1, 1979. It was amended in several important respects by the Bankruptcy Amendments and Federal Judgeship Act of 1984.

The Bankruptcy Act consists of eight odd-numbered chapters:

CHAPTER	TITLE
1	General Provisions
3	Case Administration
✳ 5	Creditors, the Debtor, and the Estate
✳ 7	Liquidation
9	Adjustment of Debts of a Municipality
✳11	Reorganization
✳13	Adjustment of Debts of an Individual with Regular Income
15	United States Trustees

Chapters 7, 9, 11, and 13 provide four different types of proceedings, whereas Chapters 1, 3, and 5 apply to all four proceedings. **Straight,** or ordinary, **bankruptcy** (Chapter 7) provides for liquidation and termination of the business of the debtor, whereas the other proceedings provide for **reorganization** and continuance of the business of the debtor.

Chapter 7 applies to *all* debtors, with the exception of railroads, insurance companies, banks, savings and loan associations, homestead associations, and credit unions. Moreover, Chapter 7 has special provisions for the liquidation of the estates of stockbrokers and commodity brokers. Any person that may be a debtor under Chapter 7 (except stockbrokers and commodity brokers) as well as railroads may be a debtor under Chapter 11. Chapter 9, however, applies only to a municipality that is generally authorized to be a debtor under that chapter, that is insolvent, and that desires to effect a plan to adjust its debts. Chapter 13 applies to individuals with regular income who owe liquidated unsecured debts of less than $100,000 and secured debts of less than $350,000.

The Act had established a new bankruptcy court system which was held by the United States Supreme Court to have been granted powers in violation of Article III of the U.S. Constitution. *Northern Pipeline Co. v. Marathon Pipe Line Co.,* 458 U.S. 50 (1982). The Bankruptcy Amendments Act of 1984 restructured the bankruptcy court system in an attempt to satisfy the constitutional considerations raised by the *Marathon* case. As amended, the Bankruptcy Act grants to U.S. district courts original and exclusive jurisdiction over all bankruptcy cases and original, but not exclusive, jurisdiction over civil proceedings arising under bankruptcy cases. The district court must abstain from related matters that, but for bankruptcy, could not have been brought in a Federal court. The district court in which a bankruptcy case is commenced has exclusive jurisdiction of all of the debtor's property. In addition, a bankruptcy court staffed by bankruptcy judges is established as a unit of each Federal district court. Bankruptcy courts are authorized to hear certain matters specified by the Act and to enter appropriate orders and judgments subject to review by the district court, or where established, a panel of three bankruptcy judges. The Circuit Court of Appeals has jurisdiction over appeals from the district court or panel. In all other matters, unless the parties assent, only the district court may issue a final order or judgment that is based upon proposed findings of fact and conclusions of law submitted to the district court by the bankruptcy judge.

Case Administration—Chapter 3

Chapter 3 of the Bankruptcy Act contains provisions dealing with the commencement of the case, the officers that administer the case, the meetings of creditors, and the administrative powers of the various officers.

Commencement of the Case

The jurisdiction of the bankruptcy court and the operation of the bankruptcy laws are begun by the filing of a voluntary or involuntary petition.

Voluntary Petitions   Most petitions are filed voluntarily. Any person eligible to be a debtor under a given bankruptcy proceeding may file a voluntary petition under that chapter. Moreover, the debtor need *not* be insolvent to file the petition. The commencement of a voluntary case constitutes an automatic **order for relief.** A voluntary petition includes a list of all creditors both secured and unsecured, a list of all property owned by the debtor, a list of property claimed by the debtor to be exempt, and a statement of the debtor's affairs.

Involuntary Petitions   An involuntary petition in bankruptcy may be filed only under Chapter 7 or 11. It may be filed (1) by three or more creditors who have unsecured claims that total $5,000 or more or (2) if there are less than twelve creditors of the debtor, by one or more creditors whose total claims equal $5,000 or more. However, an involuntary petition may not be filed against a farmer or a banking, insurance, or nonprofit corporation.

If the debtor does not contest the involuntary petition, the court will enter an order for relief against the debtor. However, if the debtor opposes the petition, the court may enter an order of relief only if (1) the debtor is generally not paying his debts as they become due or (2) within 120 days before the filing of the petition a custodian or receiver took possession of substantially all of the debtor's property to enforce a lien against that property.

Automatic Stays

The filing of a voluntary or involuntary petition operates as a stay against (that is, it prevents) attempts by creditors to begin or continue to recover claims against the debtor, to enforce judgments against the debtor, or to create or enforce liens against property of the debtor. This stay applies to both secured and unsecured creditors, although a secured creditor may petition the court to terminate the stay as to her security on showing that she lacks adequate protection in the secured property.

Trustees

The trustee is the representative of the estate and has the capacity to sue and be sued. In proceedings under Chapter 7, trustees are selected by a vote of the creditors; in all other proceedings the trustee is appointed by the court. The trustee is responsible for collecting, liquidating, and distributing the debtor's estate. The duties and powers of the trustee include (1) to use, sell, or lease property of the estate; (2) to deposit or invest money of the estate; (3) to employ attorneys, accountants, appraisers, or auctioneers, and (4) to assume or reject any executory contract or unexpired lease of the debtor.

in Ch. 7 need only to distribute assets

Meetings of Creditors

Within a reasonable time after relief is ordered, a meeting of creditors must be held. The court may not attend this meeting. The debtor must appear and submit to an examination by creditors and the trustee of his financial situation. In a proceeding under Chapter 7, qualified creditors at this meeting elect the permanent trustee.

Creditors, the Debtor, and the Estate—Chapter 5

Creditors

Creditor–any entity having a claim against the debtor

Claim–a right to payment

The Bankruptcy Act defines a creditor as any entity that has a claim against the debtor that arose at the time of or before the order for relief. A **claim** means a right to payment.

Proof of Claims Creditors may file a proof of claim. If a creditor does not do so in a timely manner, then the debtor or trustee may file a proof of such claim. Claims that are filed are allowed unless a party who has an interest objects. If an objection to a claim is made, the court determines after a hearing the amount and validity of the claim. The court will not allow any claim that (1) is unenforceable against the debtor or his property, (2) is for unmatured interest, (3) may be offset against a debt owing the debtor, or (4) is for services of an insider or attorney in excess of the reasonable value of such services. An **insider** includes a relative or general partner of a debtor as well as a partnership in which the debtor is a general partner or a corporation of which the debtor is a director, officer, or person in control.

lien - right to payment

Secured claim–claim with a lien on property of the debtor

Secured Claims An allowed claim of a creditor who has a lien on property of the estate is a secured claim to the extent of the value of the creditor's interest in the property. The creditor's claim is unsecured to the extent that the value of his interest is less than the allowed amount of his claim. Thus, if A has an allowed claim of $5,000 against the estate of debtor B and has a security interest in property of the estate that is valued at $3,000, A has a secured claim in the amount of $3,000 and an unsecured claim for $2,000.

Priority–the right of a claim to be paid before claims of lesser rank

Priority of Claims After secured claims have been satisfied, the remaining assets are distributed among creditors with unsecured claims. However, certain classes of unsecured claims have a **priority,** which means that they must be paid in full before any distribution is made to claims of lesser rank. The claims having a priority and the order of their priority are as follows:

1. **expenses of administration** of the debtor's estate, including the filing fees paid by creditors in involuntary cases; the expenses of creditors in recovering concealed assets for the benefit of the bankrupt's estate; the trustee's necessary expenses; and reasonable compensation to receivers, trustees, and their attorneys as allowed by the court

2. unsecured claims in an involuntary case arising in the ordinary course of the debtor's business after the commencement of the case but before the earlier of the appointment of the trustee or the order for relief (such claimants are referred to as **"gap" creditors**)

3. allowed, unsecured claims up to $2,000 for **wages, salaries, or commissions** earned within ninety days before the filing of the petition or the date of cessation of the debtor's business, whichever comes first

4. allowed, unsecured claims for contributions to **employee benefit plans** arising from services rendered within 180 days before the filing of the petition or the cessation of the debtor's business, whichever occurs first, but limited to $2,000 multiplied by the number of employees covered by the plan

5. allowed, unsecured claims up to $2,000 for **grain** or **fish producers** against a storage facility

6. allowed, unsecured claims up to $900 for **consumer deposits,** that is moneys deposited in connection with the purchase, lease, or rental of property or the purchase of services for personal, family, or household use

7. specified amounts owed to governmental units for income, property, employment, or excise **taxes**

After creditors with secured claims and creditors with claims having a priority have been satisfied, creditors with allowed, unsecured claims share proportionately in any remaining assets.

Subordination of Claims   In addition to statutory and contract priorities, the bankruptcy court itself can, at its discretion in proper cases, apply equitable priorities. This is accomplished through the doctrine of subordination of claims, whereby, assuming two claims of equal statutory priority, the bankruptcy court declares that one claim must be paid in full before the other claim can be paid anything. Subordination is applied in cases where allowing a claim in full would be unfair and inequitable to other creditors, such as to allow the inflated salary claims of officers in closely held corporations. In such cases, the court does not disallow the claim but merely orders it paid after all other claims are paid in full.

The claim of a parent corporation against its bankrupt subsidiary corporation may be subordinated to the claims of other creditors of the subsidiary in cases where the parent has been guilty of mismanaging the subsidiary to the detriment of its innocent creditors in a manner so unconscionable as to preclude the parent from seeking the aid of a bankruptcy court. For example, assume that corporation ABC owns all of the capital stock of corporation XYZ. Assume further that whenever XYZ shows a profit, the profit is taken out of XYZ and transferred to ABC by means of questionable intercorporate transactions; whenever XYZ shows a loss and ABC is required to put some money back into XYZ, it does so by "lending" the money to XYZ. Over a period of time, ABC takes $500,000 out of XYZ and puts $100,000 back. When XYZ goes into bankruptcy, ABC has a claim of $100,000, while outside creditors have claims aggregating $100,000. If the assets total $100,000, ABC will receive $50,000 and the other creditors $50,000. Since ABC has already received $500,000, it is clearly unfair for it to receive an additional $50,000 at the expense of the other creditors. The bankruptcy court can exercise its equity power of subordinating claims and subordinate ABC's claim to that of the other creditors, so that the other creditors will receive the entire $100,000 and ABC will receive nothing until the prior claims are paid in full.

Debtors

As indicated, the purpose of the Bankruptcy Act is to bring about an equitable distribution of the debtor's assets and to provide a discharge to the debtor. Accordingly, the Act explicitly subjects the debtor to specified duties while exempting some of his property and discharging most of his debts.

Debtor's Duties   Under the Bankruptcy Act the debtor must file a list of creditors, a schedule of assets and liabilities, and a statement of her financial affairs. In any case in which a trustee is serving, the debtor must cooperate with the trustee and surrender to the trustee all property of the estate and all records relating to property of the estate.

Debtor's Exemptions   The Bankruptcy Act exempts specified property of an individual debtor from the bankruptcy proceedings, including the following:

1. up to $7,500 in equity in property used as a residence or burial plot;

2. up to $1,200 in equity in one motor vehicle;

3. up to $200 for any particular item of household furnishings, household goods, wearing apparel, appliances, books, animals, crops, or musical instruments that are primarily for personal, family, or household use;

4. up to $500 in jewelry;

5. any property up to $400 plus any unused amount of the first exemption;

6. up to $750 in implements, professional books, or tools of the debtor's trade;

7. unmatured life insurance contracts owned by debtor other than a credit life insurance contract;

8. professionally prescribed health aids;

9. social security, veterans, and disability benefits;

10. unemployment compensation;

11. alimony and support payments, including child support;

12. payments from pension, profit-sharing, and annuity plans; and

13. payments from an award under a crime victim's reparation law, a wrongful death award, and up to $7,500, not including pain and suffering or compensation for actual pecuniary loss, from a personal injury award.

The debtor has the option of using either the exemptions provided by the Bankruptcy Act or those available under State law. Nevertheless, a State may by specific legislative action deny to its citizens the use of the Federal exemptions and limit them to the exemptions provided by State law. More than two-thirds of the States have enacted such legislation.

Discharge Discharge is the termination of all dischargeable debts of the debtor for allowed claims. Certain debts, however, are nondischargeable under the Act. A discharge of a debt voids any judgment obtained at any time concerning that debt and operates as an injunction against the commencement or continuation of any action to recover that debt.

Discharge–termination of certain allowed claims against a debtor

No private employer may terminate the employment of, or discriminate with respect to employment against, an individual who is or has been a debtor under the Bankruptcy Act solely because such debtor (1) is or has been a debtor under the Bankruptcy Act; (2) has been insolvent before the commencement of a case or during the case; or (3) has not paid a debt that is dischargeable in a case under the Bankruptcy Act.

An agreement between a debtor and a creditor permitting the creditor to enforce a discharged debt is enforceable to the extent State law permits but only if (1) the agreement was made before the discharge has been granted; (2) the debtor has not rescinded the agreement within thirty days after it becomes enforceable; (3) the court has informed a debtor who is an individual that he is not required to enter into such an agreement and explains the legal effect of the agreement; and (4) if the debt is a consumer debt, the court approves the agreement as not imposing an undue hardship on the debtor and as being in the debtor's best interest.

The following debts are **not dischargeable** in bankruptcy:

1. certain taxes and customs duties;

2. legal liabilities for obtaining money or property by false pretenses or false representations;

3. legal liability for wilful and malicious injuries to the person or property of another;

4. alimony and support of spouse or child;

5. debts not scheduled, unless the creditor knew of the bankruptcy;

6. debts created by the fraud or embezzlement of the debtor while acting in a fiduciary capacity;

7. student loans that first became due less than five years before the filing of the petition; and

8. debts that were or could have been listed in a previous bankruptcy in which the debtor waived or was denied a discharge;

9. consumer debts for luxury goods in excess of $500 per creditor if incurred by an individual debtor on or within forty days before the order for relief;

10. cash advances aggregating more than $1,000 obtained by an individual debtor under an open end credit plan within twenty days before the order for relief; and

11. liability for a court judgment based upon the debtor's operation of a motor vehicle while legally intoxicated.

To illustrate: D files a petition in bankruptcy. D owes A $1,500, B $2,500, and C $3,000. A's claim is not dischargeable in bankruptcy while B's and C's claims are. A receives $180 from the liquidation of D's bankruptcy estate, B receives $300, and C receives $360. If D receives a bankruptcy discharge, B and C will be precluded from pursuing D for the remainder of their claims

($2,200 and $2,640 respectively). A, on the other hand, because his debt is not dischargeable, may pursue D for the remaining $1,320 subject to the applicable statute of limitations. If D does *not* receive a discharge, A, B and C may all pursue D for the unpaid portion of their claims.

The Estate

Estate–all legal and equitable interests of a debtor in nonexempt property

The commencement of a bankruptcy case creates an estate consisting of all legal and equitable interests of the debtor in nonexempt property at that time. The estate also includes property that the debtor acquires within 180 days after the commencement of the case by inheritance or as a beneficiary of a life insurance policy. In addition, the estate includes property that the trustee recovers under her powers (1) as a lien creditor, (2) to avoid voidable preferences, (3) to avoid fraudulent transfers, and (4) to avoid statutory liens.

Judicial lien–interest in property to secure payment of a debt that is obtained by court action

Trustee as Lien Creditor   When the case commences, the trustee gains the rights and powers of any creditor with a judicial lien against the debtor that is returned unsatisfied, whether or not such a creditor exists. A **judicial lien** is a charge or interest in property to secure payment of a debt or performance of an obligation that is obtained by judgment, levy, or some other legal or equitable process. The trustee is made an ideal creditor possessing every right and power conferred by the law of the State on its most favored creditor who has acquired a lien by legal or equitable proceedings. The trustee does not need to locate an actual existing lien creditor, for the trustee assumes the rights and powers of a purely hypothetical lien creditor.

trustee become one of highest priority creditors

For example, Farley, the debtor, grants a security interest in goods purchased on credit to Marge, the seller. Marge fails to perfect the security interest before Farley files a voluntary petition. Angela, the trustee, would assume the status of a lien creditor who has priority over an unperfected security interest. As a consequence, Marge would be denied standing as a secured creditor and would become an unsecured creditor.

Voidable Preferences   The Bankruptcy Act invalidates certain preferential transfers from the debtor to favored creditors before the date of bankruptcy. The trustee may recover any transfer of property of the debtor

can't pay! prefer' creditor over others

1. to or for the benefit of a creditor;

2. for or on account of an antecedent debt owed by the debtor before the transfer was made;

3. made while the debtor was insolvent;

4. made on or within ninety days before the date of the filing of the petition; or, if the creditor was an "insider" as previously defined, within one year of the date of the filing of the petition; and

5. that enables such creditor to receive more than he would have received under Chapter 7.

A transfer is any means, whether direct or indirect, voluntary or involuntary, of disposing of property or an interest in property, including the retention of title as a security interest. It is presumed that the debtor has been insolvent on and during the ninety days immediately preceding the date of the filing of the petition. **Insolvency** is a financial condition of a debtor such that the sum of its debts is greater than all of its property at fair valuation.

Insolvency–financial condition where debts exceed fair value of assets

Not all transfers made within ninety days of bankruptcy are voidable, however. For example, if sixty days before the petition is filed the debtor purchases an automobile for $9,000, this transfer of property (i.e., the $9,000) is *not* voidable because it was not made for an antecedent debt but rather as a contemporaneous exchange for new value. Similarly, if within ninety days of the filing of the petition the debtor purchases a refrigerator on credit and grants the seller a security interest in the refrigerator, the transfer of that interest is not voidable if the secured party perfects within ten days after the security interest attaches. In addition, the trustee may *not* avoid a transfer made (1) in payment of a debt incurred in the ordinary course of business of the debtor and the transferee, (2) not later than forty-five days after the debt was incurred, and (3) according to ordinary business terms.

FACTS: Freelin Conn filed a voluntary petition under Chapter 7 of the Bankruptcy Code on September 30, 1980. Conn listed BancOhio National Bank as having a claim incurred in October of 1979 in the amount of $4,000 secured by a 1978 Oldsmobile Omega. The car is listed as having a market value of $3,500. During the period from June 30, 1980 to September 30, 1980, Conn made three payments totaling $439.17 to BancOhio. The net payoff balance on the installment loan was $4,015.91 on September 30 when the bankruptcy petition was filed. The trustee in bankruptcy now seeks to set aside those three payments as voidable preferences.

DECISION: Judgment for BancOhio. The trustee may avoid the transfer from Conn to BancOhio only if he can show that all five elements of a voidable preference are met. BancOhio has admitted that the first four elements are present. The trustee, however, has failed to show the final element—that the effect of the payments was to enable the creditor to obtain a greater percentage of its debt than it would receive under Chapter 7 of the Bankruptcy Code. BancOhio's claim is secured to the extent of the value of the collateral, the Omega. The market value of the car was listed at $3,500. Conn, however, claims that it is worth much more, and the trustee did not show that it was worth less than BancOhio's claim of $4,015.91. Thus, the value of the car is held to be equal to the amount of BancOhio's claim, and therefore, it has a fully secured claim. Since the trustee did not establish that the transfer enabled BancOhio to recover more on its claim than other secured creditors, the transfer is not a voidable preference, and the trustee may not recover the payments made to BancOhio.

IN RE CONN

United States Bankruptcy
Court, N.D. Ohio, 1981.
9 B.R. 431.

Fraudulent Transfers The trustee may avoid fraudulent transfers made on or within one year before the date of the filing of the petition. One type of fraudulent transfer consists of the debtor's transferring property with the actual intent to hinder, delay, or defraud any of her creditors. Another type of a fraudulent transfer is the transfer by the debtor of property for less than a reasonably equivalent consideration while she is insolvent or would become insolvent because of the transfer. For example, Carol, who is in debt, transfers title to her house to Wallace, her father, without any payment by Wallace to Carol and with the understanding that when the house is no longer in danger of seizure by creditors, Wallace will reconvey it to Carol. The transfer of the house by Carol to Wallace is a fraudulent transfer.

Statutory Liens The trustee may avoid a statutory lien on property of the debtor if the lien (1) first becomes effective when the debtor becomes insolvent *or* (2) is not perfected or enforceable on the date of the filing of the petition against a *bona fide* purchaser. A statutory lien is a lien that arises solely by force of a statute and does *not* include a security interest or judicial lien.

Statutory lien–interest in property to secure payment of a debt that arises solely by statute

Liquidation—Chapter 7

To accomplish its dual goals of distributing the debtor's property fairly and providing the debtor with a fresh start, the Bankruptcy Act has established two approaches: liquidation and adjustment of debts. Chapter 7 concerns liquidation, whereas Chapters 11 and 13, discussed below, concern the adjustment of debts. Liquidation involves the termination of the business of the debtor, distribution of his nonexempt assets, and usually a discharge of all dischargeable debts of the debtor.

Proceedings

Proceedings under Chapter 7 apply to all debtors except railroads, insurance companies, banks, savings and loan associations, homestead associations and credit unions. Once a voluntary or involuntary petition has been filed, the court must determine whether to enter an order for relief. If an order is entered, the court appoints an interim trustee, who serves until a permanent trustee is selected by the creditors. Under Chapter 7, the trustee collects and reduces to money the property of the estate; accounts for all property received; investigates the financial affairs of the debtor; examines and, if appropriate, challenges proofs of claims; opposes, if advisable, the discharge of the debtor; and makes a final report of the administration of the estate.

The creditors may also elect a committee of not fewer than three and not more than eleven unsecured creditors that may consult with the trustee, make recommendations to him, and submit questions to the court.

Distribution of the Estate

After the trustee has collected all the assets of the debtor's estate, she distributes them to the creditors and, if any assets remain, to the debtor in the following order:

1. Secured creditors are paid on their security interests.
2. Creditors entitled to a priority are paid in the order provided.
3. Payment is made to unsecured creditors who filed their claims on time.
4. Payment is made to unsecured creditors who filed their claims late.
5. Claims for multiple, exemplary, or punitive damages are paid.
6. Interest at the legal rate from the date of the filing of the petition is paid to all of the above claimants.
7. Whatever property remains is distributed to the debtor.

Claims of the same rank are paid proportionately. For example: D has filed a petition for a Chapter 7 proceeding. The total value of D's estate *after* paying the expenses of administration is $25,000. E, who is owed $15,000, has a security interest in property valued at $10,000. F has an unsecured claim of $6,000, which is entitled to a priority of $2,000. The United States has a claim for income taxes of $4,000. G has an unsecured claim of $9,000 that was filed on time. H has an unsecured claim of $12,000 that was filed on time. J has a claim of $8,000 that was not filed on time even though J was aware of the bankruptcy proceedings. The distribution would be as follows:

1. E receives $11,500
2. F receives $3,200

3. United States receives $4,000

4. G receives $2,700

5. H receives $3,600

6. J receives $0

E receives $10,000 as a secured creditor and has an unsecured claim of $5,000. F receives $2,000 on the portion of his claim entitled to a priority and has an unsecured claim of $4,000. The United States has a priority of $4,000. After paying $10,000 to E, $2,000 to F, and $4,000 to the United States, there remains $9,000 ($25,000—$10,000—$2,000—$4,000) to be distributed *pro rata* to unsecured creditors who filed on time. Their claims total $30,000 (E = $5,000, F = $4,000, G = $9,000 and H = $12,000). Therefore, each will receive $\frac{\$9,000}{\$30,000}$ or 30¢ on the dollar. Accordingly, E receives an additional $1,500, F receives an additional $1,200, G receives $2,700, and H receives $3,600. Because there were insufficient assets to pay all unsecured claimants who filed on time, J, who filed tardily, receives nothing.

Figure 38-1 summaries the collection and distribution of the debtor's estate.

Discharge

After distribution of the estate, the court will grant the debtor a discharge unless the debtor

1. is not an individual;

2. has destroyed, falsified, concealed, or failed to keep books of account and records;

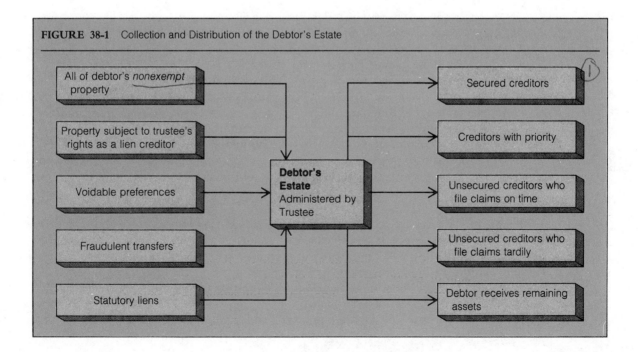

FIGURE 38-1   Collection and Distribution of the Debtor's Estate

All of debtor's *nonexempt* property

Property subject to trustee's rights as a lien creditor

Voidable preferences

Fraudulent transfers

Statutory liens

Debtor's Estate Administered by Trustee

Secured creditors

Creditors with priority

Unsecured creditors who file claims on time

Unsecured creditors who file claims tardily

Debtor receives remaining assets

3. has knowingly and fraudulently made a false oath or account, presented or used a false claim, or given or received bribes;

4. has transferred, removed, destroyed, or concealed any of his property with intent to hinder, delay, or defraud his creditors within twelve months before the filing of the bankruptcy petition;

5. has within six years before the bankruptcy been granted a discharge;

6. has refused to obey any lawful order of the court or to answer any question approved by the court;

7. has failed to explain satisfactorily any losses of assets or deficiency of assets to meet his liabilities; or

8. has executed a written waiver of discharge approved by the court.

On request of the trustee or a creditor and after notice and a hearing, the court may revoke a discharge within one year if it was obtained through the fraud of the debtor.

Reorganization—Chapter 11

Reorganization is the means by which a distressed business enterprise and its value as a going concern are preserved through the correction or elimination of the factors that brought about its distress. Chapter 11 of the Bankruptcy Act governs reorganization of eligible debtors, including partnerships and corporations, and permits restructuring of their capital structure. The main objective of a reorganization proceeding is to develop and carry out a fair, equitable, and feasible (workable) plan of reorganization. After a plan has been prepared and filed, a hearing is held before the court to determine whether or not it will be confirmed.

Proceedings

Any person that may be a debtor under Chapter 7 (except stockbrokers and commodity brokers) and railroads may be a debtor under Chapter 11. Petitions may be voluntary or involuntary.

As soon as possible after the order for relief, the court will appoint a committee of unsecured creditors. This committee usually consists of persons that hold the seven largest claims against the debtor. In addition, the court may appoint additional committees of creditors or of equity security holders if necessary to assure adequate representation. The committee may, with the court's approval, employ attorneys, accountants, and other agents to represent or perform services for the committee. The committee should consult with the debtor or trustee concerning the administration of the case and may investigate the debtor's affairs and participate in formulating a reorganization plan.

The debtor will remain in possession and management of the property of the estate unless the court appoints a trustee, who may then operate the debtor's business. The court will appoint a trustee only for cause (including fraud, dishonesty, incompetence, or gross mismanagement of the debtor's affairs) or if the appointment is in the interests of creditors or equity security holders.

The duties of a trustee in a case under Chapter 11 are

1. to be accountable for all property received;

2. to examine proof of claims;

3. to furnish information to all parties with an interest;

4. to provide the court and taxing authorities with financial reports of the business operations;

5. to make a final report and account of the administration of the estate;

6. to investigate the financial condition of the debtor and the desirability of the continuance of the debtor's business; and

7. to file a plan or a report on why there will be no plan or to recommend conversion of the case to Chapter 7.

The Bankruptcy Amendments Act added a new provision dealing with the rejection of collective bargaining agreements. It provides that subsequent to filing and prior to seeking such rejection, the trustee or debtor-in-possession must make a proposal for the necessary modifications of the labor contract that will enable reorganization of the debtor and also provide for the fair and equitable treatment of all of the parties concerned. The provision also requires that good faith meetings to reach a mutually satisfactory agreement be held between management and the union. It authorizes the court to approve rejection of the collective bargaining agreement only if the court finds that the proposal was made in accordance with these conditions, that the union refused the proposal without good cause, and that the balance of equities clearly favors rejection of such agreement.

Plan of Reorganization

The debtor may file a plan at any time and has the exclusive right to file a plan during the 120 days after the order for relief, unless a trustee has been appointed. Then other parties in interest, including the trustee or a creditors' committee, may file a plan.

A plan of reorganization must divide creditor's claims and shareholder's interests into classes, specify how each class will be treated, and deal with each class equally. After a plan has been filed, the plan and a written disclosure statement approved by the court as containing adequate information must be transmitted to each holder of a claim before seeking acceptance or rejection of the plan.

Acceptance of Plan

Each class of claims and interests has the opportunity to accept or reject the proposed plan. A **class of claims** has accepted a plan if it has been accepted by creditors that hold at least two-thirds in amount and more than one-half of the allowed claims of such class. Acceptance of a plan by a **class of interests,** such as shareholders, requires acceptance by holders of at least two-thirds in amount of the allowed interests of such class.

A class that is not impaired under a plan is deemed to have accepted the plan. Basically, a class is not impaired if the plan leaves unaltered the legal, equitable, and contractual rights to which such claim or interest entitles the holder of that claim or right.

Law In The News

Bankruptcy: No Longer a Sure Escape From Union Contracts

Courts are enforcing tough new standards that make it harder for troubled firms to ditch their labor agreements.

A financially troubled company's quickest way out of an onerous labor contract used to be to declare bankruptcy. That gambit is no longer working.

Changes made by Congress last year in the nation's bankruptcy laws now cause many companies to think twice about asking bankruptcy courts to let them scrap collective-bargaining pacts.

The reason: It's no easy matter getting out of a contract. Firms filing for bankruptcy are being scrutinized as never before by bankruptcy judges, often with rulings unfavorable to employers—

■ A commuter airline in Ohio was denied immediate relief from a union agreement because it could not show that such help was essential to staying in business.

■ A bankruptcy court in Minnesota would not let a food-products supplier repudiate its collective-bargaining agreement and reduce hourly wages from $11.50 to $8. The court said the pay cut would amount to only 2 percent of the firm's costs.

■ A New York maker of fiberglass products lost its bid for relief from a labor pact because, in the court's view, the firm's own financial analysis and revenue projections, plus the union's willingness to grant concessions, made voiding the agreement unnecessary.

Congress acted last year after Continental Airlines, Wilson Foods and other companies created uproars by entering bankruptcy and immediately abrogating labor agreements.

What emerged from Congress were stiff standards that companies had to meet in order to void a contract. The changes require that the employer bargain in good faith, proposing any "necessary modifications" to the contract in an attempt to reach an agreement. The employer must share its financial data with the union.

Failing an accord, the bankruptcy court now weighs the fairness of the company's offer to all parties, including debtors and creditors. Only if the judge finds that the union rejected the employer's proposal without a good reason and that the balance of interests clearly favors rejection of an agreement can the employer throw out the contract.

"Bankruptcy judges got the wrong message from Congress," complains Washington management attorney Walter Connolly, Jr. "I think they now believe that rejection of a collective-bargaining agreement ought to be the exception to the rule."

Disarmed. The upshot is that financially ailing companies that were considering the bankruptcy escape route are feeling increasingly trapped and without leverage to use against unions.

Robert Janowitz, a Kansas City management attorney, says the new statute is making it more difficult for companies to win concessions from unions in negotiations because a bankruptcy ultimatum no longer carries the punch that it once did.

"Now the union says, 'We'll take our chances in court,'" observes Janowitz. "Even if you prove to the bankruptcy judge that you're losing money, he still may say, 'That may be true, but as I inter-

pret the amendment, I'm still not satisfied and I'm going to require you to honor the contract anyway.'"

Unions maintain that this is as it should be. A union attorney currently negotiating with a large bankrupt industrial company says that the bankruptcy-law changes improved the tone of the talks. "Under the old law, the company would probably be systematically violating the contract," he says. "The statute makes a voluntary solution more achievable."

Legal advisers to unions say that the new law appears to be aiding organized labor. "The courts have performed better than I thought they would," says Bruce Simon, a New York attorney who represents unions. "The one thing the change in the law did was raise the consciousness of bankruptcy judges."

From labor's standpoint, the outcome isn't always satisfactory. In a recent Wyoming decision involving a freight-hauling concern, a bankruptcy judge agreed with the employer that there were sufficient reasons to justify rejection of its contract.

A major test of the new statute is pending. Wheeling-Pittsburgh Steel, which filed for protection under bankruptcy laws in April, petitioned the bankruptcy court May 31 to reject its labor pact with the United Steelworkers—a move that, if approved, would let the company set its own pay rates and working conditions.

Labor-law specialists familiar with the case think the court may side with Wheeling-Pittsburgh because lower wages for its workers would greatly aid the company's solvency.

Bankruptcy continued

Says New York attorney Harvey Miller, who represents insurance companies that are owed money by Wheeling-Pittsburgh: "Given the illness in the steel industry, I believe that Wheeling-Pittsburgh will be able to demonstrate that labor is such a significant factor in its cost of doing business that changes in this area can go a long way toward swinging the company around."

Whatever the outcome, employers anxious to shed labor contracts can no longer count on the nation's bankruptcy laws to bail them out.

By CAREY W. ENGLISH
Reprinted from *U.S. News & World Report* issue of June 17, 1985. Copyright, 1985, U.S. News & World Report, Inc.

Confirmation of Plan

A plan must be confirmed by the court before it is binding on any parties. A court will confirm a plan only if it meets all of the requirements of the Bankruptcy Act. The most important of these requirements are the following.

Good Faith   The plan must have been proposed in good faith and not by any means forbidden by law.

Feasibility   The court must find that confirmation of the plan is not likely to be followed by the liquidation or the need for further financial reorganization of the debtor. The essence of feasibility is that the reorganized entity will be able to operate economically and efficiently, will be able to compete on fairly equal terms with other companies within the industry, and is not likely to require liquidation or a second reorganization within the foreseeable future.

Cash Payments   Certain classes of creditors must have their allowed claims paid in full in cash immediately or, in some instances, on a deferred basis. These classes include the expenses of administration, gap creditors, claims for wages and salaries, and employee benefits and consumer deposits.

Acceptance by Creditors   To be confirmed, the plan must be accepted by at least *one* class of claims, and with respect to *each* class each holder must either accept the plan *or* receive not less than the amount he would have received under Chapter 7. In addition, each class must accept the plan or be unimpaired by the plan. Nonetheless, under certain circumstances the court may confirm a plan that is not accepted by all impaired classes. The court must determine that the plan does not discriminate unfairly and that it is fair and equitable. Under these circumstances a class of claims or interests may, over its objections, be involuntarily subjected to the provisions of a plan.

Effect of Reorganization

The reorganized debtor or the new entity succeeding to the debtor's properties emerges from the proceedings and begins life anew with only those obligations that are imposed on it by the plan. The plan binds the debtor and any creditor, equity security holder, or general partner of the debtor. After the entry of a final decree closing the proceedings, the debtor is discharged from all of its debts and liabilities except those that are not dischargeable. All persons who are entitled to participate in the plan of reorganization have a period of not less than five years from the date of the final decree within which to exchange their old securities for the new, as provided in the plan.

MATTER OF
LANDMARK AT PLAZA
PARK LTD.

United States Bankruptcy
Court, D.N.J., 1980. 7 B.R.
653.

FACTS: Landmark at Plaza Park, Ltd., filed a plan of reorganization under Chapter 11 of the Bankruptcy Code. Landmark is a limited partnership whose only substantial asset is a 200-unit garden apartment complex. City Federal holds the first mortgage on the property in the face amount of $2,250,000. The mortgage bears an interest rate of 9.5 percent and is due and payable on October 1, 1986.

Landmark has proposed a plan of reorganization under which the property now in possession of City Federal would be returned. Landmark will then deliver a non-recourse note, payable in three years in the face amount of $2,705,820.31 to the City in substitution of all of the partnership's existing liabilities. On the sixteenth month through the thirty-sixth month after the effective date of the plan, Landmark will make monthly interest payments at a rate of 12.5 percent computed on the value of the property of $2,260,000. Finally, the note will be secured by the existing mortgage. Landmark's theory is that the note will be paid off at the end of thirty-six months by a combination of refinancing and accumulation of cash from the project. The key is Landmark's proposal to obtain a new first mortgage in three years in the face amount of $2,400,000.

City Federal is a first mortgagee without recourse that has been collecting rents pursuant to a rent assignment agreement since the default on the mortgage in December of 1979, eleven months ago. City Federal is impaired by the plan, has rejected the plan, and seeks to complete its foreclosure action.

DECISION: Decision for City Federal. In order for Landmark's plan to be accepted over City Federal's objection, it must show that (1) City Federal has retained its lien on the property; (2) that the total stream of deferred cash payments proposed by the plan must at least total the amount of the secured claim; and (3) that the total stream of payments has a value equal to the value of the property. Landmark has shown that its plan satisfies the first two requirements, but it fails to satisfy the third. The rate of interest on the $2,260,000 loan that City Federal is supposed to make is 12.5 percent. The interest rate, however, must reflect the market rate for a loan of similar risk. A 15 percent rate of interest is appropriate here. The second step is to scrutinize the proposed plan with the 15 percent rate to determine whether it offers a reasonable prospect of success. It must be shown that confirmation of the plan is not likely to be followed by liquidation or the need for further financial reorganization of the debtor. Factors to be considered include: (1) the adequacy of the capital structure, (2) the earning potential of the business, (3) economic conditions, and (4) the ability of management. The requirement of confirmation of the plan is intended to prevent unrealistic schemes from being forced on creditors. Here, with the 15 percent interest rate factored onto realistic income and expense projections substituted for those supplied by Landmark, it appears that confirmation of the plan would likely be followed by liquidation or further reorganization proceedings. Accordingly, Landmark's request for confirmation of its plan of reorganization is denied.

Adjustment of Debts of Individuals—Chapter 13

To encourage debtors to pay their debts wherever possible, Congress enacted Chapter 13 of the Bankruptcy Act. This chapter permits an individual debtor to file a repayment plan that, if confirmed by the court, will discharge him from almost all of his debts when he completes his payments under the plan.

Proceedings

Chapter 13 provides a procedure for the adjustment of debts of an *individual* with regular income who owes liquidated, unsecured debts of less than $100,000 and secured debts of less than $350,000. Sole proprietorships are also eligible if these debt limitations are met. A case under Chapter 13 may be initiated *only* by a voluntary petition. The court appoints a trustee in every Chapter 13 case.

The Plan

The debtor files the plan and may notify it at any time before confirmation. The plan must meet three requirements:

1. It must provide for submission of all or any portion of future earnings or income of the debtor, as is necessary for the execution of the plan, to the supervision and control of the trustee.

2. It must provide for full payment on a deferred basis of all claims entitled to a priority unless a holder of a claim agrees to a different treatment of such claim.

3. If the plan classifies claims, it must provide the same treatment for each claim in the same class.

In addition, the plan *may* modify the rights of unsecured creditors and the rights of secured creditors except those secured only by a security interest in the debtor's principal residence. A plan may provide for payments on any unsecured claim to be made at the same time as payments on any secured claim.

The plan may *not* provide for payments over a period longer than three years, unless the court approves for cause a longer period not to exceed five years.

Confirmation

The plan will be confirmed by the court if certain requirements have been met. First, the plan must comply with applicable law and be proposed in good faith. Second, the value of the property to be distributed to unsecured creditors must be not less than the amount that would be paid them under Chapter 7. Third, either the secured creditors must accept the plan *or* the plan must provide that the debtor will surrender to the secured creditors the collateral *or* the plan must permit the secured creditors to retain their security interest and the value of property to be distributed to them is not less than the allowed amount of their claim. Fourth, the debtor must be able to make all payments and comply with the plan.

Discharge

After a debtor completes all payments under the plan, the court will grant him a discharge of all debts except long-term debts whose maturity extends beyond the expiration of the plan and nondischargeable debts for alimony, maintenance, and support. This discharge is considerably more extensive than that granted under Chapter 7. Moreover, a debtor who receives a discharge under Chapter 7 cannot obtain a discharge again under that chapter for six years, although a debtor discharged under Chapter 13 is not always subject to that limitation.

Even if all payments have *not* been made, the court may, after a hearing, grant a discharge if the debtor's failure to complete such payments is due to circumstances for which the debtor should not justly be held accountable, the value of property actually distributed is not less than what would have been received under Chapter 7, and modification of the plan is not practicable.

IN RE JONSON

United States Bankruptcy
Court, S.D. Indiana, 1981.
17 B.R. 78

FACTS: The debtor, Jonson, is a single, thirty-five year old male with no dependents. He works as an administrative assistant for a medical doctor and has a net income of $755.00 per month. Jonson received a Master of Music degree from Indiana University and is only 2 courses short of receiving his doctorate. His only indebtedness is a student loan in the amount of $10,250.00 from Indiana University. Jonson has made no payments on his loan which became due and payable two years ago with monthly payments of $98.98. Jonson filed an amended plan under Chapter 13 in which he proposes to make payments to the Trustee of $140.00 per month for 36 months. Jonson's proposed plan would result in a total payment of $4,036.00 to Indiana University for a $10,250.00 loan. The plaintiff, Indiana University, objected to the confirmation of Jonson's Chapter 13 plan, raising the question of "good faith" on the part of Jonson.

DECISION: Judgment for Indiana University. Before a bankruptcy court can confirm a Chapter 13 plan, it must find that the plan was proposed in good faith. Since good faith is not defined in the Act or in the legislative history, the court's duty is to fashion a meaning of that term. The major purposes of permitting the court such discretion in scrutinizing a Chapter 13 plan are: (1) to prevent debtors from abusing Chapter 13, and (2) to preserve a distinction between Chapter 7 and Chapter 13.

Here, the sole purpose of Jonson's Chapter 13 plan was to avoid Chapter 7's provisions, which would not allow a discharge of Jonson's only debt, the student loan. In addition, Jonson's plan proposed a $140 payment—$41 more than the monthly payment due on the student loan. At the end of the proposed 36 months, Jonson would have paid only $4,036 of the $10,250 student loan. Thus, Jonson's proposed payment was not a meaningful one. The avoidance of Chapter 7's provisions without a corresponding attempt to repay creditors a meaningful amount is evidence of bad faith.

Creditor's Rights and Debtor Relief Outside of Bankruptcy

The rights and remedies of debtors and creditors outside of bankruptcy are principally governed by State law. Because of the expense and notoriety associated with bankruptcy it is often in the best interests of both debtor and creditor to resolve their claims outside of a bankruptcy proceeding. Accordingly, bankruptcy is usually viewed as the last resort.

The rights and remedies of creditors outside of bankruptcy are varied. In the first part of this section we examine the basic right of *all* creditors to pursue their overdue claims to judgment and to satisfy that judgment out of property belonging to the debtor. Other rights and remedies are discussed elsewhere in this book. The second part of this section describes the various forms of non-bankruptcy compromises that have developed to provide relief to debtors who have become overextended and are unable to pay all of their creditors.

Creditors' Rights

When a debtor fails to pay a debt, the creditor may file suit to collect the debt owed. The ultimate objective is to obtain a judgment against the debtor and then to collect on that judgment.

Pre-judgment Remedies

Because litigation takes time, a creditor attempting to collect on a claim through the judicial process will almost always experience delay in obtaining judgment. To protect against the debtor's disposing of his assets the creditor may utilize, when available, certain pre-judgment remedies. The most important of these is **attachment** which is the process of seizing property, by virtue of a writ, summons, or other judicial order, and bringing the property into the custody of the court for the purpose of securing satisfaction of the judgment ultimately to be entered in the action. At common law the main objective was to coerce the defendant debtor to appear in court; today the writ of attachment is statutory and is used primarily to seize the debtor's property in the event a judgment is rendered. Most States limit attachment to specified grounds and require the opportunity for a hearing before a judge prior to the issuance of a writ of execution. Generally, attachment is limited to situations in which (a) the defendant cannot be personally served; (b) the claim is based upon fraud or the equivalent; or (c) the defendant has or is likely to transfer away his property. In addition, the plaintiff must generally post a bond to compensate the defendant for loss should the plaintiff not prevail in the cause of action.

Attachment–seizure of property to bring it under the custody of the court

Similar in purpose is the remedy of prejudgment **garnishment** which is a statutory proceeding directed at a third person who owes a debt to the debtor or has property belonging to the debtor. Garnishment is most commonly used against the employer of the debtor and the bank in which the debtor has a savings or checking account. Property garnished remains in the hands of the third party pending the outcome of the suit. For example, C brings an action against B to collect a debt that is past due. A has property belonging to B. C might garnish this property so that if C is successful in his action against B, C's judgment could be satisfied out of that property held by A. If A no longer had the property when C obtained judgment, C could recover from A.

Garnishment–proceeding by a creditor against a third person who owes money to debtor

Post-judgment Remedies

If the debtor still has not paid the claim, the creditor may proceed to trial and try to obtain a court judgment against the debtor. Obtaining a judgment, however, is only the first, although necessary, step in collecting the debt. If the debtor does not voluntarily pay the judgment the creditor will have to take additional steps to collect on the judgment. These steps are called "post-judgment remedies."

First, the judgment creditor will have the clerk issue a **writ of execution** which is served by the sheriff upon the defendant/debtor demanding payment of the judgment. Upon return of the writ "unsatisfied," the judgment creditor may post bond or other security and order a levy on and sale of specified nonexempt property belonging to the defendant/debtor which is then seized by the sheriff, advertised for sale, and sold at public sale under the writ of execution.

Writ of execution–order served by sheriff upon debtor demanding payment of a court judgment against debtor

The writ of execution is limited to property of the debtor that is not exempt. All States restrict creditors from recourse to certain property the type and amount of which varies greatly from State to State.

If the proceeds of the sale do not produce sufficient funds to pay the judgment, the creditor may institute a **supplementary proceeding** in an attempt to locate money or other property belonging to the defendant. He may also proceed by **garnishment** against the debtor's employer or a bank in which the debtor has an account in an attempt to collect the judgment.

Debtor's Relief

There are several inherent conflicts between creditors' rights and debtor relief, including: (1) the right of diligent creditors to pursue their claims to judgment and to satisfy their judgment by sale of property of the debtor; (2) the right of unsecured creditors who have refrained from suing the debtor; and (3) the social policy of giving relief to a debtor who has contracted debts beyond his ability to pay and who may be confronted by a lifetime burden. Resolving these conflicts necessarily involves a compromise under which the debtor will disclose and surrender all his assets to a trustee or other person for the benefit of his creditors and the creditors will receive fair and equal treatment.

Various forms of nonbankruptcy compromises have been developed to provide relief to debtors, some of which are less formal, such as those offered by credit agencies and adjustment bureaus. Some are founded in common law and involve simple contract and trust principles, such as compositions and assignments; others are statutory, such as statutory assignments. Some involve the intervention of a court and its officers, such as equity receiverships, and others do not.

Compositions

Composition–agreement between debtor and two or more of her creditors that each will take a portion of his claim as full payment

A common law or nonstatutory composition is an ordinary contract or agreement between the debtor and her creditors under which the creditors receive a proportional part of their claims and the debtor is discharged from the balance of the claims. As a contract it requires the formalities of a contract, such as offer, acceptance, and consideration. For example, debtor D, owing debts of $5,000 to A, $2,000 to B, and $1,000 to C, offers to settle these claims by paying a total of $4,000 to A, B, and C. If A, B, and C accept the offer, a composition results with A receiving $2,500, B $1,000, and C $500. The consideration for the promise of A to forgive the balance of his claim consists of the promises of B and C to forgive the balance of their claims. All the creditors benefit because a conflict among creditors to obtain the debtor's limited assets is avoided.

It should be noted, however, that the debtor in a composition is discharged from liability only on the claims of creditors who voluntarily consent to the composition. If, in the illustration above, C had refused to accept the offer of composition and had refused to take the $500, he could attempt to collect the full $1,000 claim. Likewise, if D owed additional debts to X, Y, and Z, these creditors would not be bound by the agreement between D and A, B, and C. Another disadvantage of the composition is the fact that any creditor can attach the assets of the debtor during the usual period of bargaining and negotiation that precedes the execution of the composition agreement. For instance, once D advised A, B and C that he was offering to compose the claims, any one of the creditors could seize D's property.

A variation of the composition is an extension agreement worked out by the debtor with her creditors providing for payment of her debts either in full or proportionately scaled down over a period of time.

Assignments For Benefit of Creditors

A common law or nonstatutory assignment for the benefit of creditors, or a general assignment, as it is sometimes called, is a voluntary transfer by the debtor of some or all of his property to a trustee, who applies the property to the payment of all of the debtor's debts. For instance, debtor D transfers title to his property to trustee T, who converts the property into money and pays it to all of the creditors on a *pro rata* basis.

The advantage of the assignment over the composition is that it prevents the debtor's assets from being attached or executed and halts the race of diligent creditors to attach. On the other hand, the common law assignment does not require the consent of the creditors, and payment by the trustee of part of the claims does not discharge the debtor from the balance of them. Thus, in the previous example, even after T pays A $2,500, B $1,000 and C $500 (and appropriate payments to all other creditors), A, B and C and the other creditors may still attempt to collect the balance of their claims.

Statutory Assignments

Because assignments benefit creditors by protecting the debtor's assets from attachment, there have been many statutory attempts to combine the idea of the assignment with a corresponding benefit to the debtor by discharging him from the balance of his debts. Since the United States Constitution prohibits a State from impairing the obligation of a contract between private citizens, it is impossible for a State to force all creditors to discharge a debtor on a *pro rata* distribution of assets, although, as previously discussed, the Federal government *does* have such power and exercises it in the Bankruptcy Act. Accordingly, the States have generally enacted assignment statutes permitting the debtor to obtain *voluntary* releases of the balance of claims from creditors who accept partial payments, thus combining the advantages of common law compositions and assignments.

Equity Receiverships

One of the oldest remedies in equity is the appointment of a receiver by the court. The receiver is a disinterested (unbiased) person appointed by the court who collects and preserves the debtor's assets and income and disposes of them at the direction of the court. The court may instruct her (1) to liquidate the assets by public or private sale; (2) to operate the business as a going concern temporarily; or (3) to conserve the assets until final disposition of the matter before the court.

A receiver will be appointed on the petition (1) of a secured creditor seeking foreclosure of his security; (2) of a judgment creditor after exhausting legal remedies to satisfy the judgment; or (3) of a shareholder of a corporate debtor where it appears that the assets of the corporation will be dissipated by fraud or mismanagement. The receiver is always appointed at the discretion of the court. Insolvency, in the equity sense of inability by the debtor to pay his debts as they mature, is one of the factors considered by the court in appointing a receiver.

CHAPTER SUMMARY

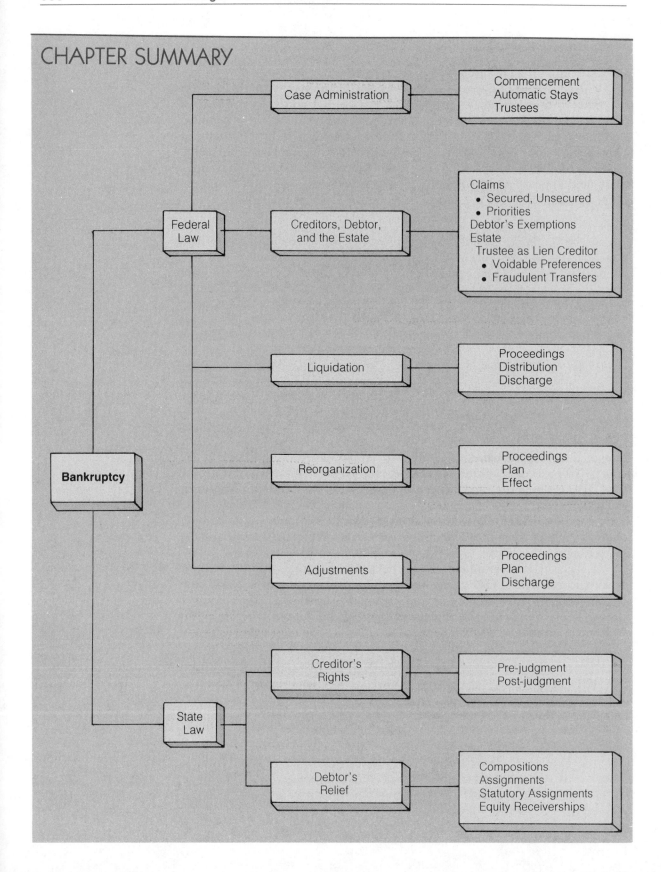

KEY TERMS

Straight bankruptcy	Debtor's exemptions	Class of claims
Reorganization	Discharge	Class of interests
Voluntary petition	Estate	Adjustment of debts
Involuntary petition	Lien creditor	Attachment
Creditor	Judicial lien	Garnishment
Claim	Voidable preference	Writ of execution
Insider	Insolvency	Composition
Secured claim	Fraudulent transfer	Assignment for benefit of creditors
Priority	Statutory lien	Statutory assignment
Subordination of claims	Liquidation	Equity

PROBLEMS

1. (a) B goes into bankruptcy. His estate has no assets. Are B's taxes discharged by the proceedings? Why or why not?

(b) B obtains property from A on credit by representing that he is solvent when in fact he knows he is insolvent. Is B's debt to A discharged by B's discharge in bankruptcy?

2. B goes into bankruptcy owing $5,000 as wages to his four employees. There is enough in his estate to pay all costs of administration and enough to pay his employees, but nothing will be left for general creditors. Do the employees take all the estate? Under what conditions? If the general creditors received nothing at all, would these debts be discharged?

3. A sold goods to B for $2,500 and retained a security interest in them. Three months later B filed a petition in bankruptcy under Chapter 7. At this time B still owed A $2,000 for the purchase price of the goods, whose value was $1,500.

(a) May the trustee invalidate A's security interest. If so, under what provision?

(b) If the security interest is invalidated, what is A's status in the bankruptcy proceeding?

(c) If the security interest is *not* invalidated, what is A's status in the bankruptcy proceeding?

4. A debtor went through bankruptcy and received his discharge. Which of the following debts were completely discharged, and which remain debts against him in the future?

(a) Claims of $900 by X and Y for wages earned within three months immediately prior to bankruptcy.

(b) A judgment of $3,000 against the debtor by C for breach of contract.

(c) Sales taxes of $1,800.

(d) $1,000 in past alimony and support money owed to his divorced wife for herself and their child.

(e) A judgment of $4,000 for injuries received because of the debtor's negligent operation of an automobile.

5. Rosinoff and his wife, who were business partners, entered bankruptcy. Objection was made to their discharge in bankruptcy by a creditor, Baldwin, on the grounds that:

(a) the partners had obtained credit from Baldwin on the basis of a false financial statement;

(b) the partners had failed to keep books of account and records from which their financial condition could be determined; and

(c) Rosinoff had falsely sworn that he had taken $70 from the partnership account when the correct amount was $700.

Were the debtors entitled to a discharge?

6. X Corporation is a debtor in a reorganization proceeding under Chapter 11 of the Bankruptcy Act. By fair and proper valuation its assets are worth $100,000. The indebtedness of the corporation is $105,000, it has outstanding preferred stock of par value of $20,000, and common stock of par value of $75,000. The plan of reorganization submitted by the trustees would eliminate the common shareholders and give bonds of the face amount of $5,000 to the creditors and common stock in the ratio of 84 percent to the creditors and 16 percent to the preferred shareholders. Should this plan be confirmed?

7. A is a wage earner with a regular income. She has unsecured debts of $42,000 and secured debts owing to B, C, D, and E totaling $120,000. E's debt is secured only by a mortgage on A's house. A files a petition under Chapter 13 and a plan providing payment as follows: (a) 60 percent of all taxes owed, (b) 35 percent of all unsecured debts, and (c) $100,000 in total to B, C, D, and E. Should the court confirm the plan? If not, how must the plan be modified and/or what other conditions must be satisfied?

8. John Bunker has assets of $130,000 and liabilities of $185,000 owed to nine creditors. Nonetheless, his cash flow is positive and he is making payment on all of his obligations as they become due. I. M. Flintheart, who is owed $22,000 by Bunker, files an involuntary petition in bankruptcy against Bunker. Bunker contests the petition. Decision?

9. D has filed a petition for a Chapter 7 proceeding. The total value of D's estate is $35,000. V, who is owed $18,000 has a security interest in property valued at $12,000. X has an unsecured claim of $9,000, which is entitled to a priority of $2,000. The United States has a claim for income taxes of $7,000. Y has an unsecured claim of $10,000 that was filed on time. Z has an unsecured claim of $17,000 that was filed on time. W has a claim of $14,000 that was not filed on time even though J was aware of the bankruptcy proceedings.

What should each of the creditors receive in a distribution under Chapter 7?

PART NINE
REGULATION OF BUSINESS

PART NINE

REGULATION OF BUSINESS

PUBLIC POLICY, SOCIAL ISSUES AND BUSINESS ETHICS

Part Nine addresses the role of government in regulating business, a role that has grown in this country to great proportions during the twentieth century. It is theoretically possible to have an economic system in which government plays no part at all; it is also conceivable to have an economy in which government exercises a totally dominant role by owning all productive property as well as deciding what is produced, where it is produced, who shall produce it, and who shall consume it. In practice, however, economic systems fall somewhere between these two extremes: our economy has less governmental involvement than the Soviet Union's or China's but more than Hong Kong's.

Our economic system is thus a "mixed economy" that has evolved from capitalism. As explained and justified by Adam Smith in *The Wealth of Nations* (1776), the capitalistic system is composed of six "institutions": economic motivation, private productive property, free enterprise, free markets, competition, and limited government. Economic motivation assumes that a person will work harder if he receives an economic return for his effort; therefore the economic system should provide greater economic rewards for those who work harder. Private property (which we discuss in Part Ten of this book) is the means by which economic motivation is exercised. It permits individuals to innovate and produce while securing to them the fruits of their efforts. Jack Behrman, in *Discourses on Ethics and Business,* has described how the four other institutions combine with these two to bring about industrialized capitalism:

Free enterprise permits the combination of properties so people can do things together that they can't do alone. Free enterprise means a capitalistic combination of factors of production under decisions of free individuals. Free enterprise is the group expression of the use of private property, and it permits greater efficiency in an industrial setting through variation in the levels and kinds of production.

. . . The free market operates to equate supply and demand—supply reflecting the ability and willingness to offer certain goods or services, and demand reflecting the consumer's *ability* and *willingness* to pay. Price is adjusted to include the maximum number of *both* bids and offers. The market, therefore, is *the* decision-making mechanism outside of the firm. It is the *means* by which basic decisions are made about the use of resources, and all factors are supposed to respond to it, however they wish.

. . .

Just in case it doesn't work out that way, there is one more institution—the *Government*—which is supposed to set rules and provide protection for the society and its members. That's all, said Smith, that it should do: it should set the rules, enforce them, and stand aside.

As long as all these constituent institutions continued to exist and operate in a balanced manner, the factors of production—land, capital, and labor—would combine to produce an efficient allocation of resources for individual consumers and for the economy as a whole. For this outcome to succeed, however, Smith's model required that a number of conditions be satisfied: "standardized products, numerous firms in markets, each firm with a small share and unable by its actions alone to exert significant influence over price, no barriers to entry, and output carried to the point where each seller's marginal cost equals the going market price." E. Singer, *Antitrust Economics and Legal Analysis.*

History has demonstrated that almost all of these assumptions have *not* been satisfied by the actual operation of the economy. More specifically, the actual competitive process falls considerably short of the assumptions of the classic economical model of perfect competition:

Competitive industries are never perfectly competitive in this sense. Many of the resources they employ cannot be shifted to other employments without substantial cost and delay. The allocation of those resources, as between industries or as to relative proportions within a single industry, is unlikely to have been made in a way that affords the best possible expenditure of economic effort. Information is incomplete, motivation confused, and decision therefore ill informed and often unwise. Variations in efficiency are not directly reflected in variations of profit. Success is derived in large part from competitive selling efforts, which in the aggregate may be wasteful, and from differentiation of products, which may be undertaken partly by methods designed to impair the opportunity of the buyer to compare quality and price. Profit is sought not only in producing or distributing goods but also in a wide variety of financial manipulations that have no fixed relationship to the productive process. Rivalry is often between a few concerns that strike at one another in a conscious effort to do injury rather than between a large number of concerns that compete anonymously and impersonally. Incentives to limit production and maintain prices are often dominant in spite of this rivalry. C. Edwards, *Maintaining Competition.*

In addition to capitalism's failure to accomplish its objective of efficient resource allocation, it cannot be relied on to achieve all of the social and public policy objectives required by a pluralistic democracy. For example, equi-

table distribution of wealth, national defense, conservation of natural resources, full employment, stability in economic cycles, protection against economic dislocations, health and safety, social security, and other important social and economic goals are simply not comprehended or addressed by the free-enterprise model. As a consequence, increased governmental intervention has occurred not only to preserve the competitive process in our mixed economic system but also to achieve social goals extrinsic to the efficient allocation of resources. Such intervention attempts (1) to regulate both "legal" monopolies such as those conferred by law through copyrights, patents, and trade symbols and "natural" monopolies such as utilities, transportation, and communications; (2) to correct imperfections in the market system to preserve competition; (3) to protect specific groups from failures of the marketplace, the most important example being labor; and (4) to promote other social goals. Successful government regulation involves a delicate balance between regulations that attempt to preserve competition and those that attempt to advance other social objectives. The latter must not undermine the basic competitive processes that are relied on to bring about an efficient allocation of economic resources.

In Part Nine we examine a number of critical areas of governmental intervention. The chapter on Trade Regulation covers antitrust and unfair competition and addresses the ways in which the government has sought to preserve a free and fair competitive system. Governmental regulation of another key factor—capital—is discussed in the chapter on Securities Regulation. Finally, in the chapter on consumer protection we deal with the attempts by government to ensure that, as Adam Smith said, "the consumer is King." In studying these chapters you should keep in mind the goals and objectives of the capitalistic system, the failures of the system in actual operation, the abuses of the system, and the economic and social reasons underlying government's intervention.

TRADE REGULATION

The economic community is best served in normal times by free competition in trade and industry. It is in the public interest that quality, price, and service in an open, competitive market for goods and services be determining factors in the business rivalry for the customer's dollar. The law of trade regulation attempts to assure such free and fair competition.

The common law has traditionally favored free and open competition in the marketplace and has held that agreements and contracts in restraint of trade are illegal and unenforceable. Antitrust statutes adopted in most of the States as well as by the Federal government to prohibit anticompetitive practices implement this policy. These statutes also seek to prevent unreasonable concentrations of economic power because they stifle or weaken competition.

In addition, practices such as imitation of a competitor's trademark, passing off one's products as those of another, betrayal of trade secrets, disloyalty of employees, interference with contracts, and false advertising are injurious to free and fair competition. To preserve fairness and to protect freedom of competition by preventing businesses from taking unfair advantage of their competitors, the courts have developed certain rules and principles. Generally referred to as the law of unfair competition, they are basically rules of fair play applied to the world of business.

Antitrust

In the last half of the nineteenth century it became apparent that concentrations of economic power in the form of trusts and combinations of business were too powerful and widespread to be effectively controlled by State action. This prompted the Congress in 1890 to enact the Sherman Antitrust Act, which was the first Federal statute in this field. Since then, Congress has enacted several other antitrust statutes, including the Clayton Act, the Robinson-Patman Act, and the Federal Trade Commission Act.

Sherman Antitrust Act

Section 1 of the Sherman Act prohibits contracts, combinations, and conspiracies that restrain trade while Section 2 outlaws monopolies and attempts to monopolize. Failure to comply with either section is a criminal violation and subjects the offender to fine or imprisonment or both. Individual offenders are subject to imprisonment up to three years and fines up to $100,000, while corporate offenders are subject to fines up to $1,000,000. Moreover, the Federal district courts are empowered to issue injunctions restraining violations, and anyone injured by a violation is entitled to recover in a civil action **treble damages,** that is, three times the amount of the actual loss sustained. It is the duty of United States district attorneys and of the Federal Trade Commission to institute appropriate enforcement proceedings other than treble damage actions.

Treble damages–three times actual loss

Contracts, Combinations, and Conspiracies in Restraint of Trade

Section 1 of the Sherman Act provides that "[e]very contract, combination in the form of trust or otherwise, or conspiracy, in restraint of trade or commerce among the several states, or with foreign nations is hereby declared to be illegal." Taken literally, this prohibition would invalidate every unperformed contract. To avoid such a broad and impractical application, the courts have interpreted this section to invalidate only *unreasonable* restraints of trade:

> The true test of legality is whether the restraint imposed is such as merely regulates and perhaps thereby promotes competition or whether it is such as may suppress or even destroy competition. To determine that question the courts must ordinarily consider the facts peculiar to the business to which the restraint is applied; its condition before and after the restraint was imposed; the nature of the restraint and its effect, actual or probable. The history of the restraint, the evil believed to exist, the reason for adopting the particular remedy, the purpose or end sought to be attained, are all relevant facts. This is not because a good intention will save an otherwise objectionable regulation or the reverse; but because knowledge of intent may help the court to interpret facts and to predict consequences.

Rule of reason–balancing the anticompetitive effects against procompetitive effects of the restraint

This standard, known as the **rule of reason test,** however, presented several problems of its own. By mandating that courts balance the *anticompetitive* effects against the *procompetitive* effects of every questioned restraint, this standard placed a substantial burden upon the judicial system. The United States Supreme Court accordingly responded by declaring certain categories of restraints to be unreasonable by their very nature and thus **illegal per se:**

Illegal per se–conclusively presumed unreasonable and therefore illegal

> [T]here are certain agreements or practices which because of their pernicious effect on competition and lack of any redeeming virtue are conclusively presumed to be unreasonable and therefore illegal without elaborate inquiry as to the precise harm they have caused or the business excuse for their use. This principle of *per se* unreasonableness not only makes the type of restraints which are proscribed by the Sherman Act more certain to the benefit of everyone concerned, but it also avoids the necessity for an incredibly complicated and prolonged economic investigation into the entire history of the industry involved, as well as related industries, in an effort to determine at large whether a particular restraint has been unreasonable—an inquiry so often wholly fruitless when undertaken.

Those restraints not categorized as illegal *per se* are judged by the rule of reason test.

In addition, restraints may be classified as either horizontal or vertical. A restraint is **horizontal** if it involves collaboration among competitors at the same level in the chain of distribution (see Figure 39-1). For example, an

Horizontal–agreements among competitors

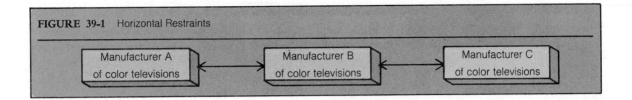

FIGURE 39-1   Horizontal Restraints

| Manufacturer A of color televisions | Manufacturer B of color televisions | Manufacturer C of color televisions |

agreement among manufacturers or among wholesalers or among retailers would be horizontal.

On the other hand, an agreement is **vertical** if it is made by parties that are not in direct competition at the same level of distribution (see Figure 39-2). Thus an agreement between a manufacturer and a wholesaler is vertical. Although the distinction between horizontal and vertical restraints can become blurred, it often determines whether a restraint is illegal *per se* or should be judged by the rule of reason test. For instance, horizontal market allocations are illegal *per se*, whereas vertical market allocations are not illegal *per se* but are subject to the rule of reason test.

> Vertical–agreements among parties at different levels of the distribution chain

Finally, Section 1 does not prohibit **unilateral** conduct; rather, it forbids **concerted** action. Thus, one person or business by itself cannot violate the section. Although concerted action usually takes the form of explicit agreements, combinations, or conspiracies, less obvious conduct has on occasion been found to violate Section 1 where there is sufficient circumstantial evidence to warrant such a finding.

Price Fixing   Price fixing is the primary and most serious example of a *per se* violation under the Sherman Act. As held in *United States v. Socony Vacuum Oil Co. all* **horizontal** price-fixing agreements are illegal *per se*. This prohibition covers any agreement between sellers to establish *maximum* prices at which certain commodities or services are offered for sale as well as *minimum* prices. The law also prohibits sellers' agreements to change the prices of certain commodities or services simultaneously or not to advertise their prices.

> Price fixing–an agreement for the purpose and effect of raising, depressing, fixing, pegging or stabilizing prices

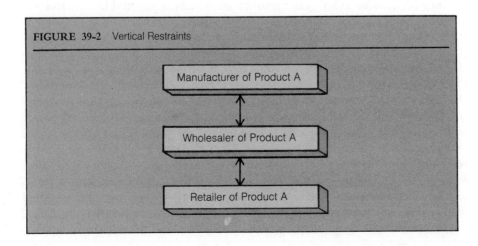

FIGURE 39-2   Vertical Restraints

Manufacturer of Product A

Wholesaler of Product A

Retailer of Product A

UNITED STATES v. SOCONY-VACUUM OIL CO.

United States Supreme Court, 1940.
310 U.S. 150, 60 S.Ct. 811, 84 L.Ed. 1129.

FACT: In the early 1930s, intense price competition characterized both the retail and the wholesale oil markets. At times, prices in the wholesale market fell below the manufacturer's cost. One cause of the volatile situation was the supply of "distress gasoline" placed on the market by seventeen independent refiners. These independent refiners had no retail sales outlets and little storage capacity, so they were forced to sell it at "distress prices." In spite of their unprofitable operations they could not afford to shut down, for if they did so, they would be apt to lose their oil connections in the field and their regular customers.

In an attempt to remedy this problem, the major oil companies entered into an informal agreement whereby each selected one or more independent refiners having distress gasoline as its "dancing partner." The major oil company would then assume responsibility for purchasing the independent's distress supply at the "fair going market price." As a result, the market price of oil rose in 1935 and 1936, and the spot market became stable. The United States then brought this criminal action against the companies charging them with horizontal price fixing in violation of the Sherman Act.

DECISION: Judgment for United States. Under the Sherman Act, a combination formed for the purpose and with the effect of raising, depressing, fixing, pegging, or stabilizing the price of a commodity in interstate or foreign commerce is illegal *per se*. Price fixing includes more than the mere establishment of uniform prices. Here, the activities of the major companies and the independent refiners had the effect of raising the market price of oil and of stabilizing the spot market. Accordingly, they acted in violation of the Sherman Act.

The conduct is *per se* illegal, and no justification will be heard. It is, therefore, irrelevant whether the prices ultimately resulting were reasonable, or that the parties acted with good intentions, or that other factors might have contributed to the price rise and market stability, or that sales on the spot market were still governed by some competition. The key is that competition was restricted. Moreover, the claim of ruinous competition is not a justification for price fixing. To allow this justification would be to allow a philosophy wholly alien to the free market system.

Similarly, it is illegal *per se* for a seller to fix the price at which its purchasers must resell the product. This **vertical** form of price fixing—usually called retail price maintenance—was allowed in some States under the "fair trade laws." However, in 1975 Congress repealed the statute authorizing these laws, and now resale price maintenance is considered a *per se* violation of Section 1. It is believed that the seller has no interest sufficient to outweigh the buyer's right to resell at a price that is responsive to the buyer's competitive conditions.

Market allocation–division of market by customers, geographic location, or products

Market Allocations   Direct price fixing is not the only method by which prices can be controlled. Competitors may agree not to compete with each other in specific markets, which may be defined by geographic area, type of customer, or class of product. Because their effects are similar to price fixing, all **horizontal** agreements to divide markets have been declared illegal *per se*. Thus, if RAC and Sonny, both manufacturers of color televisions, agree that RAC shall have the exclusive right to sell color televisions in Illinois and Iowa and that Sonny shall have the exclusive right in Minnesota and Wisconsin, RAC and Sonny have committed a *per se* violation of Section 1 of the Sherman Act. Likewise, if RAC and Sonny agree that RAC shall have the exclusive right to sell color televisions to Sears and Sonny to J.C. Penney, or that RAC shall have exclusive rights to manufacture nineteen-inch color televisions and Sonny to manufacture fifteen-inch sets, they are also in *per se* violation of Section 1 of the Sherman Antitrust Act. Horizontal market allocations may be found not only on the manufacturing level, but also on the wholesale or retail level.

Vertical territorial and customer restrictions are no longer illegal *per se* but are now judged by the rule of reason. This change in approach has resulted from a recent United States Supreme Court decision, *Continental T.V., Inc. v. GTE Sylvania, Inc.,* which mandated the lower Federal courts to balance the positive effect of vertical market restrictions on interbrand competition against the negative effects on intraband competition. Consequently, in some situations vertical territorial restrictions will be found legitimate if they, on balance, increase competition.

FACTS: As part of a corporate plan to stimulate sagging color television sales, GTE Sylvania began to phase out its wholesale distributors and began to sell its television sets directly to a smaller and more select group of franchised retailers. To this end, Sylvania limited the number of franchises granted for any given area and required each franchisee to sell Sylvania products only from the location or locations at which he was franchised. A franchise did not constitute an exclusive territory, and Sylvania retained sole discretion to increase the number of retailers in an area in light of the success or failure of existing retailers. The strategy apparently was successful, as Sylvania's national market share increased from less than 2 percent to 5 percent.

In the course of carrying out its plan, Sylvania franchised Young Brothers as a retailer of televisions at a location in San Francisco one mile from that of Continental T.V., Inc., one of Sylvania's most successful franchisees. A course of feuding began between Sylvania and Continental that reached a head when Continental requested permission to open a store in Sacramento, but Sylvania refused. Continental opened a Sacramento store anyway and began shipping merchandise there from its San Jose warehouse. Shortly thereafter, Sylvania terminated Continental's franchise.

Continental now brings this action against Sylvania, claiming that the franchise location restriction is per se violative of the Sherman Act.

DECISION: Judgment for Sylvania. In an earlier decision, this Court erroneously held that territorial and customer restrictions on sales by wholesalers in the purchasing and selling of Schwinn bicycles was *per se* illegal. *Per se* rules of illegality are appropriate, however, only when they relate to conduct that is manifestly anticompetitive. Vertical market allocation restrictions in franchise agreements are not manifestly anticompetitive, and, therefore, should be judged under the prevailing standard of analysis, the "rule of reason."

Under the rule of reason analysis, the court must weigh all of the circumstances of the case in deciding whether a restrictive practice should be prohibited as imposing an unreasonable restraint on competition. The market impact of vertical restrictions is complex because of their potential for a simultaneous reduction of intrabrand competition and stimulation of interbrand competition. On one hand, location restrictions and other vertical restraints reduce intrabrand competition by limiting the number of sellers of a particular product competing for the business of a given group of buyers. On the other hand, these vertical restrictions promote interbrand competition by allowing the manufacturer to achieve certain efficiencies in the distribution of his products. Overall, the franchise location clause imposed by Sylvania does not impose an unreasonable restraint on trade and, therefore, does not violate the Sherman Act.

CONTINENTAL T.V. v. GTE SYLVANIA

United States Supreme Court, 1977.
433 U.S. 36, 97 S.Ct. 2549, 53 L.Ed.2d 568.

Boycotts   As we noted above, Section 1 of the Sherman Act does not apply to unilateral action but only to agreements or combinations. Accordingly, the refusal of a seller to deal with any particular buyer does not violate the act. Thus a manufacturer can refuse to sell a retailer who persists in selling below the manufacturer's suggested retail price. On the other hand, **concerted refusals to deal**—group boycotts—are prohibited. Therefore, a manufacturer would violate Section 1 if it were to induce wholesalers to refuse to deal with retailers that disobeyed a suggested retail price.

Boycott–agreement among parties not to deal with a third party

For example, GE, who wishes to establish set prices for the resale of its products by both wholesalers and retailers, indicates that it will cease to deal with any wholesaler who resells at a different price. GE has *not* violated the Sherman Act; it has merely exercised its right to deal with whomever it pleases. On the other hand, if GE requires that its wholesalers refuse to deal with any retailer who does not follow its pricing policy, GE and the wholesalers have entered into an illegal concerted refusal to deal as well as an illegal vertical price-fixing scheme. Moreover, the illegality of the conduct does not depend on the express agreement of GE and its wholesalers but may be implied from the conduct of the parties. Finally, it should be noted that GE would violate the Sherman Act by engaging in vertical price fixing if it obtained an agreement from the wholesalers that they will sell at GE's set price or that they will report to GE any violations of its pricing policy.

Tying Arrangements   A seller of a product, service, or intangible (the "tying" product) may condition its sale on the buyer's purchasing a second product, service or intangible (the "tied" product) from the seller. For example, Xerox, a major manufacturer of photocopying equipment, requires that all purchasers of its photocopiers must also purchase from Xerox all of the paper they use with the copier. Xerox has tied the sale of its photocopier—the *tying* product—to the sale of paper—the *tied* product. Because tying arrangements limit the freedom of choice of buyers and may exclude competitors, the law closely scrutinizes such agreements. When the seller has considerable economic power in the tying product *or* when a not insubstantial amount of interstate commerce is affected in the tied product, the tying arrangement will be illegal *per se*. Otherwise, tying arrangements are judged by the rule of reason test.

> Tying arrangement–conditioning a sale of a desired product (tying product) on the buyer purchasing a second product (tied product)

Figure 39-3 summarizes how these Section 1 restraints on trade are judged.

Monopolies

Economic analysis indicates that a monopolist will use its power to limit production and increase prices. Therefore, a monopolistic market will produce fewer goods at a higher price than a competitive market. Addressing the problem of monopolization, Section 2 of the Sherman Act prohibits monopolies, attempts to monopolize, and conspiracies to monopolize. Thus Section

---

FIGURE 39-3   Restraints of Trade

Restraint	Standard
Price fixing	*Per se* illegal
Market allocations	Horizontal: *per se* illegal Vertical: rule of reason
Group boycotts	*Per se* illegal
Tying arrangements	*Per se* illegal*

*If seller has power in tying product or a not insubstantial amount of interstate commerce is affected in the tied product.

2 prohibits both agreements among businesses and, unlike Section 1, unilateral conduct by one firm.

Monopolization   Although the language of Section 2 appears to prohibit *all* monopolies, the courts have not interpreted it in that manner. Rather, they have required that in addition to the mere possession of market power there also must be either the unfair attainment of the monopoly power or the abusive use of that power once attained.

It is extremely rare to find an unregulated industry with only one firm, so the issue of monopoly power involves defining what degree of market dominance constitutes monopoly power. **Monopoly power** is the ability to control prices or to exclude competitors from the marketplace. The courts have grappled with this question of monopoly power and have developed a number of approaches, but the most common test is market share. A market share greater than 75 percent generally indicates monopoly power, while a share less than 50 percent does not. A 50 to 75 percent share is inconclusive.

Monopoly–ability to control price or exclude others from the marketplace

Market share is the fractional share possessed by a firm of the total relevant product and geographic markets, but defining the relevant markets is often a difficult and subjective project for the courts. The relevant *product market*, as demonstrated in the case which follows, includes products that are substitutable for the firm's product on the basis of price, quality, and adaptability for other purposes. For example, although brick and wood siding are both used in buildings as exteriors it is not likely that they would be considered as part of the same product market. On the other hand, Coca Cola and Seven-Up are both soft drinks and would be considered part of the same product market.

UNITED STATES v. E. I. du PONT De NEMOURS & CO.

United States Supreme Court, 1956. 351 U.S. 377, 76 S.Ct. 994, 100 L.Ed. 1264

FACTS: In 1923, du Pont was granted the exclusive right to make and sell cellophane in North America. In 1927, the company introduced a moistureproof brand of cellophane that was ideal for various wrapping needs. Although more expensive than most competing wrapping, it was favored for many uses because it offered a desired combination of transparency, strength, and cost. Except as to permeability to gases, however, cellophane had no qualities that were not possessed by a number of competing materials. Cellophane sales increased dramatically, and by 1950, du Pont produced almost 75 percent of the cellophane sold in the United States. Nevertheless, sales of the material constituted less than 20 percent of the sales of "flexible packaging materials."

The United States brought this action contending that by so dominating cellophane production, du Pont had monopolized a part of trade or commerce in violation of the Sherman Act. Du Pont argued that it had not monopolized in violation of the Sherman Act because it did not have the power to control the price of cellophane or to exclude competitors from the market for flexible wrapping materials.

DECISION: Judgment for du Pont. The first step in determining whether du Pont has monopolized is to determine whether the company has monopoly power in the relevant market. Monopoly power is the power to control prices or to exclude competition in the relevant market. The relevant market consists of commodities reasonably interchangeable by consumers for the same purposes. Control of the relevant market in turn depends on the availability and interchangeability of competing products. A measure of this interchangeability is the cross-elasticity of demand between cellophane and the other wrappings—that is, the responsiveness of the sales of cellophane to changes in the price of other wrapping materials. Here, the evidence shows that sales of the other materials were highly sensitive to changes in the price of cellophane, thus indicating that the products compete in the same market. In other words, the interchangeability of cellophane with other wrapping materials suffices to make the relevant market for purposes of determining whether du Pont has monopolized that for all flexible wrapping materials. Although it accounted for over 17 percent of the sales in that larger market, du Pont cannot be said by that proportion of sales to have the power to control prices or exclude competition.

The relevant *geographic market* is the territory in which the firm sells its products or services. This may be at the local, regional, or national level. For instance, the relevant geographic market for the manufacture and sale of aluminum might be national, whereas that of a taxi company would be local. The scope of the relevant geographic market will depend on such factors as transportation costs, the type of product or services, and the location of competitors and customers.

If sufficient monopoly power has been proved, it must then be shown that the firm has engaged in **unfair conduct.** The courts have not yet agreed on what constitutes unfair conduct. One judicial approach is that a firm possessing monopoly power has the burden of proving that it acquired such power passively or that it had the power "thrust" upon it. An alternative view is that monopoly power, when combined with conduct designed to exclude competitors, violates Section 1. A third approach requires monopoly power plus some type of predatory practice, such as pricing below marginal costs.

To date, however, the United States Supreme Court has not provided a definitive answer to the basic question of exactly what conduct, beyond the mere possession of monopoly power, violates Section 2. To do so, the Court must resolve the complex and conflicting policies involved. On the one hand, condemning fairly acquired monopoly power—that acquired "merely by virtue of superior skill, foresight and industry"—penalizes firms that compete effectively. On the other hand, permitting firms with monopoly power to continue provides them the opportunity to lower output and raise prices, thereby injuring consumers. For example, one case which adopted the third approach held that a firm does not violate Section 2 of the Sherman Act if it attained its market share by either (1) research, technical innovation or a superior product, or, (2) ordinary marketing methods available to all.

Attempts to Monopolize   Section 2 also prohibits attempts to monopolize. As with monopolization, the courts have experienced difficulty in developing a standard that distinguishes undesirable conduct likely to lead to monopoly from healthy, competitive conduct. The standard test applied by the courts requires proof of a specific intent to monopolize plus a dangerous probability of success. This standard leaves numerous questions unanswered, such as what conduct constitutes an attempt and how much power must be achieved. Recent cases suggest that the greater the power acquired, the less flagrant the conduct must be to constitute an attempt. These cases, however, do not specify any threshold level of market power.

Clayton Act

In 1914 Congress strengthened the Sherman Act by adopting the Clayton Act, which was expressly designed "to supplement existing laws against unlawful restraints and monopolies." The Clayton Act does not provide for criminal penalties but only for civil actions. Civil actions may be brought by private parties in Federal court for *treble* damages and attorneys' fees. In addition, the Justice Department and the Federal Trade Commission are authorized to bring civil actions, including proceedings in equity to prevent and restrict violations of the act.

The major provisions of the Clayton Act deal with price discrimination, tying contracts, exclusive dealing, and mergers. Section 2, which deals with price discrimination, was amended and rewritten by the Robinson-Patman Act, which we discuss below. The Clayton Act exempts labor, agricultural, and horticultural organizations from all antitrust laws.

Tying Contracts and Exclusive Dealing

Section 3 of the Clayton Act prohibits tying arrangements and exclusive dealing, selling, or leasing arrangements that prevent purchasers from dealing with the seller's competitors, where the effect **may** be substantially to lessen competition or **tend** to create a monopoly. This section is intended to attack anticompetitive practices when they start, before they ripen into violations of Section 1 or 2 of the Sherman Act. Unlike the Sherman Act, however, Section 3 applies only to leases or sales of goods, wares, merchandise, machinery, supplies, or other commodities.

Tying arrangements, which we discussed above, have been labeled by the Supreme Court as serving "hardly any purpose beyond the suppression of competition." Exclusive dealing arrangements are agreements by which the seller or lessor of a product conditions the agreement on the buyer's or lessor's promise not to deal in the goods of a competitor. For example, a manufacturer of razors might require that retailers wishing to sell its line of shaving equipment agree not to carry competing merchandise. Such conduct, will violate Section 3 if it tends to create a monopoly or may substantially lessen competition.

Mergers

Section 7 of the Clayton Act prohibits the merger or acquisition by a corporation of stock in another corporation or assets of another corporation where the effect may be substantially to lessen competition or tend to create a monopoly.

The current state of the law regarding horizontal, vertical, and conglomerate mergers is, particularly with respect to the last two, in a state of flux. A **horizontal merger** involves the acquisition by a company of all or part of the stock or assets of a competing company. A **vertical merger** is the acquisition by a company of one of its customers or suppliers. A vertical merger is a *forward* merger if the acquiring company purchases a *customer*, such as the purchase of Revco Discount Drug Stores by Procter and Gamble. A vertical merger is a *backward* merger if the acquiring company purchases a supplier; for example, IBM's purchase of a manufacturer of microchips. The third type of merger, the **conglomerate merger,** is a catchall category covering all other mergers.

The principal objective of antitrust law governing mergers is to maintain competition. Accordingly, horizontal mergers are scrutinized most carefully. Factors that the courts consider in reviewing the legality of a horizontal merger include the market share of each of the merging firms, the degree of industry concentration, the number of firms in the industry, entry barriers, market

Horizontal merger –acquisition by one company of a competing company

Vertical merger –acquisition by one company of one of its suppliers or customers

Conglomerate merger – an acquisition by one company of another which is not a horizontal or vertical merger

trends, the vigor and strength of other competitors in the industry, the character and history of the merging firms, market demand, and the extent of industry price competition. See *United States v. Von's Grocery Co.* below. Vertical mergers, which are far less likely to be challenged by the Justice Department or the FTC, will be attacked if the merger is likely to raise entry barriers in the industry or is likely to shut out other firms in the industry of the acquiring firm from competitively significant customers or suppliers. Finally, conglomerate mergers have been challenged only (1) where one of the merging firms is a highly likely entrant into the market of the other firm or (2) where the merged company would be disproportionately large compared with the largest competitors in its industry.

UNITED STATES v. VON'S GROCERY CO.

Supreme Court of the United States, 1966.
384 U.S. 270, 86 S.Ct. 1478, 16 L.Ed.2d 555.

FACTS: Von's Grocery, a large retail grocery chain in Los Angeles, sought to acquire Shopping Bag Food Stores, a direct competitor. At the time of the proposed merger, Von's sales ranked third in the Los Angeles area and Shopping Bag's ranked sixth. Both chains were increasing their number of stores. The merger would have resulted in the creation of the second largest grocery chain in Los Angeles, with total sales in excess of $170 million. Prior to the proposed merger, the number of owners operating single stores declined from 5,365 in 1950 to 3,590 by 1963. During this same period, the number of chains with two or more stores rose from 96 to 150. The United States brought suit against Von's to prevent the merger. It claimed that the proposed merger violated Section 7 of the Clayton Act in that it may result in the substantial lessening of competition or tend to create a monopoly.

DECISION: Judgment for the United States. The fundamental purpose behind Section 7 of the Clayton Act is to prevent economic concentration by keeping a large number of small competitors in business. The language of Section 7 looks not only to a present danger of concentration, but also to a merger's impact on future competition. Thus, to preserve competition, a trend toward concentration should be arrested in its early stages, before the market falls into the hands of a few big companies.

Here, in the Los Angeles area, the number of single owner stores was decreasing substantially while the number of chains was on a marked rise. This is the type of trend toward concentration which the Clayton Act addresses. Since the proposed merger between Von's and Shopping Bags contributes significantly to this trend, it is prohibited. Furthermore, Von's cannot argue that the two stores had to merge to save themselves from business failure or from destruction by some larger competitor. Both were already powerful companies merging in a way that would make them even more powerful.

In 1982, the Justice Department and the FTC both indicated that they will be primarily concerned with horizontal mergers in highly or moderately concentrated industries and that they question the benefits of challenging vertical and conglomerate mergers. Both have justified this policy on the basis that the latter two types of mergers are necessary to transfer assets to their most productive use and that any challenge to them would impose costs on consumers without corresponding benefits. For a discussion of the recent merger trend prompted by the Reagan administration policy see the article reprinted in Law in the News on page 705.

Robinson-Patman Act

In an attempt to limit the power of large purchasers, Congress amended Section 2 of the Clayton Act by adopting the Robinson-Patman Act, which

New Rules Breed Wasteful Mergers

By Herman Schwartz

Public policy is always fertile ground for irony. Today, for example, the economic landscape is strewn with merger fiascos, but current antitrust policy toward these combinations is increasingly lenient. "Economic efficiency" is now the "only goal" of merger policy, according to a former Justice Department official. As a result, the merger wave of the 1980's surges ahead, reaching a new peak last week with the Allied Corporation's $5 billion planned union with the Signal Companies, the largest industrial merger ever (outside the oil industry).

This preoccupation with economic efficiency ignores Congressional intent and judicial precedent. The legislative history of the antitrust laws contains almost no mention of efficiency, production or price. Rather, there is an insistent Jeffersonian concern for the small entrepreneur—for social, not economic reasons. Thus, the Supreme Court has always ruled that efficiencies cannot save an otherwise illegal merger.

Nevertheless, when the Administration took office, William F. Baxter, then the Assistant Attorney General in charge of antitrust, promptly redrew Federal guidelines to ease restrictions on mergers between competitors. The guidelines further legitimized virtually any "vertical" merger—between customer and suppliers— or between companies in neither a directly competitive nor supply relationship.

Soon, deals—such as the proposed Allied-Signal merger—were proposed "that never would have been . . . before the Reagan Administration took office," as one businessman put it. Under these guidelines, one commentator noted, the Government would not have brought over half the merger cases that it won in the Supreme Court. Last June, the Antitrust Division further softened the guidelines.

Experience shows that the supposed benefits of a merger are often illusory. Take the oil industry. "Don't leave anything sitting around on a table, or we'll buy it," one oilman joked during the fat years. Today, Mobil is trying to spin off Montgomery Ward, after pouring over $600 million into it, and is taking a $500 million charge against earnings. Exxon has written off a $1.3 billion investment in Reliance Electric.

The multibillion-dollar Chevron-Gulf, Texaco-Getty and Mobil-Superior takeovers all now seem dubious to analysts—Mobil's first-quarter 1985 profits fell 15.8 percent, partly because of $90 million in interest to pay for Superior. Chevron, Texaco and Mobil must devote huge sums to debt service and reduction, and will reduce exploration even though drilling and completion costs are low. And Arco's divestiture of its refining and retailing operations shows that vertical integration may yield not efficiencies but trouble.

Steel mergers were supposed to "rationalize" a sick industry. But LTV, for example, is having so much trouble digesting Republic that, even though LTV's own steel sales rose substantially in the first quarter of 1985, it lost $156 million and operated less efficiently than the other top steelmakers; before the merger LTV had been among the most efficient.

Elsewhere, the once-voracious ITT will spin off 12 industrial technology acquisitions in its third major asset sale in eight months, with more to follow. G.E. has shed Utah International, after a loss of perhaps $3 billion. Du Pont's acquisition of Conoco was described by one market analyst as "dead weight pulling Du Pont down all the time." And the history of railroad mergers like that of Penn Central (permitted in the name of "efficiency") is dismal: in 1979, Forbes magazine concluded that 14 out of 17 rail mergers were unsuccessful.

At least some of these deals would have been blocked by an antitrust policy more consistent with Congressional intent and established law. The oil mergers almost certainly would have drawn a challenge, while the Du Pont-Conoco, LTV-Republic and the G.M.-Toyota joint venture probably would have been challenged.

Obviously, many mergers don't sour. A large number do, however, because of communications problems, many-layered decision-making, management frictions, differing work styles and corporate cultures, labor problems, key personnel departures and more. One merger consultant estimated that 70 percent fail.

Nevertheless, "economic efficiency" remains this Administration's antitrust lodestar. Mr. Baxter claims that the acquired companies are usually "being run inefficiently." But as Harry Gray of United Technologies told Congress, acquiring companies "never go for a turnaround situation . . . We don't have a stable of management experts who [can] . . . do everything better than the people who built the business."

The elevation of efficiency *uber alles* is just a fig leaf to cover a nakedly pro-business bias that appears not just in antitrust but also in tax, labor, safety, consumer protection, environmental and other areas. In antitrust matters, it makes for a policy that harms not only the country, but business itself.

prohibits **price discrimination** in interstate commerce of commodities of similar grade and quality. To be a violation, the price discrimination must substantially lessen competition or tend to create a monopoly.

Under this act sellers of goods are prevented from granting discounts to buyers, including allowances for advertisements, counter displays, and samples, unless the same discounts are offered to all other purchasers on proportionately equal terms. The act also prohibits other types of discounts, rebates, and allowances and makes it unlawful to sell goods at unreasonably low prices for the purpose of destroying competition or eliminating a competitor. The Act further makes it unlawful for a person knowingly to "induce or receive" an illegal discrimination in price, thus imposing liability on the buyer as well as the seller. Violation of the Robinson-Patman Act, with limited exceptions, is a civil rather than a criminal wrong.

Price differentials are permitted when justified by proof of either a cost savings to the seller or a good faith price reduction to meet the lawful price of a competitor.

Cost Justification

If a seller can show that it costs less to sell a product to a particular buyer, the seller may lawfully pass along the cost savings. For example, if Sears orders goods from Wrangler by the carload, whereas retailer B orders in small quantities, Wrangler, who delivers F.O.B. buyer's warehouse, may pass along the transportation savings to Sears. Nonetheless, although it is possible to pass along transportation savings, it is extremely difficult to pass along alleged savings in manufacturing or distribution because of the complexity involved in calculating and proving such savings. Therefore, sellers rarely rely on the defense of cost justification.

Meeting Competition

A seller may lower his price in a good faith attempt to meet competition. To illustrate:

1. Manufacturer X sells its motor oil to retail outlets for 65 cents per can. Manufacturer Y approaches A, one of manufacturer X's customers, and offers to sell a comparable type of motor oil for 60 cents per can. Manufacturer X will be permitted to lower its price to A to sixty cents per can and need not lower its price to its other retail customers—B, C, and D. Manufacturer X, however, may *not* lower its price to A to 55 cents unless it also lowers its price to B, C, and D.

2. Manufacturer X will not be permitted to lower its price to A without also lowering its price to B, C and D in order to allow A to meet the lower price charged by A's competitor N selling manufacturer Y's oil. The meeting competition defense is available only to meet the competition of the seller and does not extend to the price of a competitor of a specific, individual *purchaser*. See Figure 39-4.

However, as illustrated in the following case a seller may beat its competitor's price if it does not know the competitor's price, cannot reasonably determine the competitor's price, and acts reasonably in setting its own price.

GREAT ATLANTIC &
PACIFIC TEA CO. v.
FEDERAL TRADE
COMMISSION

United States Supreme
Court, 1979.
440 U.S. 69, 99 S.Ct. 925, 59
L.Ed.2d 153.

FACTS: Great Atlantic and Pacific Tea Company desired to achieve cost savings by switching to the sale of "private label" milk. A&P asked Borden company, its longtime supplier of "brand label" milk to submit a bid to supply certain of A&P's private label dairy products. A&P was not satisfied with Borden's bid, however, and it solicited other offers. Bowman Dairy, a competitor of Borden's, submitted a lower bid. At this point, A&P contacted Borden and asked it to rebid on the private label contract. A&P included a warning that Borden would have to substantially lower its original bid in order to undercut Bowman's bid. Borden offered a bid that doubled A&P's potential annual cost savings. A&P accepted Borden's bid. The Federal Trade Commission then brought this action charging that A&P had violated the Robinson-Patman Act by knowingly inducing or receiving illegal price discriminations from Borden.

DECISION: Judgment for A&P. A buyer cannot be held liable for knowingly inducing or receiving illegal price discrimination from a seller unless the seller itself could be found liable. Here, Borden has a valid meeting competition defense. Accordingly, since A&P has done no more than accept the lower of two prices competitively offered, it did not violate the price discrimination prohibition of the Robinson-Patman Act.

Federal Trade Commission Act

In 1914 Congress enacted the Federal Trade Commission Act creating the Federal Trade Commission (FTC), which is charged with the duty to prevent

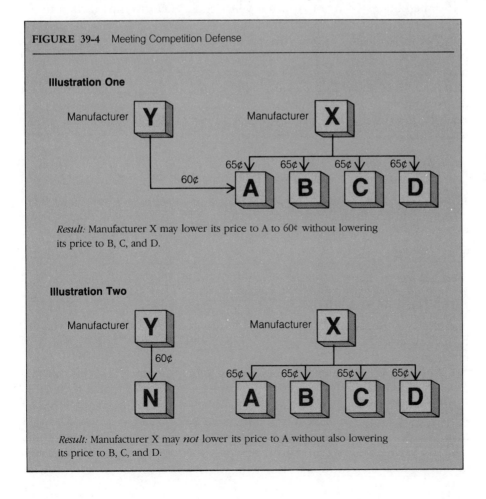

FIGURE 39-4   Meeting Competition Defense

Illustration One

Manufacturer **Y**   Manufacturer **X**

60¢   65¢ 65¢ 65¢ 65¢

A **B** **C** **D**

Result: Manufacturer X may lower its price to A to 60¢ without lowering its price to B, C, and D.

Illustration Two

Manufacturer **Y**   Manufacturer **X**

60¢   65¢ 65¢ 65¢ 65¢

N   **A** **B** **C** **D**

Result: Manufacturer X may *not* lower its price to A without also lowering its price to B, C, and D.

unfair methods of competition in commerce, and unfair or deceptive acts or practices in commerce. To this end the five-member commission is empowered to conduct appropriate investigations and hearings. It may issue cease and desist orders against violators that are enforceable in the Federal courts. Its broad power has been described as follows by the United States Supreme Court:

> The "unfair methods of competition," which are condemned by . . . the Act, are not confined to those that were illegal at common law or that were condemned by the Sherman Act. . . . It is also clear that the Federal Trade Commission Act was designed to supplement and bolster the Sherman Act and the Clayton Act . . . *to stop in their incipiency acts and practices which, when full blown, would violate those Acts.* (Emphasis added.)

Complaints may be instituted by the FTC, which after a hearing "has wide latitude for judgment and the courts will not interfere except where the remedy selected has no reasonable relation to the unlawful practices found to exist." Although the FTC most frequently enters a cease and desist order having the effect of an injunction, it may order other relief such as affirmative disclosure, corrective advertising, and the granting of licenses to patents on a reasonable royalty basis. Appeals may be taken from orders of the FTC to the United States Court of Appeals, which have exclusive jurisdiction to enforce, set aside, or modify orders of the FTC.

The work of the FTC includes not only investigation of possible violations of the antitrust laws but also unfair methods of competition, such as false and misleading advertisements, false or inadequate labeling of products, passing or palming off goods as those of a competitor, lotteries, gambling schemes, discriminatory offers of rebates and discounts, false disparagement of a competitor's goods, false or misleading descriptive names of products, use of false testimonials, and other unfair trade practices.

Unfair Competition

The law of unfair competition has been developed to prevent businesses from taking unfair advantage of their competitors. This area of law applies to trade secrets, trademarks, marks, and trade names, and copyrights and patents.

Trade Secrets

Most businesses have secret information, including lists of customers as well as contracts with suppliers and customers. Some have secret formulas, processes, and methods used in the production of goods that are vital to successful operation of the business. Sometimes designated as "trade secrets," this information must be given to certain employees employees so they can carry out their duties.

Trade secret–private business information

An employee is under a duty of loyalty to his employer, and this includes a duty not to disclose trade secrets to competitors. It is wrongful for a competitor to obtain vital secret trade information of this type from an employee by bribery or other means. The faithless employee also commits a tort by divulging secret trade information. Contracts of employment frequently contain restrictive covenants whereby the employee agrees that for a stated period of time and within a specific territory he will not directly or indirectly engage in competition with his former employer or become employed by a competitor of his former employer. These restrictive agreements, if reasonable with respect to time and area limitations, are enforced by the courts, although in some jurisdictions enforcement depends on the employee's having acquired trade secrets of his employer during the course of his employment.

In the absence of contract restriction, an employee is under no duty on termination of his employment to refrain from competing or working for a competitor of his former employer. During the period of employment he is under such a duty whether or not provided by contract. An example of unfair competition would be where one company induces employees of another company who have certain unique technical skills and secret knowledge acquired by them in the course of their employment to terminate their employment and to use their skills and secret information for the first company's benefit.

Trademarks, Marks, and Trade Names

Trademarks

A trademark is a distinctive mark, word, letter, number, design, picture, or combination in any form or arrangement that is affixed to goods and is adopted or used by a person to identify goods that she manufactures or sells. Generic and descriptive designations cannot be used as trademarks. Thus, a word that describes the ingredients, quality, purpose, function, or uses of a product may not be monopolized by a person as her proprietary trademark. "Plow" cannot be a trademark for plows, although it may be a trademark for shoes.

Trademark –distinctive insignia, word or design on a good that is used to identify the manufacturer

At common law a trademark was required to be affixed to the goods it identified. The Lanham Act, Trademark Act of 1946, relaxes this requirement by permitting trademark registration and protection of a mark placed "on the goods or their containers or the displays associated therewith or on the tags or labels affixed thereto." Trademarks may be registered in the United States Patent Office. If infringed, the owner is entitled to injunctive relief and damages. An infringement is a form of passing off one's goods or services as those of the owner of the mark, which deceives the public and constitutes unfair competition.

Service Marks, Certification Marks, and Collective Marks

Similar in function to the trademark, which identifies tangible goods and products, a **service mark** is used to identify and distinguish the services of one person from those of others. A service mark need not be affixed to goods, and when registered in the Patent Office, it is entitled to the same protection as a registered trademark.

A **certification mark** is a mark used with goods or services of persons other than the owner of the mark to certify the origin, material, mode of manufacture, quality, accuracy, or other characteristics of the goods or services or that the labor in the goods or services was performed by members of a union or other organization.

A **collective mark** is a distinctive mark or symbol used to identify or indicate membership in a trade union, trade association, fraternal society, or other organization.

Service marks, certification marks, and collective marks are protected against misuse or infringement by injunctive relief and a right of action for damages against the infringer.

Trade Names

Trade name–name used in trade or business to identify a product to a particular business or manufacturer

A trade name, like a trademark, serves as an identification of the product of a particular manufacturer or distributor. It may also designate a service or be the name under which a business is conducted. Trade names therefore have broader scope than trademarks, which only identify goods.

Descriptive and generic words as well as personal and generic names, although not proper trademarks, may become protected as trade names after acquiring a special significance in the trade. This special significance is frequently referred to as a "secondary meaning" of the name. The secondary meaning is acquired as the result of continuing and extended use in connection with specific goods or services whereby the name has lost its primary meaning to a substantial number of purchasers or users of the goods or services. A trade name for a product may be coined, such as "Kodak" or "Nylon," or it may be a popularly accepted nickname, such as "Coke."

Trade names are protected, and a person who palms off his goods or services by using the trade name of another is liable in damages and also may be enjoined from doing so.

Copyrights and Patents

Copyrights

Copyright–exclusive right to literary property

A copyright is the exclusive right to print, reprint, publish, copy, and sell books. periodicals, newspapers, dramatic and musical compositions, lectures, works of art, photographs, pictorial illustrations, and motion pictures for a period of the author's life plus an additional fifty years.

Applications for copyright are filed with the Register of Copyrights, Copyright Office, Library of Congress, Washington, D.C. Registration of the copyright is not required but is a condition of certain remedies for copyright infringement. The right is protected by the Federal Copyright Act, and remedies for infringements are available in the Federal courts.

SONY CORP. OF AMERICA v. UNIVERSAL CITY STUDIOS, INC.

Supreme Court of the United States, 1984.
   U.S.   , 104 S.Ct. 774, 78 L.Ed.2d 574.

FACTS: Sony Corporation manufactures and sells home video recorders, specifically the Betamax video tape recorders (VTR's). Universal City Studios, Inc., (Universal) owns the copyrights on some programs which had been aired on commercially sponsored television. Individual Betamax owners frequently used the device to record some of Universal's copyrighted television programs for their own noncommercial use. Universal brought suit, claiming that the sale of the Betamax VTR's to the general public violated its rights under the Copyright Act. It sought no relief against any Betamax consumer. Instead, Universal sued Sony for contributory infringement of its copyrights, seeking money damages, an equitable accounting of profits, and an injunction against the manufacture and sale of Betamax VTR's.

DECISION: Judgment for Sony. The sale of copying equipment does not constitute contributory infringement if the product is widely used for legitimate, unobjectionable purposes. The product need merely be capable of substantial noninfringing uses. Moreover, an unlicensed use of the copyright is not an infringement unless it conflicts with one of the five exclusive rights conferred by the Copyright Act. According to the Act, a "fair use" is not an infringement.

Here, the Betamax VTR's were widely used to have television programs time-shifted to suit the VTR owner's schedule. Under the "fair use" doctrine, proof that the noncommercial use of the copyrighted work would be harmful, or, if widespread, would adversely affect the potential market for the copyrighted work, is required to render the use an infringement. Sony demonstrated that substantial numbers of copyright holders of commercial television broadcasts would not object to time-shifting. Also, Universal failed to show that time-shifting would cause any substantial harm to the potential market for, or the value of, their copyrighted works. The Betamax then is capable of substantial noninfringing uses. Consequently, Sony's sale of such equipment to the general public does not constitute contributory infringement of Universal's rights.

Patents

A patent is the grant by the government of a monopoly right to an inventor to exclude others from making, using, or selling her invention for a period of seventeen years. The owner of the patent may also profit by licensing others to use the invention on a royalty basis.

Patent–exclusive right to an invention

A patent is issued by the United States Patent Office on the basis of an application containing specific claims relating to the invention, process, product, or design. Before granting a patent, the Patent Office makes a careful and thorough examination of the prior art and determines that the submitted invention has novelty and utility and does not conflict with a prior pending application or a previously issued patent. An application for a patent is confidential, and its contents will not be divulged by the Patent Office. This confidentiality ends when the patent is granted.

The granting of a patent is no guarantee of exclusive rights to make, use, or sell the alleged invention. The Patent Office is not a court and does not determine the rights of holders of patents. It may be necessary for the patentee to bring an action in the Federal court for infringement in order to determine the validity of her patent. If the court finds that the idea or invention is not novel, or is fully covered by the prior art, or that someone else had reduced the idea to practice before conception date by the patentee, the patent may be ruled invalid.

CHAPTER SUMMARY

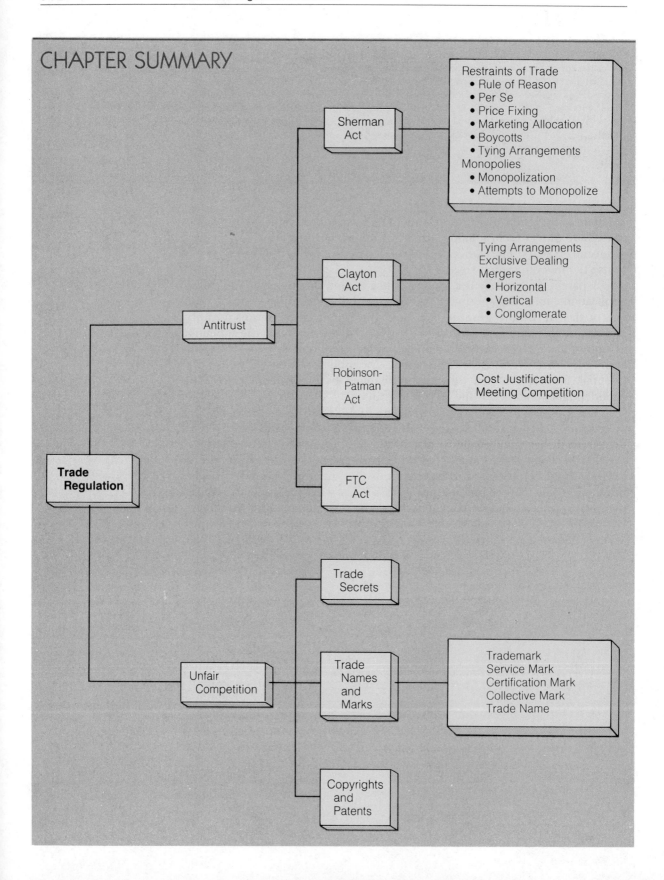

Sherman Act

Restraints of Trade
- Rule of Reason
- Per Se
- Price Fixing
- Marketing Allocation
- Boycotts
- Tying Arrangements

Monopolies
- Monopolization
- Attempts to Monopolize

Clayton Act

Tying Arrangements
Exclusive Dealing
Mergers
- Horizontal
- Vertical
- Conglomerate

Antitrust

Robinson-Patman Act

Cost Justification
Meeting Competition

FTC Act

Trade Regulation

Trade Secrets

Unfair Competition

Trade Names and Marks

Trademark
Service Mark
Certification Mark
Collective Mark
Trade Name

Copyrights and Patents

KEY TERMS

Trade regulation
Antitrust
Treble damages
Sherman Act
Rule of reason
Illegal per se
Horizontal restraint
Vertical restraint
Price fixing
Boycott
Market allocation
Exclusive dealing
Tying arrangement

Clayton Act
Monopoly power
Market share
Geographic market
Product market
Attempt to monopolize
Merger
Vertical merger
Horizontal merger
Conglomerate merger
Robinson-Patman Act
Price discrimination

Cost justification
Meeting competition
FTC Act
Trade secret
Trademark
Service mark
Certificate mark
Collection mark
Trade name
Copyright
Patent
Unfair competition

PROBLEMS

1. Discuss the validity and effect of each of the following situations:

(a) A, B, and C, manufacturers of radios, orally agree that due to the disastrous, cutthroat competition in the market, they would establish a reasonable price to charge their purchasers.

(b) A, B, C, and D, newspaper publishers, agree not to charge their customers more than thirty cents per newspaper.

(c) A, a distiller of liquor, and B, A's retail distributor, agree that B should charge a price of five dollars per bottle.

2. Discuss the validity of the following:

(a) An agreement between two manufacturers of the same type of products to allocate territories whereby neither will sell its products in the area allocated to the other.

(b) An agreement between manufacturer and distributor not to sell a dealer a particular product or parts necessary for repair of the product.

3. Universal Video sells $40 million worth of video recording equipment in the United States. The total sales of such equipment in the United States is $100 million. One-half of Universal's sales are to Giant Retailer, a company that possesses 50 percent of the retail market. Giant is presently seeking (1) to obtain an exclusive dealing arrangement with Universal or (2) to acquire Universal. Advise Giant as to the validity of its alternatives.

4. Z sells cameras to A, B, C, and D for $60.00 per camera. Y, one of Z's competitors, sells a comparable camera to A for $58.50. Z, in response to this competitive pressure from Y, lowers its price to A to $58.50. B, C, and D insist that Z lower its price to them to $58.50, but Z refuses. B, C, and D sue Z for unlawful price discrimination. Decision? Would your answer differ if Z reduced its price to A to $58.00?

5. Discount is a discount appliance chain store that continually sells goods at a price below the manufacturers' suggested retail prices. A, B, and C, the three largest manufacturers of appliances, agree that unless Discount ceases from its discount pricing, they will no longer sell to Discount. Discount refuses, and A, B, and C refuse to sell to Discount. Discount sues A, B, and C. Decision?

6. Company X produces 77 percent of all of the coal used in the United States. Coal provides 25 percent of all of the energy used in the United States. In a suit brought by the United States against X for violation of the antitrust laws, what result?

7. B, a chemist, was employed by A, a manufacturer, to work on a secret process for A's product under an exclusive three-year contract. C, a salesman, was employed by A on a week-to-week basis B and C resigned the employment with A and accepted employment in their respective capacities with D, a rival manufacturer. C began soliciting patronage from A's former customers, whose names he had memorized. What are the rights of the parties in (a) a suit by A to enjoin B from working for D and (b) a suit by A to enjoin C from soliciting A's customers?

8. X, having filed locally an affidavit required under the assumed name statute, has been operating and advertising her exclusive toy store for twenty years in Centerville, Illinois. Her advertising has consisted of large signs on her premises reading "The Toy Mart." B, after operating a store in Chicago under the name of "The Chicago Toy Mart," relocated in Centerville, Illinois and erected a large sign reading "TOY MART" with the word "Centerville" being written underneath in substantially smaller letters. Thereafter, the sales of X declined, and many of X's customers patronized B's store thinking it to be a branch of X's business. What are the rights of the parties?

SECURITIES REGULATION

The primary purpose of Federal securities regulation is to prevent fraudulent practices in the sale of securities and thereby maintain public confidence in the securities market. Federal securities law consists principally of two statutes: the Securities Act of 1933, which focuses on the issuance of securities, and the Securities Exchange Act of 1934, which deals mainly with trading in issued securities. Both Acts are administered by the Securities Exchange Commission (SEC), an independent, quasi-judicial agency. The SEC has the power to seek civil injunctions against violation of the Acts, to recommend that the Justice Department bring criminal prosecution, and to issue orders suspending or expelling broker-dealers.

The 1933 Act has two basic objectives: (1) to provide investors with material information concerning securities offered for sale to the public and (2) to prohibit misrepresentation, deceit, and other fraudulent acts and practices in the sale of securities generally, whether or not they are required to be registered.

The 1934 Act extends protection for investors to trading in securities that are already issued and outstanding. The 1934 Act also imposes disclosure requirements on publicly held corporations and regulates tender offers and proxy solicitations.

In addition to the Federal laws regulating the sale of securities, the States have their own laws regulating such sales within the State, commonly called Blue-Sky laws. These statutes all have provisions prohibiting fraud in the sale of securities. In addition, a number of States require the registration of securities, and some States also regulate brokers and dealers.

Any person who sells securities must comply with the Federal securities laws as well as with those of each State in which he intends to offer his securities. Because State securities laws vary greatly, we will discuss only the 1933 Act and the 1934 Act in this chapter.

The Securities Act of 1933

The 1933 Act, also called the "Truth in Securities Act," requires that a registration statement be filed with the SEC and become effective before any securities may be offered for sale to the public, unless either the securities or the transaction in which they are offered is exempt from registration. The

715

purpose of registration is to provide financial and other information about the issuer and those in control of it so that potential investors may consider the merits of the securities. The Act provides that potential investors must be furnished with a prospectus containing the important data set forth in the registration statement.

Regardless of whether the securities are exempt from the registration and disclosure requirements of the Act, the antifraud provisions of the Act apply to all sales of securities involving interstate commerce or the mails. Civil and criminal liability may be imposed for violations of the provisions of the Act.

Definition of a Security

The 1933 Act defines the term *security* to include any note, stock, bond, debenture, evidence of indebtedness, preorganization certificate or subscription, investment contract, voting-trust certificate, fractional undivided interest in oil, gas, or other mineral rights, or in general, any interest or instrument commonly known as a security. This definition expansively includes the many types of instruments that fall within the ordinary concept of a security. Nevertheless, even though a transaction is evidenced by an instrument labeled "stock," it may not be considered a security under the Securities Act. Accordingly, the ultimate task of determining which of the numerous financial transactions constitutes a security has fallen to the SEC and the Federal courts.

The courts have generally interpreted the statutory definition so as to expand its coverage to nontraditional forms of investments. For the purpose of the securities laws, a security is an investment of money, property, or other valuable consideration made in expectation of receiving a financial return solely from the efforts of others. Under this test, such investments as limited partnership interests, citrus groves, whiskey warehouse receipts, real estate condominiums, cattle, franchises, and pyramid schemes have been held to be securities in certain circumstances.

SECURITIES AND EXCHANGE COMM'N. v. W. J. HOWEY CO.

Supreme Court of the United States, 1970.
328 U.S. 293, 66 S.Ct. 1100, 90 L.Ed. 1244.

FACTS: W. J. Howey Co. and Howey-in-the-Hills Service, Inc., are Florida corporations under direct common control and management. The Howey Company owns large tracts of citrus acreage in Florida. The service company cultivates, harvests, and markets the crops. During the past several years Howey Company has offered one-half of its planted acreage to the public to help it "finance additional development." Each prospective customer is offered both a land sales contract and a service contract with Howey-in-the-Hills after having been told that it is not feasible to invest in the grove without a service arrangement. Upon payment of the purchase price the land is conveyed by warranty deed. The service company is given full discretion over cultivation and marketing of the crop. The purchaser has no right of entry to market the crop. The service company is also accountable only for an allocation of the net profits after the produce is pooled by the companies. The purchasers are predominantly nonresident business persons attracted by the expectation of substantial profits. Contending that this arrangement is an investment contract within the coverage of the Securities Act of 1933, the Securities and Exchange Commission brought this action against the two companies to restrain them from using the mails and instrumentalities of interstate commerce in the offer and sale of unregistered and non-exempt securities.

DECISION: Judgment for the SEC. The land sale and service contracts constitute an investment contract within the scope of the Securities Act of 1933. By including investment contracts within the Act, Congress chose a more flexible definition of a security so as to include any contract, transaction, or scheme whereby a person invests his money in a common enterprise and is led to expect profits solely from the efforts of the promoter or a third party. Such a definition fulfills the statutory purpose of compelling full and fair disclosure relative to the issuance of the many types of instruments that in the commercial world fall within the ordinary concept of a security. Furthermore, it does not matter that some of the investors choose not to accept the full offer of an investment contract by declining to enter into a service contract with Howey-in-the-Hills. The Securities Act prohibits the *offer* of unregistered non-exempt securities as well as their sale. It is enough to find a violation of the Securities Act, then, that the companies merely *offer* the essential ingredients of an investment contract.

Registration of Securities

The 1933 Act prohibits the offer or sale through the use of the mails or any means of interstate commerce of any security unless a registration statement for that security is in effect or an exemption from registration is secured. The purpose of registration is to provide **disclosure** of financial and other information on which investors may judge the merits of the securities. Registration does not insure investors against loss—the SEC does *not* make any judgment on the financial merits of any security or guarantee the accuracy of the facts presented in the registration statement.

In general, registration calls for disclosure of such information as (1) a description of the registrant's properties and business, (2) a description of the significant provisions of the security to be offered for sale and its relationship to the registrant's other capital securities, (3) information about the management of the registrant, and (4) financial statements certified by independent public accountants.

The registration statement and prospectus become public immediately on filing with the SEC, but it is unlawful to sell the securities until the effective date. However, after the filing of the registration statement, the securities may be offered orally or by certain summaries of the information in the registration statement as permitted by rules of the SEC. The ~~effective~~ date of a registration statement is the twentieth day after filing, although the commission, at its discretion, may advance the effective date.

Rule 415 of the SEC governs shelf regulations. **Shelf registrations** permit certain qualified issuers to register securities that are to be offered and sold "off the shelf" on a delayed or continuous basis in the future. This rule is a departure from the requirement that an issuer must file a registration for *every* new distribution of nonexempt securities. Rule 415 requires that the information in the original registration is kept accurate and current by updates. Shelf registrations allow issuers to respond more quickly to market conditions such as changes in stock prices and interest rates. A company issuing securities for the first time does not qualify for shelf registrations.

Exempt Securities

The 1933 Act exempts a number of specific securities from registration requirements. Exempt securities include (1) those sold under Regulation A, (2) those sold in intrastate transactions, and (3) short-term commercial paper. Because these exemptions apply to the securities themselves, the securities may be resold without registration.

Exempt security–*security not subject to registration requirements of 1933 Act*

Regulation A   Regulation A permits an issuer to offer up to $1.5 million of securities in any twelve-month period without registering them provided that the issuer files a notification and an offering circular with the SEC's regional office prior to the sale of the securities. The circular must also be provided to offerees and purchasers. Regulation A filings are less detailed and time-consuming than full registration statements, and the required financial statements are simpler and do not need to be audited. Because each purchaser must be supplied with an offering circular, securities sold under Regulation A may be freely traded after they are issued.

Intrastate Issues   The 1933 Act also exempts from registration any security that is a part of an issue offered and sold *only* to persons who live in a single state where the issuer of such security is resident and doing business. This exemption is intended to apply to local issues representing local financing by local persons and carried out through local investments. The exemption does not apply if one of the offerees, who need not be a purchaser, is not a resident of the State in which the issuer is resident.

Rule 147, promulgated by the SEC, provides a "nonexclusive safe harbor" for securing the intrastate exemption. Satisfying the rule assures the exemption, but there is no presumption that the exemption is not available for transactions that do not comply with the rule. Rule 147 requires that:

1. the issuer is incorporated or organized in the State in which the issuance occurs;

2. the issuer is principally doing business in that State, which means that 80 percent of its gross revenues must be derived from that State, 80 percent of its assets must be located in that State, and 80 percent of the net proceeds from the issue must be used in that State;

3. all of the *offerees* and purchasers are residents of that State;

4. during the period of sale and for nine months after the last sale, no resales to nonresidents are made; and

5. precautions are taken against interstate distributions. Such precautions include placing a legend on the certificate evidencing the security stating that the securities have not been registered and that resales can be made only to residents of the State and obtaining a written statement of residence from each purchaser.

Short-Term Commercial Paper   The Act exempts any note, draft, or bankers' acceptance issued for working capital that has a maturity of not more than nine months when issued. The exemption is not available if the proceeds are to be used for permanent purposes, such as the acquisition of a plant, or if the paper is sold in relatively small denominations to the public.

Other Exempt Securities   The 1933 Act also exempts the following types of securities from registration:

1. securities of domestic governments;

2. securities of domestic banks and savings and loans associations;

3. securities of nonprofit charitable organizations;

4. securities of issuers where the issuance is regulated by the Interstate Commerce Commission;

5. certificates issued by a receiver or trustee in bankruptcy with court approval;

6. insurance policies and annuity contracts issued by regulated insurance companies;

7. securities issued solely for exchange by the issuer with its existing security holders where no commission is paid; and

8. reorganization securities issued and exchanged with court or other governmental approval.

Exempt Transactions

In addition to the exemptions provided for specific types of securities, the 1933 Act also provides issuers with an exemption from the registration requirements for certain kinds of transactions. These transactions include (1) private placements, (2) limited offers not exceeding $5 million, (3) limited offers not exceeding $500,000, and (4) limited offers solely to accredited investors. These exemptions from registration apply only to the transaction in which the securities are issued and not to the securities themselves. Securities sold according to these exemptions are considered **restricted securities** and may be resold only by registration or in another transaction exempt from registration.

> **Exempt transaction**—*issuance* of securities not subject to the registration requirements of 1933 Act

> **Restricted securities**—securities issued under an exempt transaction

    An issuer who uses these exemptions must take reasonable care to assure against nonexempt, unregistered resales of restricted securities. Reasonable care includes, but is not limited to, the following: (a) making a reasonable inquiry to determine if the purchaser is acquiring the securities for herself or for other persons; (b) providing written disclosure prior to the sale to each purchaser that the securities have not been registered and therefore cannot be resold unless they are registered or an exemption from registration is available; and (c) placing a legend on the securities certificate stating that the securities have not been registered and that they are restricted securities.

Private Placements The most important exemption for issuers who wish to raise money without registration is the so-called private placement provision of the Act, which exempts "transactions by an issuer not involving any public offering." **Rule 506** of the SEC establishes a nonexclusive safe harbor for limited offers and sales without regard to the dollar amount of the offering. Securities sold under this exemption are restricted securities and may be resold only by registration or in a transaction exempt from registration. General advertising or general solicitation is not permitted. The issue may be purchased by an unlimited number of "accredited investors" and by no more than thirty-five other purchasers. **Accredited investors** include banks, insurance companies, investment companies, executive officers or directors of the issuer, any person who purchases at least $150,000 of the securities being offered so long as the total purchase price does not exceed 20 percent of the investor's net worth, any person whose net worth exceeds $1 million, and any person with an income over $200,000 in each of the last two years and who reasonably expects an income in excess of $200,000 in the current year. If the sale involves any nonaccredited investors, *all* purchasers must be given material information about the issuer, its business, and the securities being offered before the sale; otherwise such information is not required to be disclosed. The issuer must reasonably believe that each purchaser who is not an accredited investor has sufficient knowledge and experience in financial and business matters to be capable of evaluating the merits and risks of the investment or has the services of a representative who has the requisite knowledge and experience to make such an evaluation. The issuer must take precautions against nonexempt, unregistered resales and must notify the SEC of sales made under the exemption.

Limited Offers Not Exceeding $5 Million   In order to facilitate capital formation for small businesses, the SEC has promulgated **Rule 505,** which exempts from registration offerings by noninvestment company issuers that do not exceed $5 million over twelve months. Securities sold under this exemption are restricted securities and may be resold only by registration or in a transaction exempt from registration. General advertising or general solicitation is not permitted. The issue may be purchased by an unlimited number of accredited investors and by no more than thirty-five other purchasers. If the sale involves any nonaccredited investors, *all* purchasers must be given material information about the issuer, its business, and the securities being offered before the sale; otherwise, such information is not required to be disclosed. However, unlike Rule 506, the issuer is *not* required to believe reasonably that each nonaccredited investor, either alone or with his representative, has sufficient knowledge and experience in financial matters to be capable of evaluating the merits and risks of the investment. The issuer must take precautions against nonexempt, unregistered resales and must notify the SEC of sales made under the exemption.

Limited Offers Not Exceeding $500,000   The SEC's **Rule 504** provides private, noninvestment company issuers with an exemption from registration for small issues. The rule permits sales to an unlimited number of investors and does not require any information to be furnished to them. The exemption requires that:

1. the securities are offered and sold without general advertising;
2. the aggregate offering price within twelve months does not exceed $500,000;
3. the issuer takes precautions against nonexempt, unregistered resales; and
4. the issuer notifies the SEC of sales under the rule.

However, the limitations on general advertising do not apply and unregistered resales are permitted if (1) the offering is made exclusively in States that provide for the registration of the securities and require the delivery of a disclosure document before sale and (2) the securities are sold in compliance with those State provisions.

Limited Offers Solely to Accredited Investors   In 1980 Congress added **Section 4(6),** which provides an exemption for offers and sales by an issuer made *solely* to accredited investors if not in excess of $5 million. General advertising or public solicitation is not permitted. As with Rules 505 and 506, an unlimited number of accredited investors may purchase the issue; however, Section 4(6) is unlike these rules in that *no* unaccredited investors may purchase at all. No information is required to be furnished to the purchasers. Securities sold under this exemption are restricted securities and may be resold only by registration or in a transaction exempt from registration. The issuer must take precautions against nonexempt, unregistered resales and must notify the SEC of sales made under the exemption.

Resales of Restricted Securities   Transaction-based exemptions from registration do not necessarily exempt a later transaction in the same securities. Rather, those who acquire securities under Rule 506, Rule 505, Rule 504, or Section 4(6) must register any resales or find an exemption from registration, subject to the limited exception provided for some issuances under Rule 504.

Rule 144 of the SEC sets forth conditions that if met by any person selling restricted securities exempts her from registering them. The rule requires that there must be adequate current public information about the issuer, that the person selling under the rule must have owned the securities for at least two years, that she sell them only in limited amounts in unsolicited brokers' transactions, and that notice of the sale must be provided to the SEC. However, a person who is *not* an affiliate of the issuer at the time of sale of the restricted securities and has owned the securities for at least three years may sell them in unlimited amounts and is not subject to *any* of the other requirements of Rule 144.

Moreover, **Regulation A,** in addition to providing an exemption for issuers from registration for securities up to $1.5 million, also provides an exemption of up to $300,000 in any twelve-month period for all investors with a $100,000 limit for any one investor. Use of this exemption requires compliance with all of the conditions imposed on issuers by Regulation A, as we discussed above.

Figure 40-1 summarizes the exemptions from registration available under the 1933 Act, and Figure 40-2 graphically illustrates the requirements for registration and the exemptions available for various transactions.

Liability

To implement the statutory objectives of providing full disclosure and preventing fraud in the sale of securities, the 1933 Act imposes a number of sanctions for noncompliance with its requirements. The sanctions include administrative remedies by the SEC, civil liability to injured investors, and criminal penalties.

Unregistered Sales   The Act imposes civil liability for the sale of an unregistered security that is required to be registered, the sale of a registered security without delivery of a prospectus, the sale of a security by use of a prospectus that is not current, or the offer of a sale before the filing of the registration statement. Liability is absolute, as there are no defenses. The person who purchases a security sold in violation of this provision of the Act has the right to tender it back to the seller and recover the purchase price. If the purchaser no longer owns the security, he may recover monetary damages from the seller.

False Registration Statements   When securities have been sold subject to a registration statement, the Act imposes liability for the inclusion in the registration statement of any untrue statement or omission of material fact. **Material** refers to those matters to which there is a substantial likelihood that a reasonable investor would attach importance in determining whether to purchase the security registered. Liability is imposed on (1) the issuer; (2) all persons who signed the registration statement; (3) every person who was a

Material—matters to which a reasonable investor would attach importance in deciding whether to purchase a security

FIGURE 40-1   Exemptions under the 1933 Act

Exemption	Requirements	Result
Regulation A	1. Limited to $1.5 million of securities sold within 12 months 2. Proper notification and offering circular provided to SEC and offerees	Unrestricted resales
Intrastate sales	1. Issuer incorporated or organized in that State 2. Issuer principally doing business within that State 3. All offerees and purchasers are residents of that state 4. No resale for 9 months to non-residents	Freely transferable to residents; transferable to non-residents after 9 months
Private placement	1. No dollar limitation 2. Unlimited number of accredited purchasers 3. No more than 35 unaccredited but sophisticated purchasers 4. If any unaccredited purchasers must disclose material information 5. Sold without advertising 6. Notify SEC of sale	Restricted security
Limited offers not exceeding $5 million	1. Not exceed $5 million over 12 months 2. Unlimited number of accredited purchasers 3. No more than 35 unaccredited purchasers 4. If any unaccredited purchasers must disclose material information 5. Sold without advertising 6. Notify SEC of sale	Restricted security
Limited offers not exceeding $500,000	1. Not exceed $500,000 over 12 months 2. Sold without advertising 3. Notify SEC of sale	Restricted security
Limited offers solely to accredited investors	1. Not exceed $5 million 2. Unlimited number of accredited purchasers 3. No unaccredited purchasers 4. No information required 5. Sold without advertising 6. Notify SEC of sale	Restricted security

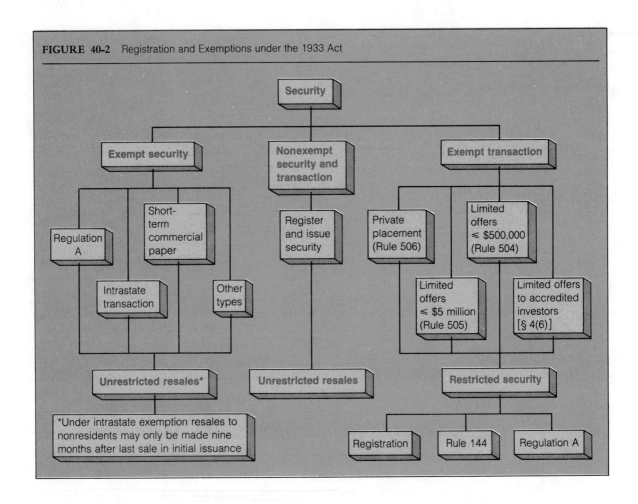

FIGURE 40-2   Registration and Exemptions under the 1933 Act

director or partner; (4) every accountant, engineer, appraiser, or expert who prepared or certified any part of the registration statement; and (5) all underwriters. These persons are jointly and severally liable to any person who acquires the security without knowledge of the untruth or omission for the amount paid for the security less either its value at the time of suit or the price for which it was sold.

However, an expert is only liable for misstatements or omissions in the portion of the registration that he prepared or certified. Moreover, any defendant, other than the issuer, may assert the defense of **due diligence.** This defense generally requires showing that the defendant had reasonable grounds to believe that there were no untrue statements or material omissions. In some instances due diligence requires that a reasonable investigation be made. In determining what constitutes a reasonable investigation and reasonable ground for belief, the standard of reasonableness is that required of a prudent man in the management of his own property.

ESCOTT v. BARCHRIS CONST. CORP.

United States District Court, Southern District of New York, 1968. 283 F.Supp. 643.

FACTS: BarChris Construction Corporation sold shares of common stock to the public in December 1959. By early 1961, BarChris needed additional working capital and sold debentures to meet this need. A registration statement was filed with the SEC in March 1961, with amendments filed in May. By the time BarChris received the net proceeds of this sale, it was experiencing financial difficulties. Eventually BarChris filed for bankruptcy. Escott, a purchaser of the debentures, brought suit under the Securities Act of 1933 against BarChris, the underwriters, the company's auditors (Peat, Marwick, Mitchell & Co.), and the persons who signed the registration, alleging that the registration statement contained material false statements and material omissions. The defendants deny the falsity of the statements and their materiality. Furthermore, all of the defendants, except BarChris, claim that they individually had exercised due diligence in connection with the statement so as to be free from liability under the statute.

DECISION: Judgment for Escott. The registration statement contained a number of false statements and omissions, many of which were material. Although the 1933 Act does provide a "due diligence" defense to all defendants other than the issuer BarChris, none of them sustained the burden of proving this defense. A non-expert (the defendants other than the auditor) is not liable for material misstatements or omissions in a registration statement not based on an expert's authority if the non-expert made a reasonable investigation from which he had reasonable grounds to believe the statement was true. A non-expert is not liable for material misstatements or omissions made on the authority of an expert if the non-expert had reasonable grounds to believe and did believe they were true. The due diligence defense for an expert, such as the auditors, requires reasonable grounds to believe that there were no material misstatements or omissions based upon a reasonable investigation. The standard of reasonableness is that of a prudent man in the management of his own property.

Antifraud Provision   The 1933 Act also contains a broad antifraud provision that applies to *all* securities, whether registered or exempt. It imposes liability on any person who offers or sells a security by means of a prospectus or oral communication that contains an untrue statement of material fact or an omission of a material fact. This liability extends only to the immediate purchaser, provided she did not know of the untruth or omission. The seller may avoid liability by proving that he did not know, and in the exercise of reasonable care could not have known, of the untrue statement or omission. The seller is liable to the purchaser for the amount paid on tender of the security. If the purchaser no longer owns the security, she may recover damages from the seller.

Criminal Sanctions   The 1933 Act imposes criminal sanctions on any person who willfully violates any of the provisions of the Act or the rules and regulations promulgated by the SEC pursuant to the Act. Conviction may carry a fine of not more than $10,000 or imprisonment of not more than five years or both.

The Securities Exchange Act of 1934

The Securities Exchange Act of 1934 deals mainly with the secondary distribution of securities. It provides protection for holders of securities listed on national exchanges as well as for holders of equity securities of companies traded over the counter if their assets exceed $3 million and they have a class of equity securities with 500 or more shareholders. Companies must register such securities and are also subject to the Act's periodic reporting requirements, the short swing profits provision, the tender offer provisions, the proxy

solicitation provisions, and the internal control and record-keeping requirements of the Foreign Corrupt Practices Act. In addition, issuers of securities,
whether registered under the 1934 Act or not, must comply with the antifraud
and the antibribery provisions of the Act (see Figure 40-3).

Registration and Periodic Reporting Requirements

The 1934 Act requires all regulated publicly held companies to register with
the SEC. These registrations are one-time registrations that apply to an entire
class of securities. Thus they differ from registrations under the Securities
Act of 1933, which relate only to securities involved in a specific offering.
Registration requires disclosure of such information as the organization, financial structure, and nature of the business; the terms, positions, rights, and
privileges of the different classes of outstanding securities; the names of the
directors, officers, and underwriters and each security holder owning more
than 10 percent of any class of nonexempt equity security; bonus and profit-
sharing arrangements; and balance sheets and profit and loss statements for
the three preceding fiscal years. Following registration, an issuer must file
specified annual and periodic reports to update the information contained in
the original registration. The Act also requires that each director, officer and
any person who owns 10 percent or more of a registered equity security file
monthly reports with the SEC stating any changes in his ownership of such
equity securities.

The 1934 Act imposes penalties for filing false statements and reports
with the SEC and imposes liability on issuers to investors who suffer losses in
the purchase or sale of registered securities because of reliance on such false
reports. Conviction may carry a fine of not more than $100,000 or impris-

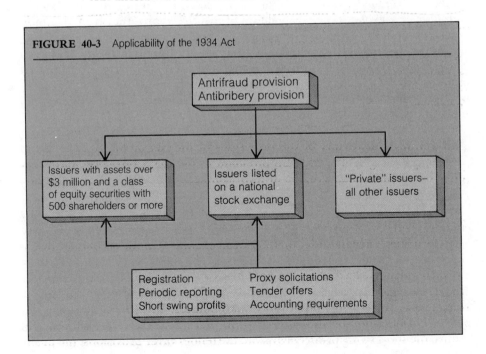

FIGURE 40-3   Applicability of the 1934 Act

onment of not more than five years or both, except no person is subject to *imprisonment* if he proves he had no knowledge of the rule or regulation.

Antifraud Provisions

Section 10(b) of the 1934 Act and SEC **Rule 10b-5** make it unlawful for any person to do any of the following when using the mails or any other facilities of interstate commerce in connection with the purchase or sale of any security:

1. employ any device, scheme, or artifice to defraud;

2. make any untrue statement of a material fact;

3. omit to state a material fact without which the information is misleading; or

4. engage in any act, practice, or course of business that operates or would operate as a fraud or deceit on any person.

Rule 10b-5 applies to any purchase or sale of **any** security, whether it is registered under the 1934 Act or not, whether it is publicly traded or closely held, whether it is listed on an exchange or sold over the counter, or whether it is part of an initial issuance or a secondary distribution. There are **no** exemptions. Unlike the liability provisions of the 1933 Act, Rule 10b-5 applies to misconduct of purchasers as well as sellers and allows both defrauded sellers and buyers to recover.

Requisites of Rule 10b-5   Recovery of damages under Rule 10b-5 requires proof of several elements, including (1) a misstatement or omission (2) that is material, (3) made with *scienter,* and (4) relied on (5) in connection with the purchase or sale of a security. Violation of this rule is different from common law fraud because the rule imposes an affirmative duty of disclosure. A misstatement or omission is material if there is a substantial likelihood that a reasonable investor would consider it important in deciding whether to purchase or sell the security. In an action for damages under Rule 10b-5, it must be shown that the violation was committed with **scienter,** which is intentional misconduct. Negligence is not sufficient.

Scienter–intentional and knowing conduct

Insider Trading   Rule 10b-5 applies to sales or purchases of securities made by an "insider" who possesses material information that is not available to the public. An insider is liable under Rule 10b-5 if he fails to disclose the material nonpublic information before trading on the information unless he waits until the information becomes public. **Insiders** for the purpose of Rule 10b-5 include directors, officers, employees, and agents of the issuer of the security as well as those with whom the issuer has entrusted information solely for corporate purposes, such as underwriters, accountants, lawyers, and consultants. In some instances, persons who receive material, nonpublic information from insiders—**"tippees"**—are also precluded from trading on that information. A tippee is under a duty not to trade on inside information when the insider has breached his fiduciary duty to the shareholders by disclosing the information to the tippee who knows or should know that there has been such a breach.

FACTS: Texas Gulf Sulphur Company (TGS) was a corporation engaged in the exploration for and mining of certain minerals. A particular tract of land in Canada looked very promising as a source of desired minerals, and a test hole was drilled by Texas Gulf on November 8, 1963. Because the core sample of the hole contained minerals of amazing quality, Texas Gulf began to acquire surrounding tracts of land. Stevens, the president of Texas Gulf, instructed all on-site personnel to keep the find a secret. Because subsequent test drillings were performed, the amount of activity surrounding the drilling had resulted in rumors as to the size and quality of the find. To counteract these rumors, Stevens authorized a press release denying the validity of the rumors and described them as excessively optimistic. The release was issued on April 12, 1964, though drilling continued through April 15. In the meantime, several officers, directors, and employees had purchased or accepted options to purchase additional Texas Gulf stock on the basis of the information concerning the drilling. They also recommended similar purchases to outsiders without divulging the inside information to the public. At 10 A.M. on April 16, an accurate report on the find was finally released to the American financial press. The SEC brought this action against Texas Gulf Sulphur and several of its officers, directors, and employees to enjoin conduct alleged to violate Section 10(b) of the Securities Act of 1934 and to compel rescission by the individual defendants of securities transactions assertedly conducted in violation of Rule 10b-5.

DECISION: Judgment for SEC. Where corporate employees learn of information which is considered material as it relates to the investment market of their corporation's securities, they have no duty to disclose that information if there is a valid business reason for nondisclosure. However, these employees may not benefit from transactions in the corporation's securities until they effectively disclose the inside information to the public. Moreover, the corporation itself may be liable under Rule 10b-5 when it issues public statements relating to material information concerning a matter which could affect its stock in the market. In these public statements, the corporation must fully and fairly state facts upon which investors can reasonably rely.

    1) Here, individual defendants had purchased TGS stock from November 12, 1963 through April 16, 1964 on the basis of material inside information concerning the results of TGS's drilling in Canada, while such information remained undisclosed to the investing public generally or to the particular sellers of the stock;

    2) Some of the defendants had divulged such inside information to others for use in purchasing TGS stock or had recommended its purchase while the information was undisclosed to the public or to sellers; and

    3) Some of the defendants had accepted options to purchase TGS stock on February 20, 1964 without disclosing the material information as to the drilling progress to either the Stock Option Committee or the TGS Board of Directors.

SECURITIES AND EXCHANGE COMM'N v. TEXAS GULF SULPHUR CO.

United States Court of Appeals, Second Circuit, 1968.
401 F.2d 833, *cert. denied* 394 U.S. 976, 89 S.Ct. 1454, 22 L.Ed.2d 756.

FACTS: In 1973, Dirks was an officer of a New York broker-dealer firm who specialized in providing investment analysis of insurance company securities to institutional investors. On March 6, Dirks received information from Ronald Secrist, a former officer of Equity Funding of America. Secrist alleged that the assets of Equity Funding, a diversified corporation primarily engaged in selling life insurance and mutual funds, were vastly overstated as the result of fraudulent corporate practices. Dirks decided to investigate the allegations. He visited Equity Funding's headquarters in Los Angeles and interviewed several officers and employees of the corporation. The senior management denied any wrongdoing, but certain corporation employees corroborated the charges of fraud. Neither Dirks nor his firm owned or traded any Equity Funding stock, but throughout his investigation he openly discussed the information he had obtained with a number of clients and investors. Some of these persons sold their holdings of Equity Funding securities, including five investment advisers who liquidated holdings of more than $16 million.

    While Dirks was in Los Angeles, he was in touch regularly with William Blundell, the *Wall Street Journal's* Los Angeles bureau chief. Dirks urged Blundell to write a story on the fraud allegations. Blundell did not believe, however, that such a massive fraud could go undetected and declined to write the story. He feared that publishing such damaging hearsay might be libelous.

DIRKS v. SECURITIES AND EXCHANGE COMMISSION

Supreme Court of the United States, 1983.
463 U.S. 646, 103 S.Ct. 3255, 77 L.Ed.2d 911.

During the two-week period in which Dirks pursued his investigation and spread word of Secrist's charges, the price of Equity Funding stock fell from $26 per share to less than $15 per share. This led the New York Stock Exchange to halt trading on March 27. Shortly thereafter California insurance authorities impounded Equity Funding's records and uncovered evidence of the fraud. Only then did the Securities and Exchange Commission (SEC) file a complaint against Equity Funding.

The SEC began an investigation into Dirks' role in the exposure of the fraud. After a hearing by an administrative law judge, the SEC found that Dirks had aided and abetted violations of § 10(b) of the Securities Exchange Act of 1934 and SEC Rule 10b-5 by repeating the allegations of fraud to members of the investment community who later sold their Equity Funding stock. Recognizing, however, that Dirks "played an important role in bringing Equity Funding's massive fraud to light," the SEC only censured him.

DECISION: Judgment for Dirks. An insider is liable under Rule 10b-5 for insider trading only when he does not disclose material non-public information before trading on it and thus makes "secret profits." This duty to disclose before trading arises from a fiduciary relationship between the insider and the shareholders of the corporation. A "tippee" assumes such a duty only if he receives information from the insider improperly. This occurs (1) when the insider has breached his fiduciary duty to the shareholders by disclosure to the tippee, and (2) the tippee knows or should know of the breach. The test is whether the insider personally will benefit from his disclosure. Absent personal gain, there is no breach of duty to the stockholders and, therefore, no derivative breach by the tippee.

Here, Dirks was a stranger to Equity Funding with no fiduciary duty to its shareholders. The insiders who provided him with the information did not intend to receive monetary gain from the disclosure. Rather, they were motivated by a desire to expose the fraud. The insiders breached no duty to the shareholders of Equity Funding. Therefore, there was no derivative breach by Dirks.

Short Swing Profits

Section 16(b) of the 1934 Act imposes liability on insiders—directors, officers and any person owning 10 percent or more of the stock of a corporation listed on a national stock exchange or registered with the SEC—for all profits resulting from their short swing trading in such stock. If any insider sells such stock within six months from the date of its purchase or purchases such stock within six months from the date of a sale of the stock, the corporation is entitled to recover any and all profit realized by the insider from these transactions. The "profit" recoverable is calculated by matching the highest sale price against the lowest purchase price within six months of each other. Losses cannot be offset against profits.

Although both Section 16(b) and Rule 10b-5 address the problem of insider trading and may apply to the same transaction, they differ in a number of respects. First, Section 16(b) applies only to transactions involving registered equity securities, whereas Rule 10b-5 applies to all securities. Second, the definition of "insider" is much broader under Rule 10b-5 and may extend beyond directors, officers, and owners of 10 percent or more of a company's stock, whereas Section 16(b) is limited to these persons. Third, Section 16(b) does *not* require that the insider possess material nonpublic information; Rule 10b-5 applies only to insider trading where such information is not disclosed. Fourth, Section 16(b) applies only to transactions within six months of each other; Rule 10b-5 has no such limitation. Finally, under Rule 10b-5 injured investors may recover damages on their own behalf, whereas under Section 16(b), although shareholders may bring suit, any recovery is on behalf of the corporation.

Insider Trading Sanctions Act

In addition to the remedies discussed above, the SEC is authorized by the Insider Trading Sanctions Act of 1984 to bring an action in a U.S. district court to have a civil penalty imposed upon any person who purchases or sells a security while in possession of material nonpublic information. Liability also extends to any person who aids and abets a violation by such person. The transaction must be on or through the facilities of a national securities exchange or from or through a broker or dealer. Purchases which are part of a public offering by an issuer of securities are not subject to this provision. The amount of the civil penalty is determined by the court in light of the facts and circumstances, but may not exceed three times the profit gained or loss avoided as a result of the unlawful purchase or sale. The penalty is payable into the Treasury of the United States. For the purpose of this provision, "profit gained" or "loss avoided" is "the difference between the purchase or sale price of the security and the value of that security as measured by the trading price of the security a reasonable period after public dissemination of the nonpublic information." An action must be brought within five years after the date of the purchase or sale.

Proxy Solicitations

A proxy is a writing signed by a shareholder of a corporation authorizing a named person to vote his shares of stock at a specified meeting of the shareholders. The 1934 Act makes it unlawful for any person to solicit any proxy concerning any registered security "in contravention of such rules and regulations as the Commission may prescribe." The rules of the SEC require the issuer to furnish security holders with a *proxy statement* describing all material facts concerning the matters being submitted to their vote together with a *proxy form* on which the security holders can indicate their approval or disapproval of each proposal to be presented. Even if a company does not solicit proxies from its shareholders but submits a matter to a shareholder vote, it must provide them with information substantially equivalent to that which would appear in a proxy statement.

Where management makes a solicitation, any security holder entitled to vote has the opportunity to communicate with other security holders. On written request, the corporation must mail the communication or, at its option, promptly furnish to that security holder a current list of security holders.

If an eligible security holder entitled to vote submits a timely proposal for action at a forthcoming meeting, management must include the proposal in its proxy statement and provide security holders with an opportunity to vote for or against it. If management opposes the proposal, it must include in its proxy materials a statement by the security holder of not more than 200 words. However, management may omit a proposal if, among other things, (1) under State law it is not a proper subject for shareholder action, (2) it is not significantly related to the business of the issuer or is beyond the issuer's power to accomplish, or (3) it relates to the conduct of the ordinary business operations of the issuer.

An issuer who distributes a false or misleading proxy statement to its security holders may be liable to any person who suffers a loss caused by purchasing or selling a security in reliance on the statement.

Law In The News

Two Inside Traders Go to Jail

As white-collar criminals go, Paul Thayer and Billy Bob Harris were strictly top drawer. Thayer, a former chairman of LTV, had served in the Reagan administration as deputy secretary of defense. Harris, a Dallas stockbroker with celebrity clients, earned upwards of $700,000 a year. As their lawyers pleaded for clemency from U.S. district judge Charles Richey last week, they might have expected to get nothing more than the customary slap on their expensively cuffed wrists. But it was their misfortune to run into a judge whose belief in "equal justice under the law" does not recognize the boundaries of the executive suite. "Yes, you defense attorneys are absolutely right in saying that the court should balance the scales of justice," Richey said. "This court has done that, and it is not going to hang a medal upon the lapel of your coats for the breach of trust, for the false statements, the perjurious statements and the obstruction of justice you have engaged in." With that, Richey hit Thayer, 65, and Harris, 45, with four years in jail and fines of $5,000 each.

Their crime was obstruction of justice—lying during a Securities Exchange Commission investigation of insider stock trading. As chairman of LTV and a director of several other companies, Thayer knew about various impending takeover and merger bids. He passed along advance information on some of them to his girl-

friend, Sandra Ryno, a former LTV employee, Harris and others—allowing them to profit by buying stock before the deals were disclosed to the public. Thayer himself made no money. U.S. Attorney Charles Roistacher suggested that Thayer benefited from Ryno's gains because he probably would otherwise have given her the same amount out of his own pocket.

The tough sentence was surprising in several respects. When Thayer and Harris pleaded guilty to the obstruction of justice charge in March, the prosecutor had agreed not to ask for a "substantial" jail term. And just a day before the sentencing, Thayer and Harris had agreed to pay $555,000 and $275,000, respectively, to settle civil charges of insider trading. The expectation was that, at most, Thayer would receive a two-year sentence—or, possibly, probation. (The four-year sentence was only one year short of the maximum.)

As additional insurance, Thayer had mustered an impressive set of character references from Gerald Ford, Barry Goldwater and Gen. John Vessey, chairman of the Joint Chiefs of Staff, and others. Harris, for his part, volunteered to perform community service—addressing other stockbrokers on the evils of insider trading—as an alternative to jail. But the judge apparently took that offer as evidence that Harris needed further instruction as to the seriousness of

his crime. "I don't see where any good is going to come," said an obviously appalled Richey, "from Billy Bob Harris going around talking to other stockbrokers. That suggestion is wholly without merit and I was shocked and surprised to receive it."

Trend: Thayer and Harris may take some comfort from the fact that they are part of a trend: more white-collar criminals are going to jail. While solid statistics are hard to come by, Justice Department figures indicate that defendants in securities cases have been sentenced to prison more frequently in recent years than they were a decade ago. The Thayer/Harris case, says Alan Bromberg, a securities expert and professor of law at Southern Methodist University in Dallas, represents "the extension of an existing trend to treat insider trading as a very serious violation." According to U.S. Attorney Joseph deGenova, the jail terms will send "a message to Wall Street offices and brokerage houses all over this country that this is . . . serious criminal behavior." Considering the number of defense contractors, financial institutions and securities dealers now facing government investigation for questionable practices, that message could not be more timely.

By Eric Gelman with Ann McDaniel.

Tender Offers

In 1968 Congress amended the 1934 Act to extend reporting and disclosure requirements to tender offers and other block acquisitions. A tender offer is a general invitation to all of the shareholders of a company to purchase their shares at a specified price.

Tender offer–general invitation to all shareholders to purchase their shares at a specified price

The Act requires any person or group that acquires or makes a tender offer for more than **5 percent** of a class of registered equity securities to file with the SEC a statement containing (1) the person's background; (2) the source of the funds used to acquire the securities; (3) the purpose of the acquisition; (4) the number of shares owned; and (5) any relevant contracts, arrangements, or understandings. A copy of the statement must be furnished to each offeree and sent to the issuer. It is unlawful for any person to make any untrue statement of material fact or omit to state any material fact or to engage in any fraudulent, deceptive, or manipulative practices in connection with any tender offer.

Shareholders who tender their shares may withdraw them during the first seven days of a tender offer or, if the offeror has not yet purchased their shares, at any time within sixty days from the time the offer was made. Moreover, all shares tendered must be purchased for the same price; if an offering price is increased, those who have already tendered receive the benefit of the increase. A tender offeror who offers to purchase less than all of the outstanding securities of the target must accept on a *pro rata* basis securities tendered during the offer.

Foreign Corrupt Practices Act

In 1977 Congress enacted the Foreign Corrupt Practices Act as an amendment to the 1934 Act. The Act imposes internal control requirements on companies with securities registered under the 1934 Act and prohibits all domestic concerns from bribing foreign governmental or political officials.

Accounting Requirements The Foreign Corrupt Practices Act requires every issuer that has a class of registered securities to

1. make and keep books that, in reasonable detail, accurately and fairly reflect the transactions and disposition of the assets of the issuer; and

2. devise and maintain internal controls to assure that transactions are executed as authorized and recorded in conformity with generally accepted accounting principles so as to provide accountability for assets and to assure that access to assets is permitted only with management's authorization.

Antibribery Provisions The Foreign Corrupt Practices Act makes it unlawful for *any* domestic concern or any of its officers, directors, employees, or agents to offer or give anything of value directly or indirectly to any foreign official, political party, or political official for the purpose of (1) influencing any act or decision of that person or party in his or its official capacity or (2) inducing that person or party to use his or its influence to affect a decision of a foreign government in order to assist the domestic concern in obtaining or retaining business. An offer or promise to make a prohibited payment is a violation even if the offer is not accepted or the promise is not performed. Violations can result in fines of up to $1 million for companies; individuals may be fined a maximum of $10,000 and imprisoned up to five years or both. Fines imposed on individuals may not be paid directly or indirectly by the domestic concern on whose behalf they acted.

Accountant's Legal Liability

An accountant is subject to potential civil liability arising from the professional services he provides to his clients and third parties. This legal liability is imposed by both the common law at the State level as well as Federal securities laws. In addition, an accountant may violate Federal and State criminal law in connection with the performance of his professional activities. In this part of the chapter we discuss accountants' legal liability under both State and Federal law.

Common Law

An accountant's legal responsibility under State law may be based on (1) contract law, (2) tort law, or (3) criminal law. In addition, the common law gives accountants certain rights and privileges, in particular, ownership of their working papers and, in some States, a limited accountant-client privilege.

Contract Liability   The employment contract between an accountant and her client is subject to the general principles of contract law. All of the requirements of a common law contract must be present for the contract to be binding, including offer and acceptance, capacity, consideration, legality, and a writing if, as is often the case, the agreement falls within the one-year provision of the Statute of Frauds.

On entering into a binding contract the accountant is bound to perform all the duties she **explicitly** agrees to provide under the contract. For example, if an accountant agrees to complete her audit of the client by October 15 to enable the client to release its annual report on time, the accountant is under a contractual obligation to do so. Likewise, if an accountant contractually promises to conduct an audit for the client to detect possible embezzlement, the accountant is under a contractual obligation to provide an audit *beyond* Generally Accepted Auditing Standards (GAAS) and must conduct an expanded audit.

By entering into a contract an accountant also **implicitly** agrees to perform the contract in a competent and professional manner. By agreeing to render professional services, an accountant is held to those standards that are generally accepted by the accounting profession.

If an accountant breaches his contract he will incur liability not only to his client but also to certain third-party beneficiaries. A **third-party beneficiary** is a noncontracting party whom the contracting parties *intended* to receive the *primary* benefit under the contract. For example, X Manufacturing Co. hires A, an accountant, to prepare X's financial statement for X to use to obtain a loan from Chemical Bank. Chemical Bank is a third-party beneficiary of the contract between X and A.

Following general contract principles, an accountant will not be entitled to any compensation if he *materially breaches* his contract. Thus, if an accountant does not perform his audit on time when time is of the essence, or if the accountant completes only 60 percent of the audit, he has materially breached the contract. On the other hand, if the accountant *substantially performs* his contractual duties he is generally entitled to be compensated for the contractually agreed-upon fee less any damages or loss his nonmaterial breach has caused the client.

Tort Liability   In performing his professional services an accountant may incur tort liability to his client or third parties for negligence or fraud. A tort, as discussed in Chapters 5 and 6, is a private or civil wrong or injury, other than a breach of contract, for which the courts will provide a remedy in the form of an action for damages.

An accountant is **negligent** if she does not exercise the degree of care a reasonably competent accountant would exercise under the circumstances. For example, A, an accountant, is engaged to audit the books of Z Corporation. During the audit O, an officer of Z Corporation, notifies A that he suspects that T, the company's treasurer, is engaged in a scheme to embezzle from the corporation. A does not pursue the matter because she was previously informed that O and T are on bad terms with each other. However, T was in fact engaged in a commonly used scheme of embezzlement. A is negligent for failing to conduct a reasonable investigation of the alleged defalcation. Nonetheless, an accountant is *not* liable for honest inaccuracies or errors of judgment so long as she exercises reasonable care in performing her duties. Moreover, an accountant is *not an insurer* of the accuracy of her reports provided she acts in a reasonably competent and professional manner.

Historically, an accountant's liability for negligence extended only to the client and to third-party beneficiaries. Under this view **privity** of contract was a requirement to a cause of action based on negligence. This approach was established in 1931 by the landmark case of *Ultramares Corp. v. Touche.* In recent years the *Ultramares* doctrine has been eroded by some courts that have in general extended the class of protected persons to include foreseeable plaintiffs. This approach has also been adopted by the Restatement of Torts. Foreseeable third parties are individuals who are members of a class that is known to the accountant or auditor to be intended recipients of the information provided or certified by the accountant. This class does not, however, include potential investors and the general public.

FACTS: Swartz, Bresenoff, Yavner & Jacobs ("Accountants") audited financial statements for its client International Trading Corporation. These statements capitalized leasehold improvements amounting to $212,000 and, therefore, showed a net profit for the corporation. The leasehold improvements were, however, fictitious. They should have been properly expensed as operating costs which would have resulted in a substantial loss on the income statement. The accountants' cover letter to the corporation expressed reservations about the fairness of the financial statements. After the Rhode Island Hospital Trust National Bank loaned the corporation an additional $126,000, it discovered that no leasehold improvements had been made. The Bank then sued to recover the balance of the loans from the accountants. It claimed that the accountants had negligently audited the financial statements and that it had relied on them in extending the loans.	**RHODE ISLAND HOSPITAL TRUST NATIONAL BANK v. SWARTZ, BRESENOFF, YAVNER & JACOBS** United States Court of Appeals, Fourth Circuit, 1972. 455 F.2d 847.

DECISION: Judgment for the bank. Generally, an accountant's liability for negligence rests on his duty to make financial reports in good faith, without fraud or collusion and with due care. An accountant owes this duty to his employer, and others whom he knows or expects to rely on the report. Here, the accountants failed to search for material costs related to the leasehold improvements and to investigate their existence. Moreover, although their disclaimer questioned the value of the improvements, it expressed no reservation about their existence. The accountants knew that Rhode Island Trust would rely on these statements. Thus, they are liable to the Bank for their negligence.

An accountant who commits a **fraudulent act** is liable to any person who the accountant *should have* reasonably foreseen would be injured by the misrepresentation and who justifiably relied on it. The required elements of fraud, which were more fully discussed in Chapter 9, are (1) a false representation (2) of fact (3) that is material (4) and made with knowledge of its falsity and with the intention to deceive (5) that is justifiably relied on. An accountant who commits fraud may be held liable for *both* compensatory and punitive damages.

Criminal Liability   An accountant's potential criminal liability in rendering professional services is primarily based on the Federal law of securities regulation and taxation. Nonetheless, an accountant would violate State criminal law if she knowingly and willfully certified false documents, altered or tampered with accounting records, used false financial reports, gave false testimony under oath, or otherwise committed forgery.

Criminal sanctions may be imposed under the Internal Revenue Code for knowingly preparing false or fraudulent tax returns or documents used in connection with a tax return. Such liability also extends to willfully assisting or advising a client or others to prepare a false return. Penalties may be a fine not to exceed $5,000 or three years imprisonment or both.

Client Information   An accountant is held to be the owner of his **working papers** but may not disclose the contents of these papers unless (1) the client consents or (2) a court orders the disclosure. Although the common law does *not* recognize an accountant-client privilege, some States have adopted statutes granting such a privilege. Nonetheless, it is generally considered to be professionally unethical for an accountant to disclose confidential communications from his client unless the disclosure is in accordance with (1) requirements of the accounting profession or of Generally Accepted Auditing Standards, (2) a court order, or (3) the client's request.

Federal Securities Law

Accountants may be both civilly and criminally liable under provisions of the 1933 and 1934 Acts. This liability is more extensive and has fewer limitations than liability under the common law.

1933 Act   Accountants are subject to **civil** liability under Section 11 of the 1933 Act if the financial statements they prepare or certify for inclusion in a registration statement contain any untrue statement or omission of material fact. This liability extends to anyone who acquires the security without knowledge of the untruth or omission. Not only is there no requirement of privity between the accountant and the purchasers, but proof of reliance on the financial statements is also usually not required under Section 11. However, an accountant will not be liable if he can prove "due diligence." The defense of **due diligence** requires that the accountant had, after reasonable investigation, reasonable grounds to believe and did believe, at the *time* the registration statement became *effective*, that the financial statements were true, complete, and accurate. The standard of reasonableness is that required of a prudent man in the management of his own property. Thus, Section 11 imposes liability on accountants for **negligence** in the conduct of the audit or the presentation of the information in the financial statements.

Moreover, if an accountant *willfully* violates this section, he may be held **criminally** liable for a fine of not more than $10,000 or imprisonment of not more than five years or both.

1934 Act   Section 18 of the 1934 Act imposes **civil** liability on an accountant if she makes or causes to be made any false or misleading statement about any material fact in any application, report, document, or registration filed with the SEC under the 1934 Act. Liability extends to any person who purchased or sold a security in reliance on that false or misleading statement and without knowing that it was false or misleading. An accountant is not liable, however, if she proves that she acted in good faith and had no knowledge that such statement was false or misleading.

Accountants may also be held **civilly** liable for violations of **Rule 10b-5.** Their liability may be for direct participation in a violation of the rule or for indirect participation resulting from their aiding and abetting others to violate the rules. Rule 10b-5, as previously discussed, is extremely broad in that it applies to *both* oral and written misstatement or omissions of material fact, and to *all* securities. This liability extends to purchasers and sellers who rely on the misstatement or omission of material fact in connection with the purchase or sale of a security. However, liability is imposed only if the accountant acted with *scienter.* Therefore, accountants are not liable under Rule 10b-5 for mere negligence, although reckless disregard of the truth *may* constitute *scienter.*

ERNST & ERNST v. HOCHFELDER

Supreme Court of the United States, 1976.
425 U.S. 185, 96 S.Ct. 1375,
47 L.Ed.2d 668.

FACTS: The defendant, Ernst & Ernst, is an accounting firm. From 1946 through 1967 it was retained by First Securities Company of Chicago, a small brokerage firm and member of the Midwest Stock Exchange and of the National Association of Securities Dealers, to perform periodic audits of the firm's books and records. In connection with these audits Ernst & Ernst prepared for filing with the Securities and Exchange Commission the annual reports required of First Securities under the 1934 Act. It also prepared for First Securities responses to the financial questionnaires of the Midwest Stock Exchange.

Hochfelder and others (plaintiffs) were customers of First Securities who invested in a fraudulent securities scheme perpetrated by Leston B. Nay, president of the firm and owner of 92% of its stock. This fraud came to light in 1968 when Nay committed suicide, leaving a note that described First Securities as bankrupt and the escrow accounts as "spurious." Plaintiffs subsequently filed this action for damages against Ernst & Ernst under § 10(b) of the 1934 Act. The complaint charged that Nay's escrow scheme violated § 10(b) and Commission Rule 10b-5, and that Ernst & Ernst had "aided and abetted" Nay's violations by its "failure" to conduct proper audits of First Securities. The plaintiffs' cause of action rests on a theory of negligent nonfeasance—that Ernst & Ernst had failed to utilize "appropriate auditing procedures" in its audits of First Securities, thereby failing to discover internal practices of the firm said to prevent an effective audit.

DECISION: Judgment for Ernst & Ernst. Section 10(b) of the 1934 Act and SEC Rule 10b-5 apply only to intentional conduct, not negligence. The legislative intent of the Act was to promote ethical standards of honesty and fair dealing by requiring regular accounting reports from corporations listed on national securities exchanges. In addition, Section 10 speaks specifically in terms of manipulation and deception and of implementing devices and contrivances. This is the commonly understood terminology of intentional wrongdoing. Based on this language and legislative history, the Supreme Court refused to expand the statute's scope to include negligent conduct. Because Ernst & Ernst's misconduct was merely negligent, not intentional, it is not liable to Hochfelder and the other shareholders.

Accountants may also be held **criminally** liable for any willful violation of Section 18 or Rule 10b-5. Conviction may carry a fine of not more than $100,000 or imprisonment for not more than five years, or both.

CHAPTER SUMMARY

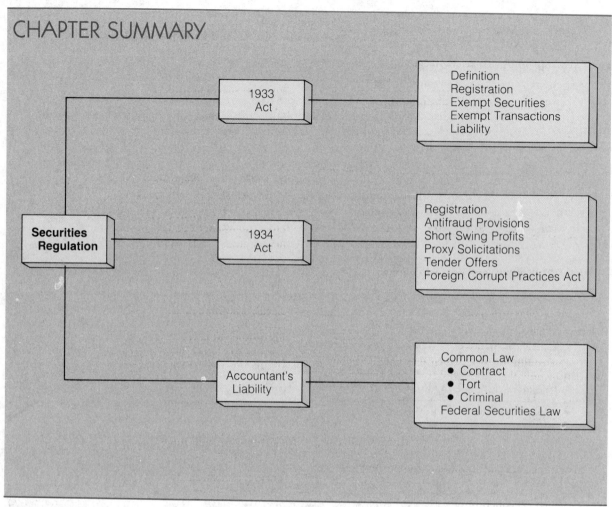

KEY TERMS

Blue Sky laws
Security
Registration statement
Prospectus
Shelf registration
Exempt securities
Offering circular
Intrastate issues
Nonexclusive safe harbor

Exempt transaction
Restricted securities
Private placement
Accredited investor
Material
Due diligence
Insider trading
Scienter

Insiders
Tippees
Short swing profits
Proxy solicitation
Proxy statement
Tender offers
Privity
Working papers

PROBLEMS

1. Acme Realty, a real estate development company, is a limited partnership organized in Georgia. It is planning to develop a 200-acre parcel of land for a regional shopping center and needs to raise $1,250,000. As part of its financing, Acme plans to offer $1,250,000 worth of limited partnership interests to about one hundred prospective investors in the southeastern United States. It anticipates that about forty to fifty private investors will purchase the limited partnership interests.

    (a) Must Acme register this offering? Why or why not?

    (b) If Acme must register but fails to do so, what are the legal consequences?

2. Bigelow Corporation has total assets of $850,000, sales of $1,350,000, one class of common stock with 375 shareholders, and a class of preferred stock with 250 shareholders, both of which are traded over the counter. Which provisions of the Securities Exchange Act of 1934 apply to Bigelow Corporation?

3. Capricorn, Inc., is planning to "go public" by offering its common stock, which had been previously owned by only three shareholders. The company intends to limit the number of purchasers to twenty-five persons resident in the State of its incorporation. All of Capricorn's business and all of its assets are located in the State of incorporation. Based on these facts, what exemptions from registration, if any, are available to Capricorn, and what conditions would each of these available exemptions impose on the terms of the offer?

4. Dryden, a certified public accountant, audited the books of Elixir, Inc., and certified incorrect financial statements in a form which was filed with the SEC. Shortly thereafter Elixer, Inc. went bankrupt. Investigation into the bankruptcy disclosed that Kraft, the president of Elixir, had engaged in an intricate and clever embezzlement scheme that siphoned off substantial sums of money that now support Kraft in a luxurious life-style in South America. Investors who purchased shares of Elixir have brought suit against Dryden under Rule 10b-5. At the trial Dryden produces evidence demonstrating that his failure to discover the embezzlements resulted merely from negligence on his part and that he had no knowledge of the fraudulent conduct. Decision?

5. Farthing is a director and vice-president of Garp, Inc. whose common stock is listed on the New York Stock Exchange. Farthing engaged in the following transactions in 1986: on January 2, Farthing sold 500 shares at thirty dollars per share; on January 15 she purchased 300 shares at thirty dollars per share; on February 1, she purchased 200 shares at forty-five dollars per share; on March 1, she purchased 300 shares at sixty dollars per share; on March 15, she sold 200 shares at fifty-five dollars per share; and on April 1, she sold 100 shares at forty dollars per share. Howell brings suit on behalf of Garp alleging that Farthing has violated the Securities Act of 1934. Farthing defends on the ground that she lost money on the transactions in question. Decision?

6. Intercontinental Widgets, Inc. had applied for a patent for a new state-of-the-art widget that, if patented, would significantly increase the value of Intercontinental's shares. On September 1, the Patent Office notified Jackson, the attorney for Intercontinental, that the patent application had been approved. After informing Kingsley, the company's president, of the good news, Jackson called his broker and purchased 1,000 shares of Intercontinental at eighteen dollars per share. He also told his partner, Lucas, who immediately proceeded to purchase 500 shares at nineteen dollars per share. Lucas then called his brother-in-law, Mammon, and told him the news. On September 3, Mammon bought 4,000 shares at twenty-one dollars per share. On September 4, Kingsley issued a press release that accurately reported that a patent had been granted to Intercontinental. On the next day Intercontinental's stock soared to thirty-eight dollars per share. A class action suit is brought against Jackson, Lucas, Mammon, and Intercontinental for violations of Rule 10b-5. Who, if anyone, is liable?

7. Nova, Inc. sought to sell a new issue of common stock. It registered the issue with the SEC but included false information in both the registration statement and the prospectus. The issue was underwritten by Omega & Sons and was sold in its entirety by Periwinkle, Rameses, and Sheffield, Inc., a securities broker-dealer. Telford purchased 500 shares at six dollars per share. Three months later the falsity of the information contained in the prospectus was made public and the price of the shares fell to one dollar per share. The following week Telford brought suit against Nova, Inc., Omega & Sons, and Periwinkle, Rameses and Sheffield, Inc. under the Securities Act of 1933.

    (a) Who, if anyone, is liable under the Act?

    (b) What defenses, if any, are available to the various defendants?

8. T, a director and officer of Deep Hole Oil Company, approached R for the purpose of buying 200 shares of Deep Hole Company stock owned by R. During the period of negotiations, T concealed his identity and did not disclose the fact that earlier in the day he had received a report of two rich oil strikes on the oil company's property. R sold his 200 shares to T for ten dollars per share. Taking into consideration the new strikes, the fair value of the stock was approximately twenty dollars per share. R sues T to recover damages. Decision?

9. Johnson Enterprises, Inc. contracted with the accounting firm of P, A & E to perform an audit of Johnson. The accounting firm performed its duty in a nonnegligent, competent manner but failed to discover a novel embezzlement scheme perpetrated by Johnson's treasurer. Shortly thereafter Johnson's treasurer disappeared with $75,000 of the company's money. Johnson now refuses to pay P, A & E its $20,000 audit fee and is seeking to recover $75,000 from P, A & E.

   (a) What are the rights and liabilities of P, A & E and Johnson? Explain.

   (b) Would your answer to (a) differ if the scheme was a common embezzlement scheme that Generally Accepted Auditing Standards should have disclosed? Explain.

10. The accounting firm of T, W & S was engaged to perform an audit of Progate Manufacturing Company. During the course of its investigation T, W & S discovered that the inventory was overvalued by the company in that it was carried on the books at the previous year's prices, which were significantly higher than current prices. When T, W & S approached Progate's president, Lehman, about the improper valuation of inventory, Lehman became enraged and told T, W & S that unless the firm accepted the valuation Progate would sue T, W & S. Although T, W & S knew that Progate's suit was frivolous and unfounded it wished to avoid the negative publicity that would arise from any suit brought against it. Therefore, on the assumption that the overvaluation would not harm anybody T, W & S accepted Progate's inflated valuation of inventory. Progate subsequently went bankrupt and T, W & S are now being sued by (1) First National Bank, a bank that relied on T, W & S's statement to loan money to Progate and (2) Thomas, an investor who purchased 20 percent of Progate's stock after receiving T, W & S's statement. What are the rights and liabilities of First National Bank, Thomas, and T, W & S?

CONSUMER PROTECTION

Consumer transactions have increased enormously since World War II, and today they amount to hundreds of billions of dollars. Although the definition of a consumer transaction varies, it is generally considered one involving goods, credit, services, or land acquired for personal, household, or family purposes. Historically, consumers were subject to the rule of *caveat emptor*— let the buyer beware. However, in recent years the law has abandoned this principle in most consumer transactions and gives greater protection to consumers. Most of this protection takes the form of statutory enactments at both the State and Federal levels, and a wide variety of governmental agencies are charged with enforcement of these statutes. Nonetheless, as pointed out in Law in the News on page 740, many contend that consumer fears and ignorance are all too frequently being exploited by charletans and that more protection is needed.

In this chapter we examine consumer protection statutes that regulate (a) unfair and deceptive trade practices; (b) consumer purchases of goods, services, and land; (c) consumer credit obligations; and (d) consumer health and safety.

Unfair and Deceptive Trade Practices

In 1914 Congress enacted the **Federal Trade Commission Act** creating the Federal Trade Commission (FTC), which is charged with the duty to prevent unfair methods of competition in commerce, and unfair or deceptive acts or practices in commerce. To this end the five-member commission is empowered to issue substantive rules and to conduct appropriate investigations and hearings. The FTC may institute complaints and after a hearing may order appropriate relief, including cease and desist orders, and under certain circumstances, recovery of civil penalties and damages for persons injured by unfair or deceptive acts or practices. Appeals may be taken from orders of the FTC to the United States Courts of Appeals, which have exclusive jurisdiction to enforce, set aside, or modify orders of the commission.

The Commission has established a Bureau of Consumer Protection, which investigates unfair methods of competition, such as false and misleading advertisements, false or inadequate labeling of products, passing or palming off goods as those of a competitor, lotteries, gambling schemes, discriminatory

Law in The News

Protecting Children From TV Commercials

Because children are especially susceptible to misleading or deceptive television advertising, particularly when it's aimed at them, consumer groups and regulatory agencies keep a sharp eye on the $600-million-a-year business. And they urge parents to do the same.

The Children's Advertising Review Unit of the Council of Better Business advises that parents keep the following questions in mind as they watch commercials aimed at children:

—Are children shown using a product in a way the average child could not?

—Does the ad suggest that a child will be superior to friends or more popular if he or she owns a certain product?

—Does the ad employ any demeaning or derogatory social stereotypes?

—Does the ad imply that one food provides all the nutrients contained in a well-balanced food plan?

—Does the ad use such words as "only" or "just" to describe the price?

—Do program hosts or characters appear in commercials within their own programs?

If the answer to any of the above questions is yes, the ad may be misleading. The same is true if the answer to any of the following questions is no:

—Is the aim of the product made clear?

—Does the ad clearly indicate what is included in the purchase price?

—If assembly is required, does the ad say so in language that a child can understand?

—In ads featuring premiums, is the product itself given more importance than the premium?

—If fantasy elements are used, is it plain that they are "just pretend"?

Reprinted by permission of The McCall Publishing Company.

offers of rebates and discounts, false disparagement of a competitor's goods, false or misleading descriptive names of products, and use of false testimonials.

The FTC is the principal Federal agency concerned with the regulation of advertising. The Commission is concerned with providing purchasers with a sufficient supply of accurate information and thus attempts to regulate misleading or deceptive advertising. Deception may occur by either false representation or material omission. The FTC Act lends some guidance by defining false advertising as it relates to foods, drugs, devices and cosmetics:

> The term "false advertisement" means an advertisement, other than labeling, which is misleading in a material respect; and in determining whether any advertisement is misleading, there shall be taken into account (among other things) not only representations made or suggested by statement, word, design, device, sound, or any combination thereof, but also the extent to which the advertisement fails to reveal facts material in the light of such representations or material with respect to consequences which may result from the use of the commodity to which the advertisement relates under the conditions prescribed in said advertisement, or under such conditions as are customary or usual.

The Commission need not prove that there was actual deception; it merely must show that the material misrepresentation or material omission has the "tendency or capacity" to deceive a significant number of consumers. Representations can be either expressed or implied and the determination of what representations have been made rests with the expertise of the Commission. Thus, a cereal advertisement which states that "no cereal has fewer calories than ours" might be considered deceptive if other cereals have equally few calories. It is unclear whether the standard for determining that an advertisement has the capacity to deceive is based upon "the average man," "the ignorant, unthinking, and the credulous," "the least-sophisticated reader," or some other standard. Nevertheless, the Commission has stated:

> True . . . the Commission's responsibility is to prevent deception of the gullible and credulous, as well as the cautious and knowledgeable. . . . [T]his principle loses its validity, however, if it is applied uncritically or pushed to an absurd extreme. An advertiser cannot be charged with liability with respect of every conceivable misconception, however outlandish, to which his representations might be subject among the foolish or feeble-minded . . . A representation does not become "false and deceptive" merely because it will be unreasonably misunderstood by an insignificant and unrepresentative segment of the class of persons to whom the representation is addressed.

Examples of deceptive practices include advertising that a certain product will save the consumer 25 percent on their automotive motor oil where the product simply replaced a quart of oil in the engine (which normally contains four quarts of oil) and was more expensive than the replaced motor oil; placing marbles in a bowl of vegetable soup in order to displace the vegetables from the bottom of the soup and therefore make it appear that the soup had more vegetables; and claiming that a drug provides greater pain relief than another named drug when there was insufficient evidence to prove the claim to the medical community.

In addition to the remedies discussed above the FTC has recently employed three other potent remedies: (1) affirmative disclosure, (2) corrective advertising, and (3) multiple product orders. **Affirmative disclosure** is frequently employed by the FTC and requires the offender to provide certain information in its advertisement in order for the ad not to be considered deceptive. In ordering such remedial action, however, the Commission must be careful not to infringe upon the advertiser's constitutional rights. For instance, the National Commission on Egg Nutrition (NCEN), an egg producers' trade association, was organized in an attempt to combat the damage being done to the egg industry by the anti-cholesterol forces. The Federal Trade Commission alleged that in its attempt to achieve this goal the NCEN had made several false and misleading statements in its advertising campaign. Principally, the FTC contended and subsequently ruled that it was an unfair trade practice for NCEN to represent "that there is no scientific evidence that eating eggs increases the risk of . . . heart and [circulatory] disease . . . ." In addition to ordering the NCEN to cease and desist from this and other representations the FTC also ordered that (1) any reference made to the relationship between cholesterol (and hence eggs) and circulatory disease be accompanied by a conspicuous statement that many medical authorities believe that eating cholesterol might increase the risk of heart or circulatory disease, and (2) any representation disparaging the scientific evidence connecting cholesterol and heart and circulatory disease is forbidden. However, the United States Court of Appeals for the Seventh Circuit amended the FTC's affirmative disclosure order on the ground that the order was an overly broad remedial decree. It held that the First Amendment prohibited a remedy "broader than that which is necessary." And, since the order directed NCEN to argue the other side of the issue rather than merely acknowledge the existence of

Affirmative disclosure– requirement that an advertiser include certain information in its advertisement so that it is not deceptive the controversy, the order unduly infringed upon NCEN's freedom of speech. The Court, nevertheless, held that: (1) the NCEN cannot disseminate any advertisement that represents that the consumption of eggs or cholesterol does not enhance the risk of heart or circulatory disease unless it conspicuously discloses that a controversy exists surrounding this connection and that the advertisement is merely stating its position and (2) that NCEN cannot disseminate any advertisement that presents scientific evidence supporting the position that the consumption of eggs and/or cholesterol does not increase the consumer's risk of heart or circulatory disease unless it conspicuously discloses that many medical authorities are of the belief that the eating of eggs (cholesterol) does, based on scientific evidence, increase one's risk of heart or circulatory ailment.

Corrective advertising goes beyond affirmative disclosure and requires that the advertiser of a deceptive claim disclose in future advertisement, that the deceptive claims made in the prior advertisements are in fact not true. For an example of this remedy *see Warner-Lambert Co. v. FTC* which follows.

Corrective advertising–disclosure in an advertisement that previous ads were deceptive

---

WARNER-LAMBERT CO. v. F.T.C.

United States Court of Appeals, District of Columbia Circuit, 1977.
562 F.2d 749.

FACTS: The F.T.C. ordered Warner-Lambert to cease and desist from advertising that its product, Listerine Antiseptic mouthwash, prevents, cures, or alleviates the common cold and sore throats. The order further required disclosure in future advertisements that: "Contrary to prior advertising, Listerine will not help prevent colds or sore throats or lessen their severity." Warner-Lambert contended that even if its past advertising claims were false, the corrective advertising portion of the order exceeds the FTC's statutory power. The FTC claims that corrective advertising is necessary in light of Warner-Lambert's 100 years of false claims and the resulting persistence of erroneous consumer beliefs.

DECISION: Judgment for the FTC. Congress intended for the FTC to have broad remedial powers in order to protect the public from deceptive trade practices. Corrective advertising represents an appropriate remedy in this case due to Warner-Lambert's long history of deceptive advertising, to the success of the advertising campaign to create a false image in the public's mind, and to the fact that this false perception would continue if not corrected.

Multiple product orders require that the deceptive advertisers not only cease and desist from any future deception in regard to the product in question but also to all products sold by the company. *See Sears, Roebuck and Co.* below. This remedy is particularly useful in dealing with companies which are repeated violators of the law.

Multiple product order–advertiser cease and desist from deceptive statements on all products it sells

---

SEARS, ROEBUCK AND CO. v. F.T.C.

United States Court of Appeals, Ninth Circuit, 1982.
676 F.2d 385.

FACTS: In the early 1970's, Sears formulated a plan to increase sales of its top of the line "Lady Kenmore" brand dishwasher. Sears' plan sought to change the Lady Kenmore's image, without the need for reengineering or any mechanical improvements in the dishwasher itself. To accomplish this, Sears undertook a four-year, $8 million advertising campaign which claimed that the Lady Kenmore completely eliminated the need for pre-rinsing and pre-scraping dishes. As a result of this campaign, sales rose by more than 300%. However, the "no scraping, no pre-rinsing" claim was not true, and Sears had no reasonable basis for asserting the claim. In addition, the Owner's Manual which customers received after they purchased the dishwasher contradicted the claim.

After a thorough investigation, the Federal Trade Commission (FTC), in 1977, filed a complaint against Sears, alleging that the advertisements were false and misleading. The final FTC order required Sears to stop making the "no scraping, no pre-rinsing" claim. The order also prevented Sears from (1) making any "performance claims" for "major home appliances" without first possessing a reasonable basis consisting of substantiating tests or other evidence; (2) misrepresenting any test, survey or demonstration regarding "major home appliances;" and (3) making any advertising statements not consistent with statements in post-purchase materials supplied to purchasers of "major home appliances." Sears contends the order is too broad, since it covers appliances other than dishwashers, as well as including "performance claims."

DECISION: Judgment for the FTC. The FTC has wide latitude for judgment in determining sanctions. Thus, courts generally will not interfere except where the remedy selected by the FTC has no reasonable relation to the discovered unlawful practices. In multi-product cases, the ultimate question is the likelihood of the wrongdoer committing the same sort of unfair practices again. Such a determination depends on the specific circumstances of the case.

Here, Sears knew its "no rinsing, no scraping" claim had no reasonable bases; it does not dispute the falsity of the advertisement. Sears' advertising campaign thus demonstrates a "blatant and utter disregard" for the law. Furthermore, the advertisements were not isolated incidents. They were part of a four-year, $8 million campaign strategy. Sears could readily transfer this selling strategy to the marketing of its other major home appliances sold nationwide. Therefore, the multi-product order and the "performance claims" provision are reasonably related to Sears' conduct and appropriate.

Numerous States have consumer protection statutes which are similar to the FTC Act and prohibit unfair and deceptive trade practices.

Consumer Purchases

A number of State and Federal regulations protect consumers in their purchases of goods, services, and real property for personal, household, or family use. The Uniform Commercial Code, which we discussed more fully in Chapters 17–21, prohibits unconscionable contractual terms and imposes implied warranties for the protection of the purchaser.

Federal Warranty Protection

To protect buyers and to prevent deception in selling, Congress in 1974 enacted the Magnuson-Moss Warranty Act, which requires that sellers of consumer products give adequate information about warranties. The FTC administers and enforces the act.

The **Magnuson-Moss Warranty Act** was enacted in order to alleviate certain reported warranty problems: (1) most warranties were not understandable; (2) most warranties disclaimed implied warranties; (3) most warranties were unfair; and (4) in some instances the warrantors did not live up to their warranties. The act was Congress's attempt to make consumer product warranties more easily understood and to help consumers enforce their claims satisfactorily. To accomplish this purpose, the act provides for:

1. disclosure in clear and understandable language of the warranty that is to be offered;

2. a description of the warranty as either "full" or "limited";

3. a prohibition against disclaiming implied warranties if a written warranty is given; and

4. an optional informal settlement mechanism.

The act applies to **consumer** products with **written warranties**. A consumer product is any item of tangible personal property that is *normally* used for family, household, or personal use and that is distributed in commerce.

Consumer product–tangible personal property normally used for family, household, or personal purpose

Commercial purchasers are *not* protected by the act, partly because they are considered to have sufficient knowledge in contracting to protect themselves. Also, they are able to employ their own attorneys to protect themselves and can spread the cost of their injuries in the marketplace.

The act contains *pre-sale disclosure* provisions that are calculated to prevent confusion and deception and to enable purchasers to make educated product comparisons. A warrantor must, "to the extent required by the rules of the Commission [Federal Trade Commission], fully and conspicuously disclose in simple and readily understood language the terms and conditions of such warranty."

The second major part of the Magnuson-Moss Warranty Act concerns the *labeling* requirement. The act divides written warranties into two categories, limited and full, one of which, for any product costing more than ten dollars, must be designated on the written warranty itself. The purpose of this provision is to alert the consumer to the legal rights under a certain warranty for purposes of initial comparison. If a warranty is designated as *full*, the warrantor must agree to repair the product without charge to conform with the warranty, no limitation may be placed on the duration of any implied warranty, the consumer must be given the option of a refund or replacement if repair is unsuccessful, and consequential damages may be excluded only if conspicuously noted.

Full warranty–warrantor will repair the product and if unsuccessful will replace or refund. Warrantor cannot disclaim or limit any implied warranty.

Most significantly, the act provides that a *written* warranty, whether full or limited, may **not** *disclaim any implied* warranty. This provision strikes at the heart of the problem, for a presidential task force report made before the act was passed revealed that most written warranties gave limited protection but in return took away the more valuable implied warranties. Hence, consumers were led to believe that the warranties they received and the warranty registration cards they promptly returned to the manufacturer were to their benefit. The act, on the other hand, provides that a full warranty must not disclaim, modify, or limit any implied warranty, and a limited warranty may not disclaim or modify any implied warranty but may limit its duration to that of the written warranty, provided that the limitation is reasonable, conscionable, and conspicuously displayed.

Limited warranty–implied warranties may be limited to a reasonable duration

For example, GE sells consumer goods to Barry for $150 and provides a written warranty regarding the quality of the goods. GE must designate the warranty as full or limited, depending on the characteristics of the warranty, and may not disclaim or modify any implied warranty. On the other hand, if GE had not provided Barry with a written warranty, then the Magnuson-Moss Act would not apply and GE could disclaim any and all implied warranties.

Finally, the act also contains a part dealing with *remedies* and the establishment, at the option of the warrantor, of an informal settlement procedure. However, the act does not provide any new or expanded remedies (see Figure 41–1).

Consumer Right of Rescission

Rescission–rescind or cancel

In most cases, a consumer is legally obligated once he has signed a contract. Many States, however, have statutes allowing a consumer a brief period of time—generally two or three days—during which he may rescind an otherwise binding credit obligation if the solicitation of the sale occurred in his home.

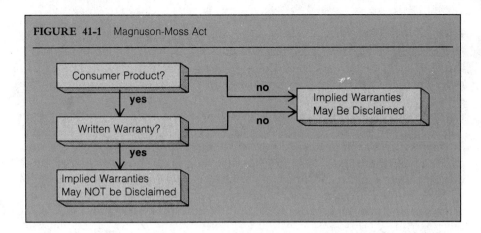

FIGURE 41-1   Magnuson-Moss Act

Moreover, the Federal Trade Commission has also set forth a trade regulation that applies to door-to-door sales of goods and services for twenty-five dollars or more, whether the sale is for cash or on credit. The regulation permits a consumer to rescind the contract within *three days* of signing.

A consumer also has a right of rescission under the Federal Consumer Credit Protection Act (discussed more fully below), which allows a consumer three days during which he may withdraw from any credit obligation secured by a mortgage on his home, unless the extension of credit was made to acquire the dwelling. After the consumer rescinds, the creditor has twenty days to return any money or property he has received from the consumer.

The **Interstate Land Sales Full Disclosure Act** applies to sales or leases of one hundred or more lots of unimproved land as part of a common promotional plan in interstate commerce. The act requires the developer to file a detailed statement of record containing specified information about the subdivision and the developer with the Department of Housing and Urban Development before offering the lots for sale or lease. The developer must provide a property report, which is a condensed version of the statement of record, to each prospective purchaser or lessee. The act provides that any contract or agreement for sale or lease may be revoked at the option of the purchaser or lessee within seven days of signing the contract, and the contract must clearly provide this right. If the property report has not been given to the purchaser or lessee before the contract was signed, the contract may be revoked within two years from the date of signing.

Consumer Credit Obligations

In the absence of special regulation, consumer credit transactions are governed by laws regulating commercial transactions generally. A consumer credit transaction is customarily defined as any credit transaction involving goods, services, or land acquired for personal, household, or family purposes. The following examples illustrate consumer credit transactions: A borrows $600 from a bank to pay a dentist bill or to take a vacation; B buys a refrigerator for her home from a department store and agrees to pay the purchase price in twelve equal monthly installments; C has an oil company credit card that he uses to purchase gasoline and tires for his family car.

Two significant developments have accelerated the legislative trend toward regulating consumer sales credit: (1) the enactment in 1968 of the **Federal Consumer Credit Protection Act** (FCCPA) and (2) the promulgation of the **Uniform Consumer Credit Code** (UCCC) in the same year. The FCCPA deals with effective disclosure of interest and finance charges, credit extension charges, and garnishment proceedings. The UCCC integrates into one document the regulation of all consumer credit transactions and gives substantially similar regulatory treatment to both credit sales and loan transactions.

Consumer credit protection has broadened considerably since the passage of the FCCPA and today includes the following areas: (1) access by creditors and consumers to the consumer credit market, (2) disclosure of information to the consumer, (3) regulation of contract terms, (4) fair reportage of credit information concerning consumers, and (5) creditors' remedies.

Access to the Market

The **Equal Credit Opportunity Act,** enacted by Congress in 1974, prohibits all businesses that regularly extend credit from discriminating in extending credit on the basis of sex, marital status, race, color, religion, national origin, or age. Under the act, creditors have thirty days after receipt of an application for credit to notify the applicant of action taken, and they must give specific reasons for a denial of credit. Although the act is administered and enforced by several Federal agencies, the FTC has overall enforcement authority. Credit applicants who are aggrieved by a violation of the act may recover actual and punitive damages, including attorneys' fees.

Disclosure Requirements

Title One of the FCCPA, also known as the **Truth-in-Lending Act,** has superseded State disclosure requirements relating to credit terms for both consumer loans and credit sales. Federal disclosure standards must be complied with in every State except those specifically exempted by the Federal Reserve Board. Such an exemption is made only if the State disclosure requirements are substantially the same as the Federal requirements and enforcement is assured. The FCCPA does not eliminate the necessity for creditor compliance with State requirements not covered by, or more stringent than, the requirements of the FCCPA, so long as the State required disclosure is not inconsistent with the FCCPA.

A creditor is required, under both State and Federal statutes, to provide certain information about contract terms to the consumer before he formally incurs the obligation. This information must be provided in a written statement presented to the consumer. Generally, the required disclosure is associated with the cost of credit, that is, interest or sales finance charges. An important requirement in the Truth-in-Lending Act is that sales finance and interest rates must be quoted in terms of an *annual percentage rate* (**APR**) and must be calculated on a uniform basis. Congress required disclosure of this information to encourage comparison of credit terms by consumers, to increase competition among financial institutions, and to facilitate economic stability. Enforcement and interpretation of the Truth-in-Lending Act was assigned to the Federal Reserve Board, which issued **Regulation Z** to carry out this responsibility.

In addition to the cost of the credit, under the Truth-in-Lending Act a creditor must inform the consumers who open revolving or open-ended credit accounts how the finance charge is computed and when it is imposed, what other charges may be levied, and whether a security interest is retained or acquired by the creditor. An **open-ended** credit account is one that permits the debtor to enter into a series of credit transactions that he may pay off in installments or in a lump sum. Examples of this type of credit include most department store credit cards, many gasoline credit cards, Visa cards, and Mastercard. With this type of credit the creditor is also required to provide a statement of account for each billing period.

Open-ended credit‗ debtor has rights to enter into a series of credit transactions

For nonrevolving or closed-end credit accounts, the creditor must provide the consumer with information about the total amount financed; the cash price; the number, amount, and due date of installments; delinquency charges; and a description of the security, if any. **Closed-end** credit is credit extended for a specified period of time during which periodic payments are generally made in an amount and at a time agreed on in advance. Examples of this type of transaction include most automobile financing agreements, most real estate purchases, and many other major purchases.

Closed-ended credit‗ credit extended to debtor for a specific period of time

FACTS: Miller purchased a used automobile from Chapman. The installment contract provided for a down payment, six weekly payments, and eighteen monthly payments. The contract, however, failed to describe the credit terms on the side of the contract on which Miller's signature appeared. The notices for Miller to read both sides of the contract were on the top and bottom of the front page, but there was no corresponding notice on the back page. Moreover, the space provided for Miller's signature was on the front page and, thus, did not follow the full content of the document. Miller made some of the payments on time but made five of the monthly payments late. Although Chapman had accepted Miller's late payments before, when the March 1975 payment became overdue, Chapman repossesed the car and notified Miller that the entire balance was then due and payable. When Miller did not pay the balance, Chapman sold the car and determined that Miller was entitled to a refund of $19.69. Miller then brought this action against Chapman for violation of the Federal Truth-in-Lending Act.

DECISION: Judgment for Miller. Chapman was required to make a disclosure of the retained security interest on a retail credit contract. The description of that retained interest, however, was located on the reverse side of the contract, while the space provided for Miller's signature was on the front page. Chapman's contract, therefore, violated the Truth-in-Lending Act. The statute requires that all disclosures be made together on the instrument on the same side of the page and above or adjacent to the place for the customer's signature. Furthermore, both sides of the contract must contain a notice for the customer to read the other side for important information, and the space for the customer's signature must follow the full content of the document. Since Chapman's document failed to satisfy all of these requirements, it violated the truth-in-lending act, and Miller is entitled to recover damages.

CHAPMAN v. MILLER

Court of Civil Appeals of Texas, 1978. 575 S.W.2d 581.

In 1975 the **Fair Credit Billing Act** went into effect to relieve some of the problems and abuses associated with billing errors. This act sets forth procedures for the consumer to follow in making complaints about specified errors in billing and requires the creditor to explain or correct such errors. Billing errors are defined to include (1) extensions of credit that were never made or were not made in the amount indicated on the billing statement; (2) undelivered or unaccepted goods or services; (3) incorrect recording of payments or credits; and (4) accounting or computational errors. Until the creditor responds to the complaint, it may not (1) take any action to collect the disputed amount, (2) restrict the use of an open-ended credit account because the disputed amount is unpaid, or (3) report the disputed amount as delinquent.

In 1974 Congress enacted the **Real Estate Settlement Procedures Act** (RESPA) to provide consumers who purchase a home with greater and more timely information on the nature and costs of the settlement process and to protect them from unncessarily high settlement charges. This act applies to all Federally related mortgage loans and requires advance disclosure to home buyers and sellers of all settlement costs, including attorneys' fees, credit reports, and title insurance. Nearly all first-mortgage loans fall within the scope of the act. RESPA prohibits kickbacks and referral fees and limits the amount home buyers are required to place in escrow accounts to insure payment of real estate taxes and insurance. The act is administered and enforced by the Secretary of Housing and Urban Development.

Contract Terms

Consumer credit is marketed on a mass basis. Contract documents are frequently printed forms containing blank spaces to be filled in by the creditor. These blank spaces relate to matters usually negotiated at the time of the extension of credit. Standardization and uniformity of contract terms facilitate transfer of the rights of the creditor, in most situations a seller, to a third party, which is usually a bank or finance company.

Almost all States impose statutory ceilings on the amount that may be charged for the extension of consumer credit. Statutes regulating rates also specify what other charges may be made. For example, charges for insurance, official fees, and taxes are usually not considered part of the finance charge. Charges that are incidental to the extension of credit are usually considered part of the finance charge, for example, a service charge or a commission for extending credit. Any charge that does not qualify as an authorized additional charge is treated as part of the finance charge and is subject to the statutory rate ceiling. Other special permitted charges include delinquency and default charges, charges incurred in connection with storing and repairing repossessed goods for sale, reasonable fees for a lawyer who is not a salaried employee of the creditor, and court costs.

Most statutes require a creditor to permit the debtor to pay her obligation in full at any time before the maturity date of the final installment. If the interest charge over the period of the loan was computed in advance and added to the principal of the loan, when making prepayment in full the debtor is entitled to a refund of the unearned interest already paid.

Aside from provisions relating to cost, the balance of a credit contract deals with the terms of repayment and the remedies of the creditor if payments are delinquent. Usually, payments must be periodic and substantially equal in amount. Balloon payments (loans in which the final payment is much larger than the regular payments; for example, monthly installments of $50 and a final installment is $1,000) may be prohibited. If they are not prohibited, the creditor may be required to refinance the loan at the same rate and with installments in the same amount as the original loan without penalty to the borrower.

In the past, certain consumer purchase transactions were financed in such way that the purchaser was legally obligated to make full payment of the price to a third party, even though the dealer from whom she bought the goods had committed fraud or the goods were defective. This occurred when the purchaser executed and delivered to the seller her negotiable promissory note and the seller negotiated it to a holder in due course, who purchased the note for value, in good faith, and without notice that it was overdue or had any defenses or claims attached to it. The buyer's defense that the goods were defective or that the seller had committed fraud, although valid against the seller, were not valid against a holder in due course of the note. To correct this situation by preserving and making available claims and defenses of consumer buyers and borrowers against holders in due course, the FTC adopted a rule that limits the rights of a holder in due course of an instrument evidencing a debt that arises out of a *consumer credit contract*. The rule applies to sellers and lessors of goods and defines consumer credit contracts to include negotiable instruments. We discuss this rule in Chapter 24.

A similar rule applies to credit card issuers under the **Fair Credit Billing Act.** The Act preserves a consumer's defense against the issuer provided the consumer had made a good faith attempt to resolve the dispute with the seller, but only if (1) the seller is controlled by the issuer or under common control with the issuer, (2) the card issuer included the seller's promotional literature in the monthly billing statement sent to the card holder, or (3) the sale involves more than fifty dollars and the consumer's billing address is in the same State as or within one hundred miles of the seller's place of business.

Moreover, under the FCCPA a card holder's liability for unauthorized use of a credit card is limited to fifty dollars. The card issuer may collect up to that amount for unauthorized use only if (1) the card has been accepted; (2) the issuer has furnished adequate notice of potential liability to the card holder; (3) the issuer has provided the card holder with a statement of the means by which the card issuer may be notified of the loss or theft of the credit card; (4) the unauthorized use occurs before the card holder has notified the card issuer of the loss or theft; and (5) the card issuer has provided a method by which the user can be identified as the person authorized to use the card.

Fair Reportage

Because consumers are usually granted credit only after an investigation into the consumer's creditworthiness, it is essential that the information on which such decisions are made is accurate and current. To this end, in 1970 Congress enacted the **Fair Credit Reporting Act,** which applies to consumer reports used for purposes of securing employment, insurance, and credit. The act prohibits including inaccurate or specified obsolete information in consumer reports. The act requires consumer reporting agencies to give written advance notice to consumers that an investigative report may be made. The consumer may request information regarding the nature and substance of all information in the consumer reporting agency's files, the source of the information, and the names of all recipients of the consumer reports furnished for employment purposes within the preceding two years and for other purposes within the preceding six months.

If the consumer notifies the reporting agency of disagreement with the accuracy and completeness of information in the file, the agency must then reinvestigate the matter within a reasonable time unless the complaint is frivolous or irrelevant. If reinvestigation proves that the information is inaccurate, it must be promptly deleted. If the dispute remains unresolved, after reinvestigation, the consumer may submit a brief statement setting forth the nature of the dispute, and this must be incorporated into the report.

Creditors' Remedies

A primary concern of creditors is their rights if a debtor defaults or is late in payment. When the credit charge is precomputed, the creditor may impose a delinquency charge for late payments, subject to statutory limits for such charges. If instead of being delinquent, the consumer defaults, the creditor may declare the entire balance of the debt immediately due and payable and may sue on the debt. What other courses of action are open to him depend on his security. Various security provisions included in consumer credit contracts are a co-signer, an assignment of wages, a security interest in the goods sold, a security interest in other real or personal property of the debtor, and a confession of judgment clause (i.e., a clause by the defendant giving the plaintiff power to enter judgment against the defendant).

However, wage assignments are prohibited by some States. In most States and under the FCCPA, a limitation is imposed on the amount that may be deducted from an individual's wages during any pay period. In addition, the FCCPA prohibits an employer from discharging an employee solely because of a creditor's exercise of an assignment of wages in connection with any one debt.

Even where assignments of wages are prohibited, the creditor may still reach the wages of the consumer through garnishment. However, garnishment is only available in a court proceeding to enforce the collection of a judgment. The FCCPA and State statutes contain exemption provisions that limit the amount of wages subject to garnishment.

In the case of credit sales, the seller may retain a security interest in the goods sold. Many States impose restrictions on other security the creditor may obtain. Where the debt is secured by property as collateral, the creditor, on default by the debtor, may take possession of the property and, subject to the provisions of the Uniform Commercial Code, either retain it in full satisfaction of the debt or sell it and, if the proceeds are less than the outstanding debt, sue the debtor for the balance and obtain a deficiency judgment. The UCC provides that where the buyer of goods has paid 60 percent of the purchase price of the goods or 60 percent of a loan secured by consumer goods, the secured creditor may not retain the property in full satisfaction but must sell the goods and pay to the buyer that part of the sale proceeds in excess of the balance due. Secured transactions are discussed in Chapter 37.

In 1977 Congress enacted the **Fair Debt Collection Practices Act** to eliminate abusive, deceptive, and unfair practices in collecting consumer debts by debt collection agencies. The act does not apply to the creditors themselves. Rather, the act provides that any debt collector who communicates with a person other than the consumer for the purpose of acquiring information about the location of the consumer may not state that the consumer owes any debt. Moreover, the act prohibits a number of abusive collection practices, including: (1) communication with the consumer at unusual or inconvenient hours; (2) communication with the consumer if she is represented by an attorney; (3) harrassing, oppressive, or abusive conduct, such as threats of violence or obscene language; (4) false, deceptive, or misleading representation or means; and (5) and unfair or unconscionable means to collect any debt. The act is enforced by the Federal Trade Commission, and consumers may recover damages from the collection agency for violations of the act.

Consumer Health and Safety

In 1972 Congress enacted the **Consumer Product Safety Act,** which has the following purposes:

1. to protect the public against unreasonable risk of injury associated with consumer products;

2. to assist consumers in evaluating the comparative safety of consumer products;

3. to develop uniform safety standards for consumer products and to minimize conflicting State and local regulations; and

4. to promote research and investigation into the causes and prevention of product-related deaths, illnesses, and injuries.

The act creates an independent regulatory Federal agency, the Consumer Product Safety Commission, consisting of five commissioners, to carry out the act's mandate.

In addition, a number of Federal statutes impose labeling and packaging requirements designed to provide the consumer with accurate information and adequate warnings about specific products. These include the Fair Packaging and Labeling Act; the Food, Drugs, and Cosmetic Act; the Fur Products Labeling Act; the Wholesome Meat Act; the Flammable Fabrics Act; the Cigarette Labeling and Advertising Act; the Wool Products Labeling Act; the Wholesome Poultry Products Act; the Special Packaging of Household Substances for the Protection of Children Act; and the Refrigerator Safety Act.

CHAPTER SUMMARY

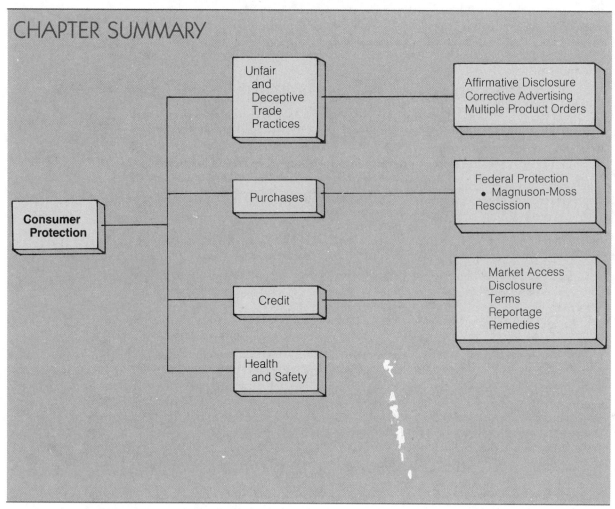

KEY TERMS

Unfair and deceptive trade
  practices
Affirmative disclosure
Corrective advertising
Multiple product order
Consumer product

Magnuson-Moss Act
Rescission
Full warranty
Limited warranty
Consumer credit

Truth-in-lending
Annual percentage rate (APR)
Open-ended credit
Closed-ended credit
Regulation Z

PROBLEMS

1. The FTC brings a deceptive trade practice action against Beneficial Finance Company based on Beneficial's use of its "instant tax refund" slogan. The FTC argues that Beneficial's advertising a tax refund loan or instant tax refund is deceptive in that the loan is not in any way connected with a tax refund but is merely Beneficial's everyday loan based on the applicant's creditworthiness. Decision?

2. B borrows $1,000 from L for one year. B agrees to pay L $200 in interest on the loan and to repay the loan in twelve monthly installments of $100. The contract that L provides and B signs specifies that the APR is 20 percent. B now contends that the contract violates the FCCPA. Decision?

3. A consumer entered into an agreement with Rent-It Corporation for the rental of a television set at a charge of seventeen dollars per week. The agreement also provides that if the renter chooses to rent the set for seventy-eight consecutive weeks, title will be transferred. The consumer now contends that the agreement is really a sales agreement and not a lease and therefore is a credit sale subject to the Truth-in-Lending Act. Decision?

4. Central Adjustment Bureau allegedly threatened Consumer with a lawsuit, service at his office, and attachment and sale of his property in order to collect a debt, although it did not intend to carry out the threat and did not have the authority to commence litigation. On some notices sent to Consumer, Central failed to disclose that it was attempting to collect a debt. In addition, Central, it is charged, sent notices demanding payment that purported to be from attorneys but were written, signed, and sent by Central. Decision?

5. The Giant Development Company undertakes a massive real estate venture to sell 9,000 one-acre unimproved lots in Utah. The company advertises the project nationally. A, a resident of New York, learns of the opportunity and requests information about the project. The company provides A with a small advertising brochure that contains no information about the developer and the land. The brochure consists of vague descriptions of the joys of home ownership and nothing else. A purchases a lot. Two weeks after entering into the agreement, A wishes to rescind the contract. Will A prevail?

6. Jane Jones, a married woman, applies for a credit card from Exxon but is refused credit. Jane is bewildered as to why she was turned down. What are her legal rights in this situation?

7. On a beautiful Saturday in October, A decides to take the twenty-mile ride from her home in New Jersey into New York City in order to do some shopping. A finds that B Retail Sales, Inc., has a terrific sale on television sets and decides to surprise her husband with a new color TV. She purchases the set from B on her American Express credit card for $450. When the set is delivered, A discovers that it does not work. B refuses to repair or replace it or to refund the money. A therefore refuses to pay American Express for the television. American Express brings a suit against A. Decision?

8. F finds A's wallet, which contains many credit cards and A's identification. By using A's identification and Visa card, F goes on a shopping spree and runs up $5,000 in charges. A does not discover that he has lost his wallet until the following day, when he promptly notifies his Visa bank. How much can Visa collect from A?

9. B applies to N National Bank for a loan. Before granting the loan, N requests that C Credit Agency provide it with a credit report on B. C reports that three years previously B had embezzled money from his employer. Based on this report, N rejects B's loan application.

   (a) B demands to know why the loan was rejected, but N refuses to divulge the information, arguing that it is privileged. Is B entitled to the information?

   (b) Assume that B obtains the information and alleges that it is inaccurate. What recourse does B have?

10. A owed B $400, which was long overdue. B decided to hire the C Collection Agency to collect the debt. After writing several letters to A, C began a campaign of calling A every hour on the hour between the hours of 8 A.M. and 8 P.M., both at work and at home. A brings suit against C and B for harassment. Decision?

PART TEN
PROPERTY

PART TEN

PROPERTY

PUBLIC POLICY, SOCIAL ISSUES
AND BUSINESS ETHICS

The concept of property is fundamental to our economic system, which is based on exchanges between units of production and consumption. The significance of property nonetheless goes beyond its immeasurable economic importance. As the eminent English jurist Blackstone stated, "There is nothing which so generally strikes the imagination, and engages the affections of mankind, as the right of property; or that sole and despotic dominion which one man claims and exercises over the external things of the world, in total exclusion of the right of any other individual in the universe."

Before inquiring further into the social and public policy issues concerning the private and public ownership of property, we must first define the term. Jeremy Bentham, in explaining the advantages of law, stated: "Property is nothing but a basis of expectation; the expectation of deriving certain advantages from a thing which we are said to possess, in consequence of the relation in which we stand towards it. . . . Property and law are born together, and die together. Before laws were made there was no property; take away laws, and property ceases." More specifically, property consists of a set of *rights* entitling one person to use and exclusively enjoy some item. R. Ely stated:

By property we mean an exclusive right to control an economic good.

By private property we mean the exclusive right of a private person to control an economic good.

By public property we mean the exclusive right of a political unit (city, state, nation, etc.) to control an economic good. . . .

. . . Speaking accurately, then, property is not a thing but the rights which extend over a thing. A less strict use of the word property makes property include the things over which the right extends. We say of a farm, this is my property, meaning the land and improvements on it and not merely the right, or rather, the land and its improvements together with the right. But, strictly speaking, property is the right, and not the object over which the right extends. R. Ely, *Property and Contract in their Relation to the Distribution of Wealth.*

No matter which sense of the word is intended—the right over the object or the object itself—there is an enormous quantity of property in the United States today. It has been estimated that as of 1980 in the United States there was $4,247 billion of real estate, $1,381 billion of stock owned, $1,112 billion of bonds and other fixed income assets, $973 billion of durables and $373 billion of cash.

The most obvious—and the most important—question regarding all of this wealth is: who should own it? This question has been answered quite differently at various times in history and today is answered just as diversely. Our economic and political system has provided for both private and public ownership of property. Moreover, it has established constitutional protections for the private ownership of property. As a result, private ownership is accepted as the norm in this country, and those who own property may assert: "To the world: Keep off unless you have my permission, which I may grant or withhold. Signed: Private citizen. Endorsed: The state." Of course, there are other views regarding the propriety of private property. For example, Karl Marx and Friedrich Engels in *The Communist Manifesto* maintained "The proletarians cannot become masters of the productive forces of society, except by abolishing their own previous mode of appropriation, and thereby also every other previous mode of appropriation. They have nothing of their own to secure and to fortify; their mission is to destroy all previous securities for, and insurances of, individual property."

Economists have set forth countless arguments supporting the notion of privately owned property. The basic one is that by allowing private property, the capitalistic system creates incentives for the efficient use and allocation of resources. The right to exclusive ownership of property encourages individuals to incur costs in order to make efficient use of their property, while the right to transfer ownership in their property provides an incentive for them to shift resources from less productive uses to more productive uses. Behrman has explained this concept as follows:

An individual must have something to be creative with. Private property can be used for private benefit, but the society as a whole should benefit, too. Each individual will greedily use property for his greatest economic benefit: he would not use it as efficiently if someone else owned it and paid him part of the fruits of his labor. Private productive property assures that each person reaps the benefit of his own efforts. If everybody works for one man, who alone has all the property, he is the only one with the ability to create. The feudal lord who owned all of the land, the cattle, stables, and so forth—he told the serfs what to do. He could be creative. But the serf who was greedy—what happened to him?

He got his hands cuffed! Private productive property is a necessary complement to individual economic motivation. It is necessary for individuals to work effectively, doing the best they can with it, responsibly, and thereby improving the whole society.

Even in our society, which constitutionally recognizes the private ownership of property, such ownership is by no means absolute. The government imposes limitations on a number of the rights embodied in ownership:

Our students of property law need, therefore, to be reminded that not only has the whole law since the industrial revolution shown a steady growth in ever new restrictions upon the use of private property, but that the ideal of absolute *laissez faire* has never in fact been completely operative. . . .

. . . There must be restrictions on the use of property not only in the interests of other property owners but also in the interests of the health, safety, religion, morals, and general welfare of the whole community. No community can view with indifference the exploitation of the needy by commercial greed. As under the conditions of crowded life the reckless or unconscionable use of one's property is becoming more and more dangerous, enlightened jurists find new doctrines to limit the abuse of ancient rights. M. Cohen, "Property and Sovereignty."

In the next six chapters we explore our legal system's answers to several questions of public policy regarding the private ownership of property. How freely should property rights be transferable? Should the government be permitted to seize privately owned property? To what extent should the government control the use of private property? Should individuals be allowed to restrict the use of property that they have transferred?

42

INTRODUCTION TO REAL AND PERSONAL PROPERTY

In our democratic and free enterprise society, the concept of property has an importance second only to the idea of liberty. Although many of our rules of property in the United States stem directly from English law, property in America occupies a unique status because of the protection expressly granted it by the Federal Constitution as well as by most State constitutions. The fifth amendment to the Federal constitution provides, in part, that "No person shall be . . . deprived of life, liberty, or property, without due process of law; nor shall private property be taken for public use, without just compensation." A similar mandate is contained in the fourteenth amendment: "No State shall . . . deprive any person of life, liberty, or property, without due process of law." This protection afforded to property owners is subject, however, to police power regulation for the public good. In addition, the private ownership of property is an essential component of our economic system. In this chapter we introduce the law governing real and personal property and then discuss personal property more specifically.

Introduction to Property

In spite of the unique place given to property in our society, uncertainties arise because the term is not easily defined. This is not all that surprising, because the term "property" includes almost every **right,** exclusive of personal liberty, that the law will protect. Property is valuable only because our law provides that certain consequences follow from the ownership of it. The right to use the property, to sell it, and to control to whom it shall pass on the death of the owner are all included within the term "propety." Accordingly, property is an interest or group of interests that is legally protected.

Property –interest that is legally protected

Thus, when a person speaks of "owning property," he may have two separate ideas in mind: (1) the *physical thing* itself, as when a home owner says, "I just bought a piece of property in Oakland," meaning complete ownership of a physically identifiable parcel of land; or (2) a *right* or *interest* in the physical object, as, for example, with respect to land, a tenant under a lease has a property interest in the leased land, although he does not own the land.

Kinds of Property

Property may be classified as (1) tangible or intangible property and (2) real or personal property (see Figure 42–1). As you will see, these classifications are not mutually exclusive.

Tangible and Intangible Property

Tangible property–physical objects

Intangible property–protected interests that are not physical

A forty-acre farm, a chair, and a household pet are *tangible* property. The group of rights of interests referred to as "title" or "ownership" are embodied in each of these *physical* objects. On the other hand, *intangible* property is property that does *not* exist in a physical form. For example, a stock certificate, a promissory note, and a deed granting Jones a right-of-way over the land of Young are intangible property. Each represents and stands for certain rights that are not capable of reduction to physical possession, but have a legal reality in the sense that they will be protected.

The same item may be the object of both tangible and intangible property rights. Suppose Ann purchases a book published by Broundsons. On the first page, there is the statement "Copyright 1986, by Broundson. Ann owns the volumes he purchased. She has the right to exclusive physical possession and use of that particular copy. It is a tangible piece of property of which she is the owner. Broundsons, however, has the exclusive right to publish copies of the book. This is a right granted it by the copyright laws. The courts will protect this intangible property of Broundson's as well as Ann's right to the particular volume.

Real and Personal Property

Real property–land and interests in land

Personal property–all property which is now real property

The most significant practical distinction between types of property is the classification into real and personal property. A simple definition would be to say that land and all interests in it are *real* property (also called realty), and every other thing or interest identified as property is *personal*. This description is adequate for most purposes, although certain physical objects that are personal property under most circumstances may, because of their attachment to land or their use in connection with land, become a form of real property called *fixtures*.

FIGURE 42-1   Kinds of Property

	Personal	**Real**
Tangible	Goods	Land Buildings Fixtures
Intangible	Commercial paper Stock certificates Contract rights Copyrights Patents	Leases Easements Mortgages

Fixtures

A fixture is an article or piece of personal property that has been attached in some manner to land or a building so that an interest in it arises under *real* property law. For example, materials for a building are clearly personal property, but when worked into a building as its construction progresses, they become real property, since buildings are part of the land. Thus, clay in its natural state is, of course, real property; when made into bricks it becomes personal property, and if the bricks are then built into the wall of a house, the "clay" once again becomes real property.

Although the question whether various items are personal property or real property may in certain instances be difficult to answer, it is only by obtaining the answer that conflicting claims to their ownership may be determined. Unless otherwise provided by agreement, personal property remains the property of the person who placed it on the real estate. On the other hand, if the property has been affixed so as to become a fixture (an actual part of the real estate), it becomes the property of the owner of the real estate.

These questions affect many persons. The apartment dweller who puts a new chandelier or a bathroom cabinet in his landlord's apartment and the shoe repairman who attaches equipment to the floor of his leased premises will not be entitled to remove them when the lease expires *if* they are held to have become part of the real estate. The seller of real estate who leaves screens on the premises will learn to his surprise that the buyer is entitled to them as part of the real estate even though they were not specifically mentioned in the deed.

In determining whether personal property becomes a fixture, the intention of the parties with conflicting claims to the property as expressed in their agreement will control. Without the binding force of an agreement, the following guides are helpful in determining whether any particular item is a fixture: (1) the physical relationship of the item to the land or building; (2) the intention of the person who attaches the item to the land or building; (3) the purpose served by the item in relation to the land or building and in relation to the person who brought it there; and (4) the interest of that person in the land or building at the time of the attachment of the item.

Although physical attachment is significant, a more important test is whether the item can be removed without material injury to the land or building on the land. If it *cannot* be so removed, it is generally held that the item has become part of the realty. The opposite is also true but to a lesser degree. Where the item may be removed without material injury to the land or building, it is generally held that it has not become part of the realty. This test, however, is not conclusive.

Rather, the courts have searched for the answer in the intention of the person who attached the item to the realty. The tests of intention are objective. One of the tests developed has been to inquire into the purpose or use of the item in relation to the land and in relation to the person who brought it there. If the use or purpose of the item is unusual for the type of realty involved (e.g., a small crane in the backyard of a country house) or peculiar to the particular individual who brought it there, then it may be reasonably concluded that the individual intended to remove the item when he leaves.

However, the courts do not regard an item as part of the realty merely because its use or purpose is usual for the type of realty involved. For example, it is usual to have beds and dressers in bedrooms and dining tables in dining rooms, but these items are not ordinarily part of the realty. The test of purpose or use applies only if the item both (a) is affixed to the realty in some way and (b) can be removed without material injury to the realty. See *Sears, Roebuck & Co. v. Seven Palms Motor Inn, Inc.*, which follows. In such a situation, if the use or purpose of the item is peculiar to the particular owner or occupant of the premises, the courts will tend to let him remove the item when he leaves. Accordingly, in the law of landlord and tenant, it is settled that the tenant may remove **trade fixtures,** that is, items used in connection with his trade, provided that this can be done without material injury to the realty. On the other hand, doors may be removed without injury to the structure, yet because they are necessary to the ordinary use of the building and not peculiar to the use of the occupant, they are considered fixtures and thus part of the real property.

SEARS, ROEBUCK & CO. v. SEVEN PALMS MOTOR INN, INC.

Supreme Court of Missouri, 1975.
530 S.W.2d 695.

FACTS: Sears had sold and installed a number of furnishings, including drapes and bedspreads, to Seven Palm Motor Inn in connection with the construction of a motel on land Seven Palms owned. Sears did not receive payment in full for the materials and labor and brought suit to recover $8,357.49 with interest and to establish a mechanic's lien on the motel and land for the unpaid portion of the furnishings. Seven Palms asserts that neither the drapes nor bedspreads are fixtures and thus Sears cannot obtain a mechanic's lien on them.

DECISION: Judgment for Sears, granting a mechanic's lien for the draperies but not the bedspreads. The characterization of an otherwise personal item as a fixture depends on: (1) the item's annexation to the realty; (2) adaption of the item to the use to which the realty is devoted; and (3) the annexor's intent that the object become a permanent accession to the realty. Here, the draperies were hung from traverse rods which were attached to the walls. The purpose of hanging the drapes was to grant the motel's guest the control of light in his room or his privacy. The traverse rod, itself, did not accomplish this purpose. Rather, the rod and drapes, as a unit, were adapted to the proper use of the motel rooms. They were placed in the rooms with the intent that they would form a part of the special purpose for which the building was designed to be used. Thus, the draperies are as much fixtures as the rods.

On the other hand, the bedspreads were not physically attached to the realty in any way. They cannot be "constructively annexed" merely because they match the drapes. The bedspreads were not essential to the use of a fixture (i.e., the drapes). In addition, it was not shown that they could not readily be used independently elsewhere. The bedspreads, therefore, are not fixtures.

Incidents of Property Ownership

The importance of the distinction between real and personal property stems primarily from very practical legal consequences that follow from the distinction. Some of these consequences are transfer of property and taxation.

Transfer of Property during Life

As we will discuss in Chapter 45, the transfer of real property during life can be accomplished only by certain formalities, including the execution and delivery of a written instrument known as a deed. Personal property, on the other hand, may be transferred with relative simplicity and informality.

Transfer of Title on Death of Owner

In many States, if a person dies without a will, title to her real property passes directly to whomever the law declares to be her heirs, whereas title to her personal property passes to her personal representative, who in turn must distribute it as the law directs. For a more detailed discussion of this topic see Chapter 46.

Taxation

Most States levy taxes on the ownership of both real property and personal property. However, the applicable tax rate depends on whether the property is classified as real property or as personal property.

Personal Property

The law concerning personal property has been largely codified. The Uniform Commercial Code includes the law of sales of goods (Article 2), as well as the law governing the transfer and negotiation of commercial paper (Article 3) and of investment securities (Article 8). But a number of issues involving the ownership and transfer of title to personal property are not covered by the Code. We address these issues in the remainder of this chapter.

Transfer of Title

The acquisition or transfer of title to real property is generally a formal affair. In contrast, title to personal property may be acquired and transferred with relative ease and with a minimum of formality. The facility with which personal property may be transferred is required by the demands of a society whose trade and industry is principally based on transactions in personal property. Stocks, bonds, merchandise, and even ideas must be sold with a minimum of delay in a free economy. It is only natural that the law will reflect these needs.

By Sale

By definition, a sale of *tangible*, personal property (goods) is a transfer of title to specified existing goods for a consideration known as the price. Title passes when the parties intend it to pass, and transfer of possession is not required for a transfer of title. For a discussion of this manner of transfer of title, see Chapter 18.

> **Sale**–transfer of property for consideration

    Sales of *intangible*, personal property also involve the transfer of title. These sales are also governed by provisions of the UCC, except for copyrights and patents which are governed by specialized Federal legislation.

By Gift

A gift is a transfer of property from one person to another without consideration. The lack of any consideration is the basic distinction between a gift and a sale. Because a gift involves no consideration or compensation, it must be completed by delivery of the gift to be effective. A gratuitous promise to make a gift is not binding. In addition, there must be intent on the part of the maker (the **donor**) of the gift to make a present transfer, and there must be acceptance by the recipient (the **donee**) of the gift.

> **Gift**–transfer of property without consideration
>
> **Donor**–maker of a gift
>
> **Donee**–recipient of a gift

Delivery   Delivery is absolutely necessary to a valid gift. The term "delivery" has a very special meaning including, but not limited to, manual transfer of the item to the donee. There can be "delivery" of a gift sufficient to make it irrevocable if the item is turned over to a third person with instructions to give it to the donee. Frequently, an item, because of its size or location or because it is intangible, is incapable of immediate manual delivery. In such cases an irrevocable gift may be effected by delivery of something symbolic of dominion over the item. This is referred to as **constructive delivery**. For example, if Joanne declares that she gives an antique desk and all its contents to Barry and hands Barry the key to the desk, in many States a valid gift has been made.

Intent   The law is also clear that there must be an intent on the part of the donor to make a present gift of the property. Thus, if Joanne leaves a packet of stocks and bonds with Barry, Barry may or may not acquire good title to them, depending on whether Joanne intended to make a gift of them or simply to place them in Barry's hands for safekeeping. Joanne voluntary, uncompensated delivery with intent to give the recipient title constitutes a gift when the donee accepts it. If these conditions are met, the donor has no further claim to the property:

COHEN v. BAYSIDE FEDERAL SAVINGS AND LOAN ASSOCIATION Supreme Court of New York, Term, 1970. 62 Misc.2d 738, 309 N.Y.S.2d 980.	**FACTS:** When Richard Rothchild became engaged to Carol Cohen, he gave her a diamond engagement ring valued at $1,000. Shortly before the wedding date, however, Richard was killed in an automobile accident. His estate then instituted this action to recover the ring. **DECISION:** Judgment for Carol Cohen. the law permits the recovery of an engagement ring "where justice so requires." For example, it is generally held that if a fiance breaks off the engagement without the fault of the donor or if it is broken by mutual consent, the ring must be returned to the donor. If the donor breaks the engagement, on the other hand, the ring may be kept. Here, Richard would have wanted Carol to keep the ring, and so she may unless she did something to prevent the marriage.

Acceptance   The final requirement of a valid gift is acceptance by the donee. In most instances, of course, the donee will accept the gift with gratitude. Accordingly, the law usually presumes that the donee has accepted. However, there are situations where a donee does not wish to accept a gift, such as when the gift imposes a burden on the donee. In such cases the law will not require the recipient to accept an unwanted gift. For example, a gift of an elephant or a wrecked car in need of extensive repairs may be prudently rejected by a donee.

By Will or Descent

Title to personal property is frequently acquired by inheritance from a person who dies, either with or without a will. We discuss this method of acquiring title in Chapter 46.

By Possession

In some instances a person may acquire title to movable personal property by taking possession of it. If the property has been intentionally **abandoned** a **finder** is entitled to the property. Moreover, under the general rule a finder

Abandoned property intentionally disposed of

is entitled to **lost** property as against everyone except the true owner. Suppose X, the owner of an apartment complex, leases a kitchenette apartment to Y. One night Z, Y's mother-in-law, is invited to sleep in the convertible bed in the living room. In the course of preparing the bed, Z finds an emerald ring caught on the springs under the mattress. The ring is turned over to the police, but diligent inquiry does not turn up the true owner. Z will be entitled to the ring because she is considered the finder.

Lost property –unintentionally left by the owner

try to find the true owner [handwritten annotation]

A different rule applies when the lost property is in the ground. Here, the owner of the land has a claim superior to that of the finder. For example, X employs Y to excavate a lateral sewer. Y uncovers old Indian relics. X, not Y, has the superior claim.

There is a further exception to the rule giving the finder first claim against all but the true owner. Most courts hold that if property has been **mislaid,** not lost, then the owner of the premises, not the finder, has first claim if the true owner is not discovered. This doctrine is involved frequently in cases where items are found on trains, buses, airplanes, and in restaurants. The true owner, it is said, did not lose the property, she simply mislaid it.

Mislaid property –intentionally placed by the owner but unintentionally left

Many States, including Illinois shown in the following case, now have statutes that provide a means of vesting title to lost property in the finder when a prescribed search for the owner is fruitless. These statutes generally do not determine the right to possession against any party other than the true owner.

FACTS: While in the examination booth in the safety deposit vault of Old Orchard Bank, Brenice Paset (plaintiff) found $6,325 in currency in the seat of a chair that was partially under the table. She notified the bank officials and turned the money over to them. They told her that they would try to locate the owner but, if unsuccessful within one year, that she, Brenice, could have the money. The bank then sent a notice to all of its safety deposit box customers asking if they had lost some property. No response was received within a year, but the bank still refused to turn over the money contending that it had to hold it for the true owner. Brenice then brought this action to establish herself as the owner of the money by her compliance with the requirements of the applicable State statute. The bank argues that the money was mislaid, and therefore the statute is not applicable.

DECISION: Judgment for Brenice Paset. Traditionally, found property could be classified as either mislaid, lost, or abandoned. Mislaid property is property that is intentionally put in a certain place and then later forgotten; at common law a finder acquires rights to mislaid property. In contrast, property is deemed lost when it is unintentionally separated from the dominion of its owner; the finder of lost property is entitled to possession against everyone except the true owner. Finally, abandoned property is that which the owner, intending to relinquish all claim to the property, leaves free to be appropriated by any other person.

Here, the money was not mislaid as the bank claims because if it was intentionally placed on the chair by someone who forgot where he left it, the bank's notice to the safety deposit box subscribers should have alerted the owner. Rather, the money was lost, and thus the statute is applicable. Since Brenice complied with the requirements of the statute and no claim to the money was made within the one-year period, she is entitled to recover it from the bank.

PASET v. OLD ORCHARD BANK AND TRUST CO.

Appellate Court of Illinois, First District, 1978. 62 Ill.App.3d 534, 19 Dec. 389, 378 N.E.2d 1264.

Concurrent Ownership

Real or personal property may be owned by one individual or by two or more persons concurrently. If title is held concurrently by two or more persons, they are generally referred to as **co-tenants,** each entitled to an undivided interest in the entire item and neither having a claim to any specific portion of it. Each may have equal undivided interests or one may have a larger undivided share than the other.

There are four ways in which personal property may be owned concurrently: (1) joint tenancy, (2) tenancy in common, (3) tenancy by the entireties, and (4) community property. We discuss these forms of concurrent ownership in Chapter 44.

[handwritten note: If property is found on another's land, it is land owner's property]

CHAPTER SUMMARY

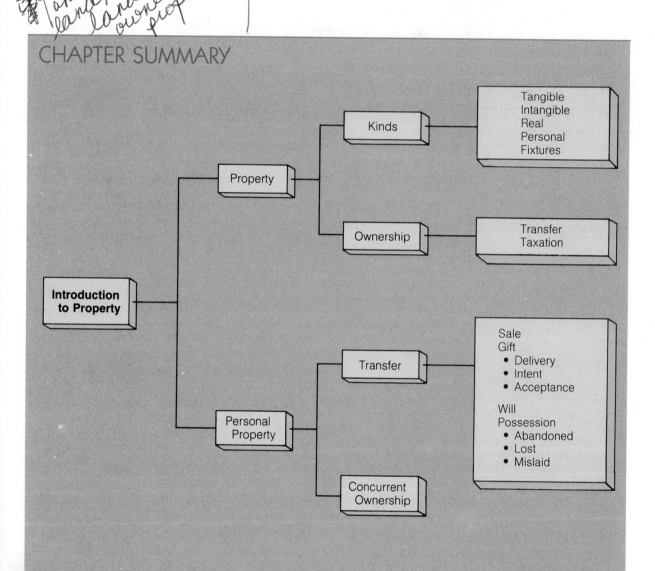

KEY TERMS

Property
Tangible property
Intangible property
Real property
Personal property
Fixture

Sale
Gift
Donor
Donee
Delivery
Acceptance

Intent
Ownership by possession
Abandoned property
Lost property
Mislaid property
Concurrent ownership

PROBLEMS

1. In January, Roger Burke loaned his favorite nephew, Jimmy White, his valuable painting by Picasso. Knowing that Jimmy would celebrate his twenty-first birthday on May 15, Burke sent a letter to Jimmy on April 14 stating:

> Dear Jimmy,
> Tomorrow I leave on my annual trip to Europe, and I want to make you a fitting birthday gift which I do by sending you my enclosed promissory note. Also I want you to keep the Picasso which I loaned you last January, and you may now consider it yours. Happy birthday!
>
> Affectionately,
> /s/ Uncle Roger

The negotiable promissory note for $5,000 sent with the letter was signed by Roger Burke, payable to Jimmy White or bearer, and dated May 15. On May 21, Burke was killed in an automobile accident while motoring in France.

First Bank was appointed administrator of Burke's estate. Jimmy presented the note to the administrator and demanded payment, which was refused. Jimmy brought an action against First Bank as administrator seeking recovery on the note. The administrator brought an action against Jimmy seeking return of the painting by Picasso.

(a) What decision in the action on the note?

(b) What decision in the action to recover the painting?

2. Several years ago P purchased a tract of land on which there was an old, vacant house. Recently, P employed F, a carpenter, to repair and remodel the house. While F was tearing out a partition for the purpose of enlarging one of the rooms, he discovered a metal box hidden in the wall of the house. F broke open the box and discovered that it contained $2,000 in gold and silver coins and old-style bills. F then took the box and its contents to P and told her where he had found it. When F handed the box and the money over to P, he said, "If you do not find the owner, I claim the money." P placed the money in an envelope and deposited it in her safe deposit box, where it is at present. No one has ever claimed the money, but P refuses to give it to F.

F brings an action against P to recover the money. Decision?

3. Gable, the owner of a lumber company, was cutting trees over the boundary line of his property and property owned by Lane. Although he realized he had crossed onto Lane's property, Gable cut trees on Lane's property of the same kind as those he had cut on his own land. While on Lane's property, he found a diamond ring on the ground, which he took home. All of the timber cut that day by Gable was commingled.

What are Lane's rights, if any, (a) in the timber and (b) in the ring?

4. Decide each of the following problems.

(a) A chimney sweep found a jewel and took it to a goldsmith, whose apprentice took the stone out and refused to return it. The chimney sweep sues the goldsmith.

(b) One of several boys walking along a railroad track found an old stocking. All started playing with it until it burst in the hands of its discoverer, revealing several hundred dollars. The original discovers claims it all; the other boys claim it should be divided equally.

(c) A traveling salesman notices a parcel of bank notes on the floor of a store as he is leaving. He picks them up and gives them to the owner of the store to keep for the true owner. After three years they have not been reclaimed, and the salesman sues the storekeeper.

(d) F is hired to clean out the swimming pool at the country club. He finds a diamond ring on the bottom of the pool. The true owner cannot be found. The country club sues F for possession of the ring.

(e) A customer found a pocketbook lying on a barber's table. He gave it to the barber to hold for the true owner, who failed to appear. The customer sues the barber.

5. Jones had 50 crates of oranges about equally divided between grades A, B, and C, grade A being the highest quality and C the lowest quality. Smith had 1,000 crates of oranges, about 90 percent of which were of grade A but some of them grades B and C, the exact quantity of each being unknown. Smith willfully mixed Jone's crates with his own so that it was impossible to identify any particular crate. Jones seized the whole lot. Smith demanded 900 crates of grade A and fifty each of grades B and C. Jones refused to give them up unless Smith could identify particular crates. This, Smith could not do. Smith brought an action against Jones to recover what he demanded or its value. Judgment for whom, and why?

6. A, the owner and operator of Blackacre, decided to cease farming operations and liquidate his holdings. A sold fifty head of yearling Merino sheep to B and sold Blackacre to C. He executed and delivered to B a bill of sale for the sheep and was paid for them. It was understood that B would send a truck for the sheep within a few days. At the same time, A executed a warranty deed conveying Blackacre to C. C took possession of the farm and brought along one hundred head of his yearling Merino sheep and turned them into the pasture, not knowing the sheep A sold B were still in the pasture. After the sheep were mixed, it was impossible to identify the fifty head belonging to B. After proper demand, B sued C to recover the fifty head of sheep. Decision?

7. O permitted S to take her very old grandfather clock on the basis of S's representations that he was skilled at repairing such clocks and restoring them to their original condition and could do the job for $60. The clock had been badly damaged for years. S immediately sold it to Fixit Shop for $30. Fixit Shop was in the business of repairing a large variety of items and also sold used articles. Three months later, O was in the Fixit Shop and clearly established that a grandfather clock Fixit Shop had for sale was the one she had given S to repair. Fixit Shop had replaced more than half of the moving parts by having exact duplicates custom made; the clock's exterior had been restored by a skilled cabinetmaker; and the clock's face had been replaced by a duplicate. All materials belonged to Fixit Shop, and the work was accomplished by its employees. Fixit Shop asserts it bought the clock in the normal course of business from S, who represented that it belonged to him. The fair market value of the clock in its damaged condition was $30, and the value of repairs made is $220.

O sued Fixit Shop for return of the clock. Fixit Shop defended that it now had title to the clock, and, in the alternative, that O must pay the value of the repairs if she is entitled to regain possession. Decision?

8. A rented a vacant lot from B for a filling station under an oral agreement and placed on it a lightly constructed building bolted to a concrete slab and storage tanks laid on the ground in a shallow excavation. Later, a lease was prepared by A, providing that A might remove the equipment at the termination of the lease. This lease was not executed, having been rejected by B because of a renewal clause it contained, but several years later another lease was prepared that both A and B did sign. This lease did not mention removal of the equipment. At the termination of this lease A removed the equipment, and B brought an action to recover possession of the equipment. What judgment?

9. A sold a parcel of real estate, describing it by its legal description and making no mention of any improvements or fixtures on it. The land had on it a residence, a barn, a rail fence, a stack of hay, some growing corn, and a windmill. The residence had a mirror built into the panel and a heating system consisting of a furnace and steam pipes and coils. There were chairs, beds, tables, and other furniture in the house. On the house was a lightning rod. In the basement were screens for the windows. Which of these things passed by the deed and which did not?

10. John Swan rented a safety deposit box at the Tenth Citizens Bank of Emanon, State of X. On December 17, 1985, Swan went to the Bank with stock certificates for placing in the safety deposit box. After he was admitted to the vault and had placed the stock certificates in the box, Swan found lying on the floor of the vault a $5,000 negotiable bearer bond issued by the State of Wisconsin with coupons attached, due June 30, 1991. Swan picked up the bond and, observing that it did not recite the name of the owner, left the vault and went to the office of the president of the bank. He told the president what had occurred and delivered the bond to the president only after obtaining his promise that, should the owner not call for the bond or become known to the bank by June 30, 1986, the bank would redeliver the bond to Swan. On July 1, Swan learned that the owner of the bond had not called for it, nor was his identity known to the bank. Swan then asked that the bond be returned to him. The bank refused, stating that it would continue to hold the bond until claimed by the owner. Swan brings an action against the bank to recover possession of the bond. Decision?

BAILMENTS AND DOCUMENTS OF TITLE

A **bailment** is the relationship created by the transfer by delivery of possession of personal property, without transfer of title, by one person called the **bailor** to another called the **bailee** for the accomplishment of a certain purpose, after which the property is to be returned by the bailee to the bailor or disposed of according to the bailor's directions. Unlike such well-known legal terms as *contract, agent, sale, partnership, corporation,* and *insurance,* the term *bailment* has not passed into common usage and thus is not familiar to the average person. Nonetheless, the word *bailment* denotes a transaction that not only is of considerable antiquity but also is one of the most common occurrences in everyday life. It is not an exaggeration to say that practically every person, whether carrying on a business or not, becomes a party to a bailment. You will easily understand this from the following common examples of bailments: keeping a car in a public garage; leaving a car, a watch, or any other article to be repaired; renting a car or truck; checking a hat or coat at a theater or restaurant; leaving wearing apparel to be laundered; delivery of jewelry or other valuables or of stocks or bonds to secure the payment of a debt; storage of goods in a warehouse; and the shipment of goods by any mode of public or private transportation.

Not only are bailments of common occurrence, but they are also of great commercial importance in their own right. As the above examples indicate, bailments include the transportation, storage, repairing, and renting of goods, which together involve billions of dollars' worth of transactions each year.

Documents of title are commonly used in bailment transactions. The most frequently used documents of title are warehouse receipts issued by warehousers and bills of lading issued by carriers.

> **Bailment**—the transfer of personal property by one party to another for the accomplishment of a certain purpose and then returned to the original party

Bailments

The benefit of a bailment may, by its terms, accrue solely to the bailor or solely to the bailee, or may accrue to both parties. A bailment may be with or without compensation. On this basis, bailments are classified as follows:

1. **Bailments for the bailor's sole benefit** include the gratuitous custody of personal property and the gratuitous services that involve personal property

> **Bailor**—transferor of the bailed property

such as repairs or transportation. For example, if Sherry stores, repairs, or transports Tim's goods without compensation, this is a bailment for the sole benefit of the bailor, Tim.

2. **Bailments for the bailee's sole benefit** are usually limited to the gratuitous loan of personal property for use by the bailee, as where Tim, without compensation, lends his car, lawn mower, or book to Sherry for her use.

3. **Bailments for the mutual benefit of both parties** include the ordinary commercial bailments, such as when goods are delivered to a repairman, jewels to a pawnbroker, or an automobile delivered to a parking lot attendant.

Bailee—possessor of the bailed property

Essential Elements of a Bailment

The basic and essential elements of a bailment are (1) delivery of possession by a bailor to a bailee; (2) the subject matter must be personal property not real property; (3) possession of the property, without ownership, by the bailee for a determinable period of time; and (4) an absolute duty on the bailee to return the property to the bailor or to dispose of it according to the bailor's directions.

In the great majority of cases, there are two simple tests by which the existence of a bailment can be determined: (1) a separation of ownership and possession of the property (possession without ownership) and (2) a duty on the party in possession to redeliver the identical property to the owner or to dispose of it according to his directions.

Delivery of Possession

The term *bailment* is derived from the French word *bailler,* meaning "to deliver." Possession by a bailee in a bailment relationship involves (1) the bailee's power to control and (2) either an intention to control or an awareness on the part of the bailee that the rightful possessor has given up physical control of the personal property. Thus, for example, where a customer in a restaurant hangs her hat or coat on a hook furnished for that purpose, the hat or coat is within an area under the physical control of the restaurant owner. However, the restaurant owner is not a bailee of the hat or coat unless he clearly signifies that he intends to exercise the power to control the hat or coat. On the other hand, where a clerk in a store helps a customer remove her coat in order to try on a new one, it is generally held that the owner of the store becomes a bailee of the old coat through the clerk, his employee. Here, the clerk has signified an intention to exercise control over the coat by taking it from the customer, and a bailment results.

The following two cases should be contrasted by the reader.

LAVAL v. LEOPOLD

Civil Court of City of New York, Special Term. 1965. 47 Misc.2d 624, 262 N.Y.S.2d 820.

FACTS: Mrs. Laval is a patient of Dr. Leopold, a practicing psychiatrist. Dr. Leopold shares an office with two associates practicing in the same field. No receptionist or other employee attends the office. Mrs. Laval placed her coat in the clothes closet in the office reception room. Later, when she returned to retrieve the coat to leave, she found it missing. Mrs. Laval then brought this action to recover $1,725, the value of her coat.

DECISION: Judgment for Mrs. Laval. The maintenance of the closet in Dr. Leopold's office created an implied invitation to Mrs. Laval to deposit her coat there. It is customary for a patient to remove her fur coat when undergoing treatment in a psychiatrist's office. Therefore, Mrs.

Laval cannot be said to be contributorily negligent in placing her coat in the closet in Dr. Leopold's reception room. It can be implied from the physician-patient relationship between the parties that Dr. Leopold became a bailee of Mrs. Laval's coat.

SEWALL v. FITZ-INN
AUTO PARKS, INC.

Court of Appeals of
Massachusetts, 1975.
3 Mass.App. 380, 330 N.E.2d
853.

FACTS: Mr. Sewall left his car in a parking lot owned by Fitz-Inn Auto Parks, Inc. The lot is approximately 100 by 200 feet in size and has a chain link fence along the rear boundary to separate the lot from a facility of the Massachusetts Bay Transportation Authority. Although the normal entrance and exit are located at the front of the lot, it is also possible to leave by way of a small side street on each side of the lot. Upon entering the lot, the driver would pay the attendant on duty a fee of twenty-five cents to park. The attendant's duties are limited to collecting money from patrons and directing them to parking spaces. Ordinarily, the attendant remained on duty until 11:00 A.M., after which time the lot was left unattended. Furthermore, a patron could remove his car from the lot at any time without interference by any employee of the parking lot.

On the morning of April 15, 1970, Sewall entered the lot, paid the twenty-five cent fee, parked his car in a space designated by the attendant, locked it, and took the keys with him. This was a practice that he had followed routinely for several years. When he returned to the unattended lot that evening, however, he found that his car was gone, apparently having been stolen by an unidentified third person. He then brought this action against Fitz-Inn, the owner of the lot, to recover the value of the car.

DECISION: Judgment for Fitz-Inn Auto Parks, Inc. The existence of a bailment is a prerequisite to Sewall's right to recover because, in the absence of such a relationship, Fitz-Inn had no duty to safeguard the car against theft. A bailment arises only upon delivery of possession of the property sought to be bailed and at least some degree of control over that property. If there has been no delivery of either possession or control, however, the intended bailee cannot be regarded as having undertaken to protect the property and owes the owner no duty to do so.

If Sewall had been required to surrender his keys to the parking lot parking facility and the sole means of exit had been staffed by an attendant responsible for checking each car leaving the facility, then a sufficient delivery of possession and control would have been present to create a bailment. Here, however, Sewall retained possession of the keys, and the attendant did not control egress from the lot. Accordingly, neither type of control over Sewall's car was exercised by the parking lot, and, thus, no bailment and its accompanying duty can be found. Rather, Sewall bore the responsibility for the theft of his car.

Personal Property

The bailment relationship can exist only with respect to personal property. The delivery of possession of real property by the owner to another is covered by real property law. It is not necessary that the bailed property be tangible. Intangible property such as promissory notes, corporate bonds, shares of stock, and life insurance policies that are evidenced by written instruments and thus capable of delivery may be and frequently are the subject matter of bailments.

Possession for a Determinable Time

To establish a bailment relationship, the person receiving possession must be under a duty to return the personal property and must not obtain title to it. Whether a particular transaction constitutes a bailment of a sale must be determined by the particular situation. A sale always involves a transfer to the buyer of *title* to specific property. If the identical property transferred is to be returned, even though in altered form, the transaction is a bailment;

however, if other property of equal value or the money value may be returned, there is a transfer of title, and the transaction is a sale.

Restoration of Possession to the Bailor

The bailee is legally obligated to restore possession of the property when the period of the bailment ends. A bailment for the mutual benefit of both parties ordinarily terminates when the purpose of the bailment is fully accomplished or when the time for which the bailment was created expires. The bailment may, of course, be terminated earlier by mutual consent of the parties. A breach by the bailee of any of his obligations gives the bailor the privilege of terminating the bailment. A bailment is also terminated by destruction of the bailed property because there can be no bailment without personal property.

Bailments for the benefit of the bailee alone or for the benefit of the bailor alone are ordinarily for a definite time or purpose. Such bailments do not terminate until the specified time expires or the purpose is accomplished. In practice, however, these bailments are often terminated at will. For example, one who has gratuitously undertaken to store his neighbor's piano for six months will most likely be able to return the piano before the expiration of that period without liability.

Normally, the bailee is required to return the identical goods bailed, although the goods may be in a changed condition because of the work that the bailee was required to perform on them. An exception to this rule obtains in the case of **fungible goods,** such as grain, where, for all practical purposes, every particle is the equivalent of every other particle, and which the bailee is expected to mingle with other like goods during the bailment. In such a case, obviously the bailee cannot be required to return the identical goods bailed. His obligation is simply to return goods of the same quality and quantity.

Fungible goods–equivalent goods, each unit being the equivalent of every other unit

Rights and Duties of Bailor and Bailee

The bailment relationship creates rights and duties on the part of the bailor and the bailee. The bailee is under a duty to exercise due care for the safety of the property and to return it to the right person. The bailee has the exclusive right to possess the property for the term of the bailment. Depending on the nature of the transaction, a bailee may have the right to compensation and reimbursement of expenses.

The law does not permit certain bailees, namely, common carriers, public warehousers, and innkeepers, to limit their liability for breach of their duties to the bailor, except as provided by statute. Other bailees, however, may vary their duties and liabilities by contract with the bailor. Where liability is limited by contract, the law requires that any such limitation be properly brought to the attention of the bailor before the property is bailed by her. This is especially true in the case of "professional bailees," such as repair garages, who make it their business to act as bailees and who deal with the public on a uniform rather than an individual basis. Thus, a variation or limitation in writing contained in a check or stub given to the bailor or posted on the walls of the bailee's place of business will ordinarily *not* bind the bailor unless the bailee (a) draws the bailor's attention to the writing and (b) informs the bailor that it contains a limitation or variation of liability.

Bailee's Duty to Exercise Due Care

The bailee must exercise due care not to permit injury to or destruction of the property by himself or third parties. The amount of recovery is discussed in *Mieske v. Bartell Drug Co.* which follows. The degree of care depends on the nature of the bailment relationship and the character of the property. Ordinarily, a bailee is *not* an insurer of the subject of the bailment. Because the failure to exercise due care for the property or intentional wrongdoing is the basis of his liability, in the absence of fault, the bailee is not liable where the property is lost, stolen, or destroyed.

MIESKE v. BARTELL DRUG CO.

Supreme Court of Washington, 1979. 92 Wash.2d 40, 593 P.2d 1308.

FACTS: Mrs. Mieske delivered thirty-two fifty-foot reels of developed movie film to the Bartell Drug Company to be spliced together into four reels for convenience of viewing. She placed the films, which contained irreplaceable pictures of their family activities over a period of years, into the order in which they were to be spliced and then delivered them to the manager of Bartell. The manager placed a film processing packet on the bag of films and gave Mrs. Mieske a receipt that stated that "We assume no responsibility beyond retail cost of film unless otherwise agreed to in writing." Although the disclaimer was not discussed, Mrs. Mieske's parting words to the store manager were "Don't lose these. They are my life."

Bartell sent the film to its processing agent, GAF Corporation, which intended to send them to another processing lab for splicing. While at the GAF laboratory, however, the film was accidently disposed of into the garbage disposal dumpster and was never recovered. Upon learning of the loss of their film, the Mieskes brought this action to recover damages from Bartell and GAF. Defendants argue that their liability is limited to the cost of the unexposed film.

DECISION: Judgment for the Mieskes. Because the negligence of both Bartell and GAF contributed to the loss of the film, both are liable as bailees to the Mieskes. The real question, however, is the proper measure of the Mieskes damages.

The general rule of recovery for destruction of personal property is as follows: (1) if the personal property that is destroyed has a market value, then the market value is the measure of damages; (2) if the property has no market value but it can be replaced or reproduced, then the measure of damages is the cost of replacement or reproduction; and (3) if the destroyed property has no market value and cannot be replaced or reproduced, then the value to the owner is to be the proper measure of damages. In the last situation, however, damages are not recoverable for the sentimental value that the owner places on the property.

Here, the property lost was thirty-two reels of film with images that had no market value and that cannot be replaced or reproduced by thirty-two reels of blank film. Therefore, the proper measure of damages is the value of the film to the Mieskes. This type of damage is difficult to ascertain and contains a subjective element, but it must be remembered that compensation for sentimental value is not allowed. With these constraints in mind, the award of $7,500 returned by the jury appears to be appropriate.

In the context of a **commercial bailment,** from which both parties derive a mutual benefit, the law requires the bailee to exercise the care that a reasonably prudent person would exercise under the same circumstances. Where the bailment is one that benefits the bailee alone, as in the case of one who gratuitously borrows a truck from another, the law requires more than reasonable care of him. On the other hand, where the bailee accepts the property for the sole benefit of the bailor, the law requires a lesser degree of care (see Figure 43-1).

It should be remembered, however, that the amount of care required to satisfy any of the standards will vary with the character of the property. A bailee required to take only slight care under the general rules mentioned

FIGURE 43-1 Bailee's Duty of Care

Type of Bailment	Duty of Care	Liability For
For sole benefit of bailor	Relaxed	Gross negligence
For sole benefit of bailee	Utmost	Slight negligence
For mutual benefit	Ordinary	Ordinary negligence

above may be liable if he does not take greater care of a $1,000 bracelet than he would have of a $20 watch. In practice, therefore, the distinctions are blurred by the fact that whatever degree of care is required in the abstract, a bailee must respond to the magnitude of the consequences that reasonably ought to have been foreseen if the property were lost or destroyed.

When the property is lost, damaged, or destroyed while in the possession of the bailee, it is often impossible for the bailor to obtain enough information to show that the loss or damage was due to the bailee's failure to exercise the required care. The law aids the bailor in this respect by *presuming* that the bailee was at fault. The bailor is merely required to show that certain property was delivered by way of bailment and that the bailee has failed to return them or that they were returned in damaged condition. The burden then rests on the bailee to prove that he exercised the degree of care required of him.

Bailee's Absolute Liability

As just discussed, the bailee is free from liability if she has exercised the degree of care required of her under the particular bailment while the property was within her control. However, this general rule has certain important exceptions that impose an absolute duty on the bailee to return the property undamaged to the proper person.

Where the bailee has an obligation by express *agreement* with the bailor or by *custom* to insure the property against certain risks, but fails to do so and the property is destroyed or damaged through such risks, she is liable for the damage or nondelivery, even though she has exercised due care.

Where the bailee uses the bailed property in a manner *not* authorized by the bailor or by the character of the bailment, and during the course of such use the property is damaged or destroyed, without fault on the part of the bailee, the bailee is absolutely liable for the damage or destruction. The reason for this is that wrongful use by the bailee automatically terminates her lawful possession, and she becomes a trespasser as to the property. For example, suppose a garage mechanic, after repairing Brown's car, takes it out for a road test, and the car is damaged in an accident that is solely the fault of someone other than the mechanic. The proprietor of the garage will not be liable as bailee for such damage, because a road test is a normal incident to this type of bailment. However, where the mechanic takes Brown's car for a joy ride or on independent business, and the car is damaged solely through the fault of someone other than the mechanic, the proprietor will be absolutely liable as bailee for the damage.

A bailee has a duty to return the property to the right person. She is not excused by delivering the property to the wrong person by mistake, even when the mistake is induced by negligence on the part of the bailor. If the bailee, by mistake or intentionally, *misdelivers* the property to someone other than the bailor who has no right to its possession, she is guilty of conversion and is liable to the bailor.

Bailor's Right to Compensation

A bailee who by express or implied agreement undertakes to perform work on or render services in connection with the bailed goods is entitled to reasonable compensation for those services or work. In most cases, the agreement between bailor and bailee fixes the amount of compensation and provides how it shall be paid. In the absence of a contrary agreement, the compensation is payable on completion of the work or the performance of the services by the bailee. If, after such completion or performance, and before the goods are redelivered to the bailor, the goods are lost or damaged without fault on the part of the bailee, the bailee is still entitled to compensation for his work and services.

Most bailees who are entitled to compensation for work and services performed in connection with bailed goods acquire a lien on the goods to secure the payment of such compensation. In most jurisdictions the bailee has a statutory right to obtain a judicial foreclosure of his lien and sale of the goods. Many statutes also provide that the bailee does not lose his lien on redelivery of the goods to the bailor, as was the case at common law. Instead, the lien continues for a specified period after redelivery by timely recording with the proper authorities an instrument claiming such a lien.

Special Types of Bailments

Although pledgees, warehousemen, and safe deposit companies are ordinarily bailees and are subject to the general principles that apply to all ordinary bailees, there are some special features about the transactions in which they respectively engage that make it desirable they be given some further consideration. In addition, innkeepers and common carriers are known as *extraordinary* bailees, whereas all other bailees are known as *ordinary* bailees. This distinction is based on the character and extent of the liability of these two classes of bailees for loss of or injury to the bailed goods. As we have seen, an **ordinary** bailee is liable for such loss or injury only where it resulted from his failure to exercise ordinary or reasonable care. The liability of the **extraordinary** bailee, on the other hand, is, in general, **absolute.** In other words, the extraordinary bailee is liable to the bailor for any loss or injury to the goods without regard to the question of his care or negligence as to their safety. As it is frequently put, an extraordinary bailee is an insurer of the safety of the goods. This simply means that just as an insurer, in general, becomes automatically liable to the insured on the happening of the hazard insured against, regardless of the cause, so does the extraordinary bailee become liable to the bailor for any loss or injury to the goods, regardless of the cause.

Ordinary bailee—must exercise due care

Extraordinary bailee—absolutely liable for the safety of the bailed property without regard to the cause of the loss

Pledges

Pledge–security interest by possession

A pledge is a bailment for security in which the owner gives possession of her personal property to another (the secured party) to secure a debt or the performance of some obligation. The secured party does not have title to the property involved but merely a possessory interest to secure a debt or some other obligation. The secured party can usually transfer and assign his special interest in the property to others, even without the consent of the debtor. Pledges of most types of personal property for security purposes are governed by Article 9 of the Uniform Commercial Code, which is discussed in Chapter 37. In most respects the secured party's duties and liabilities are the same as those of a bailee for compensation.

Warehousing

Warehouser–storer of goods for compensation

A warehouser is a bailee who receives goods to be stored in a warehouse for compensation. His duties and liabilities under the common law were in all ways the same as those of the ordinary bailee for compensation. Today, because the activities of warehousers are affected by a strong public interest, they are subject to extensive regulation by State and Federal authorities. Warehousers must also be distinguished from ordinary bailees in that the receipts they issue for storage have acquired a special status in commerce. These receipts are regarded as documents of title and are governed by Article 7 of the Uniform Commercial Code. We discuss documents of title later in this chapter.

Carriers of Goods

Carrier–transporter of goods

In the broadest sense of the term, anyone who transports goods from one place to another, either gratuitously or for compensation, is a carrier. Normally, however, a carrier engages in the business of transportation for hire or reward. The delivery of goods to a carrier for shipment creates a bailment; the carrier has the exclusive possession of the goods without ownership, and is under a duty to deliver them to the person designated by the shipper. Carriers of goods are by far the most important of all bailees. Not only are their transactions the most numerous and the largest in volume, but their function in the movement of raw materials and the distribution of manufactured and other goods of every description is also of enormous importance in our economic system.

Common carrier–carrier open to the general public

Carriers are classified primarily as common carriers and private carriers. A **common carrier** offers its services and facilities to the public on terms and under circumstances indicating that the offering is made to all persons. Common carriers of goods include railroad, steamship, aircraft, public trucking, and pipe line companies. One who carries the goods of another on isolated occasions or who serves a limited number of customers under individual contracts without offering the same or similar contracts to the public at large

Private carrier–carrier which limits its service and is not open to the general public

is **a private or contract carrier**—not a common carrier. Stated somewhat differently, the criteria for determining whether a carrier is subject to the rules applicable to common carriers are (1) the carriage must be part of its business; (2) the carriage must be for remuneration; and (3) the carrier must represent to the general public that it is willing to serve the public in the transportation of property.

The person who delivers goods to a carrier for shipment is known as the **consignor** or **shipper.** The person to whom the goods are to be delivered by the carrier is known as the **consignee.** The instrument containing the terms of the contract of transportation, which the carrier issues to the shipper, is called a **bill of lading.**

Consignor–shipper of *goods*

Consignee–person to whom the goods are to be shipped

Duty to Carry A common carrier is under a duty to serve the public to the limits of its capacity and, within those limits, to accept for carriage goods of the kind that it normally transports. A private carrier has no duty to accept goods for carriage except where it agrees to do so by contract.

Duty to Deliver to the Right Person The carrier is under an absolute duty to deliver the goods to the person to whom they are consigned by the shipper. This duty applies to both common and private carriers. Essentially, this is the duty that renders an ordinary bailee liable for misdelivery. The person to whom delivery must be made is controlled by the form of the bill of lading or other contract of carriage, as discussed later in this chapter.

Liability for Loss or Damage A private carrier, in the absence of special contract terms, is liable as a bailee for the goods it undertakes to carry. A common carrier, on the other hand, is under a stricter liability that approaches that of an insurer of the safety of the goods, except where loss or damage is caused by an act of God, an act of a public enemy, the acts or fault of the shipper, the inherent nature or defect of the goods, or an act of public authority.

In most jurisdictions the carrier is permitted to limit its liability by contract with the shipper. However, a carrier may not absolve itself of liability for its own negligence.

Innkeepers

At common law, innkeepers (today better known as hotel and motel owners or operators) are held to the same **strict or absolute liability** for their guests' belongings as are common carriers for the goods they carry. This rule of strict liability applies only to those who furnish lodging to the public for compensation as a regular business, and liability extends only to the belongings of lodgers who are "guests."

Innkeeper–hotel or motel operator

Today, in almost all jurisdictions, the old common law strict liability of the innkeeper has been substantially modified by case law and statute. Although the statutes vary in detail, they all have certain common features. They provide that the innkeeper may avoid strict liability for loss of his guests' valuables or money by providing a safe where they may be kept and by posting adequate notice of its availability. For articles that are not placed in a safe provided for this purpose or that are not articles of the kind normally kept in a safe, the statutes often limit recovery to a maximum figure that, although it varies from State to State, is generally insubstantial. However, these statutory limitations do not apply where the loss is due to the fault of the innkeeper or his employees, in which case the innkeeper is liable for the full value of the lost property.

Documents of Title

A document of title is a warehouse receipt, bill of lading, or other document evidencing a right to receive, hold, and dispose of the document *and* the goods

Document of title–instrument evidencing ownership of the document and the goods it covers

it covers. To be a document of title a document must be issued by or addressed to a bailee and cover goods in the bailee's possession that are either identified or are fungible portions of an identified mass.

Briefly, a document of title is a symbol of ownership of the goods it describes. Because of the legal characteristics of a document of title, its ownership is equivalent to the ownership or control of the goods it represents, without the necessity of the actual or physical possession of the goods. Likewise, its transfer is a transfer of the ownership or control of the goods without the necessity or inconvenience of the physical transfer of the goods themselves. For these reasons, documents of title are a convenient means of dealing with the billions of dollars' worth of goods that are transported by carriers or are stored with warehousers. Documents of title also serve a very important function in facilitating the transfer of title to goods and the creation of a security interest in goods. Article 7 of the UCC has consolidated and revised the Uniform Warehouse Receipts Act and the Uniform Bills of Lading Act and now governs the negotiation of documents of title.

Types of Documents of Title

Warehouse Receipts

Warehouse receipt–receipt issued by a person storing goods

A warehouse receipt is a receipt issued by a person engaged in the business of **storing** goods for hire.

Duties of Warehousers   A warehouser is liable for damages for loss or injury to the goods caused by his failure to exercise such care in regard to them as a reasonably careful man would exercise under the circumstances. The warehouser must deliver the goods to the person entitled to receive them under the terms of the warehouse receipt.

The liability of a warehouser, however, *may* be limited by a provision in the warehouse receipt fixing a specific maximum liability per article or item or unit of weight. This limitation as shown in the following case does not apply in the event of a conversion of the goods by the warehouseman to his own use.

I.C.C. METALS, INC. v. MUNICIPAL WAREHOUSE CO.

Court of Appeals of New York, 1980.
50 N.Y.2d 657, 431 N.Y.S.2d 372, 409 N.E.2d 849.

FACTS: In the fall of 1974, I.C.C. Metals, Inc., delivered three lots of indium, an industrial metal, to Municipal Warehouse Company for safekeeping. The indium had an aggregate weight of 845 pounds and was worth $100,000. The Warehouse supplied I.C.C. with receipts for each lot. Printed on the back of these receipts were the terms and conditions of the bailment, including an exculpatory clause limiting the liability of the Warehouse to a maximum of $50.00. For two years, the Warehouse billed I.C.C. for storage of the indium, and I.C.C. paid each invoice. In 1976, I.C.C. requested the return of the indium. For the first time, the Warehouse told I.C.C. it was unable to locate any of the indium. I.C.C. brought an action in conversion to recover the full value of the indium. The Warehouse defended on the ground that the metal had been stolen through no fault of its own; and that its liability was limited to $50.00 in accordance with the terms of the Warehouse receipts.

DECISION: Judgment for I.C.C. Absent an agreement to the contrary, a warehouse is not an insurer of goods. Thus, it may not be held liable for any injury to or loss of stolen property not due to its own fault. As a bailee, however, a warehouse must exercise reasonable care to prevent loss or damage to the bailed property. It is also required to refrain from converting the goods left in its care. If a warehouse loses bailed property due to its own negligence, it will be liable for the full value of the goods, unless the parties have agreed to limit the warehouse's liability.

A warehouse can, under certain conditions, limit its liability for its negligence. Nevertheless, if the warehouse converts the goods, liability cannot be limited. When a warehouse converts public property, it loses the protections afforded by its storage agreement.

Here, I.C.C. proved that it delivered the indium to Municipal and that it made a proper demand for its return which Municipal failed to honor. Municipal's unsupported claim that the metal was stolen does not sufficiently explain the loss. The court then determined that under these circumstances, I.C.C's action in conversion could stand. Thus, the contractual limitation on Municipal's liability is ineffective.

A warehouser is not required to keep the goods indefinitely. At the termination of the period of storage stated in the document, the warehouser may notify the person on whose account the goods are held to pay storage charges and remove the goods. If no period of time is stated in the document, the warehouser is required to give thirty days' notice to pay charges and remove the goods. A shorter time, which must be reasonable, is permitted if the goods are about to deteriorate or decline in value to less than the amount of the warehouser's lien, or if the quality or condition of the goods cause them to be a hazard to other property or to persons.

Lien of Warehouseman   To enforce the payment of his charges and necessary expenses in connection with keeping and handling the goods, a warehouser has a lien on the goods that enables him to sell them at public or private sale after notice and to apply the net proceeds of the sale to the amount of his charges.

Bills of Lading

A bill of lading is a document issued by a carrier on receipt of goods for **transportation.** It serves a threefold function: (1) as a receipt for the goods, (2) as evidence of the contract of carriage, and (3) as a document of title.

Bill of lading–terms of the shipment contract issued to the shipper by the carrier

Under the Code, bills of lading may be issued not only by common carriers but also by contract carriers, freight forwarders, or any person engaged in the business of transporting or forwarding goods.

Duties of Issuer of Bill of Lading   The carrier must deliver the goods to the person entitled to receive them under the terms of the bill of lading. The carrier's duty in this respect is similar to that of the warehouser. However, common carriers of goods are extraordinary bailees under the law and subject to a greater degree of liability than an ordinary bailee such as a warehouser.

The Code allows a carrier to limit its liability by contract in all cases where its rates are dependent on value and the shipper is given an opportunity to declare a higher value. The limitation does not apply to a conversion of the goods by the carrier to its own use.

Through Bills of Lading   A bill of lading may provide that the issuer deliver the goods to a *connecting* carrier for further transportation to destination. A bill of lading that specifies one or more connecting carriers is called a through bill of lading.

Through bill of lading– a bill of lading which specifies at least one connecting carrier

The initial or *originating* carrier, which receives the goods from the shipper and issues a through bill of lading, is liable to the holder of the document for loss or damage to the goods caused by any connecting or delivering carrier. The initial carrier has a right of reimbursement from the connecting or delivering carrier in possession of the goods when the loss or damage occurred. A carrier, however, is not required to issue through bills of lading.

Unlike the initial carrier, the liability of a connecting carrier is limited to the period while the goods are in its possession.

Lien of Carrier   The carrier has a lien on goods in its possession covered by a bill of lading for its charges and expenses necessary for preservation of the goods. As against a purchaser for value of a negotiable bill of lading, this lien is limited to charges stated in the bill or in the applicable published tariff, and if no charges are so stated, to a reasonable charge.

Negotiability of Documents of Title

The concept of negotiability has long been established in law. It is important not only in connection with documents of title but also in connection with commercial paper and investment securities treated in other chapters of this book.

Negotiability is a characteristic the law confers on instruments and documents that comply with the required statutory form. The magic words are "bearer" or "order." A promise to deliver goods to a named person is manifestly different from a promise to deliver the goods to bearer or to the order of a named person. The first promise may be safely performed by the promisor by delivery of the goods to the person named in the promise. This is typical of a straight bill of lading, that is, one issued by a carrier that undertakes to deliver the goods to a named consignee at a specific destination. In this case it is not necessary for the carrier to obtain the bill of lading on delivery of the goods at destination. The only concern of the carrier is to make sure that the person to whom it delivers the goods at destination is the person named in the straight bill of lading as the consignee. Such a bill of lading is **nonnegotiable.**

If, on the other hand, the promise of the carrier in the bill of lading is to deliver the goods to **bearer** or to the **order** of a person named in the bill, the carrier may not safely deliver the goods to anyone at destination without obtaining surrender of the original bill of lading. Anyone in possession of a bearer form document is entitled to receive the goods from the carrier. Anyone in possession of an order form document, properly indorsed, is likewise entitled to receive possession of the goods from the carrier. A bearer or order form document of title is **negotiable.** By the terms of the promise contained on its face it was intended to go to market, to pass from hand to hand, and to circulate freely through the channels of commerce.

The Code provides that a warehouse receipt, bill of lading, or other document of tile is negotiable if by its terms the goods are to be delivered to bearer or to the order of a named person or where, in overseas trade, it runs to a named person or assigns. *Any* other document is nonnegotiable.

A nonnegotiable document, such as a straight bill of lading or a warehouse receipt under which the goods are deliverable to a person named in the bill and not to the order of any person or to bearer, may be transferred by assignment but may not be negotiated. Only a negotiable document or instrument may be negotiated.

Due Negotiation

The manner in which a negotiable document of title may be negotiated and the requirements of due negotiation are set forth in the Code. An order form negotiable document of title running to the order of a named person is negotiated by her indorsement and delivery. After such indorsement in blank or to bearer, the document may be negotiated by delivery alone. A special indorsement by which the document is indorsed over to a specified person requires the indorsement of the special indorsee as well as delivery to accomplish a further negotiation.

The naming in a negotiable document of a person to be notified on the arrival of the goods does not limit the negotiability of the bill of lading or serve as a notice to any purchaser of the document that the named person has any interest in the goods.

"Due negotiation" is a term peculiar to Article 7 and requires not only that the purchaser of the negotiable document must take it in good faith without notice of any adverse claim or defense and pay value, but also that she must take it in the regular course of business or financing, and not in settlement or payment of a money obligation. Thus, a transfer for value of a negotiable document of title to a person not in business or a nonbanker, such as a college professor or student, would not be a due negotiation.

Due negotiation–transfer of a negotiable document in the regular course of business to a holder, who takes in good faith, without notice of any defense or claim, and for value

Rights Acquired by Due Negotiation   Negotiation is a form of transfer in which the transferee acquires not only the rights that the transferor had but also direct rights based on the language of the promise contained in the instrument or document. Where a property right is merely assigned, the assignee takes only those rights that the assignor had. He stands in the shoes of the assignor, and his rights are subject to all defects and infirmities in the title of the assignor. However, where a document is negotiable and is transferred by due negotiation, the transferee is one to whom the promise of the issuer runs, and he thereby acquires the direct obligation of the issuer.

The effect of due negotiation is that it creates new rights in the holder of the document. On due negotiation the transferee does not stand in the shoes of his transferor. Defects and defenses available against the transferor are not available against the new holder. His rights are newly created by the negotiation and free of such defects and defenses. This enables bankers and businesspersons to extend credit on documents of title without concern about possible adverse claims or the rights of third parties.

The rights of a holder of a negotiable document of title to whom it has been duly negotiated are that he has (1) title to the document; (2) title to the goods; (3) all rights accruing under the law of agency or estoppel, including rights to goods delivered to the bailee after the document was issued; and (4) the direct obligation of the issuer to hold or deliver the goods according to the terms of the document.

Rights Acquired in the Absence of Due Negotiation   If a nonnegotiable document is transferred or a negotiable document is transferred without due negotiation, the transferee of the document acquires all of the title and rights that the transferor had or had actual authority to convey. Prior to notification received by the bailee of the transfer, the rights of the transferee may be defeated (1) by the creditors of the transferor who could treat the sale as void; (2) by a buyer from the transferor in the ordinary course of business, if the bailee has delivered the goods to the buyer; or (3) as against the bailee by good faith dealings of the bailee with the transferor.

Warranties

A person who either negotiates or transfers a document of title for value other than a collecting bank or other intermediary incurs certain warranty obligations unless otherwise agreed. Such transferor warrants to her immediate purchaser (1) that the document is genuine, (2) that she had no knowledge of any fact that would impair its validity or worth, and (3) that her negotiation or transfer is rightful and fully effective with respect to the title to the document and the goods it represents.

Ineffective Documents of Title

It is fundamental that a thief or finder of goods may not deliver them to a warehouser or carrier in return for a negotiable document of title and thus defeat the rights of the owner by a negotiation of the document. Although such a document would be genuine and its indorsement by the thief or finder would not be a forgery, it would not represent title to the goods.

In order for a person to obtain title to goods by a negotiation to him of a document, the goods must have been delivered to the issuer of the document by the owner of the goods or by one to whom the owner has delivered or entrusted them with actual or apparent authority to ship, store, or sell them.

However, a warehouser or carrier may deliver goods according to the terms of the document that it has issued or otherwise dispose of the goods as provided in the Code without incurring liability even though the document did not represent title to the goods. It must have acted in good faith and complied with reasonable commercial standards in both the receipt and delivery or other disposition of the goods. The bailee has no liability even though the person from whom it received the goods had no authority to obtain the issuance of the document or dispose of the goods, and even though the person to whom it delivered the goods had no authority to receive them.

Thus a carrier or warehouser who receives goods from a thief or finder and later delivers them to a person to whom the thief or finder ordered them to be delivered is not liable to the true owner of the goods. Even a sale of the goods by the carrier or warehouser to enforce a lien for transportation or storage charges and expenses would not subject it to liability.

Warehousers and carriers are regarded as furnishing a service necessary to trade and commerce. They are not a link in the chain of title and do not purport to represent the owner in transactions affecting title to the goods. Consequently, this is a justifiable rule to relieve them from liability on delivery of the goods according to their contract under the document of title even though the document is ineffective against the true owner of the goods.

Lost or Missing Documents of Title

If a document has been lost, stolen, or destroyed, a claimant of the goods may apply to a court for an order directing delivery of the goods or the issuance of a substitute document. Compliance of the carrier or warehouser with the order of court relieves it of liability. The claimant must provide security approved by the court if the missing document is negotiable.

If the carrier or warehouser delivers goods to a person claiming them under a missing negotiable document without a court order, it is liable to any person who is thereby injured. Delivery to such person in good faith is not a conversion of the goods if security is posted in an amount at least double the value of the goods to indemnify any person injured by the delivery who files notice of claim within one year.

CHAPTER SUMMARY

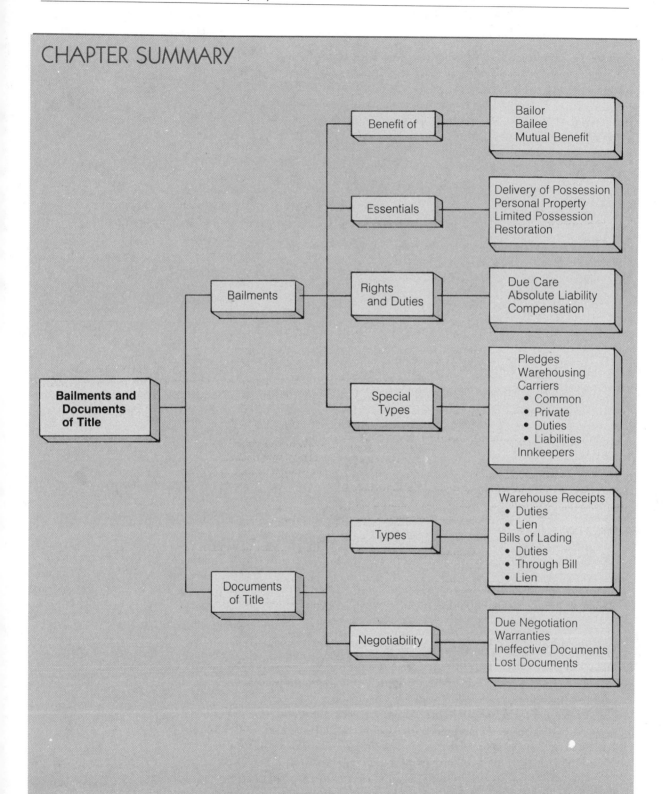

KEY TERMS

Bailment	Ordinary bailee	Innkeeper
Bailor	Extraordinary bailee	Strict liability
Bailee	Pledge	Document of title
Benefit of bailor	Warehousing	Warehouse receipt
Benefit of bailee	Carrier	Through bill
Mutual benefit	Common carrier	Originating carrier
Delivery of possession	Private carrier	Connecting carrier
Personal property	Contract carrier	Negotiable
Fungible goods	Consignor	Bearer instrument
Due care	Shipper	Order instrument
Commercial bailment	Consignee	Due negotiation
Absolute liability	Bill of lading	Warranty

PROBLEMS

1. A was the owner of a herd of twenty highly bred dairy cows. He was a prosperous farmer, but his health was very poor. On the advice of his doctor, A decided to winter in Arizona. Before he left, he made an agreement with Y under which Y was to keep the cows on Y's farm through the winter, pay A the sum of $800, and return to A the twenty cows at the close of the winter. For reasons that Y thought were good farming, Y sold six of the cows and replaced them with six other cows. After the winter was over, A returned from Arizona. When he saw that Y had replaced six cows out of the twenty originally given, he sued Y for the conversion of the original six cows. Decision?

2. Hines stored her furniture, including a grand piano, in Arnett's warehouse. Needing more space, Arnett stored Hines's piano in Butler's warehouse next door. As a result of a fire, which occurred without any fault of Arnett or Butler, both warehouses and contents were destroyed. Hines sues Arnett for the value of her piano and furniture. Decision?

3. B rented a safe deposit box from X Safe Deposit Company in which he deposited valuable securities and $4,000 in cash. Subsequently, B went to the box and found that $1,000 was missing. B brought an action against X, and at the trial the company showed that its customary procedure was as follows: that there were two keys for each box furnished to each renter; that if the key was lost, the lock was changed; also, that new keys were provided for each lock each time a box was rented; that there were two clerks in charge of the vault; and that one of the clerks was always present to open the box. X Safe Deposit Company also proved two keys were given to B at the time he

rented his box; that his box could not be opened without the use of one of the keys in his possession, and the company had issued no other keys to B's box. Decision?

4. A, B, and C each stored 5,000 bushels of yellow corn in the same bin in X's warehouse. X wrongfully sold 10,000 bushels of this corn to Y. A contends that inasmuch as his 5,000 bushels of corn were placed in the bin first, the remaining 5,000 bushels belong to him. What are the rights of the parties?

5. (a) On April 1, Mary Rich, at the solicitation of Super Fur Company, delivered a $3,000 mink coat to the company at its place of business for storage in its vaults until November 1. On the same day, she paid the company its customary charge of $20 for such storage. After Mary left the store, the general manager of the company, on finding that its storage vaults were already filled to capacity, delivered Mary's coat to Swift Trucking Company for shipment to Fur Storage Company. En route, the truck in which Mary's coat was being transported was totally damaged by fire caused by negligence on the part of the driver of the truck, and Mary's coat was totally destroyed. Is Super Fur Company liable to Mary for the value of her coat? Why?

(b) Would your answer be the same if Mary's coat had been safely delivered to Fur Storage Company and had been stolen from its storage vaults without negligence on its part? Why?

6. Rich, a club member, left his golf clubs with Bogan, the pro at the Happy Hours Country Club, to be refinished at Bogan's pro shop. The refinisher employed by Bogan suddenly left town, taking Rich's clubs with him. The refinisher had previously been above suspicion, although Bogan had never checked on the man's character references. A valuable sand wedge that Bogan had borrowed from another member, Smith, for his own use in an important tournament match was also stolen by the refinisher, as well as several pairs of golf shoes that Bogan had checked for members without charge as an accommodation. The club members concerned each made claims against Bogan for their losses. Can (a) Rich, (b) Smith, and (c) the other members compel Bogan to make good their respective losses?

7. B drove an automobile into T's garage and requested him to make repairs for which the charge would be $125. B never returned to get the automobile, and two months later C saw it in T's garage. C claimed it as his own and asserted that it had been stolen from him. T told C that he could have the automobile if he paid for the repairs and storage. One week later O appeared and proved that the automobile was hers, that it had been stolen from her, and that neither B nor C had any rights in it.

O brings an action against T for conversion of the automobile. Decision?

8. On June 1, Cain delivered his 1978 automobile to Barr, the operator of a repair shop, for necessary repairs. Barr put the car in his lot on Main Street. The lot, which is fenced on all sides except along Main Street, holds one hundred cars and is unguarded at night, although the police make periodic checks. The lot is well lighted. The cars do not have the keys in them when left out overnight. At some time during the night of June 4, the hood, starter, alternator, and gear shift were stolen from Cain's car. The car remained on the lot, and during the evening of June 5 the transmission was stolen from the car. The cost of replacement of the parts stolen in the first theft was $600 and in the second theft $500.

Cain sued Barr to recover $1,100. Decision?

9. A, in Phoenix, according to a contract with B in New York, ships to Be goods conforming to the contract and takes from the carrier a shipper's order bill of lading that A indorses in blank and forwards by mail to C, his agent in New York, with instructions to deliver the bill of lading to B on receipt of payment of the price for the goods. X, a thief, steals the bill of lading from C and transfers it for value to Y, a *bona fide* purchaser. Before the goods arrive in New York, B is petitioned into bankruptcy. What are the rights of the parties?

10. A, a Philadelphia merchant, purchased merchandise from B in Chicago. The contract of sale provided that the merchandise was sold F.O.B., Chicago, payment to be made sixty days after delivery. B delivered the goods to the railroad carrier in Chicago, took an order bill of lading in the name of A, and forwarded it to A. Before the goods arrived in Philadelphia, B learned that A had become insolvent and exercised a right of stoppage in transit by proper notice to the railroad company. Thereafter, and before the shipment reached Philadelphia, A indorsed and delivered the bill of lading to C, an innocent purchaser for value. C claimed the goods by reason of holding the bill of lading. To whom should the goods be awarded?

INTERESTS IN REAL PROPERTY

Interests in real property may be divided into ownership, possessory, and nonpossessory interests. Rights of ownership in real property are called estates and are classified to indicate the quantity, nature, and extent of the rights. The two major categories are freehold estates (those existing for an indefinite time or for the life of a person) and estates less than freehold (those that exist for a predetermined time), called leasehold estates. The ownership of property may be held by one individual or concurrently by two or more persons, each of whom is entitled to an undivided interest in the entire property. Both freehold estates and leasehold estates are regarded as possessory interests in property. In addition, there are several nonpossessory interests in property, including easements, *profits à prendre,* and licenses. We consider all of these topics in this chapter.

Freehold Estates

Of all the estates in real property, the most valuable are usually those that combine the enjoyment of immediate possession with ownership at least for life. These estates are either some form of fee estate or estates for life. In addition, it is possible that either type of estate may be created without immediate right to possession, called a future interest.

> Freehold estate–ownership of real property for an indefinite time or for the life of a person

Fee Estates

Fee estates include both fee simple and qualified fee estates.

Fee Simple Estate

When a person says that he has "bought" a house or a corporation informs its shareholders that it has "purchased" an industrial site, the property is generally held in fee simple. This means that the property is owned absolutely (possibly subject to a mortgage) and can be sold or passed on at will to heirs or successors. The absolute right of transferability and of transmitting by inheritance are basic characteristics of a fee simple estate. The estate signifies full control over the property, which is *owned absolutely* and can be sold or disposed of as desired.

> Fee simple–absolute ownership

   A fee simple is created by any words that indicate an intent to convey absolute ownership. "To B in fee simple" will accomplish the purpose, as will "to B forever." The general presumption is that a conveyance is intended to convey full and absolute title in the absence of a clear intent to the contrary.

A practical consequence of a fee simple title is that not only may it be voluntarily transferred, but it may also be levied on and sold at the instance of judgment creditors of the fee simple holder (the owner).

Qualified or Base Fee Estate

Qualified fee—ownership subject to its being taken away upon the happening of an event

It is possible to convey or will property to a person to enjoy it absolutely, *subject to* its being taken away at a later date if a certain event takes place. The estate thus created is known as a base fee, qualified fee, conditional fee, or fee simple defeasible. For example, Abe may provide in his will that his widow is to have his house and lot in "fee simple forever so long as she does not remarry." If his widow dies without remarrying, the property is transferred to her heirs as if she owned it absolutely, because the condition of remarrying did not take place. However, if Abe's widow remarries or sells the land to Ben and then remarries, the widow and Ben would respectively lose their title to the land, and it would revert to the heirs of Abe.

Life Estates

By tradition, life estates are divided into two major classes: (1) conventional life estates or those created by voluntary act and (2) those established by law, the most significant example of which is a wife's dower right in the property of her husband.

Conventional Life Estates

Life tenant—ownership for the life of a designated person

Remainder—ownership after a prior estate

A grant or a devise (grant by will) "to Alex for life" creates in Alex an estate that terminates on his death. Such a provision may stand alone, in which case the property will revert to the grantor and his heirs, or, as is more likely, it will be followed by a subsequent grant to another party such as "to Alex for life and then to Mario and his heirs." Alex is the **life tenant,** and Mario is generally described as the **remainderman.** Alex's life, however, may not be the measure of his life estate, as where an estate is granted "to Alex for the life of Bob." On Bob's death, Alex's interest terminates, and if Alex dies before Bob, Alex's interest passes to his heirs or as he directs in his will for the remainder of Bob's life.

No particular words are necessary to create a life estate. It is always a matter of determining the intent of the grantor. Life estates arise most frequently in connection with the creation of trusts, which we consider in Chapter 46.

Generally, a life tenant may make reasonable use of the property as long as he does not commit "waste." Any act or omission that does permanent injury to the realty or unreasonably changes its characteristics or value constitutes **waste.** For example, the failure to make repairs on a building, the unreasonable cutting of timber, or the neglect of an adequate conservation policy may subject the life tenant to an action by the remainderman to recover damages for waste.

A conveyance by the life tenant passes only his interest. The life tenant and the remainderman may, however, join in a conveyance to pass the entire fee to the property, or the life tenant may terminate his interest by conveying it to the remainderman.

Life Estates Established by Law

Dower Under common law, dower is a life estate that a **wife** who survives her husband has in one-third of all the real property the husband owned during the marriage. It arises by operation of law and exists regardless of the intent or wishes of the parties. However, in most States the common law has been generally modified by statute to provide the wife with a one-third interest in such real estate, rather than just a life estate in real property.

Until the death of the husband, the wife's dower is contingent or **inchoate.** During his life she cannot transfer or sell her dower interest. Dower can exist only in fee simple estates or in an estate that for practical purposes is equivalent to a fee simple estate. There is no dower in a life estate because it is not an estate of inheritance.

Although the widow does not realize her dower unless she survives her husband, her right to the dower is protected during the marriage. If the husband sells his property after he marries, the purchaser takes the property subject to the inchoate right of dower even if the purchaser did not know that the seller was married. Dower also takes precedence over any claims against the husband's estate that were not reduced to judgment or made a lien against his property before marriage. Generally, to bar dower during marriage, it is necessary that the wife expressly waive her dower, and because dower is an interest in land, such a release must be in writing. Generally, the husband must also sign the release. In most jurisdictions the wife can relinquish her dower simply by joining in a conveyance with her husband.

The incidents of dower at common law have been substantially modified by statute in most jurisdictions. In some States the widow may elect whether to take common law dower or an alternative amount given her by statute, and she has a certain period of time within which to make the election. In many jurisdictions, dower has been abolished, and a statutory share of the husband's property, generally including both real and personal, is substituted in place of it.

Curtesy At common law, the surviving **husband,** had a life estate in the real property of his wife similar to, although not identical with, the widow's dower. This estate, known as curtesy, required a valid marriage and the death of the wife before the husband. As with dower, it existed only in estates of inheritance, and there was no curtesy in a life estate. Unlike dower, curtesy did not exist unless a child were born of the marriage. However, the child did not need to survive the wife. But curtesy was like dower in that the wife could not bar the husband's claim to curtesy without his written waiver. In most States the estate of curtesy has been substantially modified or entirely abolished, and in place of it the husband in some States is given a statutory share in the estate of his deceased wife.

Future Interests

Not all interests in property are subject to immediate use and possession, even though the right and title to the interest are absolute. Thus, where property is conveyed or devised by will "to A during his life and then to B and her heirs," B has a definite, existing *interest* in the property, but she is not entitled

Dower—wife's estate in the property of her husband

Inchoate—contingent

Curtesy—husband's estate in the property of his wife

to immediate *possession*. This right and similar rights are generically referred to as future interests.

Reversions

Reversion–grantor's right to property upon termination of another estate

If Anderson conveys property "to Benson for life" and makes no disposition of the remainder of the estate, Anderson holds the reversion—the grantor's right to the property on the death of the life tenant. Thus Anderson would regain ownership to the property when Benson dies. This result is not as apparent when Anderson conveys property "to Benson for life and then to my heirs." It is arguable that there is a remainder in the grantor's next-of-kin. The common law doctrine, however, was that such a reference to the heirs of the grantor placed a reversion in the *grantor,* and his heirs took nothing except as they might inherit the reversion.

Possibility of reverter–conditional reversionary interest

handwritten: —F.S. cond. subject to condition subsequent —owner has right to reentry

A **possibility of reverter,** as the phrase suggests, exists where property may return to the grantor or his successor in interest because of the happening of an event on which a fee simple estate was to terminate. It is the possibility of a reversion what is present in the grant of a base or qualified fee as previously discussed in this chapter. Thus Karlene has a possibility of reverter if she dedicates property to a public use "so long as it is used as a park." If, in one hundred years, the city ceases to use the property for a park, the heirs of A will be entitled to the property. Unlike a reversion, which is a present estate to be enjoyed in the future, a possibility of reverter is simply an expectancy.

Remainders

handwritten: rule against perpetuities– limited time for vesting in future (21 yrs)

A remainder is an estate in property that, like a reversion, will take effect in possession, if at all, on the termination of a prior estate created by the *same instrument.* Unlike a reversion, a remainder is held by a person other than the grantor or his successors. A grant from Gwen "to Lew for his life and then to Robert and his heirs" creates a remainder in Robert. On the termination of the life estate, Robert will be entitled to possession as remainderman. Robert takes his title not from Lew but from the original grantor, Gwen.

There are two kinds of remainders, vested remainders and contingent remainders.

Vested remainder–unconditional remainder

Vested Remainders
A remainder is vested when the only contingency to the possession by the remainderman is the termination of the preceding estate. When Richard has a remainder in fee, subject only to a life estate in Laura, the only obstacle to the right of immediate possession by Robert or his heirs is Laura's life. Laura's death, no more, no less, is sufficient and necessary to place Robert in possession. The law considers this vested remainder as a fixed *present* interest to be enjoyed in the future. It is an interest in property that is transferable just as much as the preceding life estate, and it is characteristic of a vested remainder that the owner of the preceding estate can do nothing to defeat the remainder.

Contingent remainder–remainder interest, conditional upon the happening of an additional event

Contingent Remainders
A remainder is contingent if the right to possession is dependent or conditional on the happening of some event *in addition to* the termination of the preceding estate. The remainder may be conditioned on the existence of some person who does not yet exist or on the happening of an event that may never occur. A contingent remainder, by definition and

unlike a vested remainder, is *not* ready to take immediate possession simply on the termination of the preceding estate. A provision in a will "to A for life and then to his children but if he has no children then to B" creates contingent remainders both as to the children and as to B. If A marries and has a child, the remainder than vests in that child, and B's expectancy is closed out. If A dies without having fathered a child, then and only then will an estate vest in B. It is, of course, possible for a contingent remainder to become vested while possession is still in the preceding life estate, as evidenced by the birth of a child to A in the above example. Another illustration is provided by the following case.

STRICKLAND v. JACKSON

Supreme Court of North Carolina, 1963.
259 N.C. 81, 130 S.E.2d 22.

FACTS: In 1905 a deed for land in Pitt County was executed and delivered by Joel and Louisa Tyson "unto M. H. Jackson and wife Maggie Jackson, for and during the term of their natural lives and after their death to the children of the said M. H. Jackson and Maggie Jackson that shall be born to their inter-marriage as shall survive them to them and their heirs and assigns in fee simple forever." Thelma Jackson Vester, a daughter of M. H. and Maggie Jackson, died in 1957, survived by three children. M. H. Jackson, who survived his wife Maggie Jackson, died in 1958, survived by four sons. The children of Thelma Jackson Vester brought this action against M. P. Jackson, a son of and executor of the will of M. H. Jackson. The children of Vester contended that through their deceased mother they were entitled to ⅓ interest in the land conveyed by the deed of 1905. The executor contended that the deed conveyed a contingent remainder and only those children who survived the parents took an interest in the land.

DECISION: Judgment for Strickland. If those who are granted an estate cannot be determined until the happening of a stated event, the remainder is contingent. Only those able to answer the role immediately upon the happening of the event acquire any estate in the properties granted. Here, the Tysons did not grant an estate to the children of M. H. and Maggie Jackson. Rather, they specifically granted the estate to those children of the Jacksons who survived M. H. and Maggie. Thus, the estate was a contingent remainder. Since Mrs. Vester did not survive her parents, there was nothing for her children to inherit.

Leasehold Estates

No part of the law of real property affects so many persons in their daily affairs as the law of landlord and tenant. By virtue of his lease, a tenant has an estate in land, which is an interest in real property, and its primary characteristic is the right to possession. If Linda, the owner of a house and lot, rents it to Ted for a year, Linda, of course, still holds title to the property but she has sold the right to occupy the property to Ted. Ted's right to occupy the property is superior to that of Linda, and as long as Ted occupies the property according to the terms of the lease contract, he does, as a practical matter, have exclusive possession against all the world as though he were the actual owner.

Leasehold estate–right to possess real property

Creation and Duration of the Leasehold Estate

A lease is both a contract and a grant of an estate in land. It is a contract by which the owner of the land, the **landlord,** grants to another, the **tenant,** an exclusive right to use and possession of the land for a definite or ascertainable period of time or term. The possessory term thus granted is an estate in land called a **leasehold.** The landlord retains an interest in the property called a

Landlord–owner of land who grants a leasehold interest to another

Tenant–possessor of the leasehold interest

reversion. The principal characteristics of the leasehold estate are that it continues for a definite or ascertainable term and that it carries with it the obligation on the part of the tenant to pay rent to the landlord.

By statute, in most jurisdictions, leases for a term longer than a specified period of time must be in writing. The period is generally fixed at either one or three years.

Definite Term

A lease for a definite term automatically expires at the end of the term. Such a lease is frequently termed an **"estate for years,"** even though the duration may be for one year or shorter. No notice to terminate is required.

Periodic Tenancy

A periodic tenancy is a definite term lease of specified duration that is to be held over and over in the same length of time in indefinite succession. For example, a lease "to T from month to month" or "from year to year" creates a periodic tenancy. Periodic tenancies arise frequently by implication. L leases to T without stating any term in the lease. This creates a tenancy at will. If T pays rent to L at the beginning of each month and L accepts such payments, most courts hold that the tenancy at will has been transformed into a tenancy from month to month.

A periodic tenancy may be terminated by either party at the expiration of any one period but only on adequate notice to the other party. If there is no specific agreement in the lease, the common law requires six months' notice in tenancies from year to year. However, this period has been shortened in most jurisdictions by statute to periods ranging between thirty and ninety days. In periodic tenancies involving periods of less than one year, the notice required at common law is one full period in advance, but, again, this may be subject to regulation by statute.

Tenancy at Will

A lease containing a provision that either party may terminate at any time creates a tenancy at will. A lease that does not specify any duration also creates a tenancy at will. At common law such tenancies were terminable without any prior notice, but many jurisdictions now have statutes requiring a notice to terminate, usually thirty days.

Tenancy at Sufferance

One who is in possession without a valid lease is a tenant at sufferance. A tenant at sufferance is technically a trespasser, and the landlord owes him no duties except that, under the common law, a landowner has no right to willfully injure a trespasser.

The most common case of a tenancy at sufferance arises when a tenant fails to vacate the premises at the expiration of the lease. The common law gives the landlord the right to elect either to dispossess such tenant or to hold him for another term. Until the landlord makes this election, a tenancy at sufferance exists.

Transfer of Interests in a Leasehold

Both the tenant's interest in the leasehold and the landlord's reversionary interest in the property may be freely transferred in the absence of contractual

---

Margin notes:

Periodic tenancy—definite term that is to be continued

Tenancy at will—terminable at any time

Tenancy at sufferance—a tenant without a valid lease

or statutory prohibition. This general rule is subject to one major exception: the tenancy at will. Any attempt by either party to transfer her interest is usually considered as an expression of the intent to terminate the tenancy.

Transfers by Landlord

After conveying the leasehold interest, a landlord is left with a reversionary interest in the property plus the right to rent and other benefits acquired under the lease. The landlord may transfer either or both of these interests. The party to whom the reversion is transferred takes the property subject to the tenant's leasehold interest if the transferee has actual or constructive notice of the lease. For example, L leases Whiteacre to T for five years, and T records the lease with the Register of Deeds. L then sells Whiteacre to A. T's lease is still valid and enforceable against A, whose right to possession of Whiteacre begins only after the expiration of the lease.

Transfers by Tenant

A tenant may dispose of his interest either by (1) assignment or (2) sublease. In the absence of a provision in his lease, both of these rights are available to him. As a consequence, most standard leases expressly require the consent of the landlord to an assignment or subletting of the premises.

assignor can sue for breach of contract & lease; lease gives protected interest in land

Assignment If a tenant transfers *all* his interest in the leasehold so that he has no reversionary rights, he has made an assignment. This complete transfer does not simply mean the length of the time involved in the transfer. A transfer of the entire remaining period may not involve an assignment if the tenant retains any control over the premises. If there are no specific restrictions in the lease, leases are freely assignable. Many leases, however, prohibit assignment without the landlord's written consent. If the tenant assigns without such written consent, the assignment is not void, but it may be avoided by the landlord. In other words, the prohibition of assignment in a lease is only for the benefit of the landlord and cannot be relied on by the assignor to terminate an otherwise valid assignment on the ground that the landlord did not consent. If, however, the landlord accepts rent from the assignee, he will be held to have waived the restriction.

Assignment–transfer of all one's interest in the leasehold

The agreement to pay rent and certain other contractual **covenants** (express promises) pass to and obligate the assignee of the lease as long as he remains in possession of the leasehold estate. Although the assignee of the lease is thus bound to pay rent, the original tenant is *not* relieved of his contractual obligation to pay rent. If the assignee fails to pay the stipulated rent, the original tenant will have to pay. He will, of course, have a right to be reimbursed by the assignee. Thus, after an assignment of a tenant's interest, *both* the original tenant and the assignee are liable to the landlord for failure to pay rent.

Sublease A sublease differs from an assignment in that it involves the transfer by the tenant to another of *less* than all the tenant's rights in the lease. For example, T, is a tenant under a lease from L that is to terminate on December 31, 1986. If T leases the premises to SL for a shorter period than that covered by her own lease, say, until November 30, 1986, T has subleased the premises because she has transferred less than her whole interest in the lease.

Sublease–transfer of less than all of the tenant's interest in the leasehold

The legal effects of a sublease are entirely different from those of an assignment. In a sublease the sublessee, SL in the example above, has no obligation to T's landlord, L. SL's obligations run solely to T, the original tenant, and T is not relieved of any of her obligations under the lease. Thus L has no right of action against T's sublessee SL under any covenants contained in the original lease between him and T, because that lease has not been assigned to SL. T, of course, remains liable to L for the rent and for all of the other covenants in the original lease between her and L. Under the majority view, a covenant against assignment of a lease does not prohibit the tenant from subleasing the premises. Conversely, a prohibition against subleasing is not considered a restriction on the right to assign the lease (see Figure 44-1).

Tenant's Obligations

Although the leasehold estate carries with it an implied obligation on the part of the tenant to pay reasonable rent, the contract of lease almost always contains an express promise or covenant by the tenant to pay rent in specified amounts at specified times. In the absence of a specific covenant providing the amount of rental and the times for payment, the rent is a *reasonable* amount and is *payable only at the end of the term*.

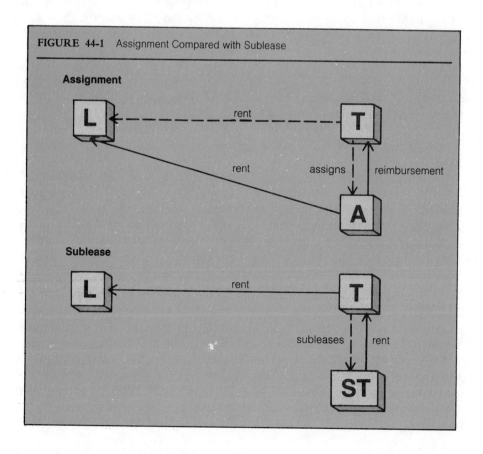

FIGURE 44-1   Assignment Compared with Sublease

Most leases contain a provision to the effect that if the tenant breaches any of the covenants in the lease, the landlord is entitled to declare the lease at an end and may regain possession of the premises. The tenant's express undertaking to pay rent thus becomes one of the covenants on which this provision can operate. Where there is no such provision in the lease, at common law the tenant's failure to pay rent when due gives the landlord only the right to recover a judgment for the amount of such rent; it does *not* give him the right to oust the tenant from the premises. However, in most jurisdictions the common law rule has been changed by statute to give the landlord the right to dispossess the tenant for nonpayment of rent, even though there is no provision for this in the lease.

A tenant is under *no* duty to make any repairs to the leased premises, unless the lease has specific provisions to the contrary. He is not obliged to repair or restore substantial or extraordinary damage occurring without his fault, nor to repair damage caused by ordinary wear and tear. However, the tenant is obliged to use the premises so that no substantial injury is caused them. The law imposes this duty on him even though it is not expressly stated in the lease. For example, a tenant who overloads a barn and thus causes it to fall is liable to the landlord, and the overloading of an electrical connection that causes damage to a wiring system will entitle a landlord to maintain an action for damages.

Destruction of the Premises

The dual character of a lease as a contract and as a grant of an estate in land is particularly evident when considering the common law rule governing the destruction of the premises by fire or other cause. Where the tenant leases land together with a building and the building is destroyed by fire or some other chance event, the common law does not relieve him of his obligation to pay rent or permit him to terminate the lease. The common law rule has been modified in some States by statute, and in most States it does not apply to tenants who occupy only a portion of the building and have no interest in the building as a whole, such as apartment tenants.

Eviction or Abandonment

The tenant's obligations also depend on whether the landlord rightfully evicts the tenant, the tenant wrongfully abandons the premises, or the landlord wrongfully evicts the tenant.

Evict—remove from the premises

Dispossession by Landlord for Breach of Covenant
When the tenant breaches one of the covenants in her lease, such as the covenant to pay rent, and the landlord evicts or dispossesses her according to a specific provision in the lease or under a statute authorizing her to do so, the lease is terminated. Because the breach of the covenant to pay rent does not involve any injury to the premises and because the landlord's action in evicting the tenant terminates the lease, the tenant is not liable to the landlord for any future installments of the rent after such an eviction. However, most long-term leases contain a **"survival clause"** providing that the eviction of the tenant for nonpayment of rent will not relieve her of liability for damages measured by

the difference between the rent specified in the lease and the rent the landlord is able to obtain when reletting the premises.

Wrongful Abandonment by Tenant　If the tenant wrongfully abandons the premises before the expiration of the term of the lease and the landlord reenters the premises or relets them to another, a majority of the courts hold that the tenant's obligation to pay rent after reentry terminates. ("Reenter" in this case means to occupy the premises.) The landlord, if he desires to hold the tenant to his obligation to pay rent, must either leave the premises vacant or must have another "survival clause" in the lease that covers this situation.

Wrongful Eviction by Landlord　If the tenant is wrongfully evicted by the landlord, the tenant's obligations under the lease are terminated, and as discussed below, the landlord is liable for breach of the tenant's right of quiet enjoyment.

Landlord's Obligations

Unless there are specific provisions in the lease, the landlord, under the common law, has few obligations to her tenant. At the beginning of the lease she must give the tenant a right to possession, but under the majority rule, she is not required to give the tenant actual possession. Thus, if the previous tenant refuses to move out at the termination of the lease, the landlord must bring dispossession proceedings to oust him, but she is not responsible to the new tenant for the delay thus brought about, and the new tenant is not relieved of the obligation to pay rent from the starting date of the lease.

Quiet Enjoyment

Quiet enjoyment—not to be evicted

The landlord may not interfere with the tenant's right to physical possession, use, and enjoyment of the premises. The landlord is bound to provide the tenant with quiet and peaceful enjoyment. This duty arises by implication and is known as the landlord's covenant of "quiet enjoyment." The landlord breaches this covenant whenever he wrongfully evicts the tenant. The law also regards the landlord as having breached this covenant if the tenant is evicted by someone having a better title than the landlord. The landlord is not responsible, however, for the wrongful acts of third parties unless they are done with his assent and under his direction.

Fitness for Use

Implied warranty of habitability—fit for ordinary residential purposes

Unless there is a specific provision in the lease, the landlord, under the common law, is under *no* obligation to maintain the premises in a livable condition or to make them fit for any purpose, since the value of the lease to the tenant was real property. Some courts, however, have abandoned this rule in residential leases by imposing an implied warranty that the leased premises are habitable, that is, fit for ordinary residential purposes. These courts have also held that the covenant to pay rent is conditioned on the landlord's performance of the **implied warranty of habitability.** Courts, as in *Javins v. First National Realty Corp.,* reaching these results have emphasized the tenant's interest in a place to live and not merely in the land. The common law assumption of the value of the leasehold being the interest in land may have been valid in an agricultural society and may even be valid in some farm leases, but it is not true in the case of a modern apartment tenant.

FACTS: By separate leases, Javins and a few others rented an apartment at the Clifton Terrace apartment complex. When they had defaulted on their rent payments, the landlord, First National Realty, brought an action to evict them. The tenants admitted to the default, but defended on the ground that the landlord had failed to maintain the premises in compliance with the Washington D.C. Housing Code. They alleged that approximately 1500 violations of this Code had arisen since the term of their lease had begun.

DECISION: Judgment for Javins and other tenants. Traditionally, a lease conveyed an interest in land. Consequently courts applied the general rules governing real property transactions to lease controversies. The rigid doctrines of real property law have inhibited the application of implied warranties to real estate transactions. However, today's tenant is not interested in land, but in a suitable place for occupation. The value of the lease for a modern apartment dweller is that it gives him a place to live which includes adequate heat, light and ventilation, servicable plumbing facilities, secure doors and windows, proper sanitation, and proper maintenance. A tenant's tenure in a specific place is often not sufficient to justify efforts at repairs. Since the lease specifies a particular period of time for the tenant to use the apartment, he may legitimately expect that it will be fit for habitation during this rental period. The landlord should then be obligated to keep the premises in a habitable condition. The court, therefore, held that a warranty of habitability, measured by housing standards regulations, is implied into leases of units covered by those regulations. In this case, the tenants' obligation to pay rent was dependent upon the landlord's performance of its obligations, which now includes the warranty to maintain the premises in a habitable condition. First National has not fulfilled its implied warranty of habitability; therefore it cannot sue for possession due to the tenants' default.

JAVINS v. FIRST NATIONAL REALTY CORP.

United States Court of Appeals, District of Columbia Circuit, 1970. 428 F.2d 1071.

A few States have statutes requiring landlords, specifically apartment landlords, to keep the premises fit for occupation. Zoning ordinances and health and safety regulations may also impose certain duties on the landlord.

For a unique way of making a landlord improve the condition of his rental property see the following Law in the News article on page 798.

Repair

Unless there is a specific provision in the lease or a statutory duty to do so, the landlord has *no* obligation to repair or restore the premises. The landlord does, however, have a duty to maintain, repair, and keep in safe condition those parts of the premises that remain under her control. For example, an apartment house owner who controls the stairways, elevators, and other common areas is liable for their maintenance and repair and is responsible for injuries that occur as a result of her failure to do so. With respect to apartment buildings, the courts presume that any portion of the premises that is not specifically leased to the tenants remains under the landlord's control. Thus, in such cases the landlord is liable for making external repairs, including repairs to the roof.

While at common law the landlord is under no duty to repair, restore, or keep the premises in a livable condition, she may and often does assume those duties in the lease. When she does, her breach of any of these obligations under the lease does *not* entitle the tenant to abandon the premises and refuse to pay rent. Unless a specific provision in the lease gives the tenant this right, the common law allows him only an action for damages.

Under the doctrine of **constructive eviction,** however, a failure by the landlord in any of her undertakings under the lease that causes a substantial and lasting injury to the tenant's beneficial enjoyment of the premises is

Law In The News _____

Surgeon-Landlord Ordered To Live Like His Tenants

LOS ANGELES (AP)—A neurosurgeon has been ordered to move from Beverly Hills for 30 days to an apartment resembling a rat-infested flat he rents to a family of seven.

The judge ordered Dr. Milton Avol to spend equal time in a clean jail cell and in one of the garbage-strewn apartments he owns after he failed to significantly improve the buildings during 36 months' probation.

For three years, Ramona Mota, her husband and five children have squeezed into a four-room, fourth-floor apartment in a building owned by Avol on South Main Street near the downtown garment district.

Rats, cockroaches, mosquitoes and flies have become almost like part of the furnishings, according to court testimony. "I set traps, but it doesn't do any good, because there are too many (rats)," Mota, 28, said Tuesday through an interpreter.

The Motas said they pay $263 a month for an apartment that lacks a reliable hot water supply, leaks when it rains, has a broken floor and requires sheets in the windows to keep the street dirt out.

Locks on doors, mailboxes and security are nonexistent.

Avol, who lives in Beverly Hills, was sentenced to spend 30 days at an even sorrier unit at one of his other complexes, also on the fringe of downtown, said Municipal

Court Judge Veronica Simmons McBeth.

Monday, she also ordered him to report for a 30-day jail term beginning Thursday. The day he is released, he will be escorted to an apartment about two miles away from Mota's, McBeth said.

In 1983, Avol was convicted of violating health, fire and building and safety codes at four of his apartment complexes, but he was given 36 months to bring the buildings into compliance with regulations.

McBeth was visiting Mota's apartment building when "I started thinking what if he had to live here. Maybe it would make him come in contact with some sense of human decency," she said.

Avol's attorney, Scott Furstman, said that Avol would not talk to reporters and that Avol had asked him not to discuss the case. But in court Monday, Avol argued that vandalism had stymied his efforts to improve the buildings.

Some 300 families live in the four buildings for which Avol was sentenced in 1983. One other building, including the site where Avol will serve his sentence, is under investigation, said Deputy City Attorney Stephanie Sautner.

She brought more than 100 photographs to court Monday showing holes in walls, rat holes, cracked or missing plaster, defective plumbing, a burned-out unit

that was left unrepaired, missing fire doors and unworkable fire extinguishers. "They are horrible places," she said.

If the vandalism was as bad as Avol described, "he should have hired a security guard or round-the-clock manager," Sautner said. "There are also no police reports of vandalism. Dr. Avol is a mystery to me. When he did make improvements, he put in inferior materials with unskilled labor."

Mota, born in Mexico, said she can't work because she must care for her five children, ages 1 to 10, and her husband, who works for a factory that makes golf bags. The family cannot afford better quarters.

For Avol, the judge selected a one-room apartment that he was offering for rent.

"It doesn't have the sense of isolation that Main Street does. But it has a torn, filthy mattress and a filthy hot plate. There are no screens on the windows, and that's the only ventilation. The bathroom is across the hall, and the shower is totally corroded," she said.

She said tenants at the building were paying $320 a month, so "it's not as though he's not making a lot of money off the building," the judge said. "I think it's suitable. It's close to the court so we can monitor his house arrest."

regarded as being, in effect, an eviction of the tenant. Under such circumstances the courts permit the tenant to abandon the premises and terminate the lease. The tenant must abandon possession within a reasonable time in order to claim that there was a constructive eviction.

FACTS: On January 1, 1966, Mrs. Irene Kern leased an apartment from Colonial Court Apartments, Inc., for a one-year term. When the lease was entered into, Mrs. Kern asked for a quiet apartment, and Colonial assured her that the assigned apartment was in a quiet, well-insulated building. In fact, however, the apartment above Mrs. Kern's was occupied by a young couple, the Lindgrens. From the start of her occupancy, Mrs. Kern complained of their twice-weekly parties and other actions that so disturbed her sleep that she had to go elsewhere for rest. After Mrs. Kern had lodged several complaints, Colonial terminated the Lindgrens' lease effective February 28, 1966. However, the termination of the lease was prolonged and Mrs. Kern vacated her apartment claiming that she was no longer able to endure the continued disturbances. Colonial then brought this action to recover rent owned by Mrs. Kern.

DECISION: Judgment for Mrs. Kern. A constructive eviction occurs when the tenant's beneficial enjoyment of the leased premises is so interfered with by the landlord as to justify an abandonment of the premises by the tenant and a termination of the lease. What constitutes a constructive eviction ordinarily depends on the circumstances of each case.

Here, the actions said to constitute the constructive eviction are those of another tenant, the Lindgrens, and not those of the landlord Colonial. Ordinarily the acts of one tenant do not constitute a constructive eviction of another tenant of the same landlord. The actions of the Lindgrens, however, materially disturbed Mrs. Kern in her use, occupancy, and enjoyment of the leased apartment and, therefore, were sufficient to constitute a constructive eviction.

COLONIAL COURT APARTMENTS, INC. v. KERN

282 Minn. 533, 163 N.W.2d 770 (1968).

Concurrent Ownership

As we have mentioned before, property may be owned by one individual or by two or more persons concurrently. Two or more persons who hold title concurrently are generally referred to as **co-tenants.** Each is entitled to an undivided interest in the entire property, and neither has a claim to any specific part of it. Each may have equal undivided interests, or one may have a larger undivided share than the other. Regardless of the particular relationships between the co-tenants, this form of ownership must be carefully distinguished from the separate ownership of specific parts of property by different persons. Thus it is possible, for example, for A, B, and C to each own distinct and separate parts of Blackstone Manor, or they may each own, as co-tenants, an undivided on-third interest in all of Blackstone Manor. Whether they are co-tenants or owners of specific portions depends on the manner and form in which they acquired their interests.

The two major types of concurrent ownership are joint tenancy and tenancy in common. They both have the characteristics of an undivided interest in the whole, the right of both tenants to possession, and the right of either to sell his interest during life and thus terminate the original relationship. Other forms of concurrent ownership of real estate are tenancy by the entireties, community property, condominiums, and cooperatives.

Joint Tenancy

The most significant feature of joint tenancy is the right of **survivorship.** On the death of one of the joint tenants, title to the entire property passes by operation of law to the survivor or survivors. Neither the heirs of the deceased joint tenant nor his general creditors have a claim to his interest, and a joint tenant cannot transfer his interest by executing a will. However, any joint tenant may sever the joint tenancy by conveying or mortgaging his interest to a third party. Further, the interest of either co-tenant is subject to levy and sale on execution. **Sever** means the right of survivorship is lost, and the tenancy becomes a tenancy in common among the remaining joint tenants and the transferee.

By statute in most States, certain words must be used to create a joint tenancy in real property. Some of those statutes provide that a grant of an estate to two or more persons in their own right is a tenancy in common unless it is specifically declared to be in joint tenancy. Thus, if a deed of conveyance is not drafted properly, the resulting ownership would be a tenancy in common.

Joint tenancy—co-ownership with the presence of the four unities and the right of survivorship

To sustain a joint tenancy, the common law requires the presence of what are known as the **four unities** of time, title, interest, and possession. The unity of time means that the interest of all the tenants must take effect at the same time; the unity of title means that all the tenants must acquire title by the same instrument; the unity of interest means that all the tenants must have identical interests as to duration and scope; and the unity of possession means that all the tenants have the same right of possession and enjoyment. The absence of any one of these four unities will prevent the creation of a joint tenancy. A failure of any one of the first three unities will result in the creation of a tenancy in common, because the only unity required of a tenancy in common is the unity of possession.

Tenancy in Common

Tenancy in common—co-ownership whereby each tenant holds an individual interest

Tenants in common, like joint tenants, are persons who hold undivided interests in the same property, each having the right to possession but neither claiming any specific portion of the property. But unlike joint tenants, they do not have the right of survivorship. Also, unlike joint tenancy, the only prerequisite for tenancy in common is the unity of possession. By statute in many States a transfer of title to two or more persons is presumed to create a tenancy in common.

A tenancy in common may be terminated either by transfer of all the co-interests to one person or by partition of the property among the tenants, making each the exclusive owner of a specific part of the entire property. **Partition** is a device recognized and regulated by law for changing undivided interests into several and exclusive interests that are proportionate to the former undivided shares.

Tenancy by the Entireties

Tenancy by the entireties—co-ownership by spouses

Tenancy by the entireties, which is less common today than in the past, is created only by a conveyance to a **husband and wife.** It is distinguished from joint tenancy by the inability of either spouse to convey separately his or her interest during life and thus destroy the right of survivorship. Likewise, the interest of either spouse cannot be attached by creditors. By the nature of the tenancy, a divorce terminates the relationship, and partition would then be available as a method of creating separate interests in the property.

Figure 44-2 compares the rights of concurrent owners in joint tenancy, tenancy in common, and tenancy by the entireties.

Community Property

In Arizona, California, Idaho, Louisiana, Nevada, New Mexico, Texas, and Washington, one-half of any property acquired by the efforts of either the

FIGURE 44-2   Rights of Concurrent Owners

	Undivided Interest	Right to Possession	Right to Sell	Right to Mortgage	Levy by Creditors	Right to Will	Right of Survivorship
Joint Tenancy	YES	YES	YES	YES	YES	NO	YES
Tenancy in Common	YES	YES	YES	YES	YES	YES	NO
Tenancy by Entireties	YES	YES	NO	NO	NO	NO	YES

husband or the wife belongs to each spouse. This system, known as "community property", originated in the civil law of continental Europe, but has been modified and affected by the common law as well as by statutes in this country.

Community property – rights by spouses in property acquired by the other during marriage

In most instances, the only property that belongs separately to either spouse is that acquired before the marriage or acquired after it by gift or inheritance. On the death of either spouse, one-half of the community property belongs outright to the survivor, and the interest of the deceased spouse in the other half may go to the heirs of the decedent or as directed by will. However, under some conditions in a few jurisdictions, the surviving spouse may also claim an interest in the decedent's one-half share of the property.

Condominiums

Condominiums are a form of concurrent ownership that have become commonplace in the United States. All States have enacted statutes authorizing the use of this form of ownership. The purchaser of a condominium acquires separate ownership to the unit and becomes a tenant in common with respect to the common facilities, such as the land on which the project is built, recreational facilities, hallways, parking areas, and spaces between the units. The common elements are maintained by a condominium association funded by assessments levied on each unit. The transfer of a condominium conveys both the separate ownership of the unit and the share in the common elements.

Cooperatives

Cooperatives involve an indirect form of common ownership. A cooperative, usually a corporation, purchases or constructs the dwelling units. The cooperative then leases the units to its shareholders as tenants, who acquire the right to use and occupy their units.

Nonpossessory Interests

Nonpossessory interests include easements, *profits à prendre*, and licenses.

Easements

An easement is a *limited right* to make use of the land of another in a specific manner that is created by the acts of the parties or by operation of law and that has all the attributes of an estate in the land itself. For example, a typical easement exists where Liz sells a part of her land to Bill and expressly provides

Easement –Limited right to use the land of another in a specific manner

in the same or a separate document that Bill, as the adjoining landowner, shall have a right-of-way over a strip of Liz's remaining parcel of land. Bill's land is said to be the **dominant** parcel, and Liz's land, which is subject to the easement, is the **servient** parcel. Easements may, of course, exist for many different types of uses, as, for example, the right to run a ditch across another's land, to lay pipe under the surface, to erect power lines, or in the case of adjacent buildings, to use a stairway or a common or "party" wall.

Because the owner of the entire servient tract retains the title to the servient parcel, she may make any use of or allow others the use of the tract as long as this use does not interfere with the easement. Thus, crops may be grown over an easement for a pipeline, but livestock could not be pastured on an easement for a driveway. Although it is the duty of the owner of the servient parcel not to interfere with the use of the easement, it is generally the responsibility of the owner of the dominant parcel to maintain the easement and keep it in repair.

Types of Easements

Easements fall into two classes: easements appurtenant and easements in gross. **Appurtenant** easements are by far the more common, and, as the name indicates, the rights and duties created by such easements pertain to the land itself and not to the particular individuals who may have created them. Therefore the easement usually stays with the land when it is sold. For example, continuing with the illustration of A and B above, if A sells her servient parcel to C, who has actual notice of the easement for the benefit of B's land or constructive notice by means of the local recording act, C takes the parcel subject to the easement. Likewise, if B sells his dominant parcel to D, it is not necessary to refer specifically to the easement in the deed from B to D in order to give to D, as the new owner of the dominant parcel, the right to use the right-of-way over the servient parcel. Because B no longer owns the dominant parcel, he has no further right to use the right-of-way. B could not, however, transfer the benefit of the easement to a party who did not acquire an interest in the dominant parcel of land. Most frequently, a deed conveying the land "together with all appurtenances" is sufficient to transfer the easement. This characteristic of an appurtenant easement is described by the statement that both the burden and the benefit of an appurtenant easement pass with the land.

The second class of easements are those that are said to be **in gross** or personal to the particular individual who received the right. They do not depend on the ownership of land and actually amount to little more than an irrevocable personal right to use.

Creation of Easements

Easements may be created in a number of different ways: (1) by express grant or reservation, (2) by implied grant or reservation, (3) by necessity, (4) by dedication, and (5) by prescription.

By Express Grant or Reservation   The most common way to create an easement is to convey it by deed. For example, when A sells part of her land to B, she may, in the same deed, expressly grant an easement to B over A's remaining property. Alternatively, A may grant an easement to B in a separate document. This document must comply with all the formalities of a deed. An easement is an interest in land subject to the Statute of Frauds.

In other instances, when an owner of land transfers it, she may wish to retain certain rights in it. In the example given, A may want to "reserve" an easement in favor of the land retained by herself over the land granted to B. A may do this by specific words reserving that right to herself in the deed of conveyance to B.

Implied Grant or Reservation   Easements by implied grant or implied reservation arise whenever an owner of adjacent properties establishes an *apparent* and *permanent* use, in the nature of an easement, and then conveys one of the properties without mention of any easement. For example, suppose that A owns two adjacent lots, 1 and 2. There is a house on each lot. Behind each house is a garage. A has constructed a driveway along the boundary between the two lots, partly on lot 1 and partly on lot 2, which leads from the street in front of the houses to the two garages in the rear. A sells lot 2 to B without any mention of the driveway. A is held to have *impliedly granted* an easement to B over that portion of the driveway that lies on A's lot 1, and she is held to have *impliedly reserved* an easement over that portion of the driveway that lies on B's lot 2.

(use = implied)

Necessity   If A conveys part of his land to B and the part conveyed to B is so situated that B would have no access to it except across A's remaining land, the law implies a grant by A to B of an easement by necessity across A's remaining land. A way by necessity will not usually arise if an alternative but circuitous approach to B's land is available.

A way by necessity may also arise by implied reservation. This would be the case where A conveys part of his land to B, and A's remaining property would be wholly landlocked unless he is given a right-of-way across the land conveyed to B.

Dedication   When an owner of land subdivides it into lots and records the plan or plat of the subdivision, she is held, both by common law and now more frequently by statute, to have dedicated *to the public* all of the streets, alleys, parks, playgrounds, and beaches shown on the plat. In addition, when the subdivider sells the lots by reference to the plat, it is now generally recognized that the purchasers acquire easements by implication over the areas shown dedicated to the public.

Prescription   An easement may arise by prescription in most States if certain required conditions are met. To obtain an easement by prescription, a person must use a portion of land owned by another in a way (1) that is adverse to the rightful owner's use, (2) that is open and generally known, and (3) that is continuous and uninterrupted for a specific period of time that varies from State to State. If the owner gives the claimant permission to use the land, no easement by prescription is acquired.

EXCEPTIVE COHEN – ownership by adverse possession

Profits À Prendre

The phrase *profit à prendre* comes from the French and means the right to remove the produce of another's land. An example would be the grant by B to A, an adjoining landowner, of the right to remove coal or fish or timber from B's land or to graze his cattle on B's land. Like an easement, a *profit à prendre* may arise by prescription, but if it comes about by an act of the parties, it must be created with all the formalities of a grant of an estate in real

Profit à prendre –right to remove the produce from the land of another property. Unless the right is clearly designated as exclusive, it is always subject to a similar use by the owner of the land. The right to take profits is frequently held even without the ownership of other land. Thus, A may have a right to remove crushed gravel from B's acreage even though A lives in another part of the county.

Licenses

It is not always easy to distinguish such real interests in property as easements or *profits à prendre* from an equally common right of use designated as a license. Permission to make use of one's land generally constitutes a license that creates no interest in the property and is usually exercised only at the will of and subject to revocation by the owner at any time. For example, if A tells B she may cut across A's land to pick hickory nuts, B has nothing but a license subject to revocation at any time. It is possible that, on the basis of a license, B may expend funds to exercise the right, and the courts may prevent A from revoking the license simply because it would be unfair to penalize B under the circumstances. In such a case, B's interest is in practice indistinguishable from an easement.

A common illustration of a license is a theater ticket or the use of a hotel or motel room. No interest is acquired in the premises; there is simply a right of use for a given length of time, subject to good behavior. No formality is required to create a license; a shopkeeper licenses persons to enter his establishment merely by being open for business.

License–permission to use another's land.

BUNN v. OFFUTT

Supreme Court of Virginia, 1976.
216 Va. 681, 222 S.E.2d 522.

FACTS: On July 9, 1962 Temco, Inc., conveyed to the Wynns certain property adjoining an apartment complex being developed at that time by Sonnett Realty Company. Although nothing to this effect was contained in the deed, the sales contract gave the purchaser of the property use of the apartment's swimming pool. Temco's sales agent also emphasized that the use of the pool would be a desirable feature in the event that the Wynns decided to sell the property.

On May 31, 1969, the Bunns contracted to buy the property from the Wynns through the latter's agent, Sonnett Realty. Although both the Wynns and Sonnett Realty's agent told the Bunns that the use of the apartment's pool went with the purchased property, neither the contract nor the deed subsequently conveyed to the Bunns so provided. When the Bunns requested passes from Temco and Offutt, the company that owned the apartments, their request was refused. The Bunns then brought this action.

DECISION: Judgment for Offutt. Whether the Bunns have a right to use the apartment's pool depends on whether the Wynns were granted a license or an easement to use it in the sales contract between the Wynns and Temco. A license is a right given by some competent authority to do some act that otherwise would be a trespass. A license, however, is personal between the licensor and the licensee and cannot be assigned.

An easement, on the other hand, runs with the land and therefore, can pass to a subsequent purchaser such as the Bunns. Easements may be created by express grant or reservation, by implication, by estoppel, or by prescription. Here, however, the deed from Temco to the Wynns was silent, and therefore, no easement by express grant or reservation can be found. Furthermore, the language in the sales contract is not sufficient to create an easement. Moreover, there is no evidence showing that an easement was created by estoppel, by necessity, or by prescription. Finally, in the absence of a showing that Temco used the pool prior to the conveyance to the Wynns or that the use of the pool is essential to the beneficial enjoyment of the land conveyed, no easement by implication was created. Therefore, the Wynns were given a mere license to use the swimming pool, and that is not an interest running with the land that could subsequently be transferred to the Bunns.

CHAPTER SUMMARY

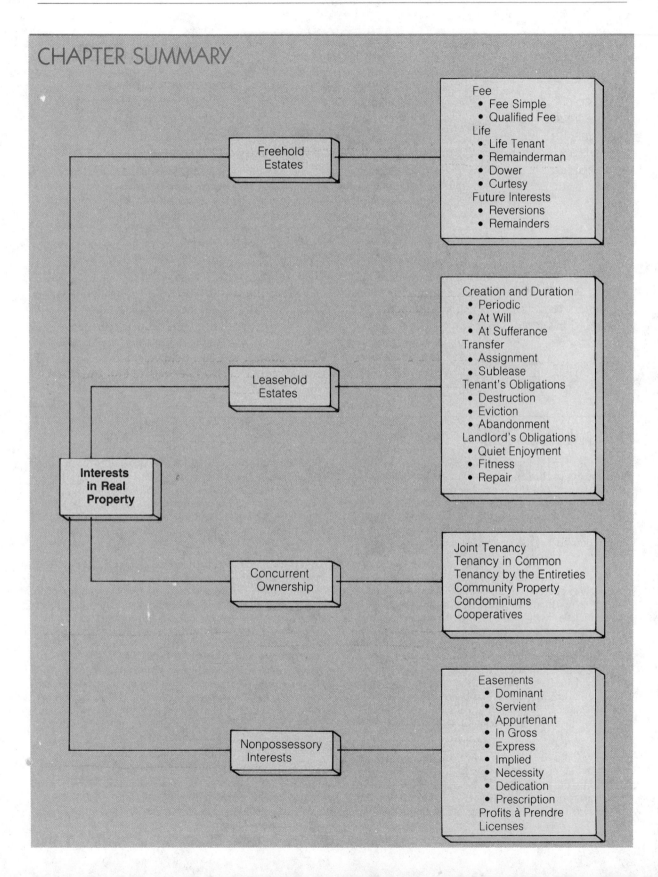

Interests in Real Property

Freehold Estates

Fee
- Fee Simple
- Qualified Fee

Life
- Life Tenant
- Remainderman
- Dower
- Curtesy

Future Interests
- Reversions
- Remainders

Leasehold Estates

Creation and Duration
- Periodic
- At Will
- At Sufferance

Transfer
- Assignment
- Sublease

Tenant's Obligations
- Destruction
- Eviction
- Abandonment

Landlord's Obligations
- Quiet Enjoyment
- Fitness
- Repair

Concurrent Ownership

Joint Tenancy
Tenancy in Common
Tenancy by the Entireties
Community Property
Condominiums
Cooperatives

Nonpossessory Interests

Easements
- Dominant
- Servient
- Appurtenant
- In Gross
- Express
- Implied
- Necessity
- Dedication
- Prescription

Profits à Prendre
Licenses

KEY TERMS

Freehold estate	Definite term	Tenancy in common
Fee simple	Periodic tenancy	Tenancy by the entireties
Qualified fee	Tenancy at will	Community property
Life estate	Tenancy at sufferance	Condominium
Life tenant	Assignment	Cooperative
Remainder	Sublease	Easement
Dower	Quiet enjoyment	Dominant
Curtesy	Fitness	Servient
Inchoate	Eviction	Appurtenant
Future interest	Implied warranty of habitability	In gross
Reversion	Constructive eviction	Express easement
Possibility of reverter	Concurrent ownership	Implied easement
Vested remainder	Co-tenants	Easement by necessity
Contingent remainder	Joint tenancy	Easement by dedication
Leasehold estate	Sever	Easement by prescription
Landlord	Four unities	Profits à prendre
Tenant	Partition	License

PROBLEMS

1. X conveyed a farm to Y to have and to hold for and during his life and on Y's death to Z. Some years thereafter, oil was discovered in the vicinity. Y thereupon made an oil and gas lease, and the oil company set up its machinery to begin drilling operations. Z then filed suit to enjoin the operations. Assuming an injunction to be the proper form of remedy, what decision?

2. S owned Blackacre in fee simple. In section 3 of a properly executed will, S devised Blackacre as follows: "I devise my farm Blackacre to my son D so long as it is used as a farm." Sections 5 and 6 of the will made gifts to persons other than D. The last clause of S's will provided: "All the remainder of my real and personal property not disposed of heretofore in this will, I devise and bequeath to the ABC University."

S died in 1984, survived by her son D. S's estate has been administered. D has been offered $100,000 for Blackacre if he can convey title to it in fee simple.

What interests in Blackacre were created by S's will?

3. A leased to B, for a term of ten years beginning May 1, certain premises located at 527–529 Main Street in the city of X. The premises were improved with a three-story building, the first floor being occupied by stores and the upper stories by apartments. On May

1 of the following year, B leased one of the apartments to C for one year. On July 5, a fire destroyed the second and third floors of the building. The first floor was not burned but was rendered unusable. Neither the lease from A to B nor the lease from B to C contained any provision in regard to the fire loss. Discuss the liabilty of B and C to continue to pay rent.

4. Ames leased an apartment to Boor for $200 a month payable the last day of each month. The term of the written lease was from January 1, 1985, through April 30, 1986. On March 15, 1985, Boor moved out, telling Ames that he disliked all the other tenants. Ames replied: "Well, you are no prize as a tenant; I probably can get more rent from someone more agreeable than you." Ames and Boor then had a minor physical altercation in which neither was injured. Boor sent the keys to the apartment to Ames by mail. Ames wrote Boor, "It will be my pleasure to hold you for every penny you owe me. I am renting the apartment on your behalf to Clay until April 30, 1986, at $175 a month." Boor had paid his rent through February 28, 1985. Clay entered the premises on April 1, 1985.

How much rent, if any, may Ames recover from Boor?

5. Jay signed a two-year lease containing a clause that expressly prohibited subletting. After six months Jay asked the landlord for permission to sublet the apartment for one year. The landlord refused. This angered Jay, and he immediately assigned his right under the lease to Kay. Kay was a distinguished gentleman, and Jay knew that everyone would consider him a desirable tenant. Is Jay's assignment of his lease to Kay valid?

6. In 1976 Roy Martin and his wife Alice, their son, Hiram, and Hiram's wife Myrna acquired title to a 240-acre farm. The deed ran to Roy Martin and Alice Martin, the father and mother, as joint tenants with the right of survivorship and to Hiram Martin and Myrna Martin, the son and his wife, as joint tenants with the right of survivorship. Alice Martin died in 1981, and in 1984 Roy Martin married Agnes Martin. By his will, Roy Martin bequeathed and devised his entire estate to Agnes Martin. When Roy Martin died in 1986, Hiram and Myrna Martin assumed complete control of the farm.

State the interest in the farm, if any, of Agnes, Hiram, and Myrna Martin on the death of Roy Martin.

7. T in her will granted a life estate to A in certain real estate, with remainder to B and C in joint tenancy. All the rest of T's estate was left to the X College. While going to T's funeral, the car in which A, B, and C were driving was wrecked. B was killed, C died a few minutes later, and A died on his way to the hospital. Who is entitled to the real estate in question?

8. Otis Olson, the owner of two adjoining city lots, A and B, built a house on each. He laid a drainpipe from lot B across lot A to the main sewer pipe under the alley beyond lot A. Olson then sold and conveyed lot A to Fred Ford. The deed, which made no mention of the drainpipe, was promptly recorded. Ford had no actual knowledge or notice of the drainpipe, although it would have been apparent to anyone making an inspection of the premises because it was only partially buried. Later, Olson sold and conveyed lot B to Luke Lane. This deed also made no reference to the drainpipe and was promptly recorded.

A few weeks later, Ford discovered the drainpipe across lot A and removed it. Did he have the right to do so?

9. At the time of his marriage to Ann, Robert owned several parcels of real estate in joint tenancy with his brother, Sam. During his marriage, Robert purchased a house and put the title in his name and his wife's name as joint tenants and not as tenants in common. Robert died; within a month of his death, Smith obtained a judgment against Robert's estate. What are the relative rights of Sam, Smith, and Ann?

10. In 1960, Ogle owned two adjoining lots numbered 6 and 7 fronting at the north on a city street. In that year she laid out and built a concrete driveway along and two feet in from what she erroneously believed to be the west boundary of lot 7. Ogle used the driveway for access to buildings situated at the southern end of both lots. Later in the same year she conveyed lot 7 to Dale, and thereafter in the same year she conveyed lot 6 to Pace. Neither deed made any reference to the driveway, and after the conveyance Dale used it exclusively for access to lot 7. In 1986 a survey by Pace established that the driveway overlapped six inches on lot 6, and he brought an appropriate action to establish his lawful ownership of the strip on which the driveway approaches, to enjoin its use by Dale, and to require Dale to remove the overlap. Decision?

TRANSFER AND CONTROL OF REAL PROPERTY

The law has always been and is still today extremely cautious about the transfer of title to real estate. Personal property may, for the most part, be easily and informally passed from owner to owner, but real property can be transferred only in compliance with a variety of formalities. This tendency is apparent in the transfer of real property at death, where the strict formalities are relaxed only with respect to personal property, and this attitude of care and formality is most evident in a transfer of land during the lifetime of the owner.

Title to land may be transferred in three principal ways: (1) by deed; (2) by will or by the law of descent on the death of the owner; and (3) by open, continuous, and adverse possession by a nonowner for a statutorily prescribed period of years. In this chapter we discuss the first and third methods of transfer, while we cover the second method in Chapter 46.

In addition to the legal restrictions placed on the transfer of real property, a number of other controls apply to the use of privately owned property. Some of these are imposed by governmental units and include zoning and eminent domain. Others are imposed by private parties through restrictive covenants. We consider these three controls in the second part of this chapter.

Transfer of Real Property

The most common way in which real property is transferred is by deed. Such transfers usually involve a contract for the sale of the land and the subsequent delivery of the deed and payment of the agreed-upon consideration. In most cases the purchase of real estate requires borrowing a part of the purchase price secured by the real property. A far less common method of transfer is called adverse possession. This unusual means of transfer of title requires no contract, deed, or other formality.

Contract of Sale

Formation

Because an oral agreement for the sale of an interest in land is not enforceable under the Statute of Frauds, the buyer and seller must put their agreement in *writing*. Neither party can enforce the agreement unless it is signed by the other party. The simplest agreement should contain (1) the names and addresses of the parties, (2) a description of the property to be conveyed, (3) the time for the conveyance (called the *closing*), (4) the type of deed to be given, and (5) the price and manner of payment. To avoid dispute and to assure adequate protection of the rights of both parties, many other points should also be covered by a properly drawn contract for the sale of land. For example, the contract should contain carefully written provisions for any and all fixtures intended to be included in the sale.

The great majority of the jurisdictions adhere to the common law rule that the risk of loss or destruction of the property is on the purchaser after the contract is formed. The contract of sale may, of course, provide that the risk of loss or destruction shall remain on the seller until conveyance of the deed to the purchaser, or it may provide that the seller will restore any structures destroyed before the deed is conveyed, that the seller will obtain insurance for the benefit of the purchaser, or any other allocation of risk agreed on by the parties.

Marketable Title

Marketable title–free from any defects or reasonable objections to one's ownership.

It is firmly established in the law of conveyancing that a contract for the sale of land carries with it an *implied* obligation on the part of the seller to transfer marketable title. Marketable title means that the title is free from (1) encumbrances (such as mortgages, easements, liens, leases, and restrictive covenants); (2) defects in the chain of title appearing in the land records (such as a prior recorded conveyance of the same property by the seller); and (3) any other defects that, although they are not sufficient to amount to encumbrances, may subject the purchaser to the inconvenience of having to defend his title in court. The significance of the seller's obligation to convey marketable title is that if the title search reveals any defect that has not been *specifically* excepted in the contract, the purchaser may refuse to take the conveyance on the date set for closing and may sue and recover damages from the seller unless the defect in title is promptly remedied.

There are two important exceptions to this rule, however. First, most courts hold that the seller's implied or express obligation to convey marketable title does not require him to convey title free from existing zoning restrictions. Second, some courts also hold that the seller's implied or express obligation to convey marketable title does not require him to convey title free from open and visible public rights of way or easements such as public roads and sewers.

Deeds

Types of Deeds

Deed–a formal document transferring an interest in land

The modern deed as authorized in American jurisdictions in a somewhat simplified version of an early English deed known as a "grant." Originally, a grant was used to transfer intangible interests in land, but its use was gradually expanded to include transfers of any type of interest in land.

Warranty deed–seller warrants good title

Warranty Deed   By a warranty deed, the **grantor** (seller) promises the **grantee** (buyer) that she has a valid title to the property. In addition, under a warranty deed the grantor, either expressly or implicitly, obliges herself to make the grantee whole if the grantee suffers any damage because the grantor's title was defective. Aside from the grantor's liability for any defects in her title, a distinct characteristic of the general warranty deed is that it will convey after-acquired title. For example, on January 30, Andrea conveys Blackacre by warranty deed to Barry. On January 30, Andrea's title to Blackacre is defective, but by February 14, Andrea has acquired a good title. Without further formalities, Barry has acquired Andrea's good title under the January 30 warranty deed.

Special Warranty Deed   Whereas a warranty deed contains a general warranty of title, a special warranty deed warrants only that the title has not been impaired, encumbered, or made defective because of any act or omission *of the grantor*. The grantor merely warrants the title so far as acts or omissions of the grantor are concerned. He does *not* warrant that the title may not be defective because of the acts or omissions of others.

> Special warranty deed–seller warrants that he has not impaired title

Quitclaim Deed   By a quitclaim deed, the grantor says no more, in effect, than, "I make no promise as to what interest I do have in this land, but whatever it is I convey it to you." Quitclaim deeds are used most frequently when it is desired that persons who appear to have an interest in land release their interest.

> Quitclaim deed–seller transfers whatever interest she has in the property

Formal Requirements

As previously noted, any transfer of an interest in land is within the Statute of Frauds if it is an interest of more than a limited duration. The transfer must therefore be in writing. Nearly all deeds, whatever the type, follow nearly the same pattern. Statutes in most States suggest that certain words of conveyance be used to make the deed effective. The words used will vary depending on whether the instrument is a warranty deed, general or special, or a quitclaim deed. A common phrase for a warranty deed is "convey and warrant," although in a number of States the phrase "grant, bargain, and sell" is used together with a covenant by the seller appearing later in the deed that she will "warrant and defend the title." A quitclaim deed will generally provide that the grantor "conveys and quitclaims" or more simply "quitclaims all interest" in the property.

Consideration   In most instances the law does not require consideration for a valid deed. A grantor may be bound by his gift of land if the deed is properly executed and delivered.

Description of the Land   The primary requirement of any description is that it is sufficiently clear and certain to permit identification of the property conveyed. The test is frequently applied in terms of whether a subsequent purchaser or a surveyor employed by him could mark off the land from the description.

Quantity of the Estate   After the property has been described, the deed will generally proceed to describe the quantity of estate conveyed to the grantee. Thus, either "to have and to hold to himself and his heirs forever" or "to have and to hold in fee simple" would vest the grantee with absolute title to the land. A deed conveying title to "X for life and to Y on X's death" would grant a life estate to X and a remainder interest to Y.

Covenants of Title   It is the practice in deeds for the grantor to make certain promises concerning her title to the land. If any one of these promises or covenants is breached, the grantee is entitled to be compensated. There are a number of these covenants, the most usual of which are of **title, against incumbrances,** of **quiet enjoyment,** and of **warranty.** These various covenants add up to an assurance that the grantee will have undisturbed possession of the land and will, in turn, be able to transfer it without adverse claims of third parties. In many States, all or many of these covenants are implied from the words of conveyance themselves—for example, "warrants" or "grant, bargain, and sell."

Execution   Deeds generally end with the signature of the grantor, a seal, and an acknowledgment before a notary public or other official authorized to verify the authenticity of documents. The signature can be made by an agent of the grantor if the agent has written authority from the grantor in a form required by law. Today the seal has lost most of its former significance, and in those jurisdictions where it is required, the seal is sufficient if the word "Seal" or the letters "L. S." appear next to the signature.

Although the notary public's acknowledgment may not be required to bind the parties to the deed, it is generally a prerequisite to recording the deed, and without an acknowledgment a deed may not be effective against third parties. In most jurisdictions a special form of acknowledgment for deeds is specified by statute.

Delivery of Deeds

A deed does not transfer title to land until it is delivered. "Delivery" means an **intent** that the deed is to take effect and is evidenced by the acts or statements of the grantor. Manual or physical transfer of the deed is usually the best evidence of this intent, but it is not necessary. For example, the act of the grantor in placing a deed in a safe deposit box may or may not constitute delivery, depending on whether the grantee did or did not have access to the box and whether the grantor acts as if the property were the grantee's. A deed conceivably may be "delivered" even when kept in the possession of the grantor, just as it would be possible that physical delivery of the deed to the grantee would not transfer title. Delivery as shown in the case which follows is not an exact ceremony to be done in one particular way. A deed is frequently turned over to a third party to hold until the grantee performs certain conditions. This is called an **escrow,** and the third party is the escrow agent. When the grantee performs the condition, the escrow agent must turn the deed over to the grantee.

Delivery–intent that the deed take effect along with acts or statements of the grantor

Escrow–third party holds the document or fund until all the conditions in the contract are fulfilled

PARRAMORE v.
PARRAMORE

Court of Appeals of Florida,
1978.
371 So.2d 123.

FACTS: In May, 1963, Fred Parramore executed four deeds, each conveying a life estate in his land to himself and his wife and a remainder interest in one-fourth of his land to each of his four children: Alney, Eudell, Bernice, and Iris. Although Fred executed and acknowledged the four deeds as part of his plan to distribute his estate at his death, he did not deliver them to his children at this time. Instead, he placed the deeds with his will in a safety deposit box and instructed the children to pick up their deeds at his death. Fred later conveyed Alney's deed to Alney, thereby vesting Alney's interest in that parcel, but Eudell, Bernice, and Iris's deeds were never handed over to them during Fred's lifetime. Fred, however, acted as if the land was beyond his control, and on one occasion told a prospective buyer that the land had already been deeded away. When Fred died in November, 1974, Alney brought this action claiming that the deeds to Eudell, Bernice, and Iris were ineffective because they had never been handed over during Fred's lifetime. Accordingly, Alney argued the remaining land should pass in equal shares to each of the four children under the residuary clause of Fred's will.

DECISION: Judgment for Eudell, Bernice and Iris affirming the validity of their deeds. The delivery of a deed is a precondition to its effectiveness. Ordinarily, it is accomplished by a physical handing over of a prepared deed with accompanying words showing an appropriate intent to relinquish control. But the grantor may also deliver a deed by placing it in the hands of a third party with instructions for that party to deliver it. If the grantor's intent to relinquish the deed is shown and his instructions are subsequently carried out, the deed is regarded as having been delivered even though it cannot be shown that the grantor could never have retrieved it from the third party.

Here, Fred Parramore, a man unsophisticated in such matters, signed deeds creating remainder interests in his four children, placed the deed beyond his immediate reach in the safe deposit box along with his will intending that they take practical effect at his death, acted as though he considered the children's remainder interests to be vested, and refrained from disturbing the contents of the box. Under the circumstances, then, Fred's actions were sufficient to constitute an effective delivery of the three remaining deeds.

Recordation

In almost all states it is not necessary to record deeds in order to pass title from grantor to grantee. However, unless the grantee has the deed recorded, a subsequent good faith purchaser of the property will acquire superior title to the grantee. Recordation consists of delivery of a duly executed and acknowledged deed to the recorder's office in the county where the property is located. There a copy of the instrument is made and inserted in the current deed book and indexed.

In some states, called **notice** states, unrecorded instruments are invalid against any subsequent purchaser without notice. In other states, called **notice-race** states, an unrecorded deed is invalid against any subsequent purchaser without notice who records first. Finally, in a few states, called **race** states, an unrecorded deed is invalid against any deed recorded before it.

Secured Transactions

The purchase of real estate usually involves a relatively large outlay of money, and few people pay cash for a house or business real estate. Most people must borrow part of the purchase price or defer payment over a period of time. In these cases, the real estate itself is used to secure the obligation, which is evidenced by a note and mortgage or trust deed. The debtor is referred to as the **mortgagor** and the creditor as the **mortgagee.**

A secured transaction includes two elements: (1) a debt or obligation to pay money and (2) an interest of the creditor in specific property that secures performance of the obligation. However, a security interest in property cannot exist apart from the debt it secures. When the debt is discharged in any manner, the security interest in the property is terminated. Transactions involving the use of real estate as security for a debt are subject to real estate law, which consists of statutes and rules developed by the common law regarding mortgages and trust deeds. The Uniform Commercial Code does *not* apply to real estate mortgages or trust deeds.

Contract

Form of Mortgages

The instrument creating a mortgage is in the form of a conveyance from the *mortgagor* to the *mortgagee* and must meet all the necessary requirements for such documents—it must be in writing, it must contain an adequate description of the property, and it must be signed, sealed, acknowledged, and delivered. The usual mortgage, however, differs from an outright conveyance of the property because it contains a provision that, on the performance of the promise by the mortgagor, the conveyance is void and of no effect. This condition is referred to as the "defeasance," and although it normally appears on the face of the mortgage, it may be in a separate document.

The concept of a mortgage as a lien on real property as security for the payment of a debt applies with equal force to transactions having the same purpose but under a different name and form. A **deed of trust** is nearly identical to a mortgage, the most striking difference being that, under a deed of trust, the property is conveyed not to the creditor as security but to a third person as trustee for the benefit of the creditor. The trust deed creates rights almost the same as those created by a mortgage. In some States it is customary to use a trust deed in lieu of the ordinary form of mortgage.

As with all interests in realty, the mortgage or deed of trust should be promptly recorded to protect the mortgagee's rights against third persons who acquire an interest in the mortgaged property without knowledge of the mortgage.

Rights and Duties

The rights and duties of the parties to a mortgage may depend on whether it is viewed as creating a lien or as transferring legal title to the mortgagee. Most States have adopted the **"lien"** theory. The mortgagor retains title and, even in the absence of any stipulation in the mortgage, is entitled to possession of the premises to the exclusion of the mortgagee even in the event of default by the mortgagor. Only by foreclosure or sale or court appointment of a receiver can the right of possession be taken from the mortgagor. Other States have adopted the common law **"title"** theory, which gives the right of ownership and possession to the mortgagee. In most cases, as a practical matter, the mortgagor retains possession because the mortgagee does not care about possession unless the mortgagor defaults.

If the mortgagor is in possession, he is entitled to the rents and profits from the land. His obligation to the mortgagee is to pay the interest and principal when due. It is occasionally stipulated in a mortgage, however, that rents and profits will be assigned to the mortgagee as additional security for the debt.

Even though the mortgagor is generally entitled to possession and to many of the attributes of unrestricted ownership, he has a responsibility to deal with the property in such a manner as not to impair the security. In most instances, *"waste"* (impairment of the security) results from the mortgagor's failure to prevent the action or threatened action of third parties against the land. For example, a failure by the debtor to pay taxes or to discharge a prior lien may seriously impair the security of the mortgagee. In such cases the mortgagee is generally permitted to pay the obligation and add it to his claim against the mortgagor.

The mortgagor has the right to relieve his mortgaged property from the lien of a mortgage by payment of the indebtedness that it secures. This right of **redemption** is characteristic of a mortgage and cannot be defeated except by operation of law. The right to redeem carries with it the obligation to pay the debt, and payment in full with interest is prerequisite to redemption.

Transfer of the Interests under the Mortgage

The interests of the original mortgagor and mortgagee can be transferred, and the rights and obligations of the assignees will depend primarily on (1) the agreement of the parties to the assignment and (2) the rules of law protecting the interest of the one who is party to the mortgage but not to the transfer.

If the mortgagor conveys the land, the purchaser is *not* personally liable for the mortgage debt unless she expressly **assumes** the mortgage. If she assumes it, she is personally obligated to pay the mortgagor's debt owing to the mortgagee. Furthermore, the mortgagee can also hold the mortgagor on his promise to pay. A transfer of mortgaged property **"subject to"** the mortgage does *not* personally obligate the transferee to pay the mortgage debt. In such a case the transferee's risk of loss is limited to the property.

A mortgagee has the right to assign the mortgage to another person without the consent of the mortgagor. An assignee of a mortgage is well advised to obtain the assignment in writing duly executed by the mortgagee and to record it promptly with the proper public official. This will protect her rights against persons who subsequently acquire an interest in the mortgaged property without knowledge of the assignment. Failure to record an assignment may cause an assignee of a mortgage note to lose her security. For example, A buys land from B, relying on a release executed and recorded by the mortgagee, C. C, however, had previously assigned the mortgage to D, who had failed to have her assignment recorded. If A had no actual knowledge of C's assignment to D, D has no claim against the property.

Foreclosure

The right to foreclose usually arises when the mortgagor fails to pay the debt. Foreclosure is an action by the mortgage holder to take the property away from the mortgagor, to end the mortgagor's rights in the property, and to sell the property to pay the mortgage debt on default by the mortgagor. However, the mortgagor's default by nonperformance of other promises in the mortgage may also give the mortgagee this right. For example, a mortgage may provide that failure of the mortgagor to pay taxes is a default that permits foreclosure. It is also a common provision in mortgages that default in payment of an installment of the debt makes the entire unpaid balance of the indebtedness immediately due and payable, permitting foreclosure for the entire amount.

Foreclosure–sale of the mortgaged property upon default to satisfy the debt

The most general method of terminating the mortgagor's right to redeem the property is by a suit in equity to obtain a judicial decree directing the sale of the property by an officer of the court, the debt being paid out of the proceeds of the sale and the excess, if any, paid to the mortgagor. In some jurisdictions the mortgagor is given a statutory right to redeem from the foreclosure sale within a specified period of time after the sale. In effect, this right is a second "right of redemption" and should not be confused with the customary right of redemption before foreclosure. In most jurisdictions a foreclosure sale is subject to approval by the court.

In States where foreclosure is not limited to a sale under judicial decree, a clause may be inserted in mortgages permitting the mortgagee to foreclose by a sale without obtaining an order of court. This power of sale in a trust deed form of mortgage is considerably less time-consuming than a judicial proceeding. The power of sale usually provides for a public auction with published notice, and frequently the mortgagee is forbidden by statute to purchase at the sale on the theory that he occupies a fiduciary relation to the mortgagor that would be breached by buying any property at a sale conducted by himself.

Whether foreclosure is by sale under judicial proceeding or by grant of power in the mortgage itself, the transaction retains its character of a procedure to obtain satisfaction of a debt. If the proceeds are sufficient to satisfy the debt in full, the debtor-mortgagor remains liable for payment of the balance of the debt. Generally, the mortgagee will obtain a *deficiency judgment* for any unsatisfied balance of the debt and may proceed to enforce payment of this amount out of other assets of the mortgagor.

Adverse Possession

Adverse possession—acquisition of title to land by open, continuous and adverse occupancy for a statutorily prescribed period

It is a possible, although very rare, event that title to land may be transferred **involuntarily** without any deed or other formality. Such an occurrence results from what the law calls adverse possession. In most States, if a person openly and continuously occupies the land of another for a statutorily prescribed period of time, typically twenty years, that person will gain title to the land. The possession must be actual. Courts have held that living on land, farming it, building on it, or maintaining structures on it are sufficient to constitute possession. However, the possession must be adverse. This means that any act of dominion by the true owner will stop the period from running. Her entry on the land or the assertion of ownership by her will break the period. The statutory period would then have to begin again from that time.

GERWITZ v. GELSOMIN

Supreme Court, Appellate Division, Fourth Department, 1979.
69 A.D.2d 992, 416 N.Y.S.2d 127.

FACTS: The Gerwitz family resides on a piece of land known as Lot #24 of the Belleville tract which they acquired by deed in 1957. Shortly thereafter, the Gerwitzs began to use the adjacent vacant Lot #25. At various times they planted grass seed, flowers, and shrubs on the land and used it for picnics and cookouts. In 1977, Gelsomin acquired Lot #25 and constructed a foundation on it so that he could place a house there. The Gerwitzs then brought this action to stop him, claiming title to Lot #25 by adverse possession.

DECISION: Judgment for Gelsomin. For a party to acquire title to land by adverse possession, it must prove that its possession of the premises has been (1) hostile and under a claim of right, (2) actual, (3) open and notorious, (4) exclusive, and (5) continuous. Here, the Gerwitzs have failed to satisfy the requirements of their claim of adverse possession because their possession of Lot #25 was neither hostile to the owner nor under a claim of right. The Gerwitzs knew they did not own the adjoining land and never asserted a claim of ownership to it. Moreover, the Gerwitzs graded their own lot and paid taxes on it but never attempted to do either on Lot #25. In addition, the Gerwitzs failed to object at the various times that owners of Lot #25 placed "For Sale" signs on the vacant premises.

In some jurisdictions, shorter periods of adverse possession have been established by statute where there is not only possession but also some other claim such as the payment of taxes for seven years and at least an apparent claim of title, even if it is not valid.

Public and Private Controls

In the exercise of its police power, the State can and does place controls on the use of privately owned land for the benefit of the community. Furthermore, the State does not pay the owner any compensation for loss or damage sustained by the owner because of such legitimate controls. The enforcement of zoning laws, which is a proper exercise of the police power, is not a taking of property but a regulation of its use. However, the taking of private property for a public use or purpose under the State's power of eminent domain is not an exercise of police power, and the owners of the property so taken are entitled to be paid its fair and reasonable value.

There are also private controls of the use of privately owned property by means of restrictive covenants, which we also consider in this section.

Zoning

Zoning is the principal method of public control over _land use._ The validity of zoning is based on the police power of the state. The police power to provide for the public health, safety, morals, and welfare is one of the inherent powers of government. Police power can be used only to **regulate** private property, never to "take" it. It is firmly established that regulation that has no reasonable relation to public health, safety, morals, or welfare is unconstitutional because it is contrary to due process of law.

Zoning–public control over private land use

Enabling Acts and Zoning Ordinances

The power to zone is generally delegated to local city and village authorities by statutes known as enabling statutes. A typical enabling statute grants the following powers to municipalities: (1) to regulate and limit the height and bulk of buildings to be erected; (2) to establish, regulate, and limit the building or setback lines on or along any street, trafficway, drive, or parkway; (3) to regulate and limit the intensity of the use of lot areas and to regulate and determine the area of open spaces within and surrounding buildings; (4) to classify, regulate, and restrict the location of trades and industries and the location of buildings designated for specified industrial, business, residential, and other uses; (5) to divide the entire municipality into districts of such number, shape, area, and such different classes as may be deemed best suited to carry out the purposes of the statute; and (6) to set standards to which buildings or structures must conform.

Under these powers the local authorities may enact zoning ordinances, which consist of a map and a text. The map divides the municipality into districts that are designated principally as industrial, commercial, or residential, with possible subclassifications. A well-drafted zoning ordinance will carefully define the uses permitted in each area.

Variance

All enabling statutes provide that the zoning authorities shall have power to grant variances in cases of "particular hardship." Mere failure to make a profit is not enough. It must affirmatively appear that the property as presently

Variance–a use differing from that provided in the zoning ordinance in order to avoid undue hardship zoned cannot yield a reasonable return on the owner's investment. The following case illustrates the point.

PURITAN-GREENFIELD
IMPROVEMENT
ASSOCIATION v. LEO

Court of Appeals of
Michigan, 1967.
7 Mich.App. 659, 153
N.W.2d 162.

FACTS: Leo owned a one-story, one-family dwelling in a single-family residential zoning district in Detroit. He attempted to sell the house with its adjoining lot for $38,500. Houses in the neighborhood generally sold for $20,000 to $25,000. Immediately to the west of Leo's property was a gasoline service station. In addition, Leo's property was located on a corner frequented with heavy traffic. Leo had not received any offers from residence-use buyers during the period of over a year that the property had been listed and offered for sale. He then applied to the board of zoning appeals for a variance to permit the use of the property as a dental and medical clinic and to use the side yard for off-street parking. The variance would be subject to certain conditions, including the preservation of the building's exterior so as to continue to appear to be a one-family dwelling. Puritan-Greenfield Improvement Association, a non-profit corporation, filed a complaint against Leo's variance request.

DECISION: Judgment for Puritan-Greenfield. Under the Detroit statute, a board of zoning appeals is authorized to grant a variance only upon a showing of practical difficulties or unnecessary hardship. However, the unnecessary hardship must be unique or peculiar to the property for which the variance is sought, rather than due to general conditions in the neighborhood. Furthermore, one seeking a variance must show that the property cannot reasonably be used in a manner consistent with existing zoning.

Here, Leo's house would not sell for $38,500 in a neighborhood where houses sell for substantially less. This is not enough to show that the property could not continue reasonably to be used as a single family residence. The fact that the property would be worth more as a doctor's clinic is immaterial. The standard is one of reasonable use, not reasonable return. Moreover, the presence of heavy traffic and the gasoline station is not unique to Loe's property, but common to the entire neighborhood. A zoning district has to end somewhere. Thus, Leo's property can continue reasonably to be used as a single family residence. Accordingly his variance request was denied.

Nonconforming Uses

Nonconforming use–
pre-existing use not in accordance with the zoning
ordinance

A zoning ordinance may not immediately terminate a lawful use that existed before it was enacted. This use must be permitted to continue as a nonconforming use for at least a reasonable time. Most ordinances provide for the elimination of nonconforming uses (1) when the use is discontinued, (2) when a nonconforming structure is destroyed or substantially damaged, or (3) when a nonconforming structure has been permitted to exist for the period of its useful life as fixed by municipal authorities.

Judicial Review of Zoning

Although the zoning process is traditionally viewed as legislative, it is subject to judicial review on a number of grounds, including the following: (1) that the zoning ordinance is invalid, (2) that the zoning ordinance has been applied unreasonably, and (3) that the zoning ordinance amounts to a confiscation or taking of property. For example, a zoning ordinance may be invalid as a whole either because it bears no reasonable relation to public health, safety, morals, or welfare or because it involves an exercise of powers that the enabling act has not granted to the municipality.

Subdivision Master Plans

A growing municipality has a special interest in regulating new housing developments so that they will harmonize with the rest of the community; so that streets within the development are integrated with existing streets or planned roads; so that adequate provision is made for open spaces for traffic, recreation, light, and air; and so that adequate provision is made for water, drainage, and sanitary facilities. Accordingly, most States have legislation enabling local authorities to require municipality approval of every land subdivision plat. These enabling statutes provide penalties for failure to secure such approval where required by local ordinance. Some statutes make it a criminal offense to sell lots by reference to unrecorded plats and provide that such plats may not be recorded unless approved by the local planning board. Other statutes provide that building permits will not be issued unless the plat is approved and recorded.

Eminent Domain

The power to take private property for public use, known as the power of eminent domain, is recognized as one of the inherent powers of government in the U.S. Constitution and in State constitutions. At the same time, however, the power is carefully circumscribed and controlled. The Fifth Amendment to the Federal Constitution provides, "Nor shall private property be taken for public use without just compensation." Similar or identical provisions are to be found in the constitutions of the States. There is, therefore, a direct constitutional prohibition against taking private property without just compensation and an implicit prohibition against taking private property for other than public use. Moreover, under both Federal and State constitutions, the individual is entitled to due process of law in connection with the taking.

Eminent domain–power to take (buy) private property for public use

Public Use

As noted, there is an implicit constitutional prohibition against taking private property for other than public use. The courts have interpreted "public use" to mean the same thing as "public purpose." Thus, it was early established that the power of eminent domain may be delegated to railroad and public utility companies. The reasonable exercise of this power by such companies to enable them to offer continued and improved service to the public is upheld as a public purpose.

As society grows more complex, other public purposes are accepted as legitimate grounds for exercise of the power of eminent domain. One is in the area of urban renewal. Most States have legislation permitting the establishment of housing authorities with power to condemn slum, blighted, and vacant areas and to finance, construct, and maintain housing projects.

Just Compensation

When the power of eminent domain is exercised, the owners of the property taken must receive just compensation. The measure of compensation is the fair market value of the property as of the time of take. The compensation award goes to holders of vested interests in the condemned property.

Private Restrictions on Land Use

The owners of lots are subject to restrictive covenants that, if actually brought to the attention of subsequent purchasers or recorded by original deed or by means of a recorded plat or separate agreement, bind purchasers of lots in the subdivision as though the restriction had been inserted in their own deed.

For example, suppose X owns a lot in a residential subdivision of a sub-urban community. On the lot are a house and a garage, and the remainder of the subdivision is either similarly improved or vacant. X decides to enlarge his living room and to extend the front of the house to within twenty feet of the front line of the lot. He knows that this is not prohibited by the zoning ordinance and that there is no limitation in the deed from his seller limiting the area of the house. He will, indeed, be astounded when a neighbor, observing the excavation, informs him that he cannot build to within twenty feet of the front line. He will be only slightly less surprised to hear that the reason he cannot do so is because of a provision in the recorded deed from the original subdivider to the original purchasers of lots in the subdivision requiring front yards of at least thirty-foot depth.

X will discover on further investigation that the entire subdivision has been subjected to a general building plan designed to benefit all the lots, and any lot owner in the subdivision has the right to enforce the restriction against a purchaser whose title descends from a common grantor.

Nature of Restrictive Covenants

Restrictive covenant–private restriction on property contained in a conveyance

Restrictive covenants of the type mentioned above are, in a sense, easements—or at least *negative* easements—to the extent that they impose a limitation on the use of the land. But unlike most easements they are not directly based on any formal grant, and the ability of any number of property owners to enforce them does not suggest the usual easement that normally is enforceable by an adjoining landowner.

If there is a clear intent that a restriction is intended to benefit an entire tract, the fact that the covenant is not formally executed will not prevent it being enforced against a subsequent purchaser of one of the lots in the tract. As long as both of the following requirements are met, the restriction will be enforced: first, that it is apparent that the restriction was intended to benefit the purchaser of any lot in the tract, and second, that the restriction appears somewhere in the chain of title to which the lot is subject.

Type and Construction of Restrictive Covenants

There are many types of restrictive covenants. The more common ones limit the use of property to residential purposes, restrict the area of the lot on which a structure can be built, or provide for a special type of architecture. Frequently a subdivider will specify a minimum size for each house in an attempt to maintain a minimum standard in the neighborhood.

Restrictive covenants, as shown in the following case, are construed strictly against the party asserting their applicability.

JOHN J. WALKER v.
ROBERT V. GROSS

Supreme Court of
Massachusetts, 1972.
362 Mass. 703, 290 N.E.2d
543.

FACTS: Gross owns certain land on which he proposes to construct an eighty-three unit apartment house. The land, however, is subject to a restriction imposed by a 1947 deed to a predecessor in title that provides that no part of the premises shall be used for any business purposes except for raising, growing, and selling live bait, fishing tackle, and sporting goods. Gross has sought a decree stating that the restriction does not prohibit the construction and operation of an apartment house.

DECISION: Judgment for Gross. The restriction itself gives no significant guidance as to what constitutes a forbidden business purpose other than expressly to permit the retail sale of fishing tackle and sporting goods. The apartment house will be used for residential purposes. That it may be owned for income-producing purposes does not make the use of the premises a use for a business purpose. The restriction is concerned with the physical activity carried on upon the land and not with the presence or absence of a profit-making motive on the part of the land-owners. Construed in this manner—strictly against the party asserting the applicability of the restriction—the resolution does not forbid Gross's construction and operation of the apartment house.

Termination of Restrictive Covenants

The principal reason for not enforcing private restrictions is long *acquiescence* by neighbors to numerous violations in the past. Evidence of *changed conditions* may be found either within the tract covered by the original covenant or in the area adjacent to or surrounding the tract. Acquiescence to one or two isolated violations in the entire tract will not, however, be a defense to a complaint for violation. In the example of X and his desire to enlarge his living room, if he is advised to proceed with his plans, it may be that the character of the neighborhood has so changed that the original purpose of the covenant (in this case, to provide front yards not less than thirty feet in depth) has no further application. If houses, apartment buildings, and even stores have been constructed in disregard of the building line restriction during the preceding decades, X may successfully maintain that the character of the area has so changed as no longer to justify enforcement of the covenant against him. To succeed, he must convince the court that the circumstances that gave rise to the covenant no longer exists.

Validity of Restrictive Covenants

Although restrictions on the use of land have never been popular in the law, if it appears that the restriction will operate to the general benefit of the owners of all the land intended to be affected, the restriction will be enforced. The usual method of enforcing such agreements is by injunction to restrain a violation.

For many decades the United States Supreme Court took the position that **private** racial restrictive agreements, regardless of their moral status, did not deny any right guaranteed by the Federal Constitution. It has been the law for many years, however, that a State or municipality cannot, under the Fourteenth Amendment to the Constitution, impose any such restrictions by statute or ordinance. In 1947, the Supreme Court held that private racial restrictive covenants cannot be enforced by State courts because the courts are an arm of the State government. This effectively invalidated private racial restrictive covenants.

CHAPTER SUMMARY

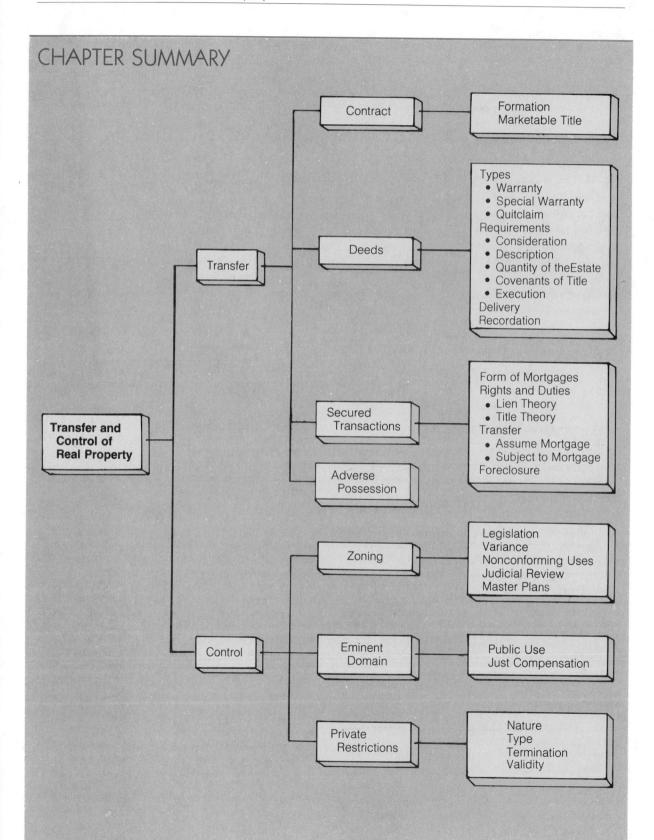

KEY TERMS

Closing	Notice state	Foreclosure
Deed	Notice-race state	Deficiency judgment
Grantor	Race state	Adverse possession
Grantee	Mortgage	Police power
Warranty deed	Mortgagor	Zoning
Special warranty deed	Mortgagee	Variance
Quitclaim deed	Deed of Trust	Nonconforming use
Quantity of the estate	Lien theory	Eminent domain
Covenant of title	Title theory	Public use
Execution	Assume mortgage	Just compensation
Delivery	Subject to mortgage	Restrictive covenant
Recordation		

PROBLEMS

1. A was the father of B, C, and D and the owner of Redacre, Blackacre, and Greenacre.

A made and executed a warranty deed conveying Redacre to B. The deed provided that "this deed shall only become effective on the death of the grantor." A retained possession of the deed and died leaving the deed in his safe deposit box.

A made and executed a warranty deed conveying Blackacre to C. The deed provided "this deed shall only become effective on the death of the grantor." A delivered the deed to C. After A died, C recorded the deed.

A made and executed a warranty deed conveying Greenacre to D. A delivered the deed to X with specific instructions to deliver the deed to D on A's death. X duly delivered the deed to D when A died.

    (a) What is the interest of B in Redacre, if any?
    (b) What is the interest of C in Blackacre, if any?
    (c) What is the interest of D in Greenacre, if any?

2. A, the owner of Redacre, executed a real estate mortgage to the Shawnee Bank and Trust Company for $10,000. After the mortgage was executed and recorded, A constructed a dwelling on the premises and planted a corn crop. After default in the payment of the mortgage debt, the bank proceeded to foreclose the mortgage. At the time of the foreclosure sale, the corn crop was mature and unharvested. A contends (a) that the value of the dwelling should be credited to him and (b) that he is entitled to the corn crop. Decision?

3. Robert and Stanley held legal title of record to adjacent tracts of land, each consisting of eighty acres. Stanley fenced his eighty acres in 1962. He placed his east fence fifteen feet onto Robert's property. Thereafter, he was in possession of this fifteen-foot strip of land and kept it fenced and cultivated continuously until he sold his tract of land to Nathan on March 1, 1967. Nathan took possession under deed from Stanley, and continued possession and cultivation of the fifteen-foot strip until May 27, 1986, when Robert, having on several occasions strenuously objected to Nathan's possession, brought suit against Nathan for trespass.

What decision?

4. A executed a mortgage of Blackacre to secure her indebtedness to Ajax Savings and Loan Association in the amount of $25,000. Later A sold Blackacre to B. The deed contained the following provision: "This deed is subject to the mortgage executed by the Grantor herein to Ajax Savings and Loan Association."

The sale price of Blackacre to B was $50,000. B paid $25,000 in cash, deducting the $25,000 mortgage debt from the purchase price. On default in the payment of the mortgage debt, Ajax brings an action against A and B to recover a judgment for the amount of the mortgage debt and to foreclose the mortgage. Decision?

5. On January 1, 1985, A and B owned Blackacre as tenants in common. On July 1, 1985, A made a written contract to sell Blackacre to C for $25,000. Pursuant to this contract, C paid A $25,000 on August 1, 1985, and A executed and delivered to C a warranty deed to Blackacre. On May 1, 1986, B quitclaimed his interest in Blackacre to A. C brings an action against A for breach of warranty of title. What judgment?

6. John Doe, for valuable consideration, agreed to convey to Richard Roe eighty acres of land. He delivered a deed, the material portions of which read:

"I, John Doe, grant and convey to Richard Roe eighty acres of land [land description]: To have and to hold unto Richard Roe, his heirs, and assigns forever.

"I, John Doe, covenant to warrant and defend the premises hereby conveyed against all persons claiming the same or any part thereof by or through me."

Thereafter, Roe conveyed "all my right, title and interest" in the eighty acres to Paul Poe. It develops that Doe had no title to the land when he conveyed it to Roe. Subsequently, Doe inherited an undivided one-half interest in the property.

What rights, if any, does Poe have against Doe and Roe?

7. B operated a retail bakery, D a drugstore, F a food store, G a gift shop, and H a hardware store in adjoining locations along one side of a single suburban village block. As the population grew, the business section developed at the other end of the village, and the establishments of B, D, F, G, and H were surrounded for at least a mile in each direction solely by residences. A zoning ordinance with the usual provisions was adopted by the village, and the area including the five stores was declared to be a "residential district for single-family dwellings." Thereafter, B tore down the frame building that housed the bakery and began to construct a modern brick bakery. D found her business increasing to such an extent that she began to build an addition on the drugstore to extend it to the rear alley. F's building was destroyed by fire, and he started to reconstruct it to restore it to its former condition. G changed the gift shop into a sporting goods store and after six months of operation has decided to go back into the gift shop business. H sold his hardware store to X.

The village building commission brings an action under the zoning ordinance to enjoin the construction work of B, D, and F to enjoin the carrying on of any business by G and X. Assume the ordinance is valid. What result?

8. A and B are residents of Unit I of Chimney Hills Subdivision. The lots owned by A and B are subject to the following restrictive covenant: "Lots shall be for single-family residence purposes only." A intends to convert the interior of her carport into a beauty shop, and B brings suit against A to enjoin her from doing so. A argues that the covenant restricts only the type of building that can be constructed, not the incidental use to which residential structures are put. Decision?

9. The City of Boston sought to condemn land in fee simple for use in constructing an entrance to an underground terminal for a subway. The owners of the land contend that no more than surface and subsurface easements are necessary for the terminal entrance and seek to retain air rights above thirty-six feet. The city argues that any building using this air space would require structural supports that would interfere with the city's plan for the terminal. The city concedes that the properties around the condemned property could be assembled and structures could be designed to span over the condemned property, in which case the air rights would be quite valuable. Decision?

46

TRUSTS AND WILLS

In previous chapters we have seen that real and personal property may be transferred in a number of ways including by sale and by gift.

In addition, an important way in which a person may convey property or allow others to use or benefit from it is through trusts and wills. See the following article in Law in the News, on page 827, concerning the use of trusts. Trusts may take effect during the transferor's lifetime, or, when used in a will, they may become effective upon his death. Wills enable individuals to control the transfer of their property at their death. Upon a person's death his or her property must pass to someone. It is almost always the best policy for individuals to decide how their property should be distributed and, except for the limitations of dower and curtesy, the law permits individuals to do so by sale, gift, trust and will. If, however, an individual dies without a will— that is, *intestate*—State law prescribes who shall be entitled to the property owned by that individual at death.

Trusts

The legal title to property may be held by one or more persons while its use, enjoyment, and benefit belong to another. This situation may arise by agreement of the parties, by a grant in a will, or by a court decree. However created, the relationship is known as a trust. The party creating the trust is the **creator** or **settlor,** the party holding the legal title to the property is the **trustee** of the trust, and the person who receives the benefit of the trust is the **beneficiary** (see Figure 46-1).

Trust–transfer of property to one party for the benefit of another

Types of Trusts

Although there are many varieties of trusts, all trusts may be divided into two major groups, express and implied. The implied trusts, which are imposed upon property by courts, are known as either "constructive" or "resulting" trusts and these two special types are explained later.

Express Trusts

The express trust is, as the name indicates, a trust established by voluntary action and is represented by a written document or, under some conditions,

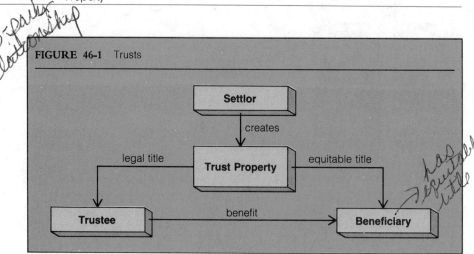

FIGURE 46-1   Trusts

[handwritten: 3-party relationship]

[handwritten: has equitable title]

an oral statement. In a majority of jurisdictions, an express trust of real property must be in writing to meet the requirements of the Statute of Frauds. No particular words are necessary to create a trust, provided that the intent of the settlor to establish a trust is unmistakable. It is not always easy to tell whether a settlor really intended to create a trust. Sometimes, words of request or recommendation are used in connection with a gift implying or hoping that the gift will be used for the purpose stated. Thus, instead of leaving property "to X for the benefit and use of Y," a settlor may leave property to X "in full confidence and with hope that he will care for Y." Such a **precatory expression** may be so definite and certain as to impose a trust upon the property for the benefit of Y. Whether it creates a trust or is nothing more than a gratuitous wish will depend on whether the court believes from all the facts that the settlor genuinely intended a trust. More frequently, courts are viewing such words as "request," "hope" and "rely" as imposing no legal obligation upon the recipient of the gift and therefore do not create a trust.

[handwritten margin note: wish, full effect, not definite]

Charitable Trusts   Almost any trusts which has for its purpose the improvement of humankind or a class of humankind is a charitable trust, unless it is so vague and indefinite that it cannot be enforced. Gifts for public museums, upkeep of parks, and to further a particular political doctrine or religious belief have been upheld as charitable.

[margin note: Charitable trust—to benefit humankind]

[handwritten margin note: beneficiary need not be specified / cy pres doctrine used / as close as possible]

Spendthrift Trusts   A settlor frequently does not believe that a beneficiary can be relied on to preserve even the limited rights granted her as beneficiary. He may then provide in the trust instrument that the beneficiary cannot, by assignment or otherwise, impair her rights to receive principal or income and that creditors of the beneficiary cannot attach the fund or the income. The term "spendthrift," as used in connection with spendthrift trusts, refers to a provision in a trust instrument under which the trust estate is removed from the beneficiary's control and disposition and from liability for her individual debts. Spendthrift provisions are generally valid. Of course, once income from the trust is actually received by the beneficiary, creditors may seize it or the beneficiary may use it as she pleases.

[margin note: Spendthrift trust—removal of the trust estate from the beneficiary's control]

[handwritten margin note: creditors also cut off]

Totten Trusts   A totten trust involves a joint bank account opened by the settlor of the trust. Typically, Sally deposits a sum of money in a savings account in

[margin note: Totten trust—a tentative trust which is a joint bank account opened by the settlor]

A Nation of Trusties

by Jane Bryant Quinn

Trusts have been long a way of having your cake while eating it too. To the wealthy, they're a sturdy defense against taxes. To the medieval clergy, they offered a way of holding monasteries so that monks could use property without violating their vows of poverty. If the rich and the holy can be trusties, why not everyone?

The Average Man trust is especially hot among parents who want to temporarily shift assets into the names of their children. It's a good tax dodge because children pay little or no income taxes on whatever interest their assets earn. With the right trust, the earnings build up virtually tax-free, and in the end you get your assets back.

Leave It to Clifford: This time-tested trust lets you give away property for a minimum of 10 years and a day. During that time, the income from the property goes to the beneficiaries—say, your children, to build up a college fund. The interest on the money is taxed in your children's low bracket instead of in your high one. When the trust expires, you get the property back. Individuals can put up to $16,275 in the trust with no gift-tax consequences; a couple, up to $32,550. It may even pay to borrow the money to fund a trust. Your loan interest will be tax deductible, while the trust's earnings will go to the child at low or no tax. Two warnings:

■ Tax reformers want to stop these trusts by forcing parents to report the income on their own tax returns. High rollers have been hustling to get Cliffords going, in hopes that Congress will leave existing trusts alone. But there's no guarantee.

■ Even today you are taxed on any trust income that is used to fulfill your own legal obligation to support your children. Tradition-ally, support meant food, clothes and lodging. But a recent Tax Court case decided that, in New Jersey, financing private school and college can also be your legal obligation—so if the trust pays, that money might have to be reported on your tax return. The same could be true in other states. You also have a legal obligation if you promised to pay for your children's college as part of a divorce settlement. (But even so, you can use a Clifford to duck taxes and enrich your child's bank account, as long as it expires before the child goes to college.)

SRT for Speedsters: The fast crowd hates Clifford trusts. Ten years and a day seem too long to be tying up money for kids, especially if they'll be out of college before the earliest day the trust can expire. So . . . enter the spousal remainder trust or SRT, a high-risk, high-wire act with quick returns.

You put money in trust, with the income—and possibly principal—payable to an account for the child. The trust expires as soon as you like, but what's left of the principal doesn't come back to you. Instead, it passes to your spouse (the property has to be given away if the trust is to last for less than 10 years). How much money you can store in these trusts gift-tax-free depends on how long the trust will last. A five-year trust can take up to $26,380 from an individual and $52,760 from a couple. So SRT's potentially yield bigger tax savings than Cliffords.

Daredevils fund these trusts with a loan from the bank, then borrow the money back out of the trust and close out the bank loan. They're left with a personal loan from the trust (usually secured with a second mortgage) on which they arrange to pay only the interest every month. Result: the trust income is banked for your child with little or no tax due, while you tax-deduct your monthly payments in full. When the trust expires, you get back your second-mortgage note and tear it up. Pretty smart.

In fact, too smart by half. I've explained this game because so many tax professionals are giving it the green light. But many other tax planners die laughing when they hear it. Three things might kill your SRT:

■ It works only if you fund the trust with your individually owned property, rather than property that is jointly owned or in which husband and wife both have a marital interest. That makes SRT's hard to qualify in community-property states and possibly in *any* state where the property owned or accumulated during a marriage belongs in some way to both spouses, says a cautious Jay Rabinowitz, head of Merrill Lynch's personal-financial-planning department. Sam Starr of Coopers & Lybrand, on the other hand, thinks it entirely possible to divide marital property and use half of it to fund an IRS-proof SRT.

■ You might be tempted to push the trust too far. Some couples, for example, are *each* setting up an SRT and naming each other as beneficiary. They might even borrow against their jointly owned house, split the cash, buy bonds in their individual names and use those bonds to fund their trusts. Will this work? Starr thinks not, because nothing has been truly given away. The spouses have merely exchanged property, with a bit of a tax dodge in the middle.

■ SRT's may also fall victim to tax reform. And even without any changes in law, the IRS could take them apart. Your minimum cost if you lose: the price of creating it ($300 to $500 or more), the ana bank in the name of "Sally, in trust for Justin." Sally may make additional deposits in the account from time to time and may withdraw money from it whenever she pleases. The courts have held this to be a tentative trust that Sally may revoke by withdrawing the fund or changing the form of the account. The transfer of ownership becomes complete only on the depositor's death.

Implied Trusts

In some cases the courts, in the absence of any expressed intent to create a trust, will impose a trust on property because the acts of the parties appear to call for such a construction. An implied trust owes its existence to the law. Implied trusts are usually divided into two classes, constructive trusts and resulting trusts.

Constructive Trusts

Constructive trust—arising by operation of law to prevent unjust enrichment

A constructive trust covers those instances where a court will impose a trust on property to rectify fraud or to prevent unjust enrichment. A constructive trust will be established where there has been abuse of a confidential relation or where actual fraud or duress is considered an equitable ground for creating the trust. The mere existence of a confidential relationship prohibits the trustee from seeking any personal benefit for himself during the course of the relationship. Business and personal affairs provide many potential situations in which constructive trusts may be implied. For example, a director of a corporation who takes advantage of a "corporate opportunity" or who makes an undisclosed profit in a transaction with the corporation will be treated as a trustee for the corporation with respect to the property or profits he acquires. Likewise, a trustee under an express trust who permits a lease held by the trust to expire and then acquires a new lease of the property in his individual capacity will be required to hold the new lease in a confidential trust for the beneficiary.

As previously indicated constructive trusts are also invoked in situations where one uses their position of friendship or marriage to their unjust advantage.

FACTS: Rodney Sharp is a fifty-six-year-old dairy farmer whose education did not go beyond the eighth grade. Upon the death of his wife of thirty-two years, Sharp developed a very close relationship with Jean Kosmalski, a school teacher sixteen years his junior. Sharp eventually proposed to Kosmalski, but when she refused, he continued to make gifts to her in hopes of changing her mind. He also gave her access to his bank account from which she withdrew substantial amounts of money, made a will naming her as sole beneficiary, and executed a deed naming her as a joint owner of his farm. Then, in September 1971, Sharp transferred his remaining joint interest in the farm to Kosmalski. In February 1973, Kosmalski ordered Sharp to move out of his home and to vacate the farm. She then took possession of both, leaving Sharp with assets of $300. Sharp brought this action to impose a constructive trust on the property transferred to Kosmalski.

DECISION: Judgment for Sharp. A constructive trust may be imposed when property has been acquired under such circumstances that the holder of the legal title may not in good conscience retain the beneficial interest. Its application requires a finding of (1) a confidential or fiduciary relation; (2) a promise; (3) a transfer in reliance on that promise; and (4) unjust enrichment.

Here a relationship of trust and confidence existed between the parties that is highlighted by the disparity in education between them. As such, Kosmalski must be charged with an obligation not to abuse the trust and confidence placed in her by Sharp. Second, an express promise or formal writing is not essential to the application of the doctrine of constructive trust, and is not likely that Sharp would have conveyed all of his property including his home to Kosmalski without at least her tacit consent that he would be allowed to continue to live on and to operate the farm. Finally it is clear that the transfer of property resulted in Kosmalski's unjust enrichment.

SHARP v. KOSMALSKI

Court of Appeals of New York, 1976.
40 N.Y.S.2d 119, 386 N.Y.S.2d 72, 351 N.E.2d 721.

Resulting Trusts   A resulting trust is different from a constructive trust in that it serves to carry out the true *intent* of the parties in those cases where the intent was inadequatly expressed rather than to rectify fraud, duress, or a breach of confidence. The most common example of a resulting trust is where A pays the purchase price for property and title is taken in the name of B. The presumption here is that the parties intended B to hold the property for the benefit of A, and B will be treated as a trustee. The difficulty is that, in many cases, it may be equally reasonable to presume that A intended to make a gift to B.

A resulting trust does not depend on contract or agreement but is founded on presumed intent that arises out of the acts of the parties. Since a resulting trust is created by implication and operation of law, it does not need to be evidenced in writing. However, if a reasonable explanation of the evidence may be made on any theory other than the existence of a resulting trust, a trust will not be declared and enforced.

Resulting trust—arises to fulfill the presumed intent of the settlor

Creation of Trusts

Each trust has (1) a creator, or settlor, (2) a "corpus," or trust property, (3) a trustee, and (4) a beneficiary. A may convey property in trust to B for the benefit of C, A may declare himself trustee for the benefit of C, or A may convey property in trust to B for the benefit of himself, A.

No particular words are necessary to create a trust, provided that the intent of the settlor to establish a trust is unmistakable. Consideration is not essential to an enforceable trust. In this respect, a trust is more like a conveyance than a contract. Trusts employed in wills are known as **testamentary trusts** because they become effective after the death of the settlor. Frequently,

Testamentary trust—established by a will

Inter vivos trust–established during the settlor's lifetime

Settlor–creator of the trust

Trustee–holder of legal title to property for the benefit of another

individuals establish trusts during their lifetime, in which case they are referred to as **inter vivos** or **"living" trusts.**

Settlor

Any person legally capable of making a contract may create a trust. However, if the settlor's conveyance would be voidable or void because of infancy, incompetency, or some other reason, a declaration of trust is also voidable or void.

Subject Matter

One of the main characteristics that sets a trust apart from other relationships, such as a debtor-creditor relationship, is the requirement of a trust corpus or *res*, which must be property that is definite and specific. A trust cannot be effective immediately for property not yet in existence or to be acquired at a later date.

The requirement of a definite and certain subject matter is, however, satisfied by the creation of a testamentary trust. Donna's will provides that she leaves to Terry, as trustee, sufficient funds to pay $300 a month to Barbara. The will takes effect on the death of Donna.

Trustee

Anyone legally capable of holding title to and dealing with property may be a trustee. The lack of a trustee will not destroy the trust. If the settlor neglects to appoint one, if the named trustee does not qualify, or if the named trustee declines to serve, the court, on request, will appoint an individual or institution to act as trustee.

Duties of the Trustee
A trustee has three primary duties: (1) to carry out the purposes of the trust; (2) to act with prudence and care in the administration of the trust; and (3) to exercise a high degree of loyalty toward the beneficiary.

No special skills are required of a trustee under ordinary circumstances. He is required to act with the same degree of care that a **prudent man** would use to carry out his personal affairs. What constitutes the care of a "prudent man" is, of course, not easy to classify in any particular case.

WITMER v. BLAIR

Missouri Court of Appeals
Western District, 1979.
588 S.W.2d 222.

FACTS: By his last will and testament, Nussbaum made a residual bequest and devise of his estate to his niece, Jane Blair, as trustee, in trust for the education of his grandchildren. If the trust could not be fulfilled, the residue would revert to Dorothy Witmer, Nussbaum's daughter. Nussbaum died in 1960. Janice Witmer, Dorothy's daughter, was the only grandchild who became a beneficiary of the trust. She was born in September, 1953. At the time of the trial she was 23 years old and had not attended a college or university. When the trustee, Blair, acquired the trust in 1961, it consisted of $1,905 in checking and savings accounts, $5,700 in certificates of deposit, and a house valued at $6,000. IN 1962, the house was sold for $4,467, which was deposited in the trust checking account, a non-interest paying account. A considerable portion of the trust funds were held in the checking account from 1962–1971. In 1972, Blair reduced the checking account balance by transfers to the savings account. The Witmers sued Blair, claiming she breached her beneficiary duty by failing to invest properly the trust corpus. Blair argues that the will failed to specify when and what investments were to be made. Thus, such matters were left to her good faith discretion. Also, she explained the large checking account balances by the fact that college for Janice "was talked about throughout high school."

DECISION: Judgment for the Witmers. It is a duty of the trustee to keep trust funds properly invested. A trustee generally cannot excuse a failure to invest funds by saying that she kept the funds to pay beneficiaries on demand. A trustee commits a breach of trust when she violates a duty in bad faith, intentionally or negligently. However, a trustee may also commit a breach because of a mistake as to the extent of her duties and powers. When in doubt, a trustee can protect herself by obtaining instructions from the court.

Here, Blair committed a breach of trust by failing to invest a large amount of the trust fund between 1962 and 1971. Her good faith mistake as to her duties is not a defense. Thus, she is liable for $2,840—the amount the money in the checking account would have earned between 1962 and 1971 in an interest bearing account. However, she is not liable for the mishandling of the trust after she transferred a substantial portion from checking to savings in 1972.

The duty of loyalty arises out of and illustrates the fiduciary character of the relationship between the trustee and the beneficiary. In all his dealings with the trust property, the beneficiary, and third parties, the trustee must act in the exclusive interest of the beneficiary. Lack of loyalty may arise from obvious self-interest, or it may be entirely innocent; in either event the trustee can be charged with lack of loyalty.

Powers of the Trustee   The powers of a trustee are determined by (1) the rules of law in the jurisdiction in which the trust is established and (2) the authority granted him by the settlor in the instrument creating the trust. State laws affecting the powers of trustees have their greatest impact on the investments a trustee may make with trust funds. Most States prescribe a list of types of securities qualified for trust investment. In some jurisdictions this list is permissive; in others it is mandatory. If the list is permissive, the trustee may invest in types of securities not listed, but he carries the burden of showing that he made a prudent choice. The trust instrument may give the trustee wide discretion as to investments, and in such an event the trustee is not bound to adhere to the list deemed advisable under the statute.

Allocation of Principal and Income   Trusts often settle a life estate in the trust corpus on one beneficiary and a remainder interest on another beneficiary. For example, on his death a man leaves his property to trustees who are instructed to pay the income from the property to his widow during her life and to distribute the property to his children when she dies. In these instances the trustee must distribute the principal to one party (the remainderman) and the income to another (the life tenant or income beneficiary). The trustee must also allocate receipts and charge expenses between the income beneficiary and the remainderman. If the trust agreement does not specify how the funds should be allocated, the trustee is provided guidance by statute, which in most States is the **Uniform Principal and Income Act.** A trustee who fails to comply with the trust agreement or the statute is personally liable for any loss.

The general rule in allocating benefits and burdens between income beneficiaries and remaindermen is that *ordinary* or current receipts and expenses are chargeable to the income beneficiary, whereas *extraordinary* receipts and expense are allocated to the remainderman. Figure 46-2 illustrates these four types of allocations.

Beneficiary

There are very few restrictions on who (or what) may be a beneficiary. Dogs, cats, horses, and a multitude of pets have at one time or another been held to be the proper objects of a settlor's bounty. Charitable uses are a common

Beneficiary–equitable owner of trust property

FIGURE 46-2 Allocation of Principal and Income

	Receipts	Expenses

Ordinary—Income Beneficiary	Rents
	Royalties
	Cash dividends
	  (regular and
	  extraordinary)
	Interest
		Interest payments
		Insurance
		Ordinary taxes
		Ordinary repairs

Extraordinary—Remainderman	Stock dividends
	Stock splits
	Proceeds for sale or
	  exchange of corpus
	Settlement of claims for
	  injury to corpus
		Extraordinary repairs
		Long-term improvements
		Principal amortization
		Costs incurred in the sale
		  or purchase of corpus
		Depreciation

[handwritten: —one who is alive (wife)]

[handwritten: kids after Dad dies]

purpose of trusts, and if the settlor's object does not outrage public policy or morals, almost any purpose that happens to strike the fancy of a settlor will be upheld.

Termination of a Trust

Unless a power of revocation is reserved by the settlor, the general rule is that a trust, once validly created, is *irrevocable*. If so reserved, the trust may be terminated at the discretion of the settlor.

Normally, the instrument creating a trust lists a termination date, and the trust terminates at the time stated without complication. A period of years may be specified, or the settlor may provide that the trust shall continue during the life of a named individual. The death of the trustee or beneficiary does not terminate the trust if neither of their lives is the measure of the duration of the trust.

Occasionally, the purpose for which a trust has been established may be regarded as fulfilled before the specified termination date. In such a case, on petition by the trustee or beneficiary the court may decree a termination of the trust. A court will usually decree a trust terminated if the beneficiary acquires legal title to the trust assets, but courts will not order the termination of a trust simply because all of the beneficiaries petition the court to do so. The court will be governed by the purposes set forth in the trust instrument by the settlor, not by the wishes of the beneficiaries.

Decedent's Estates

The assets of a person who dies leaving a valid will are to be distributed according to the directions contained in the will. A will is also called a testament; the maker of a will is called a testator; and gifts made in a will are called devises or bequests. If a person dies without leaving a will, her property will pass to her heirs and next-of-kin in the proportions provided in the applicable State statute. This is known as **intestate** (dying without a will)

Intestate–dying without a will

succession. If a person dies without a will and leaves no heirs or next-of-kin, her property *escheats* (reverts) to the State.

Wills

One major characteristic of a will sets it apart from other transactions such as deeds and contracts: a will is revocable at any time during life. There is no such thing as an irrevocable will. A document binding during life may be a contract (such as a promise to make a will) or a deed (conveying a vested remainder after a life estate in the grantor), but it is not a will. A will takes effect only on, and not until, the death of the testator.

Mental Capacity

Testamentary Capacity and Power   To make a valid will, the testator must have both the "power" and the "capacity" to do so. The *power* to make a will is granted by the State to persons who are of a class believed generally able to handle their affairs without regard to personal limitations. Thus, in most States, children under a certain age cannot make valid wills.

The *capacity* to make a will refers to the limits placed on particular persons in the class generally granted the power to make wills because of personal mental deficiencies. Underlying the notion of capacity is the premise that, for a will to be valid, a testator must *intend* a document to be his will. This required intent will be lacking if he is incompetent or suffers from delusions.

Conduct Invalidating a Will   The required intent must always be present to create a valid will. Any document appearing to be a will that reflects an intent other than the testator's is not a valid will. This is the basis for the rule that a will that transmits property as a result of *duress, undue influence,* or *fraud* is no will at all.

FACTS: In April 1961, Grace Peterson, a spinster then aged seventy-four, asked Chester Gustafson, a Minneapolis attorney, to draw a will for her. Gustafson, who had also probated Peterson's sister's estate, drew this first will and six subsequent wills and codicils free of charge because he claimed that she had no money to pay for his services. Over the five-year period during which Gustafson redrew Peterson's will, an increasing amount of property was devised to Gustafson's children until the seventh will, when Peterson's entire estate was so devised. Peterson, however, hardly knew the children except from several chance encounters ten years before. She died on February 1, 1966, without ever having changed the seventh will, and Gustafson, who was named as executor, now seeks to have the will admitted to probate.

DECISION: Judgment against Gustafson as executor. Peterson's will is the product of Gustafson's undue influence, and, therefore, it cannot be admitted to probate. Undue influence is influence that substitutes the intent of the person exerting it for that of the person making the will, thereby making the written result express the purpose of the influencing party and not that of the party making the will. In order to justify the refusal to probate the will, however, the influence must overpower the intent of the testator at the time the will is made and dominate and control its making.

Several factors in this case, taken together, support a finding of undue influence by Gustafson and justify not admitting Peterson's will to probate: (1) Gustafson had the opportunity to exercise undue influence; (2) he developed a confidential relationship with Peterson; and (3) he controlled the drafting of Peterson's wills that systematically disinherited for family and friends until her entire estate was left to his children, whom she hardly knew.

IN RE ESTATE OF PETERSON

Supreme Court of Minnesota, 1969.
283 Minn. 446, 168 N.W.2d 502.

*in testa-
die w/o a will
- falls under
state laws of
distribution*

The law is generally not as ready to invalidate or partially revise a will because of *mistake* as it is to adjust a contract based on an error. A mistake as to the identity of the instrument voids a will. But a stenographic error or a mistake in drafting may be corrected by clear evidence of the testator's intent.

Formal Requirements of a Will

By statute in all jurisdictions a will, to be valid, must comply with certain formalities. These are necessary not only to indicate that the testator understood what she was doing but also to help prevent fraud.

Writing   A basic requirement to a valid will is that it be in writing. The writing *[typed]* may be informal, as long as the basic formalities required by the statute are substantially met. Pencil, ink, and mimeograph are equally valid methods, and valid wills have been made on scratch paper and on an envelope.

It is also valid to incorporate into a will by reference another document that in itself is not a will because it was not properly executed. To incorporate a memorandum in a will by reference, the following four conditions must exist: (1) the memorandum must be in writing; (2) it must be in existence when the will is executed; (3) it must be adequately described in the will; and (4) it must be described in the will as being in existence.

Signature   A will must be signed by the testator. The signature verifies that the will has been executed and is a fundamental requirement in almost all jurisdictions. The initials "A. H." or "father" at the end of a will in the handwriting of the testator are adequate if intended as an execution.

[Holographic will—totally written by testator]

Most statutes require the signature to be at the end of the will, and even in jurisdictions where this is not specified, a signature at the end will prevent the charge that the portions of a will coming after a signature were written after its execution and therefore do not have the necessary formality of a signature.

Attestation   With the exception of a few isolated types of wills noted later that are valid in a limited number of jurisdictions, a written will must be attested, or certified, by witnesses. The number and qualification of witnesses and the manner of attestation are generally set out by statute. Usually two or three witnesses are required.

The function of witnesses is to acknowledge that the testator did execute the will and that she had the required intent and capacity. It is important that the testator sign first in the presence of all the witnesses, and it is usually essential that each witness sign in her presence and in the presence of the other witness.

The most common restriction is that a witness must not have any interest under the will. This requirement takes at least two forms under statutes. One type of statute disqualifies a witness who is also a beneficiary under the will. The other type voids the bequest or devise to the interested witness, thus making him a disinterested and qualified witness.

Revocation of a Will

By definition, a will is revocable by the testator. Under certain circumstances a will may be revoked by operation of law. This does not mean that certain formalities are not necessary to effect a revocation. In most jurisdictions the methods by which a will is revoked are specified by statute.

Destruction or Alteration   Tearing, burning, or otherwise destroying a will is a strong sign that the testator intended to revoke it and, unless it can be shown that the destruction was inadvertent, it is an effective way of revoking a will. In some States, partial revocation of a will may be accomplished by erasure or obliteration of a part of the will. But substituted or additional bequests made by insertions between the written or printed lines of a will are not effective without reexecution and reattestation.

Courts are occasionally faced with the difficult question of determining whether a will was revoked by destruction or simply mislaid. The following case deals with this problem.

[handwritten: codocils can be used to revoke]

BARKSDALE v. PENDERGRASS

Supreme Court of Alabama, 1975.
294 Ala. 526, 319 So.2d 267.

FACTS: Mamie Henry, a widow, died on October 18, 1972. She had no children, but was survived by several nieces and nephews. At first no will was found, and Joe Barksdale, a nephew, was appointed administrator of Mrs. Henry's estate. Later, Rita Pendergrass produced a copy of a will allegedly made by Mrs. Henry. The will left all of Mrs. Henry's property to Mrs. Pendergrass and appointed her as executrix. She now seeks to have the will admitted to probate. Joe Barksdale and Olen Barksdale filed a contest on the grounds that the purported will was never duly executed, or, if executed, was destroyed by Mrs. Henry prior to her death.

DECISION: Judgment for Pendergrass. In order to have an alleged lost or destroyed will admitted to probate, the one asserting its effectiveness must first establish that it is a validly executed will and second, rebut the presumption arising from the loss or destruction of the will that it was revoked by its maker. Since Mrs. Pendergrass fulfilled both of these requirements here, she is entitled to submit Mrs. Henry's will to probate.

First, Mrs. Pendergrass has established that the document was a validly executed will. It was signed by Mrs. Henry and attested by two witnesses in Mrs. Henry's presence with her express or implied knowledge or consent. Second, Mrs. Pendergrass has also succeeded in rebutting the presumption that Mrs. Henry had revoked her will by showing that Mrs. Henry wanted Mrs. Pendergrass and not her nieces and nephews to receive her property at her death.

Subsequent Will   The execution of a second will does not in itself constitute a revocation of an earlier will. The first will is revoked only to the extent that the second will is inconsistent with the first. The most certain manner of revocation is the execution of a later will containing a declaration that all former wills are revoked. In some but not all jurisdictions, a will may be revoked by a written declaration to this effect in a subsequent document, such as a letter, even though the document does not meet the formal requirements of a will.

Operation of Law   A *marriage* generally revokes a will executed before the marriage. *Divorce*, on the other hand, generally, does *not* revoke a provision in the will of one of the parties for the benefit of the other party.

The *birth* of a child after execution of a will may revoke a will at least as far as that child is concerned if it appears that the testator omitted a provision for the child. In some jurisdictions the subsequent birth of a child will not revoke the will, but the child is entitled to the same share as though the testator died without a will, unless it appears from the will that the omission was intentional.

[handwritten: preter-mitted heir]

Renunciation by the Surviving Spouse   Statutes generally provide for a right of renunciation of the will by a surviving spouse and set forth the method of accomplishing it. The purpose of such statutory provisions is to enable the spouse to elect which method of taking—under the will or under intestate succession—would be more advantageous to him or her. Where a spouse dies owning real and personal property, the surviving spouse has an interest in the decedent's estate that cannot be divested by will without the surviving spouse's consent. The right to renounce a will may be exercised only by persons designated by the statute, and the right conferred on the surviving spouse is personal. On renunciation of the will, the law of intestate succession determines the share of the estate taken by the surviving spouse.

Special Types of Wills

There are many special types of wills, including nuncupative wills, holographic wills, soldiers' and sailors' wills, conditional wills, and joint and reciprocal wills.

Nuncupative Wills   A nuncupative will is an oral declaration made before witnesses without any writing. In the few jurisdictions where authorized, it can usually be made only when the testator is in his last illness. Under most statutes permitting nuncupative wills, only limited amounts of personal property, generally under $1,000, may be passed by such wills.

Holographic Wills   In some jurisdictions a will entirely in the handwriting of the testator is a valid testamentary document even if the will is *not* witnessed. Such an instrument is referred to as a holographic will. A holographic will must comply strictly with the statutory requirements for such wills.

Soldiers' and Sailors' Wills   In the case of soldiers on active service and sailors while at sea, most statutes relax the formal requirements and permit a valid testamentary disposition regardless of the informality of the document. In most jurisdictions, however, such a will cannot pass title to real estate.

Conditional Wills   A contingent or conditional will is one that takes effect as a will only on the happening of a specified contingency, which is called a *condition precedent* to the operation of the will.

Joint and Mutual or Reciprocal Wills   A joint will is one where the same instrument is made the will of two or more persons and is signed by them jointly. Mutual or reciprocal wills are separate instruments with reciprocal terms made by two or more persons. Each testator makes a testamentary disposition in favor of the other.

Codicils

A codicil is an addition to or a revision of a will, generally by a separate instrument, in which the will is expressly referred to and, in effect, incorporated into the codicil by reference. Codicils must be executed with all the formal requirements of a will. The most frequent problem raised by codicils is the extent to which their terms, if not absolutely clear, revoke or alter provisions in the will. For the purpose of determining the testator's intent, the codicil and the will are regarded as a single instrument.

Intestate Succession

When a person dies, the title to his property must pass to someone. If the decedent leaves a valid will, his property will pass as he directs, subject only to certain limitations imposed by the State, such as the widow's right to dower

"escheats to the state"

discussed in Chapter 44. If, however, no valid will has been executed, the decedent is said to have died "intestate," and the State prescribes who shall be entitled to the property. The intestacy laws also apply to property which is not devised by a will, see *Ferguson v. Croom* below.

The rules set forth in statutes for determining, in case of intestacy, to whom the decedent's property shall be distributed not only assure an orderly transfer of title to property but also attempt to carry out what would probably be the wishes of the decedent. Nonetheless, the distribution of the estate is according to the statute and may be contrary to the clear intentions of the decedents demonstrated by the following case.

FACTS: On June 21, 1983, George W. Croom died testate. In his will Croom left various bequests of real and personal property to his children and a grandchild. Also in his will, Croom stated: "I leave nothing whatsoever to my daughter Kathryn Elizabeth Turner and my son Ernest Edward Croom." At his death, Croom left three optional share certificates in Carolina Savings & Loan Association issued to George Croom or Kimberly Croom, his minor daughter. Each of these certificates purported to create a joint account with a right of survivorship. Two of them were signed by George Croom only and the third agreement was not signed at all. None of these certificates were specifically devised by Croom's will and the will contained no residuary clause. Ferguson, as administrator of George's will, brought suit seeking a determination as to who is entitled to these certificates. Kimberly Croom contends that the share certificates should pass to her by right of survivorship. Kathryn and Ernest argue that, regardless of George's intent to leave them nothing, they are entitled to a portion of the certificates under the laws of intestate succession.

DECISION: Judgment for Kathryn and Ernest Croom. The optional share certificates did not satisfy the statutory requirements necessary to pass by joint survivorship. Thus, they became part of the Croom estate. Since there was no residuary clause, the certificates must be distributed by the laws of intestate succession. North Carolina statute 8 directs that such property must pass by intestate succession without regard to the testator's intent expressed in his will. Under the Intestate Succession Act, each of the testator's children is entitled to take an equal share of the property not disposed of by his will. Therefore, despite George's contrary intent, Kathryn and Ernest are entitled to their equal share of the certificates.

FERGUSON v. CROOM

Court of Appeals of North Carolina.
326 S.E.2d 373 (N.C.App. 1985).

Course of Descent

The rules of descent vary widely from State to State, but as a general rule and except for the specific statutory or dower rights of the widow, the intestate property passes in equal shares to each child of the decedent living at the time of his death, with the share of any child who dies before the decedent to be divided equally among that child's children. For example, if A dies intestate, leaving a widow and children, the widow will generally receive one-third of his real estate and personal property, and the remainder will pass to his children in the manner stated above. If the wife does not survive A, his entire estate passes to the children. If A dies and leaves two surviving children, B and C, and two grandchildren, D_1 and D_2, the children of a predeceased child D, the estate will go one-third to B, one-third to C, and one-sixth each to D_1 and D_2 the grandchildren dividing equally their parent's one-third share. This result is legally described by the statement that *lineal* descendants of predeceased children take property **per stirpes,** or by representation of their parent. If A had executed a will, he may have provided that all his lineal

(through the root)

descendants, regardless of generation, would share equally. In that case A's estate would be divided into four equal parts, and his descendants would be said to take the property **per capita** (see Figure 46-3).

If no children but only the widow and other relatives survive the decedent, a larger share is generally allotted the widow. She may receive all the personal property and one-half the real estate or, in some States, the entire estate.

At common law, property could not lineally ascend; parents of an intestate decedent did not share in his estate. Today, in many States, if there are no lineal descendants, the statute provides that parents are the next to share.

Most statutes make some provision for brothers and sisters in the event that no spouse, parents, or children survive the decedent. Brothers and sisters, together with nieces, nephews, aunts, and uncles, are termed *collateral* heirs. Beyond these limits most statutes provide that, if there are no survivors of the named classes, the property shall be distributed equally among the next-of-kin in equal degree.

The common law did not consider a *stepchild* as an heir or next of kin, that is, as one to whom property would descend by operation of law, and this rule prevails today. Legally *adopted* children are, however, recognized as lawful heirs of their adopting parents.

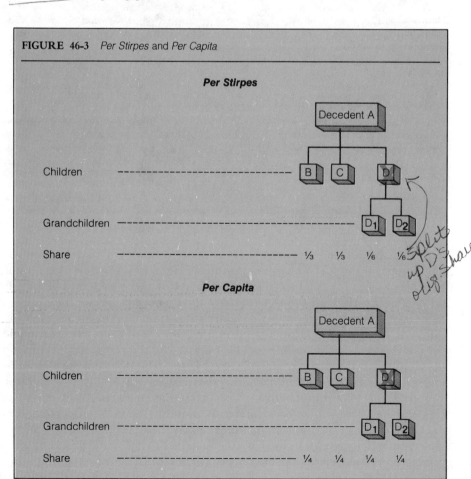

FIGURE 46-3   *Per Stirpes* and *Per Capita*

These generalities should be accepted as such; few fields of the law of property are so strictly a matter of statute, and the rights of heirs cannot be reasonably predicted without a knowledge of the exact terms of the applicable statute.

Administration of Estates

The rules and procedures controlling the management of the estate of a deceased are statutory and therefore vary somewhat from State to State. In all jurisdictions the estate is managed and finally disbursed under the supervision of a court. The procedure of managing the estates of decedents is referred to as **probate,** and the court that supervises the procedure is often designated as the Probate Court.

The first legal step after death is usually to determine whether or not the deceased left a will. If a will exists, it is probable that the testator named her executor in it.

If there is no will or if there is a will that fails to name an executor, the court will, on petition, appoint an administrator. The closest adult relative who is a resident of the State is entitled to this appointment.

Once approved or appointed by the court, the **executor** or **administrator** holds title to all the personal property of the deceased and accounts to the creditors and the beneficiaries. The estate is his responsibility.

If there is a will, it must be proved before the court by the witnesses. They will testify to the signing of the will by all signatories and as to the mental condition of the testator at the time of the execution of the will. If the witnesses are dead, proof of their handwriting is necessary. If the court is satisfied that the will is proved, a formal decree will be entered admitting the will to probate.

Soon after the admission of the will to probate, the personal representative of the decedent—the executor or administrator—must file an inventory of the estate. The personal representative will then begin her duties of collecting the assets, paying the debts, and disbursing the remainder. The executor or administrator occupies a *fiduciary* position not unlike that of a trustee, and his responsibility for investing proceeds and otherwise managing the estate is equally demanding.

In the administration of every estate, there are probate expenses as well as fees to be paid to the executor or administrator and the attorney who handles the estate. In addition, taxes are imposed at death by both the Federal and State governments. The Federal government imposes an **estate tax** on the transfer of property at death. Most State governments impose an **inheritance tax** on the privilege of an heir or beneficiary to receive the property. These taxes are separate and apart from the basic income tax that the estate must pay on income received during estate administration.

CHAPTER SUMMARY

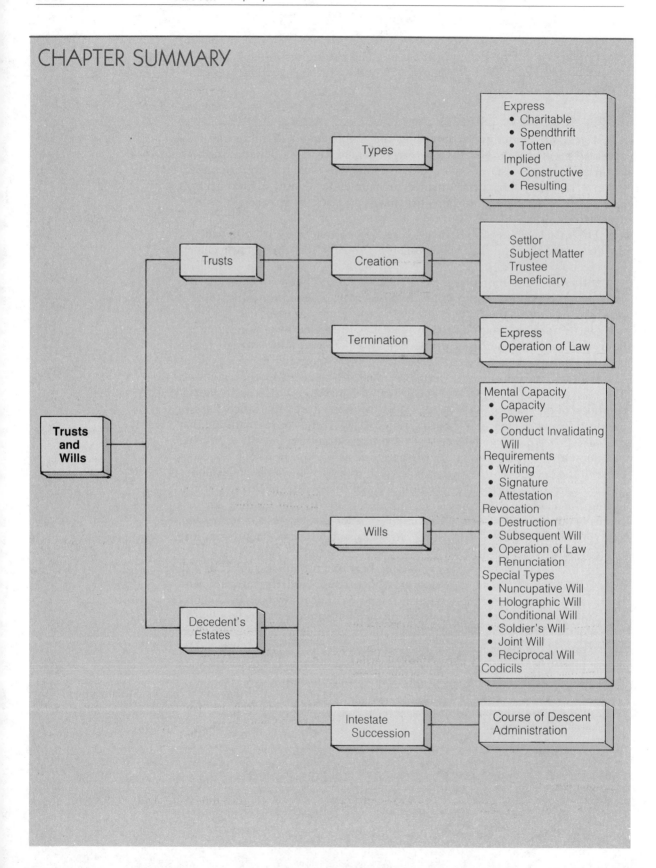

KEY TERMS

Trust	Inter vivos trust	Soldiers' will
Creator or settlor	Irrevocable trust	Conditional will
Trustee	Revocable trust	Joint will
Beneficiary	Testate	Reciprocal will
Express trust	Intestate	Codicil
Precatory trust	Testator	Per stirpes
Charitable trust	Devise	Per capita
Spendthrift trust	Bequest	Probate
Totten trust	Testamentary capacity	Executor
Constructive trust	Testamentary power	Administrator
Resulting trust	Revoked	Estate tax
Corpus	Nuncupative will	Inheritance tax
Testamentary trust	Holographic will	

PROBLEMS

1. State whether or not a trust is created in each of the following situations.

(a) A declares herself trustee of "the bulk of my securities" in trust for B.

(b) A, the owner of Blackacre, purports to convey to B in trust for C "a small part" of Blackacre.

(c) A orders B, a stockbroker, to buy 2,000 shares of American Steel or any part thereof at $20 per share. After the broker has brought 500 shares but before A knows whether any shares have been bought for him, A declares himself trustee for C of such shares of American Steel as B has bought.

(d) A owns ten bonds. He declared himself trustee for B of such five of the bonds as B may select at any time within a month.

(e) A deposits $1,000 in a savings bank. He declares himself trustee of the deposit in trust to pay B $500 out of the deposit, reserving the power to withdraw from the deposit any amounts not in excess of $500.

2. Testator gives property to T in trust for B's benefit, providing that B cannot anticipate the income by assignment or pledge. B borrows money from L, assigning his future income under the trust for a stated period. Can L obtain any judicial relief to prevent B from collecting this income?

3. Collins was trustee for Indolent under the will of Indolent's father. Indolent, a middle-aged doctor, gave little concern to the management of the trust fund, contenting himself with receiving the income paid by him by the trustee. Among the assets of the trust were one hundred shares of ABC Corporation and one hundred shares of XYZ Corporation. About two years before the termination of the trust, Collins purchased the ABC stock from the trust at a fair price and after a full explanation to Indolent. At the same time but without saying anything to Indolent, he purchased the XYZ stock at a price above its market value at the time. At the termination of the trust both stocks had advanced in market value well beyond the prices paid by Collins, and Indolent demanded that Collins either account for this advance in the value of both stocks or replace the stocks. What are Indolent's rights?

4. On September 1, 1975, Joe Brown gave $35,000 to his wife Mary with which to buy real property. They orally agreed that title to the real property should be taken in the name of Mary Brown but that she should hold the property in trust for Joe Brown. There were two witnesses to the oral agreement, both of whom are still living. Mary purchased the property on September 2, and a deed to it with Mary Brown as the grantee was delivered.

Mary died on October 5, 1986, without a will. The real property is now worth $100,000. Joe Brown is claiming the property as the beneficiary of a trust. Mary's children are claiming that the property belongs to Mary's estate and have pleaded the Statute of Limitations and the Statute of Frauds as defenses to Joe's claim. There is no evidence one way or the other as to whether Mary would have conveyed the property to Joe during her lifetime if she had been requested to do so.

What are Joe's ownership rights to this particular real property?

5. On March 10, 1986, John Carver executed his will, which was witnessed by William Hobson and Sam Witt. By his will Carver devised his farm, Stonecrest, to his nephew Roy White. The residue of his estate was given to his sister, Florence Carver.

A codicil to his will executed April 15, 1986, provided that $5,000 be given to Carver's niece, Mary Jordan, and $5,000 to Wanda White, Roy White's wife. The codicil was witnessed by Roy White and Harold Brown. John Carver died September 1, 1986, and the will and codicil were admitted to probate.

How should Carver's estate be distributed?

6. Edwin Fuller, a bachelor, prepared his will in his office. The will, which contained no residuary clause, provided that one-third of his estate would go to his nephew, Tom Fuller, one-third to the City of Emanon to be used for park improvements, and one-third to his brother Kurt.

He signed the will in his office and then went to the office of his nephew, Tom Fuller, who signed the will as a witness at Edwin's request. No other persons were available in Tom's office, so Edwin then went to the bank, where Frank Cash, the cashier, also signed as a witness at Edwin's request. In each instance Edwin stated that he had signed the document but did not state that it was his will.

Edwin returned to his office and placed the will in his safe. Subsequently, Edwin died, survived by Kurt, his only heir-at-law. How should the estate be distributed?

7. A executed a one-page will in which he devised his farm to B. Later, after a quarrel with B, A wrote the words "I hereby cancel and revoke this will /s/A" in the margin of the will but did not destroy the will. A then executed a deed to the farm, naming C as grantee, and placed the deed and will in his safe. Shortly afterward, A married D, with whom he had one child, E. A died some time later, and the deed and will were found in his safe. B, C, and E claim the farm, and D claims dower. Discuss the validity of each claim.

8. John Walker, a widower, made a will containing the following provisions:

"I give and bequeath my piano to my daughter Nancy. I give and bequeath to may daughter Jennifer the sum of $1,000. I give and bequeath to my son John the sum of $1,000 to be paid out of my account at the Tenth National Bank in the city of Erehwon. All the rest and residue of my estate I give to Nancy, Jennifer, and John, share and share alike."

After the will was executed Walker sold his piano for $2,300 and deposited the proceeds in the Citizens bank of Erehwon. He withdrew the money he had on deposit in the Tenth National Bank and purchased a new automobile.

When Walker died, he had no debts. The account in the Citizens Bank of Erehwon had a balance of $2,300, which constituted his entire net estate after all expenses of administration were paid. How should Walker's estate be distributed?

9. The validly executed will of John Dane contained the following provision: "I give and devise to my daughter, Mary, Redacre for and during her natural life and, at her death, the remainder to go to Wilmore College." The will also provided that the residue of his estate should go to Wilmore College. Thereafter, Dane sold Redacre and then added a validly executed codicil to his will, "Due to the fact that I have sold Redacre, which I previously gave to my daughter, Mary, I now give and devise Blackacre to Mary in place and instead of Redacre."

Another clause of the codicil provided: "I give my one-half interest in the oil business that I own in common with William Steele to my son, Henry." Subsequently, Dane acquired all of the interest in the oil business from his partner, Steele, and at the time of his death Dane owned the entire oil business. The will and codicil have been admitted to probate.

(a) What interest, if any, does Mary acquire in Blackacre?

(b) What interest, if any, does Henry acquire in the oil business?

INSURANCE

"Insurance" covers a vast range of contracts, all of which distribute risk among a large number of members (the **insured**) through an insurance company (the **insurer**). It is a contractual undertaking by the insurer to pay a sum of money or give something of value to the insured or a beneficiary on the happening of a contingency or fortuitous event that is beyond the control of the contracting parties.

It is literally impossible to name a commercial activity which is not affected by insurance coverage of one form or other. Tangible assets of a business can be the subject of insurance protecting it against almost any form of damage or destruction, whether from natural causes or from the accidental or improper actions of another. Insurance may also protect a business from virtually any type of liability that may be asserted against it through the negligent or intentional act of any of its representatives which, in any way, might be deemed to be the act of the business. A business may procure credit insurance to protect against losses from poor credit risks and fidelity bonds to protect it against losses incurred through defalcations of employees. If a business hires a famous pianist, it may insure the latter's hands; if it decides to present an outdoor concert, it may insure against the possibility of rain. A business may purchase life insurance on its key executives to reimburse it for the financial loss arising from their deaths, or it may purchase such life insurance payable to the families of the executives as part of an incentive compensation. A recent development of growing importance is the use of insurance to carry out pension commitments arising from bargaining agreements with unions.

The McCarran-Ferguson Act, enacted by Congress in 1945, left the regulation of insurance to the States. Each State has its own statutes that regulate its domestic insurance companies and also set forth standards that foreign (out-of-state) insurance companies must meet if they wish to do business within the State. Most State legislation relates to the incorporation, licensing, supervision, and liquidation of insurers and to the licensing and supervision of agents and brokers.

Because the insurance relationship arises from a contract of insurance between the insurer and the insured, the law of insurance is a branch of contract law. For this reason, the doctrines of offer and acceptance, consid-

3 parties involved
insured
insurer (owner)
beneficiary

eration, and other rules that apply to contracts in general also apply to insurance contracts. Beyond that, however, insurance law, like the law of sales, bailments, negotiable instruments, or other specialized types of contracts, contains many modifications and ramifications of fundamental contract law. We discuss the basics of insurance law in this chapter.

Kinds of Insurance

There are many kinds of insurance and many kinds of insurance policies. Although the listing that follows is not complete, it contains the most common kinds of insurance.

Life Insurance

Life insurance—payment of a specific sum of money to a designated beneficiary upon the death of the insured

pay premiums

Life insurance might be more accurately called "death insurance," because it is a contract by the terms of which the insurer will pay a specified sum of money on the death of the insured, provided the required premiums have been paid. The payment is made either to a named beneficiary, ordinarily a third-party donee or creditor, or to the estate of the deceased. The naming of a beneficiary is a privilege of the *owner* of the policy, but unless the right to do so is reserved in the policy, the owner has no right to change the beneficiary. Most modern policies as part of the standard form reserve to the owner of the policy the right to change beneficiaries. One person may occupy one or more of these three roles (insured, owner, and beneficiary) or each may be held by a different party.

Ordinary life—life insurance with a savings component that runs for the life of the insured

Ordinary Life   Ordinary life insurance is often considered a form of savings or investment, because the insured has a right to borrow from the insurer an amount not to exceed the **cash surrender value** of the policy, which increases the longer the policy is in force. Such a loan generally bears a low interest rate and is secured by an assignment to the insurer of the policy proceeds to the extent necessary to pay the loan in the event of death, with the remainder going to the beneficiary.

Ordinary life or whole-life insurance is designed to run for the entire life of the insured and generally requires, under a straight life policy, the payment of premiums until his death. **Limited-payment** life policies require the payment of premiums only for a fixed number of years, thus eliminating the duty of paying premiums through the later years of life when such payments may be burdensome. With **single premium** life insurance, the entire premium is prepaid in one lump sum.

Term life—life insurance issued for a limited number of years that does not have a savings component

Term Life   Term life insurance is issued for a limited number of years, with premiums payable during the period of coverage. The insurance proceeds are paid only if the insured dies within the specified time period. Term insurance, moreover, does not build up any cash surrender value or loan value, and thus the insurer may not be obligated to pay out anything on the policy. Frequently, this type of life insurance carries with it a provision to renew the policy without regard to the state of the insured's health.

Endowment and Annuity Contracts

An endowment contract is basically an agreement by the insurer to pay a lump sum of money to the insured when she reaches a certain age or to a beneficiary in the event of premature death. An annuity contract is an agreement by the insurer to pay fixed sums to the insured at periodic intervals after the insured reaches a designated age. Strictly speaking, endowment and annuity policies are not insurance contracts; however, many endowment and annuity contracts contain various provisions that are customarily found in life insurance contracts and thus the contracts are subject to regulation by State insurance departments.

Accident and Health Insurance

Accident and health insurance is really insurance against losses due to accidents and sickness and provides for the payment of certain benefits or the reimbursement of specified expenses in the event of illness or accidental injury, within the limits set forth in the policies.

Fire and Property Insurance

Fire insurance protects the owner (or another person with an insurable interest, such as a secured creditor or mortgagee) of real or personal property against loss resulting from damage to or destruction of the property by fire and certain related perils.

Fire insurance policies are standardized in the United States, either by statute or by order of the State insurance departments, but their coverage is frequently enlarged by an "endorsement" or "rider" to include other perils or to benefit the insured in ways not provided in the standard form. These policies are normally written for periods of one or three years.

Co-insurance is common in property insurance and is a means of sharing the risk between insurer and insured. For example, under the typical 80 percent co-insurance clause, the insured may recover the full amount of loss not to exceed the face amount of the policy, provided the policy is for an amount not less than 80 percent of the insurable value of the property. If the policy is for less than 80 percent the insured recovers that proportion of the loss which the amount of the policy bears up to 80 percent of the insurable value. The formula for recovery is as follows:

Co-insurance–a form of insurance in which a person insures property for less than its full or stated value and agrees to share the risk of loss

$$\text{Recovery} = \frac{\text{Fair value of policy}}{\text{Fair market value of property} \times \text{co-insurance \%}} \times \text{Loss}$$

Thus, if the co-insurance percentage is 80 percent, the value of the property is $100,000, and the policy is for $80,000 or more, the insured is protected against loss not to exceed the amount of the policy. However, if the amount of the policy is less than 80 percent of the value of the property, the insured does not receive the full amount of loss but only the proportion as determined in the formula above. Thus, in the example above, if the fire policy was for $60,000 and the property was 50 percent destroyed, the loss would be $50,000, of which the insurer would pay $37,500, which is 60,000/(100,000 × 80%) $50,000. On a total loss the recovery could not, of course, exceed the face amount of the policy. Some states, as shown in the following case do not favor co-insurance clauses and strictly construe the applicable statute against their validity.

SURRANT v. GRAIN
DEALERS MUTUAL
INSURANCE COMPANY

Court of Appeals of North
Carolina, 1985.
— N.C.App. —, 328 S.E.2d
16.

FACTS: The Surrants lost their home and personal property by fire. They sought to recover under their homeowner's insurance policy with Grain Dealers Mutual Insurance Company. The face amount of the policy was $30,000 for loss to the dwelling, $15,000 for personal property loss, and $6,000 for living expenses. The replacement cost provisions of the policy allowed the Surrants to collect the full repair or replacement costs only if they had insured their home for at least 80% of the full replacement cost. In addition, if the insurance was for less than the 80%, the Surrants were required to pay the difference between the amount of coverage and 80% of the full replacement costs. Based on these replacement provisions, Grain Dealers Mutual contends that the Surrants were underinsured. Therefore, they contend that they are only liable for the cost to repair the dwelling minus the amount the Surrants were underinsured.

DECISION: Judgment for the Surrants. The replacement provision in the Surrant policy required them to be co-insurers with Grain Dealers Mutual for a part of the loss described in the policy. It was, in effect, a co-insurance clause. According to North Carolina statute, absent the words "co-insurance contract" on the policy, a co-insurance clause is null and void. The insurer is then not entitled to any reduction of its liability under such a clause if the insured is underinsured. The Surrants' policy did not contain the words "co-insurance policy." Consequently, the replacement provision, essentially a co-insurance clause, is null and void. The Surrants, therefore, are entitled to recover the full $30,000 limit of the policy, plus amounts for living expenses and property loss within the policy's limits.

Recovery under non-life insurance policies is typically limited by "other insurance" clauses. These clauses generally require that liability be distributed *pro rata* among the various insurers. Thus, X insured his $120,000 building with A Insurance Co. for $60,000 and B Insurance Co. for $90,000. X's building is partially destroyed by fire causing X $20,000 in damages. X will collect $\frac{2}{5}\left(\frac{60,000}{150,000}\right)$ of his damages from A ($8,000) and $\frac{3}{5}\left(\frac{90,000}{150,000}\right)$ from B ($12,000).

Casualty Insurance

Casualty insurance is broad in scope but usually covers loss due to the damage or destruction of personal property by various causes other than fire or the elements. It is sometimes applied to personal injury or death or property loss due to accident.

Collision Insurance

Collision insurance protects the owner of an automobile against the risk of loss or damage due to contact with other vehicles or objects, usually subject to a deductability clause.

Liability Insurance

Liability insurance provides indemnification against loss by reason of liability of the insured for damages resulting from injuries to another's person or property. Although this kind of insurance is usually thought of in connection with automobiles, where it is often of greater interest to the injured person than to the driver who caused the injury, it is customarily carried by owners and lessees of real property to protect against public liability for injuries arising on the premises.

No-fault Insurance

A few States have legislatively adopted a system of compensating victims of automobile accidents regardless of liability. Generally, coverage is provided to the named insured, members of his household, authorized operators of the vehicle, passengers, and pedestrians for personal injury caused by a motor vehicle accident involving the insured's vehicle.

Group Insurance

Group insurance covers a number of individuals, all with some common interest, under a blanket or single policy. This insurance is usually either life or accident and health insurance. The term "group" insurance simply refers to the method of selling standard types of insurance.

Title Insurance

Title insurance provides indemnity against loss arising from defects in the title to real estate or due to liens or encumbrances on the property. An owner's title insurance policy is issued in the amount of the purchase price of the property and guarantees the owner against any loss due to defects in the title to the property or due to liens or encumbrances, except for those stated in the policy as existing at the time the policy is issued. Such policies may also be issued to mortgagees or to tenants of property to protect their interests.

Nature of Insurance Contracts

The basic principles of **contract** law apply to insurance policies. However, insurance companies engage in a large volume of business over wide areas, and therefore their policies are standardized. In some States standardization is required by statute. This usually means that the insured must accept a given policy or do without the desired insurance.

Offer and Acceptance

No matter how aggressively a life insurance agent has solicited a person to take out a policy, it is generally true that it is the applicant who makes the offer, and the contract is created when that offer is accepted by the company. The company's acceptance may be conditioned, for instance, on payment of the premium or delivery of the policy while the insured is in good health. If the company writes a policy that differs from the application, then it is the company that makes a counteroffer that the applicant may or may not choose to accept. This situation arises most frequently where the company is unwilling to write the policy that the agent proposed because of the results of a physical examination of the applicant but is willing to write a different policy based on the particular risk involved.

Life insurance agents, therefore, usually cannot bind the company to a contract with the insured, although on occasion an authorized agent may issue a **binding receipt** acknowledging payment of the premium and providing for the issuance of a standard policy effective from the date of the medical examination so long as the company has no *bona fide* reason to reject the application. In fire and casualty insurance, agents often have authority to make the insurance effective immediately, when needed, by means of a **binder.** In

[handwritten margin note: Subrogation insurer steps into shoes of insured to go after 3rd party]

[handwritten margin note: Binder—making an agreement legally binding until the completion of the formal contract]

the event of a loss before the company has actually issued a policy, the binder will be effective on the same terms and conditions the policy would have had if it had been issued.

Insurable Interest

Insurable interest—a financial interest or close personal relationship in someone's life or property that justifies insuring the life or property

The concept of insurable interest has been developed over many years, primarily to eliminate gambling and to lessen the moral hazard. If a person could obtain an enforceable insurance policy on the life of anyone or a fire insurance policy on property that he did not own or in which he had no interest, he would be in a position to profit by the death of a stranger or the destruction of property that represented no loss to him. An insurable interest is a relationship that a person has to the insured person or with respect to certain property such that the happening of a possible, specific, damage-causing contingency would result in direct loss or injury to the first person. The purpose of insurance is protection against the risk of loss resulting from such a happening, not the realization of gain or profit.

Property Insurance   Ownership obviously creates an insurable interest in the property, whether the ownership is sole or concurrent. Moreover, a right deriving from a contract concerning the property also gives rise to an insurable interest. See *Butler v. Farmers Insurance Co of Arizona* below. For instance, shareholders in a closely held corporation have been held to have an insurable interest in the corporation's property. Lessees of property also have insurable interests, as do holders of security interests, such as mortgagees or conditional sellers. The insurable interest must exist at the time the property *loss* occurs. Property insurance policies are not assignable before loss occurs but are freely assignable after the loss.

BUTLER v. FARMERS
INSURANCE COMPANY
OF ARIZONA

Supreme Court of Arizona,
1980.
126 Ariz. 371, 616 P.2d 46.

FACTS: In 1976, Butler purchased a 1967 Austin-Healy for $3,500. He received an Arizona Certificate of Title and was unaware that the vehicle had been previously stolen. Two years later, Tucson police seized the automobile and returned it to its lawful owner. Butler was insured against loss of the vehicle by Farmers Insurance Company of Arizona. When Farmers Insurance denied his claim for benefits, Butler brought suit. Farmers Insurance based its refusal to reimburse Butler upon a lack of insurable interest.

DECISION: Judgment for Butler. Noting a split of authority on the issue, the Arizona Supreme Court held that a bona fide purchaser of a stolen automobile has an interest sufficient to qualify as insurable. The insurable interest requirement is designed to discourage the intentional destruction of the covered property in order to profit from the insurance proceeds. There is no greater risk of this occurring when the insured has a financial investment in the property and believes himself the true owner, than when the insured is, in actuality, the rightful owner. Moreover, an innocent purchaser may be liable to the true owner for the destruction of the property. Thus, the purchaser has an interest in insuring the property. Consequently, Butler had an insurable interest.

Life Insurance   Only close relatives, creditors, and business associates or employers, depending generally on the particular facts involved, may take out insurance on another's life. An insured, however, may take out a policy on her own life and name anyone she chooses as beneficiary, even though that particular beneficiary may have no insurable interest in the insured's life. The insurable interest must exist at the time the *policy* is taken out and as shown in the case which follows need not exist at the time of death. An insured may assign the life policy proceeds to a third person who has no insurable interest.

SECOR v. PIONEER FOUNDRY COMPANY

Court of Appeals of
Michigan, 1969.
20 Mich.App. 30, 173
N.W.2d 780.

FACTS: Pioneer Foundry Company employed Jack Secor for a period of 9 years, 1954 to 1963. In 1960, Pioneer Foundry obtained a $50,000 insurance policy on his life; Pioneer was the applicant, the owner, and the beneficiary, and it paid the premiums on the policy. After the employment relationship ended in July, 1963, Pioneer Foundry paid the March, 1964 annual premium of $5,625. Secor died the following month. Pioneer Foundry had paid over $28,000 in premiums before he died. The insurer paid the proceeds of the policy to Pioneer Foundry in May, 1964. Jack's widow, Florence, sued Pioneer Foundry to recover these proceeds. She contends that after the termination of Secor's employment, Pioneer Foundry lost whatever insurable interest it had in Secor's life. Furthermore, she contended that to pay the insured's former employer violates the public policy against speculation on the life of another.

DECISION: Judgment for Pioneer Foundry. Generally, only an insurer can raise the defense of lack of insurable interest. In this case, the insurer paid Pioneer Foundry without raising this defense. Consequently, Florence has no standing to sue Pioneer Foundry on the issue of lack of insurable interest. Even if she could raise this issue she would not prevail. The general rule is that if an insurable interest exists when an ordinary life insurance policy is issued, the beneficiary may collect although the insurable interest subsequently terminates. Accordingly, an employer (beneficiary of a policy) insuring the life of an employee may collect the proceeds, even though the employee's death occurs after the termination of his employment. Here, Pioneer Foundry's life insurance policy on its employee, Secor was an investment, not a speculation on Jack's life. An insurable interest existed when this policy was issued. In addition, Pioneer Foundry had paid over $28,000 on the investment. To terminate its rights because Jack's employment relationship had changed would adversely affect the investment and provide the insurer with an unwarranted windfall. Therefore, Pioneer Foundry can recover the full amount of the $50,000 policy.

Premiums

Life insurance companies usually receive premiums from insured parties over periods of years. These premiums are fixed in amount and are such that the company will be able to pay the principal sum when the policy matures on the death of the insured through the accumulation of reserves. Life insurance premiums are calculated on the basis of (1) mortality rates, (2) interest, and (3) expense.

Premium –amount to be paid, often in installments, for an insurance policy

Casualty insurance policies are written only for periods of a few years at most. Long, continued liability on this type of policy is the exception rather than the rule. The rates that may be charged for fire and various kinds of casualty insurance are regulated by State law. The regulatory authorities are under a duty to require that the companies' rates be reasonable, not unfairly discriminatory, and neither excessively high nor inadequately low.

Double Indemnity

A provision found in some life insurance contracts provides for the recovery of "double indemnity," or twice the face amount of the policy, in the event of accidental death or death that results "directly and independently of all other causes from bodily injuries sustained solely from external, violent, and accidental means."

Defenses of the Insurer

In addition to the ordinary defenses to a contract, the insurer may assert the closely related defenses of misrepresentation, breach of warranty, and concealment.

Misrepresentations   A representation is a statement made by or on behalf of an applicant for insurance to induce an insurer to enter into a contract. The representation is not a part of the insurance contract, but if the application containing the representation is incorporated by reference into the contract, as in liability or burglary insurance, the representation becomes a warranty. For a representation to have legal consequences, it must have been relied on by the insurer as an inducement to enter into the contract and it mut have been substantially false when made or must have become so, to the insured's knowledge, before the contract was created. For an example see *Hawkeye-Security Insurance Co. v. Government Employees Ins. Co.* which follows. The principal remedy of the insurer on discovery of the material misrepresentation is rescission of the contract. To rescind the contract, the insurer must return to the insured all premiums that have been paid, because a rescission restores the parties to the position they were in before the contract was made. To be effective, rescission must be made as soon as possible after discovery of the misrepresentation.

HAWKEYE-SECURITY INSURANCE COMPANY v. GOVERNMENT EMPLOYEES INSURANCE CO.

Supreme Court of Virginia, 1967.
207 Va. 944, 154 S.E.2d 173.

FACTS: On August 18, 1962, Einer Mattson, Jr., was involved in a collision with an automobile driven by William Droughn. At the time, Mattson, Jr., was operating a car owned by his father Einer Mattson, Sr., and with his father's consent. Mattson, Sr. reported the accident to Government Employees Insurance Company (GEICO), the company that had issued Mattson, Sr. the liability policy on which his son was an additional insured. On November 20, 1962, GEICO wrote Mattson, Sr. advising him that his policy was null and void because of a material misrepresentation in his application as well as sending a refund of the premiums paid to date. Then, on September 22, 1964, Droughn recovered a judgment for $2,000 against Mattson, Jr., for injuries suffered in the wreck.

The alleged misrepresentation concerns Mattson's denial that any insurance company had ever refused to issue, canceled, or refused to renew a policy of insurance. In fact, a policy that Mattson, Sr. had with State Farm Mutual Insurance Company prior to the GEICO policy in question here had been canceled for "general underwriting reasons."

DECISION: Judgment for GEICO. Although Mattson, Sr., answered the question regarding prior insurance policies incorrectly, such a falsification will not bar recovery unless GEICO can show that the answer or statement was material to the risk when assumed and was untrue. A fact is material to the risk to be assumed by an insurance company if the fact would reasonably influence the company's decision whether or not to issue a policy. Here, the misrepresentation by Mattson, Sr., was clearly a false representation of a material fact since it caused GEICO to forego an opportunity to investigate why the State Farm policy was canceled. This investigation in turn would have allowed GEICO to determine whether or not the risk should be assumed as well as the premium rate applicable to the risk in the event the policy was issued. Therefore, since the misrepresentation by Mattson, Sr., was material to the risk when assumed, the policy was null and void from the outset.

Incontestability clause—the prohibition of an insurer to avoid an insurance policy after a specified period of time

Rescission may or may not be available to the life insurer, however, because of the **incontestability clause,** which generally makes the policy incontestable by the insurer after a specified period of time, generally two years, after the policy has been in effect. The incontestability clause, however, does not prevent the insurer from contesting the policy for failure to pay the premiums, for misrepresentation of age, for lack of an insurable interest by the policy owner, and for false impersonation, as, for example, when the physical examination is taken by another person. If the applicant for insurance **misstates his age,** the amount of insurance is simply reduced to that sum that the premiums paid would have purchased at the insured's correct age.

An innocent misrepresentation of a material fact (not opinion) before the running of the incontestability clause is a sufficient ground for avoidance of a policy by the insurer. Whether the fact is material or not usually depends on whether the policy would have been issued if the truth had been known. An immaterial misrepresentation, even though fraudulently made, is not a ground for avoidance of the policy.

Breach of Warranty   Warranties are of great importance in insurance contracts because they operate as conditions that *must* exist before the contract is effective or before the insurer's promise to pay is enforceable. Failure of the condition to exist or to occur relieves the insurer from any obligation to perform its promise. Broadly speaking, a condition is simply an event whose happening or failure to happen precedes the existence of a legal relationship or terminates one previously existing. Conditions are either precedent or subsequent. For example, payment of the premium is a condition precedent to the enforcement of the insurer's promise, as is the happening of the insured event. A condition subsequent is an event that ends an existing legal obligation. A provision in a policy to the effect that the insured shall not be liable unless suit is brought within twelve months from the date of the occurrence of the loss is an example of a condition subsequent.

Usually, the statements in policies that the insurer considers as express warranties can be identified by the use of such words as "warrant" or "on condition that" or "provided that." Other statements that are important to the risk assumed, such as the building address in the case where personal property at a particular location is insured against fire, are sometimes held to be informal warranties. Generally, the trend is away from allowing an insurer to avoid liability on the policy for *any* breach of a warranty by an insured; the breach must usually be material to have such an effect.

Concealment   Although rarely in life insurance, the doctrine of concealment has vitality in other fields of insurance. Concealment is simply the failure of an applicant for insurance to disclose material facts that the insurer does not know. The nondisclosure must normally be fraudulent as well as material to invalidate the policy; the applicant must have had reason to believe that the fact was material, and its disclosure must have affected the acceptance of the risk by the insurer.

Waiver and Estoppel   In certain instances, an insurer who normally would be entitled to deny liability under a policy because of a misrepresentation, breach of condition, or concealment is "estopped" from taking advantage of the defense or else is said to have "waived" the right to rely on it because of other facts.

The terms "waiver" and "estoppel" are used interchangeably, but by definition they are not synonymous. As generally defined, *waiver* is the intentional relinquishment of a known right, and *estoppel* means that a person is prevented by his own conduct from asserting a position that is inconsistent with acts of his that another person justifiably relied on.

Because a corporation such as an insurance company can act only through agents, situations involving waiver invariably are based on an agent's conduct. The higher the agent's position in the company's organization, the more likely is his conduct to bind the company, since an agent acting within the scope of his authority binds the principal. Insureds have the right to rely on representations made by the insurer's employees, and where such representations reasonably induce or cause a change of position by the insured or prevent the insured from causing a condition to occur, the insurer may not assert the failure of the condition to occur, whether the term applied to the situation is "waiver" or "estoppel." Companies have tried in many ways to limit the authority of local selling agents to bind the company through waiver or estoppel, but this is difficult to do effectively.

As a general rule, when a local agent delivers a policy with knowledge of the nonoccurrence of a condition precedent to the company's liability that would make the policy void or voidable at the company's option, the condition is waived. Although there is always a question about whether the agent had authority to waive the condition, most courts will find an effective waiver even though the condition is a delivery-in-good-health clause of the medical-treatment clause in a life insurance policy. These clauses provide that a life insurance policy shall not take effect unless delivered to the applicant while his insurability or good health continues and that the policy shall not take effect if the applicant has been treated by a physician or has been hospitalized between the date of the application and the date of delivery of the policy.

Performance and Termination

Most contracts of insurance are performed according to their terms, and due performance terminates the insurer's obligation. Normally, the insurer pays the principal sum due and the contract is thereby performed and discharged.

Cancellation   Cancellation of an insurance contract by mutual consent is another way of terminating it. Cancellation by the insurer alone means that the insurer is liable according to the terms of the policy until the time that the cancellation is effective. The right of cancellation is not always available to insurers, but where available, it is sometimes mistakenly used where rescission is preferable from the insurer's point of view. If an insurer under an accident policy elects to cancel after the occurrence of an insured event, where a right of rescission existed because of material misrepresentation, this will be taken as an admission of liability for events that occurred before cancellation. To cancel a policy, the insurer must return the unearned portion of the premium to the insured. To rescind a policy, the insurer must return all premiums received to the insured.

Notice   After the occurrence of the insured event, the owner of the policy or the insured is required to give notice to the insurer and, in the case of property insurance, proof of loss within a specified time, such as sixty days for fire insurance. In liability policies, the requirement of immediate notice is construed by the courts as notice within a "reasonable" time.

Automobile liability policies require that the insured immediately notify the insurer of any accident or occurrence that may involve liability. Notice requirements are conditions precedent to the insurer's contractual liability but may be waived by the insurer.

CHAPTER SUMMARY

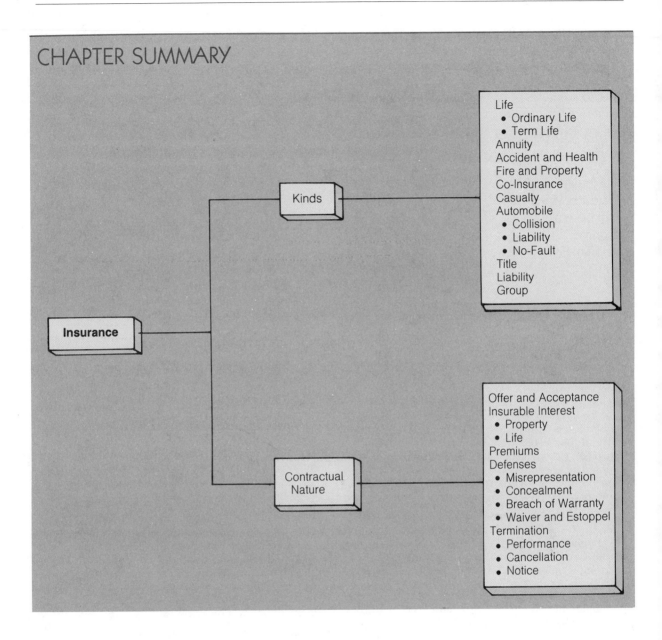

KEY TERMS

Insurance	Accident insurance	Binder
Insured	Health insurance	Insurable interest
Insurer	Fire insurance	Premium
Life insurance	Co-insurance	Double indemnity
Ordinary life	Casualty	Misrepresentation
Cash surrender value	Collision	Incontestability clause
Straight life	Liability	Warranty
Limited payment life	No-fault	Concealment
Single premium life	Group insurance	Waiver
Term life	Title	Estoppel
Endowment	Rider	Cancellation
Annuity		

PROBLEMS

1. Lile, an insurance broker, handled all insurance for X Co. Lile purchased a fire policy from Insurance Company insuring X Co's factory against fire in the amount of $150,000. Before the policy was delivered to X Co. and while it was still in Lile's hands, X Co. advised Lile to cancel the policy. But before the cancellation took effect, X Co. suffered a loss. Now X Co. makes a claim against Insurance Company on the policy. The premium had been billed to Lile but was unpaid at the time of loss. In an action by X Co. against Insurance Company, what judgment?

2. On July 15, A purchased in Chicago a Buick sedan, intending to drive it that day to St. Louis, Missouri. He telephoned a friend X who was in the insurance business and told him that he wanted liability insurance on the automobile, limited in amount to $50,000 for injuries to one person and $100,000 for any one accident. X took the order and told A over the telephone that he was covered and that his policy would be written by the Y Insurance Company. Later that same day and before X had informed the Y Insurance Company of A's application, A negligently operated the automobile and seriously injured B, who brings suit against A. Is A covered by liability insurance?

3. A owns a building having a fair market value of $120,000. She takes out a fire insurance policy with an 80 percent co-insurance clause from the B Insurance Company for $72,000. The building is damaged by fire to the extent of $48,000. How much insurance is A entitled to collect?

4. The B Automobile Insurance Company issues to A, the owner of a Mercury automobile, a liability policy with $30,000–$60,000 limits. On April 3, as the result of A's negligent operation of his car, C, D, and E are injured in a collision. C, D, and E sue A and recover judgments of $45,000, $9,000, and $6,000, respectively. To what extent is the B Company liable?

5. Arthur Heartburn, having knowledge of a bad heart condition, arranges to have his friend, Ira Impostor, represent himself as Heartburn to the medical examiner of the Taken Life Insurance Company. Impostor, posing as Heartburn, is found to be physically sound, and the Insurance Company issues a $75,000 life insurance policy to Heartburn. The policy contains a two-year incontestable clause. Twenty-six months after policy is issued Heartburn suffers a heart attack and dies. Before paying off the claim of Heartburn's widow, the beneficiary under the policy, the Insurance Company learns about Impostor's actions in helping Heartburn procure the policy. When the Taken Insurance Company refuses to pay the claim, the widow files suit on the policy. Decision?

6. Wiley, an insurance salesman, induces Glutz to purchase a $60,000 life insurance policy on the life of his best friend Doe and at the same time sells a policy to Doe insuring Glutz's life. After ten years Doe dies, and on due proof of death the insurance company denies liability. Glutz sues the company. Decision?

7. Kay was issued a $30,000 life insurance policy by Atlantic Bell Life Insurance Company. In her application Kay truthfully warranted that she was a professional actress and that she was not engaged in the employ of a railroad company or an airplane company. The policy provided that the company insured "the life of Kay so long as she engaged solely in the business of a professional actress." The policy also provided:

> This policy shall be incontestable for any cause after it shall have been in force during the life of the insured for two years from its date.

After the policy had been in effect for three years, Kay was killed while employed as a brakeman by a railroad company. Kay was so employed without the knowledge and consent of the insurance company. The beneficiary of the policy sued the company to recover the face amount of the policy. The company defended, denying liability on the ground that Kay was employed by a railroad company at the time of her death and had been so employed for six months previously. Decision?

8. Paul Poe purchased a life insurance policy in the sum of $100,000. The policy provided: "The proceeds of this policy are payable upon the death of the insured to Penelope Poe, wife of the insured." The policy also provided that Poe had the right to change the name of the beneficiary. Four years after he purchased the policy, Poe obtained a divorce from Penelope. One year later, Poe married Dora Doe, and this marriage continued until Poe's death two years later. At Poe's death the policy remained in its original form. Penelope demanded that the insurance company pay her the proceeds of the policy. When it refused, she brought an action against the company to recover $100,000. Decision?

9. Day had for some time been seeking out Short to "teach him a lesson" for taking out Day's girlfriend, and Day carried a pistol for this purpose. Eventually, Day caught up with Short at a local beer parlor and without warning, fired a shot at Short. Day's aim was not too good, for the shot only creased Short's head. Short dove at Day, and a scuffle ensued. During the scuffle Day fell to the floor, hitting his head on the bar railing. As a direct result of this blow to his head, Day died. At the time of his death, Day had in effect a policy of accidental death insurance in which the insurance company had agreed to pay the named beneficiary, Day's mother, $70,000 on the death of Day if the death were "effected solely through external, violent, and accidental means." The insurance company refused to pay the beneficiary. What are the beneficiary's rights, if any?

APPENDIX A

THE CONSTITUTION OF THE UNITED STATES OF AMERICA

We the People of the United States, in Order to form a more perfect Union, establish Justice, insure domestic Tranquility, provide for the common defense, promote the general Welfare, and secure the Blessings of Liberty to ourselves and our Posterity, do ordain and establish this Constitution for the United States of America.

Article I

Section 1

All legislative Powers herein granted shall be vested in a Congress of the United States, which shall consist of a Senate and House of Representatives.

Section 2

The House of Representatives shall be composed of Members chosen every second Year by the People of the several States, and the Electors in each State shall have the Qualifications requisite for Electors of the most numerous Branch of the State Legislature.

No Person shall be a Representative who shall not have attained to the Age of twenty five Years, and been seven Years a Citizen of the United States, and who shall not, when elected, be an Inhabitant of that State in which he shall be chosen.

Representatives and direct Taxes shall be apportioned among the several States which may be included within this Union, according to their respective Numbers, which shall be determined by adding to the whole Number of free Persons, including those bound to Service for a Term of Years, and excluding Indians not taxed, three fifths of all other Persons. The actual Enumeration shall be made within three Years after the first Meeting of the Congress of the United States, and within every subse-quent Term of ten Years, in such Manner as they shall by Law direct. The number of Representatives shall not exceed one for every thirty Thousand, but each State shall have at Least one Representative; and until such enumeration shall be made, the State of New Hampshire shall be entitled to chuse three, Massachusetts eight, Rhode Island and Povidence Plantations one, Connecticut five, New-York six, New Jersey four, Pennsylvania eight, Delaware one, Maryland six, Virginia ten, North Carolina five, South Craolina five, and Georgia three.

When vacancies happen in the Representation from any State, the Executive Authority thereof shall issue Writs of Election to fill such vacancies.

The House of Representatives shall chuse their Speaker and other Officers; and shall have the sole Power of Impeachment.

Section 3

The Senate of the United States shall be composed of two Senators from each State, chosen by the Legislature thereof, for six Years; and each Senator shall have one Vote.

Immediately after they shall be assembled in Consequence of the first Election, they shall be divided as equally as may be into three Classes. The Seats of the Senators of the first Class shall be vacated at the Expiration of the second Year, of the second Class at the Expiration of the fourth Year, and of the third Class at the Expiration of the sixth Year, so that one third may be chosen every second Year; and if Vacancies happen by Resignation, or otherwise, during the Recess of the Legislature of any State, the Executive thereof may make temporary Appointments until the next Meeting of the Legislature, which shall then fill such Vacancies.

No Person shall be a Senator who shall not have attained to the Age of thirty Years, and been nine Years a Citizen of the United States, and who shall not, when elected, be an Inhabitant of that State for which he shall be chosen.

The Vice President of the United States shall be President of the Senate, but shall have no Vote, unless they be equally divided.

The Senate shall chuse their other Officers, and also a President pro tempore, in the Absence of the Vice President, or when he shall exercise the Office of President of the United States.

The Senate shall have the sole power to try all Impeachments. When sitting for that Purpose, they shall be an Oath or Affirmation. When the President of the United States is tried, the Chief Justice shall preside: And no Person shall be convicted without the Concurrence of two thirds of the Members present.

Judgment in Cases of Impeachment shall not extend further than to removal from Office, and disqualification to hold and enjoy any Office of honor, Trust or Profit under the United States: but the Party convicted shall nevertheless be liable and subject to Indictment, Trial, Judgment and Punishment, according to Law.

Section 4

The Times, Places and Manner of holding Elections for Senators and Representatives, shall be prescribed in each State by the Legislature thereof: but the Congress may at any time by Law make or alter such Regulations, except as to the Places of chusing Senators.

The Congress shall assemble at least once in every Year, and such Meeting shall be on the first Monday in December, unless they shall by Law appoint a different Day.

Section 5

Each House shall be the Judge of the Elections, Returns and Qualifications of its own Members, and a Majority of each shall constitute a Quorum to do Business; but a smaller Number may adjourn from day to day, and may be authorized to compel the Attendance of absent Members, in such Manner, and under such Penalties as each House may provide.

Each House may determine the Rules of its Proceedings, punish its Members for disorderly Behaviour, and, with the Concurrence of two thirds, expel a Member.

Each House shall keep a Journal of its Proceedings, and from time to time publish the same, excepting such Parts as may in their Judgment require Secrecy; and the Yeas and Nays of the Members of either House on any question shall, at the Desire of one fifth of those Present, be entered on the Journal.

Neither House, during the Session of Congress, shall, without the Consent of the other, adjourn for more than three days, nor to any other Place than that in which the two Houses shall be sitting.

Section 6

The Senators and Representatives shall receive a Compensation for their Services, to be ascertained by Law, and paid out of the Treasury of the United States. They shall in all Cases, except Treason, Felony and Breach of the Peace, be privileged from Arrest during their Attendance at the Session of their respective Houses, and in going to and returning from the same; and for any Speech or Debate in either House, they shall not be questioned in any other Place.

No Senator or Representative shall, during the Time for which he was elected, be appointed to any civil Office under the Authority of the United States, which shall have been created, or the Emoluments whereof shall have been encreased during such time; and no Person holding any Office under the United States, shall be a Member of either House during his Continuance in Office.

Section 7

All Bills for raising Revenue shall originate in the House of Representatives; but the Senate may propose or concur with Amendments as on other Bills.

Every Bill which shall have passed the House of Representatives and the Senate, shall, before it become a Law, be presented to the President of the United States; If he approve he shall sign it, but if not he shall return it, with his Objections to that House in which it shall have originated, who shall enter the Objections at large on their Journal, and proceed to reconsider it. If after such Reconsideration two thirds of that House shall agree to pass the Bill, it shall be sent, together with the Objections, to the other House, by which it shall likewise be reconsidered, and if approved by two thirds of that House, it shall become a Law. But in all such Cases the Votes of both Houses shall be determined by Yeas and Nays, and the Names of the Persons voting for and against the Bill shall be entered on the Journal of each House respectively. If any Bill shall not be returned by the President within ten Days (Sundays excepted) after it shall have been presented to him, the Same shall be a Law, in like Manner as if he had signed it, unless the Congress by their Adjournment prevent its Return, in which Case it shall not be a Law.

Every Order, Resolution, or Vote to which the Concurrence of the Senate and House of Representatives may be necessary (except on a question of Adjournment) shall be presented to the President of the United States; and before the Same shall take Effect, shall be approved by him, or being disapproved by him, shall be repassed by two thirds of the Senate and House of Representatives, according to the Rules and Limitations prescribed in the Case of a Bill.

Section 8

The Congress shall have Power to lay and collect Taxes, Duties, Imposts and Excises, to pay the Debts and provide for the common Defence and general Welfare of the United States; but all Duties, Imposts and Excises shall be uniform throughout the United States;

To borrow Money on the credit of the United States;

To regulate Commerce with foreign Nations, and among the several States, and with the Indian Tribes;

To establish an uniform Rule of Naturalization, and uniform Laws on the subject of Bankruptcies throughout the United States;

To coin Money, regulate the Value thereof, and of foreign Coin, and fix the Standard of Weights and Measures;

To provide for the Punishment of counterfeiting the Securities and current Coin of the United States;

To establish Post Offices and post Roads;

To promote the Progress of Science and useful Arts, by securing for limited Times to Authors and Inventors the exclusive Right to their respective Writings and Discoveries;

To constitute Tribunals inferior to the supreme Court;

To define and punish Piracies and Felonies committed on the high Seas, and Offenses against the Law of Nations;

To declare War, grant Letters of Marque and Reprisal, and make Rules concerning Captures on Land and Water;

To raise and support Armies, but no Appropriation of Money to that Use shall be for a longer Term than two Years;

To provide and maintain a Navy;

To make Rules for the Government and Regulation of the land and naval Forces;

To provide for calling forth the Militia to execute the Laws of the Union, suppress Insurrections and repel Invasions;

To provide for organizing, arming, and disciplining, the Militia, and for governing such Part of them as may be employed in the Service of the United States, reserving to the States respectively, the Appointment of the Officers, and the Authority of training the Militia according to the discipline described by Congress;

To exercise exclusive Legislation in all Cases whatsoever, over such District (not exceeding ten Miles square) as may, by Cession of particular States, and the Acceptance of Congress, become the Seat of the Government of the United States, and to exercise like Authority over all Places purchased by the Consent of the Legislature of the State in which the Same shall be, for the Erection of Forts, Magazines, Arsenals, dock-Yards, and other needful Buildings;—And

To make all Laws which shall be necessary and proper for carrying into Execution the foregoing Powers, and all other Powers vested by this Constitution in the Government of the United States, or in any Department or Officer thereof.

Section 9

The Migration or Importation of such Persons as any of the States now existing shall think proper to admit, shall not be prohibited by the Congress prior to the Year one thousand eight hundred and eight, but a Tax or Duty may be imposed on such Importation, not exceeding ten dollars for each Person.

The Privilege of the Writ of Habeas Corpus shall not be suspended, unless when in Cases of Rebellion or Invasion the public Safety may require it.

No Bill of Attainder or ex post facto Law shall be passed.

No Capitation, or other direct, Tax shall be laid, unless in Proportion to the Census or Enumeration herein before directed to be taken.

No Tax or Duty shall be laid on Articles exported from any State.

No Preference shall be given by any Regulation of Commerce or Revenue to the Ports of one State over those of another; nor shall Vessels bound to, or from, one State, be obliged to enter, clear, or pay Duties in another.

No Money shall be drawn from the Treasury, but in Consequence of Appropriations made by Laws; and a regular Statement and Account of the Receipts and Expenditures of all public Money shall be published from time to time.

No Title of Nobility shall be granted by the United States: And no Person holding any Office of Profit or Trust under them, shall, without the Consent of the Congress, accept of any present, Emolument, Office, or Title, of any kind whatever, from any King, Prince, or foreign State.

Section 10

No State shall enter into any Treaty, Alliance, or Confederation; grant Letters of Marque and Reprisal; coin Money; emit Bills of Credit; make any Thing but gold and silver Coin a Tender in Payment of Debts; pass any Bill of Attainder, ex post facto Law, or Law impairing the Obligation of Contracts, or grant any Title of Nobility.

No State shall, without the Consent of the Congress, lay any Imposts or Duties on Imports or Exports, except what may be absolutely necessary for executing its inspection Laws: and the net Produce of all Duties and Imposts, laid by any State on Imports or Exports, shall be for the Use of the Treasury of the United States; and all such Laws shall be subject to the Revision and Controul of the Congress.

No State shall, without the Consent of Congress, lay any Duty of Tonnage, keep Troops, or Ships of War in time of Peace, enter into any Agreement or Compact with another State, or with a foreign Power, or engage in War, unless actually invaded, or in such imminent Danger as will not admit of delay.

Article II

Section 1

The executive Power shall be vested in a President of the United States of America. He shall hold his Office during the Term of four Years, and, together with the Vice President, chosen for the same Term, be elected, as follows:

Each State shall appoint, in such Manner as the Legislature thereof may direct, a Number of Electors, equal to the whole Number of Senators and Representatives to which the State may be entitled in the Congress: but no Senator or Representative, or Person holding an Office of Trust or Profit under the United States, shall be appointed an Elector.

The Electors shall meet in their respective States, and vote by Ballot for two Persons, of whom one at least shall not be an Inhabitant of the same State with themselves. And they shall make a list of all the Persons voted for, and of the Number of Votes for each; which List they shall sign and certify, and transmit sealed to the Seat of the Government of the United States, directed to the President of the Senate. The President of the Senate shall, in the presence of the Senate and House of Representatives, open all the Certificates, and the Votes shall be counted. The Person having the greatest Number of Votes shall be the President, if such Number be a Majority of the whole Number of Electors appointed; and

if there be more than one who have such Majority, and have an equal Number of Votes, then the House of Representatives shall immediately chuse by Ballot one of them for President; and if no Person have a Majority, then from the five highest on the List the said House shall in like Manner chuse the President. But in chusing the President, the Votes shall be taken by States, the Representation from each State having one Vote; A quorum for this Purpose shall consist of a Member or Members from two thirds of the States, and a Majority of all the States shall be necessary to a Choice. In every Case, after the Choice of the President, the Person having the greatest Number of Votes of the Electors shall be the Vice President. But if there should remain two or more who have equal Votes, the Senate shall chuse from them by Ballot the Vice President.

The Congress may determine the Time of Chusing the Electors, and the Day on which they shall give their Votes; which Day shall be the same throughout the United States.

No Person except a natural born Citizen, or a Citizen of the United States, at the time of the Adoption of this Constitution, shall be eligible to the Office of President; neither shall any Person be eligible to that Office who shall not have attained to the Age of thirty five Years, and been fourteen Years a Resident within the United States.

In Case of the Removal of the President from Office, or of his Death, Resignation, or Inability to discharge the Powers and Duties of the said Office, the Same shall devolve on the Vice President, and the Congress may by Law provide for the Case of Removal, Death, Resignation or Inability, both of the President and Vice President, declaring what Officer shall then act as President, and such Officer shall act accordingly, until the Disability be removed, or a President shall be elected.

The President shall, at stated Times, receive for his Services, a Compensation, which shall neither be encreased nor diminished during the Period for which he shall have been elected, and he shall not receive within that Period any other Emolument from the United States, or any of them.

Before he enter on the Execution of his Office, he shall take the following Oath or Affirmation:—"I do solemnly swear (or affirm) that I will faithfully execute the Office of President of the United States, and will to the best of my Ability, preserve, protect and defend the Constitution of the United States."

Section 2

The President shall be Commander in Chief of the Army and Navy of the United States, and of the Militia of the several States, when called into the actual Service of the United States; he may require the Opinion, in writing, of the principal Officer in each of the executive Departments, upon any Subject relating to the Duties of their respective Offices, and he shall have Power to grant Reprieves and Pardons for Offences against the United States, except in Cases of Impeachment.

He shall have Power, by and with the Advice and Consent of the Senate, to make Treaties, providing two thirds of the Senators present concur; and he shall nominate, and by and with the Advice and Consent of the Senate, shall appoint Ambassadors, other public Ministers and Consuls, Judges of the supreme Court, and all other Officers of the United States, whose Appointments are not herein otherwise provided for, and which shall be established by Law: but the Congress may by Law vest the Appointment of such inferior Officers, as they think proper, in the President alone, in the Courts of Law, or in the Heads of Departments.

The President shall have Power to fill up all Vacancies that may happen during the Recess of the Senate, by granting Commissions which shall expire at the End of their next Session.

Section 3

He shall from time to time give to the Congress Information of the State of the Union, and recommend to their Consideration such Measures as he shall judge necessary and expedient; he may, on extraordinary Occasions, convene both Houses, or either of them, and in Case of Disagreement between them, with Respect to the Time of Adjournment, he may adjourn them to such Time as he shall think proper, he shall receive Ambassadors and other public Ministers; he shall take Care that the Laws be faithfully executed, and shall Commission all the Offices of the United States.

Section 4

The President, Vice President and all civil Officers of the United States, shall be removed from Office on Impeachment for, and Conviction of, Treason, Bribery, or other high Crimes and Misdemeanors.

Article III

Section 1

The judicial Power of the United States, shall be vested in one supreme Court, and in such inferior Courts as the Congress may from time to time ordain and establish. The Judges, both of the supreme and inferior Courts, shall hold their Offices during good Behaviour, and shall,

at Times, receive for their Services, a Compensation, which shall not be diminished during their Continuance in Office.

Section 2

The judicial Power shall extend to all Cases, in Law and Equity, arising under this Constitution, the Laws of the United States, and Treaties made, or which shall be made, under their Authority;—to all Cases affecting Ambassadors, other public Ministers and Consuls;—to all Cases of admirality and maritime Jurisdiction;—to Controversies to which the United States shall be a Party;—to Controversies between two or more States;—between a State and Citizens of another State;—between Citizens of different States;—between Citizens of the same State claiming Lands under Grants of different States; and between a State, or the Citizens thereof, and foreign States, Citizens or Subjects.

In all Cases affecting Ambassadors, other public Ministers and Consuls, and those in which a State shall be Party, the supreme Court shall have original Jurisdiction. In all the other Cases before mentioned, the supreme Court shall have appellate Jurisdiction, both as to Law and Fact, with such Exceptions, and under such Regulations as the Congress shall make.

The Trial of all Crimes, except in Cases of Impeachment, shall be by Jury; and such Trial shall be held in the State where the said Crimes shall have been committed; but when not committed within any State, the Trial shall be at such Place or Places as the Congress may by Law have directed.

Section 3

Treason against the United States, shall consist only in levying War against them, or in adhering to their Enemies, giving them Aid and Comfort. No Person shall be convicted of Treason unless on the Testimony of two Witnesses to the same overt Act, or on Confession in open Court.

The Congress shall have Power to declare the Punishment of Treason, but no Attainder of Treason shall work Corruption of Blood, or Forfeiture except during the Life of the Person attainted.

Article IV

Section 1

Full Faith and Credit shall be given in each State to the public Acts, Records, and judicial Proceedings of every other State. And the Congress may by general Laws prescribe the Manner in which such Arts, Records and Proceedings shall be proved, and the Effect thereof.

Section 2

The Citizens of each State shall be entitled to all Privileges and Immunities of Citizens in the several States.

A Person charged in any State with Treason, Felony, or other Crime, who shall flee from Justice, and be found in another State, shall on Demand of the executive Authority of the State from which he fled, be delivered up, to be removed to the State having Jurisdiction of the Crime.

No Person held to Service or Labour in one State, under the Laws thereof, escaping into another, shall, in Consequence of any Law or Regulation therein, be discharged from such Service or Labour, but shall be delivered up on Claim of the Party to whom such Service or Labour may be due.

Section 3

New States may be admitted by the Congress into this Union; but no new State shall be formed or erected within the Jurisdiction of any other State; nor any State be formed by the Junction of two or more States, or Parts of States, without the Consent of the Legislatures of the States concerned as well as the Congress.

The Congress shall have Power to dispose of and make all needful Rules and Regulations respecting the Territory or other Property belonging to the United States; and nothing in this Constitution shall be so construed as to Prejudice any Claims of the United States, or of any particular State.

Section 4

The United States shall guarantee to every State in this Union a Republican Form of Government, and shall protect each of them against Invasion; and on Application of the Legislature, or of the Executive (when the Legislature cannot be convened) against domestic Violence.

Article V

The Congress, whenever two thirds of both Houses shall deem it necessary, shall propose Amendments to this Constitution, or, on the Application of the Legislatures of two thirds of the several States, shall call a Convention for proposing Amendments, which, in either Case, shall be valid to all Intents and Purposes, as Part of this Constitution, when ratified by the Legislatures of three fourths of the several States, or by Conventions in three fourths thereof, as the one or the other Mode of Ratification may be proposed by the Congress; Provided that no Amendment which may be made prior to the Year One thousand eight hundred and eight shall in any Manner affect the

first and fourth Clauses in the Ninth Section of the first Article; and that no State, without its Consent, shall be deprived of its equal Suffrage in the Senate.

Article VI

All Debts contracted and Engagements entered into, before the Adoption of this Constitution, shall be as valid against the United States under this Constitution, as under the Confederation.

This Constitution, and the Laws of the United States which shall be made in Pursuance thereof; and all Treaties made, or which shall be made, under the Authority of the United States, shall be the supreme Law of the Land; and the Judges in every State shall be bound thereby, any Thing in the Constitution or Laws of any State to the Contrary notwithstanding.

The Senators and Representatives before mentioned, and the Members of the several State Legislatures, and all executive and judicial Officers, both of the United States and of the Several States, shall be bound by Oath or Affirmation, to support this Constitution; but no religious Test shall ever be required as a Qualification to any Office or public Trust under the United States.

Article VII

The Ratification of the Conventions of nine States, shall be sufficient for the Establishment of this Constitution between the States so ratifying the Same.

Amendment I [1791]

Congress shall make no law respecting an establishment of religion, or prohibiting the free exercise thereof; or abridging the freedom of speech, or the press; or the right of the people peaceably to assemble, and to petition the Government for a redress of grievances.

Amendment II [1791]

A well regulated Militia, being necessary to the security for a free State, the right of the people to keep and bear Arms, shall not be infringed.

Amendment III [1791]

No Soldier shall, in time of peace be quartered in any house, without the consent of the Owner, nor in time of war, but in a manner to be prescribed by law.

Amendment IV [1791]

The right of the people to be secure in their persons, houses, papers, and effects, against unreasonable searches and seizures, shall not be violated, and no Warrants shall issue, but upon probable cause, supported by Oath or affirmation, and particularly describing the place to be searched, and the persons or things to be seized.

Amendment V [1791]

No person shall be held to answer for a capital, or otherwise infamous crime, unless on a presentment or indictment of a Grand Jury, except in cases arising in the land or naval forces, or in the Militia, when in actual service in time of War or public danger; nor shall any person be subject for the same offense to be twice put in jeopardy of life or limb; nor shall be compelled in any criminal case to be a witness against himself, nor be deprived of life, liberty, or property, without due process of law; nor shall private property be taken for public use, without just compensation.

Amendment VI [1791]

In all criminal prosecutions, the accused shall enjoy the right to a speedy and public trial, by an impartial jury of the State and district wherein the crime shall have been committed, which district shall have been previously ascertained by law, and to be informed of the nature and cause of the accusation; to be confronted with the Witnesses against him; to have compulsory process for obtaining witnesses in his favor, and to have the Assistance of counsel for his defence.

Amendment VII [1791]

In suits at common law, where the value in controversy shall exceed twenty dollars, the right of trial by jury shall be preserved, and no fact tried by a jury, shall be otherwise re-examined in any Court of the United States, than according to the rules of the common law.

Amendment VIII [1791]

Excessive bail shall not be required, no excessive fines imposed, nor cruel and unusual punishments inflicted.

Amendment IX [1791]

The enumeration in the Constitution, of certain rights, shall not be construed to deny or disparage others retained by the people.

Amendment X [1791]

The powers not delegated to the United States by the Constitution, nor prohibited by it to the States, are reserved to the States respectively, or to the people.

Amendment XI [1798]

The judicial power of the United States shall not be construed to extend to any suit in law or equity, commenced or prosecuted against one of the United States by Citizens of another State, or by Citizens or Subjects of any Foreign State.

Amendment XII [1804]

The Electors shall meet in their respective states and vote by ballot for President and Vice-President, one of whom, at least, shall not be an inhabitant of the same state with themselves; they shall name in their ballots the person voted for as President, and in distinct ballots the person voted for as Vice-President, and they shall make distinct lists of all persons voted for as President, and of all persons voted for as Vice-President, and of the number of votes for each, which lists they shall sign and certify, and transmit sealed to the seat of the government of the United States, directed to the President of the Senate;—The President of the Senate shall, in the presence of the Senate and House of Representatives, open all the certificates and the votes shall then be counted;—The person having the greatest number of votes for President, shall be the President, if such number be a majority of the whole number of Electors appointed; and if no person have such majority, then from the persons having the highest numbers not exceeding three on the list of those voted for as President, the House of Representatives shall choose immediately, by ballot, the President. But in choosing the President, the votes shall be taken by states, the representation from each state having one vote; a quorum for this purpose shall consist of a member or members from two-thirds of the states, and a majority of all the states shall be necessary to a choice. And if the House of Representatives shall not choose a President whenever the right of choice shall devolve upon them, before the fourth day of March next following, then the Vice-President shall act as President, as in the case of the death of other constitutional disability of the President. The person having the greatest number of votes as Vice-President, shall be the Vice-President, if such number be a majority of the whole number of Electors appointed, and if no person have a majority, then from the two highest numbers on the list, the Senate shall choose the Vice-President; a quorum for the purpose shall consist of two-thirds of the whole number of Senators, and a majority of the whole number shall be necessary to a choice. But no person constitutionally ineligible to the office of President shall be eligible to that of the Vice-President of the United States.

Amendment XIII [1865]

Section 1

Neither slavery nor involuntary servitude, except as a punishment for crime whereof the party shall have been duly convicted, shall exist within the United States, or any place subject to their jurisdiction.

Section 2

Congress shall have power to enforce this article by appropriate legislation.

Amendment XIV [1868]

All persons born or naturalized in the United States, and subject to the jurisdiction thereof, are citizens of the United States and of the State wherein they reside. No State shall make or enforce any law which shall abridge the privileges or immunities of citizens of the United States; nor shall any State deprive any person of life, liberty, or property, without due process of law; nor deny to any person within its jurisdiction the equal protection of the laws.

Section 2

Representatives shall be appointed among the several States according to their respective numbers, counting the whole number of persons in each State, excluding Indians not taxed. But when the right to vote at any election for the choice of electors for President and Vice President of the United States, Representatives in Congress, the Executive and Judicial officers of a State, or the members of the Legislature thereof, is denied to any of the male inhabitants of such State, being twenty-one years of age, and citizens of the United States, or in any way abridged, except for participation in rebellion, or other crime, the basis of representation therein shall be reduced in the proportion which the number of such male citizens shall bear the whole number of male citizens twenty-one years of age in such State.

Section 3

No person shall be a Senator or Representative in Congress, or elector of President and Vice President, or hold any office, civil or military, under the United States, or under any State, who, having previously taken an oath, as a member of Congress, or as an officer of the United States, or as a member of any State legislature, or as an executive or judicial officer of any State, to support the Constitution of the United States, shall have engaged in insurrection or rebellion against the same, or given aid or comfort to the enemies thereof. But Congress may by a vote of two-thirds of each House, remove such disability.

Section 4

The validity of the public debt of the United States, authorized by law, including debts incurred for payment of pensions and bounties for services in suppressing insurrection or rebellion, shall not be questioned. But neither the United States nor any State shall assume or pay any debt or obligation incurred in aid of insurrection of rebellion against the United States, or any claim for the loss or emancipation of any slave; but all such debts, obligations and claims shall be held illegal and void.

Section 5

The Congress shall have power to enforce, by appropriate legislation, the provisions of this article.

Amendment XV [1870]

Section 1

The right of citizens of the United States to vote shall not be denied or abridged by the United States or by any State on account of race, color, or previous condition of servitude.

Section 2

The Congress shall have power to enforce this article by appropriate legislation.

Amendment XVI [1913]

The Congress shall have power to lay and collect taxes on incomes, from whatever source derived, without apportionment among the several States, and without regard to any census or enumeration.

Amendment XVII [1913]

The Senate of the United States shall be composed of two Senators from each State, elected by the people thereof, for six years; and each Senator shall have one vote. The electors in each State shall have the qualifications requisite for electors of the most numerous branch of the State legislatures.

When vacancies happen in the representation of any State in the Senate, the executive authority of each State shall issue writs of election to fill such vacancies; *Provided,* That the legislature of any State may empower the executive thereof to make temporary appointments until the people fill the vacancies by election as the legislature may direct.

This amendment shall not be construed as to affect the election or term of any Senator chosen before it becomes valid as part of the Constitution.

Amendment XVIII [1919]

Section 1

After one year from the ratification of this article the manufacture, sale, or transportation of intoxicating liquors within, the importation thereof into, or the exportation thereof from the United States and all territory subject to the jurisdiction thereof for beverage purposes is hereby prohibited.

Section 2

The Congress and the several States shall have concurrent power to enforce this article by appropriate legislation.

Section 3

This article shall be inoperative unless it shall have been ratified as an amendment to the Constitution by the legislatures of the several States, as provided in the Constitution, within seven years from the date of the submission hereof to the States by the Congress.

Amendment XIX [1920]

The right of citizens of the United States to vote shall not be denied or abridged by the United States or by any State on account of sex.

Congress shall have power to enforce this article by appropriate legislation.

Amendment XX [1933]

Section 1

The terms of the President and Vice President shall end at noon on the 20th day of January, and the terms of Senators and Representatives at noon on the 3d day of January, of the years in which such terms would have ended if this article had not been ratified; and the terms of their successors shall then begin.

Section 2

The Congress shall assemble at least once in every year, and such meeting shall begin at noon on the 3d day of January, unless they shall by law appoint a different day.

Section 3

If, at the time fixed for the beginning of the term of the President, the President elect shall have died, the Vice President elect shall become President. If a President shall not have been chosen before the time fixed for the beginning of his term, or if the President elect shall have failed to qualify, then the Vice President elect shall act as President until a President shall have qualified; and the Congress may by law provide for the case wherein neither a President elect nor a Vice President elect shall have qualified, declaring who shall then act as President, or the manner in which one who is to act shall be selected, and such person shall act accordingly until a President or Vice President shall have qualified.

Section 4

The Congress may by law provide for the case of the death of any of the persons from whom the House of Representatives may choose a President whenever the right of choice shall have devolved upon them, and for the case of the death of any of the persons from whom the Senate may choose a Vice President whenever the right of choice shall have devolved upon them.

Section 5

Sections 1 and 2 shall take effect on the 15th day of October following the ratification of this article.

Section 6

This article shall be inoperative unless it shall have been ratified as an amendment to the Constitution by the legislatures of three-fourths of the several States within seven years from the date of its submission.

Amendment XXI [1933]

Section 1

The eighteenth article of amendment to the Constitution of the United States is hereby repealed.

Section 2

The transportation or importation into any State, Territory, or possession of the United States for delivery or use therein of intoxicating liquors, in violation of the laws thereof, is hereby prohibited.

Section 3

This article shall be inoperative unless it shall have been ratified as an amendment to the Constitution by conventions in the several States, as provided in the Constitution, within seven years from the date of the submission hereof to the States by the Congress.

Amendment XXII [1951]

Section 1

No person shall be elected to the office of the President more than twice, and no person who has held the office of President, or acted as President, for more than two years of a term to which some other person was elected President shall be elected to the office of the President more than once. But this Article shall not apply to any person holding the office of President when this Article was proposed by the Congress, and shall not prevent any person who may be holding the office of President, or acting as President, during the term within which this Article becomes operative from holding the office of President or acting as President during the remainder of such term.

Section 2

This article shall be inoperative unless it shall have been ratified as an amendment to the Constitution by the legislatures of three-fourths of the several States within seven years from the date of its submission to the States by the Congress.

Amendment XXIII [1961]

Section 1

The District constituting the seat of Government of the United States shall appoint in such manner as the Congress may direct:

A number of electors of President and Vice President equal to the whole number of Senators and Representatives in Congress to which the District would be entitled if it were a State, but in no event more than the least populous State; they shall be in addition to those appointed by the States, but they shall be considered, for the purposes of the election of President and Vice President, to be electors appointed by a State; and they shall meet in the District and perform such duties as provided by the twelfth article of amendment.

Section 2

The Congress shall have power to enforce this article by appropriate legislation.

Amendment XXIV [1964]

Section 1

The right of citizens of the United States to vote in any primary or other election for President or Vice President, for electors for President or Vice President, or for Sentor or Representative in Congress, shall not be denied or abridged by the United States or any State by reason of failure to pay any poll tax or other tax.

Section 2

The Congress shall have power to enforce this article by appropriate legislation.

Amendment XXV [1967]

Section 1

In case of the removal of the President from office or of his death or resignation, the Vice President shall become President.

Section 2

Whenever there is a vacancy in the office of the Vice President, the President shall nominate a Vice President who shall take office upon confirmation by a majority vote of both Houses of Congress.

Section 3

Whenever the President transmits to the President pro tempore of the Senate and the Speaker of the House of Representatives his written declaration that he is unable to discharge the powers and duties of his office, and until he transmits to them a written declaration to the contrary, such powers and duties shall be discharged by the Vice President as Acting President.

Section 4

Whenever the Vice President and a majority of either the principal officers of the executive departments or of such other body as Congress may by law provide, transmit to the President pro tempore of the Senate and the Speaker of the House of Representatives their written declaration that the President is unable to discharge the powers and duties of his office, the Vice President shall immediately assume the powers and duties of the office as Acting President.

Thereafter, when the President transmits to the President pro tempore of the Senate and the Speaker of the House of Representatives his written declaration that no inability exists, he shall resume the powers and duties of his office unless the Vice President and a majority of either the principal officers of the executive department or of such other body as Congress may by law provide, transmit within four days to the President pro tempore of the Senate and the Speaker of the House of Representatives their written declaration that the President is unable to discharge the powers and duties of his office. Thereupon Congress shall decide the issue, assembling within forty-eight hours for that purpose if not in session. If the Congress, within twenty-one days after receipt of the latter written declaration, or, if Congress is not in session, within twenty-one days after Congress is required to assemble, determines by two-thirds vote of both Houses that the President shall continue to discharge the same as Acting President; otherwise, the President shall resume the powers and duties of his office.

Amendment XXVI [1971]

Section 1

The right of citizens of the United States, who are eighteen years of age or older, to vote shall not be denied or abridged by the United States or by any State on account of age.

Section 2

The Congress shall have power to enforce this article by appropriate legislation.

APPENDIX B

THE UNIFORM COMMERCIAL CODE

(Adopted in 52 jurisdictions; all 50 States, although Louisiana has adopted only Articles 1, 3, 4, and 5; the District of Columbia, and the Virgin Islands.)

The Code consists of 10 Articles as follows:

Art.

1. GENERAL PROVISIONS
2. Sales
3. Commercial Paper
4. Bank Deposits and Collections
5. Letters of Credit
6. Bulk Transfers
7. Warehouse Receipts, Bills of Lading and Other Documents of Title
8. Investment Securities
9. Secured Transactions: Sales of Accounts, Contract Rights and Chattel Paper
10. Effective Date and Repealer

Article 1
GENERAL PROVISIONS

Part 1 **Short Title, Construction, Application and Subject Matter of the Act**

§ 1—101. **Short Title.**

This Act shall be known and may be cited as Uniform Commercial Code.

§ 1—102. **Purposes; Rules of Construction; Variation by Agreement.**

(1) This Act shall be liberally construed and applied to promote its underlying purposes and policies.

(2) Underlying purposes and policies of this Act are

(a) to simplify, clarify and modernize the law governing commercial transactions;

(b) to permit the continued expansion of commercial practices through custom, usage and agreement of the parties;

(c) to make uniform the law among the various jurisdictions.

(3) The effect of provisions of this Act may be varied by agreement, except as otherwise provided in this Act and except that the obligations of good faith, diligence, reasonableness and care prescribed by this Act may not be disclaimed by agreement but the parties may by agreement determine the standards by which the performance of such obligations is to be measured if such standards are not manifestly unreasonable.

(4) The presence in certain provisions of this Act of the words "unless otherwise agreed" or words of similar import does not imply that the effect of other provisions may not be varied by agreement under subsection (3).

(5) In this Act unless the context otherwise requires

(a) words in the singular number include the plural, and in the plural include the singular;

(b) words of the masculine gender include the feminine and the neuter, and when the sense so indicates words of the neuter gender may refer to any gender.

§ 1—103. **Supplementary General Principles of Law Applicable.**

Unless displaced by the particular provisions of this Act, the principles of law and equity, including the law mer-

[13]

chant and the law relative to capacity to contract, principal and agent, estoppel, fraud, misrepresentation, duress, coercion, mistake, bankruptcy, or other validating or invalidating cause shall supplement its provisions.

§ 1—104. **Construction Against Implicit Repeal.**

This Act being a general act intended as a unified coverage of its subject matter, no part of it shall be deemed to be impliedly repealed by subsequent legislation if such construction can reasonably be avoided.

§ 1—105. **Territorial Application of the Act; Parties' Power to Choose Applicable Law.**

(1) Except as provided hereafter in this section, when a transaction bears a reasonable relation to this state and also to another state or nation the parties may agree that the law either of this state or of such other state or nation shall govern their rights and duties. Failing such agreement this Act applies to transactions bearing an appropriate relation to this state.

(2) Where one of the following provisions of this Act specifies the applicable law, that provision governs and a contrary agreement is effective only to the extent permitted by the law (including the conflict of laws rules) so specified:

Rights of creditors against sold goods. Section 2—402.

Applicability of the Article on Bank Deposits and Collections. Section 4—102.

Bulk transfers subject to the Article on Bulk Transfers. Section 6—102.

Applicability of the Article on Investment Securities. Section 8—106.

Perfection provisions of the Article on Secured Transactions. Section 9—103.

§ 1—106. **Remedies to Be Liberally Administered.**

(1) The remedies provided by this Act shall be liberally administered to the end that the aggrieved party may be put in as good a position as if the other party had fully performed but neither consequential or special nor penal damages may be had except as specifically provided in this Act or by other rule of law.

(2) Any right or obligation declared by this Act is enforceable by action unless the provision declaring it specifies a different and limited effect.

§ 1—107. **Waiver or Renunciation of Claim or Right After Breach.**

Any claim or right arising out of an alleged breach can be discharged in whole or in part without consideration by a written waiver or renunciation signed and delivered by the aggrieved party.

§ 1—108. **Severability.**

If any provision or clause of this Act or application thereof to any person or circumstances is held invalid, such invalidity shall not affect other provisions or applications of the Act which can be given effect without the invalid provision or application, and to this end the provisions of this Act are declared to be severable.

§ 1—109. **Section Captions.**

Section captions are parts of this Act.

Part 2 **General Definitions and Principles of Interpretation**

§ 1—201. **General Definitions.**

Subject to additional definitions contained in the subsequent Articles of this Act which are applicable to specific Articles or Parts thereof, and unless the context otherwise requires, in this Act:

(1) "Action" in the sense of a judicial proceeding includes recoupment, counterclaim, set-off, suit in equity and any other proceedings in which rights are determined.

(2) "Aggrieved party" means a party entitled to resort to a remedy.

(3) "Agreement" means the bargain of the parties in fact as found in their language or by implication from other circumstances including course of dealing or usage of trade or course of performance as provided in this Act (Sections 1—205 and 2—208). Whether an agreement has legal consequences is determined by the provisions of this Act, if applicable; otherwise by the law of contracts (Section 1—103). (Compare "Contract".)

(4) "Bank" means any person engaged in the business of banking.

(5) "Bearer" means the person in possession of an instrument, document of title, or certified security payable to bearer or indorsed in blank.

(6) "Bill of lading" means a document evidencing the receipt of goods for shipment issued by a person engaged in the business of transporting or forwarding goods, and includes an airbill. "Airbill" means a document serving for air transportation as a bill of lading does for marine or rail transportation, and includes an air consignment note or air waybill.

(7) "Branch" includes a separately incorporated foreign branch of a bank.

(8) "Burden of establishing" a fact means the burden of persuading the triers of fact that the existence of the fact is more probable than its non-existence.

(9) "Buyer in ordinary course of business" means a person who in good faith and without knowledge that the

sale to him is in violation of the ownership rights or security interest of a third party in the goods buys in ordinary course from a person in the business of selling goods of that kind but does not include a pawnbroker. All persons who sell minerals or the like (including oil and gas) at wellhead or minehead shall be deemed to be persons in the business of selling goods of that kind. "Buying" may be for cash or by exchange of other property or on secured or unsecured credit and includes receiving goods or documents of title under a pre-existing contract for sale but does not include a transfer in bulk or as security for or in total or partial satisfaction of a money debt.

(10) "Conspicuous": A term or clause is conspicuous when it is so written that a reasonable person against whom it is to operate ought to have noticed it. A printed heading in capitals (as: NON-NEGOTIABLE BILL OF LADING) is conspicuous. Language in the body of a form is "conspicuous" if it is in larger or other contrasting type or color. But in a telegram any stated term is "conspicuous". Whether a term or clause is "conspicuous" or not is for decision by the court.

(11) "Contract" means the total legal obligation which results from the parties' agreement as affected by this Act and any other applicable rules of law. (Compare "Agreement".)

(12) "Creditor" includes a general creditor, a secured creditor, a lien creditor and any representative of creditors, including an assignee for the benefit of creditors, a trustee in bankruptcy, a receiver in equity and an executor or administrator of an insolvent debtor's or assignor's estate.

(13) "Defendant" includes a person in the position of defendant in a cross-action or counterclaim.

(14) "Delivery" with respect to instruments, documents of title, chattel paper, or certificated securities means voluntary transfer of possession.

(15) "Document of title" includes bill of lading, dock warrant, dock receipt, warehouse receipt or order for the delivery of goods, and also any other document which in the regular course of business or financing is treated as adequately evidencing that the person in possession of it is entitled to receive, hold and dispose of the document and the goods it covers. To be a document of title a document must purport to be issued by or addressed to a bailee and purport to cover goods in the bailee's possession which are either identified or are fungible portions of an identified mass.

(16) "Fault" means wrongful act, omission or breach.

(17) "Fungible" with respect to goods or securities means goods or securities of which any unit is, by nature or usage of trade, the equivalent of any other like unit.

Goods which are not fungible shall be deemed fungible for the purposes of this Act to the extent that under a particular agreement or document unlike units are treated as equivalents.

(18) "Genuine" means free of forgery or counterfeiting.

(19) "Good faith" means honesty in fact in the conduct or transaction concerned.

(20) "Holder" means a person who is in possession of a document of title or an instrument or a certificated investment security drawn, issued, or indorsed to him or his order or to bearer or in blank.

(21) To "honor" is to pay or to accept and pay, or where a credit so engages to purchase or discount a draft complying with the terms of the credit.

(22) "Insolvency proceedings" includes any assignment for the benefit of creditors or other proceedings intended to liquidate or rehabilitate the estate of the person involved.

(23) A person is "insolvent" who either has ceased to pay his debts in the ordinary course of business or cannot pay his debts as they become due or is insolvent within the meaning of the federal bankruptcy law.

(24) "Money" means a medium of exchange authorized or adopted by a domestic or foreign government as a part of its currency.

(25) A person has "notice" of a fact when

(a) he has actual knowledge of it; or

(b) he has received a notice or notification of it; or

(c) from all the facts and circumstances known to him at the time in question he has reason to know that it exists.

A person "knows" or has "knowledge" of a fact when he has actual knowledge of it. "Discover" or "learn" or a word or phrase of similar import refers to knowledge rather than to reason to know. The time and circumstances under which a notice or notification may cease to be effective are not determined by this Act.

(26) A person "notifies" or "gives" a notice or notification to another by taking such steps as may be reasonably required to inform the other in ordinary course whether or not such other actually comes to know of it. A person "receives" a notice or notification when

(a) it comes to his attention; or

(b) it is duly delivered at the place of business through which the contract was made or at any other place held out by him as the place for receipt of such communications.

(27) Notice, knowledge or a notice or notification received by an organization is effective for a particular

transaction from the time when it is brought to the attention of the individual conducting that transaction, and in any event from the time when it would have been brought to his attention if the organization had exercised due diligence. An organization exercises due diligence if it maintains reasonable routines for communicating significant information to the person conducting the transaction and there is reasonable compliance with the routines. Due diligence does not require an individual acting for the organization to communicate information unless such communication is part of his regular duties or unless he has reason to know of the transaction and that the transaction would be materially affected by the information.

(28) "Organization" includes a corporation, government or governmental subdivision or agency, business trust, estate, trust, partnership or association, two or more persons having a joint or common interest, or any other legal or commercial entity.

(29) "Party", as distinct from "third party", means a person who has engaged in a transaction or made an agreement within this Act.

(30) "Person" includes an individual or an organization (See Section 1—102).

(31) "Presumption" or "presumed" means that the trier of fact must find the existence of the fact presumed unless and until evidence is introduced which would support a finding of its non-existence.

(32) "Purchase" includes taking by sale, discount, negotiation, mortgage, pledge, lien, issue or re-issue, gift or any other voluntary transaction creating an interest in property.

(33) "Purchaser" means a person who takes by purchase.

(34) "Remedy" means any remedial right to which an aggrieved party is entitled with or without resort to a tribunal.

(35) "Representative" includes an agent, an officer of a corporation or association, and a trustee, executor or administrator of an estate, or any other person empowered to act for another.

(36) "Rights" includes remedies.

(37) "Security interest" means an interest in personal property or fixtures which secures payment or performance of an obligation. The retention or reservation of title by a seller of goods notwithstanding shipment or delivery to the buyer (Section 2—401) is limited in effect to a reservation of a "security interest". The term also includes any interest of a buyer of accounts or chattel paper which is subject to Article 9. The special property interest of a buyer of goods on identification of such goods to a contract for sale under Section 2—401 is not a "security interest", but a buyer may also acquire a "security interest" by complying with Article 9. Unless a lease or consignment is intended as security, reservation of title thereunder is not a "security interest" but a consignment is in any event subject to the provisions on consignment sales (Section 2—326). Whether a lease is intended as security is to be determined by the facts of each case; however, (a) the inclusion of an option to purchase does not of itself make the lease one intended for security, and (b) an agreement that upon compliance with the terms of the lease the lessee shall become or has the option to become the owner of the property for no additional consideration or for a nominal consideration does make the lease one intended for security.

(38) "Send" in connection with any writing or notice means to deposit in the mail or deliver for transmission by any other usual means of communication with postage or cost of transmission provided for and properly addressed and in the case of an instrument to an address specified thereon or otherwise agreed, or if there be none to any address reasonable under the circumstances. The receipt of any writing or notice within the time at which it would have arrived if properly sent has the effect of a proper sending.

(39) "Signed" includes any symbol executed or adopted by a party with present intention to authenticate a writing.

(40) "Surety" includes guarantor.

(41) "Telegram" includes a message transmitted by radio, teletype, cable, any mechanical method of transmission, or the like.

(42) "Term" means that portion of an agreement which relates to a particular matter.

(43) "Unauthorized" signature or indorsement means one made without actual, implied or apparent authority and includes a forgery.

(44) "Value". Except as otherwise provided with respect to negotiable instruments and bank collections (Sections 3—303, 4—208 and 4—209) a person gives "value" for rights if he acquires them

(a) in return for a binding commitment to extend credit or for the extension of immediately available credit whether or not drawn upon and whether or not a chargeback is provided for in the event of difficulties in collection; or

(b) as security for or in total or partial satisfaction of a pre-existing claim; or

(c) by accepting delivery pursuant to a preexisting contract for purchase; or

(d) generally, in return for any consideration sufficient to support a simple contract.

(45) "Warehouse receipt" means a receipt issued by a person engaged in the business of storing goods for hire.

(46) "Written" or "writing" includes printing, typewriting or any other intentional reduction to tangible form.

Amended in 1962, 1972 and 1977.

§ 1—202. **Prima Facie Evidence by Third Party Documents.**

A document in due form purporting to be a bill of lading, policy or certificate of insurance, official weigher's or inspector's certificate, consular invoice, or any other document authorized or required by the contract to be issued by a third party shall be prima facie evidence of its own authenticity and genuineness and of the facts stated in the document by the third party.

§ 1—203. **Obligation of Good Faith.**

Every contract or duty within this Act imposes an obligation of good faith in its performance or enforcement.

§ 1—204. **Time; Reasonable Time; "Seasonably".**

(1) Whenever this Act requires any action to be taken within a reasonable time, any time which is not manifestly unreasonable may be fixed by agreement.

(2) What is a reasonable time for taking any action depends on the nature, purpose and circumstances of such action.

(3) An action is taken "seasonably" when it is taken at or within the time agreed or if no time is agreed at or within a reasonable time.

§ 1—205. **Course of Dealing and Usage of Trade.**

(1) A course of dealing is a sequence of previous conduct between the parties to a particular transaction which is fairly to be regarded as establishing a common basis of understanding for interpreting their expressions and other conduct.

(2) A usage of trade is any practice or method of dealing having such regularity of observance in a place, vocation or trade as to justify an expectation that it will be observed with respect to the transaction in question. The existence and scope of such a usage are to be proved as facts. If it is established that such a usage is embodied in a written trade code or similar writing the interpretation of the writing is for the court.

(3) A course of dealing between parties and any usage of trade in the vocation or trade in which they are engaged or of which they are or should be aware give particular meaning to and supplement or qualify terms of an agreement.

(4) The express terms of an agreement and an applicable course of dealing or usage of trade shall be construed wherever reasonable as consistent with each other; but when such construction is unreasonable express terms control both course of dealing and usage of trade and course of dealing controls usage trade.

(5) An applicable usage of trade in the place where any part of performance is to occur shall be used in interpreting the agreement as to that part of the performance.

(6) Evidence of a relevant usage of trade offered by one party is not admissible unless and until he has given the other party such notice as the court finds sufficient to prevent unfair surprise to the latter.

§ 1—206. **Statute of Frauds for Kinds of Personal Property Not Otherwise Covered.**

(1) Except in the cases described in subsection (2) of this section a contract for the sale of personal property is not enforceable by way of action or defense beyond five thousand dollars in amount or value of remedy unless there is some writing which indicates that a contract for sale has been made between the parties at a defined or stated price, reasonably identifies the subject matter, and is signed by the party against whom enforcement is sought or by his authorized agent.

(2) Subsection (1) of this section does not apply to contracts for the sale of goods (Section 2—201) nor of securities (Section 8—319) nor to security agreements (Section 9—203).

§ 1—207. **Performance or Acceptance Under Reservation of Rights.**

A party who with explicit reservation of rights performs or promises performance or assents to performance in the manner demanded or offered by the other party does not thereby prejudice the rights reserved. Such words as "without prejudice", "under protest" or the like are sufficient.

§ 1—208. **Option to Accelerate at Will.**

A term providing that one party or his successor in interest may accelerate payment or performance or require collateral or additional collateral "at will" or "when he deems himself insecure" or in words of similar import shall be construed to mean that he shall have power to do so only if he in good faith believes that the prospect of payment or performance is impaired. The burden of establishing lack of good faith is on the party against whom the power has been exercised.

§ 1—209. **Subordinated Obligations.**

An obligation may be issued as subordinated to payment of another obligation of the person obligated, or a creditor may subordinate his right to payment of an obligation by agreement with either the person obligated or another creditor of the person obligated. Such a subordination does not create a security interest as against either the common debtor or a subordinated creditor. This section shall be construed as declaring the law as it existed prior to the enactment of this section and not as modifying it. Added 1966.

Note: *This new section is proposed as an optional provision to make it clear that a subordination agreement does not create a security interest unless so intended.*

Article 2
SALES

Part 1
Short Title, General Construction and Subject Matter

§ 2—101. **Short Title.**

This Article shall be known and may be cited as Uniform Commercial Code—Sales.

§ 2—102. **Scope; Certain Security and Other Transactions Excluded From This Article.**

Unless the context otherwise requires, this Article applies to transactions in goods; it does not apply to any transaction which although in the form of an unconditional contract to sell or present sale is intended to operate only as a security transaction nor does this Article impair or repeal any statute regulating sales to consumers, farmers or other specified classes of buyers.

§ 2—103. **Definitions and Index of Definitions.**

(1) In this Article unless the context otherwise requires

(a) "Buyer" means a person who buys or contracts to buy goods.

(b) "Good faith" in the case of a merchant means honesty in fact and the observance of reasonable commercial standards of fair dealing in the trade.

(c) "Receipt" of goods means taking physical possession of them.

(d) "Seller" means a person who sells or contracts to sell goods.

(2) Other definitions applying to this Article or to specified Parts thereof, and the sections in which they appear are:
"Acceptance". Section 2—606.
"Banker's credit". Section 2—325.
"Between merchants". Section 2—104.
"Cancellation". Section 2—106(4).
"Commercial unit". Section 2—105.
"Confirmed credit". Section 2—325.
"Conforming to contract". Section 2—106.
"Contract for sale". Section 2—106.
"Cover". Section 2—712.
"Entrusting". Section 2—403.
"Financing agency". Section 2—104.
"Future goods". Section 2—105.
"Goods". Section 2—105.
"Identification". Section 2—501.
"Installment contract". Section 2—612.
"Letter of Credit". Section 2—325.
"Lot". Section 2—105.
"Merchant". Section 2—104.
"Overseas". Section 2—323.
"Person in position of seller". Section 2—707.
"Present sale". Section 2—106.
"Sale". Section 2—106.
"Sale on approval". Section 2—326.
"Sale or return". Section 2—326.
"Termination". Section 2—106.

(3) The following definitions in other Articles apply to this Article:
"Check". Section 3—104.
"Consignee". Section 7—102.
"Consignor". Section 7—102.
"Consumer goods". Section 9—109.
"Dishonor". Section 3—507.
"Draft". Section 3—104.

(4) In addition Article 1 contains general definitions and principles of construction and interpretation applicable throughout this Article.

§ 2—104. **Definitions: "Merchant"; "Between Merchants"; "Financing Agency".**

(1) "Merchant" means a person who deals in goods of the kind or otherwise by his occupation holds himself out as having knowledge or skill peculiar to the practices or goods involved in the transaction or to whom such knowledge or skill may be attributed by his employment of an agent or broker or other intermediary who by his occupation holds himself out as having such knowledge or skill.

(2) "Financing agency" means a bank, finance company or other person who in the ordinary course of business makes advances against goods or documents of title or who by arrangement with either the seller or the buyer intervenes in ordinary course to make or collect payment due or claimed under the contract for sale, as by purchasing or paying the seller's draft or making advances against it or by merely taking it for collection whether or not documents of title accompany the draft. "Financing agency" includes also a bank or other person who similarly intervenes between persons who are in the position of seller and buyer in respect to the goods (Section 2—707).

(3) "Between merchants" means in any transaction with respect to which both parties are chargeable with the knowledge or skill of merchants.

§ 2—105. Definitions: Transferability; "Goods"; "Future" Goods; "Lot"; "Commercial Unit".

(1) "Goods" means all things (including specially manufactured goods) which are movable at the time of identification to the contract for sale other than the money in which the price is to be paid, investment securities (Article 8) and things in action. "Goods" also includes the unborn young of animals and growing crops and other identified things attached to realty as described in the section on goods to be severed from realty (Section 2—107).

(2) Goods must be both existing and identified before any interest in them can pass. Goods which are not both existing and identified are "future" goods. A purported present sale of future goods or of any interest therein operates as a contract to sell.

(3) There may be a sale of a part interest in existing identified goods.

(4) An undivided share in an identified bulk of fungible goods is sufficiently identified to be sold although the quantity of the bulk is not determined. Any agreed proportion of such a bulk or any quantity thereof agreed upon by number, weight or other measure may to the extent of the seller's interest in the bulk be sold to the buyer who then becomes an owner in common.

(5) "Lot" means a parcel or a single article which is the subject matter of a separate sale or delivery, whether or not it is sufficient to perform the contract.

(6) "Commercial unit" means such a unit of goods as by commercial usage is a single whole for purposes of sale and division of which materially impairs its character or value on the market or in use. A commercial unit may be a single article (as a machine) or a set of articles (as a suite of furniture or an assortment of sizes) or a quantity (as a bale, gross, or carload) or any other unit treated in use or in the relevant market as a single whole.

§ 2—106. Definitions: "Contract"; "Agreement"; "Contract for Sale"; "Sale"; "Present Sale"; "Conforming" to Contract; "Termination"; "Cancellation".

(1) In this Article unless the context otherwise requires "contract" and "agreement" are limited to those relating to the present or future sale of goods. "Contract for sale" includes both a present sale of goods and a contract to sell goods at a future time. A "sale" consists in the passing of title from the seller to the buyer for a price (Section 2—401). A "present sale" means a sale which is accomplished by the making of the contract.

(2) Goods or conduct including any part of a performance are "conforming" or conform to the contract when they are in accordance with the obligations under the contract.

(3) "Termination" occurs when either party pursuant to a power created by agreement or law puts an end to the contract otherwise than for its breach. On "termination" all obligations which are still executory on both sides are discharged but any right based on prior breach or performance survives.

(4) "Cancellation" occurs when either party puts an end to the contract for breach by the other and its effect is the same as that of "termination" except that the cancelling party also retains any remedy for breach of the whole contract or any unperformed balance.

§ 2—107. Goods to Be Severed From Realty: Recording.

(1) A contract for the sale of minerals or the like (including oil and gas) or a structure or its materials to be removed from realty is a contract for the sale of goods within this Article if they are to be severed by the seller but until severance a purported present sale thereof which is not effective as a transfer of an interest in land is effective only as a contract to sell.

(2) A contract for the sale apart from the land of growing crops or other things attached to realty and capable of severance without material harm thereto but not described in subsection (1) or of timber to be cut is a contract for the sale of goods within this Article whether the subject matter is to be severed by the buyer or by the seller even though it forms part of the realty at the time of contracting, and the parties can by identification effect a present sale before severance.

(3) The provisions of this section are subject to any third party rights provided by the law relating to realty records, and the contract for sale may be executed and recorded as a document transferring an interest in land and shall then constitute notice to third parties of the buyer's rights under the contract for sale.

Part 2 Form, Formation and Readjustment of Contract

§ 2—201. Formal Requirements; Statute of Frauds.

(1) Except as otherwise provided in this section a contract for the sale of goods for the price of $500 or more is not enforceable by way of action or defense unless there is some writing sufficient to indicate that a contract for sale has been made between the parties and signed by the party against whom enforcement is sought or by his authorized agent or broker. A writing is not sufficient because it omits or incorrectly states a term agreed upon

but the contract is not enforceable under this paragraph beyond the quantity of goods shown in such writing.

(2) Between merchants if within a reasonable time a writing in confirmation of the contract and sufficient against the sender is received and the party receiving it has reason to know its contents, it satisfies the requirements of subsection (1) against such party unless written notice of objection to its contents is given within ten days after it is received.

(3) A contract which does not satisfy the requirements of subsection (1) but which is valid in other respects is enforceable

(a) if the goods are to be specially manufactured for the buyer and are not suitable for sale to others in the ordinary course of the seller's business and the seller, before notice of repudiation is received and under circumstances which reasonably indicate that the goods are for the buyer, has made either a substantial beginning of their manufacture or commitments for their procurement; or

(b) if the party against whom enforcement is sought admits in his pleading, testimony or otherwise in court that a contract for sale was made, but the contract is not enforceable under this provision beyond the quantity of goods admitted; or

(c) with respect to goods for which payment has been made and accepted or which have been received and accepted (Sec. 2—606).

§ 2—202. **Final Written Expression: Parol or Extrinsic Evidence.**

Terms with respect to which the confirmatory memoranda of the parties agree or which are otherwise set forth in a writing intended by the parties as a final expression of their agreement with respect to such terms as are included therein may not be contradicted by evidence of any prior agreement or of a contemporaneous oral agreement but may be explained or supplemented

(a) by course of dealing or usage of trade (Section 1—205) or by course of performance (Section 2—208); and

(b) by evidence of consistent additional terms unless the court finds the writing to have been intended also as a complete and exclusive statement of the terms of the agreement.

§ 2—203. **Seals Inoperative.**

The affixing of a seal to a writing evidencing a contract for sale or an offer to buy or sell goods does not constitute the writing a sealed instrument and the law with respect to sealed instruments does not apply to such a contract or offer.

§ 2—204. **Formation in General.**

(1) A contract for sale of goods may be made in any manner sufficent to show agreement, including conduct by both parties which recognizes the existence of such a contract.

(2) An agreement sufficient to constitute a contract for sale may be found even though the moment of its making is undetermined.

(3) Even though one or more terms are left open a contract for sale does not fail for indefiniteness if the parties have intended to make a contract and there is a reasonably certain basis for giving an appropriate remedy.

§ 2—205. **Firm Offers.**

An offer by a merchant to buy or sell goods in a signed writing which by its terms gives assurance that it will be held open is not revocable, for lack of consideration, during the time stated or if no time is stated for a reasonable time, but in no event may such period of irrevocability exceed three months; but any such term of assurance on a form supplied by the offeree must be separately signed by the offeror.

§ 2—206. **Offer and Acceptance in Formation of Contract.**

(1) Unless other unambiguously indicated by the language or circumstances

(a) an offer to make a contract shall be construed as inviting acceptance in any manner and by any medium reasonable in the circumstances;

(b) an order or other offer to buy goods for prompt or current shipment shall be construed as inviting acceptance either by a prompt promise to ship or by the prompt or current shipment of conforming or nonconforming goods, but such a shipment of nonconforming goods does not constitute an acceptance if the seller seasonably notifies the buyer that the shipment is offered only as an accommodation to the buyer.

(2) Where the beginning of a requested performance is a reasonable mode of acceptance an offeror who is not notified of acceptance within a reasonable time may treat the offer as having lapsed before acceptance.

§ 2—207. **Additional Terms in Acceptance or Confirmation.**

(1) A definite and seasonable expression of acceptance or a written confirmation which is sent within a reasonable time operates as an acceptance even though it states terms additional to or different from those offered or agreed upon, unless acceptance is expressly made conditional on assent to the additional or different terms.

(2) The additional terms are to be construed as proposals for addition to the contract. Between merchants such terms become part of the contract unless:

(a) the offer expressly limits acceptance to the terms of the offer;

(b) they materially alter it; or

(c) notification of objection to them has already been given or is given within a reasonable time after notice of them is received.

(3) Conduct by both parties which recognizes the existence of a contract is sufficient to establish a contract for sale although the writings of the parties do not otherwise establish a contract. In such case the terms of the particular contract consist of those terms on which the writings of the parties agree, together with any supplementary terms incorporated under any other provisions of this Act.

§ 2—208. **Course of Performance or Practical Construction.**

(1) Where the contract for sale involves repeated occasions for performance by either party with knowledge of the nature of the performance and opportunity for objection to it by the other, any course of performance accepted or acquiesced in without objection shall be relevant to determine the meaning of the agreement.

(2) The express terms of the agreement and any such course of performance, as well as any course of dealing and usage of trade, shall be construed whenever reasonable as consistent with each other; but when such construction is unreasonable, express terms shall control course of performance and course of performance shall control both course of dealing and usage of trade (Section 1—205).

(3) Subject to the provisions of the next section on modification and waiver, such course of performance shall be relevant to show a waiver or modification of any term inconsistent with such course of performance.

§ 2—209. **Modification, Rescission and Waiver.**

(1) An agreement modifying a contract within this Article needs no consideration to be binding.

(2) A signed agreement which excludes modification or rescission except by a signed writing cannot be otherwise modified or rescinded, but except as between merchants such a requirement on a form supplied by the merchant must be separately signed by the other party.

(3) The requirements of the statute of frauds section of this Article (Section 2—201) must be satisfied if the contract as modified is within its provisions.

(4) Although an attempt at modification or rescission does not satisfy the requirements of subsection (2) or (3) it can operate as a waiver.

(5) A party who has made a waiver affecting an executory portion of the contract may retract the waiver by reasonable notification received by the other party that strict performance will be required of any term waived, unless the retraction would be unjust in view of a material change of position in reliance on the waiver.

§ 2—210. **Delegation of Performance; Assignment of Rights.**

(1) A party may perform his duty through a delegate unless otherwise agreed or unless the other party has a substantial interest in having his original promisor perform or control the acts required by the contract. No delegation of performance relieves the party delegating of any duty to perform or any liability for breach.

(2) Unless otherwise agreed all rights of either seller or buyer can be assigned except where the assignment would materially change the duty of the other party, or increase materially the burden or risk imposed on him by his contract, or impair materially his chance of obtaining return performance. A right to damages for breach of the whole contract or a right arising out of the assignor's due performance of his entire obligation can be assigned despite agreement otherwise.

(3) Unless the circumstances indicate the contrary a prohibition of assignment of "the contract" is to be construed as barring only the delegation to the assignee of the assignor's performance.

(4) An assignment of "the contract" or of "all my rights under the contract" or an assignment in similar general terms is an assignment of rights and unless the language or the circumstances (as in an assignment for security) indicate the contrary, it is a delegation of performance of the duties of the assignor and its acceptance by the assignee constitutes a promise by him to perform those duties. This promise is enforceable by either the assignor or the other party to the original contract.

(5) The other party may treat any assignment which delegates performance as creating reasonable grounds for insecurity and may without prejudice to his rights against the assignor demand assurances from the assignee (Section 2—609).

Part 3 **General Obligation and Construction of Contract**

§ 2—301. **General Obligations of Parties.**

The obligation of the seller is to transfer and deliver and that of the buyer is to accept and pay in accordance with the contract.

§ 2—302. **Unconscionable Contract or Clause.**

(1) If the court as a matter of law finds the contract or any clause of the contract to have been unconscionable at the time it was made the court may refuse to enforce the contract, or it may enforce the remainder of the contract without the unconscionable clause, or it may so limit the application of any unconscionable clause as to avoid any unconscionable result.

(2) When it is claimed or appears to the court that the contract or any clause thereof may be unconscionable the parties shall be afforded a reasonable opportunity to present evidence as to its commercial setting, purpose and effect to aid the court in making the determination.

§ 2—303. **Allocations or Division of Risks.**

Where this Article allocates a risk or a burden as between the parties "unless otherwise agreed", the agreement may not only shift the allocation but may also divide the risk or burden.

§ 2—304. **Price Payable in Money, Goods, Realty, or Otherwise.**

(1) The price can be made payable in money or otherwise. If it is payable in whole or in part in goods each party is a seller of the goods which he is to transfer.

(2) Even though all or part of the price is payable in an interest in realty the transfer of the goods and the seller's obligations with reference to them are subject to this Article, but not the transfer of the interest in realty or the transferor's obligations in connection therewith.

§ 2—305. **Open Price Term.**

(1) The parties if they so intend can conclude a contract for sale even though the price is not settled. In such a case the price is a reasonable price at the time for delivery if

(a) nothing is said as to price; or

(b) the price is left to be agreed by the parties and they fail to agree; or

(c) the price is to be fixed in terms of some agreed market or other standard as set or recorded by a third person or agency and it is not so set or recorded.

(2) A price to be fixed by the seller or by the buyer means a price for him to fix in good faith.

(3) When a price left to be fixed otherwise than by agreement of the parties fails to be fixed through fault of one party the other may at his option treat the contract as cancelled or himself fix a reasonable price.

(4) Where, however, the parties intend not to be bound unless the price be fixed or agreed and it is not fixed or agreed there is no contract. In such a case the buyer must

return any goods already received or if unable so to do must pay their reasonable value at the time of delivery and the seller must return any portion of the price paid on account.

§ 2—306. **Output, Requirements and Exclusive Dealings.**

(1) A term which measures the quantity by the output of the seller or the requirements of the buyer means such actual output or requirements as may occur in good faith, except that no quantity unreasonably disproportionate to any stated estimate or in the absence of a stated estimate to any normal or otherwise comparable prior output or requirements may be tendered or demanded.

(2) A lawful agreement by either the seller or the buyer for exclusive dealing in the kind of goods concerned imposes unless otherwise agreed an obligation by the seller to use best efforts to supply the goods and by the buyer to use best efforts to promote their sale.

§ 2—307. **Delivery in Single Lot or Several Lots.**

Unless otherwise agreed all goods called for by a contract for sale must be tendered in a single delivery and payment is due only on such tender but where the circumstances give either party the right to make or demand delivery in lots the price if it can be apportioned may be demanded for each lot.

§ 2—308. **Absence of Specified Place for Delivery.**

Unless otherwise agreed

(a) the place for delivery of goods is the seller's place of business or if he has none his residence; but

(b) in a contract for sale of identified goods which to the knowledge of the parties at the time of contracting are in some other place, that place is the place for their delivery; and

(c) documents of title may be delivered through customary banking channels.

§ 2—309. **Absence of Specific Time Provisions; Notice of Termination.**

(1) The time for shipment or delivery or any other action under a contract if not provided in this Article or agreed upon shall be a reasonable time.

(2) Where the contract provides for successive performances but is indefinite in duration it is valid for a reasonable time but unless otherwise agreed may be terminated at any time by either party.

(3) Termination of a contract by one party except on the happening of an agreed event requires that reasonable notification be received by the other party and an

agreement dispensing with notification is invalid if its operation would be unconscionable.

§ 2—310. Open Time for Payment or Running of Credit; Authority to Ship Under Reservation.

Unless otherwise agreed

(a) payment is due at the time and place at which the buyer is to receive the goods even though the place of shipment is the place of delivery; and

(b) if the seller is authorized to send the goods he may ship them under reservation, and may tender the documents of title, but the buyer may inspect the goods after their arrival before payment is due unless such inspection is inconsistent with the terms of the contract (Section 2—513); and

(c) if delivery is authorized and made by way of documents of title otherwise than by subsection (b) then payment is due at the time and place at which the buyer is to receive the documents regardless of where the goods are to be received; and

(d) where the seller is required or authorized to ship the goods on credit the credit period runs from the time of shipment but post-dating the invoice or delaying its dispatch will correspondingly delay the starting of the credit period.

§ 2—311. Options and Cooperation Respecting Performance.

(1) An agreement for sale which is otherwise sufficiently definite (subsection (3) of Section 2—204) to be a contract is not made invalid by the fact that it leaves particulars of performance to be specified by one of the parties. Any such specification must be made in good faith and within limits set by commercial reasonableness.

(2) Unless otherwise agreed specifications relating to assortment of the goods are at the buyer's option and except as otherwise provided in subsections (1)(c) and (3) of Section 2—319 specifications or arrangements relating to shipment are at the seller's option.

(3) Where such specification would materially affect the other party's performance but is not seasonably made or where one party's cooperation is necessary to the agreed performance of the other but is not seasonably forthcoming, the other party in addition to all other remedies

(a) is excused for any resulting delay in his own performance; and

(b) may also either proceed to perform in any reasonable manner or after the time for a material part of his own performance treat the failure to specify or to cooperate as a breach by failure to deliver or accept the goods.

§ 2—312. Warranty of Title and Against Infringement; Buyer's Obligation Against Infringement.

(1) Subject to subsection (2) there is in a contract for sale a warranty by the seller that

(a) the title conveyed shall be good, and its transfer rightful; and

(b) the goods shall be delivered free from any security interest or other lien or encumbrance of which the buyer at the time of contracting has no knowledge.

(2) A warranty under subsection (1) will be excluded or modified only by specific language or by circumstances which give the buyer reason to know that the person selling does not claim title in himself or that he is purporting to sell only such right or title as he or a third person may have.

(3) Unless otherwise agreed a seller who is a merchant regularly dealing in goods of the kind warrants that the goods shall be delivered free of the rightful claim of any third person by way of infringement or the like but a buyer who furnishes specifications to the seller must hold the seller harmless against any such claim which arises out of compliance with the specifications.

§ 2—313. Express Warranties by Affirmation, Promise, Description, Sample.

(1) Express warranties by the seller are created as follows:

(a) Any affirmation of fact or promise made by the seller to the buyer which relates to the goods and becomes part of the basis of the bargain creates an express warranty that the goods shall conform to the affirmation or promise.

(b) Any description of the goods which is made part of the basis of the bargain creates an express warranty that the goods shall conform to the description.

(c) Any sample or model which is made part of the basis of the bargain creates an express warranty that the whole of the goods shall conform to the sample or model.

(2) It is not necessary to the creation of an express warranty that the seller use formal words such as "warrant" or "guarantee" or that he have a specific intention to make a warranty, but an affirmation merely of the value of the goods or a statement purporting to be merely the seller's opinion or commendation of the goods does not create a warranty.

§ 2—314. Implied Warranty: Merchantability; Usage of Trade.

(1) Unless excluded or modified (Section 2—316), a warranty that the goods shall be merchantable is implied in a contract for their sale if the seller is a merchant with respect to goods of that kind. Under this section the serving for value of food or drink to be consumed either on the premises or elsewhere is a sale.

(2) Goods to be merchantable must be at least such as

(a) pass without objection in the trade under the contract description; and

(b) in the case of fungible goods, are of fair average quality within the description; and

(c) are fit for the ordinary purposes for which such goods are used; and

(d) run, within the variations permitted by the agreement, of even kind, quality and quantity within each unit and among all units involved; and

(e) are adequately contained, packaged, and labeled as the agreement may require; and

(f) conform to the promises or affirmations of fact made on the container or label if any.

(3) Unless excluded or modified (Section 2—316) other implied warranties may arise from course of dealing or usage of trade.

§ 2—315. **Implied Warranty: Fitness for Particular Purpose.**

Where the seller at the time of contracting has reason to know any particular purpose for which the goods are required and that the buyer is relying on the seller's skill or judgment to select or furnish suitable goods, there is unless excluded or modified under the next section an implied warranty that the goods shall be fit for such purpose.

§ 2—316. **Exclusion or Modification of Warranties.**

(1) Words or conduct relevant to the creation of an express warranty and words or conduct tending to negate or limit warranty shall be construed wherever reasonable as consistent with each other; but subject to the provisions of this Article on parol or extrinsic evidence (Section 2—202) negation or limitation is inoperative to the extent that such construction is unreasonable.

(2) Subject to subsection (3), to exclude or modify the implied warranty of merchantability or any part of it the language must mention merchantability and in case of a writing must be conspicuous, and to exclude or modify any implied warranty of fitness the exclusion must be by a writing and conspicuous. Language to exclude all implied warranties of fitness is sufficient if it states, for example, that "There are no warranties which extend beyond the description on the face hereof."

(3) Notwithstanding subsection (2)

(a) unless the circumstances indicate otherwise, all implied warranties are excluded by expressions like "as is", "with all faults" or other language which in common understanding calls the buyer's attention to the exclusion of warranties and makes plain that there is no implied warranty; and

(b) when the buyer before entering into the contract has examined the goods or the sample or model as fully as he desired or has refused to examine the goods there is no implied warranty with regard to defects which an examination ought in the circumstances to have revealed to him; and

(c) an implied warranty can also be excluded or modified by course of dealing or course of performance or usage of trade.

(4) Remedies for breach of warranty can be limited in accordance with the provisions of this Article on liquidation or limitation of damages and on contractual modification of remedy (Sections 2—718 and 2—719).

§ 2—317. **Cumulation and Conflict of Warranties Express or Implied.**

Warranties whether express or implied shall be construed as consistent with each other and as cumulative, but if such construction is unreasonable the intention of the parties shall determine which warranty is dominant. In ascertaining that intention the following rules apply:

(a) Exact or technical specifications displace an inconsistent sample or model or general language of description.

(b) A sample from an existing bulk displaces inconsistent general language of description.

(c) Express warranties displace inconsistent implied warranties other than an implied warranty of fitness for a particular purpose.

§ 2—318. **Third Party Beneficiaries of Warranties Express or Implied.**

Note: If this Act is introduced in the Congress of the United States this section should be omitted. (States to select one alternative.)

Alternative A

A seller's warranty whether express or implied extends to any natural person who is in the family or household of his buyer or who is a guest in his home if it is reasonable to expect that such person may use, consume or be affected by the goods and who is injured in person by breach of the warranty. A seller may not exclude or limit the operation of this section.

Alternative B

A seller's warranty whether express or implied extends to any natural person who may reasonably be expected to use, consume or be affected by the goods and who is injured in person by breach of the warranty. A seller may not exclude or limit the operation of this section.

Alternative C

A seller's warranty whether express or implied extends to any person who may reasonably be expected to use, consume or be affected by the goods and who is injured by breach of the warranty. A seller may not exclude or limit the operation of this section with respect to injury to the person of an individual to whom the warranty extends. As amended 1966.

§ 2—319. F.O.B. and F.A.S. Terms.

(1) Unless otherwise agreed the term F.O.B. (which means "free on board") at a named place, even though used only in connection with the stated price, is a delivery term under which

(a) when the term is F.O.B. the place of shipment, the seller must at that place ship the goods in the manner provided in this Article (Section 2—504) and bear the expense and risk of putting them into the possession of the carrier; or

(b) when the term is F.O.B. the place of destination, the seller must at his own expense and risk transport the goods to that place and there tender delivery of them in the manner provided in this Article (Section 2—503);

(c) when under either (a) or (b) the term is also F.O.B. vessel, car or other vehicle, the seller must in addition at his own expense and risk load the goods on board. If the term is F.O.B. vessel the buyer must name the vessel and in an appropriate case the seller must comply with the provisions of this Article on the form of bill of lading (Section 2—323).

(2) Unless otherwise agreed the term F.A.S. vessel (which means "free alongside") at a named port, even though used only in connection with the stated price, is a delivery term under which the seller must

(a) at his own expense and risk deliver the goods alongside the vessel in the manner usual in that port or on a dock designated and provided by the buyer; and

(b) obtain and tender a receipt for the goods in exchange for which the carrier is under a duty to issue a bill of lading.

(3) Unless otherwise agreed in any case falling within subsection (1)(a) or (c) or subsection (2) the buyer must

seasonably give any needed instructions for making delivery, including when the term is F.A.S. or F.O.B. the loading berth of the vessel and in an appropriate case its name and sailing date. The seller may treat the failure of needed instructions as a failure of cooperation under this Article (Section 2—311). He may also at his option move the goods in any reasonable manner preparatory to delivery or shipment.

(4) Under the term F.O.B. vessel or F.A.S. unless otherwise agreed the buyer must make payment against tender of the required documents and the seller may not tender nor the buyer demand delivery of the goods in substitution for the documents.

§ 2—320. C.I.F. and C. & F. Terms.

(1) The term C.I.F. means that the price includes in a lump sum the cost of the goods and the insurance and freight to the named destination. The term C. & F. or C.F. means that the price so includes cost and freight to the named destination.

(2) Unless otherwise agreed and even though used only in connection with the stated price and destination, the term C.I.F. destination or its equivalent requires the seller at his own expense and risk to

(a) put the goods into the possession of a carrier at the port for shipment and obtain a negotiable bill or bills of lading covering the entire transportation to the named destination; and

(b) load the goods and obtain a receipt from the carrier (which may be contained in the bill of lading) showing that the freight has been paid or provided for; and

(c) obtain a policy or certificate of insurance, including any war risk insurance, of a kind and on terms then current at the port of shipment in the usual amount, in the currency of the contract, shown to cover the same goods covered by the bill of lading and providing for payment of loss to the order of the buyer or for the account of whom it may concern; but the seller may add to the price the amount of the premium for any such war risk insurance; and

(d) prepare an invoice of the goods and procure any other documents required to effect shipment or to comply with the contract; and

(e) forward and tender with commercial promptness all the documents in due form and with any indorsement necessary to perfect the buyer's rights.

(3) Unless otherwise agreed the term C. & F. or its equivalent has the same effect and imposes upon the seller the same obligations and risks as a C.I.F. term except the obligation as to insurance.

(4) Under the term C.I.F. or C. & F. unless otherwise agreed the buyer must make payment against tender of the required documents and the seller may not tender nor the buyer demand delivery of the goods in substitution for the documents.

§ 2—321. C.I.F. or C. & F.: "Net Landed Weights"; "Payment on Arrival"; Warranty of Condition on Arrival.

Under a contract containing a term C.I.F. or C. & F.

(1) Where the price is based on or is to be adjusted according to "net landed weights", "delivered weights", "out turn" quantity or quality or the like, unless otherwise agreed the seller must reasonably estimate the price. The payment due on tender of the documents called for by the contract is the amount so estimated, but after final adjustment of the price a settlement must be made with commercial promptness.

(2) An agreement described in subsection (1) or any warranty of quality or condition of the goods on arrival places upon the seller the risk of ordinary deterioration, shrinkage and the like in transportation but has no effect on the place or time of identification to the contract for sale or delivery or on the passing of the risk of loss.

(3) Unless otherwise agreed where the contract provides for payment on or after arrival of the goods the seller must before payment allow such preliminary inspection as is feasible; but if the goods are lost delivery of the documents and payment are due when the goods should have arrived.

§ 2—322. Delivery "Ex-Ship".

(1) Unless otherwise agreed a term for delivery of goods "ex-ship" (which means from the carrying vessel) or in equivalent language is not restricted to a particular ship and requires delivery from a ship which has reached a place at the named port of destination where goods of the kind are usually discharged.

(2) Under such a term unless otherwise agreed

(a) the seller must discharge all liens arising out of the carriage and furnish the buyer with a direction which puts the carrier under a duty to deliver the goods; and

(b) the risk of loss does not pass to the buyer until the goods leave the ship's tackle or are otherwise properly unloaded.

§ 2—323. Form of Bill of Lading Required in Overseas Shipment; "Overseas".

(1) Where the contract contemplates overseas shipment and contains a term C.I.F. or C. & F. or F.O.B. vessel, the seller unless otherwise agreed must obtain a negoti-

able bill of lading stating that the goods have been loaded on board or, in the case of a term C.I.F. or C. & F., received for shipment.

(2) Where in a case within subsection (1) a bill of lading has been issued in a set of parts, unless otherwise agreed if the documents are not to be sent from abroad the buyer may demand tender of the full set; otherwise only one part of the bill of lading need be tendered. Even if the agreement expressly requires a full set

(a) due tender of a single part is acceptable within the provisions of this Article on cure of improper delivery (subsection (1) of Section 2—508); and

(b) even though the full set is demanded, if the documents are sent from abroad the person tendering an incomplete set may nevertheless require payment upon furnishing an indemnity which the buyer in good faith deems adequate.

(3) A shipment by water or by air or a contract contemplating such shipment is "overseas" insofar as by usage of trade or agreement it is subject to the commercial, financing or shipping practices characteristic of international deep water commerce.

§ 2—324. "No Arrival, No Sale" Term.

Under a term "no arrival, no sale" or terms of like meaning, unless otherwise agreed,

(a) the seller must properly ship conforming goods and if they arrive by any means he must tender them on arrival but he assumes no obligation that the goods will arrive unless he has caused the non-arrival; and

(b) where without fault of the seller the goods are in part lost or have so deteriorated as no longer to conform to the contract or arrive after the contract time, the buyer may proceed as if there had been casualty to identified goods (Section 2—613).

§ 2—325. "Letter of Credit" Term; "Confirmed Credit".

(1) Failure of the buyer seasonably to furnish an agreed letter of credit is a breach of the contract for sale.

(2) The delivery to seller of a proper letter of credit suspends the buyer's obligation to pay. If the letter of credit is dishonored, the seller may on seasonable notification to the buyer require payment directly from him.

(3) Unless otherwise agreed the term "letter of credit" or "banker's credit" in a contract for sale means an irrevocable credit issued by a financing agency of good repute and, where the shipment is overseas, of good international repute. The term "confirmed credit" means that the credit must also carry the direct obligation of such an agency which does business in the seller's financial market.

§ 2—326. **Sale on Approval and Sale or Return; Consignment Sales and Rights of Creditors.**

(1) Unless otherwise agreed, if delivered goods may be returned by the buyer even though they conform to the contract, the transaction is

(a) a "sale on approval" if the goods are delivered primarily for use, and

(b) a "sale or return" if the goods are delivered primarily for resale.

(2) Except as provided in subsection (3), goods held on approval are not subject to the claims of the buyer's creditors until acceptance; goods held on sale or return are subject to such claims while in the buyer's possession.

(3) Where goods are delivered to a person for sale and such person maintains a place of business at which he deals in goods of the kind involved, under a name other than the name of the person making delivery, then with respect to claims of creditors of the person conducting the business the goods are deemed to be on sale or return. The provisions of this subsection are applicable even though an agreement purports to reserve title to the person making delivery until payment or resale or uses such words as "on consignment" or "on memorandum". However, this subsection is not applicable if the person making delivery

(a) complies with an applicable law providing for a consignor's interest or the like to be evidenced by a sign, or

(b) establishes that the person conducting the business is generally known by his creditors to be substantially engaged in selling the goods of others, or

(c) complies with the filing provisions of the Article on Secured Transactions (Article 9).

(4) Any "or return" term of a contract for sale is to be treated as a separate contract for sale within the statute of frauds section of this Article (Section 2—201) and as contradicting the sale aspect of the contract within the provisions of this Article on parol or extrinsic evidence (Section 2—202).

§ 2—327. **Special Incidents of Sale on Approval and Sale or Return.**

(1) Under a sale on approval unless otherwise agreed

(a) although the goods are identified to the contract the risk of loss and the title do not pass to the buyer until acceptance; and

(b) use of the goods consistent with the purpose of trial is not acceptance but failure seasonably to notify the seller of election to return the goods is acceptance, and if the goods conform to the contract acceptance of any part is acceptance of the whole; and

(c) after due notification of election to return, the return is at the seller's risk and expense but a merchant buyer must follow any reasonable instructions.

(2) Under a sale or return unless otherwise agreed

(a) the option to return extends to the whole or any commercial unit of the goods while in substantially their original condition, but must be exercised seasonably; and

(b) the return is at the buyer's risk and expense.

§ 2—328. **Sale by Auction.**

(1) In a sale by auction if goods are put up in lots each lot is the subject of a separate sale.

(2) A sale by auction is complete when the auctioneer so announces by the fall of the hammer or in other customary manner. Where a bid is made while the hammer is falling in acceptance of a prior bid the auctioneer may in his discretion reopen the bidding or declare the goods sold under the bid on which the hammer was falling.

(3) Such a sale is with reserve unless the goods are in explicit terms put up without reserve. In an auction with reserve the auctioneer may withdraw the goods at any time until he announces completion of the sale. In an auction without reserve, after the auctioneer calls for bids on an article or lot, that article or lot cannot be withdrawn unless no bid is made within a reasonable time. In either case a bidder may retract his bid until the auctioneer's announcement of completion of the sale, but a bidder's retraction does not revive any previous bid.

(4) If the auctioneer knowingly receives a bid on the seller's behalf or the seller makes or procures such as bid, and notice has not been given that liberty for such bidding is reserved, the buyer may at his option avoid the sale or take the goods at the price of the last good faith bid prior to the completion of the sale. This subsection shall not apply to any bid at a forced sale.

Part 4 **Title, Creditors and Good Faith Purchasers**

§ 2—401. **Passing of Title; Reservation for Security; Limited Application of This Section.**

Each provision of this Article with regard to the rights, obligations and remedies of the seller, the buyer, purchasers or other third parties applies irrespective of title to the goods except where the provision refers to such title. Insofar as situations are not covered by the other provisions of this Article and matters concerning title became material the following rules apply:

(1) Title to goods cannot pass under a contract for sale prior to their identification to the contract (Section 2—501), and unless otherwise explicitly agreed the buyer acquires by their identification a special property as lim-

ited by this Act. Any retention or reservation by the seller of the title (property) in goods shipped or delivered to the buyer is limited in effect to a reservation of a security interest. Subject to these provisions and to the provisions of the Article on Secured Transactions (Article 9), title to goods passes from the seller to the buyer in any manner and on any conditions explicitly agreed on by the parties.

(2) Unless otherwise explicitly agreed title passes to the buyer at the time and place at which the seller completes his performance with reference to the physical delivery of the goods, despite any reservation of a security interest and even though a document of title is to be delivered at a different time or place; and in particular and despite any reservation of a security interest by the bill of lading.

(a) if the contract requires or authorizes the seller to send the goods to the buyer but does not require him to deliver them at destination, title passes to the buyer at the time and place of shipment; but

(b) if the contract requires delivery at destination, title passes on tender there.

(3) Unless otherwise explicitly agreed where delivery is to be made without moving the goods,

(a) if the seller is to deliver a document of title, title passes at the time when and the place where he delivers such documents; or

(b) if the goods are at the time of contracting already identified and no documents are to be delivered, title passes at the time and place of contracting.

(4) A rejection or other refusal by the buyer to receive or retain the goods, whether or not justified, or a justified revocation of acceptance revests title to the goods in the seller. Such revesting occurs by operation of law and is not a "sale".

§ 2—402. **Rights of Seller's Creditors Against Sold Goods.**

(1) Except as provided in subsections (2) and (3), rights of unsecured creditors of the seller with respect to goods which have been identified to a contract for sale are subject to the buyer's rights to recover the goods under this Article (Sections 2—502 and 2—716).

(2) A creditor of the seller may treat a sale or an identification of goods to a contract for sale as void if as against him a retention of possession by the seller is fraudulent under any rule of law of the state where the goods are situated, except that retention of possession in good faith and current course of trade by a merchant-seller for a commercially reasonable time after a sale or identification is not fraudulent.

(3) Nothing in this Article shall be deemed to impair the rights of creditors of the seller.

(a) under the provisions of the Article on Secured Transactions (Article 9); or

(b) where identification to the contract or delivery is made not in current course of trade but in satisfaction of or as security for a pre-existing claim for money, security or the like and is made under circumstances which under any rule of law of the state where the goods are situated would apart from this Article constitute the transaction a fraudulent transfer or voidable preference.

§ 2—403. **Power to Transfer; Good Faith Purchase of Goods; "Entrusting".**

(1) A purchaser of goods acquires all title which his transferor had or had power to transfer except that a purchaser of a limited interest acquires rights only to the extent of the interest purchased. A person with voidable title has power to transfer a good title to a good faith purchaser for value. When goods have been delivered under a transaction of purchase the purchaser has such power even though

(a) the transferor was deceived as to the identity of the purchaser, or

(b) the delivery was in exchange for a check which is later dishonored, or

(c) it was agreed that the transaction was to be a "cash sale", or

(d) the delivery was procured through fraud punishable as larcenous under the criminal law.

(2) Any entrusting of possession of goods to a merchant who deals in goods of that kind gives him power to transfer all rights of the entruster to a buyer in ordinary course of business.

(3) "Entrusting" includes any delivery and any acquiescence in retention of possession regardless of any condition expressed between the parties to the delivery or acquiescence and regardless of whether the procurement of the entrusting or the possessor's disposition of the goods have been such as to be larcenous under the criminal law.

(4) The rights of other purchasers of goods and of lien creditors are governed by the Articles on Secured Transactions (Article 9), Bulk Transfers (Article 6) and Documents of Title (Article 7).

Part 5 **Performance**

§ 2—501. **Insurable Interest in Goods; Manner of Identification of Goods.**

(1) The buyer obtains a special property and an insurable interest in goods by identification of existing goods as goods to which the contract refers even though the

goods so identified are nonconforming and he has an option to return or reject them. Such identification can be made at any time and in any manner explicitly agreed to by the parties. In the absence of explicit agreement identification occurs

(a) when the contract is made if it is for the sale of goods already existing and identified;

(b) if the contract is for the sale of future goods other than those described in paragraph (c), when goods are shipped, marked or otherwise designated by the seller as goods to which the contract refers;

(c) when the crops are planted or otherwise become growing crops or the young are conceived if the contract is for the sale of unborn young to be born within twelve months after contracting or for the sale of crops to be harvested within twelve months or the next normal harvest season after contracting whichever is longer.

(2) The seller retains an insurable interest in goods so long as title to or any security interest in the goods remains in him and where the identification is by the seller alone he may until default or insolvency or notification to the buyer that the identification is final substitute other goods for those identified.

(3) Nothing in this section impairs any insurable interest recognized under any other statute or rule of law.

§ 2—502. **Buyer's Right to Goods on Seller's Insolvency.**

(1) Subject to subsection (2) and even though the goods have not been shipped a buyer who has paid a part or all of the price of goods in which he has a special property under the provisions of the immediately preceding section may on making and keeping good a tender of any unpaid portion of their price recover them from the seller if the seller becomes insolvent within ten days after receipt of the first installment on their price.

(2) If the identification creating his special property has been made by the buyer he acquires the right to recover the goods only if they conform to the contract for sale.

§ 2—503. **Manner of Seller's Tender of Delivery.**

(1) Tender of delivery requires that the seller put and hold conforming goods at the buyer's disposition and give the buyer any notification reasonably necessary to enable him to take delivery. The manner, time and place for tender are determined by the agreement and this Article, and in particular

(a) tender must be at a reasonable hour, and if it is of goods they must be kept available for the period reasonably necessary to enable the buyer to take possession; but

(b) unless otherwise agreed the buyer must furnish facilities reasonably suited to the receipt of the goods.

(2) Where the case is within the next section respecting shipment tender requires that the seller comply with its provisions.

(3) Where the seller is required to deliver at a particular destination tender requires that he comply with subsection (1) and also in any appropriate case tender documents as described in subsections (4) and (5) of this section.

(4) Where goods are in the possession of a bailee and are to be delivered without being moved

(a) tender requires that the seller either tender a negotiable document of title covering such goods or procure acknowledgment by the bailee of the buyer's right to possession of the goods; but

(b) tender to the buyer of a non-negotiable document of title or of a written direction to the bailee to deliver is sufficient tender unless the buyer seasonably objects, and receipt by the bailee of notification of the buyer's rights fixes those rights as against the bailee and all third persons; but risk of loss of the goods and of any failure by the bailee to honor the nonnegotiable document of title or to obey the direction remains on the seller until the buyer has had a reasonable time to present the document or direction, and a refusal by the bailee to honor the document or to obey the direction defeats the tender.

(5) Where the contract requires the seller to deliver documents

(a) he must tender all such documents in correct form, except as provided in this Article with respect to bills of lading in a set (subsection (2) of Section 2—323); and

(b) tender through customary banking channels is sufficient and dishonor of a draft accompanying the documents constitutes non-acceptance or rejection.

§ 2—504. **Shipment by Seller.**

Where the seller is required or authorized to send the goods to the buyer and the contract does not require him to deliver them at a particular destination, then unless otherwise agreed he must

(a) put the goods in the possession of such a carrier and make such a contract for their transportation as may be reasonable having regard to the nature of the goods and other circumstances of the case; and

(b) obtain and promptly deliver or tender in due form any document necessary to enable the buyer to obtain possession of the goods or otherwise required by the agreement or by usage of trade; and

(c) promptly notify the buyer of the shipment.

Failure to notify the buyer under paragraph (c) or to make a proper contract under paragraph (a) is a ground for rejection only if material delay or loss ensues.

§ 2—505. **Seller's Shipment Under Reservation.**

(1) Where the seller has identified goods to the contract by or before shipment:

(a) his procurement of a negotiable bill of lading to his own order or otherwise reserves in him a security interest in the goods. His procurement of the bill to the order of a financing agency or of the buyer indicates in addition only the seller's expectation of transferring that interest to the person named.

(b) a non-negotiable bill of lading to himself or his nominee reserves possession of the goods as security but except in a case of conditional delivery (subsection (2) of Section 2—507) a non-negotiable bill of lading naming the buyer as consignee reserves no security interest even though the seller retains possession of the bill of lading.

(2) When shipment by the seller with reservation of a security interest is in violation of the contract for sale it constitutes an improper contract for transportation within the preceding section but impairs neither the rights given to the buyer by shipment and identification of the goods to the contract nor the seller's powers as a holder of a negotiable document.

§ 2—506. **Rights of Financing Agency.**

(1) A financing agency by paying or purchasing for value a draft which relates to a shipment of goods acquires to the extent of the payment or purchase and in addition to its own rights under the draft and any document of title securing it any rights of the shipper in the goods including the right to stop delivery and the shipper's right to have the draft honored by the buyer.

(2) The right to reimbursement of a financing agency which has in good faith honored or purchased the draft under commitment to or authority from the buyer is not impaired by subsequent discovery of defects with reference to any relevant document which was apparently regular on its face.

§ 2—507. **Effect of Seller's Tender; Delivery on Condition.**

(1) Tender of delivery is a condition to the buyer's duty to accept the goods and, unless otherwise agreed, to his duty to pay for them. Tender entitles the seller to acceptance of the goods and to payment according to the contract.

(2) Where payment is due and demanded on the delivery to the buyer of goods or documents of title, his right as against the seller to retain or dispose of them is conditional upon his making the payment due.

§ 2—508. **Cure by Seller of Improper Tender or Delivery; Replacement.**

(1) Where any tender or delivery by the seller is rejected because non-conforming and the time for performance has not yet expired, the seller may seasonably notify the buyer of his intention to cure and may then within the contract time make a conforming delivery.

(2) Where the buyer rejects a non-conforming tender which the seller had reasonable grounds to believe would be acceptable with or without money allowance the seller may if he seasonably notifies the buyer have a further reasonable time to substitute a conforming tender.

§ 2—509. **Risk of Loss in the Absence of Breach.**

(1) Where the contract requires or authorizes the seller to ship the goods by carrier

(a) if it does not require him to deliver them at a particular destination, the risk of loss passes to the buyer when the goods are duly delivered to the carrier even though the shipment is under reservation (Section 2—505); but

(b) if it does require him to deliver them at a particular destination and the goods are there duly tendered while in the possession of the carrier, the risk of loss passes to the buyer when the goods are there duly so tendered as to enable the buyer to take delivery.

(2) Where the goods are held by a bailee to be delivered without being moved, the risk of loss passes to the buyer

(a) on his receipt of a negotiable document of title covering the goods; or

(b) on acknowledgment by the bailee of the buyer's right to possession of the goods; or

(c) after his receipt of a non-negotiable document of title or other written direction to deliver, as provided in subsection (4)(b) of Section 2—503.

(3) In any case not within subsection (1) or (2), the risk of loss passes to the buyer on his receipt of the goods if the seller is a merchant; otherwise, the risk passes to the buyer on tender of delivery.

(4) The provisions of this section are subject to contrary agreement of the parties and to the provisions of this Article on sale on approval (Section 2—327) and on effect of breach on risk of loss (Section 2—510).

§ 2—510. **Effect of Breach on Risk of Loss.**

(1) Where a tender or delivery of goods so fails to conform to the contract as to give a right of rejection the risk of their loss remains on the seller until cure or acceptance.

(2) Where the buyer rightfully revokes acceptance he may to the extent of any deficiency in his effective insurance coverage treat the risk of loss as having rested on the seller from the beginning.

(3) Where the buyer as to conforming goods already identified to the contract for sale repudiates or is otherwise in breach before risk of their loss has passed to him, the seller may to the extent of any deficiency in his effective insurance coverage treat the risk of loss as resting on the buyer for a commercially reasonable time.

§ 2—511. **Tender of Payment by Buyer; Payment by Check.**

(1) Unless otherwise agreed tender of payment is a condition to the seller's duty to tender and complete any delivery.

(2) Tender of payment is sufficient when made by any means or in any manner current in the ordinary course of business unless the seller demands payment in legal tender and gives any extension of time reasonably necessary to procure it.

(3) Subject to the provisions of this Act on the effect of an instrument on an obligation (Section 3—802), payment by check is conditional and is defeated as between the parties by dishonor of the check on due presentment.

§ 2—512. **Payment by Buyer Before Inspection.**

(1) Where the contract requires payment before inspection non-conformity of the goods does not excuse the buyer from so making payment unless

(a) the non-conformity appears without inspection; or

(b) despite tender of the required documents the circumstances would justify injunction against honor under the provisions of this Act (Section 5—114).

(2) Payment pursuant to subsection (1) does not constitute an acceptance of goods or impair the buyer's right to inspect or any of his remedies.

§ 2—513. **Buyer's Right to Inspection of Goods.**

(1) Unless otherwise agreed and subject to subsection (3), where goods are tendered or delivered or identified to the contract for sale, the buyer has a right before payment or acceptance to inspect them at any reasonable place and time and in any reasonable manner. When the seller is required or authorized to send the goods to the buyer, the inspection may be after their arrival.

(2) Expenses of inspection must be borne by the buyer but may be recovered from the seller if the goods do not conform and are rejected.

(3) Unless otherwise agreed and subject to the provisions of this Article on C.I.F. contracts (subsection (3) of Section 2—321), the buyer is not entitled to inspect the goods before payment of the price when the contract provides

(a) for delivery "C.O.D." or on other like terms; or

(b) for payment against documents of title, except where such payment is due only after the goods are to become available for inspection.

(4) A place or method of inspection fixed by the parties is presumed to be exclusive but unless otherwise expressly agreed it does not postpone identification or shift the place for delivery or for passing the risk of loss. If compliance becomes impossible, inspection shall be as provided in this section unless the place or method fixed was clearly intended as an indispensable condition failure of which avoids the contract.

§ 2—514. **When Documents Deliverable on Acceptance; When on Payment.**

Unless otherwise agreed documents against which a draft is drawn are to be delivered to the drawee on acceptance of the draft if it is payable more than three days after presentment; otherwise, only on payment.

§ 2—515. **Preserving Evidence of Goods in Dispute.**

In furtherance of the adjustment of any claim or dispute

(a) either party on reasonable notification to the other and for the purpose of ascertaining the facts and preserving evidence has the right to inspect, test and sample the goods including such of them as may be in the possession or control of the other; and

(b) the parties may agree to a third party inspection or survey to determine the conformity or condition of the goods and may agree that the findings shall be binding upon them in any subsequent litigation or adjustment.

Part 6 **Breach, Repudiation and Excuse**

§ 2—601. **Buyer's Rights on Improper Delivery.**

Subject to the provisions of this Article on breach in installment contracts (Section 2—612) and unless otherwise agreed under the sections on contractual limitations of remedy (Sections 2—718 and 2—719), if the goods or the tender of delivery fail in any respect to conform to the contract, the buyer may

(a) reject the whole; or

(b) accept the whole; or

(c) accept any commercial unit or units and reject the rest.

§ 2—602. **Manner and Effect of Rightful Rejection.**

(1) Rejection of goods must be within a reasonable time after their delivery or tender. It is ineffective unless the buyer seasonably notifies the seller.

(2) Subject to the provisions of the two following sections on rejected goods (Sections 2—603 and 2—604),

(a) after rejection any exercise of ownership by the buyer with respect to any commercial unit is wrongful as against the seller; and

(b) if the buyer has before rejection taken physical possession of goods in which he does not have a security interest under the provisions of this Article (subsection (3) of Section 2—711), he is under a duty after rejection to hold them with reasonable care at the seller's disposition for a time sufficient to permit the seller to remove them; but

(c) the buyer has no further obligations with regard to goods rightfully rejected.

(3) The seller's rights with respect to goods wrongfully rejected are governed by the provisions of this Article on seller's remedies in general (Section 2—703).

§ 2—603. **Merchant Buyer's Duties as to Rightfully Rejected Goods.**

(1) Subject to any security interest in the buyer (subsection (3) of Section 2—711), when the seller has no agent or place of business at the market of rejection a merchant buyer is under a duty after rejection of goods in his possession or control to follow any reasonable instructions received from the seller with respect to the goods and in the absence of such instructions to make reasonable efforts to sell them for the seller's account if they are perishable or threaten to decline in value speedily. Instructions are not reasonable if on demand indemnity for expenses is not forthcoming.

(2) When the buyer sells goods under subsection (1), he is entitled to reimbursement from the seller or out of the proceeds for reasonable expenses of caring for and selling them, and if the expenses include no selling commission then to such commission as is usual in the trade or if there is none to a reasonable sum not exceeding ten per cent on the gross proceeds.

(3) In complying with this section the buyer is held only to good faith and good faith conduct hereunder is neither acceptance nor conversion nor the basis of an action for damages.

§ 2—604. **Buyer's Options as to Salvage of Rightfully Rejected Goods.**

Subject to the provisions of the immediately preceding section on perishables if the seller gives no instructions within a reasonable time after notification of rejection the buyer may store the rejected goods for the seller's account or reship them to him or resell them for the seller's account with reimbursement as provided in the preceding section. Such action is not acceptance or conversion.

§ 2—605. **Waiver of Buyer's Objections by Failure to Particularize.**

(1) The buyer's failure to state in connection with rejection a particular defect which is ascertainable by reasonable inspection precludes him from relying on the unstated defect to justify rejection or to establish breach

(a) where the seller could have cured it if stated seasonably; or

(b) between merchants when the seller has after rejection made a request in writing for a full and final written statement of all defects on which the buyer proposes to rely.

(2) Payment against documents made without reservation of rights precludes recovery of the payment for defects apparent on the face of the documents.

§ 2—606. **What Constitutes Acceptance of Goods.**

(1) Acceptance of goods occurs when the buyer

(a) after a reasonable opportunity to inspect the goods signifies to the seller that the goods are conforming or that he will take or retain them in spite of their nonconformity; or

(b) fails to make an effective rejection (subsection (1) of Section 2—602), but such acceptance does not occur until the buyer has had a reasonable opportunity to inspect them; or

(c) does any act inconsistent with the seller's ownership; but if such act is wrongful as against the seller it is an acceptance only if ratified by him.

(2) Acceptance of a part of any commercial unit is acceptance of that entire unit.

§ 2—607. **Effect of Acceptance; Notice of Breach; Burden of Establishing Breach After Acceptance; Notice of Claim or Litigation to Person Answerable Over.**

(1) The buyer must pay at the contract rate for any goods accepted.

(2) Acceptance of goods by the buyer precludes rejection of the goods accepted and if made with knowledge of a non-conformity cannot be revoked because of it unless the acceptance was on the reasonable assumption that

the non-conformity would be seasonably cured but acceptance does not of itself impair any other remedy provided by this Article for non-conformity.

(3) Where a tender has been accepted

(a) the buyer must within a reasonble time after he discovers or should have discovered any breach notify the seller of breach or be barred from any remedy; and

(b) if the claim is one for infringement or the like (subsection (3) of Section 2—312) and the buyer is sued as a result of such a breach he must so notify the seller within a reasonable time after he receives notice of the litigation or be barred from any remedy over for liability established by the litigation.

(4) The burden is on the buyer to establish any breach with respect to the goods accepted.

(5) Where the buyer is sued for breach of a warranty or other obligation for which his seller is answerable over

(a) he may give his seller written notice of the litigation. If the notice states that the seller may come in and defend and that if the seller does not do so he will be bound in any action against him by his buyer by any determination of fact common to the two litigations, then unless the seller after seasonable receipt of the notice does come in and defend he is so bound.

(b) if the claim is one for infringement or the like (subsection (3) of Section 2—312) the original seller may demand in writing that his buyer turn over to him control of the litigation including settlement or else be barred from any remedy over and if he also agrees to bear all expense and to satisfy any adverse judgment, then unless the buyer after seasonable receipt of the demand does turn over control the buyer is so barred.

(6) The provisions of subsections (3), (4) and (5) apply to any obligation of a buyer to hold the seller harmless against infringement or the like (subsection (3) of Section 2—312).

§ 2—608. **Revocation of Acceptance in Whole or in Part.**

(1) The buyer may revoke his acceptance of a lot or commercial unit whose non-conformity substantially impairs its value to him if he has accepted it

(a) on the reasonable assumption that its non- conformity would be cured and it has not been seasonably cured; or

(b) without discovery of such non-conformity if his acceptance was reasonably induced either by the dif-

ficulty of discovery before acceptance or by the seller's assurances.

(2) Revocation of acceptance must occur within a reasonable time after the buyer discovers or should have discovered the ground for it and before any substantial change in condition of the goods which is not caused by their own defects. It is not effective until the buyer notifies the seller of it.

(3) A buyer who so revokes has the same rights and duties with regard to the goods involved as if he had rejected them.

§ 2—609. **Right to Adequate Assurance of Performance.**

(1) A contract for sale imposes an obligation on each party that the other's expectation of receiving due performance will not be impaired. When reasonable grounds for insecurity arise with respect to the performance of either party the other may in writing demand adequate assurance of due performance and until he receives such assurance may if commercially reasonable suspend any performance for which he has not already received the agreed return.

(2) Between merchants the reasonableness of grounds for insecurity and the adequacy of any assurance offered shall be determined according to commercial standards.

(3) Acceptance of any improper delivery or payment does not prejudice the aggrieved party's right to demand adequate assurance of future performance.

(4) After receipt of a justified demand failure to provide within a reasonable time not exceeding thirty days such assurance of due performance as is adequate under the circumstances of the particular case is a repudiation of the contract.

§ 2—610. **Anticipatory Repudiation.**

When either party repudiates the contract with respect to a performance not yet due the loss of which will substantially impair the value of the contract to the other, the aggrieved party may

(a) for a commercially reasonable time await performance by the repudiating party; or

(b) resort to any remedy for breach (Section 2—703 or Section 2—711), even though he has notified the repudiating party that he would await the latter's performance and has urged retraction; and

(c) in either case suspend his own performance or proceed in accordance with the provisions of this Article on the seller's right to identify goods to the contract notwithstanding breach or to salvage unfinished goods (Section 2—704).

§ 2—611. **Retraction of Anticipatory Repudiation.**

(1) Until the repudiating party's next performance is due he can retract his repudiation unless the aggrieved party has since the repudiation cancelled or materially changed his position or otherwise indicated that he considers the repudiation final.

(2) Retraction may be by any method which clearly indicates to the aggrieved party that the repudiating party intends to perform, but must include any assurance justifiably demanded under the provisions of this Article (Section 2—609).

(3) Retraction reinstates the repudiating party's rights under the contract with due excuse and allowance to the aggrieved party for any delay occasioned by the repudiation.

§ 2—612. **"Installment Contract"; Breach.**

(1) An "installment contract" is one which requires or authorizes the delivery of goods in separate lots to be separately accepted, even though the contract contains a clause "each delivery is a separate contract" or its equivalent.

(2) The buyer may reject any installment which is nonconforming if the non-conformity substantially impairs the value of that installment and cannot be cured or if the non-conformity is a defect in the required documents; but if the non-conformity does not fall within subsection (3) and the seller gives adequate assurance of its cure the buyer must accept that installment.

(3) Whenever non-conformity or default with respect to one or more installments substantially impairs the value of the whole contract there is a breach of the whole. But the aggrieved party reinstates the contract if he accepts a non-conforming installment without seasonably notifying of cancellation or if he brings an action with respect only to past installments or demands performance as to future installments.

§ 2—613. **Casualty to Identified Goods.**

Where the contract requires for its performance goods identified when the contract is made, and the goods suffer casualty without fault of either party before the risk of loss passes to the buyer, or in a proper case under a "no arrival, no sale" term (Section 2—324) then

(a) if the loss is total the contract is avoided; and

(b) if the loss is partial or the goods have so deteriorated as no longer to conform to the contract the buyer may nevertheless demand inspection and at his option either treat the contract as voided or accept the goods with due allowance from the contract price for the deterioration or the deficiency in quantity but without further right against the seller.

§ 2—614. **Substituted Performance.**

(1) Where without fault of either party the agreed berthing, loading, or unloading facilities fail or an agreed type of carrier becomes unavailable or the agreed manner of delivery otherwise becomes commercially impracticable but a commercially reasonable substitute is available, such substitute performance must be tendered and accepted.

(2) If the agreed means or manner of payment fails because of domestic or foreign governmental regulation, the seller may withhold or stop delivery unless the buyer provides a means or manner of payment which is commercially a substantial equivalent. If delivery has already been taken, payment by the means or in the manner provided by the regulation discharges the buyer's obligation unless the regulation is discriminatory, oppressive or predatory.

§ 2—615. **Excuse by Failure of Presupposed Conditions.**

Except so far as a seller may have assumed a greater obligation and subject to the preceding section on substituted performance:

(a) Delay in delivery or non-delivery in whole or in part by a seller who complies with paragraphs (b) and (c) is not a breach of his duty under a contract for sale if performance as agreed has been made impracticable by the occurrence of a contingency the nonoccurrence of which was a basic assumption on which the contract was made or by compliance in good faith with any applicable foreign or domestic governmental regulation or order whether or not it later proves to be invalid.

(b) Where the causes mentioned in paragraph (a) affect only a part of the seller's capacity to perform, he must allocate production and deliveries among his customers but may at his option include regular customers not then under contract as well as his own requirements for further manufacture. He may so allocate in any manner which is fair and reasonable.

(c) The seller must notify the buyer seasonably that there will be delay or non-delivery and, when allocation is required under paragraph (b), of the estimated quota thus made available for the buyer.

§ 2—616. **Procedure on Notice Claiming Excuse.**

(1) Where the buyer receives notification of a material or indefinite delay or an allocation justified under the preceding section he may by written notification to the seller as to any delivery concerned, and where the prospective deficiency substantially impairs the value of the whole contract under the provisions of this Article relating to breach of installment contracts (Section 2—612), then also as to the whole,

(a) terminate and thereby discharge any unexecuted portion of the contract; or

(b) modify the contract by agreeing to take his available quota in substitution.

(2) If after receipt of such notification from the seller the buyer fails so to modify the contract within a reasonable time not exceeding thirty days the contract lapses with respect to any deliveries affected.

(3) The provisions of this section may not be negated by agreement except in so far as the seller has assumed a greater obligation under the preceding section.

Part 7 Remedies

§ 2—701. **Remedies for Breach of Collateral Contracts Not Impaired.**

Remedies for breach of any obligation or promise collateral or ancillary to a contract for sale are not impaired by the provisions of this Article.

§ 2—702. **Seller's Remedies on Discovery of Buyer's Insolvency.**

(1) Where the seller discovers the buyer to be insolvent he may refuse delivery except for cash including payment for all goods theretofore delivered under the contract, and stop delivery under this Article (Section 2—705).

(2) Where the seller discovers that the buyer has received goods on credit while insolvent he may reclaim the goods upon demand made within ten days after the receipt, but if misrepresentation of solvency has been made to the particular seller in writing within three months before delivery the ten day limitation does not apply. Except as provided in this subsection the seller may not base a right to reclaim goods on the buyer's fraudulent or innocent misrepresentation of solvency or of intent to pay.

(3) The seller's right to reclaim under subsection (2) is subject to the rights of a buyer in ordinary course or other good faith purchaser under this Article (Section 2—403). Successful reclamation of goods excludes all other remedies with respect to them.

§ 2—703. **Seller's Remedies in General.**

Where the buyer wrongfully rejects or revokes acceptance of goods or fails to make a payment due on or before delivery or repudiates with respect to a part or the whole, then with respect to any goods directly affected and, if the breach is of the whole contract (Section 2—612), then also with respect to the whole undelivered balance, the aggrieved seller may

(a) withhold delivery of such goods;

(b) stop delivery by any bailee as hereafter provided (Section 2—705);

(c) proceed under the next section respecting goods still unidentified to the contract;

(d) resell and recover damages as hereafter provided (Section 2—706);

(e) recover damages for non-acceptance (Section 2—708) or in a proper case the price (Section 2—709);

(f) cancel.

§ 2—704. **Seller's Right to Identify Goods to the Contract Notwithstanding Breach or to Salvage Unfinished Goods.**

(1) An aggrieved seller under the preceding section may

(a) identify to the contract conforming goods not already identified if at the time he learned of the breach they are in his possession or control;

(b) treat as the subject of resale goods which have demonstrably been intended for the particular contract even though those goods are unfinished.

(2) Where the goods are unfinished an aggrieved seller may in the exercise of reasonable commercial judgment for the purposes of avoiding loss and of effective realization either complete the manufacture and wholly identify the goods to the contract or cease manufacture and resell for scrap or salvage value or proceed in any other reasonable manner.

§ 2—705. **Seller's Stoppage of Delivery in Transit or Otherwise.**

(1) The seller may stop delivery of goods in the possession of a carrier or other bailee when he discovers the buyer to be insolvent (Section 2—702) and may stop delivery of carload, truckload, planeload or larger shipments of express or freight when the buyer repudiates or fails to make a payment due before delivery or if for any other reason the seller has a right to withhold or reclaim the goods.

(2) As against such buyer the seller may stop delivery until

(a) receipt of the goods by the buyer; or

(b) acknowledgment to the buyer by any bailee of the goods except a carrier that the bailee holds the goods for the buyer; or

(c) such acknowledgment to the buyer by a carrier by reshipment or as warehouseman; or

(d) negotiation to the buyer of any negotiable document of title covering the goods.

(3) (a) To stop delivery the seller must so notify as to enable the bailee by reasonable diligence to prevent delivery of the goods.

(b) After such notification the bailee must hold and deliver the goods according to the directions of the seller but the seller is liable to the bailee for any ensuing charges or damages.

(c) If a negotiable document of title has been issued for goods the bailee is not obliged to obey a notification to stop until surrender of the document.

(d) A carrier who has issued a non-negotiable bill of lading is not obliged to obey a notification to stop received from a person other than the consignor.

§ 2—706. Seller's Resale Including Contract for Resale.

(1) Under the conditions stated in Section 2—703 on seller's remedies, the seller may resell the goods concerned or the undelivered balance thereof. Where the resale is made in good faith and in a commercially reasonable manner the seller may recover the difference between the resale price and the contract price together with any incidental damages allowed under the provisions of this Article (Section 2—710), but less expenses saved in consequence of the buyer's breach.

(2) Except as otherwise provided in subsection (3) or unless otherwise agreed resale may be at public or private sale including sale by way of one or more contracts to sell or of identification to an existing contract of the seller. Sale may be as a unit or in parcels and at any time and place and on any terms but every aspect of the sale including the method, manner, time, place and terms must be commercially reasonable. The resale must be reasonably identified as referring to the broken contract, but it is not necessary that the goods be in existence or that any or all of them have been identified to the contract before the breach.

(3) Where the resale is at private sale the seller must give the buyer reasonable notification of his intention to resell.

(4) Where the resale is at public sale

(a) only identified goods can be sold except where there is a recognized market for a public sale of futures in goods of the kind; and

(b) it must be made at a usual place or market for public sale if one is reasonably available and except in the case of goods which are perishable or threaten to decline in value speedily the seller must give the buyer reasonable notice of the time and place of the resale; and

(c) if the goods are not to be within the view of those attending the sale the notification of sale must state the place where the goods are located and provide for their reasonable inspection by prospective bidders; and

(d) the seller may buy.

(5) A purchaser who buys in good faith at a resale takes the goods free of any rights of the original buyer even though the seller fails to comply with one or more of the requirements of this section.

(6) The seller is not accountable to the buyer for any profit made on any resale. A person in the position of a seller (Section 2—707) or a buyer who has rightfully rejected or justifiably revoked acceptance must account for any excess over the amount of his security interest, as hereinafter defined (subsection (3) of Section 2—711).

§ 2—707. "Person in the Position of a Seller".

(1) A "person in the position of a seller" includes as against a principal an agent who has paid or become responsible for the price of goods on behalf of his principal or anyone who otherwise holds a security interest or other right in goods similar to that of a seller.

(2) A person in the position of a seller may as provided in this Article withhold or stop delivery (Section 2—705) and resell (Section 2—706) and recover incidental damages (Section 2—710).

§ 2—708. Seller's Damages for Non-Acceptance or Repudiation.

(1) Subject to subsection (2) and to the provisions of this Article with respect to proof of market price (Section 2—723), the measure of damages for non-acceptance or repudiation by the buyer is the difference between the market price at the time and place for tender and the unpaid contract price together with any incidental damages provided in this Article (Section 2—710), but less expenses saved in consequence of the buyer's breach.

(2) If the measure of damages provided in subsection (1) is inadequate to put the seller in as good a position as performance would have done then the measure of damages is the profit (including reasonable overhead) which the seller would have made from full performance by the buyer, together with any incidental damages provided in this Article (Section 2—710), due allowance for costs reasonably incurred and due credit for payments or proceeds of resale.

§ 2—709. Action for the Price.

(1) When the buyer fails to pay the price as it becomes due the seller may recover, together with any incidental damages under the next section, the price

(a) of goods accepted or of conforming goods lost or damaged within a commercially reasonable time after risk of their loss has passed to the buyer; and

(b) of goods identified to the contract if the seller is unable after reasonable effort to resell them at a reasonable price or the circumstances reasonably indicate that such effort will be unavailing.

(2) Where the seller sues for the price he must hold for the buyer any goods which have been identified to the contract and are still in his control except that if resale become possible he may resell them at any time prior to the collection of the judgment. The net proceeds of any such resale must be credited to the buyer and payment of the judgment entitles him to any goods not resold.

(3) After the buyer has wrongfully rejected or revoked acceptance of the goods or has failed to make a payment due or has repudiated (Section 2—610), a seller who is held not entitled to the price under this section shall nevertheless be awarded damages for non-acceptance under the preceding section.

§ 2—710. Seller's Incidental Damages.

Incidental damages to an aggrieved seller include any commercially reasonable charges, expenses or commissions incurred in stopping delivery, in the transportation, care and custody of goods after the buyer's breach, in connection with return or resale of the goods or otherwise resulting from the breach.

§ 2—711. Buyer's Remedies in General; Buyer's Security Interest in Rejected Goods.

(1) Where the seller fails to make delivery or repudiates or the buyer rightfully rejects or justifiably revokes acceptance then with respect to any goods involved, and with respect to the whole if the breach goes to the whole contract (Section 2—612), the buyer may cancel and whether or not he has done so may in addition to recovering so much of the price as has been paid

(a) "cover" and have damages under the next section as to all the goods affected whether or not they have been identified to the contract; or

(b) recover damages for non-delivery as provided in this Article (Section 2—713).

(2) Where the seller fails to deliver or repudiates the buyer may also

(a) if the goods have been identified recover them as provided in this Article (Section 2—502); or

(b) in a proper case obtain specific performance or replevy the goods as provided in this Article (Section 2—716).

(3) On rightful rejection or justifiable revocation of acceptance a buyer has a security interest in goods in his possession or control for any payments made on their price and any expenses reasonably incurred in their inspection, receipt, transportation, care and custody and

may hold such goods and resell them in like manner as an aggrieved seller (Section 2—706).

§ 2—712. "Cover"; Buyer's Procurement of Substitute Goods.

(1) After a breach within the preceding section the buyer may "cover" by making in good faith and without unreasonable delay any reasonable purchase of or contract to purchase goods in substitution for those due from the seller.

(2) The buyer may recover from the seller as damages the difference between the cost of cover and the contract price together with any incidental or consequential damages as hereinafter defined (Section 2—715), but less expenses saved in consequence of the seller's breach.

(3) Failure of the buyer to effect cover within this section does not bar him from any other remedy.

§ 2—713. Buyer's Damages for Non-Delivery or Repudiation.

(1) Subject to the provisions of this Article with respect to proof of market price (Section 2—723), the measure of damages for non-delivery or repudiation by the seller is the difference between the market price at the time when the buyer learned of the breach and the contract price together with any incidental and consequential damages provided in this Article (Section 2—715), but less expenses saved in consequence of the seller's breach.

(2) Market price is to be determined as of the place for tender or, in cases of rejection after arrival or revocation of acceptance, as of the place of arrival.

§ 2—714. Buyer's Damages for Breach in Regard to Accepted Goods.

(1) Where the buyer has accepted goods and given notification (subsection (3) of Section 2—607) he may recover as damages for any non-conformity of tender the loss resulting in the ordinary course of events from the seller's breach as determined in any manner which is reasonable.

(2) The measure of damages for breach of warranty is the difference at the time and place of acceptance between the value of the goods accepted and the value they would have had if they had been as warranted, unless special circumstances show proximate damages of a different amount.

(3) In a proper case any incidental and consequential damages under the next section may also be recovered.

§ 2—715. Buyer's Incidental and Consequential Damages.

(1) Incidental damages resulting from the seller's breach include expenses reasonably incurred in inspection, receipt, transportation and care and custody of goods rightfully rejected, any commercially reasonable charges, expenses or commissions in connection with effecting cover and any other reasonable expense incident to the delay or other breach.

(2) Consequential damages resulting from the seller's breach include

(a) any loss resulting from general or particular requirements and needs of which the seller at the time of contracting had reason to know and which could not reasonably be prevented by cover or otherwise; and

(b) injury to person or property proximately resulting from any breach of warranty.

§ 2—716. Buyer's Right to Specific Performance or Replevin.

(1) Specific performance may be decreed where the goods are unique or in other proper circumstances.

(2) The decree for specific performance may include such terms and conditions as to payment of the price, damages, or other relief as the court may deem just.

(3) The buyer has a right of replevin for goods identified to the contract if after reasonable effort he is unable to effect cover for such goods or the circumstances reasonably indicate that such effort will be unavailing or if the goods have been shipped under reservation and satisfaction of the security interest in them has been made or tendered.

§ 2—717. Deduction of Damages From the Price.

The buyer on notifying the seller of his intention to do so may deduct all or any part of the damages resulting from any breach of the contract from any part of the price still due under the same contract.

§ 2—718. Liquidation or Limitation of Damages; Deposits.

(1) Damages for breach by either party may be liquidated in the agreement but only at an amount which is reasonable in the light of the anticipated or actual harm caused by the breach, the difficulties of proof of loss, and the inconvenience or nonfeasibility of otherwise obtaining an adequate remedy. A term fixing unreasonably large liquidated damages is void as a penalty.

(2) Where the seller justifiably withholds delivery of goods because of the buyer's breach, the buyer is entitled to restitution of any amount by which the sum of his payments exceeds

(a) the amount to which the seller is entitled by virtue of terms liquidating the seller's damages in accordance with subsection (1), or

(b) in the absence of such terms, twenty per cent of the value of the total performance for which the buyer is obligated under the contract or $500, whichever is smaller.

(3) The buyer's right to restitution under subsection (2) is subject to offset to the extent that the seller establishes

(a) a right to recover damages under the provisions of this Article other than subsection (1), and

(b) the amount or value of any benefits received by the buyer directly or indirectly by reason of the contract.

(4) Where a seller has received payment in goods their reasonable value or the proceeds of their resale shall be treated as payments for the purposes of subsection (2); but if the seller has notice of the buyer's breach before reselling goods received in part performance, his resale is subject to the conditions laid down in this Article on resale by an aggrieved seller (Section 2—706).

§ 2—719. Contractual Modification or Limitation of Remedy.

(1) Subject to the provisions of subsections (2) and (3) of this section and of the preceding section on liquidation and limitation of damages,

(a) the agreement may provide for remedies in addition to or in substitution for those provided in this Article and may limit or alter the measure of damages recoverable under this Article, as by limiting the buyer's remedies to return of the goods and repayment of the price or to repair and replacement of nonconforming goods or parts; and

(b) resort to a remedy as provided is optional unless the remedy is expressly agreed to be exclusive, in which case it is the sole remedy.

(2) Where circumstances cause an exclusive or limited remedy to fail of its essential purpose, remedy may be had as provided in this Act.

(3) Consequential damages may be limited or excluded unless the limitation or exclusion is unconscionable. Limitation of consequential damages for injury to the person in the case of consumer goods is prima facie unconscionable but limitation of damages where the loss is commercial is not.

§ 2—720. Effect of "Cancellation" or "Rescission" on Claims for Antecedent Breach.

Unless the contrary intention clearly appears, expressions of "cancellation" or "rescission" of the contract or the like shall not be construed as a renunciation or discharge of any claim in damages for an antecedent breach.

§ 2—721. **Remedies for Fraud.**

Remedies for material misrepresentation or fraud include all remedies available under this Article for nonfraudulent breach. Neither rescission or a claim for rescission of the contract for sale nor rejection or return of the goods shall bar or be deemed inconsistent with a claim for damages or other remedy.

§ 2—722. **Who Can Sue Third Parties for Injury to Goods.**

Where a third party so deals with goods which have been identified to a contract for sale as to cause actionable injury to a party to that contract

(a) a right of action against the third party is in either party to the contract for sale who has title to or a security interest or a special property or an insurable interest in the goods; and if the goods have been destroyed or converted a right of action is also in the party who either bore the risk of loss under the contract for sale or has since the injury assumed that risk as against the other;

(b) if at the time of the injury the party plaintiff did not bear the risk of loss as against the other party to the contract for sale and there is no arrangement between them for disposition of the recovery, his suit or settlement is, subject to his own interest, as a fiduciary for the other party to the contract;

(c) either party may with the consent of the other sue for the benefit of whom it may concern.

§ 2—723. **Proof of Market Price: Time and Place.**

(1) If an action based on anticipatory repudiation comes to trial before the time for performance with respect to some or all of the goods, any damages based on market price (Section 2—708 or Section 2—713) shall be determined according to the price of such goods prevailing at the time when the aggrieved party learned of the repudiation.

(2) If evidence of a price prevailing at the times or places described in this Article is not readily available the price prevailing within any reasonable time before or after the time described or at any other place which in commercial judgment or under usage of trade would serve as a reasonable substitute for the one described may be used, making any proper allowance for the cost of transporting the goods to or from such other place.

(3) Evidence of a relevant price prevailing at a time or place other than the one described in this Article offered by one party is not admissible unless and until he has given the other party such notice as the court finds sufficient to prevent unfair surprise.

§ 2—724. **Admissibility of Market Quotations.**

Whenever the prevailing price or value of any goods regularly bought and sold in any established commodity market is in issue, reports in official publications or trade journals or in newspapers or periodicals of general circulation published as the reports of such market shall be admissible in evidence. The circumstances of the preparation of such a report may be shown to affect its weight but not its admissibility.

§ 2—725. **Statute of Limitations in Contracts for Sale.**

(1) An action for breach of any contract for sale must be commenced within four years after the cause of action has accrued. By the original agreement the parties may reduce the period of limitation to not less than one year but may not extend it.

(2) A cause of action accrues when the breach occurs, regardless of the aggrieved party's lack of knowledge of the breach. A breach of warranty occurs when tender of delivery is made, except that where a warranty explicitly extends to future performance of the goods and discovery of the breach must await the time of such performance the cause of action accrues when the breach is or should have been discovered.

(3) Where an action commenced within the time limited by subsection (1) is so terminated as to leave available a remedy by another action for the same breach such other action may be commenced after the expiration of the time limited and within six months after the termination of the first action unless the termination resulted from voluntary discontinuance or from dismissal for failure or neglect to prosecute.

(4) This section does not alter the law on tolling of the statute of limitations nor does it apply to causes of action which have accrued before this Act becomes effective.

Article 3
COMMERCIAL PAPER

Part 1 **Short Title, Form and Interpretation**

§ 3—101. **Short Title.**

This Article shall be known and may be cited as Uniform Commercial Code—Commercial Paper.

§ 3—102. **Definitions and Index of Definitions.**

(1) In this Article unless the context otherwise requires

(a) "Issue" means the first delivery of an instrument to a holder or a remitter.

(b) An "order" is a direction to pay and must be more than an authorization or request. It must identify the person to pay with reasonable certainty. It may be addressed to one or more such persons jointly or in the alternative but not in succession.

(c) A "promise" is an undertaking to pay and must be more than an acknowledgment of an obligation.

(d) "Secondary party" means a drawer or endorser.

(e) "Instrument" means a negotiable instrument.

(2) Other definitions applying to this Article and the sections in which they appear are:

"Acceptance". Section 3—410.
"Accommodation party". Section 3—415.
"Alteration". Section 3—407.
"Certificate of deposit". Section 3—104.
"Certification". Section 3—411.
"Check". Section 3—104.
"Definite time". Section 3—109.
"Dishonor". Section 3—507.
"Draft". Section 3—104.
"Holder in due course". Section 3—302.
"Negotiation". Section 3—202.
"Note". Section 3—104.
"Notice of dishonor". Section 3—508.
"On demand". Section 3—108.
"Presentment". Section 3—504.
"Protest". Section 3—509.
"Restrictive Indorsement". Section 3—205.
"Signature". Section 3—401.

(3) The following definitions in other Articles apply to this Article:

"Account". Section 4—104.
"Banking Day". Section 4—104.
"Clearing House". Section 4—104.
"Collecting Bank". Section 4—105.
"Customer". Section 4—104.
"Depositary Bank". Section 4—105.
"Documentary Draft". Section 4—104.
"Intermediary Bank". Section 4—105.
"Item". Section 4—104.
"Midnight deadline". Section 4—104.
"Payor Bank". Section 4—105.

(4) In addition Article 1 contains general definitions and principles of construction and interpretation applicable throughout this Article.

§ 3—103. **Limitations on Scope of Article.**

(1) This Article does not apply to money, documents of title or investment securities.

(2) The provisions of this Article are subject to the provisions of the Article on Bank Deposits and Collections (Article 4) and Secured Transactions (Article 9).

§ 3—104. **Form of Negotiable Instruments; "Draft"; "Check"; "Certificate of Deposit"; "Note".**

(1) Any writing to be a negotiable instrument within this Article must

(a) be signed by the maker or drawer; and

(b) contain an unconditional promise or order to pay a sum certain in money and no other promise, order, obligation or power given by the maker or drawer except as authorized by this Article; and

(c) be payable on demand or at a definite time; and

(d) be payable to order or to bearer.

(2) A writing which complies with the requirements of this section is

(a) a "draft" ("bill of exchange") if it is an order;

(b) a "check" if it is a draft drawn on a bank and payable on demand;

(c) a "certificate of deposit" if it is an acknowledgment by a bank of receipt of money with an engagement to repay it;

(d) a "note" if it is a promise other than a certificate of deposit.

(3) As used in other Articles of this Act, and as the context may require, the terms "draft", "check", "certificate of deposit" and "note" may refer to instruments which are not negotiable within this Article as well as to instruments which are so negotiable.

§ 3—105. **When Promise or Order Unconditional.**

(1) A promise or order otherwise unconditional is not made conditional by the fact that the instrument

(a) is subject to implied or constructive conditions; or

(b) states its consideration, whether performed or promised, or the transaction which gave rise to the instrument, or that the promise or order is made or the instrument matures in accordance with or "as per" such transaction; or

(c) refers to or states that it arises out of a separate agreement or refers to a separate agreement for rights as to prepayment or acceleration; or

(d) states that it is drawn under a letter of credit; or

(e) states that it is secured, whether by mortgage, reservation of title or otherwise; or

(f) indicates a particular account to be debited or any other fund or source from which reimbursement is expected; or

(g) is limited to payment out of a particular fund or the proceeds of a particular source, if the instrument is issued by a government or governmental agency or unit; or

(h) is limited to payment out of the entire assets of a partnership, unincorporated association, trust or estate by or on behalf of which the instrument is issued.

(2) A promise or order is not unconditional if the instrument

(a) states that it is subject to or governed by any other agreement; or

(b) states that it is to be paid only out of a particular fund or source except as provided in this section.

§ 3—106. **Sum Certain.**

(1) The sum payable is a sum certain even though it is to be paid

(a) with stated interest or by stated installments; or

(b) with stated different rates of interest before and after default or a specified date; or

(c) with a stated discount or addition if paid before or after the date fixed for payment; or

(d) with exchange or less exchange, whether at a fixed rate or at the current rate; or

(e) with costs of collection or an attorney's fee or both upon default.

(2) Nothing in this section shall validate any term which is otherwise illegal.

§ 3—107. **Money.**

(1) An instrument is payable in money if the medium of exchange in which it is payable is money at the time the instrument is made. An instrument payable in "currency" or "current funds" is payable in money.

(2) A promise to order to pay a sum stated in a foreign currency is for a sum certain in money and, unless a different medium of payment is specified in the instrument, may be satisfied by payment of that number of dollars which the stated foreign currency will purchase at the buying sight rate for that currency on the day on which the instrument is payable or, if payable on demand, on the day of demand. If such an instrument specifies a foreign currency as the medium of payment the instrument is payable in that currency.

§ 3—108. **Payable on Demand.**

Instruments payable on demand include those payable at sight or on presentation and those in which no time for payment is stated.

§ 3—109. **Definite Time.**

(1) An instrument is payable at a definite time if by its terms it is payable

(a) on or before a stated date or at a fixed period after a stated date; or

(b) at a fixed period after sight; or

(c) at a definite time subject to any acceleration; or

(d) at a definite time subject to extension at the option of the holder, or to extension to a further definite time at the option of the maker or acceptor or automatically upon or after a specified act or event.

(2) An instrument which by its terms is otherwise payable only upon an act or event uncertain as to time of occurrence is not payable at a definite time even though the act or event has occurred.

§ 3—110. **Payable to Order.**

(1) An instrument is payable to order when by its terms it is payable to the order or assigns of any person therein specified with reasonable certainty, or to him or his order, or when it is conspicuously designated on its face as "exchange" or the like and names a payee. It may be payable to the order of

(a) the maker or drawer; or

(b) the drawee; or

(c) a payee who is not maker, drawer or drawee; or

(d) two or more payees together or in the alternative; or

(e) an estate, trust or fund, in which case it is payable to the order of the representative of such estate, trust or fund or his successors; or

(f) an office, or an officer by his title as such in which case it is payable to the principal but the incumbent of the office or his successors may act as if he or they were the holder; or

(g) a partnership or unincorporated association, in which case it is payable to the partnership or association and may be indorsed or transferred by any person thereto authorized.

(2) An instrument not payable to order is not made so payable by such words as "payable upon return of this instrument properly indorsed."

(3) An instrument made payable both to order and to bearer is payable to order unless the bearer words are handwritten or typewritten.

§ 3—111. **Payable to Bearer.**

An instrument is payable to bearer when by its terms it is payable to

(a) bearer or the order of bearer; or

(b) a specified person or bearer; or

(c) "cash" or the order of "cash", or any other indication which does not purport to designate a specific payee.

§ 3—112. Terms and Omissions Not Affecting Negotiability.

(1) The negotiability of an instrument is not affected by

(a) the omission of a statement of any consideration or of the place where the instrument is drawn or payable; or

(b) a statement that collateral has been given to secure obligations either on the instrument or otherwise of an obligor on the instrument or that in case of default on those obligations the holder may realize on or dispose of the collateral; or

(c) a promise or power to maintain or protect collateral or to give additional collateral; or

(d) a term authorizing a confession of judgment on the instrument if it is not paid when due; or

(e) a term purporting to waive the benefit of any law intended for the advantage or protection of any obligor; or

(f) a term in a draft providing that the payee by indorsing or cashing it acknowledges full satisfaction of an obligation of the drawer; or

(g) a statement in a draft drawn in a set of parts (Section 3—801) to the effect that the order is effective only if no other part has been honored.

(2) Nothing in this section shall validate any term which is otherwise illegal.

§ 3—113. Seal.

An instrument otherwise negotiable is within this Article even though it is under a seal.

§ 3—114. Date, Antedating, Postdating.

(1) The negotiability of an instrument is not affected by the fact that it is undated, antedated or postdated.

(2) Where an instrument is antedated or postdated the time when it is payable is determined by the stated date if the instrument is payable on demand or at a fixed period after date.

(3) Where the instrument or any signature thereon is dated, the date is presumed to be correct.

§ 3—115. Incomplete Instruments.

(1) When a paper whose contents at the time of signing show that it is intended to become an instrument is signed while still incomplete in any necessary respect it cannot be enforced until completed, but when it is completed in

accordance with authority given it is effective as completed.

(2) If the completion is unauthorized the rules as to material alteration apply (Section 3—407), even though the paper was not delivered by the maker or drawer; but the burden of establishing that any completion is unauthorized is on the party so asserting.

§ 3—116. Instruments Payable to Two or More Persons.

An instrument payable to the order of two or more persons

(a) if in the alternative is payable to any one of them and may be negotiated, discharged or enforced by any of them who has possession of it;

(b) if not in the alternative is payable to all of them and may be negotiated, discharged or enforced only by all of them.

§ 3—117. Instruments Payable With Words of Description.

An instrument made payable to a named person with the addition of words describing him

(a) as agent or officer of a specified person is payable to his principal but the agent or officer may act as if he were the holder;

(b) as any other fiduciary for a specified person or purpose is payable to the payee and may be negotiated, discharged or enforced by him;

(c) in any other manner is payable to the payee unconditionally and the additional words are without effect on subsequent parties.

§ 3—118. Ambiguous Terms and Rules of Construction.

The following rules apply to every instrument:

(a) Where there is doubt whether the instrument is a draft or a note the holder may treat it as either. A draft drawn on the drawer is effective as a note.

(b) Handwritten terms control typewritten and printed terms, and typewritten control printed.

(c) Words control figures except that if the words are ambiguous figures control.

(d) Unless otherwise specified a provision for interest means interest at the judgment rate at the place of payment from the date of the instrument, or if it is undated from the date of issue.

(e) Unless the instrument otherwise specifies two or more persons who sign as maker, acceptor or drawer or indorser and as a part of the same transaction are jointly and severally liable even though the instrument contains such words as "I promise to pay."

(f) Unless otherwise specified consent to extension authorizes a single extension for not longer than the original period. A consent to extension, expressed in the instrument, is binding on secondary parties and accommodation makers. A holder may not exercise his option to extend an instrument over the objection of a maker or acceptor or other party who in accordance with Section 3—604 tenders full payment when the instrument is due.

§ 3—119. **Other Writings Affecting Instrument.**

(1) As between the obligor and his immediate obligee or any transferee the terms of an instrument may be modified or affected by any other written agreement executed as a part of the same transaction, except that a holder in due course is not affected by any limitation of his rights arising out of the separate written agreement if he had no notice of the limitation when he took the instrument.

(2) A separate agreement does not affect the negotiability of an instrument.

§ 3—120. **Instruments "Payable Through" Bank.**

An instrument which states that it is "payable through" a bank or the like designates that bank as a collecting bank to make presentment but does not of itself authorize the bank to pay the instrument.

§ 3—121. **Instruments Payable at Bank.**

Note: If this Act is introduced in the Congress of the United States this section should be omitted.
(States to select either alternative)

Alternative A—

A note or acceptance which states that it is payable at a bank is the equivalent of a draft drawn on the bank payable when it falls due out of any funds of the maker or acceptor in current account or otherwise available for such payment.

Alternative B—

A note or acceptance which states that it is payable at a bank is not of itself an order or authorization to the bank to pay it.

§ 3—122. **Accrual of Cause of Action.**

(1) A cause of action against a maker or an acceptor accrues

(a) in the case of a time instrument on the day after maturity;

(b) in the case of a demand instrument upon its date or, if no date is stated, on the date of issue.

(2) A cause of action against the obligor of a demand or time certificate of deposit accrues upon demand, but demand on a time certificate may not be made until on or after the date of maturity.

(3) A cause of action against a drawer of a draft or an indorser of any instrument accrues upon demand following dishonor of the instrument. Notice of dishonor is a demand.

(4) Unless an instrument provides otherwise, interest runs at the rate provided by law for a judgment

(a) in the case of a maker, acceptor or other primary obligor of a demand instrument, from the date of demand;

(b) in all other cases from the date of accrual of the cause of action.

Part 2 **Transfer and Negotiation**

§ 3—201. **Transfer: Right to Indorsement.**

(1) Transfer of an instrument vests in the transferee such rights as the transferor has therein, except that a transferee who has himself been a party to any fraud or illegality affecting the instrument or who as a prior holder had notice of a defense or claim against it cannot improve his position by taking from a later holder in due course.

(2) A transfer of a security interest in an instrument vests the foregoing rights in the transferee to the extent of the interest transferred.

(3) Unless otherwise agreed any transfer for value of an instrument not then payable to bearer gives the transferee the specifically enforceable right to have the unqualified indorsement of the transferor. Negotiation takes effect only when the indorsement is made and until that time there is no presumption that the transferee is the owner.

§ 3—202. **Negotiation.**

(1) Negotiation is the transfer of an instrument in such form that the transferee becomes a holder. If the instrument is payable to order it is negotiated by delivery with any necessary indorsement; if payable to bearer it is negotiated by delivery.

(2) An indorsement must be written by or on behalf of the holder and on the instrument or on a paper so firmly affixed thereto as to become a part thereof.

(3) An indorsement is effective for negotiation only when it conveys the entire instrument or any unpaid residue. If it purports to be of less it operates only as a partial assignment.

(4) Words of assignment, condition, waiver, guaranty, limitation or disclaimer of liability and the like accom-

panying an indorsement do not affect its character as an indorsement.

§ 3—203. **Wrong or Misspelled Name.**

Where an instrument is made payable to a person under a misspelled name or one other than his own he may indorse in that name or his own or both; but signature in both names may be required by a person paying or giving value for the instrument.

§ 3—204. **Special Indorsement; Blank Indorsement.**

(1) A special indorsement specifies the person to whom or to whose order it makes the instrument payable. Any instrument specially indorsed becomes payable to the order of the special indorsee and may be further negotiated only by his indorsement.

(2) An indorsement in blank specifies no particular indorsee and may consist of a mere signature. An instrument payable to order and indorsed in blank becomes payable to bearer and may be negotiated by delivery alone until specially indorsed.

(3) The holder may convert a blank indorsement into a special indorsement by writing over the signature of the indorser in blank any contract consistent with the character of the indorsement.

§ 3—205. **Restrictive Indorsements.**

An indorsement is restrictive which either

(a) is conditional; or

(b) purports to prohibit further transfer of the instrument; or

(c) includes the words "for collection", "for deposit", "pay any bank", or like terms signifying a purpose of deposit or collection; or

(d) otherwise states that it is for the benefit or use of the indorser or of another person.

§ 3—206. **Effect of Restrictive Indorsement.**

(1) No restrictive indorsement prevents further transfer or negotiation of the instrument.

(2) An intermediary bank, or a payor bank which is not the depositary bank, is neither given notice nor otherwise affected by a restrictive indorsement of any person except the bank's immediate transferor or the person presenting for payment.

(3) Except for an intermediary bank, any transferee under an indorsement which is conditional or includes the words "for collection", "for deposit", "pay any bank", or like terms (subparagraphs (a) and (c) of Section 3—205) must pay or apply any value given by him for or on the security of the instrument consistently with the indorse-

ment and to the extent that he does so he becomes a holder for value. In addition such transferee is a holder in due course if he otherwise complies with the requirements of Section 3—302 on what constitutes a holder in due course.

(4) The first taker under an indorsement for the benefit of the indorser or another person (subparagraph (d) of Section 3—205) must pay or apply any value given by him for or on the security of the instrument consistently with the indorsement and to the extent that he does so he becomes a holder for value. In addition such taker is a holder in due course if he otherwise complies with the requirements of Section 3—302 on what constitutes a holder in due course. A later holder for value is neither given notice nor otherwise affected by such restrictive indorsement unless he has knowledge that a fiduciary or other person has negotiated the instrument in any transaction for his own benefit or otherwise in breach of duty (subsection (2) of Section 3—304).

§ 3—207. **Negotiation Effective Although It May Be Rescinded.**

(1) Negotiation is effective to transfer the instrument although the negotiation is

(a) made by an infant, a corporation exceeding its powers, or any other person without capacity; or

(b) obtained by fraud, duress or mistake of any kind; or

(c) part of an illegal transaction; or

(d) made in breach of duty.

(2) Except as against a subsequent holder in due course such negotiation is in an appropriate case subject to rescission, the declaration of a constructive trust or any other remedy permitted by law.

§ 3—208. **Reacquisition.**

Where an instrument is returned to or reacquired by a prior party he may cancel any indorsement which is not necessary to his title and reissue or further negotiate the instrument, but any intervening party is discharged as against the reacquiring party and subsequent holders not in due course and if his indorsement has been cancelled is discharged as against subsequent holders in due course as well.

Part 3 **Rights of a Holder**

§ 3—301. **Rights of a Holder.**

The holder of an instrument whether or not he is the owner may transfer or negotiate it and, except as otherwise provided in Section 3—603 on payment or satisfaction, discharge it or enforce payment in his own name.

§ 3—302. **Holder in Due Course**

(1) A holder in due course is a holder who takes the instrument

    (a) for value; and

    (b) in good faith; and

    (c) without notice that it is overdue or has been dishonored or of any defense against or claim to it on the part of any person.

(2) A payee may be a holder in due course.

(3) A holder does not become a holder in due course of an instrument:

    (a) by purchase of it at judicial sale or by taking it under legal process; or

    (b) by acquiring it in taking over an estate; or

    (c) by purchasing it as part of a bulk transaction not in regular course of business of the transferor.

(4) A purchaser of a limited interest can be a holder in due course only to the extent of the interest purchased.

§ 3—303. **Taking for Value.**

A holder takes the instrument for value

(a) to the extent that the agreed consideration has been performed or that he acquires a security interest in or a lien on the instrument otherwise than by legal process; or

(b) when he takes the instrument in payment of or as security for an antecedent claim against any person whether or not the claim is due; or

(c) when he gives a negotiable instrument for it or makes an irrevocable commitment to a third person.

§ 3—304. **Notice to Purchaser.**

(1) The purchaser has notice of a claim or defense if

    (a) the instrument is so incomplete, bears such visible evidence of forgery or alteration, or is otherwise so irregular as to call into question its validity, terms or ownership or to create an ambiguity as to the party to pay; or

    (b) the purchaser has notice that the obligation of any party is voidable in whole or in part, or that all parties have been discharged.

(2) The purchaser has notice of a claim against the instrument when he has knowledge that a fiduciary has negotiated the instrument in payment of or as security for his own debt or in any transaction for his own benefit or otherwise in breach of duty.

(3) The purchaser has notice that an instrument is overdue if he has reason to know

    (a) that any part of the principal amount is overdue or that there is an uncured default in payment of another instrument of the same series; or

    (b) that acceleration of the instrument has been made; or

    (c) that he is taking a demand instrument after demand has been made or more than a reasonable length of time after its issue. A reasonable time for a check drawn and payable within the states and territories of the United States and the District of Columbia is presumed to be thirty days.

(4) Knowledge of the following facts does not of itself give the purchaser notice of a defense or claim

    (a) that the instrument is antedated or postdated;

    (b) that it was issued or negotiated in return for an executory promise or accompanied by a separate agreement, unless the purchaser has notice that a defense or claim has arisen from the terms thereof;

    (c) that any party has signed for accommodation;

    (d) that an incomplete instrument has been completed, unless the purchaser has notice of any improper completion;

    (e) that any person negotiating the instrument is or was a fiduciary;

    (f) that there has been default in payment of interest on the instrument or in payment of any other instrument, except one of the same series.

(5) The filing or recording of a document does not of itself constitute notice within the provisions of this Article to a person who would otherwise be a holder in due course.

(6) To be effective notice must be received at such time and in such manner as to give a reasonable opportunity to act on it.

§ 3—305. **Rights of a Holder in Due Course.**

To the extent that a holder is a holder in due course he takes the instrument free from

(1) all claims to it on the part of any person; and

(2) all defenses of any party to the instrument with whom the holder has not dealt except

    *(a) infancy, to the extent that it is a defense to a simple contract; and

    (b) such other incapacity, or duress, or illegality of the transaction, as renders the obligation of the party a nullity; and

    (c) such misrepresentation as has induced the party to sign the instrument with neither knowledge nor reasonable opportunity to obtain knowledge of its character or its essential terms; and

(d) discharge in insolvency proceedings; and

(e) any other discharge of which the holder has notice when he takes the instrument.

§ 3—306. **Rights of One Not Holder in Due Course.**

Unless he has the rights of a holder in due course any person takes the instrument subject to

(a) all valid claims to it on the part of any person; and

(b) all defenses of any party which would be available in an action on a simple contract; and

(c) the defenses of want or failure of consideration, nonperformance of any condition precedent, nondelivery, or delivery for a special purpose (Section 3—408); and

(d) the defense that he or a person through whom he holds the instrument acquired it by theft, or that payment or satisfaction to such holder would be inconsistent with the terms of a restrictive indorsement. The claim of any third person to the instrument is not otherwise available as a defense to any party liable thereon unless the third person himself defends the action for such party.

§ 3—307. **Burden of Establishing Signatures, Defenses and Due Course.**

(1) Unless specifically denied in the pleadings each signature on an instrument is admitted. When the effectiveness of a signature is put in issue

(a) the burden of establishing it is on the party claiming under the signature; but

(b) the signature is presumed to be genuine or authorized except where the action is to enforce the obligation of a purported signer who has died or become incompetent before proof is required.

(2) When signatures are admitted or established, production of the instrument entitles a holder to recover on it unless the defendant establishes a defense.

(3) After it is shown that a defense exists a person claiming the rights of a holder in due course has the burden of establishing that he or some person under whom he claims is in all respects a holder in due course.

Part 4 **Liability of Parties**

§ 3—401. **Signature.**

(1) No person is liable on an instrument unless his signature appears thereon.

(2) A signature is made by use of any name, including any trade or assumed name, upon an instrument, or by any word or mark used in lieu of a written signature.

§ 3—402. **Signature in Ambiguous Capacity.**

Unless the instrument clearly indicates that a signature is made in some other capacity it is an indorsement.

§ 3—403. **Signature by Authorized Representative.**

(1) A signature may be made by an agent or other representative, and his authority to make it may be established as in other cases of representation. No particular form of appointment is necessary to establish such authority.

(2) An authorized representative who signs his own name to an instrument

(a) is personally obligated if the instrument neither names the person represented nor shows that the representative signed in a representative capacity;

(b) except as otherwise established between the immediate parties, is personally obligated if the instrument names the person represented but does not show that the representative signed in a representative capacity, or if the instrument does not name the person represented but does show that the representative signed in a representative capacity.

(3) Except as otherwise established the name of an organization preceded or followed by the name and office of an authorized individual is a signature made in a representative capacity.

§ 3—404. **Unauthorized Signatures.**

(1) Any unauthorized signature is wholly inoperative as that of the person whose name is signed unless he ratifies it or is precluded from denying it; but it operates as the signature of the unauthorized signer in favor of any person who in good faith pays the instrument or takes it for value.

(2) Any unauthorized signature may be ratified for all purposes of this Article. Such ratification does not of itself affect any rights of the person ratifying against the actual signer.

§ 3—405. **Impostors; Signature in Name of Payee.**

(1) An indorsement by any person in the name of a named payee is effective if

(a) an impostor by use of the mails or otherwise has induced the maker or drawer to issue the instrument to him or his confederate in the name of the payee; or

(b) a person signing as or on behalf of a maker or drawer intends the payee to have no interest in the instrument; or

(c) an agent or employee of the maker or drawer has supplied him with the name of the payee intending the latter to have no such interest.

(2) Nothing in this section shall affect the criminal or civil liability of the person so indorsing.

§ 3—406. **Negligence Contributing to Alteration or Unauthorized Signature.**

Any person who by his negligence substantially contributes to a material alteration of the instrument or to the making of an unauthorized signature is precluded from asserting the alteration or lack of authority against a holder in due course or against a drawee or other payor who pays the instrument in good faith and in accordance with the reasonable commercial standards of the drawee's or payor's business.

§ 3—407. **Alteration.**

(1) Any alteration of an instrument is material which changes the contract of any party thereto in any respect, including any such change in

(a) the number or relations of the parties; or

(b) an incomplete instrument, by completing it otherwise than as authorized; or

(c) the writing as signed, by adding to it or by removing any part of it.

(2) As against any person other than a subsequent holder in due course

(a) alteration by the holder which is both fraudulent and material discharges any party whose contract is thereby changed unless that party assents or is precluded from asserting the defense;

(b) no other alteration discharges any party and the instrument may be enforced according to its original tenor, or as to incomplete instruments according to the authority given.

(3) A subsequent holder in due course may in all cases enforce the instrument according to its original tenor, and when an incomplete instrument has been completed, he may enforce it as completed.

§ 3—408. **Consideration.**

Want or failure of consideration is a defense as against any person not having the rights of a holder in due course (Section 3—305), except that no consideration is necessary for an instrument or obligation thereon given in payment of or as security for an antecedent obligation of any kind. Nothing in this section shall be taken to displace any statute outside this Act under which a promise is enforceable notwithstanding lack or failure of consideration. Partial failure of consideration is a defense pro tanto whether or not the failure is in an ascertained or liquidated amount.

§ 3—409. **Draft Not an Assignment.**

(1) A check or other draft does not of itself operate as an assignment of any funds in the hands of the drawee available for its payment, and the drawee is not liable on the instrument until he accepts it.

(2) Nothing in this section shall affect any liability in contract, tort or otherwise arising from any letter of credit or other obligation or representation which is not an acceptance.

§ 3—410. **Definition and Operation of Acceptance.**

(1) Acceptance is the drawee's signed engagement to honor the draft as presented. It must be written on the draft, and may consist of his signature alone. It becomes operative when completed by delivery or notification.

(2) A draft may be accepted although it has not been signed by the drawer or is otherwise incomplete or is overdue or has been dishonored.

(3) Where the draft is payable at a fixed period after sight and the acceptor fails to date his acceptance the holder may complete it by supplying a date in good faith.

§ 3—411. **Certification of a Check.**

(1) Certification of a check is acceptance. Where a holder procures certification the drawer and all prior indorsers are discharged.

(2) Unless otherwise agreed a bank has no obligation to certify a check.

(3) A bank may certify a check before returning it for lack of proper indorsement. If it does so the drawer is discharged.

§ 3—412. **Acceptance Varying Draft.**

(1) Where the drawee's proffered acceptance in any manner varies the draft as presented the holder may refuse the acceptance and treat the draft as dishonored in which case the drawee is entitled to have his acceptance cancelled.

(2) The terms of the draft are not varied by an acceptance to pay at any particular bank or place in the United States, unless the acceptance states that the draft is to be paid only at such bank or place.

(3) Where the holder assents to an acceptance varying the terms of the draft each drawer and indorser who does not affirmatively assent is discharged.

§ 3—413. **Contract of Maker, Drawer and Acceptor.**

(1) The maker or acceptor engages that he will pay the instrument according to its tenor at the time of his engagement or as completed pursuant to Section 3—115 on incomplete instruments.

(2) The drawer engages that upon dishonor of the draft and any necessary notice of dishonor or protest he will

pay the amount of the draft to the holder or to any indorser who takes it up. The drawer may disclaim this liability by drawing without recourse.

(3) By making, drawing or accepting the party admits as against all subsequent parties including the drawee the existence of the payee and his then capacity to indorse.

§ 3—414. **Contract of Indorser; Order of Liability.**

(1) Unless the indorsement otherwise specifies (as by such words as "without recourse") every indorser engages that upon dishonor and any necessary notice of dishonor and protest he will pay the instrument according to its tenor at the time of his indorsement to the holder or to any subsequent indorser who takes it up, even though the indorser who takes it up was not obligated to do so.

(2) Unless they otherwise agree indorsers are liable to one another in the order in which they indorse, which is presumed to be the order in which their signatures appear on the instrument.

§ 3—415. **Contract of Accommodation Party.**

(1) An accommodation party is one who signs the instrument in any capacity for the purpose of lending his name to another party to it.

(2) When the instrument has been taken for value before it is due the accommodation party is liable in the capacity in which he has signed even though the taker knows of the accommodation.

(3) As against a holder in due course and without notice of the accommodation oral proof of the accommodation is not admissible to give the accommodation party the benefit of discharges dependent on his character as such. In other cases the accommodation character may be shown by oral proof.

(4) An indorsement which shows that it is not in the chain of title is notice of its accommodation character.

(5) An accommodation party is not liable to the party accommodated, and if he pays the instrument has a right of recourse on the instrument against such party.

§ 3—416. **Contract of Guarantor.**

(1) "Payment guaranteed" or equivalent words added to a signature mean that the signer engages that if the instrument is not paid when due he will pay it according to its tenor without resort by the holder to any other party.

(2) "Collection guaranteed" or equivalent words added to a signature mean that the signer engages that if the instrument is not paid when due he will pay it according to its tenor, but only after the holder has reduced his claim against the maker or acceptor to judgment and execution has been returned unsatisfied, or after the maker or acceptor has become insolvent or it is otherwise apparent that it is useless to proceed against him.

(3) Words of guaranty which do not otherwise specify guarantee payment.

(4) No words of guaranty added to the signature of a sole maker or acceptor affect his liability on the instrument. Such words added to the signature of one of two or more makers or acceptors create a presumption that the signature is for the accommodation of the others.

(5) When words of guaranty are used presentment, notice of dishonor and protest are not necessary to charge the user.

(6) Any guaranty written on the instrument is enforcible notwithstanding any statute of frauds.

§ 3—417. **Warranties on Presentment and Transfer.**

(1) Any person who obtains payment or acceptance and any prior transferor warrants to a person who in good faith pays or accepts that

(a) he has a good title to the instrument or is authorized to obtain payment or acceptance on behalf of one who has a good title; and

(b) he has no knowledge that the signature of the maker or drawer is unauthorized, except that this warranty is not given by a holder in due course acting in good faith

(i) to a maker with respect to the maker's own signature; or

(ii) to a drawer with respect to the drawer's own signature, whether or not the drawer is also the drawee; or

(iii) to an acceptor of a draft if the holder in due course took the draft after the acceptance or obtained the acceptance without knowledge that the drawer's signature was unauthorized; and

(c) the instrument has not been materially altered, except that this warranty is not given by a holder in due course acting in good faith

(i) to the maker of a note; or

(ii) to the drawer of a draft whether or not the drawer is also the drawee; or

(iii) to the acceptor of a draft with respect to an alteration made prior to the acceptance if the holder in due course took the draft after the acceptance, even though the acceptance provided "payable as originally drawn" or equivalent terms; or

(iv) to the acceptor of a draft with respect to an alteration made after the acceptance.

(2) Any person who transfers an instrument and receives consideration warrants to his transferee and if the transfer is by indorsement to any subsequent holder who takes the instrument in good faith that

(a) he has a good title to the instrument or is authorized to obtain payment or acceptance on behalf of one who has a good title and the transfer is otherwise rightful; and

(b) all signatures are genuine or authorized; and

(c) the instrument has not been materially altered; and

(d) no defense of any party is good against him; and

(e) he has no knowledge of any insolvency proceeding instituted with respect to the maker or acceptor or the drawer of an unaccepted instrument.

(3) By transferring "without recourse" the transferor limits the obligation stated in subsection (2) (d) to a warranty that he has no knowledge of such a defense.

(4) A selling agent or broker who does not disclose the fact that he is acting only as such gives the warranties provided in this section, but if he makes such disclosure warrants only his good faith and authority.

§ 3—418. **Finality of Payment or Acceptance.**

Except for recovery of bank payments as provided in the Article on Bank Deposits and Collections (Article 4) and except for liability for breach of warranty on presentment under the preceding section, payment or acceptance of any instrument is final in favor of a holder in due course, or a person who has in good faith changed his position in reliance on the payment.

§ 3—419. **Conversion of Instrument; Innocent Representative.**

(1) An instrument is converted when

(a) a drawee to whom it is delivered for acceptance refuses to return it on demand; or

(b) any person to whom it is delivered for payment refuses on demand either to pay or to return it; or

(c) it is paid on a forged indorsement.

(2) In an action against a drawee under subsection (1) the measure of the drawee's liability is the face amount of the instrument. In any other action under subsection (1) the measure of liability is presumed to be the face amount of the instrument.

(3) Subject to the provisions of this Act concerning restrictive indorsements a representative, including a depositary or collecting bank, who has in good faith and in accordance with the reasonable commercial standards applicable to the business of such representative dealt with an instrument or its proceeds on behalf of one who was not the true owner is not liable in conversion or otherwise to the true owner beyond the amount of any proceeds remaining in his hands.

(4) An intermediary bank or payor bank which is not a depositary bank is not liable in conversion solely by reason of the fact that proceeds of an item indorsed restrictively (Sections 3—205 and 3—206) are not paid or applied consistently with the restrictive indorsement of an indorser other than its immediate transferor.

Part 5 **Presentment, Notice of Dishonor and Protest**

§ 3—501. **When Presentment, Notice of Dishonor, and Protest Necessary or Permissible.**

(1) Unless excused (Section 3—511) presentment is necessary to charge secondary parties as follows:

(a) presentment for acceptance is necessary to charge the drawer and indorsers of a draft where the draft so provides, or is payable elsewhere than at the residence or place of business of the drawee, or its date of payment depends upon such presentment. The holder may at his option present for acceptance any other draft payable at a stated date;

(b) presentment for payment is necessary to charge any indorser;

(c) in the case of any drawer, the acceptor of a draft payable at a bank or the maker of a note payable at a bank, presentment for payment is necessary, but failure to make presentment discharges such drawer, acceptor or maker only as stated in Section 3—502(1)(b).

(2) Unless excused (Section 3—511)

(a) notice of any dishonor is necessary to charge any indorser;

(b) in the case of any drawer, the acceptor of a draft payable at a bank or the maker of a note payable at a bank, notice of any dishonor is necessary, but failure to give such notice discharges such drawer, acceptor or maker only as stated in Section 3—502(1)(b).

(3) Unless excused (Section 3—511) protest of any dishonor is necessary to charge the drawer and indorsers of any draft which on its face appears to be drawn or payable outside of the states, territories, dependencies, and possessions of the United States, the District of Columbia and the Commonwealth of Puerto Rico. The holder may at his option make protest of any dishonor of any other instrument and in the case of a foreign draft may

on insolvency of the acceptor before maturity make protest for better security.

(4) Notwithstanding any provision of this section, neither presentment nor notice of dishonor nor protest is necessary to charge an indorser who has indorsed an instrument after maturity.

§ 3—502. **Unexcused Delay; Discharge.**

(1) Where without excuse any necessary presentment or notice of dishonor is delayed beyond the time when it is due

(a) any indorser is discharged; and

(b) any drawer or the acceptor of a draft payable at a bank or the maker of a note payable at a bank who because the drawee or payor bank becomes insolvent during the delay is deprived of funds maintained with the drawee or payor bank to cover the instrument may discharge his liability by written assignment to the holder of his rights against the drawee or payor bank in respect of such funds, but such drawer, acceptor or maker is not otherwise discharged.

(2) Where without excuse a necessary protest is delayed beyond the time when it is due any drawer or indorser is discharged.

§ 3—503. **Time of Presentment.**

(1) Unless a different time is expressed in the instrument the time for any presentment is determined as follows:

(a) where an instrument is payable at or a fixed period after a stated date any presentment for acceptance must be made on or before the date it is payable;

(b) where an instrument is payable after sight it must either be presented for acceptance or negotiated within a reasonable time after date or issue whichever is later;

(c) where an instrument shows the date on which it is payable presentment for payment is due on that date;

(d) where an instrument is accelerated presentment for payment is due within a reasonable time after the acceleration;

(e) with respect to the liability of any secondary party presentment for acceptance or payment of any other instrument is due within a reasonable time after such party becomes liable thereon.

(2) A reasonable time for presentment is determined by the nature of the instrument, any usage of banking or trade and the facts of the particular case. In the case of an uncertified check which is drawn and payable within the United States and which is not a draft drawn by a bank the following are presumed to be reasonable periods within which to present for payment or to initiate bank collection:

(a) with respect to the liability of the drawer, thirty days after date or issue whichever is later; and

(b) with respect to the liability of an indorser, seven days after his indorsement.

(3) Where any presentment is due on a day which is not a full business day for either the person making presentment or the party to pay or accept, presentment is due on the next following day which is a full business day for both parties.

(4) Presentment to be sufficient must be made at a reasonable hour, and if at a bank during its banking day.

§ 3—504. **How Presentment Made.**

(1) Presentment is a demand for acceptance or payment made upon the maker, acceptor, drawee or other payor by or on behalf of the holder.

(2) Presentment may be made

(a) by mail, in which event the time of presentment is determined by the time of receipt of the mail; or

(b) through a clearing house; or

(c) at the place of acceptance or payment specified in the instrument or if there be none at the place of business or residence of the party to accept or pay. If neither the party to accept or pay nor anyone authorized to act for him is present or accessible at such place presentment is excused.

(3) It may be made

(a) to any one of two or more makers, acceptors, drawees or other payors; or

(b) to any person who has authority to make or refuse the acceptance or payment.

(4) A draft accepted or a note made payable at a bank in the United States must be presented at such bank.

(5) In the cases described in Section 4—210 presentment may be made in the manner and with the result stated in that section.

§ 3—505. **Rights of Party to Whom Presentment Is Made.**

(1) The party to whom presentment is made may without dishonor require

(a) exhibition of the instrument; and

(b) reasonable identification of the person making presentment and evidence of his authority to make it if made for another; and

(c) that the instrument be produced for acceptance or payment at a place specified in it, or if there be none at any place reasonable in the circumstances; and

(d) a signed receipt on the instrument for any partial or full payment and its surrender upon full payment.

(2) Failure to comply with any such requirement invalidates the presentment but the person presenting has a reasonable time in which to comply and the time for acceptance or payment runs from the time of compliance.

§ 3—506. **Time Allowed for Acceptance or Payment.**

(1) Acceptance may be deferred without dishonor until the close of the next business day following presentment. The holder may also in a good faith effort to obtain acceptance and without either dishonor of the instrument or discharge of secondary parties allow postponement of acceptance for an additional business day.

(2) Except as a longer time is allowed in the case of documentary drafts drawn under a letter of credit, and unless an earlier time is agreed to by the party to pay, payment of an instrument may be deferred without dishonor pending reasonable examination to determine whether it is properly payable, but payment must be made in any event before the close of business on the day of presentment.

§ 3—507. **Dishonor; Holder's Right of Recourse; Term Allowing Re-Presentment.**

(1) An instrument is dishonored when

(a) a necessary or optional presentment is duly made and due acceptance or payment is refused or cannot be obtained within the prescribed time or in case of bank collections the instrument is seasonably returned by the midnight deadline (Section 4—301); or

(b) presentment is excused and the instrument is not duly accepted or paid.

(2) Subject to any necessary notice of dishonor and protest, the holder has upon dishonor an immediate right of recourse against the drawers and indorsers.

(3) Return of an instrument for lack of proper indorsement is not dishonor.

(4) A term in a draft or an indorsement thereof allowing a stated time for re-presentment in the event of any dishonor of the draft by nonacceptance if a time draft or by nonpayment if a sight draft gives the holder as against any secondary party bound by the term an option to waive the dishonor without affecting the liability of the secondary party and he may present again up to the end of the stated time.

§ 3—508. **Notice of Dishonor.**

(1) Notice of dishonor may be given to any person who may be liable on the instrument by or on behalf of the holder or any party who has himself received notice, or any other party who can be compelled to pay the instrument. In addition an agent or bank in whose hands the instrument is dishonored may give notice to his principal or customer or to another agent or bank from which the instrument was received.

(2) Any necessary notice must be given by a bank before its midnight deadline and by any other person before midnight of the third business day after dishonor or receipt of notice of dishonor.

(3) Notice may be given in any reasonable manner. It may be oral or written and in any terms which identify the instrument and state that it has been dishonored. A misdescription which does not mislead the party notified does not vitiate the notice. Sending the instrument bearing a stamp, ticket or writing stating that acceptance or payment has been refused or sending a notice of debit with respect to the instrument is sufficient.

(4) Written notice is given when sent although it is not received.

(5) Notice to one partner is notice to each although the firm has been dissolved.

(6) When any party is in insolvency proceedings instituted after the issue of the instrument notice may be given either to the party or to the representative of his estate.

(7) When any party is dead or incompetent notice may be sent to his last known address or given to his personal representative.

(8) Notice operates for the benefit of all parties who have rights on the instrument against the party notified.

§ 3—509. **Protest; Noting for Protest.**

(1) A protest is a certificate of dishonor made under the hand and seal of a United States consul or vice consul or a notary public or other person authorized to certify dishonor by the law of the place where dishonor occurs. It may be made upon information satisfactory to such person.

(2) The protest must identify the instrument and certify either that due presentment has been made or the reason why it is excused and that the instrument has been dishonored by nonacceptance or nonpayment.

(3) The protest may also certify that notice of dishonor has been given to all parties or to specified parties.

(4) Subject to subsection (5) any necessary protest is due by the time that notice of dishonor is due.

(5) If, before protest is due, an instrument has been noted for protest by the officer to make protest, the protest may be made at any time thereafter as of the date of the noting.

§ 3—510. Evidence of Dishonor and Notice of Dishonor.

The following are admissible as evidence and create a presumption of dishonor and of any notice of dishonor therein shown:

(a) a document regular in form as provided in the preceding section which purports to be a protest;

(b) the purported stamp or writing of the drawee, payor bank or presenting bank on the instrument or accompanying it stating that acceptance or payment has been refused for reasons conconsistent with dishonor;

(c) any book or record of the drawee, payor bank, or any collecting bank kept in the usual course of business which shows dishonor, even though there is no evidence of who made the entry.

§ 3—511. Waived or Excused Presentment, Protest or Notice of Dishonor or Delay Therein.

(1) Delay in presentment, protest or notice of dishonor is excused when the party is without notice that it is due or when the delay is caused by circumstances beyond his control and he exercises reasonable diligence after the cause of the delay ceases to operate.

(2) Presentment or notice or protest as the case may be is entirely excused when

(a) the party to be charged has waived it expressly or by implication either before or after it is due; or

(b) such party has himself dishonored the instrument or has countermanded payment or otherwise has no reason to expect or right to require that the instrument be accepted or paid; or

(c) by reasonable diligence the presentment or protest cannot be made or the notice given.

(3) Presentment is also entirely excused when

(a) the maker, acceptor or drawee of any instrument except a documentary draft is dead or in insolvency proceedings instituted after the issue of the instrument; or

(b) acceptance or payment is refused but not for want of proper presentment.

(4) Where a draft has been dishonored by nonacceptance a later presentment for payment and any notice of dishonor and protest for nonpayment are excused unless in the meantime the instrument has been accepted.

(5) A waiver of protest is also a waiver of presentment and of notice of dishonor even though protest is not required.

(6) Where a waiver of presentment or notice or protest is embodied in the instrument itself it is binding upon all parties; but where it is written above the signature of an indorser it binds him only.

Part 6 Discharge

§ 3—601. Discharge of Parties.

(1) The extent of the discharge of any party from liability on an instrument is governed by the sections on

(a) payment or satisfaction (Section 3—603); or

(b) tender of payment (Section 3—604); or

(c) cancellation or renunciation (Section 3—605); or

(d) impairment of right of recourse or of collateral (Section 3—606); or

(e) reacquisition of the instrument by a prior party (Section 3—208); or

(f) fraudulent and material alteration (Section 3—407); or

(g) certification of a check (Section 3—411); or

(h) acceptance varying a draft (Section 3—412); or

(i) unexcused delay in presentment or notice of dishonor or protest (Section 3—502).

(2) Any party is also discharged from his liability on an instrument to another party by any other act or agreement with such party which would discharge his simple contract for the payment of money.

(3) The liability of all parties is discharged when any party who has himself no right of action or recourse on the instrument

(a) reacquires the instrument in his own right; or

(b) is discharged under any provision of this Article, except as otherwise provided with respect to discharge for impairment of recourse or of collateral (Section 3—606).

§ 3—602. Effect of Discharge Against Holder in Due Course.

No discharge of any party provided by this Article is effective against a subsequent holder in due course unless he has notice thereof when he takes the instrument.

§ 3—603. Payment or Satisfaction.

(1) The liability of any party is discharged to the extent of his payment or satisfaction to the holder even though it is made with knowledge of a claim of another person

to the instrument unless prior to such payment or satisfaction the person making the claim either supplies indemnity deemed adequate by the party seeking the discharge or enjoins payment or satisfaction by order of a court of competent jurisdiction in an action in which the adverse claimant and the holder are parties. This subsection does not, however, result in the discharge of the liability

(a) of a party who in bad faith pays or satisfies a holder who acquired the instrument by theft or who (unless having the rights of a holder in due course) holds through one who so acquired it; or

(b) of a party (other than an intermediary bank or a payor bank which is not a depositary bank) who pays or satisfies the holder of an instrument which has been restrictively indorsed in a manner not consistent with the terms of such restrictive indorsement.

(2) Payment or satisfaction may be made with the consent of the holder by any person including a stranger to the instrument. Surrender of the instrument to such a person gives him the rights of a transferee (Section 3—201).

§ 3—604. **Tender of Payment.**

(1) Any party making tender of full payment to a holder when or after it is due is discharged to the extent of all subsequent liability for interest, costs and attorney's fees.

(2) The holder's refusal of such tender wholly discharges any party who has a right of recourse against the party making the tender.

(3) Where the maker or acceptor of an instrument payable otherwise than on demand is able and ready to pay at every place of payment specified in the instrument when it is due, it is equivalent to tender.

§ 3—605. **Cancellation and Renunciation.**

(1) The holder of an instrument may even without consideration discharge any party

(a) in any manner apparent on the face of the instrument or the indorsement, as by intentionally cancelling the instrument or the party's signature by destruction or mutilation, or by striking out the party's signature; or

(b) by renouncing his rights by a writing signed and delivered or by surrender of the instrument to the party to be discharged.

(2) Neither cancellation nor renunciation without surrender of the instrument affects the title thereto.

§ 3—606. **Impairment of Recourse or of Collateral.**

(1) The holder discharges any party to the instrument to the extent that without such party's consent the holder

(a) without express reservation of rights releases or agrees not to sue any person against whom the party has to the knowledge of the holder a right of recourse or agrees to suspend the right to enforce against such person the instrument or collateral or otherwise discharges such person, except that failure or delay in effecting any required presentment, protest or notice of dishonor with respect to any such person does not discharge any party as to whom presentment, protest or notice of dishonor is effective or unnecessary; or

(b) unjustifiably impairs any collateral for the instrument given by or on behalf of the party or any person against whom he has a right of recourse.

(2) By express reservation of rights against a party with a right of recourse the holder preserves

(a) all his rights against such party as of the time when the instrument was originally due; and

(b) the right of the party to pay the instrument as of that time; and

(c) all rights of such party to recourse against others.

Part 7 **Advice of International Sight Draft**

§ 3—701. **Letter of Advice of International Sight Draft.**

(1) A "letter of advice" is a drawer's communication to the drawee that a described draft has been drawn.

(2) Unless otherwise agreed when a bank receives from another bank a letter of advice of an international sight draft the drawee bank may immediately debit the drawer's account and stop the running of interest pro tanto. Such a debit and any resulting credit to any account covering outstanding drafts leaves in the drawer full power to stop payment or otherwise dispose of the amount and creates no trust or interest in favor of the holder.

(3) Unless otherwise agreed and except where a draft is drawn under a credit issued by the drawee, the drawee of an international sight draft owes the drawer no duty to pay an unadvised draft but if it does so and the draft is genuine, may appropriately debit the drawer's account.

Part 8 **Miscellaneous**

§ 3—801. **Drafts in a Set.**

(1) Where a draft is drawn in a set of parts, each of which is numbered and expressed to be an order only if no other part has been honored, the whole of the parts constitutes one draft but a taker of any part may become a holder in due course of the draft.

(2) Any person who negotiates, indorses or accepts a single part of a draft drawn in a set thereby becomes

liable to any holder in due course of that part as if it were the whole set, but as between different holders in due course to whom different parts have been negotiated the holder whose title first accrues has all rights to the draft and its proceeds.

(3) As against the drawee the first presented part of a draft drawn in a set is the part entitled to payment, or if a time draft to acceptance and payment. Acceptance of any subsequently presented part renders the drawee liable thereon under subsection (2). With respect both to a holder and to the drawer payment of a subsequently presented part of a draft payable at sight has the same effect as payment of a check notwithstanding an effective stop order (Section 4—407).

(4) Except as otherwise provided in this section, where any part of a draft in a set is discharged by payment or otherwise the whole draft is discharged.

§ 3—802. **Effect of Instrument on Obligation for Which It Is Given.**

(1) Unless otherwise agreed where an instrument is taken for an underlying obligation

(a) the obligation is pro tanto discharged if a bank is drawer, maker or acceptor of the instrument and there is no recourse on the instrument against the underlying obligor; and

(b) in any other case the obligation is suspended pro tanto until the instrument is due or if it is payable on demand until its presentment. If the instrument is dishonored action may be maintained on either the instrument or the obligation; discharge of the underlying obligor on the instrument also discharges him on the obligation.

(2) The taking in good faith of a check which is not postdated does not of itself so extend the time on the original obligation as to discharge a surety.

§ 3—803. **Notice to Third Party.**

Where a defendant is sued for breach of an obligation for which a third person is answerable over under this Article he may give the third person written notice of the litigation, and the person notified may then give similar notice to any other person who is answerable over to him under this Article. If the notice states that the person notified may come in and defend and that if the person notified does not do so he will in any action against him by the person giving the notice be bound by any determination of fact common to the two litigations, then unless after seasonable receipt of the notice the person notified does come in and defend he is so bound.

§ 3—804. **Lost, Destroyed or Stolen Instruments.**

The owner of an instrument which is lost, whether by destruction, theft or otherwise, may maintain an action in his own name and recover from any party liable thereon upon due proof of his ownership, the facts which prevent his production of the instrument and its terms. The court may require security indemnifying the defendant against loss by reason of further claims on the instrument.

§ 3—805. **Instruments Not Payable to Order or to Bearer.**

This Article applies to any instrument whose terms do not preclude transfer and which is otherwise negotiable within this Article but which is not payable to order or to bearer, except that there can be no holder in due course of such an instrument.

Article 4
BANK DEPOSITS AND COLLECTIONS

Part 1 **General Provisions and Definitions**

§ 4—101. **Short Title.**

This Article shall be known and may be cited as Uniform Commercial Code—Bank Deposits and Collections.

§ 4—102. **Applicability.**

(1) To the extent that items within this Article are also within the scope of Articles 3 and 8, they are subject to the provisions of those Articles. In the event of conflict the provisions of this Article govern those of Article 3 but the provisions of Article 8 govern those of this Article.

(2) The liability of a bank for action or non-action with respect to any item handled by it for purposes of presentment, payment or collection is governed by the law of the place where the bank is located. In the case of action or non-action by or at a branch or separate office of a bank, its liability is governed by the law of the place where the branch or separate office is located.

§ 4—103. **Variation by Agreement; Measure of Damages; Certain Action Constituting Ordinary Care.**

(1) The effect of the provisions of this Article may be varied by agreement except that no agreement can disclaim a bank's responsibility for its own lack of good faith or failure to exercise ordinary care or can limit the measure of damages for such lack or failure; but the parties may by agreement determine the standards by which such responsibility is to be measured if such standards are not manifestly unreasonable.

(2) Federal Reserve regulations and operating letters, clearing house rules, and the like, have the effect of agreements under subsection (1), whether or not specif-

ically assented to by all parties interested in items handled.

(3) Action or non-action approved by this Article or pursuant to Federal Reserve regulations or operating letters constitutes the exercise of ordinary care and, in the absence of special instructions, action or nonac- tion consistent with clearing house rules and the like or with a general banking usage not disapproved by this Article, prima facie constitutes the exercise of ordinary care.

(4) The specification or approval of certain procedures by this Article does not constitute disapproval of other procedures which may be reasonable under the circumstances.

(5) The measure of damages for failure to exercise ordinary care in handling an item is the amount of the item reduced by an amount which could not have been realized by the use of ordinary care, and where there is bad faith it includes other damages, if any, suffered by the party as a proximate consequence.

§ 4—104. **Definitions and Index of Definitions.**

(1) In this Article unless the context otherwise requires

(a) "Account" means any account with a bank and includes a checking, time, interest or savings account;

(b) "Afternoon" means the period of a day between noon and midnight;

(c) "Banking day" means that part of any day on which a bank is open to the public for carrying on substantially all of its banking functions;

(d) "Clearing house" means any association of banks or other payors regularly clearing items;

(e) "Customer" means any person having an account with a bank or for whom a bank has agreed to collect items and includes a bank carrying an account with another bank;

(f) "Documentary draft" means any negotiable or nonnegotiable draft with accompanying documents, securities or other papers to be delivered against honor of the draft;

(g) "Item" means any instrument for the payment of money even though it is not negotiable but does not include money;

(h) "Midnight deadline" with respect to a bank is midnight on its next banking day following the banking day on which it receives the relevant item or notice or from which the time for taking action commences to run, whichever is later;

(i) "Properly payable" includes the availability of funds for payment at the time of decision to pay or dishonor;

(j) "Settle" means to pay in cash, by clearing house settlement, in a charge or credit or by remittance, or otherwise as instructed. A settlement may be either provisional or final;

(k) "Suspends payments" with respect to a bank means that it has been closed by order of the supervisory authorities, that a public officer has been appointed to take it over or that it ceases or refuses to make payments in the ordinary course of business.

(2) Other definitions applying to this Article and the sections in which they appear are:
"Collecting bank" Section 4—105.
"Depositary bank" Section 4—105.
"Intermediary bank" Section 4—105.
"Payor bank" Section 4—105.
"Presenting bank" Section 4—105.
"Remitting bank" Section 4—105.

(3) The following definitions in other Articles apply to this Article:
"Acceptance" Section 3—410.
"Certificate of deposit" Section 3—104.
"Certification" Section 3—411.
"Check" Section 3—104.
"Draft" Section 3—104.
"Holder in due course" Section 3—302.
"Notice of dishonor" Section 3—508.
"Presentment" Section 3—504.
"Protest" Section 3—509.
"Secondary party" Section 3—102.

(4) In addition Article 1 contains general definitions and principles of construction and interpretation applicable throughout this Article.

§ 4—105. **"Depositary Bank"; "Intermediary Bank"; "Collecting Bank"; "Payor Bank"; "Presenting Bank"; "Remitting Bank".**

In this Article unless the context otherwise requires:

(a) "Depositary bank" means the first bank to which an item is transferred for collection even though it is also the payor bank;

(b) "Payor bank" means a bank by which an item is payable as drawn or accepted;

(c) "Intermediary bank" means any bank to which an item is transferred in course of collection except the depositary or payor bank;

(d) "Collecting bank" means any bank handling the item for collection except the payor bank;

(e) "Presenting bank" means any bank presenting an item except a payor bank;

(f) "Remitting bank" means any payor or intermediary bank remitting for an item.

§ 4—106. **Separate Office of a Bank.**

A branch or separate office of a bank [maintaining its own deposit ledgers] is a separate bank for the purpose of computing the time within which and determining the place at or to which action may be taken or notices or orders shall be given under this Article and under Article 3.

Note: The brackets are to make it optional with the several states whether to require a branch to maintain its own deposit ledgers in order to be considered to be a separate bank for certain purposes under Article 4. In some states "maintaining its own deposit ledgers" is a satisfactory test. In others branch banking practices are such that this test would not be suitable.

§ 4—107. **Time of Receipt of Items.**

(1) For the purpose of allowing time to process items, prove balances and make the necessary entries on its books to determine its position for the day, a bank may fix an afternoon hour of two P.M. or later as a cut-off hour for the handling of money and items and the making of entries on its books.

(2) Any item or deposit of money received on any day after a cut-off hour so fixed or after the close of the banking day may be treated as being received at the opening of the next banking day.

§ 4—108. **Delays.**

(1) Unless otherwise instructed, a collecting bank in a good faith effort to secure payment may, in the case of specific items and with or without the approval of any person involved, waive, modify or extend time limits imposed or permitted by this Act for a period not in excess of an additional banking day without discharge of secondary parties and without liability to its transferor or any prior party.

(2) Delay by a collecting bank or payor bank beyond time limits prescribed or permitted by this Act or by instructions is excused if caused by interruption of communication facilities, suspension of payments by another bank, war, emergency conditions or other circumstances beyond the control of the bank provided it exercises such diligence as the circumstances require.

§ 4—109. **Process of Posting.**

The "process of posting" means the usual procedure followed by a payor bank in determining to pay an item and in recording the payment including one or more of the following or other steps as determined by the bank:

(a) verification of any signature;

(b) ascertaining that sufficient funds are available;

(c) affixing a "paid" or other stamp;

(d) entering a charge or entry to a customer's account;

(e) correcting or reversing an entry or erroneous action with respect to the item.

Part 2 **Collection of Items: Depositary and Collecting Banks**

§ 4—201. **Presumption and Duration of Agency Status of Collecting Banks and Provisional Status of Credits; Applicability of Article; Item Indorsed "Pay Any Bank".**

(1) Unless a contrary intent clearly appears and prior to the time that a settlement given by a collecting bank for an item is or becomes final (subsection (3) of Section 4—211 and Sections 4—212 and 4—213) the bank is an agent or sub-agent of the owner of the item and any settlement given for the item is provisional. This provision applies regardless of the form of indorsement or lack of indorsement and even though credit given for the item is subject to immediate withdrawal as of right or is in fact withdrawn; but the continuance of ownership of an item by its owner and any rights of the owner to proceeds of the item are subject to rights of a collecting bank such as those resulting from outstanding advances on the item and valid rights of setoff. When an item is handled by banks for purposes of presentment, payment and collection, the relevant provisions of this Article apply even though action of parties clearly establishes that a particular bank has purchased the item and is the owner of it.

(2) After an item has been indorsed with the words "pay any bank" or the like, only a bank may acquire the rights of a holder

(a) until the item has been returned to the customer initiating collection; or

(b) until the item has been specially indorsed by a bank to a person who is not a bank.

§ 4—202. **Responsibility for Collection; When Action Seasonable.**

(1) A collecting bank must use ordinary care in

(a) presenting an item or sending it for presentment; and

(b) sending notice of dishonor or non-payment or returning an item other than a documentary draft to the bank's transferor [or directly to the depositary bank under subsection (2) of Section 4—212] *(see note to Section 4—212)* after learning that the item has not been paid or accepted as the case may be; and

(c) settling for an item when the bank receives final settlement; and

(d) making or providing for any necessary protest; and

(e) notifying its transferor of any loss or delay in transit within a reasonable time after discovery thereof.

(2) A collecting bank taking proper action before its midnight deadline following receipt of an item, notice or payment acts seasonably; taking proper action within a reasonably longer time may be seasonable but the bank has the burden of so establishing.

(3) Subject to subsection (1)(a), a bank is not liable for the insolvency, neglect, misconduct, mistake or default of another bank or person or for loss or destruction of an item in transit or in the possession of others.

§ 4—203. **Effect of Instructions.**

Subject to the provisions of Article 3 concerning conversion of instruments (Section 3—419) and the provisions of both Article 3 and this Article concerning restrictive indorsements only a collecting bank's transferor can give instructions which affect the bank or constitute notice to it and a collecting bank is not liable to prior parties for any action taken pursuant to such instructions or in accordance with any agreement with its transferor.

§ 4—204. **Methods of Sending and Presenting; Sending Direct to Payor Bank.**

(1) A collecting bank must send items by reasonably prompt method taking into consideration any relevant instructions, the nature of the item, the number of such items on hand, and the cost of collection involved and the method generally used by it or others to present such items.

(2) A collecting bank may send

(a) any item direct to the payor bank;

(b) any item to any non-bank payor if authorized by its transferor; and

(c) any item other than documentary drafts to any non-bank payor, if authorized by Federal Reserve regulation or operating letter, clearing house rule or the like.

(3) Presentment may be made by a presenting bank at a place where the payor bank has requested that presentment be made.

§ 4—205. **Supplying Missing Indorsement; No Notice from Prior Indorsement.**

(1) A depositary bank which has taken an item for collection may supply any indorsement of the customer which is necessary to title unless the item contains the words "payee's indorsement required" or the like. In the absence of such a requirement a statement placed on the item by the depositary bank to the effect that the item was deposited by a customer or credited to his account is effective as the customer's indorsement.

(2) An intermediary bank, or payor bank which is not a depositary bank, is neither given notice nor otherwise affected by a restrictive indorsement of any person except the bank's immediate transferor.

§ 4—206. **Transfer Between Banks.**

Any agreed method which identifies the transferor bank is sufficient for the item's further transfer to another bank.

§ 4—207. **Warranties of Customer and Collecting Bank on Transfer or Presentment of Items; Time for Claims.**

(1) Each customer or collecting bank who obtains payment or acceptance of an item and each prior customer and collecting bank warrants to the payor bank or other payor who in good faith pays or accepts the item that

(a) he has a good title to the item or is authorized to obtain payment or acceptance on behalf of one who has a good title; and

(b) he has no knowledge that the signature of the maker or drawer is unauthorized, except that this warranty is not given by any customer or collecting bank that is a holder in due course and acts in good faith

(i) to a maker with respect to the maker's own signature; or

(ii) to a drawer with respect to the drawer's own signature, whether or not the drawer is also the drawee; or

(iii) to an acceptor of an item if the holder in due course took the item after the acceptance or obtained the acceptance without knowledge that the drawer's signature was unauthorized; and

(c) the item has not been materially altered, except that this warranty is not given by any customer or collecting bank that is a holder in due course and acts in good faith

(i) to the maker of a note; or

(ii) to the drawer of a draft whether or not the drawer is also the drawee; or

(iii) to the acceptor of an item with respect to an alteration made prior to the acceptance if the holder in due course took the item after the acceptance, even though the acceptance provided "payable as originally drawn" or equivalent terms; or

(iv) to the acceptor of an item with respect to an alteration made after the acceptance.

(2) Each customer and collecting bank who transfers an item and receives a settlement or other consideration for it warrants to his transferee and to any subsequent collecting bank who takes the item in good faith that

(a) he has a good title to the item or is authorized to obtain payment or acceptance on behalf of one who has a good title and the transfer is otherwise rightful; and

(b) all signatures are genuine or authorized; and

(c) the item has not been materially altered; and

(d) no defense of any party is good against him; and

(e) he has no knowledge of any insolvency proceeding instituted with respect to the maker or acceptor or the drawer of an unaccepted item.

In addition each customer and collecting bank so transferring an item and receiving a settlement or other consideration engages that upon dishonor and any necessary notice of dishonor and protest he will take up the item.

(3) The warranties and the engagement to honor set forth in the two preceding subsections arise notwithstanding the absence of indorsement or words of guaranty or warranty in the transfer or presentment and a collecting bank remains liable for their breach despite remittance to its transferor. Damages for breach of such warranties or engagement to honor shall not exceed the consideration received by the customer or collecting bank responsible plus finance charges and expenses related to the item, if any.

(4) Unless a claim for breach of warranty under this section is made within a reasonable time after the person claiming learns of the breach, the person liable is discharged to the extent of any loss caused by the delay in making claim.

§ 4—208. **Security Interest of Collecting Bank in Items, Accompanying Documents and Proceeds.**

(1) A bank has a security interest in an item and any accompanying documents or the proceeds of either

(a) in case of an item deposited in an account to the extent to which credit given for the item has been withdrawn or applied;

(b) in case of an item for which it has given credit available for withdrawal as of right, to the extent of the credit given whether or not the credit is drawn upon and whether or not there is a right of chargeback; or

(c) if it makes an advance on or against the item.

(2) When credit which has been given for several items received at one time or pursuant to a single agreement is withdrawn or applied in part the security interest remains upon all the items, any accompanying documents or the proceeds of either. For the purpose of this section, credits first given are first withdrawn.

(3) Receipt by a collecting bank of a final settlement for an item is a realization on its security interest in the item, accompanying documents and proceeds. To the extent and so long as the bank does not receive final settlement for the item or give up possession of the item or accompanying documents for purposes other than collection, the security interest continues and is subject to the provisions of Article 9 except that

(a) no security agreement is necessary to make the security interest enforceable (subsection (1)(b) of Section 9—203); and

(b) no filing is required to perfect the security interest; and

(c) the security interest has priority over conflicting perfected security interests in the item, accompanying documents or proceeds.

§ 4—209. **When Bank Gives Value for Purposes of Holder in Due Course.**

For purposes of determining its status as a holder in due course, the bank has given value to the extent that it has a security interest in an item provided that the bank otherwise complies with the requirements of Section 3—302 on what constitutes a holder in due course.

§ 4—210. **Presentment by Notice of Item Not Payable by, Through or at a Bank; Liability of Secondary Parties.**

(1) Unless otherwise instructed, a collecting bank may present an item not payable by, through or at a bank by sending to the party to accept or pay a written notice that the bank holds the item for acceptance or payment. The notice must be sent in time to be received on or before the day when presentment is due and the bank must meet any requirement of the party to accept or pay under Section 3—505 by the close of the bank's next banking day after it knows of the requirement.

(2) Where presentment is made by notice and neither honor nor request for compliance with a requirement under Section 3—505 is received by the close of business on the day after maturity or in the case of demand items by the close of business on the third banking day after notice was sent, the presenting bank may treat the item as dishonored and charge any secondary party by sending him notice of the facts.

§ 4—211. **Media of Remittance; Provisional and Final Settlement in Remittance Cases.**

(1) A collecting bank may take in settlement of an item

(a) a check of the remitting bank or of another bank on any bank except the remitting bank; or

(b) a cashier's check or similar primary obligation of a remitting bank which is a member of or clears through a member of the same clearing house or group as the collecting bank; or

(c) appropriate authority to charge an account of the remitting bank or of another bank with the collecting bank; or

(d) if the item is drawn upon or payable by a person other than a bank, a cashier's check, certified check or other bank check or obligation.

(2) If before its midnight deadline the collecting bank properly dishonors a remittance check or authorization to charge on itself or presents or forwards for collection a remittance instrument of or on another bank which is of a kind approved by subsection (1) or has not been authorized by it, the collecting bank is not liable to prior parties in the event of the dishonor of such check, instrument or authorization.

(3) A settlement for an item by means of a remittance instrument or authorization to charge is or becomes a final settlement as to both the person making and the person receiving the settlement

(a) if the remittance instrument or authorization to charge is of a kind approved by subsection (1) or has not been authorized by the person receiving the settlement and in either case the person receiving the settlement acts seasonably before its midnight deadline in presenting, forwarding for collection or paying the instrument or authorization,—at the time the remittance instrument or authorization is finally paid by the payor by which it is payable;

(b) if the person receiving the settlement has authorized remittance by a non-bank check or obligation or by a cashier's check or similar primary obligation of or a check upon the payor or other remitting bank which is not of a kind approved by subsection (1)(b),—at the time of the receipt of such remittance check or obligation; or

(c) if in a case not covered by sub-paragraphs (a) or (b) the person receiving the settlement fails to seasonably present, forward for collection, pay or return a remittance instrument or authorization to it to charge before its midnight deadline,—at such midnight deadline.

§ 4—212. **Right of Charge-Back or Refund.**

(1) If a collecting bank has made provisional settlement with its customer for an item and itself fails by reason of dishonor, suspension of payments by a bank or otherwise to receive a settlement for the item which is or becomes final, the bank may revoke the settlement given by it, charge back the amount of any credit given for the item to its customer's account or obtain refund from its customer whether or not it is able to return the items if by its midnight deadline or within a longer reasonable time after it learns the facts it returns the item or sends notification of the facts. These rights to revoke, charge-back and obtain refund terminate if and when a settlement for the item received by the bank is or becomes final (subsection (3) of Section 4—211 and subsections (2) and (3) of Section 4—213).

[(2) Within the time and manner prescribed by this section and Section 4—301, an intermediary or payor bank, as the case may be, may return an unpaid item directly to the depositary bank and may send for collection a draft on the depositary bank and obtain reimbursement. In such case, if the depositary bank has received provisional settlement for the item, it must reimburse the bank drawing the draft and any provisional credits for the item between banks shall become and remain final.]

Note: Direct returns is recognized as an innovation that is not yet established bank practice, and therefore, Paragraph 2 has been bracketed. Some lawyers have doubts whether it should be included in legislation or left to development by agreement.

(3) A depositary bank which is also the payor may charge-back the amount of an item to its customer's account or obtain refund in accordance with the section governing return of an item received by a payor bank for credit on its books (Section 4—301).

(4) The right to charge-back is not affected by

(a) prior use of the credit given for the item; or

(b) failure by any bank to exercise ordinary care with respect to the item but any bank so failing remains liable.

(5) A failure to charge-back or claim refund does not affect other rights of the bank against the customer or any other party.

(6) If credit is given in dollars as the equivalent of the value of an item payable in a foreign currency the dollar amount of any charge-back or refund shall be calculated on the basis of the buying sight rate for the foreign currency prevailing on the day when the person entitled to the charge-back or refund learns that it will not receive payment in ordinary course.

§ 4—213. **Final Payment of Item by Payor Bank; When Provisional Debits and Credits Become Final; When Certain Credits Become Available for Withdrawal.**

(1) An item is finally paid by a payor bank when the bank has done any of the following, whichever happens first:

(a) paid the item in cash; or

(b) settled for the item without reserving a right to revoke the settlement and without having such right under statute, clearing house rule or agreement; or

(c) completed the process of posting the item to the indicated account of the drawer, maker or other person to be charged therewith; or

(d) made a provisional settlement for the item and failed to revoke the settlement in the time and manner permitted by statute, clearing house rule or agreement.

Upon a final payment under subparagraphs (b), (c) or (d) the payor bank shall be accountable for the amount of the item.

(2) If provisional settlement for an item between the presenting and payor banks is made through a clearing house or by debits or credits in an account between them, then to the extent that provisional debits or credits for the item are entered in accounts between the presenting and payor banks or between the presenting and successive prior collecting banks seriatim, they become final upon final payment of the item by the payor bank.

(3) If a collecting bank receives a settlement for an item which is or becomes final (subsection (3) of Section 4—211, subsection (2) of Section 4—213) the bank is accountable to its customer for the amount of the item and any provisional credit given for the item in an account with its customer becomes final.

(4) Subject to any right of the bank to apply the credit to an obligation of the customer, credit given by a bank for an item in an account with its customer becomes available for withdrawal as of right

(a) in any case where the bank has received a provisional settlement for the item,—when such settlement becomes final and the bank has had a reasonable time to learn that the settlement is final;

(b) in any case where the bank is both a depositary bank and a payor bank and the item is finally paid,— at the opening of the bank's second banking day following receipt of the item.

(5) A deposit of money in a bank is final when made but, subject to any right of the bank to apply the deposit to an obligation of the customer, the deposit becomes available for withdrawal as of right at the opening of the bank's next banking day following receipt of the deposit.

§ 4—214. **Insolvency and Preference.**

(1) Any item in or coming into the possession of a payor or collecting bank which suspends payment and which item is not finally paid shall be returned by the receiver, trustee or agent in charge of the closed bank to the presenting bank or the closed bank's customer.

(2) If a payor bank finally pays an item and suspends payments without making a settlement for the item with its customer or the presenting bank which settlement is or becomes final, the owner of the item has a preferred claim against the payor bank.

(3) If a payor bank gives or a collecting bank gives or receives a provisional settlement for an item and thereafter suspends payments, the suspension does not prevent or interfere with the settlement becoming final if such finality occurs automatically upon the lapse of certain time or the happening of certain events (subsection (3) of Section 4—211, subsections (1)(d), (2) and (3) of Section 4—213).

(4) If a collecting bank receives from subsequent parties settlement for an item which settlement is or becomes final and suspends payments without making a settlement for the item with its customer which is or becomes final, the owner of the item has a preferred claim against such collecting bank.

Part 3 **Collection of Items: Payor Banks**

§ 4—301. **Deferred Posting; Recovery of Payment by Return of Items; Time of Dishonor.**

(1) Where an authorized settlement for a demand item (other than a documentary draft) received by a payor bank otherwise than for immediate payment over the counter has been made before midnight of the banking day of receipt the payor bank may revoke the settlement and recover any payment if before it has made final payment (subsection (1) of Section 4—213) and before its midnight deadline it

(a) returns the item; or

(b) sends written notice of dishonor or nonpayment if the item is held for protest or is otherwise unavailable for return.

(2) If a demand item is received by a payor bank for credit on its books it may return such item or send notice of dishonor and may revoke any credit given or recover the amount thereof withdrawn by its customer, if it acts within the time limit and in the manner specified in the preceding subsection.

(3) Unless previous notice of dishonor has been sent an item is dishonored at the time when for purposes of dishonor it is returned or notice sent in accordance with this section.

(4) An item is returned:

(a) as to an item received through a clearing house, when it is delivered to the presenting or last collecting bank or to the clearing house or is sent or delivered in accordance with its rules; or

(b) in all other cases, when it is sent or delivered to the bank's customer or transferor or pursuant to his instructions.

§ 4—302. Payor Bank's Responsibility for Late Return of Item.

In the absence of a valid defense such as breach of a presentment warranty (subsection (1) of Section 4—207), settlement effected or the like, if an item is presented on and received by a payor bank the bank is accountable for the amount of

(a) a demand item other than a documentary draft whether properly payable or not if the bank, in any case where it is not also the depositary bank, retains the item beyond midnight of the banking day of receipt without settling for it or, regardless of whether it is also the depositary bank, does not pay or return the item or send notice of dishonor until after its midnight deadline; or

(b) any other properly payable item unless within the time allowed for acceptance or payment of that item the bank either accepts or pays the item or returns it and accompanying documents.

§ 4—303. When Items Subject to Notice, Stop-Order, Legal Process or Setoff; Order in Which Items May Be Charged or Certified.

(1) Any knowledge, notice or stop-order received by, legal process served upon or setoff exercised by a payor bank, whether or not effective under other rules of law to terminate, suspend or modify the bank's right or duty to pay an item or to charge its customer's account for the item, comes too late to so terminate, suspend or modify such right or duty if the knowledge, notice, stop-order or legal process is received or served and a reasonable time for the bank to act thereon expires or the setoff is exercised after the bank has done any of the following:

(a) accepted or certified the item;

(b) paid the item in cash;

(c) settled for the item without reserving a right to revoke the settlement and without having such right under statute, clearing house rule or agreement;

(d) completed the process of posting the item to the indicated account of the drawer, maker or other person to be charged therewith or otherwise has evidenced by examination of such indicated account and by action its decision to pay the item; or

(e) become accountable for the amount of the item under subsection (1)(d) of Section 4—213 and Section 4—302 dealing with the payor bank's responsibility for late return of items.

(2) Subject to the provisions of subsection (1) items may be accepted, paid, certified or charged to the indicated account of its customer in any order convenient to the bank.

Part 4 Relationship Between Payor Bank and Its Customer

§ 4—401. When Bank May Charge Customer's Account.

(1) As against its customer, a bank may charge against his account any item which is otherwise properly payable from that account even though the charge creates an overdraft.

(2) A bank which in good faith makes payment to a holder may charge the indicated account of its customer according to

(a) the original tenor of his altered item; or

(b) the tenor of his completed item, even though the bank knows the item has been completed unless the bank has notice that the completion was improper.

§ 4—402. Bank's Liability to Customer for Wrongful Dishonor.

A payor bank is liable to its customer for damages proximately caused by the wrongful dishonor of an item. When the dishonor occurs through mistake liability is limited to actual damages proved. If so proximately caused and proved damages may include damages for an arrest or prosecution of the customer or other consequential damages. Whether any consequential damages are proximately caused by the wrongful dishonor is a question of fact to be determined in each case.

§ 4—403. Customer's Right to Stop Payment; Burden of Proof of Loss.

(1) A customer may by order to his bank stop payment of any item payable for his account but the order must be received at such time and in such manner as to afford the bank a reasonable opportunity to act on it prior to any action by the bank with respect to the item described in Section 4—303.

(2) An oral order is binding upon the bank only for fourteen calendar days unless confirmed in writing within that period. A written order is effective for only six months unless renewed in writing.

(3) The burden of establishing the fact and amount of loss resulting from the payment of an item contrary to a binding stop payment order is on the customer.

§ 4—404. Bank Not Obligated to Pay Check More Than Six Months Old.

A bank is under no obligation to a customer having a checking account to pay a check, other than a certified check, which is presented more than six months after its date, but it may charge its customer's account for a payment made thereafter in good faith.

§ 4—405. Death or Incompetence of Customer.

(1) A payor or collecting bank's authority to accept, pay or collect an item or to account for proceeds of its collection if otherwise effective is not rendered ineffective by incompetence of a customer of either bank existing at the time the item is issued or its collection is undertaken if the bank does not know of an adjudication of incompetence. Neither death nor incompetence of a customer revokes such authority to accept, pay, collect or account until the bank knows of the fact of death or of an adjudication of incompetence and has reasonable opportunity to act on it.

(2) Even with knowledge a bank may for ten days after the date of death pay or certify checks drawn on or prior to that date unless ordered to stop payment by a person claiming an interest in the account.

§ 4—406. Customer's Duty to Discover and Report Unauthorized Signature or Alteration.

(1) When a bank sends to its customer a statement of account accompanied by items paid in good faith in support of the debit entries or holds the statement and items pursuant to a request or instructions of its customer or otherwise in a reasonable manner makes the statement and items available to the customer, the customer must exercise reasonable care and promptness to examine the statement and items to discover his unauthorized signature or any alteration on an item and must notify the bank promptly after discovery thereof.

(2) If the bank establishes that the customer failed with respect to an item to comply with the duties imposed on the customer by subsection (1) the customer is precluded from asserting against the bank

(a) his unauthorized signature or any alteration on the item if the bank also establishes that it suffered a loss by reason of such failure; and

(b) an unauthorized signature or alteration by the same wrongdoer on any other item paid in good faith by the bank after the first item and statement was available to the customer for a reasonable period not exceeding fourteen calendar days and before the bank receives notification from the customer of any such unauthorized signature or alteration.

(3) The preclusion under subsection (2) does not apply if the customer establishes lack of ordinary care on the part of the bank in paying the item(s).

(4) Without regard to care or lack of care of either the customer or the bank a customer who does not within one year from the time the statement and items are made available to the customer (subsection (1)) discover and report his unauthorized signature or any alteration on the face or back of the item or does not within three years from that time discover and report any unauthorized indorsement is precluded from asserting against the bank such unauthorized signature or indorsement or such alteration.

(5) If under this section a payor bank has a valid defense against a claim of a customer upon or resulting from payment of an item and waives or fails upon request to assert the defense the bank may not assert against any collecting bank or other prior party presenting or transferring the item a claim based upon the unauthorized signature or alteration giving rise to the customer's claim.

§ 4—407. Payor Bank's Right to Subrogation on Improper Payment.

If a payor bank has paid an item over the stop payment order of the drawer or maker or otherwise under circumstances giving a basis for objection by the drawer or maker, to prevent unjust enrichment and only to the extent necessary to prevent loss to the bank by reason of its payment of the item, the payor bank shall be subrogated to the rights

(a) of any holder in due course on the item against the drawer or maker; and

(b) of the payee or any other holder of the item against the drawer or maker either on the item or under the transaction out of which the item arose; and

(c) of the drawer or maker against the payee or any other holder of the item with respect to the transaction out of which the item arose.

Part 5 Collection of Documentary Drafts

§ 4—501. Handling of Documentary Drafts; Duty to Send for Presentment and to Notify Customer of Dishonor.

A bank which takes a documentary draft for collection must present or send the draft and accompanying documents for presentment and upon learning that the draft has not been paid or accepted in due course must seasonably notify its customer of such fact even though it may have discounted or bought the draft or extended credit available for withdrawal as of right.

§ 4—502. Presentment of "On Arrival" Drafts.

When a draft or the relevant instructions require presentment "on arrival", "when goods arrive" or the like, the collecting bank need not present until in its judgment a reasonable time for arrival of the goods has expired. Refusal to pay or accept because the goods have not arrived is not dishonor; the bank must notify its transferor of such refusal but need not present the draft again until it is instructed to do so or learns of the arrival of the goods.

§ 4—503. Responsibility of Presenting Bank for Documents and Goods; Report of Reasons for Dishonor; Referee in Case of Need.

Unless otherwise instructed and except as provided in Article 5 a bank presenting a documentary draft

(a) must deliver the documents to the drawee on acceptance of the draft if it is payable more than three days after presentment; otherwise, only on payment; and

(b) upon dishonor, either in the case of presentment for acceptance or presentment for payment, may seek and follow instructions from any referee in case of need designated in the draft or if the presenting bank does not choose to utilize his services it must use diligence and good faith to ascertain the reason for dishonor, must notify its transferor of the dishonor and of the results of its effort to ascertain the reasons therefor and must request instructions.

But the presenting bank is under no obligation with respect to goods represented by the documents except to follow any reasonable instructions seasonably received; it has a right to reimbursement for any expense incurred in following instructions and to prepayment of or indemnity for such expenses.

§ 4—504. Privilege of Presenting Bank to Deal With Goods; Security Interest for Expenses.

(1) A presenting bank which, following the dishonor of a documentary draft, has seasonably requested instructions but does not receive them within a reasonable time may store, sell, or otherwise deal with the goods in any reasonable manner.

(2) For its reasonable expenses incurred by action under subsection (1) the presenting bank has a lien upon the goods or their proceeds, which may be foreclosed in the same manner as an unpaid seller's lien.

Article 5
LETTERS OF CREDIT
(omitted)

Article 6
BULK TRANSFERS
(Omitted)

Article 7
WAREHOUSE RECEIPTS, BILLS OF LADING AND OTHER DOCUMENTS OF TITLE
(Omitted)

Article 8
INVESTMENT SECURITIES
(Omitted)

Article 9
Secured Transactions; Sales of Accounts and Chattel Paper

Note: *The adoption of this Article should be accompanied by the repeal of existing statutes dealing with conditional sales, trust receipts, factor's liens where the factor is given a non-possessory lien, chattel mortgages, crop mortgages, mortgages on railroad equipment, assignment of accounts and generally statutes regulating security interests in personal property.*

Where the state has a retail installment selling act or small loan act, that legislation should be carefully examined to determine what changes in those acts are needed to conform them to this Article. This Article primarily sets out rules defining rights of a secured party against persons dealing with the debtor; it does not prescribe regulations and controls which may be necessary to curb abuses arising in the small loan business or in the financing of consumer purchases on credit. Accordingly there is no intention to repeal existing regulatory acts in those fields by enactment or re-enactment of Article 9. See Section 9—203(4) and the Note thereto.

Part 1 **Short Title, Applicability and Definitions**

§ 9—101. Short Title.

This Article shall be known and may be cited as Uniform Commercial Code—Secured Transactions.

§ 9—102. Policy and Subject Matter of Article.

(1) Except as otherwise provided in Section 9—104 on excluded transactions, this Article applies

(a) to any transaction (regardless of its form) which is intended to create a security interest in personal property or fixtures including goods, documents, instruments, general intangibles, chattel paper or accounts; and also

(b) to any sale of accounts or chattel paper.

(2) This Article applies to security interests created by contract including pledge, assignment, chattel mortgage, chattel trust, trust deed, factor's lien, equipment trust, conditional sale, trust receipt, other lien or title retention contract and lease or consignment intended as security. This Article does not apply to statutory liens except as provided in Section 9—310.

(3) The application of this Article to a security interest in a secured obligation is not affected by the fact that the obligation is itself secured by a transaction or interest to which this Article does not apply. Amended in 1972.

§ 9—103. **Perfection of Security Interest in Multiple State Transactions**

(1) Documents, instruments and ordinary goods.

(a) This subsection applies to documents and instruments and to goods other than those covered by a certificate of title described in subsection (2), mobile goods described in subsection (3), and minerals described in subsection (5).

(b) Except as otherwise provided in this subsection, perfection and the effect of perfection or non-perfection of a security interest in collateral are governed by the law of the jurisdiction where the collateral is when the last event occurs on which is based the assertion that the security interest is perfected or unperfected.

(c) If the parties to a transaction creating a purchase money security interest in goods in one jurisdiction understand at the time that the security interest attaches that the goods will be kept in another jurisdiction, then the law of the other jurisdiction governs the perfection and the effect of perfection or non-perfection of the security interest from the time it attaches until thirty days after the debtor receives possession of the goods and thereafter if the goods are taken to the other jurisdiction before the end of the thirty-day period.

(d) When collateral is brought into and kept in this state while subject to a security interest perfected under the law of the jurisdiction from which the collateral was removed, the security interest remains perfected, but if action is required by Part 3 of this Article to perfect the security interest,

(i) if the action is not taken before the expiration of the period of perfection in the other jurisdiction or the end of four months after the collateral

is brought into this state, whichever period first expires, the security interest becomes unperfected at the end of that period and is thereafter deemed to have been unperfected as against a person who became a purchaser after removal;

(ii) if the action is taken before the expiration of the period specified in subparagraph (i), the security interest continues perfected thereafter;

(iii) for the purpose of priority over a buyer of consumer goods (subsection (2) of Section 9—307), the period of the effectiveness of a filing in the jurisdiction from which the collateral is removed is governed by the rules with respect to perfection in subparagraphs (i) and (ii).

(2) Certificate of title.

(a) This subsection applies to goods covered by a certificate of title issued under a statute of this state or of another jurisdiction under the law of which indication of a security interest on the certificate is required as a condition of perfection.

(b) Except as otherwise provided in this subsection, perfection and the effect of perfection or non-perfection of the security interest are governed by the law (including the conflict of laws rules) of the jurisdiction issuing the certificate until four months after the goods are removed from that jurisdiction and thereafter until the goods are registered in another jurisdiction, but in any event not beyond surrender of the certificate. After the expiration of that period, the goods are not covered by the certificate of title within the meaning of this section.

(c) Except with respect to the rights of a buyer described in the next paragraph, a security interest, perfected in another jurisdiction otherwise than by notation on a certificate of title, in goods brought into this state and thereafter covered by a certificate of title issued by this state is subject to the rules stated in paragraph (d) of subsection (1).

(d) If goods are brought into this state while a security interest therein is perfected in any manner under the law of the jurisdiction from which the goods are removed and a certificate of title is issued by this state and the certificate does not show that the goods are subject to the security interest or that they may be subject to security interests not shown on the certificate, the security interest is subordinate to the rights of a buyer of the goods who is not in the business of selling goods of that kind to the extent that he gives value and receives delivery of the goods after issuance of the certificate and without knowledge of the security interest.

(3) Accounts, general intangibles and mobile goods.

(a) This subsection applies to accounts (other than an account described in subsection (5) on minerals) and general intangibles (other than uncertificated securities) and to goods which are mobile and which are of a type normally used in more than one jurisdiction, such as motor vehicles, trailers, rolling stock, airplanes, shipping containers, road building and construction machinery and commercial harvesting machinery and the like, if the goods are equipment or are inventory leased or held for lease by the debtor to others, and are not covered by a certificate of title described in subsection (2).

(b) The law (including the conflict of laws rules) of the jurisdiction in which the debtor is located governs the perfection and the effect of perfection or non-perfection of the security interest.

(c) If, however, the debtor is located in a jurisdiction which is not a part of the United States, and which does not provide for perfection of the security interest by filing or recording in that jurisdiction, the law of the jurisdiction in the United States in which the debtor has its major executive office in the United States governs the perfection and the effect of perfection or non-perfection of the security interest through filing. In the alternative, if the debtor is located in a jurisdiction which is not a part of the United States or Canada and the collateral is accounts or general intangibles for money due or to become due, the security interest may be perfected by notification to the account debtor. As used in this paragraph, "United States" includes its territories and possessions and the Commonwealth of Puerto Rico.

(d) A debtor shall be deemed located at his place of business if he has one, at his chief executive office if he has more than one place of business, otherwise at his residence. If, however, the debtor is a foreign air carrier under the Federal Aviation Act of 1958, as amended, it shall be deemed located at the designated office of the agent upon whom service of process may be made on behalf of the foreign air carrier.

(e) A security interest perfected under the law of the jurisdiction of the location of the debtor is perfected until the expiration of four months after a change of the debtor's location to another jurisdiction, or until perfection would have ceased by the law of the first jurisdiction, whichever period first expires. Unless perfected in the new jurisdiction before the end of that period, it becomes unperfected thereafter and is deemed to have been unperfected as against a person who became a purchaser after the change.

(4) Chattel paper.

The rules stated for goods in subsection (1) apply to a possessory security interest in chattel paper. The rules stated for accounts in subsection (3) apply to a non-possessory security interest in chattel paper, but the security interest may not be perfected by notification to the account debtor.

(5) Minerals.

Perfection and the effect of perfection or non-perfection of a security interest which is created by a debtor who has an interest in minerals or the like (including oil and gas) before extraction and which attaches thereto as extracted, or which attaches to an account resulting from the sale thereof at the wellhead or minehead are governed by the law (including the conflict of laws rules) of the jurisdiction wherein the wellhead or minehead is located.

(6) Uncertificated securities.

The law (including the conflict of laws rules) of the jurisdiction of organization of the issuer governs the perfection and the effect of perfection or non-perfection of a security interest in uncertificated securities.

Amended in 1972 and 1977.

§ 9—104. **Transactions Excluded From Article.**

This Article does not apply

(a) to a security interest subject to any statute of the United States, to the extent that such statute governs the rights of parties to and third parties affected by transactions in particular types of property; or

(b) to a landlord's lien; or

(c) to a lien given by statute or other rule of law for services or materials except as provided in Section 9—310 on priority of such liens; or

(d) to a transfer of a claim for wages, salary or other compensation of an employee; or

(e) to a transfer by a government or governmental subdivision or agency; or

(f) to a sale of accounts or chattel paper as part of a sale of the business out of which they arose, or an assignment of accounts or chattel paper which is for the purpose of collection only, or a transfer of a right to payment under a contract to an assignee who is also to do the performance under the contract or a transfer of a single account to an assignee in whole or partial satisfaction of a preexisting indebtedness; or

(g) to a transfer of an interest in or claim in or under any policy of insurance, except as provided with respect to proceeds (Section 9—306) and priorities in proceeds (Section 9—312); or

(h) to a right represented by a judgment (other than a judgment taken on a right to payment which was collateral); or

(i) to any right of set-off; or

(j) except to the extent that provision is made for fixtures in Section 9—313, to the creation or transfer of an interest in or lien on real estate, including a lease or rents thereunder; or

(k) to a transfer in whole or in part of any claim arising out of tort; or

(l) to a transfer of an interest in any deposit account (subsection (1) of Section 9—105), except as provided with respect to proceeds (Section 9—306) and priorities in proceeds (Section 9—312).

Amended in 1972.

§ 9—105. **Definitions and Index of Definitions**

(1) In this Article unless the context otherwise requires:

(a) "Account debtor" means the person who is obligated on an account, chattel paper or general intangible;

(b) "Chattel paper" means a writing or writings which evidence both a monetary obligation and a security interest in or a lease of specific goods, but a charter or other contract involving the use or hire of a vessel is not chattel paper. When a transaction is evidenced both by such a security agreement or a lease and by an instrument or a series of instruments, the group of writings taken together constitutes chattel paper;

(c) "Collateral" means the property subject to a security interest, and includes accounts and chattel paper which have been sold;

(d) "Debtor" means the person who owes payment or other performance of the obligation secured, whether or not he owns or has rights in the collateral, and includes the seller of accounts or chattel paper. Where the debtor and the owner of the collateral are not the same person, the term "debtor" means the owner of the collateral in any provision of the Article dealing with the collateral, the obligor in any provision dealing with the obligation, and may include both where the context so requires;

(e) "Deposit account" means a demand, time, savings, passbook or like account maintained with a bank, savings and loan association, credit union or like organization, other than an account evidenced by a certificate of deposit;

(f) "Document" means document of title as defined in the general definitions of Article 1 (Section 1—201), and a receipt of the kind described in subsection (2) of Section 7—201;

(g) "Encumbrance" includes real estate mortgages and other liens on real estate and all other rights in real estate that are not ownership interests;

(h) "Goods" includes all things which are movable at the time the security interest attaches or which are fixtures (Section 9—313), but does not include money, documents, instruments, accounts, chattel paper, general intangibles, or minerals or the like (including oil and gas) before extraction. "Goods" also includes standing timber which is to be cut and removed under a conveyance or contract for sale, the unborn young of animals, and growing crops;

(i) "Instrument" means a negotiable instrument (defined in Section 3—104), or a certificated security (defined in Section 8—102) or any other writing which evidences a right to the payment of money and is not itself a security agreement or lease and is of a type which is in ordinary course of business transferred by delivery with any necessary indorsement or assignment;

(j) "Mortgage" means a consensual interest created by a real estate mortgage, a trust deed on real estate, or the like;

(k) An advance is made "pursuant to commitment" if the secured party has bound himself to make it, whether or not a subsequent event of default or other event not within his control has relieved or may relieve him from his obligation;

(l) "Security agreement" means an agreement which creates or provides for a security interest;

(m) "Secured party" means a lender, seller or other person in whose favor there is a security interest, including a person to whom accounts or chattel paper have been sold. When the holders of obligations issued under an indenture of trust, equipment trust agreement or the like are represented by a trustee or other person, the representative is the secured party;

(n) "Transmitting utility" means any person primarily engaged in the railroad, street railway or trolley bus business, the electric or electronics communications transmission business, the transmission of goods by pipeline, or the transmission or the production and transmission of electricity, steam, gas or water, or the provision of sewer service.

(2) Other definitions applying to this Article and the sections in which they appear are:

"Account". Section 9—106.
"Attach". Section 9—203.
"Construction mortgage". Section 9—313(1).
"Consumer goods". Section 9—109(1).
"Equipment". Section 9—109(2).
"Farm products". Section 9—109(3).

"Fixture". Section 9—313(1).
"Fixture filing". Section 9—313(1).
"General intangibles". Section 9—106.
"Inventory". Section 9—109(4).
"Lien creditor". Section 9—301(3).
"Proceeds". Section 9—306(1).
"Purchase money security interest". Section 9—107.
"United States". Section 9—103.

(3) The following definitions in other Articles apply to this Article:
"Check". Section 3—104.
"Contract for sale". Section 2—106.
"Holder in due course". Section 3—302.
"Note". Section 3—104.
"Sale". Section 2—106.

(4) In addition Article 1 contains general definitions and principles of construction and interpretation applicable throughout this Article.

Amended in 1966, 1972 and 1977.

§ 9—106. Definitions: "Account"; "General Intangibles".

"Account" means any right to payment for goods sold or leased or for services rendered which is not evidenced by an instrument or chattel paper, whether or not it has been earned by performance. "General intangibles" means any personal property (including things in action) other than goods, accounts, chattel paper, documents, instruments, and money. All rights to payment earned or unearned under a charter or other contract involving the use or hire of a vessel and all rights incident to the charter or contract are accounts. Amended in 1966, 1972.

§ 9—107. Definitions: "Purchase Money Security Interest".

A security interest is a "purchase money security interest" to the extent that it is

(a) taken or retained by the seller of the collateral to secure all or part of its price; or

(b) taken by a person who by making advances or incurring an obligation gives value to enable the debtor to acquire rights in or the use of collateral if such value is in fact so used.

§ 9—108. When After-Acquired Collateral Not Security for Antecedent Debt.

Where a secured party makes an advance, incurs an obligation, releases a perfected security interest, or otherwise gives new value which is to be secured in whole or in part by after-acquired property his security interest in the after-acquired collateral shall be deemed to be taken for new value and not as security for an antecedent debt if the debtor acquires his rights in such collateral either

in the ordinary course of his business or under a contract of purchase made pursuant to the security agreement within a reasonable time after new value is given.

§ 9—109. Classification of Goods; "Consumer Goods"; "Equipment"; "Farm Products"; "Inventory".

Goods are

(1) "consumer goods" if they are used or bought for use primarily for personal, family or household purposes;

(2) "equipment" if they are used or bought for use primarily in business (including farming or a profession) or by a debtor who is a non-profit organization or a governmental subdivision or agency or if the goods are not included in the definitions of inventory, farm products or consumer goods;

(3) "farm products" if they are crops or livestock or supplies used or produced in farming operations or if they are products of crops or livestock in their unmanufactured states (such as ginned cotton, woolclip, maple syrup, milk and eggs), and if they are in the possession of a debtor engaged in raising, fattening, grazing or other farming operations. If goods are farm products they are neither equipment nor inventory;

(4) "inventory" if they are held by a person who holds them for sale or lease or to be furnished under contracts of service or if he has so furnished them, or if they are raw materials, work in process or materials used or consumed in a business. Inventory of a person is not to be classified as his equipment.

§ 9—110. Sufficiency of Description.

For purposes of this Article any description of personal property or real estate is sufficient whether or not it is specific if it reasonably identifies what is described.

§ 9—111. Applicability of Bulk Transfer Laws.

The creation of a security interest is not a bulk transfer under Article 6 (see Section 6—103).

§ 9—112. Where Collateral Is Not Owned by Debtor.

Unless otherwise agreed, when a secured party knows that collateral is owned by a person who is not the debtor, the owner of the collateral is entitled to receive from the secured party any surplus under Section 9—502(2) or under Section 9—504(1), and is not liable for the debt or for any deficiency after resale, and he has the same right as the debtor

(a) to receive statements under Section 9—208;

(b) to receive notice of and to object to a secured party's proposal to retain the collateral in satisfaction of the indebtedness under Section 9—505;

(c) to redeem the collateral under Section 9—506;

(d) to obtain injunctive or other relief under Section 9—507(1); and

(e) to recover losses caused to him under Section 9—208(2).

§ 9—113. **Security Interests Arising Under Article on Sales.**

A security interest arising solely under the Article on Sales (Article 2) is subject to the provisions of this Article except that to the extent that and so long as the debtor does not have or does not lawfully obtain possession of the goods

(a) no security agreement is necessary to make the security interest enforceable; and

(b) no filing is required to perfect the security interest; and

(c) the rights of the secured party on default by the debtor are governed by the Article on Sales (Article 2).

§ 9—114. **Consignment.**

(1) A person who delivers goods under a consignment which is not a security interest and who would be required to file under this Article by paragraph (3)(c) of Section 2—326 has priority over a secured party who is or becomes a creditor of the consignee and who would have a perfected security interest in the goods if they were the property of the consignee, and also has priority with respect to identifiable cash proceeds received on or before delivery of the goods to a buyer, if

> (a) the consignor complies with the filing provision of the Article on Sales with respect to consignments (paragraph (3)(c) of Section 2—326) before the consignee receives possession of the goods; and

> (b) the consignor gives notification in writing to the holder of the security interest if the holder has filed a financing statement covering the same types of goods before the date of the filing made by the consignor; and

> (c) the holder of the security interest receives the notification within five years before the consignee receives possession of the goods; and

> (d) the notification states that the consignor expects to deliver goods on consignment to the consignee, describing the goods by item or type.

(2) In the case of a consignment which is not a security interest and in which the requirements of the preceding subsection have not been met, a person who delivers goods

to another is subordinate to a person who would have a perfected security interest in the goods if they were the property of the debtor.

Added in 1972.

Part 2 Validity of Security Agreement and Rights of Parties Thereto

§ 9—201. **General Validity of Security Agreement.**

Except as otherwise provided by this Act a security agreement is effective according to its terms between the parties, against purchasers of the collateral and against creditors. Nothing in this Article validates any charge or practice illegal under any statute or regulation thereunder governing usury, small loans, retail installment sales, or the like, or extends the application of any such statute or regulation to any transaction not otherwise subject thereto.

§ 9—202. **Title to Collateral Immaterial.**

Each provision of this Article with regard to rights, obligations and remedies applies whether title to collateral is in the secured party or in the debtor.

§ 9—203. **Attachment and Enforceability of Security Interest; Proceeds; Formal Requisites**

(1) Subject to the provisions of Section 4—208 on the security interest of a collecting bank, Section 8—321 on security interests in securities and Section 9—113 on a security interest arising under the Article on Sales, a security interest is not enforceable against the debtor or third parties with respect to the collateral and does not attach unless:

> (a) the collateral is in the possession of the secured party pursuant to agreement, or the debtor has signed a security agreement which contains a description of the collateral and in addition, when the security interest covers crops growing or to be grown or timber to be cut, a description of the land concerned;

> (b) value has been given; and

> (c) the debtor has rights in the collateral.

(2) A security interest attaches when it becomes enforceable against the debtor with respect to the collateral. Attachment occurs as soon as all of the events specified in subsection (1) have taken place unless explicit agreement postpones the time of attaching.

(3) Unless otherwise agreed a security agreement gives the secured party the rights to proceeds provided by Section 9—306.

(4) A transaction, although subject to this Article, is also subject to . . . .*, and in the case of conflict between the provisions of this Article and any such statute, the provisions of such statute control. Failure to comply with any applicable statute has only the effect which is specified therein.

Amended in 1972 and 1977.

Note: *At * in subsection (4) insert reference to any local statute regulating small loans, retail installment sales and the like.*

> *The foregoing subsection (4) is designed to make it clear that certain transactions, although subject to this Article, must also comply with other applicable legislation.*
>
> *This Article is designed to regulate all the "security" aspects of transactions within its scope. There is, however, much regulatory legislation, particularly in the consumer field, which supplements this Article and should not be repealed by its enactment. Examples are small loan acts, retail installment selling acts and the like. Such acts may provide for licensing and rate regulation and may prescribe particular forms of contract. Such provisions should remain in force despite the enactment of this Article. On the other hand if a retail installment selling act contains provisions on filing, rights on default, etc., such provisions should be repealed as inconsistent with this Article except that inconsistent provisions as to deficiencies, penalties, etc., in the Uniform Consumer Credit Code and other recent related legislation should remain because those statutes were drafted after the substantial enactment of the Article and with the intention of modifying certain provisions of this Article as to consumer credit.*

§ 9—204. After-Acquired Property; Future Advances.

(1) Except as provided in subsection (2), a security agreement may provide that any or all obligations covered by the security agreement are to be secured by after-acquired collateral.

(2) No security interest attaches under an after-acquired property clause to consumer goods other than accessions (Section 9—314) when given as additional security unless the debtor acquires rights in them within ten days after the secured party gives value.

(3) Obligations covered by a security agreement may include future advances or other value whether or not the advances or value are given pursuant to commitment (subsection (1) of Section 9—105).

Amended in 1972.

§ 9—205. Use or Disposition of Collateral Without Accounting Permissible.

A security interest is not invalid or fraudulent against creditors by reason of liberty in the debtor to use, commingle or dispose of all or part of the collateral (including returned or repossessed goods) or to collect or compromise accounts or chattel paper, or to accept the return of goods or make repossessions, or to use, commingle or dispose of proceeds, or by reason of the failure of the

secured party to require the debtor to account for proceeds or replace collateral. This section does not relax the requirements of possession where perfection of a security interest depends upon possession of the collateral by the secured party or by a bailee.

Amended in 1972.

§ 9—206. Agreement Not to Assert Defenses Against Assignee; Modification of Sales Warranties Where Security Agreement Exists.

(1) Subject to any statute or decision which establishes a different rule for buyers or lessees of consumer goods, an agreement by a buyer or lessee that he will not assert against an assignee any claim or defense which he may have against the seller or lessor is enforceable by an assignee who takes his assignment for value, in good faith and without notice of a claim or defense, except as to defenses of a type which may be asserted against a holder in due course of a negotiable instrument under the Article on Commercial Paper (Article 3). A buyer who as part of one transaction signs both a negotiable instrument and a security agreement makes such an agreement.

(2) When a seller retains a purchase money security interest in goods the Article on Sales (Article 2) governs the sale and any disclaimer, limitation or modification of the seller's warranties.

Amended in 1962.

§ 9—207. Rights and Duties When Collateral is in Secured Party's Possession.

(1) A secured party must use reasonable care in the custody and preservation of collateral in his possession. In the case of an instrument or chattel paper reasonable care includes taking necessary steps to preserve rights against prior parties unless otherwise agreed.

(2) Unless otherwise agreed, when collateral is in the secured party's possession

(a) reasonable expenses (including the cost of any insurance and payment of taxes or other charges) incurred in the custody, preservation, use or operation of the collateral are chargeable to the debtor and are secured by the collateral;

(b) the risk of accidental loss or damage is on the debtor to the extent of any deficiency in any effective insurance coverage;

(c) the secured party may hold as additional security any increase or profits (except money) received from the collateral, but money so received, unless remitted to the debtor, shall be applied in reduction of the secured obligation;

(d) the secured party must keep the collateral identifiable but fungible collateral may be commingled;

(e) the secured party may repledge the collateral upon terms which do not impair the debtor's right to redeem it.

(3) A secured party is liable for any loss caused by his failure to meet any obligation imposed by the preceding subsections but does not lose his security interest.

(4) A secured party may use or operate the collateral for the purpose of preserving the collateral or its value or pursuant to the order of a court of appropriate jurisdiction or, except in the case of consumer goods, in the manner and to the extent provided in the security agreement.

§ 9—208. Request for Statement of Account or List of Collateral.

(1) A debtor may sign a statement indicating what he believes to be the aggregate amount of unpaid indebtedness as of a specified date and may send it to the secured party with a request that the statement be approved or corrected and returned to the debtor. When the security agreement or any other record kept by the secured party identifies the collateral a debtor may similarly request the secured party to approve or correct a list of the collateral.

(2) The secured party must comply with such a request within two weeks after receipt by sending a written correction or approval. If the secured party claims a security interest in all of a particular type of collateral owned by the debtor he may indicate that fact in his reply and need not approve or correct an itemized list of such collateral. If the secured party without reasonable excuse fails to comply he is liable for any loss caused to the debtor thereby; and if the debtor has properly included in his request a good faith statement of the obligation or a list of the collateral or both the secured party may claim a security interest only as shown in the statement against persons misled by his failure to comply. If he no longer has an interest in the obligation or collateral at the time the request is received he must disclose the name and address of any successor in interest known to him and he is liable for any loss caused to the debtor as a result of failure to disclose. A successor in interest is not subject to this section until a request is received by him.

(3) A debtor is entitled to such a statement once every six months without charge. The secured party may require payment of a charge not exceeding $10 for each additional statement furnished.

Part 3 Rights of Third Parties; Perfected and Unperfected Security Interests; Rules of Priority

§ 9—301. Persons Who Take Priority Over Unperfected Security Interests; Rights of "Lien Creditor".

(1) Except as otherwise provided in subsection (2), an unperfected security interest is subordinate to the rights of

(a) persons entitled to priority under Section 9—312;

(b) a person who becomes a lien creditor before the security interest is perfected;

(c) in the case of goods, instruments, documents, and chattel paper, a person who is not a secured party and who is a transferee in bulk or other buyer not in ordinary course of business or is a buyer of farm products in ordinary course of business, to the extent that he gives value and receives delivery of the collateral without knowledge of the security interest and before it is perfected;

(d) in the case of accounts and general intangibles, a person who is not a secured party and who is a transferee to the extent that he gives value without knowledge of the security interest and before it is perfected.

(2) If the secured party files with respect to a purchase money security interest before or within ten days after the debtor receives possession of the collateral, he takes priority over the rights of a transferee in bulk or of a lien creditor which arise between the time the security interest attaches and the time of filing.

(3) A "lien creditor" means a creditor who has acquired a lien on the property involved by attachment, levy or the like and includes an assignee for benefit of creditors from the time of assignment, and a trustee in bankruptcy from the date of the filing of the petition or a receiver in equity from the time of appointment.

(4) A person who becomes a lien creditor while a security interest is perfected takes subject to the security interest only to the extent that it secures advances made before he becomes a lien creditor or within 45 days thereafter or made without knowledge of the lien or pursuant to a commitment entered into without knowledge of the lien.

Amended in 1972.

§ 9—302. When Filing Is Required to Perfect Security Interest; Security Interests to Which Filing Provisions of This Article Do Not Apply

(1) A financing statement must be filed to perfect all security interests except the following:

(a) a security interest in collateral in possession of the secured party under Section 9—305;

(b) a security interest temporarily perfected in instruments or documents without delivery under Section 9—304 or in proceeds for a 10 day period under Section 9—306;

(c) a security interest created by an assignment of a beneficial interest in a trust or a decedent's estate;

(d) a purchase money security interest in consumer goods; but filing is required for a motor vehicle required to be registered; and fixture filing is required for priority over conflicting interests in fixtures to the extent provided in Section 9—313;

(e) an assignment of accounts which does not alone or in conjunction with other assignments to the same assignee transfer a significant part of the outstanding accounts of the assignor;

(f) a security interest of a collecting bank (Section 4—208) or in securities (Section 8—321) or arising under the Article on Sales (see Section 9—113) or covered in subsection (3) of this section;

(g) an assignment for the benefit of all the creditors of the transferor, and subsequent transfers by the assignee thereunder.

(2) If a secured party assigns a perfected security interest, no filing under this Article is required in order to continue the perfected status of the security interest against creditors of and transferees from the original debtor.

(3) The filing of a financing statement otherwise required by this Article is not necessary or effective to perfect a security interest in property subject to

(a) a statute or treaty of the United States which provides for a national or international registration or a national or international certificate of title or which specifies a place of filing different from that specified in this Article for filing of the security interest; or

(b) the following statutes of this state; [list any certificate of title statute covering automobiles, trailers, mobile homes, boats, farm tractors, or the like, and any central filing statute.]; but during any period in which collateral is inventory held for sale by a person who is in the business of selling goods of that kind, the filing provisions of this Article (Part 4) apply to a security interest in that collateral created by him as debtor; or

(c) a certificate of title statute of another juris- diction under the law of which indication of a security interest on the certificate is required as a condition of perfection (subsection (2) of Section 9—103).

(4) Compliance with a statute or treaty described in subsection (3) is equivalent to the filing of a financing statement under this Article, and a security interest in property subject to the statute or treaty can be perfected only by compliance therewith except as provided in Section 9—103 on multiple state transactions. Duration and renewal of perfection of a security interest perfected by compliance with the statute or treaty are governed by the provisions of the statute or treaty; in other respects the security interest is subject to this Article.

Amended in 1972 and 1977.

§ 9—303. **When Security Interest Is Perfected; Continuity of Perfection.**

(1) A security interest is perfected when it has attached and when all of the applicable steps required for perfection have been taken. Such steps are specified in Sections 9—302, 9—304, 9—305 and 9—306. If such steps are taken before the security interest attaches, it is perfected at the time when it attaches.

(2) If a security interest is originally perfected in any way permitted under this Article and is subsequently perfected in some other way under this Article, without an intermediate period when it was unperfected, the security interest shall be deemed to be perfected continuously for the purposes of this Article.

§ 9—304. **Perfection of Security Interest in Instruments, Documents, and Goods Covered by Documents; Perfection by Permissive Filing; Temporary Perfection Without Filing or Transfer of Possession**

(1) A security interest in chattel paper or negotiable documents may be perfected by filing. A security interest in money or instruments (other than certificated securities or instruments which constitute part of chattel paper) can be perfected only by the secured party's taking possession, except as provided in subsections (4) and (5) of this section and subsections (2) and (3) of Section 9—306 on proceeds.

(2) During the period that goods are in the possession of the issuer of a negotiable document therefor, a security interest in the goods is perfected by perfecting a security interest in the document, and any security interest in the goods otherwise perfected during such period is subject thereto.

(3) A security interest in goods in the possession of a bailee other than one who has issued a negotiable document therefor is perfected by issuance of a document in the name of the secured party or by the bailee's receipt of notification of the secured party's interest or by filing as to the goods.

(4) A security interest in instruments (other than certificated securities) or negotiable documents is perfected without filing or the taking of possession for a period of 21 days from the time it attaches to the extent that it

arises for new value given under a written security agreement.

(5) A security interest remains perfected for a period of 21 days without filing where a secured party having a perfected security interest in an instrument (other than a certificated security), a negotiable document or goods in possession of a bailee other than one who has issued a negotiable document therefor

(a) makes available to the debtor the goods or documents representing the goods for the purpose of ultimate sale or exchange or for the purpose of loading, unloading, storing, shipping, transshipping, manufacturing, processing or otherwise dealing with them in a manner preliminary to their sale or exchange, but priority between conflicting security interests in the goods is subject to subsection (3) of Section 9—312; or

(b) delivers the instrument to the debtor for the purpose of ultimate sale or exchange or of presentation, collection, renewal or registration of transfer.

(6) After the 21 day period in subsections (4) and (5) perfection depends upon compliance with applicable provisions of this Article.

Amended in 1972 and 1977.

§ 9—305. **When Possession by Secured Party Perfects Security Interest Without Filing**

A security interest in letters of credit and advices of credit (subsection (2)(a) of Section 5—116), goods, instruments (other than certificated securities), money, negotiable documents, or chattel paper may be perfected by the secured party's taking possession of the collateral. If such collateral other than goods covered by a negotiable document is held by a bailee, the secured party is deemed to have possession from the time the bailee receives notification of the secured party's interest. A security interest is perfected by possession from the time possession is taken without a relation back and continues only so long as possession is retained, unless otherwise specified in this Article. The security interest may be otherwise perfected as provided in this Article before or after the period of possession by the secured party.

Amended in 1972 and 1977.

§ 9—306. **"Proceeds"; Secured Party's Rights on Disposition of Collateral.**

(1) "Proceeds" includes whatever is received upon the sale, exchange, collection or other disposition of collateral or proceeds. Insurance payable by reason of loss or damage to the collateral is proceeds, except to the extent that it is payable to a person other than a party to the security agreement. Money, checks, deposit accounts, and

the like are "cash proceeds". All other proceeds are "non-cash proceeds".

(2) Except where this Article otherwise provides, a security interest continues in collateral notwithstanding sale, exchange or other disposition thereof unless the disposition was authorized by the secured party in the security agreement or otherwise, and also continues in any identifiable proceeds including collections received by the debtor.

(3) The security interest in proceeds is a continuously perfected security interest if the interest in the original collateral was perfected but it ceases to be a perfected security interest and becomes unperfected ten days after receipt of the proceeds by the debtor unless

(a) a filed financing statement covers the original collateral and the proceeds are collateral in which a security interest may be perfected by filing in the office or offices where the financing statement has been filed and, if the proceeds are acquired with cash proceeds, the description of collateral in the financing statement indicates the types of property constituting the proceeds; or

(b) a filed financing statement covers the original collateral and the proceeds are identifiable cash proceeds; or

(c) the security interest in the proceeds is perfected before the expiration of the ten day period.

Except as provided in this section, a security interest in proceeds can be perfected only by the methods or under the circumstances permitted in this Article for original collateral of the same type.

(4) In the event of insolvency proceedings instituted by or against a debtor, a secured party with a perfected security interest in proceeds has a perfected security interest only in the following proceeds:

(a) in identifiable non-cash proceeds and in separate deposit accounts containing only proceeds;

(b) in identifiable cash proceeds in the form of money which is neither commingled with other money nor deposited in a deposit account prior to the insolvency proceedings;

(c) in identifiable cash proceeds in the form of checks and the like which are not deposited in a deposit account prior to the insolvency proceedings; and

(d) in all cash and deposit accounts of the debtor in which proceeds have been commingled with other funds, but the perfected security interest under this paragraph (d) is

(i) subject to any right to set-off; and

(ii) limited to an amount not greater than the amount of any cash proceeds received by the debtor within ten days before the institution of the insolvency proceedings less the sum of (I) the payments to the secured party on account of cash proceeds received by the debtor during such period and (II) the cash proceeds received by the debtor during such period to which the secured party is entitled under paragraphs (a) through (c) of this subsection (4).

(5) If a sale of goods results in an account or chattel paper which is transferred by the seller to a secured party, and if the goods are returned to or are repossessed by the seller or the secured party, the following rules determine priorities:

(a) If the goods were collateral at the time of sale, for an indebtedness of the seller which is still unpaid, the original security interest attaches again to the goods and continues as a perfected security interest if it was perfected at the time when the goods were sold. If the security interest was originally perfected by a filing which is still effective, nothing further is required to continue the perfected status; in any other case, the secured party must take possession of the returned or repossessed goods or must file.

(b) An unpaid transferee of the chattel paper has a security interest in the goods against the transferor. Such security interest is prior to a security interest asserted under paragraph (a) to the extent that the transferee of the chattel paper was entitled to priority under Section 9—308.

(c) An unpaid transferee of the account has a security interest in the goods against the transferor. Such security interest is subordinate to a security interest asserted under paragraph (a).

(d) A security interest of an unpaid transferee asserted under paragraph (b) or (c) must be perfected for protection against creditors of the transferor and purchasers of the returned or repossessed goods.

Amended in 1972.

§ 9—307. **Protection of Buyers of Goods.**

(1) A buyer in ordinary course of business (subsection (9) of Section 1—201) other than a person buying farm products from a person engaged in farming operations takes free of a security interest created by his seller even though the security interest is perfected and even though the buyer knows of its existence.

(2) In the case of consumer goods, a buyer takes free of a security interest even though perfected if he buys without knowledge of the security interest, for value and for his own personal, family or household purposes unless prior to the purchase the secured party has filed a financing statement covering such goods.

(3) A buyer other than a buyer in ordinary course of business (subsection (1) of this section) takes free of a security interest to the extent that it secures future advances made after the secured party acquires knowledge of the purchase, or more than 45 days after the purchase, whichever first occurs, unless made pursuant to a commitment entered into without knowledge of the purchase and before the expiration of the 45 day period. Amended in 1972.

§ 9—308. **Purchase of Chattel Paper and Instruments.**

A purchaser of chattel paper or an instrument who gives new value and takes possession of it in the ordinary course of his business has priority over a security interest in the chattel paper or instrument

(a) which is perfected under Section 9—304 (permissive filing and temporary perfection) or under Section 9—306 (perfection as to proceeds) if he acts without knowledge that the specific paper or instrument is subject to a security interest; or

(b) which is claimed merely as proceeds of inventory subject to a security interest (Section 9—306) even though he knows that the specific paper or instrument is subject to the security interest.

Amended in 1972.

§ 9—309. **Protection of Purchasers of Instruments, Documents and Securities**

Nothing in this Article limits the rights of a holder in due course of a negotiable instrument (Section 3—302) or a holder to whom a negotiable document of title has been duly negotiated (Section 7—501) or a bona fide purchaser of a security (Section 8—302) and the holders or purchasers take priority over an earlier security interest even though perfected. Filing under this Article does not constitute notice of the security interest to such holders or purchasers.

Amended in 1977.

§ 9—310. **Priority of Certain Liens Arising by Operation of Law.**

When a person in the ordinary course of his business furnishes services or materials with respect to goods subject to a security interest, a lien upon goods in the possession of such person given by statute or rule of law for such materials or services takes priority over a perfected security interest unless the lien is statutory and the statute expressly provides otherwise.

§ 9—311. Alienability of Debtor's Rights: Judicial Process.

The debtor's rights in collateral may be voluntarily or involuntarily transferred (by way of sale, creation of a security interest, attachment, levy, garnishment or other judicial process) notwithstanding a provision in the security agreement prohibiting any transfer or making the transfer constitute a default.

§ 9—312. Priorities Among Conflicting Security Interests in the Same Collateral

(1) The rules of priority stated in other sections of this Part and in the following sections shall govern when applicable: Section 4—208 with respect to the security interests of collecting banks in items being collected, accompanying documents and proceeds; Section 9—103 on security interests related to other jurisdictions; Section 9—114 on consignments.

(2) A perfected security interest in crops for new value given to enable the debtor to produce the crops during the production season and given not more than three months before the crops become growing crops by planting or otherwise takes priority over an earlier perfected security interest to the extent that such earlier interest secures obligations due more than six months before the crops become growing crops by planting or otherwise, even though the person giving new value had knowledge of the earlier security interest.

(3) A perfected purchase money security interest in inventory has priority over a conflicting security interest in the same inventory and also has priority in identifiable cash proceeds received on or before the delivery of the inventory to a buyer if

(a) the purchase money security interest is perfected at the time the debtor receives possession of the inventory; and

(b) the purchase money secured party gives notification in writing to the holder of the conflicting security interest if the holder had filed a financing statement covering the same types of inventory (i) before the date of the filing made by the purchase money secured party, or (ii) before the beginning of the 21 day period where the purchase money security interest is temporarily perfected without filing or possession (subsection (5) of Section 9—304); and

(c) the holder of the conflicting security interest receives the notification within five years before the debtor receives possession of the inventory; and

(d) the notification states that the person giving the notice has or expects to acquire a purchase money security interest in inventory of the debtor, describing such inventory by item or type.

(4) A purchase money security interest in collateral other than inventory has priority over a conflicting security interest in the same collateral or its proceeds if the purchase money security interest is perfected at the time the debtor receives possession of the collateral or within ten days thereafter.

(5) In all cases not governed by other rules stated in this section (including cases of purchase money security interests which do not qualify for the special priorities set forth in subsections (3) and (4) of this section), priority between conflicting security interests in the same collateral shall be determined according to the following rules:

(a) Conflicting security interests rank according to priority in time of filing or perfection. Priority dates from the time a filing is first made covering the collateral or the time the security interest is first perfected, whichever is earlier, provided that there is no period thereafter when there is neither filing nor perfection.

(b) So long as conflicting security interests are unperfected, the first to attach has priority.

(6) For the purposes of subsection (5) a date of filing or perfection as to collateral is also a date of filing or perfection as to proceeds.

(7) If future advances are made while a security interest is perfected by filing, the taking of possession, or under Section 8—321 on securities, the security interest has the same priority for the purposes of subsection (5) with respect to the future advances as it does with respect to the first advance. If a commitment is made before or while the security interest is so perfected, the security interest has the same priority with respect to advances made pursuant thereto. In other cases a perfected security interest has priority from the date the advance is made.

Amended in 1972 and 1977.

§ 9—313. Priority of Security Interests in Fixtures.

(1) In this section and in the provisions of Part 4 of this Article referring to fixture filing, unless the context otherwise requires

(a) goods are "fixtures" when they become so related to particular real estate that an interest in them arises under real estate law

(b) a "fixture filing" is the filing in the office where a mortgage on the real estate would be filed or recorded of a financing statement covering goods which are or are to become fixtures and conforming to the requirements of subsection (5) of Section 9—402

(c) a mortgage is a "construction mortgage" to the extent that it secures an obligation incurred for the construction of an improvement on land including the acquisition cost of the land, if the recorded writing so indicates.

(2) A security interest under this Article may be created in goods which are fixtures or may continue in goods which become fixtures, but no security interest exists under this Article in ordinary building materials incorporated into an improvement on land.

(3) This Article does not prevent creation of an encumbrance upon fixtures pursuant to real estate law.

(4) A perfected security interest in fixtures has priority over the conflicting interest of an encumbrancer or owner of the real estate where

(a) the security interest is a purchase money security interest, the interest of the encumbrancer or owner arises before the goods become fixtures, the security interest is perfected by a fixture filing before the goods become fixtures or within ten days thereafter, and the debtor has an interest of record in the real estate or is in possession of the real estate; or

(b) the security interest is perfected by a fixture filing before the interest of the encumbrancer or owner is of record, the security interest has priority over any conflicting interest of a predecessor in title of the encumbrancer or owner, and the debtor has an interest of record in the real estate or is in possession of the real estate; or

(c) the fixtures are readily removable factory or office machines or readily removable replacements of domestic appliances which are consumer goods, and before the goods become fixtures the security interest is perfected by any method permitted by this Article; or

(d) the conflicting interest is a lien on the real estate obtained by legal or equitable proceedings after the security interest was perfected by any method permitted by this Article.

(5) A security interest in fixtures, whether or not perfected, has priority over the conflicting interest of an encumbrancer or owner of the real estate where

(a) the encumbrancer or owner has consented in writing to the security interest or has disclaimed an interest in the goods as fixtures; or

(b) the debtor has a right to remove the goods as against the encumbrancer or owner. If the debtor's right terminates, the priority of the security interest continues for a reasonable time.

(6) Notwithstanding paragraph (a) of subsection (4) but otherwise subject to subsections (4) and (5), a security interest in fixtures is subordinate to a construction mortgage recorded before the goods become fixtures if the goods become fixtures before the completion of the construction. To the extent that it is given to refinance a construction mortgage, a mortgage has this priority to the same extent as the construction mortgage.

(7) In cases not within the preceding subsections, a security interest in fixtures is subordinate to the conflicting interest of an encumbrancer or owner of the related real estate who is not the debtor.

(8) When the secured party has priority over all owners and encumbrancers of the real estate, he may, on default, subject to the provisions of Part 5, remove his collateral from the real estate but he must reimburse any encumbrancer or owner of the real estate who is not the debtor and who has not otherwise agreed for the cost of repair of any physical injury, but not for any diminution in value of the real estate caused by the absence of the goods removed or by any necessity of replacing them. A person entitled to reimbursement may refuse permission to remove until the secured party gives adequate security for the performance of this obligation. Amended in 1972.

§ 9—314. **Accessions.**

(1) A security interest in goods which attaches before they are installed in or affixed to other goods takes priority as to the goods installed or affixed (called in this section "accessions") over the claims of all persons to the whole except as stated in subsection (3) and subject to Section 9—315(1).

(2) A security interest which attaches to goods after they become part of a whole is valid against all persons subsequently acquiring interests in the whole except as stated in subsection (3) but is invalid against any person with an interest in the whole at the time the security interest attaches to the goods who has not in writing consented to the security interest or disclaimed an interest in the goods as part of the whole.

(3) The security interests described in subsections (1) and (2) do not take priority over

(a) a subsequent purchaser for value of any interest in the whole; or

(b) a creditor with a lien on the whole subsequently obtained by judicial proceedings; or

(c) a creditor with a prior perfected security interest in the whole to the extent that he makes subsequent advances

if the subsequent purchase is made, the lien by judicial proceedings obtained or the subsequent advance under the prior perfected security interest is made or contracted for without knowledge of the security interest and before it is perfected. A purchaser of the whole at a foreclosure sale other than the holder of a perfected security interest purchasing at his own foreclosure sale is a subsequent purchaser within this section.

(4) When under subsections (1) or (2) and (3) a secured party has an interest in accessions which has priority over the claims of all persons who have interests in the whole, he may on default subject to the provisions of Part 5 remove his collateral from the whole but he must reimburse any encumbrancer or owner of the whole who is not the debtor and who has not otherwise agreed for the cost of repair of any physical injury but not for any diminution in value of the whole caused by the absence of the goods removed or by any necessity for replacing them. A person entitled to reimbursement may refuse permission to remove until the secured party gives adequate security for the performance of this obligation.

§ 9—315. Priority When Goods Are Commingled or Processed.

(1) If a security interest in goods was perfected and subsequently the goods or a part thereof have become part of a product or mass, the security interest continues in the product or mass if

(a) the goods are so manufactured, processed, assembled or commingled that their identity is lost in the product or mass; or

(b) a financing statement covering the original goods also covers the product into which the goods have been manufactured, processed or assembled.

In a case to which paragraph (b) applies, no separate security interest in that part of the original goods which has been manufactured, processed or assembled into the product may be claimed under Section 9—314.

(2) When under subsection (1) more than one security interest attaches to the product or mass, they rank equally according to the ratio that the cost of the goods to which each interest originally attached bears to the cost of the total product or mass.

§ 9—316. Priority Subject to Subordination.

Nothing in this Article prevents subordination by agreement by any person entitled to priority.

§ 9—317. Secured Party Not Obligated on Contract of Debtor.

The mere existence of a security interest or authority given to the debtor to dispose of or use collateral does not impose contract or tort liability upon the secured party for the debtor's acts or omissions.

§ 9—318. Defenses Against Assignee; Modification of Contract After Notification of Assignment; Term Prohibiting Assignment Ineffective; Identification and Proof of Assignment.

(1) Unless an account debtor has made an enforceable agreement not to assert defenses or claims arising out of a sale as provided in Section 9—206 the rights of an assignee are subject to

(a) all the terms of the contract between the account debtor and assignor and any defense or claim arising therefrom; and

(b) any other defense or claim of the account debtor against the assignor which accrues before the account debtor receives notification of the assignment.

(2) So far as the right to payment or a part thereof under an assigned contract has not been fully earned by performance, and notwithstanding notification of the assignment, any modification of or substitution for the contract made in good faith and in accordance with reasonable commercial standards is effective against an assignee unless the account debtor has otherwise agreed but the assignee acquires corresponding rights under the modified or substituted contract. The assignment may provide that such modification or substitution is a breach by the assignor.

(3) The account debtor is authorized to pay the assignor until the account debtor receives notification that the amount due or to become due has been assigned and that payment is to be made to the assignee. A notification which does not reasonably identify the rights assigned is ineffective. If requested by the account debtor, the assignee must seasonably furnish reasonable proof that the assignment has been made and unless he does so the account debtor may pay the assignor.

(4) A term in any contract between an account debtor and an assignor is ineffective if it prohibits assignment of an account or prohibits creation of a security interest in a general intangible for money due or to become due or requires the account debtor's consent to such assignment or security interest.

Amended in 1972.

Part 4 Filing

§ 9—401. Place of Filing; Erroneous Filing; Removal of Collateral.

First Alternative Subsection (1)

(1) The proper place to file in order to perfect a security interest is as follows:

(a) when the collateral is timber to be cut or is minerals or the like (including oil and gas) or accounts subject to subsection (5) of Section 9—103, or when the financing statement is filed as a fixture filing (Section 9—313) and the collateral is goods which are or are to become fixtures, then in the office where a mortgage on the real estate would be filed or recorded;

(b) in all other cases, in the office of the [Secretary of State].

Second Alternative Subsection (1)

(1) The proper place to file in order to perfect a security interest is as follows:

(a) when the collateral is equipment used in farming operations, or farm products, or accounts or general intangibles arising from or relating to the sale of farm products by a farmer, or consumer goods, then in the office of the . . . . in the county of the debtor's residence or if the debtor is not a resident of this state then in the office of the . . . . in the county where the goods are kept, and in addition when the collateral is crops growing or to be grown in the office of the . . . . in the county where the land is located;

(b) when the collateral is timber to be cut or is minerals or the like (including oil and gas) or accounts subject to subsection (5) of Section 9—103, or when the financing statement is filed as a fixture filing (Section 9—313) and the collateral is goods which are or are to become fixtures, then in the office where a mortgage on the real estate would be filed or recorded;

(c) in all other cases, in the office of the [Secretary of State].

Third Alternative Subsection (1)

(1) The proper place to file in order to perfect a security interest is as follows:

(a) when the collateral is equipment used in farming operations, or farm products, or accounts or general intangibles arising from or relating to the sale of farm products by a farmer, or consumer goods, then in the office of the . . . . in the county of the debtor's residence or if the debtor is not a resident of this state then in the office of the . . . . in the county where the goods are kept, and in addition when the collateral is crops growing or to be grown in the office of the . . . . in the county where the land is located;

(b) when the collateral is timber to be cut or is minerals or the like (including oil and gas) or accounts subject to subsection (5) of Section 9—103, or when the financing statement is filed as a fixture filing (Section 9—313) and the collateral is goods which are or are to become fixtures, then in the office where a mortgage on the real estate would be filed or recorded;

(c) in all other cases, in the office of the [Secretary of State] and in addition, if the debtor has a place of business in only one county of this state, also in the office of . . . . of such county, or, if the debtor

has no place of business in this state, but resides in the state, also in the office of . . . . of the county in which he resides.

Note: *One of the three alternatives should be selected as subsection (1).*

(2) A filing which is made in good faith in an improper place or not in all of the places required by this section is nevertheless effective with regard to any collateral as to which the filing complied with the requirements of this Article and is also effective with regard to collateral covered by the financing statement against any person who has knowledge of the contents of such financing statement.

(3) A filing which is made in the proper place in this state continues effective even though the debtor's residence or place of business or the location of the collateral or its use, whichever controlled the original filing, is thereafter changed.

Alternative Subsection (3)

[(3) A filing which is made in the proper county continues effective for four months after a change to another county of the debtor's residence or place of business or the location of the collateral, whichever controlled the original filing. It becomes ineffective thereafter unless a copy of the financing statement signed by the secured party is filed in the new county within said period. The security interest may also be perfected in the new county after the expiration of the four-month period; in such case perfection dates from the time of perfection in the new county. A change in the use of the collateral does not impair the effectiveness of the original filing.]

(4) The rules stated in Section 9—103 determine whether filing is necessary in this state.

(5) Notwithstanding the preceding subsections, and subject to subsection (3) of Section 9—302, the proper place to file in order to perfect a security interest in collateral, including fixtures, of a transmitting utility is the office of the [Secretary of State]. This filing constitutes a fixture filing (Section 9—313) as to the collateral described therein which is or is to become fixtures.

(6) For the purposes of this section, the residence of an organization is its place of business if it has one or its chief executive office if it has more than one place of business.

Amended in 1962 and 1972.

Note: *Subsection (6) should be used only if the state chooses the Second or Third Alternative Subsection (1).*

§ 9—402. **Formal Requisites of Financing Statement; Amendments; Mortgage as Financing Statement.**

(1) A financing statement is sufficient if it gives the names of the debtor and the secured party, is signed by the debtor, gives an address of the secured party from which

information concerning the security interest may be obtained, gives a mailing address of the debtor and contains a statement indicating the types, or describing the items, of collateral. A financing statement may be filed before a security agreement is made or a security interest otherwise attaches. When the financing statement covers crops growing or to be grown, the statement must also contain a description of the real estate concerned. When the financing statement covers timber to be cut or covers minerals or the like (including oil and gas) or accounts subject to subsection (5) of Section 9—103, or when the financing statement is filed as a fixture filing (Section 9—313) and the collateral is goods which are or are to become fixtures, the statement must also comply with subsection (5). A copy of the security agreement is sufficient as a financing statement if it contains the above information and is signed by the debtor. A carbon, photographic or other reproduction of a security agreement or a financing statement is sufficient as a financing statement if the security agreement so provides or if the original has been filed in this state.

(2) A financing statement which otherwise complies with subsection (1) is sufficient when it is signed by the secured party instead of the debtor if it is filed to perfect a security interest in

(a) collateral already subject to a security interest in another jurisdiction when it is brought into this state, or when the debtor's location is changed to this state. Such a financing statement must state that the collateral was brought into this state or that the debtor's location was changed to this state under such circumstances; or

(b) proceeds under Section 9—306 if the security interest in the original collateral was perfected. Such a financing statement must describe the original collateral; or

(c) collateral as to which the filing has lapsed; or

(d) collateral acquired after a change of name, identity or corporate structure of the debtor (subsection (7)).

(3) A form substantially as follows is sufficient to comply with subsection (1):

Name of debtor (or assignor) ....
Address ....
Name of secured party (or assignee) ....
Address ....
1. This financing statement covers the following types (or items) of property:
    (Describe) ....
2. (If collateral is crops) The above described crops are growing or are to be grown on:
    (Describe Real Estate) ....

3. (If applicable) The above goods are to become fixtures on *
*Where appropriate substitute either "The above timber is standing on . . . ." or "The above minerals or the like (including oil and gas) or accounts will be financed at the wellhead or minehead of the well or mine located on . . . ."
    (Describe Real Estate) ....
and this financing statement is to be filed [for record] in the real estate records. (If the debtor does not have an interest of record) The name of a record owner is ....
4. (If products of collateral are claimed) Products of the collateral are also covered.

(use ....
whichever   Signature of Debtor (or Assignor)

is ....
applicable)   Signature of Secured Party
                   (or Assignee)

(4) A financing statement may be amended by filing a writing signed by both the debtor and the secured party. An amendment does not extend the period of effectiveness of a financing statement. If any amendment adds collateral, it is effective as to the added collateral only from the filing of the amendment. In this Article, unless the context otherwise requires, the term "financing statement" means the original financing statement and any amendments.

(5) A financing statement covering timber to be cut or covering minerals or the like (including oil and gas) or accounts subject to subsection (5) of Section 9—103, or a financing statement filed as a future filing (Section 9—313) where the debtor is not a transmitting utility, must show that it covers this type of collateral, must recite that it is to be filed [for record] in the real estate records, and the financing statement must contain a description of the real estate [sufficient if it were contained in a mortgage of the real estate to give constructive notice of the mortgage under the law of this state]. If the debtor does not have an interest of record in the real estate, the financing statement must show the name of a record owner.

(6) A mortgage is effective as a financing statement filed as a fixture filing from the date of its recording if

(a) the goods are described in the mortgage by item or type; and

(b) the goods are or are to become fixtures related to the real estate described in the mortgage; and

(c) the mortgage complies with the requirements for a financing statement in this section other than a recital that it is to be filed in the real estate records; and

(d) the mortgage is duly recorded.

No fee with reference to the financing statement is required other than the regular recording and satisfaction fees with respect to the mortgage.

(7) A financing statement sufficiently shows the name of the debtor if it gives the individual, partnership or corporate name of the debtor, whether or not it adds other trade names or names of partners. Where the debtor so changes his name or in the case of an organization its name, identity or corporate structure that a filed financing statement becomes seriously misleading, the filing is not effective to perfect a security interest in collateral acquired by the debtor more than four months after the change, unless a new appropriate financing statement is filed before the expiration of that time. A filed financing statement remains effective with respect to collateral transferred by the debtor even though the secured party knows of or consents to the transfer.

(8) A financing statement substantially complying with the requirements of this section is effective even though it contains minor errors which are not seriously misleading. Amended in 1972.

Note: *Language in brackets is optional.*

Note: *Where the state has any special recording system for real estate other than the usual grantor-grantee index (as, for instance, a tract system or a title registration or Torrens system) local adaptations of subsection (5) and Section 9—403(7) may be necessary. See Mass.Gen.Laws Chapter 106, Section 9—409.*

§ 9—403. **What Constitutes Filing; Duration of Filing; Effect of Lapsed Filing; Duties of Filing Officer.**

(1) Presentation for filing of a financing statement and tender of the filing fee or acceptance of the statement by the filing officer constitutes filing under this Article.

(2) Except as provided in subsection (6) a filed financing statement is effective for a period of five years from the date of filing. The effectiveness of a filed financing statement lapses on the expiration of the five year period unless a continuation statement is filed prior to the lapse. If a security interest perfected by filing exists at the time insolvency proceedings are commenced by or against the debtor, the security interest remains perfected until termination of the insolvency proceedings and thereafter for a period of sixty days or until expiration of the five year period, whichever occurs later. Upon lapse the security interest becomes unperfected, unless it is perfected without filing. If the security interest becomes unperfected upon lapse, it is deemed to have been unperfected as against a person who became a purchaser or lien creditor before lapse.

(3) A continuation statement may be filed by the secured party within six months prior to the expiration of the five year period specified in subsection (2). Any such continuation statement must be signed by the secured party, identify the original statement by file number and state that the original statement is still effective. A continuation statement signed by a person other than the secured party of record must be accompanied by a separate written statement of assignment signed by the secured party of record and complying with subsection (2) of Section 9—405, including payment of the required fee. Upon timely filing of the continuation statement, the effectiveness of the original statement is continued for five years after the last date to which the filing was effective whereupon it lapses in the same manner as provided in subsection (2) unless another continuation statement is filed prior to such lapse. Succeeding continuation statements may be filed in the same manner to continue the effectiveness of the original statement. Unless a statute on disposition of public records provides otherwise, the filing officer may remove a lapsed statement from the files and destroy it immediately if he has retained a microfilm or other photographic record, or in other cases after one year after the lapse. The filing officer shall so arrange matters by physical annexation of financing statements to continuation statements or other related filings, or by other means, that if he physically destroys the financing statements of a period more than five years past, those which have been continued by a continuation statement or which are still effective under subsection (6) shall be retained.

(4) Except as provided in subsection (7) a filing officer shall mark each statement with a file number and with the date and hour of filing and shall hold the statement or a microfilm or other photographic copy thereof for public inspection. In addition the filing officer shall index the statement according to the name of the debtor and shall note in the index the file number and the address of the debtor given in the statement.

(5) The uniform fee for filing and indexing and for stamping a copy furnished by the secured party to show the date and place of filing for an original financing statement or for a continuation statement shall be $. . . . . . . if the statement is in the standard form prescribed by the [Secretary of State] and otherwise shall be $. . . . . . ., plus in each case, if the financing statement is subject to subsection (5) of Section 9—402, $. . . . . . . The uniform fee for each name more than one required to be indexed shall be $. . . . . . . The secured party may at his option show a trade name for any person and an extra uniform indexing fee of $. . . . . . . shall be paid with respect thereto.

(6) If the debtor is a transmitting utility (subsection (5) of Section 9—401) and a filed financing statement so states, it is effective until a termination statement is filed. A real estate mortgage which is effective as a fixture filing

under subsection (6) of Section 9—402 remains effective as a fixture filing until the mortgage is released or satisfied of record or its effectiveness otherwise terminates as to the real estate.

(7) When a financing statement covers timber to be cut or covers minerals or the like (including oil and gas) or accounts subject to subsection (5) of Section 9—103, or is filed as a fixture filing, [it shall be filed for record and] the filing officer shall index it under the names of the debtor and any owner of record shown on the financing statement in the same fashion as if they were the mortgagors in a mortgage of the real estate described, and, to the extent that the law of this state provides for indexing of mortgages under the name of the mortgagee, under the name of the secured party as if he were the mortgagee thereunder, or where indexing is by description in the same fashion as if the financing statement were a mortgage of the real estate described. Amended in 1972.

Note: *In states in which writings will not appear in the real estate records and indices unless actually recorded the bracketed language in subsection (7) should be used.*

§ 9—404. **Termination Statement.**

(1) If a financing statement covering consumer goods is filed on or after . . . ., then within one month or within ten days following written demand by the debtor after there is no outstanding secured obligation and no commitment to make advances, incur obligations or otherwise give value, the secured party must file with each filing officer with whom the financing statement was filed, a termination statement to the effect that he no longer claims a security interest under the financing statement, which shall be identified by file number. In other cases whenever there is no outstanding secured obligation and no commitment to make advances, incur obligations or otherwise give value, the secured party must on written demand by the debtor send the debtor, for each filing officer with whom the financing statement was filed, a termination statement to the effect that he no longer claims a security interest under the financing statement, which shall be identified by file number. A termination statement signed by a person other than the secured party of record must be accompanied by a separate written statement of assignment signed by the secured party of record complying with subsection (2) of Section 9—405, including payment of the required fee. If the affected secured party fails to file such a termination statement as required by this subsection, or to send such a termination statement within ten days after proper demand therefor, he shall be liable to the debtor for one hundred dollars, and in addition for any loss caused to the debtor by such failure.

(2) On presentation to the filing officer of such a termination statement he must note it in the index. If he has received the termination statement in duplicate, he shall return one copy of the termination statement to the secured party stamped to show the time of receipt thereof. If the filing officer has a microfilm or other photographic record of the financing statement, and of any related continuation statement, statement of assignment and statement of release, he may remove the originals from the files at any time after receipt of the termination statement, or if he has no such record, he may remove them from the files at any time after one year after receipt of the termination statement.

(3) If the termination statement is in the standard form prescribed by the [Secretary of State], the uniform fee for filing and indexing the termination statement shall be $. . . . ., and otherwise shall be $. . . . ., plus in each case an additional fee of $. . . . . . . for each name more than one against which the termination statement is required to be indexed. Amended in 1972.

Note: *The date to be inserted should be the effective date of the revised Article 9.*

§ 9—405. **Assignment of Security Interest; Duties of Filing Officer; Fees.**

(1) A financing statement may disclose an assignment of a security interest in the collateral described in the financing statement by indication in the financing statement of the name and address of the assignee or by an assignment itself or a copy thereof on the face or back of the statement. On presentation to the filing officer of such a financing statement the filing officer shall mark the same as provided in Section 9—403(4). The uniform fee for filing, indexing and furnishing filing data for a financing statement so indicating an assignment shall be $. . . . . . . if the statement is in the standard form prescribed by the [Secretary of State] and otherwise shall be $. . . . ., plus in each case an additional fee of $. . . . . . . for each name more than one against which the financing statement is required to be indexed.

(2) A secured party may assign of record all or part of his rights under a financing statement by the filing in the place where the original financing statement was filed of a separate written statement of assignment signed by the secured party of record and setting forth the name of the secured party of record and the debtor, the file number and the date of filing of the financing statement and the name and address of the assignee and containing a description of the collateral assigned. A copy of the assignment is sufficient as a separate statement if it complies with the preceding sentence. On presentation to the filing officer of such a separate statement, the filing officer shall mark such separate statement with the date

and hour of the filing. He shall note the assignment on the index of the financing statement, or in the case of a fixture filing, or a filing covering timber to be cut, or covering minerals or the like (including oil and gas) or accounts subject to subsection (5) of Section 9—103, he shall index the assignment under the name of the assignor as grantor and, to the extent that the law of this state provides for indexing the assignment of a mortgage under the name of the assignee, he shall index the assignment of the financing statement under the name of the assignee. The uniform fee for filing, indexing and furnishing filing data about such a separate statement of assignment shall be $...... if the statement is in the standard form prescribed by the [Secretary of State] and otherwise shall be $......, plus in each case an additional fee of $...... for each name more than one against which the statement of assignment is required to be indexed. Notwithstanding the provisions of this subsection, an assignment of record of a security interest in a fixture contained in a mortgage effective as a fixture filing (subsection (6) of Section 9—402) may be made only by an assignment of the mortgage in the manner provided by the law of this state other than this Act.

(3) After the disclosure or filing of an assignment under this section, the assignee is the secured party of record. Amended in 1972.

§ 9—406. **Release of Collateral; Duties of Filing Officer; Fees.**

A secured party of record may by his signed statement release all or a part of any collateral described in a filed financing statement. The statement of release is sufficient if it contains a description of the collateral being released, the name and address of the debtor, the name and address of the secured party, and the file number of the financing statement. A statement of release signed by a person other than the secured party of record must be accompanied by a separate written statement of assignment signed by the secured party of record and complying with subsection (2) of Section 9—405, including payment of the required fee. Upon presentation of such a statement of release to the filing officer he shall mark the statement with the hour and date of filing and shall note the same upon the margin of the index of the filing of the financing statement. The uniform fee for filing and noting such a statement of release shall be $...... if the statement is in the standard form prescribed by the [Secretary of State] and otherwise shall be $......, plus in each case an additional fee of $...... for each name more than one against which the statement of release is required to be indexed. Amended in 1972.

[§ 9—407. **Information From Filing Officer].**

[(1) If the person filing any financing statement, termination statement, statement of assignment, or statement of release, furnishes the filing officer a copy thereof, the filing officer shall upon request note upon the copy the file number and date and hour of the filing of the original and deliver or send the copy to such person.]

[(2) Upon request of any person, the filing officer shall issue his certificate showing whether there is on file on the date and hour stated therein, any presently effective financing statement naming a particular debtor and any statement of assignment thereof and if there is, giving the date and hour of filing of each such statement and the names and addresses of each secured party therein. The uniform fee for such a certificate shall be $...... if the request for the certificate is in the standard form prescribed by the [Secretary of State] and otherwise shall be $....... Upon request the filing officer shall furnish a copy of any filed financing statement or statement of assignment for a uniform fee of $...... per page.] Amended in 1972.

Note: *This section is proposed as an optional provision to require filing officers to furnish certificates. Local law and practices should be consulted with regard to the advisability of adoption.*

§ 9—408. **Financing Statements Covering Consigned or Leased Goods.**

A consignor or lessor of goods may file a financing statement using the terms "consignor," "consignee," "lessor," "lessee" or the like instead of the terms specified in Section 9—402. The provisions of this Part shall apply as appropriate to such a financing statement but its filing shall not of itself be a factor in determining whether or not the consignment or lease is intended as security (Section 1—201(37)). However, if it is determined for other reasons that the consignment or lease is so intended, a security interest of the consignor or lessor which attaches to the consigned or leased goods is perfected by such filing. Added in 1972.

Part 5 **Default**

§ 9—501. **Default; Procedure When Security Agreement Covers Both Real and Personal Property.**

(1) When a debtor is in default under a security agreement, a secured party has the rights and remedies provided in this Part and except as limited by subsection (3) those provided in the security agreement. He may reduce his claim to judgment, foreclose or otherwise enforce the security interest by any available judicial procedure. If the collateral is documents the secured party may proceed either as to the documents or as to the goods covered thereby. A secured party in possession has the rights, remedies and duties provided in Section 9—207. The

rights and remedies referred to in this subsection are cumulative.

(2) After default, the debtor has the rights and remedies provided in this Part, those provided in the security agreement and those provided in Section 9—207.

(3) To the extent that they give rights to the debtor and impose duties on the secured party, the rules stated in the subsections referred to below may not be waived or varied except as provided with respect to compulsory disposition of collateral (subsection (3) of Section 9—504 and Section 9—505) and with respect to redemption of collateral (Section 9—506) but the parties may by agreement determine the standards by which the fulfillment of these rights and duties is to be measured if such standards are not manifestly unreasonable:

(a) subsection (2) of Section 9—502 and subsection (2) of Section 9—504 insofar as they require accounting for surplus proceeds of collateral;

(b) subsection (3) of Section 9—504 and subsection (1) of Section 9—505 which deal with disposition of collateral;

(c) subsection (2) of Section 9—505 which deals with acceptance of collateral as discharge of obligation;

(d) Section 9—506 which deals with redemption of collateral; and

(e) subsection (1) of Section 9—507 which deals with the secured party's liability for failure to comply with this Part.

(4) If the security agreement covers both real and personal property, the secured party may proceed under this Part as to the personal property or he may proceed as to both the real and the personal property in accordance with his rights and remedies in respect of the real property in which case the provisions of this Part do not apply.

(5) When a secured party has reduced his claim to judgment the lien of any levy which may be made upon his collateral by virture of any execution based upon the judgment shall relate back to the date of the perfection of the security interest in such collateral. A judicial sale, pursuant to such execution, is a foreclosure of the security interest by judicial procedure within the meaning of this section, and the secured party may purchase at the sale and thereafter hold the collateral free of any other requirements of this Article. Amended in 1972.

§ 9—502. Collection Rights of Secured Party.

(1) When so agreed and in any event on default the secured party is entitled to notify an account debtor or the obligor on an instrument to make payment to him whether or not the assignor was theretofore making collections on the collateral, and also to take control of any proceeds to which he is entitled under Section 9—306.

(2) A secured party who by agreement is entitled to charge back uncollected collateral or otherwise to full or limited recourse against the debtor and who undertakes to collect from the account debtors or obligors must proceed in a commercially reasonable manner and may deduct his reasonable expenses of realization from the collections. If the security agreement secures an indebtedness, the secured party must account to the debtor for any surplus, and unless otherwise agreed, the debtor is liable for any deficiency. But, if the underlying transaction was a sale of accounts or chattel paper, the debtor is entitled to any surplus or is liable for any deficiency only if the security agreement so provides. Amended in 1972.

§ 9—503. Secured Party's Right to Take Possession After Default.

Unless otherwise agreed a secured party has on default the right to take possession of the collateral. In taking possession a secured party may proceed without judicial process if this can be done without breach of the peace or may proceed by action. If the security agreement so provides the secured party may require the debtor to assemble the collateral and make it available to the secured party at a place to be designated by the secured party which is reasonably convenient to both parties. Without removal a secured party may render equipment unusable, and may dispose of collateral on the debtor's premises under Section 9—504.

§ 9—504. Secured Party's Right to Dispose of Collateral After Default; Effect of Disposition.

(1) A secured party after default may sell, lease or otherwise dispose of any or all of the collateral in its then condition or following any commercially reasonable preparation or processing. Any sale of goods is subject to the Article on Sales (Article 2). The proceeds of disposition shall be applied in the order following to

(a) the reasonable expenses of retaking, holding, preparing for sale or lease, selling, leasing and the like and, to the extent provided for in the agreement and not prohibited by law, the reasonable attorneys' fees and legal expenses incurred by the secured party;

(b) the satisfaction of indebtedness secured by the security interest under which the disposition is made;

(c) the satisfaction of indebtedness secured by any subordinate security interest in the collateral if written notification of demand therefor is received before distribution of the proceeds is completed. If requested by the secured party, the holder of a subordinate security interest must seasonably furnish reasonable proof of his interest, and unless he does so, the secured party need not comply with his demand.

(2) If the security interest secures an indebtedness, the secured party must account to the debtor for any surplus, and, unless otherwise agreed, the debtor is liable for any deficiency. But if the underlying transaction was a sale of accounts or chattel paper, the debtor is entitled to any surplus or is liable for any deficiency only if the security agreement so provides.

(3) Disposition of the collateral may be by public or private proceedings and may be made by way of one or more contracts. Sale or other disposition may be as a unit or in parcels and at any time and place and on any terms but every aspect of the disposition including the method, manner, time, place and terms must be commercially reasonable. Unless collateral is perishable or threatens to decline speedily in value or is of a type customarily sold on a recognized market, reasonable notification of the time and place of any public sale or reasonable notification of the time after which any private sale or other intended disposition is to be made shall be sent by the secured party to the debtor, if he has not signed after default a statement renouncing or modifying his right to notification of sale. In the case of consumer goods no other notification need be sent. In other cases notification shall be sent to any other secured party from whom the secured party has received (before sending his notification to the debtor or before the debtor's renunciation of his rights) written notice of a claim of an interest in the collateral. The secured party may buy at any public sale and if the collateral is of a type customarily sold in a recognized market or is of a type which is the subject of widely distributed standard price quotations he may buy at private sale.

(4) When collateral is disposed of by a secured party after default, the disposition transfers to a purchaser for value all of the debtor's rights therein, discharges the security interest under which it is made and any security interest or lien subordinate thereto. The purchaser takes free of all such rights and interests even though the secured party fails to comply with the requirements of this Part or of any judicial proceedings

   (a) in the case of a public sale, if the purchaser has no knowledge of any defects in the sale and if he does not buy in collusion with the secured party, other bidders or the person conducting the sale; or

   (b) in any other case, if the purchaser acts in good faith.

(5) A person who is liable to a secured party under a guaranty, indorsement, repurchase agreement or the like

and who receives a transfer of collateral from the secured party or is subrogated to his rights has thereafter the rights and duties of the secured party. Such a transfer of collateral is not a sale or disposition of the collateral under this Article. Amended in 1972.

§ 9—505. Compulsory Disposition of Collateral; Acceptance of the Collateral as Discharge of Obligation.

(1) If the debtor has paid sixty per cent of the cash price in the case of a purchase money security interest in consumer goods or sixty per cent of the loan in the case of another security interest in consumer goods, and has not signed after default a statement renouncing or modifying his rights under this Part a secured party who has taken possession of collateral must dispose of it under Section 9—504 and if he fails to do so within ninety days after he takes possession the debtor at his option may recover in conversion or under Section 9—507(1) on secured party's liability.

(2) In any other case involving consumer goods or any other collateral a secured party in possession may, after default, propose to retain the collateral in satisfaction of the obligation. Written notice of such proposal shall be sent to the debtor if he has not signed after default a statement renouncing or modifying his rights under this subsection. In the case of consumer goods no other notice need be given. In other cases notice shall be sent to any other secured party from whom the secured party has received (before sending his notice to the debtor or before the debtor's renunciation of his rights) written notice of a claim of an interest in the collateral. If the secured party receives objection in writing from a person entitled to receive notification within twenty-one days after the notice was sent, the secured party must dispose of the collateral under Section 9—504. In the absence of such written objection the secured party may retain the collateral in satisfaction of the debtor's obligation. Amended in 1972.

§ 9—506. Debtor's Right to Redeem Collateral.

At any time before the secured party has disposed of collateral or entered into a contract for its disposition under Section 9—504 or before the obligation has been discharged under Section 9—505(2) the debtor or any other secured party may unless otherwise agreed in writing after default redeem the collateral by tendering fulfillment of all obligations secured by the collateral as well as the expenses reasonably incurred by the secured party in retaking, holding and preparing the collateral for disposition, in arranging for the sale, and to the extent provided in the agreement and not prohibited by law, his reasonable attorneys' fees and legal expenses.

§ 9—507. Secured Party's Liability for Failure to Comply With This Part.

(1) If it is established that the secured party is not proceeding in accordance with the provisions of this Part disposition may be ordered or restrained on appropriate terms and conditions. If the disposition has occurred the debtor or any person entitled to notification or whose security interest has been made known to the secured party prior to the disposition has a right to recover from the secured party any loss caused by a failure to comply with the provisions of this Part. If the collateral is consumer goods, the debtor has a right to recover in any event an amount not less than the credit service charge plus ten per cent of the principal amount of the debt or the time price differential plus 10 per cent of the cash price.

(2) The fact that a better price could have been obtained by a sale at a different time or in a different method from that selected by the secured party is not of itself sufficient to establish that the sale was not made in a commercially reasonable manner. If the secured party either sells the collateral in the usual manner in any recognized market therefor or if he sells at the price current in such market at the time of his sale or if he has otherwise sold in conformity with reasonable commercial practices among dealers in the type of property sold he has sold in a commercially reasonable manner. The principles stated in the two preceding sentences with respect to sales also apply as may be appropriate to other types of disposition. A disposition which has been approved in any judicial proceeding or by any bona fide creditors' committee or representative of creditors shall conclusively be deemed to be commercially reasonable, but this sentence does not indicate that any such approval must be obtained in any case nor does it indicate that any disposition not so approved is not commercially reasonable.

Article 10
EFFECTIVE DATE AND REPEALER

(Omitted)

Article 11
(REPORTERS' DRAFT) EFFECTIVE DATE AND TRANSITION PROVISIONS

(Omitted)

APPENDIX C

THE UNIFORM PARTNERSHIP ACT

(Adopted in 48 States, all except Georgia and Louisiana; the District of Columbia, the Virgin Islands, and Guam. The adoptions by Alabama and Nebraska do not follow the official text in every respect, but are substantially similar, with local variations.)

The Act consists of 7 Parts as follows:

I. Preliminary Provisions

II. Nature of Partnership

III. Relations of Partners to Persons Dealing with the Partnership

IV. Relations of Partners to One Another

V. Property Rights of a Partner

VI. Dissolution and Winding Up

VII. Miscellaneous Provisions

An Act to make uniform the Law of Partnerships

Be it enacted, etc.:

Part I Preliminary Provisions

This act may be cited as Uniform Partnership Act.

Sec. 2. **Definition of Terms**

In this act, "Court" includes every court and judge having jurisdiction in the case.

"Business" includes every trade, occupation, or profession.

"Person" includes individuals, partnerships, corporations, and other associations.

"Bankrupt" includes bankrupt under the Federal Bankruptcy Act or insolvent under any state insolvent act.

"Conveyance" includes every assignment, lease, mortgage, or encumbrance.

"Real property" includes land and any interest or estate in land.

Sec. 3. **Interpretation of Knowledge and Notice**

(1) A person has "knowledge" of a fact within the meaning of this act not only when he has actual knowledge thereof, but also when he has knowledge of such other facts as in the circumstances shows bad faith.

(2) A person has "notice" of a fact within the meaning of this act when the person who claims the benefit of the notice:

(a) States the fact to such person, or

(b) Delivers through the mail, or by other means of communication, a written statement of the fact to such person or to a proper person at his place of business or residence.

Sec. 4. **Rules of Construction**

(1) The rule that statutes in derogation of the common law are to be strictly construed shall have no application to this act.

(2) The law of estoppel shall apply under this act.

(3) The law of agency shall apply under this act.

(4) This act shall be so interpreted and construed as to effect its general purpose to make uniform the law of those states which enact it.

(5) This act shall not be construed so as to impair the obligations of any contract existing when the act goes into effect, nor to affect any action or proceedings begun or right accrued before this act takes effect.

Sec. 5. **Rules for Cases Not Provided for in this Act.**

In any case not provided for in this act the rules of law and equity, including the law merchant, shall govern.

Part II **Nature of Partnership**

Sec. 6. **Partnership Defined**

(1) A partnership is an association of two or more persons to carry on as co-owners a business for profit.

(2) But any association formed under any other statute of this state, or any statute adopted by authority, other than the authority of this state, is not a partnership under this act, unless such association would have been a partnership in this state prior to the adoption of this act; but this act shall apply to limited partnerships except in so far as the statutes relating to such partnerships are inconsistent herewith.

Sec. 7. **Rules for Determining the Existence of a Partnership**

In determining whether a partnership exists, these rules shall apply:

(1) Except as provided by Section 16 persons who are not partners as to each other are not partners as to third persons.

(2) Joint tenancy, tenancy in common, tenancy by the entireties, joint property, common property, or part ownership does not of itself establish a partnership, whether such co-owners do or do not share any profits made by the use of the property.

(3) The sharing of gross returns does not of itself establish a partnership, whether or not the persons sharing them have a joint or common right or interest in any property from which the returns are derived.

(4) The receipt by a person of a share of the profits of a business is prima facie evidence that he is a partner in the business, but no such inference shall be drawn if such profits were received in payment:

(a) As a debt by installments or otherwise,

(b) As wages of an employee or rent to a landlord,

(c) As an annuity to a widow or representative of a deceased partner,

(d) As interest on a loan, though the amount of payment vary with the profits of the business.

(e) As the consideration for the sale of a good-will of a business or other property by installments or otherwise.

Sec. 8. **Partnership Property**

(1) All property originally brought into the partnership stock or subsequently acquired by purchase or otherwise, on account of the partnership, is partnership property.

(2) Unless the contrary intention appears, property acquired with partnership funds is partnership property.

(3) Any estate in real property may be acquired in the partnership name. Title so acquired can be conveyed only in the partnership name.

(4) A conveyance to a partnership in the partnership name, though without words of inheritance, passes the entire estate of the grantor unless a contrary intent appears.

Part III **Relations of Partners to Persons Dealing with the Partnership**

Sec. 9. **Partner Agent of Partnership as to Partnership Business**

(1) Every partner is an agent of the partnership for the purpose of its business, and the act of every partner, including the execution in the partnership name of any instrument, for apparently carrying on in the usual way the business of the partnership of which he is a member binds the partnership, unless the partner so acting has in fact no authority to act for the partnership in the particular matter, and the person with whom he is dealing has knowledge of the fact that he has no such authority.

(2) An act of a partner which is not apparently for the carrying on of the business of the partnership in the usual way does not bind the partnership unless authorized by the other partners.

(3) Unless authorized by the other partners or unless they have abandoned the business, one or more but less than all the partners have no authority to:

(a) Assign the partnership property in trust for creditors or on the assignee's promise to pay the debts of the partnership,

(b) Dispose of the good-will of the business,

(c) Do any other act which would make it impossible to carry on the ordinary business of a partnership,

(d) Confess a judgment,

(e) Submit a partnership claim or liability to arbitration or reference.

(4) No act of a partner in contravention of a restriction on authority shall bind the partnership to persons having knowledge of the restriction.

Sec. 10. **Conveyance of Real Property of the Partnership**

(1) Where title to real property is in the partnership name, any partner may convey title to such property by a conveyance executed in the partnership name; but the partnership may recover such property unless the part-

ner's act binds the partnership under the provisions of paragraph (1) of section 9 or unless such property has been conveyed by the grantee or a person claiming through such grantee to a holder for value without knowledge that the partner, in making the conveyance, has exceeded his authority.

(2) Where title to real property is in the name of the partnership, a conveyance executed by a partner, in his own name, passes the equitable interest of the partnership, provided the act is one within the authority of the partner under the provisions of paragraph (1) of section 9.

(3) Where title to real property is in the name of one or more but not all the partners, and the record does not disclose the right of the partnership, the partners in whose name the title stands may convey title to such property, but the partnership may recover such property if the partners' act does not bind the partnership under the provisions of paragraph (1) of section 9, unless the purchaser or his assignee, is a holder for value, without knowledge.

(4) Where the title to real property is in the name of one or more or all the partners, or in a third person in trust for the partnership, a conveyance executed by a partner in the partnership name, or in his own name, passes the equitable interest of the partnership, provided the act is one within the authority of the partner under the provisions of paragraph (1) of section 9.

(5) Where the title to real property is in the names of all the partners a conveyance executed by all the partners passes all their rights in such property.

Sec. 11. **Partnership Bound by Admission of Partner**

An admission or representation made by any partner concerning partnership affairs within the scope of his authority as conferred by this act is evidence against the partnership.

Sec. 12. **Partnership Charged with Knowledge of or Notice to Partner**

Notice to any partner of any matter relating to partnership affairs, and the knowledge of the partner acting in the particular matter, acquired while a partner or then present to his mind, and the knowledge of any other partner who reasonably could and should have communicated it to the acting partner, operate as notice to or knowledge of the partnership, except in the case of a fraud on the partnership committed by or with the consent of that partner.

Sec. 13. **Partnership Bound by Partner's Wrongful Act**

Where, by any wrongful act or omission of any partner acting in the ordinary course of the business of the part-

nership or with the authority of his co-partners, loss or injury is caused to any person, not being a partner in the partnership, or any penalty is incurred, the partnership is liable therefor to the same extent as the partner so acting or omitting to act.

Sec. 14. **Partnership Bound by Partner's Breach of Trust**

The partnership is bound to make good the loss:

(a) Where one partner acting within the scope of his apparent authority receives money or property of a third person and misapplies it; and

(b) Where the partnership in the course of its business receives money or property of a third person and the money or property so received is misapplied by any partner while it is in the custody of the partnership.

Sec. 15. **Nature of Partner's Liability**

All partners are liable

(a) Jointly and severally for everything chargeable to the partnership under sections 13 and 14.

(b) Jointly for all other debts and obligations of the partnership; but any partner may enter into a separate obligation to perform a partnership contract.

Sec. 16. **Partner by Estoppel**

(1) When a person, by words spoken or written or by conduct, represents himself, or consents to another representing him to any one, as a partner in an existing partnership or with one or more persons not actual partners, he is liable to any such person to whom such representation has been made, who has, on the faith of such representation, given credit to the actual or apparent partnership, and if he has made such representation or consented to its being made in a public manner he is liable to such person, whether the representation has or has not been made or communicated to such person so giving credit by or with the knowledge of the apparent partner making the representation or consenting to its being made.

   (a) When a partnership liability results, he is liable as though he were an actual member of the partnership.

   (b) When no partnership liability results, he is liable jointly with the other persons, if any, so consenting to the contract or representation as to incur liability, otherwise separately.

(2) When a person has been thus represented to be a partner in an existing partnership, or with one or more persons not actual partners, he is an agent of the persons consenting to such representation to bind them to the same extent and in the same manner as though he were a partner in fact, with respect to persons who rely upon

the representation. Where all the members of the existing partnership consent to the representation, a partnership act or obligation results; but in all other cases it is the joint act or obligation of the person acting and the persons consenting to the representation.

Sec. 17. **Liability of Incoming Partner**

A person admitted as a partner into an existing partnership is liable for all the obligations of the partnership arising before his admission as though he had been a partner when such obligations were incurred, except that this liability shall be satisfied only out of partnership property.

Part IV   Relations of Partners to One Another

Sec. 18. **Rules Determining Rights and Duties of Partners**

The rights and duties of the partners in relation to the partnership shall be determined, subject to any agreement between them, by the following rules:

(a) Each partner shall be repaid his contributions, whether by way of capital or advances to the partnership property and share equally in the profits and surplus remaining after all liabilities, including those to partners, are satisfied; and must contribute towards the losses, whether of capital or otherwise, sustained by the partnership according to his share in the profits.

(b) The partnership must indemnify every partner in respect of payments made and personal liabilities reasonably incurred by him in the ordinary and proper conduct of its business, or for the preservation of its business or property.

(c) A partner, who in aid of the partnership makes any payment or advance beyond the amount of capital which he agreed to contribute, shall be paid interest from the date of the payment or advance.

(d) A partner shall receive interest on the capital contributed by him only from the date when repayment should be made.

(e) All partners have equal rights in the management and conduct of the partnership business.

(f) No partner is entitled to remuneration for acting in the partnership business, except that a surviving partner is entitled to reasonable compensation for his services in winding up the partnership affairs.

(g) No person can become a member of a partnership without the consent of all the partners.

(h) Any difference arising as to ordinary matters connected with the partnership business may be decided by a majority of the partners; but no act in contravention of any agreement between the partners may be done rightfully without the consent of all the partners.

Sec. 19. **Partnership Books**

The partnership books shall be kept, subject to any agreement between the partners, at the principal place of business of the partnership, and every partner shall at all times have access to and may inspect and copy any of them.

Sec. 20. **Duty of Partners to Render Information**

Partners shall render on demand true and full information of all things affecting the partnership to any partner or the legal representative of any deceased partner or partner under legal disability.

Sec. 21. **Partner Accountable as a Fiduciary**

(1) Every partner must account to the partnership for any benefit, and hold as trustee for it any profits derived by him without the consent of the other partners from any transaction connected with the formation, conduct, or liquidation of the partnership or from any use by him of its property.

(2) This section applies also to the representatives of a deceased partner engaged in the liquidation of the affairs of the partnership as the personal representatives of the last surviving partner.

Sec. 22. **Right to an Account**

Any partner shall have the right to a formal account as to partnership affairs:

(a) If he is wrongfully excluded from the partnership business or possession of its property by his co-partners,

(b) If the right exists under the terms of any agreement,

(c) As provided by section 21,

(d) Whenever other circumstances render it just and reasonable.

Sec. 23. **Continuation of Partnership Beyond Fixed Term**

(1) When a partnership for a fixed term or particular undertaking is continued after the termination of such term or particular undertaking without any express agreement, the rights and duties of the partners remain the same as they were at such termination, so far as is consistent with a partnership at will.

(2) A continuation of the business by the partners or such of them as habitually acted therein during the term, without any settlement or liquidation of the partnership affairs, is prima facie evidence of a continuation of the partnership.

Part V Property Rights of a Partner

Sec. 24. Extent of Property Rights of a Partner

The property rights of a partner are (1) his rights in specific partnership property, (2) his interest in the partnership, and (3) his right to participate in the management.

Sec. 25. Nature of a Partner's Right in Specific Partnership Property

(1) A partner is co-owner with his partners of specific partnership property holding as a tenant in partnership.

(2) The incidents of this tenancy are such that:

(a) A partner, subject to the provisions of this act and to any agreement between the partners, has an equal right with his partners to possess specific partnership property for partnership purposes; but he has no right to possess such property for any other purpose without the consent of his partners.

(b) A partner's right in specific partnership property is not assignable except in connection with the assignment of rights of all the partners in the same property.

(c) A partner's right in specific partnership property is not subject to attachment or execution, except on a claim against the partnership. When partnership property is attached for a partnership debt the partners, or any of them, or the representatives of a deceased partner, cannot claim any right under the homestead or exemption laws.

(d) On the death of a partner his right in specific partnership property vests in the surviving partner or partners, except where the deceased was the last surviving partner, when his right in such property vests in his legal representative. Such surviving partner or partners, or the legal representative of the last surviving partner, has no right to possess the partnership property for any but a partnership purpose.

(e) A partner's right in specific partnership property is not subject to dower, curtesy, or allowances to widows, heirs, or next of kin.

Sec. 26. Nature of Partner's Interest in the Partnership

A partner's interest in the partnership is his share of the profits and surplus, and the same is personal property.

Sec. 27. Assignment of Partner's Interest

(1) A conveyance by a partner of his interest in the partnership does not of itself dissolve the partnership, nor, as against the other partners in the absence of agreement, entitle the assignee, during the continuance of the partnership, to interfere in the management or administration of the partnership business or affairs, or to require any information or account of partnership transactions, or to inspect the partnership books; but it merely entitles the assignee to receive in accordance with his contract the profits to which the assigning partner would otherwise be entitled.

(2) In case of a dissolution of the partnership, the assignee is entitled to receive his assignor's interest and may require an account from the date only of the last account agreed to by all the partners.

Sec. 28. Partner's Interest Subject to Charging Order

(1) On due application to a competent court by any judgment creditor of a partner, the court which entered the judgment, order, or decree, or any other court, may charge the interest of the debtor partner with payment of the unsatisfied amount of such judgment debt with interest thereon; and may then or later appoint a receiver of his share of the profits, and of any other money due or to fall due to him in respect of the partnership, and make all other orders, directions, accounts and inquiries which the debtor partner might have made, or which the circumstances of the case may require.

(2) The interest charged may be redeemed at any time before foreclosure, or in case of a sale being directed by the court may be purchased without thereby causing a dissolution:

(a) With separate property, by any one or more of the partners, or

(b) With partnership property, by any one or more of the partners with the consent of all the partners whose interests are not so charged or sold.

(3) Nothing in this act shall be held to deprive a partner of his right, if any, under the exemption laws, as regards his interest in the partnership.

Part VI Dissolution and Winding up

Sec. 29. Dissolution Defined

The dissolution of a partnership is the change in the relation of the partners caused by any partner ceasing to be associated in the carrying on as distinguished from the winding up of the business.

Sec. 30. Partnership not Terminated by Dissolution

On dissolution the partnership is not terminated, but continues until the winding up of partnership affairs is completed.

Sec. 31. Causes of Dissolution

Dissolution is caused:

(1) Without violation of the agreement between the partners,

(a) By the termination of the definite term or particular undertaking specified in the agreement,

(b) By the express will of any partner when no definite term or particular undertaking is specified,

(c) By the express will of all the partners who have not assigned their interests or suffered them to be charged for their separate debts, either before or after the termination of any specified term or particular undertaking.

(d) By the expulsion of any partner from the business bona fide in accordance with such a power conferred by the agreement between the partners;

(2) In contravention of the agreement between the partners, where the circumstances do not permit a dissolution under any other provision of this section, by the express will of any partner at any time;

(3) By any event which makes it unlawful for the business of the partnership to be carried on or for the members to carry it on in partnership;

(4) By the death of any partner;

(5) By the bankruptcy of any partner or the partnership;

(6) By decree of court under section 32.

Sec. 32. Dissolution by Decree of Court

(1) On application by or for a partner the court shall decree a dissolution whenever:

(a) A partner has been declared a lunatic in any judicial proceeding or is shown to be of unsound mind,

(b) A partner becomes in any other way incapable of performing his part of the partnership contract,

(c) A partner has been guilty of such conduct as tends to affect prejudicially the carrying on of the business,

(d) A partner wilfully or persistently commits a breach of the partnership agreement, or otherwise so conducts himself in matters relating to the partnership business that it is not reasonably practicable to carry on the business in partnership with him,

(e) The business of the partnership can only be carried on at a loss,

(f) Other circumstances render a dissolution equitable.

(2) On the application of the purchaser of a partner's interest under sections 28 or 29 [should read 27 or 28]:

(a) After the termination of the specified term or particular undertaking,

(b) At any time if the partnership was a partnership at will when the interest was assigned or when the charging order was issued.

Sec. 33. General Effect of Dissolution on Authority of Partner

Except so far as may be necessary to wind up partnership affairs or to complete transactions begun but not then finished, dissolution terminates all authority of any partner to act for the partnership,

(1) With respect to the partners,

(a) When the dissolution is not by the act, bankruptcy or death of a partner; or

(b) When the dissolution is by such act, bankruptcy or death of a partner, in cases where section 34 so requires.

(2) With respect to persons not partners, as declared in section 35.

Sec. 34. Rights of Partner to Contribution from Co-partners After Dissolution

Where the dissolution is caused by the act, death or bankruptcy of a partner, each partner is liable to his copartners for his share of any liability created by any partner acting for the partnership as if the partnership had not been dissolved unless

(a) The dissolution being by act of any partner, the partner acting for the partnership had knowledge of the dissolution, or

(b) The dissolution being by the death or bankruptcy of a partner, the partner acting for the partnership had knowledge or notice of the death or bankruptcy.

Sec. 35. Power of Partner to Bind Partnership to Third Persons After Dissolution

(1) After dissolution a partner can bind the partnership except as provided in Paragraph (3).

(a) By any act appropriate for winding up partnership affairs or completing transactions unfinished at dissolution;

(b) By any transaction which would bind the partnership if dissolution had not taken place, provided the other party to the transaction

(I) Had extended credit to the partnership prior to dissolution and had no knowledge or notice of the dissolution; or

(II) Though he had not so extended credit, had nevertheless known of the partnership prior to dissolution, and, having no knowledge or notice of dissolution, the fact of dissolution had not been advertised in a newspaper of general circulation in the place (or in each place if more than one) at which the partnership business was regularly carried on.

(2) The liability of a partner under paragraph (1b) shall be satisfied out of partnership assets alone when such partner had been prior to dissolution

(a) Unknown as a partner to the person with whom the contract is made; and

(b) So far unknown and inactive in partnership affairs that the business reputation of the partnership could not be said to have been in any degree due to his connection with it.

(3) The partnership is in no case bound by any act of a partner after dissolution

(a) Where the partnership is dissolved because it is unlawful to carry on the business, unless the act is appropriate for winding up partnership affairs; or

(b) Where the partner has become bankrupt; or

(c) Where the partner has no authority to wind up partnership affairs; except by a transaction with one who

(I) Had extended credit to the partnership prior to dissolution and had no knowledge or notice of his want of authority; or

(II) Had not extended credit to the partnership prior to dissolution, and, having no knowledge or notice of his want of authority, the fact of his want of authority has not been advertised in the manner provided for advertising the fact of dissolution in paragraph (1bII).

(4) Nothing in this section shall affect the liability under Section 16 of any person who after dissolution represents himself or consents to another representing him as a partner in a partnership engaged in carrying on business.

Sec. 36. **Effect of Dissolution on Partner's Existing Liability**

(1) The dissolution of the partnership does not of itself discharge the existing liability of any partner.

(2) A partner is discharged from any existing liability upon dissolution of the partnership by an agreement to that effect between himself, the partnership creditor and the person or partnership continuing the business; and such agreement may be inferred from the course of dealing between the creditor having knowledge of the dissolution and the person or partnership continuing the business.

(3) Where a person agrees to assume the existing obligations of a dissolved partnership, the partners whose obligations have been assumed shall be discharged from any liability to any creditor of the partnership who, knowing of the agreement, consents to a material alteration in the nature or time of payment of such obligations.

(4) The individual property of a deceased partner shall be liable for all obligations of the partnership incurred while he was a partner but subject to the prior payment of his separate debts.

Sec. 37. **Right to Wind Up**

Unless otherwise agreed the partners who have not wrongfully dissolved the partnership or the legal representative of the last surviving partner, not bankrupt, has the right to wind up the partnership affairs; provided, however, that any partner, his legal representative or his assignee, upon cause shown, may obtain winding up by the court.

Sec. 38. **Rights of Partners to Application of Partnership Property**

(1) When dissolution is caused in any way, except in contravention of the partnership agreement, each partner, as against his co-partners and all persons claiming through them in respect of their interests in the partnership, unless otherwise agreed, may have the partnership property applied to discharge its liabilities, and the surplus applied to pay in cash the net amount owing to the respective partners. But if dissolution is caused by expulsion of a partner, bona fide under the partnership agreement and if the expelled partner is discharged from all partnership liabilities, either by payment or agreement under section 36(2), he shall receive in cash only the net amount due him from the partnership.

(2) When dissolution is caused in contravention of the partnership agreement the rights of the partners shall be as follows:

(a) Each partner who has not caused dissolution wrongfully shall have,

(I) All the rights specified in paragraph (1) of this section, and

(II) The right, as against each partner who has caused the dissolution wrongfully, to damages for breach of the agreement.

(b) The partners who have not caused the dissolution wrongfully, if they all desire to continue the business in the same name, either by themselves or jointly with others, may do so, during the agreed term for the partnership and for that purpose may possess the partnership property, provided they secure the payment by bond approved by the court, or pay to any partner who has caused the dissolution wrongfully, the value of his interest in the partnership at the dissolution, less any damages recoverable under clause (2a II) of the section, and in like manner indemnify him against all present or future partnership liabilities.

(c) A partner who has caused the dissolution wrongfully shall have:

(I) If the business is not continued under the provisions of paragraph (2b) all the rights of a partner under paragraph (1), subject to clause (2a II), of this section,

(II) If the business is continued under paragraph (2b) of this section the right as against his co-partners and all claiming through them in respect of their interests in the partnership, to have the value of his interest in the partnership, less any damages caused to his co-partners by the dissolution, ascertained and paid to him in cash, or the payment secured by bond approved by the court, and to be released from all existing liabilities of the partnership; but in ascertaining the value of the partner's interest the value of the good-will of the business shall not be considered.

Sec. 39. Rights Where Partnership is Dissolved for Fraud or Misrepresentation

Where a partnership contract is rescinded on the ground of the fraud or misrepresentation of one of the parties thereto, the party entitled to rescind is, without prejudice to any other right, entitled,

(a) To a lien on, or right of retention of, the surplus of the partnership property after satisfying the partnership liabilities to third persons for any sum of money paid by him for the purchase of an interest in the partnership and for any capital or advances contributed by him; and

(b) To stand, after all liabilities to third persons have been satisfied, in the place of the creditors of the partnership for any payments made by him in respect of the partnership liabilities; and

(c) To be indemnified by the person guilty of the fraud or making the representation against all debts and liabilities of the partnership.

Sec. 40. Rules for Distribution

In settling accounts between the partners after dissolution, the following rules shall be observed, subject to any agreement to the contrary:

(a) The assets of the partnership are:

(I) The partnership property,

(II) The contributions of the partners necessary for the payment of all the liabilities specified in clause (b) of this paragraph.

(b) The liabilities of the partnership shall rank in order of payment, as follows:

(I) Those owing to creditors other than partners,

(II) Those owing to partners other than for capital and profits,

(III) Those owing to partners in respect of capital,

(IV) Those owing to partners in respect of profits.

(c) The assets shall be applied in the order of their declaration in clause (a) of this paragraph to the satisfaction of the liabilities.

(d) The partners shall contribute, as provided by section 18(a) the amount necessary to satisfy the liabilities; but if any, but not all, of the partners are insolvent, or, not being subject to process, refuse to contribute, the other parties shall contribute their share of the liabilities, and, in the relative proportions in which they share the profits, the additional amount necessary to pay the liabilities.

(e) An assignee for the benefit of creditors or any person appointed by the court shall have the right to enforce the contributions specified in clause (d) of this paragraph.

(f) Any partner or his legal representative shall have the right to enforce the contributions specified in clause (d) of this paragraph, to the extent of the amount which he has paid in excess of his share of the liability.

(g) The individual property of a deceased partner shall be liable for the contributions specified in clause (d) of this paragraph.

(h) When partnership property and the individual properties of the partners are in possession of a court for distribution, partnership creditors shall have priority on partnership property and separate creditors on individual property, saving the rights of lien or secured creditors as heretofore.

(i) Where a partner has become bankrupt or his estate is insolvent the claims against his separate property shall rank in the following order:

(I) Those owing to separate creditors,

(II) Those owing to partnership creditors,

(III) Those owing to partners by way of contribution.

Sec. 41. Liability of Persons Continuing the Business in Certain Cases

(1) When any new partner is admitted into an existing partnership, or when any partner retires and assigns (or the representative of the deceased partner assigns) his rights in partnership property to two or more of the partners, or to one or more of the partners and one or more third persons, if the business is continued without liquidation of the partnership affairs, creditors of the

first or dissolved partnership are also creditors of the partnership so continuing the business.

(2) When all but one partner retire and assign (or the representative of a deceased partner assigns) their rights in partnership property to the remaining partner, who continues the business without liquidation of partnership affairs, either alone or with others, creditors of the dissolved partnership are also creditors of the person or partnership so continuing the business.

(3) When any partner retires or dies and the business of the dissolved partnership is continued as set forth in paragraphs (1) and (2) of this section, with the consent of the retired partners or the representative of the deceased partner, but without any assignment of his right in partnership property, rights of creditors of the dissolved partnership and of the creditors of the person or partnership continuing the business shall be as if such assignment had been made.

(4) When all the partners or their representatives assign their rights in partnership property to one or more third persons who promise to pay the debts and who continue the business of the dissolved partnership, creditors of the dissolved partnership are also creditors of the person or partnership continuing the business.

(5) When any partner wrongfully causes a dissolution and the remaining partners continue the business under the provisions of section 38(2b), either alone or with others, and without liquidation of the partnership affairs, creditors of the dissolved partnership are also creditors of the person or partnership continuing the business.

(6) When a partner is expelled and the remaining partners continue the business either alone or with others, without liquidation of the partnership affairs, creditors of the dissolved partnership are also creditors of the person or partnership continuing the business.

(7) The liability of a third person becoming a partner in the partnership continuing the business, under this section, to the creditors of the dissolved partnership shall be satisfied out of partnership property only.

(8) When the business of a partnership after dissolution is continued under any conditions set forth in this section the creditors of the dissolved partnership, as against the separate creditors of the retiring or deceased partner or the representative of the deceased partner, have a prior right to any claim of the retired partner or the representative of the deceased partner against the person or partnership continuing the business, on account of the retired or deceased partner's interest in the dissolved

partnership or on account of any consideration promised for such interest or for his right in partnership property.

(9) Nothing in this section shall be held to modify any right of creditors to set aside any assignment on the ground of fraud.

(10) The use by the person or partnership continuing the business of the partnership name, or the name of a deceased partner as part thereof, shall not of itself make the individual property of the deceased partner liable for any debts contracted by such person or partnership.

Sec. 42. **Rights of Retiring or Estate of Deceased Partner When the Business is Continued**

When any partner retires or dies, and the business is continued under any of the conditions set forth in section 41 (1, 2, 3, 5, 6), or section 38(2b) without any settlement of accounts as between him or his estate and the person or partnership continuing the business, unless otherwise agreed, he or his legal representative as against such persons or partnership may have the value of his interest at the date of dissolution ascertained, and shall receive as an ordinary creditor an amount equal to the value of his interest in the dissolved partnership with interest, or, at his option or at the option of his legal representative, in lieu of interest, the profits attributable to the use of his right in the property of the dissolved partnership; provided that the creditors of the dissolved partnership as against the separate creditors, or the representative of the retired or deceased partner, shall have priority on any claim arising under this section, as provided by section 41(8) of this act.

Sec. 43. **Accrual of Actions**

The right to an account of his interest shall accrue to any partner, or his legal representative, as against the winding up partners or the surviving partners or the person or partnership continuing the business, at the date of dissolution, in the absence of any agreement to the contrary.

Part VII **Miscellaneous Provisions**

Sec. 44. **When Act Takes Effect**

This act shall take effect on the ___ day of ___ one thousand nine hundred and ___.

Sec. 45. **Legislation Repealed**

All acts or parts of acts inconsistent with this act are hereby repealed.

APPENDIX D

THE MODEL BUSINESS CORPORATION ACT (Selected Provisions)

[By the Editor] The Model Business Corporation Act prepared by the Committee on Corporate Laws (Section of Corporation, Banking and Business Law) of the American Bar Association was originally patterned after the Illinois Business Corporation Act of 1933. It was first published as a complete act in 1950. In subsequent years several revisions, addenda and optional or alternative provisions were added. The Act was substantially revised and renumbered in 1969.

This Act should be distinguished from the Model Business Corporation Act promulgated in 1928 by the Commissioners on Uniform State Laws under the name "Uniform Business Corporation Act" and renamed Model Business Corporation Act in 1943. This Uniform Act was withdrawn in 1957.

The Model Business Corporation Act has been influential in the codification of corporation statutes in more than 35 states. However, there is no state that has totally adopted it in its current form. Moreover, since the Model Act itself has been substantially modified from time to time, there is considerable variation among the statutes of the states that used this Act as a model.

§ 1. Short Title

This Act shall be known and may be cited as the ".... . . Business Corporation Act."

§ 2. Definitions

As used in this Act, unless the context otherwise requires, the term:

(a) "Corporation" or "domestic corporation" means a corporation for profit subject to the provisions of this Act, except a foreign corporation.

(b) "Foreign corporation" means a corporation for profit organized under laws other than the laws of this State for a purpose or purposes for which a corporation may be organized under this Act.

(c) "Articles of incorporation" means the original or restated articles of incorporation or articles of consolidation and all amendments thereto including articles of merger.

(d) "Shares" means the units into which the proprietary interests in a corporation are divided.

(e) "Subscriber" means one who subscribes for shares in a corporation, whether before or after incorporation.

(f) "Shareholder" means one who is a holder of record of shares in a corporation. If the articles of incorporation or the by-laws so provide, the board of directors may adopt by resolution a procedure whereby a shareholder of the corporation may certify in writing to the corporation that all or a portion of the shares registered in the name of such shareholder are held for the account of a specified person or persons. The resolution shall set forth (1) the classification of shareholder who may certify, (2) the purpose or purposes for which the certification may be made, (3) the form of certification and information to be contained therein, (4) if the certification is with respect to a record date or closing of the stock transfer books within which the certification must be received by the corporation and (5) such other provisions with respect to the procedure as are deemed necessary or desirable. Upon receipt by the corporation of a certification complying with the procedure, the persons specified in the certification shall be deemed, for the purpose or purposes set forth in the certification, to be the holders of record of the number of shares specified in place of the shareholder making the certification.

(g) "Authorized shares" means the shares of all classes which the corporation is authorized to issue.

[95]

(h) "Employee" includes officers but not directors. A director may accept duties which make him also an employee.

(i) "Distribution" means a direct or indirect transfer of money or other property (except its own shares) or incurrence of indebtedness, by a corporation to or for the benefit of any of its shareholders in respect of any of its shares, whether by dividend or by purchase, redemption or other acquisition of its shares, or otherwise.

§ 3. Purposes

Corporations may be organized under this Act for any lawful purpose or purposes, except for the purpose of banking or insurance.

§ 4. General Powers

Each corporation shall have power:

(a) To have perpetual succession by its corporate name unless a limited period of duration is stated in its articles of incorporation.

(b) To sue and be sued, complain and defend, in its corporate name.

(c) To have a corporate seal which may be altered at pleasure, and to use the same by causing it, or a facsimile thereof, to be impressed or affixed or in any other manner reproduced.

(d) To purchase, take, receive, lease, or otherwise acquire, own, hold, improve, use and otherwise deal in and with, real or personal property, or any interest therein, wherever situated.

(e) To sell, convey, mortgage, pledge, lease, exchange, transfer and otherwise dispose of all or any part of its property and assets.

(f) To lend money and use its credit to assist its employees.

(g) To purchase, take, receive, subscribe for, or otherwise acquire, own, hold, vote, use, employ, sell, mortgage, lend, pledge, or otherwise dispose of, and otherwise use and deal in and with, shares or other interests in, or obligations of, other domestic or foreign corporations, associations, partnerships or individuals, or direct or indirect obligations of the United States or of any other government, state, territory, governmental district or municipality or of any instrumentality thereof.

(h) To make contracts and guarantees and incur liabilities, borrow money at such rates of interest as the corporation may determine, issue its notes, bonds, and other obligations, and secure any of its obligations by mortgage or pledge of all or any of its property, franchises and income.

(i) To lend money for its corporate purposes, invest and reinvest its funds, and take and hold real and personal property as security for the payment of funds so loaned or invested.

(j) To conduct its business, carry on its operations and have offices and exercise the powers granted by this Act, within or without this State.

(k) To elect or appoint officers and agents of the corporation, and define their duties and fix their compensation.

(l) To make and alter by-laws, not inconsistent with its articles of incorporation or with the laws of this State, for the administration and regulation of the affairs of the corporation.

(m) To make donations for the public welfare or for charitable, scientific or educational purposes.

(n) To transact any lawful business which the board of directors shall find will be in aid of governmental policy.

(o) To pay pensions and establish pension plans, pension trusts, profit sharing plans, stock bonus plans, stock option plans and other incentive plans for any or all of its directors, officers and employees.

(p) To be a promoter, partner, member, associate, or manager of any partnership, joint venture, trust or other enterprise.

(q) To have and exercise all powers necessary or convenient to effect its purposes.

§ 5. Indemnification of Directors and Officers

(a) As used in this section:

(1) *Director* means any person who is or was a director of the corporation and any person who, while a director of the corporation, is or was serving at the request of the corporation as a director, officer, partner, trustee, employee or agent of another foreign or domestic corporation, partnership, joint venture, trust, other enterprise or employee benefit plan.

(2) *Corporation* includes any domestic or foreign predecessor entity of the corporation in a merger, consolidation or other transaction in which the predecessor's existence ceased upon consummation of such transaction.

(3) *Expenses* include attorneys' fees.

(4) *Official capacity* means

(A) when used with respect to a director, the office of director in the corporation, and

(B) when used with respect to a person other than a director, as contemplated in subsection (i), the elective or appointive office in the corporation held by the officer or the employment or agency relationship undertaken by the employee or agent in behalf of the corporation,

but in each case does not include service for any other foreign or domestic corporation or any partnership, joint venture, trust, other enterprise, or employee benefit plan.

(5) *Party* includes a person who was, is, or is threatened to be made, a named defendant or respondent in a proceeding.

(6) *Proceeding* means any threatened, pending or completed action, suit or proceeding, whether civil, criminal, administrative or investigative.

(b) A corporation shall have power to indemnify any person made a party to any proceeding by reason of the fact that he is or was a director if

(1) he conducted himself in good faith; and

(2) he reasonably believed

(A) in the case of conduct in his official capacity with the corporation, that his conduct was in its best interests, and

(B) in all other cases, that his conduct was at least not opposed to its best interests; and

(3) in the case of any criminal proceeding, he had no reasonable cause to believe his conduct was unlawful.

Indemnification may be made against judgments, penalties, fines, settlements and reasonable expenses, actually incurred by the person in connection with the proceeding; except that if the proceeding was by or in the right of the corporation, indemnification may be made only against such reasonable expenses and shall not be made in respect of any proceeding in which the person shall have been adjudged to be liable to the corporation. The termination of any proceeding by judgment, order, settlement, conviction, or upon a plea of nolo contendere or its equivalent, shall not, of itself, be determinative that the person did not meet the requisite standard of conduct set forth in this subsection (b).

(c) A director shall not be indemnified under subsection (b) in respect of any proceeding charging improper personal benefit to him, whether or not involving action in his official capacity, in which he shall have been adjudged to be liable on the basis that personal benefit was improperly received by him.

(d) Unless limited by the articles of incorporation,

(1) a director who has been wholly successful, on the merits or otherwise, in the defense of any proceeding referred to in subsection (b) shall be indemnified against reasonable expenses incurred by him in connection with the proceeding; and

(2) a court of appropriate jurisdiction, upon application

of a director and such notice as the court shall require, shall have authority to order indemnification in the following circumstances:

(A) if it determines a director is entitled to reimbursement under clause (1), the court shall order indemnification, in which case the director shall also be entitled to recover the expenses of securing such reimbursement; or

(B) if it determines that the director is fairly and reasonably entitled to indemnification in view of all the relevant circumstances, whether or not he has met the standard of conduct set forth in subsection (b) or has been adjudged liable in the circumstances described in subsection (c), the court may order such indemnification as the court shall deem proper, except that indemnification with respect to any proceeding by or in the right of the corporation or in which liability shall have been adjudged in the circumstances described in subsection (c) shall be limited to expenses.

A court of appropriate jurisdiction may be the same court in which the proceeding involving the director's liability took place.

(e) No indemnification under subsection (b) shall be made by the corporation unless authorized in the specific case after a determination has been made that indemnification of the director is permissible in the circumstances because he has met the standard of conduct set forth in subsection (b). Such determination shall be made:

(1) by the board of directors by a majority vote of a quorum consisting of directors not at the time parties to the proceeding; or

(2) if such a quorum cannot be obtained, then by a majority vote of a committee of the board, duly designated to act in the matter by a majority vote of the full board (in which designation directors who are parties may participate), consisting solely of two or more directors not at the time parties to the proceeding; or

(3) by special legal counsel, selected by the board of directors or a committee thereof by vote as set forth in clauses (1) or (2) of this subsection (e), or, if the requisite quorum of the full board cannot be obtained therefor and such committee cannot be established, by a majority vote of the full board (in which selection directors who are parties may participate); or

(4) by the shareholders.

Authorization of indemnification and determination as to reasonableness of expenses shall be made in the same manner as the determination that indemnification is permissible, except that if the determination that indemnification is permissible is made by special legal counsel, authorization of indemnification and determination as to reasonableness of expenses shall be made in a manner specified in clause (3) in the preceding sentence for the selection of such counsel. Shares held by directors who are parties to the proceeding shall not be voted on the subject matter under this subsection (e).

(f) Reasonable expenses incurred by a director who is a party to a proceeding may be paid or reimbursed by the corporation in advance of the final disposition of such proceeding upon receipt by the corporation of

(1) a written affirmation by the director of his good faith belief that he has met the standard of conduct necessary for indemnification by the corporation as authorized in this section, and

(2) a written undertaking by or on behalf of the director to repay such amount if it shall ultimately be determined that he has not met such standard of con- duct, and after a determination that the facts then known to those making the determination would not preclude indemnification under this section. The undertaking required by clause (2) shall be an unlimited general obligation of the director but need not be secured and may be accepted without reference to financial ability to make repayment. Determinations and authorizations of payments under this subsection (f) shall be made in the manner specified in subsection (e).

(g) No provision for the corporation to indemnify or to advance expenses to a director who is made a party to a proceeding, whether contained in the articles of incorporation, the by-laws, a resolution of shareholders or directors, an agreement or otherwise (except as contemplated by subsection (j)), shall be valid unless consistent with this section or, to the extent that indemnity hereunder is limited by the articles of incorporation, consistent therewith. Nothing contained in this section shall limit the corporation's power to pay or reimburse expenses incurred by a director in connection with his appearance as a witness in a proceeding at a time when he has not been made a named defendant or respondent in the proceeding.

(h) For purposes of this section, the corporation shall be deemed to have requested a director to serve an employee benefit plan whenever the performance by him of his duties to the corporation also imposes duties on, or otherwise involves services by, him to the plan or participants or beneficiaries of the plan; excise taxes assessed on a director with respect to an employee benefit plan pursuant to applicable law shall be deemed "fines"; and action taken or omitted by him with respect to an employee benefit plan in the performance of his duties for a purpose reasonably believed by him to be in the interest of the participants and beneficiaries of the plan shall be deemed to be for a purpose which is not opposed to the best interests of the corporation.

(i) Unless limited by the articles of incorporation,

(1) an officer of the corporation shall be indemnified as and to the same extent provided in subsection (d) for a director and shall be entitled to the same extent as a director to seek indemnification pursuant to the provisions of subsection (d);

(2) a corporation shall have the power to indemnify and to advance expenses to an officer, employee or agent of the corporation to the same extent that it may indemnify and advance expenses to directors pursuant to this section; and

(3) a corporation, in addition, shall have the power to indemnify and to advance expenses to an officer, employee or agent who is not a director to such further extent, consistent with law, as may be provided by its articles of incorporation, by-laws, general or specific action of its board of directors, or contract.

(j) A corporation shall have power to purchase and maintain insurance on behalf of any person who is or was a director, officer, employee or agent of the corporation, or who, while a director, officer, employee or agent of the corporation, is or was serving at the request of the corporation as a director, officer, partner, trustee, employee or agent of another foreign or domestic corporation, partnership, joint venture, trust, other enterprise or employee benefit plan, against any liability asserted against him and incurred by him in any such capacity or arising out of his status as such, whether or not the corporation would have the power to indemnify him against such liability under the provisions of this section.

(k) Any indemnification of, or advance of expenses to, a director in accordance with this section, if arising out of a proceeding by or in the right of the corporation, shall be reported in writing to the shareholders with or before the notice of the next shareholders' meeting.

§ 6. Power of Corporation to Acquire Its Own Shares

A corporation shall have the power to acquire its own shares. All of its own shares acquired by a corporation shall, upon acquisition, constitute authorized but unissued shares, unless the articles of incorporation provide that they shall not be reissued, in which case the authorized shares shall be reduced by the number of shares acquired.

If the number of authorized shares is reduced by an acquisition, the corporation shall, not later than the time it files its next annual report under this Act with the Secretary of State, file a statement of cancellation showing the reduction in the authorized shares. The statement of cancellation shall be executed in duplicate by the corporation by its president or a vice president and by its secretary or an assistant secretary, and verified by one of the officers signing such statement, and shall set forth:

(a) The name of the corporation.

(b) The number of acquired shares cancelled, itemized by classes and series.

(c) The aggregate number of authorized shares, itemized by classes and series, after giving effect to such cancellation.

Duplicate originals of such statement shall be delivered to the Secretary of State. If the Secretary of State finds that such statement conforms to law, he shall, when all fees and franchise taxes have been paid as in this Act prescribed:

(1) Endorse on each of such duplicate originals the word "Filed", and the month, day and year of the filing thereof.

(2) File one of such duplicate originals in his office.

(3) Return the other duplicate original to the corporation or its representative.

§ 7. Defense of Ultra Vires

No act of a corporation and no conveyance or transfer of real or personal property to or by a corporation shall be invalid by reason of the fact that the corporation was without capacity or power to do such act or to make or receive such conveyance or transfer, but such lack of capacity or power may be asserted:

(a) In a proceeding by a shareholder against the corporation to enjoin the doing of any act or the transfer of real or personal property by or to the corporation. If the unauthorized act or transfer sought to be enjoined is being, or is to be, performed or made pursuant to a contract to which the corporation is a party, the court may, if all of the parties to the contract are parties to the proceeding and if it deems the same to be equitable, set aside and enjoin the performance of such contract, and in so doing may allow to the corporation or to the other parties to the contract, as the case may be, compensation for the loss or damage sustained by either of them which may result from the action of the court in setting aside and enjoining the performance of such contract, but anticipated profits to be derived from the performance of the contract shall not be awarded by the court as a loss or damage sustained.

(b) In a proceeding by the corporation, whether acting directly or through a receiver, trustee, or other legal representative, or through shareholders in a representative suit, against the incumbent or former officers or directors of the corporation.

(c) In a proceeding by the Attorney General, as provided in this Act, to dissolve the corporation, or in a proceeding by the Attorney General to enjoin the corporation from the transaction of unauthorized business.

§ 8. Corporate Name

The corporate name:

(a) Shall contain the word "corporation," "company," "incorporated" or "limited," or shall contain an abbreviation of one of such words.

(b) Shall not contain any word or phrase which indicates or implies that it is organized for any purpose other than one or more of the purposes contained in its articles of incorporation.

(c) Shall not be the same as, or deceptively similar to, the name of any domestic corporation existing under the laws of this State or any foreign corporation authorized to transact business in this State, or a name the exclusive right to which is, at the time, reserved in the manner provided in this Act, or the name of a corporation which has in effect a registration of its corporate name as provided in this Act, except that this provision shall not apply if the applicant files with the Secretary of State either of the following: (1) the written consent of such other corporation or holder of a reserved or registered name to use the same or deceptively similar name and one or more words are added to make such name distinguishable from such other name, or (2) a certified copy of a final decree of a court of competent jurisdiction establishing the prior right of the applicant to the use of such name in this State.

A corporation with which another corporation, domestic or foreign, is merged, or which is formed by the reorganization or consolidation of one or more domestic or foreign corporations or upon a sale, lease or other disposition to or exchange with, a domestic corporation of all or substantially all the assets of another corporation, domestic or foreign, including its name, may have the same name as that used in this State by any of such corporations if such other corporation was organized under the laws of, or is authorized to transact business in, this State.

§ 9. Reserved Name

The exclusive right to the use of a corporate name may be reserved by:

(a) Any person intending to organize a corporation under this Act.

(b) Any domestic corporation intending to change its name.

(c) Any foreign corporation intending to make application for a certificate of authority to transact business in this State.

(d) Any foreign corporation authorized to transact business in this State and intending to change its name.

(e) Any person intending to organize a foreign corporation and intending to have such corporation make application for a certificate of authority to transact business in this State.

The reservation shall be made by filing with the Secretary of State an application to reserve a specified corporate name, executed by the applicant. If the Secretary of State finds that the name is available for corporate use, he shall reserve the same for the exclusive use of the applicant for a period of one hundred and twenty days.

The right to the exclusive use of a specified corporate name so reserved may be transferred to any other person or corporation by filing in the office of the Secretary of State a notice of such transfer, executed by the applicant for whom the name was reserved, and specifying the name and address of the transferee.

§ 10. Registered Name

Any corporation organized and existing under the laws of any state or territory of the United States may register its corporate name under this Act, provided its corporate name is not the same as, or deceptively similar to, the name of any domestic corporation existing under the laws of this State, or the name of any foreign corporation authorized to transact business in this State, or any corporate name reserved or registered under this Act.

Such registration shall be made by:

(a) Filing with the Secretary of State (1) an application for registration executed by the corporation by an officer thereof, setting forth the name of the corporation, the state or territory under the laws of which it is incorporated, the date of its incorporation, a statement that it is carrying on or doing business, and a brief statement of the business in which it is engaged, and (2) a certificate setting forth that such corporation is in good standing under the laws of the state or territory wherein it is organized, executed by the Secretary of State of such state or territory or by such other official as may have custody of the records pertaining to corporations, and

(b) Paying to the Secretary of State a registration fee in the amount of . . . . for each month, or fraction thereof, between the date of filing such application and December 31st of the calendar year in which such application is filed.

Such registration shall be effective until the close of the calendar year in which the application for registration is filed.

§ 11. Renewal of Registered Name

(Omitted)

§ 12. Registered Office and Registered Agent

Each corporation shall have and continuously maintain in this State:

(a) A registered office which may be, but need not be, the same as its place of business.

(b) A registered agent, which agent may be either an individual resident in this State whose business office is identical with such registered office, or a domestic corporation, or a foreign corporation authorized to transact business in this State, having a business office identical with such registered office.

§ 13. Change of Registered Office or Registered Agent

(Omitted)

§ 14. Service of Process on Corporation

The registered agent so appointed by a corporation shall be an agent of such corporation upon whom any process, notice or demand required or permitted by law to be served upon the corporation may be served.

Whenever a corporation shall fail to appoint or maintain a registered agent in this State, or whenever its registered agent cannot with reasonable diligence be found at the registered office, then the Secretary of State shall be an agent of such corporation upon whom any such process, notice, or demand may be served. Service on the Secretary of State of any such process, notice, or demand shall be made by delivering to and leaving with him, or with any clerk having charge of the corporation department of his office, duplicate copies of such process, notice or demand. In the event any such process, notice or demand is served on the Secretary of State, he shall immediately cause one of the copies thereof to be forwarded by registered mail, addressed to the corporation at its registered office. Any service so had on the Secretary of State shall be returnable in not less than thirty days.

The Secretary of State shall keep a record of all processes, notices and demands served upon him under this section, and shall record therein the time of such service and his action with reference thereto.

Nothing herein contained shall limit or affect the right to serve any process, notice or demand required or permitted by law to be served upon a corporation in any other manner now or hereafter permitted by law.

§ 15. Authorized Shares

Each corporation shall have power to create and issue the number of shares stated in its articles of incorporation. Such shares may be divided into one or more classes with such designations, preferences, limitations, and relative rights as shall be stated in the articles of incorporation. The articles of incorporation may limit or deny the voting rights of or provide special voting rights for the shares of any class to the extent not inconsistent with the provisions of this Act.

Without limiting the authority herein contained, a corporation, when so provided in its articles of incorporation, may issue shares of preferred or special classes:

(a) Subject to the right of the corporation to redeem any of such shares at the price fixed by the articles of incorporation for the redemption thereof.

(b) Entitling the holders thereof to cumulative, noncumulative or partially cumulative dividends.

(c) Having preference over any other class or classes of shares as to the payment of dividends.

(d) Having preference in the assets of the corporation over any other class or classes of shares upon the voluntary or involuntary liquidation of the corporation.

(e) Convertible into shares of any other class or into shares of any series of the same or any other class, except a class having prior or superior rights and preferences as to dividends or distribution of assets upon liquidation.

§ 16. Issuance of Shares of Preferred or Special Classes in Series

If the articles of incorporation so provide, the shares of any preferred or special class may be divided into and issued in series. If the shares of any such class are to be issued in series, then each series shall be so designated as to distinguish the shares thereof from the shares of all other series and classes. Any or all of the series of any such class and the variations in the relative rights and preferences as between different series may be fixed and determined by the articles of incorporation, but all shares of the same class shall be identical except as to the following relative rights and preferences, as to which there may be variations between different series:

(A) The rate of dividend.

(B) Whether shares may be redeemed and, if so, the redemption price and the terms and conditions of redemption.

(C) The amount payable upon shares in the event of voluntary and involuntary liquidation.

(D) Sinking fund provisions, if any, for the redemption or purchase of shares.

(E) The terms and conditions, if any, on which shares may be converted.

(F) Voting rights, if any.

If the article of incorporation shall expressly vest authority in the board of directors, then, to the extent that the articles of incorporation shall not have established

series and fixed and determined the variations in the relative rights and preferences as between series, the board of directors shall have authority to divide any or all of such classes into series and, within the limitations set forth in this section and in the articles of incorporation, fix and determine the relative rights and preferences of the shares of any series so established.

In order for the board of directors to establish a series, where authority so to do is contained in the articles of incorporation, the board of directors shall adopt a resolution setting forth the designation of the series and fixing and determining the relative rights and preferences thereof, or so much thereof as shall not be fixed and determined by the articles of incorporation.

Prior to the issue of any shares of a series established by resolution adopted by the board of directors, the corporation shall file in the office of the Secretary of State a statement setting forth:

(a) The name of the corporation.

(b) A copy of the resolution establishing and designating the series, and fixing and determining the relative rights and preferences thereof.

(c) The date of adoption of such resolution.

(d) That such resolution was duly adopted by the board of directors.

Such statement shall be executed in duplicate by the corporation by its president or a vice president and by its secretary or an assistant secretary, and verified by one of the officers signing such statement, and shall be delivered to the Secretary of State. If the Secretary of State finds that such statement conforms to law, he shall, when all franchise taxes and fees have been paid as in this Act prescribed:

(1) Endorse on each of such duplicate originals the word "Filed," and the month, day, and year of the filing thereof.

(2) File one of such duplicate originals in his office.

(3) Return the other duplicate original to the corporation or its representative.

Upon the filing of such statement by the Secretary of State, the resolution establishing and designating the series and fixing and determining the relative rights and preferences thereof shall become effective and shall constitute an amendment of the articles of incorporation.

§ 17. Subscriptions for Shares

A subscription for shares of a corporation to be organized shall be irrevocable for a period of six months, unless otherwise provided by the terms of the subscription agreement or unless all of the subscribers consent to the revocation of such subscription.

Unless otherwise provided in the subscription agreement, subscriptions for shares, whether made before or after the organization of a corporation, shall be paid in full at such time, or in such installments and at such times, as shall be determined by the board of directors. Any call made by the board of directors for payment on subscriptions shall be uniform as to all shares of the same class or as to all shares of the same series, as the case may be. In case of default in the payment of any installment or call when such payment is due, the corporation may proceed to collect the amount due in the same manner as any debt due the corporation. The by-laws may prescribe other penalties for failure to pay installments or calls that may become due, but no penalty working a forfeiture of a subscription, or of the amounts paid thereon, shall be declared as against any subscriber unless the amount due thereon shall remain unpaid for a period of twenty days after written demand has been made therefor. If mailed, such written demand shall be deemed to be made when deposited in the United States mail in a sealed envelope addressed to the subscriber at his last post-office address known to the corporation, with postage thereon prepaid. In the event of the sale of any shares by reason of any forefeiture, the excess of proceeds realized over the amount due and unpaid on such shares shall be paid to the delinquent subscriber or to his legal representative.

§ 18. Issuance of Shares

Subject to any restrictions in the articles of incorporation:

(a) Shares may be issued for such consideration as shall be authorized by the board of directors establishing a price (in money or other consideration) or a minimum price or general formula or method by which the price will be determined; and

(b) Upon authorization by the board of directors, the corporation may issue its own shares in exchange for or in conversion of its outstanding shares, or distribute its own shares, pro rata to its shareholders or the shareholders of one or more classes or series, to effectuate stock dividends or splits, and any such transaction shall not require consideration; provided, that no such issuance of shares of any class or series shall be made to the holders of shares of any other class or series unless it is either expressly provided for in the articles of incorporation, or is authorized by an affirmative vote or the written consent of the holders of at least a majority of the outstanding shares of the class or series in which the distribution is to be made.

§ 19. Payment for Shares

The consideration for the issuance of shares may be paid, in whole or in part, in money, in other property, tangible or intangible, or in labor or services actually performed for the corporation. When payment of the consideration for which shares are to be issued shall have been received by the corporation, such shares shall be non-assessable.

Neither promissory notes nor future services shall constitute payment or part payment for the issuance of shares of a corporation.

In the absence of fraud in the transaction, the judgment of the board of directors or the shareholders, as the case may be, as to the value of the consideration received for shares shall be conclusive.

§ 20. Stock Rights and Options

Subject to any provisions in respect thereof set forth in its articles of incorporation, a corporation may create and issue, whether or not in connection with the issuance and sale of any of its shares or other securities, rights or options entitling the holders thereof to purchase from the corporation shares of any class or classes. Such rights or options shall be evidenced in such manner as the board of directors shall approve and, subject to the provisions of the articles of incorporation, shall set forth the terms upon which, the time or times within which and the price or prices at which such shares may be purchased from the corporation upon the exercise of any such right or option. If such rights or options are to be issued to directors, officers or employees as such of the corporation or of any subsidiary thereof, and not to the shareholders generally, their issuance shall be approved by the affirmative vote of the holders of a majority of the shares entitled to vote thereon or shall be authorized by and consistent with a plan approved or ratified by such a vote of shareholders. In the absence of fraud in the transaction, the judgment of the board of directors as to the adequacy of the consideration received for such rights or options shall be conclusive.

§ 21. Determination of Amount of Stated Capital

[Repealed in 1979].

§ 22. Expenses of Organization, Reorganization and Financing

The reasonable charges and expenses of organization or reorganization of a corporation, and the reasonable expenses of and compensation for the sale or underwriting of its shares, may be paid or allowed by such corporation out of the consideration received by it in payment for its shares without thereby rendering such shares assessable.

§ 23. Shares Represented by Certificates and Uncertified Shares

The shares of a corporation shall be represented by certificates or shall be uncertificated shares. Certificates shall be signed by the chairman or vice-chairman of the board of directors or the president or a vice president and by the treasurer or an assistant treasurer or the secretary or an assistant secretary of the corporation, and may be sealed with the seal of the corporation or a facsimile thereof. Any of or all the signatures upon a certificate may be a facsimile. In case any officer, transfer agent or registrar who has signed or whose facsimile signature has been placed upon such certificate shall have ceased to be such officer, transfer agent or registrar before such certificate is issued, it may be issued by the corporation with the same effect as if he were such officer, transfer agent or registrar at the date of its issue.

Every certificate representing shares issued by a corporation which is authorized to issue shares of more than one class shall set forth upon the face or back of the certificate, or shall state that the corporation will furnish to any shareholder upon request and without charge, a full statement of the designations, preferences, limitations, and relative rights of the shares of each class authorized to be issued, and if the corporation is authorized to issue any preferred or special class in series, the variations in the relative rights and preferences between the shares of each such series so far as the same have been fixed and determined and the authority of the board of directors to fix and determine the relative rights and preferences of subsequent series.

Each certificate representing shares shall state upon the face thereof:

(a) That the corporation is organized under the laws of this State.

(b) The name of the person to whom issued.

(c) The number and class of shares, and the designation of the series, if any, which such certificate represents.

(d) The par value of each share represented by such certificate, or a statement that the shares are without par value.

No certificate shall be issued for any share until such share is fully paid.

Unless otherwise provided by the articles of incorporation or by-laws, the board of directors of a corporation may provide by resolution that some or all of any or all classes and series of its shares shall be uncertificated shares, provided that such resolution shall not apply to shares represented by a certificate until such certificate is surrendered to the corporation. Within a reasonable time after the issuance or transfer of uncertificated shares, the corporation shall send to the registered owner thereof a written notice containing the information required to be set forth or stated on certificates pursuant to the second and third paragraphs of this section. Except as otherwise expressly provided by law, the rights and obligations of the holders of uncertificated shares and the rights and obligations of the holders of certificates representing shares of the same class and series shall be identical.

§ 24. Fractional Shares

A corporation may (1) issue fractions of a share, either represented by a certificate or uncertificated, (2) arrange for the disposition of fractional interests by those entitled thereto, (3) pay in money the fair value of fractions of a share as of a time when those entitled to receive such fractions are determined, or (4) issue scrip in registered or bearer form which shall entitle the holder to receive a certificate for a full share or an uncertificated full share upon the surrender of such scrip aggregating a full share. A certificate for a fractional share or an uncertificated fractional share shall, but scrip shall not unless otherwise provided therein, entitle the holder to exercise voting rights, to receive dividends thereon, and to participate in any of the assets of the corporation in the event of liquidation. The board of directors may cause scrip to be issued subject to the condition that it shall become void if not exchanged for certificates representing full shares or uncertificated full shares before a specified date, or subject to the condition that the shares for which scrip is exchangeable may be sold by the corporation and the proceeds thereof distributed to the holders of scrip, or subject to any other conditions which the board of directors may deem advisable.

§ 25. Liability of Subscribers and Shareholders

A holder of or subscriber to shares of a corporation shall be under no obligation to the corporation or its creditors with respect to such shares other than the obligation to pay to the corporation the full consideration for which such shares were issued or to be issued.

Any person becoming an assignee or transferee of shares or of a subscription for shares in good faith and without knowledge or notice that the full consideration therefor has not been paid shall not be personally liable to the corporation or its creditors for any unpaid portion of such consideration.

An executor, administrator, conservator, guardian, trustee, assignee for the benefit of creditors, or receiver shall not be personally liable to the corporation as a holder of or subscriber to shares of a corporation but the estate and funds in his hands shall be so liable.

No pledgee or other holder of shares as collateral security shall be personally liable as a shareholder.

§ 26. Shareholders' Preemptive Rights

The shareholders of a corporation shall have no preemptive right to acquire unissued shares of the corporation, or securities of the corporation convertible into or carrying a right to subscribe to or acquire shares, except to the extent, if any, that such right is provided in the articles of incorporation.

§ 26A. Shareholders' Preemptive Rights [Alternative]

Except to the extent limited or denied by this section or by the articles of incorporation, shareholders shall have a preemptive right to acquire unissued shares or securities convertible into such shares or carrying a right to subscribe to or acquire shares.

Unless otherwise provided in the articles of incorporation,

(a) No preemptive right shall exist

(1) to acquire any shares issued to directors, officers or employees pursuant to approval by the affirmative vote of the holders of a majority of the shares entitled to vote thereon or when authorized by and consistent with a plan theretofore approved by such a vote of shareholders; or

(2) to acquire any shares sold otherwise than for money.

(b) Holders of shares of any class that is preferred or limited as to dividends or assets shall not be entitled to any preemptive right.

(c) Holders of shares of common stock shall not be entitled to any preemptive right to shares of any class that is preferred or limited as to dividends or assets or to any obligations, unless convertible into shares of common stock or carrying a right to subscribe to or acquire shares of common stock.

(d) Holders of common stock without voting power shall have no preemptive right to shares of common stock with voting power.

(e) The preemptive right shall be only an opportunity to acquire shares or other securities under such terms and conditions as the board of directors may fix for the purpose of providing a fair and reasonable opportunity for the exercise of such right.

§ 27. By-Laws

The initial by-laws of a corporation shall be adopted by its board of directors. The power to alter, amend or repeal the by-laws or adopt new by-laws, subject to repeal or change by action of the shareholders, shall be vested in the board of directors unless reserved to the shareholders by the articles of incorporation. The by-laws may contain any provisions for the regulation and management of the affairs of the corporation not inconsistent with law or the articles of incorporation.

§ 27A. By-Laws and Other Powers in Emergency [Optional]

(Omitted)

§ 28. Meetings of Shareholders

Meetings of shareholders may be held at such place within or without this State as may be stated in or fixed in accordance with the by-laws. If no other place is stated or so fixed, meetings shall be held at the registered office of the corporation.

An annual meeting of the shareholders shall be held at such time as may be stated in or fixed in accordance with the by-laws. If the annual meeting is not held within any thirteen-month period the Court of . . . . may, on the application of any shareholder, summarily order a meeting to be held.

Special meetings of the shareholders may be called by the board of directors, the holders of not less than one-tenth of all the shares entitled to vote at the meeting, or such other persons as may be authorized in the articles of incorporation or the by-laws.

§ 29. Notice of Shareholders' Meetings

Written notice stating the place, day and hour of the meeting and, in case of a special meeting, the purpose or purposes for which the meeting is called, shall be delivered not less than ten nor more than fifty days before the date of the meeting, either personally or by mail, by or at the direction of the president, the secretary, or the officer or persons calling the meeting, to each shareholder of record entitled to vote at such meeting. If mailed, such notice shall be deemed to be delivered when deposited in the United States mail addressed to the shareholder at his address as it appears on the stock transfer books of the corporation, with postage thereon prepaid.

§ 30. Closing of Transfer Books and Fixing Record Date

For the purpose of determining shareholders entitled to notice of or to vote at any meeting of shareholders or any adjournment thereof, or entitled to receive payment of any dividend, or in order to make a determination of shareholders for any other proper purpose, the board of directors of a corporation may provide that the stock transfer books shall be closed for a stated period but not to exceed, in any case, fifty days. If the stock transfer books shall be closed for the purpose of determining shareholders entitled to notice of or to vote at a meeting of shareholders, such books shall be closed for at least ten days immediately preceding such meeting. In lieu of closing the stock transfer books, the by-laws, or in the absence of an applicable by-law the board of directors, may fix in advance a date as the record date for any such determination of shareholders, such date in any case to be not more than fifty days and, in case of a meeting of shareholders, not less than ten days prior to the date on which the particular action, requiring such determination of shareholders, is to be taken. If the stock transfer books are not closed and no record date is fixed for the determination of shareholders entitled to notice of or to vote at a meeting of shareholders, or shareholders entitled to receive payment of a dividend, the date on which notice of the meeting is mailed or the date on which the resolution of the board of directors declaring such dividend is adopted, as the case may be, shall be the record date for such determination of shareholders. When a determination of shareholders entitled to vote at any meeting of shareholders has been made as provided in this section, such determination shall apply to any adjournment thereof.

§ 31. Voting Record

The officer or agent having charge of the stock transfer books for shares of a corporation shall make a complete record of the shareholders entitled to vote at such meeting or any adjournment thereof, arranged in alphabetical order, with the address of and the number of shares held by each. Such record shall be produced and kept open at the time and place of the meeting and shall be subject to the inspection of any shareholder during the whole time of the meeting for the purposes thereof.

Failure to comply with the requirements of this section shall not affect the validity of any action taken at such meeting.

An officer or agent having charge of the stock transfer books who shall fail to prepare the record of shareholders, or produce and keep it open for inspection at the meeting, as provided in this section, shall be liable to any shareholder suffering damage on account of such failure, to the extent of such damage.

§ 32. Quorum of Shareholders

Unless otherwise provided in the articles of incorporation, a majority of the shares entitled to vote, represented in person or by proxy, shall constitute a quorum at a meeting of shareholders, but in no event shall a quorum consist of less than one-third of the shares entitled to vote at the meeting. If a quorum is present, the affirmative vote of the majority of the shares represented at the meeting and entitled to vote on the subject matter shall be the act of the shareholders, unless the vote of a greater number or voting by classes is required by this Act or the articles of incorporation or by-laws.

§ 33. Voting of Shares

Each outstanding share, regardless of class, shall be entitled to one vote on each matter submitted to a vote at a meeting of shareholders, except as may be otherwise provided in the articles of incorporation. If the articles of incorporation provide for more or less than one vote for any share, on any matter, every reference in this Act to a majority or other proportion of shares shall refer to

such a majority or other proportion of votes entitled to be cast.

Shares held by another corporation if a majority of the shares entitled to vote for the election of directors of such other corporation is held by the corporation, shall not be voted at any meeting or counted in determining the total number of outstanding shares at any given time.

A shareholder may vote either in person or by proxy executed in writing by the shareholder or by his duly authorized attorney-in-fact. No proxy shall be valid after eleven months from the date of its execution, unless otherwise provided in the proxy.

[Either of the following prefatory phrases may be inserted here: "The articles of incorporation may provide that" or "Unless the articles of incorporation otherwise provide"] . . . at each election for directors every shareholder entitled to vote at such election shall have the right to vote, in person or by proxy, the number of shares owned by him for as many persons as there are directors to be elected and for whose election he has a right to vote, or to cumulate his votes by giving one candidate as many votes as the number of such directors multiplied by the number of his shares shall equal, or by distributing such votes on the same principle among any number of such candidates.

Shares standing in the name of another corporation, domestic or foreign, may be voted by such officer, agent or proxy as the by-laws of such other corporation may prescribe, or, in the absence of such provision, as the board of directors of such other corporation may determine.

Shares held by an administrator, executor, guardian or conservator may be voted by him, either in person or by proxy, without a transfer of such shares into his name. Shares standing in the name of a trustee may be voted by him, either in person or by proxy, but no trustee shall be entitled to vote shares held by him without a transfer of such shares into his name.

Shares standing in the name of a receiver may be voted by such receiver, and shares held by or under the control of a receiver may be voted by such receiver without the transfer thereof into his name if authority so to do be contained in an appropriate order of the court by which such receiver was appointed.

A shareholder whose shares are pledged shall be entitled to vote such shares until the shares have been transferred into the name of the pledgee, and thereafter the pledgee shall be entitled to vote the shares so transferred.

On and after the date on which written notice of redemption of redeemable shares has been mailed to the holders thereof and a sum sufficient to redeem such shares has been deposited with a bank or trust company with irrevocable instruction and authority to pay the redemption price to the holders thereof upon surrender of certificates therefor, such shares shall not be entitled to vote on any matter and shall not be deemed to be outstanding shares.

§ 34. Voting Trusts and Agreements Among Shareholders

Any number of shareholders of a corporation may create a voting trust for the purpose of conferring upon a trustee or trustees the right to vote or otherwise represent their shares, for a period of not to exceed ten years, by entering into a written voting trust agreement specifying the terms and conditions of the voting trust, by depositing a counterpart of the agreement with the corporation at its registered office, and by transferring their shares to such trustee or trustees for the purposes of the agreement. Such trustee or trustees shall keep a record of the holders of voting trust certificates evidencing a beneficial interest in the voting trust, giving the names and addresses of all such holders and the number and class of the shares in respect of which the voting trust certificates held by each are issued, and shall deposit a copy of such record with the corporation at its registered office. The counterpart of the voting trust agreement and the copy of such record so deposited with the corporation shall be subject to the same right of examination by a shareholder of the corporation, in person or by agent or attorney, as are the books and records of the corporation, and such counterpart and such copy of such record shall be subject to examination by any holder of record of voting trust certificates, either in person or by agent or attorney, at any reasonable time for any proper purpose.

Agreements among shareholders regarding the voting of their shares shall be valid and enforceable in accordance with their terms. Such agreements shall not be subject to the provisions of this section regarding voting trusts.

§ 35. Board of Directors

All corporate powers shall be exercised by or under authority of, and the business and affairs of a corporation shall be managed under the direction of, a board of directors except as may be otherwise provided in this Act or the articles of incorporation. If any such provision is made in the articles of incorporation, the powers and duties conferred or imposed upon the board of directors by this Act shall be exercised or performed to such extent and by such person or persons as shall be provided in the articles of incorporation. Directors need not be residents of this State or shareholders of the corporation unless the articles of incorporation or by-laws so require. The articles of incorporation or by-laws may prescribe other qualifications for directors. The board of directors shall have authority to fix the compensation of directors unless otherwise provided in the articles of incorporation.

A director shall perform his duties as a director, including his duties as a member of any committee of the board upon which he may serve, in good faith, in a manner he reasonably believes to be in the best interests of the corporation, and with such care as an ordinarily prudent person in a like position would use under similar circumstances. In performing his duties, a director shall be entitled to rely on information, opinions, reports or statements, including financial statements and other financial data, in each case prepared or presented by:

(a) one or more officers or employees of the corporation whom the director reasonably believes to be reliable and competent in the matters presented,

(b) counsel, public accountants or other persons as to matters which the director reasonably believes to be within such person's professional or expert competence, or

(c) a committee of the board upon which he does not serve, duly designated in accordance with a provision of the articles of incorporation or the by-laws, as to matters within its designated authority, which committee the director reasonably believes to merit confidence,

but he shall not be considered to be acting in good faith if he has knowledge concerning the matter in question that would cause such reliance to be unwarranted. A person who so performs his duties shall have no liability by reason of being or having been a director of the corporation.

A director of a corporation who is present at a meeting of its board of directors at which action on any corporate matter is taken shall be presumed to have assented to the action taken unless his dissent shall be entered in the minutes of the meeting or unless he shall file his written dissent to such action with the secretary of the meeting before the adjournment thereof or shall forward such dissent by registered mail to the secretary of the corporation immediately after the adjournment of the meeting. Such right to dissent shall not apply to a director who voted in favor of such action.

§ 36. Number and Election of Directors

The board of directors of a corporation shall consist of one or more members. The number of directors shall be fixed by, or in the manner provided in, the articles of incorporation or the by-laws, except as to the number constituting the initial board of directors, which number shall be fixed by the articles of incorporation. The number of directors may be increased or decreased from time to time by amendment to, or in the manner provided in, the articles of incorporation or the by-laws, but no decrease shall have the effect of shortening the term of any incumbent director. In the absence of a by-law providing for the number of directors, the number shall be the same as that provided for in the articles of incorporation. The names and addresses of the members of the first board of directors shall be stated in the articles of incorporation. Such persons shall hold office until the first annual meeting of shareholders, and until their successors shall have been elected and qualified. At the first annual meeting of shareholders and at each annual meeting thereafter the shareholders shall elect directors to hold office until the next succeeding annual meeting, except in case of the classification of directors as permitted by this Act. Each director shall hold office for the term for which he is elected and until his successor shall have been elected and qualified.

§ 37. Classification of Directors

When the board of directors shall consist of nine or more members, in lieu of electing the whole number of directors annually, the articles of incorporation may provide that the directors be divided into either two or three classes, each class to be as nearly equal in number as possible, the term of office of directors of the first class to expire at the first annual meeting of shareholders after their election, that of the second class to expire at the second annual meeting after their election, and that of the third class, if any, to expire at the third annual meeting after their election. At each annual meeting after such classification the number of directors equal to the number of the class whose term expires at the time of such meeting shall be elected to hold office until the second succeeding annual meeting, if there be two classes, or until the third succeeding annual meeting, if there be three classes. No classification of directors shall be effective prior to the first annual meeting of shareholders.

§ 38. Vacancies

Any vacancy occurring in the board of directors may be filled by the affirmative vote of a majority of the remaining directors though less than a quorum of the board of directors. A director elected to fill a vacancy shall be elected for the unexpired term of his predecessor in office. Any directorship to be filled by reason of an increase in the number of directors may be filled by the board of directors for a term of office continuing only until the next election of directors by the shareholders.

§ 39. Removal of Directors

At a meeting of shareholders called expressly for that purpose, directors may be removed in the manner provided in this section. Any director or the entire board of directors may be removed, with or without cause, by a vote of the holders of a majority of the shares then entitled to vote at an election of directors.

In the case of a corporation having cumulative voting, if less than the entire board is to be removed, no one of the directors may be removed if the votes cast against his removal would be sufficient to elect him if then cumulatively voted at an election of the entire board of directors, or, if there be classes of directors, at an election of the class of directors of which he is a part.

Whenever the holders of the shares of any class are entitled to elect one or more directors by the provisions of the articles of incorporation, the provisions of this section shall apply, in respect to the removal of a director or directors so elected, to the vote of the holders of the outstanding shares of that class and not to the vote of the outstanding shares as a whole.

§ 40. Quorum of Directors

A majority of the number of directors fixed by or in the manner provided in the by-laws or in the absence of a by-law fixing or providing for the number of directors, then of the number stated in the articles of incorporation, shall constitute a quorum for the transaction of business unless a greater number is required by the articles of incorporation or the by-laws. The act of the majority of the directors present at a meeting at which a quorum is present shall be the act of the board of directors, unless the act of a greater number is required by the articles of incorporation or the by-laws.

§ 41. Director Conflicts of Interest

No contract or other transaction between a corporation and one or more of its directors or any other corporation, firm, association or entity in which one or more of its directors are directors or officers or are financially interested, shall be either void or voidable because of such relationship or interest or because such director or directors are present at the meeting of the board of directors or a committee thereof which authorizes, approves or ratifies such contract or transaction or because his or their votes are counted for such purpose, if:

(a) the fact of such relationship or interest is disclosed or known to the board of directors or committee which authorizes, approves or ratifies the contract or transaction by a vote or consent sufficient for the purpose without counting the votes or consents of such interested directors; or

(b) the fact of such relationship or interest is disclosed or known to the shareholders entitled to vote and they authorize, approve or ratify such contract or transaction by vote or written consent; or

(c) the contract or transaction is fair and reasonable to the corporation.

Common or interested directors may be counted in determining the presence of a quorum at a meeting of the board of directors or a committee thereof which authorizes, approves or ratifies such contract or transaction.

§ 42. **Executive and Other Committees**

If the articles of incorporation or the by-laws so provide, the board of directors, by resolution adopted by a majority of the full board of directors, may designate from among its members an executive committee and one or more other committees each of which, to the extent provided in such resolution or in the articles of incorporation or the by-laws of the corporation, shall have and may exercise all the authority of the board of directors, except that no such committee shall have authority to (i) authorize distributions, (ii) approve or recommend to shareholders actions or proposals required by this Act to be approved by shareholders, (iii) designate candidates for the office of director, for purposes of proxy solicitation or otherwise, or fill vancancies on the board of directors or any committee thereof, (iv) amend the by-laws, (v) approve a plan of merger not requiring shareholder approval, (vi) authorize or approve the reacquisition of shares unless pursuant to a general formula or method specified by the board of directors, or (vii) authorize or approve the issuance or sale of, or any contract to issue or sell, shares or designate the terms of a series of a class of shares, provided that the board of directors, having acted regarding general authorization for the issuance or sale of shares, or any contract therefor, and, in the case of a series, the designation thereof, may, pursuant to a general formula or method specified by the board by resolution or by adoption of a stock option or other plan, authorize a committee to fix the terms of any contract for the sale of the shares and to fix the terms upon which such shares may be issued or sold, including, without limitation, the price, the dividend rate, provisions for redemption, sinking fund, conversion, voting or preferential rights, and provisions for other features of a class of shares, or a series of a class of shares, with full power in such committee to adopt any final resolution setting forth all the terms thereof and to authorize the statement of the terms of a series for filing with the Secretary of State under this Act.

Neither the designation of any such committee, the delegation thereto of authority, nor action by such committee pursuant to such authority shall alone constitute compliance by any member of the board of directors, not a member of the committee in question, with his responsibility to act in good faith, in a manner he reasonably believes to be in the best interests of the corporation, and with such care as an ordinarily prudent person in a like position would use under similar circumstances.

§ 43. **Place and Notice of Directors' Meetings; Committee Meetings**

Meetings of the board of directors, regular or special, may be held either within or without this State.

Regular meetings of the board of directors or any committee designated thereby may be held with or without notice as prescribed in the by-laws. Special meetings of the board of directors or any committee designated thereby shall be held upon such notice as is prescribed in the by-laws. Attendance of a director at a meeting shall constitute a waiver of notice of such meeting, except where a director attends a meeting for the express purpose of objecting to the transaction of any business because the meeting is not lawfully called or convened. Neither the business to be transacted at, nor the purpose of, any regular or special meeting of the board of directors or any committee designated thereby need be specified in the notice or waiver of notice of such meeting unless required by the by-laws.

Except as may be otherwise restricted by the articles of incorporation or by-laws, members of the board of directors or any committee designated thereby may participate in a meeting of such board or committee by means of a conference telephone or similar communications equipment by means of which all persons participating in the meeting can hear each other at the same time and participation by such means shall constitute presence in person at a meeting.

§ 44. **Action by Directors Without a Meeting**

Unless otherwise provided by the articles of incorporation or by-laws, any action required by this Act to be taken at a meeting of the directors of a corporation, or any action which may be taken at a meeting of the directors or of a committee, may be taken without a meeting if a consent in writing, setting forth the action so taken, shall be signed by all of the directors, or all of the members of the committee, as the case may be. Such consent shall have the same effect as a unanimous vote.

§ 45. **Distributions to Shareholders**

Subject to any restrictions in the articles of incorporation, the board of directors may authorize and the corporation may make distributions, except that no distribution may be made if, after giving effect thereto, either:

(a) the corporation would be unable to pay its debts as they become due in the usual course of its business; or

(b) the corporation's total assets would be less than the sum of its total liabilities and (unless the articles of incorporation otherwise permit) the maximum amount that then would be payable, in any liquidation, in respect of all outstanding shares having preferential rights in liquidation.

Determinations under subparagraph (b) may be based upon (i) financial statements prepared on the basis of accounting practices and principles that are reasonable in the circumstances, or (ii) a fair valuation or other method that is reasonable in the circumstances.

In the case of a purchase, redemption or other acquisition of a corporation's shares, the effect of a distribution shall be measured as of the date money or other property is transferred or debt is incurred by the corporation, or as of the date the shareholder ceases to be a shareholder of the corporation with respect to such shares, whichever is earlier. In all other cases, the effect of a distribution shall be measured as of the date of its authorization if payment occurs 120 days or less following the date of authorization, or as of the date of payment if payment occurs more than 120 days following the date of authorization.

Indebtedness of a corporation incurred or issued to a shareholder in a distribution in accordance with this Section shall be on a parity with the indebtedness of the corporation to its general unsecured creditors except to the extent subordinated by agreement.

§ 46. Distributions from Capital Surplus

[Repealed in 1979].

§ 47. Loans to Employees and Directors

A corporation shall not lend money to or use its credit to assist its directors without authorization in the particular case by its shareholders, but may lend money to and use its credit to assist any employee of the corporation or of a subsidiary, including any such employee who is a director of the corporation, if the board of directors decides that such loan or assistance may benefit the corporation.

§ 48. Liability of Directors in Certain Cases

In addition to any other liabilities, a director who votes for or assents to any distribution contrary to the provisions of this Act or contrary to any restrictions contained in the articles of incorporation, shall, unless he complies with the standard provided in this Act for the performance of the duties of directors, be liable to the corporation, jointly and severally with all other directors so voting or assenting, for the amount of such dividend which is paid or the value of such distribution in excess of the amount of such distribution which could have been made without a violation of the provisions of this Act or the restrictions in the articles of incorporation.

Any director against whom a claim shall be asserted under or pursuant to this section for the making of a distribution and who shall be held liable thereon, shall be entitled to contribution from the shareholders who accepted or received any such distribution, knowing such distribution to have been made in violation of this Act, in proportion to the amounts received by them.

Any director against whom a claim shall be asserted under or pursuant to this section shall be entitled to contribution from any other director who voted for or assented to the action upon which the claim is asserted and who did not comply with the standard provided in this Act for the performance of the duties of directors.

§ 49. Provisions Relating to Actions by Shareholders

No action shall be brought in this State by a shareholder in the right of a domestic or foreign corporation unless the plaintiff was a holder of record of shares or of voting trust certificates therefor at the time of the transaction of which he complains, or his shares or voting trust certificates thereafter devolved upon him by operation of law from a person who was a holder of record at such time.

In any action hereafter instituted in the right of any domestic or foreign corporation by the holder or holders of record of shares of such corporation or of voting trust certificates therefor, the court having jurisdiction, upon final judgment and a finding that the action was brought without reasonable cause, may require the plaintiff or plaintiffs to pay to the parties named as defendant the reasonable expenses, including fees of attorneys, incurred by them in the defense of such action.

In any action now pending or hereafter instituted or maintained in the right of any domestic or foreign corporation by the holder or holders of record of less than five per cent of the outstanding shares of any class of such corporation or of voting trust certificates therefor, unless the shares or voting trust certificates so held have a market value in excess of twenty-five thousand dollars, the corporation in whose right such action is brought shall be entitled at any time before final judgment to require the plaintiff or plaintiffs to give security for the reasonable expenses, including fees of attorneys, that may be incurred by it in connection with such action or may be incurred by other parties named as defendant for which it may become legally liable. Market value shall be determined as of the date that the plaintiff institutes the action or, in the case of an intervenor, as of the date that he becomes a party to the action. The amount of such security may from time to time be increased or decreased, in the discretion of the court, upon showing that the security provided has or may become inadequate or is excessive. The corporation shall have recourse to such security in such amount as the court having jurisdiction shall determine upon the termination of such action, whether or not the court finds the action was brought without reasonable cause.

§ 50. Officers

The officers of a corporation shall consist of a president, one or more vice presidents as may be prescribed by the by-laws, a secretary, and a treasurer, each of whom shall be elected by the board of directors at such time and in such manner as may be prescribed by the by-laws. Such other officers and assistant officers and agents as may be deemed necessary may be elected or appointed by the board of directors or chosen in such other manner as may be prescribed by the by-laws. Any two or more offices may be held by the same person, except the offices of president and secretary.

All officers and agents of the corporation, as between themselves and the corporation, shall have such authority and perform such duties in the management of the corporation as may be provided in the by-laws, or as may be determined by resolution of the board of directors not inconsistent with the by-laws.

§ 51. Removal of Officers

Any officer or agent may be removed by the board of directors whenever in its judgment the best interests of the corporation will be served thereby, but such removal shall be without prejudice to the contract rights, if any, of the person so removed. Election or appointment of an officer or agent shall not of itself create contract rights.

§ 52. Books and Records: Financial Reports to Shareholders; Examination of Records

Each corporation shall keep correct and complete books and records of account and shall keep minutes of the proceedings of its shareholders and board of directors and shall keep at its registered office or principal place of business, or at the office of its transfer agent or registrar, a record of its shareholders, giving the names and addresses of all shareholders and the number and class of the shares held by each. Any books, records and minutes may be in written form or in any form capable of being converted into written form within a reasonable time.

Any person who shall have been a holder of record of shares or of voting trust certificates therefor at least six months immediately preceding his demand or shall be the holder of record of, or the holder of record of voting trust certificates for, at least five percent of all the outstanding shares of the corporation, upon written demand stating the purpose thereof, shall have the right to examine, in person, or by agent or attorney, at any reasonable time or times, for any proper purpose its relevant books and records of account, minutes, and record of shareholders and to make extracts therefrom.

Any officer or agent who, or a corporation which, shall refuse to allow any such shareholder or holder of voting trust certificates, or his agent or attorney, so to examine and make extracts from its books and records of account, minutes, and record of shareholders, for any proper purpose, shall be liable to such shareholder or holder of voting trust certificates in a penalty of ten per cent of the value of the shares owned by such shareholder, or in respect of which such voting trust certificates are issued, in addition to any other damages or remedy afforded him by law. It shall be a defense to any action for penalties under this section that the person suing therefor has within two years sold or offered for sale any list of shareholders or of holders of voting trust certificates for shares of such corporation or any other corporation or has aided or abetted any person in procuring any list of shareholders or of holders of voting trust certificates for any such purpose, or has improperly used any information secured through any prior examination of the books and records of account, or minutes, or record of shareholders or of holders of voting trust certificates for shares of such corporation or any other corporation, or was not acting in good faith or for a proper purpose in making his demand.

Nothing herein contained shall impair the power of any court of competent jurisdiction, upon proof by a shareholder or holder of voting trust certificates of proper purpose, irrespective of the period of time during which such shareholder or holder of voting trust certificates shall have been a shareholder of record or a holder of record of voting trust certificates, and irrespective of the number of shares held by him or represented by voting trust certificates held by him, to compel the production for examination by such shareholder or holder of voting trust certificates of the books and records of account, minutes and record of shareholders of a corporation.

Upon the written request of any shareholder or holder of voting trust certificates for shares of a corporation, the corporation shall mail to such shareholder or holder of voting trust certificates its most recent financial statements showing in reasonable detail its assets and liabilities and the results of its operations.

Each corporation shall furnish to its shareholders annual financial statements, including at least a balance sheet as of the end of each fiscal year and a statement of income for such fiscal year, which shall be prepared on the basis of generally accepted accounting principles, if the corporation prepares financial statements for such fiscal year on that basis for any purpose, and may be consolidated statements of the corporation and one or more of its subsidiaries. The financial statements shall be mailed by the corporation to each of its shareholders within 120 days after the close of each fiscal year and, after such mailing and upon written request, shall be mailed by the corporation to any shareholder (or holder of a voting trust certificate for its shares) to whom a copy of the most recent annual financial statements has not previously been mailed. In the case of statements audited by a public accountant, each copy shall be accompanied by a report setting forth his opinion thereon; in other cases, each copy shall be accompanied by a statement of the president or the person in charge of the corporation's financial accounting records (1) stating his reasonable belief as to whether or not the financial statements were prepared in accordance with generally accepted accounting principles and, if not, describing the basis of presentation, and (2) describing any respects in which the financial statements were not prepared on a basis consistent with those prepared for the previous year.

§ 53. Incorporators

One or more persons, or a domestic or foreign corporation, may act as incorporator or incorporators of a corporation by signing and delivering in duplicate to the Secretary of State articles of incorporation for such corporation.

§ 54. Articles of Incorporation

The articles of incorporation shall set forth:

(a) The name of the corporation.

(b) The period of duration, which may be perpetual.

(c) The purpose or purposes for which the corporation is organized which may be stated to be, or to include, the transaction of any or all lawful business for which corporations may be incorporated under this Act.

(d) The aggregate number of shares which the corporation shall have authority to issue and, if such shares are to be divided into classes, the number of shares of each class.

(e) If the shares are to be divided into classes, the designation of each class and a statement of the preferences, limitations and relative rights in respect of the shares of each class.

(f) If the corporation is to issue the shares of any preferred or special class in series, then the designation of each series and a statement of the variations in the relative rights and preferences as between series insofar as the same are to be fixed in the articles of incorporation, and a statement of any authority to be vested in the board of directors to establish series and fix and determine the variations in the relative rights and preferences as between series.

(g) If any preemptive right is to be granted to shareholders, the provisions therefor.

(h) The address of its initial registered office, and the name of its initial registered agent at such address.

(i) The number of directors constituting the initial board of directors and the names and addresses of the persons who are to serve as directors until the first annual meeting of shareholders or until their successors be elected and qualify.

(j) The name and address of each incorporator.

In addition to provisions required therein, the articles of incorporation may also contain provisions not inconsistent with law regarding:

(1) the direction of the management of the business and the regulation of the affairs of the corporation;

(2) the definition, limitation and regulation of the powers of the corporation, the directors, and the shareholders, or any class of the shareholders, including restrictions on the transfer of shares;

(3) the par value of any authorized shares or class of shares;

(4) any provision which under this Act is required or permitted to be set forth in the by-laws.

It shall not be necessary to set forth in the articles of incorporation any of the corporate powers enumerated in this Act.

§ 55. Filing of Articles of Incorporation

Duplicate originals of the articles of incorporation shall be delivered to the Secretary of State. If the Secretary of State finds that the articles of incorporation conform to law, he shall, when all fees have been paid as in this Act prescribed:

(a) Endorse on each of such duplicate originals the word "Filed," and the month, day and year of the filing thereof.

(b) File one of such duplicate originals in his office.

(c) Issue a certificate of incorporation to which he shall affix the other duplicate original.

The certificate of incorporation, together with the duplicate original of the articles of incorporation affixed thereto by the Secretary of State, shall be returned to the incorporators or their representative.

§ 56. Effect of Issuance of Certificate of Incorporation

Upon the issuance of the certificate of incorporation, the corporate existence shall begin, and such certificate of incorporation shall be conclusive evidence that all conditions precedent required to be performed by the incorporators have been complied with and that the corporation has been incorporated under this Act, except as against this State in a proceeding to cancel or revoke the certificate of incorporation or for involuntary dissolution of the corporation.

§ 57. Organization Meeting of Directors

After the issuance of the certificate of incorporation an organization meeting of the board of directors named in the articles of incorporation shall be held, either within or without this State, at the call of a majority of the directors named in the articles of incorporation, for the purpose of adopting by-laws, electing officers and transacting such other business as may come before the meeting. The directors calling the meeting shall give at least three days' notice thereof by mail to each director so named, stating the time and place of the meeting.

§ 58. **Right to Amend Articles of Incorporation**

A corporation may amend its articles of incorporation, from time to time, in any and as many respects as may be desired, so long as its articles of incorporation as amended contain only such provisions as might be lawfully contained in original articles of incorporation at the time of making such amendment, and, if a change in shares or the rights of shareholders, or an exchange, reclassification or cancellation of shares or rights of shareholders is to be made, such provisions as may be necessary to effect such change, exchange, reclassification or cancellation.

In particular, and without limitation upon such general power of amendment, a corporation may amend its articles of incorporation, from time to time, so as:

(a) To change its corporate name.

(b) To change its period of duration.

(c) To change, enlarge or diminish its corporate purposes.

(d) To increase or decrease the aggregate number of shares, or shares of any class, which the corporation has authority to issue.

(e) To provide, change or eliminate any provision with respect to the par value of any shares or class of shares.

(f) To exchange, classify, reclassify or cancel all or any part of its shares, whether issued or unissued.

(g) To change the designation of all or any part of its shares, whether issued or unissued, and to change the preferences, limitations, and the relative rights in respect of all or any part of its shares, whether issued or unissued.

(h) To change the shares of any class, whether issued or unissued [sic] into a different number of shares of the same class or into the same or a different number of shares of other classes.

(i) To create new classes of shares having rights and preferences either prior and superior or subordinate and inferior to the shares of any class then authorized, whether issued or unissued.

(j) To cancel or otherwise affect the right of the holders of the shares of any class to receive dividends which have accrued but have not been declared.

(k) To divide any preferred or special class of shares, whether issued or unissued, into series and fix and determine the designations of such series and the variations in the relative rights and preferences as between the shares of such series.

(l) To authorize the board of directors to establish, out of authorized but unissued shares, series of any preferred or special class of shares and fix and determine the relative rights and preferences of the shares of any series so established.

(m) To authorize the board of directors to fix and determine the relative rights and preferences of the authorized but unissued shares of series theretofore established in respect of which either the relative rights and preferences have not been fixed and determined or the relative rights and preferences theretofore fixed and determined are to be changed.

(n) To revoke, diminish, or enlarge the authority of the board of directors to establish series out of authorized but unissued shares of any preferred or special class and fix and determine the relative rights and preferences of the shares of any series so established.

(o) To limit, deny or grant to shareholders of any class the preemptive right to acquire additional shares of the corporation, whether then or thereafter authorized.

§ 59. **Procedure to Amend Articles of Incorporation**

Amendments to the articles of incorporation shall be made in the following manner:

(a) The board of directors shall adopt a resolution setting forth the proposed amendment and, if shares have been issued, directing that it be submitted to a vote at a meeting of shareholders, which may be either the annual or a special meeting. If no shares have been issued, the amendment shall be adopted by resolution of the board of directors and the provisions for adoption by shareholders shall not apply. If the corporation has only one class of shares outstanding, an amendment solely to change the number of authorized shares to effectuate a split of, or stock dividend in, the corporation's own shares, or solely to do so and to change the number of authorized shares in proportion thereto, may be adopted by the board of directors; and the provisions for adoption by shareholders shall not apply, unless otherwise provided by the articles of incorporation. The resolution may incorporate the proposed amendment in restated articles of incorporation which contain a statement that except for the designated amendment the restated articles of incorporation correctly set forth without change the corresponding provisions of the articles of incorporation as theretofore amended, and that the restated articles of incorporation together with the designated amendment supersede the original articles of incorporation and all amendments thereto.

(b) Written notice setting forth the proposed amendment or a summary of the changes to be effected thereby shall be given to each shareholder of record entitled to vote thereon within the time and in the manner provided in this Act for the giving of notice of meetings of shareholders. If the meeting be an annual meeting, the proposed amendment of such summary may be included in the notice of such annual meeting.

(c) At such meeting a vote of the shareholders entitled to vote thereon shall be taken on the proposed amendment. The proposed amendment shall be adopted upon receiving the affirmative vote of the holders of a majority of the shares entitled to vote thereon, unless any class of shares is entitled to vote thereon as a class, in which event the proposed amendment shall be adopted upon receiving the affirmative vote of the holders of a majority of the shares of each class of shares entitled to vote thereon as a class and of the total shares entitled to vote thereon.

Any number of amendments may be submitted to the shareholders, and voted upon by them, at one meeting.

§ 60. Class Voting on Amendments

The holders of the outstanding shares of a class shall be entitled to vote as a class upon a proposed amendment, whether or not entitled to vote thereon by the provisions of the articles of incorporation, if the amendment would:

(a) Increase or decrease the aggregate number of authorized shares of such class.

(b) Effect an exchange, reclassification or cancellation of all or part of the shares of such class.

(c) Effect an exchange, or create a right of exchange, of all or any part of the shares of another class into the shares of such class.

(d) Change the designations, preferences, limitations or relative rights of the shares of such class.

(e) Change the shares of such class into the same or a different number of shares of the same class or another class or classes.

(f) Create a new class of shares having rights and preferences prior and superior to the shares of such class, or increase the rights and preferences or the number of authorized shares, of any class having rights and preferences prior or superior to the shares of such class.

(g) In the case of a preferred or special class of shares, divide the shares of such class into series and fix and determine the designation of such series and the variations in the relative rights and preferences between the shares of such series, or authorize the board of directors to do so.

(h) Limit or deny any existing preemptive rights of the shares of such class.

(i) Cancel or otherwise affect dividends on the shares of such class which have accrued but have not been declared.

§ 61. Articles of Amendment

The articles of amendment shall be executed in duplicate by the corporation by its president or a vice president and by its secretary or an assistant secretary, and verified by one of the officers signing such articles, and shall set forth:

(a) The name of the corporation.

(b) The amendments so adopted.

(c) The date of the adoption of the amendment by the shareholders, or by the board of directors where no shares have been issued.

(d) The number of shares outstanding, and the number of shares entitled to vote thereon, and if the shares of any class are entitled to vote thereon as a class, the designation and number of outstanding shares entitled to vote thereon of each such class.

(e) The number of shares voted for and against such amendment, respectively, and, if the shares of any class are entitled to vote thereon as a class, the number of shares of each such class voted for and against such amendment, respectively, or if no shares have been issued, a statement to that effect.

(f) If such amendment provides for an exchange, reclassification or cancellation of issued shares, and if the manner in which the same shall be effected is not set forth in the amendment, then a statement of the manner in which the same shall be effected.

§ 62. Filing of Articles of Amendment

Duplicate originals of the articles of amendment shall be delivered to the Secretary of State. If the Secretary of State finds that the articles of amendment conform to law, he shall, when all fees and franchise taxes have been paid as in this Act prescribed:

(a) Endorse on each of such duplicate originals the word "Filed," and the month, day and year of the filing thereof.

(b) File one of such duplicate originals in his office.

(c) Issue a certificate of amendment to which he shall affix the other duplicate original.

The certificate of amendment, together with the duplicate original of the articles of amendment affixed thereto by the Secretary of State, shall be returned to the corporation or its representative.

§ 63. Effect of Certificate of Amendment

Upon the issuance of the certificate of amendment by the Secretary of State, the amendment shall become effective and the articles of incorporation shall be deemed to be amended accordingly.

No amendment shall affect any existing cause of action in favor of or against such corporation, or any pending suit to which such corporation shall be a party, or the existing rights of persons other than shareholders; and, in the event the corporate name shall be changed by amendment, no suit brought by or against such corporation under its former name shall abate for that reason.

§ 64. Restated Articles of Incorporation

A domestic corporation may at any time restate its articles of incorporation as theretofore amended, by a resolution adopted by the board of directors.

Upon the adoption of such resolution, restated articles of incorporation shall be executed in duplicate by the corporation by its president or a vice president and by its secretary or assistant secretary and verified by one of the officers signing such articles and shall set forth all of the operative provisions of the articles of incorporation as theretofore amended together with a statement that the restated articles of incorporation correctly set forth without change the corresponding provisions of the articles of incorporation as theretofore amended and that the restated articles of incorporation supersede the original articles of incorporation and all amendments thereto.

Duplicate originals of the restated articles of incorporation shall be delivered to the Secretary of State. If the Secretary of State finds that such restated articles of incorporation conform to law, he shall, when all fees and franchise taxes have been paid as in this Act prescribed:

(1) Endorse on each of such duplicate originals the word "Filed," and the month, day and year of the filing thereof.

(2) File one of such duplicate originals in his office.

(3) Issue a restated certificate of incorporation, to which he shall affix the other duplicate original.

The restated certificate of incorporation, together with the duplicate original of the restated articles of incorporation affixed thereto by the Secretary of State, shall be returned to the corporation or its representative.

Upon the issuance of the restated certificate of incorporation by the Secretary of State, the restated articles of incorporation shall become effective and shall supersede the original articles of incorporation and all amendments thereto.

§ 65. Amendment of Articles of Incorporation in Reorganization Proceedings

Whenever a plan of reorganization of a corporation has been confirmed by decree or order of a court of competent jurisdiction in proceedings for the reorganization of such corporation, pursuant to the provisions of any applicable statute of the United States relating to reorganizations of corporations, the articles of incorporation of the corporation may be amended, in the manner provided in this section, in as many respects as may be necessary to carry out the plan and put it into effect, so long as the articles of incorporation as amended contain only such provisions as might be lawfully contained in original articles of incorporation at the time of making such amendment.

In particular and without limitation upon such general power of amendment, the articles of incorporation may be amended for such purpose so as to:

(A) Change the corporate name, period of duration or corporate purposes of the corporation;

(B) Repeal, alter or amend the by-laws of the corporation;

(C) Change the aggregate number of shares or shares of any class, which the corporation has authority to issue;

(D) Change the preferences, limitations and relative rights in respect of all or any part of the shares of the corporation, and classify, reclassify or cancel all or any part thereof, whether issued or unissued;

(E) Authorize the issuance of bonds, debentures or other obligations of the corporation, whether or not convertible into shares of any class or bearing warrants or other evidences of optional rights to purchase or subscribe for shares of any class, and fix the terms and conditions thereof; and

(F) Constitute or reconstitute and classify or reclassify the board of directors of the corporation, and appoint directors and officers in place of or in addition to all or any of the directors or officers then in office.

Amendments to the articles of incorporation pursuant to this section shall be made in the following manner:

(a) Articles of amendment approved by decree or order of such court shall be executed and verified in duplicate by such person or persons as the court shall designate or appoint for the purpose, and shall set forth the name of the corporation, the amendments of the articles of incorporation approved by the court, the date of the decree or order approving the articles of amendment, the title of the proceedings in which the decree or order was entered, and a statement that such decree or order was entered by a court having jurisdiction of the proceedings for the reorganization of the corporation pursuant to the provisions of an applicable statute of the United States.

(b) Duplicate originals of the articles of amendment shall be delivered to the Secretary of State. If the Secretary of State finds that the articles of amendment conform to law, he shall, when all fees and franchise taxes have been paid as in this Act prescribed:

> (1) Endorse on each of such duplicate originals the word "Filed," and the month, day and year of the filing thereof.

> (2) File one of such duplicate originals in his office.

> (3) Issue a certificate of amendment to which he shall affix the other duplicate original.

The certificate of amendment, together with the duplicate original of the articles of amendment affixed thereto by the Secretary of State, shall be returned to the corporation or its representative.

Upon the issuance of the certificate of amendment by the Secretary of State, the amendment shall become effective and the articles of incorporation shall be deemed to be amended accordingly, without any action thereon by the directors or shareholders of the corporation and with the same effect as if the amendments had been adopted by unanimous action of the directors and shareholders of the corporation.

§ 66. **Restriction on Redemption or Purchase of Redeemable Shares**

[Repealed in 1979].

§ 67. **Cancellation of Redeemable Shares by Redemption or Purchase**

[Repealed in 1979].

§ 68. **Cancellation of Other Reacquired Shares**

[Repealed in 1979].

§ 69. **Reduction of Stated Capital in Certain Cases**

[Repealed in 1979].

§ 70. **Special Provisions Relating to Surplus and Reserves**

[Repealed in 1979].

§ 71. **Procedure for Merger**

Any two or more domestic corporations may merge into one of such corporations pursuant to a plan of merger approved in the manner provided in this Act.

The board of directors of each corporation shall, by resolution adopted by each such board, approve a plan of merger setting forth:

(a) The names of the corporations proposing to merge, and the name of the corporation into which they propose to merge, which is hereinafter designated as the surviving corporation.

(b) The terms and conditions of the proposed merger.

(c) The manner and basis of converting the shares of each corporation into shares, obligations or other securities of the surviving corporation or of any other corporation or, in whole or in part, into cash or other property.

(d) A statement of any changes in the articles of incorporation of the surviving corporation to be effected by such merger.

(e) Such other provisions with respect to the proposed merger as are deemed necessary or desirable.

§ 72. **Procedure for Consolidation**

Any two or more domestic corporations may consolidate into a new corporation pursuant to a plan of consolidation approved in the manner provided in this Act.

The board of directors of each corporation shall, by a resolution adopted by each such board, approve a plan of consolidation setting forth:

(a) The names of the corporations proposing to consolidate, and the name of the new corporation into which they propose to consolidate, which is hereinafter designated as the new corporation.

(b) The terms and conditions of the proposed consolidation.

(c) The manner and basis of converting the shares of each corporation into shares, obligations or other securities of the new corporation or of any other corporation or, in whole or in part, into cash or other property.

(d) With respect to the new corporation, all of the statements required to be set forth in articles of incorporation for corporations organized under this Act.

(e) Such other provisions with respect to the proposed consolidation as are deemed necessary or desirable.

§ 72A. **Procedure for Share Exchange**

All the issued or all the outstanding shares of one or more classes of any domestic corporation may be acquired through the exchange of all such shares of such class or classes by another domestic or foreign corporation pursuant to a plan of exchange approved in the manner provided in this Act.

The board of directors of each corporation shall, by resolution adopted by each such board, approve a plan of exchange setting forth:

(a) The name of the corporation the shares of which are proposed to be acquired by exchange and the name of the corporation to acquire the shares of such corporation in the exchange, which is hereinafter designated as the acquiring corporation.

(b) The terms and conditions of the proposed exchange.

(c) The manner and basis of exchanging the shares to be acquired for shares, obligations or other securities of the acquiring corporation or any other corporation, or, in whole or in part, for cash or other property.

(d) Such other provisions with respect to the proposed exchange as are deemed necessary or desirable.

The procedure authorized by this section shall not be deemed to limit the power of a corporation to acquire all or part of the shares of any class or classes of a corporation through a voluntary exchange or otherwise by agreement with the shareholders.

§ 73. Approval by Shareholders

(a) The board of directors of each corporation in the case of a merger or consolidation, and the board of directors of the corporation the shares of which are to be acquired in the case of an exchange, upon approving such plan of merger, consolidation or exchange, shall, by resolution, direct that the plan be submitted to a vote at a meeting of its shareholders, which may be either an annual or a special meeting. Written notice shall be given to each shareholder of record, whether or not entitled to vote at such meeting, not less than twenty days before such meeting, in the manner provided in this Act for the giving of notice of meetings of shareholders, and, whether the meeting be an annual or a special meeting, shall state that the purpose or one of the purposes is to consider the proposed plan of merger, consolidation or exchange. A copy or a summary of the plan of merger, consolidation or exchange, as the case may be, shall be included in or enclosed with such notice.

(b) At each such meeting, a vote of the shareholders shall be taken on the proposed plan. The plan shall be approved upon receiving the affirmative vote of the holders of a majority of the shares entitled to vote thereon of each such corporation, unless any class of shares of any such corporation is entitled to vote thereon as a class, in which event, as to such corporation, the plan shall be approved upon receiving the affirmative vote of the holders of a majority of the shares of each class of shares entitled to vote thereon as a class and of the total shares entitled to vote thereon. Any class of shares of any such corporation shall be entitled to vote as a class if any such plan contains any provision which, if contained in a proposed amendment to articles of incorporation, would entitle such class of shares to vote as a class and, in the case of an exchange, if the class is included in the exchange.

(c) After such approval by a vote of the shareholders of each such corporation, and at any time prior to the filing of the articles of merger, consolidation or exchange, the merger, consolidation or exchange may be abandoned pursuant to provisions therefor, if any, set forth in the plan.

(d) (1) Notwithstanding the provisions of subsections (a) and (b), submission of a plan of merger to a vote at a meeting of shareholders of a surviving corporation shall not be required if:

(i) the articles of incorporation of the surviving corporation do not differ except in name from those of the corporation before the merger,

(ii) each holder of shares of the surviving corporation which were outstanding immediately before the effective date of the merger is to hold the same number of shares with identical rights immediately after,

(iii) the number of voting shares outstanding immediately after the merger, plus the number of voting shares issuable on conversion of other securities issued by virtue of the terms of the merger and on exercise of rights and warrants so issued, will not exceed by more than 20 percent the number of voting shares outstanding immediately before the merger, and

(iv) the number of participating shares outstanding immediately after the merger, plus the number of participating shares issuable on conversion of other securities issued by virtue of the terms of the merger and on exercise of rights and warrants so issued, will not exceed by more than 20 percent the number of participating shares outstanding immediately before the merger.

(2) As used in this subsection:

(i) "voting shares" means shares which entitle their holders to vote unconditionally in elections of directors;

(ii) "participating shares" means shares which entitle their holders to participate without limitation in distribution of earnings or surplus.

§ 74. Articles of Merger, Consolidation or Exchange

(a) Upon receiving the approvals required by Sections 71, 72 and 73, articles of merger or articles of consolidation shall be executed in duplicate by each corporation by its president or a vice president and by its secretary or an assistant secretary, and verified by one of the officers of each corporation signing such articles, and shall set forth:

(1) The plan of merger or the plan of consolidation;

(2) As to each corporation, either (i) the number of shares outstanding, and, if the shares of any class are entitled

to vote as a class, the designation and number of outstanding shares of each such class, or (ii) a statement that the vote of shareholders is not required by virtue of subsection 73(d);

(3) As to each corporation the approval of whose shareholders is required, the number of shares voted for and against such plan, respectively, and, if the shares of any class are entitled to vote as a class, the number of shares of each such class voted for and against such plan, respectively.

(b) Duplicate originals of the articles of merger, consolidation or exchange shall be delivered to the Secretary of State. If the Secretary of State finds that such articles conform to law, he shall, when all fees and franchise taxes have been paid as in this Act prescribed:

(1) Endorse on each of such duplicate originals the word "Filed," and the month, day and year of the filing thereof.
(2) File one of such duplicate originals in his office.
(3) Issue a certificate of merger, consolidation or exchange to which he shall affix the other duplicate original.

(c) The certificate of merger, consolidation or exchange together with the duplicate original of the articles affixed thereto by the Secretary of State, shall be returned to the surviving, new or acquiring corporation, as the case may be, or its representative.

§ 75. Merger of Subsidiary Corporation

Any corporation owning at least ninety per cent of the outstanding shares of each class of another corporation may merge such other corporation into itself without approval by a vote of the shareholders of either corporation. Its board of directors shall, by resolution, approve a plan of merger setting forth:

(A) The name of the subsidiary corporation and the name of the corporation owning at least ninety per cent of its shares, which is hereinafter designated as the surviving corporation.

(B) The manner and basis of converting the shares of the subsidiary corporation into shares, obligations or other securities of the surviving corporation or of any other corporation or, in whole or in part, into cash or other property.

A copy of such plan of merger shall be mailed to each shareholder of record of the subsidiary corporation.

Articles of merger shall be executed in duplicate by the surviving corporation by its president or a vice president and by its secretary or an assistant secretary, and verified by one of its officers signing such articles, and shall set forth:

(a) The plan of merger;

(b) The number of outstanding shares of each class of the subsidiary corporation and the number of such shares of each class owned by the surviving corporation; and

(c) The date of the mailing to shareholders of the subsidiary corporation of a copy of the plan of merger.

On and after the thirtieth day after the mailing of a copy of the plan of merger to shareholders of the subsidiary corporation or upon the waiver thereof by the holders of all outstanding shares duplicate originals of the articles of merger shall be delivered to the Secretary of State. If the Secretary of State finds that such articles conform to law, he shall, when all fees and franchise taxes have been paid as in this Act prescribed:

(1) Endorse on each of such duplicate originals the word "Filed," and the month, day and year of the filing thereof,

(2) File one of such duplicate originals in his office, and

(3) Issue a certificate of merger to which he shall affix the other duplicate original.

The certificate of merger, together with the duplicate original of the articles of merger affixed thereto by the Secretary of State, shall be returned to the surviving corporation or its representative.

§ 76. Effect of Merger, Consolidation or Exchange

Upon the issuance of the certificate of merger or the certificate of consolidation by the Secretary of State, the merger or consolidation shall be effected.

When such merger or consolidation has been effective:

(a) The several corporations parties to the plan of merger or consolidation shall be a single corporation, which, in the case of a merger, shall be that corporation designated in the plan of merger as the surviving corporation, and, in the case of a consolidation, shall be the new corporation provided for in the plan of consolidation.

(b) The separate existence of all corporations parties to the plan of merger or consolidation, except the surviving or new corporation, shall cease.

(c) Such surviving or new corporation shall have all the rights, privileges, immunities and powers and shall be subject to all the duties and liabilities of a corporation organized under this Act.

(d) Such surviving or new corporation shall thereupon and thereafter possess all the rights, privileges, immunities, and franchises, of a public as well as of a private nature, of each of the merging or consolidating corporations; and all property, real, personal and mixed, and all debts due on whatever account, including subscriptions to shares, and all other choses in action, and all and every other interest of or belonging to or due to each of the corporations so merged or consolidated, shall be taken and deemed to be transferred to and vested in such single corporation without further act or deed; and the title to any real estate, or any interest therein, vested in any of such corporations shall not revert or be in any way impaired by reason of such merger or consolidation.

(e) Such surviving or new corporation shall thenceforth be responsible and liable for all the liabilities and obligations of each of the corporations so merged or consolidated; and any claim existing or action or proceeding pending by or against any of such corporations may be prosecuted as if such merger or consolidation had not taken place, or such surviving or new corporation may be substituted in its place. Neither the rights of creditors nor any liens upon the property of any such corporation shall be impaired by such merger or consolidation.

(f) In the case of a merger, the articles of incorporation of the surviving corporation shall be deemed to be amended to the extent, if any, that changes in its articles of incorporation are stated in the plan of merger; and, in the case of a consolidation, the statements set forth in the articles of consolidation and which are required or permitted to be set forth in the articles of incorporation of corporations organized under this Act shall be deemed to be the original articles of incorporation of the new corporation.

§ 77. **Merger, Consolidation or Exchange of Shares Between Domestic and Foreign Corporations**

One or more foreign corporations and one or more domestic corporations may be merged or consolidated in the following manner, if such merger or consolidation is permitted by the laws of the state under which each such foreign corporation is organized:

(a) Each domestic corporation shall comply with the provisions of this Act with respect to the merger or consolidation, as the case may be, of domestic corporations and each foreign corporation shall comply with the applicable provisions of the laws of the state under which it is organized.

(b) If the surviving or new corporation, as the case may be, is to be governed by the laws of any state other than this State, it shall comply with the provisions of this Act with respect to foreign corporations if it is to transact business in this State, and in every case it shall file with the Secretary of State of this State:

(1) An agreement that it may be served with process in this State in any proceeding for the enforcement of any obligation of any domestic corporation which is a party to such merger or consolidation and in any proceeding for the enforcement of the rights of a

dissenting shareholder of any such domestic corporation against the surviving or new corporation;

(2) An irrevocable appointment of the Secretary of State of this State as its agent to accept service of process in any such proceeding; and

(3) An agreement that it will promptly pay to the dissenting shareholders of any such domestic corporation the amount, if any, to which they shall be entitled under the provisions of this Act with respect to the rights of dissenting shareholders.

The effect of such merger or consolidation shall be the same as in the case of the merger or consolidation of domestic corporations, if the surviving or new corporation is to be governed by the laws of this State. If the surviving or new corporation is to be governed by the laws of any state other than this State, the effect of such merger or consolidation shall be the same as in the case of the merger or consolidation of domestic corporations except insofar as the laws of such other state provide otherwise.

At any time prior to the filing of the articles of merger or consolidation, the merger or consolidation may be abandoned pursuant to provisions therefor, if any, set forth in the plan of merger or consolidation.

§ 78. **Sale of Assets in Regular Course of Business and Mortgage or Pledge of Assets**

The sale, lease, exchange, or other disposition of all, or substantially all, the property and assets of a corporation in the usual and regular course of its business and the mortgage or pledge of any or all property and assets of a corporation whether or not in the usual and regular course of business may be made upon such terms and conditions and for such consideration, which may consist in whole or in part of cash or other property, including shares, obligations or other securities of any other corporation, domestic or foreign, as shall be authorized by its board of directors; and in any such case no authorization or consent of the shareholders shall be required.

§ 79. **Sale of Assets Other Than in Regular Course of Business**

A sale, lease, exchange, or other disposition of all, or substantially all, the property and assets, with or without the good will, of a corporation, if not in the usual and regular course of its business, may be made upon such terms and conditions and for such consideration, which may consist in whole or in part of cash or other property, including shares, obligations or other securities of any other corporation, domestic or foreign, as may be authorized in the following manner:

(a) The board of directors shall adopt a resolution recommending such sale, lease, exchange, or other disposition and directing the submission thereof to a vote at a meeting of shareholders, which may be either an annual or a special meeting.

(b) Written notice shall be given to each shareholder of record, whether or not entitled to vote at such meeting, not less than twenty days before such meeting, in the manner provided in this Act for the giving of notice of meetings of shareholders, and, whether the meeting be an annual or a special meeting, shall state that the purpose, or one of the purposes is to consider the proposed sale, lease, exchange, or other disposition.

(c) At such meeting the shareholders may authorize such sale, lease, exchange, or other disposition and may fix, or may authorize the board of directors to fix, any or all of the terms and conditions thereof and the consideration to be received by the corporation therefor. Such authorization shall require the affirmative vote of the holders of a majority of the shares of the corporation entitled to vote thereon, unless any class of shares is entitled to vote thereon as a class, in which event such authorization shall require the affirmative vote of the holders of a majority of the shares of each class of shares entitled to vote as a class thereon and of the total shares entitled to vote thereon.

(d) After such authorization by a vote of shareholders, the board of directors nevertheless, in its discretion, may abandon such sale, lease, exchange, or other disposition of assets, subject to the rights of third parties under any contracts relating thereto, without further action or approval by shareholders.

§ 80. Right of Shareholders to Dissent and Obtain Payment for Shares

(a) Any shareholder of a corporation shall have the right to dissent from, and to obtain payment for his shares in the event of, any of the following corporate actions:

(1) Any plan of merger or consolidation to which the corporation is a party, except as provided in subsection (c);

(2) Any sale or exchange of all or substantially all of the property and assets of the corporation not made in the usual or regular course of its business, including a sale in dissolution, but not including a sale pursuant to an order of a court having jurisdiction in the premises or a sale for cash on terms requiring that all or substantially all of the net proceeds of sale be distributed to the shareholders in accordance with their respective interests within one year after the date of sale;

(3) Any plan of exchange to which the corporation is a party as the corporation the shares of which are to be acquired;

(4) Any amendment of the articles of incorporation which materially and adversely affects the rights appurtenant to the shares of the dissenting shareholder in that it:

(i) alters or abolishes a preferential right of such shares;

(ii) creates, alters or abolishes a right in respect of the redemption of such shares, including a provision respecting a sinking fund for the redemption or repurchase of such shares;

(iii) alters or abolishes a preemptive right of the holder of such shares to acquire shares or other securities;

(iv) excludes or limits the right of the holder of such shares to vote on any matter, or to cumulate his votes, except as such right may be limited by dilution through the issuance of shares or other securities with similar voting rights; or

(5) Any other corporate action taken pursuant to a shareholder vote with respect to which the articles of incorporation, the bylaws, or a resolution of the board of directors directs that dissenting shareholders shall have a right to obtain payment for their shares.

(b) (1) A record holder of shares may assert dissenters' rights as to less than all of the shares registered in his name only if he dissents with respect to all the shares beneficially owned by any one person, and discloses the name and address of the person or persons on whose behalf he dissents. In that event, his rights shall be determined as if the shares as to which he has dissented and his other shares were registered in the names of different shareholders.

(2) A beneficial owner of shares who is not the record holder may assert dissenters' rights with respect to shares held on his behalf, and shall be treated as a dissenting shareholder under the terms of this section and section 31 if he submits to the corporation at the time of or before the assertion of these rights a written consent of the record holder.

(c) The right to obtain payment under this section shall not apply to the shareholders of the surviving corporation in a merger if a vote of the shareholders of such corporation is not necessary to authorize such merger.

(d) A shareholder of a corporation who has a right under this section to obtain payment for his shares shall have no right at law or in equity to attack the validity of the corporate action that gives rise to his right to obtain payment, nor to have the action set aside or rescinded, except when the corporate action is unlawful or fraudulent with regard to the complaining shareholder or to the corporation.

§ 81. **Procedures for Protection of Dissenters' Rights**

(a) As used in this section:

(1) "Dissenter" means a shareholder or beneficial owner who is entitled to and does assert dissenters' rights under section 80, and who has performed every act required up to the time involved for the assertion of such rights.

(2) "Corporation" means the issuer of the shares held by the dissenter before the corporate action, or the successor by merger or consolidation of that issuer.

(3) "Fair value" of shares means their value immediately before the effectuation of the corporate action to which the dissenter objects, excluding any appreciation or depreciation in anticipation of such corporate action unless such exclusion would be inequitable.

(4) "Interest" means interest from the effective date of the corporate action until the date of payment, at the average rate currently paid by the corporation on its principal bank loans, or, if none, at such rate as is fair and equitable under all the circumstances.

(b) If a proposed corporate action which would give rise to dissenters' rights under section 80(a) is submitted to a vote at a meeting of shareholders, the notice of meeting shall notify all shareholders that they have or may have a right to dissent and obtain payment for their shares by complying with the terms of this section, and shall be accompanied by a copy of sections 80 and 81 of this Act.

(c) If the proposed corporate action is submitted to a vote at a meeting of shareholders, any shareholder who wishes to dissent and obtain payment for his shares must file with the corporation, prior to the vote, a written notice of intention to demand that he be paid fair compensation for his shares if the proposed action is effectuated, and shall refrain from voting his shares in approval of such action. A shareholder who fails in either respect shall acquire no right to payment for his shares under this section or section 80.

(d) If the proposed corporate action is approved by the required vote at a meeting of shareholders, the corporation shall mail a further notice to all shareholders who gave due notice of intention to demand payment and who refrained from voting in favor of the proposed action. If the proposed corporate action is to be taken without a vote of shareholders, the corporation shall send to all shareholders who are entitled to dissent and demand payment for their shares a notice of the adoption of the plan of corporate action. The notice shall (1) state where and when a demand for payment must be sent and certificates of certificated shares must be deposited in order to obtain payment, (2) inform holders of uncertificated shares to what extent transfer of shares will be restricted from the time that demand for payment is received, (3) supply a form for demanding payment which includes a request for certification of the date on which the shareholder, or the person on whose behalf the shareholder dissents, acquired beneficial ownership of the shares, and (4) be accompanied by a copy of sections 80 and 81 of this Act. The time set for the demand and deposit shall be not less than 30 days from the mailing of the notice.

(e) A shareholder who fails to demand payment, or fails (in the case of certificated shares) to deposit certificates, as required by a notice pursuant to subsection (d) shall have no right under this section or section 80 to receive payment for his shares. If the shares are not represented by certificates, the corporation may restrict their transfer from the time of receipt of demand for payment until effectuation of the proposed corporate action, or the release of restrictions under the terms of subsection (f). The dissenter shall retain all other rights of a shareholder until these rights are modified by effectuation of the proposed corporate action.

(f) (1) Within 60 days after the date set for demanding payment and depositing certificates, if the corporation has not effectuated the proposed corporate action and remitted payment for shares pursuant to paragraph (3), it shall return any certificates that have been deposited, and release uncertificated shares from any transfer restrictions imposed by reason of the demand for payment.

(2) When uncertificated shares have been released from transfer restrictions, and deposited certificates have been returned, the corporation may at any later time send a new notice conforming to the requirements of subsection (d), with like effect.

(3) Immediately upon effectuation of the proposed corporate action, or upon receipt of demand for payment if the corporate action has already been effectuated, the corporation shall remit to dissenters who have made demand and (if their shares are certificated) have deposited their certificates the amount which the corporation estimates to be the fair value of the shares, with interest if any has accrued. The remittance shall be accompanied by:

(i) the corporation's closing balance sheet and statement of income for a fiscal year ending not more than 16 months before the date of remittance, together with the latest available interim financial statements;

(ii) a statement of the corporation's estimate of fair value of the shares; and

(iii) a notice of the dissenter's right to demand supplemental payment, accompanied by a copy of sections 80 and 81 of this Act.

(g) (1) If the corporation fails to remit as required by subsection (f), or if the dissenter believes that the amount remitted is less than the fair value of his shares, or that the interest is not correctly determined, he may send the corporation his own estimate of the value of the shares or of the interest, and demand payment of the deficiency.

(2) If the dissenter does not file such an estimate within 30 days after the corporation's mailing of its remittance, he shall be entitled to no more than the amount remitted.

(h) (1) Within 60 days after receiving a demand for payment pursuant to subsection (g), if any such demands for payment remain unsettled, the corporation shall file in an appropriate court a petition requesting that the fair value of the shares and interest thereon be determined by the court.

(2) An appropriate court shall be a court of competent jurisdiction in the county of this state where the registered office of the corporation is located. If, in the case of a merger or consolidation or exchange of shares, the corporation is a foreign corporation without a registered office in this state, the petition shall be filed in the county where the registered office of the domestic corporation was last located.

(3) All dissenters, wherever residing, whose demands have not been settled shall be made parties to the proceeding as in an action against their shares. A copy of the petition shall be served on each such dissenter; if a dissenter is a nonresident, the copy may be served on him by registered or certified mail or by publication as provided by law.

(4) The jurisdiction of the court shall be plenary and exclusive. The court may appoint one or more persons as appraisers to receive evidence and recommend a decision on the question of fair value. The appraisers shall have such power and authority as shall be specified in the order of their appointment or in any amendment thereof. The dissenters shall be entitled to discovery in the same manner as parties in other civil suits.

(5) All dissenters who are made parties shall be entitled to judgment for the amount by which the fair value of their shares is found to exceed the amount previously remitted, with interest.

(6) If the corporation fails to file a petition as provided in paragraph (1) of this subsection, each dissenter who made a demand and who has not already settled his claim against the corporation shall be paid by the corporation the amount demanded by him, with interest, and may sue therefor in an appropriate court.

(i) (1) The costs and expenses of any proceeding under subsection (h), including the reasonable compensation and expenses of appraisers appointed by the court, shall be determined by the court and assessed against the corporation, except that any part of the costs and expenses may be apportioned and assessed as the court may deem equitable against all or some of the dissenters who are parties and whose action in demanding supplemental payment the court finds to be arbitrary, vexatious, or not in good faith.

(2) Fees and expenses of counsel and of experts for the respective parties may be assessed as the court may deem equitable against the corporation and in favor of any or all dissenters if the corporation failed to comply substantially with the requirements of this section, and may be assessed against either the corporation or a dissenter, in favor of any other party, if the court finds that the party against whom the fees and expenses are assessed acted arbitrarily, vexatiously, or not in good faith in respect to the rights provided by this Section and Section 80.

(3) If the court finds that the services of counsel for any dissenter were of substantial benefit to other dissenters similarly situated, and should not be assessed against the corporation, it may award to these counsel reasonable fees to be paid out of the amounts awarded to the dissenters who were benefitted.

(j) (1) Notwithstanding the foregoing provisions of this section, the corporation may elect to withhold the remittance required by subsection (f) from any dissenter with respect to shares of which the dissenter (or the person on whose behalf the dissenter acts) was not the beneficial owner on the date of the first announcement to news media or to shareholders of the terms of the proposed corporate action. With respect to such shares, the corporation shall, upon effectuating the corporate action, state to each dissenter its estimate of the fair value of the shares, state the rate of interest to be used (explaining the basis thereof), and offer to pay the resulting amounts on receiving the dissenter's agreement to accept them in full satisfaction.

(2) If the dissenter believes that the amount offered is less than the fair value of the shares and interest determined according to this section, he may within 30 days after the date of mailing of the corporation's offer, mail the corporation his own estimate of fair value and interest, and demand their payment. If the dissenter fails to do so, he shall be entitled to no more than the corporation's offer.

(3) If the dissenter makes a demand as provided in paragraph (2), the provisions of subsections (h) and (i) shall apply to further proceedings on the dissenter's demand.

§ 82. Voluntary Dissolution by Incorporators

A corporation which has not commenced business and which has not issued any shares, may be voluntarily dissolved by its incorporators at any time in the following manner:

(a) Articles of dissolution shall be executed in duplicate by a majority of the incorporators, and verified by them, and shall set forth:

(1) The name of the corporation.

(2) The date of issuance of its certificate of incorporation.

(3) That none of its shares has been issued.

(4) That the corporation has not commenced business.

(5) That the amount, if any, actually paid in on subscriptions for its shares, less any part thereof disbursed for necessary expenses, has been returned to those entitled thereto.

(6) That no debts of the corporation remain unpaid.

(7) That a majority of the incorporators elect that the corporation be dissolved.

(b) Duplicate originals of the articles of dissolution shall be delivered to the Secretary of State. If the Secretary of State finds that the articles of dissolution conform to law, he shall, when all fees and franchise taxes have been paid as in this Act prescribed:

(1) Endorse on each of such duplicate originals the word "Filed," and the month, day and year of the filing thereof.

(2) File one of such duplicate originals in his office.

(3) Issue a certificate of dissolution to which he shall affix the other duplicate original.

The certificate of dissolution, together with the duplicate original of the articles of dissolution affixed thereto by the Secretary of State, shall be returned to the incorporators or their representative. Upon the issuance of such certificate of dissolution by the Secretary of State, the existence of the corporation shall cease.

§ 83. Voluntary Dissolution by Consent of Shareholders

A corporation may be voluntarily dissolved by the written consent of all of its shareholders.

Upon the execution of such written consent, a statement of intent to dissolve shall be executed in duplicate by the corporation by its president or a vice president and by its secretary or an assistant secretary, and verified by one of the officers signing such statement, which statement shall set forth:

(a) The name of the corporation.

(b) The names and respective addresses of its officers.

(c) The names and respective addresses of its directors.

(d) A copy of the written consent signed by all shareholders of the corporation.

(e) A statement that such written consent has been signed by all shareholders of the corporation or signed in their names by their attorneys thereunto duly authorized.

§ 84. Voluntary Dissolution by Act of Corporation

A corporation may be dissolved by the act of the corporation, when authorized in the following manner:

(a) The board of directors shall adopt a resolution recommending that the corporation be dissolved, and directing that the question of such dissolution be submitted to a vote at a meeting of shareholders, which may be either an annual or a special meeting.

(b) Written notice shall be given to each shareholder of record entitled to vote at such meeting within the time and in the manner provided in this Act for the giving of notice of meetings of shareholders, and, whether the meeting be an annual or special meeting, shall state that the purpose, or one of the purposes, of such meeting is to consider the advisability of dissolving the corporation.

(c) At such meeting a vote of shareholders entitled to vote thereat shall be taken on a resolution to dissolve the corporation. Such resolution shall be adopted upon receiving the affirmative vote of the holders of a majority of the shares of the corporation entitled to vote thereon, unless any class of shares is entitled to vote thereon as a class, in which event the resolution shall be adopted upon receiving the affirmative vote of the holders of a majority of the shares of each class of shares entitled to vote thereon as a class and of the total shares entitled to vote thereon.

(d) Upon the adoption of such resolution, a statement of intent to dissolve shall be executed in duplicate by the corporation by its president or a vice president and by its secretary or an assistant secretary, and verified by one of the officers signing such statement, which statement shall set forth:

(1) The name of the corporation.

(2) The names and respective addresses of its officers.

(3) The names and respective addresses of its directors.

(4) A copy of the resolution adopted by the shareholders authorizing the dissolution of the corporation.

(5) The number of shares outstanding, and, if the shares of any class are entitled to vote as a class, the designation and number of outstanding shares of each such class.

(6) The number of shares voted for and against the resolution, respectively, and, if the shares of any class are entitled to vote as a class, the number of shares of each such class voted for and against the resolution, respectively.

§ 85. Filing of Statement of Intent to Dissolve

Duplicate originals of the statement of intent to dissolve, whether by consent of shareholders or by act of the corporation, shall be delivered to the Secretary of State. If the Secretary of State finds that such statement conforms to law, he shall, when all fees and franchise taxes have been paid as in this Act prescribed:

(a) Endorse on each of such duplicate originals the word "Filed," and the month, day and year of the filing thereof.

(b) File one of such duplicate originals in his office.

(c) Return the other duplicate original to the corporation or its representative.

§ 86. Effect of Statement of Intent to Dissolve

Upon the filing by the Secretary of State of a statement of intent to dissolve, whether by consent of shareholders or by act of the corporation, the corporation shall cease to carry on its business, except insofar as may be necessary for the winding up thereof, but its corporate existence shall continue until a certificate of dissolution has been issued by the Secretary of State or until a decree dissolving the corporation has been entered by a court of competent jurisdiction as in this Act provided.

§ 87. Procedure after Filing of Statement of Intent to Dissolve

After the filing by the Secretary of State of a statement of intent to dissolve:

(a) The corporation shall immediately cause notice thereof to be mailed to each known creditor of the corporation.

(b) The corporation shall proceed to collect its assets, convey and dispose of such of its properties as are not to be distributed in kind to its shareholders, pay, satisfy and discharge its liabilities and obligations and do all other acts required to liquidate its business and affairs, and, after paying or adequately providing for the payment of all its obligations, distribute the remainder of its assets, either in cash or in kind, among its shareholders according to their respective rights and interests.

(c) The corporation, at any time during the liquidation of its business and affairs, may make application to a court of competent jurisdiction within the state and judicial subdivision in which the registered office or principal place of business of the corporation is situated, to have the liquidation continued under the supervision of the court as provided in this Act.

§ 88. Revocation of Voluntary Dissolution Proceedings by Consent of Shareholders

(Omitted)

§ 89. Revocation of Voluntary Dissolution Proceedings by Act of Corporation

(Omitted)

§ 90. Filing of Statement of Revocation of Voluntary Dissolution Proceedings

(Omitted)

§ 91. Effect of Statement of Revocation of Voluntary Dissolution Proceedings

(Omitted)

§ 92. Articles of Dissolution

If voluntary dissolution proceedings have not been revoked, then when all debts, liabilities and obligations of the corporation have been paid and discharged, or adequate provision has been made therefor, and all of the remaining property and assets of the corporation have been distributed to its shareholders, articles of dissolution shall be executed in duplicate by the corporation by its president or a vice president and by its secretary or an assistant secretary, and verified by one of the officers signing such statement, which statement shall set forth:

(a) The name of the corporation.

(b) That the Secretary of State has theretofore filed a statement of intent to dissolve the corporation, and the date on which such statement was filed.

(c) That all debts, obligations and liabilities of the corporation have been paid and discharged or that adequate provision has been made therefor.

(d) That all the remaining property and assets of the corporation have been distributed among its shareholders in accordance with their respective rights and interests.

(e) That there are no suits pending against the corporation in any court, or that adequate provision has been made for the satisfaction of any judgment, order or decree which may be entered against it in any pending suit.

§ 93. Filing of Articles of Dissolution

Duplicate originals of such articles of dissolution shall be delivered to the Secretary of State. If the Secretary of State finds that such articles of dissolution conform to law, he shall, when all fees and franchise taxes have been paid as in this Act prescribed:

(a) Endorse on each of such duplicate originals the word "Filed," and the month, day and year of the filing thereof.

(b) File one of such duplicate originals in his office.

(c) Issue a certificate of dissolution to which he shall affix the other duplicate original.

The certificate of dissolution, together with the duplicate original of the articles of dissolution affixed thereto by the Secretary of State, shall be returned to the representative of the dissolved corporation. Upon the issuance of such certificate of dissolution the existence of the corporation shall cease, except for the purpose of suits, other proceedings and appropriate corporate action by shareholders, directors and officers as provided in this Act.

§ 94. Involuntary Dissolution

A corporation may be dissolved involuntarily by a decree of the . . . . court in an action filed by the Attorney General when it is established that:

(a) The corporation has failed to file its annual report within the time required by this Act, or has failed to pay its franchise tax on or before the first day of August of the year in which such franchise tax becomes due and payable; or

(b) The corporation procured its articles of incorporation through fraud; or

(c) The corporation has continued to exceed or abuse the authority conferred upon it by law; or

(d) The corporation has failed for thirty days to appoint and maintain a registered agent in this State; or

(e) The corporation has failed for thirty days after change of its registered office or registered agent to file in the office of the Secretary of State a statement of such change.

§ 95. Notification to Attorney General

The Secretary of State, on or before the last day of December of each year, shall certify to the Attorney General the names of all corporations which have failed to file their annual reports or to pay franchise taxes in accordance with the provisions of this Act, together with the facts pertinent thereto. He shall also certify, from time to time, the names of all corporations which have given other cause for dissolution as provided in this Act, together with the facts pertinent thereto. Whenever the Secretary of State shall certify the name of a corporation to the Attorney General as having given any cause for dissolution, the Secretary of State shall concurrently mail to the corporation at its registered office a notice that such certification has been made. Upon the receipt of such certification, the Attorney General shall file an action in the name of the State against such corporation for its dissolution. Every such certificate from the Secretary of State to the Attorney General pertaining to the failure of a corporation to file an annual report or pay

a franchise tax shall be taken and received in all courts as prima facie evidence of the facts therein stated. If, before action is filed, the corporation shall file its annual report or pay its franchise tax, together with all penalties thereon, or shall appoint or maintain a registered agent as provided in this Act, or shall file with the Secretary of State the required statement of change of registered office or registered agent, such fact shall be forthwith certified by the Secretary of State to the Attorney General and he shall not file an action against such corporation for such cause. If, after action is filed, the corporation shall file its annual report or pay its franchise tax, together with all penalties thereon, or shall appoint or maintain a registered agent as provided in this Act, or shall file with the Secretary of State the required statement of change of registered office or registered agent, and shall pay the costs of such action, the action for such cause shall abate.

§ 96. Venue and Process

Every action for the involuntary dissolution of a corporation shall be commenced by the Attorney General either in the . . . . court of the county in which the registered office of the corporation is situated, or in the . . . . court of . . . . county. Summons shall issue and be served as in other civil actions. If process is returned not found, the Attorney General shall cause publication to be made as in other civil cases in some newspaper published in the county where the registered office of the corporation is situated, containing a notice of the pendency of such action, the title of the court, the title of the action, and the date on or after which default may be entered. The Attorney General may include in one notice the names of any number of corporations against which actions are then pending in the same court. The Attorney General shall cause a copy of such notice to be mailed to the corporation at its registered office within ten days after the first publication thereof. The certificate of the Attorney General of the mailing of such notice shall be prima facie evidence thereof. Such notice shall be published at least once each week for two successive weeks, and the first publication thereof may begin at any time after the summons has been returned. Unless a corporation shall have been served with summons, no default shall be taken against it earlier than thirty days after the first publication of such notice.

§ 97. Jurisdiction of Court to Liquidate Assets and Business of Corporation

The . . . . courts shall have full power to liquidate the assets and business of a corporation:

(a) In an action by a shareholder when it is established:

(1) That the directors are deadlocked in the management of the corporate affairs and the shareholders are unable to break the deadlock, and that irreparable injury to the corporation is being suffered or is threatened by reason thereof; or

(2) That the acts of the directors or those in control of the corporation are illegal, oppressive or fraudulent; or

(3) That the shareholders are deadlocked in voting power, and have failed, for a period which includes at least two consecutive annual meeting dates, to elect successors to directors whose terms have expired or would have expired upon the election of their successors; or

(4) That the corporate assets are being misapplied or wasted.

(b) In an action by a creditor:

(1) When the claim of the creditor has been reduced to judgment and an execution thereon returned unsatisfied and it is established that the corporation is insolvent; or

(2) When the corporation has admitted in writing that the claim of the creditor is due and owing and it is established that the corporation is insolvent.

(c) Upon application by a corporation which has filed a statement of intent to dissolve, as provided in this Act, to have its liquidation continued under the supervision of the court.

(d) When an action has been filed by the Attorney General to dissolve a corporation and it is established that liquidation of its business and affairs should precede the entry of a decree of dissolution.

Proceedings under clause (a), (b) or (c) of this section shall be brought in the county in which the registered office or the principal office of the corporation is situated.

It shall not be necessary to make shareholders parties to any such action or proceeding unless relief is sought against them personally.

§ 98. **Procedure in Liquidation of Corporation by Court**

In proceedings to liquidate the assets and business of a corporation the court shall have power to issue injunctions, to appoint a receiver or receivers pendente lite, with such powers and duties as the court, from time to time, may direct, and to take such other proceedings as may be requisite to preserve the corporate assets wherever situated, and carry on the business of the corporation until a full hearing can be had.

After a hearing had upon such notice as the court may direct to be given to all parties to the proceedings and to any other parties in interest designated by the court, the court may appoint a liquidating receiver or receivers with authority to collect the assets of the corporation, including all amounts owing to the corporation by subscribers on account of any unpaid portion of the consideration for the issuance of shares. Such liquidating receiver or receivers shall have authority, subject to the order of the court, to sell, convey and dispose of all or any part of the assets of the corporation wherever situated, either at public or private sale. The assets of the corporation or the proceeds resulting from a sale, conveyance or other disposition thereof shall be applied to the expenses of such liquidation and to the payment of the liabilities and obligations of the corporation, and any remaining assets or proceeds shall be distributed among its shareholders according to their respective rights and interests. The order appointing such liquidating receiver or receivers shall state their powers and duties. Such powers and duties may be increased or diminished at any time during the proceedings.

The court shall have power to allow from time to time as expenses of the liquidation compensation to the receiver or receivers and to attorneys in the proceeding, and to direct the payment thereof out of the assets of the corporation or the proceeds of any sale or disposition of such assets.

A receiver of a corporation appointed under the provisions of this section shall have authority to sue and defend in all courts in his own name as receiver of such corporation. The court appointing such receiver shall have exclusive jurisdiction of the corporation and its property, wherever situated.

§ 99. **Qualifications of Receivers**

A receiver shall in all cases be a natural person or a corporation authorized to act as receiver, which corporation may be a domestic corporation or a foreign corporation authorized to transact business in this State, and shall in all cases give such bond as the court may direct with such sureties as the court may require.

§ 100. **Filing of Claims in Liquidation Proceedings**

In proceedings to liquidate the assets and business of a corporation the court may require all creditors of the corporation to file with the clerk of the court or with the receiver, in such form as the court may prescribe, proofs under oath of their respective claims. If the court requires the filing of claims it shall fix a date, which shall be not less than four months from the date of the order, as the last day for the filing of claims, and shall prescribe the notice that shall be given to creditors and claimants of the date so fixed. Prior to the date so fixed, the court may extend the time for the filing of claims. Creditors and claimants failing to file proofs of claim on or before the date so fixed may be barred, by order of court, from participating in the distribution of the assets of the corporation.

§ 101. Discontinuance of Liquidation Proceedings

The liquidation of the assets and business of a corporation may be discontinued at any time during the liquidation proceedings when it is established that cause for liquidation no longer exists. In such event the court shall dismiss the proceedings and direct the receiver to redeliver to the corporation all its remaining property and assets.

§ 102. Decree of Involuntary Dissolution

In proceedings to liquidate the assets and business of a corporation, when the costs and expenses of such proceedings and all debts, obligations and liabilities of the corporation shall have been paid and discharged and all of its remaining property and assets distributed to its shareholders, or in case its property and assets are not sufficient to satisfy and discharge such costs, expenses, debts and obligations, all the property and assets have been applied so far as they will go to their payment, the court shall enter a decree dissolving the corporation, whereupon the existence of the corporation shall cease.

§ 103. Filing of Decree of Dissolution

In case the court shall enter a decree dissolving a corporation, it shall be the duty of the clerk of such court to cause a certified copy of the decree to be filed with the Secretary of State. No fee shall be charged by the Secretary of State for the filing thereof.

§ 104. Deposit with State Treasurer of Amount Due Certain Shareholders

Upon the voluntary or involuntary dissolution of a corporation, the portion of the assets distributable to a creditor or shareholder who is unknown or cannot be found, or who is under disability and there is no person legally competent to receive such distributive portion, shall be reduced to cash and deposited with the State Treasurer and shall be paid over to such creditor or shareholder or to his legal representative upon proof satisfactory to the State Treasurer of his right thereto.

§ 105. Survival of Remedy after Dissolution

The dissolution of a corporation either (1) by the issuance of a certificate of dissolution by the Secretary of State, or (2) by a decree of court when the court has not liquidated the assets and business of the corporation as provided in this Act, or (3) by expiration of its period of duration, shall not take away or impair any remedy available to or against such corporation, its directors, officers, or shareholders, for any right or claim existing, or any liability incurred, prior to such dissolution if action or other proceeding thereon is commenced within two years after the date of such dissolution. Any such action or proceeding by or against the corporation may be prosecuted or defended by the corporation in its corporate name. The shareholders, directors and officers shall have power to take such corporate or other action as shall be appropriate to protect such remedy, right or claim. If such corporation was dissolved by the expiration of its period of duration, such corporation may amend its articles of incorporation at any time during such period of two years so as to extend its period of duration.

§ 106. Admission of Foreign Corporation

No foreign corporation shall have the right to transact business in this State until it shall have procured a certificate of authority so to do from the Secretary of State. No foreign corporation shall be entitled to procure a certificate of authority under this Act to transact in this State any business which a corporation organized under this Act is not permitted to transact. A foreign corporation shall not be denied a certificate of authority by reason of the fact that the laws of the state or country under which such corporation is organized governing its organization and internal affairs differ from the laws of this State, and nothing in this Act contained shall be construed to authorize this State to regulate the organization or the internal affairs of such corporation.

Without excluding other activities which may not constitute transacting business in this State, a foreign corporation shall not be considered to be transacting business in this State, for the purposes of this Act, by reason of carrying on in this State any one or more of the following activities:

(a) Maintaining or defending any action or suit or any administrative or arbitration proceeding, or effecting the settlement thereof or the settlement of claims or disputes.

(b) Holding meetings of its directors or shareholders or carrying on other activities concerning its internal affairs.

(c) Maintaining bank accounts.

(d) Maintaining offices or agencies for the transfer, exchange and registration of its securities, or appointing and maintaining trustees or depositaries with relation to its securities.

(e) Effecting sales through independent contractors.

(f) Soliciting or procuring orders, whether by mail or through employees or agents or otherwise, where such orders require acceptance without this State before becoming binding contracts.

(g) Creating as borrower or lender, or acquiring, indebtedness or mortgages or other security interests in real or personal property.

(h) Securing or collecting debts or enforcing any rights in property securing the same.

(i) Transacting any business in interstate commerce.

(j) Conducting an isolated transaction completed within a period of thirty days and not in the course of a number of repeated transactions of like nature.

§ 107. Powers of Foreign Corporation

A foreign corporation which shall have received a certificate of authority under this Act shall, until a certificate of revocation or of withdrawal shall have been issued as provided in this Act, enjoy the same, but no greater, rights and privileges as a domestic corporation organized for the purposes set forth in the application pursuant to which such certificate of authority is issued; and, except as in this Act otherwise provided, shall be subject to the same duties, restrictions, penalties and liabilities now or hereafter imposed upon a domestic corporation of like character.

§ 108. Corporate Name of Foreign Corporation

No certificate of authority shall be issued to a foreign corporation unless the corporate name of such corporation:

(a) Shall contain the word "corporation," "company," "incorporated," or "limited," or shall contain an abbreviation of one of such words, or such corporation shall, for use in this State, add at the end of its name one of such words or an abbreviation thereof.

(b) Shall not contain any word or phrase which indicates or implies that it is organized for any purpose other than one or more of the purposes contained in its articles of incorporation or that it is authorized or empowered to conduct the business of banking or insurance.

(c) Shall not be the same as, or deceptively similar to, the name of any domestic corporation existing under the laws of this State or any foreign corporation authorized to transact business in this State, or a name the exclusive right to which is, at the time, reserved in the manner provided in this Act, or the name of a corporation which has in effect a registration of its name as provided in this Act except that this provision shall not apply if the foreign corporation applying for a certificate of authority files with the Secretary of State any one of the following:

(1) a resolution of its board of directors adopting a fictitious name for use in transacting business in this State which fictitious name is not deceptively similar to the name of any domestic corporation or of any foreign corporation authorized to transact business in this State or to any name reserved or registered as provided in this Act, or

(2) the written consent of such other corporation or holder of a reserved or registered name to use the same or deceptively similar name and one or more words are added to make such name distinguishable from such other name, or

(3) a certified copy of a final decree of a court of competent jurisdiction establishing the prior right of such foreign corporation to the use of such name in this State.

§ 109. Change of Name by Foreign Corporation

(Omitted)

§ 110. Application for Certificate of Authority

A foreign corporation, in order to procure a certificate of authority to transact business in this State, shall make application therefor to the Secretary of State, which application shall set forth:

(a) The name of the corporation and the state or county under the laws of which it is incorporated.

(b) If the name of the corporation does not contain the word "corporation," "company," "incorporated," or "limited," or does not contain an abbreviation of one of such words, then the name of the corporation with the word or abbreviation which it elects to add thereto for use in this State.

(c) The date of incorporation and the period of duration of the corporation.

(d) The address of the principal office of the corporation in the state or country under the laws of which it is incorporated.

(e) The address of the proposed registered office of the corporation in this State, and the name of its proposed registered agent in this State at such address.

(f) The purpose or purposes of the corporation which it proposes to pursue in the transaction of business in this State.

(g) The names and respective addresses of the directors and officers of the corporation.

(h) A statement of the aggregate number of shares which the corporation has authority to issue, itemized by classes and series, if any, within a class.

(i) A statement of the aggregate number of issued shares, itemized by class and by series, if any, within each class.

(j) An estimate, expressed in dollars, of the value of all property to be owned by the corporation for the following year, wherever located, and an estimate of the value of the property of the corporation to be located within this State during such year, and an estimate, expressed in dollars of the gross amount of business which will be transacted by the corporation during such year, and an estimate of the gross amount thereof which will be transacted by the corporation at or from places of business in this State during such year.

(k) Such additional information as may be necessary or appropriate in order to enable the Secretary of State to determine whether such corporation is entitled to a certificate of authority to transact business in this State and to determine and assess the fees and franchise taxes payable as in this Act prescribed.

Such application shall be made on forms prescribed and furnished by the Secretary of State and shall be executed in duplicate by the corporation by its president or a vice president and by its secretary or an assistant secretary, and verified by one of the officers signing such application.

§ 111. Filing of Application for Certificate of Authority

(Omitted)

§ 112. Effect of Certificate of Authority

Upon the issuance of a certificate of authority by the Secretary of State, the corporation shall be authorized to transact business in this State for those purposes set forth in its application, subject, however, to the right of this State to suspend or to revoke such authority as provided in this Act.

§ 113. Registered Office and Registered Agent of Foreign Corporation

Each foreign corporation authorized to transact business in this State shall have and continuously maintain in this State:

(a) A registered office which may be, but need not be, the same as its place of business in this State.

(b) A registered agent, which agent may be either an individual resident in this State whose business office is identical with such registered office, or a domestic corporation, or a foreign corporation authorized to transact business in this State, having a business office identical with such registered office.

§ 114. Change of Registered Office or Registered Agent of Foreign Corporation

(Omitted)

§ 115. Service of Process on Foreign Corporation

The registered agent so appointed by a foreign corporation authorized to transact business in this State shall be an agent of such corporation upon whom any process, notice or demand required or permitted by law to be served upon the corporation may be served.

Whenever a foreign corporation authorized to transact business in this State shall fail to appoint or maintain a registered agent in this State, or whenever any such registered agent cannot with reasonable diligence be found at the registered office, or whenever the certificate of authority of a foreign corporation shall be suspended or revoked, then the Secretary of State shall be an agent of such corporation upon whom any such process, notice, or demand may be served. Service on the Secretary of State of any such process, notice or demand shall be made by delivering to and leaving with him, or with any clerk having charge of the corporation department of his office, duplicate copies of such process, notice or demand. In the event any such process, notice or demand is served on the Secretary of State, he shall immediately cause one of such copies thereof to be forwarded by registered mail, addressed to the corporation at its principal office in the state or country under the laws of which it is incorporated. Any service so had on the Secretary of State shall be returnable in not less than thirty days.

The Secretary of State shall keep a record of all processes, notices and demands served upon him under this section, and shall record therein the time of such service and his action with reference thereto.

Nothing herein contained shall limit or affect the right to serve any process, notice or demand, required or permitted by law to be served upon a foreign corporation in any other manner now or hereafter permitted by law.

§ 116. Amendment to Articles of Incorporation of Foreign Corporation

(Omitted)

§ 117. Merger of Foreign Corporation Authorized to Transact Business in This State

(Omitted)

§ 118. Amended Certificate of Authority

(Omitted)

§ 119. Withdrawal of Foreign Corporation

(Omitted)

§ 120. Filing of Application for Withdrawal

(Omitted)

§ 121. Revocation of Certificate of Authority

(Omitted)

§ 122. Issuance of Certificate of Revocation

(Omitted)

§ 123. Application to Corporations Heretofore Authorized to Transact Business in this State

(Omitted)

§ 124. Transacting Business Without Certificate of Authority

No foreign corporation transacting business in this State without a certificate of authority shall be permitted to maintain any action, suit or proceeding in any court of this State, until such corporation shall have obtained a certificate of authority. Nor shall any action, suit or proceeding be maintained in any court of this State by any successor or assignee of such corporation on any right, claim or demand arising out of the transaction of business by such corporation in this State, until a certificate of authority shall have been obtained by such corporation or by a corporation which has acquired all or substantially all of its assets.

The failure of a foreign corporation to obtain a certificate of authority to transact business in this State shall not impair the validity of any contract or act of such corporation, and shall not prevent such corporation from defending any action, suit or proceeding in any court of this State.

A foreign corporation which transacts business in this State without a certificate of authority shall be liable to this State, for the years or parts thereof during which it transacted business in this State without a certificate of authority, in an amount equal to all fees and franchise taxes which would have been imposed by this Act upon such corporation had it duly applied for and received a certificate of authority to transact business in this State as required by this Act and thereafter filed all reports required by this Act, plus all penalties imposed by this Act for failure to pay such fees and franchise taxes. The Attorney General shall bring proceedings to recover all amounts due this State under the provisions of this Section.

§ 125. Annual Report of Domestic and Foreign Corporations

Each domestic corporation, and each foreign corporation authorized to transact business in this State, shall file, within the time prescribed by this Act, an annual report setting forth:

(a) The name of the corporation and the state or country under the laws of which it is incorporated.

(b) The address of the registered office of the corporation in this State, and the name of its registered agent in this State at such address, and, in case of a foreign corporation, the address of its principal office in the state or country under the laws of which it is incorporated.

(c) A brief statement of the character of the business in which the corporation is actually engaged in this State.

(d) The names and respective addresses of the directors and officers of the corporation.

(e) A statement of the aggregate number of shares which the corporation has authority to issue, itemized by class and series, if any, within each class.

(f) A statement of the aggregate number of issued shares, itemized by class and series, if any, within each class.

(g) A statement, expressed in dollars, of the value of all the property owned by the corporation, wherever located, and the value of the property of the corporation located within this State, and a statement, expressed in dollars, of the gross amount of business transacted by the corporation for the twelve months ended on the thirty-first day of December preceding the date herein provided for the filing of such report and the gross amount thereof transacted by the corporation at or from places of business in this State. If, on the thirty-first day of December preceding the time herein provided for the filing of such report, the corporation had not been in existence for a period of twelve months, or in the case of a foreign corporation had not been authorized to transact business in this State for a period of twelve months, the statement with respect to business transacted shall be furnished for the period between the date of incorporation or the date of its authorization to transact business in this State, as the case may be, and such thirty-first day of December.

If all the property of the corporation is located in this State and all of its business is transacted at or from places of business in this State, then the information required by this subparagraph need not be set forth in such report.

(h) Such additional information as may be necessary or appropriate in order to enable the Secretary of State to determine and assess the proper amount of franchise taxes payable by such corporation.

Such annual report shall be made on forms prescribed and furnished by the Secretary of State, and the information therein contained shall be given as of the date of the execution of the report, except as to the information required by subparagraphs (g) and (h) which shall be given as of the close of business on the thirty-first day of December next preceding the date herein provided for the filing of such report. It shall be executed by the corporation by its president, a vice president, secretary, an assistant secretary, or treasurer, and verified by the officer executing the report, or, if the corporation is in the hands of a receiver or trustee, it shall be executed on behalf of the corporation and verified by such receiver or trustee.

§ 126. Filing of Annual Report of Domestic and Foreign Corporations

(Omitted)

§ 127. Fees, Franchise Taxes and Charges to be Collected by Secretary of State

(Omitted)

§ 128. Fees for Filing Documents and Issuing Certificates

(Omitted)

§ 129. Miscellaneous Charges

(Omitted)

§ 130. License Fees Payable by Domestic Corporations

(Omitted)

§ 131. License Fees Payable by Foreign Corporations

(Omitted)

§ 132. Franchise Taxes Payable by Domestic Corporations

(Omitted)

§ 133. Franchise Taxes Payable by Foreign Corporations

(Omitted)

§ 134. Assessment and Collection of Annual Franchise Taxes

(Omitted)

§ 135. Penalties Imposed Upon Corporations

Each corporation, domestic or foreign, that fails or refuses to file its annual report for any year within the time prescribed by this Act shall be subject to a penalty of ten per cent of the amount of the franchise tax assessed against it for the period beginning July 1 of the year in which such report should have been filed. Such penalty shall be assessed by the Secretary of State at the time of the assessment of the franchise tax. If the amount of the franchise tax as originally assessed against such corporation be thereafter adjusted in accordance with the provisions of this Act, the amount of the penalty shall be

likewise adjusted to ten per cent of the amount of the adjusted franchise tax. The amount of the franchise tax and the amount of the penalty shall be separately stated in any notice to the corporation with respect thereto.

If the franchise tax assessed in accordance with the provisions of this Act shall not be paid on or before the thirty-first day of July, it shall be deemed to be delinquent, and there shall be added a penalty of one per cent for each month or part of month that the same is delinquent, commencing with the month of August.

Each corporation, domestic or foreign, that fails or refuses to answer truthfully and fully within the time prescribed by this Act interrogatories propounded by the Secretary of State in accordance with the provisions of this Act, shall be deemed to be guilty of a misdemeanor and upon conviction thereof may be fined in any amount not exceeding five hundred dollars.

§ 136. Penalties Imposed Upon Officers and Directors

Each officer and director of a corporation, domestic or foreign, who fails or refuses within the time prescribed by this Act to answer truthfully and fully interrogatories propounded to him by the Secretary of State in accordance with the provisions of this Act, or who signs any articles, statement, report, application or other document filed with the Secretary of State which is known to such officer or director to be false in any material respect, shall be deemed to be guilty of a misdemeanor, and upon conviction thereof may be fined in any amount not exceeding .... dollars.

§ 137. Interrogatories by Secretary of State

(Omitted)

§ 138. Information Disclosed by Interrogatories

(Omitted)

§ 139. Powers of Secretary of State

The Secretary of State shall have the power and authority reasonably necessary to enable him to administer this Act efficiently and to perform the duties therein imposed upon him.

§ 140. Appeal from Secretary of State

(Omitted)

§ 141. Certificates and Certified Copies to be Received in Evidence

(Omitted)

§ 142. Forms to be Furnished by Secretary of State

(Omitted)

§ 143. Greater Voting Requirements

Whenever, with respect to any action to be taken by the shareholders of a corporation, the articles of incorporation require the vote or concurrence of the holders of a greater proportion of the shares, or of any class or series thereof, than required by this Act with respect to such action, the provisions of the articles of incorporation shall control.

§ 144. Waiver of Notice

Whenever any notice is required to be given to any shareholder or director of a corporation under the provisions of this Act or under the provisions of the articles of incorporation or by-laws of the corporation, a waiver thereof in writing signed by the person or persons entitled to such notice, whether before or after the time stated therein, shall be equivalent to the giving of such notice.

§ 145. Action by Shareholders Without a Meeting

Any action required by this Act to be taken at a meeting of the shareholders of a corporation, or any action which may be taken at a meeting of the shareholders, may be taken without a meeting if a consent in writing, setting forth the action so taken, shall be signed by all of the shareholders entitled to vote with respect to the subject matter thereof.

Such consent shall have the same effect as a unanimous vote of shareholders, and may be stated as such in any articles or document filed with the Secretary of State under this Act.

§ 146. Unauthorized Assumption of Corporate Powers

All persons who assume to act as a corporation without authority so to do shall be jointly and severally liable for all debts and liabilities incurred or arising as a result thereof.

§ 147. Application to Existing Corporations

(Omitted)

§ 148. Application to Foreign and Interstate Commerce

(Omitted)

§ 149. Reservation of Power

The ....* shall at all times have power to prescribe such regulations, provisions and limitations as it may deem advisable, which regulations, provisions and limitations shall be binding upon any and all corporations subject to the provisions of this Act, and the ....* shall have power to amend, repeal or modify this Act at pleasure.

*Insert name of legislative body.

§ 150. Effect of Repeal of Prior Acts

(Omitted)

§ 151. Effect of Invalidity of Part of this Act

(Omitted)

§ 152. Exclusivity of Certain Provisions [Optional]

(Omitted)

§ 153. Repeal of Prior Acts

Close Corporations

In view of the increasing importance of close corporations, both for the small family business and for the larger undertakings conducted by some small number of other corporations, this liberalizing trend has now been followed by the 1969 Amendments to the Model Act. The first sentence of section 35, providing that the business of the corporation shall be managed by a board of directors, was supplemented by a new clause "except as may be otherwise provided in the articles of incorporation." This permits the shareholders to take over and exercise the functions of the directors by appropriate provision to that effect in the articles, or to allocate functions between the directors and shareholders in such manner as may be desired. Taken with other provisions of the Model Act, which are here enumerated for convenience, this rounds out the adaptability of the Model Act for all the needs of a close corporation:

(1) By section 4(*l*) the by-laws may make any provision for the regulation of the affairs of the corporation that is not inconsistent with the articles or the laws of the incorporating state.

*Insert name of legislative body.

(2) By section 15 shares may be divided into several classes and the articles may limit or deny the voting rights of or provide special voting rights for the shares of any class to the extent not inconsistent with the Model Act. The narrow limits of this exception are revealed by section 33 which provides that each outstanding share, regardless of class, shall be entitled to one vote on each matter submitted to a vote at a meeting of the shareholders "except as may be otherwise provided in the articles of incorporation," thus expressly authorizing more than one vote per share or less than one vote per share, either generally or in respect to particular matters.

(3) By section 16 item (F) the shares of any preferred or special class may be issued in series and there may be variations between different series in numerous respects, including specifically the matter of voting rights, if any.

(4) By section 32 the articles may reduce a quorum of shareholders to not less than one-third of the shares en-

titled to vote, or leave the quorum at the standard of a majority or, as confirmed by section 143, increase the number to any desired point.

(5) By section 34 agreements among shareholders regarding the voting of their shares are made valid and enforceable in accordance with their terms without limitation in time. These could relate to the election or compensation of directors or officers or the creation of various types of securities for new financing or the conduct of business of various kinds or dividend policy or mergers and consolidations or other transactions without limit.

(6) The flexibility permitted by the revision of section 35 in the distribution or reallocation of authority among directors and stockholders has already been mentioned.

(7) Under section 36 the number of directors may be fixed by the by-laws at one or such greater number as may best serve the interests of the shareholders and that number may be increased or decreased from time to time by amendment to, or in the manner provided in, the articles or the by-laws, subject to any limiting provision adopted pursuant to law, such as an agreed requirement for a unanimous vote by directors for any such change or a requirement that amendments to the by-laws be made by shareholder vote. Similarly, under section 53, the incorporation may be effected by a single incorporator or by more as may be desired.

(8) By section 37 directors may be classified. While this relates to directors classified in such manner that the term of office of a specified proportion terminates in each year, the Model Act does not forbid the election of separate directors by separate classes of stock.

(9) Section 40 permits the articles or the by-laws to require more than a majority of the directors to constitute a quorum for the transaction of business and also permits the articles or by-laws to require the act of a greater number than a majority of those present at a meeting where a quorum is present before any specified business may be transacted. Or a unanimous vote of all directors may be required. This may be utilized to confer a right of veto on any designated class in order to protect its special interests.

(10) By section 50 the authority and duties of the respective officers and agents of the corporation may be tailored and prescribed in the by-laws, or consistently with the by-laws, in such manner as the needs of the shareholders may indicate.

(11) By section 54 the articles may include any desired provision for the regulation of the internal affairs of the corporation, including, in particular, "any provision restricting the transfer of shares." This expressly validates agreements for prior offering of shares to the corpora-

tion or other shareholders. All such restrictions must, of course, be clearly shown on the stock certificate as required by the Uniform Commercial Code. A similarly broad provision for the contents of the by-laws is contained in section 27.

(12) By sections 60, 73 and 79, respectively, a class vote may be required for an amendment to the articles, for any merger or consolidation or for a sale of assets other than in the regular course of business.

(13) Section 143 permits the articles to require, for any particular action by the shareholders, the vote or concurrence of the holders of a greater proportion of the shares, or of any class or series thereof, than the Model Act itself requires.

(14) Section 44 permits action by directors without a meeting and section 145 permits the same for shareholders, while section 144 contains a broad provision on waiver of notice. Thus the formality of meetings may, where desired, be eliminated in whole or in part, except for the annual meeting required by section 28.

Under these provisions protection may be afforded for a great diversity of interests. By way of illustration, the shares may be divided into different classes with different voting rights and each class may be permitted to elect a different director. Or some classes may be permitted to vote on certain transactions, but not all. Even more drastically, some classes may be denied all voting rights whatever. Thus a family could provide for equal participation in the profits of the venture, but restrict the power of management to selected members. The advantages of having a known group of business associates may be safeguarded by restrictions on the transfer of shares. Most commonly this takes the form of a requirement for *pro rata* offering to the other shareholders before selling to an outsider. Or the other shareholders may be given an option, in the event of death or a proposed transfer, to buy the stock *pro rata*. The same option may be given to the corporation. The purchase price may be fixed by any agreed formula, such as adjusted book value or some multiple of recent earnings. Or stockholder agreements may be used to assure that, at least for a limited number of years, all shares will be voted for certain directors and officers, or in a certain way on other corporate matters. Cumulative voting may be provided for, by which each shareholder has a number of votes equal to the number of his shares multiplied by the number of directors to be elected, with the privilege of casting all of his votes for a single candidate, or dividing them as he may wish. This helps minorities obtain representation on the board of directors. Thus the holder of one-fourth of the shares voting, plus one share, is sure of electing one of three directors. The preemptive right is another important protection in the case of close corporations, since it assures each stockholder a right to maintain his proportionate interest. Still more definite protection is afforded by provisions in the articles that prohibit particular transactions except with the assent of a specified percentage of all outstanding shares or of each class of shares. Much the same protection can sometimes be obtained by requiring a specially large quorum for the election of directors, or a specially large vote, or even unanimous vote, by directors for the authorization of particular transactions. Quite the opposite situation exists if one of the participants is to be an inactive investor, for whom non-voting preferred stock, with its prior right to a return from earnings, may be sufficient. But even here he may require a veto power over major transactions, such as the issuance of debt, the issuance of additional preferred shares or mergers or consolidations. Or the preferred shareholders may be given as a class the right to elect one or more of the directors, particularly in the event that dividends should be in arrears.

These possibilities are listed merely as illustrations and not in any sense as exhausting the variations permissible under the Model Act.

DICTIONARY OF LEGAL TERMS

A

acceptance   *Commercial paper* Acceptance is the drawee's signed engagement to honor the draft as presented. It becomes operative when completed by delivery or notification. U.C.C. § 3–410.

Contracts Compliance by offeree with terms and conditions of offer.

Sale of goods U.C.C. § 2–606 provides three ways a buyer can accept goods: (1) by signifying to the seller that the goods are conforming or that he will accept them in spite of their nonconformity, (2) by failing to make an effective rejection, and (3) by doing an act inconsistent with the seller's ownership.

acceptor   Drawee upon acceptance of an instrument.

accession   An addition to one's property by increase of the original property or by production from such property. E.g., A innocently converts the wheat of B into bread. U.C.C. § 9–315 changes the common law where a perfected security interest is involved.

accommodation   An arrangement made as a favor to another, usually involving a loan of money or commercial paper. While a party's intent may be to aid a maker of note by lending his credit, if he seeks to accomplish thereby legitimate objects of his own, and not simply to aid the maker, the act is not for accommodation.

accommodation indorser   Signer not in the chain of title.

accommodation party   A person who signs commercial paper in any capacity for the purpose of lending his name to another party to an instrument. U.C.C. § 3–415.

accord and satisfaction   A method of discharging a claim whereby the parties agree to accept something in settlement, the "accord" being the agreement and the "satisfaction" its execution or performance. It is a new contract that is substituted for an old contract, which is thereby discharged, or for an obligation or cause of action and that must have all of the elements of a valid contract.

account   Any account with a bank, including a checking, time, interest or savings account. U.C.C. § 4–194. Also, any right to payment, for goods or services, that is not evidenced by an instrument or chattel paper. E.g., account receivable.

accounting   Equitable proceeding for a complete settlement of all partnership affairs.

actual authority   Power conferred upon agent by actual consent given by principal.

actual express authority   Actual authority derived from written or spoken words of principal.

actual implied authority   Actual authority inferred from words or conducted manifested to agent by principal.

actual notice   Knowledge actually and expressly communicated.

actus reas   Wrongful act.

adhesion contract   Standard "form" contract, usually between a large retailer and a consumer, in which the weaker party has no realistic choice or opportunity to bargain.

*Many of the definitions are abridged and adapted from *Black's Law Dictionary*, 5th Edition.

[135]

adjudication   The giving or pronouncing of a judgment in a case; also the judgment given.

administrative law   Law dealing with the establishment, duties and powers of agencies in the executive branch of government.

administrator   A person appointed by the court to manage the assets and liabilities of an intestate (person dying without a will). A person who is named in the will by testator (person dying with a will) is called the executor. Female designations are administratrix and executrix.

adversary system   System in which opposing parties initiate and present their case.

adverse possession   A method of acquisition of title to real property by possession for a statutory period under certain conditions. There may be different periods of time, depending on whether the adverse possessor has color of title.

affidavit   A written statement of facts, made voluntarily, confirmed by oath or affirmation of party making it, and taken before an authorized officer.

affirmative action   Active recruitment of minority applicants.

affirmative defense   A response that attacks the plaintiff's legal right to bring an action as opposed to attacking the truth of the claim. E.g., accord and satisfaction; assumption of risk; contributory negligence; duress; estoppel.

affirmative disclosure   Requirement that an advertiser include certain information in its advertisement so that it is not deceptive.

after acquired property   Property the debtor may acquire at some time in the future.

agency   Relation in which one person acts for or represents another by the latter's authority.
   Actual agency   Exists where the agent is really employed by the principal.
   Agency by estoppel   One created by operation of law and established by proof of such acts of the principal as reasonably lead to the conclusion of its existence.
   Implied agency   One created by acts of parties and deduced from proof of other facts.

allegation   A statement of a party setting out what he expects to prove.

allonge   Piece of paper firmly affixed to the instrument.

annul   To annul a judgment or judicial proceeding is to deprive it of all force and operation.

answer   The answer is the formal written statement made by a defendant setting forth the ground of his defense.

antecedent debt   Preexisting obligation.

anticipatory breach of contract   (or **anticipatory repudiation**). The unjustified assertion by a party that he will not perform an obligation that he is contractually obligated to perform at a future time. See U.C.C. §§ 610 & 611.

apparent authority   Such principal power that a reasonable person would assume an agent has in light of the principal's conduct.

appeal   Resort to a superior (appellate) court to review the decision of an inferior (trial) court or administrative agency.

appeal by right   Mandatory review by a higher court.

appellant   A party who takes an appeal from one court to another. He may be either the plaintiff or defendant in the original court proceeding.

appellee   The party in a cause against whom an appeal is taken; that is, the party who has an interest adverse to setting aside or reversing the judgment. Sometimes also called the "respondent."

appropriation   Unauthorized use of another person's name or likeness for one's own benefit.

appurtenances   Things appurtenant pass as incident to the principal thing. Sometimes an easement consisting of a right of way over one piece of land will pass with another piece of land as being appurtenant to it.

arbitration   The reference of a dispute to an impartial (third) person chosen by the parties who agree in advance to abide by the arbitrator's award issued after a hearing at which both parties have an opportunity to be heard.

articles of incorporation (or **certificate of incorporation**).   The instrument under which a corporation is formed. The contents are prescribed in the particular state's general incorporation statute.

articles of partnership   A written agreement by which parties enter into a partnership, to be governed by the terms set forth therein.

as is   Disclaimer of implied warranties.

assault   Unlawful attempted battery; intentional infliction of apprehension of immediate bodily harm or offensive contact.

assignee   Party to whom contract rights are assigned.

assignment   A transfer of the rights to real or personal property, usually intangible property such as rights in a lease, mortgage, sale agreement or partnership.

assignment of rights   Voluntary transfer to a third party of the rights arising from a contract.

assignor   Party making an assignment.

assumption of risk   Plaintiff's express or implied consent to encounter a known danger.

attachment   The process of seizing property, by virtue of a writ, summons, or other judicial order, and bringing the same into the custody of the court for the purpose of securing satisfaction of the judgment ultimately to be entered in the action. While formerly the main objective was to coerce the defendant debtor to appear in court, today the writ of attachment is used primarily to seize the debtor's property in the event a judgment is rendered.

Distinguished from execution   See **execution.**

Also, the process by which a security interest becomes enforceable. Attachment may occur upon the taking of possession or upon the signing of a security agreement by the person who is pledging the property as collateral.

authority   Power of an agent to change the legal status of his principal.

award   The decision of an arbitrator.

B

bad checks   Issuing a check with insufficient funds to cover the check.

bailee   The party to whom personal property is delivered under a contract of bailment.

Extraordinary bailee   Absolutely liable for the safety of the bailed property without regard to the cause of the loss.

Ordinary bailee   Must exercise due care.

bailment   A delivery of personal property in trust for the execution of a special object in relation to such goods, beneficial either to the bailor or bailee or both, and upon a contract to either redeliver the goods to the bailor or otherwise dispose of the same in conformity with the purpose of the trust.

bailor   The party who delivers goods to another in the contract of bailment.

bankrupt   The state or condition of one who is unable to pay his debts as they are, or become, due.

bankruptcy act   The Act was substantially revised in 1978, effective October 1, 1979. Straight bankruptcy is in the nature of a liquidation proceeding and in-

volves the collection and distribution to creditors of all the bankrupt's non-exempt property by the trustee in the manner provided by the Act. The debtor rehabilitation provisions of the Act (Chapters 11 and 13) differ however from straight bankruptcy in that the debtor looks to rehabilitation and reorganization, rather than liquidation, and the creditor looks to future earnings of the bankrupt, rather than property held by the bankrupt to satisfy their claims.

bargain   Negotiated exchange.

battery   Unlawful touching of another; intentional infliction of harmful or offensive bodily contact.

bearer   Person in possession of an instrument.

beneficiary   One who benefits from act of another. See also **third party beneficiary.**

Incidental   A person who may derive benefit from performance on contract, though he is neither the promisee nor the one to whom performance is to be rendered. Since the incidental beneficiary is not a donee or creditor beneficiary (see **third party beneficiary**), he has no right to enforce the contract.

Intended beneficiary   Third party intended by the two contracted parties to receive a benefit from their contract.

Trust   As it relates to trust beneficiaries, includes a person who has any present or future interest, vested or contingent, and also includes the owner of an interest by assignment or other transfer and, as it relates to a charitable trust, includes any person entitled to enforce the trust.

beyond a reasonable doubt   Evidence which is entirely convincing.

bill of lading   Document evidencing receipt of goods for shipment issued by person engaged in business of transporting or forwarding goods and it includes airbill. U.C.C. § 1–201(6).

Through bill of lading   A bill of lading which specifies at least one connecting carrier.

bill of sale   A written agreement, formerly limited to one under seal, by which one person assigns or transfers his right to or interest in goods and personal chattels to another.

binder   A written memorandum of the important terms of contract of insurance which gives temporary protection to insured pending investigation of risk by insurance company or until a formal policy is issued.

blue law   Prohibition of certain types of commercial activity on Sunday.

blue sky laws   A popular name for state statutes providing for the regulation and supervision of securities offerings and sales, for the protection of citizen-investors from investing in fraudulent companies.

bona fide   Latin. In good faith.

bond   A certificate or evidence of a debt on which the issuing company or governmental body promises to pay the bondholders a specified amount of interest for a specified length of time, and to repay the loan on the expiration date. In every case a bond represents debt—its holder is a creditor of the corporation and not a part owner as is the shareholder.

boycott   Agreement among parties not to deal with a third party.

breach   Wrongful failure to perform the terms of a contract.

Material breach   Nonperformance which significantly impairs the aggrieved party's rights under the contract.

bribery   Offering property to a public official to influence the official's decision.

bulk transfer   Transfer not in the ordinary course of the transferor's business of a major part of his inventory.

burglary   Breaking and entering the home of another at night with intent to commit a felony.

business trust   A trust (managed by a trustee for the benefit of a beneficiary) established to conduct a business for a profit.

buyer in ordinary course of business   Person who buys in ordinary course, in good faith, and without knowledge that the sale to him is in violation of anyone's ownership rights.

by-laws   Regulations, ordinances, rules of laws adopted by an association or corporation for its government.

C

cancellation   Putting an end to a contract by one party because of a breach by other party.

capital   Accumulated goods, possessions, and assets, used for the production of profits and wealth. Owners' equity in a business. Often used equally correctly to mean the total assets of a business. Sometimes used to mean capital assets.

carrier   Transporter of goods.

cause of action   The ground on which an action may be sustained.

caveat emptor   Latin. Let the buyer beware. This maxim is more applicable to judicial sales, auctions, and the like, than to sales of consumer goods where strict liability, warranty, and other laws protect.

certificate of deposit   A written acknowledgment by a bank or banker of a deposit with promise to pay to depositor, to his order, or to some other person or to his order. U.C.C. § 3–104(2)(c).

certification   Acceptance of a check by a drawee bank.

certification of incorporation   See **articles of incorporation**.

certiorari   Latin. To be informed of. A writ of common law origin issued by a superior to an inferior court requiring the latter to produce a certified record of a particular case tried therein. It is most commonly used to refer to the Supreme Court of the United States, which uses the writ of certiorari as a discretionary device to choose the cases it wishes to hear.

chancery   Equity; equitable jurisdiction; a court of equity; the system of jurisprudence administered in courts of equity.

charging order   Judicial lien against a partner's interest in the partnership.

charter   An instrument emanating from the sovereign power, in the nature of a grant. A charter differs from a constitution in that the former is granted by the sovereign, while the latter is established by the people themselves.

Corporate law   An act of a legislature creating a corporation, or creating and defining the franchise of a corporation. Also a corporation's constitution or organic law; that is to say, the articles of incorporation taken in connection with the law under which the corporation was organized.

chattel mortgage   A pre-Uniform Commercial Code security device whereby a security interest was taken by the mortgagee in personal property of the mortgagor. Such security device has generally been superseded by other types of security agreements under U.C.C. Article 9 (Secured Transactions).

chattel paper   Writings that evidence both a debt and a security interest.

check   A draft drawn upon a bank and payable on demand, signed by the maker or drawer, containing an unconditional promise to pay a sum certain in money to the order of the payee. U.C.C. § 3–104(2)(b).

Cashier's check   A bank's own check drawn on itself and signed by the cashier or other authorized official. It is a direct obligation of the bank.

C. & F.   Cost, insurance, and freight.

C.I.F.   Cost, insurance, and freight.

civil law Laws concerned with civil or private rights and remedies, as contrasted with criminal laws.

The system of jurisprudence administered in the Roman empire, particularly as set forth in the compilation of Justinian and his successors, as distinguished from the common law of England and the canon law. The civil law (Civil Code) is followed by Louisiana.

claim A right to payment.

close corporation See **corporation.**

closed-ended credit Credit extended to debtor for a specific period of time.

C.O.D. Collect on delivery.

code A compilation of all permanent laws in force consolidated and classified according to subject matter. Many states have published official codes of all laws in force, including the common law and statutes as judicially interpreted, which have been compiled by code commissions and enacted by the legislatures.

codicil A supplement or an addition to a will; it may explain, modify, add to, subtract from, qualify, alter, restrain or revoke provisions in existing will. It must be executed with the same formalities as a will.

cognovit judgment Written authority by debtor for entry of judgment against him in the event he defaults in payment. Such provision in a debt instrument on default confers judgment against the debtor.

collateral Secondarily liable, only liable if the party with primary liability does not perform.

collateral (security) Personal property subject to security interest. A security given in addition to the direct security, and subordinate to it, intended to guaranty its validity or convertibility or insure its performance.

Banking Some form of security in addition to the personal obligation of the borrower.

collecting bank Any bank handling the item for collection except the payor bank. U.C.C. § 4–105(d).

commerce power Exclusive power granted by the U.S. Constitution to the Federal government to regulate commerce with foreign countries and among the States.

commercial impracticability Performance can only be accomplished at unforeseen and unjust hardship.

commercial law A phrase used to designate the whole body of substantive jurisprudence (*e.g.* Uniform Commercial Code; Truth in Lending Act) applicable to the rights, intercourse, and relations of persons engaged in commerce, trade, or mercantile pursuits. See **uniform commercial code.**

commercial paper Bills of exchange (*i.e.* drafts), promissory notes, bank-checks, and other negotiable instruments for the payment of money, which, by their form and on their face, purport to be such instruments. U.C.C. Article 3 is the general law governing commercial paper.

commercial speech Expression related to the economic interests of the speaker and its audience.

common carrier Carrier open to the general public.

common law Body of law originating in England and derived from judicial decisions. As distinguished from statutory law created by the enactment of legislatures, the common law comprises the judgments and decrees of the courts recognizing, affirming, and enforcing usages and customs of immemorial antiquity.

community property Rights by spouses in property acquired by the other during marriage.

comparative negligence Under comparative negligence statutes or doctrines, negligence is measured in terms of percentage, and any damages allowed shall be diminished in proportion to amount of negligence attributable to the person for whose injury, damage or death recovery is sought.

complainant One who applies to the courts for legal redress by filing complaint (*i.e.* plaintiff).

complaint The pleading which sets forth a claim for relief. Such complaint (whether it be the original claim, counterclaim, cross-claim, or third-party claim) shall contain: (1) a short and plain statement of the grounds upon which the court's jurisdiction depends, unless the court already has jurisdiction and the claim needs no new grounds of jurisdiction to support it, (2) a short and plain statement of the claim showing that the pleader is entitled to relief, and (3) a demand for judgment for the relief to which he deems himself entitled. Fed.R. Civil P. 8(a). The complaint, together with the summons, is required to be served on the defendant. Rule 4.

composition Agreement between debtor and two or more of her creditors that each will take a portion of his claim as full payment.

concurrent jurisdiction Authority of more than one court to hear the same case.

condition An uncertain event which affects the duty of performance.

Concurrent conditions Performance by the parties are to occur simultaneously.

Express condition Performance is contingent on the happening of a stated event.

condition precedent An event which must occur or not occur before performance is due; event or events (presentment, dishonor, notice of dishonor) which must occur to hold a secondary party liable to commercial paper.

condition subsequent An event which terminates a duty of performance.

conditional acceptance An acceptance of an offer based upon the acceptance of an additional or different term.

confession of judgment Written agreement by debtor authorizing creditor to obtain a court judgment in the event debtor defaults. See also **cognovit judgment.**

conflict of laws That branch of jurisprudence, arising from the diversity of the laws of different nations, states or jurisdictions, that reconciles the inconsistency, or decides which law is to govern in the particular case.

confusion Results when goods belonging to two or more owners become intermixed to the point where the property of any of them no longer can be identified except as part of a mass of like goods.

consanguinity Kinship; blood relationship; the connection or relation of persons descended from the same stock or common ancestor.

conservator Appointed by court to manage affairs of incompetent or to liquidate business.

consideration The cause, motive, price, or impelling influence which induces a contracting party to enter into a contract. Some right, interest, profit or benefit accruing to one party, or some forbearance, detriment, loss, or responsibility, given, suffered, or undertaken by the other.

consignee One to whom a consignment is made. Person named in bill of lading to whom or to whose order the bill promises delivery. U.C.C. § 7–102(b).

consignment Ordinarily implies an agency and denotes that property is committed to the consignee for care or sale.

consignor One who sends or makes a consignment; a shipper of goods. The person named in a bill of lading as the person from whom the goods have been received for shipment. U.C.C. § 7–102(c).

consolidation In *corporate law*, the combination of two or more corporations into a newly created corporation. Thus, A Corporation and B Corporation combine to form C Corporation.

constitution Fundamental law of a government establishing its powers and limitations.

constructive That which is established by the mind of the law in its act of *construing* facts, conduct, circumstances, or instruments. That which has not the character assigned to it in its own essential nature, but acquires such character in consequence of the way in which it is regarded by a rule or policy of law; hence, inferred, implied, or made out by legal interpretation; the word "legal" being sometimes used here in lieu of "constructive."

constructive assent An assent or consent imputed to a party from a construction or interpretation of his conduct; as distinguished from one which he actually expresses.

constructive conditions Conditions in contracts which are neither expressed nor implied but are rather imposed by law to meet the ends of justice.

constructive delivery Term comprehending all those acts which, although not truly conferring a real possession of the vendee, have been held by construction of law to be the equivalent to acts of real delivery.

constructive notice Knowledge imputed by law.

constructive trust Arising by operation of law to prevent unjust enrichment. See also trustee.

consumer goods Tangible personal property used for personal, family or household purposes.

contract An agreement between two or more persons which creates an obligation to do or not to do a particular thing. Its essentials are competent parties, subject matter, a legal consideration, mutuality of agreement, and mutuality of obligation.

Destination contract Seller is required to tender delivery of the goods at a particular destination; seller bears the expense and risk of loss.

Executed contract Fully performed by all of the parties.

Executory contract Contract partially or entirely unperformed by one or more of the parties.

Express contract Agreement of parties that is expressed in words either in writing or orally.

Formal contract Agreement which is legally binding because of its particular form or mode or expression.

Implied in fact contract Contract where agreement of the parties is inferred from their conduct.

Informal contract All oral or written contracts other than formal contracts.

Installment contract Goods are delivered in separate lots.

Integrated contract Complete and total agreement.

Output contract A contract in which one party agrees to sell his entire output and the other agrees to buy it; it is not illusory, though it may be indefinite.

Quasi contract Obligation not based upon contract that is imposed to avoid injustice.

Requirements contract A contract in which one party agrees to purchase his total requirements from the other party and hence it is binding and not illusory.

Substituted contract An agreement between the parties to rescind their old contract and replace it with a new contract.

Unconscionable contract One which no sensible man not under delusion, duress, or in distress would make, and such as no honest and fair man would accept. A contract the terms of which are excessively unreasonable, overreaching and one-sided.

Unenforceable contract Contract for the breach of which the law does not provide a remedy.

Unilateral and bilateral A unilateral contract is one in which one party makes an express engagement or undertakes a performance, without receiving in return any express engagement or promise of performance from the other. Bilateral (or reciprocal) contracts are those by which the parties expressly enter into mutual engagements.

contribution Payment from cosureties of their proportionate share.

contributory negligence The act or omission amounting to want of ordinary care on part of complaining party, which, concurring with defendant's negligence, is proximate cause of injury.

The defense of contributory negligence is an absolute bar to any recovery in some states; because of this, it has been replaced by the doctrine of comparative negligence in many other states.

conversion Unauthorized and wrongful exercise of dominion and control over another's personal property, to exclusion of or inconsistent with rights of the owner.

copyright Exclusive right granted by Federal government to authors of original works including literary, musical, dramatic, pictorial, graphic, sculptural, and film works.

corporation A legal entity ordinarily consisting of an association of numerous individuals. Such entity is regarded as having a personality and existence distinct from that of its several members and is vested with the capacity of continuous succession, irrespective of changes in its membership, either in perpetuity or for a limited term of years.

Closely held corporation Corportion that is owned by few shareholders and whose shares are not actively traded.

Domestic corporation Corporation created under the laws of a given State.

Foreign corporation Corporation created under the laws of any other State.

Subsidiary and parent Subsidiary corporation is one in which another corporation (called parent corporation) owns at least a majority of the shares, and thus has control.

Close corporation A corporation whose shares, or at least voting shares, are held by a single shareholder or closely-knit group of shareholders.

Corporation de facto One existing under color of law and in pursuance of an effort made in good faith to organize a corporation under the statute. Such a corporation is not subject to collateral attack.

Corporation de jure That which exists by reason of full compliance with requirements of an existing law permitting organization of such corporation.

Subchapter S corporation A small business corporation which, under certain conditions, may elect to have its undistributed taxable income taxed to its shareholders. I.R.C. § 1371 *et seq.* Of major significance is the fact that Subchapter S status usually avoids the corporate income tax, and corporate losses can be claimed by the shareholders.

corrective advertising Disclosure in an advertisement that previous ads were deceptive.

costs A pecuniary allowance, made to the successful party (and recoverable from the losing party), for his expenses in prosecuting or defending an action or a distinct proceeding within an action. Fed.R.Civil P. 54(d); Fed.R.App.P. 39. Generally, "costs" do not include attorney fees unless such fees are by a statute denominated costs or are by statute allowed to be recovered as costs in the case.

counter offer A statement by the offeree which has the legal effect of rejecting the offer and of proposing a new offer to the offeror. However, the provisions of U.C.C. § 2–207(2) modifies this principle by providing that the "additional terms are to be construed as proposals for addition to the contract."

counterclaim A claim presented by a defendant in opposition to or deduction from the claim of the plaintiff.

course of dealing A sequence of previous acts and conduct between the parties to a particular transaction which is fairly to be regarded as establishing a common basis of understanding for interpreting their expressions and other conduct. U.C.C. § 1–205(1).

course of performance Conduct between the parties concerning performance of the particular contract.

court above—court below In appellate practice, the "court above" is the one to which a cause is removed for review, whether by appeal, writ of error, or certiorari; while the "court below" is the one from which the case is being removed.

covenant Used primarily with respect to promises in conveyances or other instruments dealing with real estate.

Covenant of warranty An assurance by the grantor of an estate that the grantee shall enjoy the same without interruption by virtue of paramount title.

Covenant running with land A covenant which goes with the land, as being annexed to the estate, and which cannot be separated from the land, and transferred without it. A covenant is said to run with the land when not only the original parties or their representatives, but each successive owner of the land, will be entitled to its benefit, or be liable (as the case may be) to its obligation. Such a covenant is said to be one which "touches and concerns" the land itself, so that its benefit or obligation passes with the ownership. Essentials are that the grantor and grantee must have intended that the covenant run with the land, the covenant must affect or concern the land with which it runs, and there must be privity of estate between party claiming the benefit and the party who rests under the burden.

Covenants against incumbrances A stipulation against all rights to or interests in the land which may subsist in third persons to the diminution of the value of the estate granted.

Covenant appurtenant A covenant which is connected with land of the grantor, and not in gross. A covenant running with the land and binding heirs, executors and assigns of the immediate parties.

Covenant for further assurance An undertaking, in the form of a covenant, on the part of the vendor of real estate to do such further acts for the purpose of perfecting the purchaser's title as the latter may reasonably require.

Covenant for possession A covenant by which the grantee or lessee is granted possession.

Covenant for quiet enjoyment An assurance against the consequences of a defective title, and of any disturbances thereupon.

Covenants for title Covenants usually inserted in a conveyance of land, on the part of the grantor, and binding him for the completeness, security, and continuance of the title transferred to the grantee. They comprise covenants for seisin, for right to convey, against incumbrances, or quiet enjoyment, sometimes for further assurance, and almost always of warranty.

Covenant in gross Such as do not run with the land.

Covenant of right to convey An assurance by the convenantor that the grantor has sufficient capacity and title to convey the *estate* which he by his deed undertakes to convey.

Covenant of seisin An assurance to the purchaser that the grantor has the very estate in quantity and quality which he purports to convey.

cover Buyer's purchase of goods in substitution for those not delivered by breaching seller.

credit beneficiary See **third party beneficiary.**

creditor Any entity having a claim against the debtor.

crime An act or omission in violation of a public law and punishable by the government.

criminal duress Coercion by threat of serious bodily injury.

criminal intent Desired or virtually certain consequences of one's conduct.

criminal law The law that involves offenses against the entire community.

cure The right of a seller under U.C.C. to correct a non-conforming delivery of goods to buyer within the contract period. § 2–508.

cy-pres As near as (possible). Rule for the construction of instruments in equity, by which the intention of the party is carried out *as near as may be,* when it would be impossible or illegal to give it literal effect.

D

damage Loss, injury, or deterioration, caused by the negligence, design, or accident of one person to another, in respect of the latter's person or property. The word is to be distinguished from its plural, "damages", which means a compensation in money for a loss or damage.

damages Money sought as a remedy for breach of contract or for tortious acts.

Actual damages Real, substantial and just damages, or the amount awarded to a complainant in compensation for his actual and real loss or injury, as opposed on the one hand to "nominal" damages, and on the other to "exemplary" or "punitive" damages. Synonymous with "compensatory damages" and with "general damages."

Benefit-of-the-bargain damages Difference between the value received and the value of the fraudulent party's performance as represented.

Compensatory damages Compensatory damages are such as will compensate the injured party for the injury sustained, and nothing more; such as will simply make good or replace the loss caused by the wrong or injury.

Consequential damages Such damage, loss or injury as does not flow directly and immediately from the act of the party, but only from some of the consequences or results of such act. Consequential damages resulting from a seller's breach of contract include any loss resulting from general or particular requirements and needs of which the seller at the time of contracting had reason to know and which could not reasonably be prevented by cover or otherwise, and injury to person or property proximately resulting from any breach of warranty. U.C.C. § 2–715(2).

Exemplary or punitive damages Damages other than compensatory damages which may be awarded against person to punish him for outrageous conduct.

Expectancy damages Calculable by subtracting the injured party's actual dollar position as a result of the breach from that party's projected dollar position had performance occurred.

Foreseeable damages Loss that the party in breach had reason to know of when the contract was made.

Incidental damages Under U.C.C. § 2–710, such damages include any commercially reasonable charges, expenses or commissions incurred in stopping delivery, in the transportation, care and custody of goods after the buyer's breach, in connection with the return or resale of the goods or otherwise resulting from the breach. Also, such damages, resulting from a seller's breach of contract, include expenses reasonably incurred in inspection, receipt, transportation and care and custody of goods rightfully rejected, any commercially reasonable charges, expenses or commissions in connection with effecting cover and any other reasonable expense incident to the delay or other breach. U.C.C. § 2–715(1).

Irreparable damages In the law pertaining to injunctions, damages for which no certain pecuniary standard exists for measurement.

Liquidated damages and penalties Damages for breach by either party may be liquidated in the agreement but only at an amount which is reasonable in the light of the anticipated or actual harm caused by the breach, the difficulties of proof of loss, and the inconvenience or nonfeasibility of otherwise obtaining an adequate remedy. A term fixing unreasonably large liquidated damages is void as a penalty. U.C.C. § 2–718(1).

Mitigation of damages A plaintiff may not recover damages for the effects of an injury which reasonably could have been avoided or substantially ameliorated. This limitation on recovery is generally denominated as "mitigation of damages" or "avoidance of consequences."

Nominal damages A small sum awarded where a contract has been breached but the loss is negligible or unproven.

Out-of-pocket damages Difference between the value received and the value given.

Reliance damages Contract damages placing the injured party in as good a position as he would have been in had the contract not been made.

Treble damages Three times actual loss.

decree Decision of a court of equity.

de facto In fact, in deed, actually. This phrase is used to characterize an officer, a government, a past action, or a state of affairs which must be accepted for all practical purposes, but is illegal or illegitimate. See also **corporation,** *corporation de facto.*

de jure Descriptive of a condition in which there has been total compliance with all requirements of law. In this sense it is the contrary of *de facto.* See also **corporation,** *corporation de jure.*

de novo Anew; afresh; a second time.

debenture Unsecured bond.

debt security Any form of corporate security reflected as debt on the books of the corporation in contrast to equity securities such as stock; *e.g.* bonds, notes and debentures are debt securities.

debtor Person who owes payment or obligation.

deceit A fraudulent and cheating misrepresentation, artifice, or device, used to deceive and trick one who is ignorant of the true facts, to the prejudice and damage of the party imposed upon. See also **fraud; misrepresentation.**

deed A conveyance of realty; a writing signed by grantor, whereby title to realty is transferred from one to another.

defamation Injury of a person's reputation by publication of false statements.

defendant The party against whom relief or recovery is sought in an action or suit.

delectus personae Partner's right to choose who may become a member of the partnership.

delegatee Third party to whom the delegator's duty is delegated.

delegation of duties Transferring all or part of one's duties arising under a contract to another.

delegator Party delegating his duty to a third party.

delivery The physical or constructive transfer of an instrument or of goods from the hands of one person to those of another. See also **constructive delivery.**

demand paper Payable on request.

demurrer An allegation of a defendant that, even if the facts as stated in the pleading to which objection is taken be true, yet their legal consequences are not such as to put the demurring party to the necessity of answering them or proceeding further with the cause.

The Federal Rules of Civil Procedure do not provide for the use of a demurrer, but provide an equivalent to a general demurrer in the motion to dismiss for failure to state a claim on which relief may be granted. Fed.R. Civil P. 12(b).

deposition The testimony of a witness taken upon interrogatories, not in court, but intended to be used in court. See also **discovery.**

depository bank The first bank to which an item is transferred for collection even though it may also be the payor bank. U.C.C. § 4–105(a).

descent Succession to the ownership of an estate by inheritance, or by any act of law, as distinguished from "purchase."

Descents are of two sorts, *lineal* and *collateral.* Lineal descent is descent in a direct or right line, as from father or grandfather to son or grandson. Collateral descent is descent in a collateral or oblique line, that is, up to the common ancestor and then down from him, as from brother to brother, or between cousins.

design defect Inadequate plans or specifications to insure the products' safety.

devise A testamentary disposition of land or realty; a gift of real property by the last will and testament of the donor. When used as a noun, means a testamentary disposition of real or personal property and when used as a verb, means to dispose of real or personal property by will.

dictum Generally used as an abbreviated form of *obiter dictum,* "a remark by the way;" that is, an observation or remark made by a judge which does not embody the resolution or determination of the court and which is made without argument or full consideration of the point.

directed verdict In a case in which the party with the burden of proof has failed to present a prima facie case for jury consideration, the trial judge may order the entry of a verdict without allowing the jury to consider it, because, as a matter of law, there can be only one such verdict. Fed.R. Civil P. 50(a).

disaffirmance Avoidance of the contract.

discharge Termination of certain allowed claims against a debtor.

disclaimer Negation of warranty.

discount A discount by a bank means a drawback or deduction made upon its advances or loans of money, upon negotiable paper or other evidences of debt payable at a future day, which are transferred to the bank.

discovery The pre-trial devices that can be used by one party to obtain facts and information about the case from the other party in order to assist the party's preparation for trial. Under Federal Rules of Civil Procedure tools of discovery include: depositions upon oral and written questions, written interrogatories, production of documents or things, permission to enter upon land or other property, physical and mental examinations and requests for admission. Rules 26–37.

dishonor To refuse to accept or pay a draft or to pay a promissory note when duly presented. U.C.C. § 3–507(1); § 4–210. See also **protest.**

disparagement Publication of false statements resulting in harm to another's monetary interests.

dissenting shareholder One who opposes a fundamental change and has the right to receive the fair value of her shares.

dissolution The dissolution of a partnership is the relation of the partners caused by any partner ceasing to be associated in the carrying on as distinguished from the winding up of the business. See also **winding up.**

distribution Transfer of partnership property from the partnership to a partner; transfer of property from a corporation to any of its shareholders.

dividend The payment designated by the board of directors of a corporation to be distributed pro rata among a class or classes of the shares outstanding.

document Document of title.

document of title Instrument evidencing ownership of the document and the goods it covers.

domicile That place where a person has his true, fixed, and permanent home and principal establishment, and to which whenever he is absent he has the intention of returning.

donee Recipient of a gift.

donee beneficiary See **third party beneficiary.**

donor Maker of a gift.

dower A species of life-estate which a woman is, by law, entitled to claim on the death of her husband, in the lands and tenements of which he was seised in fee during the marriage, and which her issue, if any, might by possibility have inherited.

Dower has been abolished in the majority of the states and materially altered in most of the others.

draft A written order by the first party, called the drawer, instructing a second party, called the drawee (such as a bank) to pay a third party, called the payee. An order to pay a sum certain in money, signed by a drawer, payable on demand or at a definite time, and to order or bearer. U.C.C. § 3–104.

drawee A person to whom a bill of exchange or draft is directed, and who is requested to pay the amount of money therein mentioned. The drawee of a check is the bank on which it is drawn.

When drawee accepts, he engages that he will pay the instrument according to its tenor at the time of his engagement or as completed. U.C.C. § 3–413(1).

drawer The person who draws a bill or draft. The drawer of a check is the person who signs it.

The drawer engages that upon dishonor of the draft and any necessary notice of dishonor or protest, he will pay the amount of the draft to the holder or to any indorser who takes it up. The drawer may disclaim this liability by drawing without recourse, U.C.C. § 3–413(2).

due negotiation Transfer of a negotiable document in the regular course of business to a holder, who takes in good faith, without notice of any defense or claim, and for value.

duress Unlawful constraint exercised upon a person, whereby he is forced to do some act against his will.

Physical duress Coercion involving physical force or the threat of physical force.

E

earned surplus Undistributed net profits, income, gains and losses.

earnest The payment of a part of the price of goods sold, or the delivery of part of such goods, for the purpose of binding the contract.

easement A right in the owner of one parcel of land, by reason of such ownership, to use the land of another for a special purpose not inconsistent with a general property in the owner. This right is distinguishable from a "license" which merely confers personal privilege to do some act on the land.

Affirmative easement One where the servient estate must permit something to be done thereon, as to pass over it, or to discharge water on it.

Appurtenant easement An incorporeal right which is attached to a superior right and inheres in land to which it is attached and is in the nature of a covenant running with the land.

Easement by necessity Such arises by operation of law when land conveyed is completely shut off from access to any road by land retained by grantor or by land of grantor and that of a stranger.

Easement by prescription A mode of acquiring title to property by immemorial or long-continued enjoyment, and refers to personal usage restricted to claimant and his ancestors or grantors.

Easement in gross An easement in gross is not appurtenant to any estate in land or does not belong to any person by virtue of ownership of estate in other land but is mere personal interest in or right to use land of another; it is purely personal and usually ends with death of grantee.

Easement of access Right of ingress and egress to and from the premises of a lot owner to a street appurtenant to the land of the lot owner.

ejectment An action of which the purpose is to determine whether the title to certain land is in the plaintiff or is in the defendant.

electronic fund transfer A transaction with a financial institution by means of computer, telephone or electronic instrument.

emancipation The act by which an infant is set at liberty from the control of parent or guardian and made his own master.

embezzlement The taking in violation of a trust the property of one's employer.

emergency Sudden, unexpected event calling for immediate action.

eminent domain Right of the people or government to take private property for public use upon giving of a fair consideration.

employment relationship One in which employer has right to control the physical conduct of employee.

entirety Used to designate that which the law considers as one whole, and not capable of being divided into parts.

entrapment Induced into committing a crime by a government official.

equipment Goods used primarily in business.

equitable Just, fair, and right. Existing in equity; available or sustainable only in equity, or only upon the rules and principles of equity.

equity Justice administered according to fairness as contrasted with the strictly formulated rules of common law. It is based on a system of rules and principles which originated in England as an alternative to the harsh rules of common law and which were based on what was fair in a particular situation.

equity of redemption   The right of the mortgagor of an estate to redeem the same after it has been forfeited, at law, by a breach of the condition of the mortgage, upon paying the amount of debt, interest and costs.

equity securities   Stock or similar security, in contrast to debt securities such as bonds, notes and debentures.

error   A mistake of law, or false or irregular application of it, such as vitiates the proceedings and warrants the reversal of the judgment.

Harmless error   In appellate practice, an error committed in the progress of the trial below which was not prejudicial to the rights of the party assigning it and for which, therefore, the court will not reverse the judgment.

Reversible error   In appellate practice, such an error as warrants the appellate court in reversing the judgment before it.

escrow   A system of document transfer in which a deed, bond, or funds is delivered to a third person to hold until all conditions in a contract are fulfilled; *e.g.* delivery of deed to escrow agent under installment land sale contract until full payment for land is made.

estate   The degree, quantity, nature, and extent of interest which a person has in real and personal property. An estate in lands, tenements, and hereditaments signifies such interest as the tenant has therein.

Also, the total property of whatever kind that is owned by a decedent prior to the distribution of that property in accordance with the terms of a will, or, when there is no will, by the laws of inheritance in the state of domicile of the decedent.

Future estate   An estate limited to commence in possession at a future day, either without the intervention of a precedent estate, or on the determination by lapse of time, or otherwise, of a precedent estate created at the same time. Examples include reversions and remainders.

estoppel   A bar or impediment raised by the law, which precludes a man from alleging or from denying a certain fact or state of facts, in consequence of his previous allegation or denial or conduct or admission, or in consequence of a final adjudication of the matter in a court of law. See also **waiver.**

eviction   Dispossession by process of law; the act of depriving a person of the possession of lands which he has held, in pursuance of the judgment of a court.

evidence   Any species of proof, or probative matter, legally presented at the trial of an issue, by the act of the parties and through the medium of witnesses, records, documents, concrete objects, etc., for the purpose of inducing belief in the minds of the court or jury as to their contention.

exception   A formal objection to the action of the court, during the trial of a cause, in refusing a request or overruling an objection; implying that the party excepting does not acquiesce in the decision of the court, but will seek to procure its reversal, and that he means to save the benefit of his request or objection in some future proceeding.

exclusionary rule   Prohibition of illegally obtained evidence.

exclusive dealing   Sole right to sell goods in a defined market.

exclusive jurisdiction   Such jurisdiction that permits only one court to hear a case.

exculpatory clause   Excusing oneself from fault or liability.

execution   *Execution of contract* includes performance of all acts necessary to render it complete as an instrument and imports idea that nothing remains to be done to make complete and effective contract.

Execution upon a money judgment   is the legal process of enforcing the judgment, usually by seizing and selling property of the debtor.

executor   A person appointed by a testator to carry out the directions and requests in his will, and to dispose of the property according to his testamentary provisions after his decease. The f male designation is executrix. A person appointed by the court in an intestacy situation is called the administrator(rix).

executory   That which is yet to be executed or performed; that which remains to be carried into operation or effect; incomplete; depending upon a future performance or event. The opposite of executed.

executory contract   See **contracts.**

exemplary damages   See **damages.**

exoneration   Relieved of liability.

express   Manifested by direct and appropriate language, as distinguished from that which is inferred from conduct. The word is usually contrasted with "implied."

express warranty   Explicitly made contractual promise regarding property or contract rights transferred; in a sale of goods affirmation of fact or promise about the goods or a description, including sample, of goods which becomes part of the basis of the bargain.

ex-ship Risk of loss passes to buyer upon the goods leaving the ship. See U.C.C. § 2–322. See also **F.A.S.**

extortion Making threats to obtain property.

F

F.A.S. Free alongside. Term used in sales price quotations, indicating that the price includes all costs of transportation and delivery of the goods alongside the ship. See U.C.C. § 2–319(2).

false imprisonment Intentional interference with a person's freedom of movement by unlawful confinement.

false light Offensive publicity placing another in a false light.

false pretenses Intentional misrepresentation of fact for purpose to cheat.

farm products Crops, livestock, or stock used or produced in farming.

federal preemption First right of the Federal government to regulate matters within its powers to the possible exclusion of State regulation.

federal question Any case arising under the Constitution, statutes or treaties of the United States.

fee simple

Absolute A fee simple absolute is an estate that is unlimited as to duration, disposition, and descendibility. It is the largest estate and most extensive interest that can be enjoyed in land.

Conditional Type of transfer in which grantor conveys fee simple on condition that something be done or not done.

Defeasible Type of fee grant which may be defeated on the happening of an event. An estate which may last forever, but which may end upon the happening of a specified event, is a "fee simple defeasible".

Determinable Created by conveyance which contains words effective to create a fee simple and, in addition, a provision for automatic expiration of estate on occurrence of stated event.

fee tail An estate of inheritance, descending only to a certain class or classes or heirs; e.g., an estate is conveyed or devised "to A. and the heirs of his body," or "to A. and the heirs male of his body," or "to A., and the heirs female of his body." State statutes have dealt variously with estates tail, some converting them into estates in fee simple.

fellow servant rule Common law defense relieving employer for liability to an employee for injuries caused by negligence of fellow employee.

felony Serious crime.

fiduciary A person or institution who manages money or property for another and who must exercise a standard of care in such management activity imposed by law or contract; *e.g.* executor of estate; receiver in bankruptcy; trustee.

fiduciary duty Duty of utmost loyalty and good faith owed by a fiduciary such as an agent owes to her principal.

field warehouse Secured party takes possession of the goods while the pledgor has access to the goods.

final credit Payment of the instrument by the payor.

financing statement Under the Uniform Commercial Code, a financing statement is used under Article 9 to reflect a public record that there is a security interest or claim to the goods in question to secure a debt. The financing statement is filed by the security holder with the Secretary of State, or similar public body, and as such becomes public record. See also **secured transaction.**

firm offer Irrevocable offer to sell or buy goods by a merchant in a signed writing which gives assurance that it will not be rescinded for up to three months.

fitness for a particular purpose Goods are fit for a stated purpose provided the seller selects the product knowing the buyer's intended use and that the buyer is relying on the seller's judgment.

fixture An article in the nature of personal property which has been so annexed to realty that it is regarded as a part of the land. Examples include a furnace affixed to a house or other building, counters permanently affixed to the floor of a store, a sprinkler system installed in a building. U.C.C. § 9–313(1)(a).

Trade fixtures Such chattels as merchants usually possess and annex to the premises occupied by them to enable them to store, handle, and display their goods, which are generally removable without material injury to the premises.

F.O.B. Free on board some location (for example, FOB shipping point; FOB destination); the invoice price includes delivery at seller's expense to that location. Title to goods usually passes from seller to buyer at the FOB location. U.C.C. § 2–319(1).

foreclosure Procedure by which mortgaged property is sold on default of mortgagor in satisfaction of mortgage debt.

forgery   Intentional falsification of a document with intent to defraud.

franchise   A privilege granted or sold, such as to use a name or to sell products or services. The right given by a manufacturer or supplier to a retailer to use his products and name on terms and conditions mutually agreed upon.

fraud   Elements include: false representation; of a present or past fact; made by defendant; action in reliance thereon by plaintiff; damage resulting to plaintiff from such misrepresentation.

fraud in the execution   Misrepresentation that deceives the other party as to the nature of a document evidencing the contract.

fraud in the inducement   Misrepresentation regarding the subject matter of a contract and inducing the other party to enter into it.

freehold   An estate for life or in fee. It must possess two qualities: (1) immobility, that is, the property must be either land or some interest issuing out of or annexed to land; and (2) indeterminate duration.

frustration of purpose doctrine   Excuses a promisor in certain situations when the objectives of contract have been utterly defeated by circumstances arising after formation of agreement, and performance is excused under this rule even though there is no impediment to actual performance.

fungibles   With respect to goods or securities, those of which any unit is, by nature or usage of trade, the equivalent of any other like unit. U.C.C. § 1–201(17); *e.g.*, a bushel of wheat or other grain.

future estate   See **estate**

G

garnishment   A statutory proceeding whereby a person's property, money, or credits in the possession or control of another are applied to payment of the former's debt to a third person.

general intangible   Catch-all category of collateral not otherwise covered.

general partner   Member of either a general or limited partnership with unlimited liability for its debts, full management powers and a right to share in the profits.

gift   A voluntary transfer of property to another made gratuitously and without consideration. Essential requisites of "gift" are capacity of donor, intention of donor to make gift, completed delivery to or for donee, and acceptance of gift by donee.

gift causa mortis   A gift in view of death is one which is made in contemplation, fear, or peril of death, and with intent that it shall take effect only in case of the death of the giver.

good faith   Honesty in fact in conduct or a transaction.

good faith purchaser   Buyer who acts honestly, gives value, and takes the goods without notice or knowledge of any defect in the title of his transferor.

goods   A term of variable content and meaning. It may include every species of personal property or it may be given a very restricted meaning. Sometimes the meaning of "goods" is extended to include all tangible items, as in the phrase "goods and services."

All things (including specially manufactured goods) which are movable at the time of identification to the contract for sale other than the money in which the price is to be paid, investment securities and things in action. U.C.C. § 2–105(1).

grantor   A transferor of property. The creator of a trust is usually designated as the grantor of the trust.

guaranty   A promise to answer for the payment of some debt, or the performance of some duty, in case of the failure of another person, who, in the first instance, is liable to such payment or performance.

The terms *guaranty* and *suretyship* are sometimes used interchangeably; but they should not be confounded. The distinction between contract of suretyship and contract of guaranty is whether or not the undertaking is a joint undertaking with the principal or a separate and distinct contract; if it is the former it is one of "suretyship", and if the latter, it is one of "guaranty". See also **surety**.

guardianship   The relationship under which a person (the guardian) is appointed by a court to preserve and control the property of another (the ward).

H

heir   A person who succeeds, by the rules of law, to an estate in lands, tenements, or hereditaments, upon the death of his ancestor, by descent and right of relationship.

holder   Person who is in possession of a document of title or an instrument or an investment security drawn, issued or endorsed to him or to his order, or to bearer or in blank. U.C.C. § 1–201(20).

holder in due course   A holder who takes an instrument for value, in good faith, and without notice that it is overdue or has been dishonored or of any defense against or claim to it on the part of any person.

holograph A will or deed written entirely by the testator or grantor with his own hand and not witnessed (attested). State laws vary with respect to the validity of the holographic will.

homicide Unlawful taking of another's life.

horizontal Agreements among competitors.

horizontal privity Who may bring a cause of action.

I

identified goods Designated goods as a part of a particular contract.

illegal per se Conclusively presumed unreasonable and therefore illegal.

implied-in-fact condition Contingencies understood but not expressed by the parties.

implied-in-law condition Contingency that arises from operation of law.

implied warranty Obligation imposed by law upon the transferor of property or contract rights; implicit in the sale arising out of certain circumstances.

implied warranty of habitability Fit for ordinary residential purposes.

impossibility Performance that can not be done.

in personam Against the person. Action seeking judgment against a person involving his personal rights and based on jurisdiction of his person, as distinguished from a judgment against property (*i.e.* in rem).

in personam jurisdiction Jurisdiction based on claims against a person in contrast to jurisdiction over his property.

in re In the affair; in the matter of; concerning; regarding. This is the usual method of entitling a judicial proceeding in which there are not adversary parties, but merely some *res* concerning which judicial action is to be taken, such as a bankrupt's estate, an estate in the probate court, a proposed public highway, etc.

in rem A technical term used to designate proceedings or actions instituted *against the thing*, in contradistinction to personal actions, which are said to be *in personam*.

Quasi in rem A term applied to proceedings which are not strictly and purely *in rem*, but are brought against the defendant personally, though the real object is to deal with particular property or subject property to the discharge of claims asserted; for example, foreign attachment, or proceedings to foreclose a mortgage, remove a cloud from title, or effect a partition.

in rem jurisdiction Jurisdiction based on claims against property.

incidental beneficiary Third party whom the two parties to a contract have no intention of benefitting by their contract.

incontestability clause The prohibition of an insurer to avoid an insurance policy after a specified period of time.

indemnification Duty owed by principal to agent to pay agent for losses incurred while acting as directed by principal.

indemnify To reimburse one for a loss already incurred.

indenture A written agreement under which bonds and debentures are issued, setting forth maturity date, interest rate, and other terms.

independent contractor Person who contracts with another to do a particular job and is not subject to the control of the other.

indicia Signs; indications. Circumstances which point to the existence of a given fact as probable, but not certain.

indictment Grand jury charge that the defendant should stand trial.

indispensable paper Chattel paper, instruments and documents.

indorsee The person to whom a negotiable instrument, promissory note, bill of lading, etc., is assigned by indorsement.

indorsement The act of a payee, drawee, accommodation indorser, or holder of a bill, note, check, or other negotiable instrument, in writing his name upon the back of the same, with or without further or qualifying words, whereby the property in the same is assigned and transferred to another. U.C.C. § 3–202 *et seq.*

Blank indorsement No indorsee is specified.

Qualified indorsement Without recourse, limiting one's liability of the instrument.

Restrictive indorsement Limits the rights of the indorser in some manner.

Special indorsement Designates an indorsee to be paid.

infliction of emotional distress Extreme and outrageous conduct intentionally or recklessly causing severe emotional distress.

injunction An equitable remedy forbidding the party defendant from doing some act which he is threatening or attempting to commit, or restraining him in the continuance thereof, such act being unjust and inequitable, injurious to the plaintiff, and not such as can be adequately redressed by an action at law.

innkeeper   Hotel or moteloperator.

inquisitorial system   System in which the judiciary initiates, conducts and decides cases.

insolvency   Under U.C.C., a person is insolvent who either has ceased to pay his debts in the ordinary course of business or cannot pay his debts as they fall due or is insolvent within the meaning of the Federal Bankruptcy Law. U.C.C. § 1–201(23).
  Insolvency (bankruptcy)   Total liabilities exceed total value of assets.
  Insolvency (equity)   Inability to pay debts in ordinary course of business or as they become due.

inspection   Examination of the goods to determine whether they conform to the contract.

instrument   Negotiable instruments, stocks, bonds, and other investment securities.

insurable interest   Exists where insured derives pecuniary benefit or advantage by preservation and continued existence of property or would sustain pecuniary loss from its destruction.

insurance   A contract whereby, for a stipulated consideration, one party undertakes to compensate the other for loss on a specified subject by specified perils. The party agreeing to make the compensation is usually called the "insurer" or "underwriter"; the other, the "insured" or "assured"; the written contract, a "policy"; the events insured against, "risks" or "perils"; and the subject, right, or interest to be protected, the "insurable interest." Insurance is a contract whereby one undertakes to indemnify another against loss, damage, or liability arising from an unknown or contingent event.
  Co-insurance   A form of insurance in which a person insures property for less than its full or stated value and agrees to share the risk of loss.
  Life insurance   Payment of a specific sum of money to a designated beneficiary upon the death of the insured.
  Ordinary life   Life insurance with a savings component that runs for the life of the insured.
  Term life   Life insurance issued for a limited number of years and does not have a savings component.

intangible property   Protected interests that are not physical.

intangibles   Accounts and general intangibles.

intent   Desire to cause the consequences of an act or knowledge that the consequences are substantially certain to result from the act.

inter alia   Among other things.

inter se or **inter sese**   Latin. Among or between themselves; used to distinguish rights or duties between two or more parties from their rights or duties to others.

interest in land   Any right, privilege, power or immunity in real property.

interest in partnership   Partner's share in the partnership's profits and surplus.

interference with contractual relations   Intentionally causing one of the parties to a contract not to perform the contract.

intermediary bank   Any bank to which an item is transferred in the course of collection except the depositary or payor bank. U.C.C. § 4–105(c).

interpretation   Construction or meaning of the contract.

interpretative rules   Statements issued by an administrative agency indicating its construction of its governing statute.

intestate   A person is said to die intestate when he dies without making a will. The word is also often used to signify the person himself. *Compare* **testator.**

intrusion   Unreasonable and highly offensive interference with the seclusion of another.

inventory   Goods held for sale or lease.

invitee   A person is an "invitee" on land of another if (1) he enters by invitation, express or implied, (2) his entry is connected with the owner's business or with an activity the owner conducts or permits to be conducted on his land and (3) there is mutuality of benefit or benefit to the owner.

J

joint and several liability   Liability where creditor may sue obligors jointly as a group or separately as individuals.

joint liability   Liability where creditor must sue all of the obligors as a group.

joint stock company   A general partnership with some corporate attributes.

joint tenancy   See **tenancy.**

joint venture   An association of two or more persons to carry on a single business enterprise for profit.

judgment   The official and authentic decision of a

court of justice upon the respective rights and claims of the parties to an action or suit therein litigated and submitted to its determination.

judgment in personam A judgment against a particular person, as distinguished from a judgment against a thing or a right or *status*.

judgment in rem An adjudication pronounced upon the status of some particular thing or subject matter, by a tribunal having competent authority.

judgment n. o. v. Judgment non obstante verdicto in its broadest sense is a judgment rendered in favor of one party notwithstanding the finding of a verdict in favor of the other party.

judicial lien Interest in property to secure payment of a debt that is obtained by court action.

judicial review Authority of the courts to determine the constitutionality of legislative and executive acts.

jurisdiction The right and power of a court to adjudicate concerning the subject matter in a given case.

jurisdiction over the parties Power of a court to bind the parties to a suit.

jury (From the Latin jurare, to swear). A body of persons selected and summoned by law and sworn to try the facts of a case and to find according to the law and the evidence. In general, the province of the jury is to find the facts in a case, while the judge passes upon pure questions of law. As a matter of fact, however, the jury must often pass upon mixed questions of law and fact in determining the case, and in all such cases the instructions of the judge as to the law become very important.

L

labor dispute Any controversy concerning terms or conditions of employment or union representation.

laches Based upon maxim that equity aids the vigilant and not those who slumber on their rights. It is defined as neglect to assert right or claim which, taken together with lapse of time and other circumstances causing prejudice to adverse party, operates as bar in court of equity.

landlord He who, being the owner of an estate in land, or a rental property, has leased it to another person, called the "tenant." Also called "lessor."

larceny Trespassory taking and carrying away the goods of another with the intent to permanently deprive.

lease Any agreement which gives rise to relationship of landlord and tenant (real property) or lessor and lessee (real or personal property).

The person who conveys is termed the "lessor," and the person to whom conveyed, the "lessee;" and when the lessor conveys land or tenements to a lessee, he is said to lease, demise, or let them.

Sublease, or underlease One executed by the lessee of an estate to a third person, conveying the same estate for a shorter term than that for which the lessee holds it.

leasehold An estate in realty held under a lease. The four principal types of leasehold estates are the estate for years, periodic tenancy, tenancy at will, and tenancy at sufferance.

legacy "Legacy" is a gift or bequest by will of personal property, whereas a "devise" is a testamentary disposition of real estate.

Demonstrative legacy A bequest of a certain sum of money, with a direction that it shall be paid out of a particular fund. It differs from a specific legacy in this respect: that, if the fund out of which it is payable fails for any cause, it is nevertheless entitled to come on the estate as a general legacy. And it differs from a general legacy in this: that it does not abate in that class, but in the class of specific legacies.

General legacy A pecuniary legacy, payable out of the general assets of a testator.

Residuary legacy A bequest of all the testator's personal estate not otherwise effectually disposed of by his will.

Specific legacy One which operates on property particularly designated. A legacy or gift by will of a particular specified thing, as of a horse, a piece of furniture, a term of years, and the like.

legal aggregate A group of individuals not having a legal existence separate from its members.

legal benefit Obtaining something you had no legal right to.

legal detriment Doing an act not legally obligated to do or not doing an act which one has a legal right to do.

legal entity An organization having a separate legal existence from its members.

legal sufficiency Benefit to promisor or detriment to promisee.

legislative rules Substantive rules issued by an administrative agency under the authority delegated to it by the legislature.

letter of credit An engagement by a bank or other person made at the request of a customer that the issuer will honor drafts or other demands for payment upon compliance with the conditions specified in the credit.

letters of administration Formal document issued by probate court appointing one an administrator of an estate.

letters testamentary The formal instrument of authority and appointment given to an executor by the proper court, empowering him to enter upon the discharge of his office as executor. It corresponds to letters of administration granted to an administrator.

levy To assess; raise; execute; exact; tax; collect; gather; take up; seize. Thus, to levy (assess, exact, raise, or collect) a tax; to levy an execution, *i.e.*, to levy or collect a sum of money on an execution.

libel Defamation communicated by writing, television, radio or the like.

license License with respect to real property is a privilege to go on premises for a certain purpose, but does not operate to confer on, or vest in, licensee any title, interest, or estate in such property.

licensee Person privileged to enter or remain on land by virtue of the consent of the lawful possessor.

lien A qualified right of property which a creditor has in or over specific property of his debtor, as security for the debt or charge or for performance of some act.

lien creditor A creditor who has acquired a lien on the property by attachment.

life estate An estate whose duration is limited to the life of the party holding it, or some other person. Upon the death of the life tenant, the property will go to the holder of the remainder interest or to the grantor by reversion.

limited liability Liability limited to amount invested in a business enterprise.

limited partner Member of a limited partnership with liability for its debts only to the extent of her capital contribution.

limited partnership See **partnership.**

limited partnership association A partnership which closely resembles a corporation.

liquidated Ascertained; determined; fixed; settled; made clear or manifest. Cleared away; paid; discharged.

liquidated damages See **damages.**

liquidated debt Certain in amount.

liquidation The settling of financial affairs of a business or individual, usually by liquidating (turning to cash) all assets for distribution to creditors, heirs, etc. It is to be distinguished from dissolution.

lost property Property which the owner has involuntary parted with and does not know where to find or recover it, not including property which he has intentionally concealed or deposited in a secret place for safe-keeping. Distinguishable from mislaid property which has been deliberately placed somewhere and forgotten.

M

McNaughton test Right/wrong test for criminal insanity.

main purpose rule Where object of promisor/surety is to provide an economic benefit for herself, the promise is considered outside of the Statute of Frauds.

maker One who makes or executes; as the maker of a promissory note. One who signs a check; in this context, synonymous with drawer. See **draft.**

mala in se Morally wrong.

mala prohibita Wrong by law.

mandamus Latin, we command. A legal writ compelling the defendant to do an official duty.

manslaughter Unlawful taking of another's life without malice.
  Involuntary manslaughter Taking the life of another by criminal negligence or during the course of a misdemeanor.
  Voluntary manslaughter Intentional killing of another under extenuating circumstances.

manufacturing defect Not produced according to specifications.

market allocations Division of market by customers, geographic location, or products.

marketable title Free from any defects or reasonable objections to one's ownership.

marshaling of assets Segregating the assets and liabilities of the partnership separately from the assets and liabilities of the individual partners.

master See **principal.**

material Matters to which a reasonable investor would attach importance in deciding whether to purchase a security.

material alteration Any change that changes the contract of any party to the instrument.

maturity The date at which an obligation, such as the principal of a bond or a note, becomes due.

maxim A general legal principle.

mechanic's lien A claim created by state statutes for the purpose of securing priority of payment of the price or value of work performed and materials furnished in erecting or repairing a building or other structure, and as such attaches to the land as well as buildings and improvements erected thereon.

mens reas Criminal intent.

mentally incompetent Unable to understand the nature and effect of one's acts.

mercantile law An expression substantially equivalent to commercial law. It designates the system of rules, customs, and usages generally recognized and adopted by merchants and traders, and which, either in its simplicity or as modified by common law or statutes, constitutes the law for the regulation of their transactions and the solution of their controversies. The Uniform Commercial Code is the general body of law governing commercial or mercantile transactions.

merchant A person who deals in goods of the kind or otherwise by his occupation holds himself out as having knowledge or skill peculiar to the practices or goods involved in the transaction or to whom such knowledge or skill may be attributed by his employment of an agent or broker or other intermediary who by his occupation holds himself out as having such knowledge or skill. U.C.C. § 2–104(1).

merchantability Merchant seller guarantees that the goods are fit for their ordinary purpose.

merger The fusion or absorption of one thing or right into another. In corporate law, the absorption of one company by another, latter retaining its own name and identity and acquiring assets, liabilities, franchises, and powers of former, and absorbed company ceasing to exist as separate business entity. It differs from a consolidation wherein all the corporations terminate their existence and become parties to a new one.

Conglomerate merger An acquisition by one company of another which is not horizontal or vertical.

Horizontal merger Merger between business competitors, such as manufacturers of the same type products or distributors selling competing products in the same market area.

Short-form merger Merger of a 90 percent subsidiary into its parent.

Vertical merger Union with corporate customer or supplier.

midnight deadline Midnight of the next banking day after receiving an item.

mining partnership A specific type of partnership for the purpose of extracting raw minerals.

minor Under full legal age (usually 18).

mirror image rule An acceptance cannot deviate from the terms of the offer.

misdemeanor Less serious crime.

mislaid property Property which an owner has put deliberately in a certain place but owner is unable to remember where he put it, as distinguished from lost property which the owner leaves unwittingly in a place, forgetting its location. See also **lost property.**

misrepresentation Any manifestation by words or other conduct by one person to another that, under the circumstances, amounts to an assertion not in accordance with the facts. A "misrepresentation" that justifies the rescission of a contract is a false statement of a substantive fact, or any conduct which leads to a belief of a substantive fact material to proper understanding of the matter in hand. See also **deceit; fraud.**

Fraudulent misrepresentation False statement made with knowledge of its falsity and intent to mislead.

Innocent misrepresentation Misrepresentation made without knowledge of its falsity but with due care.

Negligent misrepresentation Misrepresentation made without due care in ascertaining its falsity.

money Medium of exchange issued by a government body.

monopoly Ability to control price or exclude others from the marketplace.

mortgage A mortgage is an interest in land created by a written instrument providing security for the performance of a duty or the payment of a debt.

multiple product order Order requiring an advertiser to cease and desist from deceptive statements on all products it sells.

murder Unlawful and premeditated taking of another's life.

mutual mistake Where both parties have a common but erroneous belief forming the basis of a contract.

N

necessary Goods or services required to maintain one's station in life.

negligence The omission to do something which a reasonable man, guided by those ordinary considerations which ordinarily regulate human affairs, would do, or the doing of something which a reasonable and prudent man would not do.

Culpable negligence Greater than ordinary negligence but less than gross negligence.

negligence per se Conclusive on the issue of negligence (duty of care and breach).

negotiable Legally capable of being transferred by endorsement or delivery. Usually said of checks and notes and sometimes of stocks and bearer bonds.

negotiable instrument Signed document (such as a check or promissory note) containing an unconditional promise to pay a "sum certain" of money at a definite time to order or bearer.

negotiation Transferee becomes a holder.

net assets Total assets minus total debts.

nonconforming use Pre-existing use not in accordance with the zoning ordinance.

nonsuit Action in form of a judgment taken against a plaintiff who has failed to appear to prosecute his action or failed to prove his case.

note See **promissory note.**

novation A novation substitutes a new party and discharges one of the original parties to a contract by agreement of all three parties. A new contract is created with the same terms as the original one but only the parties are changed.

nuisance Nuisance is that activity which arises from unreasonable, unwarranted or unlawful use by a person of his own property, working obstruction or injury to right of another, or to the public, and producing such material annoyance, inconvenience and discomfort that law will presume resulting damage.

O

obiter dictum See **dictum**

objective standard What a reasonable man under the circumstances would reasonably believe or do.

obligee Party to whom a duty of performance is owed.

obligor Party owing a duty.

offer A manifestation of willingness to enter into a bargain, so made as to justify another person in understanding that his assent to that bargain is invited and will conclude it. Restatement, Second, Contracts, § 24.

offeree Recipient of the offer.

offeror Person making the offer.

open-ended credit Credit arrangement under which debtor has rights to enter into a series of credit transactions.

option Contract which provides that an offer will stay open for a specified period of time.

output contract See **contracts.**

P

parent corporation Corporation which controls another corporation.

parol evidence Literally oral evidence, but now includes prior to and contemporaneous, oral and written evidence.

parol evidence rule Under this rule, when parties put their agreement in writing, all previous oral agreements merge in the writing and a contract as written cannot be modified or changed by parol evidence, in the absence of a plea of mistake or fraud in the preparation of the writing. But rule does not forbid a resort to parol evidence not inconsistent with the matters stated in the writing. Also, as regards sales of goods, such written agreement may be explained or supplemented by course of dealing or usage of trade or by course of conduct, and by evidence of consistent additional terms unless the court finds the writing to have been intended also as a complete and exclusive statement of the terms of the agreement. U.C.C. § 2–202.

part performance In order to establish part performance taking an oral contract for the sale of realty out of the statute of frauds, the acts relied upon as part performance must be of such a character that they can reasonably be naturally accounted for in no other way than that they were performed in pursuance of the contract, and they must be in conformity with its provisions. See U.C.C. § 2–201(3).

partial assignment Transfer of a portion of contractual rights to one or more assignees.

partition The dividing of lands held by joint tenants, coparceners, or tenants in common, into distinct portions, so that they may hold them in severalty.

partnership An association of two or more persons to carry on, as co-owners, a business for profit.

Partnerships are treated as a conduit and are, therefore, not subject to taxation. The various items of partnership income, gains, and losses, etc. flow through to the individual partners and are reported on their personal income tax returns.

Limited partnership Type of partnership comprised of one or more general partners who manage business and who are personally liable for partnership debts, and one or more limited partners who contribute capital and share in profits but who take no part in running business and incur no liability with respect to partnership obligations beyond contribution.

partnership capital Total money and property contributed by partners for permanent use by the partnership.

partnership property Sum of all of the partnership's assets.

patent Exclusive right to an invention.

payee The person in whose favor a bill of exchange, promissory note, or check is made or drawn.

payer, or **payor** One who pays, or who is to make a payment; particularly the person who is to make payment of a check, bill or note. Correlative to "payee."

payor bank A bank by which an item is payable as drawn or accepted. U.C.C. § 4–105(b).

per capita This term, derived from the civil law, is much used in the law of descent and distribution, and denotes that method of dividing an intestate estate by which an equal share is given to each of a number of persons, all of whom stand in equal degree to the decedent, without reference to their stocks or the right of representation. It is the opposite of *per stirpes*

per stirpes This term, derived from the civil law, is much used in the law of descents and distribution, and denotes that method of dividing an intestate estate where a class or group of distributees take the share which their deceased would have been entitled to, taking thus by their right of representing such ancestor, and not as so many individuals. It is the opposite of *per capita*

perfect tender rule Seller's tender of delivery must conform exactly to the contract.

perfection of security interest Acts required of a secured party in the way of giving at least constructive notice so as to make his security interest effective at least against lien creditors of the debtor. See U.C.C. §§ 9–302 through 9–306. In most cases, the secured party may obtain perfection either by filing with Secretary of State or by taking possession of the collateral.

performance Fulfillment of one's contractual obligations. See also **part performance; specific performance.**

personal defenses Contractual defenses which are good against holders but not holders in due course.

personal property Generally, all property other than real estate.

plaintiff The party who complains or sues in a civil action and is so named on the record.

pleadings The formal allegations by the parties of their respective claims and defenses.

Rules or Codes of Civil Procedure Unlike the rigid technical system of common law pleading, pleadings under federal and state rules or codes of civil procedure have a far more limited function, with determination and narrowing of facts and issues being left to discovery devices and pre-trial conferences. In addition, the rules and codes permit liberal amendment and supplementation of pleadings.

Under rules of civil procedure the pleadings consist of a complaint, an answer, a reply to a counterclaim, an answer to a cross-claim, a third party complaint, and a third party answer. Fed.R.Civil P. 7(a).

pledge A bailment of goods to a creditor as security for some debt or engagement.

Much of the law of pledges has been replaced by the provisions for secured transactions in Article 9 of the U.C.C.

possibility of reverter The interest which remains in a grantor or testator after the conveyance or devise of a fee simple determinable and which permits the grantor to be revested automatically of his estate on breach of the condition.

possibility test Under the Statute of Frauds could performance possibly be completed within one year.

power of appointment A power of authority conferred by one person by deed or will upon another (called the "donee") to appoint, that is, to select and nominate, the person or persons who are to receive and enjoy an estate or an income therefrom or from a fund, after the testator's death, or the donee's death, or after the termination of an existing right or interest.

power of attorney An instrument authorizing a person to act as the agent or attorney of the person granting it.

power of termination The interest left in the grantor or testator after the conveyance or devise of a fee simple on condition subsequent or conditional fee.

precedent An adjudged case or decision of a court, considered as furnishing an example or authority for an identical or similar case afterwards arising or a similar question of law. See also **stare decisis.**

pre-emptive right The privilege of a stockholder to maintain a proportionate share of ownership by purchasing a proportionate share of any new stock issues.

preference The act of an insolvent debtor who, in distributing his property or in assigning it for the benefit of his creditors, pays or secures to one or more creditors the full amount of **their claims or** a larger amount than they would be entitled to receive on a *pro rata* distribution. The treatment of such preferential payments in bankruptcy is governed by Bankruptcy Act, § 547.

premium   The price for insurance protection for a specified period of exposure.

preponderance of the evidence   Greater weight of the evidence; standard used in civil cases.

prescription   Acquisition of a personal right to use a way, water, light and air by reason of continuous usage. See also **easement**.

presenter's warranty   Warranties given to any payor or acceptor of an instrument.

presentment   The production of a negotiable instrument to the drawee for his acceptance, or to the drawer or acceptor for payment; or of a promissory note to the party liable, for payment of the same. U.C.C. § 3–504(1).

presumption   A presumption is a rule of law, statutory or judicial, by which finding of a basic fact gives rise to existence of presumed fact, until presumption is rebutted. A presumption imposes on the party against whom it is directed the burden of going forward with evidence to rebut or meet the presumption, but does not shift to such party the burden of proof in the sense of the risk of nonpersuasion, which remains throughout the trial upon the party on whom it was originally cast.

price discrimination   Price differential.

price fixing   Any agreement for the purpose and effect of raising, depressing, fixing, pegging or stabilizing prices.

prima facie   Latin. At first sight; on the first appearance; on the face of it; so far as can be judged from the first disclosure; presumably; a fact presumed to be true unless disproved by some evidence to the contrary.

primary liability   Absolute obligation to pay the instrument.

principal   *Law of agency*   The term "principal" describes one who has permitted or directed another (*i.e.* agent or servant) to act for his benefit and subject to his direction and control. Principal includes in its meaning the term "master" or employer, a species of principal who, in addition to other control, has a right to control the physical conduct of the species of agents known as servants or employees, as to whom special rules are applicable with reference to harm caused by their physical acts.

Disclosed principal   One whose existence and identity is known.

Partially disclosed principal   One whose existence is known but whose identity is not known.

Undisclosed principal   One whose existence and identity are not known.

principal debtor   Person whose debt is being supported by a surety.

priority   Precedence in order of right.

private carrier   Carrier which limits its service and is not open to the general public.

private law   The law involving relationships among individuals and entities.

privity   Contractual relationship.

privity of contract   That connection or relationship which exists between two or more contracting parties. The absence of privity as a defense in actions for damages in contract and tort actions is generally no longer viable with the enactment of warranty statutes (*e.g.* U.C.C. § 2–318), acceptance by states of doctrine of strict liability and court decisions which have extended the right to sue to third party beneficiaries and even innocent bystanders.

probate   Court procedure by which a will is proved to be valid or invalid; though in current usage this term has been expanded to generally include all matters and proceedings pertaining to administration of estates, guardianships, etc.

procedural due process   Requirement that governmental action depriving a person of life, liberty or property be done through a fair procedure.

procedural law   Rules for enforcing substantive law.

procedural rules   Rules issued by an administrative agency establishing its organization, method of operation and rules of conduct for practice before it.

proceeds   Consideration for the sale, exchange or other disposition of the collateral.

process   *Judicial process*   In a wide sense, this term may include all the acts of a court from the beginning to the end of its proceedings in a given cause; but more specifically it means the writ, summons, mandate, or other process which is used to inform the defendant of the institution of proceedings against him and to compel his appearance, in either civil or criminal cases.

Legal process   This term is sometimes used as equivalent to "lawful process." Thus, it is said that legal process means process not merely fair on its face, but in fact valid. But properly it means a summons, writ, warrant, mandate, or other process issuing from a court.

Profit à prendre Right to make some use of the soil of another, such as a right to mine metals, and it carries with it the right of entry and the right to remove.

promisee Person to whom a promise is made.

promisor Person making a promise.

promissory estoppel Arises where there is a promise which promisor should reasonably expect to induce action or forbearance on part of promisee and which does induce such action or forbearance, and where injustice can be avoided only by enforcement of the promise.

promissory note An unconditional written promise to pay a specified sum of money on demand or at a specified date. Such a note is negotiable if signed by the maker and containing an unconditional promise to pay a sum certain in money either on demand or at a definite time and payable to order or bearer. U.C.C. § 3–104.

promoters In the law relating to corporations, those persons are called the "promoters" of a company who first associate themselves together for the purpose of organizing the company, issuing its prospectus, procuring subscriptions to the stock, securing a charter, etc.

property Interest that is legally protected.
Abandoned property Intentionally disposed of.
Lost property Unintentionally left by the owner.
Mislaid property Intentionally placed by the owner but unintentionally left.

prosecute To bring a criminal proceeding.

protest A formal declaration made by a person interested or concerned in some act about to be done, or already performed, whereby he expresses his dissent or disapproval, or affirms the act against his will. The object of such a declaration is generally to save some right which would be lost to him if his implied assent could be made out, or to exonerate himself from some responsibility which would attach to him unless he expressly negatived his assent.
Notice of protest A notice given by the holder of a bill or note to the drawer or indorser that the bill has been protested for refusal of payment or acceptance. U.C.C. § 3–509.

provisional credit Tentative credit for the deposit of an instrument until final credit is given.

proximate cause Where the act or omission played a substantial part in bringing about or actually causing the injury or damage and where the injury or damage was either a direct result or a reasonably probable consequence of the act or omission.

proxy (Contracted from procuracy.) Written authorization given by one person to another so that the second person can act for the first, such as that given by a shareholder to someone else to represent him and vote his shares at a shareholders' meeting.

public disclosure of private facts Offensive publicity given to private information about another person.

public law The law dealing with the relationship between government and individuals.

puffery Sales talk.

punitive damages Damages awarded in excess of normal compensation to punish a defendant for a serious civil wrong.

purchase money security interest A seller of goods who retains a security interest in goods purchased with the loaned money.

Q

quantum meruit Expression "quantum meruit" means "as much as he deserves" and it is an expression that describes the extent of liability on a contract implied by law. Essential elements of recovery under quantum meruit are: (1) valuable services were rendered or materials furnished, (2) for person sought to be charged, (3) which services and materials were accepted by person sought to be charged, used and enjoyed by him, and (4) under such circumstances as reasonably notified person sought to be charged that plaintiff, in performing such services, was expected to be paid by person sought to be charged.

quasi Latin. As if; almost as it were; analogous to. It negatives idea of identity, but points out that the conceptions are sufficiently similar for one to be classed as the equal of the other.

quasi contract Legal fiction invented by common law courts to permit recovery by contractual remedy in cases where, in fact, there is no contract, but where circumstances are such that justice warrants a recovery as though there had been a promise.

quasi in rem See **in rem**.

quasi in rem jurisdiction Jurisdiction over property not based on claims against it.

quitclaim deed A deed of conveyance operating by way of release; that is, intended to pass any title, interest, or claim which the grantor may have in the premises, but not professing that such title is valid, nor containing any warranty or covenants for title.

quorum When a committee, board of directors, meeting of shareholders, legislature or other body of persons cannot act unless a certain number at least of them are present.

R

rape Unlawful and unconsented to sexual intercourse.

ratification In a broad sense, the confirmation of a previous act done either by the party himself or by another; as, confirmation of a voidable act.

In the law of principal and agent, the adoption and confirmation by one person with knowledge of all material facts, of an act or contract performed or entered into in his behalf by another who at the time assumed without authority to act as his agent.

real defenses Defenses that are valid against all holders, including holders in due course.

real property Land, and generally whatever is erected or growing upon or affixed to land. Also rights issuing out of, annexed to, and exercisable within or about land. See also **fixture.**

reasonable man standard Duty of care required to avoid being negligent; one who is careful, dililgent and prudent.

receiver A fiduciary of the court, appointed as an incident to other proceedings wherein certain ultimate relief is prayed. He is a trustee or ministerial officer representing court, and all parties in interest in litigation, and property or fund intrusted to him.

recognizance Formal acknowledgment of indebtedness made in court.

redemption The realization of a right to have the title of property restored free and clear of the mortgage; performance of the mortgage obligation being essential for that purpose.

Repurchase by corporation of its own shares.

reformation Equitable remedy used to reframe written contracts to reflect accurately real agreement between contracting parties when, either through mutual mistake or unilateral mistake coupled with actual or equitable fraud by other party, the writing does not embody contract as actually made.

regulatory license Requirement to protect the public interest.

reimbursement Duty owed by principal to pay back authorized payments agent has made on principal's

behalf. Duty owed by a principal debtor to repay surety who pays principal debtor's obligation.

rejection The refusal to accept an offer; manifestation of an unwillingness to accept the goods (sales).

release The relinquishment, concession, or giving up of a right, claim, or privilege, by the person in whom it exists or to whom it accrues, to the person against whom it might have been demanded or enforced.

remainder An estate limited to take effect and be enjoyed after another estate is determined.

remand To send back. The sending by the appellate court of the cause back to the same court out of which it came, for purpose of having some further action taken on it there.

remedy The means by which the violation of a right is prevented, redressed, or compensated. Though a remedy may be by the act of the party injured, by operation of law, or by agreement between the injurer and the injured, we are chiefly concerned with one kind of remedy, the judicial remedy, which is by action or suit.

rent Consideration paid for use or occupation of property. In a broader sense, it is the compensation or fee paid, usually periodically, for the use of any property, land, buildings, equipment, etc.

replevin An action whereby the owner or person entitled to repossession of goods or chattels may recover those goods or chattels from one who has wrongfully distrained or taken or who wrongfully detains such goods or chattels.

reply Plaintiff's pleading in response to the defendant's answer.

repudiation Repudiation of a contract means refusal to perform duty or obligation owed to other party.

requirements contract See **contracts.**

res ipsa loquitur "The thing speaks for itself"; permits the jury to infer both negligent conduct and causation.

rescission An equitable action in which a party seeks to be relieved of his obligations under a contract on the grounds of mutual mistake, fraud, impossibility, etc.

residuary Pertaining to the residue; constituting the residue; giving or bequeathing the residue; receiving or entitled to the residue. See also **legacy,** *residuary legacy.*

respondeat superior Latin. Let the master answer.

This maxim means that a master or employer is liable in certain cases for the wrongful acts of his servant or employee, and a principal for those of his agent.

respondent In equity practice, the party who makes an answer to a bill or other proceeding in equity. In appellate practice, the party who contends against an appeal; *i.e.* the appellee. The party who appeals is called the "appellant."

restitution An equitable remedy under which a person who has rendered services to another seeks to be reimbursed for the costs of his acts (but not his profits) even though there was never a contract between the parties.

restraint on alienation A provision in an instrument of conveyance which prohibits the grantee from selling or transferring the property which is the subject of the conveyance. Many such restraints are unenforceable as against public policy and the law's policy of free alienability of land.

restrictive covenant Private restriction on property contained in a conveyance.

revenue license Requirement to raise money.

reverse An appellate court uses the term "reversed" to indicate that it annuls or avoids the judgment, or vacates the decree, of the trial court.

reversion The term reversion has two meanings, first, as designating the estate left in the grantor during the continuance of a particular estate and also the residue left in grantor or his heirs after termination of particular estate. It differs from a remainder in that it arises by act of the law, whereas a remainder is by act of the parties. A reversion, moreover, is the remnant left in the grantor, while a remainder is the remnant of the whole estate disposed of, after a preceding part of the same has been given away.

revocation The recall of some power, authority, or thing granted, or a destroying or making void of some deed that had existence until the act of revocation made it void.

revocation of acceptance Rescission of one's acceptance of goods based upon the nonconformity of the goods which substantially impairs their value.

right of entry The right of taking or resuming possession of land by entering on it in a peaceable manner.

right of redemption The right (granted by statute only) to free property from the encumbrance of a foreclosure or other judicial sale, or to recover the title passing thereby, by paying what is due, with interest, costs, etc. Not to be confounded with the "equity of redemption," which exists independently of statute but must be exercised before sale. See also **equity of redemption.**

risk of loss Placement of loss between seller and buyer where the goods have been damaged, destroyed or lost.

robbery Larceny from the person by force or threat of force.

rule against perpetuities Principle that no interest in property is good unless it must vest, if at all, not later than 21 years, plus period of gestation, after some life or lives in being at time of creation of interest.

rule of reason Balancing the anticompetitive effects against procompetitive effects of the restraint.

S

sale Transfer of ownership from seller to buyer.

sale on approval Transfer of possession without title to buyer for trial period.

sale or return Sale where buyer has option to return goods to seller.

sanction Means of enforcing legal judgments.

satisfaction The discharge of an obligation by paying a party what is due to him (as on a mortgage, lien, or contract) or what is awarded to him, by the judgment of a court or otherwise. Thus, a judgment is satisfied by the payment of the amount due to the party who has recovered such judgment, or by his levying the amount. See also **accord and satisfaction.**

scienter Latin. Knowingly.

seal Symbol that authenticates a document.

secondary liability Obligation to pay is subject to the conditions of presentment, dishonor, notice of dishonor, and sometimes protest.

secured claim Claim with a lien on property of the debtor.

secured party Creditor who possesses a security interest in collateral.

secured transaction A transaction which is founded on a security agreement. Such agreement creates or provides for a security interest. U.C.C. § 9–105(h).

securities Stocks, bonds, notes, convertible debentures, warrants, or other documents that represent a share in a company or a debt owed by a company.

Certificated security Security represented by a certificate.

Exempt security   Security not subject to registration requirements of 1933 Act.

Exempt transaction   Issuance of securities not subject to the registration requirements of 1933 Act.

Restricted securities   Securities issued under an exempt transaction.

Uncertified security   Security not represented by a certificate.

security agreement   Agreement that grants a security interest.

security interest   Right in personal property securing payment or performance of an obligation.

seisin   Possession with an intent on the part of him who holds it to claim a freehold interest.

self-defense   Force to protect oneself against attack.

separation of powers   Allocation of powers among the legislative, executive and judicial branches of government.

set-off   A counter-claim demand which defendant holds against plaintiff, arising out of a transaction extrinsic of plaintiff's cause of action.

settlor   Creator of the trust.

severance   The destruction of any one of the unities of a joint tenancy. It is so called because the estate is no longer a joint tenancy, but is severed.

Term may also refer to cutting of the crops, such as corn, wheat, etc., or the separating of anything from the realty.

share   A proportionate ownership interest in a corporation.

Shelley's case, rule in   Where a person takes an estate of freehold, legally, or equitably, under a deed, will, or other writing, and in the same instrument there is a limitation by way of remainder of any interest of the same legal or equitable quality to his heirs, or heirs of his body, as a class of persons to take in succession from generation to generation, the limitation to the heirs entitles the ancestor to the whole estate.

The rule was adopted as a part of the common law of this country, though it has long since been abolished by most states.

shelter rule   Transferee gets rights of transferor.

shipment contract   Seller is authorized or required only to bear the expense of placing goods with the common carrier and bears the risk of loss only up to such point.

short swing profits   Profits made by insider through sale or other disposition of the corporate stock within six months after purchase.

sight draft   An instrument payable on presentment.

slander   Oral defamation.

sole proprietorship   A form of business in which one person owns all the assets of the business in contrast to a partnership and corporation.

specific performance   The doctrine of specific performance is that, where damages would be an inadequate compensation for the breach of an agreement, the contractor or vendor will be compelled to perform specifically what he has agreed to do; *e.g.* ordered to execute a specific conveyance of land.

With respect to sale of goods, specific performance may be decreed where the goods are unique or in other proper circumstances. The decree for specific performance may include such terms and conditions as to payment of the price, damages, or other relief as the court may deem just. U.C.C. §§ 2–711(2)(b), 2–716.

standardized business form   A preprinted contract.

stare decisis   Doctrine that, when court has once laid down a principle of law as applicable to a certain state of facts, it will adhere to that principle, and apply it to all future cases, where facts are substantially the same; regardless of whether the parties and property are the same.

state action   Actions by governments as opposed to actions taken by private individuals.

Statute of Frauds   A celebrated English statute, passed in 1677, and which has been adopted, in a more or less modified form, in nearly all of the United States. Its chief characteristic is the provision that no action shall be brought on certain contracts unless there be a note or memorandum thereof in writing, signed by the party to be charged or by his authorized agent.

statute of limitation   A statute prescribing limitations to the right of action on certain described causes of action; that is, declaring that no suit shall be maintained on such causes of action unless brought within a specified period after the right accrued.

statutory lien   Interest in property to secure payment of a debt that arises solely by statute.

stock   "Stock" is distinguished from "bonds" and, ordinarily, from "debentures," in that it gives right of ownership in part of assets of corporation and right to interest in any surplus after payment of debt. "Stock" in a corporation is an equity, and it represents an ownership interest, and it is to be distinguished from obligations such as notes or bonds which are not equities and represent no ownership interest.

Capital stock   See **capital.**

Common stock   Securities which represent an ownership interest in a corporation. If the company has also issued preferred stock, both common and preferred have ownership rights. Claims of both common and preferred stockholders are junior to claims of bondholders or other creditors of the company. Common stockholders assume the greater risk, but generally exercise the greater control and may gain the greater reward in the form of dividends and capital appreciation.

Convertible stock   Stock which may be changed or converted into common stock.

Cumulative preferred   A stock having a provision that if one or more dividends are omitted, the omitted dividends must be paid before dividends may be paid on the company's common stock.

Preferred stock   is a separate portion or class of the stock of a corporation, which is accorded, by the charter or by-laws, a preference or priority in respect to dividends, over the remainder of the stock of the corporation, which in that case is called *common stock.*

Stock warrant   A certificate entitling the owner to buy a specified amount of stock at a specified time(s) for a specified price. Differs from a stock option only in that options are granted to employees and warrants are sold to the public.

Treasury stock   Shares reacquired by a corporation.

stock option   Contractual right to purchase stock from a corporation.

stop payment   Order for a drawee not to pay an instrument.

strict liability   A concept applied by the courts in product liability cases in which a seller is liable for any and all defective or hazardous products which unduly threaten a consumer's personal safety. This concept applies to all members involved in the manufacturing and selling of any facet of the product.

subagent   Person appointed by agent to perform agent's duties.

subject matter jurisdiction   Authority of a court to decide a particular kind of case.

subpoena   A subpoena is a command to appear at a certain time and place to give testimony upon a certain matter. A subpoena duces tecum requires production of books, papers and other things.

subrogation   The substitution of one thing for another, or of one person into the place of another with respect to rights, claims, or securities.

Subrogation denotes the putting a third person who has paid a debt in the place of the creditor to whom he has paid it, so that he may exercise against the debtor all the rights which the creditor, if unpaid, might have done.

subscribe   Literally to write underneath, as one's name. To sign at the end of a document. Also, to agree in writing to furnish money or its equivalent, or to agree to purchase some initial stock in a corporation.

subscriber   Person who agrees to purchase initial stock in a corporation.

subsidiary corporation   Corporation controlled by another corporation.

substantial performance   Equitable doctrine protects against forfeiture for technical inadvertence or trivial variations or omissions in performance.

substantive due process   Requirement that governmental action be compatible with individual liberties.

substantive law   The basic law of rights and duties (contract law, criminal law, tort law, law of wills, etc.) as opposed to procedural law (law of pleading, law of evidence, law of jurisdiction, etc.).

sue   To begin a lawsuit in a court.

suit   "Suit" is a generic term, of comprehensive signification, and applies to any proceeding in a court of justice in which the plaintiff pursues, in such court, the remedy which the law affords him for the redress of an injury or the recovery of a right.

Derivative suit   Suit brought by a shareholder on behalf of the corporation to enforce a right belonging to the corporation.

Direct suit   Suit brought by a shareholder against the corporation based upon his ownership of shares.

summary judgment   Rule of Civil Procedure 56 permits any party to a civil action to move for a summary judgment on a claim, counterclaim, or cross-claim when he believes that there is no genuine issue of material fact and that he is entitled to prevail as a matter of law.

summons   Writ or process directed to the sheriff or other proper officer, requiring him to notify the person named that an action has been commenced against him in the court from where the process issues, and that he is required to appear, on a day named, and answer the complaint in such action.

surety   One who undertakes to pay money or to do any other act in event that his principal debtor fails therein.

suretyship   A guarantee of debts of another.

surplus   Excess of net assets over stated capital.

T

tangible property   Physical objects.

tenancy   Possession or occupancy of land or premises under lease.

Joint tenancy   Joint tenants have one and the same interest, accruing by one and the same conveyance, commencing at one and the same time, and held by one and the same undivided possession. The primary incident of joint tenancy is survivorship, by which the entire tenancy on the decease of any joint tenant remains to the survivors, and at length to the last survivor.

Tenancy at sufferance   Only naked possession which continues after tenant's right of possession has terminated.

Tenancy at will   Possession of premises by permission of owner or landlord, but without a fixed term.

Tenancy by the entirety   A tenancy which is created between a husband and wife and by which together they hold title to the whole with right of survivorship so that, upon death of either, other takes whole to exclusion of deceased heirs. It is essentially a "joint tenancy," modified by the common law theory that husband and wife are one person.

Tenancy for a period   A tenancy for years or for some fixed period.

Tenancy in common   A form of ownership whereby each tenant (*i.e.,* owner) holds an undivided interest in property. Unlike a joint tenancy or a tenancy by the entirety, the interest of a tenant in common does not terminate upon his or her prior death (*i.e.,* there is no right of survivorship).

tenancy in partnership   Type of joint ownership that determines partners' rights in specific partnership property.

tender   An offer of money; the act by which one produces and offers to a person holding a claim or demand against him the amount of money which he considers and admits to be due, in satisfaction of such claim or demand, without any stipulation or condition.

Also, there may be a tender of performance of a duty other than the payment of money.

tender of delivery   Seller makes available to buyer goods conforming to the contract and so notifies the buyer.

tender offer   General invitation to all shareholders to purchase their shares at a specified price.

testator   One who makes or has made a testament or will; one who dies leaving a will.

third party beneficiary   One for whose benefit a promise is made in a contract but who is not a party to the contract

Creditor beneficiary   Where performance of a promise in a contract will benefit a person other than the promisee, that person is a creditor beneficiary if no purpose to make a gift appears from the terms of the promise in view of the accompanying circumstances and performance of the promise will satisfy an actual or supposed or asserted duty of the promisee to the beneficiary.

Donee beneficiary   The person who takes the benefit of the contract even though there is no privity between him and the contracting parties. A third party beneficiary who is not a creditor beneficiary. See also **beneficiary.**

time paper   Payable at definite time.

title   The means whereby the owner of lands or of personalty has the just possession of his property.

tort   A private or civil wrong or injury, other than breach of contract, for which the court will provide a remedy in the form of an action for damages.

Three elements of every tort action are: Existence of legal duty from defendant to plaintiff, breach of duty, and damage as proximate result.

tort-feasor   One who commits a tort.

trade acceptance   A draft drawn by a seller which is presented for signature (acceptance) to the buyer at the time goods are purchased and which then becomes the equivalent of a note receivable of the seller and the note payable of the buyer.

trade name   Name used in trade or business to identify a particular business or manufacturer.

trade secrets   Private business information.

trademark   Distinctive insignia, word or design of a good that is used to identify the manufacturer.

transferor's warranty   Warranties given by any person who transfers an instrument and receives consideration.

trespass   At common law, trespass was a form of action brought to recover damages for any injury to one's person or property or relationship with another.

Trespass to chattels or personal property An unlawful and serious interference with the possessory rights of another to personal property.

Trespass to land At common law, every unauthorized and direct breach of the boundaries of another's land was an actionable trespass. The present prevailing position of the courts finds liability for trespass only in the case of intentional intrusion, or negligence, or some "abnormally dangerous activity" on the part of the defendant. Compare **nuisance**.

trespasser Person who enters or remains on the land of another without permission or privilege to do so.

trust Any arrangement whereby property is transferred with intention that it be administered by trustee for another's benefit.

A trust, as the term is used in the Restatement, when not qualified by the word "charitable," "resulting" or "constructive," is a fiduciary relationship with respect to property, subjecting the person by whom the title to the property is held to equitable duties to deal with the property for the benefit of another person, which arises as a result of a manifestation of an intention to create it. Restatement, Second, Trusts § 2.

Charitable trust To benefit humankind.

Constructive trust Wherever the circumstances of a transaction are such that the person who takes the legal estate in property cannot also enjoy the beneficial interest without necessarily violating some established principle of equity, the court will immediately raise a *constructive trust*, and fasten it upon the conscience of the legal owner, so as to convert him into a trustee for the parties who in equity are entitled to the beneficial enjoyment.

Intervivos trust Established during the settlor's lifetime.

Resulting trust One that arises by implication of law, where the legal estate in property is disposed of, conveyed, or transferred, but the intent appears or is inferred from the terms of the disposition, or from the accompanying facts and circumstances, that the beneficial interest is not to go or be enjoyed with the legal title.

Spendthrift trust Removal of the trusts estate from the beneficiary's control.

Testamentary trust Established by a will.

Totten trust A tentative trust which is a joint bank account opened by the settlor.

Voting trust A trust which holds the voting rights to stock in a corporation. It is a useful device when a majority of the shareholders in a corporation cannot agree on corporate policy.

trustee In a strict sense, a "trustee" is one who holds the legal title to property for the benefit of another, while, in a broad sense, the term is sometimes applied to anyone standing in a fiduciary or confidential relation to another, such as agent, attorney, bailee, etc.

trustee in bankruptcy Representative of the estate in bankruptcy who is responsible for collecting, liquidating, and distributing the debtor's assets.

tying arrangements Conditioning a sale of a desired product (tying product) on the buyer's purchasing a second product (tied product).

U

ultra vires Acts beyond the scope of the powers of a corporation, as defined by its charter or laws of state of incorporation. By doctrine of ultra vires a contract made by a corporation beyond the scope of its corporate powers is unlawful.

unconscionable contract See **contracts**

underwriter Any person, banker, or syndicate that guarantees to furnish a definite sum of money by a definite date to a business or government in return for an issue of bonds or stock. In insurance, the one assuming a risk in return for the payment of a premium.

undue influence Term refers to conduct by which a person, through his power over mind of testator, makes the latter's desires conform to his own, thereby overmastering the violition of the testator.

unenforceable Neither party can recover under the contract.

Uniform Commercial Code One of the Uniform Laws drafted by the National Conference of Commissioners on Uniform State Laws governing commercial transactions (sales of goods, commercial paper, bank deposits and collections, letters of credit, bulk transfers, warehouse receipts, bills of lading, investment securities, and secured transactions).

unilateral mistake Erroneous belief on the part of only one of the parties to a contract.

unliquidated debt Uncertain or contested in amount.

unreasonably dangerous Danger beyond that which the ordinary consumer contemplates.

usage of trade A usage of trade is any practice or method of dealing having such regularity of observance in a place, vocation or trade as to justify an expectation that it will be observed with respect to the transaction in question.

usury Collectively, the laws of a jurisdiction regulating the charging of interest rates. A usurious loan is one whose interest rates are determined to be in excess of those permitted by the usury laws.

V

value   The performance of legal consideration, the forgiveness of an antecedent debt, the giving of a negotiable instrument, or the giving of an irrevocable commitment to a third party. U.C.C. § 1–201(44).

variance   A use differing from that provided in the zoning ordinance in order to avoid undue hardship.

vendee   A purchaser or buyer; one to whom anything is sold. See also **vendor.**

vendor   The person who transfers property by sale, particularly real estate; "seller" being more commonly used for one who sells personalty. See also **vendee.**

venue   "Jurisdiction" of the court means the inherent power to decide a case, whereas "venue" designates the particular county or city in which a court with jurisdiction may hear and determine the case.

verdict   The formal and unanimous decision or finding of a jury, impaneled and sworn for the trial of a cause, upon the matters or questions duly submitted to them upon the trial.

vertical   Agreements among parties at different levels of the distribution chain.

vertical privity   Who is liable to the plaintiff.

vested   Fixed; accrued; settled; absolute. To be "vested," a right must be more than a mere expectation based on an anticipation of the continuance of an existing law; it must have become a title, legal or equitable, to the present or future enforcement of a demand, or a legal exemption from the demand of another.

vicarious liability   Indirect legal responsibility; for example, the liability of an employer for the acts of an employee, or, a principal for torts and contracts of an agent.

void   Null; ineffectual; nugatory; having no legal force or binding effect; unable, in law, to support the purpose for which it was intended.

There is this difference between the two words "void" and "voidable": *void* in the strict sense means that an instrument or transaction is nugatory and ineffectual so that nothing can cure it; *voidable* exists when an imperfection or defect can be cured by the act or confirmation of him who could take advantage of it.

Frequently the word "void" is used and construed as having the more liberal meaning of "voidable."

voidable   Capable of being made void. See also **void.**

voir dire   Preliminary examination of potential jurors.

voluntary   Resulting from free choice. The word, especially in statutes, often implies knowledge of essential facts.

W

waiver   Terms "estoppel" and "waiver" are not synonymous; "waiver" means the voluntary, intentional relinquishment of a known right, and "estoppel" rests upon principle that, where anyone has done an act, or made a statement, which would be a fraud on his part to controvert or impair, because other party has acted upon it in belief that what was done or said was true, conscience and honest dealing require that he not be permitted to repudiate his act or gainsay his statement. See also **estoppel.**

ward   An infant or insane person placed by authority of law under the care of a guardian.

warehouse receipt   Receipt issued by a person storing goods.

warehouser   Storer of goods for compensation.

warrant, *v.*   In contracts, to engage or promise that a certain fact or state of facts, in relation to the subject-matter, is, or shall be, as it is represented to be.

In conveyancing, to assure the title to property sold, by an express covenant to that effect in the deed of conveyance.

warranty   A warranty is a statement or representation made by seller of goods, contemporaneously with and as a part of contract of sale, though collateral to express object of sale, having reference to character, quality, or title of goods, and by which seller promises or undertakes to insure that certain facts are or shall be as he then represents them.

The general statutory law governing warranties on sales of goods is provided in U.C.C. § 2–312 *et seq.* The three main types of warranties are: (1) express warranty; (2) implied warranty of fitness; (3) implied warranty of merchantability.

warranty deed   Deed in which grantor warrants good clear title. The usual covenants of title are warranties of seisin, quiet enjoyment, right to convey, freedom from encumbrances and defense of title as to all claims.

Special warranty deed   Seller warrants that he has not impaired title.

white collar crime   Corporate crime.

will   A written instrument executed with the formalities required by statutes, whereby a person makes a disposition of his property to take effect after his death.

winding up   To settle the accounts and liquidate the assets of a partnership or corporation, for the purpose of making distribution and terminating the concern.

without reserve   Auctioneer may not withdraw the goods from the auction.

writ of certiorari   Discretionary review by a higher court. See also **certiorari.**

writ of execution   Order served by sheriff upon debtor demanding payment of a court judgment against debtor.

Z

zoning   Public control over land use.

INDEX